PRINCIPLES OF INTERNATIONAL ENVIRONMENTAL LAW

Second edition

This second edition of Philippe Sands' leading textbook on international environmental law provides a clear and authoritative introduction to the subject, revised to 1 January 2003. It updates existing topics and addresses important new topics, such as the Kyoto Protocol, genetically modified organisms, and foreign investment and environmental protection. It will remain the most comprehensive account of the international principles and rules relating to environmental protection and the conservation of natural resources. In addition to the key material from the 1992 Rio Conference and the 2002 Johannesburg Conference and subsequent developments, Sands covers topics including the legal and institutional framework, the field's historic development and standards for general application. This will continue to be an invaluable resource for students, scholars and practitioners.

PHILIPPE SANDS QC is Professor of Laws and Director of the Centre for International Courts and Tribunals at University College London. He was a co-founder of FIELD (Foundation for International Environmental Law and Development), and as Legal Director established programmes on Climate Change and Sustainable Development. As a practising barrister Professor Sands has extensive experience litigating cases before the International Court of Justice, the International Tribunal for the Law of the Sea, the WTO Dispute Settlement Body, and the World Bank's International Centre for Settlement of Investment Disputes. He also frequently acts as an advisor to governments, international organisations and non-state actors on aspects of international law.

PRINCIPLES OF INTERNATIONAL ENVIRONMENTAL LAW

Second edition

PHILIPPE SANDS QC

Professor of Laws and Director, Centre for International Courts
and Tribunals, University College London
Barrister-at-Law, Middle Temple

CAMBRIDGE
UNIVERSITY PRESS

PUBLISHED BY THE PRESS SYNDICATE OF THE UNIVERSITY OF CAMBRIDGE
The Pitt Building, Trumpington Street, Cambridge, United Kingdom

CAMBRIDGE UNIVERSITY PRESS
The Edinburgh Building, Cambridge CB2 2RU, UK
40 West 20th Street, New York, NY 10011–4211, USA
477 Williamstown Road, Port Melbourne, VIC 3207, Australia
Ruiz de Alarcón 13, 28014 Madrid, Spain
Dock House, The Waterfront, Cape Town 8001, South Africa

http://www.cambridge.org

Printed in the United Kingdom at the University Press, Cambridge

Typeface Minion 10/12 pt.   *System* LaTeX 2_ε [TB]

A catalogue record for this book is available from the British Library

Library of Congress cataloguing in publication data
Sands, Philippe, 1960–
Principles of international environmental law / Philippe Sands. – 2nd ed.
p.   cm.
Rev. ed. of: Principles of international environmental law. c1994–c1995.
Includes bibliographical references and index.
ISBN 0-521-81794-3 (hb.) – ISBN 0-521-52106-8 (pb.)
1. Environmental law, International.   I. Principles of international environmental law.
II. Title.
K3585.S265   2003
341.7′62 – dc21   2003046122

ISBN 0 521 81794 3 hardback
ISBN 0 521 52106 8 paperback

For Natalia

CONTENTS

Foreword   *page* xiii

Preface and acknowledgments to the first edition   xvii

Preface and acknowledgments to the second edition   xxi

Table of cases   xxiv

Table of treaties and other international instruments   xxxv

List of abbreviations   cxxiv

PART I **The legal and institutional framework**

1 The environment and international society: issues, concepts and definitions   3
The environmental challenge   3
The basis for decision-making: science, economics and other
   values   5
The international legal order   11
The environment and international law: defining terms   15
Further reading   18

2 History   25
Introduction   25
From early fisheries conventions to the creation of the
   United Nations   26
From the creation of the United Nations to Stockholm:
   1945–1972   30
From Stockholm to Rio: 1972–1992   40
UNCED   52
Beyond UNCED: trends and directions   63
Conclusions   69

vii

3   Governance: states, international organisations and non-state
    actors   70
    Introduction   70
    States   71
    International organisations   72
    Non-state actors   112
    Conclusions   120

4   International law-making and regulation   123
    Introduction   123
    Treaties   125
    Other international acts   140
    Customary international law   143
    General principles of international law   150
    Subsidiary sources   153
    Introduction to regulatory approaches   154
    Direct regulation   155
    Economic instruments   158
    Integrated pollution control   167
    Conclusions   169

5   Compliance: implementation, enforcement,
    dispute settlement   171
    Introduction   171
    Implementation   174
    International enforcement   182
    International conflict resolution (settlement of disputes)   200
    UNCED   225
    Conclusions   227

PART II   **Principles and rules establishing standards**

6   General principles and rules   231
    Introduction   231
    Sovereignty over natural resources and the responsibility not to
        cause damage to the environment of other states or to areas
        beyond national jurisdiction   235
    Principle of preventive action   246
    Co-operation   249
    Sustainable development   252
    Precautionary principle   266
    Polluter-pays principle   279

Principle of common but differentiated responsibility   285
Conclusions   289

7   Human rights and armed conflict   291
International human rights   291
War and armed conflict   307
Conclusions   316

8   Atmosphere   317
Introduction   317
Urban and transboundary air pollution   322
Ozone depletion   342
Climate change   357
Outer space   382
UNCED   385
Conclusions   389

9   Oceans and seas   391
Introduction   391
The treaty regime   395
Pollution by dumping   415
Pollution from land-based sources including through the
    atmosphere   427
Pollution from vessels   438
Pollution from seabed activities   445
Environmental emergencies   448
Liability and compensation   454
UNCED   455
Conclusions   457

10   Freshwater resources   459
Introduction   459
Customary law   461
Regional rules   477
UNCED and WSSD   494
Conclusions   497

11   Biological diversity   499
Introduction   499
General instruments of global application   505
General instruments of regional and sub-regional application   523
Regulation of particular habitats or species   543
Conclusions   615

12 Hazardous substances and activities   618
    Introduction   618
    Accident prevention, preparedness and response   620
    Chemicals, pesticides and other dangerous substances   625
    The working environment   638
    Radioactive substances   641
    Biotechnology   651
    Other hazardous activities   662
    UNCED and WSSD   670
    Conclusions   673

13 Waste   675
    Introduction   675
    Prevention and treatment   681
    Disposal   684
    Recycling and re-use   688
    International movement (including trade) in waste   690
    UNCED   705
    Conclusions   708

14 The polar regions: Antarctica and the Arctic   710
    Introduction   711
    The Antarctic Treaty regime   712
    The Arctic   727
    Conclusions   730

15 European Community environmental law   732
    Introduction   732
    Sources and institutions   734
    Historical development   740
    Principles and rules   749
    Conclusions   794

PART III Techniques for implementing international
          principles and rules

16 Environmental impact assessment   799
    Introduction   799
    Non-binding instruments   801
    Treaties and other binding instruments   803
    Conclusions   824

17 Environmental information   826
    Introduction   826
    Information exchange   829
    Reporting and provision of information   832
    Consultation   838
    Notification of emergency situations   841
    Monitoring and other information gathering   847
    Access to environmental information   852
    Public education and awareness   859
    Eco-labelling   860
    Eco-auditing and accounting   862
    Conclusions   866

18 Liability for environmental damage   869
    Introduction   869
    State liability   871
    Civil liability for environmental damage under international law   904
    Conclusions   938

19 International trade and competition   940
    Introduction   940
    Trade measures in international environmental agreements   942
    Unilateral environmental measures and international trade   946
    Competition and subsidies   1010
    Conclusions   1017

20 Financial resources, technology and intellectual
    property   1020
    Introduction   1020
    Financial resources and mechanisms   1021
    Technology transfer and technical assistance   1037
    Intellectual property   1043
    Conclusions   1053

21 Foreign investment   1056
    Introduction   1056
    Investment treaties   1057
    Insurance   1071
    Conclusions   1072

    Index   1074

FOREWORD

It is with pleasure that I write a foreword to this timely exposition and analysis of the system of environmental law as a whole, and as it stands after the Rio Conference. If it seems a little bold to call environmental law a 'system', it is assuredly not so bold as it would have been before the publication of Philippe Sands' important work. A main purpose of academic writing should be to perceive and portray patterns and relations in a body of legal rules so as to make it manageable, teachable, comprehensible and usable. The present work succeeds in doing this to a remarkable degree.

The author's statement that environmental law has a 'longer history than some might suggest' might be thought to border on understatement. When something is taken up as a modish 'concern', there is often a strong temptation to think of it as a discovery by a newly enlightened generation. It is, therefore, a useful antidote to be reminded that, of the two pioneering decisions, both still leading and much-cited cases, one was the *Bering Sea* arbitration, of a century ago, and the other, the *Trail Smelter* arbitration, of half a century ago. Nevertheless, the present-day need for law to protect the environment and to preserve resources is of a scale and urgency far beyond the imagining of the early pioneers.

Seeing these questions, however, in a proper historical perspective does help to warn against the dangers of treating environmental law as a specialisation, which can be made a separate study; or, on the other hand, of regarding environmental law – and here I borrow Philippe's words – as a 'marginal part of the existing legal order'. A perusal of this book will readily reveal to the reader the fallacy of both of these attitudes. Part I of the book – which is entitled 'The legal and institutional framework' – comprises illuminating treatments of such basic subjects of international law as the legal nature of states, international organisations, non-governmental organisations, treaties and other international acts such as resolutions of the General Assembly and other international bodies, EC regulations and directives, the nature and uses of customary law, the general principles of law, and general problems of compliance, implementation and enforcement, and dispute settlement. These pages amply demonstrate that the environmental lawyer has to be equipped with a good basic knowledge of general international law before he can even get properly started on the study of environmental law. Likewise, the general student of international law will, in these pages, find illumination in plenty on these basic questions of general public international law; and indeed also of EC law. He will also find, in the later pages, valuable light upon such difficult questions as 'sovereignty over natural resources', the *actio popularis*, 'standards' and 'soft law'; techniques to encourage compliance, such as reporting; the position in war and armed conflict; general principles of liability and reparation, as well as specifically environmental notions such as the so-called 'polluter pays' principle.

It is in Part II of the book that the author broaches the immense task of setting out, and analysing in some detail, the developing substantive law for the protection of the environment and for the conservation of resources, and of biological diversity. Here, again, when it comes to classifying the areas for purposes of exposition, some of the general headings are familiar to every international lawyer: the atmosphere and outer space; oceans and seas; freshwater resources; hazardous substances and activities; waste; the polar regions; and European Community environmental law. It is in itself a valuable lesson to be able thus to see the shape and dimensions of environmental law as a whole. To establish the boundaries of a subject is an important step towards its intellectual comprehension.

It is a trite observation that environmental problems, though they closely affect municipal laws, are essentially international; and that the main structure of control can therefore be no other than that of international law. Yet one result of this study of environmental law as a whole is to show that the environmental factor has already so infiltrated so many of the traditional areas of public international law that it is no longer possible adequately to study many of the main headings of public international law without taking cognisance of the modifying influence in that particular respect of the principles, laws and regulations of environmental law. There are many instances; one that might not be the first possibility that comes to mind is the law concerning foreign investment. Many readers will remember the controversies of the 1960s and 1970s over the efforts to strike some sort of balance between the principle of national sovereignty over a nation's natural resources, and the competing principles limiting the sovereign rights of expropriation without proper compensation for the foreign investment in those resources. At the present time, this is an area of the law which can no longer be appreciated without adding the considerable factor of the need to protect the environment and therefore the need to limit certain kinds of exploitation, whether foreign or domestic, which cause international waste and harm. The problem of the destruction of tropical rainforests is probably the most dramatic and best known example of a national resource itself becoming an international problem.

Another matter that needs to be thought about is how to make the law of the environment more efficient. The existing principles, laws, case law, regulations, standards, resolutions and so on, already constitute a vast and complicated apparatus of paper and of powers conferred upon certain bodies or persons. When it is considered that the existing law is, however, also seemingly quite inadequate to the problem and that much more may be needed, one is bound to ask questions about how much of the world's resources, wealth, energy and intellect is to be spent on this task of regulation and control. Pollution resulting from an excess of the complication and sheer number of laws, regulations and officials is by no means the least of the threats to our living environment. This book is an important first step towards rationalisation, for it does, by its very able and effective exposition, enable one to see the dimensions of the problem and to get some sort of conspectus of the existing legal apparatus.

Another matter of concern is the need to keep laws and regulations in this area reasonably flexible and open when necessary to changes of direction. Good laws on the environment are driven, or should be driven, by the lessons to be learned from the natural sciences and from technology. But scientists are not by any means always in agreement. It is reasonable to assume, moreover, that the enormous sums spent upon further scientific and technological research imply that the scene of scientific 'fact' is liable to change importantly and even suddenly; for, if not, it is difficult to see what this expensive endeavour is about. For an example of this kind of effect, it is necessary only to mention how new scientific knowledge of the dangers from dioxins have put into a wholly new perspective erstwhile schemes for conserving non-renewable sources of energy using instead the combustion of mixed wastes. We need, therefore, a law of the environment that can change with the changes in the scientific world; otherwise it will quickly and most damagingly be enforcing outmoded science. But to achieve change in international regulations, without thereby merely adding more layers of regulation, is technically by no means an easy task or even always a possible one.

But the matter goes deeper than these preoccupations, important as they are. Humanity is faced with a multifaceted dilemma. There seems to be an urgent need for more and more complex regulation and official intervention; yet this is, in our present system of international law and relations, extremely difficult to bring about in a timely and efficient manner. The fact of the matter surely is that these difficulties reflect the increasingly evident inadequacy of the traditional view of international relations as composed of pluralistic separate sovereignties, existing in a world where pressures of many kinds, not least of scientific and technological skills, almost daily make those separate so-called sovereignties, in practical terms, less independent and more and more interdependent. What is urgently needed is a more general realisation that, in the conditions of the contemporary global situation, the need to create a true international society must be faced. It needs in fact a new vision of international relations and law. This is a matter that takes us beyond the scope of this book. But those who doubt the need for radical changes in our views of, and uses of, international law should read Philippe Sands' book and then tell us how else some of these problems can be solved. After all, this is not just a question of ameliorating the problems of our civilisation but of our survival.

Sir Robert Jennings QC
Former Judge and President of the International Court of Justice; sometime Whewell Professor of International Law in the University of Cambridge; Honorary Bencher of Lincoln's Inn; former President of the Institut de Droit International

PREFACE AND ACKNOWLEDGMENTS TO THE FIRST EDITION

Principles of International Environmental Law marks the culmination of that aspect of my professional activities which was triggered by the accident at the Chernobyl nuclear power plant, on 26 April 1986. At that time I was a research fellow at the Research Centre for International Law at Cambridge University, working on international legal aspects of contracts between states and non-state actors, and not involved in environmental issues. With the active support of the Research Centre's Director, Eli Lauterpacht, I began to examine the international legal implications of the Chernobyl accident, which indicated that the legal aspects of international environmental issues were of intellectual and political interest, and still in an early phase of development. This led to several research papers, a book and various matters involving the provision of legal advice on international environmental issues. My interest having been aroused, the implications of environmental issues for public international law provided a rich seam which has sustained me for several years, and resulted in my founding, with James Cameron, what is now the Foundation for International Environmental Law and Development (FIELD). That, in turn, has provided me with the fortunate opportunity to participate in a number of international negotiations, most notably those preparatory to UNCED and the Climate Change Convention, and to develop an international legal practice which is varied, unpredictable, entertaining, often challenging and occasionally frustrating.

This book, together with the accompanying volumes of international documents (Volumes IIA and IIB) and EC documents (Volume III), is intended to provide a comprehensive overview of those rules of public international law which have as their object the protection of the environment. I hope that it will be of some use to lawyer and non-lawyer alike, whether working for government, international organisations, non-governmental organisations and the private sector, or having an academic or other perspective. Its structure and approach reflect my belief that international environmental efforts will remain marginal unless they are addressed in an integrated manner with those international economic endeavours which retain a primary role in international law-making and institutional arrangements, and unless the range of actors participating in the development and application of international environmental law continues to expand. In that regard, it is quite clear that international environmental law remains, as a branch of general public international law, at an early stage of practical development, in spite of the large body of instruments and a burgeoning literature. Over the past decade the body of law has increased dramatically, and only the best equipped researchers will be able to keep up with all developments as they occur. I have sought to state the law as it was on 1 January 1993, although the diligent reader will note that on some aspects more recent developments have also been treated.

Principles of International Environmental Law therefore marks the culmination of an initial phase of my endeavours as an academic and practitioner. Its roots run deep and wide, and it is impossible to acknowledge here all the sources of input and generous support which I have received over the past several years. It seems to me to be quite appropriate, however, to acknowledge those teachers, colleagues and friends who have exercised particular influence, directly or indirectly.

The fact that I became interested in international law at all is largely due to my first teacher of international law, Robbie Jennings, then in his final year at Cambridge before moving to The Hague: I am hugely grateful for his inspiring encouragement and support ever since, particularly for taking the view that the environment was, even several years ago, properly a subject for consideration in its international legal aspect. Eli Lauterpacht gave me my first professional 'break' and taught me, in particular, the value of a practical approach and the importance of rigour. Even at a distance, Philip Allott constantly reminds me of the need to think about the bigger picture. And lest I should slip, David Kennedy has been a critical inspiration in reminding me that there is another way.

Colleagues at London University (particularly Ian Kennedy at King's College and Peter Slinn at the School of Oriental and African Studies) have provided great support in allowing me the flexibility to combine teaching with practical efforts. I would also like to record my debt to Tom Franck for introducing me to New York University Law School, and to Dean John Sexton for giving me a more regular perch from which to base my forays to the United Nations.

I am tremendously indebted to all my colleagues at FIELD. I would like to thank the Board of Trustees, and especially John Jopling, the Chairman, for allowing me to devote considerable time to this project, as well as Marian Bloom, Frances Connelly, Rona Udall and Roger Wilson for their administrative support. Many FIELD interns provided long hours of patient assistance, and I want especially to thank Carolyn d'Agincourt, Mary Beth Basile and Kiran Kamboj for going way beyond the call of duty during their extended internships, and Joanna Jenkyn-Jones, Hugo Jolliffe and Penny Simpson for helping me to get over the final hurdles more easily. But it is to FIELD's lawyers that I extend especially warm thanks for helping me to fulfil my other obligations and for always being available to provide information and critical insights on those areas in which they are expert. James Cameron is an inspirational friend, colleague and co-founder of FIELD, and I feel fortunate to have found a working partner who is able to provide me with the space and support to get on with my own efforts whilst reminding me that I also have, in all senses, broader responsibilities. Greg Rose (now at the Australian Department of Foreign Affairs and Trade), Jake Werksman and Farhana Yamin have been outstanding colleagues and friends. Richard Tarasofsky and Mary Weiss, my collaborators on Volumes II and III, assisted also in the preparation of this volume. FIELD's many supporters have also contributed, indirectly but significantly, to the production of this book, and I would like to thank, in particular, Janet Maughan (Ford Foundation), Mike Northrop (Rockefeller Brothers Fund), Ruth Hennig (John Merck Fund) and Marianne Lais Ginsburg (German Marshall Fund) for supporting FIELD's efforts and enabling me to participate in some of the important international legal developments since 1989. At my chambers, I want to thank Ailsa Wall for her magnificent typing efforts, and Paul Cooklin for his accommodation of my rather peripatetic needs.

For their efforts on a day-to-day basis my deepest gratitude, however, is reserved for two individuals without whose support it is unimaginable that this book could have been completed. Louise Rands has run my office for the past two and a half years with the greatest efficiency, effectiveness and humour anyone could hope to benefit from, maintaining order (and priorities) in the maelstrom of activities and obligations that frequently engulf FIELD's offices. Natalia Schiffrin has been absolutely fabulous in putting up with the demands that the book placed on our daily routine, and reminding me of what is important in life and what isn't.

I must also acknowledge the assistance of numerous other individuals, who enabled me to obtain access to information or to participate in various meetings, in particular: Andronico Adede (Office of Legal Affairs, United Nations); Raymondo Arnaudo and Genevieve Ball (United States Department of State); Dr John Ashe (Permanent Mission of Antigua and Barbuda to the United Nations); Cath Baker, A. M. Forryan and Susan Halls (UK Foreign and Commonwealth Office); Germaine Barikako (OAU); William Berenson (OAS); Giselle Bird (Department of Foreign Affairs and Trade, Australia); Celine Blais (External Affairs and International Trade, Canada); Dan Bodansky (University of Washington School of Law); Laurence Boisson de Chazournes (Institut des Hautes Etudes, Geneva); M. Borel (Departement Federal des Affaires Etrangeres, Switzerland); Jo Butler and Michael Zammit-Cutajar (Climate Change Convention Interim Secretariat); G. de Proost (Ministere des Affaires Etrangeres, Belgium); Juan-Manuel Dias-Pache Pumareda (Ministerio de Asuntos Exteriores, Spain); Dr Emonds (Bundesministerium fur Umwelt, Naturschutz und Reaktorsicherheit, Germany); Philip Evans (Council of the European Communities); Denis Fada (FAO); Dr Antonio Fernandez (International Commission for the Conservation of Atlantic Tunas); Dr Charles Flemming (Permanent Representative of St Lucia to the United Nations); Nigel Fyfe and Paul Keating

(New Zealand Ministry of External Affairs and Trade); Dr R. Gambell (International Whaling Commission); John Gavitt (CITES Secretariat); Professor Gunther Handl (Editor, *Yearbook of International Environmental Law*); Beatrice Larre (OECD); Howard Mann (Environment Canada); Norma Munguia (Mexican Embassy, Washington DC); Lincoln Myers (formerly Minister of Environment, Trinidad and Tobago); Boldiszar Nagy (Associate Professor, Eotvos Lorand University); Bernard Noble (Deputy Registrar, International Court of Justice); Manoel Pereyra (ICAO); Amelia Porges (GATT); Marie-Louise Quere-Messing (United Nations); N. Raja Chandran (Ministry of Foreign Affairs, Malaysia); Patrick Reyners (OECD-NEA); Keith Richmond (FAO); Stan Sadowski (Paris/Oslo Commissions); Candice Stevens (OECD); Wouter Sturms (IAEA); Patrick Szell (UK Department of Environment); Dr Alexandre Timoshenko (UNEP); Eduardo Valencia Ospina (Registrar, International Court of Justice); Robert van Lierop (formerly Permanent Representative of Vanuatu to the United Nations); Makareta Waqavonova (South Pacific Forum); and Linda Young (IMO).

Finally, I would like to thank Vaughan Lowe for encouraging me to write this textbook (and the supporting volumes of documents), for providing clear intellectual guidance and support, and for introducing me to Manchester University Press. At the Press, Richard Purslow has been as patient and supportive an editor as one could possibly hope to find, and his colleagues Jane Hammond Foster, Elaine White and Celia Ashcroft have provided enormous assistance. Needless to say, such errors or omissions as might have crept in remain my full responsibility.

Philippe Sands
London
1 November 1994

PREFACE AND ACKNOWLEDGMENTS TO THE SECOND EDITION

The second edition of *Principles of International Environmental Law* indicates that the legal aspects of international environmental issues are of growing intellectual and political interest, and that they have moved beyond the situation I described nearly ten years ago as reflecting 'an early phase of development'. It is apparent from the new material which this edition treats – new conventions, new secondary instruments, new (or newly recognised) norms of customary law, and a raft of new judicial decisions – that international environmental law is now well established and is a central part of the international legal order. It is also clear that international environmental law has reached new levels of complexity, in particular as it has become increasingly integrated into other social objectives and subject areas, particularly in the economic field. The burgeoning case law, and the increased involvement of practitioners, suggests that it can no longer be said that international environmental law is, as a branch of general public international law, at an early stage of practical development.

Like the first edition, this edition (together with the accompanying volume of international documents for students) is intended to provide a comprehensive overview of those rules of public international law which have as their object the protection of the environment. Those rules have become more numerous and complex, but also more accesible: the advent of the Internet often means that material which was previously difficult to track down – for example, information as to the status, signature and ratification of treaties, and acts and decisions of conferences of the parties and susbidiary bodies – is now relatively easy to obtain. But the Internet also increases the danger of becoming overwhelmed by the sheer quantity of material that is now available, a risk which is exacerbated by the very extensive (and growing) secondary literature which is produced every year, only a small proportion of which may really be said to indicate real insights into new developments. This background necessarily means that what is gained on breadth may be lost – at least in some areas – on depth. This comprehensive account cannot address all of the details that now dominate specific areas – trade, fisheries and climate change spring immediately to mind – and the reader will need to refer to more detailed accounts of particular sectors, and the websites of various conventions, to obtain many of the details. Over the past decade, the body of law has again increased dramatically; I have sought to state the law as it was on 1 January 2003.

This second edition has largely been inspired by my endeavours as an academic and practitioner over the last eight years, in particular contact with my academic colleagues at London and New York Universities and professional contact in connection with the various international cases I have been fortunate to be involved in. Again, it is impossible to acknowledge here all the sources of input and generous support received since 1995. It is appropriate, however, to acknowledge those colleagues and friends who have exercised particular influence, directly or indirectly. At London University, Matt Craven and Michael Anderson have provided great support, as have many other colleagues at SOAS, together with Richard McCrory, Jane Holder and Jeffrey Jowell at my new home at University College London, with help too from Ray Purdue and Helen Ghosh. At New York University, I could not have wished for greater collegiality and friendship than that offered by Dick Stewart, together with the support offered over many years by Tom Franck, Andy Lowenfeld, Eleanor Fox, Iqbal Ishar, Norman Dorsen, Ben Kingsbury, Radu Popa, Vicki Been and Ricky Revesz, as well as Jane Stewart, and for heaps of administrative support from Jennifer Larmour. At the Project on International Courts and Tribunals, Shep Forman, Ruth Mackenzie, Cesare Romano, Thordis Ingadottir and Noemi Byrd have also provided unstinting support. My former colleagues at FIELD have continued to provide support and assistance, including Jake Werksman, Farhana Yamin, Jurgen Lefevre, Alice Palmer and Beatrice Chaytor.

Many of my students and former students at London and New York Universities have provided long hours of patient assistance. Two colleagues have provided particular support, to whom I extend special thanks and appreciation: Jacqueline Peel, now at the Melbourne University Faculty of Law, who has expended great efforts in assisting with research and in drafting of the highest quality and who, I hope, might become the co-author of this book in its third edition; and Paolo Galizzi, now at Imperial College London, who is co-authoring the student edition of basic documents to accompany this volume. Thanks also go to Valeria Angelini, Lauren Godshall, Ed Grutzmacher, Victoria Hallum, Miles Imwalle, Jimmy Kirby, Lawrence Lee, Bruce Monnington, Lillian Pinzon, Katarina Kompari, Denise Ryan, Anna-Lena Sjolund, Eva Stevens-Boenders and Mimi Yang. Thanks also go to Tim Walsh for electronic wizardry, and – once again – to Louise Rands in deepest Devon for helping to bring the manuscript in on time.

In other places – courts and tribunals and conferences – I have benefited inestimably from the learning and experience offered to me by James Crawford and Pierre-Marie Dupuy, and from Boldizsar Nagy, Vaughan Lowe, Chris Thomas, Laurence Boisson de Chazournes and Adriana Fabra. My colleagues at Matrix Chambers have created an environment which encourages ideas to be generated and tested, supportive of both the environmental law and the international law elements which make up this book and the experience it reflects.

Finally, I would like to thank Finola O'Sullivan and Jennie Rubio at Cambridge University Press. Needless to say, such errors or omissions as might have crept in remain my full responsibility.

For her efforts on a day-to-day basis – and every day – my greatest thanks are to Natalia Schiffrin, for all her help, and for continuing to remind me of what is important in life and what isn't. And of course this time she has had a little help from Leo, Lara and Katya, each of whom has contributed uniquely over the last eight years.

Philippe Sands
1 June 2003
Faculty of Laws
University College London
Bentham House
London WC1H 0EG

TABLE OF CASES

Permanent Court of International Justice

Chorzow Factory (Germany v. Poland), PCIJ Series A, No. 17, 29   152, 873, 882–3

Diversion of the Waters from the Meuse (Netherlands v. Belgium), PCIJ Series A/B, No. 70, 76–7   152, 217

Frontier Between Turkey and Iraq, PCIJ Series B, No. 12   132

Jurisdiction of the Courts of Danzig (Poland, Advisory Opinion), PCIJ Series B. No. 15   152

Legal Status of Eastern Greenland (Denmark v. Norway), PCIJ Series A/B, No. 53, 49   131

The Lotus (France/Turkey), PCIJ Series A, No. 10   239

Mosul Case, PCIJ Series B. No. 12, 32   152

Territorial Jurisdiction of the International Commission of the River Oder [1929] (Czechoslovakia, Denmark, France, Germany, Great Britain, Sweden, Poland), PCIJ Series A, No. 23, 27   217, 462, 471, 474

The Wimbledon (Great Britain, France, Italy, Japan, and Poland (Intervening) v. Germany), PCIJ Series A, No. 1   185

International Court of Justice

Asylum (Colombia/Peru) (1950) ICJ Reports 266   149

Barcelona Traction, Light and Power Company Limited (Second Application) (Belgium v. Spain) (1970) ICJ Reports 3   188

Certain Phosphate Lands in Nauru (Nauru v. Australia) (1992) ICJ Reports 240   94–5, 142, 144, 174, 217, 248, 666–9, 877, 879, 887

Continental Shelf (Libyan Arab Jamahiriya/Malta) (1985) ICJ Reports 13   145

Corfu Channel (United Kingdom v. Albania) (1949) ICJ Reports 4   152, 153, 243, 249, 471, 842, 881

Estai Case (Canada v. Spain) (1998) ICJ Reports 432   567–8, 578–80

Fisheries Jurisdiction (Federal Republic of Germany v. Iceland) (Jurisdiction) (1983) ICJ Reports 96; (Merits) (1974) ICJ Reports 175   14, 173, 567–8

Fisheries Jurisdiction (*Estai*) (Spain v. Canada) (1998) ICJ Reports 432 216, 217, 239, 567–8, 578–80

Fisheries Jurisdiction (United Kingdom v. Iceland) (Jurisdiction) (1973) ICJ Reports 3; (Merits) (1974) ICJ Reports 3 14, 152, 153, 218, 262, 561, 567–8

Fisheries Jurisdiction (United Kingdom v. Norway) (1951) ICJ Reports 116 149

Frontier Dispute (Burkina Faso/Republic of Mali) (1986) ICJ Reports 554 150–1

Gabcikovo-Nagymaros (Hungary/Slovakia) (1997) ICJ Reports 7 7, 9, 11, 65, 94–5, 106, 132, 134, 145, 146, 152, 153, 173, 174, 184, 217, 247, 249–51, 254–5, 257, 263, 274–5, 462, 469–77, 822–4, 873, 875, 877, 883, 889

Gulf of Maine Case (Canada/United States) (1984) ICJ Reports 246 152

Kasiliki/Sedulu Island (Botswana/Namibia) (1999) ICJ Reports 1045 250, 462, 467

Legality of the Threat or Use of Nuclear Weapons (1996) ICJ Reports 226 4, 95, 99, 145, 148, 153, 257, 310, 315, 649

Legality of the Use of Force (Yugoslavia v. United Kingdom) (1999) ICJ Reports 218

Military and Paramilitary Activities In and Against Nicaragua (Nicaragua v. United States) (1986) ICJ Reports 14 106, 145–7, 150–2, 842

North Sea Continental Shelf (Federal Republic of Germany/Denmark; Federal Republic of Germany/Netherlands) (1969) ICJ Reports 3 145–9, 152, 153, 201, 251

Nottebohm (Liechtenstein v. Guatemala) (Judgment) (1955) ICJ Reports 4 146

Nuclear Tests (Australia v. France) (Interim Protection) (1973) ICJ Reports 99; (Judgment) (1974) ICJ Reports 253 33, 120–1, 141, 144, 151, 153, 184–5, 188, 190, 218, 241–2, 248, 317, 319–21, 649, 877, 879, 881, 887

Nuclear Tests (New Zealand v. France) (Interim Protection) (1973) ICJ Reports 135; (Judgment) (1974) ICJ Reports 457 33, 120–1, 141, 144, 151, 153, 184–5, 218, 318–21, 649, 877, 881, 887

Passage Through the Great Belt (Finland v. Denmark) (Provisional Measures) (1991) ICJ Reports 12 218

Reparation for Injuries Suffered in the Service of the United Nations (1949) ICJ Reports 174 131, 191, 1024

Request for an Examination of the Situation in Accordance with Paragraph 63 of the Court's Judgment of 20 December 1974 in the Nuclear Tests (New Zealand v. France) (1995) ICJ Reports 288 95–6, 173, 187, 217, 244–5, 273–4, 310, 813–14

Reservations to the Convention on the Prevention and Punishment of the Crime of Genocide (1951) ICJ Reports 15 135

South West Africa (Preliminary Objections), (1966) ICJ Reports 47 187

International Tribunal for the Law of the Sea

Mox Plant, 3 December 2001   7, 138, 173, 174, 184, 213, 251, 276, 436, 806–7, 828, 838, 857

Southern Bluefin Tuna (Australia and New Zealand v. Japan), 4 August 2002, 39 ILM 1359 (2000)   7, 137–8, 173, 185, 220, 275–6, 561, 580–1, 828

Volga Case (Russia v. Australia) 22 December 2002   220

Awards of international arbitral tribunals

Azinian, Davitian and Baca v. Mexico, 1 November 1998, 5 ICSID Reports 269   1064

Bering Sea Fur Seals Fisheries Arbitration (Great Britain v. United States) *Moore's International Arbitration* (1893) 755   29–30, 150–1, 153, 173, 185, 190, 213, 238, 253, 256, 561–6, 588

Compania del Desarrollo de Santa Elena SA v. Costa Rica, 17 February 2000, 39 ILM 1317 (2000)   1070–1

Ethyl Corporation v. Canada, Jurisdiction phase, 38 ILM 708 (1999)   1064–5

Feldman (Marvin) v. Mexico, 9 December 2002, ICSID Case ARB(AF)/99/1   1069

Gentini Case (Italy v. Venezuela) MCC (1903)   232, 234

Gut Dam Arbitration, 8 ILM 118 (1969)   486–7

Kuwait v. American Independent Oil Co., 21 ILM 976 (1982)   237

Lac Lanoux Arbitration (France v. Spain) 24 ILR 101 (1957)   34, 153, 173, 184, 202, 213, 243, 248, 250, 463–4, 838, 877, 881

Metalclad Corporation v. Mexico, 25 August 2000, 40 ILM 35 (2001)   173, 1066–9

Methanex v. United States of America, 15 January 2001   200, 1069–70

OSPAR (Article 9), 2 July 2003   857

Palmas Case 2 HCR 84 (PCA 1928)   241

People of Enewetak (Marshall Islands Nuclear Claims Tribunal, 13 April 2000), 39 ILM 1214 (2000)   889–90, 910

Pope and Talbot v. Canada, 26 June 2000   1069

Rainbow Warrior (New Zealand v. France) 82 ILR 500   883

S. D. Myers v. Canada   1065–6

Texaco Overseas Petroleum Co. and California Asiatic Oil Co. v. Libya, 53 ILR 389 (1977)   237, 305, 317–19

Trail Smelter Arbitration (United States v. Canada) 16 April 1938, 11 March 1941; 3 RIAA 1907 (1941)   4, 30, 150–1, 153, 173, 184, 213, 241–2, 248, 249, 321–5, 471, 877, 879, 881, 885–6

Waste Management Inc. v. Mexico, 2 June 2000, 5 ICSID Reports 443   1064

GATT Panel Decisions

Canada – Measures Affecting Exports of Unprocessed Herring and Salmon, BISD/35S/98 (1988)   953

Thailand – Restriction on Importation of and Internal Taxes on Cigarettes, BISD/37S/200 (1990)   953

Tuna/Dolphin I, 30 ILM 1594 (1991)   953, 955, 960–1

Tuna/Dolphin II, 33 ILM 839 (1991)   953, 958–61

US – Chemicals Tax, BISD/34S/160 (1987)   285, 953

US – Measures on Yellow-Fin Tuna Imports, GATT Doc. DS21/R (1991)   132, 158, 173, 185, 189, 190, 238, 1002

US – Tuna Import Measures, BISD/29S/91 (1982)   953

WTO Cases

Australia – Measures Affecting Importation of Salmon, WT/DS18/R, 12 June 1998 and WT/DS18/AB/R, 20 October 1998   981–3, 985

EC – Measures Affecting Asbestos and Asbestos-Containing Products, WT/DS135/R, 18 September 2000 and WT/DS135/AB/R, 12 March 2001   10, 222, 973–7

EC – Measures concerning Meat and Meat Products (Hormones), WT/DS48/AB/R, 16 January 1998; WT/DS26/R/USA and WT/DS48/CAN, 18 August 1997   7, 222, 277–8, 979–81, 985, 1019

Japan – Measures Affecting Agricultural Products, WT/DS76/R, 27 October 1998 and WT/DS76/AB/R, 22 February 1999   983–4

Swordfish Case (Chile v. EC), DS193, 12 December 2000   561, 582–3

US – Import Prohibition of Certain Shrimp and Shrimp Products, 12 October 1998, 38 ILM 118 (1999)   9, 11, 132, 173, 190, 200, 222, 238, 255, 290, 944, 945, 961–73, 977, 1009

US – Reformulated Gasoline, 35 ILM 603 (1996)   961–5, 977

World Bank Administrative Tribunal

De Merode v. World Bank, WBAT Reports [1987] Decision No. 1   734

European Court of Justice

Aher-Waggon GmbH v. Germany (Case C-389/96) [1998] ECR I-4473   783, 992–3

Alpharma Inc. v. Council (Case T-70/99) [1999] ECR II-2077   272

Arcaro (Case C-168/95) [1996] ECR I-4705   737

Arco Chemie Nederland Ltd (Cases 418/419/97) [2000] ECR I-4475   788

Association Greenpeace and Others v. Ministère de l'Agriculture et de la Pêche (Case C-6/99) [2000] ECR I-1651   272

Bund Naturschutz in Bayern eV and Others v. Freistaat Bayern (Case C-396/92) [1994] ECR I-3717   810

Burgemeester v. Holland (Case C-81/96) [1998] ECR I-3923   810

Cali v. Servizi Ecologici Porto di Genova SpA (Case C-343/95) [1997] ECR I-1547   1016

Chemische Afvalstoffen Düsseldorp BV and Others v. Minister van Volkshuisvesting (Case C-203/96) [1998] ECR I-4075   699, 789

Comitato di Difesa della Cava (Case C-236/92) [1994] ECR I-483   737

Commission v. Belgium (Case 68/81) [1982] ECR 153   792

Commission v. Belgium (Case 69/81) [1982] ECR 163   787

Commission v. Belgium (Case 71/81) [1982] ECR 175   792

Commission v. Belgium (Case 72/81) [1982] ECR 183   772

Commission v. Belgium (Case 73/81) [1982] ECR 189   771

Commission v. Belgium (Case 239/85) [1986] ECR 3645   790

Commission v. Belgium (Case 247/85) [1987] ECR 3029   604

Commission v. Belgium (Case 1/86) [1987] ECR 2797   775

Commission v. Belgium (Case 134/86) [1988] ECR 2415   222, 768

Commission v. Belgium (Case C-162/89) [1990] ECR I-2391   760

Commission v. Belgium (Case C-42/89) [1990] ECR I-2821   771, 772

Commission v. Belgium (Case C-2/90) [1993] 1 CMLR 365   150, 987, 990–2

Commission v. Belgium (Case C-174/91) [1993] ECR I-2275   775

Commission v. Belgium (Case C-133/94) [1996] ECR I-2323   811

Commission v. Belgium (Cases C-218/219/220/221/222/96) [1996] ECR I-6817   784

Commission v. Belgium (Case C-207/97) [1999] ECR I-275   774

Commission v. Belgium (Case C-347/97) [1999] ECR I-309   792

Commission v. Belgium (Case C-79/98) [1999] ECR I-5187   785

Commission v. Belgium (Case C-217/99) [2000] ECR I-10251   994–5

Commission v. Belgium (Case C-236/99) [2000] ECR I-5657   778

Commission v. Council (Case C-300/89) [1991] ECR I-2687   223, 744

Commission v. Council (Case C-155/91) [1993] ECR I-939   223, 745

Commission v. Denmark (Case 278/85) [1987] ECR 4069   785

Commission v. Denmark (Case 302/86) [1989] 1 CMLR 619   689, 987

Commission v. France (Case 252/85) [1988] ECR 2243   604

Commission v. France (Case C-182/89) [1990] ECR I-4337   223

Commission v. France (Case C-166/97) [1999] ECR I-1719   604

Commission v. France (Case C-97/98) [1999] ECR I-08531   604

Chemission v. France (Case C-374/98) [2000] ECR I-10799   604

Commission v. France (Case C-38/99) [2000] ECR I-10941   604

Commission v. France (Case C-220/99) [2001] ECR I-5831   537

Commission v. France (Case C-320/99) [2000] ECR I-10453   760
Commission v. France (Case C-147/00) [2001] ECR I-2387   773
Commission v. Germany (Case 208/85) [1987] ECR 4045   785
Commission v. Germany (Case 412/85) [1987] ECR 3503   604
Commission v. Germany (Case C-131/88) [1991] ECR I-825   775
Commission v. Germany (Case C-288/88) [1990] ECR I-2721   604
Commission v. Germany (Case C-57/89) [1991] ECR I-883   605
Commission v. Germany (Case C-57/89 R) [1989] ECR 2849   194
Commission v. Germany (Case C-237/90) [1992] ECR I-5937   772
Commission v. Germany (Case C-422/92) [1995] ECR I-1097   790
Commission v. Germany (Case C-431/92) [1995] ECR I-2189   808, 810
Commission v. Germany (Case C-61/94) [1996] ECR I-3989   536, 762
Commission v. Germany (Case C-262/95) [1996] ECR I-5729   774
Commission v. Germany (Case C-297/95) [1996] ECR I-6739   778
Commission v. Germany (Case C-298/95) [1996] ECR I-6747   775
Commission v. Germany (Case C-301/95) [1998] ECR I-6135   811
Commission v. Germany (Case C-137/96) [1997] ECR I-6749   786
Commission v. Germany (Case C-184/97) [1999] ECR I-7837   774
Commission v. Germany (Case C-198/97) [1999] ECR I-3257   772
Commission v. Germany (Case C-217/97) [1999] ECR I-5087   855
Commission v. Germany (Case C-71/99) [2002] ECR I-5811   537
Commission v. Greece (Case C-45/91) [1992] ECR I-2509   789
Commission v. Greece (Case C-161/95) [1996] ECR I-1979   778
Commission v. Greece (Cases C-232/233/95) [1998] ECR I-3343   774
Commission v. Greece (Case C-380/95) [1996] ECR I-4837   786
Commission v. Greece (Case C-387/97) [2000] ECR I-5047   788, 929
Commission v. Greece (Case C-103/00) [2002] ECR I-1147   539
Commission v. Greece (Case C-64/01) [2002] ECR I-2523   755
Commission v. Ireland (Case C-392/96) [1999] ECR I-5901   811
Commission v. Ireland (Case C-67/99) [2001] ECR I-5757   537
Commission v. Ireland (Case C-117/00) [2002] ECR I-5335   538
Commission v. Italy (Case 91/79) [1980] ECR 1099   175, 738, 986
Commission v. Italy (Case 92/79) [1980] ECR 1115   738, 760, 986
Commission v. Italy (Cases 30–34/81) [1981] ECR 3379   222, 771, 772, 787, 791, 792
Commission v. Italy (Case 262/85) [1987] ECR 3073   604
Commission v. Italy (Case 309/86) [1988] ECR 1237   768
Commission v. Italy (Case 322/86) [1988] ECR 3995   775
Commission v. Italy (Case C-360/87) [1991] ECR I-791   775
Commission v. Italy (Case C-291/93) [1994] ECR I-859   775
Commission v. Italy (Case C-238/95) [1996] ECR I-1451   785
Commission v. Italy (Case C-302/95) [1996] ECR I-6765   778
Commission v. Italy (Case C-225/96) [1997] ECR I-6887   776

Commission v. Italy (Case C-365/97) [1999] ECR I-7773   789
Commission v. Italy (Case C-159/99) [2001] ECR I-4007   604
Commission v. Italy (Case C-65/00) [2002] ECR I-1795   791
Commission v. Luxembourg (Case C-313/93) [1994] ECR I-1279   810
Commission v. Netherlands (Case 96/81) [1982] ECR 1791   772
Commission v. Netherlands (Case 97/81) [1982] ECR 1819   223, 772
Commission v. Netherlands (Case 291/84) [1987] ECR 3483   223, 775
Commission v. Netherlands (Case 236/85) [1987] ECR 3989   604
Commission v. Netherlands (Case C-339/87) [1993] 2 CMLR 360   604
Commission v. Netherlands (Case C-3/96) [1998] ECR I-3031   604
Commission v. Netherlands (Case C-152/98) [2001] ECR I-3463   774
Commission v. Portugal (Case C-150/97) [1999] ECR I-259   810
Commission v. Portugal (Case C-183/97) [1998] ECR I-4005   775
Commission v. Portugal (Case C-208/97) [1998] ECR I-4017   773
Commission v. Portugal (Case C-213/97) [1998] ECR I-3289   773
Commission v. Portugal (Case C-435/99) [2000] ECR I-1179   774
Commission v. Spain (Santona Marshes) (Case C-355/90) [1993] ECR
    I-4221   602–3
Commission v. Spain (Case C-92/96) [1998] ECR I-505   772
Commission v. Spain (Case C-29/01) [2002] ECR I-2503   755
Commission v. United Kingdom (Case C-337/89) [1992] ECR I-6103   772
Commission v. United Kingdom (Case C-56/90) [1993] ECR I-4109   223,
    772
Commission v. United Kingdom (Case C-340/96) [1999] ECR I-2023   772
Commission v. United Kingdom (Case C-35/00) [2002] ECR I-953   791
Commission v. United Kingdom (Case C-39/01) [2002] ECR I-2513   755
Criminal Proceedings Against Giacomo Caldana (Case 187/84) [1985] ECR
    3013   785
Criminal Proceedings Against Gourmetterie van den Burg (Case C-169/89)
    [1990] ECR 2143   604, 990
Criminal Proceedings Against Tombesi and Others (Cases C-242/304/330/94
    and 224/95) [1997] ECR I-3561   678, 788
Danish Bees (Criminal Proceedings Against Bluhme) (Case C-67/97) [1998]
    ECR I-8033   993–4
Dassonville (Case 8/74) [1974] ECR 837   996
Enichem Base and Others v. Commune di Cinisello Balsamo (Case C-380/87)
    [1989] ECR 2491   224, 787
Fornasar (Case C-318/98) [2000] ECR I-4785   791
France v. United Kingdom (Case 141/78) [1979] ECR 2923   185
Francovich and Another v. Italy (Case C-6/9/90) [1993] 2 CMLR 66   928–9
Gianni Bettati v. Safety Hi-Tech Srl (Case C-341/95) [1998] ECR I-4355   762
Greenpeace and Others v. Commission (Case C-321/95) [1998] ECR
    I-6151   177

Groupement d'Interêt Economique 'Rhone Alpes Huiles' and Others v. Syndicat National des Fabricants d'Huile de Graissage and Others (Case 295/82) [1984] ECR 575   791, 990

Handelskwekerij G. J. Bier v. Mines de Potasse d'Alsace (Case 21/76) [1976] ECR 1735   198

Inter-Environment Wallonie ASBL v. Région Wallone (Case C-129/96) [1997] ECR I-7411   678, 738, 788

Kemikalienspektionen v. Toolex Alpha AB (Case C-473/98) [2000] ECR I-5681   995–6

Kraaijeveld (Case C-72/95) [1996] ECR I-5403   737, 811

Luxembourg v. Berthe Linster EA (Case C-287/98) [2000] ECR I-6917   738, 808

Ministère Public v. Oscar Traen and Others (Cases 372/373/374/85) [1987] ECR 2141   789

Netherlands v. European Parliament and EU Council (Case C-377/98) [2001] ECR I-7079   516, 1047, 1051–2

Palin Granit and Vehmassalon kansanternveystyon kuntayhtyman hallitus (Case C-9/00) [2002] ECR I-3533   678

Pretore di Salo v. Persons Unknown (Case 14/86) [1987] ECR 2545   775

Preussen Elektra AG v. Schleswag AG (Case C-379/98) [2001] ECR I-2099   996–7

Procureur de la République v. Association de Défense des Brûleurs d'Huiles Usagées (Case 240/83) [1985] ECR 531   133, 742, 987

R. v. Secretary of State for the Environment and Ministry of Agriculture, Fisheries and Food, ex parte H. A. Stanley and Others and D. G. Metson and Others (Case C-293/97) [1999] ECR I-2603   284

R. v. Secretary of State for the Environment, Transport and the Regions, ex parte First Corporate Shipping Ltd (Case C-371/98) [2000] ECR I-9235   224, 537

Reference for a Preliminary Ruling: Rechtbank van Eerste Aanleg Turnhout – Belgium (Criminal Proceedings Against Brandsma) (Case C-293/94) [1996] ECR I-3159   992

Saarland and Others v. Ministry of Industry and Others (Case C-187/87) [1988] ECR 5013   793

Simmenthal (Case 107/77) [1978] ECR 629   738

Sydhavnens Sten & Grus (Case C-209/98) [2000] ECR I-3743   789

Syndicat National des Fabricants d'Huile de Graissage v. Groupement d'Intérêt Economique Inter-Huiles (Case 172/82) [1983] ECR 555   791, 987

Unilever Italia SpA v. Central Food SpA (Case C-443/98) [2000] ECR I-7535   738

Union de Pequenos Agricultores v. Council (Case C-50/00 P) [2002] 3 CMLR 1   177

United Kingdom v. Commission (Case C-180/96) [1998] ECR I-2265   272
Van Gend and Loos (Case 26/62) [1963] ECR 3   734, 737
Vessaso and Zanetti (Cases C-206/207/88) [1990] ECR I-1461   677, 788
Wilhelm Mecklenburg v. Kreis Pinneberg (Case C-321/96) [1998] ECR
    I-3809   855
WWF and Others v. Autonome Provinz Bozen and Others (Case C-435/97)
    [1999] ECR I-5613   808, 811
Zanetti and Others (Case C-359/88) [1990] ECR I-1509   677, 788

Court of First Instance

Jego Quere et Cie SA v. Commission (Case T-177/01) [2002] 2 CMLR 44   177

European Patent Office

Harvard College, Case T19/90, [1990] 12 OJEPO 476   1048
Hormone Relaxin, Case T272/95, [1995] 6 OJEPO 388   1048
Lubrizol Genetics Inc, Case T320/87, [1990] 3 OJEPO 71   1047–8
Oncomouse, Application No. 85 304 490.7, [1992] OJEPO 589   1048–9
Plant Genetic Systems, Case T356/93, [1995] 8 OJEPO 545   7, 1048

European Court/Commission of Human Rights

Arondelle v. United Kingdom (1982) 26 DR 5   300–1
Balmer-Schafroth v. Switzerland (1998) 25 EHRR 598   277–8, 306
Bladet Tromso and Stensas v. Norway (2000) 29 EHRR 125   306
Church of X v. UK, Application No. 3798/68   225
Fredin v. Sweden, Judgment of 18 February 1991, ECHR Series A, No. 192,
    14   303
Guerra and Others v. Italy (1998) 26 EHRR 357   301–2, 306, 853
Hatton and Others v. United Kingdom (2002) 34 EHRR 1   302–3
Klass v. Germany (1978) 2 EHRR 214   225
Lopez-Ostra v. Spain, ECHR Series A, No. 303-C, (1995) 20 EHRR 277   301
Matos e Silva v. Portugal (1997) 24 EHRR 573   303
Oerlemans v. Netherlands, ECHR Series A, No. 219, (1993) 15 EHRR
    561   303
Pine Valley Developments Ltd and Others v. Ireland, ECHR Series A, No. 222,
    (1992) 14 EHRR 319   303–4
Powell and Rayner v. United Kingdom, ECHR Series A, No. 172, (1990) 12
    EHRR 355   302, 306
X and Y v. Federal Republic of Germany, Application No. 7407/76, Decision of
    13 May 1976 on the Admissibility of the Application, 5 DR 161 (1976)   299
X v. Federal Republic of Germany, Application No. 9234/81, 26 DR 270   306

Inter-American Commission on Human Rights

Mayagna (Sumo) Awas Tingni Community v. Nicaragua, Judgment of 31 August 2001, Inter-AmCtHR Series C, No. 79   304

Yanomami v. Brazil, Case No. 7615 of 5 March 1985, OAS Doc. OAE/Ser.L/ VII.66.doc.10 rev.1, 24 (1985)   304

Decisions of national courts

Australia

Commonwealth of Australia v. State of Tasmania and Others, 68 ILR 266   612–14

Belgium

Count Lippens v. Etat Belge, 47 ILR 336   601

India

Narmada Bachao Andolan v. Union of India and Others, Supreme Court of India, 18 October 2000   279

Vellore Citizens' Welfare Forum v. Union of India and Others, Writ Petition (C) No. 914 of 1991   279

Italy

Joined Cases 676/86 and 337 and Others, General Nation Maritime Transport Company and Others v. Patmos Shipping Company and Others, Court of Messina, 1st Civil Division, 30 July 1986   919

United Kingdom

Kincardine and Deeside DC v. Forestry Commissioners, 1992 SLT 1180; 1991 SCLR 729; [1994] 2 CMLR 869; [1993] Env LR 151   811

R. v. Secretary of State for Foreign Affairs, ex parte World Development Movement Ltd [1995] 1 All ER 611   1023

R. v. Secretary of State for the Environment, ex parte Kingston upon Hull City Council and ex parte Bristol City Council and Another [1996] Env LR 248; (1996) 8 Admin LR 509   777

R. v. Secretary of State for the Environment, Transport and the Regions and Another, ex parte Alliance Against the Birmingham Northern Relief Road and Others (No. 1) [1999] Env LR 447; [1999] JPL 231   855

R. v. Secretary of State for Trade and Industry, ex parte Greenpeace, unreported,
      5 November 1999   200
R. v. Secretary of State for Trade and Industry, ex parte Greenpeace (No. 2)
      [2002] 2 CMLR 94; [2000] Env LR 221   537
R. v. Swale Borough Council, ex parte Royal Society for the Protection of Birds
      (1990) 2 Admin LR 790; [1991] 1 PLR 6; [1991] JPL 39   811
Rylands v. Fletcher (1868) LR 3 HL 330   882
Twyford Parish Council and Others v. Secretary of State for Transport [1992]
      1 CMLR 276; [1993] Env LR 37   811

United States

Beanal v. Freeport-McMoran, 969 F Supp 362 (US District Court of Louisiana,
      1997)   279
Dow Chemical Co. v. Alfara, 768 SW 2d 674 (Texas 1990)   239
Laker Airways v. Pan American World Airways, 23 ILM 748 (1984)
Timberlane Lumber Co. v. Bank of America, 66 ILR 270 (1976–7)   240

TABLE OF TREATIES AND OTHER INTERNATIONAL INSTRUMENTS

Treaties

1867

Convention Between France and Great Britain Relative to Fisheries (Paris) 11 November 1867, in force 18 January 1868; 21 IPE 1   27

1869

Convention Establishing Uniform Regulations Concerning Fishing in the Rhine Between Constance and Basel (Berne) 9 December 1869; 9 IPE 4695   479

1882

International Phylloxera Convention, with a Final Protocol (Berne) 23 June 1882; 4 IPE 1571   28

Treaty for the Regulation of the Police of the North Sea Fisheries (Overfishing Convention), S.Ex. Doc. 106, 50 Congress, 2 Sess. 97   27

1887

Convention Designed to Remove the Danger of Epizootic Diseases in the Territories of Austria-Hungary and Italy (Rome) 7 December 1887; 4 IPE 1586   29

1891

Agreement Between the Government of the United States of America and the Government of Her Britannic Majesty for a Modus Vivendi in relation to Fur Seal Fisheries in the Bering Sea (Washington) 15 June 1891; 8 IPE 3655   30

1892

Convention Between the Government of the United States of America and the Government of Her Britannic Majesty for the Renewal of the Existing Modus Vivendi in the Bering Sea (Washington) 18 April 1892; 4 IPE 3656   30

Treaty Between Great Britain and the United States submitting to Arbitration the Questions Relating to the Seal Fisheries in the Bering Sea (Washington) 29 February 1892; 176 CTS 447   562

1899

International Convention with respect to the Laws and Customs of War by Land (**Hague II**) 29 July 1899, in force 4 September 1900; 26 Martens (2nd)   311

1900

Convention Between the Riverine States of the Rhine Respecting Regulations Governing the Transport of Corrosive and Poisonous Substances (Mannheim) 11 May 1900; 25 IPE 214   29

Convention destinée à assurer la conservation des diverses espèces vivant à l'état sauvage en Afrique qui sont utiles à l'homme ou inoffensives (London) 19 May 1900; 4 IPE 1607 (**1900 London Convention**)   28, 524

1902

Convention concernant l'exploitation et la conservation des pêcheries dans la partie-frontière du Danube, Belgrade, 15 January 1902; 190 CTS 344   27

Convention for the Protection of Birds Useful to Agriculture (Paris) 19 March 1902, in force 20 April 1908; 4 IPE 1615   27

1907

Convention Concerning the Laws and Customs of War on Land (The Hague) 18 October 1907, in force 26 January 1910; 3 Martens (3rd) 461 (**1907 Hague Convention IV**)   311

Convention Relative to the Laying of Automatic Submarine Contact Mines (The Hague) 18 October 1907, in force 26 January 1910; 3 Martens (3rd) 580 (**Hague Convention VIII**)   312

Hague Convention on the Pacific Settlement of International Disputes (The Hague) 18 October 1907   212

1909

Treaty Relating to the Boundary Waters and Questions Arising Along the Boundary Between the United States and Canada (Washington) 11 January 1909, in force 5 May 1910; 10 IPE 5158 (**1909 Boundary Water Treaty**)   28, 203, 485–6

    Art. IV   486
    Art. VII   486
    Arts. VIII–X   486
    Art. IX   486

1911

Convention Between the United States of America, the United Kingdom of Great Britain and Northern Ireland, and Russia, for the Preservation and

Protection of Fur Seals (Washington) 7 July 1911, in force 15 December 1911; 8 IPE 3682   30, 565

1913

Act of Foundation of a Consultative Committee for the International Protection of Nature (Berne) 19 November 1913; 4 IPE 1631   29

1916

Convention for the Protection of Migratory Birds in the United States and Canada (Washington) 16 August 1916; 4 IPE 1638   28, 601

1920

Convention Regarding the Organisation of the Campaign Against Locusts (Rome) 31 October 1920; 4 IPE 1642   29

1923

Convention for the Preservation of the Halibut Fishery of the North Pacific Ocean, 2 March 1923; 32 LNTS 93   565

Convention Relative to the Development of Hydraulic Power Affecting More than One State (Geneva) 9 December 1923; 36 LNTS 76   463

1924

International Agreement for the Creation of an International Office for Dealing with Contagious Diseases of Animals (Paris) 25 January 1924   29

1925

Protocol for the Prohibition of the Use in War of Asphyxiating, Poisonous or Other Gases, and of Bacteriological Methods of Warfare (Geneva) 17 June 1925, in force 8 February 1928; 94 LNTS 65   312

1930

Convention for the Preservation of the Halibut Fishery of the North Pacific Oceans and the Bering Sea, 9 May 1930; 121 LNTS 209   565

1931

Convention for the Regulation of Whaling (Geneva) 24 September 1931, in force 16 January 1935; 155 LNTS 349   27

1933

Convention Relative to the Preservation of Fauna and Flora in their Natural State (London) 8 November 1933, in force 14 January 1936; 172 LNTS 241 (**1933 London Convention**)   28, 524

Art. 5 833
Art. 8 830, 833
Art. 9 236–7, 830, 942
Art. 12 248, 250, 830
Montevideo Convention on the Rights and Duties of States; 165 LNTS 19 71

1935
Convention for the Final Settlement of the Difficulties Arising Through the Complaints of Damage Done in the State of Washington by Fumes Discharged from the Smelter of the Consolidated Mining and Smelting Company, Trail, British Columbia, 15 April 1935; 162 LNTS 73 318, 885
Treaty on the Protection of Artistic and Scientific Institutions and Historic Monuments, in force 26 August 1935; 167 LNTS 289 611

1936
Convention for the Protection of Migratory Birds and Game Mammals (Mexico–United States), 7 February 1936; 178 LNTS 309 601

1937
International Agreement for the Regulation of Whaling (London) 8 June 1937; 190 LNTS 79 (Protocol, London, 24 June 1938, 196 LNTS 131) 592

1940
Convention on Nature Protection and Wildlife Preservation in the Western Hemisphere (Washington) 12 October 1940, in force 1 May 1942; 161 UNTS 193 (**1940 Western Hemisphere Convention**) 28, 107, 200, 527–9, 1071
Preamble 528
Art. I 943
Art. II(1) 528
Art. III 528
Art. IV 155, 528
Arts. V–VIII 528
Art. VI 250, 830
Art. VII 260
Art. IX 528, 942
Art. V 155
Annex 528

1942
Provisional Fur Seal Treaty; 156 UNTS 363 (1942) 565

1944

Treaty Relating to the Utilization of the Colorado and Tijuana Rivers, and the Rio Grande (Rio Bravo) from Fort Quitman (Texas) to the Gulf of Mexico (Washington) 3 February 1944; 3 UNTS 314   485

1946

International Convention for the Regulation of Whaling (Washington) 2 December 1946, in force 10 November 1948; 161 UNTS 72 (as amended 19 November 1956, 338 UNTS 336) (**1946 International Whaling Convention**)   16, 110, 127, 140, 181, 200, 592–5

Preamble	256, 258, 592
Art. I	592
Art. III	592
Art. V	593
Art. V(1)	141
Art. V(2)	258, 268
Art. V(3)	141
Art. VI	141
Art. VII	834
Art. VIII	593, 834
Art. VIII(1)	180
Art. VIII(3)	181
Art. IX	593, 834
Art. IX(1)	176
Art. IX(3)	176
Art. IX(4)	181
Schedule	593–5, 849

1947

General Agreement on Tariffs and Trade (Geneva) 30 October 1947, not yet in force; 55 UNTS 194 (in force provisionally since 1 January 1948 under the 1947 Protocol of Application, 55 UNTS 308) (**GATT**)   31, 136–8, 222, 944–85

1979 TBT Agreement	949–51, 974
Art. III	948, 955–60, 973–6, 998, 1000
Art. V	582
Art. VI(1)	1016–17
Art. IX	955–60
Art. XI	582, 948, 953, 955–60, 966, 973–6, 998, 1000
Art. XIII	955–60
Art. XVI(1)	1015
Art. XX	945, 948, 962, 966, 974–7, 998, 1000, 1018

Art. XX(g)   255, 582, 955–60, 998–9
Art. XXIII   973–6
Art. XXIV   999
Annex 1A   947
Annex 1B   947
Annex 1C   947
Annex 2   947

1949
Convention IV for the Protection of War Victims, Concerning Protection of
   Civilians in Time of War (Geneva) 12 August 1949, in force 21 October 1950;
   75 UNTS 287 (**1949 Geneva Convention IV**)   312
FAO Agreement for the Establishment of a General Fisheries Council for the
   Mediterranean (Rome) 24 September 1949, in force 3 December 1963;
   126 UNTS 237 (as amended 1963) (**1949 FAO Mediterranean Fisheries
   Agreement**)   95–6
   Art. IV(a)   261
   Art. IV(h)   248
   Art. XIII   203
Washington Convention for the Establishment of an Inter-American Tropical
   Tuna Commission (Washington) 30 May 1949, in force 3 March 1950; 80
   UNTS 3 (**1949 Tropical Tuna Convention**)   111, 598
   Preamble   258, 286
   Art. I(2)   833
   Art. I(16)   830
   Art. II(1)   851

1950
European Convention for the Protection of Human Rights and Fundamental
   Freedoms (Rome) 4 November 1950, in force 3 September 1953; 213 UNTS
   221 (**1950 ECHR**)   106, 225–6, 245, 294
   Art. 1   303
   Art. 2   299, 305
   Art. 3   299, 305
   Art. 5   299
   Art. 6   278, 306
   Art. 8   225, 300–3, 306
   Art. 10   302, 306
   Art. 11   306
   Art. 13   300, 305
   Art. 24   185
   Art. 28   204

Art. 31   204
Art. 33   225
Art. 34   198, 225
Protocol 1, Art. 1   225, 300, 303, 306
Protocol 9   225
International Convention for the Protection of Birds (Paris) 18 October 1950,
    in force 17 January 1963; 638 UNTS 185 (**1950 Birds Convention**)   601–2
Art. 3   942
Art. 4   942
Art. 9   942
Protocol to Establish a Tripartite Standing Committee on Polluted Waters
    (Brussels) 8 April 1950, in force 8 April 1950; 66 UNTS 285   478

1951

FAO International Plant Protection Convention (Rome) 6 December 1951,
    in force 3 April 1952; 150 UNTS 67 (**1951 International Plant Protection
    Convention**)   96, 551
    Preamble   243
    Art. I   248, 943
    Art. V   830
    Art. VI   834, 943
    Art. VII   835
    Art. IX   203
International Convention for the Establishment of the European and Mediter-
    ranean Plant Protection Organization (Paris) 18 April 1951, in force
    1 November 1953; UKTS 44 (1956) (**1951 European Plant Protection
    Convention**)   96, 551, 831
Treaty Establishing the European and Steel Community, 18 April 1951, 261
    UNTS 140   734

1952

International Convention for the High Seas Fisheries of the North Pacific Ocean
    (Tokyo) 9 May 1952, in force 12 June 1953; 205 UNTS 65 (**1952 North Pacific
    Fisheries Convention**)   111, 585
    Preamble   258
    Art. III(1)   835
    Art. IV(1)(b)   258
    Art. IV(2)   309
    Art. VIII   830
    Protocol, para. 4   203
    Protocol, para. 5   203

1953

Convention on the International Right of Correction, 16 December 1952, entered into force 24 August 1962; 435 UNTS 191   847

1954

Convention for the Protection of Cultural Property in the Event of Armed Conflict (The Hague) 14 May 1954, in force 7 August 1956; 249 UNTS 215 (**1954 Hague Convention**)   312

European Cultural Convention (Paris) 19 December 1954, in force 5 May 1955; 218 UNTS 139   611

International Convention for the Prevention of Pollution of the Sea by Oil (London) 12 May 1954, in force 26 July 1958; 327 UNTS 3 (**1954 Oil Pollution Convention**)   33, 97, 393

   Preamble   248
   Art. VI(3)   834
   Art. VIII(3)   835
   Art. IX(5)   850
   Art. XIX(1)   309

Phyto-Sanitary Convention for Africa South of the Sahara (London) 29 July 1954, in force 15 June 1956; 1 SMTE 115 (**1954 African Phyto-Sanitary Convention**)   551

   Preamble   943
   Art. 3(b)   831, 833
   Art. 9   831

1956

FAO Plant Protection Agreement for South-East Asia and the Pacific Region (Rome) 27 February 1956, in force 2 July 1956; 247 UNTS 400   96, 551

   Preamble   943
   Art. II(1)   834
   Art. III   850
   Art. IV   943
   Art. V   850
   Appendix B   943

1957

European Agreement Concerning the International Carriage of Goods by Road (Geneva) 30 September 1957, in force 20 January 1968; 619 UNTS 77, 1297 UNTS 406 (**1957 ADR**)   637, 702

Interim Convention on Conservation of North Pacific Fur Seals (Washington) 9 February 1957, in force 14 October 1957; 314 UNTS 105   565

Treaty Establishing the European Atomic Energy Authority (Rome) 25 March
     1957, in force 1 January 1958; 298 UNTS 167 (**1957 EURATOM**)   734,
     793
Treaty Establishing the European Economic Community (Rome) 25 March
     1957, in force 1 January 1958; 2989 UNTS 11 (**1957 EEC Treaty**)   734

Art. 2	748
Art. 3(8)	735
Art. 6	748, 986, 997
Art. 7	736
Art. 28	986, 987, 990–3, 995–7
Art. 30	986, 990, 995
Arts. 32–38	735, 781
Art. 36	994
Arts. 39–42	735
Arts. 43–48	735
Arts. 49–55	735
Arts. 56–69	735
Arts. 70–80	735
Art. 81	1015–16
Arts. 81–86	735
Art. 82	1016
Art. 87	1011–14
Arts. 87–89	735
Arts. 90–92	736
Art. 94	741, 742
Art. 95	744, 748, 986
Arts. 99–111	736
Arts. 131–135	736
Art. 161	746
Art. 171	789
Art. 174	743, 746, 748–50, 1037
Art. 174(1)	682
Art. 174(2)	232, 247, 271, 283, 682, 743, 991
Art. 174(5)	283
Arts. 174–176	743, 986
Art. 175	743–6, 748–50, 987
Art. 175(5)	288
Art. 176	743, 987
Art. 211	193, 736
Art. 220	222
Art. 226	194, 222, 987, 990, 994
Arts. 226–227	738
Art. 227	185, 186
Art. 228	194, 929

Art. 230   223, 224
Arts. 230–232   738
Art. 234   224, 738, 990
Art. 235   224, 738
Art. 243   194
Art. 249   175, 737
Art. 266   1029
Art. 267   1029
Art. 288   738
Art. 308   741

1958

Agreement Concerning the Adoption of Uniform Conditions of Approval for
    Motor Vehicle Equipment and Parts (Geneva) 20 March 1958, in force 20
    June 1959; 35 UNTS 211   324
Convention Concerning Fishing in the Waters of the Danube (Bucharest) 29
    January 1958, in force 20 December 1958; 339 UNTS 23 (**1958 Danube
    Convention**)   191
    Preamble   260
    Art. 7   248
    Art. 8   260, 830
    Art. 12   830
Convention on Fishing and Conservation of the Living Resources of the High
    Sea (Geneva) 29 April 1958, in force 20 March 1966; 559 UNTS 285 (**1958
    High Seas Conservation Convention**)   33, 393
    Art. 2   258
    Art. 9   200, 212
    Art. 12   212
    Art. 25   248, 684
Convention on the Continental Shelf (Geneva) 29 April 1958, in force 10 June
    1964; 499 UNTS 311 (**1958 Continental Shelf Convention**)   393
    Art. 5(5)   834, 837
    Art. 6   147, 148
Convention on the High Seas (Geneva) 29 April 1958, in force 30 September
    1962; 450 UNTS 82   33, 393, 566–7

1959

Agreement Concerning Co-operation in the Quarantine of Plants and
    their Protection Against Pests and Diseases (Sofia) 14 December 1959, in force
    19 October 1960; 1 SMTE 153 (**1959 Plant Protection Agreement**)   551,
    684
    Art. II   842
    Art. IV   830
    Art. VIII   831

Agreement for the Establishment on a Permanent Basis of a Latin American
   Forest Research and Training Institute (Rome) 18 November 1959, in force
   16 November 1960; 1 SMTE 143 (**1959 Latin American Forest Research
   Agreement**)   96, 261
Antarctic Treaty (Washington) 1 December 1959, in force 23 June 1961;
   402 UNTS 71 (**1959 Antarctic Treaty**) (*see* 1991 Antarctic Environmental
   Protocol)   33, 712–13
    Art. I(1)   310
    Art. III   830
    Art. V(1)   688
    Art. VII   848–9
    Art. VIII   839
    Art. XI(2)   216
Convention Concerning Fishing in the Black Sea (Varna) 7 July 1959, in force 21
   March 1960; 377 UNTS 203 (**1959 Black Sea Fishing Convention**)   260
North-East Atlantic Fisheries Convention (London) 24 January 1959, in force
   27 June 1963; 486 UNTS 157 (**1959 NEAFC**)   260

1960

Convention on the Protection of Lake Constance Against Pollution (Steckborn)
   27 October 1960, in force 10 November 1961; 620 UNTS 191   478
ILO Convention (No. 115) Concerning the Protection of Workers Against Ionising Radiation (Geneva) 22 June 1960, in force 17 June 1962; 431 UNTS 41
   (**1960 Radiation Convention**)   98, 646
    Art. 1   840
    Art. 3(1)   248, 268
    Art. 11   850
OECD Convention on Third Party Liability in the Field of Nuclear Energy
   (Paris) 29 July 1960, in force 1 April 1968; 956 UNTS 251 (**1960 Paris
   Convention**)   103, 281, 906–8
    Art. 1   906
    Art. 2   906
    Art. 3(a)   906
    Art. 4   907
    Art. 7(b)   907
    Art. 8   907
    Art. 9   309
    Art. 10   907
    Art. 13   197, 907

1961
European Social Charter (Turin) 18 October 1961, in force 26 February 1965;
   529 UNTS 89   106, 294, 297

Art. 3   297
Art. 11   304

International Convention for the Protection of New Varieties of Plants (Brussels) 2 December 1961, in force 10 August 1968; 15 UNTS 89 (**UPOV Convention**)   1044

Protocol Concerning the Constitution of an International Commission for the Protection of the Mosel Against Pollution (Paris) 20 December 1961, in force 1 July 1962; 940 UNTS 211   34, 478

1962

Convention Concerning the Protection of the Waters of Lake Geneva Against Pollution (Paris) 16 November 1962, in force 1 November 1963; 922 UNTS 49   478

Convention on the African Migratory Locust Organization (Kano) 25 May 1962; 486 UNTS 103 (**1962 African Migratory Locust Convention**)–
Art. 4(4)   851
Art. 7(2)(a)   833

Convention on the Liability of Operators of Nuclear Ships (Brussels) 25 May 1962, not in force; 57 AJIL 268 (1963)   906

1963

Act Regarding Navigation and Economic Co-operation Between the States of the Niger Basin (Niamey) 26 October 1963, in force 1 February 1966; 587 UNTS 9 (**1963 Niger Basin Act**)   261, 489–90

Agreement Concerning the International Commission for the Protection of the Rhine Against Pollution (Berne) 29 April 1963, in force 1 May 1965; 994 UNTS 3 (amended Bonn, 3 December 1976; IELMT 976:91) (**1963 Rhine Convention**)   34, 110, 479–80

Agreement for the Establishment of a Commission for Controlling the Desert Locust in the Eastern Region of its Distribution Area in South-West Asia (Rome) 3 December 1963, in force 15 December 1964; 1 SMTE 190 (**1963 South West Asia Locust Agreement**)   96, 831

Convention on Civil Liability for Nuclear Damage (Vienna) 29 May 1963, in force 12 November 1977; 1063 UNTS 265 (**1963 Vienna Convention**)   100, 281, 882
Art. I   908
Art. III   203
Art. IV   309, 908
Art. V   908
Art. VI   908
Art. VII   908
Art. X(1)   197
Art. XII   908

Art. XIV 908
Art. XVIII 908
Art. XL 908
Optional Protocol, Art. I 216
Nordic Mutual Emergency Assistance Agreement in Connection with Radiation Accidents, 17 October 1963, 525 UNTS 75 648
OECD Agreement supplementary to the Paris Convention of 1960 on Third Party Liability in the Field of Nuclear Energy (Brussels) 31 January 1963, in force 4 December 1974; 1041 UNTS 358 (as amended by 1964 Protocol) (**1963 Brussels Supplementary Convention**) 907
Art. 13 835
Art. 16 839
Treaty Banning Nuclear Weapon Tests in the Atmosphere, in Outer Space and under Water (Moscow) 5 August 1963, in force 10 October 1963; 480 UNTS 43 (**1963 Nuclear Test Ban Treaty**) 33, 100, 127, 319, 438, 649
Art. 1(1) 243, 248

1964

Agreement Concerning the Niger River Commission and the Navigation and Transport on the River Niger (Niamey) 25 November 1964, in force 12 April 1966; 587 UNTS 21 489

1965

Agreement for the Establishment of a Commission for Controlling the Desert Locust in the Near East (Rome) 96
Treaty Establishing a Single Council and a Single Commission of the European Communities, 8 April 1965; 4 ILM 776 (1965) 736

1966

Belgium–France Convention on Radiological Protection Relating to the Installations at the Ardennes Nuclear Power Station, 23 September 1966; 988 UNTS 288 837
International Convention for the Conservation of Atlantic Tunas (Rio de Janeiro) 14 May 1966, in force 21 March 1969; 37 UNTS 63 (**1966 Atlantic Tuna Convention**) 111, 598–9
Art. III(9) 833
Art. IV(2) 258, 830
International Convention on Load Lines (London) 5 April 1966, in force 21 July 1968; 640 UNTS 133 (Protocol of 11 November 1988, in force 3 February 2000) 444
International Covenant on Civil and Political Rights, 16 December 1966, in force 23 March 1976; Annex to UNGA Res. 2200(XXI); 6 ILM 368 (1967) (**1966 ICCPR**) 91

Art. 1(2)   297
Art. 3   305
Art. 6(1)   305
Art. 7   305
Art. 14(1)   306
Art. 17   306
Art. 25   306

International Covenant on Economic, Social and Cultural Rights, 16 December
    1966, in force 3 January 1976; Annex to UNGA Res. 2200 (XXI); 6 ILM 360
    (1967) (**1966 ICESCR**)   91
Art. 1(2)   297
Art. 7(b)   297
Art. 10(3)   297
Art. 11(1)   297
Art. 12(1)   297
Art. 12(2)(b)   297
Art. 15(1)(b)   297
Art. 17   297

1967

Agreement Between France and Belgium on Radiological Protection Concern-
    ing the Installations of the Nuclear Power Station of the Ardennes, 7 March
    1967; 588 UNTS 227   646
Treaty for the Prohibition of Nuclear Weapons in Latin America (Tlatelolco)
    14 February 1967, in force 22 April 1968; 6 ILM 52 (1967)   650
Treaty on Principles Governing the Activities of States in the Exploration and
    Use of Outer Space, including the Moon and Other Celestial Bodies (London,
    Moscow, Washington) 27 January 1967, in force 10 October 1967; 610 UNTS
    205 (**1967 Outer Space Treaty**)   178, 382–3
Art. I   286, 383
Art. II   383
Art. III   383
Art. IV   383
Art. VI   383
Art. VII   897–8
Art. VIII   383

1968

African Convention on the Conservation of Nature and Natural Resource
    (Algiers) 15 September 1968, in force 9 October 1969; 1001 UNTS 4 (**1968
    African Nature Convention**)   28, 34, 106, 524–6
Preamble   256, 258
Art. II   260, 525

Art. IV	525, 555
Art. V	525, 840
Art. VI	525
Art. VII	261, 525
Art. VIII	525
Art. IX	525, 942
Arts. XII–XV	525
Art. XIV(3)	202
Art. XVI(1)	243, 250
Art. XVII	525
Art. XVIII	203
Art. XL	525
Annex	525

Convention on Jurisdiction and Enforcement of Judgments in Civil and Commercial Matters (Brussels) 27 September 1968, in force 1 February 1973; 8 ILM 229 (1969)   197

European Convention for the Protection of Animals During International Transport (Paris) 13 December 1968; IELMT 968:92   105

European Convention on the Restriction of the Use of Certain Detergents in Washing and Cleaning Products (Strasbourg) 16 September 1968, in force 16 February 1971; 788 UNTS 181   105

Intergovernmental Conference of Experts on the Scientific Basis for the Rational Use and Conservation of the Resources of the Biosphere (**1968 Biosphere Conference**); *Yearbook of the United Nations* (1968), 958   35

Treaty on the Non-Proliferation of Nuclear Weapons (London, Moscow, Washington) 1 July 1968, in force 5 March 1970; 729 UNTS 161 (**1968 Non-Proliferation Treaty**)   641

1969

Agreement for Co-operation in Dealing with Pollution of the North Sea by Oil and other Harmful Substances (Bonn) 9 June 1969, in force 9 August 1969; 704 UNTS 3 (**1969 Bonn Agreement**)   408, 452–3

Art. 1	452
Art. 4	453
Art. 5	453, 842
Art. 6	453
Art. 7	453
Art. 8	835

American Convention on Human Rights (San Jose) 22 November 1969, in force 18 July 1978; 9 ILM 673 (1970) (**1969 ACHR**)   107, 294

Art. 4(1)	305
Art. 5	305
Art. 11	306

Art. 21 306
Art. 23 306
Art. 24 305
Art. 44 198
Art. 45 198
Convention on the Law of Treaties (Vienna) 23 May 1969, in force 27 January 1980; 8 ILM 679 (1969) (**1969 Vienna Convention**)   130
    Art. 2(1)(a) 126
    Art. 18 134
    Art. 19 135
    Art. 30 137
    Art. 30(3) 137
    Art. 30(4) 137
    Art. 31 130
    Art. 31(2) 131
    Art. 31(3) 131
European Convention on the Protection of the Archaeological Heritage (London) 6 May 1969, in force 20 November 1970; 788 UNTS 227   105, 611, 830
FAO Convention on the Conservation of the Living Resources of the South-East Atlantic (Rome) 23 October 1969, in force 24 October 1971; 801 UNTS 101 (**1969 South-East Atlantic Convention**)   96, 111
    Preamble 260
    Art. VIII 834
    Art. X(1) 175, 176
    Art. X(3) 191
International Convention on Civil Liability for Oil Pollution Damage (Brussels) 29 November 1969, in force 19 June 1975; 973 UNTS 3 (**1969 CLC**)   135, 394, 729
    Art. I(7) 248
    Art. III 202, 309
    Art. V(2) 281
    Art. IX(1) 197
International Convention Relating to Intervention on the High Seas in Cases of Oil Pollution Damage (Brussels) 29 November 1969, in force 6 May 1975; 9 ILM 25 (1970) (**1969 Intervention Convention**)   97, 394, 449, 729
    Preamble 449
    Art. I 268, 449
    Art. II 449, 919
    Art. III 449
    Art. IV 449
    Art. V 268, 449
    Art. VI 449

Art. VII	449
Art. VIII	212
Annex	212

1970

Agreement for the Establishment of a Commission for Controlling the Desert
Locust in Northwest Africa   96

Benelux Convention on the Hunting and Protection of Birds (Brussels) 10
June 1970, in force 1 July 1972; 847 UNTS 255 (**1970 Benelux Birds
Convention**)   602, 850

Patent Co-operation Treaty (Washington DC), 19 June 1970, in force 24 January
1978, 9 ILM 978   1044

1971

Agreement Concerning International Patent Classification (Strasbourg) 24
March 1971, in force 7 October 1975; UKTS 113 (1975) Cmnd 6238   1044

Convention Concerning Protection Against Hazards of Poisons arising from
Benzene (Geneva) 23 June 1971, in force 27 July 1973 (**1971 ILO Benzene
Convention**)   98, 638, 833

International Convention on the Establishment of an International Fund for
Compensation for Oil Pollution Damage (Brussels) 18 December 1971,
in force 16 October 1978; 11 ILM 284 (1972) (**1971 Oil Pollution Fund
Convention**)   133, 394, 729

Preamble	281
Art. 4(2)(a)	309
Art. 5(1)	139
Art. 15(2)	834
Protocol 1984	133

Ramsar Convention on Wetlands of International Importance especially as
Waterfowl Habitat (Ramsar) 2 February 1971, in force 21 December 1975;
996 UNTS 245 (**Ramsar Convention**); Protocol, 3 December 1982, in force
10 October 1986, 22 ILM 698 (1982); Protocol, 28 May 1987, not in force;
IELMT 997:9/13   33, 97, 110, 127, 543–5, 1030–1

Preamble	286, 607
Art. 1	543, 545
Art. 2(1)	544
Art. 2(2)	544
Art. 2(3)	237, 544
Art. 2(4)	544
Art. 2(5)	544
Art. 2(6)	261, 544
Art. 3	545
Art. 4(1)	545

Art. 4(2) 544
Art. 4(3) 545
Art. 4(4) 545
Art. 4(5) 545
Art. 5 545, 840
Art. 6(2)(d) 261
Art. 6(3) 545
Art. 7(2) 545
Art. 8 545
Treaty on the Prohibition of the Emplacement of Nuclear Weapons and Other Weapons of Mass Destruction on the Seabed and the Ocean Floor and in the Subsoil thereof, 11 February 1971, in force 18 May 1972; 955 UNTS 115 (**1971 Nuclear Weapons Treaty**) 649
Art. III(2) 839
Art. III(4) 193
Art. III(6) 847

1972

Agreement Between the United States and Canada Concerning the Water Quality of the Great Lakes (Ottawa) 15 April 1972, in force 25 April 1972; 11 ILM 694 (1972) 487, 844
Convention for the Conservation of Antarctic Seals (London) 1 June 1972, in force 11 March 1978; 11 ILM 251 (1972), 417 (**1972 Antarctic Seals Convention**) 713–14
Preamble 258
Art. 3(1) 260
Art. 6 840
Annex 268, 834
Convention for the Prevention of Marine Pollution by Dumping from Ships and Aircraft (Oslo) 15 February 1972, in force 7 April 1974; 932 UNTS 3 (**1972 Oslo Convention**) (*see* 1992 OSPAR Convention) 34, 109, 143, 394, 395, 408, 423–5
Art. 1 248
Art. 2 423
Art. 5 424
Art. 6 424
Art. 7 424
Art. 8 424
Art. 8(3) 424
Art. 9 424
Art. 10 424, 850
Art. 11 424, 835
Art. 12 424

Art. 13	424
Art. 14	424
Art. 15(1)	176
Art. 15(2)	835
Art. 15(3)	176
Art. 19(1)	423
Art. 19(2)	423
Annex IV, Rule 2	424
Annex IV, Rules 3–7	424
Annex IV, Rules 8–9	424

Convention for the Protection of Birds and Birds in Danger of Extinction and their Environment (Japan–US) (Tokyo) 4 March 1972, 25 UST 3329 601

Convention for the Protection of the World Cultural and Natural Heritage (Paris) 16 November 1972, in force 17 December 1975; 27 UST 37, 11 ILM 1358 (1972) (**1972 World Heritage Convention**) 41, 97, 111, 127, 312, 611–15

Preamble	268, 286
Art. 1	612
Art. 2	612
Art. 4	256, 612–14
Art. 5	612–14
Art. 6	243, 612
Art. 8	262, 614
Art. 11	612, 615, 834
Art. 13	615
Art. 14	614
Art. 15	1030
Arts. 15–18	615
Art. 16	614
Arts. 19–20	615
Art. 29	180, 612

Convention on International Liability for Damage Caused by Space Objects (London, Moscow, Washington) 29 March 1972, in force 1 September 1972; 961 UNTS 187 (**1972 Space Liability Convention**) 202, 896–8

Art. II	881
Art. IX	202

Convention on the International Regulations for Preventing Collisions at Sea (London) 20 October 1972, in force 15 July 1977; UKTS 77 (1977), Cmnd 6962 444

Convention on the Preservation of Marine Pollution by Dumping of Wastes and Other Matter (London, Mexico City, Moscow, Washington DC) 29 December 1972, in force 30 August 1975; 1046 UNTS 120 (**1972 London Convention**) 40, 97, 110, 127, 128, 140, 141, 181, 244, 416–22, 685, 729

Art. I	248, 416
Art. II	288
Art. III	417, 677
Art. IV(1)(a)	417
Art. IV(1)(b)	417
Art. IV(1)(c)	417
Art. V	202, 417, 840
Art. VI(1)	418, 849
Art. VI(2)	418
Art. VI(3)	418
Art. VI(4)	180, 835
Art. VII(1)	175
Art. VII(2)	176
Art. VII(3)	835
Art. VII(4)	310, 417
Art. VIII	416
Art. IX	418
Art. X	418, 455, 871, 924
Art. XI	418
Art. XII	418
Art. XIV	418
Art. XV	139, 141, 268, 418, 419
Annex I	417, 419
Annex I, para. 8	417
Annex I, para. 10	417, 686
Annex II	417, 419
Annex III	418

Convention on the Prohibition of the Development, Production and Stockpiling of Bacteriological (Biological) and Toxic Weapons, and on their Destruction (London, Washington, Moscow) 10 April 1972, in force 28 March 1975; 1015 UNTS 163 (**1972 Biological and Toxic Convention**)   193, 312

1973

Agreement Concerning the Permanent and Definitive Solution to the International Problems of the Salinity of the Colorado River, 30 August 1973; 915 UNTS 203   485

Agreement on the Conservation of Polar Bears (Oslo) 15 November 1973, in force 26 May 1976; 13 ILM 13 (1974) (**1973 Polar Bears Agreement**)   605–6, 830

Convention on Fishing and Conservation of the Living Resources in the Baltic Sea and the Belts (Gdansk) 13 September 1973, in force 28 July 1974; 12 ILM 1291 (1973) (**Baltic Sea Convention**). Amendment Protocol (Warsaw) 11 November 1982, in force 10 February 1984; 22 ILM 704   260, 263, 585

Convention on International Trade in Endangered Species of Wild Fauna and
   Flora (Washington) 3 March 1973, in force 1 July 1975; 993 UNTS 243
   (**1973 CITES**); Protocol (Bonn), 27 June 1979, in force April 1987. Protocol
   (Gabonne), 30 April 1983, not in force   8, 41, 110, 127, 128, 130, 140, 157,
   181, 505–15
      Preamble   256
      Art. I   507, 508
      Art. II   508, 509
      Art. III   508, 943
      Arts. III–V   942
      Art. IV   508, 943
      Art. V   509, 942, 943
      Art. VI   513
      Art. VII   511
      Art. VIII(1)   176, 514
      Art. IX   508
      Art. X   512, 943
      Art. XI   141, 506, 507, 509
      Art. XII   506, 507, 833
      Art. XIII   192, 515
      Art. XIV   508
      Art. XV   141, 509, 512
      Art. XVI(2)   512
      Art. XVIII   202
      Art. XXIII   511, 512
      Art. XVI(2)   512
      Art. XVIII   213
      Annex 1   510
      Annex 2a   510
      Annex 2b   510
      Annex 4   510
      Annex 6   510
      Appendix I   42, 508–9, 591
      Appendix II   508–9
      Appendix III   508–9
Convention on the Conservation of the Living Resources of the Southeast
   Atlantic (Rome) 23 October 1969, in force 24 October 1971; 801 UNTS
   101   585
Convention on the Grant of European Patents (Munich) 5 October 1973, in
   force 7 October 1977; 13 ILM 270 (1974)   1044, 1047–51
International Convention for the Prevention of Pollution by Ships (London)
   2 November 1973, not in force; 12 ILM 1319 (1973), 1434 (**MARPOL 73**)
   (*see* MARPOL 73/78)   394, 395

Art. 4(3)   834
Art. 8   835
Protocol I   835
Protocol Relating to Intervention on the High Seas in Cases of Marine Pollution
    by Substances other than Oil (London) 2 November 1973, in force 30 March
    1983; UKTS 27 (1983), Cmnd 8924 (**1973 Intervention Protocol**)   449–50
    Art. 1(1)   449
    Art. 1(2)   449
    Art. 1(3)   450
Treaty Concerning La Plata River and its Maritime Limits, 19 November 1973;
    13 ILM 251 (1974)   485

1974

Convention on the Prevention of Marine Pollution from Land-Based Sources
    (Paris) 4 June 1974, in force 6 May 1978; 13 ILM 352 (1974) (**1974 Paris
    Convention**) (*see* 1992 OSPAR Convention)   64, 109, 142, 143, 395, 408,
    428, 430–4, 728, 729, 742
        Art. 1   248
        Art. 3(c)   431
        Art. 4(1)(a)   431
        Art. 4(1)(b)   431
        Art. 4(2)   162
        Art. 4(2)(a)   431
        Art. 4(2)(b)   431
        Art. 4(3)   431
        Art. 4(4)   268, 431
        Art. 5   431
        Art. 6(2)(d)   265
        Arts. 6–11   432
        Art. 9(1)   202
        Art. 11   849
        Art. 12   176
        Art. 13   432
        Art. 15   432
        Art. 16   432
        Art. 17   432
        Art. 18(3)   432
        Art. 18(4)   432
        Art. 21   203, 212
        Annex B   212
Convention on the Protection of the Marine Environment of the Baltic Sea Area
    (Helsinki) 22 March 1974, in force 3 May 1980; 13 ILM 546 (1974) (**Baltic
    Sea Convention**)   109, 111, 395, 408, 413, 428, 728

Art. 3(2)	167
Art. 5	413
Art. 6(2)	413
Art. 6(3)	413
Art. 6(4)	835
Art. 6(6)	413
Arts. 6–10	413
Art. 18(1)	202, 213
Art. 18(2)	216

ILO Convention (No. 139) Concerning Prevention and Control of Occupational Hazards caused by Carcinogenic Substances and Agents (Geneva) 26 June 1974, in force 10 June 1976; IELMT 974:48　　638

International Convention for the Safety of Life at Sea (London) 1 November 1974, in force 25 May 1980, 1184 UNTS 2 (**1974 SOLAS**)　　444

Nordic Convention on the Protection of the Environment (Stockholm) 19 February 1974, in force 5 October 1976; 13 ILM 511 (1974) (**1974 Nordic Environmental Protection Convention**)–

Art. 3	196
Art. 4	197
Art. 5	830
Art. 6	804
Art. 10	197, 850
Art. 11	202, 205, 840
Art. 12	205
Art. 62	17

1975

Convention for the European Patent for the Common Market (Luxembourg) 15 December 1975, not in force, 15 ILM 5 (1975)　　1044

Convention on the Registration of Objects Launched to Outer Space, 14 January 1975, in force 15 September 1976; 28 UST 695 (**1975 Outer Space Registration Convention**)　　382

1976

Convention for the Protection of the Mediterranean Sea Against Pollution (Barcelona) 16 February 1976, in force 12 February 1978; 15 ILM 290 (1976) (**1976 Barcelona Convention**)　　130, 142, 214, 400, 401

Art. 2	406, 426
Art. 3	426
Arts. 3–11	454
Arts. 4–11	406
Art. 10	849
Art. 11(3)	288

Art. 12	407, 454, 455
Art. 13	407
Art. 15	407
Art. 17	407
Art. 22	213
Annex A	213, 454

Convention for the Protection of the Rhine River Against Chemical Pollution (Bonn) 3 December 1976, in force 1 February 1979; 1124 UNTS 375 (**1976 Rhine Chemical Convention**) 192, 479

Art. 2	479
Art. 3	479
Art. 4	479, 842
Art. 5	479
Art. 6	479
Art. 7(2)	479
Art. 10	849, 851
Arts. 10–12	479
Art. 15	212
Annex B	212
Annex III	479

Convention on Conservation of Nature in the South Pacific (Apia) 12 June 1976, in force 28 June 1990; IELMT 976:45 (**Apia Convention**) 108, 531–2

Preamble	257, 258, 531
Art. II	258, 260, 531
Art. III	531
Art. IV	531
Art. V	258, 261, 531, 532
Art. VI	531
Art. VII	531
Art. VIII	532
Art. XI	258
Art. XII	202

Convention on the Protection of the Rhine River Against Pollution by Chlorides (Bonn) 3 December 1976, in force 5 July 1985; 16 ILM 265 (1977) (**1976 Rhine Chloride Convention**) 285, 480

Art. 2	480
Art. 3	480, 834
Art. 4	480
Art. 5	480
Art. 7	480
Art. 9	480
Art. 11	480
Art. 12	480

Art. 13   213
Annex B   213
Annex I   480
Protocol   480–1

European Convention for the Protection of Animals Kept for Farming Purposes
(Strasbourg) 10 March 1976, in force 10 September 1978; UKTS 70 (1979),
Cmnd 7684   105, 203, 669

Protocol for Co-operation in Combating Pollution of the Mediterranean Sea
by Oil and Other Harmful Substances in Cases of Emergency (Barcelona)
16 February 1976, in force 12 February 1978 (**1976 Barcelona Oil Pollution
Protocol**)   400, 401, 453

Protocol for the Prevention of Pollution of the Mediterranean Sea by Dumping
from Ships and Aircraft (Barcelona) 16 February 1976, in force 12 February
1978 (**1976 Barcelona Dumping Protocol**)   400, 401, 426
Art. 7   427
Art. 10(2)   427
Art. 12   427
Art. 14   427
Arts. 4–7   427
Arts. 8–9   427
Annex I   310
Annex III   804

1977

Convention on Civil Liability for Oil Pollution Damage Resulting from Exploration for and Exploration of Seabed Mineral Resources (London) 1 May
1977, not yet in force; 16 ILM 1450 (1977) (**1977 CLC**)   281, 309, 923–4

Convention on the Prohibition of Military or Any Other Hostile Use of En-
vironmental Modification Techniques (New York) 18 May 1977, in force 5
October 1978; 1108 UNTS 151 (**1977 ENMOD Convention**)   111
Preamble   257
Art. 1   248, 313–14
Art. 2   17, 313–14
Art. 3   313–14, 830
Art. 5   202, 839
Annex   202

Denmark–Federal Republic of Germany Agreement Relating to Exchange of
Information on Construction of Nuclear Installations along the Border, 4
July 1977; 17 ILM 274 (1978)   646

ILO Convention Concerning the Protection of Workers Against Occupational
Hazards in the Working Environment due to Air Pollution, Noise and Vibra-
tion (Geneva) 20 June 1977, in force July 1979; 28 IPE 335 (**1977 Working
Environment Convention**)   98, 638–9

Protocol I (Additional to the 1949 Geneva Conventions) Relating to the Protection of Victims of International Armed Conflicts (Geneva) 8 June 1977, in force 7 December 1978; 16 ILM 1391 (1977) (**1977 Additional Protocol**)   311, 312, 314–15

    Art. 35   314–15
    Art. 55   314–15
    Art. 56(2)   313
    Art. 85   313

Treaty on the International Recognition of the Deposit of Micro-organisms for the Purpose of Patent Procedure (Budapest) 28 April 1977, in force 19 August 1980; 17 ILM 285 (1977)   1044

1978

Agreement Between the United States and Canada on the Water Quality of the Great Lakes (Ottawa) 22 November 1978, in force 22 November 1978; 30 UST 1383 (**1978 Great Lakes Water Quality Agreement**); Protocol signed and in force 16 October 1983; TIAS 10798   487–9

Convention on Future Multilateral Co-operation in the North-West Atlantic Fisheries (Ottawa) 24 October 1978, in force 1 January 1979; 2 SMTE 60 (**1978 Northwest Atlantic Fisheries Convention**)   111, 585

    Art. II(1)
    Art. VI(1)   839
    Art. XI(4)   850
    Art. XI(5)   84, 191, 260

Convention on the Protection of the Archaeological, Historical and Artistic Heritage of the American Nations (Santiago) 16 June 1976, in force 30 June 1978, 15 ILM 1350 (1976)   611

Federal Republic of Germany and Luxembourg Agreement on the Exchange of Information in case of Accidents which could have Radiological Consequences, 2 March 1978; 29 IPE 251   647

Kuwait Protocol Concerning Co-operation in Combating Pollution by Oil and Other Harmful Substances in Cases of Emergency (Kuwait) 23 April 1978, in force 1 July 1979; 17 ILM 526 (1978) (**Kuwait Emergency Protocol**)   402

    Art. I   453
    Arts. II–XII   454
    Art. XIII   454
    Appendix A   454

Kuwait Regional Convention for Co-operation on the Protection of the Marine Environment from Pollution (Kuwait) 23 April 1978, in force 1 July 1979; 1140 UNTS 133 (**1978 Kuwait Convention**)   402

    Preamble   256, 265
    Art. I(a)   406

Arts. III–IX	406
Art. X	407, 849
Art. XI	407, 804
Art. XII	407
Art. XIII	455, 871
Art. XVI	407
Art. XVII	407
Art. XVIII	407
Art. XXIII	407

Protocol Relating to the Convention for the Prevention of Pollution from Ships (London) 17 February 1978, in force 2 October 1983; 17 ILM 246 (1978) (**MARPOL 73/78**)   41, 97, 110, 127, 181, 440–5, 703, 729

Art. 1	248, 440
Art. 2	440
Art. 2(2)	440
Art. 2(3)	
Art. 3	440, 441
Art. 5(1)	441
Art. 5(2)	441, 850
Art. 5(4)	441
Art. 6	441, 850
Art. 8	441
Art. 10	202, 212, 441
Art. 11	441
Art. 14	441
Art. 17	441
Annex I	441–2
Annex II	442–3
Annex III	443
Annex IV	443
Annex V	443–4
Annex VI	444
Protocol I	441
Protocol II	212, 441

Treaty for Amazonian Co-operation (Brasilia) 3 July 1978, in force 2 February 1980; 17 ILM 1045 (1978) (**1978 Amazonian Treaty**)   529–30

Preamble	263, 265
Art. I	260, 529
Art. IV	244, 529
Art. V	261
Art. VII	260, 529
Art. XXV	529
Arts. XX–XXIV	529

1979

Agreement Governing the Activities of States on the Moon and Other Celestial
 Bodies (New York) 5 December 1979, in force 11 July 1984; 18 ILM 1434
 (1979) (**1979 Moon Treaty**)   382, 384

   Art. 1(1)   384
   Art. 3(1)   384
   Art. 4(1)   384
   Art. 7   384
   Art. 11   384
   Art. 12(1)   178
   Art. 14   178, 384

Convention for the Conservation and Management of the Vicuna (Lima) 20
 December 1979, in force 19 March 1982; IELMT 979:94   606

Convention on Long-Range Transboundary Air Pollution (Geneva) 13 November 1979, in force 16 March 1983; 18 ILM 1442 (1979) (**1979 LRTAP
 Convention**)   41, 109, 128, 130, 134, 244, 324–36, 728, 899

   Art. 1   325, 877
   Art. 2   248, 321–5
   Art. 3   325
   Art. 4   325
   Art. 5   202, 325, 840
   Art. 6   158, 326
   Art. 7   17, 325
   Art. 8   131, 326, 831, 899, 1039
   Art. 9   326, 849
   Art. 10   326
   Art. 11   326
   Art. 13   202
   Annex III   899

Convention on the Conservation of European Wildlife and Natural Habitats
 (Berne) 19 September 1979, in force 1 June 1982; UKTS 56 (1982), Cmnd
 8738 (**Berne Convention**)   27, 41, 106, 110, 532, 970

   Art. 1   533
   Art. 2   533
   Art. 3   533, 830
   Art. 4   533
   Art. 5   533
   Art. 6   533
   Art. 7   534
   Art. 8   534
   Art. 9(1)   534, 540
   Art. 10   533
   Art. 11   533
   Art. 12   534

Art. 13   534
Art. 14   193, 534
Art. 15   535, 833
Art. 17   535
Art. 18   213
Convention on the Conservation of Migratory Species of Wild Animals (Bonn)
    23 June 1979, in force 1 November 1983; 19 ILM 15 (1980) (**1979 Bonn
    Convention**)   41, 110, 607–11
        Preamble   257, 287, 607, 608
        Art. I(1)   608
        Art. II(1)   608
        Art. III(1)   608
        Art. III(2)   268, 608
        Art. III(4)   248, 608
        Art. III(5)   608
        Art. III(7)   608
        Art. IV   608
        Art. V   608
        Art. VI   610, 834
        Art. VII   610
        Arts. VII–IX   610
        Art. XI   268, 610
South Pacific Forum Fisheries Convention (Honiara) 10 July 1978, in force 9
    August 1979; IEL 979:57   585

1980
Agreement Between Spain and Portugal on Co-operation in Matters affecting
    the Safety of Nuclear Installation in the vicinity of the Frontier, 31 March
    1980, in force 13 July 1981   646, 837
Athens Protocol for the Protection of the Mediterranean Sea Against Pollution
    from Land-Based Resources (Athens) 17 May 1980, in force 17 June 1983;
    19 ILM 869 (1980) (**1980 Athens LBS Protocol**)   401, 436
        Art. 4(1)(b)   437
        Art. 5   436
        Art. 6   436
        Art. 9   1040
        Art. 10   1040
        Art. 12(1)   839
        Annex III   436
Convention Creating the Niger Basin Authority (Faranah) 21 November 1980,
    in force 3 December 1982; IELMT 980:86   489, 834
Convention on Future Multilateral Co-operation in the North-East Atlantic
    Fisheries (London) 18 November 1989, in force 17 March 1982; 2 SMTE
    107   111, 586

Convention on Prohibitions or Restrictions on the Use of Certain Conventional Weapons which may be Deemed to be Excessively Injurious or to have Indiscriminate Effects, 10 April 1980; 19 ILM 1523 (1980) (**1980 Inhuman Weapons Convention**)   312
    Protocol III, Art. 2(4)   312
Convention on the Conservation of Antarctic Marine Living Resources (Canberra) 20 May 1980, in force 7 April 1982; 19 ILM 841 (1980) (**1980 CCAMLR**)   111, 157, 714–15, 730
    Art. II   261
    Art. XV(2)   804
    Art. XXIV   848–9
    Art. XXV   213
    Annex   213
Convention on the Physical Protection of Nuclear Material (Vienna and New York) 3 March 1980, in force 8 February 1987; 18 ILM 1419 (1979)   100, 645
    Art. 4(5)   835
    Art. 5   830
    Art. 6   830
    Art. 17(2)   216
European Outline Convention on Transfrontier Co-operation Between Territorial Communities or Authorities (Madrid) 21 May 1980, in force 22 December 1981; ETS 106   106

1981
African Charter on Human and Peoples' Rights (Banjul) 27 June 1981, in force 21 October 1986; 21 ILM 59 (1982) (**1981 African Charter**)   106, 198
    Art. 3(2)   305
    Art. 4   305
    Art. 5   305
    Art. 7(1)   305
    Art. 9(1)   306
    Art. 13   306
    Art. 14   306
    Art. 16(1)   297
    Art. 20(1)   297
    Art. 21   297
    Art. 24   298
    Art. 26   305
Agreement for the Protection and Conservation of the Vicuna (Buenos Aires) 2 February 1981   606
Agreement on Regional Co-operation in Combating Pollution of the South-East Pacific by Hydrocarbon or Other Harmful Substances in Cases

of Emergency (Lima) 12 November 1981, in force 14 July 1986; IELMT
981:85   403

    Art. I   453
    Art. III   453
    Arts. IV–XI   454
    Art. XII   454
    1983 Protocol   403
Convention for Co-operation in the Protection and Development of the Marine
and Coastal Environment of the West and Central African Region (Abidjan)
23 March 1981, in force 5 August 1984; 20 ILM 746 (1981) (**1981 Abidjan
Convention**)   403

    Art. 2(1)   406
    Art. 4(1)   261, 288, 407
    Art. 10   406
    Art. 11   407
    Art. 13   407, 804
    Art. 14   261, 407
    Art. 15   455
    Art. 16   407
    Art. 17   407
    Art. 22   407
Convention for the Protection of the Marine Environment and Coastal Area
of the South-East Pacific (Lima) 12 November 1981, in force 19 May 1986;
IELMT 981:85 (**1981 Lima Convention**)   403

    Art. 2(a)   406
    Art. 3(1)   261
    Art. 3(5)   244
    Arts. 3–6   406
    Art. 5   406
    Art. 8   804
    Art. 11   455
    Art. 12   407
    Art. 13   407
ILO Convention Concerning Occupational Safety and Health and the Working
Environment (Geneva) 22 June 1981, in force 11 August 1983; 2 SMTE 126
(**1981 ILO Occupational Safety Convention**)   98, 840, 850
Protocol Concerning Co-operation in Combating Pollution in Cases of Emergency (Abidjan) 23 March 1981, in force 5 August 1584; 20 ILM 756 (1981)
(**1981 Abidjan Emergency Protocol**)   403

    Art. 1   453
    Arts. 4–10   454
    Art. 7   835
    Art. 10(1)(b)   840

Art. 11   454
Annex   835

1982

Austria–Czechoslovakia Agreement on Questions of Common Interest in relation to Nuclear Facilities, 18 November 1982, in force 1 June 1984   837

Benelux Convention on Nature Conservation and Landscape Protection and
Natural Resources (Brussels) 8 June 1982, in force 1 October 1983; 2 SMTE
163 (**1982 Benelux Conservation Convention**)   535

Convention for the Protection of Salmon in the North Atlantic Ocean (Reykjavik) 2 March 1982, in force 1 October 1983; EEC OJ (1982) L 378   111,
191, 260, 586

Protocol Concerning Mediterranean Specially Protected Areas (Geneva) 3
April 1982, in force 23 March 1986; IELMT 982:26 (**1982 Geneva SPA
Protocol**)   401, 840, 860

Protocol Concerning Regional Co-operation in Combating Pollution by Oil
and Other Harmful Substances in Case of Emergency (Jeddah) 14 February
1982, in force 20 August 1985; IELMT 982:14 (**1982 Jeddah Emergency
Protocol**)   404

Art. I(1)   453
Art. I(5)   453
Arts. II–XI   454
Art. XIII   454

Regional Convention for the Conservation of the Red Sea and Gulf of Aden
Environment (Jeddah) 14 February 1982, in force 20 August 1985; 9 EPL 56
(1982) (**1982 Jeddah Convention**)   204, 403

Art. I   256, 261, 406
Arts. III–IX   406
Art. X   407
Art. XI   407, 804
Art. XII   407
Art. XIII   455, 871
Arts. XVI–XX   408
Art. XXII   407

United Nations Convention on the Law of the Sea (Montego Bay) 10 December 1982, in force 16 November 1994; 21 ILM 1261 (1982) (**1982
UNCLOS**)   41, 110, 127, 130, 134, 395–9, 416, 428, 445, 454, 568–73,
712, 729

Preamble   260, 287, 288, 396
Art. 1   179, 398, 877, 900
Art. 2   13, 569
Art. 3   569
Art. 5   17

Art. 8	13
Art. 16	137
Art. 19(2)	569
Art. 21	397, 569, 860
Art. 24	860
Art. 33	14
Art. 42(1)(b)	397
Art. 48	13
Art. 49	570
Art. 51(1)	570
Art. 52(1)	570
Art. 54	397
Art. 56	397, 570
Art. 58(1)	397
Art. 61	258, 260, 570, 831
Art. 62	260, 570, 571
Art. 63	571
Art. 64	258, 571, 583
Art. 65	571, 573, 591, 596
Art. 66	571
Art. 67	571
Art. 68	571
Art. 69	571
Art. 70	571
Art. 76	14
Art. 77	14, 570
Art. 78	570
Art. 87	583
Art. 89	583
Art. 92	565
Art. 116	572
Arts. 116–119	582
Art. 117	572
Art. 118	572
Art. 119	260, 572
Art. 120	571, 573, 591
Art. 123	250, 251, 398
Art. 136	179
Art. 139	180, 899
Art. 142(2)	840
Art. 143	831
Art. 145	180, 446
Art. 150(b)	260

Art. 161(1)(e)	263
Art. 162	192, 446–7
Art. 165(2)	192, 839
Art. 169(1)	839
Art. 176	192
Arts. 186–191	219
Art. 187	220
Art. 192	397
Arts. 192–237	726
Art. 193	244–5, 397
Art. 194	183
Art. 194(1)	248, 397
Art. 194(2)	244, 398
Art. 194(3)	17, 398
Art. 194(5)	398
Art. 195	167, 398
Art. 196	398
Art. 197	250, 251, 398
Art. 198	398, 842
Art. 199	398
Art. 200	398, 831
Art. 202	398, 1040
Art. 203	398
Art. 204(1)	849
Arts. 204–206	398
Art. 205	805–6
Art. 206	805–6
Art. 207	288, 429
Arts. 207–212	398
Art. 208(5)	445
Art. 210	416
Art. 211	397, 439
Art. 212	437, 438
Art. 213	175
Arts. 213–233	399
Art. 214	175
Art. 216	175
Art. 217	178
Art. 218	178, 179
Art. 219	178, 179
Art. 220	178, 179
Art. 221	179
Art. 222	175

Art. 226(1)	850
Art. 235	399, 900, 939
Art. 235(2)	175
Art. 235(3)	871
Art. 236	399
Art. 237	399
Art. 244	831
Art. 266	1040
Art. 268	1040
Art. 269	1040
Arts. 270–278	1040
Art. 281(1)	138
Art. 284	203
Art. 287	219
Art. 292	220
Art. 297	219
Art. 298	219
Art. 309	134
Art. 310	136
Annex III	446, 899
Annex V	203
Annex VI	219
Annex VII	213

1983

Agreement Between the Federal Republic of Germany and the German Democratic Republic on Principles Covering Damage at the Border, September 1983   844

Agreement for Co-operation in Dealing with Pollution of the North Sea by Oil and other Harmful Substances (Bonn) 13 September 1983, in force 1 September 1989; Misc 26 (1983) 9104   408, 453

Art. 1	453
Art. 3(2)	453
Art. 4(e)	453
Art. 5(3)	453
Arts. 9–15	453
Art. 19(2)	453

Convention for the Protection and Development of the Marine Environment of the Wider Caribbean Region (Cartagena de Indias) 24 March 1983, in force 11 October 1986; 22 ILM 221 (1983) (**1983 Cartagena Convention**)   404

Arts. 3–11	406
Art. 4(1)	261
Art. 12	407, 804

Art. 13   407, 1040
Art. 14   455, 871
Art. 15   407
Art. 16   407
Art. 22   407
Art. 23   213
Annex   213
International Tropical Timber Agreement (Geneva) 18 November 1983, in force
  1 April 1985; UN Doc. TD/TIMBER/II/Rev.1 (1984) (**1983 ITTA**)–
Art. 1   237, 258
Art. 14(1)   839
Art. 27   834
Art. 28   833
Protocol Concerning Co-operation in Combating Oil Spills in the Wider
  Caribbean Region (Cartagena de Indias) 24 March 1983, in force 11 Oc-
  tober 1986; 22 ILM 240 (1983) (**Cartagena Oil Spills Protocol**)   404
Preamble   256
Art. 1   453
Art. 2   453
Arts. 3–9   454
Art. 4   830
Art. 10   454
Protocol for the Protection of the South East Pacific Against Pollution from
  Land Based Sources (Quito) 22 July 1983, in force 23 September 1986; IELMT
  983:54   403, 436
Arts. I–III   454
Art. II   437
Art. IV   436
Art. V   436
Arts. VI–XII   437
Art. IX   830
Art. XII   839
Art. XV   437
Art. XL   244
Annex III   436

1984

International Convention on Standards of Training, Certification and Watchkeeping for Seafarers (London) 7 July 1978, in force 28 April 1984, UKTS 50
  (1984) Cmnd 9266   445
Protocol for Long Term Financing of the Co-operative Programmes for Monitoring and Evaluating the Long-Range Transmission of Air Pollutants in
  Europe (EMEP) (Geneva) 28 September 1984, in force 28 January 1988; 2
  SMTE 285 (**1984 EMEP Protocol**)   326–7

Art. 2	327
Art. 3	327
Art. 4	327
Annex	327

1985

Agreement of Co-operation Between the United States of America and the United Mexican States Regarding Pollution of the Environment along the Inland International Boundary by Discharges of Hazardous Substances, 18 July 1985, in force 29 November 1985; 26 ILM 19 (1987)   621

Association of South East Asian Nations Agreement on the Conservation of Nature and Natural Resources (Kuala Lumpur) 9 July 1985, not in force; 15 EPL 64 (1985) (**1985 ASEAN Agreement**)   46, 108, 133, 540–2

Preamble	257
Art. 1	258, 541
Art. 2	265, 541
Art. 3	541
Art. 4	541
Art. 5	541
Art. 6	541, 542
Arts. 6–9	541
Art. 7	555
Art. 9	258
Art. 10	284, 542
Art. 11	248, 408, 542
Art. 12(1)	258
Arts. 12–14	542
Art. 13	408, 542
Art. 14(1)	804
Arts. 15–17	542
Art. 16	860
Art. 18(2)	839
Arts. 18–19	542
Art. 19(2)	542, 840
Art. 20	199, 542, 843
Art. 21	542
Arts. 21–23	542
Art. 25	542
Art. 26	542

Convention for the Protection, Management and Development of the Marine and Coastal Environment of the East African Region (Nairobi) 21 June 1985, not in force; IELMT 985:46 (**1985 Nairobi Convention**)   404

Preamble	257
Art. 2(b)	406

Arts. 3–12	406
Art. 4(1)	261
Art. 10	407
Art. 12	407
Art. 13	407, 804, 840
Art. 14	407, 1040
Art. 15	455
Art. 16	407
Art. 17	407
Art. 23	407

Convention for the Protection of the Ozone Layer (Vienna) 22 March 1985, in force 22 September 1988; 26 ILM 1529 (1985) (**1985 Vienna Convention**) (*see* 1987 Montreal Protocol)   6, 83, 109, 127, 128, 130, 133, 244, 343–5

Preamble	268, 288
Art. 1	18, 344, 877
Art. 2(1)	344, 345
Art. 2(2)	248, 250, 288, 345, 532
Art. 2(3)	345
Art. 3	345, 849
Art. 4	345, 1041
Art. 5	345
Art. 6	345
Art. 6(4)	345
Art. 7	345
Art. 8	139, 345
Art. 9	139, 345
Art. 10	345
Art. 10(2)	140
Art. 10(3)	140
Art. 11	201, 204, 213
Art. 11(1)	202
Art. 11(2)	203
Art. 11(3)	136, 216
Art. 11(4)	203
Art. 11(5)	203
Art. 16(1)	345
Art. 18	134
Art. 73	308
Annex I	345, 849
Annex II	345, 1041

ILO Convention No. 155 Concerning Occupational Health Services (Geneva) 22 June 1985, in force 17 February 1988, 2 SMTE 126   98, 639, 804, 854

Protocol Concerning Co-operation in Combating Pollution in Cases of Emergency (Nairobi) 21 June 1985, not in force; IELMT 985:48 (**1985 Nairobi Emergency Protocol**)   405
> Art. 1(d)–(g)   454
> Art. 2   454
> Arts. 3–9   454
> Art. 10   454

Protocol Concerning Protected Areas and Wild Fauna and Flora in the Eastern African Region (Nairobi) 21 June 1985, not in force; IELMT 985:47 (**1985 Nairobi Protocol**)   404, 526–7

Protocol to the 1979 Convention on LRTAP on the Reduction of Sulphur Emissions or their Transboundary Fluxes by at Least 30 Per Cent (Helsinki) 8 July 1985, in force 2 September 1987; 27 ILM 1077 (1987)   51, 64, 156, 478
> Art. 2   327, 878
> Art. 4   327, 834
> Art. 5   327
> Art. 6   327

South Pacific Nuclear Free Zone Treaty (Rarotonga) 6 August 1985, in force 11 December 1986; 24 ILM 1142 (1985) (**1985 Rarotonga Treaty**)   108, 205, 427, 650–1, 685, 839

1986

Canada–US Agreement Concerning the Transboundary Movement of Hazardous Waste (Ottawa) 28 October 1986, in force 8 November 1986; TIAS 11099   680, 691, 697, 1065

Convention for the Protection of the Natural Resources and Environment of the South Pacific Region (Noumea) 25 November 1986, in force 22 August 1990; 26 ILM 38 (1987) (**1986 Noumea Convention**)   108, 405, 426
> Art. 2   426
> Art. 2(b)   426
> Art. 2(c)   426
> Art. 2(f)   406
> Art. 2(g)   407
> Arts. 3–9   454
> Arts. 4–6   427
> Arts. 4–9   406
> Art. 5(1)   248
> Arts. 9–10   427
> Art. 10   310, 407, 454, 840
> Art. 11   407, 688
> Art. 12   407
> Art. 13   406

Art. 14   407
Art. 15   406
Art. 16   407, 804, 813
Art. 17   407, 1040
Art. 18   407, 1040
Art. 19   407
Art. 20   455, 871
Art. 21   407
Art. 22   407
Art. 26   213
Annex   213, 310
Convention on Assistance in the Case of a Nuclear Accident or Radiological
    Emergency (Vienna) 26 September 1986, in force 26 February 1987; 25 ILM
    1377 (1986) (**IAEA Assistance Convention**)   100, 448, 647–8
    Art. 2   840
    Art. 6(2)   853
    Art. 11   840
    Art. 13   213
Convention on Early Notification of Nuclear Accidents (Vienna) 26 September
    1986, in force 27 October 1986; 25 ILM 1370 (1986) (**1986 Notification
    Convention**)   100, 448, 845–7, 853
    Art. 6   840
    Art. 11   213
European Convention for the Protection of Animals during International
    Transport (Paris) 30 December 1986, ETS No. 65; Protocol (Strasbourg)
    10 May 1979, ETS No. 103   669
ILO Convention No. 162 Concerning Safety in the Use of Asbestos (Geneva)
    24 June 1986, in force 16 June 1989, 2 SMTE 359 (**1986 ILO Asbestos
    Convention**)   98, 639, 684
    Art. 1(2)   804
    Art. 20   850, 854
    Art. 22   860
Mexico–United States Agreement for Co-operation on Environmental Pro-
    grammes and Transboundary Problems (Washington), 12 November 1986,
    in force 29 January 1987; 26 ILM 25 (1987)   680, 697
Protocol Concerning Co-operation in Combating Pollution Emergencies
    (Noumea) 25 November 1986, in force 22 August 1990; IELMT 986:87B
    (**1986 Noumea Pollution Emergencies Protocol**)   405, 454
Protocol for the Prevention of Pollution of the South Pacific Region by Dumping
    (Noumea) 25 November 1986, in force 22 August 1990; IELMT 986:87A
    (**1986 Noumea Dumping Protocol**)   405
    Art. 7   427
    Art. 8   427
    Art. 11(2)   427

Art. 14	427
Art. 16	427
Annex IV	427

Single European Act (Luxembourg) 17 February 1986 (The Hague) 28 February 1986, in force 1 July 1987; 25 ILM 503 (1986) (**1986 SEA**)   739, 742–5

1987

Agreement on the Action Plan for the Environmentally Sound Management of the Common Zambezi River System (Harare) 28 May 1987, in force 28 May 1987; 27 ILM 1109 (**1987 Zambezi Action Plan Agreement**)   490–1

Finland and USSR Agreement on Early Notification of a Nuclear Accident and on Exchange of Information Relating to Nuclear Facilities, 7 January 1987; IAEA LegSer No. 15   647

Protocol on Substances that deplete the Ozone Layer (Montreal) 16 September 1987, in force 1 January 1989; 26 ILM 154 (1987) (**Montreal Protocol**)   6, 9, 51, 78, 83, 109, 127, 128, 141, 157, 181, 187, 343, 345–57

Preamble	248, 263, 268, 346
Art. 1P	289
Art. 1T	180
Art. 2	348
Art. 2(1)	348, 351
Art. 2(2)	349
Art. 2(3)	351
Art. 2(4)	351
Art. 2(5)	351
Art. 2(6)	351
Art. 2(7)	162
Art. 2(8)	352
Art. 2(9)	348
Art. 2A(3)	349
Art. 2A(4)	349
Art. 2A(5)	349
Art. 2A(6)	349
Art. 2A(7)	349
Art. 2A(8)	349
Art. 2B(1)	349
Art. 2B(2)	349
Art. 2B(3)	349
Art. 2B(4)	349
Art. 2C	349, 350
Art. 2D	350
Art. 2E	350
Art. 2F	350, 351
Art. 2G	351

Art. 2H   351
Art. 3   346
Art. 4   352, 353, 942, 943, 945
Art. 4(1)   136
Art. 4(2)   352
Art. 4(3)   352
Art. 4(4)   352
Art. 4(5)   352
Art. 4(6)   352
Art. 4(7)   352
Art. 4(8)   352
Art. 4B   353
Art. 5   354
Art. 5(1)   289, 351, 354
Art. 6   348
Art. 7   180, 356, 834
Art. 8   357
Art. 9   1041
Art. 9(1)   689, 831
Art. 9(2)   859–60
Art. 9(a)   139
Art. 9(c)   139
Art. 9(d)   139
Art. 10   354–6, 1031–2, 1041
Art. 10A   1041
Art. 10(a)   139
Art. 10(b)   139
Art. 11   356
Art. 12   357
Art. 14   131
Art. 16(1)   133
Art. 18   134
Annex A   348
Annex B   348
Annex C   348
Annex D   348
Annex E   348

1988

Additional Protocol to the ACHR on Economic, Social and Cultural Rights
   (San Salvador) 17 November 1988, not in force; 28 ILM 161 (1989)   294,
   298

Agreement on the Network of Aquaculture Centres in Asia and the
   Pacific   204

Canada–US Free Trade Agreement (Ottawa) 2 January 1988, in force 1 January
1989; 27 ILM 281 (1988)   107, 997–9

Convention Concerning Safety and Health in Construction (Geneva) 20 June
1988, in force 11 January 1991; 2 SMTE 440   639–40, 684, 860

Convention on Jurisdiction and Enforcement of Judgments in Civil and Commercial Matters (Lugano) 16 September 1988, in force 1 January 1992; OJ
1988 L 319/9   198

Convention on the Regulation of Antarctic Mineral Resource Activities
(Wellington) 2 June 1988, not in force; 27 ILM 868 (1988) (**1988
CRAMRA**)   41, 133, 665, 716–21, 900, 931–2

Art. 1	716, 718, 876–7, 931
Art. 2	310, 716, 717, 804
Art. 4	717, 804
Art. 5	716, 717
Art. 7	175, 192
Art. 8	881, 931–2
Art. 8(2)	719, 900
Art. 8(4)	309
Art. 8(10)	178, 721
Art. 10	193
Art. 11	193, 849
Art. 12	192, 193, 720, 849
Art. 13	717
Art. 15	718
Art. 16	720
Art. 18(2)	718
Arts. 18–22	718
Art. 19(2)	719
Art. 21(1)	718, 721
Art. 23(2)	718
Arts. 23–27	718
Art. 25(3)	721
Art. 26	717
Art. 28	718
Art. 29(2)	718
Arts. 29–32	718
Art. 31(1)	192
Art. 33	718
Art. 34	721
Art. 37	717–19, 721
Art. 38(1)	719
Art. 39	717, 719
Art. 41	719
Art. 43	720

Art. 44 717, 720

Art. 47 720, 721

Art. 48 720

Art. 49 720

Art. 51 720

Art. 52 720, 851

Art. 53 717, 720, 721

Art. 54 720

Arts. 55–59 213, 721

Art. 57 839

Art. 62(1) 716

Annex 721

Joint Protocol Relating to the Application of the Vienna Convention and the Paris Convention (Vienna) 21 September 1988, in force 27 April 1992; 42 *Nuclear Law Bulletin* 56 (1988) (**1988 Joint Protocol**) 912

Protocol Concerning the Control of Emissions of Nitrogen Oxides or their Transboundary Fluxes (Sofia) 31 October 1988, in force 14 February 1991; 28 ILM 214 (1988) (**1988 NO^x Protocol**) 181, 328–9

Preamble 328

Art. 2 156, 158

Art. 2(1) 328

Art. 2(2) 328

Art. 2(3)(a) 329

Art. 2(3)(b) 329

Art. 2(4) 329

Art. 3 329, 830, 1039

Art. 4 329, 834

Art. 6 329, 804

Art. 7 329

Art. 8 329

Art. 9 329

Art. 10 328

Technical Annex 328

Sweden–USSR Agreement on Early Notification of a Nuclear Accident and on Exchange of Information Relating to Nuclear Facilities, 1 January 1988, IAEA LegSer No. 15, 407 647

1989

African, Caribbean and Pacific States–European Community: Fourth Lomé Convention (Lomé) 15 December 1989, in force 1 September 1991; 29 ILM 783 (1990) (**1989 Lomé Convention**) 41, 691, 695, 753

Art. 4 259, 265, 437, 1022

Arts. 7–13 437

Art. 14   250, 437
Art. 15   437
Art. 33   254
Art. 34   265
Art. 35   247
Art. 39   680, 943
Convention for the Prohibition of Fishing with Long Driftnets in the South
    Pacific (Wellington) 24 November 1989, in force 17 May 1991; 29 ILM 1454
    (1990) (**1989 Wellington Convention**)   108, 157, 588–9
Convention on Civil Liability for Damage caused during Carriage of Dangerous
    Goods by Road, Rail and Inland Navigation Vessels (Geneva) 10 October
    1989, not in force; UN Doc. ECE/TRANS/79 (**1989 CRTD**)   930
Convention on the Control of Transboundary Movement of Hazardous Wastes
    and their Disposal (Basel) 22 March 1989, in force 1992; 28 ILM 657 (1989)
    (**Basel Convention**)   83, 111, 127, 128, 133, 135, 207, 631, 691–5, 712,
    992, 1065
Art. 1   679–80
Art. 2   158, 677, 682
Art. 3   834
Art. 4   692–3, 834, 943
Art. 4(1)   943
Art. 4(2)   158, 682, 804
Art. 4(4)   175, 176
Art. 4(6)   726
Art. 4A   695
Art. 5   175
Art. 6   693, 696
Art. 7   696
Art. 8   693
Art. 9   176, 696
Art. 10   682, 689, 860
Art. 11   694
Art. 12   694, 905
Art. 13   694, 834
Art. 13(1)   835, 843
Art. 13(2)   181
Art. 13(3)   180
Art. 14   1030
Art. 15   694
Art. 16   694
Art. 17   139
Art. 19   187
Art. 20   201, 213, 216

Art. 26(1)   134
Annex IV(B)   689
Annex V(A)   804
Annex VI   213
Annex VII   695
Convention on the Rights of the Child (New York) 20 November 1989, in force 2 September 1990; 29 ILM 1340 (1990)   299, 859–60
ILO Convention (No. 169) Concerning Indigenous and Tribal Peoples in Independent Countries (Geneva) 27 June 1989, not yet in force; 28 ILM 1382 (1989)–
Art. 2   299
Art. 3   299
Art. 4(1)   299
Art. 6   306
Art. 7   299, 306
Art. 11   306
International Convention on Salvage (London) 28 April 1989, not yet in force; IMO/LEG/Conf.7/27   450–1
Art. 9   450
Art. 12   450
Art. 13(1)(b)   450
Art. 14   450–1
Lima Convention for the Establishment of a Latin American Tuna Organization or Convention Establishing the Eastern Pacific Tuna Organization (Lima) 21 July 1989, not yet in force   598
Protocol Concerning Marine Pollution resulting from Exploration and Exploitation of the Continental Shelf (Kuwait) 29 March 1989, in force 17 February 1990 (**Kuwait Exploration Protocol**)   402, 448
Protocol for the Conservation and Management of Protected Marine and Coastal Areas of the South-East Pacific (Paipa) 21 September 1989, in force 1994 IELMT 989:71 (**1989 Paipa SPA Protocol**)   403
Protocol for the Protection of the South-East Pacific Against Radioactive Contamination (Paipa) 21 September 1989, not in force; IELMT 989:70 (**1989 Paipa Radioactive Contamination Protocol**)   403, 426

1990

Adjustments and Amendments to the 1987 Montreal Protocol (London) 29 June 1990, in force 10 August 1992; 30 ILM 537 (1991) (**1990 Montreal Amendments and Adjustments**)   131, 344, 346–7
Preamble   347
Art. 1(4)   347
Art. 1(5)   347
Art. 1(9)   347

Art. 4(1)   353
Art. 4(1bis)   353
Art. 4(2)   353
Art. 4(3)   137
Art. 4(4bis)   137
Art. 4(9)   353
Annex B   348
Annex C   348
Agreement Establishing the European Bank for Reconstruction and Development (London) 29 May 1990, in force 1991; 29 ILM 1077 (1990)   831, 833
Agreement on Conservation of Seals in the Wadden Sea Area (Bonn), 16 October 1990, in force 1 October 1991   605, 609
Convention Concerning Safety in the use of Chemicals at Work (ILO No. 170) (Geneva) 25 June 1990, not in force   98, 626, 640–1, 684
Convention of the International Commission for the Protection of the Elbe (Magdeburg) 8 October 1990; IELMT 990:75   478
International Convention on Oil Pollution Preparedness, Response and Co-operation (London) 30 November 1990, in force 13 May 1995; 30 ILM 733 (1991) (**Oil Pollution Preparedness Convention**)   97, 451–2, 729
  Preamble   284, 451
  Art. 1(1)   451
  Art. 3   451
  Art. 4   451
  Art. 5   451
  Art. 6   451
  Art. 7   451
  Art. 11   452
  Annex   452
Protocol Concerning Pollution from Land-Based Sources (Kuwait) 20 February 1990, in force 1993 (**1990 Kuwait LBS Protocol**)   402, 436
Protocol Concerning Specially Protected Areas and Wildlife in the Wider Caribbean Region (Kingston) 18 January 1990, in force 18 June 2000; 1 *Yearbook of International Environmental Law* 441 (1990) (**1990 Kingston SPA Protocol**)   404, 530–1

1991

Agreement Between the Government of the United States of America and the Government of Canada on Air Quality (Ottawa) 13 March 1991, in force 13 March 1991; 30 ILM 676 (1991)   339–1
  Art. II   339
  Art. III(1)   339
  Art. IV(2)   340

Art. V   341
Art. VI   341
Art. VII   341
Art. VIII   341
Art. IX   341
Art. XI   341
Art. XIV(3)   341
Annex I, section 1A   340
Annex I, section 1B   340
Annex I, section 2A   340
Annex I, section 2B   340
Annex I, section 3   340
Annex I, section 4   340
Annex II   341
Agreement on the Conservation of Populations of European Bats (London)
    4 December 1991, in force 16 January 1994   609
Convention on Environmental Impact Assessment in a Transboundary Context
    (Espoo) 25 February 1991, in force 10 September 1997; 30 ILM 802 (1991)
    (**1991 Espoo Convention**)   42, 111, 134, 187, 471, 803, 814–17
    Preamble   248
    Art. 1   17, 814
    Art. 2   248, 814, 815, 817
    Art. 3   205, 815, 837
    Art. 4   816
    Art. 5   816, 840
    Art. 6   816
    Art. 16   733
    Art. 17   733
    Art. 18(2)   733
    Appendix I   687, 815
    Appendix II   816
    Appendix IV   205, 816
Convention on the Ban of Import into Africa and the Control of Transboundary
    Movement and Management of Hazardous Wastes within Africa (Bamako)
    29 January 1991, in force April 1998 30 ILM 775 (1991) (**1991 Bamako
    Convention**)   106, 111, 631, 691, 695
    Art. 1   677, 683
    Art. 2   637, 680
    Art. 4   943
    Art. 4(1)   637, 696
    Art. 4(2)   685, 686
    Art. 4(3)   158, 270, 683, 696, 924–6
    Art. 5(4)   696

Art. 6(6)   696
Art. 7   696
Art. 9   176, 696
Art. 10   689
Art. 15   696
Art. 16   696
Art. 19   696
Art. 20   696
Convention on the Protection of the Alps (Salzburg) 7 November 1991, not in
    force; 31 ILM 767 (1992)   535–6
    Art. 2(1)   250, 284
    Art. 2(d)   247
    Protocol   555
Protocol on Environmental Protection to the Antarctic Treaty (Madrid)
    4 October 1991, in force 14 January 1998; 30 ILM 1461 (1991)   131, 157,
    665, 721–6, 731, 804, 818–19, 932
    Preamble   723
    Art. 2   723
    Art. 3   17, 723, 819
    Art. 4   723, 819
    Art. 7   722
    Art. 8   723, 818
    Art. 9(1)   723
    Art. 10   725
    Art. 11   725
    Art. 12   725
    Art. 13   175, 726
    Art. 14   849
    Art. 15   726
    Art. 16   726, 932
    Art. 17   726
    Arts. 18–20   726
    Art. 24   721
    Art. 25   722
    Annex I   723, 818
    Annex II   723
    Annex III   687, 688, 723–4
    Annex IV   724
    Annex V   724–5
Protocol on the Control of Emissions of Volatile Organic Compounds and their
    Transboundary Fluxes (Geneva) 18 November 1991, in force 29 September
    1997; 31 ILM 568 (1992)   207, 288, 329–32
    Art. 2   878

Art. 2(2) 136
Art. 2(2)(a) 330
Art. 2(2)(b) 330
Art. 2(2)(c) 330
Art. 2(3)(a) 331
Art. 2(3)(b) 331
Art. 2(4) 331
Art. 2(5) 331
Art. 2(6) 331
Art. 2(7) 331
Art. 3(1) 331
Art. 3(2) 331
Art. 3(3) 332
Art. 4 332, 1039
Art. 5 332
Art. 6 332
Art. 7 332
Art. 8 332
Annex II 331
Annex III 331
Annex IV 331
Treaty Establishing the African Economic Community (Abuja) 3 June 1991, not in force; 30 ILM 1241 (1991)   1007–8

1992
Adjustments and Amendments to the 1987 Montreal Protocol (Copenhagen) 23–25 November 1992, not yet in force; 32 ILM 874 (1993)   344
Agreement on the Conservation of Small Cetaceans of the Baltic and North Seas (New York) 17 March 1992, in force 29 March 1994 (**1992 ASCOBANS**)   595–6, 609
Agreement on the European Economic Area (Oporto) 20 May 1992, in force 1 January 1994; OJ L1, 3 January 1994, 3 (**1992 EEA Agreement**)   252, 283, 733, 747
Agreement on the North Atlantic Marine Mammals Conservation Organization (NAMMCO) (Nuuk, Greenland), 9 April 1992, in force 7 July 1992   596
Convention for the Conservation of Anadromous Fish Stocks in the North Pacific Ocean (Moscow) 11 February 1992, in force 16 February 1993   585
Convention for the Protection of the Marine Environment of the North-East Atlantic (Paris) 22 September 1992, not in force; 32 ILM 1068 (1993) (**1992 OSPAR Marine Environment Convention**)   18, 109, 110, 127, 129, 300, 395, 408–12, 425–6, 428, 434–6, 447
    Preamble 258, 410, 569

Art. 1(o)	425, 678
Art. 2	232
Art. 2(1)	410
Art. 2(2)	271, 284, 411
Art. 2(3)(b)	158, 411
Art. 3	434
Art. 3(2)	426, 685
Art. 3(3)(a)	426
Art. 3(3)(b)	426
Art. 3(3)(c)	426
Arts. 3–7	411
Art. 3(a)	410
Art. 4	425, 426
Art. 5	426, 447
Art. 6	411, 849
Art. 7	426
Art. 8	411, 425, 447
Art. 9	213, 411, 447, 856–7
Art. 10	411, 426, 447
Art. 11(1)	113
Art. 11(2)	113
Art. 11(3)	113
Art. 12	411
Art. 13	411
Art. 21(2)	411
Art. 22	411, 834
Art. 23	193, 411
Art. 24	411
Art. 32	213, 411
Annex I	434
Annex I, Art. 1	435
Annex I, Art. 2	435
Annex I, Art. 3	435
Annex II	425–6
Annex II, Art. 3	273
Annex III	425, 447
Annex IV	849
Annex IV, Art. 1	411, 848
Annex IV, Art. 2	411
Annex IV, Art. 3	412
Appendix 1	158
Appendix 2	435

Convention on Biological Diversity (Rio de Janeiro) 5 June 1992, in force 29 December 1993; 31 ILM 822 (1992) (**Biodiversity Convention**)   9, 28, 53, 83, 110, 127, 128, 180, 182, 263, 515, 652, 819–20

Preamble	249, 257, 258, 270, 287, 289
Art. 1	249, 258, 262, 516
Art. 2	18, 516, 518, 652
Art. 3	54, 136, 232, 244, 517
Art. 4(a)	517
Art. 4(b)	517
Art. 5	250, 517, 653, 970
Art. 6	265, 517, 653
Art. 7	517, 654, 819, 834, 849
Art. 8	258, 654
Art. 8(a)	518
Art. 8(b)	518
Art. 8(c)	518
Art. 8(d)	518
Art. 8(g)	518
Art. 8(h)	518
Art. 8(j)	518, 1053
Art. 9	519, 654
Art. 10	519, 655
Art. 11	160, 258, 655
Art. 12	258, 518, 656, 860
Art. 13	518, 860
Art. 14	519, 656, 819, 843
Art. 15	237, 262, 519, 655
Art. 16	258, 520–1, 656, 1041, 1045–6
Art. 17	258, 518, 657, 831
Art. 18	258, 518, 657
Art. 19	521–2
Art. 19(3)	653
Art. 19(4)	653
Art. 20	136, 266, 289, 523, 657, 1035, 1041, 1042
Art. 21	136, 523, 657
Art. 22	657, 1045
Art. 23	523, 1036
Art. 24	523, 656, 657
Art. 25	523, 657
Art. 26	834
Art. 27	201–4, 213, 216, 523
Art. 28	516
Art. 29	139, 516, 658

Arts. 29–31   658
Art. 30   139, 516
Art. 33   658
Arts. 34–35   658
Art. 36   134
Art. 37   134, 516
Art. 40   523
Annex II   201, 517–18, 523
Annex II, Part 1   213
Annex II, Part 2   203
Convention on the Protection and Use of Transboundary Watercourses and
International Lakes (Helsinki) 17 March 1992, in force 6 October 1996; 31
ILM 1312 (1992) (**1992 Watercourses Convention**)   42, 110, 134, 454,
471, 482–5
Art. 1   17, 482, 483, 879
Art. 2   232, 483
Art. 2(1)   248, 482
Art. 2(2)   248, 482
Art. 2(2)(b)   261
Art. 2(5)   257, 270, 284
Art. 2(6)   483
Art. 2(8)   483
Art. 3(1)   483, 804
Art. 3(2)   483
Art. 3(3)   483
Art. 4   483
Arts. 4–8   483
Art. 5   483
Art. 6   483
Art. 7   871
Art. 8   483
Art. 9(1)   484
Art. 9(2)   484, 804
Arts. 10–12   484
Art. 11   849
Arts. 13–14   484
Art. 14   837
Arts. 14–15   484
Art. 16   484
Arts. 17–19   484
Art. 22   213, 216
Annex I   483
Annex II   483

Convention on the Protection of the Black Sea Against Pollution (and Protocols)
(Bucharest) 21 April 1992, in force 15 January 1994; 32 ILM 1101 (1992)
(**Black Sea Convention**)   405, 436, 924

    Art. 3(3)   158
    Art. XI(1)   448
    Art. XVI   924
    Annex II   158

Convention on the Protection of the Marine Environment of the Baltic Sea
Area (Helsinki) 9 April 1992, in force 17 January 2000; BNA 35: 0401 (**Baltic
Sea Convention**)   244, 395, 408, 413–14, 428

    Art. 2(2)   437
    Art. 3   158, 174, 232, 271, 284, 414
    Art. 4   414
    Art. 5   414
    Art. 6   414
    Art. 7   415
    Art. 8   414
    Art. 9   415
    Art. 10   414
    Art. 11   414
    Art. 12   414, 448
    Art. 13   415
    Art. 14   415
    Art. 15   415
    Art. 16   415
    Art. 17   415
    Art. 18   415
    Art. 19(5)   413
    Art. 20   413
    Art. 25   871
    Annex I   414
    Annex II   158, 174
    Annex III   414
    Annex IV   414
    Annex V   414
    Annex VI   414, 448

International Convention on Civil Liability for Oil Pollution Damage 1992,
29 November 1969, in force 19 June 1975; 973 UNTS 3; amended by the
1976 Protocol, 19 November 1976, in force 8 April 1981, 16 ILM 617 (1977);
1984 Protocol, 25 May 1984, not in force; 23 ILM 177 (1984); and 1992
Protocol, 27 November 1992, in force 1996 (**1992 CLC Convention**), IMO
LEG/CONF.9.15   913

North American Free Trade Agreement (Washington, Ottawa, Mexico City) 17 December 1992, in force 1 January 1994; 32 ILM 289 (1993) and 32 ILM 605 (1993) (**NAFTA**)   115, 999–7, 1059–60, 1062, 1064–70

Protocol to the 1969 CLC (London) 27 November 1992, not in force; BNA 21: 1551   97, 676–7, 914, 915

Protocol to the 1971 Oil Pollution Fund Convention (London) 27 November 1992, not in force; BNA 21: 1751   97, 110, 454, 915–22

Art. 1	916
Art. 2	192, 916, 918
Art. 4	916
Art. 6	917
Art. 7	197, 917
Art. 10	917
Art. 12	917
Arts. 16–30	918
Art. 17	918
Art. 22	262, 918
Art. 26	917, 918
Arts. 32–33	918
Art. 33	917

Treaty on European Union, Maastricht, 17 February 1992, in force 1 November 1993; 31 ILM 247 (1992) (**Maastricht Treaty**)   259, 739, 745–6, 751

UNECE Convention on the Transboundary Effects of Industrial Accidents (Helsinki) 17 March 1992, in force 19 April 2000; 31 ILM 1330 (1992) (**Industrial Accidents Convention**)   42, 64, 111, 623–5

Preamble	249, 284
Art. 1	17, 623, 879
Art. 2(2)	623
Art. 3	232, 624
Art. 4	623, 804, 837, 840
Art. 6	624
Art. 7	624
Art. 8	624
Art. 9	624, 853
Art. 10	624
Art. 11	624
Arts. 12–16	625
Art. 13	871
Arts. 17–20	625
Art. 21	213, 216
Annex I	623
Annex III	623, 804

Annex IV 624
Annex V 624
Annex VI 624
Annex VIII 624, 853
Annex IX 624
Annexes X–XI 625
Annex XII 625

United Nations Framework Convention on Climate Change (New York) 9 May 1992, in force 24 March 1994; 31 ILM), 849 (1992) (**1992 Climate Change Convention**) 6, 9, 12, 53, 109, 127–30, 133, 170, 182, 263, 359–68, 756, 900–1, 944

Preamble 244–5, 265, 266, 287, 288
Art. 1 131
Art. 1(1) 362, 877
Art. 1(2) 361
Art. 1(3) 18, 361
Art. 2 156, 249, 361, 878
Art. 3 8, 232–3, 362
Art. 3(1) 257, 262, 286
Art. 3(2) 288
Art. 3(3) 271
Art. 3(4) 258, 266
Art. 3(5) 1009
Art. 4 233, 289, 362–4, 849, 1042
Art. 4(1) 250, 369, 805, 831, 834, 835, 860
Art. 4(2) 364–5
Art. 4(2)(a) 162, 262, 369
Art. 4(2)(b) 162, 369
Art. 4(2)(e) 160
Art. 4(3) 180, 366, 1035
Art. 4(4) 366, 900
Art. 4(5) 367
Art. 4(6) 366
Art. 4(7) 266, 289, 1035
Art. 4(8) 367
Art. 4(9) 367
Art. 4(10) 366
Art. 7 193, 367, 1036
Arts. 7–11 367
Art. 9(1) 367
Art. 10 78, 201, 367, 836
Art. 11 1035
Art. 11(1) 367

Art. 11(2)   368
Art. 11(3)   368
Art. 12   289, 366, 834
Art. 12(1)   180, 834
Art. 12(2)   363
Art. 12(3)   363
Art. 12(5)   181, 363
Art. 12(8)   364
Art. 12(9)   364, 853
Art. 12(10)   364, 853
Art. 13   201, 206, 368
Art. 14   201–3, 213, 216, 368
Art. 15   139
Art. 16   139
Art. 21   368, 1036
Art. 23   134
Art. 24   134, 368
Annex I   360
Annex II   360

1993

Agreement Concerning the Establishment of a Border Environment Co-operation Commission and a North American Development Bank, 18 November 1993, in force 1 January 1994; 32 ILM 1545 (1993)   1007

Agreement for the Establishment of the Indian Ocean Tuna Commission (Rome) 25 November 1993, in force 27 March 1996   599–600

Agreement for the Establishment of the Near East Plant Protection Organization, Rabat, 18 February 1993, not yet in force   551

Agreement to Promote Compliance with International Conservation and Management Measures by Fishing on the High Seas, November 1993 (FAO Res. 15/93)   572

Convention for the Conservation of Southern Bluefin Tuna, 10 May 1993, in force 30 May 1994; 1819 UNTS 360   580, 600

Convention on Civil Liability for Damage Resulting from Activities Dangerous to the Environment (Lugano) 21 June 1993, not in force; 32 ILM 1228 (1993) (**1993 Lugano Convention**)   64, 106, 857, 876, 877, 933–7
        Preamble   284
        Art. 1   933
        Art. 2   620, 894, 934, 935
        Art. 4   933
        Art. 5   934
        Art. 6   934
        Art. 7   934, 935

Art. 8   879, 935
Art. 9   936
Art. 10   936
Art. 12   934
Art. 13   857
Arts. 13–16   933
Art. 14   857
Art. 15
Art. 16
Art. 17   937
Art. 18   177, 936
Art. 19   936, 937
Arts. 20–23   937
Art. 25   933
Arts. 26–31   937
Art. 32   933
Art. 33   933
Art. 35   134
Annex I   620

ILO Convention (No. 174) on the Prevention of Major Industrial Accidents
   (Geneva) 22 June 1993, in force 3 January 1996 (**1993 ILO Accidents
   Convention**)   98, 620, 621
North American Agreement on Environmental Co-operation (Washington,
   Ottawa, Mexico City), 8, 9, 12, 14 September 1993, in force 1 January 1994;
   32 ILM 1480 (1993)   1005–6

1994
Agreement Establishing the World Trade Organization, Marrakesh, 15 April
   1994, in force 1 January 1995, 33 ILM 1125 (1994)   136, 946–85
   Preamble   259
   Annex 1A   977–82, 984
   Annex 2   670
Agreement on the Trade-Related Aspects of Intellectual Property Rights, in
   force 1 January 1995; 33 ILM 81 (**1994 TRIPs Agreement**)   1050–2
Agreements on the Protection of the Rivers Meuse and Scheldt (Charleville
   Mézières) 26 April 1994, in force 1 March 1995, 34 ILM 851 (1995)   284,
   478
Convention on Co-operation for the Protection and Sustainable Use of the
   Danube River (Sofia) 29 June 1994, in force 22 October 1998 (**1994 Danube
   Convention**)   213, 270, 284, 478
Convention on Nuclear Safety (Vienna) 20 September 1994, in force 24 October
   1996, 33 ILM 1514 (**Nuclear Safety Convention**)   100, 643–4, 647

Convention to Combat Desertification in those Countries Experiencing Serious Drought and/or Desertification, particularly in Africa (Paris) 17 June 1994, in force 26 December 1996, 33 ILM 1328 (1994) (**1994 Desertification Convention**)   180, 557–8

Art. 18	1040
Art. 21	1035

Energy Charter Treaty and Energy Charter Protocol on Energy Efficiency and Related Environmental Aspects (Lisbon) 17 December 1994, in force 16 April 1998, 33 ILM 360 (1995)   271, 284, 664–5

Art. 3(7)	804
Art. 9	804
Art. 10(1)	1060
Art. 13(1)	1061
Art. 19	804
Art. 26	1062

International Tropical Timber Agreement (Geneva) 26 January 1994, in force 1 January 1997, 33 ILM 1014 (1994)   237, 547–8

Lusaka Agreement on Co-operative Enforcement Operations Directed at Illegal Trade in Wild Fauna and Flora (Lusaka) 8 September 1994, in force 10 December 1996, UNEP Doc. No. 94/7929   525–6

North American Agreement on Environmental Co-operation   1065

Protocol for the Protection of the Mediterranean Sea Against Pollution resulting from Exploration and Exploitation of the Continental Shelf and the Seabed and its Subsoil (Madrid) 14 October 1994, not yet in force (**1994 Mediterranean Offshore Protocol**)   401, 448

Protocol to the 1979 Convention on Long Range Transboundary Air Pollution on Further Reduction of Sulphur Emissions (Oslo), 14 June 1994, in force 5 August 1998, 33 ILM 1540 (1998) (**1994 LRTAP Sulphur Protocol**)   207, 332–3, 478

Art. 2(1)	332
Art. 2(2)	332
Art. 2(3)	332
Art. 2(4)	332
Art. 2(5)	333
Art. 2(6)	332
Art. 2(7)	332
Art. 2(8)	332
Art. 3	333
Art. 4	333
Art. 5	333
Art. 6	333
Art. 7	333

Annex II   332
Annex IV   332

1995
Agreement for the Conservation of African–Eurasian Migratory Waterbirds
  (The Hague) 16 June 1995, in force 1 November 1999, 6 *Yearbook of Inter-
  national Environmental Law* 306 (1995)   609
Agreement for the Implementation of the Provisions of the United Nations
  Convention on the Law of the Sea of 10 December 1982 Relating to the Con-
  servation and Management of Straddling Fish Stocks and Highly Migratory
  Fish Stocks (New York) 4 December 1995, in force 11 December 2001, 34
  ILM 1542 (1995) (**1995 Straddling Stocks Agreement**)   6, 64, 127, 249,
  258, 574–8
    Art. 2   258
    Art. 5   271, 575, 576
    Art. 6   271, 575, 576
    Art. 7   575, 576
    Art. 8   577
    Arts. 8–10   577
    Arts. 11–13   577
    Art. 14   850
    Arts. 15–16   577
    Art. 17   577
    Art. 18(1)   577
    Art. 19   176, 178
    Art. 20   186
    Art. 21   186
    Art. 42   575
    Annex II   271, 576, 850
Agreement on Co-operation for the Sustainable Development of the Mekong
  River Basin (Chiang Rai, Thailand) 5 April 1995   490–1
Protocol on Shared Watercourse Systems in the Southern African Development
  Community (Johannesburg) 28 August 1995, in force 29 September 1998
  (**1995 SADC Water Protocol**)   213, 490–1

1996
Agreement on the Conservation of the Cetaceans of the Black Sea, Mediterranean Sea and Contiguous Atlantic Area (Monaco) 24 November 1996, in
  force 1 June 2001 (**1996 ACCOBAMS**); 36 ILM 777 (1997)   596, 609
Bangladesh/India Treaty on Sharing the Waters of the Ganges River, New Delhi,
  12 December 1996, 36 ILM 519   492–3
Comprehensive Test Ban Treaty (New York) 24 September 1996, not yet in
  force, 35 ILM 1439 (1996)   649

India/Nepal Treaty on Sharing the Waters of the Mahakali River, New Delhi, 12 February 1996, 36 ILM 519　　492

International Convention on Liability and Compensation for Damage in Connection with the Carriage of Hazardous and Noxious Substances by Sea (London) 3 May 1996, not yet in force, 25 ILM 1406 (1996) (**1996 HNS Convention**)　　97, 454, 930–1

Israel–Jordan Peace Treaty, 34 ILM 46 (1995)　　494

Protocol on the Prevention of Pollution of the Mediterranean Sea by Transboundary Movements of Hazardous Wastes and their Disposal (Izmir) 1 October 1996, not yet in force, UN Doc. UNEP (OCA)/MED/IG.9/4 Annexes (1996) (**1996 Mediterranean Hazardous Wastes Protocol**)　　401, 691

Protocol to the Convention on the Prevention of Marine Pollution by Dumping of Wastes and Other Matter (London) 7 November 1996, not yet in force, 36 ILM 1 (1997) (**1996 Protocol to the London Convention**)　　422–3, 686
    Art. 1(8)　　678
    Art. 2　　422
    Art. 3　　271, 284, 423
    Art. 4　　423
    Art. 5　　423
    Art. 6　　423
    Art. 7(2)　　423
    Art. 9(4)　　180
    Art. 10　　176
    Art. 11　　207, 423
    Art. 13　　423
    Art. 15　　871, 924
    Art. 16　　213
    Art. 25(1)　　422
    Art. 26　　423

Treaty on the Nuclear-Weapon-Free Zone in Africa (Cairo) 1 April 1996, not yet in force, 35 ILM 698 (1996) (**Pelindaba Treaty**)　　651

1997

Amsterdam Treaty, amending Treaty on European Union and EC Treaty, 2 October 1997, in force 1 May 1999, 37 ILM 56 (1998)　　735, 748–9

Convention on Supplementary Compensation for Nuclear Damage (Vienna) 12 September 1997, not yet in force 36 ILM 1473 (1997) (**1997 Supplementary Compensation Convention**)　　906

Convention on the Law of Non-Navigational uses of International Watercourses (New York) 21 May 1997, 36 ILM 700 (1997)　　134, 460, 466–8
    Art. 1(1)　　466
    Art. 2(b)　　466

Art. 3	466
Art. 4	466
Art. 7	467
Art. 9	467
Art. 10	467
Arts. 11–14	467
Art. 12	804, 837
Arts. 15–19	467
Art. 17	839
Art. 20	467
Art. 21	467
Art. 22	467
Art. 23	468
Art. 24	468
Arts. 25–26	468
Arts. 29–32	468
Art. 33(2)	204, 468
Art. 33(3)	204
Art. 33(4)–(6)	468
Art. 33(7)	468
Art. 33(10)	468
Art. 43(8)	468

Convention on the Prohibition of the Development, Production, Stockpiling and Use of Chemical Weapons (Paris) 13 January 1993, in force 29 April 1997; 32 ILM 800 (1993)   628

Joint Convention on the Safety of Spent Fuel Management and on the Safety of Radioactive Waste Management (Vienna) 5 September 1997, in force 18 June 2001, 36 ILM 1431 (1997) (**1997 Joint Safety Convention**)   644–5, 647, 712

Protocol to Amend the Vienna Convention on Civil Liability for Nuclear Damage (Vienna) 12 September 1997, not yet in force, 36 ILM 1454 (1997) (**Protocol to the 1963 Vienna Convention**)   906, 910–11

Protocol to the United Nations Framework Convention on Climate Change (Kyoto) 11 December 1997, not yet in force, 37 ILM 22 (1998) (**1997 Kyoto Protocol**)   6, 64, 109, 139, 170, 289, 368–81, 756, 944

Art. 2	372, 901
Art. 3	373, 836
Art. 3(1)	371, 378, 379, 381
Art. 3(2)	371
Art. 3(3)	374
Art. 3(4)	374, 380–1
Art. 3(5)	371
Art. 3(9)	371

Art. 4   162, 375
Art. 5   162, 375, 378
Art. 6   373, 380
Art. 7   180, 375–6, 378, 836
Art. 8   378
Art. 8(1)   376
Art. 8(3)   376
Art. 8(5)   376
Art. 8(6)   376
Art. 10   375
Art. 12   373–4
Art. 13(3)   371
Art. 15   201
Art. 16   201
Art. 17   373
Art. 18   207–8, 376
Art. 19   201
Art. 21(7)   371
Art. 25(1)   133
Annex A   372
Annex B   371
Annex I   207–8

1998

Convention on Access to Information, Public Participation and Decision-
Making and Access to Justice in Environmental Matters (Aarhus)
25 June 1998, in force 30 October 2001, 38 ILM 517 (1999) (**1998 Aarhus
Convention**)   15, 64, 111, 120–1, 196, 297, 307, 316, 827, 858–9, 1072
Preamble   292
Art. 1   118, 292
Art. 2   119, 178, 858
Art. 3(7)   118
Art. 4   858
Art. 5   858–9, 861
Art. 6   119
Art. 6(1)–(4)   119
Art. 6(2)   805
Art. 6(5)–(9)   119
Art. 6(7)   838
Art. 6(10)   119
Art. 7   119
Art. 8   119, 838
Art. 9(1)   119

Art. 9(2)   119, 178
Art. 9(3)   119, 178
Art. 9(4)   120, 178
Art. 9(5)   120, 178
Art. 10(5)   113
Annex I   805

Convention on Co-operation for the Protection and Sustainable Use of the Waters of the Luso-Spanish River Basins, 30 November 1998, in force 17 January 2000   478

Convention on the Prior Informed Consent Procedure for Certain Hazardous Chemicals and Pesticides in International Trade (Rotterdam) 11 September 1998, not yet in force, 38 ILM 1 (1999) (**1998 Chemicals Convention**)   66, 83, 94–5, 111, 127, 134, 635–6, 827, 943

Art. 1   249
Art. 2   635
Art. 3   635
Art. 4   635
Art. 5   636
Art. 6   636
Art. 7   636
Art. 8   636
Art. 9   636
Art. 10   841
Art. 12   636, 841
Art. 13   636
Art. 14   832
Arts. 14–16   636
Art. 15   175, 1018
Art. 17   207
Arts. 17–19   636
Art. 20   203, 216
Arts. 21–22   636
Art. 22(5)(b)   636
Annex II   636
Annex IV   636

Convention on the Protection of the Environment through Criminal Law (Strasbourg) 4 November 1998, not yet in force, 38 ILM 259 (1999)   106, 896

Protocol on the Control of Marine Transboundary Movements and Disposals of Hazardous Wastes (Kuwait), not yet in force (**1998 Hazardous Wastes Protocol**)   402, 691

Protocol to the 1979 Convention on Long Range Transboundary Air Pollution on Heavy Metals (Aarhus) 24 June 1998, not yet in force (**1998 LRTAP Heavy Metals Protocols**)   333–4

Art. 3(1)   333
Art. 3(2)   334
Art. 3(3)   334
Art. 3(4)   334
Art. 4   334
Art. 5   334
Art. 6   334
Art. 7   334, 834
Art. 9   334
Annex I   333
Annex III   334
Annex VI   334
Annex VII   334
Protocol to the 1979 Convention on Long Range Transboundary Air Pollution
   on Persistent Organic Pollutants (Aarhus) 24 June 1998, not yet in force, 37
   ILM 505 (1998) (**1998 LRTAP POPs Protocol**)   334–5, 628
Art. 3(1)   334
Art. 3(3)   334
Art. 3(5)(a)   334
Art. 3(5)(b)   334
Art. 4   334
Arts. 5–8   335
Art. 6   860
Art. 9   335, 834
Art. 11   335
Annex IV   334
Annex V   334

1999

Agreement Concerning the Creation of a Marine Mammal Sanctuary in the
   Mediterranean (Rome) 25 November 1999   596
Convention on the Protection of the Rhine (Bern) 12 April 1999, OJ L289, 16
   November 2000, 30   481
Protocol Concerning Pollution from Land-Based Sources and Activities to the
   Cartagena Convention (Oranjestad, Aruba) 6 October 1999, not yet in force
   (**1999 LBS Protocol**)   404, 436
Protocol on Liability and Compensation for Damage resulting from
   Transboundary Movements of Hazardous Wastes and their Disposal
   (Basel) 10 December 1999, not yet in force (**1999 Basel Liability
   Protocol**)   924–6
Protocol on Water and Health to the 1992 Convention on the Protection and Use
   of Transboundary Watercourses and International Lakes (London) 17 June
   1999, not yet in force, 38 ILM 1708 (1999) (**1999 Health Protocol**)   484–5,
   804, 860

Protocol to the 1979 Convention on Long Range Transboundary Air Pollution
   to Abate Acidification, Eutrophication and Ground-Level Ozone (Gothenburg) 30 November 1999, not yet in force, UN Doc. EB.AIR/1999 (**1999
   LRTAP Acidification Protocol**)   335–6

Art. 2	335
Art. 3	336
Art. 4	336
Art. 5	336, 860
Art. 6	336
Art. 7	336, 834
Art. 8	336
Art. 9	336
Annex IX	336

Wildlife Conservation and Law Enforcement Protocol to the Treaty Establishing
   the Southern African Development Community (Maputo) 18 August 1999,
   not yet in force   527

2000

Cartagena Protocol on Biosafety to the Convention on Biological Diversity
   (Montreal) 29 January 2000, in force 11 September 2003, 39 ILM 1027
   (**Biosafety Protocol**)   6, 7, 12, 64, 83, 110, 157, 653–8, 820–1

Art. 1	249, 258, 271, 653
Art. 2	653, 1018
Art. 4	653
Art. 7	841
Art. 8	841
Arts. 8–12	943
Art. 9	841
Art. 10	270–1, 942, 943
Art. 11	270–1, 841, 942, 943
Art. 13	841
Art. 15	270–1, 820
Art. 17(1)	843
Art. 18(2)	861
Art. 19	175
Art. 20(3)	832
Art. 23	180, 860
Art. 25(1)	176
Art. 26(1)	10
Art. 27	871
Art. 28	1035
Art. 34	207
Annex III	270–1, 820

Convention on the Conservation and Management of Highly Migratory Fish Stocks in the Western and Central Pacific Ocean, 5 September 2002, not yet in force; 40 ILM 277 (2001)   586

Cotonou Agreement (Cotonou, Benin) 23 June 2000, not yet in force   695–6, 753

Art. 32   247, 254, 259, 265

European Landscape Convention (Florence), 20 October 2000, not yet in force, ETS 176   106, 611

Framework Agreement for the Conservation of the Living Marine Resources of the High Seas of the South Pacific, 14 August 2000, not yet in force (**Galapagos Agreement**)   586

Protocol to the OPRC Convention on Preparedness, Response and Co-operation to Pollution Incidents by Hazardous and Noxious Substances (**HNS Protocol**) (London), 15 March 2000, not yet in force   452

Revised Protocol on Shared Watercourses in the Southern African Development Community (Windhoek) 7 August 2000, not yet in force, 40 ILM 321 (2001) (**2000 SADC Revised Water Protocol**)   213

2001

Agreement on the Conservation of Albatrosses and Petrels (Canberra) 19 June 2001, not yet in force   610

Convention on Persistent Organic Pollutants (Stockholm) 22 May 2001, not yet in force, 40 ILM 532 (2001) (**2001 POPs Convention**)   9, 66, 83, 111, 127, 139, 180, 628–30, 691

Preamble	271
Art. 1	249, 271
Art. 3	942, 943
Art. 3(1)	628, 683
Art. 3(2)	629
Art. 3(3)	629
Art. 3(4)	629
Art. 6	688
Art. 7	629
Art. 8	630
Art. 9(5)	832
Arts. 9–12	629
Art. 10(1)	860
Art. 12	1040
Art. 13	629, 1036
Art. 15	180, 629, 834
Art. 16	630
Art. 17	207, 629, 871, 942
Art. 18	203, 216
Arts. 19–20	630

Arts. 21–22   630

Annex A   628

Annex B   628

Convention on the Conservation and Management of the Fishery Resources in the Southeast Atlantic Ocean (Windhoek) 20 April 2001, not yet in force   585, 586

Convention on the Protection of the Underwater Cultural Heritage (Paris) 6 November 2001, not yet in force, 41 ILM 40 (2002)   97, 611

ILO Convention on Safety and Health in Agriculture, adopted by the International Labor Conference at its 89th session, Geneva, 21 June 2001   98

IMO International Convention on Civil Liability for Bunker Oil Pollution Damage (London) 27 March 2001, not yet in force, 40 ILM 1493 (2001)   97, 454, 922

International Convention on the Control of Harmful Anti-Fouling Systems on Ships, 5 October 2001   97

International Treaty on Plant Genetic Resources for Food and Agriculture (Rome) 3 November 2001, not yet in force, www.fao.org/biodiversity/cgrfa (**2001 Treaty on Plant Genetic Resources**)   95, 1046

Art. 12   1046

Art. 13   1046

Art. 18   1035

Art. 19   1035

Art. 22   204

Treaty Establishing the East African Community, 30 November 1998   247, 296

Treaty of Nice Amending the Treaty on European Union, the Treaties Establishing the European Communities and Certain Related Acts, Nice, 26 February 2001, 10 March 2001, 12   736, 737, 739

2002

Convention for Co-operation in the Protection and Sustainable Development of the Marine and Coastal Environment of the North-East Pacific (Antigua, Guatemala) 18 February 2002, not yet in force (**2002 North-East Pacific Convention**)   271, 280, 405

2003

Protocol on Strategic Environmental Assessment (Kiev) 21 May 2003, not yet in force   817

United Nations

1972 UN Conference on the Human Environment, Declaration of Principles

Principle 1   38, 257, 294

Principle 2   16–17, 39, 501–2, 826
Principle 3   39, 259, 501–2
Principle 4   39, 257, 261, 501–2
Principle 5   39, 259
Principle 6   39, 247, 619
Principle 7   39, 247, 501–2
Principle 8   39, 394
Principle 9   39
Principle 10   39
Principle 11   39, 1038
Principle 12   39
Principle 13   39
Principle 14   39
Principle 15   39, 247
Principle 16   39
Principle 17   39
Principle 18   39, 247
Principle 19   39
Principle 20   39, 829, 1038
Principle 21   34, 38, 40, 44, 51, 145, 148, 189, 231, 232,
                                  235–7, 241–6, 310, 471, 881
Principle 22   38, 40, 870
Principle 23   38, 287
Principle 24   38, 247, 249
Principle 26   309

1992 Rio Declaration on Environment and Development   4–5, 15, 54–7
Principle 1   54, 293
Principle 2   54, 189, 231, 232, 236–7, 241–6, 310, 881
Principle 3   55, 265–6, 307, 969
Principle 4   55, 264, 266, 941, 969, 1023
Principle 5   259–60
Principle 6   288, 675
Principle 7   259–60, 280, 285–6
Principle 8   259–60
Principle 9   829, 1043
Principle 10   64, 118, 154, 196, 226, 307, 853, 859
Principle 11   56, 247, 249, 288, 1017
Principle 12   240, 259–60, 970, 1009, 1018
Principle 13   64, 870, 881, 938
Principle 14   247, 676
Principle 15   56, 247, 268, 471
Principle 16   56, 154, 280–1, 863, 1017

Principle 17	795, 800, 803
Principle 18	842
Principle 19	837, 839
Principle 20	307
Principle 21	54, 307
Principle 22	307
Principle 24	309
Principle 25	74
Principle 26	226
Principle 27	10, 53, 54, 249, 259–60
Agenda 21	11, 15, 57–9
para. 2	58, 88
para. 2.3	941–6
para. 2.22	970
para. 3	58, 88
para. 4	58, 88
para. 5	58, 88
para. 6	58, 88
para. 7	58, 88
para. 7.41(b)	803
para. 8	58, 60–1, 88
para. 8.4	803
para. 8.5(b)	803
para. 8.32	1011
para. 9	58, 88, 384–8
para. 9.12(b)	803
para. 10	58, 88
para. 10.8(b)	803
para. 11	58, 88, 547
para. 11.12(e)	546
para. 11.24(a)	803
para. 12	58, 88, 556
para. 12.2	556
para. 13	58, 88
para. 13.17(a)	803
para. 14	58, 88
para. 15	58, 88, 502, 654
para. 15.5(k)	803
para. 16	58, 88
para. 16.1	652
para. 16.39	670
para. 16.41	671

para. 16.44(b)	671
para. 16.45(c)	803
para. 17	58, 88, 455–7, 575, 1017
para. 17.1	396
para. 17.5(d)	803
para. 17.22	396
paras. 17.44–17.69	569
paras. 17.44–17.88	561
para. 17.45	573
para. 17.46	573
para. 17.47	573
paras. 17.49–17.54	573
para. 17.58	589
para. 17.61	597
para. 17.62	597
paras. 17.69–17.95	561
para. 17.73–17.74	573
para. 17.74	573
para. 17.85	573
para. 18	58, 88, 495–6
para. 18.22(c)	803
para. 19	58, 88, 670
para. 19.1	625
para. 19.11	625
para. 19.13	671
para. 19.14	671
para. 19.17	671
para. 19.21(d)	803
para. 19.27	671
para. 19.29	671
para. 19.38	671
para. 19.48	671
para. 19.49	671
para. 19.52	672
para. 19.56	672
para. 19.61	672
paras. 19.66–19.76	672
para. 20	59, 88, 705–6
para. 21	59, 88, 706–7
para. 21.31(a)	803
para. 22	59, 88, 707–8
para. 22.4(d)	803
para. 22.5(b)	421

para. 22.5(c)	422
para. 23.2	803
para. 23.3	854
paras. 23–32	59, 88
para. 27	114
para. 27.9(a)	113
para. 27.9(b)	113
para. 27.10	113
para. 27.12	112, 113
para. 27.13	113, 196
para. 30	115
para. 31	113
para. 33	88, 1021
para. 33.15	1022
para. 33.16	1034
paras. 33–40	59
para. 34	88
para. 34.10	1045
para. 34.14	1042–43
para. 34.18	1039, 1045
para. 35	88
para. 36	88, 859
para. 37	88
para. 38	59–60, 75, 84, 88
para. 38.9	81
para. 38.10	91
para. 38.13(f)	226
para. 38.16	80
para. 38.17	80
para. 38.21	85
para. 38.22	85, 830
para. 38.24	226
para. 38.25(a)	226
para. 38.42	112
para. 38.43	112
para. 38.44	112
para. 39	53, 59, 62–3, 88
para. 39.1	10
para. 39.1(a)	10
para. 39.2	10
para. 39.3(d)	241, 1008
para. 39.3(e)	226
para. 39.3(h)	226

para. 39.6(a)	316
para. 39.7	226
para. 39.9	226
para. 40	59, 88, 851–2
para. 40.1	827

Security Council Resolutions

(1991) 687/1991	93, 315, 878
(2001) S/RES/1355	94
(2001) S/RES/1376	94

General Assembly Resolutions

(1947) 174 (II)	86
(1948) 217 (III)	293
(1950) 523 (VI)	236
(1952) 626 (VII)	236
(1954) 837 (IX)	236
(1954) 900 (IX)	33
(1955) 912 (X)	33
(1955) 913 (X)	33
(1955) 913 (X)	90
(1957) 1147 (XII)	33
(1958) 1252 (XIII)	33
(1958) 1314 (XIII)	236
(1959) 1379 (XIV)	33
(1959) 1402 (XIV)	33
(1959) 1472 (XIV)	90
(1961) 1629 (XVI)	243
(1961) 1649 (XVI)	33
(1961) 1714 (XVI)	94–5
(1962) 1803 (XVII)	81, 236
(1962) 1831 (XVII)	34
(1963) 1934 (XVIII)	90
(1964) 1995 (XIX)	55, 89
(1965) 2029 (XX)	85
(1965) 2033 (XX)	651
(1966) 2200 (XXI)	293
(1966) 2211 (XXI)	90
(1967) 2347 (XXII)	667
(1968) 2398 (XXII)	82, 294
(1968) 2414 (XXII)	394
(1968) 2467B (XXIII)	81

(1968) 23983 (XXIII)	36
(1969) 2566 (XXIV)	81, 394
(1970) 2625 (XXV)	13
(1970) 2749 (XXV)	287
(1971) 2847 (XXVI)	142
(1971) 2849 (XXVI)	82, 237, 265
(1972) 2849 (XXIV)	243
(1972) 2994 (XXVII)	40
(1972) 2995 (XXVII)	40, 801
(1972) 2996 (XXVII)	40, 243
(1972) 2997 (XXVII)	40, 82, 1030
(1972) 2998 (XXVII)	40
(1972) 2999 (XXVII)	40
(1972) 3000 (XXVII)	40
(1972) 3001 (XXVII)	40
(1972) 3002 (XXVII)	40
(1972) 3003 (XXVII)	40
(1972) 3004 (XXVII)	40
(1973) 3129 (XXVIII)	43
(1973) 3133 (XXVIII)	81
(1974) 3129	82
(1974) 3201	288
(1974) 3281	244
(1979) 34/188	82
(1980) 35/8	82, 257
(1982) 37/7	45, 82, 627
(1982) 37/137	82
(1982) 37/215	312
(1982) 37/250	82
(1983) 37/137	630
(1983) 38/149	627
(1983) 38/161	50
(1984) 39/229	627
(1987) 42/183	691
(1987) 42/184	802
(1987) 42/186	50
(1987) 42/187	52, 82
(1987) 42/430	90
(1987) 44/228	52
(1988) 43/53	287, 359
(1988) 43/75	684
(1988) 43/75Q	684
(1988) 43/75T	684

(1988) 43/76	650
(1988) 43/196	52
(1989) 44/207	287, 359
(1989) 44/224	82, 621
(1989) 44/225	82, 589
(1989) 44/226	691
(1989) 44/228	10, 82
(1990) 44/224	79
(1990) 44/226	631
(1990) 45/53	651
(1990) 45/94	295
(1990) 45/197	589
(1990) 45/212	82, 287
(1990) 45/221	359
(1991) 46/214	1039
(1991) 46/215	589
(1991) 46/235	91
(1992) 47/68	384–5
(1992) 47/188	63, 82, 557
(1992) 47/189	64, 129
(1992) 47/190	54, 57, 64
(1992) 47/191	64, 74–6, 86, 87, 226, 307, 833, 834, 838
(1992) 47/192	64, 574
(1992) 47/591	316
(1993) 47/68	382
(1993) 48/167	1039
(1993) 48/194	82
(1994) 49/80	712
(1994) 49/116	589
(1994) 49/118	589
(1995) 50/24	82
(1995) 50/25	589
(1996) 51/36	589
(1996) 51/45J	684
(1996) 51/56	712
(1996) 51/122	382
(1997) 52/29	589
(1997) 52/229	82
(1998) 53/33	589
(1998) 53/77C	684
(1999) 54/33	82
(1999) 54/45	712
(1999) 54/54C	684

(2000) 55/8   589
(2000) 55/199   82
(2001) 56/13   82
(2002) 56/206   90
(2002) 5733   82

ECOSOC Resolutions

(1946) 5 (I)   93
(1946) 9 (II)   199
(1946) 10 (II)   93
(1946) 13 (III)   79
(1947) 32 (IV)   32
(1947) 36 (IV)   92
(1947) 37 (IV)   92
(1948) 106 (VI)   92
(1948) 150 (VII)   93
(1958) 671 (XXV)   92
(1959) 537A (XVIII)   394
(1965) 1079 (XXXIX)   93
(1966) 139 (XLI)   93
(1966) 1763 (LIV)   90
(1968) 1310 (XLIV)   36
(1968) 1346 (XLV)   36
(1973) 1818 (LV)   92
(1974) 1895 (LVII)   92
(1974) 1913 (LVII)   93
(1975) 87 (LVII)   93
(1985) 1985/69   92
(1988) 1988/4   199
(1989) 1989/87   52
(1991) 645 (XXIII)   637
(1995) 1995/55   93
(1996) 1996/7   93
(1998) 1998/4   93
(1998) 1998/46   93
(2000) 2000/22   93
(2000) 2000/35   92, 550

UNEP Governing Council Decisions

(1975) 24/3   84
(1975) 44 (III)   43
(1978) 6/11   556

(1978) 6/14	43
(1981) 10/5	44
(1982) 10/14 (VI)	84, 555, 665
(1982) 10/21	84
(1984) 12/12	555
(1985) 13/19 (II)	84
(1987) 14/17	676
(1987) 14/25	84
(1987) 14/27	84, 630–3
(1987) 14/30	676
(1989) 15/3	52
(1989) 15/28	626
(1989) 15/30	84, 630–3
(1991) 16/9	84, 621
(1993) 17/5	67, 556
(2001) 21/17	621
(2001) 21/22	69
(2001) 21/23	84

UNEP Draft Principles on Shared National Resources   43–4, 568

Principle 1	44, 247, 262
Principle 2	44
Principle 3	44, 244
Principle 4	44
Principle 5	44, 801
Principle 6	44, 837
Principle 7	44, 250, 829, 838
Principle 8	44
Principle 9	44
Principle 10	44
Principle 12	44, 873
Principle 13	44
Principle 14	44
Principle 15	44

UNEP London Guidelines   157, 630, 633–5, 841, 943

Specialised agencies of the United Nations and related bodies

FAO

International Undertaking on Plant Genetic Resource   552–4, 1053

Pesticide Guidelines   627, 943

World Bank

Operational Directive 4.00	211, 821
Operational Directive 4.01	211, 620, 821–2, 1027
Operational Directive 4.02	1027
Operational Directive 4.04	1027
Operational Directive 4.09	1027
Operational Directive 4.12	1026
Operational Directive 4.20	211, 1026
Operational Directive 4.36	1027
Operational Directive 4.37	1027
Operational Directive 7.50	1027
Operational Directive 14.70	1026

Treaty organisations

Consultative Meetings of the 1972 London Convention (Resolutions)

LDC 5(12)	417, 418
LDC 5(111)	419
LDC 6(III)	418
LDC 10(15)	417
LDC 10(V)	418
LDC 11(14)	417, 418
LDC 12(16)	418
LDC 14(7)	419
LDC 21(9)	419, 420
LDC 22(9)	419
LDC 23(10)	419
LDC 24(10)	417
LDC 28(10)	420
LDC 29(10)	419
LDC 31(11)	417
LDC 33(11)	686
LDC 35(11)	419, 686
LDC 39(13)	682, 686
LDC 41(13)	419, 422
LDC 43(13)	419
LDC 44(14)	419
LDC 51(16)	419, 421, 682
LDC 52(18)	419, 685

CITES Conference of the Parties (1973)

Conf. Res. 1.1 (1976)	509
Conf. Res. 2.18 (1979)	507

Conf. Res. 2.20 (1979)	507
Conf. Res. 3.9 (1981)	514
Conf. Res. 3.15 (1981)	513
Conf. Res. 4.8 (1983)	507
Conf. Res. 4.11 (1983)	511
Conf. Res. 4.23 (1983)	512
Conf. Res. 4.24 (1983)	507
Conf. Res. 4.25 (1983)	513
Conf. Res. 5.4 (1985)	512
Conf. Res. 5.9 (1985)	507, 511
Conf. Res. 5.11 (1985)	78, 131, 511
Conf. Res. 5.12(h) (1985)	512
Conf. Res. 5.16(j) (1985)	512
Conf. Res. 6.3 (1987)	512, 514
Conf. Res. 6.4 (1987)	515
Conf. Res. 6.8 (1987)	511
Conf. Res. 6.16 (1987)	508
Conf. Res. 6.22 (1987)	513
Conf. Res. 6.23 (1987)	513
Conf. Res. 6.18 (1989)	508
Conf. Res. 7.9 (1989)	507
Conf. Res. 7.11 (1989)	513
Conf. Res. 7.13 (1989)	507
Conf. Res. 8.4 (1992)	514
Conf. Res. 8.11 (1992)	513
Conf. Res. 8.15 (1992)	513
Conf. Res. 8.16 (1992)	511
Conf. Res. 8.17 (1992)	16, 508
Conf. Res. 8.20 (1992)	510
Conf. Res. 8.22 (1992)	513
Conf. Res. 9.6 (1994)	508
Conf. Res. 9.19 (1994)	511
Conf. Res. 9.21 (1994)	513
Conf. Res. 9.24 (1994)	271, 510, 514
Conf. Res. 10.2 (1997)	514
Conf. Res. 10.6 (1997)	511
Conf. Res. 10.9 (1997)	507
Conf. Res. 10.14 (1997)	513
Conf. Res. 10.16 (1997)	511
Conf. Res. 10.20 (1997)	511
Conf. Res. 11.1 (2000)	506
Conf. Res. 11.3 (2000)	515
Conf. Res. 11.9 (2000)	515

Conf. Res. 11.15 (2000)   511
Conf. Res. 11.16 (2000)   513

Regional organisations

OSCOM Decisions
85/1   424
88/1   425
89/1   425, 685
90/1   425
90/2   425, 686

PARCOM Recommendations
88/4   432
88/5   432
89/1   269, 432
89/2   432
90/1   432
90/2   432
90/4   432
91/4   432
91/5   433
93/5   433–4

OECD Council Decisions and Recommendations
C(71)73   104
C(71)83   104
C(72)128   103, 281
C(73)1   105, 627
C(73)172   105
C(74)16   104, 664
C(74)215   105
C(74)216   103, 802
C(74)217   105, 663
C(74)219   104
C(74)220   104, 465
C(74)221   104, 465
C(74)222   104, 664
C(74)223   103, 282, 1011
C(74)224   104, 837
C(76)55   104, 196
C(76)155   104, 676

C(76)162	104, 664
C(77)28	104, 196, 837
C(77)97	105
C(77)109	104, 664
C(77)115	104
C(78)4	104, 465
C(78)8	104, 689
C(78)73	105, 663
C(78)77	104
C(79)114	104
C(79)115	105, 670
C(79)116	103, 802
C(79)117	104
C(79)218	104, 689
C(81)30	105, 627
C(82)196	105, 627
C(83)95	105
C(83)96	105
C(83)97	105
C(83)98	105
C(83)180	104, 691
C(84)37	105
C(85)100	104, 691
C(85)101	104
C(85)102	104, 664
C(85)103	105, 663
C(85)104	103, 802, 1023
C(86)64	104, 691
C(88)84	105
C(88)85	621, 854
C(89)88	103, 282
C(90)163	105
C(90)164	103, 167
C(90)165	104, 879
C(90)177	103, 160
C(90)178	104
C(92)1	627
C(92)39	104, 689, 691, 699
C(94)154	691
C(96)41	44, 104, 627
C(98)67	104, 854
C(2001)107	104
C(2002)3	104

European Communities Council Regulations

437/75	742
348/81	779
3626/82	223, 780
170/83	781–2
1707/86	880
3094/86	781
3528/86	766
3954/87/EURATOM	794
1734/88	785
428/89	785
1615/89	781
2218/89	794
2219/89	794
2496/89	779
737/90	794
1210/90	739
3926/90	781
594/91	761
880/92	861
2157/92	781
2158/92	781
2455/92	637, 785
3760/92	782–3
259/93	699–703, 787, 788, 943
792/93	1037
793/93	786
1493/93/EURATOM	794
1164/94	284, 1037
3093/94	761
384/96	1017
338/97	780
939/97	780
1181/98	782
933/1999	739
1260/1999	284
1264/1999	284, 1037
1267/1999	284
1430/1999	794
1334/2000	637
1655/2000	1037
1980/2000	861
2037/2000	761

2494/2000	781
44/2001	197
761/2001	866
2555/2001	783

European Communities Directives

67/548	620, 626, 741, 784, 785, 935
70/157	783
70/220	758
72/306	759
73/404	768
75/439	791
75/440	769, 771
75/441	767
75/442	677, 682, 754, 787–9, 929, 990
Art. 1(a)	677, 678
Art. 2(1)	678
Art. 3(1)	689
Art. 15	283
75/716	760
76/160	772–3
76/403	791
76/464	769, 773
76/769	785
78/176	792
78/319	677, 788–90
78/659	769, 775–6
78/1015	783
79/113	783, 784
79/117	17
79/409 (Wild Birds Directive)	194, 602–5, 607, 990
79/831	785
79/869	771
79/923	769, 776
80/51	783
80/68	223, 769, 774–5
80/778	742, 771
80/779	762, 763
80/836	704
80/836/EURATOM	794
82/176	773
82/217	766
82/242	768

82/459	767
82/883	792
82/884	760, 763
83/129	779
83/513	773
84/63	699, 926, 990–1
84/156	773
84/360	158, 763
84/467/EURATOM	794
84/491	773
84/532–538	784
84/533	783
84/534	783
84/535	783
84/536	783
84/537	783
84/538	783
85/203	762, 763
85/210	760
85/337	17, 185, 803, 807–11
85/339	792
85/536	760
86/94	768
86/278	555, 670, 792
86/280	773
86/594	783
86/609	779
86/662	784
87/18	785
87/217	785
87/441	760
88/77	759
88/320	785
88/347	773
88/379	785, 935
88/609	336–7
Art. 3(1)	337
Art. 3(2)	337
Art. 3(3)	337
Art. 3(4)	337
Art. 4(1)	338
Art. 4(2)	338
Art. 4(3)	338

Art. 16	181
Annex I	337
Annex IX	337
89/369	764–5
89/428	223, 744
89/429	765
89/458	758
89/552	743
89/618/EURATOM	794
89/629	783
90/219	658–9
90/220	10, 272, 658
90/313	854–6
90/415	773
91/76	771
91/156	678, 682, 689, 745, 787, 788
91/157	785, 792
91/271	273, 771, 776–8
91/414	786
91/441	758, 766
91/542	759
91/676	773
91/689	680, 682, 689, 788, 790
91/692	689
92/3/EURATOM	441, 699, 700, 703–5, 711, 794
92/14	783
92/43 (Habitats Directive)	536–40, 607
Preamble	537
Art. 1(a)	536
Art. 1(b)	536
Art. 1(d)	538
Art. 1(f)	536
Art. 2(3)	537
Art. 3(1)	537
Art. 4(1)	537
Art. 4(2)	538
Art. 4(3)	538
Art. 5	537
Art. 6(2)	538
Art. 6(3)	538
Art. 6(4)	539
Art. 8	539
Art. 9	539

Art. 11	539
Art. 12	539
Art. 13	540
Art. 15	540
Art. 16	540
Art. 17	181
Arts. 17–21	540
Art. 22	540
92/72	766
92/112	792
93/12	760
93/59	758
93/67	785
93/76	767
94/12	758
94/31	689
94/62	682, 689, 792
94/63	766
94/67	283, 764, 765, 792
96/1	759
96/22	979
96/29/EURATOM	794
96/44	758
96/59	791
96/61	771, 834
96/61 (IPPC Directive)	163, 754–5, 764, 774
96/62	756–7, 767
96/82 (Seveso Directive)	622–3
96/92	997
96/350	682, 689
97/11	17, 807, 808
97/24	783
97/62	536
97/68	759
98/8	786
98/15	778
98/44	1048, 1051–2
98/69	758
98/70	760
98/83	772
98/618/EURATOM	794
99/13	766
99/22	780

99/26	759
99/30	757, 763
99/31 (Landfill Directive)	284, 682, 684, 687, 792
99/45	785
99/94	768
99/102	758
2000/3	766
2000/14	784
2000/53	792
2000/59	283
2000/60	283, 769–71, 775
2000/69	757
2000/76	682, 686, 765, 792
2000/80	757
2001/18	658–62
2001/27	759
2001/42	807, 812–13
2001/63	760
2001/80	336
Art. 2(7)	337
Art. 3(2)	337
Art. 4(1)	338
Art. 4(2)	338
Art. 4(3)	338
Art. 4(5)	339
Art. 4(6)	338
Art. 4(7)	339
Art. 5	339
Art. 7	339
Art. 8	339
Art. 9	339
Art. 10	338
Art. 11	339
Art. 12	339
Art. 13	339
Art. 15	339
2001/81	757
2002/??	164
2002/3	757

European Communities Council Decisions

75/406/EURATOM	794
75/437/EEC	778

77/585/EEC	779
77/795/EEC	771
80/372/EEC	761
81/420/EEC	779
81/462/EEC	762
81/691/EEC	780
82/72/EEC	780
82/461/EEC	780
82/795/EEC	761
83/101/EEC	779
84/132/EEC	779
84/358/EEC	779
85/613/EEC	778
86/277/EEC	762
86/569/EEC	785
87/57/EEC	778
87/600/EURATOM	794
88/540/EEC	761
93/350/EURATOM/ESC/EEC	224
93/361/EEC	762
93/389/EEC	767
93/626/EEC	780
94/69/EEC	767
94/156/EEC	778
94/157/EEC	778
94/493/EEC	780
95/308/EEC	779
97/101/EEC	767
98/216/EEC	780
98/249/EEC	779
98/392/EEC	779
98/685/EEC	785
99/296/EEC	767
99/337/EEC	779
99/575/EEC	779
2000/532/EEC	790
2000/706/EEC	779
2000/1753/EEC	768
2000/2850/EEC	283, 779
2001/379/EEC	762
2001/2455/EEC	770
2002/628/EEC	785

European Communities Council Recommendations
75/436/EURATOM/ESC/EEC   283

European Communities Commission Regulations
82/3626   512
90/770/EURATOM   794
97/120   702
99/1547   794
1997/120   699
2001/2557   699, 702

European Communities Commission Decisions
85/71   785
91/155   785
92/316   1013
94/322   1016
97/266   537
98/2179   751
99/272   284
99/816   699, 702
2000/532   680, 689
2000/728   861
2000/729   861
2000/730   861
2000/731   861
2001/118   689
2002/18   861
2002/1600   752

European Communities Commission Recommendations
1982/74/EURATOM   794
1999/125/EC   166
1999/829/EURATOM   793
2000/303/EC   166
2000/304/EC   166, 759

ABBREVIATIONS

AAU	assigned amounts unit
ACAP	Arctic Council Action Plan (to Eliminate Pollution of the Arctic)
ACC	Administrative Committee on Co-ordination
ACCIS	Advisory Committee for the Co-ordination of Information Systems
ACEA	Association des constructeurs européens d'automobiles
ACHR	1969 American Convention on Human Rights
ACP	African-Caribbean-Pacific
ADB	Asian Development Bank
AEPS	Arctic Environmental Protection Strategy
AFDI	*Annuaire Francais de Droit International*
AIDI	*Annuaire de l'Institut de Droit International*
AJIL	*American Journal of International Law*
AMAP	Arctic Monitoring and Assessment Programme
AOSIS	Alliance of Small Island States
APEC	Asia Pacific Economic Co-operation
ASEAN	Association of South East Asian Nations
ATCM	Antarctic Treaty Consultative Meeting
BATNEEC	best available technology not entailing excessive cost
BCICLR	*Boston College International and Comparative Law Review*
BFSP	*British and Foreign State Papers*
BISD	*Basic Instruments and Selected Documents* (GATT)
BIT	bilateral investment treaty
BPIL	*British Practice in International Law*
BYIL	*British Yearbook of International Law*
CCAMLR	1980 Convention on the Conservation of Antarctic Marine Living Resources
CCSBT	1993 Convention for the Conservation of Southern Bluefin Tuna
CDM	Clean Development Mechanism
CERs	certified emissions reductions

CFC	chlorofluorocarbon
CFI	Court of First Instance (of the European Communities)
CGIAR	Consultative Group on International Agricultural Research
CH_4	methane
CITES	1973 Convention on International Trade in Endangered Species
CLC	1969 Convention on Civil Liability for Oil Pollution
CMLR	*Common Market Law Reports*
Cmnd	Command Paper (UK)
CO	carbon monoxide
CO_2	carbon dioxide
COPUOS	Committee on Peaceful Uses of Outer Space
CRAMRA	1988 Convention on the Regulation of Antarctic Mineral Resource Activities
CRTD	1989 Geneva Convention on Civil Liability for Damage Caused During Carriage of Dangerous Goods by Road, Rail and Inland Navigation Vessels
CSCE	Conference on Security and Co-operation in Europe
CSD	Commission on Sustainable Development
CTS	*Consolidated Treaty Series*
CYIL	*Canadian Yearbook of International Law*
DJILP	*Denver Journal of International Law and Policy*
DPCIA	Dolphin Protection Consumer Information Act (US)
DR	*Decisions and Reports of the European Commission on Human Rights*
DSB	Dispute Settlement Body (WTO)
DSU	Dispute Settlement Understanding (WTO)
EBRD	European Bank for Reconstruction and Development
ECA	(UN) Economic Commission for Africa
ECE	(UN) Economic Commission for Europe
ECHR	European Convention on Human Rights
ECJ	European Court of Justice
ECOSOC	(UN) Economic and Social Council
ECR	*European Court Reports*
ECSC	European Coal and Steel Community
EEA	European Economic Area
EEZ	exclusive economic zone
EFTA	European Free Trade Area
EHRR	*European Human Rights Reports*
EIA	environmental impact assessment
EIB	European Investment Bank
EJIL	*European Journal of International Law*

ELJ	*European Law Journal*
EMEP	European Monitoring and Evaluation Programme (UNECE/UNEP/WMO)
EPA	Environmental Protection Agency (US)
EPL	*Environmental Policy and Law*
EPO	European Patent Office
EPPO	European and Mediterranean Plant Protection Organization
ERU	emissions reduction unit
ESCAP	UN Economic and Social Commission on Asia and the Pacific
ETS	*European Treaty Series*
EURATOM	European Atomic Energy Agency
FAO	Food and Agriculture Organization
FIELD	Foundation for International Environmental Law and Development
FTA	free trade area
GAOR	*General Assembly Official Records*
GATS	General Agreement on Trade in Services
GATT	General Agreement on Tariffs and Trade
GEF	Global Environment Facility
GEMS	Global Environmental Monitoring System
GESAMP	Group of Experts on Scientific Aspects of Marine Pollution
GMM	genetically modified micro-organism
GMO	genetically modified organism
GPA	1995 Global Programme of Action (for the Protection of the Marine Environment from Land-Based Activities)
GYIL	*German Yearbook of International Law*
HCFC	hydrochlorofluorocarbon
HLW	high-level waste
HNS	hazardous and noxious substances
IACSD	Inter-Agency Committee on Sustainable Development
IAEA	International Atomic Energy Agency
IATTC	Inter-American Tropical Tuna Commission
IBRD	International Bank for Reconstruction and Development
ICAO	International Civil Aviation Organization
ICCAT	International Commission for the Conservation of Atlantic Tunas
ICCPR	1966 International Covenant on Civil and Political Rights
ICESCR	1966 International Covenant on Economic, Social and Cultural Rights
ICJ	International Court of Justice
ICLQ	*International and Comparative Law Quarterly*
ICRP	International Commission on Radiological Protection

ICSID	International Centre for Settlement of Investment Disputes
ICSU	International Council of Scientific Unions
IDA	International Development Agency
IDI	Institut de Droit International
IELMT	*International Environmental Legal Materials and Treaties*
IFC	International Finance Corporation
IGPRAD	Intergovernmental Panel of Experts on Radioactive Wastes
IJECL	*International Journal of Estuarine and Coastal Law*
IJMCL	*International Journal of Marine and Coastal Law*
ILA	International Law Association
ILC	International Law Commission
ILM	*International Legal Materials*
ILO	International Labor Organization
ILR	*International Law Reports*
ILW	intermediate-level waste
IMDG Code	International Maritime Dangerous Goods Code
IMF	International Monetary Fund
IMO	International Maritime Organization
INC/FCCC	Intergovernmental Negotiating Committee for a Framework Convention on Climate Change
INFOTERRA	International Referral System for Sources of Environmental Information (UNEP)
IOC	International Oceanographic Commission
IOPC Fund	International Oil Pollution Compensation Fund
IPCC	Intergovernmental Panel on Climate Change
IPE	B. Ruster and B. Simma, *International Protection of the Environment: Treaties and Related Document* (vols. I–XXXI, 1975–83)
IPPC	integrated pollution prevention and control
ISAR	International Standards on Accounting and Reporting
ISO	International Standards Organization
ITLOS	International Tribunal for the Law of the Sea
ITTA	1983 International Tropical Timber Agreement
ITTC	International Tropical Timber Council
ITTO	International Tropical Timber Organization
IUCN	International Union for the Conservation of Nature
IWC	International Whaling Commission
JDI	*Journal de Droit International*
JEL	*Journal of Environmental Law*
JENRL	*Journal of Energy and Natural Resources Law*
JIWLP	*Journal of International Wildlife Law and Policy*
JPL	*Journal of Public Law*

JWT	*Journal of World Trade*
JWTL	*Journal of World Trade Law*
LBS	land-based source
LDC	1972 London Dumping Convention
LIFE	Financial Instrument for the Environment (EC)
LLW	low-level waste
LMCLQ	*Lloyd's Maritime and Commercial Law Quarterly*
LMO	living modified organism
LMO-FFP	living modified organism intended for use as food or feed, or for processing
LNTS	*League of Nations Treaty Series*
LRTAP	long range transboundary air pollution
LULUCF	land-use, land-use change and forestry
MAI	multilateral agreement on investment
MARPOL	International Convention for the Prevention of Pollution from Ships
MCC	Mixed Claims Commission
MEA	multilateral environmental agreement
MEPC	Marine Environment Protection Committee (IMO)
MIGA	Multilateral Investment Guarantee Agency
MLR	*Modern Law Review*
MMPA	1972 Marine Mammal Protection Act (US)
MOU	Memorandum of Understanding
MOX	mixed oxide
MSY	maximum sustainable yield
NAFO	North Atlantic Fisheries Organization
NAFTA	North American Free Trade Agreement
NAMMCO	North Atlantic Marine Mammals Conservation Organization
NATO	North Atlantic Treaty Organization
NEAFC	North-East Atlantic Fisheries Commission
NGO	non-governmental organisation
NO_2	nitrogen dioxide
NO_X	nitrogen oxide
NYIL	*Netherlands Yearbook of International Law*
NYUELJ	*New York University Environmental Law Journal*
NYUJILP	*New York University Journal of International Law and Policy*
NYULR	*New York University Law Review*
O_3	ozone
OAS	Organization of American States
OAU	Organization of African Unity
OECD	Organization for Economic Co-operation and Development

OEEC	Organization for European Economic Co-operation
OJ	*Official Journal of the European Communities*
OJEPO	*Official Journal of the European Patent Office*
OPEC	Organization of Petroleum Exporting Countries
Oppenheim	R. Jennings and A. Watts (eds.), *Oppenheim's International Law* (1992, 9th edn), vol. I
OSCE	Organization for Security and Co-operation in Europe
OSCOM	Commission of the 1972 Oslo Convention for the Prevention of Marine Pollution by Dumping from Ships and Aircraft
OSPAR	1992 Convention for the Protection of the Marine Environment of the North-East Atlantic
PARCOM	Commission of the 1974 Paris Convention for the Prevention of Marine Pollution from Land-Based Sources
PCA	Permanent Court of Arbitration
PCB	polychlorinated biphenyl
PCIJ	Permanent Court of International Justice
PCT	polychlorinated terphenyl
POP	persistent organic pollutant
RBDI	*Revue Belge de Droit International*
RdC	*Receuil des Cours*
RECIEL	*Review of European Community and International Environmental Law*
REDI	*Revue Egyptienne de Droit International*
RGDIP	*Revue Générale de Droit International Public*
RIAA	*Reports of International Arbitral Awards*
RMU	removal unit
SADC	Southern African Development Community
SCAR	Scientific Committee on Antarctic Research
SDRs	special drawing rights
SEAFO	South-East Atlantic Fisheries Organization
SMTE	*Selected Multilateral Treaties on the Environment* (A. Kiss (ed.), vol. 1, 1983; I. Rummel-Bulska and S. Osafa (eds.), vol. 2, 1991)
SO_2	sulphur dioxide
SOLAS	1974 Convention for the Safety of Life at Sea
SO_x	oxides of sulphur
SPA	specially protected areas
SPREP	South Pacific Regional Environment Programme
TAC	total allowable catch
TBT	Technical Barriers to Trade
TED	turtle excluder device
TIAS	*Treaties and Other International Acts*
TNC	transnational corporation

TREMs	trade-related environmental measures
TRIPs	Agreement on Trade-Related Aspects of Intellectual Property Rights (WTO)
UBCLR	*University of British Columbia Law Review*
UDHR	Universal Declaration of Human Rights
UKTS	*United Kingdom Treaty Series*
UNCCUR	1949 United Nations Conference on the Conservation and Utilisation of Resources
UNCED	United Nations Conference on Environment and Development
UNCITRAL	United Nations Commission for International Trade Law
UNCLOS	1982 United Nations Convention on the Law of the Sea
UNCTAD	United Nations Conference on Trade and Development
UNCTC	United Nations Centre for Transnational Corporations
UNDP	United Nations Development Programme
UNECE	United Nations Economic Commission for Europe
UNEP	United Nations Environment Programme
UNESCO	United Nations Educational, Scientific and Cultural Organization
UNGA	United Nations General Assembly
UNIDO	United Nations Industrial Development Organization
UNITAR	United Nations Institute on Training and Research
UNTS	*United Nations Treaty Series*
UPOV	International Union for the Protection of New Varieties of Plants
USC	United States Code
UST	*US Treaties and Other International Agreements*
VOC	volatile organic compound
WBAT	World Bank Administrative Tribunal
WCED	World Commission on Environment and Development
WCMC	World Conservation Monitoring Centre
WHO	World Health Organization
WICEM	World Industry Conference on Environmental Management
WIPO	World Intellectual Property Organization
WLR	*Weekly Law Reports*
WMO	World Meteorological Organization
WRI	World Resources Institute
WSSD	World Summit on Sustainable Development (2002)
WWF	World Wide Fund for Nature
ZACPLAN	Action Plan for the Environmental Management of the Common Zambezi River System
ZaöRV	*Zeitschrift für ausländisches öffentliches Recht und Völkerrecht*

PART I

The legal and institutional framework

The environment and international society: issues, concepts and definitions

Given that the land – and the sea – and the air-spaces of planet Earth are shared, and are not naturally distributed among the states of the world, and given that world transforming activities, especially economic activities, can have effects directly or cumulatively, on large parts of the world environment, how can international law reconcile the inherent and fundamental interdependence of the world environment? How could legal control of activities adversely affecting the world environment be instituted, given that such activities may be fundamental to the economies of particular states?[1]

The environmental challenge

It is now widely recognised that the planet faces a diverse and growing range of environmental challenges which can only be addressed through international co-operation. Acid rain, ozone depletion, climate change, loss of biodiversity, toxic and hazardous products and wastes, pollution of rivers and depletion of freshwater resources are some of the issues which international law is being called upon to address. Since the mid-1980s, the early international legal developments which addressed aspects of the conservation of natural resources have crystallised into an important and growing part of public international law. The conditions which have contributed to the emergence of international environmental law are easily identified: environmental issues are accompanied by a recognition that ecological interdependence does not respect national boundaries and that issues previously considered to be matters of domestic concern have international implications. The implications, which may be bilateral, sub-regional, regional or global, can frequently only be addressed by international law and regulation.

The growth of international environmental issues is reflected in the large body of principles and rules of international environmental law which apply bilaterally, regionally and globally, and reflects international interdependence

---

[1] P. Allott, *Eunomia: A New Order for a New World* (1990), para. 17.52.

in a 'globalising' world.[2] Progress in developing international legal control of activities has been gradual, piecemeal and often reactive to particular incidents or the availability of new scientific evidence. It was not until the late nineteenth century that communities and states began to recognise the transboundary consequences of activities which affected shared rivers or which led to the destruction of wildlife, such as fur seals, in areas beyond national jurisdiction. In the 1930s, the transboundary consequences of air pollution were acknowledged in the litigation leading to the award of the arbitral tribunal in the *Trail Smelter* case. In the 1950s, the international community legislated on international oil pollution in the oceans. By the 1970s, the regional consequences of pollution and the destruction of flora and fauna were obvious, and by the late 1980s global environmental threats were part of the international community's agenda as scientific evidence identified the potential consequences of ozone depletion, climate change and loss of biodiversity. Local issues were recognised to have transboundary, then regional, and ultimately global consequences. In 1996, the International Court of Justice recognised, for the first time, that there existed rules of general international environmental law, and that a 'general obligation of States to ensure that activities within their jurisdiction and control respect the environment of other States or of areas beyond national control is now part of the corpus of international law relating to the environment'.[3] Since then, specific treaty rules have become more complex and technical, environmental issues have been increasingly integrated into other subject areas (including trade, investment, intellectual property, human rights, and armed conflict), and international environmental jurisprudence has become less exceptional as the case law of international courts and tribunals expands.

The 1992 UN Conference on Environment and Development (UNCED) provided an opportunity for the international community to prioritise environmental issues and consolidate a vast and unwieldy patchwork of international legal commitments. The treaties and other international acts adopted before, at and since UNCED reflect the growing range of economic activities which are a legitimate concern of the international community and properly subject to international legal regulation. UNCED agreed environmental priorities which were essentially divided into two categories: those relating to the protection of various environmental media, and those relating to the regulation of particular activities or products. The first category identified the following priorities for the protection and conservation of particular environmental media:

- protection of the atmosphere, in particular by combating climate change, ozone depletion and ground-level and transboundary air pollution;
- protection of land resources;
- halting deforestation;

[2] P. Sands, 'Turtles and Torturers: The Transformation of International Law', 33 NYUJILP 527–58 (2001).
[3] (1996) ICJ Reports 226 at 242.

- conservation of biological diversity;
- protection of freshwater resources; and
- protection of oceans and seas (including coastal areas) and marine living resources.

The second category of major issues identified the products and by-products of human technological and industrial innovation which are considered to be particularly harmful to the environment, and which therefore require international regulation. These include:

- biotechnology;
- toxic chemicals, including their international trade;
- agricultural practices;
- hazardous wastes, including their international trade;
- solid wastes and sewage-related issues; and
- radioactive wastes.

For both categories, the international legal issues are complex, and cannot be considered or addressed properly without taking account of political, cultural, economic and scientific concerns. What level of environmental protection should those standards seek to establish? Should the standards be set on a uniform basis or should they be differentiated to take account of political, economic and ecological circumstances? What regulatory and other techniques exist to apply those standards? How are the standards to be enforced domestically and internationally? What happens if a dispute arises over non-compliance?

In addressing these questions, it is clear that the environment represents a complex system of interconnections, that to understand the evolution and character of a particular environment it is necessary to consider a broad range of apparently unrelated factors, and that these factors should be understood as interacting with each other in a number of ways which do not permit them to be treated as discrete.[4] The interdependence of environmental issues poses legal challenges: how to develop and apply a comprehensive and effective set of legal requirements aimed at preventing environmental damage by addressing the sources without taking measures which will cause harm elsewhere? Current efforts to develop environmentally-sound energy policies reflect the full extent of this challenge, and require international law-making to respond to environmental complexity.

The basis for decision-making: science, economics and other values

International environmental law is influenced by a range of non-legal factors. The likelihood of achieving an agreement increases with: greater scientific consensus about the cause and seriousness of a problem; increased public concern;

[4] A. Goudie, *The Nature of the Environment* (3rd edn, 1993), 367–8.

a perception on the part of the negotiating states that other partners are doing their 'fair' share to address the problem; an increase in short-term political benefits; and the existence of previous, related multilateral agreements.[5] Factors which lessen the likelihood of reaching agreement include the upward costs of environmental controls and the increases in the number of states negotiating a treaty or other instrument. Other relevant considerations include the existence of appropriate international fora for the negotiation of the agreement and the nature of arrangements for dealing with non-compliance. Of all these factors, two have been particularly influential: the impact of science, and the economic costs. Since the first edition of this book, greater attention has also been given to other values, representing neither scientific nor economic considerations.

Science

The strong concern of states to ensure that their economic interests are taken into account in the development and application of international environmental law has been matched by an equally firm view that environmental regulations should only be adopted where there is compelling scientific evidence that action is required to prevent environmental damage. This has brought diplomats and international lawyers together with the scientific community in ways not often seen in other areas of international law. The ease with which an international lawyer is able to present a cogent case for international legislation will often turn upon the ability to show that the lack of action by the international community is likely to result in significant adverse effects. Within the past decade the task may have been made substantially less onerous by the broad acceptance and application of the precautionary principle, which provides a basis for action to be taken even in the face of significant scientific uncertainty. The 1985 Vienna Convention (and its 1987 Montreal Protocol), the 1992 Climate Change Convention (and its 1997 Kyoto Protocol), the 1995 Straddling Stocks Agreement and the 2000 Cartagena Protocol on Biosafety may be cited as examples of the numerous international environmental treaties establishing obligations in the face of scientific uncertainty and in the absence of an international consensus on the existence of environmental harm.[6] To these may be added a series of international judicial decisions informed by 'prudence and caution'.[7]

Since the first edition of this book was published in 1995, the place of science in international environmental decision-making has been the subject of vigorous debate, largely focusing around competing claims concerning the lawfulness of restrictions on the use of, and international trade in, modified

---

[5] R. Hahn and K. Richards, 'The Internationalisation of Environmental Regulation', 30 *Harvard International Law Journal* 421 at 433–40 (1989).
[6] See chapter 6, pp. 266–79 below on the precautionary principle.
[7] ITLOS. See chapter 10, pp. 469–77 and chapter 11, pp. 580–3 below.

foodstuffs, including genetically modified organisms. Disputes under various World Trade Organization (WTO) agreements (relating to beef hormones[8] and asbestos[9]) and the negotiations leading to the adoption of the Cartagena Protocol on Biosafety[10] have provided opportunities for an airing of states' views as to the degree of scientific evidence and certainty that is required to justify restrictions (as well as the economic and other implications of such decisions, and the extent to which non-scientific and non-economic considerations may be applied in decision-making, on which see below).[11] As to science, in large part the issues have been driven by differences of perspective between the United States and the European Union, with the former strongly in favour of decision-making which is based on 'hard science' and strictly limiting the circumstances in which restrictions may be permitted in the face of uncertainty as to consequences. The extent of the difference – and its implications for the legal order more generally – are reflected in views expressed by one official of the US State Department:

> the increasing efforts from within the EU . . . could weaken the scientific basis for regulatory decisions that affect trade. This trend poses a challenge not only to US interests but also to the rules-based, global trading system that we have spent the past 50 years building.[12]

The contrary position – adopted by the European Union – would allow decision-makers a greater 'margin of appreciation' in the face of scientific uncertainty, and is reflected in its arguments to the WTO Appellate Body in the *Beef Hormones* case, and in its Communication on the use of the precautionary principle.[13] The tension in the two approaches has not been resolved at the level of international legislation, and will fall to international adjudicators to determine on a case-by-case basis. The approaches of the International Court of Justice (in the *Gabcikovo-Nagymaros* case), the International Tribunal for the Law of the Sea (in the *Southern Bluefin Tuna* and *MOX* cases), the WTO Appellate Body (in the *Beef Hormones* case) and the European Patent Office (in the *Plant Genetic Systems* case) merit attention and comparison, indicating

---

[8] See chapter 18, pp. 979–81 below.
[9] See chapter 18, pp. 973–7 below.   [10] See chapter 11, pp. 521–3 below.
[11] For an excellent overview, see T. Christoforou, 'Science, Law and Precaution in Dispute Resolution on Health and Environmental Protection: What Role for Scientific Experts?', in J. Bourrinet and S. Maljean-Dubois (eds.), *Le Commerce international des organismes génétiquement modifiés* (2002).
[12] Quoted in M. Geistfeld, 'Reconciling Cost-Benefit Analysis with the Principle that Safety Matters More than Money', 76 *New York University Law Review* 114 at 176 (2001). The same article quotes an editorial in the *Wall Street Journal* (on 10 February 2000): 'The precautionary "principle" is an environmentalist neologism, invoked to trump scientific evidence and move directly to banning things they don't like – biotech, wireless technology, hydrocarbon emissions.'
[13] Respectively at chapter 18, pp. 979–81; and chapter 6, pp. 266–79.

a reluctance to move away from traditional approaches, but tempered with a growing recognition as to some appropriate role for precautionary measures.[14] Of particular note, in this regard, is the recognition of a greater role for early 'risk assessment', beyond traditional use of environmental impact assessment.[15]

Economics

The progress of international environmental law reflects the close relationship between environmental protection and economic development. Over the short term, laws adopted to protect the environment can impose potentially significant economic costs. Moreover, certain developed countries will be well placed to benefit from the adoption of stringent environmental standards, including the advantages gained from the sale of environmentally sound technology, while others will be concerned about the threat to their economic competitiveness which results from the failure of other countries to adopt similar stringent standards and may, some argue, relax their environmental standards.[16]

Most environmental treaties do not provide for financial resources to be made available to compensate for the additional costs of protective measures, partly because, it must be said, at the time of their negotiation their economic consequences were not fully considered. The Convention on the International Trade in Endangered Species (CITES), for example, did not provide compensation to African states for the loss of revenue resulting from the 1989 ban on international trade in ivory. This may have limited the desire of many developing countries to support similar measures subsequently. There is also concern that the move towards harmonisation might lead to a lowering of environmental standards to ensure that economic costs can be borne, as reflected in efforts to introduce a principle of 'cost-effectiveness' to guide decision-making under some environmental agreements.[17] Accordingly, some treaties, such as the EC Treaty (as amended since 1992), required certain EC secondary legislation to include a safeguard clause which allows member states to adopt provisional measures for 'non-economic environmental reasons'.[18]

---

[14] Respectively at chapter 10, pp. 469–77; chapter 11, pp. 580–1; chapter 6, p. 276; chapter 19, pp. 979–81; and chapter 20, p. 1048.

[15] See e.g. 2000 Biosafety Protocol, chapter 12, pp. 653–8; 1998 Chemicals Convention, chapter 12, pp. 635–6.

[16] See D. Esty, 'Revitalizing Environmental Federalism', 95 *Michigan Law Review* 570 (1996). For a compelling alternative view, see R. Revesz, 'Rehabilitating Interstate Competition: Rethinking the "Race to the Bottom" Rationale for Federal Environmental Regulation', 67 *New York University Environmental Law Review* 1210 (1992) and R. Revesz, 'The Race to the Bottom and Federal Environmental Regulation: A Response to Critics', 82 *Minnesota Law Review* 535 (1997). In the context of the NAFTA rules on direct foreign investment, and the failed OECD negotiation for a Multilateral Agreement on Investment, see chapter 20, pp. 1058–64.

[17] 1992 Climate Change Convention, Art. 3.   [18] Chapter 15, pp. 734–54.

It is hardly surprising, therefore, that in recent years environmental concerns have become interconnnected with economic considerations. Aside from the question of the potential use of economic instruments to achieve environmental objectives,[19] two issues have become particularly acute in recent negotiations. Developing countries have sought to make their acceptance of environmental obligations dependent upon the provision of financial assistance, and some developed countries, in order to prevent the competitive economic advantages which might flow from non-compliance, have striven to ensure that environmental treaties establish effective institutions to verify and ensure that the contracting parties comply with their environmental obligations.

These two features have resulted in environmental treaties breaking new ground in the development of international legal techniques. Some environmental treaties, such as the 1987 Montreal Protocol, the 1992 Climate Change Convention, the 1992 Biodiversity Convention and the 2001 POPs Convention, now provide for 'compensatory' finance to be made available to developing countries to enable them to meet certain 'incremental costs' of implementing their obligations, and provide for subsidiary bodies to verify compliance and implementation. This linkage has in turn led to the creation of specialised funding arrangements within existing institutions, in particular the World Bank and the regional development banks, such as the Global Environment Facility (GEF).[20]

The integration of environmental protection and economic development could make international environmental law less marginal. On the other hand, the integration of environmental concerns into international economic arrangements may merely serve to subsume environmental considerations and perpetuate an approach to international economic practices and arrangements which may encourage certain environmental problems. This concern refers to the integration of environment and development which has led to the emergence of the concept of sustainable development, now reflected in many international instruments[21] and the decisions of some international courts.[22]

Other social objectives

Science and economics are not the only factors which influence international environmental decision-making, or international adjudication of decisions premised on environmental arguments. Within the past five years, there has been increasing recognition of a place for social and other values as legitimate factors influencing environmental decision-making. This is reflected, initially,

---

[19] Chapter 4, pp. 158–67.   [20] Chapter 20, pp. 1032–4.   [21] Chapter 6, pp. 252–66.
[22] E.g. the ICJ in the *Case Concerning the Gabcikovo-Nagymaros Project* (1997) ICJ Reports 7, at para. 140 (chapter 10, pp. 469–77); the WTO Appellate Body, in the *Shrimp/Turtle* case, chapter 19, pp. 965–73.

in the EC rules which emerged in 1992 to permit (on a temporary basis) exceptional measures based on non-economic considerations (see above), which were relied upon (in Directive 90/220) by some EC member states to justify temporary bans on the placing on the market of genetically modified maize and oil rapeseed products.[23] More recently, however, it has been taken up in other contexts. The 2000 Biosafety Protocol allows parties, in reaching decisions under the Protocol, to

> take into account, consistent with their international obligations, socio-economic considerations arising from the impact of living modified organisms on the conservation and sustainable use of biological diversity, especially with regard to the value of biological diversity to indigenous and local communities.[24]

In a similar vein, in its decision in the *Asbestos* case, also in 2000, the WTO Appellate Body confirmed that an importing state was entitled to take into account (among other factors) consumer tastes and habits in respect of a particular product in order to determine whether it was 'like' another product.[25] This recognises, apparently for the first time, that the characteristics of a product go beyond economic and physical (scientific) considerations.

Sustainable development

The concept of sustainable development may be found expressly or implicitly in many environmental treaties and other instruments in the period prior to the publication of the Brundtland Report in 1987.[26] Nevertheless, the Brundtland Report is commonly viewed as the point at which sustainable development became a broad global policy objective and set the international community on the path which led to UNCED and the body of rules referred to as 'international law in the field of sustainable development',[27] but distinguished from international environmental law.[28] Is there any difference between international law in the field of sustainable development and international environmental law?

The Brundtland Report defined sustainable development as 'development that meets the needs of the present without compromising the ability of future generations to meet their own needs'. Two key concepts are contained within this definition: the concept of needs, in particular the essential needs of the present generation, and the idea of limitations imposed by the state of technology and social organisation on the environment's ability to meet present

---

[23] Chapter 12, pp. 658–62.

[24] Art. 26(1); see R. H. Khawa, 'Socio-Economic Considerations', in C. Bail, R. Falkner and H. Marquard, *The Cartagena Protocol on Biosafety* (2002), 361.

[25] Chapter 19, pp. 973–7.   [26] Chapter 6, pp. 260–1, notes 166–82.

[27] Rio Declaration, Principle 27; Agenda 21, Chapter 39, para. 39.1.

[28] UNGA Res. 44/228 (1989), para. 15(e); Agenda 21, paras. 39.1(a) and 39.2.

and future needs.[29] The Brundtland Report identified critical objectives for environment and development policies reflected in the concept of sustainable development:

- reviving growth and changing its quality;
- meeting essential needs for jobs, food, energy, water and sanitation;
- ensuring a sustainable level of population;
- conserving and enhancing the resource base;
- reorienting technology and managing risk; and
- merging environment and economics in decision-making.[30]

The forty chapters of Agenda 21 elaborate upon these issues. Taken together they constitute the framework for international law in the field of sustainable development, now confirmed as an international legal term by the ICJ in the *Gabcikovo-Nagymaros* case and as having practical legal consequences by the WTO Appellate Body in the *Shrimp/Turtle* case.[31] Agenda 21 has been confirmed and, to a limited extent, taken a step further by the Plan of Implementation adopted by the World Summit on Sustainable Development, in September 2002. Only fourteen chapters of Agenda 21 address issues which are primarily 'environmental', and they provide the subject matter of this book. The international law of sustainable development is therefore broader than international environmental law; apart from environmental issues, it includes the social and economic dimension of development, the participatory role of major groups, and financial and other means of implementation.[32] International environmental law is part of the international law of sustainable development, but is narrower in scope. And, as will be seen in subsequent chapters, the integration of environmental considerations with other social objectives has led to the development of a human rights/environment jurisprudence[33] and the integration of environment into matters such as armed conflict and criminal law (reflected, in a limited way, in the Statute of the International Criminal Court).[34]

The international legal order

Environmental issues pose challenges for the traditional international legal order, in at least three ways. They pose challenges, first, for the legislative, administrative and adjudicative functions of international law; secondly, for the manner in which international legal arrangements are currently organised (i.e.

---

[29] WCED, *Our Common Future* (1987), 43.   [30] *Ibid.*, 49–65.
[31] Chapter 6, pp. 252–66. See generally P. Sands, 'International Courts and the Application of the Concept of "Sustainable Development"', 3 *Max Planck Yearbook of United Nations Law* 389–407 (1999).
[32] Sections I, III and IV of Agenda 21.   [33] Chapter 7, pp. 291–307.
[34] Chapter 18, pp. 894–6.

along territorial lines); and, thirdly, for the various actors who are considered to be members of the international community and participants in the various processes and practices of the international legal order.[35] The ability of the international legal order to address these three aspects, in the context of environmental issues, will determine whether international law is up to the task of taking on these new global challenges, or whether it will become 'the faithful friend of a family overtaken by time'.[36] It remains to be seen whether a diminishing conception of sovereignty in the face of a more assertive international judiciary, together with a more inclusive, accessible and diverse international legal order, leads to any greater protection of the environment.[37]

The functions of international law

International law and institutions serve as the principal framework for international co-operation and collaboration between members of the international community in their efforts to protect the local, regional and global environment. At each level, the task becomes progressively more complex as new actors and interests are drawn into the legal process: whereas just two states negotiated the nineteenth-century fishery conservation conventions, more than 150 states negotiated the 1992 Climate Change Convention and the 2000 Biosafety Protocol.

In both cases, however, the principles and rules of public international law and international organisations serve similar functions: to provide a framework within which the various members of the international community may co-operate, establish norms of behaviour and resolve their differences. The proper functions of international law are legislative, administrative and adjudicative functions. The legislative function, which is considered in chapter 4, provides for the creation of legal principles and rules which impose binding obligations requiring states and other members of the international community to conform to certain norms of behaviour. These obligations place limits upon the activities which may be conducted or permitted because of their actual or potential impact upon the environment. The impact might be felt within the borders of a state, or across the boundaries of two or more states, or in areas beyond the jurisdiction and control of any state.

The administrative function of international law allocates tasks to various actors to ensure that the standards imposed by the principles and rules

---

[35] For a more complete exploration of these issues, see P. Sands, *Vers une transformation du droit international? Institutionaliser le doute* (Editions A. Pedone, Paris, 2000).

[36] Allott, *Eunomia*, para. 16.3.

[37] P. Sands, 'Turtles and Torturers: The Transformation of International Law', 33 NYUJILP 527 at 558 (2001).

of international environmental law are applied. The adjudicative function of international law aims to provide mechanisms or fora to prevent and peacefully settle differences or disputes which arise between members of the international community involving the use of natural resources or the conduct of activities which will impact upon the environment. As will be seen, since the mid-1990s the adjudicative function has assumed increasing importance in interpreting and applying – and even developing – the rules of international law in the field of the environment.

Sovereignty and territory

The international legal order regulates the activities of an international community comprising states, international organisations and non-state actors. States have the primary role in the international legal order, as both international law-makers and holders of international rights and obligations. Under international law states are sovereign and have equal rights and duties as members of the international community, notwithstanding differences of an economic, social, political or other nature.[38] The doctrine of the sovereignty and equality of states has three principal corollaries, namely, that states have:

> (1) a jurisdiction, prima facie exclusive, over a territory and a permanent population living there; (2) a duty of non-intervention in the area of exclusive jurisdiction of other states; and (3) the dependence of obligations arising from customary law and treaties on the consent of obligor.[39]

The sovereignty and exclusive jurisdiction of the 200 or so states over their territory means, in principle, that they alone have the competence to develop policies and laws in respect of the natural resources and the environment of their territory, which comprises:

1. the land within its boundaries, including the subsoil;
2. internal waters, such as lakes, rivers and canals;[40]
3. the territorial sea, which is adjacent to the coast, including its seabed, subsoil and the resources thereof;[41] and
4. the airspace above its land, internal waters and territorial sea,[42] up to the point at which the legal regime of outer space begins.[43]

---

[38] Declaration on Principles of International Law Concerning Friendly Relations and Cooperation Among States in Accordance with the Charter of the United Nations, UNGA Res. 2625 (XXV) (1970).

[39] I. Brownlie, *Principles of Public International Law* (1990, 4th edn), 287.

[40] 1982 UNCLOS, Art. 8.

[41] 1982 UNCLOS, Art. 2. On archipelagic waters as national territory, see 1982 UNCLOS, Art. 48.

[42] Oppenheim, vol. 1, 650–61.   [43] Oppenheim, vol. 1, 826–45.

Additionally, states have limited sovereign rights and jurisdiction over other areas, including: a contiguous zone adjacent to the territorial seas;[44] the resources of the continental shelf, its seabed and subsoil;[45] certain fishing zones;[46] and the 'exclusive economic zone'.[47] It follows that certain areas fall outside the territory of any state, and in respect of these no state has exclusive jurisdiction. These areas, which are sometimes referred to as the 'global commons', include the high seas and its seabed and subsoil, outer space, and, according to a majority of states, the Antarctic. The atmosphere is also sometimes considered to be a part of the global commons. This apparently straightforward international legal order worked satisfactorily as an organising structure until technological developments permeated national boundaries. This structure does not, however, co-exist comfortably with an environmental order which consists of a biosphere of interdependent ecosystems which do not respect artificial national territorial boundaries. Many natural resources and their environmental components are ecologically shared. The use by one state of natural resources within its territory will invariably have consequences for the use of natural resources and their environmental components in another state.[48] This is evident where a river runs through two or more countries, or where living resources migrate between two or more sovereign territories. What has only recently become clear is that apparently innocent activities in one country, such as the release of chlorofluorocarbons or (possibly) genetically modified organisms, can have significant effects upon the environment of other states or in areas beyond national jurisdiction. Ecological interdependence poses a fundamental problem for international law, and explains why international co-operation and the development of international environmental standards are increasingly indispensable: the challenge for international law in the world of sovereign states is to reconcile the fundamental independence of each state with the inherent and fundamental interdependence of the environment.

An additional but related question arises as a result of existing territorial arrangements which leave certain areas outside any state's territory: how can international law ensure the protection of areas beyond national jurisdiction? While it is clear that under international law each state may have environmental obligations to its citizens and to other states which may be harmed by its activities, it is less clear whether such an obligation is owed to the international community as a whole.[49]

---

[44] 1982 UNCLOS, Art. 33.

[45] 1982 UNCLOS, Arts. 76 and 77.

[46] *Fisheries Jurisdiction Cases* (1974) ICJ Reports 3, at para. 52.

[47] 1982 UNCLOS, Arts. 55 and 56; chapter 5, pp. 178–9; and chapter 11, pp. 570–2.

[48] On 'shared natural resources', see chapter 2, p. 43, n. 113, and accompanying text.

[49] On the enforcement of international rights owed to the international community as a whole, see chapter 5, pp. 184–91.

International actors

A second salient issue concerns the membership of the international community and the participation of actors in the development and application of the principles and rules of international environmental law. In the environmental field it is clear that international law is gradually moving away from an approach which treats international society as comprising a community of states, and is increasingly encompassing the persons (both legal and natural) within and among those states. This is reflected in developments both in relation to law-making and law enforcement. This feature is similar to that which applies in the field of international human rights law, where non-state actors and international organisations also have an expanded role. This reality is reflected in many international legal instruments. The Rio Declaration and Agenda 21 recognise and call for the further development of the role of international organisations and non-state actors in virtually all aspects of the international legal process which relate to environment and development.[50] The 1998 Aarhus Convention provides clear rules on the rights of participation of non-state actors, in relation to access to information and justice, and the right to participate in environmental decision-making.[51] Although the Convention's requirements are intended to apply at the national level, there is no reason why this rationale should not equally apply at the international level, including in the EU context.

The environment and international law: defining terms

International environmental law comprises those substantive, procedural and institutional rules of international law which have as their primary objective the protection of the environment. Dictionaries define 'environment' as 'the objects or the region surrounding anything'.[52] Accordingly, the term encompasses both the features and the products of the natural world and those of human civilisation. On this definition, the environment is broader than, but includes, 'nature', which is concerned only with features of the world itself.[53] 'Ecology', on the other hand, is a science related to the environment and to nature which is concerned with animals and plants, and is 'that branch of biology which deals with the relations of living organisms to their surroundings, their habits and modes of life'.[54] The 'ecosystem' is 'a unit of ecology . . . which includes the plants and animals occurring together plus that part of their environment over which they have an influence'.[55]

The legal definition of the 'environment' and related concepts is important at two levels. At a general level, it defines the scope of the legal subject and the competence of, say, international organisations. Thus, the failure of the

---

[50] Chapter 3, pp. 72–120.   [51] Chapter 5, pp. 209–10.
[52] *Compact Oxford English Dictionary* (1991, 2nd edn), 523.
[53] *Ibid.*, 1151.   [54] *Ibid.*, 494.   [55] *Ibid.*

1946 International Whaling Convention to define the term 'whale' has led to protracted disputes over whether the International Whaling Commission has competence over dolphins;[56] and the text of CITES was unclear as to whether its provisions applied to artificially propagated plants grown under controlled conditions in a 'non-natural environment'.[57] More specifically, the definition of the 'environment' assumes particular significance in relation to efforts to establish rules governing liability for damage to the environment.[58]

Legal definitions of the 'environment' reflect scientific categorisations and groupings, as well as political acts which incorporate cultural and economic considerations. A scientific approach will divide environmental issues into 'compartments'. These include the atmosphere, atmospheric deposition, soils and sediments, water quality, biology and humans.[59] Scientific definitions are transformed by the political process into the legal definitions found in treaties; although 'environment' does not have a generally accepted usage as a term of art under international law, recent agreements have consistently identified the various media included in the term.

The approaches to defining the 'environment' do nevertheless vary. Early treaties tended to refer to 'flora and fauna' rather than the environment,[60] thus restricting the scope of their application. Article XX(b) and (g) of the General Agreement on Tariffs and Trade (GATT) refers not to the environment but to 'human, animal or plant life or health' and to the 'conservation of exhaustible natural resources', and these terms are considered by some to have limited the scope of permissible exceptions to the rules of free trade, particularly in the context of the narrow construction given to the terms used by GATT Dispute Settlement Panels.[61] Although the 1972 Stockholm Declaration does not include a definition of the environment, Principle 2 refers to the natural resources of the earth as including 'air, water, land, flora and fauna and . . . natural ecosystems'. The Stockholm Declaration also recognises, as the Preamble makes clear, that the environment of natural resources should be distinguished from the man-made environment, which includes in particular the living and working environment. The 1982 World Charter for Nature similarly does not define the 'environment', but addresses the need to respect nature through principles

---

[56] Chapter 11, p. 592.   [57] CITES Conf. Res. 8.17 (1992).

[58] The definition of 'environment' and 'environmental resources' is also important for economists. In 1974, the Norwegian Department of Natural Resources developed and introduced a system of natural resource accounting and budgeting which divided resources into two categories: material resources and environmental resources. Material resources included minerals (minerals, hydrocarbons, stone, gravel and sand), biological resources (in the air, water, on land and in the ground) and inflowing resources (solar radiation, hydrological cycle, wind, ocean currents). Environmental resources are air, water, soil and space. See D. Pearce *et al.* (eds.), *Blueprint for a Green Economy* (1989).

[59] UNEP, *Environmental Data Report* (1992), 3.

[60] Chapter 2, pp. 25–6.   [61] Chapter 19, pp. 948–9.

which are applicable to all life forms, habitats, all areas of the earth, ecosystems and organisms, and land, marine and atmospheric resources.

Those treaties which do refer to the environment and seek to include some form of working definition tend to adopt broad definitions. Under the 1974 Nordic Convention, 'environmentally harmful activities' are those which result in discharges 'into water courses, lakes or the sea, and the use of land, the sea bed, buildings or installations'.[62] Under the 1977 ENMOD Convention, 'environmental modification' refers to changing the 'dynamics, composition or structure of the earth, including its biota, lithosphere, hydrosphere and atmosphere, or of outer space'.[63] As used in the 1979 LRTAP Convention, the environment includes 'agriculture, forestry, materials, aquatic and other natural ecosystems and visibility'.[64] Under the 1991 Espoo Convention and the 1992 Watercourses Convention, the 'environment', which is defined in terms of impacts, includes 'human health and safety, flora, fauna, soil, air, water, climate, landscape and historical monuments or other physical structures or the interaction among these factors'.[65] In similar terms, the 1991 Antarctic Environment Protocol protects the climate and weather patterns; air and water quality; atmospheric, terrestrial (including aquatic), glacial or marine environments; fauna and flora; and areas of biological, scientific, historic, aesthetic or wilderness significance.[66] Under EC law, the environment comprises 'the relationship of human beings with water, air, land and all biological forms'.[67] EC Council Directive 85/337 (as amended by Directive 97/11), on environmental impact assessment, includes in the scope of information to be provided the likely effect of projects on human beings, fauna and flora, soil, water, air, climate and the landscape, and material assets and cultural heritage.[68] The 1990 EC Directive on freedom of access to information on the environment includes information on the state of 'water, air, soil, fauna, flora, land and natural sites',[69] and the 2000 Directive on eco-labelling establishes an 'Indicative Environmental Matrix' which requires pollution and contamination in eleven environmental fields to be taken into account (air, water, soil, waste, energy savings, natural resources consumption, global warming prevention, ozone layer protection, environmental safety, noise, and biodiversity) when deciding whether to grant an eco-label to a particular product.[70] Other agreements which use the term 'environment' do not define it. The 1982 United Nations Convention on the Law of the Sea does not define 'marine environment', although it appears to

---

[62] Art. 1.   [63] Art. II.   [64] Art. 7(d).

[65] 1991 Espoo Convention, Art. 1(vii); and 1997 Watercourses Convention, Art. 1(2).

[66] Art. 3(2).   [67] Directive 79/117, Art. 2(10). See chapter 14.

[68] 583, Art. 3. See chapter 16, pp. 807–11. The same reference is used by the 1992 Industrial Accidents Convention, Art. 1(c).

[69] Art. 2(a). See chapter 17, pp. 853–6.

[70] Chapter 17, p. 861. The original 1992 Directive provided for eight fields.

include ecosystems, habitats, threatened or endangered species and other forms of marine life, and atmospheric pollution.[71]

More specific international legal terms are being used and are subject to carefully negotiated definition. Recent examples include definitions of biological resources,[72] the climate system,[73] and the ozone layer.[74] Other terms frequently used in international agreements relating to environmental matters and for which specific legal definitions have been established include 'pollution',[75] 'conservation',[76] 'damage',[77] adverse effects'[78] and 'sustainable use' or 'management'.[79]

Further reading[80]

International environmental law: texts, articles and history

An extensive literature on international environmental law developed in the mid-1980s, although the first treatises appeared only in 1989 (Alexandre Kiss) and 1992 (Patricia Birnie and Alan Boyle), followed in 1994 by the first edition of this book. Earlier works addressed specific aspects of international environmental protection and the conservation of natural resources, and little of the early literature addressed economic aspects.

E. D. Brown, 'The Conventional Law of the Environment', 13 *Natural Resources Journal* 203 (1973)

L. B. Sohn, 'The Stockholm Declaration on the Human Environment', 14 *Harvard International Law Journal* 423 (1973)

Academie de Droit International de la Haye, Colloque, *The Protection of the Environment and International Law* (1973)

J. Barros and D. M. Johnston, *The International Law of Pollution* (1974)

---

[71] Art. 194(3)(a) and (5). Cf. the 1992 OSPAR Convention, which appears to distinguish between the 'marine environment' and the 'flora and fauna which it supports': Preamble.

[72] '[G]enetic resources, organisms or parts thereof, populations, or any other biotic component of ecosystems with actual or potential use or value for humanity': 1992 Biodiversity Convention, Art. 2; see also the definition of biological diversity, chapter 11, p. 516, n. 91.

[73] '[T]he totality of the atmosphere, hydrosphere, biosphere and geosphere and their interactions': 1992 Climate Change Convention, Art. 1(3).

[74] '[T]he layer of atmospheric ozone above the planetary boundary layer': 1985 Vienna Convention, Art. 1(1).

[75] Chapter 8, p. 325; chapter 9, pp. 398, 406 and chapter 18, p. 876.

[76] Chapter 6, p. 260; chapter 11, p. 518.

[77] Chapter 18, p. 876.

[78] Chapter 18, p. 877.

[79] Chapter 6, p. 324; chapter 9, p. 400; and chapter 11, p. 519.

[80] There exists an extensive literature on general and specialised aspects of international environmental law. The list which follows is intended to be indicative only, and any ommissions should not be taken to indicate a qualitative judgment on that work.

L. A. Teclaff and A. E. Utton (eds.), *International Environmental Law* (1974)

R. A. Falk, 'The Global Environment and International Law: Challenge and Response', 23 *Kansas Law Review* 385 (1975)

A. L. Springer, 'Towards a Meaningful Concept of Pollution in International Law', 26 *International and Comparative Law Quarterly* 531 (1977)

J. Schneider, *World Public Order of the Environment: Towards an Ecological Law and Organisation* (1979)

R. M. M'Gonigle and M. W. Zacher, *Pollution, Politics and International Law: Tankers at Sea* (1979)

R. S. Bock, *International Protection of the Environment* (1983)

A. L. Springer, *The International Law of Pollution: Protecting the Global Environment in a World of Sovereign States* (1983)

R. J. Dupuy, *The Future International Law of the Environment* (1985)

S. Lyster, *International Wildlife Law: An Analysis of International Treaties Concerned with the Conservation of Wildlife* (1985)

UN World Commission on Environment and Development, R. D. Munro and J. G. Lammers (eds.), *Environmental Protection and Sustainable Development: Legal Principles and Recommendations* (1987)

W. Lang, *Internationaler Umweltschutz* (1989)

P. Sands, 'The Environment, Community and International Law', 30 *Harvard International Law Journal* 393 (1989)

M. Bothe and L. Gundling, *Neuere Tendenzen des Umweltrechts im Internationalen Vergleich* (1990)

M. Lachs, 'The Challenge of the Environment', 39 *International and Comparative Law Quarterly* 663 (1990)

P. Sand, *Lessons Learned in Global Environmental Governance* (1990)

C. De Casadevante Romani, *La Protection del Medio Ambiente en Derecho Internacional Derecho Comunitario Europeo y Derecho Espanol* (1991)

O. Schachter, 'The Emergence of International Environmental Law', 44 *Journal of International Affairs* 457 (1991)

W. Lang, H. Neuhold and K. Zemanek (eds.), *Environmental Protection and International Law* (1991)

D. B. Magraw (ed.), *International Law and Pollution* (1991)

J. L. Mathieu, *La protection internationale de l'environnement* (1992)

P. Sand (ed.), *The Effectiveness of International Environmental Agreements – A Survey of Existing Legal Instruments* (1992)

P. Sands (ed.), *Greening International Law* (1993)

C. Stone, *The Gnat is Older than Man: Global Environment and Human Agenda* (1993)

E. Brown Weiss (ed.), *Environmental Change and International Law* (1993)

A. Kiss, *Droit international de l'environnement* (1994, 2nd edn)

A. Kiss and F. Burhenne-Guilmin (eds.), *A Law for the Environment: Essays in Honour of Wolfgang E. Burhenne* (1994)

S. Murase, 'Perspectives from International Economic Law on Transnational Environmental Issues', 253 *Recueil des Cours* 283 (1995)

P. Dupuy, 'Ou en est le droit international de l'environnement à la fin du siecle?', RGDIP 873 (1997)

A. Boyle and D. Freestone, *International Law and Sustainable Development* (1999)

A. Kiss and D. Shelton, *International Environmental Law* (1999, 2nd edn)

J. Juste Ruiz, *Derecho Internacional del Medio Ambiente* (1999)

A. Gillespie, *International Environmental Law, Ethics and Policy* (2001)

D. Hunter, J. Salzman and D. Zaelke (eds.), *International Environmental Law and Policy (Casebook)* (2001, 2nd edn)

P. Birnie and A. Boyle, *International Law and the Environment* (2002, 2nd edn)

M. Fitzmaurice, 'International Protection of the Environment', 293 RdC 9 (2001)

T. Kuokkanen, *International Law and the Environment: Variations on a Theme* (2002)

Sources of international environmental law
Primary materials

Beyond the general sources of international law (see the works cited in chapter 4, p. 123 **et seq.** below) a specialised literature now addresses the primary sources of international environmental law. The Internet is now the leading source of treaties, acts of international organisations (including conferences of the parties), case law of international courts and tribunals, and other primary materials (see below). Apart from the useful collections of selected materials, the works edited by Burhenne and by Rüster and Simma provide comprehensive sources of information on treaties and other international acts. Certain primary sources nevertheless remain obscure: early bilateral agreements are frequently only available directly from the countries or organisations involved in their promulgation.

W. E. Burhenne (ed.), *International Environmental Law: Multilateral Treaties* (looseleaf, 1974–)

B. Rüster and B. Simma (eds.), *International Protection of the Environment: Treaties and Related Documents* (vols. I–XXXI, 1975–1983)

B. Rüster and B. Simma, *International Protection of the Environment: Treaties and Related Documents* (looseleaf, 1990–)

UNEP, *Selected Multilateral Treaties in the Field of the Environment* (vol. 1, A. C. Kiss (ed.), 1983; vol. 2, I. Rummel-Bulska and S. Osafo (eds.), 1991)

H. Hohmann (ed.), *Basic Documents of International Environmental Law* (1992)

T. Scovazzi and T. Treves (eds.), *World Treaties for the Protection of the Environment* (1992)

E. Brown Weiss, P. C. Szasz and D. B. Magraw, *International Environmental Law – Basic Instruments and References* (1992)

A. O. Adede, *International Environmental Law Digest: Instruments for International Responses to Problems of Environment and Development* (1993)

W. E. Burhenne (ed.), *International Environmental Soft Law: Collection of Relevant Instruments* (1993)

P. Sands, R. Tarasofsky and M. Weiss, *Documents in International Environmental Law* (1994, 2 vols.)

P. Sands and R. Tarasofsky, *Documents in EC Environmental Law* (1994)

P. Birnie and A. Boyle, *Basic Documents on International Law and the Environment* (1995)

L. Boisson de Chazournes, R. Desgagné and C. Romano (eds.), *Protection international de l'environnement: recueil d'instruments juridiques* (1998)

C. Dommen and P. Cullet, *Droit international de l'environnement: textes de bases et références* (1998)

D. Hunter, J. Salzman and D. Zaelke (eds.), *International Environmental Law and Policy: Treaty Supplement* (2001)

P. Sands and P. Galizzi, *Basic Documents in International Environmental Law* (2003)

International environmental jurisprudence

C. Robb (ed.), *International Environmental Law Reports 1: Early Decisons* (1999)

C. Robb (ed.), *International Environmental Law Reports 2: Trade and Environment* (2001)

C. Robb (ed.), *International Environmental Law Reports 3: Human Rights and Environment* (2001)

Journals

The following academic and practitioners' journals provide sources of information on important international legal developments, and articles on specific aspects of international environmental law. The *Yearbook of International Environmental Law* is an especially useful source for annual developments, including materials on municipal practice (including the implementation of international legal obligations).

International law generally

American Journal of International Law
European Journal of International Law
International and Comparative Law Quarterly
International Legal Materials
Revue General de Droit International Public

International environmental law

Colorado Journal of International Environmental Law and Policy
Ecology Law Quarterly
Environmental Law and Policy
Georgetown International Environment Law Review

International Environment Reporter
International Journal of Marine and Coastal Law
Journal of Environmental Law
Journal of Environment and Natural Resources Law
Natural Resources Journal
New York University Environmental Law Journal
Review of European Community and International Environmental Law
Yearbook of International Environmental Law

International environmental negotiations

Earth Negotiations Bulletin (available at: http://www.iisd.ca/linkages/)

International environmental co-operation and policy

R. Carson, *Silent Spring* (1963)

J. E. Harf and B. Trout, *The Politics of Global Resources: Population, Food, Energy, and Environment* (1971)

B. Ward and R. Dubos, *Only One Earth: The Care and Maintenance of a Small Planet* (1972)

R. Falk, *This Endangered Planet: Prospects and Proposals for Human Survival* (1971)

W. T. Blackstone (ed.), *Philosophy and the Environmental Crisis* (1974)

J. Busterud, 'International Environmental Relations', 7 *Natural Resources Law* 325 (1974)

J. Passmore, *Man's Responsibility for Nature: Ecological Problems and Western Traditions* (1980)

D. Kay and H. Jacobson (eds.), *Environmental Protection: The International Dimension* (1982)

M. Nicholson, *The New Environmental Age* (1987)

UN World Commission on Environment and Development, *Our Common Future* (1987)

J. E. Carrol (ed.), *International Environmental Diplomacy: The Management and Resolution of Transfrontier Environmental Problems* (1987)

J. McCormick, *Reclaiming Paradise: The Global Environmental Movement* (1989)

R. F. Mash, *The Rights of Nature: A History of Environmental Ethics* (1989)

L. K. Caldwell, *International Environmental Policy: Emergence and Dimensions* (1990, 2nd edn)

L. Starke, *Signs of Hope: Working Towards Our Common Future* (1990)

H. Cleveland, *The Global Commons: Policy for the Planet* (1990)

B. Commoner, *Making Peace with the Planet* (1990)

J. R. Engel and J. G. Engel, *Ethics of Environment and Development: Global Challenge and International Response* (1990)

J. MacNeill, P. Winsemius and T. Yakushiji, *Beyond Interdependence: The Meshing of the World's Economy and the Earth's Ecology* (1991)

IUCN, UNEP and WWF, *Caring for the Earth* (1991)

A. Hurrell and B. Kingsbury, *The International Politics of the Environment, Actors, Interests and Institutions* (1992)

S. Johnson (ed.), *The Earth Summit: The United Nations Conference on Environment and Development (UNCED)* (1993)

L. Susskind, *Environmental Diplomacy* (1994)

J. Atik, 'Science and International Regulatory Convergence', 17 *Northwestern Journal of International Law and Business* 336 (1996–7)

UNDP, *Human Development Report 2001* (2001)

World Bank, *World Development Report 2003: Sustainable Development in a Dynamic World* (2002)

Science and the state of the environment

G. H. Dury, *An Introduction to Environmental Systems* (1981)

L. K. Caldwell, *Between Two Worlds: Science, the Environmental Movement, and Policy Choice* (1990)

B. L. Turner, W. C. Clark, R. Kates *et al.*, *The Earth as Transformed by Human Action: Global and Regional Changes Over the Past 300 Years* (1990)

UNEP, *State of the Environment: 1972–1992* (1992)

WCMC, *Global Biodiversity 1992: The Status of the Earth's Living Resources* (1992)

WHO, *World Health Statistics Annual 1997–9* (2000)

S. Andresen *et al.* (eds.), *Science and Politics in International Environmental Regimes* (2000)

A. Goudie, *The Human Impact on the Natural Environment* (2000, 5th edn)

A. Goudie, *The Nature of the Environment* (2001, 4th edn)

D. Botkin, *Environmental Science: Earth as a Living Planet* (2002)

UNEP, *Global Environment Outlook 3 (GEO 3)* (2002)

L. Brown *et al.* (eds.), *State of the World 2002* (2002) (published annually by the Worldwatch Institute)

WRI, *World Resources 2002–2004: A Guide to the Global Environment* (2003) (published bi-annually)

For a more sceptical view, see B. Lomborg, *The Skeptical Environmentalist* (2001).

Environmental economics and development

C. Howe, *Natural Resource Economics* (1979)

P. Bartelmus, *Environment and Development* (1986)

R. Goodland and G. Ledec, 'Neo-classical Economics and Principles of Sustainable Development', 38 *Ecological Modelling* 36 (1987)

M. Redclift, *Sustainable Development* (1987)

R. K. Turner (ed.), *Sustainable Environmental Management* (1988)

D. W. Pearce, A. Markandya and E. Barbier, *Blueprint for a Green Economy* (1989)

O. R. Young, 'The Politics of International Regime Formation: Managing Natural Resources and the Environment', 43 *International Organization* 349 (1989)

O. R. Young, *International Co-operation: Building Regimes for Natural Resources and the Environment* (1989)

W. M. Adams, *Green Development: Environment and Sustainability in the Third World* (1990)

D. W. Pearce, E. Barbier and A. Markandya, *Sustainable Development: Economics and Environment in the Third World* (1990)

D. Pearce (ed.), *Blueprint 2: The Greening of the World Economy* (1991)

R. Eckersley, *Environmentalism and Political Theory* (1992)

D. Pearce (ed.), *Blueprint 3: Measuring Sustainable Devleopment* (1994)

D. Pearce and E. Barbier (eds.), *Blueprint 4: Capturing Global Developmental Value* (1995)

D. Pearce and E. Barbier, *Blueprint for a Sustainable Economy* (2000)

T. Tietenberg, *Environmental and Natural Resource Economics* (2000, 3rd edn)

P. Rao, *International Environmental Law and Economics* (2001)

Websites

Every international organisation and most international environmental agreements have their own sites on the Internet. These are indicated in the text at appropriate sections.

There is no single website which provides one-stop shopping for international environmental law. Of particular use, however, is www.google.com, which provides easy access to international environmental agreements, decisions and other acts of international organisations, and municipal and international court decisions. It also provides some guidance to literature sources.

2

History

See literature cited in Chapter 1, 'Further reading', pp. 18 **et seq**. See also: R. Carson, *Silent Spring* (1963); G. Hardin, 'The Tragedy of the Commons', 162 *Science* 3859 (1968); B. Ward and R. Dubos, *Only One Earth* (1972); and M. Nicholson, *The New Environmental Age* (1987).

Introduction

Modern international environmental law can be traced directly to international legal developments which took place in the second half of the nineteenth century. Thus, although the current form and structure of the subject has become recognisable only since the mid-1980s, a proper understanding of modern principles and rules requires a historic sense of earlier scientific, political and legal developments. International environmental law has evolved over at least four distinct periods, reflecting developments in scientific knowledge, the application of new technologies and an understanding of their impacts, changes in political consciousness and the changing structure of the international legal order and institutions.[1]

The first period began with bilateral fisheries treaties in the nineteenth century, and concluded with the creation of the new international organisations in 1945. During this period, peoples and nations began to understand that the process of industrialisation and development required limitations on the exploitation of certain natural resources (flora and fauna) and the adoption of appropriate legal instruments. The second period commenced with the creation of the UN and culminated with the UN Conference on the Human Environment, held in Stockholm in June 1972. Over this period, a range of international organisations with competence in environmental matters was created, and legal instruments were adopted, at both the regional and global level, which addressed particular sources of pollution and the conservation of general and particular environmental resources, such as oil pollution, nuclear testing, wetlands, the marine environment and its living resources, the quality

---

[1] For another approach, identifying traditional, modern and post-modern eras, see T. Kuokkanen, *International Law and the Environment: Variations on a Theme* (2002).

of freshwaters, and the dumping of waste at sea. The third period ran from the 1972 Stockholm Conference and concluded with the UN Conference on Environment and Development (UNCED) in June 1992. During this period, the UN tried to put in place a system for co-ordinating responses to international environmental issues, regional and global conventions were adopted, and for the first time the production, consumption and international trade in certain products was banned at the global level. The fourth period was set in motion by UNCED, and may be characterised as the period of integration: when environmental concerns should, as a matter of international law and policy, be integrated into all activities. This has also been the period in which increased attention has been paid to compliance with international environmental obligations, with the result that there has been a marked increase in international jurisprudence.

In tracing the development of the subject, general tendencies and themes may be discerned. First, the development of principles and rules of international environmental law – through treaties, other international acts and custom – has tended to react to events or incidents or the availability of scientific evidence, rather than anticipate general or particular environmental threats and put in place an anticipatory legal framework. Secondly, developments in science and technology have played a significant catalytic role: without the availability of scientific evidence, new rules of law are unlikely to be put in place. Thirdly, as is reflected throughout this book, the principles and rules of international law have developed as a result of a complex interplay between governments, non-state actors and international organisations. The extent to which a particular area is subject to legal rules will depend upon pressure being imposed by non-state actors, the existence of appropriate institutional fora in which rules can be developed, and sufficient will on the part of states to transform scientific evidence and political pressures into legal obligations. And, fourthly, it is only very recently – within the past decade – that issues of international environmental law have become a regular subject of international adjudication, and that international courts have begun to contribute to the definition and application of the subject.

From early fisheries conventions to the creation of the United Nations

Early attempts to develop international environmental rules focused on the conservation of wildlife (fisheries, birds and seals) and, to a limited extent, on the protection of rivers and seas. International legal developments followed the research efforts of scientists in the late eighteenth and nineteenth centuries, including: the work of Count Buffon which contrasted the appearance of inhabited life with uninhabited life; the studies by Fabre and Surrell of flooding, siltation, erosion and the division of watercourses brought about by deforestation in the Alps; and the conclusions of de Saussure and von Humboldt that deforestation had lowered water levels of lakes in the Alps and in Venezuela.[2] By the mid-eighteenth century, the relationship between deforestation and the drying-up of water basins was widely observed. In the island of Ascension,

> there was an excellent spring situated at the foot of the mountain originally covered with wood; the spring became scanty and dried up after the trees which covered the mountain had been felled. The loss of the spring was rightly ascribed to the cutting down of the timber. The mountain was therefore planted anew. A few years afterwards the spring reappeared by degrees, and by and by flowed with its former abundance.[3]

Concern for flora and fauna coincided with industrialisation and the use of mineral resources. This led to the adoption of early environmental legislation at the national level.

The adoption of treaties was *ad hoc*, sporadic and limited in scope. Bilateral fisheries conventions were adopted in the mid-nineteenth century to halt overexploitation. Examples include a convention to conserve oysters by prohibiting fishing outside certain dates,[4] and instruments to protect fisheries, usually in rivers or lakes or in or around territorial waters, from over-exploitation.[5] The first whaling convention was adopted in 1931.[6]

Migratory birds also required international co-operation to ensure their conservation. In 1872, Switzerland proposed an international regulatory commission for the protection of birds. This led to consideration of the matter by the non-governmental International Ornithological Congress and the creation in 1884 of an International Ornithological Committee, which formulated a treaty proposal,[7] and the adoption in 1902 of the Convention to Protect Birds Useful to Agriculture.[8] The Convention relied upon regulatory techniques still used today, such as the grant of absolute protection to certain birds, a prohibition on their killing or the destruction or taking of their nests, eggs or breeding places, and the use of certain methods of capture or destruction. The 1902 Birds Convention allowed exceptions, such as scientific research and repopulation, which continue to be reflected in more modern instruments, such as the 1979 Berne

---

[2] A. Goudie, *The Human Impact: Man's Role in Environmental Change* (1981), 2.

[3] J. B. Boussingault, *Rural Economy* (1845, 2nd edn), cited in Goudie, *The Human Impact*, 3.

[4] Convention Between France and Great Britain Relative to Fisheries, Art. XI, Paris, 11 November 1867, 21 IPE 1.

[5] North Sea Fisheries (Overfishing Convention), 1882, UN Doc. ST/LEG/SER.B/6, 1957, 695; Convention Concernant l'Exploitation et la Conservation des Pêcheries dans la Partie-Frontière du Danube, Belgrade, 15 January 1902. For other examples, see 9 IPE 4319–792.

[6] Convention for the Regulation of Whaling, Geneva, 24 September 1931, 155 LNTS 351.

[7] L. K. Caldwell, *International Environmental Policy* (1990, 2nd edn), 32.

[8] Paris, 19 March 1902.

Convention and the 1992 Biodiversity Convention. 1916 saw the adoption of the first bilateral treaty for the protection of migratory birds.[9] The founding in 1922 of the International Committee (later Council) for Bird Protection (later Preservation) (ICBP) reflected the recognition that substantive rules needed to be accompanied by new institutional arrangements. The ICBP was created to strengthen links between American and European bird protection groups, and its aim of encouraging 'transnational co-ordination rather than international integration' reflected a reluctance to go too far in impinging upon the sovereignty of states.[10]

The first treaty aimed at the protection of wildlife in a particular region was the 1900 Convention Destinée à Assurer la Conservation des Diverses Espèces Animales Vivant à l'Etat Sauvage en Afrique qui sont Utiles à l'Homme ou Inoffensive.[11] It sought to ensure the conservation of wildlife in the African colonies of European states, including the use of trade restrictions on the export of certain skins and furs,[12] reflecting a desire to combine regulatory techniques with economic incentives.[13] The 1900 Convention was replaced by the 1933 Convention on the Preservation of Fauna and Flora in their Natural State,[14] which was itself superseded by a new instrument in 1968 following the attainment of independence by these former colonial territories of Africa.[15] Like other early conventions, the 1933 Convention did not create any institutional arrangements for administering its provisions, monitoring compliance or ensuring implementation. During this first period, the only other region to adopt a treaty for the protection of wildlife was the Americas.[16]

It was not only fisheries and wildlife that attracted the attentions of the international legislators. The 1909 Water Boundaries Treaty between the United States and Canada was the first to commit its parties to preventing pollution,[17] and under the auspices of its International Joint Commission a draft Treaty on Pollution Prevention was drawn up in 1920, but not adopted. Another draft instrument prepared in this period, also not adopted, sought to prevent oil pollution of the seas.[18] Treaties were adopted to limit the spread of phylloxera[19]

---

[9] Convention Between the United States and Great Britain for the Protection of Migratory Birds in the United States and Canada, Washington, 7 December 1916, 4 IPE 1638.

[10] C. McCormick, *Reclaiming Paradise* (1989), 23.

[11] London, 19 May 1900, 4 IPE 1607.   [12] Art. II.

[13] On trade and environmental law, see chapter 19, pp. 940–1009 below.

[14] London, 8 November 1933, 172 LNTS 242.

[15] See 1968 African Nature Convention; see chapter 11, pp. 524–6 below.

[16] 1940 Western Hemisphere Convention; see chapter 11, pp. 527–9 below.

[17] 11 IPE 5704.

[18] Final Act and Draft Convention of the Preliminary Conference on Oil Pollution of Navigable Waters, Washington, June 1926, 19 IPE 9585; Draft Convention and Draft Final Act on Pollution of the Sea by Oil, 21–25 October 1935, 19 IPE 9597.

[19] International Phylloxera Convention, with a Final Protocol, Berne, 23 June 1882, 4 IPE 1571.

and epizootic diseases,[20] and to prevent damage from corrosive and poisonous substances.[21] Developments relating to the creation of international environmental organisations were limited. The first international institution to address nature protection arose from the 1909 meeting of the International Congress for the Protection of Nature, in Paris, which proposed the creation of an international nature protection body.[22] In 1913, an Act of Foundation of a Consultative Committee for the International Protection of Nature was signed in Berne by seventeen countries, with the task of collecting, classifying and publishing information on the international protection of nature.[23] The outbreak of the First World War laid the Commission to rest. Rudimentary international organisations were created at this time to address locust infestation[24] and contagious animal diseases.[25]

It is evident that many of the developments during this period were inspired by the efforts of private individuals, scientists and environmental organisations in Europe and the United States.[26] Lawyers were also active: in 1911 the Institut de Droit International, a private association of lawyers, adopted International Regulations Regarding the Use of International Watercourses for Purposes Other than Navigation. Although these were not binding, they declared that 'neither [riparian] state may, on its own territory, utilise or allow the utilisation of the water in such a way as seriously to interfere with its utilisation by the other state or by individuals, corporations, etc. thereof'.[27]

During this period, two environmental disputes were submitted to international arbitration. Both awards set forth principles which influenced subsequent developments and included regulatory provisions governing the conduct of future activities. In the *Pacific Fur Seal Arbitration*, the dispute between the United States and Great Britain concerned the latter's alleged over-exploitation of fur seals in areas beyond national jurisdiction.[28] The award rejected the argument that states had the right to assert jurisdiction over natural resources outside their jurisdiction to ensure their conservation, and set forth regulations for the 'proper protection and preservation' of fur seals outside jurisdictional limits.

---

[20] Convention Designed to Remove the Danger of Epizootic Diseases in the Territories of Austria-Hungary and Italy, Rome, 7 December 1887, 4 IPE 1586.

[21] Convention Between the Riverine States of the Rhine Respecting Regulations Governing the Transport of Corrosive and Poisonous Substances, Mannheim, 11 May 1900, 25 IPE 214.

[22] McCormick, *Reclaiming Paradise*, 22.   [23] Berne, 19 November 1913, 4 IPE 1631.

[24] Convention Regarding the Organisation of the Campaign Against Locusts, Rome, 31 October 1920, 4 IPE 1642.

[25] International Agreement for the Creation of an International Office for Dealing with Contagious Diseases of Animals, Paris, 25 January 1924, 4 IPE 1646.

[26] McCormick, *Reclaiming Paradise*, 1–23.   [27] 20 April 1911, 11 IPE 5702.

[28] 1 *Moore's International Arbitral Awards* (1893) 755; see chapter 11, pp. 561–6 below.

The regulations reflected earlier treaty provisions,[29] and provided a basis for a convention prohibiting pelagic sealing in the North Pacific Ocean and the importation of sealskins.[30] The episode provided early evidence of the potential for disputes over valuable natural resources lying beyond the national jurisdiction of any state, as well as evidence of the role international law might play in resolving disputes and establishing a framework for the conduct of activities.

The second arbitral award of this period is the better known. The *Trail Smelter* case arose out of a dispute between the United States and Canada over the emission of sulphur fumes from a smelter situated in Canada which caused damage in the state of Washington.[31] The Tribunal applied the principle that under international law 'no state has the right to use or permit the use of its territory in such a manner as to cause injury by fumes in or to the territory of another or the properties or persons therein, when the case is of serious consequence and the injury is established by clear and convincing evidence'.[32] The award of the Tribunal and its finding on the state of international law on air pollution in the 1930s has come to represent a crystallising moment for international environmental law which has influenced subsequent developments in a manner which undoubtedly exceeds its true value as an authoritative legal determination.

These two arbitral awards, together with the treaties and organisations which were brought into being, established early foundations. Institutional arrangements to address environmental matters were limited, and international rules were sparse in terms of both the subject matter they addressed and the regions they covered. However, there was a growing awareness that the exploitation of natural resources could not occur on an unlimited basis, that industrialisation and technological developments brought with them pollution and associated problems, and that international measures were needed to address these matters.

From the creation of the United Nations to Stockholm: 1945–1972

The second phase in the development of international environmental law began with the creation of the UN and its specialised agencies in 1945.[33] It was a period characterised by two features: international organisations at the regional and

---

[29] Agreement Between the Government of the United States of America and the Government of Her Britannic Majesty for a Modus Vivendi in Relation to Fur Seal Fisheries in the Bering Sea, Washington, 15 June 1891, 8 IPE 3655; Convention Between the Government of the United States of America and the Government of Her Britannic Majesty for the Renewal of the Existing Modus Vivendi in the Bering Sea, Washington, 18 April 1892, 4 IPE 3656.

[30] Convention Between the United States of America, the United Kingdom of Great Britain and Northern Ireland, and Russia, for the Preservation and Protection of Fur Seals, Washington, 7 July 1911, 8 IPE 3682, Arts. I–III.

[31] 3 RIAA 1905 (1941); see chapter 8, pp. 318–19 below.

[32] 35 AJIL 716 (1941); 9 ILR 317.

[33] On the structure of the UN, see chapter 3, pp. 78–83 below.

global level began to address environmental issues; and the range of environmental concerns addressed by international regulatory activity broadened to include a focus on the causes of pollution resulting from certain ultra-hazardous activities. A third feature was the limited recognition of the relationship between economic development and environmental protection.

Despite attempts by certain individuals to push conservation onto the international agenda following the Second World War, the UN Charter did not include provisions on environmental protection or the conservation of natural resources.[34] Nevertheless, the UN's purposes include the achievement of international co-operation in solving international problems of an economic, social, cultural or humanitarian character, and this has provided the basis for the subsequent environmental activities of the UN.[35] No environment or nature conservation body was established among the specialised agencies. However, the constituent instruments of the Food and Agriculture Organization (FAO) and the United Nations Educational, Scientific and Cultural Organization (UNESCO) included provisions with an environmental or conservationist aspect, and the instrument establishing the General Agreement on Tariffs and Trade (GATT) permits certain measures relating to 'the conservation of exhaustible natural resources' as exceptions to the rules establishing free trade obligations.[36]

In October 1948, governments and non-governmental actors established the first major international organisation to address environmental issues. A conference convened with the assistance of UNESCO, which was attended by representatives of eighteen governments, seven international organisations and 107 national organisations, established the International Union for the Protection of Nature (IUPN), to promote the preservation of wildlife and the natural environment, public knowledge, education, scientific research and legislation.[37] The IUCN is a unique organisation whose members are governments and non-governmental actors, and which has played an important role in developing treaties to protect wildlife and conserve natural resources.

UNCCUR

The seeds of intergovernmental environmental action were sown in 1947 by the UN, with the Economic and Social Council (ECOSOC) resolution convening the 1949 United Nations Conference on the Conservation and Utilisation of Resources (UNCCUR). The origins of this resolution have been traced to the

[34] For reasons, see McCormick, *Reclaiming Paradise*, 25–7.

[35] UN Charter, San Francisco, 26 June 1945, in force 24 October 1945, 1 UNTS xvi, Art. 1(3); see chapter 3, pp. 78–83 below.

[36] See respectively chapter 3, pp. 95–7, and chapter 19, pp. 944–9 below.

[37] 1977 Statutes, 18 IPE 8960; on the creation of the IUCN, see McCormick, *Reclaiming Paradise*, 31–6. In 1956, the IUPN was renamed the International Union for the Conservation of Nature and Natural Resources (IUCN).

initiative of Presidents Franklin D. Roosevelt and Harry S. Truman.[38] The resolution reflected an awareness of the need for international action to establish a balanced approach to the management and conservation of natural resources. The resolution emphasised the importance of the world's natural resources and their importance to the reconstruction of devastated areas; it also recognised the need for the 'continuous development and widespread application of the techniques of resource conservation and utilisation'.[39] The resolution determined the competence of the UN over environmental matters and ultimately resulted in the 1972 Stockholm Conference and the 1992 UNCED, as well as other UN action on the environment.

UNCCUR provided a modest start. It had a limited scope, having been convened to exchange information on 'techniques in this field, their economic costs and benefits, and their interrelations' and being devoted to the exchange of ideas and experience.[40] It had no mandate to adopt any recommendations. Held from 17 August to 6 September 1949 in New York State, it was attended by over 1,000 individuals from more than fifty countries, some 500 having been selected by the UN Secretary General upon the nomination of governments, non-governmental organisations and the Preparatory Committee. UNCCUR addressed six issues: minerals, fuels and energy, water, forests, land, and wildlife and fish. The main topics addressed included:

- the world resource situation;
- a world review of critical shortages;
- the interdependence of resources;
- the use and conservation of resources;
- the development of new resources by applied technology;
- education for conservation;
- resource techniques for less developed countries; and
- the integrated development of river basins.[41]

If UNCCUR's accomplishments were limited, the topics were similar to those addressed at UNCED nearly half a century later. Even at this early stage, the relationship between conservation and development was a central theme, with discussions focusing on the relationship between conservation and use, on the need to develop standards to ensure conservation and on the relationship between conservation and development.[42]

Following the 1949 UNCCUR, environmental action by the UN and its specialised agencies addressed issues relating to the conservation of flora and fauna. In 1954, the General Assembly convened a major Conference on the

---

[38] Caldwell, *International Environmental Policy*, 42.
[39] ECOSOC Resolution 32 (IV) (1947), Preamble.   [40] *Ibid.*
[41] *Yearbook of the UN* (1948–9), 481–2. See also UNCCUR Proceedings, vol. 1: Plenary Meetings (E/Conf.7/7).
[42] *Ibid.*

Conservation of the Living Resources of the Sea,[43] which led to the conservation rules adopted in the 1958 Geneva Conventions. The major new development was the attention given by the General Assembly to the effects of atmospheric nuclear tests and oil pollution. The fact that these subjects were debated, and resolutions adopted, signalled a shift in emphasis, away from the protection of flora and fauna and towards international action addressing products and processes associated with industrial and military activity. With hindsight, it is easy to see how significant these developments were, although at the time it was probably not foreseeable that the implications of intergovernmental environmental action would be far-reaching. In 1955, the General Assembly adopted the first of a number of resolutions on the use of atomic energy and the effects of atomic radiation,[44] which led to the adoption of the Test Ban Treaty in 1963,[45] and provided the political context for Australia and New Zealand to bring actions before the International Court of Justice (ICJ) calling on France to stop all atmospheric nuclear tests.[46]

In 1954, under the auspices of the International Maritime Organization (IMO), the first global convention for the prevention of oil pollution was adopted (building on the text of the earlier drafts of 1926 and 1935),[47] to be followed fifteen years later by treaties permitting intervention to combat the effects of oil pollution,[48] establishing rules of civil liability for oil pollution damage[49] and creating an oil pollution compensation fund.[50] These were adopted in response to specific incidents resulting in large-scale oil pollution which caused damage to the marine environment and to people and property. Other global conventions were the 1958 High Seas Fishing and Conservation Convention which established innovative provisions on conservation of marine living resources,[51] and the 1958 Convention on the High Seas which committed contracting parties to preventing oil pollution and the dumping of radioactive wastes.[52] The 1971 Ramsar Convention was the first environment treaty to establish rules addressing the conservation of a particular type of ecosystem.[53]

At this time, notable regional developments were occurring to prohibit or regulate activities previously beyond the scope of international law. The 1959 Antarctic Treaty committed parties to peaceful activities in that region, and

---

[43] See UNGA Res. 900 (IX) (1954). The Conference Report is at 8 IPE 3696.
[44] See e.g. UNGA Res. 912 (X) (1955); Res. 913 (X) (1955); Res. 1147 (XII) (1957); Res. 1252 (XIII) (1958); Res. 1379 (XIV) (1959); Res. 1402 (XIV) (1959); Res. 1649 (XVI) (1961).
[45] See chapter 8, pp. 319–21; and chapter 11, p. 649 below.
[46] See chapter 8, pp. 319–21 below (and New Zealand's subsequent application in 1995, at chapter 8 below).
[47] 1954 International Convention for the Prevention of Pollution of the Sea by Oil, London, 12 May 1954, in force 26 July 1958, 327 UNTS 3.
[48] See chapter 9, pp. 452–3 below.   [49] See chapter 18, pp. 913–15 below.
[50] See chapter 18, pp. 915–18 below.   [51] See chapter 11, pp. 566–7 below.
[52] See chapter 9, p. 393 below.   [53] See chapter 11, pp. 543–5 below.

prohibited nuclear explosions or the disposal of radioactive waste.[54] The United Nations Economic Commission for Europe (UNECE) promulgated harmonising regulations on emissions from motor vehicles,[55] and the Committee of Ministers of the Council of Europe adopted the first international act dealing with general aspects of air pollution.[56] In 1967, the European Community (EC) adopted its first environmental act, on the packaging and labelling of dangerous goods, despite the absence of express environmental provisions in the 1957 Treaty of Rome.[57] In relation to wildlife conservation, the 1968 African Nature Convention went beyond the limited approach to conservation of fauna and flora by aiming at the 'conservation, utilisation and development of soil, water, flora and fauna resources in accordance with scientific principles and with due regard to the best interests of the people'.[58] In early 1972, shortly before the Stockholm Conference, the Oslo Dumping Convention became the first treaty to prohibit the dumping of a wide range of hazardous substances at sea.[59] During this period, treaties sought to protect the quality of rivers[60] and, under the auspices of the International Labor Organization (ILO), the quality of the working environment.[61]

Other developments were noteworthy. In 1949, the International Court of Justice (ICJ) confirmed 'every state's obligation not to allow knowingly its territory to be used for acts contrary to the rights of other states', a *dictum* which was to contribute significantly to the emergence of Principle 21 of the Stockholm Conference.[62] In 1957, in the *Lac Lanoux Arbitration*, the Tribunal affirmed principles concerning limitations on the right of states in their use of shared rivers and informing the meaning of co-operation in international law.[63] However, the substantive commitments adopted in these treaties were not accompanied by the adoption of guiding principles of general application. What was looming, however, was the broader issue of the relationship between environment and development, which had been identified by the 1949 UNCCUR; in 1962, the General Assembly adopted a resolution on the relationship between economic development and environmental protection.[64]

By 1972, there was, therefore, an emerging body of international environmental rules at the regional and global levels, and international organisations were addressing international environmental issues. Limitations on the right of states to treat their natural resources as they wished were being established.

---

[54] See chapter 14, pp. 712–13 below.   [55] See chapter 8, pp. 324–5 below.
[56] Resolution (66) 23 Air Pollution (1966), 15 IPE 7521.
[57] Chapter 12 below; on the EC see generally chapter 14 below.
[58] Chapter 11, pp. 524–6 below.   [59] Chapter 9, pp. 423–5 below.
[60] Protocol Concerning the Constitution of an International Commission for the Protection of the Mosel Against Pollution, Paris, 20 December 1961, in force July 1962, 940 UNTS 211; Agreement Concerning the International Commission for the Protection of the Rhine Against Pollution, Berne, 29 April 1963, 914 UNTS 3.
[61] Chapter 3, p. 98 below; and chapter 12, pp. 638–41 below.   [62] (1949) ICJ Reports 4.
[63] Chapter 10, pp. 463–4 below.   [64] UNGA Res. 1831 (XVII) (1962).

Nevertheless, these treaty and institutional developments were developing in a piecemeal fashion, and the lack of co-ordination hampered efforts to develop a coherent international environmental strategy. Moreover, no international organisation had overall responsibility for co-ordinating international environmental policy and law, and few had a specific environmental mandate. International procedures for ensuring the implementation of, and compliance with, international environmental standards were virtually non-existent. The regulatory techniques available for addressing a growing range of issues were limited, and no rules had yet been developed on procedural obligations, such as environmental impact assessment or the dissemination of and access to environmental information. The 1972 Stockholm Conference must be seen in this context.

The 1972 Stockholm Conference can be traced to an Intergovernmental Conference of Experts on the Scientific Basis for Rational Use and Conservation of the Resources of the Biosphere convened by UNESCO in 1968 (the 1968 Biosphere Conference). The Conference considered the impact of human activities on the biosphere, including the effects of air and water pollution, overgrazing, deforestation and the drainage of wetlands, and adopted twenty recommendations reflecting themes adopted at the 1972 Stockholm Conference.[65] The scale of the task facing the international community was reflected in the final report of the 1968 Biosphere Conference:

> Until this point in history the nations of the world have lacked considered, comprehensive policies for managing the environment. Although changes have been taking place for a long time, they seem to have reached a threshold recently that has made the public aware of them. This awareness is leading to concern, to the recognition that to a large degree, man now has the capability and the responsibility to determine and guide the future of his environment, and to the beginnings of national and international corrective action . . . It has become clear, however, that earnest and bold departures from the past will have to be taken nationally and internationally if significant progress is to be made.[66]

The 1972 United Nations Conference on the Human Environment

Report of the UN Conference on the Human Environment, Stockholm, 5–16 June 1972, UN Doc. A/CONF.48/14/Rev.1; W. Kennett, 'The Stockholm Conference on the Human Environment', 48 *International Affairs* 33 (1972); A. C. Kiss and J. D. Sciault, 'La Conference des Nations Unies sur l'Environnement', AFDI 603 (1972);

---

[65] See *Yearbook of the UN* (1968), 958; UNESCO, *Use and Conservation of the Biosphere: Proceedings of the Intergovernmental Conference of Experts on the Scientific Basis for Rational Use and Conservation of the Resources of the Biosphere* (1970); and McCormick, *Reclaiming Paradise*, 88–90.

[66] Cited in Caldwell, *International Environmental Policy*, 45.

A. C. Kiss and J. D. Sciault, 'Post Stockholm: Influencing National Environmental Law and Practice Through International Law and Policy', 66 *Proceedings of the American Society of International Law* 1 (1972); L. Sohn, 'The Stockholm Declaration on the Human Environment', 14 *Harvard International Law Journal* 423 (1973); A. Kiss, 'Dix Ans Après Stockholm, Une Decénnie de Droit International de l'Environnement', 28 AFDI 784 (1982); A. Kiss, 'Ten Years After Stockholm: International Environmental Law', 77 *Proceedings of the American Society of International Law* 411 (1983).

The Stockholm Conference was convened in December 1968 by the United Nations General Assembly.[67] This followed the adoption in July 1968 of a resolution, first proposed by Sweden, noting 'the continuing and accelerating impairment of the quality of the human environment', and recommending that the General Assembly consider the desirability of convening a UN Conference.[68] The Conference was held in Stockholm on 5–16 June 1972, under the chairmanship of Maurice Strong, a Canadian, and was attended by 114 states and a large number of international institutions and non-governmental observers. The Conference adopted three non-binding instruments: a resolution on institutional and financial arrangements, a Declaration containing twenty-six Principles, and an Action Plan containing 109 recommendations.[69] The Conference did not adopt any binding obligations and formal decisions had to await the twenty-seventh session of the UN General Assembly the following autumn. The Conference was generally considered to have been successful, largely because the preparatory process had allowed agreement to be reached on most issues prior to the Conference.[70] According to one commentator, 'Stockholm enlarged and facilitated means toward international action previously limited by inadequate perception of environmental issues and by restrictive concepts of national sovereignty . . . There were significant elements of innovation in (1) the redefinition of international issues, (2) the rationale for co-operation, (3) the approach to international responsibility, and (4) the conceptualisation of international organisational relationships.'[71] Although the infusion of new international law was not dramatic, trends underway before Stockholm relating to marine pollution, transboundary air and water pollution, and the protection

---

[67] UNGA Res. 2398 (XXIII) (1968).

[68] ECOSOC Res. 1346 (XLV) (1968). Two months earlier, ECOSOC had taken note of a report by the World Health Organisation (WHO) on environmental pollution and its control, and a report by UNESCO and FAO on the conservation and rational utilisation of the environment: ECOSOC Res. 1310 (XLIV) (1968).

[69] *Report of the UN Conference on the Human Environment,* UN Doc. A/CONF.48/14 at 2–65, and Corr.1 (1972); 11 ILM 1416 (1972). For an excellent account of the Conference and the Declaration, see Louis B. Sohn, 'The Stockholm Declaration on the Human Environment', 14 *Harvard International Law Journal* 423 (1973).

[70] *Ibid.,* 424.   [71] Caldwell, *International Environmental Policy,* 55 and 60.

of endangered species were reinforced by the Stockholm resolutions.[72] From a legal perspective, the significant developments were the recommendations for the creation of new institutions and the establishment of co-ordinating mechanisms among existing institutions (the Action Plan), the definition of a framework for future actions to be taken by the international community (the Recommendations), and the adoption of a set of general guiding principles (the Principles).

The recommendation on institutional and financial arrangements proposed that action be taken by the UN General Assembly to establish four institutional arrangements: an intergovernmental Governing Council for Environmental Programmes to provide policy guidance for the direction and co-ordination of environmental programmes; an Environment Secretariat headed by an Executive Director; an Environment Fund to provide financing for environmental programmes; and an inter-agency Environmental Co-ordinating Board to ensure co-operation and co-ordination among all bodies concerned in the implementation of environmental programmes in the United Nations system. The Action Plan comprised 109 recommendations. These were generally accepted by consensus, and reflected an agenda which identified six main subject areas:

1. planning and management of human settlements for environmental quality;
2. environmental aspects of natural resources management;
3. identification and control of pollutants and nuisances of broad international significance;
4. educational, informational, social and cultural aspects of environmental issues;
5. development and environment; and
6. international organisational implications of action proposals.[73]

The Action Plan included proposals on environmental assessment (by the establishment of Earthwatch, which was to include a Global Environmental Monitoring System (GEMS) and an International Referral System (subsequently INFOTERRA)); on natural resources management; and on supporting measures related to training and education and the provision of information. Consensus was virtually complete, although some reservations were made. The United States would not accept the principle of additionality, according to which an increase in its foreign aid budget would be required to cover costs imposed by environmental protection measures on development projects (Recommendation 109),[74] and Japan refused to observe the recommendation calling for a ten-year moratorium on commercial whaling (Recommendation 33).[75]

---

[72] *Ibid.*, 60.   [73] *Ibid.*, 61.
[74] This principle was, in effect, accepted at UNCED in 1992 and in the Climate Change and Biodiversity Conventions.
[75] Caldwell, *International Environmental Policy*, 62.

The Declaration of Principles for the Preservation and Enhancement of the Human Environment was based on a draft Declaration prepared by the Preparatory Committee. It was intended to provide 'a common outlook and . . . common principles to inspire and guide the peoples of the world in the preservation and enhancement of the human environment'.[76] The twenty-six Principles reflected a compromise between those states which believed it should stimulate public awareness of, and concern for, environmental issues, and those states which wanted the Declaration to provide specific guidelines for future governmental and intergovernmental action.

From a legal perspective, the most relevant provisions are Principles 24, 21, 22 and 23. Principle 24 called for international co-operation 'to effectively control, prevent, reduce and eliminate adverse environmental effects resulting from activities conducted in all spheres, in such a way that due account is taken of the sovereignty and interests of all states'. Principle 21 affirmed the responsibility of states to ensure that activities within their jurisdiction or control do not cause damage in another state or beyond national jurisdiction, such as in outer space or on the high seas. This responsibility is said to extend also to activities under a state's 'control', such as those carried out by its nationals or by or on ships or aircraft registered in its territory.[77]

Principle 22 required states to co-operate in developing international environmental law. This is a substantially weakened version of an earlier proposal, which would have required states to pay compensation for all environmental damage caused by activities carried on within their territory. The earlier proposal failed because of concerns that it implied acceptance of a no-fault or 'strict' standard of liability for environmental harm. Certain states made clear their view that liability to pay compensation would only exist where there had been negligence attributable to the state concerned.[78] Principle 23 foresaw a limited role for international regulation and suggested that certain standards would 'have to be determined nationally' on the basis of the value systems applying in each country and their social costs, and in accordance with the need for different environmental standards in different countries. The Stockholm Principles are weak on techniques for implementing environmental standards, such as environmental impact assessment, access to environmental information and the availability of administrative and judicial remedies. Principle 24 simply calls for international organisations to play a co-ordinated, efficient and dynamic role.

The other Stockholm Principles were couched in non-legal language. Principle 1 linked environmental protection to human rights norms, stating that man

---

[76] UN Doc. A/CONF.48/PC.17.
[77] For the background to Principle 21 and its subsequent development, see chapter 6, pp. 235–6 below.
[78] UN Doc. A/CONF.48/PC.12, Annex 1, at 15 (1971).

has 'the fundamental right to freedom, equality and adequate conditions of life, in an environment of a quality that permits a life of dignity and well-being, and he bears a solemn responsibility to protect and improve the environment for present and future generations'.[79] Other Principles can be grouped into themes. Principles 2, 3 and 5 set forth general guidelines for the natural resources of the earth to be safeguarded for the benefit of present and future generations, and for the maintenance, restoration and improvement of vital renewable resources and the non-exhaustion of non-renewable resources. Principles 4, 6 and 7 identified specific environmental threats, recalling the special responsibility of man to safeguard and wisely manage the heritage of wildlife and habitat, halt the discharge of toxic and other substances and heat which cause serious or irreversible damage to the ecosystem, and prevent pollution of the seas or harm to living resources and marine life. Principles 8–15 addressed issues which reflected the relationship between development and the environment: they recognised the relationship between economic and social development and environmental quality; they called for 'accelerated development' through the transfer of financial and technological assistance and stable and adequate prices for commodities and raw materials; and they supported an integrated and co-ordinated approach to rational development planning which is compatible with protecting and improving the human environment. Principles 16–20 recognised the need for appropriate demographic policies; supported the development of national institutions to manage environmental resources; called for the application of science and technology; and encouraged education and scientific research and development.[80]

The draft Declaration prepared by the Preparatory Committee had included a third important legal principle, originally entitled 'Principle 20', which would have provided that:

> relevant information must be supplied by states on activities or developments within their jurisdiction or under their control whenever they believe, or have reason to believe, that such information is needed to avoid the risk of significant adverse effects on the environment in areas beyond their national jurisdiction.[81]

This Principle was not agreed at the Conference following the objections of a number of developing states, which maintained that the obligation to consult might be abused by developed states to impede development projects. As will be seen, this requirement is now recognised by the International Law Commission, and by many conventions, as a basic requirement.

---

[79] See chapter 7, p. 293 below.

[80] When the Stockholm Declaration was adopted, fewer than six states had national authorities specifically responsible for the environment. Today, few states do not have such a body.

[81] UN Doc. A/CONF.48/4, Annex, para. 20, at 4 (1972).

Stockholm follow-up

The Report of the Stockholm Conference was considered by the UN General Assembly at its twenty-seventh session, which adopted eleven resolutions. Resolution 2994 (XXVII) noted with satisfaction the Conference Report.[82] Resolution 2995 (XXVII) was a partial revival of the Preparatory Committee's original 'Principle 20', providing that technical information on proposed works should be supplied to other states where there is a risk of significant transboundary environmental harm, but that this information should be received in good faith and not used to delay or impede development of natural resources.[83] Resolution 2996 (XXVII) affirmed that Resolution 2995 was not to be construed as limiting Principles 21 and 22 of the Stockholm Declaration,[84] and Resolutions 2997 to 3004 addressed institutional and financial arrangements for international environmental co-operation, including the creation of the United Nations Environment Programme.[85]

From Stockholm to Rio: 1972–1992

The Stockholm Conference set the scene for international activities at the regional and global level, and influenced legal and institutional developments up to and beyond UNCED. Developments in this period are of two types: those directly related to Stockholm and follow-up actions; and those indirectly related thereto. The period was marked by: a proliferation of international environmental organisations (including those established by treaty) and greater efforts by existing institutions to address environmental issues; the development of new sources of international environmental obligations from acts of such organisations; new environmental norms established by treaty; the development of new techniques for implementing environmental standards, including environmental impact assessment and access to information; and the formal integration of environment and development, particularly in relation to international trade and development assistance.

Post-Stockholm: treaties and other international acts

The creation of the United Nations Environment Programme (UNEP) and the adoption of Principle 21 were the most significant achievements of the Stockholm Conference. UNEP has been responsible for the establishment and implementation of the Regional Seas Programme, including some thirty regional treaties,[86] as well as important global treaties addressing ozone depletion, trade in hazardous waste and biodiversity.[87] In the period immediately after

---

[82] *Yearbook of the UN* (1972), 330.   [83] *Ibid.*, 330–1.   [84] *Ibid.*, 331.
[85] *Ibid.*, 331–7. On UNEP, see chapter 3, pp. 83–5 below.
[86] Chapter 9, pp. 399–400 below.   [87] Chapter 3, pp. 83–5 below.

Stockholm, several other treaties of potentially global application were adopted outside UNEP but within the UN system, to address the dumping of waste at sea,[88] pollution from ships,[89] the trade in endangered species[90] and the protection of world cultural heritage.[91] The most important, viewed over time, is likely to be the United Nations Convention on the Law of the Sea (UNCLOS) which established a comprehensive framework for the establishment of global rules on the protection of the marine environment and marine living resources, including detailed and important institutional arrangements and provisions on environmental assessment, technology transfer, liability and dispute settlement.[92] Many of the techniques subsequently adopted in other environmental treaties may be traced directly to UNCLOS.

The Stockholm Conference was followed by important regional developments, including the adoption of EC environmental protection rules,[93] and the creation of an Environment Committee at the OECD.[94] Other notable regional developments included: multilateral treaties dedicated to the protection of all migratory species;[95] the protection of habitats;[96] the prevention of transboundary air pollution;[97] the regulation and prohibition of commercial mineral activities in the Antarctic,[98] and rules on environmental co-operation and behaviour in a compact on development assistance between developed and developing countries.[99]

Towards the end of this period, UN economic and financial organisations began to be faced with the practical implications which national and international environmental law might have for their respective activities. In 1971, the General Agreement on Tariffs and Trade (GATT) had established a Group on Environmental Measures and International Trade (which did not meet until 1991), and as an organisation found itself increasingly faced with environmental issues, including the question of the circumstances in which unilateral trade restrictions adopted in the name of environmental protection could be justified under GATT rules.[100] In the face of increasing public and governmental pressure, the World Bank and the regional development

---

[88] 1972 London Convention; see chapter 9, pp. 416–20 below.

[89] MARPOL 73/78; see chapter 9, pp. 440–5 below.

[90] 1973 CITES; see chapter 11, pp. 505–15 below.

[91] 1972 World Heritage Convention; see chapter 11, pp. 611–15 below.

[92] See chapter 5; chapter 10; chapter 17 below; and chapter 19 below.

[93] Chapter 15, pp. 732–98 below.   [94] Chapter 3, p. 103 below.

[95] 1979 Bonn Convention; see chapter 11, pp. 607–11 below.

[96] 1979 Berne Convention; see chapter 11, pp. 532–5 below.

[97] 1979 LRTAP Convention and Protocols; see chapter 8, pp. 324–6 below.

[98] 1988 CRAMRA and 1991 Environmental Protocol to the 1959 Antarctic Treaty; see chapter 14, pp. 716–21 below.

[99] 1989 Lomé Convention; see chapter 20, p. 1022 below.

[100] Chapter 19, pp. 946–85 below. The same issue had arisen in the regional context of the EC as early as 1980: see chapter 19, pp. 985–97 below.

banks were called upon to integrate environmental considerations into their loan-making processes. This led to the establishment of an Environment Department in the World Bank and the adoption of limited environmental impact assessment requirements by most multilateral development banks.[101] Amongst the most significant reflection of the changing times was the integration of environmental obligations into the 1990 Articles establishing the European Bank for Reconstruction and Development.[102] In 1991, the World Bank, UNEP and the United Nations Development Programme established the Global Environmental Facility to provide financial resources to support projects which benefited the global commons. At the same time, the GATT decided to reactivate its long-dormant Group on Environmental Measures and International Trade.

Prior to UNCED, treaties were adopted in areas not previously subject to international regulation. Under the auspices of the UNECE, treaties addressed environmental impact assessment,[103] the transboundary impacts of industrial accidents,[104] and the protection and use of international watercourses.[105] The International Law Commission (ILC) completed a first reading of its draft Articles on the law of non-navigational uses of international watercourses, while the UN Security Council declared that ecological issues could constitute threats to international peace and security. The UN General Assembly adopted a resolution prohibiting the use of driftnets, the first time that body had adopted a normative rule seeking to establish a worldwide standard.

This was also the period in which the impact of acts of international organisations began to be felt. Many organisations had the power to adopt binding or non-binding decisions, resolutions, recommendations or other acts, and these organisations served as fora in which new international environmental legislation could be proposed, adopted and implemented. There are several examples of such acts which are noteworthy for their consequences on industrial and other economic activity, but three in particular reflect the scale of the changes which had occurred. These were: the moratorium on commercial whaling adopted by resolution of the International Whaling Commission in 1982;[106] the 1983 moratorium on commercial whaling adopted by resolution of the Consultative Meeting of the parties to the 1972 London Convention;[107] and the decision by the 1989 conference of the parties to the 1973 CITES which placed African elephant ivory on Appendix 1 to the Convention and banned the international trade in ivory.[108] Each of these acts followed public pressure and politico-legal strategies adopted at the national and international levels

[101] Chapter 20, pp. 1025–7 below.   [102] Chapter 20, pp. 1028–9 below.
[103] 1991 Espoo Convention; see chapter 16, pp. 814–17 below.
[104] 1992 Industrial Accidents Convention; see chapter 12, pp. 623–5 below.
[105] 1992 Watercourses Convention; see chapter 10, pp. 466–8 below.
[106] Chapter 11, pp. 592–5 below.   [107] Chapter 9, pp. 416–22 below.
[108] Chapter 11, pp. 505–14 below.

over several years. Despite strong efforts to reverse these acts, they remained effective in 2002, although their economic impact, and their effect on the activities of indigenous peoples, focused attention on the broader economic and social implications of adopting international environmental regulations.

Several non-binding instruments were adopted under the auspices of inter-governmental and non-governmental organisations. Three such instruments have played an influential role: the 1978 UNEP draft Principles, the 1981 Monte-video Programme, and the 1982 World Charter for Nature. Non-governmental efforts lay behind two other initiatives whose impact has been substantial: the collaboration between IUCN, UNEP and the Worldwide Fund for Nature (WWF) which led to the 1980 World Conservation Strategy; and the 1991 document entitled 'Caring for the Earth: A Strategy for Sustainable Living'.

1978 UNEP draft Principles

One of the first acts to be adopted by UNEP in the field of international law led to the 1978 draft 'Principles of Conduct in the Field of the Environment for the Guidance of States in the Conservation and Harmonious Utilisation of Natural Resources Shared by Two or More States' (the UNEP draft Principles).[109] The draft Principles resulted from the efforts of an Intergovernmental Working Group established by the UNEP Governing Council in 1976,[110] pursuant to a request by the UN General Assembly.[111] The Working Group agreed to limit the effort to the preparation of principles and guidelines which would not be taken as creating legally binding obligations. This is reflected in the Explanatory Note to the Principles, which states that 'the language used throughout does not seek to prejudice whether or to what extent the conduct envisaged in the principles is already prescribed by existing principles of general international law'. The UNEP draft Principles were annexed to the final report of the Working Group which was adopted by the UNEP Governing Council in May 1978 but never submitted to the General Assembly for its consideration.[112]

The UNEP draft Principles comprise fifteen principles to govern the use of 'shared natural resources', a concept which is not defined but which is understood from the Report of the UNEP Executive Director to mean something other than the 'global commons'.[113] The fifteen Principles include language

---

[109] 17 ILM 1097 (1978); see also A. O. Adede, 'Utilisation of Shared Natural Resources: Towards a Code of Conduct', 5 *Environmental Policy and Law* 66 at 67–8 (1979).

[110] UNEP Governing Council Decision 44 (III) (1975).

[111] UNGA Res. 3129 (XXVIII) (1973).

[112] UNEP Governing Council Decision 6/14 (1978).

[113] Co-operation in the Field of the Environment Concerning National Resources Shared by Two or More States, Report of the Executive Director, UNEP/GC/44, 20 February 1975, which cites five illustrative examples: (1) an international water system, including both surface and ground water; (2) an air-shed or air mass above the territories of a limited number of states; (3) enclosed or semi-enclosed seas and adjacent coastal waters;

presciently similar to some of the provisions which were endorsed by the whole of the international community, fourteen years later at UNCED. Principles 1 and 2 recognise the duty of states to co-operate to control, prevent, reduce and eliminate adverse environmental effects, and requires them, to that end, to endeavour to conclude bilateral or multilateral agreements to secure specific regulation of their conduct. Principle 21 of the Stockholm Declaration, broadly followed by Principles 3 and 4, introduces a requirement that states 'make environmental assessments' before engaging in certain activities. Principles 5 and 6 relate to information exchange, consultation and notification, which are elements of the principle of good faith and good neighbourliness elaborated by Principle 7. The draft Principles include principles on scientific studies and assessments (Principle 8), emergency action (Principle 9) and the use of the 'services' of international organisations (Principle 10). The settlement of disputes and responsibility and liability are addressed by Principles 12 and 13, and Principles 13 and 14 elaborate upon the objectives of non-discrimination and the rights of persons in other jurisdictions who may be adversely affected by environmental damage to the equal right of access to administrative and judicial proceedings. Principle 15 provides that the UNEP draft Principles should be interpreted and applied 'to enhance and not to affect adversely development and the interests of all countries, and in particular the developing countries'.

1981 Montevideo Programme

Three years later, an *ad hoc* meeting of senior government officials expert in environmental law was held in Montevideo under UNEP auspices, and the Programme for the Development and Periodic Review of Environmental Law (the Montevideo Programme) was prepared.[114] The Programme was adopted by the UNEP Governing Council in May 1982 and influenced UNEP's legal activities in the period 1982–92, resulting in the development of regional and global treaties and 'soft law' instruments.[115] The Montevideo Programme has also been integrated into the UN System-Wide Medium-Term Environment Programmes (1984–9 and 1990–5). In 1993 and again in 2001, the UNEP Governing Council adopted new Programmes.[116]

The original Montevideo Programme was divided into three parts. The first part proposed that guidelines, principles or agreements should be developed

---

(4) migratory species which move between the waters or territories of several states; and
(5) a special ecosystem spanning the frontiers between two or more states, such as a series of mountains, forests or areas of special nature conservation; *Ibid.*, 40–1. See chapter 1 above.

[114] Report, UNEP/GC.10/5/Add.2, Annex, chapter II (1981); 8 *Environmental Policy and Law* 31 (1982).

[115] Governing Council Decision 10/21, 31 May 1982. On UNEP-sponsored legal developments, see chapter 3, pp. 83–5 below.

[116] See pp. 67–9 below.

to address: marine pollution from land-based sources; protection of the strato-spheric ozone layer; and the transport, handling and disposal of toxic and dangerous wastes. The second part proposed that action should be taken to address eight priority subject areas:

- international co-operation in environmental emergencies;
- coastal zone management;
- soil conservation;
- transboundary air pollution;
- international trade in potentially harmful chemicals;
- the protection of rivers and other inland waters against pollution;
- legal and administrative measures for the prevention and redress of pollution damage; and
- environmental impact assessment.

The third programme area proposed work of a general nature to promote the development of environmental law, including research, writing and teaching of theoretical and practical aspects of environmental law and the dissemination of information.

1982 World Charter for Nature

Ten years after the Stockholm Conference, the UN General Assembly adopted the World Charter for Nature, which set forth 'principles of conservation by which all human conduct affecting nature is to be guided and judged'.[117] The Charter, which is divided into three sections, is a non-binding instrument drafted in general language. The Charter differs from the Stockholm Declaration and the UNEP draft Principles in substance and form: it is an avowedly ecological instrument. Whereas the earlier instruments were anthropocentric and focused on the protection of nature for the benefit of mankind, the Charter emphasises the protection of nature as an end in itself. The explanation for this lies in part in its origins – the Twelfth General Assembly of the IUCN held in Zaire in 1975 – and in its subsequent elaboration by IUCN and an international group of independent experts. The Charter was strongly supported by developing countries, marking a change from the general reluctance which many of these countries had expressed at Stockholm ten years earlier for international environmental policy. The Charter is not binding, and has been characterised as 'an important symbolic expression of an intent among nations to achieve a more harmonious and sustainable relationship between humanity and the rest of the biosphere – between mankind and earth'.[118] As a standard of ethical conduct, however, many of its provisions are now reflected in treaties.

---

[117] UNGA Res. 37/7, 28 October 1982. The Charter was adopted by a vote of 111 in favour, eighteen abstentions and one vote against (United States); 23 ILM 455 (1983).

[118] Caldwell, *International Environmental Policy*, 92.

Section I, entitled 'General Principles', contains aspirational language calling for the respect of nature and its essential processes: safeguarding habitats and ensuring the survival of all life forms; providing special protection for unique areas, ecosystems and habitats of endangered species; maintaining 'optimum sustainable productivity' of natural resources without endangering other ecosystems or species; and securing nature against degradation from warfare.[119] Section II, entitled 'Functions', is more operational in character. It calls for the integration of nature into the planning and implementation of development activities, taking into account the long-term capacity of natural systems and the physical constraints, biological productivity and diversity and natural beauty of different areas.[120] The Charter includes 'rules' governing the use of natural resources which pre-date the concept of sustainable development first used in the 1985 ASEAN Agreement and endorsed by the Brundtland Report in 1987. Living resources should not be used in excess of their natural capacity for regeneration; the productivity of soils should be maintained; resources should be reused or recycled, and non-renewable resources should be used with restraint.[121] The Charter includes language on environmental impact assessment and distinguishes between three activities in the light of such assessments: (1) activities which are likely to cause irreversible damage to nature (which should be avoided); (2) activities which are likely to pose a significant risk to nature (which should be preceded by an exhaustive examination); and (3) activities which may disturb nature (which should be preceded by an assessment of their consequences).[122] The approach is now broadly reflected in international practice. The Charter supports an approach which combines the prevention of natural disasters, the avoidance of discharge of pollutants, and the rehabilitation of degraded areas.[123]

Section III, entitled 'Implementation', includes elements of the approaches endorsed and applied by subsequent environmental treaties and instruments. These techniques include: the dissemination of knowledge of nature, particularly by ecological education; the formulation of conservation strategies and environmental assessments; public access to information for consultation and participation; the provision of funds and administrative structures; scientific research; and early detection of degradation.[124] Implementation includes: co-operation among and between the various actors in the international community (states, public authorities, international organisations, individuals, groups and corporations); the establishment of standards for products and manufacturing processes; the implementation of applicable international legal provisions, and measures to ensure that activities do not cause damage to natural systems within other states or in areas beyond the limits of national

---

[119] Paras. 1–5.   [120] Paras. 7–9.   [121] Para. 10.   [122] Para. 11.
[123] Paras. 11(e), 12 and 13.   [124] Paras. 15–19.

jurisdiction.[125] The Charter recognises the place of non-state actors, including their right and duties relating to participation in the formulation of decisions, access to means of redress when their environment suffers damage, and the responsibility to act in accordance with the provisions of the Charter.[126]

1980 World Conservation Strategy/1991 'Caring for the Earth' Strategy

The 1980 World Conservation Strategy was prepared by IUCN, UNEP, WWF, UNESCO and FAO. The Strategy gave currency to the term 'sustainable development', and has led to the preparation of national and sub-national conservation strategies in most states. It has subsequently influenced international legal developments. The 1980 Strategy emphasised three objectives stressing the interdependence of conservation and development:

1. essential ecological processes and life-support systems must be maintained;
2. genetic diversity must be preserved; and
3. any use of species or ecosystems must be sustainable.

It identified six main obstacles to the fulfilment of these objectives:

1. the failure to recognise that living resource conservation is a process that cuts across all sectors;
2. the failure to integrate conservation with development;
3. a development process that is inadequate in environmental planning and management;
4. lack of capacity to conserve due to inadequate legislation and lack of enforcement;
5. lack of awareness of the benefit of conservation; and
6. the inability to deliver conservation-based development where it is most needed, including rural areas of developing countries.[127]

In 1991, the 'Caring for the Earth' Strategy restated the thinking about conservation and development with two aims: securing a commitment to sustainable living; and translating its principles into practice.[128] The text defines Principles and Additional Actions for Sustainable Living, and proposes guidelines to allow adaptation of the Strategy to needs and capabilities and to implement it. The Strategy includes a commitment to national and international law as essential tools for achieving sustainability by the establishment of standards of social behaviour and the establishment of permanent policies. Specific recommendations include:

---

[125] Para. 21.   [126] Paras. 23–24.
[127] Caldwell, *International Environmental Policy*, 322–3.
[128] IUCN, UNEP and WWF, *Caring for the Earth: A Strategy for Sustainable Living* (1991).

1. establishing a constitutional commitment to the principles of a sustainable society;
2. establishing a comprehensive system for environmental law, and providing for its implementation and enforcement;
3. reviewing the adequacy of legal and administrative controls and of implementation and enforcement mechanisms;
4. making information on the environment more accessible; and
5. subjecting projects, programmes and policies to environmental impact assessment.[129]

National legal measures specifically recommended include: the development of standards; the application of the precautionary principle and the use of best available technology; a liability system that provides for compensation not only for economic losses suffered by other users of the environmental resource in question but also for ecological and intangible losses, and the capacity to require the restoration of damaged ecosystems, or punitive damages where restoration is impossible. Also recommended were strict liability for accidents involving hazardous substances; granting citizens' groups standing in judicial and administrative procedures in order to contribute to enforcement of the law and remedies for environmental damage; and making agencies that are responsible for the implementation and enforcement of environmental law accountable for their actions.[130] The Strategy seeks the development of international law by strengthening existing international agreements, concluding new international agreements to achieve global sustainability, and preparing and adopting a Universal Declaration and Covenant on Sustainability.[131]

The Brundtland Report and the Report of the Legal Experts Group

The World Commission on Environment and Development (WCED), chaired by Norwegian Prime Minister Gro Harlem Brundtland, was established in 1983 by the UN General Assembly, and its report (the Brundtland Report) was published in 1987.[132] The Commission was established as an independent body, linked to, but outside the control of, governments and the UN system. It had three objectives: to re-examine critical environment and development issues and formulate realistic proposals for dealing with them; to propose new forms of international co-operation on these issues that would influence policies and events in the direction of needed changes; and to raise levels of understanding and commitment to action of individuals, voluntary organisations, businesses, institutions and governments. Drawing on previous work such as the World Conservation Strategy, the Brundtland Report was a catalyst for UNCED and the five instruments there adopted. The Brundtland

---

[129] *Ibid.*, 66–73.   [130] *Ibid.*, 68–9.   [131] *Ibid.*, 79–81.
[132] *Our Common Future* (1987).

Report signalled changes in the way we look at the world. It provided support for expanding the role of sustainable development, proposed a UN programme on sustainable development, and identified the central legal and institutional issues.

> Until recently, the planet was a large world in which human activities and their effects were neatly compartmentalised within nations, within sectors (energy, agriculture, trade) and within broad areas of concern (environmental, economic, social). These compartments have begun to dissolve. This applies in particular to the global 'crises' that have seized public concern, particularly over the last decade. These are not separate crises: an environmental crisis, a development crisis, an energy crisis. They are all one.[133]

On policy matters the Commission focused attention on population, food security, the loss of species and genetic resources, energy, industry and human settlements, recognising that these are connected and cannot be treated in isolation from each other. On international co-operation and institutional reform the focus included: the role of the international economy; managing the global commons; the relationship between peace, security, development and the environment; and institutional and legal change. The Report made specific recommendations in respect of each of these matters that identify challenges for the development of international law, including the impact of national sovereignty and the management of the 'global commons'. The Brundtland Report identified six priority areas for legal and institutional change, and identified the existing legal order as part of the problem. First, governments, regional organisations and international bodies and agencies were called upon to support development which would be economically and ecologically sustainable, to integrate the environment fully into their goals and activities, and to improve co-ordination and co-operation. Secondly, it sought a reinforcement of the roles and capacities of environmental protection and resource management agencies to deal with effects, including a strengthened UNEP as the principal source for environmental data, assessment and reporting and the principal advocate and agent for change and international co-operation. Thirdly, it called for an extension of the capacity of the international community to identify, assess and report on global risks of irreversible environmental damage, including a new international programme for co-operation among non-governmental organisations, scientific bodies and industry groups. Fourthly, it recognised the need to expand the rights, roles and participation in development planning, decision-making and project implementation of an informed public, non-governmental organisations, the scientific community, and industry.

---

[133] *Ibid.*, 4.

Fifthly, in recognising that 'international law is being rapidly out-distanced by the accelerating pace and expanding scale of impacts on the ecological basis of development', the Brundtland Report called on governments to fill gaps in national and international law related to the environment in order to find ways to recognise and protect the rights of present and future generations to an environment adequate for their health and well-being, to prepare under UN auspices a universal declaration on environmental protection and sustainable development and a subsequent convention, and to strengthen procedures for avoiding or resolving disputes on environment and resource management issues. Finally, the Report recognised the need to invest in pollution control by providing financial assistance through the World Bank, the IMF and other regional development banks. The Report also called for a UN Programme on Sustainable Development and an international conference to review progress and to promote follow-up arrangements. Each of these proposals received support from governments at UNCED.

An Experts Group on Environmental Law was established alongside UNCED. It proposed Legal Principles and Recommendations on Environmental Protection and Sustainable Development (1986 WCED Legal Principles),[134] set out in twenty-two Articles, which are intended to reflect the basic obligations of states based on an assessment of treaties, soft law instruments, and some state practice. The WCED Legal Principles fall into three categories, including 'general principles, rights and responsibilities', and 'principles, rights and obligations governing transboundary natural resources and environmental interference'. These are addressed below.

Environmental Perspective to the Year 2000 and Beyond

In 1987 the United Nations General Assembly adopted the 'Environmental Perspective to the Year 2000 and Beyond' as a framework to guide national action and international co-operation in policies and programmes aimed at achieving environmentally sound development.[135] The Perspective had been prepared by a UNEP intergovernmental preparatory committee pursuant to a request from the General Assembly,[136] and focused on the same six key sectoral issues as the Brundtland Commission: population; food and agriculture; energy; industry; health and human settlements; and international economic relations. The Perspective identified four further issues which it considered to be of global concern: oceans and seas; outer space; biological diversity; and security and the environment. For legislation and environmental law, the Perspective identified issues requiring attention:

---

[134] Reprinted in R. D. Munro and J. G. Lammers (eds.), *Environmental Protection and Sustainable Development* (1987), 7.

[135] Res. 42/186, 11 December 1987.   [136] UNGA Res. 38/161, 19 December 1983.

- the need to conclude conventions for hazards relating to chemicals, the treatment and international transport of hazardous wastes, industrial accidents, climate change, protection of the ozone layer, protection of the marine environment from pollution from land-based sources, and protection of biological diversity; and
- the establishment of legal regimes at international and national levels to improve the environmental management of rivers, lakes and forests.[137]

The Perspective noted, in opaque language which reflected the lack of consensus over future directions, that the 'progressive emergence of general environmental norms and principles and the codification of existing agreements could lead to a global convention on the protection and enhancement of the environment'.[138] It also noted that the International Court of Justice, the Permanent Court of Arbitration and regional mechanisms should facilitate the peaceful settlement of environmental disputes.[139]

Conclusions

By 1990, preparations for UNCED were under way and significant political and legal changes were in place. There was now a discrete area of law called international environmental law. At the global and regional level this included a large number of substantive rules limiting the rights of states to engage in activities which were harmful to the environment. International environmental law was no longer focused on the protection of wildlife. Standards had been adopted and applied for the protection of the marine environment and freshwater resources, the atmosphere and the ozone layer, and the disposal of hazardous and other wastes. New techniques for the implementation of those standards, such as environmental impact assessment and access to environmental information, were being developed and applied. Environmental protection was being addressed in the context of economic matters, such as trade and development lending. Developing countries had succeeded in establishing the principle that financial resources should be made available to help them meet the incremental costs of implementing their international environmental obligations. Differential standards were accepted in the 1985 SO_2 Protocol to the 1979 LRTAP Convention and the 1987 Montreal Protocol. New institutions had been created to address regional and global environmental issues, and existing institutions were beginning to integrate environmental considerations into their activities. Subsidiary bodies were being established to ensure innovative implementation and compliance techniques. Principle 21 was broadly considered to reflect a rule of customary international law, and new principles were emerging, such as the polluter-pays principle and the precautionary principle. Perhaps most significantly, in respect of the standards being adopted, and in respect of monitoring

[137] *Ibid.*, Annex, 38, paras. 100–2.   [138] *Ibid.*, para. 138.   [139] *Ibid.*, para. 103.

and implementation, new international actors, including non-governmental organisations from developed and developing countries, were participating in the international legal process.

UNCED

Report of the UN Conference on Environment and Development, Rio de Janeiro, 3–14 June 1992, UN Doc. A/CONF.151/26/Rev.1 (vols. I–III); A. Adede, 'International Environmental Law from Stockholm to Rio: an Overview of Past Lessons and Future Challenges', 22 *Environmental Policy and Law* 88 (1992); A. C. Kiss and S. Doumbe-Bille, 'La Conference des Nations Unies sur l'Environnement et le Developpement', AFDI 823 (1992); I. M. Porras, 'The Rio Declaration: A New Basis for International Co-operation', 1 RECIEL 245 (1992); G. Speth, 'A Post Rio Compact', 88 *Foreign Policy* 145 (1992); M. Pallemaerts, 'International Environmental Law from Stockholm to Rio: Back to the Future?' 1 RECIEL 254 (1992); P. Sand, 'UNCED and the Development of International Environmental Law', 3 *Yearbook of International Enviromental Law* 3 (1992); N. Robinson (ed.), *International Protection of the Environment: Agenda 21 and the UNCED Proceedings* (1992); D. Freestone, 'The Road from Rio: International Environmental Law after the Earth Summit', 6 JEL 193 (1994); H. Smets, 'The Polluter-Pays Principle in the Early 1990s', in L. Campiglio *et al.* (eds.), *The Environment After Rio* (1994), 131.

In December 1987, the UN General Assembly noted the Brundtland Report,[140] and the following year called for a UN conference on environment and development.[141] In December 1989, General Assembly Resolution 44/228 convened a UN Conference on Environment and Development for June 1992 in Brazil. The purpose of the Conference was to 'elaborate strategies and measures to halt and reverse the effects of environmental degradation in the context of strengthened national and international efforts to promote sustainable and environmentally sound development in all countries'.[142]

UNCED was held in Rio de Janeiro, Brazil, on 3–14 June 1992, and was attended by 176 states, more than fifty intergovernmental organisations, and several thousand corporations and non-governmental organisations. UNCED adopted three non-binding instruments: the Rio Declaration on Environment and Development (the Rio Declaration); a Non-Legally Binding Authoritative Statement of Principles for a Global Consensus on the Management, Conservation and Sustainable Development of All Types of Forest (the UNCED Forest

---

[140] UNGA Res. 42/187 (1987).
[141] UNGA Res. 43/196 (1988). See also UNEP Governing Council Decision 15/3 (1989); ECOSOC Res. 1989/87 (1989); Report of the Secretary General, UN Doc. A/44/256-E/1989/66 and Corr.1 and Add.1 and 2 (1989).
[142] UNGA Res. 44/228, para. 3.

Principles);[143] and Agenda 21. Two treaties were also opened for signature: the Convention on Biological Diversity;[144] and the UN Framework Convention on Climate Change.[145]

UNCED was the culmination of three separate but related negotiating processes, one of which was the Preparatory Committee for UNCED (PrepComm) which met four times between August 1990 and May 1992. The other two were the Intergovernmental Negotiating Committee for a Framework Convention on Climate Change (INC/FCCC) which held five sessions between February 1991 and May 1992, and the Intergovernmental Negotiating Committee for a Convention on Biological Diversity (INC/CBD) which held five sessions between June 1991 and May 1992. It was also, however, an opportunity to take stock of developments which had taken place in regional and global organisations, in public and private initiatives, and in bilateral, regional and global treaties. It provided an opportunity for the international community to translate initiatives such as the Brundtland Report and the Strategy for Sustainable Living, as well as the many regional preparatory conferences which had taken place, into a coherent strategy of international environmental policy and law for the twenty-first century. UNCED's contribution to international law will emerge over time, and is likely to include the Commission on Sustainable Development, the endorsement of a new topic area known as the 'international law of sustainable development' (of which international environmental law forms a significant part),[146] a number of the Rio Declaration principles, and the framework established by Agenda 21. It has been suggested that UNCED's endorsement of sustainable development could undermine 'the autonomy of environmental law as a body of rules and standards designed to restrain and prevent the environmentally destructive effects of certain kinds of economic activity', and there might be some reason to fear that the Rio Conference constituted 'the beginning of the decline of international environmental law as an autonomous branch of international law'.[147] This has not been borne out by subsequent developments.

UNCED was concerned with the balance between environmental protection and economic development. Environmental concerns have been marginal in the broader scheme of international legal and institutional arrangements. For them to affect and influence behaviour in significant ways they must be integrated into economic and development activities, without their being overwhelmed by the more powerful rules of international economic co-operation.

---

[143] A/CONF.151/6/Rev.1, 13 June 1992. See chapter 11, pp. 548–51 below.
[144] Chapter 11, pp. 515–23 below.   [145] Chapter 8, pp. 359–68 below.
[146] Rio Declaration, Principle 27. Agenda 21, paras. 39.1 and 39.2.
[147] Marc Pallemaerts, 'International Environmental Law from Stockholm to Rio: Back to the Future?', 1 RECIEL 254 at 264 (1992); and D. Wirth, 'The Rio Declaration on Environment and Development: Two Steps Forward and One Step Back, or Vice Versa', 29 *Georgetown Law Review* 599 (1995).

The Rio Declaration

The Rio Declaration represents a series of compromises between developed and developing countries and a balance between the objectives of environmental protection and economic development.[148] The text was completed at the Fourth PrepComm in April 1992 and was not reopened for negotiation at UNCED, despite threats from a number of countries to do so, and was 'endorsed' by the UN General Assembly in December 1992.[149] It comprises twenty-seven Principles which set out the basis upon which states and people are to co-operate and further develop 'international law in the field of sustainable development' (Principle 27). Although it is non-binding, some provisions reflect rules of customary law, others reflect emerging rules, and yet others provide guidance as to future legal developments. A number of the Principles have been referred to with regularity by national and international courts. The Rio Declaration provides a benchmark to measure future developments, and provides a basis for defining 'sustainable development' and its application. It attempts to achieve an acceptable balance between environment and development. The Rio Declaration lost its original title ('Earth Charter'), mainly at the insistence of developing countries, and it bears little resemblance to the Universal Declaration of Human Rights, or to the Universal Covenant which the Brundtland Report had called for.

Principle 1 of the Rio Declaration reflects a shift towards an anthropocentric approach to environmental and developmental issues, declaring that human beings are 'at the centre of concerns for sustainable development', and that they are 'entitled to a healthy and productive life in harmony with nature'; this falls short of recognising a right to a clean and healthy environment. The Rio Declaration reaffirmed Principle 21 of the Stockholm Declaration with one addition. As amended, Principle 2 provides that:

> States have, in accordance with the Charter of the United Nations and the principles of international law, the sovereign right to exploit their own resources pursuant to their own environmental and developmental policies, and the responsibility to ensure that activities within their jurisdiction or control do not cause damage to the environment of other states or of areas beyond the limits of national jurisdiction.

The addition of the words 'and developmental' (which is not reflected in Article 3 of the Biodiversity Convention or Principle 2(a) of the Forest Principles), in the context of a negotiation of a document adopted by consensus by 176 states, arguably reflects an 'instant' change in the rule of customary international law which is widely considered to be set forth in Principle 21. It has been

---

[148] 31 ILM 874 (1992). For an account of the negotiating history of the Rio Declaration, and an excellent interpretative guide, see Ileana Porras, 'The Rio Declaration: A New Basis for International Co-operation', 1 RECIEL 245 (1992).

[149] UNGA Res. 47/190 (1992), para. 2.

suggested that the addition of these two words reveals a 'skilfully masked step backwards' which by its stronger emphasis on development 'upsets the delicate balance struck in Stockholm between the sovereign use of natural resources and the duty of care for the environment'.[150] In fact, a careful reading suggests that the additional words merely affirm that states are entitled to pursue their own development policies. The introduction of these words may even expand the scope of the responsibility not to cause environmental damage to apply to national development policies as well as national environment policies. In practice, the modest amendment has not been identified as having been relied upon by states.[151]

The heart of the Rio Declaration is found in Principles 3 and 4, which should be read together to understand the political context in which they were negotiated and the trade-off they represent. Both Principles were initially controversial. Principle 3 provides that '[t]he right to development must be fulfilled so as to equitably meet developmental and environmental needs of present and future generations'. It represents something of a victory for developing countries and the Group of 77, being the first time that the 'right to development' has been affirmed in an international instrument adopted by consensus.[152] The nature and extent of that right is left open, as is the question of whether such a right attaches to states, peoples or individuals. In return for Principle 3, the developed countries extracted Principle 4, which provides that '[i]n order to achieve sustainable development, environmental protection shall constitute an integral part of the development process and cannot be considered in isolation from it'. This reflects a commitment to moving environmental considerations and objectives from the periphery of international relations to its economic core. In practical terms, Principle 4 can be read as permitting, or requiring, the attachment of environmental conditionalities to all development lending by states and multilateral development banks, and the integration of environmental considerations into all economic and other development.

The Rio Declaration recognises a principle of 'common but differentiated responsibility'. Principle 7 notes the different contributions of countries to regional and global environmental degradation, and provides that:

> [i]n view of the different contributions to global environmental degradation, States have common but differentiated responsibilities. The developed countries acknowledge the responsibility that they bear in the international pursuit of sustainable development in view of the pressures their societies place on the global environment and of the technologies and financial resources they command.[153]

---

[150] Pallemaerts, 'International Environmental Law', 256.

[151] See chapter 6, pp. 252–66 below.

[152] Cf. the written statement by the United States, which 'does not, by joining consensus . . . change its longstanding opposition to the so-called "right to development"': A/CONF.151/26/Rev.1 (vol. II), 17 (1992).

[153] See chapter 6, pp. 285–9 below.

This principle of 'common but differentiated responsibilities' crystallises the provisions in earlier instruments which encourage universal participation in agreements by providing incentives in the form of differentiated standards and 'grace periods', and the provision of financial incentives to subsidise at least some of the incremental costs incurred in fulfilling treaty obligations. The United States rejected an interpretation 'that would imply a recognition or acceptance by the United States of any international obligations or liabilities, or any diminutions in the responsibilities of developing countries.[154]

Principle 11 of the Rio Declaration commits all states to enact 'effective environmental legislation', although the standards, objectives and priorities 'should reflect the environmental and developmental context to which they apply'.[155] Principle 11 also recognises that standards applied by some countries 'may be inappropriate and of unwarranted economic and social cost to other countries, in particular developing countries'.

The Rio Declaration develops general principles of the international law of sustainable development. The 'precautionary approach' is endorsed by Principle 15, and the polluter-pays principle is implicitly recognised in Principle 16. The Rio Declaration takes several steps beyond the Stockholm Declaration by supporting the development of 'procedural' techniques for implementing international standards (including the provision of, and access to, information relating to environmental matters, and recognising the need for participation of concerned citizens) supporting environmental impact assessments, and calling for notification, information exchange and consultation.

Other matters addressed by the Rio Declaration include: the relationship between environmental protection and free trade obligations; the development of national and international law regarding liability and compensation for the victims of pollution and other environmental damage; the need to eradicate poverty and decrease disparities in standards of living; and the reduction and elimination of 'unsustainable patterns of production and consumption'. It promotes 'appropriate demographic policies', endogenous capacity-building and scientific understanding, as well as the transfer of technologies. The Rio Declaration supports the full participation of women, youth and indigenous people and their communities, recognises that war is 'inherently destructive of sustainable development', that peace, development and environmental protection are 'interdependent and indivisible', and that there is a need for the peaceful resolution of environmental disputes.

As a package, the Rio Declaration includes provisions which are more specific than those adopted in the Stockholm Declaration. It provides a framework for the development of environmental law at the national and international level which will serve as an important point of reference to guide decision-making. Its

---

[154] A/CONF.151/26/Rev.1 (vol. II), 18 (1993).   [155] Principle 11.

contribution to the development of rules of customary law has become clearer over time, although many of its provisions were already found in treaties and other international acts and reflected in the domestic practice of many states.

Agenda 21

Agenda 21 is a non-binding blueprint and action plan for a global partnership for sustainable development.[156] It was conceived as a plan of action by and for the whole of the international community, designed to integrate environment and development concerns for 'the fulfilment of basic needs, improved living standards for all, better protected and managed ecosystems and a safer, more prosperous future.[157] Agenda 21 comprises forty chapters and hundreds of programme areas, the indicative cost of each having been estimated by the UNCED secretariat. The average annual cost of implementing the activities in Agenda 21 was estimated at US$600 billion in the period 1993–2000.

Agenda 21 was negotiated over two years, and 'reflects a global consensus and political commitment at the highest level' towards the implementation of national strategies, plans, policies and processes to be supported and supplemented by international co-operation.[158] The implementation of Agenda 21 is the responsibility of governments, with key roles to be played by the UN system, other international, regional and sub-regional organisations, and with broad public participation and the active involvement of non-governmental organisations.[159] It constitutes an extensive series of programme areas setting out 'the basis for action, objectives, activities and means of implementation' which will be carried out

> by the various actors according to the different situations, capacities and priorities of countries and regions in full respect of all the principles contained in the Rio Declaration on Environment and Development. It could evolve over time in the light of changing needs and circumstances. This process marks the beginning of a new global partnership for sustainable development.[160]

What contribution has Agenda 21 made to international law? The tangible developments which flow directly from the text are limited. It recommended the creation of a Commission on Sustainable Development, and new

---

[156] UNCED Report, A/CONF.151/26/Rev.1 (vol. I) (1993).

[157] Chapter 1, para. 1.1. UNGA Res. 47/190 (1992) called upon 'all concerned' to implement the commitments and recommendations without specifically endorsing Agenda 21.

[158] Chapter 1, para. 1.2. For the draft negotiating texts, see N. Robinson *et al.* (eds.), *The United Nations Conference on Environment and Development*, Agenda 21 and the UNCED Proceedings (1992). Although it was adopted by consensus, written statements were submitted by the United States, Saudi Arabia, Argentina, Kuwait, Philippines, France and the delegation from Palestine: A/CONF.151/26/Rev.1 (vol. II), 18–22 (1993).

[159] *Ibid.*   [160] Chapter 1, para. 1.5.

co-ordinating mechanisms among UN and other bodies. It proposed a Convention on Drought and Desertification (which was adopted in 1994), but could not agree on a possible international agreement on forests (which remains an unachieved goal for some states). It proposed two intergovernmental follow-up conferences, on 'straddling stocks' of marine living resources (a convention was adopted in 1995) and on the sustainable development of small island states. It endorsed a partnership role for all members of the international community (states, international organisations, non-state actors) in the development and implementation of law and policy on environment and development. And it established programme areas of variable quality and likely effect to cover virtually all human activity. Its contribution to international law can be considered at three levels. First, as a consensus document negotiated by the international community over a period of two years, it provides the only agreed global framework for the development and application of international legal instruments, including 'soft law' instruments, and the activities of international organisations. Secondly, limited parts of Agenda 21 might be considered to reflect rules of 'instant' customary law.[161] Thirdly, it reflected a consensus on principles, practices and rules which might contribute to the development of new rules of conventional and customary law.

Agenda 21 comprises a Preamble (Chapter 1) and four sections. Section 1 (Chapters 2–8) addresses 'Social and Economic Dimensions'. The seven chapters in this section provide for national and international action in relation to international co-operation, poverty, consumption patterns, population, human health, sustainable human settlement and the integration of environment and development in decision-making. Section II (Chapters 9–22) is concerned with 'Conservation and Management of Resources for Development'. Its fourteen chapters address substantive issues for the protection and sustainable use of natural resources in various sectors:

- protection of the atmosphere (Chapter 9);
- planning and management of land resources (Chapter 10);
- deforestation (Chapter 11);
- desertification and drought (Chapter 12);
- sustainable mountain development (Chapter 13);
- sustainable agriculture and rural development (Chapter 14);
- conservation of biological diversity (Chapter 15);
- management of biotechnology (Chapter 16);
- protection of oceans, seas, coastal areas, and the protection, use and development of their living resources (Chapter 17);
- protection of the quality and supply of freshwater resources (Chapter 18);
- management of toxic chemicals (Chapter 19);

[161] See e.g. the provision limiting the storage or disposal of radioactive waste near the sea: Agenda 21, para. 22.5(c); see chapter 9, p. 455 and chapter 12, p. 619 below.

- management of hazardous wastes (Chapter 20);
- management of solid and sewage wastes (Chapter 21); and
- management of radioactive wastes (Chapter 22).

Section III (Chapters 23–32) provides for 'Strengthening the Role of Major Groups'. The section recognises that '[o]ne of the fundamental prerequisites for the achievement of sustainable development is broad public participation in decision-making', including new forms of participation.[162] In a chapter devoted to each, it identifies key groups for the implementation of Agenda 21 and proposes their roles at the national and international levels: women; children and youth; indigenous people and their communities; non-governmental organisations; local authorities; workers and their trade unions; business and industry; the scientific and technological community; and farmers.[163] Finally, Section IV (Chapters 33–40) identifies 'Means of Implementation'. The eight chapters in this section identify actions relating to financial resources and mechanisms (Chapter 33), technology transfer, co-operation and capacity-building (Chapter 34), science (Chapter 35), education, public awareness and training (Chapter 36), capacity-building in developing countries (Chapter 37), international institutional arrangements (Chapter 38), international legal instruments and mechanisms (Chapter 39), and information for decision-making (Chapter 40).

A comprehensive assessment of Agenda 21 lies beyond the scope of this chapter. The provisions of Section II, as well as those of Chapters 38, 39 and 40 on financial resources, technology transfer, institutions, legal instruments and mechanisms, and information and education may provide useful points of reference. Agenda 21 aims at developing the concept of the international law of sustainable development, and calls on competent intergovernmental and non-state actors to co-operate

> to provide governments and legislators, upon request, with an integrated programme of environment and development law (sustainable development law) services, carefully adapted to the specific requirements of the recipient legal and administrative systems.[164]

Institutions

Chapter 38 of Agenda 21 proposes a framework for institutional arrangements to implement Agenda 21, and calls for the establishment of a new commission to ensure effective follow-up of UNCED, to enhance international co-operation and to rationalise the intergovernmental decision-making capacity for the integration of environmental and development issues.[165] The underlying principles

---

[162] Agenda 21, Preamble, paras. 23.1–23.2.   [163] *Ibid.*, Chapters 24–32.
[164] *Ibid.*, para. 8.19.   [165] *Ibid.*, para. 38.11; see chapter 3, pp. 75 and 87 below.

to guide institutional arrangements, in the context of reform and revitalisation of the UN system, are an 'action- and result-oriented approach' based on 'universality, democracy, transparency, cost-effectiveness and accountability'.[166] In fulfilling the task of integrating environment and development issues, institutional arrangements in the UN system are called upon: to ensure the implementation of Agenda 21; to adopt concrete programmes to strengthen co-operation and co-ordination; to strengthen institutional capabilities; to establish effective co-operation and exchange of information; to respond to continuing and emerging issues; and to ensure that any new institutional arrangements support revitalisation, clearly divide responsibilities, and avoid duplication.[167] Specific proposals are made for the UN and its organs and bodies, as well as UN specialised agencies, related organisations and other relevant intergovernmental organisations, and regional and sub-regional organisations.[168] Chapter 38 also identifies the need for partnership with non-governmental organisations and calls for their 'expanded role'.[169] The development of environmental law is addressed in two chapters: Chapter 8, Part B, deals with environmental law at the national level; and Chapter 39 deals with international law.

National law

Chapter 8 identifies limitations in legal and regulatory arrangements at the national level, and recognises that the enactment and enforcement of laws and regulations at the regional, national, state/provincial or local/municipal levels are 'essential for the implementation of most international agreements in the field of environment and development'.[170] The survey of existing agreements undertaken in UNCED preparations indicated problems of compliance with international agreements; according to Chapter 8, this was due, in part, to the fact that law-making in many countries appeared to be 'ad hoc and piecemeal, or . . . not endowed with the necessary institutional machinery and authority for enforcement and timely adjustment'.[171] The basis for national legal and regulatory arrangements was summarised thus:

> it is essential to develop and implement integrated, enforceable and effective laws and regulations that are based upon sound social, ecological, economic and scientific principles. It is equally critical to develop workable programmes to review and enforce compliance with the laws, regulations

---

[166] Agenda 21, para. 38.2.   [167] *Ibid.*, para. 38.8.
[168] *Ibid.*, paras. 38.9–38.35; see chapter 3, p. 75 below.
[169] Agenda 21, paras. 38.42–38.44; see chapter 3, pp. 112–20 below.
[170] Agenda 21, para. 8.14.
[171] *Ibid.*, paras. 8.13 and 8.15; see P. Sand (ed.), *The Effectiveness of International Environmental Agreements: A Survey of Existing Legal Instruments* (1992).

and standards that are adopted. Technical support may be needed for many countries to accomplish these goals. Technical co-operation requirements in this field include legal information, advisory services, and specialised training and institutional capacity-building.[172]

Chapter 8, Part B, in effect recognises that national legal and regulatory arrangements are international matters. Three specific objectives are proposed to address international aspects:

1. the dissemination of information on effective legal and regulatory innovations;
2. supporting country requests to modernise and strengthen the legal framework; and
3. encouraging the development and implementation of national, state, provincial and local programmes to assess and promote compliance and respond to non-compliance.[173]

To give effect to these objectives, six activities are proposed:

1. governments and international organisations are called upon to assess their laws and regulations and institutional and administrative machinery;
2. judicial and administrative procedures should be established 'for legal redress and remedy of actions affecting environment and development that may be unlawful or infringe on rights under the law, and should provide access to individuals, groups and organisations with a recognised legal interest';
3. international organisations and non-governmental organisations should provide governments and legislators with an 'integrated programme of environment and development law (sustainable development law) services';
4. international and academic institutions should provide postgraduate programmes and in-service training facilities in environment and development law;
5. countries should develop strategies to maximise compliance with their laws and regulations, with assistance from international organisations and other countries (including: enforceable laws incorporating sanctions designed to punish violations, obtain redress and act as deterrence; mechanisms for promoting compliance; collecting data; and involving individuals and groups in the development and enforcement of laws); and
6. parties to international agreements should improve practice and procedures for collecting information on the legal and regulatory measures taken.[174]

---

[172] Agenda 21, para. 8.14.   [173] *Ibid.*, para. 8.15.   [174] *Ibid.*, paras. 8.15–8.22.

International law

Chapter 39 addresses the further development of international law on sustainable development. Its provisions are limited compared to the specific proposals put forward in, *inter alia*, the Brundtland Report, the WCED Legal Principles, the Perspective 2000 Plan adopted by the UN General Assembly, and the WCN/UNEP/WWF document, *Caring for the Earth*. The UNCED Preparatory Committee had also examined areas for the further development of international environmental law, in light of the need to integrate environment and development and taking into account the needs and concerns of developing countries,[175] and had before it the conclusions of the 1990 Siena Forum on International Law of the Environment,[176] the Beijing Symposium on Developing Countries and International Environmental Law,[177] the Report of the Meeting of Experts for the Review of the Montevideo Programme,[178] and relevant comments by governments and international organisations in the context of the United Nations Decade of International Law.[179] The proposals in Chapter 39 are premised on: the need to clarify and strengthen the relationship between existing international agreements; the importance of participation from all countries; the need for technical assistance; the work of the International Law Commission; and the need for universality.[180] The overall objective is:

> to evaluate and to promote the efficacy of that law and to promote the integration of environment and development policies through effective international agreements or instruments taking into account both universal principles and the particular and differentiated needs and concerns of all countries.[181]

Eight specific objectives are identified:

1. addressing the difficulties which prevent some states, in particular developing countries, from participating in or implementing international agreements;
2. setting priorities for future law-making at the global, regional or sub-regional level;
3. promoting the participation of all countries in the negotiation, implementation, review and governance of international agreements;

---

[175] Terms of Reference of Working Group III, Decision 2/3, A/46/48, vol. I, Annex I (1992).
[176] A/45/66 (1990).
[177] 12–14 August 1991, 2 *Yearbook of International Environmental Law* 304 (1991).
[178] UNEP/Env.Law/2/3 (1991).
[179] Report of the UN Secretary General, A/46/372 (1992).   [180] Agenda 21, para. 39.1.
[181] *Ibid.*, para. 39.2. In this regard, and for reasons which appear to be related to a transcribing or editing error, the relevant law is identified as 'international environmental law' rather than the 'international law of sustainable development'.

4. gradually promoting international environmental standards;
5. ensuring effective, full and prompt implementation of legally binding instruments;
6. improving the effectiveness of administrative arrangements;
7. identifying and preventing conflicts; and
8. providing for the identification, avoidance and settlement of international disputes in the field of sustainable development.[182]

To the extent that the international community has a blueprint for the development of the international law of sustainable development (including international environmental law), this is it. Chapter 39 is short on substance, and there was no agreement on the need for a binding instrument of general application, although it was agreed that it would be useful to examine 'the feasibility of elaborating general rights and obligations of states . . . in the field of sustainable development'.[183] Specific activities to be undertaken include: the review and assessment of the performance and effectiveness of agreements and priorities for future law-making on sustainable development; further consideration by the General Assembly of armed conflict and 'large-scale destruction of the environment that cannot be justified under international law'; and efforts to conclude a nuclear safety convention under the International Atomic Energy Agency (IAEA).[184] Chapter 39 also calls for the promotion and review of the effective, full and prompt implementation of international agreements (including by establishing efficient and practical reporting systems and enhancing the contribution of international bodies such as UNEP), and the provision of technical and financial assistance, particularly to developing countries, to ensure their effective participation.[185] The measures proposed to ensure the avoidance and settlement of disputes call for further study and consideration of existing techniques, and are disappointing in the context of the more specific proposals which were put forward.[186]

Beyond UNCED: trends and directions

The UN General Assembly adopted five follow-up resolutions to UNCED. These established a negotiating committee to elaborate a convention on drought and desertification;[187] convened a global conference on the sustainable development

---

[182] Agenda 21, para. 39.3.

[183] *Ibid.*, para. 39.5; by implication, the Rio Declaration is therefore something other than an elaboration of such rights and obligations.

[184] Agenda 21, paras. 39.5 and 39.6; see chapter 12, pp. 643–4 below.

[185] Agenda 21, paras. 39.7–39.8; on reporting, see chapter 17, pp. 832–8 below; on financial and technical support, see chapter 20, pp. 1021 **et seq**. below.

[186] Agenda 21, para. 39.9; on dispute settlement, see chapter 5, pp. 212–26 below.

[187] UNGA Res. 47/188 (1992); see chapter 11, pp. 557–8 below.

of small island states;[188] noted the report of UNCED, endorsed the Rio Declaration and the Forest Principles and called for effective follow-up action and the implementation of all commitments, agreements and recommendations;[189] established new institutional arrangements to follow up UNCED, including the Commission on Sustainable Development;[190] and convened a conference on straddling and highly migratory fish stocks.[191]

Since UNCED, a number of important new instruments have been adopted and the negotiation of others continues. There is no sign that the rate of legislative activity is dropping off. A treaty was signed to replace the 1972 Oslo Dumping Convention and the 1974 Paris LBS Convention, incorporating many of the principles (precaution, polluter-pays) and legal techniques (environmental impact assessment, access to information, economic instruments) which were endorsed at UNCED.[192] In 1995, a global Agreement on Straddling Fish Stocks was adopted by parties to the 1982 UNCLOS.[193] The parties to the 1969 CLC and the 1971 Fund Convention adopted 1992 Protocols which introduced significant legal changes;[194] and the Council of Europe adopted a convention on civil liability for environmental damage which incorporates many of the recommendations on procedural matters referred to in the Rio Declaration, including access to information and national legal remedies.[195] The Kyoto Protocol to the 1992 Climate Change Convention was adopted in 1997,[196] and the Biosafety Protocol to the 1992 Biodiversity Convention was adopted in 2000:[197] both instruments reflect new thinking in the approach to international regulation and the role of various actors, including the private sector. In 1998, under the auspices of the UNECE, states adopted the Aarhus Convention, the first treaty to address in a comprehensive fashion the rights of participation reflected in Principle 10 of the Rio Declaration.[198] Other treaties which have been adopted include an IAEA nuclear safety convention;[199] amendments to the 1960 and 1963 nuclear liability conventions;[200] a convention on desertification and drought under the auspices of the General Assembly;[201] an International Labor Organization convention on the prevention of industrial disasters;[202] revisions to the 1985 SO$_2$ Protocol to the 1979 LRTAP Convention and the adoption of Protocols concerning other matters;[203] a liability protocol to the 1989 Basel Convention;[204] global conventions on chemicals and pesticides

---

[188] UNGA Res. 47/189 (1992).   [189] UNGA Res. 47/190 (1992).
[190] UNGA Res. 47/191 (1992); see chapter 3, pp. 74–6 below.
[191] UNGA Res. 47/192 (1992); see chapter 11, p. 574 below.
[192] 1992 OSPAR Convention; see chapter 9, pp. 409–12 below.
[193] Chapter 11, pp. 574–8 below.   [194] Chapter 18, pp. 913–18 below.
[195] 1993 Lugano Convention; see chapter 18, pp. 933–7 below, noting Principle 13 of the Rio Declaration.
[196] Chapter 8, pp. 368–81 below.   [197] Chapter 12, pp. 653–8 below.
[198] Chapter 5, pp. 209–10 below; and chapter 17, pp. 859–61 below.
[199] Chapter 12, pp. 644–5 below.   [200] Chapter 18, pp. 905–12 below.
[201] Chapter 11, pp. 556–8 below.   [202] Chapter 12, pp. 623–5 below.
[203] Chapter 8, pp. 324–36 below.   [204] Chapter 18, pp. 924–6 below.

and on persistent organic pollutants;[205] and a convention on liability for hazardous and noxious substances under the auspices of the International Maritime Organization.[206] Important new treaties have also been adopted in relation to international watercourses, at the global, regional and bilateral levels.[207]

International organisations have continued to address a wide range of environmental issues. Recent developments include: the maintenance by the International Whaling Commission of its moratorium on commercial whaling;[208] the maintenance of the prohibition on trade in African elephant ivory;[209] further adjustments and amendments to the Montreal Protocol bringing forward the phaseout of certain substances and adopting a non-compliance procedure which provides for sanctions;[210] the adoption of the EC's Sixth Environmental Action Programme;[211] and the OSPAR Commission Decisions on reprocessing activities.[212] In the meantime, the International Law Commission has concluded its work on state responsibility,[213] and transformed its work on liability for injurious consequences arising out of acts not prohibited by international law.[214]

The decade since UNCED has been notable for the significant increase in international litigation on international environmental issues, reflecting a willingness on the part of states to bring international claims and a growing receptiveness on the part of the courts to give effect to environmental considerations. The International Court of Justice has addressed the environment in three important cases, including the dispute between Hungary and Slovakia concerning the Gabcikovo-Nagymaros project on the Danube River.[215] Important decisions have been handed down by other international courts and tribunals, including the WTO Appellate Body,[216] the International Tribunal for the Law of the Sea,[217] the European Court of Human Rights,[218] and international arbitral tribunals.[219] As increased attention is given to compliance with environmental obligations, states have also established new non-compliance mechanisms.[220] There is also considerable evidence that national courts are increasingly willing to apply international environmental obligations.[221]

---

[205] Chapter 12, pp. 628–30 below.   [206] Chapter 18, pp. 912–18 below.
[207] Chapter 10, pp. 466–8 below.   [208] Chapter 11, pp. 592–5 below.
[209] Chapter 11, pp. 509–11 below; and chapter 5 below.
[210] Chapter 8, pp. 348–53 below; and chapter 5, pp. 198–9 below.
[211] Chapter 15, pp. 750–3 below.   [212] Chapter 9, pp. 411–12 below.
[213] Chapter 18, pp. 873–5 below.   [214] Chapter 18, pp. 828–9 below.
[215] See respectively chapter 10, pp. 469–77 below, and chapter 5, p. 173 below.
[216] Chapter 19, pp. 952–85 below.   [217] Chapter 11, pp. 578–83 below.
[218] Chapter 7, pp. 300–5 below.
[219] Chapter 5, p. 225 below; and chapter 17, p. 857 below.
[220] Chapter 5, pp. 212–14 below.
[221] Chapter 11, pp. 205–10 below; see generally M. Anderson and P. Galizzi, *International Environmental Law in National Courts* (2002).

World Summit on Sustainable Development

To mark the tenth anniversary of UNCED, the World Summit on Sustainable Development (WSSD) was held in Johannesburg in September 2002.[222] The WSSD did not adopt any conventions or a statement of principles, and was generally focused on the eradication of poverty. The Johannesburg Declaration on Sustainable Development notes that the global environment continues to suffer, but proposes no specific actions beyond a general commitment to sustainable development.[223] The WSSD Plan of Implementation is long on general commitments and aspiration, but short on specific actions to be taken.[224] Such soft targets and timetables as are proposed are intended to build on post-UNCED achievements and expedite the realisation of UNCED's goals. Among the relatively more specific undertakings are commitments to:

- halve, by 2015, the proportion of the world's people whose income is less than US$1 a day and the proportion of people who suffer from hunger;
- halve, by 2015, the proportion of people without access to safe drinking water;
- halve, by 2015, the proportion of people who do not have access to basic sanitation;
- encourage and promote the development of a ten-year framework of programmes to accelerate the shift towards sustainable consumption and production;
- diversify energy supply and substantially increase the global share of renewable energy sources in order to increase its contribution to total energy supply;
- establish domestic programmes for energy efficiency with the support of the international community, and accelerate the development and dissemination of energy-efficiency and energy-conservation technologies, including the promotion of research and development;
- aim, by 2020, to use and produce chemicals in ways that do not lead to significant adverse effects on human health and the environment;
- promote the ratification and implementation of relevant international instruments on chemicals and hazardous waste, including the 1998 Chemicals Convention so that it can enter into force by 2003 and the 2001 POPs Convention so that it can enter into force by 2004;
- encourage countries to implement the new globally harmonised system for the classification and labelling of chemicals as soon as possible, with a view to having the system fully operational by 2008;
- develop integrated water resources management and water efficiency plans by 2005;

---

[222] In 1997, a five-year review conference was held: see D. Osborn and T. Bigg, *Earth Summit II: Outcomes and Analysis* (1998); and chapter 2 below.

[223] Available at http://www.un.org/jsummit/html/documents/ summit_docs/1009wssd_pol_declaration.htm.

[224] Available at http://www.un.org/jsummit/html/documents/ summit_docs/2309_planfinal.htm.

- encourage the application by 2010 of the ecosystem approach for the sustainable development of the oceans;
- on an urgent basis and where possible by 2015, maintain or restore depleted fish stocks to levels that can produce the maximum sustainable yield;
- put into effect the FAO international plans of action for the management of fishing capacity by 2005, and to prevent, deter and eliminate illegal, unreported and unregulated fishing by 2004;
- establish by 2004 a regular process under the UN for the global reporting and assessment of the state of the marine environment;
- eliminate subsidies that contribute to illegal, unreported and unregulated fishing and to over-capacity;
- achieve, by 2010, a significant reduction in the current rate of loss of biological diversity;
- adopt new measures to strengthen institutional arrangements for sustainable development at international, regional and national levels;
- enhance the role of the Commission on Sustainable Development, including through reviewing and monitoring progress in the implementation of Agenda 21 and fostering the coherence of implementation, initiatives and partnerships.

A potentially more useful indicator of future international legal developments are reflected in the revisions to the Montevideo Programme. A first revision had been completed by government experts from eighty-one countries (with input from observers from one country, one national liberation movement and twelve international organisations, but no non-governmental organisations) in September 1992. This was endorsed by the UNEP Governing Council in May 1993.[225] A second revision – the Programme for the Development and Periodic Review of Environmental Law for the First Decade of the Twenty-first Century – was completed by government experts from seventy countries (with input from observers, a national liberation movement and international organisations, but no non-governmental organisations) in October 2000. The Programme is divided into three parts. Part I addresses the effectiveness of environmental law, and focuses on:

- achieving effective implementation of, compliance with and enforcement of environmental law;
- strengthening the regulatory and institutional capacity of developing countries to develop and implement environmental law;
- strengthening measures to prevent environmental damage, and to mitigate such damage when it occurs;
- improving the effectiveness of measures and methods for avoiding and settling international environmental disputes;

---

[225] UNEP/GC.17/5 (1993).

- strengthening and further developing international environmental law, building on the existing foundations;
- promoting appropriate harmonised approaches to the development and implementation of environmental law and promoting co-ordination between relevant institutions;
- improving decision-making in environmental matters through increased transparency, access to information and public participation;
- improving the development, content, effectiveness and awareness of environmental law through the use of new and existing information technology; and
- improving the effectiveness of environmental law through the application of innovative approaches.

Part II seeks to enhance conservation and management, in particular by:

- enhancing the conservation, protection, integrated management and sustainable use of freshwater resources, both ground and surface water;
- improving the management, conservation and sustainable use of coastal and marine resources and ecosystems;
- improving the conservation, rehabilitation and sustainable use of soils;
- enhancing the conservation and sustainable use of all types of forests;
- enhancing the conservation of biological diversity, the sustainable use of its components, and the fair and equitable sharing of benefits arising out of the utilisation of genetic resources;
- strengthening and expanding existing, and developing new, legal instruments to prevent, reduce and control environmental pollution, to minimise the generation of wastes and to achieve their safe disposal, and to achieve the environmentally sound and safe management of hazardous substances;
- improving the sustainability of ecosystems through adequate patterns of production and consumption; and
- improving the ability of the international community to prevent and respond to environmental emergencies arising from man-made and natural disasters.

Part III addresses the relationship between environmental issues and other fields, and focuses on three areas:

- securing environmental protection objectives in international trade, investment and financial laws and policies in order to achieve sustainable development;
- promoting the integration of the environmental dimension into traditional concepts of international and national security; and
- reducing the harmful effects of military activities on the environment and encouraging a positive role for the military sector in environmental protection.

The Programme was adopted by the UNEP Governing Council in February 2001, and will be reviewed in 2005.[226]

Conclusions

It is apparent that over the past decade the rules of international law have become increasingly complex and technical, as environmental considerations are increasingly addressed in economic and other social fields, in particular human rights. While UNCED and its follow-up (the World Summit on Sustainable Development) have not provided a clear sense of direction as to likely future developments, one feature emerges as international environmental law moves into its next phase: international environmental law is no longer exclusively concerned with the adoption of normative standards to guide behaviour, but increasingly addresses techniques of implementation which are practical, effective, equitable and acceptable to most members of the international community. Two consequences follow. First, the focus on implementation means that international environmental law will increasingly be concerned with procedural, constitutional and institutional issues: environmental impact assessment; access to and dissemination of environmental information; techniques of law-making and issues of international governance, including accountability and transparency in decision-making; the participation or representation of the different members of the international community in the international legal process; new compliance mechanisms (including appropriate national judicial and administrative remedies), and new techniques of regulation (including economic instruments). Secondly, as environmental issues are increasingly integrated into aspects of economic and development institutions and law (in particular trade, development lending and intellectual property), the field in which international environmental law has developed will continue to broaden, creating new challenges for the subject and for lawyers and others involved in its development and application.

[226] UNEP/GC.21/22 (9 February 2001).

3

Governance: states, international organisations and non-state actors

K. Dahlberg, A. Feraru and M. Soroos (eds.), *Environment and the Global Arena: Actors, Values, Policies, Futures* (1983); P. Sands, 'The Environment, Community and International Law', 30 *Harvard International Law Journal* 393 (1989); P. Sand, *Lessons Learned in Global Environmental Governance* (1990); J. Tuchman-Mathews (ed.), *Preserving the Global Environment: The Challenge of Shared Leadership* (1990); A. Hurrell and B. Kingsbury (eds.), *The International Politics of the Environment: Actors, Interests and Institutions* (1992); Commission on Global Governance, *Our Global Neighborhood* (1995); K. Ginther, E. Denters and P. De Waart (eds.), *Sustainable Development and Good Governance* (1995); D. Bodansky, 'The Legitimacy of International Governance: A Coming Challenge for International Environmental Law?', 93 AJIL 596 (1999).

Introduction

A wide range of actors participate in those aspects of the international legal order which address environmental issues, including the negotiation, implementation and enforcement of international environmental agreements. Apart from state delegations, which play the central role, a visitor to ozone or climate change negotiations would find international organisations and non-state actors actively involved. International environmental law is characterised by this phenomenon which, with the possible exception of the human rights field, renders it unique. Various reasons explain this state of affairs. States are involved because they are still the pre-eminent international legal persons. International organisations participate because they have been created by states to address particular environmental issues. Of the various non-state participants, the scientific community is involved because, to a great extent, international environmental law is driven by scientific considerations; business is involved because of the significant implications which decisions taken at the global level can now have even for individual companies; and environmental non-governmental organisations (NGOs) are involved because their membership increasingly drives them into the international arena as the distinction between local, national and global issues disintegrates. The participation of non-state actors in international environmental law has an established history, and is now widely encouraged and accepted.

The various actors have different roles and functions, both as subjects and objects of international environmental law, including: participating in the law-making process; monitoring implementation, including reporting; and ensuring implementation and enforcement of obligations. The role of each actor turns upon its international legal personality and upon the rights and obligations granted to it by general international law and the rules established by particular treaties and other rules. The Rio Declaration and Agenda 21, as well as an increasing number of international environmental agreements, support an expanded role for international organisations and non-state actors in virtually all aspects of the international legal process.[1]

States

OECD, *Transfrontier Pollution and the Role of States* (1981); T. M. Franck, *The Power of Legitimacy Among Nations* (1990); R. Jennings and A. Watts, *Oppenheim's International Law* (1992, 9th edn), chapter 2 (especially pp. 110–26); B. Simma, 'From Bilateralism to Community Interest in International Law', 250 RdC 217 (1994); U. Beyerlin, 'State Community Interests and Institution Building in International Environmental Law', 56 ZaöRV 602 (1996); P. Daillier and A. Pellet, *Droit International Public* (2002, 7th edn), 407–514.

States are the primary subjects of international law. This remains the case in spite of the incursions made by international organisations into previously sovereign spheres of activity and the expanded role of non-state actors. It is still states which create, adopt and implement international legal principles and rules, establish international organisations, and permit the participation of other actors in the international legal process. There are currently 191 member states of the UN, another five states which are not members and numerous entities which do not possess the full characteristics of statehood, including dependent territories and non-self-governing territories.[2] The role played by the 191 UN member states in the development and application of international law depends on the subject being addressed and on the relationship of their vital interests to that subject, and on a complex blend of economic, political, cultural, geographical and ecological considerations. Broadly speaking, states are divided by international, legal and institutional arrangements into developed countries, developing countries, and economies in transition. Developed

---

[1] See pp. 112–20 below.

[2] The four characteristics which must traditionally obtain before an entity can exist as a state are: (a) a permanent population; (b) a defined territory; (c) a government; and (d) a capacity to enter into relations with other states: see 1933 Montevideo Convention on the Rights and Duties of States, Art. 1, 165 LNTS 19; see also Oppenheim, vol. 1, 120–3.

countries include the thirty member states of the OECD. The twenty-seven states which previously formed part of the 'Soviet bloc' are generally referred to as 'economies in transition'.[3]

The rest of the world, comprising some 134 states, are the developing states which form the Group of 77.[4] The Group of 77 often works as a single negotiating bloc within the framework of the UN, although in relation to environmental matters their perspectives vary widely. Within the UN system, states are also arranged into regional groupings, usually for the purpose of elections to UN bodies. The five groupings are: the Latin American and Caribbean Group; the African Group; the Asian Group; the Western European and Others Group; and the Central and Eastern European Group (although this grouping is increasingly less tenable with the prospect of EC membership for seven states in 2004). Frequently in environmental negotiations these distinctions tend to break down as states pursue what they perceive to be their vital national interests, including their strategic alliances, which may be unrelated to environmental matters. The UNCED negotiations – and more recently those relating to the 2000 Biosafety Protocol – have illustrated the extent of the differences which existed between and among developed states and developing states on particularly contentious issues: atmospheric emissions, production and trade in living modified organisms, conservation of marine mammals, protection of forests, institutional arrangements and financial resources.[5]

International organisations

National Academy of Sciences, *Institutional Arrangements for International Environmental Co-operation* (1972); J. Hargrove (ed.), *Law, Institutions and the Global Environment* (1972) (especially A. Chayes, 'International Institutions for the Environment'); J. Schneider, *World Public Order of the Environment: Towards an International Ecological Law and Organisation* (1979); R. Boardman, *International Organisation and the Conservation of Nature* (1981); E. Ostrom, *Governing the Commons: The Evolution of Institutions for Collective Action* (1990); 'Institutional Arrangements', in 'Developments – International Environmental Law', 104 *Harvard Law Review* 1484 at 1580 (1991); P. Thacher, 'Multilateral Co-operation

---

[3] For an indicative list of developed countries and 'economies in transition', see Appendix 1 to the 1992 Climate Change Convention, and Appendix 2 for a list of OECD members; see chapter 8, p. 275 below. Poland, Hungary, the Czech Republic and Slovakia, all formerly part of the 'Soviet bloc', have now joined the OECD and can now be considered developed countries. For a list of countries currently considered by the UN to be 'economies in transition', see the report of the Secretary General, 'Integration of the Economies in Transition into the World Economy', 9 September 2002, A/57/288.

[4] The G77, as it is known, does not include all developing countries; China is not a member of the Group, although it frequently participates in its activities.

[5] See C. Bail *et al.*, *The Cartagena Protocol on Biosafety* (2002), Part II.

and Global Change', 44 *Journal of International Affairs* 433 (1991); UNCED, *International Institutions and Legal Instruments* (Research Paper No. 10, 1991); A. Boyle, 'Saving the World: Implementation and Enforcement of International Environmental Law Through International Institutions', 3 *Journal of Environmental Law* 229 (1991); L. A. Kimball, *Forging International Agreement: Strengthening Inter-Governmental Institutions for Environment and Development* (1992); L. A. Kimball, 'Towards Global Environmental Management: The Institutional Setting', 3 *Yearbook of International Environmental Law* 18 (1992); H. French, *After the Earth Summit: The Future of Global Environmental Governance* (1992); P. Haas, R. Keohane and M. Levy (eds.), *Institutions for the Earth: Sources of Effective Environmental Protection* (1993); J. Werksman (ed.), *Greening International Institutions* (1996); N. Desai, 'Revitalizing International Environmental Institutions: The UN Task Force Report and Beyond', 40 *Indian Journal of International Law* 455 (2000); P. Sands and P. Klein, *Bowett's Law of International Institutions* (2001, 5th edn).

Introduction

International organisations involved in environmental law are established at the global, regional, sub-regional and bilateral levels. Almost all international organisations today have some competence or responsibility for the development, application or enforcement of international environmental obligations, including functions related to standard-setting. The decentralised nature of international organisations in the environmental field makes it difficult to assess their role by reference to any functional, sectoral or geographic criteria. They can be divided into three general categories: global organisations associated with the UN and its specialised agencies; regional organisations outside the UN system; and organisations established by environmental and other treaties. Within these categories, there are of course overlaps, since many of the organisations established in the third category were created by acts of the UN or its specialised agencies.[6]

History of international organisational arrangements

The role of international organisations has developed in a somewhat *ad hoc* manner. Early environmental agreements did not generally establish standing bodies to administer, or ensure implementation of, their provisions. Since 1945, the number of international environmental organisations has flourished, and they have usually been established at the sub-regional, regional or global level either to deal with specific environmental issues or, as is more often the case, by formally or informally adapting existing organisations to endow them

---

[6] See e.g. the Conference of the Parties to the 1987 Montreal Protocol (UNEP); the 1989 Basic Convention (UNEP); the 1992 Climate Change Convention (UNGA); the 1992 Biodiversity Convention (UNEP); and the Intergovernmental Panel on Climate Change (WMO/UNEP).

with competence in the area of environmental issues. The Stockholm Conference and UNCED provided opportunities to establish more orderly and coherent arrangements for international organisations in addressing environmental matters. The Stockholm Declaration recognised that the growing global and regional environmental problems required 'extensive co-operation among nations and action by international organisations in the common interest'.[7] Its Principle 25 called on states to 'ensure that international organisations play a co-ordinated, efficient and dynamic role for the protection and improvement of the environment'. Following the Stockholm Conference, the UN General Assembly established the United Nations Environment Programme (UNEP), an environment secretariat and fund, and an Environment Co-ordination Board to co-ordinate UN environment activities.[8]

Between Stockholm and UNCED, the environmental activities of global and regional organisations proliferated, and many new organisations were created by environmental treaties and acts. The proliferation did not occur in the context of a coherent strategy, and there was little effort to ensure effective co-operation or co-ordination between them. Moreover, significant gaps existed, and many activities considered to be particularly harmful to the environment remained outside the scope of formal international institutional authority. Activities relating to the energy, mining and transport (other than air transport) sectors are examples of areas for which no single UN body yet has overall responsibility. The Brundtland Report recognised the gaps and in 1989 a group of twenty-four developed and developing states adopted the Hague Declaration calling for the development of a new institutional authority, within the framework of the UN, with responsibility for preserving the earth's atmosphere.[9] The Hague Declaration even called for decisions of the new institutional authority to be subject to control by the International Court of Justice. UNCED reflected the unwillingness of states to institute such far-reaching changes.

UNCED

The UN General Assembly recognised the gaps, overlapping activities and lack of co-ordination in international environmental arrangements. In 1990, UNCED was called upon to review and examine the role of the UN system in dealing with the environment, to promote the development of regional and global organisations, and to promote international co-operation within the UN system in monitoring, assessing and anticipating environmental threats.[10]

---

[7] Preambular para. 7.   [8] See pp. 83–5 below.
[9] Declaration of the Hague, 11 March 1989, 28 ILM 1308 (1989). See also J. Ayling, 'Serving Many Voices: Progressing Calls for an International Environmental Organization', 9 JEL 243 (1997).
[10] UNGA Res. 44/228, para. 15(q), (r) and (t) (1990).

During the UNCED negotiations, many proposals were put forward by states, international organisations and non-governmental actors. Three main issues needing international attention were identified: the role of institutions for environment and development within the UN system; institutional follow-up arrangements after UNCED, especially regarding Agenda 21; and the relationship of the UN system to other institutions in the field of environment and development.[11] During the UNCED negotiations, specific institutional proposals related to five functions and responsibilities: functions related to technical and operational matters; responsibilities for policy-making; co-ordinating functions; responsibilities for financial matters; and functions relating to the administration and implementation of international law.[12] Proposals on technical and operational functions focused on UNEP, the development of regional institutions in the UN system, and new technical functions, particularly environmental assessment, early warning and emergency response, and energy management.[13]

Chapter 38 of Agenda 21 proposed the framework for institutional arrangements. The underlying principles and tasks to guide such arrangements were identified in chapter 2 above. With regard to specific institutions, UNCED proposed the establishment of a UN Commission on Sustainable Development and the further development of UNEP and the United Nations Development Programme (UNDP). It affirmed the central role of the UN General Assembly and the Economic and Social Council (ECOSOC), and provided limited guidance on co-operative mechanisms between UN bodies, and between UN bodies and regional organisations and international financial organisations. Overall, it appears that UNCED missed the opportunity to set in motion a wholesale and effective review of activities and operations. UN General Assembly Resolution 47/191 (1992) endorsed the Agenda 21 recommendations on international institutional arrangements to follow up on UNCED and took the following decisions:

- requested ECOSOC to set up a high-level Commission on Sustainable Development;
- requested all UN specialised agencies and related organisations of the UN system to strengthen and adjust their activities, programmes and plans in line with Agenda 21;
- invited the World Bank and other international, regional and sub-regional financial and development institutions, including the Global Environment Facility, to submit regularly to the Commission on Sustainable Development reports on their activities and plans to implement Agenda 21;

---

[11] 'Institutional Proposals: Report by the Secretary General of the Conference' A/CONF.151/PC/102 (1991).

[12] *Ibid.*, 5–54.   [13] *Ibid.*, 21–6.

- requested UNEP, UNDP, the United Nations Conference on Trade and Development (UNCTAD), the UN Sudano-Sahelian Office and the regional economic commissions to submit reports of their plans to implement Agenda 21 to the Commission on Sustainable Development; and
- endorsed the view of the UN Secretary General concerning the establishment of a High Level Advisory Board.

UNCED received its first major review at the World Summit on Sustainable Development (WSSD) in Johannesburg in 2002. The main outcomes relating to the institutional framework to support sustainable development were recommendations to:

- adopt new measures to strengthen institutional arrangements for sustainable development at international, regional and national levels;
- facilitate and promote the integration of the environmental, social and economic dimensions of sustainable development into the work programmes of UN regional commissions;
- establish an effective, transparent and regular inter-agency co-ordination mechanism on ocean and coastal issues within the UN system;
- enhance the role of the Commission on Sustainable Development, including through reviewing and monitoring progress in the implementation of Agenda 21 and fostering coherence of implementation, initiatives and partnerships; and
- take immediate steps to make progress in the formulation and elaboration of national strategies for sustainable development and begin their implementation by 2005.[14]

The function and role of international organisations

International organisations perform a range of different functions and roles in the development and management of international legal responses to environmental issues which are of a judicial, legislative or administrative nature. The function of each organisation depends upon the powers granted to it by its constituent instrument as subsequently interpreted and applied by the practice of the organisation and the parties to it. Apart from very specific functions required of some particular organisations, international organisations perform five main functions.

First, they provide a forum for co-operation and co-ordination between states on matters of international environmental management. The participation of states in the activities of international organisations is the principal means for consultation and the informal sharing of ideas and information which contribute towards building an international consensus for regional and global action. Thus, the formal negotiation of the 1992 Climate Change Convention

---

[14] WSSD Plan of Implementation, paras. 120–40.

followed extensive 'consciousness-raising' activities by a number of international organisations, including the UN General Assembly, the World Health Organization (WHO), the World Meteorological Organization (WMO) and the Intergovernmental Panel on Climate Change (IPCC), as well as the less formal settings of the World Climate Conferences held in 1979 and 1990.[15] International organisations thus contribute to developing the international agenda on environmental matters, broadening the participation of interested states, and encouraging technical research and development. Such organisations also play an important role in liaising with non-state actors.

The second function of international organisations is more formal, and relates to the provision of information. International organisations receive and disseminate information, facilitate information exchange, and provide for formal and informal consultation between states, and between states and the organisation. They also act as a conduit for notification of emergencies and other urgent matters.[16] In the case of certain highly developed organisations, such as the EC Commission and various international human rights bodies, the information function may include a formal fact-finding role.[17]

A third function of international organisations is to contribute to the development of international legal obligations, including 'soft law'. This function may take place informally, where the organisation acts as a catalyst for the development of legal and other obligations outside the organisation itself. Alternatively, it may take place formally and within the organisation, where the organisation adopts acts and decisions which can create legal obligations or which may contribute to the subsequent development of legal obligations.[18] International organisations develop policy initiatives and standards, may adopt rules which establish binding obligations or reflect customary law, and can establish new and subsidiary institutional arrangements.[19]

Once environmental and other standards and obligations have been established, institutions increasingly play a role in ensuring implementation of and compliance with these standards and obligations. Assisting in implementation takes a number of forms. It may be limited to receiving information from parties or other persons on an informal and *ad hoc* basis, or it may entail the regular receipt and consideration of reports or periodic communications from parties to international environmental treaties as a means of reviewing progress in implementation.[20] Assisting in implementation also takes place

---

[15] See chapter 8, pp. 357–61 below.
[16] See chapter 17, pp. 841–7 below.   [17] See chapter 5, pp. 180–2 and 203–5 below.
[18] See chapter 4, pp. 140–3 below, for a discussion of the legal effects of acts of international institutions.
[19] Such as the creation of UNEP and the Commission on Sustainable Development by the UN General Assembly, the Marine Environment Protection Committee by the IMO Assembly, and the European Environment Agency by the EC.
[20] See chapter 5, pp. 180–2 below.

through the provision of advice on technical, legal and administrative or institutional matters. Under the 1987 Montreal Protocol, the parties seek to ensure implementation through the work of a non-compliance procedure including an Implementation Committee;[21] and the 1992 Climate Change Convention provides for the establishment of a Subsidiary Body for Implementation to assist the conference of the parties in the assessment and review of the implementation of the Convention.[22] There are now a growing number of such institutional arrangements, as described in chapter 5 below.

A fifth function of international institutions is to provide an independent forum, or mechanism, for the settlement of disputes, usually disputes between states. This may occur through the work of bodies with general competence, such as a conference or meeting of the parties to an environment agreement, adopting an authoritative interpretation of a provision,[23] or by the reference of an issue to a body created specifically to assist in dispute settlement through a judicial or quasi-judicial function, such as the International Court of Justice, the International Tribunal for the Law of the Sea, the European Court of Justice, human rights courts, or WTO Dispute Settlement Panels.[24] Finally, some organisations are granted enforcement or compliance functions. To date, the only institution which has been granted extensive powers and international legal personality to engage in enforcement activities is the EC Commission, which has brought more than two hundred cases to the European Court of Justice against member states alleging non-compliance with their environmental obligations.[25]

Global organisations

United Nations (www.un.org)

The UN, its specialised agencies, and subsidiary bodies, organs and programmes are the focal point for international law and institutions in the field of the environment. The UN Charter does not expressly provide the UN with competence over environmental matters. The relevant purposes of the UN include the maintenance of international peace and security, the adoption of measures to strengthen universal peace, and the achievement of co-operation in solving international economic, social, cultural or humanitarian problems.[26] Since the

---

[21] See chapter 5, pp. 205–7 below; and chapter 8, pp. 345–7 below. The approach has been taken up by other conventions.

[22] Art. 10. The first meeting of the Subsidiary Body for Implementation was held in Geneva on 31 August 1995.

[23] See e.g. CITES conference of the parties Res. 5.11 on the meaning of the words 'pre-Convention' specimen; see chapter 10, pp. 507–15 below.

[24] See chapter 5, pp. 214–25 below; and pp. 94–101 below (WTO) (ICJ, ECJ etc.).

[25] See chapter 5, pp. 193–5 below.

[26] Charter of the United Nations, Art. 1(1), (2) and (3).

late 1960s, however, the practice of the organisation through its principal organs, in particular the General Assembly and the Economic and Social Council (ECOSOC), has been to interpret and apply these broad purposes as including the protection of the environment and the promotion of sustainable development. The UN is the principal forum for global environmental law-making and has played a central role in the development of international environmental law, its universal character making it the only 'appropriate forum for concerted political action on global environmental problems'.[27] Apart from the Secretariat, the UN has five principal organs: the General Assembly, the Security Council, ECOSOC, the Trusteeship Council and the International Court of Justice.[28] Each organ has, to differing degrees, addressed international environmental issues.

Co-ordination   From 1977 until recently, co-ordination between the various UN organs and bodies at the Secretariat level took place under the Administrative Committee on Co-ordination (ACC) (co-ordination at the political level is a responsibility of ECOSOC), which was established in 1946 to supervise the implementation of the agreements between the UN and the specialised agencies and to ensure that the activities of the various bodies are co-ordinated.[29] The ACC comprised the heads of the specialised agencies and related bodies and organs who met several times a year under the chairmanship of the Secretary General. Together with an inter-agency board of Designated Officials on Environmental Matters, the ACC deliberated and adopted recommendations on the co-ordination of all environment-related programmes which are carried on by the participating agencies and bodies, and prepared an annual report to the UNEP Governing Council.

In October 1992, an Inter-Agency Committee on Sustainable Development (IACSD) was established to make recommendations to the ACC and to improve co-operation and co-ordination between the various UN bodies and organs on issues related to sustainable development, including environmental matters. The IACSD, attended by the senior officials of UN bodies most closely involved in the issues,[30] was established to rationalise subsidiary mechanisms for co-ordination, allocate and share responsibilities for implementing Agenda 21, monitor financial matters, and assess reporting requirements. In December 1992, the UN Secretary General established a new Department for Policy Co-ordination and Sustainable Development (DPCSD) in the

[27] UNGA Res. 44/224 (1990); G. Smith, 'The United Nations and the Environment: Sometimes a Great Notion?', 19 *Texas International Law Journal* 335 (1984).

[28] The role of the ICJ is discussed in chapter 5, pp. 215–18 below.

[29] ECOSOC Res. 13 (111) (1946).

[30] Senior officials from the following bodies participated: FAO, UNESCO, WMO, WHO, ILO, World Bank, IAEA, UNEP and UNDP; any other ACC member could also take part in discussions on relevant topics.

Department of Economic and Social Development which provided support to ECOSOC and to the Commission on Sustainable Development. This was later consolidated with other departments to form the Department of Economic and Social Affairs which continues to act as the central co-ordinating mechanism for policy and programme development on sustainable development issues, including co-operative relationships with international organisations, NGOs, the academic community and the corporate sector. Agenda 21 recognised the important role of the Secretary General, and the need for the further development of the co-ordination mechanism under the ACC.[31]

The operation of the ACC has recently been reformed as part of the Secretary General's wider reform efforts. The ACC has been renamed the UN System Chief Executives Board for Co-ordination (CEB), a title which is intended to emphasise the high-level nature of the body and the shift to a more collegial body whose participants share a collective responsibility over an integrated system. The reforms have also involved a transformation of the subsidiary structures. The previous multi-layered and rigid arrangements of inter-agency committees have been transformed and streamlined into two high-level committees, the High Level Committee on Programmes and the High-Level Committee on Management, complemented by flexible 'networks' of specialists in different areas of common concern, along with time-bound task-oriented inter-agency arrangements.[32] These changes have involved the abolition of the previous subsidiary bodies, including the IACSD, and its subcommittees. The exact shape of future inter-agency co-ordination in the area of sustainable development has been caught up in the recommendations of the WSSD and their implementation by the General Assembly, but it is interesting to note that, in one area at least, the shift from standing committees has been resisted: the WSSD recommended the establishment of an effective, transparent and regular inter-agency co-ordination mechanism on ocean and coastal issues within the United Nations system,[33] presumably to replace the abolished ACC Sub-Committee on Oceans and Coastal Areas.

UN General Assembly

The UN General Assembly, which is the principal policy-making organ on UNCED follow-up, has the power to discuss any questions or matters within the scope of the UN Charter, to make recommendations to the member states or to the Security Council on any such questions or matters, and to promote international co-operation in the political, economic, social, cultural, educational

---

[31] Agenda 21, paras. 38.16 and 38.17.
[32] Annual Overview Report of the United Nations System Chief Executives Board for Co-ordination for 2001: E/200/5/55.
[33] WSSD Plan of Implementation, para. 29(c).

and health fields and the progressive development of international law and its codification.[34] Although it does not have a specific environmental mandate, its role over the past two decades has led to its being identified by Agenda 21 as 'the principal policy-making and appraisal organ' on UNCED follow-up, having a regular review function with the possibility of convening an overall review and appraisal of Agenda 21 no later than 1997.[35] This review was conducted by a Special Session of the General Assembly convened in June 1997 (UNGASS-19), which produced a Programme for the Further Implementation of Agenda 21.[36] The Programme of Implementation adopted by the WSSD affirmed the need for the General Assembly to adopt sustainable development as a key element of the overarching framework for United Nations activities and its role in giving overall political direction to the implementation of Agenda 21 and its review.[37]

Although its resolutions are not formally binding, the General Assembly has taken decisions which have created new bodies, convened conferences, endorsed principles and substantive rules, and recommended actions. Its contribution to the development of international environmental law is not to be underestimated. The General Assembly has long been involved in natural resource issues: the 1962 resolution on permanent sovereignty over natural resources was a landmark instrument in the development of international law, and has continued to influence debate and practice on the nature and extent of limitations imposed on states for environmental reasons.[38] It was only in the late 1960s, however, that the General Assembly began to address the protection of the environment and the conservation of natural resources, and since 1968 it has adopted a large number of resolutions contributing directly or indirectly to the development of substantive legal obligations and new institutional arrangements.

The General Assembly's early interest in environmental matters related to the protection of the marine environment,[39] the relationship between

---

[34] UN Charter, Arts. 10 and 13(1).   [35] Agenda 21, para. 38.9.

[36] A/RES/S-19/2. This included a five-year work plan for the Commission on Sustainable Development. The General Assembly also acknowledged the need for greater coherence and better policy co-ordination at the intergovernmental level, particularly given the increasing number of decision-making bodies and international conventions concerned. UNEP was identified as the appropriate organisation to take the lead on this. The Programme also recommended the strengthening of the Inter-Agency Committee on Sustainable Development of the Administrative Committee on Co-ordination to enhance system-wide intersectoral co-operation. These issues were further considered at the World Summit on Sustainable Development held in Johannesburg, South Africa, in August 2002.

[37] WSSD Plan of Implementation, para. 125.

[38] UNGA Res. 1803/62; see chapter 6, p. 236 below.

[39] UNGA Res. 2467B (XXIII) (1968); UNGA Res. 2566 (XXIV) (1969); and UNGA Res. 3133 (XXVIII) (1973).

environment and development,[40] and co-operation on shared natural re-
sources.[41] The General Assembly convened the 1972 UN Conference on the
Human Environment,[42] and created UNEP later that year.[43] Other bodies
created by the General Assembly include the United Nations Development
Programme (UNDP), the International Law Commission, UNCED and the
Commission on Sustainable Development. Other relevant bodies established
by the UN, which are conspicuous by their more limited actions, include the
Committee on the Development and Utilisation of New and Renewable Sources
of Energy.[44] More recently, and at a more informal level, the General Assembly
has also created the Open-Ended Informal Consultative Process on Oceans and
the Law of the Sea established on the recommendation of the Commission on
Sustainable Development to facilitate the General Assembly's annual review of
ocean affairs.[45]

Amongst the General Assembly resolutions on broad principles are those:
declaring the historical responsibility of states for the preservation of nature;[46]
noting the 1978 UNEP draft Code of Conduct;[47] adopting the 1982 World
Charter for Nature;[48] requesting the UN Secretary General to prepare and regularly update a consolidated list of products whose consumption or sale has
been banned, withdrawn, severely restricted or not approved by governments;[49]
endorsing the Brundtland Report;[50] and seeking to improve co-operation in the
monitoring and assessment of environmental threats.[51] The General Assembly
has also convened UNCED,[52] the negotiations of the framework Convention
on Climate Change,[53] the Convention on Drought and Desertification,[54] the
negotiations leading to the 1995 Straddling Stocks Agreement,[55] and, more
recently, the WSSD.[56] In 1997, it adopted the Watercourses Convention.[57] The
General Assembly has only on a few occasions adopted resolutions on substantive matters, examples being the recommendation that moratoria should be
imposed on all large-scale pelagic driftnet fishing on the high seas by the end of
1993,[58] and support for the precautionary approach to the conservation, management and exploitation of straddling fish stocks and highly migratory fish
stocks.[59] The General Assembly's 1994 request for an advisory opinion on the
legality of the use of nuclear weapons resulted in the ICJ affirming the existence

---

[40] UNGA Res. 2849 (XXVI) (1971).
[41] UNGA Res. 3129 (XXIX) (1974).   [42] UNGA Res. 2398 (XXII) (1968).
[43] UNGA Res. 2997 (XXVII) (1972).   [44] UNGA Res. 37/250 (1982).
[45] UNGA Res. 54/33 (1999) and 57/33 (2002).   [46] UNGA Res. 35/8 (1980).
[47] UNGA Res. 34/188 (1979).   [48] UNGA Res. 37/7 (1982).
[49] UNGA Res. 37/137 (1982).   [50] UNGA Res. 42/187 (1987).
[51] UNGA Res. 44/224 (1989).   [52] UNGA Res. 44/228 (1989).
[53] UNGA Res. 45/212 (1990).   [54] UNGA Res. 47/188 (1992).
[55] UNGA Res. 48/194 (1993); and UNGA Res. 50/24 (1995).
[56] UNGA Res. 55/199 (2000).   [57] UNGA Res. 52/229 (1997).
[58] UNGA Res. 44/225 (1989).   [59] UNGA Res. 56/13 (2001).

of a general obligation of states not to cause transboundary environmental harm.[60]

UN Environment Programme (www.unep.org)

UNEP was established in 1972 by General Assembly Resolution 2997 following the Stockholm Conference, and it has played a significant catalytic role in the development of treaties and soft law rules. It is based in Nairobi and comprises a Governing Council of fifty-eight members elected by the General Assembly (which meets bi-annually at the headquarters in Nairobi and reports to the General Assembly through ECOSOC) and an Environment Secretariat headed by the UNEP Executive Director. Following UNCED and WSSD, it remains the only UN body exclusively dedicated to international environmental matters. Its constituent instrument commits it to promote international environmental co-operation; to provide policy guidance for the direction and co-ordination of environmental programmes within the UN system; to receive and review reports from UNEP's Executive Director on the implementation of the UN's environment programmes; to review the world environment situation; to promote scientific knowledge and information and contribute to technical aspects of environmental programmes; and to maintain under review the impact of national and international environmental policies on developing countries.[61]

Despite its limited status as a UN programme (rather than a specialised agency or body) and its limited financial resources, few observers would dispute that UNEP has made an important contribution to the development and application of international environmental law. UNEP promoted the Regional Seas Programme, which now includes more than thirty environmental treaties and numerous regional Action Plans,[62] including the Zambezi Agreement and Action Plan, and has been responsible for the development of several global environmental treaties, including the 1985 Vienna Convention and 1987 Montreal Protocol (Ozone), the 1989 Basel Convention (Hazardous Waste), the 1992 Biodiversity Convention, the 2000 Biosafety Protocol, and the 2001 POPs Convention. UNEP provides secretariat functions to these treaties and performs a supportive role in relation to several others including the 1998 Chemicals Convention (with FAO). UNEP has also been responsible for sponsoring numerous soft law instruments, including the 1978 draft Principles on

---

[60] Chapter 6, p. 241 below.

[61] UNGA Res. 2997 (XXVII) (1972), section I, para. 2. See generally C. A. Petsonk, 'The Role of the United Nations Environment Programme in the Development of International Environmental Law', 5 *American University Journal of International Law and Policy* 351 (1990).

[62] The Programme is administered by the UNEP Ocean and Coastal Areas Programme Activity Centre (OCA/PAC); see chapter 9, p. 399 below.

shared natural resources, offshore mining and drilling;[63] and instruments on land-based marine pollution;[64] the management of hazardous wastes;[65] environmental impact assessment;[66] and the international trade in chemicals.[67] UNEP has focused attention on the inadequacy of existing international legal instruments in the field of the environment and has sought to further develop international environmental law in a variety of ways. Among its most important initiatives has been the regular convening of the experts group which led to the Programme for the Development and Periodic Review of Environmental Law (Montevideo Programme).[68] This formed the basis for many of its activities in the field of environmental law over the following decade.

Resolutions of the UNEP Governing Council guide the development of UNEP's contribution to international law. UNEP Governing Council resolutions are supplemented by the activities of the Environmental Law Branch of the Division of Policy Development, which publishes the *Register of International Treaties and Other Agreements in the Field of the Environment.*[69] The Division of Environmental Policy Implementation is responsible for issues relating to compliance and enforcement. UNEP also participates in the Global Environmental Monitoring System (GEMS) and collaborates in the operation of INFOTERRA.[70] UNEP has also established, on an experimental basis, the UN Centre for Urgent Environmental Assistance, focusing on assessment of and responses to man-made environmental emergencies.[71]

Although UNEP was not significantly strengthened by UNCED, its increasingly focused and enhanced role is reflected in the decision granting it co-management responsibilities, with UNDP and the World Bank, of the Global Environment Facility.[72] The need to enhance and strengthen the policy and co-ordination role of UNEP was recognised by UNCED in Chapter 38 of Agenda 21.

---

[63] 1982 Guidelines Concerning the Environment Related to Offshore Mining and Drilling Within the Limits of National Jurisdiction, UNEP GC Dec. 10/14/(VI) (1982).

[64] 1985 Montreal Guidelines for the Protection of the Marine Environment Against Pollution from Land-Based Sources, adopted by UNEP GC Dec. 13/18(II) (1985); see chapter 9, p. 000 below.

[65] 1987 Cairo Guidelines for the Environmentally Sound Management of Hazardous Wastes, UNEP GC Dec. 14/30 (1987); see chapter 13, p. 676 below.

[66] 1987 Goals and Principles of Environmental Impact Assessment, adopted by UNEP GC Dec. 14/25 (1987); see chapter 16, p. 802 below.

[67] 1987 London Guidelines for the Exchange of Information on Chemicals in International Trade, adopted by UNEP GC Dec. 14/27 (1987) and amended by UNEP GC Dec. 15/30 (1989); see chapter 12, p. 633 below.

[68] First adopted by UNEP GC Dec. 10/21 (1982), and most recently UNEP GC 21/23 (2001); see chapter 2, pp. 67–9 above.

[69] Initiated by UNEP GC Dec. 24/3 (1975). An updated version of this register is due to be published in 2003 and should be available on the UNEP website, www.unep.org.

[70] Chapter 17, p. 848 below.   [71] UNEP GC Dec. 16/9 (1991).

[72] Chapter 20, pp. 1032–4 below.

The priority areas for UNEP set out in Agenda 21 include: strengthening its 'catalytic role', through the development of techniques such as natural resource accounting and environmental economics; promoting environmental monitoring and assessment; co-ordinating scientific research; disseminating information and raising general awareness; further developing international environmental law, including promoting implementation and co-ordinating functions; further developing environmental impact assessment; and providing technical, legal and institutional advice.[73] UNEP's present priorities include: environmental information, assessment and research, including environmental emergency response capacity and strengthening of early warning and assessment functions; enhanced the co-ordination of environmental conventions and development of policy instruments; fresh water; technology transfer and industry; and support to African states.

UN Development Programme (www.undp.org)

The UN General Assembly established the UN Development Programme (UNDP) in 1965.[74] It is the principal channel for multilateral technical and investment assistance to developing countries. It is active in all economic and social sectors and has addressed environmental issues since the early 1970s. UNDP receives voluntary contributions from participating states, as well as donor co-financing, and additional finance from the business sector, foundations and NGOs, and in 2002 had a total budget of approximately US$2.58 billion. The role of UNDP in environmental programmes has been strengthened by its participation in the management of important programmes and institutions, such as the Tropical Forestry Action Plan and the Global Environment Facility. In 2001, UNDP adopted major reforms which realigned its global network around six thematic practice areas, including energy and environment, the focus of which is on building developing country capacity to protect natural resources wisely, acquire them affordably and use them sustainably. UNDP's role is to help developing countries strengthen their capacity to deal with these challenges at global, national and community levels, seeking out and sharing best practices, providing policy advice and linking partners through practical pilot projects on the ground. UNDP's work in this area is supported by two trust funds: the Energy for Sustainable Development Trustfund and the Environment Trustfund.[75] UNDP also administers several special-purpose funds which are relevant to environmental matters,[76] and is particularly active in translating international efforts into grass-roots programmes and activities.

[73] Agenda 21, paras. 38.21 and 38.22.
[74] UNGA Res. 2029 (XX) (1965).   [75] UNDP Annual Report 2002.
[76] Including the UN Resolving Fund for Natural Resources Exploration, the UNDP Energy Account, and the UN Trust Fund for Sudano-Sahelian Activities.

International Law Commission (www.un.org/law/ilc/)

The International Law Commission (ILC) was established by the General Assembly in 1947 to promote the 'progressive development of international law and its codification'.[77] Since 1981, it has had thirty-four members, who are persons of recognised competence in the field of international law elected by the UN General Assembly (the original membership of fifteen was raised to twenty-one in 1956 and to twenty-two in 1961). Since 1949, the ILC has worked on more than thirty topics. Apart from its important contribution to the development of general aspects of international law, including the law of treaties, state responsibility, and treaties between states and international organisations and between two or more international organisations, the ILC has also addressed environmental issues and contributed significantly to the development of international environmental law.[78] Its draft articles on the legal regime of the high seas and territorial waters led to the development of the 1958 Geneva Conventions, which include provisions which have influenced the development of environmental law. The ILC's draft articles on the Law of the Non-Navigational Uses of International Watercourses, completed in 1994, led to the adoption of the 1997 Watercourses Convention. In 2001, the ILC adopted Draft Articles on the Responsibility of States for Internationally Wrongful Acts and Draft Articles on the Prevention of Transboundary Harm from Hazardous Activities.[79] In 2002, the ILC decided to resume work on the liability aspects of the long-standing topic of International Liability for Injurious Consequences Arising out of Acts Not Prohibited by International Law, and established a new project on Shared Natural Resources.[80]

UN Commission on Sustainable Development (www.un.org/esa/sustdev/csd.htm)

In 1992, pursuant to its mandate in Agenda 21, the General Assembly and ECOSOC established the UN Commission on Sustainable Development (CSD).[81] The CSD comprises representatives of fifty-three states elected by ECOSOC with due regard to equitable geographical distribution, and on the basis of representation at a high level including ministerial participation.[82]

---

[77] UNGA Res. 174 (II) (1947), as subsequently amended, at Art. 1. In this context, the 'progressive development of international law' means the 'preparation of draft conventions on subjects which have not yet been regulated by international law or in regard to which the law has not yet been sufficiently developed in the practice of States', and 'codification' means 'the more precise formulation and systematisation of rules of international law in fields where there already has been extensive state practice, precedent and doctrine': Art. 15.

[78] See generally G. Hafner and H. Pearson, 'Environmental Issues in the Work of the ILC', 11 *Yearbook of International Environmental Law* 3 (2000).

[79] Chapter 18, pp. 873–5 below; chapter 6, p. 234 below; and chapter 17, p. 828 below.

[80] Chapter 18, p. 902 below.   [81] UNGA Res. 47/191 (1992).   [82] Para. 6.

Other member states of the UN and its specialised agencies and other observers of the UN are able to participate as observers, and international organisations (including the EC) participate to assist and advise the Commission in the performance of its functions; non-governmental organisations are also entitled to 'participate effectively' in the Commission's work and contribute to its deliberations.[83] The CSD is assisted by a secretariat based in New York and meets annually in New York.[84] The Commission makes recommendations to ECOSOC and, through it, to the General Assembly. The Commission's objectives are to

> ensure the effective follow-up of [UNCED], as well as to enhance international co-operation and rationalise the intergovernmental decision-making capacity for the integration of environment and development issues and to examine the progress of the implementation of Agenda 21 at the national, regional and international levels, fully guided by the principles of the Rio Declaration on Environment and Development and all other aspects of the Conference, in order to achieve sustainable development.[85]

The CSD is the UN body primarily responsible for sustainable development issues and has ten enumerated environmental functions. From an international legal perspective, the most significant are those requiring it to monitor progress in the implementation of Agenda 21 and the integration of environmental and developmental goals; to consider information provided by governments, including periodic communications or reports; to consider information regarding the progress made in the implementation of environmental conventions, which is provided by relevant conferences of the parties; and to make recommendations to the General Assembly on the implementation of Agenda 21.[86]

The Commission can 'receive and analyse relevant input from competent non-governmental organisations', a function representing a compromise between those states which sought to deny NGOs any role in the activities of the Commission, and those states which envisaged NGOs providing regular information, and even complaints, along the lines of the procedures established by the UN Human Rights Committee.[87] In practice, the involvement of non-state actors is organised around the categories of 'major groups' recognised in Section III of Agenda 21.[88] The Commission is recognised as being open, transparent and accessible to non-state actors. The Commission's other functions include: reviewing progress towards the UN target of 0.7 per cent

---

[83] Paras. 7 and 8.

[84] UNGA Res. 47/191 provided for the possibility of future sessions being held in Geneva, but to date all substantive sessions have been held in New York.

[85] Para. 2.   [86] Para. 3(a), (b), (h) and (i).

[87] Para. 3(f). On human rights generally, see chapter 7, pp. 291–316 below.

[88] The 'major groups' recognised in Agenda 21 are: women; children and youth; indigenous people; non-governmental organisations; local authorities; workers and trade unions; business and industry; scientific and technological communities; and farmers.

of the gross national product of developed countries for official development assistance; reviewing the adequacy of funding and mechanisms; enhancing dialogue with NGOs and other entities outside the UN system; and considering the results of reviews by the Secretary General of all the recommendations of UNCED.[89]

The CSD divided its work programme into three areas: the first addresses financial resources and mechanisms, transfer of technology and other cross-sectoral issues; the second reviews the implementation of Agenda 21, taking into account progress in the implementation of relevant environmental conventions; and the third is a high-level meeting to consider the implementation of Agenda 21 on an integrated basis, to consider emerging policy issues, and to provide the necessary political impetus to implement the decisions and commitments of UNCED.[90] Since its first session, in June 1993, the Commission has organised its work around thematic clusters of topics and a multi-year thematic programme of work.[91] The thematic clusters are based upon the various chapters of Agenda 21, and address the following themes:

- critical elements of sustainability;[92]
- financial resources and mechanisms;[93]
- education, science, transfer of environmentally sound technologies, co-operation and capacity-building;[94]
- decision-making structures;[95]
- the roles of major groups;[96]
- health, human settlement and freshwater;[97]
- land, desertification, forests and biodiversity;[98]
- atmosphere, oceans and all kinds of seas;[99] and
- toxic chemicals and hazardous wastes.[100]

Under the multi-year thematic programme of work, the CSD has annually reviewed various aspects of these clusters, on the basis of information submitted by governments in the form of periodic communications or national reports. These reports are used by the secretariat to prepare analytical reports comprising an annual overview report on the progress made in the implementation of Agenda 21, and thematic reports corresponding to the Agenda 21 sectoral

---

[89] Para. 3(c), (d), (e), (g) and (j). The resolution also recommends the Commission to promote the incorporation of the Rio Declaration and the Forest Principles, to monitor progress in technology transfer and to consider issues related to the provision of financial resources: paras. 4 and 5.

[90] Para. 14.

[91] Report of the Commission on Sustainable Development on its First Session, E/CN.17/1993/3/Add.1, 30 June 1993.

[92] Agenda 21, Chapters 2, 3, 4 and 5.   [93] Chapter 33.   [94] Chapters 16 and 34–7.

[95] Chapters 8 and 38–40.   [96] Chapters 23–32.   [97] Chapters 6, 7, 18 and 21.

[98] Chapters 10–15.   [99] Chapters 9 and 17.   [100] Chapters 19–22.

clusters in accordance with the multi-year programme of work. The information provided by governments includes the following:

- policies and measures adopted to meet the objectives of Agenda 21;
- institutional mechanisms to address sustainable development issues;
- assessments of progress to date;
- measures taken and progress achieved to reach sustainable production and consumption patterns and lifestyles, to combat poverty and to limit population growth;
- the impact of environmental measures on the national economy;
- experience gained and progress in strategies to improve social conditions and environmental sustainability;
- specific problems and constraints encountered;
- the adverse impact on sustainable development of trade-restrictive and distortive policies, and measures and progress in making trade and environment mutually supportive;
- assessments of capacity;
- assessments of needs and priorities for external assistance;
- implementation of Agenda 21 commitments related to finance;
- assessments of the effectiveness of activities and projects of international organisations; and
- other relevant environment and development activities.

WSSD reviewed the functioning of the Commission and concluded that, although its original mandate remained valid, the Commission needed to be strengthened and more emphasis needed to be placed on reviewing and monitoring the implementation of Agenda 21 and on fostering the coherence of implementation, initiatives and partnerships. To this end, WSSD recommended that the Commission should limit the number of issues addressed in each session and limit negotiations to every two years.

Other subsidiary bodies established by the General Assembly

The General Assembly has established numerous other bodies with less direct responsibility for environmental issues. The UN Conference on Trade and Development (UNCTAD) was established by the General Assembly in 1964 as one of its organs.[101] UNCTAD's functions include promoting international trade with a view to accelerating the economic growth of developing countries, and formulating and implementing principles and policies on international trade and the related problems of economic development. The eighth session of UNCTAD, held in 1992, adopted 'A New Partnership for Development: The Cartagena Commitment', which commits UNCTAD to a programme of ensuring that growth and development, poverty alleviation, rural development and

---

[101] UNGA Res. 1995 (XIX) (1964); www.unctad.org.

the protection of the environment are 'mutually reinforcing'.[102] UNCTAD has convened international commodity conferences which have led to the nego-tiation and adoption of international agreements on individual commodities, under the Integrated Programme for Commodities.[103] The Bangkok Declara-tion and Programme of Action, adopted in February 2000 at the tenth session of UNCTAD,[104] provide the main thrust for the current work of UNCTAD, as the focal point for the integrated treatment of development and the interrelated issues of trade, finance, investment, technology and sustainable development. The Bangkok Programme of Action made a number of specific recommen-dations on the focus of UNCTAD's work on trade and the environment.[105] Other bodies created by the General Assembly which play a role in interna-tional environmental issues include: the United Nations Institute on Training and Research (UNITAR), whose role is to carry out training programmes and initiate research programmes;[106] the UN Population Fund, which promotes awareness of the social, economic and environmental implications of national and international population problems;[107] the Committee on Peaceful Uses of Outer Space (COPUOS) to review international co-operation in peaceful uses of outer space and study associated legal problems;[108] the Scientific Com-mittee on Effects of Atomic Radiation (UNSCEAR) to consider the effects of radiation levels and radiation on humans and their environment;[109] and the United Nations Human Settlements Programme, known as UN-Habitat, which has a mandate to promote sustainable human settlements development in all countries with due regard for the carrying capacity of the environment in ac-cordance with the Habitat Agenda adopted at the Habitat II Conference held in Istanbul in 1996.[110] Additionally, several human rights treaties have established

---

[102] TD (VIII)/MISC.4 (1992), para. 63. See also paras. 118–23 (environment and devel-opment finance, and resource allocation and sustainable development); paras. 151–5 (environment and trade); and para. 208 (commodities and sustainable development).

[103] Commodity agreements have been established for bauxite, cocoa, coffee, cotton, jute, olive oil, rice, rubber, silk, sugar, tin and wheat.

[104] Bangkok Declaration (TD/387) and Bangkok Programme of Action (TD/386), both adopted 18 February 2000.

[105] TD/386, para 147.   [106] UNGA Res. 1934 (XVIII) (1963); www.unitar.org.

[107] UNGA Res. 2211 (XXI) (1966); ECOSOC Res. 1763 (LIV) (1966); renamed by UNGA Res. 42/430 (1987); www.unfpa.org.

[108] UNGA Res. 1472 (XIV) (1959); the Committee's work has led to the negotiation and adoption of, *inter alia*, the 1967 Outer Space Treaty, the 1972 Space Liability Convention, the 1979 Moon Treaty and the 1992 Outer Space Principles: see chapter 7, pp. 000–0 below; www.oosa.unvienna.org/COPUOS/copuos.html.

[109] UNGA Res. 913 (X) (1955); www.unscear.org.

[110] See now UNGA Res. 56/206 (2002) transforming former Commission on Human Settlements and its secretariat, the United Nations Centre for Human Settlements (Habitat), including the United Nations Habitat and Human Settlements Foundation into the United Nations Human Settlements Programme, to be known as UN-Habitat; www.unhabitat.org.

committees to monitor implementation which report on their activities to parties and to the General Assembly. Of particular relevance to environmental matters are the Human Rights Committee (established under the 1966 International Covenant on Civil and Political Rights) and the Committee on Economic, Social and Cultural Rights (established under the 1966 International Covenant on Economic, Social and Cultural Rights).[111] In November 2002, the Committee on Economic, Social and Cultural Rights issued a 'General Comment recognising access to safe drinking water and sanitation as a human right, which stresses that water is a limited natural resource and a public commodity fundamental to life and health'.[112]

Economic and Social Council (ECOSOC)

The Economic and Social Council (ECOSOC), which has fifty-four members serving three-year terms, has competence over international economic, social, cultural, educational and health issues, and related matters. Although it does not have an express mandate over environmental issues, it has addressed a broad range of topics which are directly related to the environment. ECOSOC makes recommendations with respect to the General Assembly, to the UN members and to specialised agencies, and it can also prepare draft conventions.[113] ECOSOC has responsibility for co-ordinating the activities of specialised agencies, including UNEP and the CSD, and obtaining regular reports from them.[114] This co-ordinating function was underlined by UNCED which called for ECOSOC to assist the General Assembly by 'overseeing system-wide co-ordination, overview on the implementation of Agenda 21 and making recommendations'.[115]

ECOSOC has contributed to the development of international environmental law. In 1946, it convened the 1949 UN Scientific Conference on the Conservation and Utilisation of Resources (UNCCUR), the predecessor to the Stockholm and Rio Conferences.[116] It receives the reports of the UNEP Governing Council and the CSD, which are passed on to the General Assembly. Since it does not have any committees which focus exclusively on the environment, it has not itself served as a forum for important decisions on these matters. It has, however, established subsidiary bodies relevant to the environment.

The five Regional Economic Commissions, established under Article 68 of the UN Charter, have contributed significantly to the development of international environmental law.[117] Under the auspices of the UN Economic

---

[111] Chapter 7, pp. 294–7 below.

[112] United Nations Commitee on Economic, Social and Cultural Rights, General Comment No. 15, adopted 26 November 2002.

[113] UN Charter, Art. 62(1) and (3).   [114] *Ibid.*, Arts. 63(2) and 64(1).

[115] Agenda 21, para. 38.10.

[116] *UN Yearbook 1946–47* (1947), 491; see chapter 2, pp. 31–5 above.

[117] See UNGA Res. 46/235 (1991).

Commission for Europe (UNECE),[118] regional treaties have been adopted on: transboundary air pollution;[119] environmental impact assessment;[120] industrial accidents;[121] protection of watercourses;[122] and public access and participation in environmental decision making.[123] The UNECE Group of Senior Advisers to UNECE Governments on Environmental and Water Problems has also adopted numerous recommendations on water issues and biodiversity conservation, as well as a draft UNECE Charter on Environmental Rights and Obligations.[124] In 1995, the UNECE ministers adopted the Environmental Programme for Europe, the first attempt to set long-term environmental priorities at the pan-European level and to make Agenda 21 more operational in the European context. It covers a broad range of issues and contains some 100 recommendations.[125]

The other UN Regional Economic Commissions are responsible for Asia and the Pacific (ESCAP),[126] Africa (ECA),[127] Latin America and the Caribbean (ECLAC)[128] and West Asia.[129] Although the Regional Economic Commissions have not yet promoted the negotiation of international environmental agreements, they play some role in developing 'soft' instruments and the regional preparatory arrangements for international conferences and meetings.

ECOSOC recently established the UN Forum on Forests with a mandate to promote the management, conservation and sustainable development of all types of forests and to strengthen long-term political commitment to this end.[130] Over the first five years of its operation, in addition to its more generalised activities, the Forum is to work on a mandate for developing a legal framework for all types of forests.

---

[118] ECOSOC Res. 36 (IV) (1947). Its members are the European members of the UN, the US, Canada, Switzerland and Israel; www.unece.org.

[119] 1979 LRTAP Convention and Protocols; see chapter 8, pp. 324–6 below.

[120] 1991 Espoo Convention; see chapter 16, pp. 814–17 below.

[121] See 1992 Industrial Accidents Convention; see chapter 12, pp. 623–5 below.

[122] 1992 Watercourses Convention; see chapter 10, pp. 482–5 below.

[123] 1998 Aarhus Convention; see chapter 5, p. 209 below; and chapter 17, pp. 858–9 below.

[124] Chapter 10, p. 482 below.

[125] Environmental Programme for Europe, adopted at the 1995 Sofia Ministerial Conference on Environment for Europe.

[126] ECOSOC Res. 37 (IV) (1947), as the Economic Commission for Asia and the Far East; the name was changed to ESCAP by ECOSOC Res. 1895 (LVII) (1974); www.unescap.org.

[127] ECOSOC Res. 671 (XXV) (1958) to develop 'concerted action for the economic development of Africa, including its social aspects, with a view to raising the level of economic activity and levels of living in Africa'; www.un.org/depts/eca/.

[128] ECOSOC Res. 106 (VI) (1948); www.eclac.cl.

[129] ECOSOC Res. 1818 (LV) (1973) as the Economic Commission for West Asia; ECOSOC Res. 1985/69 to ESCWA; www.escwa.org.lb.

[130] ECOSOC Res. 2000/35.

Other relevant ECOSOC subsidiary bodies include: the newly established Permanent Forum on Indigenous Issues, an expert advisory body with a mandate to consider indigenous issues relating to economic and social development, culture, the environment, education, health and human rights;[131] the Commission on Population and Development;[132] the Commission on Social Development;[133] the Commission on Human Rights;[134] the Committee on Energy and Natural Resources for Development;[135] and the Standing Committee for Development Policy.[136] The now-disbanded Commission on Transnational Corporations carried out useful work examining the relationship between transnational corporations and international environmental obligations.[137]

Security Council

The Security Council, which has primary responsibility in the UN system for the maintenance of international peace and security,[138] has only recently addressed international environmental issues. Its five permanent members and ten members elected for a period of two years can adopt legally binding resolutions which give it the potential to develop a significant role.[139]

The Security Council's first foray into environmental affairs was in 1991, when it adopted a resolution holding Iraq liable for, *inter alia*, damage to the environment resulting from the invasion of Kuwait.[140] In the following years it met for the first time at the level of heads of government or state, and adopted a declaration which affirmed that 'non-military sources of instability in the economic, social, humanitarian and ecological fields have become threats to peace and security'.[141] In recognising the link between environment and security, the Security Council has opened the door to further consideration of significant environmental matters, and over time it is increasingly likely

---

[131] ECOSOC Res. 2000/22.

[132] ECOSOC Res. 150 (VII) (1948), Res. 87 (LVII) (1975) and Res. 1995/55.

[133] ECOSOC Res. 10 (II) (1946), Res. 1139 (XLI) (1966) and Res. 1996/7.

[134] ECOSOC Res. 5 (I) (1946) (as well as the Sub-Commission on Prevention of Discrimination and Protection of Minorities and the Working Group on the Right to Development); see chapter 7, p. 298 below.

[135] ECOSOC Res. 1998/46; which merged the previous Committee on New and Renewable Sources of Energy for Development and the Committee on Natural Resources; www.un.org/esa/sustdev/enrcom.htm.

[136] ECOSOC Res. 1998/46 which renamed the former Committee on Development Planning originally established by ECOSOC Res. 1079 (XXXIX) (1965); www.un.org/esa/analysis/devplan/.

[137] ECOSOC Res. 1913 (LVII) (1974); see p. 116 below; and chapter 17, pp. 863–5 below.

[138] Charter, Art. 24(1).   [139] Art. 25.   [140] Security Council Res. 687/1991 (1991).

[141] Note by the President of the Security Council on 'The Responsibility of the Security Council in the Maintenance of International Peace and Security', UN Doc. S/23500, 31 January 1992, 2.

that the Council will address issues relating to environmental emergencies and their consequences. More recently, the Security Council has addressed the link between the illegal exploitation of natural resources and armed conflict in Africa.[142]

Trusteeship Council

The Trusteeship Council assists the Security Council and the General Assembly in performing the UN's functions under the International Trusteeship System of Chapter XII of the UN Charter. The Trusteeship Council has one administering power (US) and four non-administering powers (China, France, Russia and the United Kingdom). Its basic objectives include the promotion of political, economic, social and educational advancement of the inhabitants of trust territories, without specifying environmental objectives.[143] Although the Trusteeship Council has not played a direct role in the development of international environmental law, its obligation to respect these basic objectives provides a role in natural resource issues, including conservation. The role of the Trusteeship Council was therefore indirectly at issue in the case concerning *Certain Phosphate Lands in Nauru*, where Nauru asked the ICJ to declare Australia's responsibility for breaches of international law relating to phosphate mining activities, including, *inter alia*, breaches of Article 76 of the UN Charter and the Trusteeship Agreement between Australia, New Zealand and the United Kingdom.[144]

As the number of international trusteeships has steadily declined, alternative functions for the Trusteeship Council have been proposed. One idea, put forward by President Gorbachev of the Soviet Union in 1990, was to expand the trusteeship function to include responsibility for environmental protection in areas beyond national jurisdiction, the global commons. Although the suggestion received widespread attention, it was rejected at UNCED, and has not since been revived.

International Court of Justice (www.icj-cij.org)

The environmentally-related activities of the International Court of Justice (ICJ) are considered in more detail in chapter 5 below. Through its judgments and advisory opinions, the ICJ has contributed to the development of international environmental law through general principles and rules elaborated in non-environmental cases and in cases concerned directly with environmental issues. Recent cases raising significant environmental issues include those relating to *Certain Phosphate Lands in Nauru*, the *Gabcikovo-Nagymaros Project*

---

[142] Report of the Panel of Experts on the Illegal Exploitation of Natural Resources and Other Forms of Wealth of the Democratic Republic of the Congo: S/2001/357 and Security Council Resolutions S/RES/1355 (2001) and S/RES/1376 (2001).

[143] See UN Charter, Art. 76.   [144] Chapter 12, pp. 666–9 below.

(Hungary/Slovakia), the *Advisory Opinion on the Legality of the Use or Threat of Nuclear Weapons* and the *Request for an Examination of the Situation in Accordance with Paragraph 63 of the Court's Judgment of 20 December 1974 in the Nuclear Tests (New Zealand v. France)*. In July 1993, the ICJ established a seven-member Chamber for Environmental Matters, in view of the developments in the field of environmental law and protection which had taken place in the past few years.

United Nations specialised agencies and related organisations

The UN specialised agencies and related international organisations were established before environmental matters became an issue for the international community. It is therefore not surprising that none was designed to deal with, or given express competence over, environmental matters, and that consequently the environment has tended to play a somewhat peripheral role in their affairs. Since the specialised agencies were designed to deal with issues of concern to the international community in the post-war period, there are numerous significant gaps in their competence, including in particular energy, mining and transport matters.

Food and Agriculture Organization (www.fao.org)

The Food and Agriculture Organization (FAO), which is based in Rome, was established in 1945 to collect, analyse, interpret and disseminate information on nutrition, food and agriculture (including fisheries, marine products, forestry and primary forest products), to promote national and international action, and to provide technical and other assistance.[145] The FAO is the only specialised agency with an environmental mandate in its constitution, namely, to promote the 'conservation of natural resources and the adoption of improved methods of agricultural production'.[146] The FAO Conference and Council may initiate and approve conventions and agreements on food and agriculture,[147] and the FAO has developed soft law, including the operation with WHO of the World Food Programme,[148] the operation of a Global System on Plant Genetic Resources,[149] and the adoption and operation of the 1985 International Code of Conduct on the Distribution and Use of Pesticides.[150] The FAO also established (with WHO) the *Codex Alimentarius* Commission (discussed below). Additionally, the FAO has sponsored numerous international treaties[151] and created a number of international organisations in, for example, the fields of

---

[145] Constitution, Art. I.   [146] Art. I(2)(c).   [147] Art. XIV.

[148] FAO Conference Resolution 1/16 of 24 November 1961; and UNGA Res. 1714 (XVI) (1961).

[149] Chapter 11, pp. 551–4 below.   [150] Chapter 12 below.

[151] Most recently, the 1998 Chemicals Convention (see chapter 12, p. 631 below), and the 2001 Plant Genetic Resources Treaty (see chapter 11, p. 553 below).

fisheries,[152] plant protection,[153] forest research[154] and locust control.[155] It has addressed forest issues, and in 1985 established the Tropical Forestry Action Plan.[156] The FAO convenes international conferences which have led to the adoption and development of international action plans and strategies, some of which have subsequently led to binding international obligations. Examples include the 1981 World Soil Charter,[157] the 1984 World Soil Policy and Plan of Action,[158] the 1991 Strategy and Agenda for Action for Sustainable Agriculture and Rural Development,[159] and the 1995 World Food Summit. Recent international plans of action of importance to the environment are the 1999 Plans of Action on seabirds, sharks and fishing capacity and the 2001 Plan of Action on illegal unreported and unregulated fishing.[160]

United Nations Education and Scientific Organization
(www.unesco.org)

The United Nations Education and Scientific Organization (UNESCO), which is based in Paris, was established in 1945 to contribute to peace and security by promoting international collaboration through education, science and culture, including the conservation and protection of historic and scientific monuments and recommending necessary international conventions.[161] UNESCO played a role in convening and hosting the 1948 UNCCUR and has established institutions and programmes such as the Intergovernmental Oceanographic Commission in 1960, and the Man and the Biosphere Programme (under which the 1985 Action Plan for Biosphere Reserves was adopted).[162]

---

[152] 1949 Agreement for the Establishment of a General Fisheries Council for the Mediterranean; 1969 Convention on the Conservation of the Living Resources of the Southeast Atlantic.

[153] 1951 Convention for the Establishment of the European and Mediterranean Plant Protection Organization; 1951 International Plant Protection Convention; 1956 Plant Protection Agreement for the South East Asia and Pacific Region.

[154] 1959 Agreement for the Establishment on a Permanent Basis of a Latin American Forest Research and Training Institute.

[155] 1963 Agreement for the Establishment of a Commission for Controlling the Desert Locust in the Eastern Region of its Distribution Area in South-West Asia; 1965 Agreement for the Establishment of a Commission for Controlling the Desert Locust in the Near East; and 1970 Agreement for the Establishment of a Commission for Controlling the Desert Locust in Northwest Africa.

[156] Chapter 11, p. 548 below.   [157] Chapter 11, p. 555 below.

[158] *Ibid.*, and chapter 12, p. 669 below.   [159] Chapter 12, p. 669 below.

[160] The International Plan of Action for Reducing Incidental Catch of Seabirds in Longline Fisheries International Plan of Action for the Conservation and Management of Sharks; the International Plan of Action for the Management of Fishing Capacity; and the International Plan of Action to Prevent, Deter and Eliminate Illegal, Unreported and Unregulated Fishing.

[161] Constitution, Art. I(2)(c).

[162] See generally B. Von Droste, 'UNESCO's Man and the Biosphere Programme: Two Decades of Sustainable Development', 2 *Colorado Journal of International Environmental Law*

UNESCO was responsible for the adoption of, and performs secretariat functions for, the 1971 Ramsar Convention, the 1972 World Heritage Convention[163] and the 2001 Convention on the Protection of Underwater Cultural Heritage.[164]

International Maritime Organization (www.imo.org)

The International Maritime Organization (IMO, formerly known as the Intergovernmental Maritime Consultative Organisation) is based in London and was established in 1948. Its objectives, which originally did not refer to marine pollution, include: the provision of machinery for co-operation among governments on regulation and practice relating to technical matters of all kinds affecting shipping engaged in international trade; encouraging the general adoption of the highest practical standards in matters concerning maritime safety; and ensuring the efficiency of navigation and the prevention and control of marine pollution from ships.[165] IMO activities relating to marine pollution are mainly carried out through the Legal Committee and the Marine Environment Protection Committee (MEPC), established by the IMO Assembly in 1975.[166] The MEPC has broad powers to consider any matter to do with the prevention and control of marine pollution from ships, including the power to propose regulations and develop recommendations and guidelines.[167] The IMO has supported the negotiation and conclusion of a number of important environmental treaties, for which it provides secretariat functions. These relate to oil pollution,[168] pollution from ships,[169] civil liability and compensation for oil pollution damage,[170] and emergency preparedness.[171] The IMO also acts as Secretariat to the 1972 London Convention and has contributed to soft law

---

and Policy 295 (1991); see also chapter 11, p. 505, n. 23 below; and chapter 2, p. 35 above.

[163] Chapter 11, pp. 543–5 and 611–15 below.

[164] Chapter 11, p. 678 below.   [165] Constitution, Art. 1(a), as amended.

[166] Assembly Resolution A.358 (1975); L. de la Fayette, 'The Marine Environment Protection Committee: Conjunction of the Law of the Sea and International Environmental Law', 16 IJMCL 163 (2001).

[167] Constitution, Part IX, Arts. 38–42.

[168] 1954 International Convention for the Prevention of Pollution of the Sea by Oil; 1969 High Seas Intervention Convention (and a 1973 Protocol); see chapter 9, pp. 440 and 449 below.

[169] MARPOL 73/78; see chapter 9, pp. 440–5 below; 2001 International Convention on the Control of Harmful Anti-Fouling Systems on Ships.

[170] 1992 CLC (chapter 18, pp. 913–15 below); 1992 Fund Convention (chapter 18, pp. 915–18 below); 1996 HNS Convention (chapter 18 below); and the 2001 Bunker Liability Convention (chapter 18, p. 922 below).

[171] 1990 Oil Pollution Preparedness Convention; see chapter 9, pp. 451–2 below; 2000 Protocol on Preparedness, Response and Co-operation to Pollution Incidents by Hazardous and Noxious Substances.

by adopting non-binding guidelines, standards and codes relating to maritime safety and the protection of the marine environment.[172]

International Labor Organization (www.ilo.org)

The purposes of the International Labor Organization (ILO), which is based in Geneva and was originally established in 1919, include the protection of workers against sickness, disease and injury arising out of employment, and the adoption of humane conditions of labour.[173] To this end, the ILO has adopted a number of conventions which set international standards for environmental conditions in the workplace, including occupational safety and health[174] as well as numerous non-binding recommendations and guidelines.[175]

World Meteorological Organization (www.wmo.ch)

The World Meteorological Organization (WMO) was established in 1947 and is based in Geneva. Its purposes are: to facilitate worldwide co-operation in meteorological observation and hydrological and other geophysical observations related to meteorology; to promote the establishment and maintenance of meteorological centres and the rapid exchange of meteorological information; to promote the standardisation and uniform publication of observations and statistics; and to encourage research and training.[176] The WMO operates the World Weather Watch,[177] the World Climate Programme[178] and the Atmospheric Research and Environment Programme. The World Climate Programme supports the Global Climate Observing System (GCOS) which is sponsored jointly by the WMO, UNESCO's International Oceanographic

---

[172] See e.g. the 1997 Guidelines to Assist Flag States in the Implementation of IMO Instruments, Assembly Res. A.847(20); and the 2002 Revised GESAMP Hazard Evaluation Procedure for Chemical Substances Carried by Ships (adopted by IMO/FAO/UNESCO-IOC/WMO/WHO/IAEA/UN/UNEP Joint Group of Experts on the Scientific Aspects of Marine Environmental Protection, GESAMP Reports and Studies No. 64).

[173] Constitution, Preamble.

[174] 1960 Ionising Radiations Convention; 1971 Benzene Convention; 1977 Occupational Hazards Convention; 1981 Occupational Safety Convention; 1985 Occupational Health Services Convention; 1986 Asbestos Convention; 1990 Chemicals Convention (see chapter 12, p. 626 below); 1993 Prevention of Major Industrial Accidents Convention; and 2001 Safety and Health in Agriculture Convention.

[175] 1991 Code of Practice on the Prevention of Major Industrial Accidents; *International Encyclopedia of Occupational Health and Safety* (2000, 4th edn); and 1995 Safety and Health in Mines Recommendation.

[176] Constitution, Art. 2.

[177] The World Weather Watch provides up-to-the-minute worldwide weather information through member-operated observation systems and telecommunications links.

[178] The objectives of the World Climate Programme are: to use existing climate information to improve economic and social planning; to improve the understanding of climate processes through research; and to detect and warn governments of impending climate variations or changes which may significantly affect human activities.

Commission, UNEP and the ICSU. In 1988, the WMO, with UNEP, established the Intergovernmental Panel on Climate Change (IPCC), an intergovernmental body providing scientific, technical and socio-economic advice on climate change issues, and has contributed to the establishment of the legal regimes for ozone depletion, climate change and transboundary atmospheric pollution. The Atmospheric Research and Environment Programme incorporates the Global Atmosphere Watch (GAW) and is the vehicle for the WMO's involvement in the GCOS.

International Civil Aviation Organization (www.icao.int)

The International Civil Aviation Organization (ICAO), based in Montreal, was established in 1947. Its objectives include the promotion of safe, efficient and economical air transport and generally the development of all aspects of international civil aeronautics.[179] To that end, it has adopted several relevant instruments, including international standards and recommended practices on aircraft engine emissions and on noise pollution.[180]

World Health Organization (www.who.int)

The World Health Organization (WHO) was established in 1946 to ensure 'the attainment by all peoples of the highest possible level of health'.[181] It is based in Geneva. The WHO Assembly can adopt conventions or agreements for any matters within the competence of the organisation,[182] as well as regulations on sanitary and quarantine requirements, and on the standards, advertising and labelling of biological, pharmaceutical and similar products placed on international markets.[183] It may also make recommendations,[184] and non-binding standards have been adopted for drinking water and air quality.[185] In 1990, the WHO established the WHO Commission on Health and Environment which played a key role in ensuring that environmental health considerations were incorporated in Agenda 21. In 1993, the WHO Assembly requested an Advisory Opinion from the International Court of Justice on the legality of nuclear weapons use, in the context of its work on the effects of nuclear weapons on health and the environment.[186]

The WHO administers the Food Standard Programme with the FAO, which is administered by the *Codex Alimentarius* Commission.[187] The *Codex Alimentarius* Commission was established in 1963 with the purposes of making proposals to the FAO and the WHO on all matters relating to the

---

[179] Constitution, Art. 44(d) and (i).   [180] Arts. 37 and 38; see chapter 8, p. 341 below.

[181] Constitution, Art. 1.   [182] Art. 19.

[183] Art. 21; 1969 International Health Regulations.   [184] Art. 23.

[185] 1993 Guidelines for Drinking Water Quality and 1999 Air Quality Guidelines.

[186] Chapter 5, p. 218 below (the Court's opinion was that the request fell outside the competence of the organisation).

[187] www.codexalimentarius.net; chapter 12, p. 627 below.

implementation of the Joint FAO/WHO Food Standards Programme, the purpose of which are: to protect the health of consumers and to ensure fair practices in the food trade; to promote the co-ordination of all food standards work undertaken by international governmental and non-governmental organisations; to guide the preparation of and finalise standards and, after acceptance by governments, to publish them in a *Codex Alimentarius* either as regional or worldwide standards; and to amend published standards in the light of developments.[188] Over 160 states are members of the Commission, which has adopted commodity standards and general standards for a very large number of foodstuffs, including in relation to additives, pesticide residues and labelling. In varying degrees, the *Codex* standards are recognised and applied in international trade regimes, including by the WTO, NAFTA, the EC, APEC and MERCOSUR.

International Atomic Energy Agency (www.iaea.org)

The International Atomic Energy Agency (IAEA), which is based in Vienna, was established in 1956 to develop the peaceful uses of atomic energy.[189] The IAEA is autonomous and not formally a specialised agency of the United Nations, but sends reports to the General Assembly and other UN organs. It is the only member of the UN 'family' dedicated to the energy sector, although its dual promotional and regulatory function appears anomalous. Under the 1963 Treaty on the Non-Proliferation of Nuclear Weapons, the IAEA has responsibilities for safeguarding nuclear materials in non-nuclear weapon states parties to it. The IAEA has also sponsored, and provides secretariat functions for, international conventions relating to liability,[190] the protection of nuclear material,[191] nuclear accidents,[192] and the safety of nuclear installations.[193] The IAEA has also adopted numerous non-binding standards and recommendations on basic safety standards relating to, *inter alia*, radioactive discharges into the environment[194] and the disposal and transboundary movement of radioactive wastes.[195]

---

[188] Statute, Art. 1.   [189] Constitution, Art. II.
[190] 1963 IAEA Civil Liability Convention, Protocol and Supplementary Convention; chapter 18, pp. 909–10 below.
[191] 1980 Convention on the Physical Protection of Nuclear Material; chapter 12, p. 645 below.
[192] 1986 Convention on Early Notification of a Nuclear Accident, and the 1986 Convention on Assistance in the Event of Nuclear Accident or Radiological Emergency; chapter 12, p. 647 below.
[193] 1994 Convention on Nuclear Safety; chapter 12, pp. 643–4 below.
[194] Regulatory Control of Radioactive Discharges to the Environment (2000), Safety Guide No. WS-2-G.3.
[195] Near Surface Disposal of Radioactive Waste (1999), Requirements, WS-R-1; 1990 Code of Practice on International Transboundary Movement of Radioactive Wastes and Regulations for the Safe Transport of Radioactive Material (1996 revised edition), Requirements, TS-R-1, chapter 13, pp. 697–9 below.

World Bank, International Monetary Fund, and World Trade Organization

The World Bank (comprising the International Bank for Reconstruction and Development (IBRD), the International Development Association (IDA) and the International Finance Corporation (IFC)), the IMF and the WTO are central players in international environmental law. They and their activities are considered in chapters 19 and 20 below.

Co-operative arrangements

Apart from the subsidiary bodies of the specialised agencies which are referred to above, two others bodies merit special mention on account of their contribution to the negotiation and adoption of international legal instruments: the Joint Group of Experts on Scientific Aspects of Marine Pollution (GESAMP)[196] and the Intergovernmental Panel on Climate Change (IPCC).[197] GESAMP (which is jointly run by the UN, UNEP, FAO, UNESCO, WHO, WMO, IMO and IAEA) has a mandate to conduct research and carry out assessments on the state of the marine environment, and to make appropriate recommendations, and has produced numerous reports since 1982.[198] The IPCC was established to assess the available scientific information on climate change, to assess the environmental and socio-economic impacts of climate change, and to formulate response strategies. Its efforts are organised under three working groups (Science, Impact and Adaptation, and Mitigation) and a task force (on National Greenhouse Gas Inventories). It has produced three Assessment Reports on Climate Change (1990, 1995 and 2001), contributing to the ongoing intergovernmental negotiations around the 1992 Climate Change Convention and its 1997 Kyoto Protocol, and a number of special reports on particular aspects, such as aviation and land-use.

Other global institutions

Beyond the activities of the UN and specialised agencies, in law of the sea matters, the 1982 UN Convention on the Law of the Sea (UNCLOS) established two new international institutions which address environmental aspects of the law of the sea. These are the International Tribunal for the Law of the Sea (ITLOS), which has already made a significant contribution to maritime environmental law,[199] and the International Seabed Authority, which has recently promulgated regulations which establish environmental conditions for deep sea-bed prospecting.[200]

---

[196] www.gesamp.imo.org.   [197] www.ipcc.ch.
[198] Most recently, 'Protecting the Oceans from Land-Based Activities', GESAMP Reports and Studies No. 71 (2001); and 'A Sea of Troubles', GESAMP Reports and Studies No. 70 (2001). See chapter 9, pp. 392–3 below.
[199] Chapter 5, pp. 218–20 below.   [200] Chapter 9, pp. 445–7 below.

Regional and sub-regional organisations

Regional organisations outside the UN system also play a growing role in the development of international environmental law. In application of the principle that different environmental standards could be applied to different geopolitical regions, the role of regional organisations is likely to increase significantly. They are frequently able to provide the flexibility needed to accommodate special regional concerns, as was recognised by the Brundtland Report's call for regional organisations to do more to integrate environmental concerns into their activities.[201] As the regional rules of international environmental law and institutional arrangements are particularly well developed in the Antarctic and in the European Communities, organisations related to those developments are considered in more detail in chapters 14 and 15 below.

Some international organisations are not regional, in a strict geographic sense, and are not UN agencies, bodies or programmes. These include the Commonwealth Secretariat, the Organization of the Islamic Conference, the League of Arab States whose members are in Africa and Asia, and the Organization of Petroleum Exporting Countries. Although each maintains an interest in environmental matters, none has adopted rules of international environmental law or ensured their enforcement, although they provide assistance to states on environmental matters.

Europe and the OECD

In the European context, apart from the EU, three organisations play an important role in the development of regional rules: the Council of Europe, the Organization for Economic Co-operation and Development (OECD) and the Conference on Security and Co-operation in Europe (CSCE). More recently, the European Bank for Reconstruction and Development (EBRD) has emerged as an innovative contributor to European environmental law and policy; it is noteworthy, in a broader global context, as the first multilateral development bank to have a constituent instrument which expressly requires it to fulfil environmental protection and sustainable development objectives.[202]

OECD (www.oecd.org)

The OECD (formerly the Organization for European Economic Co-operation, OEEC) was established in 1960 to promote policies designed to achieve in its member countries the highest sustainable economic growth, sound economic expansion in the process of economic development, and the expansion of world trade.[203] Seven of its thirty members are not European states. In 1974, the members of the OECD established an International Energy Agency,[204] the Nuclear

---

[201] Chapter 15, pp. 732–54 below.
[202] Chapter 20, pp. 1028–9 below.   [203] Convention on the OECD, Art. 1.
[204] 1974 Agreement on an International Energy Programme Including Establishment of the International Energy Agency, Paris, 18 November 1974, 27 UST 1685 at Chapter IX.

Energy Agency having been established in 1957.[205] The OECD Convention does not specify environmental protection among its functions, but the organisation began to address environmental issues in 1970 following the decision to create an Environment Committee as a subsidiary body to the Executive Committee, which is itself subordinate to the OECD Council. The OECD became involved in environmental issues for three reasons. First, certain environmental issues were recognised to be intrinsically international; secondly, differences among member countries' environmental standards were considered to have implications for trade and economic and political relations; and, thirdly, it was felt that some member countries might be insufficiently prepared to address certain environmental problems.

The OECD Council may adopt two types of act: decisions, which are binding on its members; and recommendations, which are non-binding. Both acts are usually adopted with the support of all members.[206] Since 1972, the OECD Council has adopted a large number of environmental measures, and has promulgated a treaty on liability for nuclear damage.[207] These environmental acts have influenced the development of national environmental legislation in the member countries, and have often provided a basis for international environmental standards and regulatory techniques in other regions and at the global level. The OECD Council has frequently been at the forefront of developments in international environmental policy, focusing on the relationship between economic and environmental policies;[208] defining and endorsing the 'polluter-pays' principle;[209] providing early support for the development and use of environmental assessment techniques;[210] promoting economic instruments;[211] endorsing the use of integrated pollution prevention and control;[212]

---

[205] EEC Decision of 20 December 1957, subsequently approved by OECD Decision of 30 September 1961.

[206] Arts. 5(a) and (b) and 6(1).

[207] 1960 Convention on Third Party Liability in the Field of Nuclear Energy; see chapter 18, pp. 906–8 below.

[208] 1972 Guiding Principles Concerning International Economic Aspects of Environmental Policies, Recommendation, C(72)128; see chapter 6, p. 281 below.

[209] 1974 Recommendation on the Implementation of the Polluter-Pays Principle, C(74)223; 1989 Recommendation on the Application of the Polluter-Pays Principle to Accidental Pollutions, C(89)88(Final), 28 ILM 1320 (1989); see chapter 6, pp. 279–85 below.

[210] 1974 Recommendation on the Analysis of the Environmental Consequences of Significant Public and Private Projects, C(74)216; 1979 Recommendation on the Assessment of Projects with Significant Impacts on the Environment, C(79)116; 1985 Recommendation on Environmental Assessment of Development Assistance Projects and Programmes, C(85)104; 1985 and 1986 Joint Recommendations on the Environmental Assessment of Development Assistance Projects and Programmes, see chapter 16, pp. 801–2 below.

[211] 1991 Recommendation on Use of Economic Instruments in Environmental Policy, C(90)177; see chapter 4, p. 160 below.

[212] 1990 Recommendation on Integrated Pollution Prevention and Control, C(90)164; see chapter 4, pp. 167–9 below.

using pollutant release and transfer registers;[213] and 'greening' public procurement.[214] The OECD Council has also supported the broad use of techniques for ensuring the availability of environmental information,[215] and for developing co-operation on transfrontier pollution.[216] Substantive issues have also been addressed, and the OECD Council has developed a broad range of decisions or recommendations on many sectors of environmental protection, including air quality,[217] water quality,[218] energy,[219] waste,[220] chemicals,[221] noise,[222] tourism[223] and multinational enterprises.[224]

---

[213] 1996 Recommendation, C(96)41.   [214] 2002 Recommendation, C(2002)3.

[215] 1979 Recommendation on Reporting on the State of the Environment, C(79)114; 1991 Recommendation on Environmental Indicators and Information, C(90)165; 1998 Recommendation on Environmental Information, C(98)67.

[216] 1974 Recommendation on Principles Concerning Transfrontier Pollution, C(74)224; 1976 Recommendation on Equal Right of Access in Relation to Transfrontier Pollution, C(76)55 (Final); 1977 Recommendation on Implementation of a Regime of Equal Right of Access and Non-Discrimination in Relation to Transfrontier Pollution, C(77)28 (Final); 1978 Recommendation on Strengthening International Co-operation on Environmental Protection in Transfrontier Regions, C(78)77 (Final).

[217] 1974 Recommendation on Guidelines for Action to Reduce Emissions of Sulphur Oxides and Particulate Matter from Fuel Combustion in Stationary Sources, C(74)16 (Final); 1974 Recommendation on Measures Required for Further Air Pollution Control, C(74)219; 1985 Recommendation on Control of Air Pollution from Fossil Fuel Combustion, C(85)101.

[218] 1971 Recommendation on the Determination of the Biodegradability of Anionic Synthetic Surface Active Agents, C(71)83 (Final); 1974 Recommendation on the Control of Eutrophication of Waters, C(74)220; 1974 Recommendation on Strategies for Specific Water Pollutants Control, C(74)221; 1978 Recommendation on Water Management Policies and Instruments, C(78)4 (Final).

[219] 1974 Recommendation on Energy and the Environment, C(74)222; 1976 Recommendation on Reduction of Environmental Impacts from Energy Production and Use, C(76)162 (Final); 1977 Recommendation on the Reduction of Environmental Impacts from Energy Use in the Household and Commercial Sectors, C(77)109 (Final); 1979 Recommendation on Coal and the Environment, C(79)117; 1985 Recommendation on Environmentally Favourable Energy Options and their Implementation, C(85)102.

[220] 1976 Recommendation on a Comprehensive Waste Management Policy, C(76)155 (Final); 1977 Recommendation on Multilateral Consultation and Surveillance Mechanisms for Sea Dumping of Radioactive Waste, C(77)115 (Final); 1978 Recommendation on the Re-Use and Recycling of Beverage Containers, C(78)8 (Final); 1980 Recommendation on Waste Paper Recovery, C(79)218 (Final); 1984 Decision and Recommendation on Transfrontier Movements of Hazardous Waste, C(83)180 (Final); 1985 Resolution on International Co-operation Concerning Transfrontier Movements of Hazardous Waste, C(85)100; 1986 Decision/Recommendation on Exports of Hazardous Wastes from the OECD Area, C(86)64 (Final); 1991 Decision/Recommendation on Reduction of Transfrontier Movements of Waste, C(90)178; 1992 Decision on the Control of Transfrontier Movements of Wastes Destined for Recovery Operations, C(92)39 (Final) (amended by C(2001)107).

[221] 1971 Resolution on Procedures for Notification and Consultation on Measures for Control of Substances Affecting Man and His Environment, C(71)73 (Final); 1973 and 1987 Decisions on Protection of the Environment by Control of Polychlorinated Biphenyls,

Council of Europe (www.coe.int)

The Council of Europe was established in 1949 to achieve greater unity between members 'for safeguarding and realising their ideals and principles which are their common heritage and facilitating their economic and social progress'.[225] The Council of Europe now has forty-one members across the whole of Europe. Without an explicit environmental mandate, the Council of Europe has adopted a number of acts and policies relating to environmental protection through its organs, the Committee of Ministers and the Consultative Assembly. The Parliamentary Assembly has adopted many non-binding recommendations on environmental issues.[226] The Council of Europe's contributions include several treaties: apart from an early environmental treaty restricting the use of detergents,[227] the Council of Europe has adopted treaties on: the protection of animals;[228] the protection of archaeological heritage;[229] the conservation

---

C(73)1 (Final); 1973 Recommendation on Measures to Reduce All Man-Made Emissions of Mercury to the Environment, C(73)172 (Final); 1974 Recommendation on the Assessment of the Potential Environmental Effects of Chemicals, C(74)215; 1979 Recommendation on Guidelines in Respect of Procedures and Requirements for Anticipating the Effects of Chemicals on Man and in the Environment, C(77)97 (Final); 1981 Decision on the Mutual Acceptance of Data in the Assessment of Chemicals, C(81)30 (Final); 1982 Decision on the Minimum Pre-Marketing Set of Data in the Assessment of Chemicals, C(82)196 (Final); 1983 Recommendation on the Mutual Recognition of Compliance with Good Laboratory Practice, C(83)95 (Final); 1983 Recommendation on the Protection of Proprietary Rights to Data Submitted in Notifications of New Chemicals, C(83)96 (Final); 1983 Recommendation on the Exchange of Confidential Data on Chemicals, C(83)97 (Final); 1983 Recommendation on the OECD List of Non-Confidential Data on Chemicals, C(83)98 (Final); 1984 Recommendation on Information Exchange Related to Export of Banned or Severely Restricted Chemicals, C(84)37 (Final); 1988 Decisions on the Exchange of Information Concerning Accidents Capable of Causing Transfrontier Damage, C(88)84 (Final); 1991 Decision on the Co-operative Investigation and Risk Reduction of Existing Chemicals, C(90)163.

[222] 1974 Recommendation on Noise Prevention and Abatement, C(74)217; 1978 Recommendation on Noise Abatement Policies, C(78)73 (Final); 1985 Recommendation on Strengthening Noise Abatement Policies, C(85)103.

[223] 1979 Recommendation on Environment and Tourism, C(79)115.

[224] Updated most recently in 2000; see p. 116 below.

[225] Statute of the Council of Europe, as amended, Art. 1(a).

[226] These relate to general environmental policy (see Recommendations 888 (1980), 910 (1981), 937 (1982), 958 (1983), 998 (1984), 1078 (1988), 1130 (1990), 1131 (1991)); marine pollution (Recommendations 585 (1970), 946 (1982), 997 (1984), 1003 (1985), 1015 (1985), 1079 (1988)); fisheries (Recommendations 913 (1981), 825 (1984), 842 (1985)); biodiversity (Recommendations 966 (1983), 978 (1984), 1033 (1986), 1048 (1987)); freshwater resources (Recommendations 1052 (1987), 1128 (1990)); and air pollution (Recommendations 977 (1984), 1006 (1985), 926 (1989)).

[227] 1968 European Agreement on the Restriction of the Use of Certain Detergents in Washing and Cleaning Products, Strasbourg, 16 September 1968.

[228] 1968 European Convention for the Protection of Animals During International Transport; 1976 European Convention for the Protection of Animals Kept for Farming Purposes.

[229] 1969 European Convention on the Protection of the Archaeological Heritage.

of wildlife;[230] transfrontier co-operation;[231] civil liability for environmental damage;[232] the protection of the environment through criminal law;[233] and landscape.[234] The European Convention on Human Rights and the European Social Charter, both of which have contributed to environmental jurisprudence and policy, were also adopted under the auspices of the Council of Europe.[235]

Organization for Security and Co-operation in Europe (www.osce.org)

The Final Act of the 1975 Conference on Security and Co-operation in Europe (CSCE) encompassed co-operation on the protection and improvement of the environment, and the institutions established thereunder may accordingly address matters relating to the environment.[236] The 1990 Charter of Paris for a New Europe affirmed the close relationship between economic liberty, social justice and environmental responsibility.[237] In 1994, the CSCE was renamed the OSCE, and its institutions now comprise a Ministerial Council, a Senior Council, a Permanent Council, and a Conflict Prevention Centre.[238] So far, these institutions do not appear to have been apprised of a security issue arising out of an environmental conflict, although there was some suggestion that the dispute between Hungary and Slovakia over the Gabcikovo-Nagymaros Project might be referred to CSCE procedures.

Africa

The principal African organisation which addresses environmental matters is the African Union (formerly the Organization of African Unity (OAU)), which was established in 1963 to promote the unity and solidarity of African states and to co-ordinate co-operation to achieve a better life for the peoples of Africa.[239] To that end, the OAU has supported the adoption of a treaty on the conservation of nature and natural resources,[240] and a treaty on the trade in and management of hazardous waste.[241] The OAU also sponsored the 1981 African

---

[230] 1979 Berne Convention; see chapter 11, p. 532 below.

[231] 1980 European Outline Convention on Transfrontier Co-operation Between Territorial Communities or Authorities; and Protocols (1995 and 1998).

[232] 1993 Convention on Civil Liability for Damage Resulting from Activities Dangerous to the Environment; see chapter 18, pp. 933–7 below.

[233] 1998 Convention on the Protection of the Environment Through Criminal Law; see chapter 18, p. 896 below.

[234] 2000 European Landscape Convention; see chapter 9 below.

[235] Chapter 7, p. 294 below.

[236] 14 ILM 1292 (1975). The ICJ has held that support for the Helsinki Final Act constitutes an expression of *opinio juris*: see *Military and Paramilitary Activities Case In and Against Nicaragua* (1986) ICJ Reports 3 at 100 and 107.

[237] 30 ILM 190 (1991).   [238] Chapter 5, p. 174, n. 15 below.

[239] Charter of the OAU, Art. II(1); www.africa-union.org.

[240] 1968 African Nature Convention; see chapter 11, pp. 524–6 below.

[241] 1991 Bamako Convention; see chapter 13, p. 680 below.

Charter on Human Right and Peoples' Rights[242] and the 1991 African Economic Community,[243] both of which have environmental provisions. Apart from the UN Economic Commission for Africa, other organisations having environmental responsibilities and activities include the African Development Bank, the Arab Bank for Economic Development in Africa,[244] the Economic Community of Central African States,[245] the Economic Community of West African States,[246] and the Intergovernmental Authority on Drought and Development. The Southern African Development Community was established in 1992 and has adopted protocols on shared watercourses, wildlife conservation and law enforcement.[247] Regional bodies have also been established to manage shared natural resources.

Americas and the Caribbean

The Organization of American States (OAS), whose purposes include promoting the economic, social and cultural development of its members,[248] has played a limited role in international environmental law. As the successor organisation to the Pan American Union, the OAS has responsibility for the dormant 1940 Western Hemisphere Convention,[249] and has been responsible for the adoption of just one convention, with passing relevance for environmental protection.[250] Other organisations with a higher environmental profile include the Inter-American Development Bank, the Caribbean Development Bank,[251] the Central American Commission on Environment and Development,[252] and the American Convention on Human Rights, which is the only such instrument to state expressly that people have a right to a clean and healthy environment.[253] Neither the Caribbean Community nor the Organization of Eastern Caribbean States has played a particularly active role, save in the field of fisheries. Regional free trade agreements have played a catalytic role in developing regional rules of environmental protection, particularly the Canada–United States Free Trade Agreement and the North American Free Trade Agreement.[254] At the bilateral level, the Canada–United States International Joint Commission, established in 1909, is significant,[255] and important bilateral arrangements also exist between Mexico and the United States.[256]

---

[242] Chapter 7, p. 294 below.

[243] Chapter 19, pp. 1007–8 below.   [244] Chapter 20 below.

[245] Chapter 19 below.   [246] Chapter 19 below.

[247] 32 ILM 116 (1993); chapter 10, pp. 490–1 below; chapter 11, p. 527 below.

[248] Charter of the OAS, Art. 2(e); www.oas.org.   [249] Chapter 11, pp. 527–9 below.

[250] 1976 Convention on the Protection of the Archaeological, Historical and Artistic Heritage of the American Nations; see chapter 11 below.

[251] Chapter 20, p. 1028 below.

[252] 1 *Yearbook of International Environmental Law* 229 (1990).

[253] Chapter 7, p. 294 below.   [254] Chapter 19, pp. 999–1007 below.

[255] Chapter 10 below.   [256] See e.g. chapter 10 below.

Asia

Asia has taken only limited measures towards establishing regional environmental organisations.[257] Given the rapid industrialisation which is occurring in many countries in the region, the important role of Japan, and the size and significance of China and India, shared environmental problems and the need to conserve natural resources will inevitably lead to the creation of such organisations. In the short term, developments are likely to focus on giving existing organisations greater environmental competence, and on the relationship between economic commitments (free trade and investment) and environmental standards.

One of the few regional organisations to have already made a significant contribution is the Association of South East Asian Nations (ASEAN), under whose auspices the 1985 ASEAN Convention was adopted.[258] The Asian Development Bank integrates environmental considerations into its decision-making process,[259] and the South Asian Association for Regional Co-operation (SAARC)[260] may ultimately be granted a role in the development of regional rules.

Regional organisations in Oceania are more active, including in the negotiation of multilateral environmental agreements.[261] The South Pacific Commission has promulgated at least two treaties for the protection of natural resources.[262] At the annual meetings of the South Pacific Forum, regional and global environmental issues are high on the agenda, and the Forum has taken decisions which led to the negotiation and adoption of a nuclear free zone treaty[263] and the prohibition of driftnet fishing.[264] The South Pacific Regional Environment Programme (SPREP) became an independent and autonomous regional organisation in 1991, and has recently adopted an Action Strategy for Nature Conservation in the Pacific Islands Region.[265]

Organisations established by environmental treaties

The third type of organisation is that established by environmental treaty, most of which establish institutional arrangements for their implementation, development and review. The institutional arrangements have a variety of names and forms, and have not attracted a great deal of scholarly or practical

---

[257] See generally B. Boer, R. Ramsay and D. Rothwell, *International Environmental Law in the Asia Pacific* (1998).

[258] Chapter 11, pp. 540–2 below.   [259] Chapter 20, p. 1028 below.

[260] Charter of SAARC, Dhaka, 8 December 1985.

[261] Pacific island states, together with Caribbean states, are active in the the Alliance of Small Island States, in the climate change negotiations.

[262] 1976 Apia Convention, see chapter 11, p. 685 below; and 1986 Noumea Convention, see chapter 11, p. 531 below; www.forumsec.org.fj.

[263] 1985 Rarotonga Treaty; see chapter 12, p. 650 below.

[264] 1989 Driftnet Convention; see chapter 11, pp. 588–9 below.   [265] www.sprep.org.ws.

attention.[266] They range from the standing Commission established by the 1992 OSPAR Convention (replacing the Commissions established by the 1972 Oslo Convention and the 1974 Paris Convention), to the *ad hoc* conferences or meetings of the parties to a wide range of agreements. Each treaty organisation will also have a secretariat. These institutional arrangements are, in effect, international organisations. They have international legal status, rules of procedure and membership, and have enumerated powers relating to decision-making and dispute settlement and, occasionally, enforcement powers. A large number of treaty organisations are highly active and have made significant contributions to the development of international environmental law, much of which is not collectively well documented and assessed. The reporting arrangements established under the Commission on Sustainable Development should have provided an opportunity for improved co-ordination of the activities of these organisations and the consequential rationalisation.

A detailed list of these organisations is beyond the scope of this section: where appropriate, they are identified in relevant sections of the book. As will be seen, they may, through their acts, impose obligations on states which range from the legally binding to recommendations with no legal consequences. Certain treaty organisations at the regional and global level are, or are likely to become, noteworthy in respect of particular environmental issues, and these are listed below.

Atmosphere

Transboundary air pollution

- 1979 LRTAP Convention (and Protocols), Executive Body (meets annually)

Ozone

- 1985 Vienna Convention, conference of the parties (as necessary)
- 1987 Montreal Protocol, meetings of the parties (at regular intervals)

Climate change

- 1992 Climate Change Convention and 1997 Kyoto Protocol, Conference of the Parties (every year unless decided otherwise)

Oceans and seas

General

- UNEP Regional Seas Conventions, various
- 1974 Baltic Convention, Helsinki Commission (at least annually)

---

[266] See now R. Churchill and G. Ulfstein, 'Autonomous Institutional Arrangements in Multilateral Environmental Agreements: A Little Noticed Phenomenon in International Law', 94 AJIL 623 (2000).

- 1982 UNCLOS, Assembly of the International Sea-Bed Authority (annually)
- 1992 OSPAR Convention, OSPAR Commission (at regular intervals)

Dumping

- 1972 London Convention, consultative meetings (annually)

Pollution from ships

- MARPOL 1973/78, IMO Assembly (annually)

Compensation and liability

- 1992 Oil Pollution Fund Convention, Assembly and Executive Committee (annually/at least every two years)

Freshwaters

- 1963 Rhine Convention, International Commission
- 1992 Watercourses Convention, meeting of the parties (at least every three years)

Biological diversity

General

- 1979 Berne Convention, Standing Committee
- 1992 Biodiversity Convention and 2000 Biosafety Protocol, conference of the parties (at regular intervals)

Trade in endangered species

- 1973 CITES, conference of the parties (at least once every three years, in practice every two years)

Wetlands

- 1971 Ramsar Convention, conferences (as necessary)

Whales

- 1946 International Whaling Convention, Commission (meets annually)

Migratory species

- 1979 Bonn Convention, conference of the parties (at least every three years)

Fisheries

- 1949 Tropical Tuna Convention, Commission
- 1952 North Pacific Fisheries Convention, Commission (annually)
- 1966 Atlantic Tuna Convention, Commission (every two years)
- 1969 South East Atlantic Convention, Commission (at least every two years)
- 1973 Baltic Fishing Convention, Commission (every two years unless decided otherwise)
- 1978 Northwest Atlantic Fisheries Convention, General Council of the Northwest Atlantic Fisheries Organisation (annually)
- 1979 South Pacific Forum Fisheries Agency, Committee (annually)
- 1980 North-East Atlantic Fisheries Convention, Commission (annually unless decided otherwise)
- 1980 Convention for the Conservation of Antarctic Marine Living Resources, Commission (annually)
- 1982 North Atlantic Salmon Conservation Organization, Council (annually)

World heritage

- 1972 World Heritage Convention, World Heritage Committee

Waste

- 1989 Basel Convention, conference of the parties (at regular intervals)
- 1991 Bamako Convention, conference of the parties (at regular intervals)

Chemicals

- 1998 Chemicals Convention, conference of the parties (at regular intervals)
- 2001 POPs Convention, conference of the parties (at regular intervals)

Environmental impact assessment, accidents

- 1991 Espoo Convention, meeting of the parties (as necessary)
- 1992 Industrial Accidents Convention, conference of the parties (annually)

Public participation

- 1998 Aarhus Convention, meeting of the parties (at least once every two years)

War and environment

- 1977 ENMOD Convention, conference of the parties (usually every five years)

Non-state actors

P. Lowe and J. Goyder, *Environmental Groups in Politics* (1983); M. Bettati and P. Dupuy (eds.), *Les ONG et le droit international* (1986); R. Branes Ballesteros, *Aspectos institucionales y juridicos del medio ambiente, includia la participacion de las organizaciones no gubernamentales en la gestion ambiental* (Inter-American Development Bank, 1991); M. Garner, 'Transnational Alignment of Non-Governmental Organisations for Global Environmental Action', 24 *Vanderbilt Journal of Transnational Law* 653 (1991); S. Charnovitz, 'Two Centuries of Participation: NGOs and International Governance', 18 *Michigan Journal of International Law* 183 (1997); P. Sands, 'International Law, the Practitioner and Non-State Actors', in C. Wickremasinghe (ed.), *The International Lawyer as Practitioner* (2000).

Non-state actors have played a central role in developing international environmental law. They remain highly influential. Since the latter half of the nineteenth century, the scientific community and environmental groups have mobilised the forces of public opinion, and have sought to contribute to the progressive development of international law. The corporate sector has also fought to ensure that its voice is heard, especially as international rules expand and touch directly upon industrial and other economic activities. At the international level, non-state actors play a formal role in several ways. They identify issues requiring international legal action; they participate as observers in international organisations, and in treaty negotiations; and they participate, formally and informally, in the national and international implementation of principles and rules adopted at the regional and global levels.

Over the past two decades, six categories of non-state actors have emerged as important actors: the scientific community; non-profit-making environmental groups and associations (NGOs); private companies and business concerns; legal organisations; the academic community; and individuals.[267] The Rio Declaration and Agenda 21 affirm the important partnership role of non-governmental organisations and call for their 'expanded role'.[268] Agenda 21 declared that:

> [t]he organisations of the United Nations system and other intergovernmental organisations and forums, bilateral programmes and the private sector as appropriate, will need to provide increased financial and administrative support for non-governmental organisations and their self-organised networks, in particular those based in developing countries, contributing to the monitoring and evaluation of Agenda 21 programmes, and provide training for non-governmental organisations . . . to enhance their partnership role in programme design and implementation.[269]

[267] Agenda 21, Section III, entitled 'Strengthening the Role of Major Groups', identifies the following 'major groups': women, children and youth, indigenous people, non-governmental organisations, local authorities, workers and trade unions, business and industry, the scientific and technological community, and farmers.

[268] Agenda 21, paras. 38.42–38.44.   [269] *Ibid.*, para. 27.12.

Agenda 21 also calls on the UN system, including international finance and development agencies and all intergovernmental organisations, to take measures to enhance the contribution of non-governmental organisations to 'policy design, decision-making, implementation and evaluation at the individual agency level, in inter-agency discussions and in United Nations conferences'.[270] This objective is to be achieved by, *inter alia*: augmenting their role as partners in project and programme implementation; ensuring their participation in the processes to review and evaluate the implementation of Agenda 21; providing them with access to accurate and timely data and information; and providing them with increased administrative and financial support.[271] Agenda 21 urges governments to take similar measures at the national level and to take:

> any legislative measures necessary to enable the establishment by non-governmental organisations of consultative groups, and to ensure the right of non-governmental organisations to protect the public interest through legal action.[272]

Non-state actors have for many years been able to participate as observers in the activities of international organisations, such rights being granted expressly in the treaty establishing the organisation, or by its rules of procedures, or by practice. The 1992 OSPAR Convention included, for the first time, a treaty provision for observers which does not distinguish between states, international governmental organisations and non-governmental organisations with respect to the conditions of the granting of observer status, save that the non-governmental organisations must carry out activities which are related to the Convention.[273] Moreover, once observer status has been granted, each observer appears to have identical rights, namely, to present to the Commission any information or reports relevant to the objectives of the Convention but not the right to vote.[274] Even more far-reaching is the 1998 Aarhus Convention which, no doubt because of its subject matter, entitles non-governmental organisations to participate in the meeting of the parties and – uniquely – to nominate candidates for election to the Convention's implementation committee.[275]

Scientific community[276]

Often, the driving force behind international environmental law is science, a feature which distinguishes this from other areas of public international law where developments are frequently initiated by political, economic or commercial imperatives. The important place for science introduces an objective

---

[270] *Ibid.*, para. 27.9(a).   [271] *Ibid.*, paras. 27.9(b) to (g) and 27.12.

[272] *Ibid.*, paras. 27.10 and 27.13.   [273] Art. 11(1).

[274] Art. 11(2). Under Art. 11(3), conditions for admission and participation are to be set in the Rules of Procedure.

[275] 1998 Convention, Art. 10(5); Meeting of the Parties, Decision I/7, Annex, para. 4 (2002).

[276] Agenda 21, Chapter 31; see chapter 1, p. 6 above.

element over which governments have less control. As one commentator has noted, this has two effects: the 'environmental movement has been powerfully affected by the consequences of science misused to the detriment of the living world, but even more importantly by what advancing science has revealed about the structure and process of nature'.[277] Non-state actors rely upon scientific evidence generated from different sources, including that which emerges from international processes such as the IPCC and GESAMP, from government departments, and from non-state sources. The last-mentioned have long played a role in the development of international environmental law. Early efforts leading to international legal developments include the work of individual members of the scientific community in the eighteenth century and the scientific congresses of the late nineteenth century.[278] Today the principal co-ordinating force for the non-governmental activities of individual researchers and academics, and university and commercial research centres and institutes is the International Council of Scientific Unions (ICSU), a co-ordinating federation of twenty or so constituent unions. ICSU committees address particular issues, of which the following are among the more influential: the Scientific Committees on Oceanic Resources (SCOR, 1957), on Space Research (COSPAR, 1958) on Antarctic Research (SCAR, 1958) and on Problems of the Environment (SCOPE, 1969).[279] SCOPE serves as a non-governmental, interdisciplinary and international council of scientists, and provides advice for governments and non-governmental bodies on environmental problems. It is often through the activities of environmental organisations that this scientific work is brought to the attention of governments and international organisations, supporting calls for further international action and providing the basis for political lobbying in intergovernmental negotiating fora.

Environmental and developmental organisations[280]

Internationally, a number of environmental and developmental organisations have played a particularly important role in developing international environmental law. The International Union for the Conservation of Nature (IUCN), established in 1948, has developed policy initiatives and has prepared texts of draft instruments which have served as the basis for the negotiation of the 1971 Ramsar Convention, the 1973 CITES and the 1992 Biodiversity Convention. Together with UNEP and WWF, IUCN was also instrumental in drawing up the 1980 World Conservation Strategy and the 1990 World Conservation Strategy II. WWF, Greenpeace and Friends of the Earth are other international non-governmental organisations which have played an active role in developing treaty language and other international standards, and in acting as watchdogs in the implementation of treaty commitments, together with groups such as

---

[277] L. K. Caldwell, *International Environmental Policy* (1990, 2nd edn), 9.
[278] *Ibid.*, 32.   [279] *Ibid.*, 114.   [280] See Agenda 21, Chapter 27.

Oxfam and Action Aid.[281] This extends to the filing of international cases, where rules permit,[282] or intervening as *amicus curiae*.[283] Grassroots environmental and consumer organisations have also influenced the development of international environmental law, including through domestic litigation. Often, they participate in global networks which focus on specific issues, such as the Climate Action Network and the Pesticides Action Network; similar global networks have been established to address environmental issues relating to matters such as the GATT Uruguay Round and NAFTA, as well as policies and projects funded by the multilateral development banks. At UNCED, a large group of non-governmental organisations prepared their own draft treaties on a range of international legal issues relating to sustainable development.

Legal groups

Private groups and associations of lawyers have long played a role in the progressive development of international environmental law. Since the Institut de Droit International adopted its 1911 Resolution on International Regulations Regarding the Role of International Watercourses for Purposes Other Than Navigation,[284] it and the International Law Association have developed model international rules on a range of environmental issues, including transboundary water resources and atmospheric pollution. The IUCN Environmental Law Centre and the IUCN Commission on Environmental Law have prepared important draft treaties which have formed the basis of formal negotiations. Other private organisations contributing significantly to the field include environmental law groups based in the United States, such as the Natural Resources Defense Council (NRDC), Earthjustice and the Environmental Defense Fund (EDF), which play an advocacy role in the development of international environmental law. The International Council on Environmental Law and university-based organisations, such as the Foundation for International Environmental Law and Development (FIELD) at University College London, and the Center for International Environmental Law (CIEL) in Washington DC, have provided international legal assistance to developing countries and non-governmental organisations. Many national academic institutions have also contributed to the domestic implementation of international environmental obligations.

Corporate sector[285]

In the private sector, associations such as the International Chamber of Commerce and the Business Council for Sustainable Development have sought to

---

[281] Chapter 5, p. 199 below.   [282] Chapter 5, p. 199 below.
[283] Chapter 5, p. 199 below.   [284] See chapter 2, p. 29 above.
[285] See Agenda 21, Chapter 30.

ensure that the interests of the business community are taken into account. To that end, they, and others, have developed proposals for the development of international environmental law, such as the Business Charter on Sustainable Development, the Declaration of the World Industry Conference on Environmental Management (WICEM II) and the Valdez Principles (in the United States).[286] In 2000, the UN established a Global Compact as a 'voluntary corporate citizenship initiative' intended to provide 'a contextual framework to encourage innovation, creative solutions, and good practices among participants'.[287] The Global Compact commits its corporate participants to adhere to nine principles, of which three relate to the environment and commit businesses to:

- support a precautionary approach to environmental challenges;
- undertake initiatives to promote greater environmental responsibility; and
- encourage the development and diffusion of environmentally friendly technologies.

The WSSD Plan of Implementation commits states to 'enhance corporate environmental and social responsibility and accountability' including actions at all levels to encourage industry:

> [t]o improve social and environmental performance through voluntary initiatives, including environmental management systems, codes of conduct, certification and public reporting on environmental and social issues, taking into account such initiatives as the International Organization for Standardization (ISO) standards and Global Reporting Initiative guidelines on sustainability reporting, bearing in mind Principle 11 of the Rio Declaration.[288]

The corporate sector also participates as observers in international legal negotiations where it is perceived that issues affecting their interests are likely to be legislated on. At negotiations relating to the 1987 Montreal Protocol, the 1992 Climate Change Convention and the 2000 Biosafety Protocol, among others, individual companies, trade associations and other industry groups have been particularly active. Their participation reflects the growing relevance of public international law to the business community. Transnational corporations have also been the subject of international regulatory efforts in relation to activities which may entail harmful consequences. The OECD Guidelines for multinational enterprises were introduced in 1976 as the first internationally agreed

---

[286] Business Charter on Sustainable Development, adopted by the 64th session of the board of the International Chamber of Commerce; Official Report of the Second World Industry Conference on Environmental Management, Rotterdam, 10–12 April 1991; L. M. Thomas, 'The Business Charter for Sustainable Development: Action Beyond UNCED', 1 RECIEL 325 (1992).

[287] www.unglobalcompact.org/Portal/.

[288] Para. 17(a). On the Global Reporting Initiative see www.globalreporting.org.

framework for co-operation in the field of international direct investment and multinational enterprises,[289] and updated most recently in 2000.[290] Part V of the 2000 Guidelines (on the environment) provides that:

> Enterprises should, within the framework of laws, regulations and adminis-
> trative practices in the countries in which they operate, and in consideration
> of relevant international agreements, principles, objectives, and standards,
> take due account of the need to protect the environment, public health and
> safety, and generally to conduct their activities in a manner contributing
> to the wider goal of sustainable development.[291]

Individuals and indigenous communities

Individual citizens have traditionally expressed their involvement in the de-velopment and application of international environmental law through the activities of environmental organisations. However, the growing relationship between human rights and environmental discourse at the international level has led to individuals having recourse to international human rights norms and procedures including, where available, the right to complain to international bodies.[292] International law also increasingly recognises the special interests and rights of indigenous communities, for example in relation to land rights and traditional knowledge associated with the conservation of biodiversity.[293] As citizens of nation-states, individuals are responsible for the implementation

---

[289] Annexed to the Declaration of 21 June 1976 by governments of OECD member countries in international investment and multinational enterprises, as amended in 1979, 1982 and 1984: 15 ILM 969 (1976), 31 ILM 494 (1992).

[290] DAFFE/IME(2000)20, Annex. The Guidelines propose that enterprises should, in the countries in which they operate, contribute to 'economic, social and environmental progress with a view to achieving sustainable development' ('General', para. 1).

[291] The Guidelines indicate, *inter alia*, the following minimum requirements for enterprises: to establish and maintain a system of environmental management appropriate to the enterprise; to provide adequate and timely information on the potential environment, health and safety impacts of the activities of the enterprise; to assess and address the fore-seeable environmental, health and safety-related impacts associated with the processes, goods and services of the enterprise over their full lifecycle (preparing appropriate envi-ronmental impact assessment); not to use the lack of full scientific certainty as a reason for postponing cost-effective measures to prevent or minimise such damage; to main-tain contingency plans for preventing, mitigating and controlling serious environmental and health damage from their operations; and to seek continually to improve corporate environmental performance.

[292] Chapter 7, pp. 300–5 below.

[293] D. Shelton, 'Fair Play, Fair Pay: Preserving Traditional Knowledge and Biological Re-sources', 5 *Yearbook of International Environmental Law* 77 (1994); R. Gupta, 'Indige-nous Peoples and the International Environmental Community: Accommodating Claims Through a Co-operative Legal Process', 74 *New York University Law Review* 1741 (1999); chapter 11, p. 557 below; chapter 20, p. 1052 below.

of international obligations; their role will be enhanced if they are able to report violations by governments of international legal obligations to environmental organisations, to national public authorities and, in the case of the EC and international human rights organisations, to international organisations. It is in regard to the latter that individuals have acquired rights under international law: the increased availability of complaint procedures – such as the Inspection Panel of the World Bank and the non-compliance mechanism established under the 1998 Aarhus Convention[294] – provides formal mechanisms.

Potentially important developments took place at UNCED, as reflected in the Rio Declaration, which recognises the rights of individual citizens to participate in decision-making processes, to have access to information, and to have access to judicial and administrative remedies. Principle 10 of the Rio Declaration provides that:

> [e]nvironmental issues are best handled with the participation of all concerned citizens, at the relevant level. At the national level, each individual shall have appropriate access to information concerning the environment that is held by public authorities, including information on hazardous materials and activities in their communities, and the opportunity to participate in decision-making processes. States shall facilitate and encourage public awareness and participation by making information widely available. Effective access to judicial and administrative proceedings, including redress and remedy, shall be provided.

Although Principle 10 is not binding *per se*, it has provided an international benchmark against which the compatibility of national standards can be compared. Building on the human rights model, these developments foresee the creation of a new range of procedural rights which may be granted to individuals by international law, and which would be exercisable at the national and, possibly, international levels.[295] Principle 10 has inspired the adoption of the first international convention – the 1998 Aarhus Convention – to require parties to guarantee the rights of access to information, public participation in decision-making and access to justice in environmental matters, and to promote the Convention's principles in international environmental decision-making and within international organisations.[296] Article 6 of the Convention requires parties to inform the public concerned – early

---

[294] Chapter 5, p. 177 below.

[295] On access to information, see chapter 17, pp. 852–9 below; on participation in environmental impact assessments, see chapter 16, pp. 810 and 815 below; on access to national remedies, see chapter 5, pp. 195–8 below.

[296] Aarhus, 25 June 1998, in force 30 October 2001, Arts. 1 and 3(7). The rights established by the Convention are to be applied without discrimination as to citizenship, nationality or domicile or place of registration/effective centre of activities: Art. 3(9). On access to and dissemination of information under Arts. 4 and 5, see chapter 17, pp. 858–9 below.

in the decision-making process – of proposed activities listed in Annex I to the Convention and other activities which may have a significant effect on the environment, and to ensure early public participation in decision-making.[297] The right to participate includes access to information relevant to decision-making (subject to certain exceptions), the right to submit comments, information, analyses or opinions considered relevant, the requirement that account is taken of the outcome of the public participation, and the requirement to inform the public of the decision.[298] These rights are to apply equally in respect of the reconsideration or updating of operating conditions.[299] Article 7 obliges parties to enable the public to participate in the preparation of plans and programmes relating to the environment within a 'transparent and fair framework'. Article 8 requires parties to 'strive to promote' public participation during the preparation of executive regulations and other generally applicable, legally binding rules that may have a significant effect on the environment.

Article 9 governs access to justice. In respect of the right to environmental information, parties must provide access to remedies before a court or other independent and impartial body established by law.[300] In respect of decisions, acts or omissions subject to Article 6, parties must ensure that a member of the public having a sufficient interest or maintaining impairment of a right has access to a review procedure or a court of law or other independent and impartial body established by law to challenge its substantive and procedural legality.[301] The Convention provides that 'sufficient interest' and 'impairment of a right' are to be determined in accordance with national law and are to be consistent with the objective of giving the public concerned wide access to justice, and that non-governmental organisations meeting certain requirements will be deemed to have a sufficient interest.[302] In respect of decisions, acts or omissions subject to other relevant provisions of the Convention (i.e. Articles 7 and 8) the matter is governed by national law.[303] Further, in accordance with criteria (if any) laid down in national law, members of the public are to have access to administrative or judicial procedures to challenge acts or omissions by private persons and public authorities which contravene national law relating to the environment.[304] All of the procedures are to provide adequate and

---

[297] Art. 6(1)–(4).   [298] Art. 6(5)–(9).   [299] Art. 6(10).

[300] Art. 9(1). Where a party provides for review by a court, it must also ensure that a person has access to 'an expeditious procedure established by law that is free of charge or inexpensive for reconsideration by a public authority or an independent and impartial body other than a court': *ibid.*

[301] Art. 9(2).

[302] *Ibid.* (the rule is without prejudice to any 'preliminary review procedure' which may exist under national law). Art. 2(5) defines the requirements to be met by NGOs: to promote environmental protection and meet any requirements under national law.

[303] *Ibid.*   [304] Art. 9(3).

effective remedies, including injunctive relief (as appropriate), and must be fair, equitable, timely and not prohibitively expensive.[305]

The media

Whilst the contribution of the media to international environmental law should not be overstated, there is little doubt that it plays an important informal role in various aspects of international environmental law. The media is able to place a spotlight on particular international legal issues which excite public interest and which can serve to change the public (or private) position of states. The media also provides an opportunity for governments to make statements which may have legal consequences. In the *Nuclear Tests* cases, the International Court of Justice held that it did not have to decide on the Australian and New Zealand claims, after the French Prime Minister made a statement at a press conference that France no longer intended to conduct atmospheric nuclear tests after 1974.[306]

Conclusions

The discussion in this chapter confirms that 'relationships among global, regional, national and local organisations – governmental and non-governmental – are an expanding web of international governance that will grow increasingly interconnected in the future'.[307] The discussion indicates that the range of actors involved in the development and application of international environmental law is broad and that the involvement of non-state actors is recognised as legitimate, and is increasingly being encouraged, at both national and international levels. International law has three interrelated challenges: first, to ensure that all states are able to participate in the response of the international community to the growing range of environmental challenges which require an international legal response; Secondly, to strengthen the role of international organisations, and their effectiveness, by rationalising their activities and endowing them with increased functions; and, thirdly, to ensure that the role of non-state actors is properly harnessed, by providing them with sufficient international status to participate effectively in the international legal process and to make the link that governments and international organisations seem to find so difficult: translating global obligations into domestic action and implementation.

---

[305] Art. 9(4). Parties must also consider the establishment of appropriate assistance mechanisms to remove or reduce financial and other barriers to access to justice: Art. 9(5).

[306] (1974) ICJ Reports 253, para. 37. Other statements were made by the Minister of Defence on French television and at press conferences, and by the Minister of Foreign Affairs at the UN; on the legal effect of unilateral acts of this type, see chapter 4, pp. 144–5 below.

[307] L. Kimball, *Forging International Agreement: Strengthening Intergovernmental Institutions for Environment and Development* (WRI, 1992), 2.

These three challenges are closely interconnected, and each will require the further elaboration of rules of participation and procedure; the amendment of the constitutions of most international organisations; and a rethink about the limits of sovereignty. Beginning with the participation of states, it has become ever clearer that most developing states are not able to participate as fully and effectively in the law-making process as they should, because they frequently have insufficient financial and human resources. This is not a comment on their lack of insight, ability, inspiration or commitment; it simply reflects the explosion in the number of centres of international environmental legislation which has occurred in the past twenty years. Without effective participation in the law-making process, there can be little expectation that countries, particularly developing countries, will be able to translate their international commitments into domestic action. International law is increasingly complex and technical, both to negotiate and to apply, and significant effort needs to be made to develop the human capacities, including developing international legal knowledge. The UNCED process made an important start by ensuring that the funds were available to allow most developing countries at least to attend the negotiations, and it is a testament to their skills that they achieved as much as they did without the resources available to other, more affluent countries.

The process of rationalisation of the activities of international organisations is closely linked to the effective participation of states. The proliferation of organisations, including treaty-based environmental organisations, has brought with it a proliferation of secretariats, most of which would be able to function far more efficiently if they could share experiences and expertise. Rationalisation would allow the functions of the organisations and the secretariats to be more efficiently undertaken, and might then provide them with a stronger basis to engage in the sorts of activities which are clearly needed, for which they are well equipped, and which they should be undertaking: preparing documentation, synthesising national implementation reports, encouraging compliance, conducting verification and sponsoring new agreements.[308]

Many international organisations already rely heavily on the efforts and activities of non-state actors, either informally or formally. These actors need to be given a strengthened role, and as implementation and enforcement becomes increasingly important their participation in the process as observers could be supplemented by allowing them to provide information of a general nature or, more specifically, on non-compliance by states with their international obligations. This has now happened under the non-compliance procedure of the 1998 Aarhus Convention. The model provided by the human rights field is a useful one which could be further extended into the environmental field;

---

[308] See House of Commons (UK), Select Committee on Environment, Transport and Regional Affairs, Sixteenth Report, 'Multilateral Environmental Agreements' (1999), paras. 67–8.

this is perhaps the direction which UNEP or the Commission on Sustainable Development should be encouraged to take, if they are provided with sufficient authority and resources. UNEP, in particular, has been given a broad mandate to ensure the progressive development of international environmental law, and it should be encouraged to develop that mandate in an expansive manner.

4

International law-making and regulation

Introduction

R. Hahn and K. Richards, 'The Internationalisation of Environmental Regulation',
30 *Harvard International Law Journal* 421 (1989); O. Schachter, 'The Emergence
of International Environmental Law', 44 *Journal of International Affairs* 457 (1991);
W. Lang, 'Diplomacy and International Environmental Law-Making: Some Observations', 3 *Yearbook of International Environmental Law* 108 (1992); U. Beyerlin
and T. Marauhn, 'Law Making and Law-Enforcement in International Environmental Law after the 1992 Rio Conference' (Berichte 4/1997); P. Sands, 'The New
Architecture of International Environmental Law', 30 RBDI 512 (1997); A. Ahmad,
*Cosmopolitan Orientation of the Process of International Environmental Lawmaking:
An Islamic Law Genre* (2001).

This chapter identifies the sources of international legal obligation in the field
of the environment, and the regulatory techniques used to give effect to these
obligations. International law is traditionally stated to comprise 'the body of
rules which are legally binding on states in their intercourse with each other'.[1]
These rules derive their authority, in accordance with Article 38(1) of the Statute
of the International Court of Justice (ICJ), from four sources: treaties, international custom, general principles of law, and subsidiary sources (decisions
of courts and tribunals and the writings of jurists and groups of jurists). It is
to these sources that the ICJ would look in determining whether a particular
legally binding principle or rule of international environmental law existed.
The list of sources identified in Article 38(1) does not wholly reflect the sources
of obligation, broadly understood, which have arisen in international environmental law. A list of sources of international environmental law is more
properly reflected in the list proposed by the International Law Commission
(ILC) in 1989, which included those identified in Article 38(1) as well as binding decisions of international organisations, and judgments of international
courts or tribunals.[2]

---

[1] Oppenheim, vol. 1, 4.
[2] International Law Commission, Draft Articles on State Responsibility, Part 2, Art. 5(1),
'Report of the ILC to the United Nations General Assembly', UN Doc. A/44/10, 218 (1989).

Beyond these sources of 'hard law', which establish legally binding obligations, there are also so-called rules of 'soft law', which are not binding *per se* but which in the field of international environmental law have played an important role; they point to the likely future direction of formally binding obligations, by informally establishing acceptable norms of behaviour, and by 'codifying' or possibly reflecting rules of customary law.[3] It is also worth recalling that, although the rules of public international law primarily govern relations between states, it is now widely accepted that states are no longer the only subjects of international law, and that the rules of international law can, and do, impose obligations upon other members of the international community, in particular international organisations and, to a more limited extent, non-state actors, including individuals and corporations.

The traditional sources of international law, together with acts of international organisations and taking account of hard and soft law, have given rise to a large body of international legal obligations which relate, directly or indirectly, to the protection of the environment. These have arisen without a central legislative authority: the international law-making function is decentralised and fragmented. Accordingly, the rules and principles of international environmental law which have developed at the global, regional and bilateral levels comprise a complex network of bilateral and multilateral legal relations. With the exception of some of the general rules and principles identified in chapter 6 below, and the particular rules established by each individual treaty, there exists no 'level playing field' which subjects all states and other members of the international community to identical standards. As treaties increasingly apply differentiated standards, the precise rules applicable to any state will depend on the treaties to which it is a party, and the acts of international organisations and the customary and other rules which are binding upon it. Disparities exist between countries and groups of countries, regions and sub-regions, and within regions and sub-regions.

UNCED attempted to propose a rationalisation of the law-making process by allocating particular functions to the regional and global levels, and by seeking to specify the roles of regional and global international organisations. The effort was not successful, having failed to address the root causes of legal and institutional fragmentation,[4] although it did focus attention on the limitations

---

[3] See C. M. Chinkin, 'The Challenge of Soft Law: Development and Change in International Law', 38 *International and Comparative Law Quarterly* 850 (1989); A. Nollkaemper, 'The Distinction Between Non-Legal Norms and Legal Norms in International Affairs: An Analysis with Reference to the North Sea', 13 IJMCL 355 (1998); A. Boyle, 'Some Reflections on the Relationship of Soft Law and Treaties', 48 *International and Comparative Law Quarterly* 901 (1999).

[4] The causes are complex, but include a lack of political will on the part of states to establish more effective and efficient arrangements, as well as a degree of bureaucratic resistance within some treaty secretariats.

of the existing international law-making process in the field of environment and development.

Three limitations of an institutional or procedural nature dominate:

- the need to improve the mechanisms for identifying critical issues and legislative priorities;
- the need to ensure that all relevant actors participate in the law-making process (in particular, developing countries), including the negotiation, implementation, review and governance of international environmental. agreements; and
- rationalising the law-making process by improving co-ordination between international organisations, including those established by environmental agreements.[5]

These limitations are reflected in most activities relating to treaty-making and acts of international organisations, although they may also be relevant to developing rules of customary law which can be subjected to 'consciously directed adjustment' even if they are not as 'easily and unambiguously manufactured'.[6]

Treaties

The main collections of treaties are the *Consolidated Treaty Series* (C. Parry (ed.), 1648–1918); the *League of Nations Treaty Series* (205 volumes, 1920–46); and the *United Nations Treaty Series* (since 1946). Relevant national collections include the *United Kingdom Treaty Series* (since 1892), the *European Communities Treaty Series* (since 1974) and the United States' *Treaties and Other International Agreements Series* (13 volumes, 1776–1949 and annually thereafter). Apart from the collections of international environmental treaties cited in the 'Further reading' section in chapter 1 (especially those edited by Burhenne and by Rüster and Simma), important environmental treaties are regularly reproduced in *International Legal Materials*.

A. D. McNair, *The Law of Treaties* (1961, revised edn); S. Rosenne, *The Law of Treaties* (1970); E. D. Brown, 'The Conventional Law of the Environment', 13 *Natural Resources Journal* 203 (1973); T. O. Elias, *The Modern Law of Treaties* (1974);

---

[5] See House of Commons Select Committee Report on Multilateral Environmental Agreements, 21 July 1999, www.parliament.the-stationery-office.co.uk/pa/cm199899/cmselect/cmenvtra/307r/30702.htm.

[6] P. Szasz, 'International Norm-Making', in E. Brown Weiss (ed.), *Environmental Change and International Law: New Challenges and Dimensions* (1992), 41 at 43. On the negotiation of international environmental agreements, see B. I. Spector (ed.), *International Environmental Negotiation: Insights for Practice* (1992); and V. A. Kremenyuk and W. Lang, 'The Political, Diplomatic and Legal Background', in G. Sjöstedt (ed.), *International Environmental Negotiation* (1993), 3–16.

I. M. Sinclair, *The Vienna Convention on the Law of Treaties* (1984, 2nd edn);
P. Reuter, *Introduction to the Law of Treaties* (English trans., 1989); T. Gehring,
'International Environmental Regimes: Dynamic Sectoral Legal Systems', 1 *Yearbook
of International Environmental Law* 35 (1990); D. Caron, 'Protection of the Stratospheric Ozone Layer and the Structure of International Environmental Law-
making', 14 *Hastings. International and Comparative Law Review* 755 (1991);
A. Flournay, 'Legislative Inaction: Asking the Wrong Questions in Protective
Environmental Decisionmaking', 15 *Harvard Environmental Law Review* 327
(1991); A. Aust, *Modern Treaty Law and Practice* (2000).

Treaties (also referred to as conventions, accords, agreements and protocols)
are the primary source of international legal rights and obligations in relation
to environmental protection. A treaty can be adopted bilaterally, regionally or
globally, and is defined by the 1969 Vienna Convention on the Law of Treaties
(1969 Vienna Convention)[7] as 'an international agreement concluded between
states in written form and governed by international law, whether embodied
in a single instrument or in two or more related instruments and whatever
its particular designation'.[8] At the heart of this definition is the idea that the
instrument is intended to create international legal rights and obligations between the parties. Whether an instrument is intended to create such binding
obligations will usually be clear from its characteristics and the circumstances
in which it was adopted. The 1972 Stockholm Declaration, the 1978 UNEP
Draft Principles of Conduct, the 1982 World Charter for Nature, the 1992 Rio
Declaration and the 2002 WSSD Plan of Implementation were not intended to
create legal rights and obligations; the fact that they are not treaties, however,
does not preclude the possibility that they may reflect rules of international
law or contribute to the development of such rules, other than by operation of
treaty law.[9]

Numerous attempts have been made to classify treaties in one form or another, such as whether they are bilateral or multilateral, or of general or universal
effect. These efforts frequently have not shed a great deal of light on the practical
consequences of a particular treaty. Certain treaties nevertheless have greater
authority than others, and may assume the quality of 'law-making treaties' in
the sense that they have been concluded for the purpose of laying down general
rules of conduct among a large number of states. Factors which are relevant

---

[7] Vienna, 23 May 1969, in force 27 January 1980, 8 ILM 679 (1969).
[8] Art. 2(1)(a). Treaties may also be adopted by international organisations: see the 1986
Convention on the Law of Treaties Between States and International Organisations, 25 ILM
543 (1986).
[9] See pp. 147–8 below. On occasion they are referred to by international courts and tribunals
to confirm the existence of a rule or finding: see e.g. *The Legality of the Threat or Use of
Nuclear Weapons* (1996) ICJ Reports 226 at 242, para. 30, referring to Principle 24 of the
Rio Declaration.

in assessing the authority of a treaty include: the subject-matter it addresses; the number and representativity of states participating in its negotiation, and signing it or becoming parties; the commitments it establishes; and practice prior to and following its entry into force. In relation to environmental obligations, certain treaties of potentially global application might be considered to have 'law-making' characteristics, particularly where they have attracted a large number of ratifications. These include the 1946 International Whaling Convention, the 1963 Test Ban Treaty, the 1971 Ramsar Convention, the 1972 London Convention, the 1972 World Heritage Convention, MARPOL 73/78, the 1973 CITES, the 1982 UNCLOS, the 1985 Vienna Convention, the 1987 Montreal Protocol (as amended), the 1989 Basel Convention and the 1995 Straddling Stocks Agreement. The 1992 Climate Change Convention and the 1992 Biodiversity Convention can also be considered 'law-making' treaties since their provisions lay down basic rules of general conduct, as may the 1998 Chemicals Convention and the 2001 POPs Convention after they have come into force.

Regional arrangements and treaties can also have a general law-making role for those regions; examples include the UNEP Regional Seas Conventions, the 1992 OSPAR Convention, the 1959 Antarctic Treaty and the rules of EC environmental law.

The number of treaties relating to the environment has increased dramatically in the past two decades. UNEP's 1989 Register of Environmental Agreements listed a total of 139 treaties.[10] The emergence and rapid recent development of international environmental law is evidenced by the number of treaties adopted in each decade of this century: according to the UNEP Register, the number of such treaties was six by 1950, eighteen in the 1950s and twenty-six in the 1960s. The 1970s saw a jump, following the Stockholm Conference, to forty-seven treaties, and a further forty-one treaties in the 1980s. The table of treaties in this book reflects a similar rate of increase during the 1990s and into the opening years of the twenty-first century.

To the UNEP Register list of treaties must be added those treaties which were not adopted primarily to address environmental issues but which nevertheless establish environmental obligations. Primary examples include agreements relating to trade and other international economic matters, such as the GATT/WTO, regional free trade agreements, the EC Treaty, the agreements establishing the World Bank and the regional multilateral development banks, and the multilateral development assistance agreements such as the 1989 Lomé Convention. To this list might now also be added bilateral and other agree-

---

[10] UNEP, 'Register of International Treaties and Other Agreements in the Field of the Environment', UN Doc. UNEP/GC. 15/Inf.2 (1989); see also B. Rüster, B. Simma and M. Bock (eds.), *International Protection of the Environment – Treaties and Related Documents* (1975–82; and 2nd Series, 1990); see also the list of agreements and instruments in UNCED Doc. A/CONF.151/PC/77.

ments relating to the protection of foreign investments.[11] Additionally, there also exists a huge body of bilateral environmental agreements which have contributed significantly to the development of international environmental law. More than 2,000 such treaties have apparently been adopted since the mid-eighteenth century.[12]

Environmental treaties

Environmental treaties share the same general characteristics as other treaties, and are subject to the general rules reflected in the 1969 Vienna Convention and customary law. Nevertheless, certain special features exist, even if a standard format has not yet emerged. When regulating regional or global environmental problems, a framework treaty is frequently adopted. This sets out general obligations, creates the basic institutional arrangements, and provides procedures for the adoption of detailed obligations in a subsequent protocol.[13] Frequently, a framework agreement or protocol will have one or more annexes or appendices, which include scientific, technical or administrative provisions (such as dispute settlement or information exchange),[14] but which might also list the species, substances or activities which are regulated,[15] or the parties to which one or more substantive obligations will apply.[16] This three-tiered approach (framework agreement, protocol, annex/appendices) introduces flexibility by allowing legal amendments or other changes in accordance with political, scientific or economic developments.

The treaty-making process

The adoption and entry into force of an environmental treaty is preceded by a series of steps which will frequently take place over a lengthy period of time. Once two or more states have identified an environmental issue as requiring international legislation, they will identify the forum or institution to serve as a legislative forum. If the subject is already covered by a framework treaty, the new legal obligation could be developed in a protocol or by amendments to an

---

[11] Chapter 21, pp. 1057–61 below.

[12] For an extensive list of environmental agreements, including bilateral agreements, see B. Rüster and B. Simma (eds.), *International Protection of the Environment* (30 vols., and looseleaf service, 1975–93).

[13] Framework treaties allowing for protocols include the conventions adopted under the UNEP Regional Seas Programme (see chapter 9, pp. 399–408 below); the 1979 LRTAP Convention; the 1985 Vienna Convention; the 1989 Basel Convention; the 1992 Climate Change Convention; and the 1992 Biodiversity Convention.

[14] 1985 Vienna Convention.

[15] 1972 London Convention; 1973 CITES; 1987 Montreal Protocol; 1989 Basel Convention.

[16] 1992 Climate Change Convention.

existing protocol; in such cases, the appropriate forum will be the conference of the parties or equivalent institution established by the framework agreement. If the international legislation can appropriately be dealt with by an international act other than a treaty, it may be addressed simply by a binding decision, or resolution, or other act of an international organisation or the conference of the parties of an environmental treaty. If a new treaty is required, the states involved will need to determine which organisation shall conduct the negotiation of the treaty. This decision can be controversial. Thus, although the 1992 Biodiversity Convention was negotiated under the auspices of UNEP, developing countries insisted that the UN General Assembly, rather than UNEP, be responsible for the Climate Change Convention. This was due to the view that developing countries were better represented in the UN General Assembly than at UNEP and better able to participate in negotiations. Similar considerations lay behind the failure of the UN General Assembly in December 1992 to agree whether the UN Commission on Sustainable Development should meet in Geneva (where many developing countries are not represented) or New York (where all developing countries are represented), or in both places.[17]

Once the forum for negotiations is agreed, that body will establish a negotiating process. This could be anything from an informal *ad hoc* group of governmental experts (such as was established by the UNEP Governing Council for what became the 1985 Vienna Ozone Convention), to a formal institutional structure (such as the Intergovernmental Negotiating Committee for a Framework Convention on Climate Change (INC/FCCC), established by UN General Assembly Resolution 44/212). Similar arrangements apply in the negotiation of protocols under framework agreements. An alternative approach is for an international organisation to establish a subsidiary body to 'prepare' a text for consideration and adoption by an Intergovernmental Diplomatic Conference (such as the establishment by the Governing Body of the IAEA of a Standing Committee on Nuclear Liability to prepare draft amendments to the 1963 Vienna Convention).

Negotiations may be open-ended in time or established for a limited period. Examples of the former include the negotiations of the 1985 Vienna Convention (which took place over five years) and the 1982 UN Convention on the Law of the Sea (UNCLOS) (which took nearly twenty years). On the other hand, formal negotiations of the 1992 Climate Change Convention and the 1992 Biodiversity Convention were concluded in just fifteen months, the negotiators having been asked to prepare a text in time for signature at UNCED. Once the draft text has

---

[17] UNGA Res. 47/189 (1992) recommended that the first substantive session would be held in New York 'without prejudice to the venue of its future session': para. 9. The secretariat to the Commission on Sustainable Development is based in New York, and the normal practice is for a meeting of an institution to be held in the place in which its secretariat is based.

been negotiated, it will be adopted and opened for signature. It will then enter into force in accordance with its provisions on entry into force.[18]

The 1969 Vienna Convention and legal issues relating to treaties

The international law of treaties is governed by customary law, the 1969 Vienna Convention and the 1986 Vienna Convention. The 1969 Vienna Convention, large parts of which reflect rules of customary international law, provides the basis for considering many of the legal issues which arise in relation to treaties. With respect to 'environmental' treaties, certain legal issues merit particular attention: these include: the effect of treaties on third parties; the proper approach to interpreting the terms of a treaty; the consequences of conflict between two or more treaties; the legal effect of reservations and interpretative declarations; and the legal effect, if any, of unratified treaties. Each of these issues raises complex legal points, the resolution of which will always turn on the particular facts of a matter. Accordingly, the discussion which follows should be considered as introductory.

Interpretation

The techniques used to interpret treaties and other international acts can have important practical consequences. A restrictive approach to interpretation will limit the scope and effect of a rule, whereas a broad approach may identify an obligation where none was thought to exist. Most environmental treaties include definitions of some of the key words or phrases used in the treaty, but invariably there will be words for which states could not reach an agreed definition[19] or for which no definition was thought necessary at the time of negotiation.[20] Different treaties may define the same word or words differently.[21]

The rules governing the interpretation of treaties are set out in Articles 31 and 32 of the 1969 Vienna Convention. Article 31 establishes the primary rule that a treaty is to be interpreted 'in good faith in accordance with the ordinary meaning to be given to the terms of the treaty in their context and

---

[18] See M. Fitzmaurice, 'Expression of Consent to be Bound by a Treaty as Developed in Some Environmental Treaties', in J. Klabbers and R. Lefeber (eds.), *Essays on the Law of Treaties* (1997), 59.

[19] See e.g. the failure to reach agreement on the definition of 'forest' in the 1992 Climate Change Convention, chapter 8, p. 360 below.

[20] See e.g. the difficulties caused by the failure of the 1973 CITES to define 'pre-Convention specimen': chapter 11, p. 512 below.

[21] See e.g. the different definitions of 'pollution' in the 1979 LRTAP Convention (chapter 8, p. 325 below), the 1976 Barcelona Convention and the 1982 UNCLOS (chapter 9, pp. 401 and 398 below respectively); of 'waste' (see chapter 13, pp. 677–81 below), and 'adverse effects' in the 1985 Vienna Convention and the 1992 Climate Change Convention (see chapter 18, p. 877 below).

in the light of its object and purpose'. From this general approach certain consequences follow. A person seeking to rely on a special meaning for the terms of a treaty, as opposed to the ordinary meaning, will have to prove that special meaning.[22] The context of a treaty includes the whole of its text, the preamble, annexes and, in the case of at least two environmental treaties, footnotes.[23] Any agreement made between all the parties in connection with the conclusion of the treaty and any instrument made by one or more parties relating to the conclusion of the treaty and accepted by the other parties as such are included in understanding the treaty's context.[24] Examples of the latter include a protocol adopted after the conclusion of a framework treaty. In relation to environmental treaties, this happens frequently and is usually specifically provided for in the treaty, and a protocol may incorporate certain parts of a framework treaty.[25] Finally, apart from the context, Article 31(3) of the 1969 Vienna Convention provides that account is also to be taken of certain factors which are extrinsic to the treaty: subsequent agreement between the parties regarding the interpretation or application of the treaty; subsequent practice in application of the treaty which establishes the agreement of the parties regarding its interpretation;[26] and any relevant rules of international law applicable in the relations between the parties.[27] A notable development in recent years has been the willingness of international courts charged with the interpretation and application of an international agreement to have regard to rules of international environmental law arising outside the treaty which is

[22] *Legal Status of Eastern Greenland Case*, PCIJ (1933), Ser. A/B No. 53, 49, as to the meaning of the term 'Greenland'.

[23] 1979 LRTAP Convention, Art. 8(f); and 1992 Climate Change Convention, Art. 1, which states that 'Titles of articles are included solely to assist the reader'. The latter footnote raises the question of the legal effect, if any, of titles to individual Articles, and was inserted at the instigation of the US delegation in an attempt to downplay the legal effect of Article 3, which is entitled 'Principles'.

[24] 1969 Vienna Convention, Art. 31(2). See e.g. Final Act of the Eleventh Antarctic Treaty Special Consultative Meeting, 4 October 1991, noting that the harvesting of ice was not considered to be an Antarctic mineral resource activity under the 1991 Antarctic Environment Protocol; see chapter 14, p. 713 below.

[25] 1987 Montreal Protocol, Art. 14.

[26] Decisions and acts of the institutions established by treaties, even if they are not binding, may thus assume a particular importance. See e.g. CITES Conf. Res. 5.11, concerning the meaning of 'pre-Convention specimen', chapter 10, p. 512 below; and Appendix I to Decision II/8, adopted at the second meeting of the parties to the Montreal Protocol establishing an indicative list of categories of incremental cost to be used by the Financial Mechanism, UNEP/OzL. Pro. 2/3, 41, 29 June 1990.

[27] On the interpretation of treaties by reference to customary international law, see the *Reparations for Injuries Case* (1949) ICJ Reports 174 at 182. The European Court of Human Rights has held that the reference to 'relevant rules of international law' includes general principles of law, 57 ILR 201 at 217 (1975). See generally P. Sands, 'Treaty, Custom and the Cross-Fertilisation of International Law', 1 *Yale Human Rights and Development Law Journal* (1998) (www.diana.law.yale.edu/yhrdlj/vol01iss01/sands_philippe_article.htm).

being interpreted.[28] Related to this approach is the recognition by the ICJ that it is appropriate, in interpreting and applying environmental norms, including those reflected in treaties, to have regard to new norms and standards which may have been developed in the period after a treaty has been adopted:

> Such new norms have to be taken into consideration, and such new standards given proper weight, not only when States contemplate new activities but also when continuing with activities begun in the past.[29]

If the application of the approach laid down by Article 31 produces a result which is not clear or which is ambiguous, Article 32 allows recourse to be had to supplementary means of interpretation, which may also be used to confirm a meaning already established. The principal supplementary means are the *travaux préparatoires* of a treaty, including the minutes of formal negotiations, reports of sessions, and prior drafts of a text. Other supplementary means include the circumstances of a treaty's conclusion, and the application of certain principles of interpretation, such as *in dubio mitius*,[30] and *expressio unius est exclusio alterius*.[31] The reliance on supplementary means of interpretation at a later date means that states will ensure during the negotiation of a text that they are alert to the possible consequences of adding or removing language, or of opposing or failing to oppose language. In the negotiation of recent instruments, such as the Climate Change Convention and the Biodiversity Convention, the number of states involved was so large that it proved impossible to keep detailed formal records of all aspects of proceedings, although informal records may be kept. This will make recourse to *travaux préparatoires* less feasible.

In practice, international bodies which are required to interpret and apply the language of a treaty apply widely differing approaches. One example of a 'restrictive' approach to treaty interpretation is the GATT Panel decision in the yellow-fin tuna dispute between Mexico and the United States, where the Panel interpreted Article XX(b) and (g) of the GATT to exclude the possibility of allowing an importer to take into account the environmental effects of a process leading to a product's final state when considering whether a product's

---

[28] See e.g. WTO Appellate Body, *US – Import Prohibition of Certain Shrimp and Shrimp Products*, 12 October 1998, paras. 129–34, 38 ILM 118 (1999); and P. Sands, 'International Courts and the Application of the Concept of "Sustainable Development"', 3 *Max Planck Yearbook of UN Law* 389–407 (1999).

[29] *Case Concerning the Gabcikovo-Nagymaros Project* (1997) ICJ Reports 7 at 78, para. 140. This has been referred to as the 'principle of contemporaneity' by Judge Weeramantry: *ibid.*, at 113 *et seq.*

[30] The PCIJ recognised the principle as meaning that 'if the wording of a treaty provision is not clear, in choosing between several admissible interpretations, the one which involves the minimum of obligations for the parties should be adopted': *Frontier Between Turkey and Iraq* (1925 PCIJ) Ser. B No. 12, 25.

[31] Oppenheim, vol. 1, 1279, s. 633, describes it as an 'essentially grammatical' rule.

import could be prohibited.[32] An example of a more 'expansive' approach to treaty interpretation is the holding by the European Court of Justice (ECJ) that environmental protection was one of the EU's 'essential objectives', even in the absence of any express reference to environmental protection in the original Treaty of Rome.[33]

Entry into force

Treaties provide expressly for the circumstances in which they will enter into force. This is usually upon ratification by a certain number of states.[34] In the field of environmental law, global treaties have tended to require a low number of ratifications for entry into force.[35] In some instances, entry into force depends upon the participation of certain states or states representing a certain percentage of a particular activity. Examples include the 1971 Oil Pollution Fund Convention (entry into force upon ratification by eight states importing 750 million tons of contributing oil),[36] the 1987 Montreal Protocol (entry into force upon eleven ratifications representing at least two-thirds of the 1986 estimated global consumption of substances controlled by the Montreal Protocol)[37] and the 1997 Kyoto Protocol (entry into force upon ratification by fifty-five states, incorporating developed states accounting for 55 per cent of total carbon dioxide emissions from developed states as at 1990).[38]

Establishing a link between entry into force and the participation of particular states or all states which negotiated the agreement is designed to ensure the fullest participation of key states. However, it is liable to make entry into force hostage to the decision of just one or two states, as has happened with the 1984 Protocols to the Oil Fund Convention and the Civil Liability Convention. Other environmental agreements which have not entered into force because of the participation requirements include the 1985 ASEAN Agreement and the 1988 CRAMRA. Concerns about delay and the difficulty of agreeing applicable criteria prevented the participation of certain states or categories of states from being required in the Climate Change Convention. No agreement could

---

[32] Chapter 19, pp. 955–8 below. The approach has not been followed by the WTO Appellate Body: see. n. 28 above and the accompanying text.

[33] ECJ, Case 240/83 *Procureur de la Republique* v. *Association de défense des brûleurs d'huiles vsagées* [1985] ECR 531, chapter 15, p. 742 below.

[34] Use of the term 'ratification' here includes the acceptance of, approval of or accession to a treaty.

[35] See e.g. the twenty states required for the entry into force of the 1985 Vienna Convention and the 1989 Basel Convention.

[36] Chapter 18, n. 261, p. 915, and n. 68, p. 139 below. The 1984 Protocol has not entered into force because the required number of ratifications have not been achieved: *ibid.*

[37] Art. 16(1). Cf. entry into force of the 1990 amendments to the Montreal Protocol, which require at least twenty ratifications: 1990 amendments, Art. 2(1).

[38] Art. 25(1).

be reached on which greenhouse gases or their proportions should establish a threshold for entry into force.

As environmental agreements increasingly affect national economic interests, and where a large number of states have been involved in the negotiation process, the number of states required to ratify to bring a treaty into force has increased. The Biodiversity Convention and the Climate Change Convention respectively require the ratification of thirty and fifty states.[39] UNCLOS, which required sixty ratifications, only entered into force twelve years after its conclusion. Treaties which have not entered into force may nevertheless have certain legal consequences. Under the 1969 Vienna Convention, signatory states must refrain from acts which would defeat the objects and purposes of the treaty they have signed (unless they have indicated an intention not to become a party),[40] and, partly with this in mind, arrangements have been made to allow for the provisional application of a treaty or part of a treaty, prior to its entry into force.[41] Moreover, a treaty which has not yet entered into force may also contribute to the development of customary international law,[42] or reflect in clearer terms pre-existing customary international law.

Reservations and interpretative declarations

Most recent international environmental agreements do not allow reservations.[43] A few are silent on the matter,[44] and some permit reservations only in strict accordance with specific provisions of the treaty.[45] The general tendency to prohibit the use of reservations is intended to avoid a proliferation of bilateral legal relations. There are two principal reasons for this in the environmental field. First, many environmental treaties are framework agreements providing general structures and guidelines, rather than specific commitments

[39] 1992 Biodiversity Convention, Art. 36; 1992 Climate Change Convention, Art. 23.

[40] Art. 18. An example of a state indicating its intention not to become a party to a convention which it has signed is the United States in relation to the 1997 Kyoto Protocol.

[41] See e.g. Resolutions 2 and 3 of the Conference adopting the 1990 Oil Pollution Preparedness Act calling for implementation of the Convention pending entry into force, including in particular Art. 12: Final Act, OPPR/CONF/24, 29 November 1990, reprinted in 1 *Yearbook of International Environmental Law* 546 at 569–70 (1990). See also the particular transitional arrangements in relation to the 1998 Chemicals Convention, chapter 12, p. 635 below.

[42] In the *Gabcikovo-Nagymaros* case, the ICJ referred to the adoption of the 1997 Watercourses Convention as evidence of the 'modern development of international law' notwithstanding (1) the fact that the Convention was adopted between the close of pleadings in the case and the Court's judgment, and (2) Slovakia had abstained in the adoption of the Convention: (1997) ICJ Reports 7 at 56, para. 85.

[43] 1985 Vienna Convention, Art. 18; 1987 Montreal Protocol, Art. 18; 1989 Basel Convention, Art. 26(1); 1992 Biodiversity Convention, Art. 37; 1992 Climate Change Convention, Art. 24.

[44] 1979 LRTAP Convention; 1991 Espoo Convention; 1992 Watercourses Convention.

[45] 1982 UNCLOS, Art. 309; 1993 Civil Liability Convention, Art. 35.

with implications for a particular activity or practice. Secondly, where a treaty does deal with particularly sensitive or controversial matters, especially where important economic interests are involved, the negotiated text will often represent a series of delicate compromises which would be undermined by allowing one or more states to opt out of certain provisions. Flexibility is intended to be built into the text itself. Reservations or other forms of opt-out are usually permitted in respect of 'secondary legislation', such as an act adopted by the institutions established under an environmental agreement. Examples include the reservations entered by the former Soviet Union, Norway, Iceland and Japan to the 1983 International Whaling Convention moratorium on commercial whaling,[46] and the reservation originally entered by the United Kingdom to the decision at CITES to uplist the African elephant from Appendix II to Appendix I and exclude for a limited period the operation of the decision to the territory of Hong Kong.[47] Where reservations are either expressly allowed or not prohibited, either for treaties or acts of institutions adopted under treaties, customary international law and the 1969 Vienna Convention provide certain guidance on the conditions in which they will be permitted.[48] Parties are free to object to reservations which have been entered, which usually happens when the reservation is considered to be incompatible with the objects and purposes of the treaty or another rule of international law.[49]

The trend towards limiting the permissibility of reservations has not prevented states, when signing or ratifying environmental treaties, from entering statements or 'interpretative declarations' explaining an understanding of a particular provision. Recent examples include: the declaration by the then Federal Republic of Germany to the 1989 Basel Convention;[50] the declaration entered by four small island states (Fiji, Kiribati, Nauru and Tuvalu) to the 1992 Climate Change Convention;[51] and the declaration entered by the United Kingdom in

---

[46] Chapter 11, p. 592 below.   [47] Chapter 11, p. 509 below.

[48] 1969 Vienna Convention, Art. 19; see also the *Case Concerning Reservations to the Convention on the Prevention and Punishment of the Crime of Genocide* (1951) ICJ Reports 15.

[49] See e.g. the numerous objections to the reservations entered by the former USSR under the 1969 CLC (which includes no provision on reservations), purporting to exclude the application of certain jurisdictional rules under the Convention from being applied in respect of state-owned ships; see T. Scovazzi and T. Treves (eds.), *World Treaties for the Protection of the Environment* (1992), 642.

[50] The declaration provides, *inter alia*, that 'nothing in this Convention shall be deemed to require the giving of notice to or the consent of any state for the passage of hazardous wastes on a vessel under the flag of a party exercising its right of innocent passage through the territorial sea or the freedom of navigation in an exclusive economic zone under international law': see Scovazzi and Treves, *World Treaties*, 464.

[51] The states declare their 'understanding that signature of the Convention shall in no way constitute a renunciation of any rights under international law concerning state responsibility for the adverse effects of climate change and that no provisions in the Convention can be interpreted as derogating from the principles of general international law'.

respect of the 1992 Biodiversity Convention.[52] The legal effect of such interpretative declarations remains an open question for which there are no settled general rules. On the other hand, some treaties expressly require declarations to be entered in respect of procedural matters[53] or a choice among substantive options available under a treaty,[54] or allow generally for declarations or statements.[55] The majority are silent as to declarations.

Relations between international agreements

The proliferation of environmental treaties has raised the possibility of overlap or conflict between two or more treaties. This issue is particularly important for the relationship between the growing number of environmental treaties which prohibit trade in certain goods and the WTO, which seeks to restrict non-tariff barriers to trade, including national or, possibly, internationally agreed environmental protection measures. Potential conflict between environmental agreements also exists where regional and global agreements have been adopted for the same subject-matter, such as those for the protection of the marine environment (which might adopt different rules on the dumping of wastes)[56] and the international trade in waste (which might regulate rather than prohibit such trade).[57]

The relationship between WTO rules and the 1987 Montreal Protocol illustrates the potential for conflict. Parties to the 1987 Montreal Protocol are under an obligation to prohibit the import of controlled substances from any state not party to the Protocol, a requirement which may conflict with earlier GATT obligations, if both the countries concerned were parties to the GATT.[58] The 1990 amendments to the Protocol may be problematic, since they ban imports

---

[52] The declaration states, *inter alia*, 'the understanding that Article 3 of the Convention sets out a guiding principle to be taken into account in the implementation of the Convention', and that 'nothing in Article 20 or Article 21 authorises the Conference of the Parties to take decisions concerning the amount, nature, frequency or size of the contributions of the Parties under the Convention'; on these provisions, see chapter 10, p. 000 below; and chapter 19, pp. 000–0 below.

[53] 1985 Vienna Convention, Art. 11(3), providing for declarations concerning the acceptance of compulsory means of dispute settlement.

[54] 1991 VOC Protocol, Art. 2(2), requiring declarations to express a choice between three possible options setting dates and amounts for future emissions of volatile organic compounds.

[55] 1982 UNCLOS, Art. 310, allowing declarations or statements 'however phrased or named, with a view, *inter alia*, to the harmonisation of its laws and regulations with the provisions of this Convention, provided that such declarations or statements do not purport to exclude or to modify the legal effect of the provisions of this Convention in their application to that state'.

[56] Chapter 8, pp. 000–0 below.

[57] Chapter 12, pp. 000–0 below; although the GATT was only of provisional application, the issues posed are useful to illustrate the problem.

[58] 1987 Montreal Protocol, Art. 4(1). The matter is now further complicated by the adoption of the new WTO rules, including GATT 1994, which post-date the 1987 Montreal Protocol.

from third parties of products *containing* controlled substances (such as refrigerators).[59] In the event that a party to the Montreal Protocol were to ban the import of refrigerators containing CFCs from a third state, where both states were party to the GATT, which obligation would prevail?

Article 30 of the 1969 Vienna Convention sets forth rules governing the situation where states are parties to treaties relating to the same subject-matter (in this case, trade). Article 30(2) provides that, when a treaty specifies that it is subject to, or not incompatible with, an earlier or later treaty, then the provisions of the other treaty will prevail. Under Article 30(3), if all the parties to the earlier treaty are also parties to the later treaty, and the earlier treaty continues in force, then only those provisions of the earlier treaty which are compatible with the later treaty will apply. Finally, Article 30(4) governs the likely situations when the parties to the later treaty do not include all the parties to the earlier treaty. It provides that (a) as between states party to both treaties the same rule applies as in Article 30(3); and (b) as between a state party to both treaties and a state party to only one of the treaties, the treaty to which both states are parties governs their mutual rights and obligations.

The application of Article 30(4) would appear to lead to the following result: in the event of a conflict between the GATT (signed in 1947) (assuming that its obligations are to be considered treaty obligations) and the 1987 Montreal Protocol, where two states are parties to the GATT but only one state is a party to the Montreal Protocol, then the provisions of the GATT would appear to prevail, without taking into account any permissible exceptions under the GATT. However, if both states are parties to both instruments, then the later in time (the Montreal Protocol) will prevail.[60]

With the growing number of environmental agreements touching upon the same subject matter, the question has also arisen as to the conditions under which a party is entitled to invoke the dispute settlement provisions under one treaty as opposed to another. This may be a particularly complex issue where one treaty sets forth general rules and another more specialised rules, as is the case with the 1982 UNCLOS and more specific marine pollution or fisheries conservation agreements. The issue arose in the *Southern Bluefin Tuna* cases, which Australia and New Zealand chose to litigate under the 1982 UNCLOS rather than the (regional) 1993 Convention on the Conservation of Southern-Bluefin Tuna.[61] Japan argued that the UNCLOS Annex VII arbitral tribunal did not have jurisdiction, on the grounds *inter alia* that the 1993 Convention governed the dispute and Article 16 of that Convention (on dispute settlement) excluded the application of the procedures on dispute settlement under Part XV of UNCLOS.[62] By four votes to one, the UNCLOS arbitral

---

[59] 1990 amendment, Art. 4(3)–(4*bis*).
[60] See further chapter 19, p. 940 below.   [61] Chapter 11, pp. 580–1 below.
[62] Art. 281(1) of UNCLOS provides: 'If the States Parties which are parties to a dispute concerning the interpretation or application of this Convention have agreed to seek settlement

tribunal accepted the argument: although Article 16 of the 1993 Convention did not expressly exclude any further procedure under Part XV of UNCLOS, the 'intent of Article 16 [was] to remove proceedings under that Article from the reach of the compulsory procedures of section 2 of Part XV of UNCLOS'.[63] The award declining jurisdiction has not been received with broad approval.[64] It should not be assumed that it will be followed,[65] particularly having regard to the approach taken by the International Tribunal for the Law of the Sea (ITLOS) the following year in the provisional measures phase of the *MOX* case, which raised a related, but distinguishable, issue.[66] The ITLOS rejected an argument by the United Kingdom to the effect that ITLOS did not have jurisdiction since the dispute was centred upon other conventions (and EC law) with their own dispute provisions, noting that:

> even if the OSPAR Convention, the EC Treaty and the Euratom Treaty contain rights or obligations similar to or identical with the rights or obligations set out in the Convention, the rights and obligations under those agreements have a separate existence from those under the Convention . . . the application of international law rules on interpretation of treaties to identical or similar provisions of different treaties may not yield the same results, having regard to, *inter alia*, differences in the respective contexts, objects and purposes, subsequent practice of parties and *travaux préparatoires*.[67]

The approach may be of particular importance for the interpretation and application of international environmental agreements, which often contain the same or similar language imposing substantive obligations, but which may have been negotiated or subsequently applied in a particular context.

Amendment

The need for expedited amendment processes for environmental agreements (to take into account changes of a scientific, economic or political nature) has led to the adoption of innovative approaches. Almost all environmental treaties

of the dispute by peaceful means of their own choice, the procedures provided for in this Part apply only where no settlement has been reached by recourse to such means and the agreement between the parties does not exclude any further procedure.'

[63] Arbitral Award of 4 August 2000, para. 57, 39 ILM 1359 (2000).

[64] See e.g. B. Oxman, 'Complementary Agreements and Compulsory Jurisdiction', 95 AJIL 277 (2001).

[65] See P. Sands, 'ITLOS: An International Lawyer's Perspective', in M. H. Nordquist and J. Norton Moore (eds.), *Twenty-Fifth Annual Conference: Current Marine Environmental Issues and the International Tribunal for the Law of the Sea* (2001)

[66] ITLOS, *MOX Plant* case, Order of 3 December 2001.

[67] Paras. 50 and 51. In June 2003 the Annex VII Tribunal in the *MOX* case suspended the proceedings pending clarification of jurisdictional issues relating to EC competence: see order No. 3, 24 June 2003 (available at www.pca-cpa.org).

make express provision for a formal amendment process by the adoption of a further treaty between the parties.[68] Informal amendment may also take place orally or by tacit agreement of the parties, including decisions or acts of organs established under a treaty which may amount to a *de facto* amendment.

The provisions of the 1985 Vienna Convention and the 1987 Montreal Protocol illustrate new techniques, which have been subsequently followed.[69] The 1985 Vienna Convention is a framework treaty with two annexes and provision for protocols.[70] To date, the only protocol is the 1987 Montreal Protocol, which was amended and adjusted in 1990, 1992, 1997 and 1999. The 1985 Vienna Convention establishes the rules for its own amendment as well as that of any protocols: as a last resort, amendments to the 1985 Vienna Convention may be adopted by a 'three-fourths majority vote of the parties present and voting' at a meeting of the conference of the parties; amendments to protocols require only a 'two-thirds majority of the parties to that protocol present and voting' at a meeting of the parties to the protocol.[71] The 1987 Montreal Protocol also provides an alternative to formal amendment by the adoption of 'adjustments and reductions' by the parties; adjustment may be made to the ozone-depleting potential of controlled substances identified in Annexes to the Protocol, as well as production or consumption levels of controlled substances.[72] As a last resort, adjustments and reductions are adopted by a two-thirds majority of the parties present and voting which represent at least 50 per cent of the total consumption of the controlled substances, and these are binding on all parties without the possibility of objection.[73] The Protocol also allows the parties to add or remove any substances from any Annex to the Protocol and decide on the mechanism, scope and timing of the control measures that should apply to such substances.[74] Such decisions become effective provided they have been accepted by a two-thirds majority of the parties present and voting, without specifying the manner of acceptance or the effect of any objection of a party outside the two-thirds majority.[75] Adjustments under Article 9 and decisions under Article 10 are made on the basis of assessments under Article 6. This procedure has been used to adopt adjustments at the second and fourth meetings of the parties to the Protocol.[76] Amendments to the Annexes to the 1985

---

[68] 1971 Fund Convention, Art. V(1); 1972 London Dumping Convention, Art. XV; 1989 Basel Convention, Art. 17; 1992 Biodiversity Convention, Arts. 29 and 30; 1992 Climate Change Convention, Arts. 15 and 16. See generally M. Bowman, 'The Multilateral Treaty Amendment Process: A Case Study', 66 ICLQ 540 (1995).

[69] See e.g. 1997 Kyoto Protocol; 2001 POPs Convention.   [70] Art. 8.

[71] Art. 9. Amendments which have been adopted will then need to be ratified, approved or accepted before entering into force, by three-fourths of the parties to the Convention or two-thirds of the parties to the Protocol unless otherwise provided by the Protocol: Art. 9(5). The Convention has not been amended, but the Protocol was amended in 1990 and 1992: see chapter 8, pp. 346–7 below.

[72] Art. 9(a).   [73] Art. 9(c) and (d).   [74] Art. 10(a).

[75] Art. 10(b).   [76] Chapter 8, pp. 346–7 below.

Vienna Convention or the 1987 Montreal Protocol are adopted in the same way as amendments to the Convention or Protocol.[77] However, the procedure for entry into force of an Annex amendment differs: it requires a party which objects to such an amendment to opt out, by notifying the depositary within six months of its adoption, failing which it will bind any state which has not objected.[78]

Other international acts

Other international acts include those adopted by international organisations (which may be binding or non-binding), and by states in the form of non-binding declarations or Action Plans. Non-binding acts are sometimes referred to as 'soft law'. Although not legally binding, they may contribute to the development of customary law or lead to the adoption of binding obligations by treaty or an act of an international organisation.

Acts of international organisations

Acts of international organisations, sometimes referred to as secondary legislation, provide an important source of international law: they may be legally binding *per se*, or they may amend treaty obligations, or they may authoritatively interpret treaty obligations.[79] Since binding acts of international organisations derive their legal authority from the treaty on which they were based, they can be considered as part of treaty law.

Many far-reaching decisions affecting the use of natural resources result from acts of international organisations. Examples include: the 1983 decision of the IWC to adopt a moratorium on commercial whaling;[80] the 1985 resolution of the consultative meeting of the parties to the 1972 London Convention adopting a moratorium on the dumping of radioactive waste at sea;[81] the 1989 decision by the CITES conference of the parties to ban the international trade in African elephant products;[82] and the 1991 Security Council resolution reaffirming the liability of Iraq for the environmental damage caused by its unlawful invasion of Kuwait.[83]

The legal effect of an act of an international organisation depends upon the treaty basis of the organisation, as the following examples illustrate. Usually, the treaty will specify the intended legal consequences. Under Article 25 of the UN Charter, UN General Assembly resolutions are 'only recommendatory',

---

[77] Art. 10(2) and (3).   [78] Art. 10(2)(b).

[79] See generally P. Sands and P. Klein, *Bowett's Law of International Institutions* (2001, 5th edn), 275–92.

[80] Chapter 11, p. 593 below.   [81] Chapter 9, p. 417 below.

[82] Chapter 11, p. 509 below.   [83] Chapter 7, p. 315 below.

whereas resolutions of the Security Council are binding 'on all states';[84] Regulations, Directives and Decisions of the EU (the EC, ECSC and Euratom) are legally binding on member states and can create rights and obligations which are directly enforceable in the national legal systems of the member states.[85] Acts of organisations established by environmental treaties may be binding or non-binding. Such institutions often have a choice. Thus, the IWC can adopt regulations which are 'effective' for parties not presenting an objection, or it can adopt recommendations which are not legally binding.[86] The consultative meetings of the parties to the 1972 London Convention can amend the Annexes to the Convention, which enter into force either upon notification by a party or after a stated period of time, unless a party declares that it is not able to accept an amendment.[87] The CITES conference of the parties adopts amendments to Appendices I and II to the Convention which 'enter into force' for all parties except those making a reservation.[88] And the meeting of the parties to the 1987 Montreal Protocol may adopt amendments and adjustments which can bind even parties not accepting them.[89] In each case, a majority of the parties to a treaty may adopt binding acts, although the minority is usually free to opt out.

In other cases, an international organisation may adopt an act (which might be called a resolution, recommendation or decision), without a clear provision in the treaty establishing the legal consequences of that act. The legal effect of resolutions adopted under the 1972 London Convention is less clear (such as the resolution on the dumping of radioactive wastes at sea adopted by the ninth consultative meeting which agreed to a 'suspension of all dumping at sea of radioactive wastes and other radioactive matter').[90] Such resolutions, addressing substantive matters, are not binding *per se*, although they may contribute to the development of customary international law, or may set forth an authoritative interpretation of the international agreement under which it was adopted. Examples of such acts include the resolutions adopted by the Governing Council of UNEP which adopt or endorse principles, guidelines or recommended practices addressed to states and other members of the international community.[91] The resolution or act could also bind those states supporting it through the operation of some general principle of law, such as the principle of estoppel.[92] Where the act is an internal act of the organisation

---

[84] This categorisation may be somewhat misleading, however, since certain resolutions of the General Assembly can have 'definitive legal effect': see n. 93 below.

[85] Chapter 15, p. 734 below.

[86] 1946 International Whaling Convention, Arts. V(1) and (3) and VI.

[87] Art. XV(2).   [88] Arts. XI(3)(b) and XV.

[89] See pp. 138–40 above.   [90] Chapter 9, p. 418 below.

[91] See e.g. the 1985 Montreal Guidelines for the Protection of the Marine Environment Against Pollution from Land-Based Sources; and the 1987 London Guidelines for the Exchange of Information on Chemicals in International Trade.

[92] See *Nuclear Tests* cases, discussed at p. 151 below; see also P. Klein, *Bowett's Law of International Institutions* (5th edn, 2001), 289.

(adopting a budget or procedural rules, or establishing a subsidiary organ), the resolution may bind all members of the organisation as a matter of the internal law of the organisation.[93]

A further issue is the legal effect, if any, of an act of one international organisation upon another, to the extent that it is arguable that there exists a 'common law of international organisations'.[94] This would allow a measure, or interpretative act, adopted by one international organisation, to be relied upon by or have consequences for, another. The proliferation of international organisations addressing environmental issues increases the need for legal consistency and certainty. In practice, organisations do take account of each other's activities, in relation to both procedural and substantive matters, and precedents may be followed on an informal basis. Examples include: the emerging rules and practices governing the participation of non-state actors in the activities of international organisations; the definition of 'best available technology' adopted by the meeting of the parties to the 1974 Paris LBS Convention;[95] and the definition of the 'precautionary principle' adopted by the parties to the 1976 Barcelona Convention or the 1974 Paris LBS Convention.[96]

Conference declarations and other acts

Many intergovernmental conferences are convened every year to address environmental issues and issues linking environment and development. Many adopt declarations, statements or other non-binding acts, which may contribute to the development of international environmental law even if they are not binding as treaties or as formal acts of international organisations. The most important international conferences have been the 1949 UNCCUR, the 1972 Stockholm Conference, the 1992 UNCED and the 2002 WSSD. Each adopted non-binding acts, of which the Stockholm Declaration, the Rio Declaration and Agenda 21 include important elements which now reflect, or are contributing to the development of, customary international law. They continue to provide a significant influence on the development of new treaties and acts of international organisations.[97]

Other conferences have addressed specific, or sectoral, issues. These too can contribute to the development of binding international rules over time. Examples of declarations which have influenced international legislation include the 1990 Ministerial Declaration of the Second World Climate Conference, the Declaration adopted by the 1990 UNECE Bergen Conference

---

[93] The ICJ affirmed that resolutions of the General Assembly can have 'definitive legal effect': *Case Concerning Certain Phosphate Lands in Nauru* (1992) ICJ Reports 251 (concerning UNGA Res. 2847).
[94] See *de Merode*, WBAT Reports 1987, Decision No. 1, paras. 26 and 28.
[95] Chapter 9, p. 432 below.   [96] Chapter 6, p. 268 below; chapter 9, p. 432 below.
[97] Chapter 8, p. 385 below; chapter 6, pp. 262–3 and 235 below.

on Sustainable Development, and regional conferences on environment and development. These contributed to the consensus at UNCED and the negotiations of the Climate Change and Biodiversity Conventions. The 1992 Rio Declaration may be the single most significant such declaration, in terms of its contribution to the development of international environmental rules and jurisprudence. Other conference declarations have led to acts of international organisations which are then followed by the adoption of a new treaty rule incorporating in binding terms the original conference act or objective. One such example is the 1990 Third Ministerial Declaration on the North Sea, elements of which were incorporated into resolutions of the Commissions established under the 1972 Oslo and 1974 Paris Conventions, and are now reflected in the 1992 OSPAR Convention.[98] A more recent example is the 1998 Sintra Ministerial Declaration on the prevention of pollution of the north-east Atlantic by radioactive substances.[99]

Another act frequently adopted by international conferences (or by international organisations) is the 'Action Plan', which also frequently forms the basis or context for the subsequent adoption of treaty rules. Examples include: the Recommendations adopted by the 1972 Stockholm Conference; the various Regional Action Plans adopted under the UNEP Regional Seas Programme; Agenda 21; and the WSSD Plan of Implementation. Action Plans have also been adopted on a range of sectoral issues, such as water resources, drought and desertification, national parks, and the conservation of biodiversity.

Customary international law

A. D'Amato, *The Concept of Custom in International Law* (1971); H. W. A. Thirlway, *International Customary Law and Codification* (1972); M. Akehurst, 'Custom as a Source of International Law', 47 BYIL 1 (1974–5); M. E. Villiger, *Customary International Law and Treaties* (1985); M. Mendelson, 'The Formation of Customary International Law', 272 RdC 155 (1998); International Law Association, *London Statement of Principles Relating to the Formation of General Customary International Law* (2000); I. Brownlie, 'A Survey of International Customary Rules of Environmental Protection', 13 *Natural Resources Journal* 179 (1973); P. M. Dupuy, 'Overview of Existing Customary Legal Regime Regarding International Pollution', in D. Magraw (ed.), *International Law and Pollution* (1991); D. Bodansky, 'Customary (and Not So Customary) International Environmental Law', 3 *Indiana Journal of Global Legal Studies* 105 (1995).

Customary law rules have played a secondary role in international environmental law, although they can establish binding obligations for states and other members of the international community and may be relied upon in the

---

[98] Chapter 6, p. 271 below; chapter 13, p. 686 below.   [99] Chapter 9, p. 426 below.

codification of obligations in treaties and other binding acts. The significance of custom lies in the fact that it creates obligations for all states (or all states within a particular region) except those which have persistently objected to a practice and its legal consequences. Moreover, a customary rule may exist alongside a conventional rule, can inform the content and effect of a conventional rule, and can give rise to a distinct cause of action for dispute settlement purposes.

However, the process of developing rules of customary law cannot really be considered as part of a formal legislative process, and the existence of a customary rule may be difficult to prove.[100] Proving customary international law requires evidence of consistent state practice, which practice will only rarely provide clear guidance as to the precise context or scope of any particular rule. Nevertheless, 'customary law can be somewhat shaped and directed, because the practices of states can be consciously affected by various international actions',[101] including the non-binding acts of international organisations and the intergovernmental statements and declarations discussed above. Article 38(1)(b) of the Statute of the International Court of Justice identifies the two elements of customary international law: state practice and *opinio juris.*

State practice

State practice is notoriously difficult to prove, and little empirical research has been carried out on state practice relating to international environmental obligations.[102] State practice can be discerned from several sources, including: ratification of treaties; participation in treaty negotiations and other international meetings; national legislation; the decisions of national courts; votes and other acts in the UN General Assembly and other international organisations; statements by ministers and other governmental and diplomatic representatives; formal diplomatic notes; and legal opinions by government lawyers.[103] Preparatory materials to these sources can also provide useful evidence of state practice. Other sources include the pleadings of states before national and international courts and tribunals, parliamentary debates, collections of diplomatic materials and the records and *travaux préparatoires* of international conferences and treaty negotiations. Useful pleadings include those relating to the *Nuclear Tests* cases and the *Case Concerning Certain Phosphate Lands in Nauru.*

---

[100] As reflected in the fact that national courts in different countries may reach diametrically opposed conclusions as to the customary status of a rule or principle of international law: see e.g. the precautionary principle, at chapter 6, pp. 278–9 below.

[101] P. Szasz, 'International Norm-Making', in E. Brown Weiss (ed.), *Issues in International Law* (1992), 41 at 67.

[102] Useful sources of evidence of state practice in relation to environment matters include national reports prepared for UNCED by participating states; and the country/region reports in Part 2 (the Year in Review) of the *Yearbook of International Environmental Law.*

[103] See *Yearbook of the International Law Commission* (1950-II), 368–72.

The pleadings in New Zealand's resumed *Nuclear Tests* case (1995),[104] the ICJ's Advisory Opinion on the legality of the use of nuclear weapons[105] and the *Gabcikovo-Nagymaros Project* case are also likely to repay careful consideration. It is important to bear in mind that the failure of a state to act can also provide evidence of state practice: mutual toleration of certain levels of pollution, or of activities which cause environmental degradation, can provide evidence that states accept such levels and activities as being compatible with international law.

For state practice to contribute to the development of a rule of law, the practice must be general, although this does not mean that it requires the participation of all states across the globe or in a particular region. The ICJ has stated that:

> it might be that, even without the passage of any considerable period of time, a very widespread and representative participation in the convention might suffice of itself, provided it included states whose interests were specifically affected.[106]

More recently, the ICJ deemed it sufficient that the conduct of states should, in general, be consistent with such rules, and that instances of state conduct inconsistent with a given rule should generally have been treated as breaches of that rule, not as indications of the recognition of a new rule.[107]

In both cases, the ICJ was concerned with customary law arising in the context of treaty rules. The relationship between treaty and custom is close, often based upon elements of mutual interdependence. A treaty might codify or further develop a rule of customary law, as was the case in the 1982 UNCLOS. Alternatively, the conclusion and implementation of a treaty may reflect the existence of a rule of customary law. In the *North Sea Continental Shelf* cases, the ICJ found that state practice since the conclusion of the 1958 Geneva Convention on the Continental Shelf, including signature and ratification of the convention, could create a rule of customary law. In the *Military and Paramilitary Activities* case, the ICJ again considered the relationship between treaties and custom, finding that multilateral conventions 'may have an important role to play in recording and defining rules deriving from custom. or indeed in developing them'.[108] The frequent reference to, and incorporation of, Principle 21 of the Stockholm Declaration in the text of treaties is an example of treaties contributing to development of custom.[109] In 1996, the

---

[104] For a summary of the pleadings, see P. Sands, 'Year in Review: International Court of Justice', 6 *Yearbook of International Environmental Law* 531 (1995).
[105] *Ibid.*, 533.
[106] *North Sea Continental Shelf* Cases (1969) ICJ Reports 3, para. 73.
[107] *Military and Paramilitary Activities* Case (1986) ICJ Reports 98.
[108] (1986) ICJ Reports 97; and *Libya/Malta Continental Shelf* Case (1985) ICJ Reports 29.
[109] See chapter 6, pp. 231–4 below.

ICJ confirmed the customary status of the norm reflected in Principle 21,[110] but without addressing the extent or uniformity of state practice. It appears to have taken a similarly flexible approach the following year, in its judgment in the *Gabcikovo-Nagymaros* case, where it cited with approval the principle of 'equitable utilisation' referred to in Article 5(2) of the 1997 Watercourses Convention.[111] This suggests that in the environmental field the ICJ may well be conscious of the 'Herculean task' of deducing rules of customary international law directly from state practice,[112] and will divine the existence of such rules by more flexible and pragmatic means.

Opinio juris

The second element of customary law, *opinio juris sive necessitatis*, requires evidence that a state has acted in a particular way because it believes that it is required to do so by law. The ICJ in the *North Sea Continental Shelf* cases identified the content and role of *opinio juris*:

> Not only must the acts concerned amount to a settled practice, but they must also be such, or be carried out in such a way, as to be evidence of a belief that this practice is rendered obligatory by the existence of a rule of law requiring it. The need for such a belief, i.e. the existence of a subjective element, is implicit in the very notion of the *opinio juris sive necessitatis*. The states concerned must therefore feel that they are conforming to what amounts to a legal obligation. The frequency, or even habitual character of the acts is not in itself enough. There are many intentional acts, e.g. in the field of ceremonial and protocol, which are performed almost invariably, but which are motivated only by considerations of courtesy, convenience or tradition, and not by any sense of legal duty.[113]

Proving the existence of *opinio juris* will always be a difficult task, since it requires consideration of the motives underlying state activity. It has been suggested that it can be found from a number of sources, including: expressions of beliefs regarding acts of international organisations and other international meetings;[114] statements made by representatives of states;[115] and the conclusion of treaties.[116] Given the difficulties of proving *opinio juris*, there is a certain attraction in the view of Sir Hersch Lauterpacht, who proposed that the accurate principle consists in 'regarding all uniform conduct of Governments (or, in

---

[110] Chapter 6, p. 236 below.   [111] Chapter 10, pp. 469–77 below.

[112] See D. Bodansky, 'Customary (and Not So Customary) International Environmental Law', 3 *Indiana Journal of Global Legal Studies* 105 at 113 (1995).

[113] (1969) ICJ Reports 3 at 44.

[114] *Military and Paramilitary Activities* Case (1986) ICJ Reports 99–101.

[115] *Ibid.*, 100–1.   [116] *Nottebohm* Case (1955) ICJ Reports 22–3.

appropriate cases, abstention therefrom) as evidencing the *opinio necessitatis juris* except when it is shown that the conduct in question was not accompanied by any such intention'.[117] Such an approach, which shifts the burden of proof but which is not universally shared, would make the acceptance of principles and rules set out in treaties more likely to contribute to the development of custom.

Treaties and custom

State practice in treaty-making and in accordance with obligations under treaties can contribute to the development of customary law. Moreover, as the ICJ recognised in the *Military and Paramilitary Activities* case, customary rules may emerge which are identical to those of treaty law, and which exist simultaneously with treaty obligations.[118] In the *North Sea Continental Shelf* cases, the ICJ had to decide whether the principle of equidistance for delimitation of the continental shelf found in Article 6 of the 1958 Convention on the Continental Shelf constituted a rule of customary international law. The ICJ found that it was necessary to examine the status of a principle as it stood when a treaty was drawn up, as it resulted from the effect of the treaty, and in the light of state practice subsequent to the treaty.[119] The ICJ held that at the time of its conclusion the principle set out in Article 6 of the 1958 Convention was a treaty rule and not regarded as *lege lata* or as an emerging rule of customary international law. The ICJ then considered whether the principle found in Article 6 had passed into the general *corpus* of international law, and was accepted as such by *opinio juris*, so as to be binding even for countries which were not parties to the Convention: such a process was 'a perfectly possible one which does from time to time occur, although it could not be a result lightly regarded as having been attained'.[120] The ICJ identified the conditions to be fulfilled for a new rule of customary international law to be formed as a result of a treaty:

> It would in the first place be necessary that the provision concerned should, at all events potentially, be of a fundamentally norm-creating character such as could be regarded as forming the basis of a general rule . . . With respect to the other elements usually regarded as necessary before a conventional rule can be considered to have become a general rule of international law, it might be that, even without the passage of any considerable period of time, a very widespread and representative participation in the convention might suffice of itself, provided it included that of states whose interests were specially affected.[121]

---

[117] Sir Hersch Lauterpacht, *The Development of International Law by the International Court* (1958), 380.

[118] (1986) ICJ Reports 14.   [119] (1969) ICJ Reports 37.   [120] *Ibid.*   [121] *Ibid.*, 41–2.

In this case, the number of ratifications was respectable but insufficient. As to the time element:

> [a]lthough the passage of only a short period of time is not necessarily, or of itself, a bar to the formation of a new rule of customary international law on the basis of what was originally a purely conventional rule, an indispensable requirement would be that within the period in question, short though it might be, state practice, including that of states whose interests are specially affected, should have been both extensive and virtually uniform in the sense of the provision invoked; and should moreover have occurred in such a way as to show a general recognition that a rule of law or legal obligation is involved.[122]

The ICJ held on the facts of the case that state practice was insufficient to transform the treaty obligation under Article 6 of the 1958 Convention into a customary obligation.

However, it should not be assumed that the mere fact that a large number of states are party to a treaty establishes a customary norm for all. For example, the ICJ declined to indicate that the rule prohibiting widespread and significant environmental harm in armed conflict reflected a customary rule.[123] For environmental treaties, provisions of a fundamentally norm-creating character which are capable of being considered as rules of customary law include those of a substantive nature, as well as principles which inform and guide decision-making. Examples of substantive obligations reflected in many treaties include: Principle 21 of the Stockholm Declaration; the obligation to co-operate on environmental problems associated with shared natural resources; the obligation to adopt general measures to protect the marine environment from significant damage; and the obligation to take measures to ensure the conservation of, and prevention of harm to, endangered species of flora and fauna. More specific examples of treaty rules which can be considered as having a 'fundamentally norm-creating character' arguably include: the obligation to use a shared international watercourse in an 'equitable and reasonable' manner; the obligation not to dump high-level radioactive waste in the marine environment; the obligation not to engage in commercial whaling; and the general obligation of developed states to limit emissions of gases such as sulphur dioxide. Guiding principles which may, through treaty practice, reflect existing or emerging norms of customary law might include the polluter-pays principle, the principle of precautionary action, and the principle of common but differentiated responsibilities of developed and developing countries. Procedural obligations which may be binding under customary law, at least within certain regions, include consultation, the provision of information on the environment and the obligation to carry out an environmental impact assessment for activities likely to cause significant environmental damage.

[122] *Ibid.*, 43.   [123] (1996) ICJ Reports 226 at 242, para. 31.

Persistent objector

Since a rule of customary law may develop without the express or active support of all states in the international community, the silence or failure of a state to act will not necessarily prevent such a rule from becoming binding upon it, as is clear from the judgments of the ICJ in the *North Sea Continental Shelf* cases. However, a state can avoid being bound by a rule if it persistently objects to that rule. This was one of the issues in the *Anglo-Norwegian Fisheries* case, where the United Kingdom argued the unlawfulness of the Norwegian practice of drawing straight base-lines across the mouths of bays to measure the width of the territorial sea, and where both states accepted the existence of the 'persistent objector' principle.[124] An example of persistent objection in the environmental field is provided by the clear and consistent objection of the United States to the view that the 'right to development' exists as a legal rule.[125] Another example may perhaps be seen in the ICJ's 1996 opinion that environmental obligations under the 1977 Geneva Protocol I did not, at least at that time, reflect customary law in view of the unwillingness of certain states to recognise the application of the Protocol to nuclear weapons.[126] Closely related to the principle of the persistent objector is the operation of acquiescence, according to which the failure of a state to protest against the practice of other states over time will operate to limit or prevent a state from subsequently protesting against the fact that the practice is permitted as a matter of international law. The ICJ considered the principle of acquiescence in the *Anglo-Norwegian Fisheries* case, holding that the 'notoriety of the facts, the general toleration of the international community, Great Britain's position in the North Sea, her own interest in the question, and her prolonged abstention would in any case warrant Norway's enforcement of her system against the United Kingdom'.[127]

Regional custom

Rules of customary international law may also develop at the regional level. This was recognised by the ICJ in the *Asylum* case, holding that regional or local custom peculiar to Latin American states could be established where the rule invoked can be proved to be 'in accordance with a constant and uniform usage practised by the states in question'.[128] This is important in the field of environmental protection, where global regimes have been the exception rather than the rule, and in respect of which some regions (Europe and the Antarctic)

---

[124] *Anglo-Norwegian Fisheries* Case (1951) ICJ Reports 131.
[125] Chapter 6, pp. 265–6 below.
[126] See n. 9 above and the accompanying text.   [127] (1951) ICJ Reports 139.
[128] *Asylum* Case (*Colombia* v. *Peru*) (1950) ICJ Reports 266; in this case, the Court found that Colombia had not proved the existence of regional or local custom due to the uncertainty, contradiction, fluctuation, discrepancy and inconsistency in practice, which had also been influenced by political expediency.

are particularly well developed. A regional approach allows flexibility in encouraging groups of countries to develop rules which reflect their particular interests, needs and capacities. The Pacific region has been particularly active in developing international treaty rules prohibiting the presence of radioactive materials and the use of driftnet fishing practices in the region, both of which may now reflect rules of customary law for that region. A similar conclusion may be drawn from state practice supporting efforts adopted by African states to limit and prohibit the import of hazardous and other waste onto the African continent, or in respect of certain mineral activities in the Antarctic.

General principles of international law[129]

B. Cheng, *General Principles of Law as Applied by International Courts and Tribunals* (1953); A. McNair, 'The General Principles of Law Recognised by Civilised Nations', 33 BYIL 1 (1957); G. Herczegh, *General Principles of Law and the International Legal Order* (1969); E. Zoller, *La Bonne Foi en Droit International Public* (1977); M. Akehurst, 'The Application of General Principles of Law by the Court of Justice of the European Communities', 52 BYIL 29 (1981); B. Vitanyi, 'Les Positions Doctrinals Concernant le Sens de la Notion de "Principes Généraux de Droit Reconnus par les Nations Civilisées"', 86 RGDIP 48 (1982)

The inclusion of 'general principles of law recognised by civilised nations' in Article 38 is widely believed to have been intended to allow the ICJ to consider and apply general principles of municipal law, and in practice they are occasionally relied upon when gaps need to be filled. The ICJ has only rarely relied on general principles, although other international tribunals, such as the ECJ, have relied on general principles of municipal law to assist in reaching conclusions.[130]

The general principles relating to good faith in the exercise of rights and prohibitions on the abuse by a state of a right which it enjoys under international law have been invoked by the ICJ and arbitral tribunals which have considered international environmental issues.[131] The principle of good faith appears to have been relied upon by the President of the Tribunal in the *Fur Seal Arbitration* in finding that the exercise of a right for the sole purpose of causing injury to another (abuse of rights) is prohibited.[132] The award in the *Trail Smelter* case is also cited as an example of reliance upon the principle of

---

[129] General principles of the type discussed in this section should be distinguished from the general obligations and principles which have emerged specifically in relation to international environmental law and are addressed in chapter 6 below.

[130] See Case C-2/90, *EC Commission v. Belgium* [1993] 1 CMLR 365, chapter 19, pp. 990–1 below.

[131] On abuse of rights, see Oppenheim, vol. I, 407–10; B. Cheng, *General Principles of Law as Applied by International Tribunals* (1951), 121–36.

[132] Chapter 11, pp. 561–6 below.

good faith which governs the exercise of rights, to ensure that a proper balance is struck between a state's rights and obligations and a 'recognition of the interdependence of a person's rights and obligations'.[133] The abuse of rights doctrine is also considered to provide the basis for the rule that a state must not interfere with the flow of a river to the detriment of other riparian states,[134] and is related to the principle requiring respect for mutual interests which is now reflected in Principle 21 of the Stockholm Declaration and Principle 2 of the Rio Declaration, namely, *sic utere tuo ut alienum non laedas*. The principle of 'good faith' was relied upon by the ICJ in the *Nuclear Tests* cases to enable it to reach its conclusion on the legal effect of a French unilateral declaration that it would cease atmospheric nuclear tests. In recognising that unilateral declarations could have the effect of creating legal obligations which are binding 'if given publicly, and with an intent to be bound, even though not made within the context of international negotiations', the Court stated that:

> One of the basic principles governing the creation and performance of legal obligations, whatever their source, is the principle of good faith. Trust and confidence are inherent in international co-operation, in particular in an age when this co-operation in many fields is becoming increasingly essential. just as the very rule of *pacta sunt servanda* in the law of treaties is based on good faith, so also is the binding character of an international obligation assumed by unilateral declaration. Thus interested states may take cognisance of unilateral declarations and place confidence in them, and are entitled to require that the obligation thus created be respected.[135]

The ICJ held that a number of communications made by senior government officers speaking for France created binding legal obligations for that country. States which make unilateral declarations may establish binding environmental obligations. Examples include: the declaration by the UK that it would cease to permit the disposal of sewage sludge in the North Sea by the end of 1998;[136] the joint declaration by the EC and its member states that they would stabilise their emissions of carbon dioxide at 1990 levels by the year 2000;[137] and the declaration by Japan that it would prohibit driftnet fishing by the end of 1993.[138] It is important to recall, however, that these and other such declarations need to be considered carefully, as they are often drafted to allow discretion in the act required by a state, or may only be intended to have political or domestic effects.[139] Other 'general principles' which have relevance for environmental

---

[133] B. Cheng, *General Principles*, 130.

[134] Oppenheim, vol. I, 408 and 585; see generally chapter 10 below.

[135] *Nuclear Tests* Cases (1974) ICJ Reports 267, 268.   [136] Chapter 9, p. 426 below.

[137] Chapter 15, p. 758 below.   [138] See generally chapter 11, especially pp. 588–9 below.

[139] *Military and Paramilitary Activities* Case (1986) ICJ Reports 132, holding that a governmental statement did not involve a legally binding commitment; see also the *Case Concerning the Frontier Dispute (Burkina Faso and Mali)* (1986) ICJ Reports 554, 573 and 876.

matters include: the obligation to make reparation for the breach of an engagement;[140] the principle that a person may not plead his or her own wrong;[141] the principle that no one may be a judge in his or her own suit;[142] and 'elementary considerations of humanity'[143] and 'fundamental general principles of humanitarian law'.[144]

Equity

It is also important to consider the role of 'equity', which allows the international community to take into account considerations of justice and fairness in the establishment, operation or application of a rule of international law. In the *North Sea Continental Shelf* cases, the ICJ described the concept of equity as being a 'direct emanation of the idea of justice' and a 'general principle directly applicable as law' which should be applied as part of international law 'to balance up the various considerations which it regards as relevant in order to produce an equitable result'.[145] In that case, the ICJ held there were no rigid rules as to the exact weight to be attached to each element in a case, and that equity was not an exercise of discretion or conciliation or the operation of distributive justice.[146] The ICJ has linked equity with acquiescence and estoppel,[147] and applied it to the conservation of fishery resources to achieve an 'equitable solution derived from the applicable law'.[148]

Equity can therefore operate as a part of international law to inform the application of a particular rule. It may also be applied by the ICJ to decide a case *ex aequo et bono*, if the parties to a dispute agree, in application of Article 38(2) of the Statute of the Court, although no such judgment has yet been given by the ICJ. As described in chapter 6 below, many environmental treaties refer to or incorporate equity or equitable principles.[149] In applying equity in these treaties, it will be proper to establish its meaning in the context of its use in a particular treaty. Since, however, treaties rarely provide a working definition of equity, states, international organisations and international courts and tribunals may, ultimately, have to refer back to the general concept as interpreted and applied by the ICJ and other international tribunals.

---

[140] *Chorzow Factory* case and *Gabcikovo-Nagymaros* case, chapter 18, p. 873 below.

[141] *Jurisdiction of the Courts of Danzig*, PCIJ Ser. B, No. 15, 27.

[142] *Mosul* Case, PCIJ Ser. B, No. 12, 32.   [143] *Corfu Channel* Case (1949) ICJ Reports 22.

[144] *Military and Paramilitary Activities* Case (1986) ICJ Reports 113–15 and 129–30.

[145] (1982) ICJ Reports 18. See also the Individual Opinion of Judge Hudson in the *Diversion of the Waters from the Meuse* Case, recognising equity as 'a part of international law': (1937) PCIJ Ser. A/B, No. 70, 76–7.

[146] *Ibid.*   [147] *Gulf of Maine* Case (1984) ICJ Reports 246 at 305.

[148] *Fisheries Jurisdiction* Cases (1974) ICJ Reports 3 at 33; chapter 11, pp. 567–8 below.

[149] Chapter 6, pp. 261–3 below.

Subsidiary sources

R. Jennings and A. Watts (eds.), *Oppenheim's International Law* (1992, 9th edn),
vol. I; M. Shaw, *International Law* (1997, 4th edn); P. Daillier and A. Pellet, *Droit
International Public* (2002, 7th edn); I. Brownlie, *Principles of Public International
Law* (2003, 6th edn); P.-M. Dupuy, *Droit International Public* (2002, 6th edn)

The main subsidiary sources are the decisions of courts and tribunals and the
writings of jurists. The ICJ has only recently come to deal with the substantive
aspects of international environmental protection: in the *Nuclear Tests* cases
the dispute was settled by the ICJ before the merits could be addressed. The
ICJ has considered the conservation of fisheries resources (*Icelandic Fisheries*
cases), guiding principles of general application (*Corfu Channel* case, *North
Sea Continental Shelf* cases), the protection of the environment in times of war
and armed conflict (Advisory Opinion on *The Legality of the Threat or Use of
Nuclear Weapons*) and general norms of international environmental law and
principles governing the law of shared watercourses (*Gabcikovo-Nagymaros*
case).[150] Other international courts dealing with environmental issues are the
European Court of Justice (which has been called upon to interpret and apply
EC environmental law and international agreements such as 1973 CITES, the
1979 Berne Convention and the GATT), the European Court of Human Rights,
the WTO Appellate Body and the International Tribunal for the Law of the Sea,
as well as panels established under the Canada–US Free Trade Agreement.[151]
Awards of international arbitral tribunals have also contributed to the development of international environmental law. Four stand out in particular: the
1893 decision in the *Pacific Fur Seals Arbitration*, the 1941 decision in the much
cited *Trail Smelter* case, the 1957 award of the *Lac Lanoux Arbitration*, and the
2003 award in the *OSPAR Information* case.[152] National courts and tribunals are
increasingly faced with the task of interpreting international obligations in this
field, and the jurisprudence of these tribunals is becoming an increasingly important source of reference in the development of international environmental
law and policy.[153]

The writings of jurists have played a less significant role in developing international environmental law. The *Trail Smelter* case relied on the writings of
Professor Eagleton, and there is some evidence that international jurisprudence
on environmental issues has been influenced by academic and other writings.[154]

---

[150] Chapter 10, pp. 469–77 below.
[151] Chapter 5, p. 203 below; chapter 19, pp. 952–85 below.
[152] Chapter 11, pp. 561–6 below; chapter 8, pp. 318–19 below; chapter 10, pp. 463–4 below;
chapter 17, pp. 857–8 below. At the time of writing, proceedings are also pending before
an UNCLOS Annex VII arbitral tribunal (the *MOX* case).
[153] Chapter 8, pp. 318–19 below.
[154] See e.g. the opinions of Judge Weeramantry in the *Nuclear Tests* case (1995) ICJ Reports
34 *et seq.* and in the *Gabcikovo-Nagymaros* Case (1997) ICJ Reports 92–4.

Resolutions of groups of international jurists acting through the International Law Association and the Institut de Droit International have contributed in important ways to the development of subsequent treaty obligations, particularly in the field of water and atmospheric pollution, as will be seen in the chapters which follow.

Introduction to regulatory approaches

The principles and rules of international environmental law established by treaty and other sources of international law are applied to a range of regulatory techniques. These can be divided into two types: traditional forms of direct regulation (frequently referred to as 'command-and-control'), and techniques which make use of economic incentives (referred to as 'economic instruments').[155] Awareness of the limited effectiveness of international environmental regulation has resulted in numerous proposals for a new regulatory approach, referred to as integrated pollution prevention (or control), which aims to adopt a more comprehensive approach to regulation. It is beginning to gain favour at the national level and, at least in Europe, at the international level also.

The techniques relied upon are themselves the subject of political and ideological differences. The 1990 Ministerial Declaration of the Second World Climate Conference illustrates the tensions which exist as to the proper balance to be achieved in the use of two types of regulation, stating that:

> Appropriate economic instruments may offer the potential for achieving environmental improvements in a cost-effective manner. The adoption of any form of economic or regulatory measures would require careful and substantive analyses. We *recommend* that relevant policies make use of economic instruments appropriate to each country's socio-economic conditions in conjunction with a balanced mix of regulatory approaches.

The Rio Declaration also reflects support for a balanced approach. Principle 10 indicates that states should enact effective environmental legislation, and that 'environmental standards, management objectives and priorities should reflect the environmental and developmental context to which they apply'. Principle 16, the use of economic instruments, suggests only that national authorities should 'endeavour to promote' their use. It is therefore likely that the international use of command-and-control regulation will remain the primary approach, as reflected in recent instruments such as the Climate Change and

---

[155] For an illustrative list of regulatory technique, see Annex II to the 1985 Montreal Guidelines on Land-Based Sources of Pollution, chapter 8, p. 430 below. See also D. Driesen, 'Choosing Environmental Instruments in a Transnational Context', 27 *Ecology Law Quarterly* 1 (2001).

Biodiversity Conventions, and supplemented (where a consensus exists) with economic instruments.

Direct regulation

Under direct regulation ('command-and-control') the state instructs environmental protection or pollution control bodies to adopt and apply standards which are generally applicable in a uniform manner to their addressees. Once they have been 'commanded', the standards are enforced (or controlled) by public authorities (or, in some jurisdictions, by private persons as well). The environmental standards fall into four categories: environmental quality standards; product standards; emission standards; and technology or process standards.

Environmental quality standards

Environmental quality standards prescribe the levels of pollution, nuisance or environmental interference which are permitted and which must not be exceeded in a given environment or particular environmental media. International treaties and other acts frequently use this approach to environmental regulation. The earliest environmental treaties relating to the protection of flora and fauna provide for the designation of areas which are protected from environmental interference. Under the 1940 Western Hemisphere Convention, for example, 'strict wilderness reserves' are to be kept virtually inviolate and the quality of their flora and fauna are to be kept, as far as practicable, pristine.[156] National parks, on the other hand, may be subjected to some environmental interference, although commercial activity is not allowed.[157] International environmental law establishes a range of environmental quality standards which vary from the absolute prohibition of particular activities in order to maintain environmental and natural resources free from any change, to the more limited acceptance that certain changes in the quality of a given environment are inevitable and may be tolerated as a matter of law. Examples of international acts intended to maintain the environment or parts of it absolutely free from further interference by particular substances or activities include: the prohibitions on the dumping of certain hazardous substances at sea;[158] the moratorium on dumping of all radioactive waste at sea;[159] the moratorium on the killing or taking of whales for commercial purposes;[160] and the prohibitions on mining and related activities in the Antarctic,[161] interference with flora and fauna in certain protected areas,[162] the production and consumption of certain ozone-depleting substances,[163] the production and consumption of certain chemicals,[164]

[156] Art. IV.   [157] Art. III.   [158] Chapter 9, pp. 416–23 and 423–5 below.
[159] Chapter 9, p. 420 below.   [160] Chapter 11, pp. 592–5 below.
[161] Chapter 14, pp. 721–6 below.   [162] See generally chapter 11 below.
[163] Chapter 8, pp. 345–57 below.   [164] Chapter 12, pp. 628–30 below.

incineration at sea,[165] and the import of hazardous waste into Africa and other parts of the developing world.[166]

Other environmental quality standards recognise that certain levels of environmental interference are the inevitable consequence of human activity. Rather than prohibit the activity and attempt to establish absolute protection of the environment at its existing level, these standards aim to establish a level beyond which pollution, nuisance or environmental interference is not permitted. Early examples of this approach include the limited protection given to certain areas under wildlife treaties. More recently, the same approach sets targets for acceptable levels of environmental interference by setting 'critical loads' which can be translated into individual country targets.[167] Other examples include: 30 per cent cuts in atmospheric emissions of sulphur dioxide for all EC states;[168] differentiated cuts of sulphur dioxide emissions of up to 70 per cent by EC member states;[169] the general objective of stabilising levels of greenhouse gas concentrations in the atmosphere at 'a level that would prevent dangerous anthropogenic interference with the climate system';[170] and maximum admissible levels of concentrations in the marine environment.[171] A different approach to achieving the same objective is reflected in the 1993 Lugano Convention which imposes strict liability for an operator carrying out certain hazardous activities, but allows a defence where the operator can prove that damage was caused 'by pollution at tolerable levels under local relevant circumstances'. Implicit in this approach is the recognition that environmental quality standards will have been maintained until a threshold of intolerability has been reached. The Convention does not provide guidance as to when such a threshold will be crossed.

Product standards

Product standards establish levels for pollutants or nuisances which must not be exceeded in the manufacture or emissions of a product, or specify the properties or characteristics of design of a product, or are concerned with the ways in which a product is used. This approach was only infrequently applied, as it required a degree of specificity which would have been unusual for an international treaty. Recently, however, there has been an increased tendency to target specific industrial activities even at the international level. Examples of

---

[165] Chapter 9, pp. 409–12 below; chapter 13, pp. 686–7 below.
[166] Chapter 13, pp. 695–6 below.
[167] 1988 NO$_x$ Protocol, Art. 2; chapter 8, pp. 328–9 below.
[168] 1985 SO$_2$ Protocol; chapter 8, pp. 332–3 below.
[169] 1988 EC Large Combustion Directive, chapter 8, pp. 336–9 below.
[170] 1992 Climate Change Convention, Art. 2, chapter 8, pp. 357–68 below.
[171] EC Water Quality Directives, chapter 15, pp. 768–79 below; 1998 Sintra Ministerial Declaration (radioactive substances), chapter 9, p. 435 below.

product standards in international agreements include: the permitted use of certain ozone-depleting substances in manufacture;[172] the use of parts of endangered species in manufacturing;[173] and the construction of new oil tankers with 'double hulls'.[174] Product standards also include specifications relating to testing, packaging, marking, labelling and distribution.[175]

Emission standards

Emission standards set levels for pollutants or nuisances which are not to be exceeded in emissions from installations or activities. Examples of their international use include atmospheric emissions from aircraft,[176] automobiles[177] and large industrial utilities.[178]

Process standards

Process standards can be developed and applied to fixed installations and to mobile installations and activities. Two types are frequently used: 'installation design standards', which determine the requirements to be met in the design and construction of installations to protect the environment; and 'operating standards', which determine the requirements to be met in the course of activities and the operation of installations. Examples of process standards in international agreements include: processes for the treatment of municipal waste[179] and the incineration of hazardous waste;[180] methods and means of conducting fisheries activities[181] (such as driftnet fishing)[182] and the development of biotechnology.[183] 'Process standards' involve the application of particular types of technology, technique and practice. Many international environmental agreements require their use, although the permissibility of applying national standards to processes carried out beyond a state's jurisdiction is subject to

---

[172] 1987 Montreal Protocol, chapter 8, pp. 345–57 below.

[173] 1973 CITES, chapter 11, pp. 505–15 below.

[174] 1991 amendments to MARPOL 73/78, chapter 9, pp. 440–5 below.

[175] Chapter 12, pp. 626–7 below; 1985 UNEP London Guidelines, chapter 12, pp. 633–5 below.

[176] Chapter 8, pp. 341–2 below.

[177] ECE Regulations Concerning Gaseous Pollutant Emissions from Motor Vehicles, chapter 8, p. 324 below; see chapter 15, pp. 758–60 below.

[178] Chapter 8, pp. 336–9 below.

[179] 1991 EC Urban Waste Water Directive, chapter 15, pp. 776–8 below.

[180] 1991 Antarctic Environment Protocol, chapter 14, pp. 721–6 below.

[181] 1980 CCAMLR, Chapter 14, pp. 714–15 below. See also the views of the WTO Appellate Body, chapter 19, pp. 965–73 below.

[182] 1989 Driftnet Convention, chapter 11, pp. 588–9 below.

[183] EC Directives, chapter 12, pp. 658–62 below; 2000 Biosafety Protocol, chapter 12, pp. 653–8 below.

limits under WTO law.[184] Examples of obligations imposed upon states include the requirement that they ensure the use of: 'best available techniques';[185] or 'best environmental practice';[186] or 'best available technology';[187] or 'best available technology not entailing excessive cost';[188] or 'clean production methods';[189] or environmentally sound management;[190] or best available technology which is economically feasible.[191]

The techniques for implementing these four types of standard at the national level demand a central role for public authorities. It is they who must set the standards (increasingly by implementing international standards), and implement them through authorising, permitting, licensing and receiving information from potential users. Public authorities are also required, under many international environmental agreements, to enforce international standards at the national level through appropriate administrative, judicial and other means.[192] Environmental impact assessment and the broad dissemination of information are other techniques which are increasingly used to ensure the implementation of environmental quality, process and product standards.

Economic instruments[193]

OECD, *Economic Instruments for Environmental Protection* (1989); 'Report of the Working Group of Experts from the Member States on the Use of Economic and Fiscal Instruments in EC Environmental Policy (1990)', 14 *Boston College International and Comparative Law Review* 447 (1991); R. Hahn and R. Stavins, 'Incentive-Based Environmental Regulation: A New Era from an Old Idea?', 18 *Ecology Law Quarterly* 1 (1991); OECD, *Guidelines for the Application of Economic Instruments in Environmental Policy* (1991); E. Rehbinder, 'Environmental Regulation Through Fiscal and Economic Incentives in a Federalist System', 20 *Ecology Law Quarterly* 57 (1993); R. Wolfrum (ed.), *Enforcing Environmental Standards: Economic Mechanisms as Viable Means* (1996); P. Galizzi, 'Economic Instruments as Tools

---

[184] See GATT Panel Decision in *Yellow-Fin Tuna* Case, 1991, chapter 19, pp. 953–61 below.
[185] 1992 OSPAR Convention, Art. 2(3)(b) and Appendix 1.
[186] 1992 OSPAR Convention, Art. 2(3)(b) and Appendix 1; 1992 Black Sea Convention, Art. 3(3) and Annex II.
[187] 1992 Baltic Convention, Art. 3(3) and Annex II.
[188] Council Directive 84/360/EEC on the combating of air pollution from industrial plants, OJ L188, 16 July 1984, 20, Art. 4.
[189] 1991 Bamako Convention, Art. 4(3)(g); 1992 OSPAR Convention, Art. 2(3)(b).
[190] 1989 Basel Convention, Arts. 2(8) and 4(2)(b).
[191] 1979 LRTAP Convention, Art. 6; 1988 NO$_x$ Protocol, Art. 2.
[192] Chapter 5, p. 176 below. Sometimes, non-state actors are also granted an enforcement role: *ibid.*
[193] For an early initiative, see 'Report of the Working Group of Experts from the EC Member States on the Use of Economic and Fiscal Instruments in EC Environmental Policy', 14 BCICLR 447 (1991).

for the Protection of the International Environment', 6 *European Environmental Law Review* 155 (1997); K. Bosselmann and B. Richardson, *Environmental Justice and Market Mechanisms* (1999); R. Stewart and P. Sands, 'The Legal and Institutional Framework for a Plurilateral Greenhouse Gas Emissions Trading System', in UNCTAD, *Greenhouse Gas Market Perspectives, Trade and Investment Implications of Climate Change* (2001), 82; R. Stewart, 'The Importance of Law and Economics for European Environmental Law', 2 *Yearbook of European Environmental Law* 856 (2002).

The use of economic policy instruments to protect the environment has been under discussion for several years as the international community addresses the fact that many environmental regulations have not resulted in environmentally cleaner behaviour, technologies or products. It is believed that current mechanisms have failed to provide adequate economic incentives to limit activities which are environmentally damaging and have failed to achieve their environmental objectives. The use of economic instruments is premised on a belief that the market can be used to provide incentives to guide human behaviour:

> If environmental resources are properly valued, the costs of using the environment will be taken fully into account in private economic decision-making. This implies that environmental resources are used in 'sustainable' quantities, provided that their prices are based on their scarcity and place an appropriate value on non-renewable resources. Economic instruments are meant to correct current market prices by internalising environmental costs which are treated by the market mechanisms as external.[194]

Economic instruments 'affect through the market mechanism costs and benefits of alternative actions open to economic agents, with the effect of influencing behaviour in a way which is favourable for the environment'.[195]

The use of economic instruments at the international level to supplement, or supplant, regulatory approaches to environmental protection is supported, at least in principle, by a growing number of states. The practical application is nevertheless limited. In so far as economic instruments are defined by reference to their attempts to use the market to internalise environmental costs, the polluter-pays principle first developed by the OECD and the EC in the early 1970s can be seen as a precursor to more recent discussions and proposals.[196] Explicit references in international acts to 'economic instruments' is a relatively recent phenomenon. In April 1990, the Presidency of the EC Environment Council concluded that EC Ministers 'acknowledged the value of supplementing existing regulatory instruments . . . by the use of economic and

---

[194] *Ibid.*, 453–4.   [195] *Ibid.*, 455.
[196] Chapter 6, pp. 279–84 below. On subsidies and competition, see chapter 19, pp. 1010–16 below.

fiscal instruments'.[197] The following month, the UNECE Bergen Ministerial Declaration stated that to support sustainable development it would be necessary 'to make more extensive use of economic instruments in conjunction with . . . regulatory approaches'.[198] By November 1990, the Ministerial Declaration of the Second World Climate Conference had found support for similar language at the global level.

Support for the use of economic instruments can also be found in other regional and global declarations such as the Rio Declaration. Agenda 21 refers frequently to the need to develop economic instruments. Support for the use of economic instruments is also reflected in soft law instruments and treaties. Examples include the 1992 Climate Change Convention, which requires developed country parties to co-ordinate relevant economic instruments,[199] and the 1992 Biodiversity Convention, which although it does not specifically mention economic instruments, calls on parties to 'adopt economically and socially sound measures that act as incentives for the conservation and sustainable use of components of biological diversity'.[200]

What are the different types of economic instruments available? The 1991 OECD Council Recommendation on the Use of Economic Instruments in Environmental Policy provided the clearest guidance yet adopted at the international level on the types of instrument the use of which is being envisaged in future years.[201] It recommends that member countries make greater use of economic instruments, improve the allocation and efficient use of natural and environmental resources, and make efforts to reach further agreement at an international level on the use of economic instruments.[202] The different types of economic instruments envisaged are set out in the Guidelines and Considerations for the Use of Economic Instruments in Environmental Policy contained in the Annex to the Recommendation. They include charges and taxes, marketable permits, deposit-refund systems and financial assistance. Other types of economic instrument not dealt with in the Recommendation include enforcement incentives, administrative charges, liability and compensation for damage, trade measures and consumer information incentives, as well as non-compliance fees and performance bonds. The permissibility of subsidies for environmentally beneficial activities is also premised upon an economic approach to environmental regulation.

---

[197] Quoted in 'Report of the Working Group of Experts from the EC Member States on the use of Economic and Fiscal Instruments in EC Environmental Policy', 14 BCICLR 447 at 448 (1991).

[198] 7 May 1990; see also 1985 Montreal Guidelines, Annex II.

[199] Art. 4(2)(e).   [200] Art. 11.

[201] C(90)177 (1991). See also the Report of the Working Party on Economic and Environmental Policy Integration, 'Economic Instruments for Pollution Control and Natural Resources Management in OECD Countries: A Survey' (1999), ENV/EPOC/ GEEI(98)35/REV1/FINAL.

[202] Para. I(i)–(iii).

Charges and taxes

The rationale behind charges and taxes is that they create an incentive for polluters to limit activities which can be harmful to the environment, such as emissions, the generation of waste, and the excessive use of natural resources. The difference between a charge and a tax reflects the different way in which the revenues are allocated: tax revenues are added to the general public budget, while charge revenues are used specifically to finance environmental measures. Charges can also have different purposes. Emission charges, which are levied on all dischargers, can be levied on discharges of effluents and gases and can be calculated on the basis of the quality and/or quantity of the pollution load. User charges are paid for services rendered by authorities, such as the collection and removal of municipal waste water and solid and hazardous wastes, and are only paid by persons who receive, or are associated with, the services.

Although widely used at the national level, charges and taxes have not yet been the subject of international legal measures. In May 1992, the first international environmental tax was proposed by the EC, to contribute to the implementation of its commitment to stabilise carbon dioxide emissions by the year 2000 at 1990 levels. The EC Commission proposal was to harmonise the introduction in the EC member states of a tax on certain fossil fuel products (coal, lignite, peat, natural gas, mineral oils, ethyl and methyl alcohol, electricity and heat),[203] levying the tax on the basis of carbon dioxide emissions and energy content.[204] The introduction of the tax was, however, conditional upon the introduction by the other OECD members of similar taxes or of measures having a financial impact equivalent to the draft Directive, and was to take account of issues of international competitiveness. The Directive was not adopted.

Joint implementation and tradeable permits

The suggestion that international law might encourage the use of tradeable permits is drawn from developments in the United States under the 1990 amendments to the Clean Air Act.[205] According to this approach, regions or utilities are granted a limited number of pollution rights; if they manage to use less than the amount allocated to them, they may sell their excess to another region or utility. Although the idea has generated some interest, the first international scheme was only adopted in 2002, by the EC. Early environmental agreements

---

[203] EC Commission Proposal for a Council Directive Introducing a Tax on Carbon Dioxide Emissions and Energy, COM (92) 226 final, 30 June 1992, Arts. 1(1) and 3(1) and (2). The draft excludes certain products: *ibid.*, Art. 3.

[204] *Ibid.*, Arts. 1(1) and 9(1).

[205] USC §§ 7401–671 (1988) and amendments in Supp. III to USC (1991). See J. Nash and R. Revesz, 'Markets and Geography: Designing Marketable Permit Schemes to Control Local and Regional Pollutants', 28 *Ecology Law Quarterly* 569 (2001).

allowed parties jointly to implement programmes and measures without specifying any criteria or conditions according to which this is to be achieved,[206] and
since they did not establish specific pollution limits there was no intention for
inter-state trading. The first elements of possible trading can be found in certain fisheries agreements (under which 'trade' in quotas may take place) and in
Article 2(7) of the 1987 Montreal Protocol, which allows member states of a regional economic integration organisation (which currently might only include
the EC) to agree to 'jointly fulfil their obligations respecting consumption' of
certain ozone-depleting substances provided that their total combined calculated level of consumption does not exceed the levels required by the Montreal
Protocol. The 1992 Climate Change Convention allows developed country parties and other parties included in Annex 1 to implement policies and measures
required under Articles 4(2)(a) and (b) 'jointly with other parties', subject to
decisions taken by the conference of the parties at its first session 'regarding
criteria for joint implementation'.[207] The language is unclear on a number of
points. Is it envisaged that parties with specific targets and timetables under
Article 4(2)(a) and (b) should be able to implement their commitments with
parties which have no such targets? And may joint implementation under the
Convention proceed in the absence of criteria established by the conference of
the parties? Interpretation of these provisions on the basis of an effort to ensure
the long-term effectiveness of the Convention suggests that the answer to both
questions should be no. A positive answer to the first question would, in effect,
allow developed country parties to bypass their targets by supporting efforts in
countries with no targets. While this may, over the short term, be cost-effective
for developed countries, it may not, over the longer term, meet the commitment to be guided by principles of equity or to meet the ultimate objective of
the Convention, as set out in Article 2. These questions have been overtaken
by the 1997 Kyoto Protocol, which provides more detailed provisions on joint
implementation.[208] The Kyoto Protocol also provides for the emergence of a
system of tradeable permits (emission reduction units), the details of which
will be elaborated by the conference of the parties at its first meeting.[209]

---

[206] 1974 Paris Convention, Art. 4(2).

[207] Art. 4(2)(a) and (d); see chapter 8, pp. 357–68 below.

[208] Art. 4; see A. Gosseries, 'The Legal Architecture of Joint Implementation', 7 NYUELJ 49,
(1999).

[209] Art. 5. See generally J. C. Fort and C. A. Faur, 'Can Emissions Trading Work Beyond a
National Program?: Some Practical Observations on the Available Tools', 18 *University of
Pennsylvania Journal of International Economic Law* 463 (1997); J. R. Nash, 'Too Much
Market? Conflict Between Tradeable Pollution Allowances and the "Polluter Pays"
Principle', 24 *Harvard Environmental Law Review* 465 (2000); R. B. Stewart, J. L.
Connaughton and L. C. Foxhall, 'Designing an International Greenhouse Gas Emis-
sions Trading System', 15 *Natural Resources and Environment* 160 (2001); J. Yelin-Kefer,
'Warming Up to an International Greenhouse Gas Market: Lessons from the US Acid
Rain Experience', 20 *Stanford Environmental Law Journal* 221 (2001).

In March 2003, the EC Council adopted a common position on a Directive establishing a scheme for greenhouse gas emission allowance trading within the EC, which is intended 'to promote reductions of greenhouse gas emissions in a cost-effective and economically efficient manner' and which it would be desirable to link with project-based mechanisms under the Kyoto Protocol, including joint implementation and the Clean Development Mechanism.[210] When it enters into force in December 2003, the Directive will establish the first international trading arrangement. The Directive demonstrates the potential complexities – and degree of intrusion – which will underlie the operation of such arrangements. Its operation is premised on the allocation of allowances[211] to operators of installations involving designated activities and resulting in emissions of certain greenhouse gases.[212] It requires each member state to en-sure that with effect from 1 January 2005 all designated activities resulting in the emission of the designated gases must be authorised by a permit granted by a competent authority, which will be subject to certain conditions.[213] Each member state must develop a national allocation plan stating the total quan-tity of allowances it will allocate for a three-year period from 1 January 2005 and for a five-year period beginning 1 January 2008 (and subsequent five-year periods), consistent with its obligations to limit its emissions pursuant to the 1997 Kyoto Protocol and implementing EC law, and in accordance with the criteria set forth in Article 9.[214] Allowances for the first period (three years) will be allocated free of charge, and 90 per cent of allowances for the first five-year period are to be allocated free of charge, and will be valid for emissions during the period in which they are issued.[215] The allowances will be trans-ferable between persons within the EU, and between persons within the EU and third countries listed in Annex B to the Kyoto Protocol which have rati-fied the Protocol and which have entered into agreements with the EU on the mutual recognition of allowances.[216] Provision is made for a certain number of

---

[210] 9 December 2002, http://europa.eu.int/comm/environment/climat/
030318commonposition_en.pdf, Arts. 1 and 26(3).

[211] An allowance is 'an allowance to emit one tonne of carbon dioxide equivalent during a specified period' valid only for the purposes of the Directive and transferable only in accordance with the Directive: Art. 3(a).

[212] Art. 2. The activities are: energy; production and processing of ferrous metals; the mineral industry; and other activities (production of pulp and paper) (Annex I); the gases are carbon dioxide, methane, nitrous oxide, hydrofluorocarbons, perfluorocarbons and sul-phur hexafluoride (Annex II). Provision is made for the unilateral inclusion of additional activities and gases (Art. 23(a)) and for pooling of installations (Art. 25(b)).

[213] Arts. 4–7. Art. 8 provides for co-ordination with Directive 96/61 on integrated pollution control (chapter 15, pp. 754–5 below). In accordance with Art. 25(a), certain installations may be temporarily excluded.

[214] Arts. 9(1) and 11, and Annex III, para. 1. Specific reference is made to the requirements of EC competition law: see chapter 20, p. 1010 below.

[215] Arts. 10 and 13(1).   [216] Arts. 12(1) and 24.

allowances to be surrendered (and cancelled) each year by the operator of each installation (to cover emissions during the previous year), and for the cancellation of allowances which are no longer valid.[217] The EC Commission will adopt guidelines on the monitoring and reporting of emissions, and member states will be required to ensure that emissions are duly monitored and that reports submitted by operators are verified.[218] Member states will lay down rules on penalties for infringements of implementing provisions, which must be effective, proportionate and dissuasive, as well as payment of an excess emissions penalty where an operator does not surrender sufficient allowances by 30 April each year to cover its emissions during the previous year.[219] Each member state is required to designate a competent authority, and to establish a registry to ensure the accurate accounting of the issue, holding, transfer and cancellation of allowances, and the Commission will designate a central authority to maintain an independent transaction log in relation to allowances, and to conduct automated checks.[220] The Commission may make a proposal to amend the list of activities and gases by 31 December 2004, and must report on the application of the Directive by 30 June 2006.

Deposit-refund systems

Deposit-refund systems require a deposit to be paid on potentially polluting products, such as batteries. bottles and other packaging. The return of the product or its residuals is intended to avoid pollution and is compensated by a refund of the deposit. The system is frequently used at the national level but has not yet been used at the international level. In the *Danish Bottles* case, a Danish deposit-and-return system was challenged by the EC Commission and other member states as incompatible with the rules on the free movement of goods. The ECJ upheld the deposit-and-return system as having lawful objectives of environmental protection despite its limitation on the application of the EC rules on free movement of goods (Article 30).[221]

Subsidies

Governments often seek to justify the grant of subsidies which might otherwise be unlawful on the grounds that they bring environmental benefits. They can nevertheless distort competition and run against the inherent purpose of the polluter-pays principle and may, on those grounds, fall foul of international

---

[217] Arts. 12(3) and 13(2) and (3).   [218] Arts. 14 and 15 and Annexes IV and V.

[219] Art. 16. In the first three-year period, the excess emissions penalty is 40 euros per tonne of carbon dioxide equivalent emitted, rising to 100 euros per tonne in the first five-year period: Art. 16(3) and (4).

[220] Arts. 19 and 20.   [221] Chapter 19, pp. 987–90 below.

competition and trade rules. International practice (in the EC and under the WTO) on the environmental aspects of subsidies is considered in chapter 19 below.

Enforcement incentives

Enforcement incentives, such as non-compliance fees and performance bonds, are closely linked to fiscal regulation. Non-compliance fees penalise polluters who exceed prescribed environmental standards, and performance bonds are payments to authorities which are returned when the polluter performs in accordance with its licence. Enforcement incentives have not been the subject of international legal measures, although recent developments suggest that they may be emerging. In November 1992, the parties to the Montreal Protocol adopted an indicative list of measures that might be taken by a meeting of the parties in respect of non-compliance with the Protocol which included, *inter alia*, suspending specific rights and privileges under the Protocol such as those relating to the receipt of funds under the financial mechanism.[222] The approach has been followed in other multilateral environmental agreements.[223]

Liability and compensation for damage

One of the objectives of the rules of international law establishing civil and state liability for environmental and related damage is the establishment of economic incentives for complying with international environmental obligations. As will be seen in chapter 18, however, the limited state of development of the rules of state liability, and the low financial limits on liability established by most of the international civil liability conventions do not properly fulfil the incentive functions.

Trade measures

Regulations and prohibitions on international trade were among the first economic instruments to be used at the international level in aid of environmental protection objectives, and they are considered in detail in chapter 19 below. They are designed to influence behaviour (i.e. not killing endangered species or not producing or consuming certain harmful substances) by limiting the availability of markets for certain products or by making the availability of markets dependent upon participation in an international regulatory arrangement. Despite their evident attractiveness to government environmental departments

---

[222] Fourth Report of the Parties to the Montreal Protocol. UNEP/OzL.Pro.4/15, 25 November 1992, 48 (Annex V); see chapter 5, pp. 203–5 below.

[223] Chapter 5, p. 205 below.

as an efficient and effective means to achieve environmental objectives, trade measures remain controversial, and are subject to a trade regime under the WTO which raises questions as to the circumstances in which they may be relied upon.

Investment incentives

More recently, increased attention is being given to identifying incentives for directing investment in clean technologies towards developing countries and countries with economies in transition. The most elaborate arrangement is the Clean Development Mechanism established under the Kyoto Protocol, which will provide credits to states whose companies invest in certain greenhouse gas reduction activities abroad.[224] Other arrangements aim to provide financial resources to developing countries to invest in certain clean technologies pursuant to the ozone and other international agreements.[225]

Environmental agreements

Alongside legislative and economic instruments, there has also been a growing use of 'environmental agreements', i.e. voluntary agreements between industrial undertakings which supplement regulatory requirements. A leading example is the agreement between associations of European, Japanese and Korean car manufacturers on the reduction of carbon dioxide emissions from passenger cars, which has been acknowledged by EC Commission recommendations.[226] In 1996, the EC Commission published a Communication on Environmental Agreements, which identified potential benefits as including a pro-active approach by industry, cost-effectiveness and tailor-made solutions, and the faster achievement of environmental objectives.[227] In 1999, the OECD published a survey of environmental agreements, identifying more than 300 in the EU alone.[228] In 2002, the EC Commission published a further Communication, identifying substantive and procedural criteria for the use of environmental agreements at the EU level, in the context of self-regulation (where economic and other actors establish on a voluntary basis in order to regulate and organise their activities) and co-regulation (where the legislator establishes the essential elements of the regulation and the economic and other actors then agree on the means for giving effect to it).[229]

---

[224] Chapter 8, p. 373 below.   [225] Chapter 20, p. 1021 below.

[226] Recommendations 1999/125/EC, 2000/303/EC and 2000/304/EC.

[227] COM (96) 561 final, 2 July 1996.

[228] OECD, *Voluntary Approaches for Environment Policy – An Assessment* (1999).

[229] Environmental Agreements at the Community Level, COM (2002) 412 final, 17 July 2002. The substantive criteria include: cost-effectiveness, representativeness, quantified and staged objectives, involvement of civil society, monitoring and reporting, sustainability, and incentive compatibility.

Consumer information incentives

Consumer information incentives, which set out the environmental performance of companies, such as eco-labelling and eco-auditing, are designed to capitalise on the perception that many consumers take environmental considerations into account when buying products and services. In 1991, the EC adopted the first international eco-labelling scheme,[230] and the compatibility of national eco-labelling schemes with WTO rules and other international trade agreements is under consideration at the WTO and has been the subject of an early GATT case.[231]

Integrated pollution control

The continuous increase in pollution levels and environmental degradation provides evidence of the fundamental failure of traditional law-making to change human behaviour and patterns of production and consumption. The traditional approach to environmental regulation has been to address particular activities, substances or environmental media (air, water, soil and biota), and to focus pollution control and prevention efforts on each environmental medium. In reality, different substances and activities can move among, and have effects upon, a range of environmental media as they travel along a 'pathway' from a particular source to a particular receptor, and in that process may accumulate in the environment. The regulation and establishment of controls over releases of a substance to one environmental medium can lead to that substance being shifted to another environmental medium. This is recognised by a number of international environmental agreements which include provisions requiring parties not to transfer pollution or environmental damage elsewhere in the implementation of their treaty obligations.[232]

In the early 1990s, some states recognised that efforts to address each environmental medium separately may not be an efficient or effective way to protect the environment. Beginning at the national level, some began to rely upon 'integrated pollution prevention (or control)', which was defined in 1991 by the OECD Council as:

> taking into account the effects of activities and substances on the environment as a whole and the whole commercial and environmental life-cycles of substances when assessing the risks they pose and when developing and implementing controls to limit their release.[233]

---

[230] Chapter 17, pp. 860–2 below.
[231] Chapter 19, pp. 953–61 below; chapter 17, pp. 860–2 below.
[232] 1974 Baltic Convention, Art. 3(2); 1982 UNCLOS, Art. 195.
[233] OECD Council Recommendation on Integrated Pollution Prevention and Control, C(90)164/FINAL (1991), para. I(a).

This broader holistic approach to environmental regulation and protection is now reflected in a number of international instruments, including the attempts by the EC to take a 'cradle-to-grave' approach to eco-labelling and to address 'waste streams' in its developing waste prevention policy.[234] In 1992, the Oslo and Paris Commissions endorsed this approach by addressing particular industrial sectors and activities.[235] In 1996, the EU adopted the first international rules on integrated pollution control.[236]

The EU rules are premised on the approach recommended in the 1991 OECD Council Recommendation, which called on OECD member countries to support integrated pollution prevention and control by addressing impediments to an integrated approach, removing those impediments, and adopting appropriate new laws and regulations, taking account of the Guidance on Integrated Pollution Prevention and Control set out in the Appendix to the Recommendation.[237] The Guidance set out, for the first time in an international instrument, a detailed approach to implementing integrated pollution prevention and control and preventing or minimising the risk of harm to the environment taken as a whole; it recognises the integrated nature of the environment by taking account of the substances or activities on all the environmental media (air, water, soil), the living organisms (including people) that these media support, and the stock of cultural and aesthetic assets.[238] The Guidance identified five important elements of an integrated approach: the 'cradle-to-grave' concept; the anticipation of effects in all environmental media of substances and activities; the minimisation of waste quantity and harmfulness; the use of a common means to estimate and compare environmental problems (such as risk assessment); and the complementary use of effects-oriented measures (environmental quality objectives) and source-oriented measures (emission limits).[239]

The OECD Recommendation also recognised that certain policies were 'essential to an effective integrated approach', including sustainable development, the use of no- or low-waste technology and recycling strategies, cleaner technologies and safer substances, precautionary action, public information, the integration of environmental considerations into private and public decision-making, and consistent and effective compliance and enforcement policies.[240] Under the Recommendation, an integrated approach would shift the focus of decision-making, to a combination of the substances, the sources (including processes, products and economic sectors) and the geographical regions; it would provide for the use of a range of legislative forms such as mineral

---

[234] Chapter 15, pp. 789–91 below. The EC Commission has also proposed a draft Directive on Integrated Pollution Prevention and Control: COM (93) 423, 14 September 1993.

[235] 1992 Action Plan of the Oslo and Paris Commissions, Appendix A, in LDC 15/INF.11, Annex 3, 2 October 1992.

[236] Chapter 15, pp. 754–5 below.   [237] Note 233 above, para. I(b) and (c).

[238] Guidance, para. 1.   [239] *Ibid.*   [240] *Ibid.*, para. 2.

rights, development aid and taxes.[241] The Recommendation recognised that an integrated approach would require changes in institutional arrangements, management instruments and technical methods. New institutional arrangements would require the establishment of co-ordinating mechanisms within and among government bodies and international co-operative arrangements within and among different levels of government within countries.[242] Proposals relating to management instruments included the following: issuing single permits which cover all releases and processes; linking environmental instruments with land-use planning and natural resource management; undertaking environmental impact assessments for policy proposals and projects; establishing integrated inspection and enforcement authorities; using economic instruments; encouraging and/or subsidising cleaner technologies; and covering whole life cycle issues in the development of industry management plans.[243] An integrated approach to technical methods would encompass such things as life cycle analysis (from design through manufacture to disposal), analysis of multiple pathways of exposure, the use of inventories of releases and inputs, and more effective monitoring of the condition of environmental media, the biota they support, and the condition of cultural and aesthetic assets.[244] The necessity for such changes remains equally apparent with regard to international institutions, in respect of both their internal practices and their external relations.

Conclusions

From the discussion in this chapter of the different sources of international legal obligation, it will be evident that the principles and rules of international environmental law are set forth or are reflected in thousands of acts adopted at the national, bilateral, sub-regional, regional and global levels. There is no international legal text which sets out the principles and rules which are of general application, and it is unlikely that one will be adopted in the foreseeable future, despite the efforts of the IUCN Commission on Environmental Law in the 1990s. The lack of a central legislative authority, or of a coherent set of international legislative arrangements, has resulted in a law-making process and a body of rules which are *ad hoc*, piecemeal and fragmented. The limitations of existing arrangements are well known. Although existing international arrangements have apparently not limited the international community's environmental law-making over the past decade, there remains a real need to establish a coherent framework for the co-ordination of existing rules and the development of new rules. The UNCED process could have contributed to such a framework, by addressing three priority needs: to establish improved mechanisms for identifying critical issues and priorities for law-making; to ensure that

[241] *Ibid.*, paras. 3 and 4.   [242] *Ibid.*, para. 5.   [243] *Ibid.*, para. 6.   [244] *Ibid.*, para. 7.

all relevant actors are able to participate fully and effectively in the international law-making process (in particular developing countries), including the negotiation, implementation, review and governance of international environmental agreements or instruments; and to rationalise the international law-making process by improving co-ordination between international organisations and their secretariats, in particular those established by environmental agreements. In the ten years since UNCED, however, it has become apparent that there is an absence of the political will which would be required to overhaul existing international structures.

It will also be clear from this chapter that the limitations and inadequacies of existing techniques for applying standards established by international principles and rules (principally by so-called 'command-and-control' methods) are, and should continue to be, the subject of critical international scrutiny. Developments since UNCED confirm that environmental protection will not be achieved merely by the adoption of a vast body of regulatory obligations. These regulations need fine-tuning, and they may need to be supplemented by introducing and applying a broad range of equitable and effective economic instruments which can provide incentives to improve compliance without exacerbating social injustice and which take account of the need to ensure that the poorer members of the international community are not disproportionately affected. So far, however, there has been little practical experience at the international level with the use of economic instruments, with the exception of trade instruments and the emerging efforts of the EC, and more work of a theoretical nature needs to be done to explore the implications and practical consequences of the various proposed arrangements. The limited experience of efforts to devise a system of 'joint implementation' under the 1992 Climate Change Convention suggests that legal and institutional issues of considerable complexity arise when economic theories are to be translated into practical, acceptable and effective international legal obligations and arrangements. That experience suggests that, although it may yet be premature to embark on a broad effort at adopting and applying economic instruments, international law may be about to embark on new efforts which selectively support such arrangements. In this regard, developments under the 1997 Kyoto Protocol will be of singular importance, even if – for the time being at least – traditional regulatory approaches will continue to be the primary approach. Efforts to devise new economic approaches will no doubt continue, supplemented by the obviously necessary move away from single-sector environmental regulation towards a more integrated approach to pollution prevention and control which seeks to address all environmental media on a comprehensive basis, and all products on a cradle-to-grave basis. Each of these new initiatives poses challenges to the international legal order.

5

Compliance: implementation, enforcement, dispute settlement

R. Bilder, 'The Settlement of Disputes in the Field of the International Law of the Environment', 144 RdC 139 (1975); E. Somers, 'The Role of the Courts in the Enforcement of Environmental Rules', 5 *International Journal of Estuarine and Coastal Law* 193 (1990); M. Koskenniemi, 'Peaceful Settlement of Environmental Disputes', 60 *Nordic Journal of International Law* 73 (1991); K. Sachariew, 'Promoting Compliance with International Environmental Standards: Reflections on Monitoring and Reporting Mechanisms', 2 *Yearbook of International Environmental Law* 31 (1991); P. Sands, 'Enforcing Environmental Security: the Challenges of Compliance with International Obligations', 15 *Journal of International Affairs* 46 (1993); A. and A. H. Chayes, *The New Sovereignty: Compliance with International Regulatory Regimes* (1995); J. Cameron, J. Werksman and P. Roderick (eds.), *Improving Compliance with International Environmental Law* (1995); W. Lang, 'Compliance Control in International Environmental Law', 56 ZaöRV 685 (1996); A. Kiss, 'Compliance with International and European Environmental Obligations', *Hague Yearbook of International Environmental Law* 45 (1996); E. Brown Weiss and H. Jacobson (eds.), *Engaging Countries: Strengthening Compliance with International Accords* (1998); R. Wolfrum, 'Means of Ensuring Compliance with and Enforcement of International Environmental Law', 272 *Recueil des Cours* 9 (1998); J. Collier and V. Lowe, *The Settlement of Disputes in International Law* (1999); C. Romano, *The Peaceful Settlement of International Environmental Disputes: A Pragmatic Approach* (2000); M. Ehrmann, *Erfüllungskontrolle im Umweltvölkerrecht* (2000).

Introduction

Ensuring compliance by members of the international community with their international environmental obligations continues to be a matter of increasing concern. This is evident not only from the attention which the issue received during UNCED, as well as in the negotiation and implementation of recent environmental agreements, but also in the growing number of environmental disputes which have been brought to international judicial bodies. The relevance of environmental concerns to international peace and security was affirmed by the UN Security Council in January 1992 when its members declared that 'non-military sources of instability in the . . . ecological fields have become threats to international peace and security'.[1] The response to those concerns has included the development of existing mechanisms for implementation, enforcement and dispute settlement (such as the 1993 decision of the ICJ to establish a Chamber for Environmental Matters), as well as new approaches such as the non-compliance mechanisms established under a number of environmental agreements, and the role given to the UN Compensation Commission over environmental claims,[2] and the specialised rules for arbitrating environmental disputes which were promulgated by the Permanent Court of Arbitration in 2001.

Of the reasons proffered for renewed efforts, at least three are especially relevant. First, it is apparent that states are taking on ever more international environmental commitments which are increasingly stringent and which must be complied with. Secondly, the growing demands on access to finite natural resources provides fertile conditions for conflicts over the use of natural resources. And, thirdly, as international environmental obligations increasingly intersect with economic interests, states which do not comply with their environmental obligations are perceived to gain economic advantage from non-compliance. Non-compliance is therefore seen to be important because it limits the effectiveness of legal commitments, undermines the international legal process, and can lead to conflict and instability in the international order. Plainly, non-compliance occurs for different reasons,[3] and it is widely recognised that the underlying causes require further attention so that existing and new international legal obligations are crafted to ensure their effective implementation. At UNCED, attention was focused on mechanisms to *prevent* disputes and to resolve them peacefully when they arise. Subsequent efforts have reflected a desire to address enforcement and dispute settlement in a non-contentious and non-adversarial manner.

Non-compliance can include a failure to give effect to substantive norms (e.g. to limit atmospheric emission of sulphur dioxide or greenhouse gases as required by treaty or to allow transboundary emissions of hazardous substances or gases in violation of any rules of customary law); or to fulfil procedural requirements (e.g. to carry out an environmental impact assessment or to consult with a neighbouring state on the construction of a new plant); or to fulfil an institutional obligation (e.g. to submit an annual report to an international organisation). Non-compliance raises three distinct but related issues relating to implementation, enforcement, and conflict resolution (traditionally referred to by international lawyers as 'dispute settlement'). These are:

[1] Note by the President of the Security Council, 31 January 1992, UN Doc. S23500, 2 (1992).
[2] Chapter 18, p. 890 below.
[3] Non-compliance may occur for a variety of reasons, including a lack of institutional, financial or human resources, and differing interpretations as to the meaning or requirements of a particular obligation. On the practice of the ECJ, see pp. 222–4 below.

1. What formal or informal steps must be taken to implement a state's international legal obligations?
2. What legal or natural person may enforce international environmental obligations of other states?
3. What techniques, procedures and institutions exist under international law to resolve conflicts or settle disputes over alleged non-compliance with international environmental obligations?

Over the years, a range of techniques have been adopted and used to improve compliance with environmental obligations, drawing upon other developments in international law. Today, techniques and practices specific to environmental matters are being developed. Despite the emergence of the concept of 'environmental security',[4] the legal issues relating to the environment concerning implementation, enforcement and conflict resolution are not dissimilar to those of one hundred years ago.[5] Since the *Fur Seals Arbitration* of 1893, numerous environmental disputes have been submitted to international dispute resolution arrangements, and the rate of submission appears to have increased significantly within the past decade. These disputes have addressed a broad range of issues, including: transboundary air pollution;[6] the diversion of the flow of international rivers;[7] conservation of fisheries resources;[8] protection of the marine environment;[9] import restrictions adopted to enforce domestic conservation standards;[10] the relationship between environmental laws and foreign investment protection treaties;[11] access to environmental information;[12] environmental impact assessment;[13] and responsibility for rehabilitation of

---

[4] See e.g. J. T. Matthews, 'Redefining Security', 68 *Foreign Affairs* 163 (1989); M. Renner, *National Security: The Economic and Environmental Dimensions* (Worldwatch Paper, 1989), 89; A. Timoshenko, 'Ecological Security: Global Change Paradigm', 1 *Colorado Journal of International Environmental Law and Policy* 127 (1990); S. Vinogradov, 'International Environmental Security: The Concept and its Implementation', in A. Carter and G. Danilenko (eds.), *Perestroika and International Law* (1990), 196; G. Handl, 'Environmental Security and Global Change: The Challenge to International Law', 1 *Yearbook of International Environmental Law* 3 (1990).

[5] See the *Fur Seals* Arbitration *(Great Britain v. United States)* (1893), chapter 11, pp. 561–6 below.

[6] *Trail Smelter* case, chapter 8, pp. 318–19 below.

[7] *Lac Lanoux Arbitration* (1957), chapter 10, pp. 463–4 below, *Gabcikovo-Nagymaros Project* case, chapter 10, pp. 469–77 below.

[8] *Fisheries Jurisdiction* case (1974), chapter 11, pp. 567–8 below; *Southern Bluefin Tuna* cases, chapter 11, pp. 580–1 below.

[9] *New Zealand v. France* (1995), chapter 8, pp. 319–21 below; *MOX* case, chapter 9, p. 436 below.

[10] *Yellow-Fin Tuna* decision (1991), chapter 19, pp. 955–61 below; *Shrimp/Turtle* case, chapter 19, pp. 961–73 below.

[11] *Metalclad* v. *Mexico*, chapter 21, pp. 1066–9 below.

[12] *MOX* case, chapter 9, p. 436 below.

[13] *Gabcikovo-Nagymaros* case, chapter 10, pp. 469–77 below; *MOX* case, chapter 9, p. 436 below.

mined lands.[14] Recent cases illustrate the availability of a growing range of fora for the resolution of disputes over environment and natural resources. In the context of the dispute over the Gabcikovo-Nagymaros barrages, Hungary and Slovakia had explored a range of enforcement and dispute settlement options including unilateral reference to the ICJ, arbitration, conciliation by the EC Commission, and the emergency procedures of the Conference on Security and Co-operation in Europe (CSCE) before they agreed to settle the dispute at the ICJ.[15] The dispute between Ireland and the United Kingdom concerning the MOX plant at Sellafield has been litigated at ITLOS and two separate arbitration tribunals (OSPAR and UNCLOS), and other fora (including the ECJ, the ECHR and the ICJ) were also available. Historically, the available mechanisms were under-utilised, leaving it unclear whether they would be able to deal with the growing range of environmental issues which may require resolution. In the past decade, however, there has been an increasing willingness on behalf of states to invoke these traditional procedures, which have demonstrated an ability to contribute to the resolution of contentious disputes and, in the process, to the development of the rules of international environmental law.

Implementation

States implement their international environmental obligations in three distinct phases. First, by adopting national implementing measures; secondly, by ensuring that national measures are complied with by those subject to their jurisdiction and control; and, thirdly, by fulfilling obligations to the relevant international organisations, such as reporting the measures taken to give effect to international obligations.[16]

---

[14] *Certain Phosphate Lands in Nauru* case, chapter 12, pp. 666–9 below.

[15] A mechanism for consultation and co-operation in emergency situations was adopted by the Berlin Meeting of the CSCE Council in June 1991. The mechanism comprises a process of exchange of information between the states involved, which if unsuccessful may lead to a special meeting of the Committee of Senior Officials, who may then refer the matter to a meeting at ministerial level. If the process does not resolve the situation the dispute may be referred to the Procedure for Peaceful Settlement of Disputes, involving the Conflict Prevention Centre: see Summary of Conclusion, 30 ILM 1348 (1991), Annexes 2 and 3.

[16] See generally D. Victor, K. Raustiala and E. Skolnikoff (eds.), *The Implementation and Effectiveness of International Environmental Commitments* (1998); T. Zhenghua and R. Wolfrum, *Implementing International Environmental Law in Germany and China* (2001). See also G. Handl, 'Controlling Implementation of and Compliance with International Environmental Commitments: The Rocky Road from Rio', 5 *Colorado Journal of International Environmental Law and Policy* 305 (1994); L. Boisson de Chazournes, 'La mise en oeuvre du droit international dans le domaine de l'environnement', 99 RGDIP 37 (1995); P. Sand, 'Institution Building to Assist Compliance with International Environmental Law: Perspectives', 56 ZaöRV 754 (1996).

National law

Once a state has formally accepted an international environmental obligation, usually following the entry into force of a treaty which it has ratified or the act of an international organisation by which it is bound, it will usually need to develop, adopt or modify relevant national legislation, or give effect to national policies, programmes or strategies by administrative or other measures. Some treaties expressly require parties to take measures to ensure the implementation of obligations,[17] or to take appropriate measures within their competence to ensure compliance with the convention and any measures in effect pursuant to it.[18] Numerous agreements require parties to designate a competent national authority or focal point for international liaison purposes to ensure domestic implementation.[19] The 1982 UNCLOS provides a typical example, its provisions being drawn from different precedents in the field of marine pollution. It includes provisions on implementation of pollution requirements from different sources, and provides specifically for the enforcement by states of their laws and regulations adopted in accordance with the Convention and the implementation of applicable international rules and standards.[20] It also requires states to ensure that recourse is available under their legal system for prompt and adequate compensation for damage caused by marine pollution by persons under their jurisdiction.[21]

Treaty obligations which have not been implemented domestically will usually be difficult to enforce in national courts. EC law provides a notable exception, since it can create rights and obligations enforceable before national courts without being implemented provided that they fulfil certain conditions, such as being clear and unconditional.[22] The failure by EC members to adopt measures implementing EC environmental law has been the subject of enforcement measures taken at the ECJ.[23] In dealing with these cases the ECJ has rejected different arguments by states seeking to justify domestic non-implementation.[24]

---

[17] 1969 Southeast Atlantic Convention, Art. X(1); 1972 London Convention, Art. VII(1); 1989 Basel Convention, Art. 4(4); 1991 Antarctic Environment Protocol, Art. 13.

[18] 1988 CRAMRA, Art. 7(1). The 1998 Chemicals Convention identifies possible measures to include the establishment of national registers and databases, the encouragement of initiatives by industry, and the promotion of voluntary agreements: Art. 15(1).

[19] 1989 Basel Convention, Art. 5; 2001 Biosafety Protocol, Art. 19.

[20] 1982 UNCLOS, Arts. 213, 214, 216 and 222.   [21] Art. 235(2).

[22] EC Treaty, Art. 249 (formerly Article 189); chapter 15, pp. 736–9 below.

[23] See p. 222 below. R. Wagenbaur, 'The European Community's Policy on Implementation of Environmental Directives', 14 *Fordham International Law Journal* 455 (1990); L. Krämer, 'The Implementation of Community Environmental Directives Within Member States: Some Implications of Direct Effect Doctrine', 3 *Journal of Environmental Law* 39 (1991).

[24] See e.g. Case 91/79, *EC Commission* v. *Italy* [1980] ECR 1099, rejecting Italy's defences that the national legislation already contained provisions which to a large extent secured the realisation of the objects of the Directive, that the Directive was *ultra vires*, and that implementation was 'thwarted by the vicissitudes which were a feature of the brief existence

National compliance

Once an obligation has been domestically implemented, the party must ensure that it is complied with by those within its jurisdiction and control. Numerous treaties expressly require parties to ensure such compliance,[25] or to apply sanctions for failing to implement measures.[26] Others specifically provide for the application of criminal penalties or for the 'punishment' of violations.[27] Ensuring national compliance is a matter for the public authorities of each state, although there is much evidence to suggest that domestic compliance with environmental obligations is inadequate and that compliance with international obligations needs to be enhanced.[28] National judges meeting shortly before the World Summit on Sustainable Development adopted the Johannesburg 'Principles on the Role of Law and Sustainable Development', which affirmed their adherence to the 1992 Rio Declaration which laid down the basic principles of sustainable development, affirmed that members of the judiciary, as well as those contributing to the judicial process at the national, regional and global levels, are 'crucial partners for promoting compliance with, and the implementation and enforcement of, international and national environmental law', and recognised that 'the rapid evolution of multilateral environmental agreements, national constitutions and statutes concerning the protection of the environment increasingly require the courts to interpret and apply new legal instruments in keeping with the principles of sustainable development'.[29]

Recognising that public authorities in many countries may not be able to ensure compliance, because of a lack of resources or commitment, and

---

of the seventh legislature of the Italian Parliament, and particularly its premature end': *ibid.*, at 1105.

[25] 1972 Oslo Convention, Art. 15(1); 1973 CITES, Art. VIII(1); 1974 Paris Convention, Art. 12; 1996 Protocol to the London Convention, Art. 10; 1995 Straddling Stocks Agreement, Art. 19.

[26] 1946 International Whaling Convention, Art. IX(1) and (3); 1969 Southeast Atlantic Convention, Art. X(1); 1972 Oslo Convention, Art. 15(3); 1972 London Convention, Art. VII(2); 1989 Basel Convention, Art. 4(4).

[27] 1974 Paris Convention, Art. 12(1); 1989 Basel Convention, Art. 9(5); 1991 Bamako Convention, Art. 9; 2001 Biosafety Protocol, Art. 25(1); ILC Draft Code of Crimes Against the Peace and Security of Mankind, Arts. 22(2)(d) and 26 (chapter 18, pp. 894–6 below; see also Resolution on the Role of Criminal Law in the Protection of Nature and the Environment, 8th UN Congress on the Prevention of Crime and the Treatment of Offenders, UN Doc. A/CONF/144/7, paras. 456–62 (1990).

[28] Agenda 21, Chapter 39, para. 39.3(d) and (e); EC Commission, Fifth Environmental Action Programme (1992); chapter 15, n. 107, p. 750 below.

[29] 20 August 2002, available at www.inece.org/wssd_principles.html. The Principles also express the judges' view that 'there is an urgent need to strengthen the capacity of judges, prosecutors, legislators and all persons who play a critical role at national level in the process of implementation, development and enforcement of environmental law, including multilateral environmental agreements (MEAs), especially through the judicial process'.

that individuals, groups and business can play a role in ensuring compliance, increasing numbers of states are encouraging private enforcement of national environmental obligations. These are sometimes referred to as 'citizen suits', allowing citizens (and businesses) to enforce national environmental obligations in the public interest. The importance of national remedies to challenge acts which damage the environment or violate environmental obligations has been recognised and is being addressed internationally. Principle 10 of the Rio Declaration states that '[e]ffective access to judicial and administrative proceedings, including redress and remedy, shall be provided'. The EC Commission has recognised that individuals and public interest 'groups should have practicable access to the courts in order to ensure that their legitimate interests are protected and that prescribed environmental measures are effectively enforced and illegal practices stopped',[30] although the ECJ has not been willing to move away from its traditional and restrictive approach to recognising the rights of individuals and other non-state actors to challenge EC legislative and administrative acts.[31] The 1993 Lugano Convention was the first international agreement to elaborate rules governing access to national courts to allow enforcement of environmental obligations in the public interest: Article 18 requires standing to be granted to environmental organisations to allow them to bring certain enforcement proceedings before national courts.[32]

The 1998 Aarhus Convention goes a great deal further, giving concrete effect to the requirements of Principle 10 of the Rio Declaration on access to justice. Its Article 9(2) establishes an obligation on parties to ensure that members of the public which have a 'sufficient interest' or who claim an 'impairment of a right' shall have access 'to a review procedure before a court of law and/or another independent and impartial body established by law, to challenge the substantive and procedural legality of any decision, act or omission' which is subject to the Convention's Article 6. The Convention provides that 'sufficient interest' and 'impairment of a right' are to be determined in accordance with national law and 'consistently with the objective of giving the public concerned wide access to justice', and expressly provides that non-governmental organisations fulfilling certain conditions are deemed to have a 'sufficient interest' and rights capable

[30] EC Commission, Fifth Environmental Action Programme (1992), chapter 15, n. 107, p. 750 below.
[31] See Case C-321/95P, *Greenpeace* v. *EC Commission* 1998 ECR I-6151 (individuals and associations not 'individually concerned' by a Commission decision dispensing structural funds, and no account is to be taken of the 'nature and specific characteristics of the environmental interests' at stake). The Court of First Instance has indicated a desire to adopt a more flexible approach (see Case T-177/01, *Jego-Quere et Cie SA* v. *Commission* [2002] 2 CMLR 44, but the ECJ has rejected the approach (see Case C-50/00P, *Union de Pequenos Agricultores* v. *Council*, [2002] 3 CMLR 1). It may be that the requirements of the 1998 Aarhus Convention (see below) modify the approach taken by the ECJ, or that the matter might be addressed in the constitutional reforms which are underway in 2002–3.
[32] Chapter 18, pp. 933–7 below.

of being impaired.[33] The Convention also provides that members of the public should be able to challenge acts and omission by private persons and public authorities which contravene national provisions relating to the environment, and that all the procedures available should provide adequate and effective remedies (including injunctive relief) and be fair, equitable, timely and 'not prohibitively expensive'.[34]

The question of which state may or must ensure implementation is a difficult one where the environmental obligation relates to a shared natural resource or the global commons.[35] This can lead to conflicts between states over which has jurisdiction over a particular activity or violation.[36] Some treaties allocate enforcement obligations to particular states, and in respect of marine pollution the 1982 UNCLOS is notable for the detailed provisions on national enforcement responsibilities of flag states, port states or coastal states, depending on where a pollution incident occurred.[37] No equivalent treaty rules apply for other matters, such as atmospheric pollution. However, under the 1979 Moon Treaty, the state of registration retains jurisdiction and control over personnel and equipment and is responsible for ensuring that 'national activities are carried out in conformity with the provisions' of the treaty.[38] And under the 1988 CRAMRA each party would have been required to ensure that recourse was available in its national courts for adjudicating liability claims under Article 8 of the Convention (and consistently with Article 7), including the adjudication of claims against any operator it had sponsored.[39]

The UNCLOS rules are detailed and may provide a model for enforcement jurisdiction in other matters. Generally the flag state will be responsible for ensuring that vessels flying its flag or of its registry comply with applicable international pollution rules and standards, and with laws and regulations adopted in accordance with UNCLOS, and for the effective enforcement of such measures 'irrespective of where a violation occurs'.[40] Port states also have important enforcement functions. They may investigate and institute proceedings in respect of a vessel voluntarily within its port or at an offshore terminal for harmful discharges from that vessel outside the internal waters, territorial sea or exclusive economic zone (EEZ) in violation of international rules and

---

[33] Art. 9(2). Art. 2(5) establishes the conditions for non-governmental organisations, requiring merely that they promote environmental protection and meet 'any requirements under national law'.

[34] Art. 9 (3) and (4). By Art. 9(5) the parties are also to consider establishing appropriate assistance mechanisms to reduce barriers to access to justice.

[35] Chapter 6, p. 240 below (global commons), and p. 238 below (shared natural resources).

[36] On extra-territorial jurisdiction, see chapter 6, pp. 237–41 below.

[37] 1982 UNCLOS, Arts. 217–220.

[38] Arts. 12(1) and 14(1), see chapter 8 below. Similar provisions apply under the 1967 Outer Space Treaty, chapter 8, p. 383 below, Arts. VI and VIII.

[39] Art. 8(10); chapter 14, pp. 716–21 below.

[40] Art. 217(1). See also 1995 Straddling Stocks Agreement, Art. 19.

standards.[41] And they must take measures to prevent vessels from sailing where they have ascertained that the vessel is in violation of applicable international rules and standards relating to seaworthiness which may threaten the marine environment.[42] A coastal state may institute proceedings against vessels within its port for violations of its laws and regulations adopted in accordance with UNCLOS or applicable international rules and standards for environmental violations occurring in its territorial sea or EEZ.[43] Where there are grounds for believing that there is a 'substantial discharge causing or threatening significant pollution of the marine environment', the coastal state also has the right to investigate and institute proceedings against vessels navigating in its territorial sea, to obtain information from vessels navigating in its EEZ, and to undertake inspections of vessels in its EEZ. The coastal state may also institute proceedings – with sanctions including detention – against vessels in its territorial sea or EEZ if there is 'clear, objective evidence' that violation of applicable international rules and standards has occurred which results 'in a discharge causing major damage or threat of major damage to the coastline or related interests of the coastal state, or to any resources of its territorial sea or exclusive economic zone.[44] UNCLOS does not prejudice the rights of states under international law to take and enforce measures to protect their coastlines or related interests from pollution or a threat of pollution. Such pollution may result from a maritime casualty, including collision or stranding, which may reasonably be expected to have major harmful consequences.[45]

With regard to the sea-bed and ocean floor and its subsoil, beyond the limits of national jurisdiction (known as the 'Area') and which constitutes the 'common heritage of mankind',[46] state parties must ensure that their activities, or the activities of their nationals or those effectively controlled by them or their nationals, are carried out in conformity with Part XI of UNCLOS. State parties will also be subject to rules adopted by the International Sea-bed Authority

---

[41] Art. 218(1). Proceedings in respect of violations taking place in the internal waters, the territorial sea or the EEZ of another state are, however, subject to certain limitations: see Art. 218(2).

[42] Art. 219. See in this regard the various understandings and agreements on port state controls, including: the 1982 Paris Memorandum of Understanding on Port State Control, as amended (http://www.parismou.org); the 1992 Latin American Agreement on Port State Control of Vessels (http://200.45.69.62/index_i.htm); and the 1994 Memorandum of Understanding on Port State Control in the Asia-Pacific Region (www.tokyo-mou.org/memoran.htm). See generally E. Molenaar, *Coastal State Jurisdiction over Vessel-Source Pollution* (1998); D. Anderson, 'Port States and Environmental Protection', in A. Boyle and D. Freestone (eds.), *International Law and Sustainable Development* (1999), 325; T. Keselj, 'Port State Jurisdiction in Respect of Pollution from Ships: the 1982 UNCLOS and the MOU', 30 *Ocean Development and International Law* 127 (1999).

[43] Art. 220(1).   [44] Art. 220(1), (2), (3), (5) and (6).   [45] Art. 221.

[46] Arts. 1(1) and 136. These provisions are not affected by the 1994 Agreement Implementing Part XI of UNCLOS.

concerning pollution and other hazards to the marine environment. and the protection and conservation of natural resources.[47]

The allocation of detailed enforcement powers to ensure compliance is not well developed in respect of many other environmental media involving shared resources. In the absence of specific treaty provisions, the applicable principles arise from general rules of international law concerning enforcement jurisdiction. Given the failure of many states, particularly developing states, to implement their international obligations by reason of lack of financial and other resources, an important development is the linkage now established between the extent to which developing countries meet their treaty obligations, and the provision to them of financial resources. The 1990 amendments to the 1987 Montreal Protocol established a mechanism to 'meet all agreed incremental costs' of developing country parties 'to enable their compliance with the control measures of the Protocol'.[48] The 1992 Climate Change Convention goes further by requiring developed country parties 'to meet the agreed full costs incurred by developing country parties in complying with their [reporting requirements and] agreed full incremental costs' needed by developing country parties for implementing their substantive obligations under the Convention.[49] Similar provisions exist in other agreements, including the 1992 Biodiversity Convention, the 1994 Desertification Convention and the 2001 POPs Convention.[50]

Reporting[51]

The third element of national compliance arises from the requirement that states must usually report national implementing measures. Most environmental agreements expressly require parties to report certain information to the international organisation designated by the agreement. The information to be reported typically includes: statistical information on production, imports and exports;[52] information on emissions or discharges;[53] information on the grant of permits or authorisations[54] including criteria;[55] information on implementation measures which have been adopted;[56] details of decisions taken by

---

[47] Arts. 139(1) and 145.
[48] Art. I(T) replacing Art. 10 of the 1987 Montreal Protocol, chapter 20, pp. 1031–2 below.
[49] Art. 4(3); chapter 20, pp. 1035–6 below.   [50] Chapter 20, p. 1034 below.
[51] Chapter 20, p. 1034 below.
[52] 1987 Montreal Protocol, Art. 7, as amended; 2001 POPs Convention, Art. 15.
[53] 1997 Kyoto Protocol, Art. 7(1).
[54] 1946 International Whaling Convention, Art. VIII(1).
[55] 1972 London Convention, Art. VI(4); 1996 LDC Protocol, Art. 9(4).
[56] 1972 World Heritage Convention, Art. 29(1); 1989 Basel Convention, Art. 13(3)(c); 1992 Climate Change Convention, Art. 12(1); 2000 Biosafety Protocol, Art. 23; 2001 POPs Convention, Art. 15.

national authorities;[57] scientific information;[58] and information on breaches or violations by persons under the jurisdiction or control of the party.[59] Most EC Directives and Regulations also require the EC member states to provide regular information on measures taken to implement their obligations.[60]

These reports may be required annually or bi-annually, or according to some other timeframe.[61] They allow the international organisation and the other parties to assess the extent to which parties are implementing their obligations. It is clear, however, that many states fail to fulfil the basic reporting obligation, which suggests that more substantive obligations may also remain unimplemented. One report considered six environmental treaties requiring periodic reports, and found wide variations in compliance in the early 1990s.[62] Some treaties revealed a strong record: all six parties to the International Whaling Convention required to submit information on their 1989 whale harvests did so,[63] and sixteen of the seventeen parties to the 1988 NO_x Protocol submitted their 1990 report on their emissions in 1987 or another year.[64] By October 1990, fifty-two of the then sixty-five parties to the 1987 Montreal Protocol had responded to the requirement to report information on their consumption of controlled substances in 1986, of which twenty-nine (representing 85 per cent of world consumption) submitted complete data.[65] At the other end of the scale, however, only nineteen of the sixty-four parties to the 1972 London Convention reported on the number and types of dumping permits they issued in 1987,[66] and only thirteen of the fifty-seven parties to MARPOL 73/78 (representing only about 27 per cent of the world's gross shipping tonnage) submitted reports summarising violations and penalties they had imposed in 1989.[67] Finally, just twenty-five of the 104 parties to the 1973 CITES submitted reports summarising their 1989 import and export

---

[57] 1989 Basel Convention, Art. 13(2)(c) and (d).
[58] 1946 International Whaling Convention, Art. VIII(3).   [59] *Ibid.*, Art. IX(4).
[60] Directive 88/609 (large combustion plants), Art. 16; Directive 92/43 (habitats), Art. 17.
[61] See also 1992 Climate Change Convention, requiring initial reports to be submitted within six months of entry into force by OECD countries, within three years of entry into force or upon the availability of financial resources by developing countries, and at their discretion by least-developed countries: Art. 12(5); chapter 8, p. 363 below.
[62] See United States General Accounting Office, 'International Environment: International Agreements Are Not Well Monitored', Report to Congressional Requesters, GAO/RCED-92-43 (1992).
[63] *Ibid.*, 26.
[64] *Ibid.*, 25. This high rate of reporting occurred even though the Protocol did not enter into force until February 1991.
[65] *Ibid.*, 24–5. Concern on lack of reporting led to the establishment in June 1990 of an Ad Hoc Group of Experts on the Reporting of Data: cited in GAO Report, n. 62 above. Reasons found by the Group for incomplete reporting include lack of financial and technical resources, inability to use customs records to track imports and exports because they do not distinguish between different substances, and confidentiality of information.
[66] *Ibid.*, 26.   [67] *Ibid.*, 26–7.

certificates for listed endangered species.[68] These figures suggest the limited ability of many countries, particularly developing countries, to meet their reporting requirements. There is no evidence that the situation is improving, although steps are being taken to address the problem. Under the Biodiversity and Climate Change Conventions, financial resources are required to be made available to meet the incremental costs for developing countries of fulfilling their reporting requirements, and this has gone some way towards improving compliance.[69]

International enforcement

Once evidence is available that a state, or a party to a treaty, has failed to implement an international environmental obligation, the question arises as to which persons having international legal personality may enforce that obligation internationally. In this context, 'enforcement' is understood as the right to take measures to ensure the fulfilment of international legal obligations or to obtain a ruling by an appropriate international court, tribunal or other body, including an international organisation, that obligations are not being fulfilled. International enforcement may occur at the instigation of one or more states, or an international organisation, or by non-state actors. In practice, international enforcement usually involves a combination of the three, each acting in different capacities. The extent to which any of these actors may invoke enforcement measures depends on the nature and legal basis of the alleged violation, the subject matter involved, and the international legal obligations at issue. This aspect of enforcement is essentially about the standing required to bring international claims.

Enforcement by states

As the principal subjects of international law, states have the primary role in enforcing rules of international environmental law. To be in a position to enforce a rule of international environmental law, a state must have standing, and to have standing it must be able to show that it is, in the words of the International Law Commission (ILC), an 'injured state'. Article 42 of the ILC's 2001 Articles on State Responsibility provides:

> A State is entitled as an injured State to invoke the responsibility of another State if the obligation breached is owed to:
> (a) that State individually; or
> (b) a group of States including that State, or the international community as a whole, and the breach of the obligation:

---

[68] *Ibid.*, 27–8.   [69] Chapter 20, pp. 1034–6 below.

(i) Specially affects that State; or

(ii) Is of such a character as radically to change the position of all the other States to which the obligation is owed with respect to the further performance of the obligation.[70]

The rights concerning the first category include those arising from: a bilateral treaty; a multilateral treaty where particular performance is incumbent under the treaty as between one party and another; a unilateral commitment made by one state to another; or a rule of general international law which may give rise to individual obligations as between two states (for example, rules concerning riparian states and the non-navigational uses of international watercourses).[71] Rights arising under the second category are considered by the ILC to include a case of pollution of the high seas in breach of Article 194 of UNCLOS which may particularly impact on one or several states whose beaches may be polluted by toxic residues or whose coastal fisheries may be closed and hence considered to be specially affected,[72] or a nuclear free zone treaty or any other treaty 'where each parties' performance is effectively conditioned upon and requires the performance of each of the others'.[73]

The ILC Articles also envisage that a state other than an 'injured state' is entitled to invoke the responsibility of another state if:

(a) The obligation breached is owed to a group of states including that state, and is established for the protection of a collective interest of the group; or

(b) The obligation breached is owed to the international community as whole.[74]

In cases involving environmental damage, at least three situations are to be distinguished. The first is where a state permits activities which cause damage to its own environment; the second is where a state permits activities which cause damage to the environment of another state; and the third is where a state permits or causes damage to the environment in an area beyond national jurisdiction.[75]

---

[70] ILC Articles on State Responsibility, Pt 2, Art. 5(1), *Report of the ILC to the United Nations General Assembly,* UN Doc. A/56/10 (2001). See also the commentary in J. Crawford, *The ILC's Articles on State Responsibility* (2002), 255–60.

[71] See Commentaries on the Articles, Report of the International Law Commission on the Work of its Fifty-Third Session, *Official Records of the General Assembly, Fifty-Sixth Session, Supplement No. 10* (A/56/10), chap.IV.E.1, Art. 42 (p. 297).

[72] *Ibid.,* at 299.   [73] *Ibid.*

[74] Art. 48. The remedy which a non-injured state may make is limited to cessation of the internationally wrongful act, assurances and guarantees of non-repetition, and the performance of the obligation of reparation in the interest of the injured state or of the beneficiaries of the obligation breached: see Art. 49(2).

[75] For a most helpful discussion (and table), see C. Stone, *The Gnat is Older than Man: Global Environment and Human Agenda* (1993), 33 *et seq.*

Damage to a state's own environment

A number of international environmental agreements commit parties to protect environmental resources located exclusively within their territory, for example the conservation of non-migratory species[76] or habitats[77] or watercourses[78] located within their territories. In these circumstances, other parties to the agreement could claim to be an injured state such as to allow them – at least in theory – to bring an international claim. In practice, this has not happened: it is only where the interference with the environmental resource crosses a national boundary that one or more states have felt compelled to act. Exceptionally, in the EU context the EC Commission will institute proceedings for non-compliance with EC environmental rules even in the absence of transboundary consequences.[79]

Damage to the environment of another state

In situations involving damage to its environment, or consequential damage to its people or their property or other economic loss, a state will not find it difficult to claim that it is an 'injured state' and that it may bring an international claim. In the *Trail Smelter* case, the United States invoked its right not to be subjected to the consequences of transboundary air pollution from sulphur emissions in Canada and to bring a claim against Canada for having violated its rights. As a riparian state and a party to an international agreement with France, in the *Lac Lanoux Arbitration* Spain relied upon *prima facie* rights to challenge France over proposed works which it alleged would violate its right to use the waters of the River Carol under certain conditions.[80] Similar considerations apply in respect of the *Gabcikovo-Nagymaros* dispute submitted by Hungary and Slovakia to the ICJ for a determination of rights on the basis of a bilateral treaty between those two states and 'principles of general international law'.[81] Australia, in the *Nuclear Tests* case, argued that French nuclear tests deposited radioactive fallout on Australian territory which violated its sovereignty and impaired its independent right to determine the acts which should take place within its territory.[82] And Ireland, in the *MOX* case, claimed that it was injured by transboundary movements of radioactive substances introduced into the Irish Sea by the United Kingdom in violation of its international commitments.[83]

Damage to the environment in areas beyond national jurisdiction

Not all cases will be as straightforward as the *Trail Smelter* case, however. In the *Nuclear Tests* cases, brought by Australia and New Zealand against France calling on the latter to halt its atmospheric nuclear testing in the South Pacific

---

[76] Chapter 11, below.   [77] Chapter 11 below.
[78] Chapter 10 below.   [79] See pp. 193–5 below.
[80] Chapter 10, pp. 463–4 below.   [81] Chapter 10, pp. 469–77 below.
[82] Chapter 8, pp. 319–21 below.   [83] Chapter 9, p. 436 below.

region, the claim raised a more complicated legal question than the allegation of a violation of sovereignty by the deposit of radioactive fallout in its territory: did Australia and New Zealand have the right to bring a claim to the ICJ on the basis of a violation of an obligation owed *erga omnes* to all members of the international community to be free from nuclear tests generally or in violation of the freedom of the high seas?[84] Similar issues had been raised in the *Fur Seals* case.[85] Both cases raised the issue of whether a state had standing to bring an environmental claim to prevent damage to an area beyond national jurisdiction, even if it had not itself suffered any material damage. This raises the possibility of bringing an action on the basis of obligations which are owed *erga omnes*, either on the basis of a treaty or on the basis of customary law. As a general matter, where one party to a treaty or agreement believes that another party is in violation of its obligations under that treaty or agreement, it will have the right, under the treaty or agreement, to seek to enforce the obligations of the party alleged to be in violation, even if it has not suffered material damage.[86] In most cases involving a violation of a treaty obligation, however, the applicant state is likely to have been induced into bringing a claim because it has suffered some form of material damage and not because it wishes to bring a claim to protect the interests of the international community.[87] Such an example was Mexico's claim against the United States under the GATT over the US import ban on yellow-fin tuna caught by Mexican vessels on the high seas in violation of United States fisheries laws.[88]

For breaches of treaty obligations, the right of a state to enforce obligations will usually be settled by the terms of the treaty. Various human rights treaties permit any party to enforce the obligations of any other party by bringing a claim before the relevant treaty organs.[89] The EC Treaty allows a member state which considers that another member state has failed to fulfil an EC obligation, including an environmental obligation, to bring the matter before the ECJ.[90] Although this right has been relied upon on numerous occasions to threaten court proceedings, it appears to have resulted in a decision by the ECJ on just one occasion, when France successfully brought proceedings against the United Kingdom for unlawfully having enforced domestic legislation setting a minimum mesh size for prawn fisheries.[91] Under EC law, there is also no need to show that the claimant state has suffered damage: the mere violation of EC law is sufficient to allow standing. Thus a failure by a member state to carry out an environmental impact assessment as required under Directive

---

[84] See p. 188 below.   [85] Chapter 11, pp. 561–6 below.

[86] *The Wimbledon* (1923) PCIJ Ser. A, No. 1.

[87] See for example the proceedings brought by Australia and New Zealand against Japan in the *Southern Bluefin Tuna* cases, chapter 11, pp. 580–1 below.

[88] Chapter 19, pp. 955–61 below.   [89] ECHR, Art. 24, chapter 7, p. 299 below.

[90] EC Treaty, Art. 227 (formerly Article 170); see p. 223 below.

[91] Case 141/78, *France* v. *United Kingdom* [1979] ECR 2923.

85/337 would allow any other member state to bring an action to the ECJ in accordance with Article 227 (formerly Article 170) of the EC Treaty even if the environmental consequences might not be noticed beyond the country required to carry out the assessment. Under EC law, each member state has an actionable legal interest in the proper fulfilment by every other member state of its environmental obligations. Given that the environment is, in many instances, a shared natural resource in the protection of which each member of the international community has an interest, compelling policy arguments can be raised to apply the rationale underlying the EC approach to the international legal protection of the environment generally.

The 1995 Straddling Stocks Agreement has introduced innovative and far-reaching provisions in its Part VI (on compliance and enforcement). Article 19 requires flag states to ensure compliance with sub-regional and regional conservation and management measures for straddling fish stocks and highly migratory fish stocks.[92] Article 20 establishes arrangements for international co-operation in enforcement. These include the requirement that, where a vessel is alleged to have been engaged in unauthorised fishing in an area under the jurisdiction of a coastal state, the flag state must, at the request of the coastal state concerned, 'immediately and fully' investigate the matter.[93] Moreover, state parties which are members of a regional or sub-regional fisheries management organisation or participants in regional or sub-regional management arrangements may take action to deter vessels which have engaged in activities which undermine or violate the conservation measures established by the organisation or arrangement from fishing on the high seas until appropriate action is taken by the flag state.[94] Article 21 addresses sub-regional and regional co-operation in enforcement. It provides that a state party which is a member of a regional or sub-regional fisheries management organisation or a participant in a regional or sub-regional management arrangement may board and inspect fishing vessels flying the flag of another party to the 1995 Agreement (whether or not that party is a member of the organisation or a participant in the arrangement) in any high seas area covered by an organisation or arrangement, for the purpose of ensuring compliance with conservation and management measures.[95] Article 21 goes on to provide detailed rules on the enforcement obligations of the flag state and the rights of the state party to the 1995 Agreement, particularly with regard to 'serious violations', including the requirement that actions taken other than by flag states must be proportionate to the seriousness of the violation.[96]

---

[92] The flag state is required, *inter alia*, to enforce measures irrespective of where violations occur and ensure that where serious violations have been established the vessel involved does not engage in high seas fishing operations until all outstanding sanctions have been complied with.

[93] 1995 Straddling Stocks Agreement, Art. 20(7).   [94] Art. 20(8).   [95] Art. 21(1).

[96] Art. 21(16). 'Serious violations' are defined in Art. 21(11).

The situation in general international law is less well developed, although there is a move in the direction taken by the EC under some recent environmental treaties and in international practice. Thus, New Zealand's 1995 application to the ICJ challenging France's resumption of underground nuclear tests was premised on the view that it would be unlawful for France to conduct such tests before it had carried out an environmental impact assessment as required (it was argued) by international law.[97] A failure by a party to the 1987 Montreal Protocol to fulfil its obligations under that treaty entitles any other party to the Protocol to enforce the obligation by invoking the non-compliance or dispute settlement mechanisms under the Protocol, without having to show that it had suffered material damage as a result of the alleged failure.[98] The 1989 Basel Convention similarly provides that any party 'which has reason to believe that another party is acting or has acted in breach of its obligations' under the Convention may inform the Secretariat and the party against whom the allegations are made.[99] Most other environmental treaties are less explicit, establishing dispute settlement mechanisms which will settle the question of enforcement rights in accordance with the provisions available under that treaty or related instruments. Some treaties specifically preclude their application to the global commons. The 1991 Espoo Convention, for example, precludes parties from requesting an environmental impact assessment or other measures in respect of harm to the global commons.[100]

Whether a state has, in the absence of a specific treaty right such as those under the Montreal Protocol, a general legal interest in the protection of the environment in areas beyond its national jurisdiction such as to allow it to exercise rights of legal protection on behalf of the international community as a whole (sometimes referred to as *actio popularis*) is a question which remains difficult to answer in the absence of state practice. This may happen in a situation where the activities of a state were alleged to be causing environmental damage to the global commons, such as the high seas, the seabed beyond national jurisdiction, outer space or perhaps the Antarctic, or to living resources found in or passing through those areas. In such cases, the question is which states, if any, have the right to enforce such international legal obligations as may exist to avoid causing environmental damage to an area of the global commons?

The matter has been considered in passing by the ICJ on two occasions, and by some of the ICJ judges in a third case. In the *South West Africa (Preliminary Objections)* case, the ICJ stated that, 'although a right of this kind [*actio popularis*] may be known to certain municipal systems of law, it is not known to international law as it stands at present; nor is the Court able to regard it as

---

[97] *Request for an Examination of the Situation* (1995) ICJ Reports 288 at 291.
[98] See pp. 198–9 below.
[99] 1989 Basel Convention, Art. 19; the information is then to be submitted to the parties.
[100] Chapter 16, pp. 814–17 below.

imported by the "general principles of law" referred to in Article 38, paragraph 1(c), of its Statute'.[101] However, a majority of judges in the *Barcelona Traction* case implicitly recognised the possibility of what might be considered to be an *actio popularis* under international law where an obligation exists *erga omnes*. The ICJ held that:

> an essential distinction should be drawn between the obligations of a state towards the international community as a whole, and those arising vis-à-vis another state in the field of diplomatic protection. By their very nature the former are the concern of all states. In view of the importance of the rights involved, all states can be held to have a legal interest in their protection; they are obligations *erga omnes*.[102]

In the *Nuclear Tests* cases, four judges in their joint Dissenting Opinion (Judges Ortyeama, Dillard, Jimenez de Arechega and Sir Humphrey Waldock) identified the conditions in which the *actio popularis* might be argued:

> If the materials adduced by Australia were to convince the Court of the existence of a general rule of international law, prohibiting atmospheric nuclear tests, the Court would at the same time have to determine what is the precise character and content of that rule and, in particular, whether it confers a right on every state individually to prosecute a claim to secure respect for the rule. In short, the question of 'legal interest' cannot be separated from the substantive legal issue of the existence and scope of the alleged rule of customary international law. Although we recognise that the existence of a so-called *actio popularis* is a matter of controversy, the observations of this Court in the *Barcelona Traction, Light and Power Company, Limited* Case suffice to show that the question is one that may be considered as capable of rational legal argument and a proper subject of litigation before this Court.[103]

Despite the fact that the notion of *actio popularis* and rights and obligations *erga omnes* may be treated as distinct but related concepts, this Dissenting Opinion suggests that the two are closely linked. There has been little judicial consideration of what rights and obligations exist *erga omnes*, although the lists cited usually include obligations arising from the outlawing of acts of aggression and of genocide and relating to the protection of fundamental human rights.[104] Some support has been expressed by commentators for the view that obligations owed *erga omnes* might extend to environmental damage in areas beyond

---

[101] *South West Africa* case (1966) ICJ Reports 47.

[102] *Barcelona Traction Company* case (*Belgium* v. *Spain*) (1970) ICJ Reports 4 at 32.

[103] *Nuclear Test* case, (1974) ICJ Reports 253 at 369–70. Cf. Judge De Castro: 'The Applicant has no legal title authorizing it to act as spokesman for the international community and ask the Court to condemn France's conduct': *ibid.*, 390. See also Judge Gros (*Ibid.*, 290) and Judge Petren (*ibid.*, 224).

[104] See Oppenheim, vol. I, 5; and M. Ragazzi, *The Concept of International Obligation Erga Omnes* (1997).

national jurisdiction,[105] and support for this view might also be found in the ILC's previous classification of a 'massive pollution' of the atmosphere or of the seas as an international crime.[106] It has also been suggested that obligations *erga omnes* could be created by the actions of a limited number of states.[107]

There thus appears to be some support favouring the right of a state to bring an action in its capacity as a member of the international community to prevent significant damage from occurring to the environment in areas beyond its national jurisdiction. Although most discussions focus on damage occurring in the global commons, there may be equally compelling policy reasons for allowing the *actio populd* concept to apply also in respect of damage occurring to the environment within another state's jurisdiction. To the extent, then, that a rational legal argument can be made in favour of the *actio populaus*, in respect of which international environmental obligations could it be relied upon? At this stage, it is most likely to be successfully invoked in a case involving very significant damage to the environment, perhaps even at the level of 'massive pollution' or harm. Likely candidates would probably include those environmental obligations that have been associated with the 'common concern' or 'common heritage' principles.[108] They might therefore include the protection of the global environment from significant harm (Principle 21 of the Stockholm Declaration and Principle 2 of the Rio Declaration) and rights established by treaty which relate to, *inter alia*, protection of the high seas, the climate system, the ozone layer, biodiversity (including fisheries), plant genetic resources and, to a lesser extent, wetlands and cultural property, as well as in respect of environmental matters which are associated with human rights obligations.

On a more cautious note, it should be remembered that not all international organisations or their non-compliance bodies are likely to favour the *actio populaus* concept. The GATT Dispute Settlement Panel in the *Yellow-Fin Tuna*

---

[105] See Brownlie, calling for a liberal approach to the standing issue in such circumstances: I. Brownlie, 'A Survey of International Customary Rules of Environmental Protection', in L. Teclaff and A. Utton (eds.), *International Environmental Law* (1975), 5; J. Charney, 'Third State Remedies for Environmental Damage to the World's Common Spaces', in F. Francioni and T. Scovazzi, *International Responsibility for Environmental Harm*, (1991) 149 at 157; K. Leigh, 'Liability for Damage to the Global Commons' (paper presented at an OECD Symposium on Liability for Nuclear Damage, Helsinki, September 1992), 25. On the suggestion that a coastal state is obliged to the world at large to prevent pollution of the territorial sea, see D. O'Connell, *The International Law of the Sea* (1984), vol. 2, 988–9.

[106] Draft Articles on State Responsibility, Art. 19, Pt I, *Yearbook of the International Law Commission* (1980-II), Pt 2, 30; see chapter 18, pp. 874–5 below. See also 1998 Statute of the International Criminal Court, Art. 8(b)(iv).

[107] See Oppenheim, vol. 1, 5, citing the *Reparations for Injuries* case (1949) ICJ Reports 185, and the *Namibia* case (1971) ICJ Reports 56.

[108] On 'common concern' and related concepts, see chapter 6, p. 287 below.

case specifically rejected the claim by the United States that it was entitled to take measures to protect dolphins on the high seas, although in that case the Panel applied GATT law and not public international law, and no evidence was presented by the United States that the dolphins were protected or endangered under international law.[109] The decision of the WTO Appellate Body in the *Shrimp/Turtle* case, recognising that the United States had a legitimate interest in migratory sea-turtles which were internationally endangered, marks a shift towards recognition of the *actio popularis* concept, although in that case it is important to recall that the species of sea turtle in question (if not the turtles actually harmed) were known to be located from time to time in United States waters.[110] International law is in this respect still finding its centre of gravity, and states have not generally sought to assert a legal right to act on behalf of the whole international community in the protection of environmental issues on the basis of customary law or national law. Prior to the *Shrimp/Turtle* case, where they have sought to assert a legal right to act on behalf of the whole international community, as in the early *Fur Seals Arbitration* and the *Yellow-Fin Tuna* case, they have been rebuffed on the ground that they were seeking to apply *national* laws extra-territorially. In both of the latter cases, the result might have been different if the complainant states had relied upon, and could prove the existence of, a rule of customary international law, as Australia and New Zealand sought to do in 1973 in the *Nuclear Tests* cases.

In many respects, the discussion of *actio popularis* at the international level is similar to that which is taking place at the national level. In international affairs, the function of a state might be compared to that of an attorney general in national law. These national discussions suggest a further limitation on the likelihood of actions being brought by public authorities to enforce the environmental rights of the community as a whole. The views of one scholar on the clear limitations of an attorney general's ability to enforce rules to protect the environment on behalf of the community as a whole are equally applicable to international matters:

> Their statutory powers are limited and sometimes unclear. As political creatures, they must exercise the discretion they have with an eye towards advancing and reconciling a broad variety of important social goals, from preserving morality to increasing their jurisdiction's tax base. The present state of our environment, and the history of cautious application and development of environmental protection laws long on the books, testifies that the burdens of an attorney general's broad responsibility have apparently not left much manpower for the protection of nature.[111]

---

[109] Chapter 19, pp. 955–61 below.   [110] Chapter 19, pp. 961–73 below.
[111] C. Stone, 'Should Trees Have Standing? – Towards Legal Rights for Natural Objects', 45 *Southern California Law Review* 450 (1972).

The reluctance of states to enforce obligations towards the protection of the environment is, regrettably, supported by many examples. One leading example is the failure of any state to seek to enforce compliance by the former USSR with its international legal obligations arising out of the consequences of the accident at the Chernobyl nuclear power plant in 1986.[112] This and other examples suggest that it is unlikely that the same states would seek to enforce obligations owed to the global commons, the violation of which may only lead to indirect or nominal harm to the state. This suggests the need for an increased enforcement role for international organisations, or other members of the international community, particularly where the mere attempt to enforce obligations may establish a precedent which could subsequently apply to the enforcing state.

Enforcement by international organisations

Whilst international organisations play an important legislative role in the development of international environmental law, their enforcement function is limited. International organisations are international legal persons which may seek to protect their own rights and enforce the obligations that others have towards them.[113] Sovereign interests have, however, led states to be unwilling to transfer too much enforcement power to international organisations and their secretariats, although there are some indications that this reluctance is being overcome.

Early examples of limited enforcement roles granted to international organisations include: the right of the River Danube Mixed Commission to 'work out agreed measures' for the regulation of fishing in the Danube;[114] the right of certain international fisheries institutions to 'recommend' international enforcement measures or systems;[115] and the right of the International Commission for the Protection of the Rhine Against Pollution to regularly compare the draft national programmes of the parties to ensure that 'their aims and

---

[112] Chapter 18, pp. 887–9 below.

[113] See *Reparations for Injuries* case, (1949) ICJ Reports, 174, where in an advisory opinion the ICJ determined that the UN had an 'undeniable right' to 'demand that its Members fulfil the obligations entered into by them in the interest of the good working of the Organisation' and the capacity to claim adequate reparation for a breach of these obligations, and held that 'fifty states, representing the vast majority of the members of the international community, had the power, in conformity with international law, to bring into being an entity possessing objective international personality and not merely personality recognised by them alone, together with the capacity to bring international claims'.

[114] 1958 Danube Fishing Convention, Art. 12(1).

[115] 1969 Southeast Atlantic Convention, Art. X(3); 1978 Northwest Atlantic Fisheries Convention, Art. XI(5); 1982 Convention for the Conservation of Salmon in the North Atlantic Ocean, Art. 4(2).

means coincide'.[116] Marginally more ambitious is the obligation of the CITES Secretariat, when it is satisfied that information it has received indicates that certain endangered species are being affected adversely by trade in specimens, to communicate that information to the relevant party or parties, which may then lead to the matter being reviewed by the next conference of the parties, which may make whatever recommendations it deems appropriate.[117]

Developments for the protection of the marine environment and the Antarctic environment foresee an enhanced enforcement role for international organisations. The approach of the 1992 Oil Fund Convention is particularly ambitious, since it establishes and endows the Fund with legal personality in the laws of each party and gives it rights and obligations, including being a party in legal and enforcement proceedings before the national courts of that party.[118] The 1982 UNCLOS also introduces innovative arrangements by endowing some of its institutions with a range of enforcement powers. Thus, the Council of the International Sea-Bed Authority can: 'supervise and co-ordinate the implementation' of Part XI of UNCLOS and 'invite the attention of the Assembly to cases of non-compliance'; institute proceedings on behalf of the Authority before the Sea-Bed Disputes Chamber in case of non-compliance; issue emergency orders 'to prevent serious harm to the marine environment arising out of activities in the Area'; and direct and supervise inspectors to ensure compliance.[119] A Legal and Technical Commission, one of the Council's organs, will be entitled to make recommendations to the Council on the institution of proceedings and the measures to be taken following any decision by the Sea-Bed Disputes Chamber.[120]

The Antarctic Mineral Resources Commission, which would have been established under the 1988 CRAMRA, could draw to the attention of all parties any activity which affected the implementation of CRAMRA or compliance by any party, as well as any activities by a non-party which affected implementation.[121] The Commission could also designate observers,[122] and 'ensure the effective application' of the provisions in the Convention concerning notification, reporting of mineral prospecting, and keeping under review the conduct of Antarctic mineral resource activities with a view to safeguarding the protection of the Antarctic environment in the interest of all mankind.[123]

---

[116] 1976 Rhine Chemical Convention, Art. 6(3).

[117] 1973 CITES, Art. XIII.   [118] 1992 Oil Pollution Fund Convention, Art. 2(2).

[119] 1982 UNCLOS, Art. 162(2)(a), (u), (v), (w) and (z); the Authority is granted international legal personality and such legal capacity as may be necessary for the exercise of its functions and the fulfilment of its purposes: Art. 176.

[120] Art. 165(2)(i) and (j).

[121] Art. 7(7) and (8); chapter 14, pp. 716–21 below.   [122] Art. 12(1)(b).

[123] Art. 21 (1)(f) and (x). The 1988 CRAMRA also provides for the establishment of regulatory committees, the functions of which relate, *inter alia*, to monitoring and inspection of exploration and development activities: Art. 31(1)(d) and (f).

The 1988 CRAMRA will not come into force since being 'replaced' by the 1991 Antarctic Environment Protocol, the main environmental institution for which there is a Committee for Environmental Protection.[124] The Committee's enforcement role under the 1991 Protocol is more limited than that envisaged for the Commission under CRAMRA: its Committee will provide advice and adopt recommendations on matters such as the effectiveness of measures taken, the application and implementation of environmental impact assessment procedures, and the state of the Antarctic environment.[125] The advice and recommendations are to be drawn upon fully by the Antarctic Treaty Consultative Meetings in adopting measures under the 1959 Antarctic Treaty for implementation of the Protocol.[126] The Committee is not, however, granted any formal enforcement powers.

The 1992 OSPAR Convention also goes some way towards establishing a limited role for the Commission it creates to ensure compliance. Under Article 23, entitled 'Compliance', the Commission has two functions. First, it must 'assess' compliance with the Convention by parties, and make any decisions and recommendations on the basis of the reports submitted by the parties.[127] Secondly, when appropriate, the Commission may:

> decide upon and call for steps to bring about full compliance with the Convention, and decisions adopted thereunder, and promote the implementation of recommendations, including measures to assist a contracting party to carry out its obligations.[128]

Although these provisions do not allow the Commission to take measures such as court proceedings in national courts, or arbitration proceedings, they go beyond the provisions of many other international environmental agreements. Other arrangements endow particular organisations with enforcement or quasi-enforcement functions. In relation to weapons agreements, the UN Security Council may 'take action in accordance with the [UN] Charter' if the consultation and co-operation procedure established under the relevant treaties does not remove doubts concerning fulfilment of obligations under certain nuclear weapons treaties.[129] More generally, many of the institutions established by environmental treaties are required, as their primary task, to keep under review the relevant treaty and to promote its effective implementation.[130] This general function could be interpreted, over time and under the right conditions, to allow institutions to play an enforcement role.

No discussion of international enforcement powers would be complete without mention of the EC Commission, which must, under Article 211 (formerly

---

[124] Art. 11; see chapter 14, pp. 721–6 below.   [125] Art. 12(1)(a), (d) and (j).
[126] Art. 10(1) and (2).   [127] Art. 23(a); see chapter 9, pp. 411–12 below.   [128] Art. 23(b).
[129] 1971 Nuclear Weapons Treaty, Art. III(4); 1972 Biological and Toxic Weapons Convention, Art. VI.
[130] 1979 Berne Convention, Art. 14(1); 1992 Climate Change Convention, Art. 7(2).

Article 155) of the EC Treaty, ensure that the provisions of the EC Treaty and the measures taken by the institutions (i.e. secondary legislation) are applied. Article 226 (formerly Article 169) of the EC Treaty provides that:

> If the Commission considers that a member state has failed to fulfil an obligation under this Treaty, it shall deliver a reasoned opinion on the matter after giving the state concerned the opportunity to submit its observations.

If the member state concerned does not comply with the opinion within the period laid down by the Commission, the Commission may bring the matter before the European Court of Justice (ECJ). It has done so on many occasions.

Before the Commission can bring a member state before the ECJ it must first present its case and evidence to the member state and request observations. The member state then has an opportunity to make observations, following which the Commission will deliver a 'reasoned opinion'. This allows a full airing of the differences between the Commission and the member state and often allows the matter to be resolved before the case is actually brought to the ECJ. In environmental matters, the Commission has frequently and controversially used its powers under Article 226 (formerly Article 169). In 1982, the Commission commenced sixteen infringement proceedings against member states under the former Article 169; by 1990, that number had risen to 217 infringement proceedings.[131] In 2001, the Commission brought seventy-one cases to the ECJ against member states under Articles 226 and 228, and delivered 197 reasoned opinions.[132] At any one time, the Commission is likely to have several dozen matters pending under Article 226, and has to date brought more than two hundred cases to the ECJ alleging violations of EC environmental laws.[133]

The Commission can also apply to the ECJ for interim measures under Article 243 (formerly Article 186) of the EC Treaty – a form of interlocutory relief well established in EC jurisprudence and quite often employed, for example, in competition and anti-trust cases. The Commission must show that it has a good arguable case, that the need for relief is urgent and that irreparable damage to the EC interest will be done if the order is not granted. The member state can defend itself by establishing that it will suffer irreparable harm if the order is made. The Commission does not have to give a cross-undertaking in damages in the event that it ultimately loses the case. In Case 57/89, *EC Commission* v. *Germany*, the ECJ considered the circumstances in which it would be prepared to prescribe necessary interim measures in environmental cases.[134] The case concerned the construction in Germany of a reservoir and related site, and the Commission sought a declaration that the construction violated Article 4(1) of

---

[131] See EC Commission, Eighth Report to the European Parliament on the Enforcement of Community Law (1991).

[132] EC Commission, Third Annual Survey on the Implementation and Enforcement of Community Environmental Law (2001), 6 (http://europa.eu.int/comm/environment/law/third_annual_survey_en.pdf).

[133] See p. 222 below.   [134] [1989] ECR 2849.

the 1979 Wild Birds Directive, and the adoption of interim measures to suspend the work until the ECJ had given its decision on the main application. The ECJ held that for a measure of this type to be ordered the application must state the circumstances giving rise to the urgency and the factual and legal grounds establishing a *prima facie* case for the interim measures.[135] The ECJ rejected the application on the grounds that the Commission had failed to prove urgency: the application had been submitted after the project was well under way and the interim measures had not been sought until a large part of the work had already been partially completed, and it could not be shown that 'it [was] precisely the next stage in the construction work which will cause serious harm to the protection of birds'.[136]

Enforcement by non-state actors[137]

According to traditional rules of public international law, non-state actors are not international legal persons except within the limited confines of international human rights law and its associated fields. It is still difficult to find many textbooks on international law which make any reference to the role of environmental and other non-state actors in the international environmental legal process, although it is widely recognised that they have become in many areas, and particularly in the field of international environmental law, *de facto* international actors who are, in limited circumstances, endowed with *de jure* rights. In practice, non-state actors play a central role in the development and application of international environmental law.[138] Environmental organisations have been involved in the international implementation and enforcement process although their primary role continues to be at the national level, through political means or by recourse to administrative or judicial procedures for enforcing national measures adopted by a state in implementing its international treaty and other obligations.[139]

Enforcement in the national courts

'Judicial Application of International Environmental Law', 7 RECIEL 1–67 (1998) (special issue); M. Anderson and P. Galizzi, *International Environmental Law in National Courts* (2001).

UNCED endorsed a stronger role for the non-governmental sector in enforcing national environmental laws and obligations before national courts and

---

[135] *Ibid.*, 2854.   [136] *Ibid.*, 2855.

[137] D. Shelton, 'The Participation of NGOs in International Judicial Proceedings', 88 AJIL 611 (1994); P. Sands, 'International Law, the Practitioner and "Non-State Actors"', in C. Wickremasinghe (ed.), *The International Lawyer as Practitioner* (2000), 103–24; P. Kalas, 'International Environmental Dispute Resolution and the Need for Access by Non-State Entities', 12 *Colorado Journal of International Environmental Law and Policy* 191 (2001).

[138] Chapter 3, p. 112 above.   [139] See below.

tribunals, as reflected in Agenda 21 and the Rio Declaration,[140] and now applied in the 1998 Aarhus Convention.[141] This occurred in the context of earlier treaties and agreements which recognised and encouraged their role, particularly where individuals were the victims of pollution or environmental damage in a transboundary context. These earlier efforts sought either to establish principles governing equal access to national courts by victims of transfrontier pollution, or to establish the jurisdiction of courts in the event of transboundary incidents.[142] The 1974 OECD Council Recommendation on Principles Concerning Transfrontier Pollution prepared the ground for the adoption of more detailed principles to ensure the legal protection of persons who suffer transfrontier pollution damage.[143] The 1976 OECD Council Recommendation on Equal Right of Access in Relation to Transfrontier Pollution identified the constituent elements of a system of equal right of access.[144] According to the Recommendation, these were a set of rights recognised by a country in favour of persons who are affected or likely to be affected in their personal or proprietary interests by transfrontier pollution originating in that country. They include rights relating to access to information and participation in hearings and enquiries, and 'recourse to and standing in administrative and judicial procedures' to prevent pollution, have it abated, or obtain compensation for the damage caused.[145] These general rights were further elaborated the following year by a more detailed OECD Council Recommendation for the Implementation of a Regime of Equal Right of Access and Non-Discrimination in Relation to Transfrontier Pollution.[146]

The non-binding OECD instruments are supplemented by a range of treaty obligations which address equal access or the jurisdiction of courts over transboundary disputes. The 1974 Nordic Environmental Protection Convention allows any person who is affected or may be affected by a nuisance caused by 'environmentally harmful activities' in another contracting state to bring before the appropriate court or administrative authority of that state the question of the permissibility of such activities, including the questions of compensation and measures to prevent damage.[147] The 1974 Nordic Convention also provides for the appointment of a supervisory authority in each state 'to be entrusted with the task of safeguarding general environmental interests in so

---

[140] Agenda 21, Chapter 27, para. 27.13; Principle 10, Rio Declaration.

[141] See p. 176 above.

[142] A distinct aspect is the situation in which a transnational corporation headquartered or based in one state is challenged for the environmental or health consequences of its acts in another state, even where no transboundary pollution (in the classical sense) has occurred. For a review of three such cases (*Ok Tedi*, *Thor Chemicals* and *Connelly*), see J. Cameron and R. Ramsey, 'Transnational Environmental Disputes', 1 *Asia Pacific Journal of Environmental Law* 5 (1996).

[143] OECD Doc. C(74)224.   [144] OECD Doc. C(76)55 (Final) (1976).

[145] Annex, paras. 1 and 2.   [146] OECD Doc. C(77)28 (Final) (1977).   [147] Art. 3.

far as regards nuisances arising out of environmentally harmful activities in another contracting state', including the right to institute proceedings before or be heard by the courts or administrative authority of another contracting state.[148] The supervisory authority of the state in which damage occurs is also required to facilitate on-site inspections to determine such damage.[149]

An enforcement role for individuals is envisaged by several treaties establishing international rules on civil liability. In relation to the jurisdiction of national courts, these fall into two categories: those treaties requiring victims to bring proceedings before the courts of the state in which the transboundary pollution originated, and those allowing victims to choose either the court of the state in which the pollution originated or the courts of the state in which the damage was suffered. The nuclear liability conventions adopted in the 1960s fall into the former category.[150] They require victims of nuclear damage to make their claims before courts which may be several thousands of miles away from the area where the damage occurred, thus imposing an onerous burden. Moreover, they do not expressly allow for claims for environmental damage, although negotiations are currently underway to extend the definition of damage to include environmental damage.[151] The oil pollution conventions adopted a decade or so later also provide support for the enforcement role of individuals, and are more accessible to individuals since they allow victims to claim before the courts of any contracting state in which an incident has caused pollution damage.[152]

The second category of conventions ensuring a role for non-state enforcement establish private international law rules allocating jurisdiction to national courts over a range of civil and commercial matters, including disputes arising out of the law of tort. These generally allow victims a choice of courts. Although they were not prepared with environmental pollution and disputes in mind, they can apply to transboundary environmental disputes. The 1968 Brussels Convention on Jurisdiction and Enforcement of Judgments in Civil and Commercial Matters (1968 Brussels Convention), to which EC member states alone may become parties, has a number of purposes, including the free circulation of judgments throughout the EC, and has established jurisdiction rules for civil and commercial matters.[153] Under Article 5(3) of the Convention (and now Regulation 44/2001), jurisdiction in matters 'relating to tort, delict

---

[148] Art. 4.   [149] Art. 10.

[150] 1960 Paris Convention, Art. 13; 1963 Vienna Convention, Art. XI(1); see chapter 18, pp. 906–12 below.

[151] Chapter 18, pp. 906 and 908 below.

[152] 1969 CLC (as amended), Art. IX(1); 1992 Oil Pollution Fund Convention, as amended, Art. 7(1); chapter 18, pp. 913 and 915 below.

[153] Brussels, 27 September 1968, in force 1 February 1973;, OJ C189, 28 July 1990, 2, 77, Art. 1; 8 ILM 229 (1969). See now Council Regulation 44/2001 (EC) on jursidiction and enforcement of judgments in civil and commercial matters, OJ L12, 16 January, 1.

or quasi-delict' is conferred on the courts of the place 'where the harmful event occurred'. In *Handelskwekerij GJ Bier* v. *Mines de Potasses d'Alsace*, the ECJ was asked to interpret 'where the harmful event occurred' in a case in which the defendant was alleged to have discharged over 10,000 tonnes of chloride every twenty-four hours into the Rhine River in France but the damage was suffered by horticultural businesses in the Netherlands.[154] The Dutch plaintiffs wished to bring proceedings in the Netherlands rather than in France. On an Article 177 preliminary reference request from the Appeal Court of The Hague, the ECJ held that Article 5(3) should be interpreted 'in such a way as to acknowledge that the plaintiff has an option to commence proceedings either at the place where the damage occurred or the place of the event giving rise to it'.[155] This allows victims of transboundary pollution in EC member states to choose the jurisdiction in which they wish to bring environmental cases which could be classified as tortious, delictual or quasi-delictual in nature. In 1988, the Brussels Convention was supplemented by the Lugano Convention on Jurisdiction and Enforcement of Judgments in Civil and Commercial Matters, which applies similar rules to relations between EC and EFTA countries.[156]

International enforcement

At the international level, opportunities for non-state actors to play an enforcement role are limited. Under some regional human rights treaties, individual victims, including non-governmental organisations, may bring complaints directly to an international body. Thus, the European Convention on Human Rights allows any person, non-governmental organisation or group of individuals claiming to be the victim of a violation of the rights in the Convention by one of the parties to bring a case to the European Court of Human Rights.[157]

Similar provisions exist in the Optional Protocol to the 1966 International Covenant on Civil and Political Rights for communications by individuals to the Human Rights Committee, alleging breaches of the Covenant.[158] The International Covenant on Economic, Social and Cultural Rights, however, does

---

[154] Case 21/76, *Handelskwekerij G. J. Bier* v. *Mines de Potasse d'Alsace* [1976] ECR 1735.

[155] *Ibid.*

[156] 16 September 1988, in force 1 January 1992, 28 ILM 620 (1989); Art. 5(3) is in the same terms as Art. 5(3) of the Brussels Convention. On the relationship between the EC and EFTA states, see chapter 15, p. 747 below.

[157] Art. 34 of the ECHR (as amended by the Eleventh Protocol) (formerly 1950 ECHR, Art. 25(1)); all parties to the Convention have now accepted the right of individual petition. See also the 1969 American Convention on Human Rights, Arts. 44 and 45 and the 1981 African Charter on Human and Peoples' Rights, Art. 55. On the relationship between these human rights instruments and the protection of the environment, see chapter 7, pp. 293–305 below.

[158] *Ibid.*

not grant individuals and non-governmental organisations such rights.[159] The UN Commission on Human Rights[160] cannot receive individual complaints concerning human rights violations, although its subsidiary Sub-Commission on the Prevention of Discrimination and Protection of Minorities can receive complaints about a consistent pattern of gross and reliably attested violations of human rights, and then refer them to the Commission on Human Rights.[161]

Non-governmental organisations and individuals have played an active role in supporting the enforcement role of the EC Commission, usually by submitting complaints to that institution concerning the non-implementation by member states of their environmental obligations. In 1991, for example, more than four hundred complaints were received by the EC Commission concerning non-compliance with environmental obligations, leading to a number of formal investigations by the Commission.

It is in their capacity as watchdogs that environmental organisations play an important role in the development, application and enforcement of international environmental law. Environmental organisations have long been active in monitoring and seeking to enforce compliance by states of international environmental laws and standards. In this context, development, application and enforcement are so closely intertwined that it may be misleading to attempt to separate the tasks. In practice, environmental organisations seek to influence government positions at the national and international levels, to participate in international decision-making and law-making, and to enforce rules of international environmental law (at both the national and international levels).[162] Examples of the way in which these actors have sought to promote or give effect to international obligations include – at the international level – their role in bringing about requests from the WHO and the UN General Assembly for an advisory opinion on the legality of the use of nuclear weapons from the ICJ,[163] and informal assistance to states in the preparation (and even presentation) of a case.[164] At the national level, environmental organisations are increasingly active in bringing legal proceedings to enforce international environmental

---

[159] Chapter 7, p. 293 below. However, under ECOSOC Council Res. 1988/4, non-governmental organisations in consultative status with the ECOSOC may submit to the Committee on Economic and Social Rights written statements which might contribute to the full and universal realisation of the rights under the Covenant.

[160] Chapter 7, p. 295 below.

[161] *Ibid.*; established by the Commission on Human Rights under the authority of ECOSOC Res. 9(II) (1946).

[162] P. Sands, 'International Law, the Practitioner and "Non-State Actors"', in C. Wickremasinghe (ed.), *The International Lawyer as Practitioner* (2000), 103–24.

[163] Chapter 6, p. 236 below.

[164] For example, the 1995 request to the ICJ by New Zealand to examine the resumption by France of nuclear testing ((1995) ICJ Reports 288) was brought by the government in part as a result of public and NGO pressure, including the preparation by at least one NGO of draft pleadings.

obligation.[165] In recent years, they have also gained a degree of access to some international proceedings from which they were previously excluded, in the sense that they may be able to file *amicus curiae* submissions.[166]

International conflict resolution (settlement of disputes)

Introduction

A range of international procedures and mechanisms are available to assist in the pacific settlement of environmental disputes. Article 33 of the UN Charter identifies the traditional mechanisms, including negotiation, enquiry, mediation, conciliation, arbitration, judicial settlement, resort to regional agencies or arrangements, or other peaceful means of the parties' own choice.[167]

These techniques can be divided into two broad categories: diplomatic means according to which the parties retain control over the dispute insofar as they may accept or reject a proposed settlement (negotiation, consultation, mediation, conciliation); and legal means which result in legally binding decisions for the parties to the dispute (arbitration and judicial settlement). Recourse to regional arrangements and international organisations as mediators and conciliators provides something of a middle way: the legal consequences of any decision taken by the institution will depend on the treaty establishing the institution. Many of the earliest environmental treaties did not provide for any dispute settlement mechanisms whether of a diplomatic or legal nature, or of a voluntary or mandatory character.[168] Initially, the trend was towards the use of informal and non-binding mechanisms, such as negotiation and consultation, supplemented by the use of more formal mechanisms, such as conciliation, arbitration and judicial settlement. More recently, there has been a move towards the development of new techniques to establish non-contentious mechanisms. Recent treaties provide parties with a range of options for settling disputes and encouraging implementation. The 1992 Climate Change Convention

---

[165] See e.g. *R. v. Secretary of State for Trade and Industry, ex parte Greenpeace* [2000] 2 CMLR 94 (ruling that the 1992 Habitats Directive applies beyond UK territorial seas to areas over which the UK exercises sovereign rights).

[166] *United States – Import of Certain Shrimp and Shrimp Products*, AB-1998-4, 12 October 1998, para. 110 (Appellate Body overturning a ruling by a WTO panel that 'accepting non-requested information from non-governmental sources is incompatible with the [WTO Dispute Settlement Understanding]', at para. 110; *Methanex v. United States of America*, Decision of the Tribunal on Petitions from Third Persons to Intervene as 'Amici Curiae', 15 January 2001 (Tribunal ruling that by Art. 15(1) of the UNCITRAL rules it has power to accept written *amicus* submissions), at www.iisd.org/pdf/methanex_tribunal_first_amicus_decision.pdf.

[167] The 1958 High Seas Conservation Convention, Art. 9(1), specifically refers to Art. 33 of the UN Charter.

[168] 1940 Western Hemisphere Convention; 1946 International Whaling Convention.

envisages no fewer than three mechanisms to assist in dispute resolution or non-implementation: a Subsidiary Body for Implementation, to provide assistance in implementation; a multilateral consultative process to address questions regarding implementation in a non-confrontational way; and the settlement of remaining disputes in more traditional ways by negotiation, submission to arbitration or the ICJ, or international conciliation.[169]

Diplomatic means of dispute settlement

Negotiation and consultation

The technique of negotiation has been used to resolve a number of environmental disputes. In the *Fisheries Jurisdiction* case, the ICJ set forth the basic objectives underlying negotiation as an appropriate method for the resolution of a dispute. The ICJ held that the objective of negotiation should be:

> the delimitation of the rights and interests of the parties, the preferential rights of the coastal state on the one hand and the rights of the applicant on the other, to balance and regulate equitably questions such as those of catch-limitation, share allocations and 'related restrictions concerning areas closed to fishing, number and type of vessels allowed and forms of control of the agreed provisions'.[170]

The ICJ also set out conditions establishing that future negotiations should be conducted:

> on the basis that each must in good faith pay reasonable regard to the legal rights of the other . . . thus bringing about an equitable apportionment of the fishing resources based on the facts of the particular situation, and having regard to the interests of other states which have established fishing rights in the area. It is not a matter of finding simply an equitable solution, but an equitable solution derived from the applicable law.[171]

Environmental treaties refer, more or less as a matter of standard practice, to the need to ensure that parties resort to negotiation and other diplomatic channels to resolve their disputes before making use of other more formal

---

[169] 1992 Climate Change Convention, Arts. 10, 13 and 14. See also 1985 Vienna Convention, Art. 11; 1989 Basel Convention, Art. 20; 1992 Biodiversity Convention, Art. 27 and Annex II. See also the 1997 Kyoto Protocol, Arts. 15, 16 and 19; in addition, Art. 18 of the Kyoto Protocol provides for approval of procedures and mechanisms to address cases of non-compliance: see below.

[170] (1974) ICJ Reports 3 at 31.

[171] *Ibid.*, 33. The ICJ also invoked its earlier statement in the *North Sea Continental Shelf* cases, that 'it is not a question of applying equity simply as a matter of abstract justice, but of applying a rule of law which itself requires the application of equitable principles': *ibid.*, 47.

methods.[172] Since negotiations of this type invariably take place behind closed doors, it is difficult to identify specific examples involving the successful resolution of claims and disputes by negotiation. One case involved the settlement between Canada and the USSR concerning damage caused by the disintegration over Canada of Cosmos 954, a nuclear-powered satellite launched by the USSR. The negotiated settlement was agreed in the context of the USSR's consideration of the question of damage 'in strict accordance with the provisions' of the 1972 Space Liability Convention to which both countries were parties.[173]

Consultation between states is also encouraged by environmental treaties as a technique to avert and resolve disputes and potential disputes between states. In the *Lac Lanoux* case, the arbitral tribunal held that France had a duty to consult with Spain over certain projects likely to affect its interests, and that, in this context,

> the reality of the obligations thus undertaken is incontestable and sanctions can be applied in the event, for example, of an unjustified breaking off of the discussions, abnormal delays, disregard of the agreed procedures, systematic refusals to take into consideration adverse proposals or interests, and, more generally, in cases of violation of the rules of good faith.[174]

Specific examples of environmental treaties requiring consultation in certain situations include: development plans which may affect the natural resources of another state;[175] measures to prevent the pollution of coastlines from oil pollution incidents on the high seas;[176] the authorisation of ocean dumping in emergency situations;[177] pollution by certain substances from land-based sources;[178] the permissibility of environmentally harmful activities;[179] and generally problems in applying a treaty or the need for and nature of remedial measures for breaches of obligation.[180] The 1979 LRTAP Convention requires early consultations to be held between parties 'actually affected by or exposed to a significant risk of long-range transboundary air pollution' and the parties in which a significant contribution to such pollution originates.[181]

---

[172] 1973 CITES, Art. XVIII; MARPOL 73/78, Art. 10; 1972 Space Liability Convention, Art. IX; 1974 Baltic Convention, Art. 18(1); 1979 LRTAP Convention, Art. 13; 1985 Vienna Convention, Art. 11(1) and (2); 1992 Climate Change Convention, Art. 14; 1992 Biodiversity Convention, Art. 27(1).

[173] By a protocol dated 2 April 1981, the USSR agreed to pay, and Canada agreed to accept, C\$3 million in final settlement: chapter 18, pp. 896–8 below.

[174] *Lac Lanoux Arbitration*, 24 ILR 101 at 128 (1957).

[175] 1968 African Nature Convention, Art. XIV(3).   [176] 1969 CLC, Art. III(a).

[177] 1972 London Convention, Art. V(2).   [178] 1974 Paris Convention, Art. 9(1).

[179] 1974 Nordic Environmental Protection Convention, Art. 11.

[180] 1976 Pacific Fur Seals Convention, Art. XII; 1976 ENMOD Convention, Art. V(1) and Annex, providing for the establishing of a Consultative Committee of Experts.

[181] 1979 LRTAP Convention, Art. 5.

Mediation, conciliation, fact-finding and international institutions

Where negotiations and consultations fail, a number of environmental treaties endorse mediation[182] and conciliation[183] (or the establishment of a committee of experts[184]) to resolve disputes, all of which involve the intervention of a third person. In the case of mediation, the third person is involved as an active participant in the interchange of proposals between the parties to a dispute, and may even offer informal proposals. There are few reported examples of mediation being relied upon to resolve environmental disputes. Of recent note, however, is the outcome of a mediation conducted under the auspices of the OAS, relating to a long-standing territorial dispute between Guatemala and Belize. In September 2002, the two facilitators appointed by the OAS put forward proposals, approved by the two states and Honduras, for a resolution of the dispute, including the establishment of an ecological park and a tri-state sub-regional fisheries commission.[185]

In the case of conciliation, the third person assumes a more formal role and often investigates the details underlying the dispute and makes formal proposals for the resolution of the dispute. Examples of conciliation include the role of the International Joint Commission established by Canada and the United States in the 1909 Boundary Waters Treaty,[186] which fulfils a combination of quasi-judicial, investigative recommendatory and co-ordinating functions. The now defunct European Commission on Human Rights also performed conciliation functions: once a petition had been referred to it, it was required to ascertain the facts, to place itself at the disposal of the parties concerned with a view to securing a friendly settlement of the matter on the basis of respect for human rights as defined in the Convention, and, where no such friendly settlement was reached, to draw up a report on the facts and state its opinion as to whether the facts found disclosed a breach of obligations under the

---

[182] 1968 African Nature Convention, Art. XVIII (referring disputes to the Commission of Mediation, Conciliation and Arbitration of the OAU); 1976 European Convention for the Protection of Animals Kept for Farming Purposes, Art. 10; 1982 UNCLOS, Art. 284 and Annex V, Section 1; 1985 Vienna Convention, Art. 11(2).

[183] 1963 Vienna Convention, Optional Protocol Concerning the Compulsory Settlement of Disputes, Art. III; 1974 Paris LBS Convention, Art. 21 (conciliation by a Commission); 1985 Vienna Convention, Art. 11(4) and (5) (providing for the establishment of a conciliation commission); 1992 Biodiversity Convention, Art. 27(4) and Annex II, Part 2; 1992 Climate Change Convention, Art. 14(5) to (7); 1998 Chemicals Convention, Art. 20; 2001 POPs Convention, Art. 18. See also the Permanent Court of Arbitration, Optional Rules for Conciliation of Diputes Relating to Natural Resources and the Environment, 16 April 2002 (http://pca-cpa.org/PDF/envconciliation.pdf).

[184] 1949 FAO Mediterranean Fisheries Agreement, Art. XIII; 1951 International Plant Protection Convention, Art. IX; 1952 North Pacific Fisheries Convention, Protocol, paras. 4 and 5 (special committee of scientists).

[185] Available at www.caricom.org/belize-guatemala.htm.

[186] 1909 Boundary Waters Treaty, especially Arts. VIII and IX.

Convention.[187] The Dispute Settlement Panels established under the GATT performed a similar function of conciliation.[188] Under Article XXIII(2) of the GATT, the Panels assisted the parties to a dispute to reach a solution and, failing that, made an objective assessment of the matter before them, including an objective assessment of the facts of the case and the applicability of and conformity with the GATT.[189] If requested by the contracting parties, the Panels made such other findings, including recommendations, as would assist them in making recommendations or in giving rulings.

The 1997 Watercourses Convention provides that where negotiation fails to lead to a successful outcome the parties may jointly seek the good offices of, or request mediation or conciliation by, a third party, or make use, as appropriate, of any joint watercourse institutions that may have been established by them.[190] Where a dispute has not been settled within six months of a request for negotiations, any of the parties to the dispute may submit the dispute to impartial fact-finding in accordance with the Convention, unless the parties otherwise agree, and the fact-finding commission is to submit its report to the parties concerned setting forth its findings (with reasons) and such recommendations as it deems appropriate for an equitable resolution of the dispute, which the parties concerned must consider in good faith.[191] Under the 1985 Vienna Convention, the 1992 Biodiversity Convention and the 2001 Treaty on Plant Genetic Resources, conciliation will be used if the parties to the dispute have not accepted compulsory dispute settlement procedures by arbitration or the ICJ.[192]

The political organs of international institutions and regional agencies also play an important role in the settlement of disputes. Such organs may be granted an express mandate to consider disputes between two or more parties to the treaty.[193] Alternatively, they may attempt to resolve disputes between parties in the absence of a specific mandate to do so. Examples of the latter include the 1985 decision of the conference of the parties to CITES concerning the application of the Convention to endangered species acquired prior to the entry into force of the Convention,[194] and the 1991 decision of the Executive Committee of the 1971 Oil Pollution Fund Convention to exclude claims by Italy against the Fund for non-quantifiable damage to the marine environment.[195]

---

[187] 1950 ECHR, Arts. 28 and 31(1).

[188] See also dispute settlement under the NAFTA, chapter 19 below.

[189] See BISD 26S/210, Understanding Regarding Notification, Consultation, Dispute Settlement and Surveillance, adopted 28 November 1979. On panel decisions relating to environmental matters, see chapter 19, pp. 952–85 below.

[190] Art. 33(2).   [191] Art. 33(3).

[192] 1985 Vienna Convention, Art. 11; 1992 Biodiversity Convention, Art. 27; 2001 Treaty on Plant Genetic Resources, Art. 22.

[193] See e.g. 1982 Jeddah Convention, Art. XXIV(2); 1988 Agreement on the Network of Aquaculture Centres in Asia and the Pacific, Art. 19(1).

[194] See chapter 10, p. 514 below.   [195] See *The Haven Incident*, chapter 18, pp. 920–2 below.

Another example of this approach includes the 1974 Nordic Environmental Protection Convention, which provides for the establishment of a Commission upon the demand of any party to give an opinion on the permissibility of environmentally harmful activities which entail considerable nuisance in another party.[196] The 1985 South Pacific Nuclear Free Zone Treaty establishes a control system which includes a complaints procedure involving the possible convening of a Consultative Committee to consider complaints and evidence of breach of obligations, with certain inspection powers, and the right to report fully to members of the South Pacific Forum and to give its decision as to whether a breach of obligation has occurred.[197] Under the 1991 Espoo Convention, if the parties cannot agree on whether a proposed activity is likely to result in a 'significant adverse transboundary impact', any party involved in the disagreement may submit that question to an Inquiry Commission.[198] The Inquiry Commission, comprising three members, will advise and prepare an opinion based on 'accepted scientific principles' on the likelihood of significant adverse transboundary impact, and may take all appropriate measures to carry out its functions.[199] Finally, the procedure established under the Conference on Security and Co-operation in Europe provides an alternative means of achieving conciliation.[200]

Non-compliance procedures

E. Barratt-Brown, 'Building a Monitoring and Compliance Regime Under the Montreal Protocol', 16 *Yale Journal of International Law* 519 (1991); M. Koskenniemi, 'Breach of Treaty or Non-Compliance: Reflections on the Enforcement of the Montreal Protocol', 3 *Yearbook of International Environmental Law* 123 (1992); J. Werksman, 'Compliance and Transition: Russia's Non-Compliance Tests the Ozone Regime', 36 ZaöRV 750 (1996); J. Werksman, 'Compliance and the Kyoto Protocol', 9 *Yearbook of International Environmental Law* 48 (1998); O. Yoshida, 'Soft Enforcement of Treaties: The Montreal Non-Compliance Procedure and the Functions of the Internal International Institutions', 10 *Colorado Journal of International Environmental Law and Policy* 95 (1999); M. Fitzmaurice and C. Redgwell, 'Environmental Non-Compliance Procedures and International Law', 31 NYIL 35 (2000); P. Kalas and A. Herwig, 'Dispute Resolution under the Kyoto Protocol', 27 *Ecology Law Quarterly* 53 (2001)

One of the most significant developments in the field of international environmental law has been the emergence of non-compliance procedures under various multilateral environmental agreements, occupying a function between conciliation and traditional dispute settlement. Since the early 1990s, a significant number of treaties have established subsidiary bodies to deal with compliance and disputes over non-compliance. The first was the

---

[196] Arts. 11 and 12.   [197] Art. 8 and Annex 4.   [198] Art. 3(7).
[199] Appendix IV.   [200] See n. 15 above.

non-compliance procedure established under the 1987 Montreal Protocol, including the Implementation Committee established by the second meeting of the parties to the Protocol.[201] Under the non-compliance procedure, any party which has reservations about another party's implementation of its obligations under the Protocol may submit its concerns in writing to the secretariat, with corroborating information.[202] The secretariat will then determine, with the assistance of the party alleged to be in violation, whether it is unable to comply with its obligations under the Protocol, and will transmit the original submission, its reply and other information to the Implementation Committee.[203] The Implementation Committee has a membership of ten parties (originally five) elected by the meeting of the parties on the basis of equitable geographical distribution for a two-year period. Its functions are to receive, consider and report on submissions made by any party regarding another party's implementation of its obligations under the Protocol, and any information or observations forwarded by the secretariat in connection with the preparation of reports based on information submitted by the parties pursuant to their obligations under the Protocol.[204] The Committee may, at the invitation of the party concerned, undertake information gathering in the territory of that party, and will also maintain an exchange of information with the Executive Committee of the Multilateral Fund related to the provisions of financial and technical co-operation to developing country parties.[205] The Committee is to try to secure 'an amicable resolution of the matter on the basis of respect for the provisions of the Protocol' and report to the meeting of the parties, which may decide upon and call for steps to bring about full compliance with the Protocol.[206] The fourth meeting of the parties also adopted an indicative list of measures that might be taken by a meeting of the parties in respect of non-compliance, which comprise:

- appropriate assistance;
- issuing cautions; and
- suspension (in accordance with the applicable rules of international law concerning the suspension of the operation of a treaty) of specific rights and privileges under the Protocol.[207]

---

[201] See Decision II/5 (non-compliance), Report of the Second Meeting of the Parties to the Montreal Protocol on Substances that Deplete the Ozone Layer, UNEP/OzL.Pro.2/3, 29 June 1990; see now Decision IV/5 and Annexes IV and V, adopting the non-compliance procedure; Report of the Fourth Meeting of the Parties, UNEP/OzL.Pro.4/15, 25 November 1992, 32 ILM 874 (1993); see chapter 8, pp. 356–7 below. The 1992 Climate Change Convention provides for the possible establishment of a 'multilateral consultative process, available to the parties on their request, for the resolution of questions regarding the implementation of the Convention': Art. 13.

[202] Annex IV, para. 1.   [203] Paras. 2 to 4.

[204] Para. 7(a) and (b). Decision IV/5 and Annex IV; see n. 201 above.

[205] Para. 7(d) and (e).   [206] Paras. 8 and 9.

[207] Fourth Meeting of the Parties to the 1987 Montreal Protocol, n. 201 above. Decision IV/5.

The Committee's report must not contain confidential information and is to be made available to any person upon request.[208] Significantly, resort to the non-compliance procedure does not prejudice the dispute settlement provisions available under Article 11 of the 1985 Vienna Convention, which include negotiation, good offices, mediation, arbitration, submission to the ICJ and the establishment of a conciliation commission.[209]

Following the developments under the Montreal Protocol, non-compliance procedures have been established (or are in the process of being established) under other multilateral environmental agreements, including the 1989 Basel Convention,[210] the 1991 VOC and 1994 Sulphur Protocols to the LRTAP Convention,[211] the 1996 Protocol to the London Convention,[212] the 1998 Chemicals Convention,[213] the 2000 Biosafety Protocol,[214] and the 2001 POPs Convention.[215] The two most significant arrangements, however, are reflected in the mechanisms established under the 1997 Kyoto Protocol and the 1998 Aarhus Convention.

Article 18 of the Kyoto Protocol calls on the conference of the parties serving as the meeting of the parties to the Kyoto Protocol to approve, at its first session, 'appropriate and effective procedures and mechanisms to address cases of non-compliance', with the caveat that any procedures and mechanisms entailing binding consequences 'shall be adopted by means of an amendment to [the] Protocol'. In 2001, at the seventh conference of the parties, the parties adopted a decision on the compliance regime for the Kyoto Protocol, which is among the most comprehensive and rigorous established thus far.[216] The compliance regime consists of a Compliance Committee made up of two branches: a Facilitative Branch and an Enforcement Branch. The Facilitative Branch aims to provide advice and assistance to parties to promote compliance; the Enforcement Branch has the power to apply consequences to parties not meeting their commitments. Both branches are to be composed of ten members, including one representative from each of the five official UN regions, one from the small island developing states, and two each from Annex I and non-Annex I parties. Decisions of the Facilitative Branch may be taken by a three-quarters majority, but decisions of the Enforcement Branch require, in addition, a double majority of both Annex I and non-Annex I parties. The Committee also meets in a plenary composed of members of both branches, and a Bureau supports its

---

[208] Paras. 15 and 16.

[209] M. Koskenniemi, 'Breach of a Treaty or Non-Compliance? Reflections on Enforcement of the Montreal Protocol', 3 *Yearbook of International Environmental Law* 123 (1992).

[210] See COP Decision V/16, Mechanism for promoting implementation and compliance of the Basel Convention, UNEP/CH.5/29, 10 December 1999.

[211] Decision 1997/2, LRTAP Convention Executive Body (http://www.unece.org/env/lrtap/conv/report/eb53_a3.htm). For examples of decisions of the Implementation Committee, see Executive Body decisions 2001/3 (Italy), 2001/2 (Finland), 2001/1 (Norway), 2000/1 (Slovenia).

[212] Art. 11.   [213] Art. 17.   [214] Art. 34.   [215] Art. 17.

[216] Decision 24/CP.7, FCCC/CP/2001/13/Add.3, 10 November 2001.

work. Certain commitments fall under the remit of one or the other branch. The requirement, for example, of the flexibility mechanisms[217] to be 'supplemental' to domestic action is under the purview of the Facilitative Branch, as is the commitment of Annex I parties to strive to minimise adverse impacts on developing countries. The Facilitative Branch also provides 'early-warning' of cases where a party is in danger of not complying with its emission targets. In response to problems, the Facilitative Branch can make recommendations and also mobilise financial and technical resources to help parties comply. The Enforcement Branch, for its part, is responsible for determining whether an Annex I party is not complying with its emission targets or reporting requirements, or has lost its eligibility to participate in the mechanisms. It can also decide whether to adjust a party's inventory or correct the compilation and accounting database, in the event of a dispute between a party and the expert review team. The remedies it may decide on are to be aimed at the 'restoration of compliance to ensure environmental integrity'. In the case of compliance with emission targets, Annex I parties are granted 100 days after the expert review of their final annual emissions inventory has finished to remedy any shortfall in compliance. If, at the end of this period, a party's emissions are still greater than its assigned amount, it must make up the difference in the second commitment period, plus a penalty of 30 per cent. It will also be barred from 'selling' under emissions trading and, within three months, it must develop a compliance action plan detailing the action it will take to ensure that its target is met in the next commitment period. Any party not complying with reporting requirements must develop a similar plan, and parties that are found not to meet the criteria for participating in the mechanisms will have their eligibility withdrawn. In all cases, the Enforcement Branch will make a public declaration that the party is in non-compliance and will also make public the consequences to be applied. A potential compliance problem can be raised either by an expert review team, or by a party about its own compliance, or by a party raising concerns about another party. After a preliminary examination, the matter will be considered in the relevant branch of the Compliance Committee. The Compliance Committee will base its deliberations on reports from expert review teams, the subsidiary bodies, parties and other official sources.[218] Competent intergovernmental and non-governmental organisations may submit relevant factual and technical information to the relevant branch.

---

[217] Chapter 8, p. 372 below.

[218] The Marrakesh Accords set out more detailed additional procedures with specific timeframes for the Enforcement Branch, including the opportunity for a party facing the Compliance Committee to make formal written submissions and request a hearing where it can present its views and call on expert testimony. In the case of non-compliance with emission targets, the party can also lodge an appeal to the conference of the parties/meeting of the parties if that party believes it has been denied due process.

In October 2002, the parties to the Aarhus Convention established a Compliance Committee to review compliance by the parties with their obligations under the Convention.[219] The Committee consists of eight members, elected from candidates nominated by parties and signatories and – innovatively – non-governmental organisations. The functions of the Committee are to consider any submission, referral or communication made to it, to prepare a report on compliance with or implementation of the provisions of the Convention, and to monitor, assess and facilitate the implementation of and compliance with reporting requirements. In consultation with the party concerned, the Committee may provide advice and facilitate assistance to individual parties regarding the implementation of the Convention. Subject to agreement with the party concerned the Committee may also:

- make recommendations to the party concerned;
- request the party concerned to submit a strategy to the Committee regarding the achievement of compliance with the Convention and to report on the implementation of this strategy; and
- in cases of communications from the public, make recommendations to the party concerned on specific measures to address the matter raised by the member of the public.

The meeting of the parties may, upon consideration of a report and any recommendations of the Committee, decide upon appropriate measures to bring about full compliance with the Convention, including declarations of non-compliance, issuing cautions, suspending special rights and privileges under the Convention, and taking such other non-confrontational, non-judicial and consultative measures as may be appropriate. The Committee may receive submissions from parties and referrals from the secretariat. Breaking new ground, the Committee may also receive communications from the public.[220] Communications from the public are to be addressed in writing to the Committee through the secretariat and supported by corroborating information. In language which will be familiar to human rights lawyers, the Committee is to consider any such communication unless it determines that the communication is anonymous, or an abuse of the right to make such communications, or manifestly unreasonable, or incompatible with the provisions of the decision establishing the Committee or with the Convention. Although there is no rule requiring exhaustion of local remedies, the Committee 'should at all relevant stages take into account any available domestic remedy unless the application of the remedy is unreasonably prolonged or obviously does not provide an effective and sufficient means of redress'.[221] The Committee must bring any

[219] Decision I/7, 23 October 2002.
[220] Parties may notify the depositary that they will not accept consideration of such communications, but only up to a maximum period of four years: para. 18.
[221] Para. 21.

communications so submitted to the attention of the party alleged to be in non-compliance, and the party must within five months after any communication is brought to its attention by the Committee submit to the Committee a written statement clarifying the matter and describing any response that it may have made. The Committee may hold hearings.

Inspection procedures of multilateral development banks

I. Shihata, *The World Bank Inspection Panel* (1994); S. Schlemmer-Schulte, 'The World Bank's Experience with Its Inspection Panel', 58 ZaöRV 353 (1998); L. Boisson de Chazournes, 'Le Panel d'inspection de la Banque mondiale: à propos de la complexification de l'espace public international', RGDIP 145 (2001); G. Afredsson and R. Ring (eds.), *The World Bank Inspection Panel* (2001).

In September 1993, the World Bank became the first multilateral development bank to create an Inspection Panel to receive and review requests for inspection from a party which claimed to be affected by a World Bank project, including claims in respect of environmental harm.[222] This innovation was followed by similar arrangements established at the Inter-American Development Bank (an Independent Investigation Mechanism, established in 1994)[223] and the Asian Development Bank (1995).[224] These new mechanisms provide substantive and independent review of the activities of these banks and have enhanced access to international remedies for non-state actors.

The World Bank Inspection Panel became operational in late 1994. An affected party (or, in limited cases, its representatives) may request an inspection if it can

> demonstrate that its rights or interests have been or are likely to be directly affected by an action or omission of the Bank as a result of a failure of the Bank to follow its operational policies and procedures with respect to the design, appraisal and/or implementation of a project financed by the Bank . . . provided in all cases that such failure has had, or threatens to have, a material adverse effect.[225]

The Panel, which consists of three members, may make a recommendation to the Executive Directors as to whether a matter complained of should be investigated, having been provided by evidence from the management of the Bank

---

[222] Resolution of the Executive Directors No. IBRD 93-10 and IDA 93-6, 22 September 1993. The resolutions have been subject to Clarifications, adopted on 17 October 1996 and 20 April 1999. See http://wbln0018.worldbank.org/ipn/ipnweb.nsf.

[223] See www.iadb.org/cont/poli/investig.htm.

[224] *ADB's Inspection Policy: A Guidebook* (1996); see also www.adb.org/Inspection/default.asp. Inspection is carried out by three persons from a roster of sixteen experts.

[225] *Ibid.*, para. 12. 'Operational policies and procedures' consist of the Bank's Operational Policies, Bank Procedures and Operational Directives, and similar documents issued before these series were started. They do not include Guidelines and Best Practices or similar documents or statements: *ibid.*

as to its compliance with the Bank's policies and procedures.[226] If the Executive Directors decide to investigate the matter, one or more members of the Panel (the Inspector(s)) will conduct an inspection and report to the Panel, which will then submit its report to the Executive Directors on whether the Bank has complied with its relevant policies and procedures.[227] This new review body represents an important development in international law, creating for the first time within a multilateral development bank an administrative procedure to permit review of the institution's compliance with its internal law at the instigation of third parties other than employees. The well-developed practice of administrative tribunals addressing employment and contractual matters for Bank staff is, in effect, extended into the fields of environmental and social review. By October 2002, the Panel had received twenty-seven requests, the largest number concerning compliance with the operational directive on environmental assessment (OD 4.01).[228] Requests have also addressed the environmental policy for dam and reservoir projects (OD 4.00), environmental aspects of Bank work (OMS 2.36), indigenous peoples (OD 4.20), water resource and management (OP 4.07), wildlands (OPN 11.02) and natural habitats (OP/BP 4.04).[229]

NAFTA Commission on Environmental Co-operation

Citizen access to an independent fact-finding mechanism is available under the NAFTA: the secretariat of NAFTA's Commission on Environmental Co-operation may receive and consider submissions from any non-governmental organisation or person asserting that a party is 'failing to effectively enforce its environmental law', and may request a response from the party concerned if it determines that the submission so merits.[230] The Secretariat may be instructed by the Council, by a two-thirds vote, to prepare a 'factual record' which may be made public by the Council.[231] Since 1996, the secretariat has received submissions in respect of thirty-six matters, of which twelve are currently active. The

---

[226] *Ibid.*, paras. 18 and 19.

[227] *Ibid.*, paras. 20 and 22. The 1999 Clarifications provide that if the Panel so recommends the Board will authorise an investigation without making a judgment on the merits of the claimant's request: para. 9.

[228] See e.g. Request No. 19 (Lake Victoria Environmental Management Project), in which the Panel found that Managament was not in full compliance with OD 4.01, where Managament had made no prior review of the environmental consequences of water disposal, and that environmental and other data necessary for subsequent assessments had not been obtained; and Request No. 22 (Chad–Cameroon Pipeline Projects), failing to comply with the requirement to carry out a regional environmental assessment.

[229] See Annual Report, 1 August 2001 to 30 June 2002.

[230] Agreement on Environment Co-operation, Art. 14; see chapter 19, pp. 1005–6 below. See generally www.cec.org/citizen/index.cfm?varlan=english; and Commission for Environmental Co-operation, *Bringing the Facts to Light: A Guide to Articles 14 and 15 of the NAEEC* (2000).

[231] Art. 15. The procedure has been used by NGOs in all three of the NAFTA state parties to raise issues of non-compliance with environmental laws. Factual records have been

secretariat has published factual records in respect of three matters: *Cozumel* (24 October 1997);[232] *BC Hydro* (11 June 2000);[233] and *Metales y Derivados* (11 February 2002).[234]

Legal means of dispute settlement

Mediation and conciliation do not produce legally binding decisions. If the parties to a dispute seek such a result, they must opt for arbitration or recourse to an international court.[235]

Arbitration

International arbitration has been described as having 'for its object the settlement of disputes between states by judges of their own choice and on the basis of respect for the law. Recourse to arbitration implies an engagement to submit in good faith to the award.'[236] In recent years, states negotiating environmental treaties have favoured the inclusion of specific provisions for the establishment of an arbitration tribunal, with the power to adopt binding and final decisions. Early examples providing for the establishment of a body to take binding decisions include the 'special commission' to be established at the request of any of the parties to disputes relating to high seas fishing and conservation,[237] and the detailed provisions on the establishment of an arbitration tribunal in the Annex to the 1969 Oil Pollution Intervention Convention.[238] Other environmental treaties include provisions, including annexes or protocols, for the submission of disputes to arbitration at the instigation of one party to a dispute[239] or both

---

produced in several cases but as yet no arbitral panel has been established to hear a complaint. Records of the submissions made, factual reports and responses of NAFTA parties are made available by the Commission for Environmental Co-operation on its website, www.cec.org/citizen/index.cfm?varlan=english.

[232] *Cozumel*, SEM-96-001, 24 October 1997.

[233] *BC Hydro*, SEM-97-001, 11 June 2000.

[234] *Metales y Derivados*, SEM-98-007, 11 February 2002 (experts who have studied the site in question concur that the site must be remediated and that, given the volume of contaminated material and lead concentrations there present, it is urgent to forestall the dispersal of pollutants and limit access to the site so as to prevent adverse health effects on people living or working in its proximity).

[235] For an assessment of the composition of a court or tribunal on substantive environmental outcomes (in the US Court of Appeals for the District of Columbia), see R. Revesz, 'Environmental Regulation, Ideology and the DC Circuit', 83 *Virginia Law Review* 1717 (1997); and R. Revesz, 'Congressional Influence on Judicial Behaviour? An Empirical Examination of Challenges to Agency Action in the DC Circuit', 76 NYULR 1100 (2001).

[236] 1907 Hague Convention on the Pacific Settlement of International Disputes, Art. 37.

[237] 1958 High Seas Conservation Convention, Arts. 9 to 12.

[238] Art. VIII and Annex, Chapter II.

[239] MARPOL 73/78, Art. 10 and Protocol 11; 1974 Paris Convention, Art. 21 and Annex B; 1976 Rhine Chemical Pollution Convention, Art. 15 and Annex B; 1976 Convention

parties.[240] Other treaties refer simply to the possibility of submitting disputes to arbitration without providing details on the establishment of such a body or its working arrangements.[241] Certain environmental treaties provide for the submission of disputes to arbitration by mutual consent of the relevant parties[242] or allow a party to declare, at the time of signature or ratification, that it is not bound by parts of the dispute settlement provisions, including submission to arbitration,[243] or provide for a party to declare, at the time of signature or ratification, or at any time thereafter, its acceptance of compulsory recourse to arbitration and/or the ICJ.[244]

The *Pacific Fur Seals Arbitration* (1893),[245] the *Trail Smelter* case (1935/41)[246] and the *Lac Lanoux* case (1957)[247] reflect the historical importance played by arbitration in the development of international environmental law, in inter-state cases. More recently, there is growing evidence to support the view that states view arbitration as an attractive means of resolving international disputes. Within the past few years, the 1982 UNCLOS Annex VII arbitration procedure has been invoked on two occasions: in 1998 by Australia and New Zealand against Japan, in relation to a dispute concerning the conservation of southern bluefin tuna;[248] and in 2001 by Ireland against the United Kingdom, in the dispute concerning the authorisation of the MOX plant.[249] Additionally, France and the Netherlands have submitted a dispute to arbitration in relation to a dispute under the 1976 Rhine Chloride Convention and its 1991 Protocol, and Ireland initiated arbitration proceedings against the United Kingdom in relation to freedom of information under Article 9 of the 1992 OSPAR Convention.[250] Against that background, the Permanent Court of Arbitration (which has served as the registry in most of these disputes) has sponsored the adoption of arbitration rules specifically designed to address needs arising from the arbitration of disputes relating to the environment and natural

on the Protection of the Rhine Against Pollution by Chlorides, Art. 13 and Annex B; 1979 Berne Convention, Art. 18; 1988 CRAMRA, Arts. 55 to 59 and Annex; 1992 OSPAR Convention, Art. 32(2); 1994 Danube Convention, Art. 24; 1995 SADC Water Protocol, Art. 7; 1996 LDC Protocol, Art. 16; 1998 Rhine Convention, Art. 16; 2000 SADC Revised Water Protocol, Art. 7.

[240] 1976 Barcelona Convention, Art. 22 and Annex A; 1980 CCAMLR, Art. XXV and Annex; 1983 Cartagena Convention, Art. 23 and Annex; 1986 Noumea Convention, Art. 26 and Annex.

[241] 1974 Baltic Convention, Art. 18; 1985 Vienna Convention, Art. 11.

[242] 1973 CITES, Art. XVIII (to the Permanent Court of Arbitration at The Hague); 1989 Basel Convention, Art. 20 and Annex VI.

[243] 1986 Early Notification Convention, Art. 11; 1986 Assistance Convention, Art. 13.

[244] 1992 Biodiversity Convention, Art. 27 and Annex II, Part 1; 1992 Climate Change Convention, Art. 14; 1992 Watercourses Convention, Art. 22; 1992 Industrial Accident Convention, Art. 21.

[245] Chapter 11, pp. 561–6 below.   [246] Chapter 8, pp. 318–19 below.
[247] Chapter 10, pp. 463–4 below.   [248] Chapter 11, pp. 580–1 below.
[249] Chapter 9, p. 436 below.   [250] Chapter 17, p. 857 below.

resources.[251] The growing role of arbitration is also reflected in the case law of arbitral tribunals in investor/state disputes involving allegations of interference with foreign investments occasioned by municipal concerns to protect the environment.[252]

International courts

The settlement of international disputes may also be referred to an international court, which is a permanent tribunal competent to deliver a legally binding decision. In the environmental field, a number of international courts have assumed particular importance, namely, the ICJ, the ITLOS, the WTO Appellate Body (and panels), the ECJ, and the courts created by regional human rights treaties. In addition, several non-governmental efforts aim to establish 'international courts' to address international environmental issues. While not creating binding arrangements, these provide a useful way to bring environmental issues to the attention of the public.[253] Notwithstanding certain calls for its creation, there is as yet no international environmental court, and none is likely to emerge in the foreseeable future.[254]

---

[251] Adopted 19 June 2001; available at www.pca-cpa.org/EDR/ENRrules.htm. The Rules are available for the use of all parties who have agreed to use them; states, intergovernmental organisations, non-governmental organisations and private entities. The Rules provide for the *optional* use of a panel of arbitrators with experience and expertise in environmental or conservation of natural resources law nominated by the member states and the Secretary General, respectively (Art. 8(3)), and a panel of environmental scientists nominated by the member states and the Secretary General, respectively, who can provide expert scientific assistance to the parties and the arbitral tribunal (Art. 27(5)). The Rules also make provision for the submission to the arbitral tribunal of a document agreed to by the parties, summarising and providing background to any scientific or technical issues which the parties may wish to raise in their memorials or at oral hearings (Art. 24(4)), and empower the arbitral tribunal to order any interim measures necessary to prevent serious harm to the environment, inless the parties agree otherwise (Art. 26). Recognising that time may be an important element in disputes concerning natural resources and the environment, the Rules provide for arbitration in a shorter period of time than under previous PCA Optional Rules or the UNCITRAL Rules. The PCA Rules have been recommended for use by the Facilitators in the Belize/Guatemala matter (see n. 142 above and the accompanying text).

[252] See chapter 21 (involving arbitration proceedings under ICSID, ICSID (Additional Facility) and UNCITRAL rules).

[253] The International Water Tribunal, based in the Netherlands; the International Court for the Protection of the Environment (established by the International Juridical Organisation for Environment and Development, Rome, in relation to the 1976 Barcelona Convention). See also A. Postiglione, 'A More Efficient International Law on the Environment and Setting Up an International Court for the Environment within the United Nations', 20 *Environmental Law* 321 (1990).

[254] See A. Postiglione, 'An International Court for the Environment?', 23 *Environmental Policy and Law* 73 (1993); A. Rest, 'An International Court for the Environment: The Role of the PCA', 4 *Asia Pacific Journal of Environmental Law* 107 (1999); P. Sands, 'International

International Court of Justice

S. Rosenne, *The Law and Practice of the* ICJ (1965); S. Rosenne, *Procedure in the International Court: A Commentary on the 1978 Rules of the ICJ* (1983); S. Rosenne, *The World Court: What It Is and How It Works* (1989); R. Jennings, 'The Role of the International Court of Justice in the Development of International Environment Protection Law', 1 RECIEL 240 (1992); R. Ranjeva, 'L'environnement, la cour internationale de justice et sa chambre speciale pour les questions d'environnement', AFDI 433 (1994); V. Coussirat-Coustere, 'La reprise des éssais nucléaires francais devant la cour internationale de justice (observations sur l'ordonnance du 22 septembre 1995)', AFDI 355 (1995); M. Fitzmaurice, 'Environmental Law and the International Court of Justice', in V. Lowe and M. Fitzmaurice (eds.), *Fifty Years of the International Court of Justice* (1996), 293; L. Boisson de Chazournes and P. Sands, *International Law, the International Court of Justice and Nuclear Weapons* (1999); P. Sands, 'International Courts and the Application of the Concept of "Sustainable Development"', 3 *Max Planck Yearbook of UN Law* (1999), 389; B. Kwiatkowska, 'The Contribution of the ICJ to the Development of the Law of the Sea and Environmental Law', 8 RECIEL 10 (1999).

The ICJ, sometimes referred to as the World Court or the Hague Court, is the UN's principal judicial organ. It was established as a successor (although not formally the legal successor) to the Permanent Court of International Justice (PCIJ) in 1945. Jurisdiction of the ICJ over a dispute depends on whether the Court has been invoked in a contentious case between two or more states, or asked to give an advisory opinion on a question of law at the request of states or certain international organisations.[255]

In July 1993, the ICJ established a seven-member Chamber for Environmental Matters. This decision followed previous consideration by the ICJ on the possible formation of such a chamber, and was taken in view of the developments in the field of environmental law which have taken place in the last few years and the need to be prepared to the fullest possible extent to deal with any environmental case falling within its jurisdiction.[256]

Contentious cases The contentious jurisdiction of the ICJ can arise in at least two ways. First, under Article 36(1) of its Statute, the ICJ has jurisdiction by agreement between the parties to the dispute, either by a special agreement

Environmental Litigation and Its Future', 32 *University of Richmond Law Review* 1619 (1999); E. Hey, *Reflections on an International Environmental Court* (2000).

[255] In relation to contentious cases, 'only states may be parties in cases before the Court': UN Charter, Art. 34(1).

[256] ICJ, Communiqué 93/20, 19 July 1993. The Chamber was established under Art. 26(1) of the Statute of the ICJ; seven judges are elected by secret ballot to serve on the Chamber, which has not yet been utilised.

whereby two or more states agree to refer a particular dispute and defined matter to the ICJ, or by a compromissory clause in a multilateral or bilateral treaty. The treaty could be a general treaty for the peaceful settlement of disputes, a treaty dealing with the general relations between the states, or a treaty regulating a specific topic, such as environmental protection. Many environmental treaties provide for possible recourse to the ICJ to settle disputes. Occasionally, they recognise its compulsory jurisdiction,[257] but more usually the reference of a dispute to the ICJ requires the consent, in each case, of all parties to the dispute.[258] Recent practice in environmental treaties allows parties at the time of signature, ratification or accession, or at any time thereafter, to accept compulsory dispute settlement by recourse to arbitration or to the ICJ.[259] Few parties accept this option.

A second way in which contentious cases come before the ICJ is under Article 36(2) of its Statute (the 'Optional Clause'), under which parties to the Statute may declare that they recognise its compulsory jurisdiction, in relation to other states accepting the same obligation, in all legal disputes concerning the interpretation of a treaty; any question of international law; the existence of any fact which, if established, would constitute a breach of an international obligation; and the nature or extent of the reparation to be made for the breach of an international obligation.[260] Acceptance of the jurisdiction of the ICJ under Article 36(2) may be made unconditionally, or on condition of reciprocity, or for a limited period of time.[261] Additionally, the practice of the ICJ has been to accept reservations or conditions to declarations made under the Optional Clause, as happened in the *Fisheries Jurisdiction* case (*Spain v. Canada*).[262]

Unlike its predecessor, the PCIJ, the ICJ has now been presented with opportunities to address international environmental disputes – raising matters concerning environment and conservation – and has given judgments which establish – or imply – important general principles. Relevant cases before the

---

[257] 1963 Vienna Convention, Optional Protocol Concerning the Compulsory Settlement of Disputes, Art. 1 (not in force); 1980 Convention on the Physical Protection of Nuclear Materials, Art. 17(2).

[258] 1959 Antarctic Treaty, Art. XI(2); 1974 Baltic Convention, Art. 18(2).

[259] 1985 Vienna Convention, Art. 11(3); 1989 Basel Convention, Art. 20(3); 1992 Climate Change Convention, Art. 14(2); 1992 Biodiversity Convention, Art. 27(3); 1992 Industrial Accidents Convention, Art. 21; 1992 Watercourses Convention, Art. 22; 1998 Chemicals Convention, Art. 20(2); 2001 POPs Convention, Art. 18(2).

[260] Statute of the ICJ, Art. 36(2). As of 1 January 2002, sixty-five states have accepted the Optional Clause.

[261] Art. 36(3).

[262] (1998) ICJ Reports 432, giving effect to (and finding that the dispute was covered by) Canada's reservation (made in its Declaration of 10 May 1994 under Art. 36(2)) excluding from the jurisdiction of the Court 'disputes arising out of or concerning conservation and management measures taken by Canada with respect to vessels fishing in the NAFO Regulatory Area . . . and the enforcement of such measures'. On the dispute, see chapter 11, pp. 567–8 below.

PCIJ include the *Diversion of the Waters of the River Meuse*[263] and the *Territorial Jurisdiction of the International Commission of the River Oder.*[264] Early cases before the ICJ which have influenced the development of international environmental law include the *Corfu Channel* case, where the ICJ affirmed 'every state's obligation not to allow knowingly its territory to be used for acts contrary to the rights of other states';[265] the *Fisheries Jurisdiction* case, where the ICJ set forth basic principles governing consultations and other arrangements concerning the conservation of shared natural resources;[266] and the *Nuclear Tests* cases.[267] The ICJ has since had a number of cases before it which it considers as having important implications for international law 'on matters relating to the environment': the *Certain Phosphate Lands in Nauru* case, concerning the obligation, if any, of trustee states for, *inter alia*, the physical destruction of the island as a unit of self-determination accompanied by a failure to rehabilitate the land, as well as the nature and extent of obligations relating to permanent sovereignty over natural resources and entitlement to the costs of rehabilitation;[268] the *Gabcikovo-Nagymaros Project (Hungary/Slovakia)* case, addressing, *inter alia*, the use of international watercourses and international environmental law in relation to an agreement for the construction of two barrages which would result in the diversion of the Danube river;[269] the *Request for an Examination of the Situation*, brought by New Zealand in relation to the resumption of underground nuclear tests by France;[270] and the *Fisheries Jurisdiction* case, where Spain challenged the enforcement of fisheries conservation measures taken by Canada in areas beyond its exclusive economic zone.[271]

Advisory opinions   The UN Charter allows the General Assembly or the Security Council to request the ICJ to give an advisory opinion on any legal question,[272] and allows other organs of the UN and specialised agencies authorised by the General Assembly to request advisory opinions of the ICJ on legal questions arising within the scope of their activities.[273] Advisory opinions are not binding in law upon the requesting body, although in practice they are accepted and acted upon by that body. Although no legal question on an

---

[263] PCIJ Ser. A/B, No. 70.
[264] Chapter 10, p. 462 below.   [265] Chapter 6, p. 243, n. 39 below.
[266] Chapter 11, pp. 567–8 below.   [267] Chapter 8, pp. 319–21 below.
[268] Chapter 12, pp. 666–9 below; the case was settled in September 1993.
[269] Chapter 10, pp. 469–77 below.
[270] Chapter 9, pp. 578–80 below; chapter 15 below.
[271] Chapter 11, pp. 567–8 below.   [272] UN Charter, Art. 96(1).
[273] Art. 96(2). ECOSOC, the Trusteeship Council and fifteen of the specialised agencies have been authorised by the General Assembly, as have the IAEA, the Interim Committee of the General Assembly and the Committee for Applications for Review of the UN Administrative Tribunal. UNEP and the Commission on Sustainable Development have not been so authorised by the General Assembly.

environmental issue has been the subject of a request for an advisory opinion, this route could provide a useful and non-contentious way of obtaining independent international legal advice on environmental matters. In July 1996, the ICJ gave an advisory opinion on the legality of the use of nuclear weapons in the context of their effects on human health and the environment, arguably the most significant of the ICJ's pronouncements on international environmental law.[274]

Interim measures of protection   If it considers that the circumstances so require, the ICJ has the power to indicate interim measures of protection to preserve the rights of the parties to a dispute.[275] The irreparability of serious environmental damage could make interim measures particularly important in cases concerning environmental protection. During the preliminary phase of the *Nuclear Tests* cases, the ICJ indicated interim measures of protection, asking the parties to ensure that no action should be taken which might aggravate or extend the dispute or prejudice the rights of another party, and calling on France to 'avoid nuclear tests causing the deposit of radio-active fall-out on Australian territory'.[276] Interim measures of protection were also indicated in the *Fisheries Jurisdiction* cases,[277] but were refused by the ICJ in the *Passage Through the Great Belt* case.[278] They were also refused by the ICJ in ten cases brought by the Federal Republic of Yugoslavia to bring a halt to a bombing campaign. It was argued, *inter alia*, that attacks on oil refineries and chemical plants were having 'serious environmental effects on cities, towns and villages in the Federal Republic of Yugoslavia'.[279]

UNCLOS and ITLOS

A. O. Adede, *The System for Settlement of Disputes under the UNCLOS* (1987); S. Rosenne, 'Establishing the International Tribunal for the Law of the Sea', 89 AJIL 806 (1995); J. I. Charney, 'The Implications of Expanding International Dispute Settlement Systems: The 1982 Convention on the Law of the Sea', 90 AJIL 69 (1996); T. Treves, 'The Jurisdiction of the International Tribunal for the Law of the Sea', 37 *Indian Journal of International Law* 396 (1997); A. Boyle, 'Problems of Compulsory

---

[274] Chapter 7, p. 310 below.
[275] Statute of the ICJ, Art. 41. The ICJ has ruled that its provisional measures are legally binding: *Lagrand* case (*Germany* v. *United States*) (2001) ICJ Reports 000, 40 ILM 1069 (2001).
[276] Order for Interim Measures, (1973) ICJ Reports 99; (*New Zealand* v. *France*), Order for Interim Measures, (1973) ICJ Reports 135.
[277] *UK* v. *Iceland*, Order for Interim Measures, (1972) ICJ Reports 12; *Federal Republic of Germany* v. *Iceland*, (1972) ICJ Reports 30.
[278] *Finland* v. *Denmark*, (1991) ICJ Reports 9.
[279] E.g. *Case Concerning the Legality of the Use of Force* (*Yugoslavia* v. *United Kingdom*) (1999) ICJ Reports 826, para. 3.

Jurisdiction and the Settlement of Disputes Relating to Straddling Fish Stocks',
14 IJMCL 1 (1999); J. Noyes, 'The International Tribunal for the Law of the Sea',
32 *Cornell International Law Journal* 109 (1998); G. Eirikkson, *The International
Tribunal for the Law of the Sea* (2000).

Part XV of the 1982 UNCLOS addresses compulsory dispute settlement, allowing states at the time of signature, ratification or accession or at any time
thereafter to designate any of the following dispute settlement procedures: the
International Tribunal for the Law of the Sea (established in accordance with
Annex VI to UNCLOS); the ICJ; an arbitral tribunal (constituted in accordance
with Annex VII to UNCLOS); and a special arbitral tribunal (constituted in
accordance with Annex VIII to UNCLOS).[280] A state which does not designate
one of these means is deemed to have designated arbitration in accordance with
Annex VII, and where two or more states have designated different means the
dispute will go to arbitration (unless the parties agree otherwise).[281]

The compulsory dispute settlement procedure is limited to certain disputes
under the Convention. The exercise by a coastal state of its sovereign rights
or jurisdiction under UNCLOS is only subject to the compulsory procedures
when it is alleged that a coastal state has violated certain UNCLOS provisions,
including internationally lawful uses of the exclusive economic zone (EEZ) or
specified international rules and standards for the protection and preservation
of the marine environment which are applicable to that state and which are
established under UNCLOS or by a competent international organisation or
diplomatic conference.[282] Fisheries disputes will be subject to the compulsory
procedure, except for disputes over the sovereign right of a coastal state regarding the living resources of the EEZ (including the discretionary powers for
determining allowable catch, harvesting capacity, the allocation of surpluses
and the terms and conditions of its conservation and management laws and
regulations).[283] Such disputes may be submitted to the conciliation procedure
if it is alleged that the coastal state has manifestly failed to comply with its
obligations to maintain the living resources in the EEZ.[284] Parties may also
optionally declare that the compulsory procedures do not apply to disputes
concerning boundary delimitations, military activities, and those in respect of
which the Security Council is exercising its functions.[285]

Disputes relating to the exploration and exploitation of the international
seabed and ocean floor (known as the 'Area') and its resources are subject to
special, and rather complex, dispute settlement procedures, which will generally
involve disputes going to a Seabed Disputes Chamber of the International
Tribunal for the Law of the Sea.[286] The Seabed Disputes Chamber will have
jurisdiction over a wide range of disputes, including environmental disputes

---

[280] 1982 UNCLOS, Art. 287(1).   [281] Art. 287(3) and (5).   [282] Art. 297(1).
[283] Art. 297(3)(a).   [284] Art. 297(3)(b)(i).   [285] Art. 298.
[286] Arts. 186–191, and Annex VI, Arts. 35–40.

involving those engaged in activities in the Area (states parties, the Authority, state enterprises, legal or natural persons, and prospective contractors).[287]

The jurisdiction of ITLOS may also be invoked in certain circumstances where the parties to UNCLOS have not designated its use. Article 290(5) of the Convention provides that ITLOS may prescribe provisional measures pending the constitution of an arbitral tribunal to which a dispute is submitted. This provision has been invoked on two occasions: in 1998, Australia and New Zealand requested – and obtained – provisional measures from IT-LOS in respect of fishing for southern bluefin tuna by Japanese vessels;[288] and in 2001 ITLOS prescribed a provisional measure requiring Ireland and the United Kingdom to co-operate pending the constitution of the Annex VI arbitral tribunal.[289] Additionally, ITLOS has jurisdiction pursuant to Article 292 of UNCLOS to order the 'prompt' release of vessels apprehended by a coastal state.

ITLOS has given judgment on the merits in four cases, all of which involved vessels alleged to have been engaged in illegal fishing activities. In addressing these cases, ITLOS has sought to avoid expressing views on the underlying merits of the case, although in the most recent case – involving the Volga (*Russia* v. *Australia*) – its judgment expressed understanding as to 'international concerns about illegal, unregulated and unreported fishing' and appreciation as to the objectives 'behind the measures taken by states, including the states parties to CCAMLR, to deal with the problem'.[290]

Dispute Settlement Body of the World Trade Organization

P. Pescatore, W. Davey and A. Lowenfeld, *Handbook of GATT Dispute Settlement* (1991); E. Petersmann, 'International Trade Law and International Environmental Law – Prevention, and Settlement of International Disputes in GATT', 27 *Journal of World Trade* 43 (1993); E. U. Petersmann, 'The Dispute Settlement System of the World Trade Organization and the Evolution of the GATT Dispute Settlement System Since 1948', 31 CMLR 1157 (1994); A. Lowenfeld, 'Remedies Along with Rights: Institutional Reform in the New GATT', 88 AJIL 477 (1994); John H. Jackson, *The World Trading System: Law and Policy of International Economic Relations* (1997, 2nd edn); J. Cameron and K. Campbell (eds.), *Dispute Resolution in the World Trade Organization* (1998).

The 1994 WTO Agreement introduced as an Annex the 'Understanding on Rules and Procedures Governing the Settlement of Disputes' (DSU). The DSU

---

[287] Art. 187. Certain disputes, at the request of the relevant parties, may be submitted to the International Tribunal for the Law of the Sea, to an *ad hoc* chamber of the Sea-Bed Disputes Chamber, or to commercial arbitration under UNCITRAL rules: *ibid.*, Art. 188.

[288] Chapter 11, p. 581 below.   [289] Chapter 9, p. 436 below.

[290] Judgment of 22 December 2002, para. 68. See also the 'Camouco' case (*Panama* v. *France*), Judgment, 7 February 2000; the 'Monte Cafourco' case (*Seychelles* v. *France*), Judgment, 18 December 2000; the 'Grand Prince' case (*Belize* v. *France*), Judgment, 20 April 2001.

is intended to prevent and resolve disputes arising under the WTO Agreement and related instruments. It replaces the arrangements which had emerged in the context of the GATT, principally a system of panels with the power to make non-binding recommendations. Under the prior system, the adoption of panel recommendations could be blocked by any single contracting party. One of the principal innovations of the new WTO system is that panel decisions (as well as those of the Appellate Body) will be adopted and become legally binding unless these is a consensus to the contrary. The new WTO system therefore constitutes a system of compulsory third party adjudication with binding effects for its members. In this sense, it has potentially the most far-reaching and important jurisdiction of any of the global bodies. Its first eight years of operation suggest that it could significantly influence the development of international environmental law.

The DSU establishes a dispute settlement system consisting of three bodies – the Dispute Settlement Body (DSB), *ad hoc* panels and the Appellate Body – all based in Geneva. The DSB is a political body, comprising representatives of all WTO members. It administers the dispute settlement process. The WTO system establishes a detailed 'road map' for intergovernmental dispute settlement, characterised by its speed and relative procedural clarity. In the event of a dispute between members of the WTO over their respective trade-related obligations, one party may request the other to enter into consultations and notify the DSB of this request. If the consultations fail, each party may propose that other traditional dispute settlement procedures (good offices, conciliation or mediation) be employed, with the possible assistance of the WTO Director General. If this fails to settle the dispute, the DSB may be asked to establish an *ad hoc* panel. Once established, a panel will conduct hearings and issue a non-binding report on the merits of the case. The recommendations of a panel become binding only after they have been adopted by the DSB (adoption is automatic, unless there is a consensus against it in the DSB). Unlike the old GATT system, the panel report may be appealed on legal grounds to a permanent seven-member Appellate Body. The appeal is heard before a three-judge division of the Appellate Body, which may uphold, modify or reverse the legal findings of the panel. The report of the Appellate Body is then adopted by the DSB and given binding force, unless the DSB unanimously decides otherwise.

The WTO dispute settlement system is governed principally by Articles III and IV of the WTO Agreement and the DSU. Working Procedures have been adopted for panel and Appellate Body proceedings,[291] as have Rules of Conduct.[292] The substantive law to be applied by the panels and the

---

[291] Working Procedures for Appellate Review (as amended), WTO Doc. WT/AB/WP/3, 28 February 1997.

[292] Rules of Conduct for the Understanding on Rules and Procedures Governing the Settlement of Disputes, WTO Doc. WT/DSB/RdC/1, 11 December 1996.

Appellate Body is to be found in the 1994 WTO Agreement,[293] and in the various multilateral and plurilateral side-agreements to the GATT (including the Multilateral Agreement on Trade in Services, the General Agreement on Trade in Services and the Agreement on Trade-Related Aspects of Intellectual Property Rights).[294] In its first decision, the Appellate Body stated that these trade rules were 'not to be read in clinical isolation from public international law'.[295] It has subsequently referred to – and applied – principles and rules of international environmental law in the *Beef Hormones* case (precautionary principle), the *Shrimp/Turtle* case (including sustainable developments, fisheries conventions, the 1973 CITES, the 1992 Biodiversity Convention and the 1982 UNCLOS), and the *Asbestos* case.[296]

European Court of Justice[297]

> N. Brown and F. Jacobs, *The Court of Justice of the European Communities* (1989); H. G. Schermers and D. Waelbroeck, *Judicial Protection in the European Communities* (1992); K. P. E. Lasok, *The European Court of Justice – Practice and Procedure* (1994 2nd edn); D. Anderson, *References to the European Court* (1995); N. March Hunnings, *The European Courts* (1996).

The ECJ is the judicial institution of the EC and is required to ensure that in the interpretation and application of the EC Treaty 'the law is observed'.[298] Environmental cases reach the ECJ in a number of ways. The most frequent route is under Article 226 (formerly Article 169) of the EC Treaty,[299] and since 1980 the EC Commission has brought more than two hundred cases to the ECJ alleging the failure of a member state to comply with its environmental obligations, most of which have been successful. Its judgments have determined that member states may not plead circumstances existing in their internal legal system to justify a failure to comply with an environmental obligation;[300] that administrative practices which may be altered at the whim of the administration do

---

[293] General Agreement on Tariffs and Trade, Geneva, 30 October 1947, as revised on 15 April 1994, 33 ILM 28 (1994).

[294] DSU, Appendix 1.

[295] Case AB-1996-1, *US – Standards for Reformulated and Conventional Gasoline*, Report of the Appellate Body, 29 April 1996, at 18, WTO Doc. WT/DS2/9.

[296] Chapter 19, pp. 965, 979 and 973 below.

[297] R. Macrory, 'The Enforcement of Community Environmental Laws: Some Critical Issues', 29 *Common Market Law Review* 347 (1992); P. Sands, 'European Community Environmental Law: Legislation, the European Court of Justice and Common Interest Groups', 53 MLR 685 (1990); P. Sands, 'The European Court of Justice: An Environmental Tribunal?', in H. Somsen (ed.) *Enforcing EC Environmental Law: The National Dimension* (1996), 23–35.

[298] EC Treaty, Art. 220 (formerly Art. 164). The ECJ also has competence in relation to the interpretation and application of the 1950 ECSC and 1957 Euratom Treaties.

[299] (1973) ICJ Reports 99; chapter 8, p. 320, n. 11 below.

[300] Cases 30–41/81, *EC Commission v. Italian Republic* [1981] ECR 3379; Case 134/86, *EC Commission v. Belgium* [1987] ECR 2415.

not constitute the proper fulfilment of an environmental obligation under a Directive;[301] that the legal obligations imposed on a member state by an environmental Directive are limited to those dangerous substances specifically listed in the Directive and not to other unlisted dangerous substances as well;[302] and that member states should achieve an 'environmental result' when implementing the Drinking Water Directive.[303] The ECJ has also addressed the legality of national environmental measures and trade obligations[304] and the failure to execute its judgment in an environmental case.[305] The ECJ also has the power to impose fines for non-compliance with its judgments, which it did for the first time (in an environmental case) in 2000.[306] Under Article 227 (formerly Article 170) of the EC Treaty, a member state which believes another member state has breached its obligations has a similar right to bring a matter before the ECJ.[307]

Under Article 230 (formerly Article 173) of the EC Treaty, the ECJ may review the legality of certain acts of the EC Council, Commission, Parliament and European Central Bank on the grounds of lack of competence, infringement of an essential procedural requirement, infringement of the EC Treaty or any rule relating to its application, or misuse of powers. Actions may be brought by a member state or by a Community institution, other than the institution complained against, or by any legal or natural person provided that the act concerned is a decision addressed to that person or is of direct or individual concern to it.[308] Under this head, the ECJ has considered the legality of the treaty basis of EC environmental legislation,[309] and received applications from environmental groups alleging violations by the EC Commission of its legal obligations under the EC Treaty.[310] The ECJ also has jurisdiction under

---

[301] Cases 96, 97/81, *Commission of the European Communities* v. *Netherlands* [1982] ECR 1791 and 1819.

[302] Case 291/84, *Commission of the European Communities* v. *Netherlands* [1989] 1 CMLR 479 (concerning the failure to implement into national law Directive 80/68/EEC on the protection of groundwater against pollution by certain dangerous substances).

[303] Case C-56/90, *Commission* v. *United Kingdom* [1993] ECR I-4019.

[304] Case C-182/89, *Commission of the European Communities* v. *France* [1990] ECR I-4337, where the ECJ held that France had infringed Art. 10(1)(b) of Council Regulation 3626/82 (on the implementation of CITES) by granting import licences for skins of certain feline animals originating in Bolivia.

[305] Case C-75/91, *Commission* v. *Netherlands* [1992] ECR I-549 (wild birds).

[306] Chapter 18, p. 929 below.   [307] See below.

[308] EC Treaty, Art. 230 (formerly Art. 173). On the restrictive approach to *locus standi* for non-privileged applicants, see below and the accompanying text.

[309] Case C-300/89, *EC Commission* v. *Council* [1991] ECR I-2867 (judgment of 11 June 1991), declaring void Council Directive 89/428/EEC of 21 June 1989 for harmonising the programmes for the reduction and eventual elimination of pollution caused by waste from the titanium dioxide industry, on the ground that the Council adopted the Directive on the basis of the wrong treaty provision; but see more recently Case C-155/91, *EC Commission* v. *Council* [1993] ECR I-939; see chapter 15, p. 745 below.

[310] Chapter 16, p. 810 below.

Article 232 (formerly Article 175) under conditions similar to those governing Article 230, to challenge the failure of the Community institutions (in particular the Council or Commission) to act in pursuance of its environmental obligations under the EC Treaty. To date no environmental case appears to have been brought under this provision.

Finally, the ECJ has also considered environmental questions on the basis of its jurisdiction under Article 234 (formerly Article 177), the 'preliminary reference procedure'. Under this provision, the national courts of the EC member states may refer to the ECJ questions concerning the interpretation of the EC Treaty and the validity and interpretation of acts of the EC institutions, provided that a decision on the question is necessary to enable the national court to give a ruling on the question. Preliminary references from national courts to the ECJ are used when a dispute before the national courts raises a complex question of EC law or where the dispute turns on the EC law point and no appeal lies against the decision of the national court. The Article 234 procedure has been used on many occasions in relation to environmental matters, for example the disposal of waste from a nuclear power plant,[311] the compatibility with EC law of the ban by an Italian municipality on the sale and distribution of plastic bags and other non-biodegradable packaging material,[312] and the circumstances in which a member state may take account of economic, social and cultural requirements or regional and local characteristics when selecting and defining the boundaries of sites to be proposed to the Commission as eligible for identification as sites of Community importance, for the purposes of the 1992 Habitats Directive.[313]

Court of First Instance of the European Union   In 1988, the EC Council, acting under an amendment to the EC Treaty introduced by the 1986 Single European Act, established the Court of First Instance (CFI) with limited jurisdiction (over staff and competition cases and cases arising under the 1957 ECSC Treaty) and a right of appeal on points of law to the ECJ.[314] In 1993, following the amendments to the EC Treaty made by the 1992 Treaty on European Union, the competence of the CFI was extended and it may now hear environmental cases brought under, *inter alia*, Articles 230 and 232 of the EC Treaty, although it cannot hear and determine preliminary references requested under Article 234 (formerly Article 177). Appellate review on points of law is to the ECJ.[315]

---

[311] Chapter 15, p. 739 below.

[312] Case C-380/87, *Enichem Base et al.* v. *Commune of Cinisello Balsamo* [1989] ECR 2491.

[313] Case C-371/98, *R.* v. *Secretary of State for the Environment, Transport and the Regions, ex parte First Corporate Shipping Ltd* [2000] ECR I-9235.

[314] EC Treaty, Art. 225 (formerly Art. 168a), and Decision 88/591, OJ C251, 21 August 1988, 1.

[315] Decision 93/350/Euratom, ECSC, EEC, OJ L144, 18 June 1993, 21.

Human rights courts

The human rights courts established under regional human rights conventions[316] may also have jurisdiction over environmental matters, although so far only the European Court of Human Rights appears to have addressed such issues in a sustained manner.[317] From 1950 to 1998, the European Convention's machinery consisted of two organs, a Commission and a Court. Following the entry into force in November 1998 of the Eleventh Protocol to the Convention, the Commission was abolished and most of its functions transferred to the Court. As a result, claimants (whether state parties or individuals) now submit applications directly to the Court. The Court provides for traditional inter-state dispute resolution, as well as the rights of recourse by victims of violations. By Article 33, any state party may bring to the Court a case against any other state party which is alleged to have breached the provisions of the Convention or its Protocols. In fact, very few inter-state cases have been brought. Individuals, NGOs and groups of individuals, who claim to have been victims of a human rights violation[318] may also bring a case against the state party which has committed the alleged violation.[319] In the past few years, the Court has given far-reaching judgments in relation to Article 8 (privacy) and Article 1 of the First Protocol (property rights).

UNCED

Whereas the 1972 Stockholm Conference did not really address the compliance issue, the subject was clearly an important one for UNCED. UN General Assembly Resolution 44/228 determined that UNCED should 'assess the capacity of the United Nations system to assist in the prevention and settlement of disputes in the environmental sphere and to recommend measures in this field, while respecting existing bilateral and international agreements that provide for the

---

[316] The relevant courts are the European Court of Human Rights and the Inter-American Court of Human Rights. In the future, the African Court of Human and Peoples' Rights may also become important.

[317] Chapter 7, pp. 299–304 below.

[318] The European Human Rights Court and Commission have construed the term 'victim' narrowly. The Court has held that an individual cannot bring an *actio popularis* against a law *in abstracto*: *Klass* v. *Germany*, 2 EHRR 214 (1978). In addition, the Commission has declined on several occasions to regard organisations, bringing complaints on behalf of their members, specific persons or the general public, as 'victims' under the Convention. See e.g., *Church of X* v. *UK*, App. No. 3798/68, 12 *Yearbook of the European Convention on Human Rights* 306 (1969).

[319] ECHR, Art. 34. Under the old system, complaints presented to the Commission by individuals could be brought to the Court by the Commission, or an interested state party. Only individuals from states parties to the Ninth Protocol could forward the complaint to the Court after it had been dealt with by the Commission. 1950 ECHR, Art. 48; Protocol No. 9 to the European Convention for the Protection of Human Rights and Fundamental Freedoms, 6 November 1990, ETS 140 (1994).

settlement of such disputes'. This task was only partly fulfilled. Principles 10 and 26 of the Rio Declaration call on states to provide, at the national level, 'effective access to judicial and administrative proceedings, including redress and remedy', and internationally to 'resolve all their environmental disputes peacefully and by appropriate means and in accordance with the Charter of the United Nations'. Agenda 21 recognises the limitations of existing arrangements, including the inadequate implementation by parties of their obligations, the need to involve international institutions and environmental organisations in the implementation process, and the gaps in dispute settlement mechanisms. Chapter 39 of Agenda 21 ('International legal instruments and mechanisms') addresses some of the needs. The international community is called upon to ensure 'the full and prompt implementation of legally binding instruments',[320] and parties to international agreements are instructed to 'consider procedures and mechanisms to promote and review their effective, full and prompt implementation', including the establishment of 'efficient and practical reporting systems on the effective, full and prompt implementation of international legal instruments' and consideration of the ways in which international bodies might contribute towards the further development of such mechanisms.[321] The enhanced role of international institutions is endorsed. UNEP is called upon to promote the implementation of international environmental law; UNDP will play a lead role in support of the implementation of Agenda 21 and capacity-building at the country, regional, inter-regional and global levels; and the UN Commission on Sustainable Development is required to consider information regarding the implementation of environmental conventions made available by the relevant conferences of the parties.[322] On dispute settlement, the international community is called upon to consider broadening and strengthening the capacity of mechanisms in the UN system to identify, avoid and settle international disputes in the field of sustainable development, taking into account existing bilateral and multilateral agreements for the settlement of such disputes.[323] Specifically, this includes:

> mechanisms and procedures for the exchange of data and information, notification and consultation regarding situations that might lead to disputes with other states in the field of sustainable development and for effective peaceful means of dispute settlement in accordance with the Charter of the United Nations including, where appropriate, recourse to the International Court of Justice, and their inclusion in treaties relating to sustainable development.[324]

---

[320] Agenda 21, Chapter 39, para. 39.3(e).   [321] *Ibid.*, para. 39.7.
[322] *Ibid.*, Chapter 38, paras. 38.13(f), 38.22(h), 38.24 and 38.25(a); see also UNGA Res. 47/191 (1992).
[323] Agenda 21, Chapter 39, para. 39.3(h).   [324] *Ibid.*, para. 39.9.

Conclusions

As this chapter shows, the increased attention being given to compliance has generated new measures in the environmental field which supplement those measures available under general international law. The decision by the ICJ to establish an Chamber for Environmental Matters marked a further recognition that the effectiveness of the growing body of principles and rules required the availability of appropriate dispute settlement mechanisms. The limitations inherent in international arrangements for ensuring compliance with international environmental obligations should be apparent. Developments in international law alone will not be sufficient to overcome the political, economic and social reasons lying behind non-compliance. Nevertheless, the law, processes and institutions can make a difference, and recent developments suggest that changes in the importance attached by the international community to compliance reflect the changing structure of the traditional international legal order. Important developments within the past decade include the broadening and strengthening of non-compliance mechanisms under various multilateral environmental agreements, the Permanent Court of Arbitration's new rules on arbitration of environmental disputes, the 'environmental justice' provisions of the 1998 Aarhus Convention, and a significant body of environmental jurisprudence at the ICJ, ITLOS and the WTO Appellate Body.

Addressing compliance will require a comprehensive effort to develop rules and institutional arrangements at three levels: implementation, enforcement, and dispute settlement. First, with regard to implementation, the provision of technical, financial and other assistance to states, particularly developing states, points to the growing 'internationalisation' of the domestic implementation and legal process, and an awareness that international environmental law will not achieve its objectives if it does not also take account of the need, and techniques available, for improving domestic implementation of international environmental obligations.

Secondly, with regard to enforcement, states have been unwilling, for a variety of reasons, to bring international claims to enforce environmental rights and obligations. Within the past decade, however, it appears that this reluctance is being replaced by an increasing willingness by states to have resort to international adjudicatory mechanisms to enforce international environmental obligations, and important decisions have been handed down by the ICJ, ITLOS and the WTO Appellate Body. Nevertheless, the role of states can be reinforced by the supplementary role of international organisations and, to a lesser extent, non-state actors in the international enforcement process. Broadening the category of persons formally entitled to identify violations and to take measures to remedy them is a process which is underway and which should be further encouraged if states and other members of the international community are to be subjected to the sorts of pressure that will lead them to improve compliance with their obligations.

Thirdly, as the disputes before various international courts have shown, the availability of a broad and growing range of mechanisms for dispute settlement, including the compulsory jurisdiction of certain regional and sectoral courts and other international bodies, suggests an important and growing role for independent international adjudication. Finally, Principle 10 of the Rio Declaration and the adoption of the 1998 Aarhus Convention reflect the recognition that ensuring effective access to national judicial and administrative proceedings, including redress and remedies, is appropriately a matter for regulation by the international community.

PART II

Principles and rules establishing standards

6

General principles and rules

Introduction

This chapter describes the general principles and rules of international environmental law as reflected in treaties, binding acts of international organisations, state practice, and soft law commitments. These principles are general in the sense that they are potentially applicable to all members of the international community across the range of activities which they carry out or authorise and in respect of the protection of all aspects of the environment. From the large body of international agreements and other acts, it is possible to discern general rules and principles which have broad, if not necessarily universal, support and are frequently endorsed in practice. These are:

1. the obligation reflected in Principle 21 of the Stockholm Declaration and Principle 2 of the Rio Declaration, namely, that states have sovereignty over their natural resources and the responsibility not to cause transboundary environmental damage;
2. the principle of preventive action;
3. the principle of co-operation;
4. the principle of sustainable development;
5. the precautionary principle;
6. the polluter-pays principle; and
7. the principle of common but differentiated responsibility.

In the absence of judicial authority and in view of the conflicting interpretations under state practice, it is frequently difficult to establish the parameters or the precise international legal status of each general principle or rule. The application of each principle in relation to a particular activity or incident, and its consequences, must be considered on the facts and circumstances of each case, having regard to several factors including: the source of the principle; its textual content and language; the particular activity at issue; the environmental and other consequences of the activity; and the circumstances in which it occurs (including the actors and the geographical region). Some general principles or rules reflect customary law, others may reflect emerging legal obligations, and yet others might have a less developed legal status. In each case, however, the principle or rule has broad support and is reflected in extensive state practice through repetitive use or reference in an international legal context.

Of these general principles and rules, Principle 21/Principle 2 and the co-operation principle are sufficiently well established to provide the basis for an international cause of action; that is to say, to reflect an international customary legal obligation the violation of which would give rise to a free-standing legal remedy. The same may now be said generally in respect of the precautionary principle in the European context, and perhaps also more globally in respect of particular activities or subject areas. The status and effect of the other principles is less clear, although they may bind as treaty obligations or, in particular contexts, as customary obligations. Whether they give rise to actionable obligations of a general nature is open to question. Finally, the principles and rules described in this chapter should be distinguished from the general principles described in chapter 4,[1] as well as the substantive rules establishing environmental standards (i.e. air and water quality, conservation of biodiversity) and rules establishing techniques for implementing those standards (i.e. environmental impact assessment, participation in decision-making, access to information, economic instruments).

Principles and rules

References to principles and rules of general application have long been found in the preambular sections of treaties and other international acts, and in the jurisprudence of international courts and tribunals. More recently, however, principles of general or specific application have been incorporated into the operative part of some treaties. Article 3 of the 1992 Climate Change Convention lists 'Principles' intended to guide the parties '[i]n their actions to achieve the objective of the Convention and to implement its provisions'. Article 3 of the 1992 Biodiversity Convention introduces the text of Principle 21 of the Stockholm Declaration as the sole 'Principle'. The EC Treaty, as amended in 1986, 1992 and 1997, sets forth principles and rules of general application in Article 174(2) (formerly Article 130r). Other treaties follow a similar approach.[2]

What consequences flow from the characterisation of a legal obligation as a legal principle or a legal rule? This question has hardly been addressed in detail by international courts and tribunals, and apparently not at all in the context of environmental principles. The Umpire in the *Gentini* case, in 1903 adopted

---

[1] See chapter 4, pp. 150–2 above.
[2] See e.g. 1992 OSPAR Convention, Art. 2 (General obligations); 1992 Baltic Convention, Art. 3 (Fundamental principles and obligations); 1992 Watercourses Convention, Art. 2 (General provisions); 1992 Industrial Accidents Convention, Art. 3 (General provisions).

the following distinction, which may provide some guidance about the legal effect of principles and their relationship to rules:

> A 'rule' . . . 'is essentially practical and, moreover, binding . . . [T]here are rules of art as there are rules of government' while principle 'expresses a general truth, which guides our action, serves as a theoretical basis for the various acts of our life, and the application of which to reality produces a given consequence'.[3]

In this sense, positive rules of law may be treated as the 'practical formulation of the principles', and the 'application of the principle to the infinitely varying circumstances of practical life aims at bringing about substantive justice in every case'.[4] This view suggests that principles and rules

> point to particular decisions about legal obligations in particular circumstances, but they differ in the character of the direction they give. Rules are applicable in an all-or-nothing fashion . . . [A principle] states a reason that argues in one direction, but does not necessitate a particular decision. . . . All that is meant, when we say that a particular principle is a principle of our law, is that the principle is one which officials must take into account, if it is relevant, as a consideration inclining in one way or another.[5]

This distinction finds some support in the practice of international courts[6] and allows the conclusion that principles 'embody legal standards, but the standards they contain are more general than commitments and do not specify particular actions', unlike rules.[7] The fact that legal principles, like rules, can have international legal consequences has focused attention on their content while being elaborated in recent treaties. The negotiations of the 1992 Climate Change Convention reflected differing views on the need to adopt a section on 'Principles' at all: generally, developing countries supported the inclusion of principles, whereas developed countries opposed them. The US and some other 'common law' delegations were concerned that the requirements included in Article 3 might be subject to the Convention's dispute settlement provisions or create specific commitments beyond those set out in Article 4 and elsewhere. Although the US failed in their efforts to have the whole of Article 3 deleted, or for the text to be amended to make clear that Article 3

---

[3] *Gentini* case (*Italy* v. *Venezuela*) M.C.C. (1903), J. H. Ralston and W. T. S. Doyle, *Venezuelan Arbitrations of 1903 etc.* (1904), 720, 725, cited in B. Cheng, *General Principles of Law as Applied by International Courts and Tribunals* (1953), 376.

[4] *Ibid.*, 376.   [5] R. Dworkin, *Taking Rights Seriously* (1977), 24, 26.

[6] Case C-2/90, *EC Commission* v. *Belgium* [1993] 1 CMLR 365, where the ECJ relied on the principle that environmental damage should as a priority be rectified at the source (EC Treaty, Art. 130r(2)) and the principles of self-sufficiency and proximity (in the Basel Convention) to help it justify a conclusion: *ibid.*, paras. 34–5; see chapter 19, p. 990, n. 235 below.

[7] D. Bodansky, 'The United Nations Framework Convention on Climate Change: A Commentary', 18 *Yale Journal of International Law* 451 at 501 (1993).

could not be subject to the dispute settlement provisions, the US amendments were accepted to limit the application of principles to informing obligations under the Convention. A similar concern to limit the scope of application of a principle was reflected by the UK declaration made upon signature of the 1992 Biodiversity Convention, declaring the understanding that 'Article 3 of the Convention . . . sets out a guiding principle to be taken into account in the implementation of the Convention', implying that no legal consequences arose outside the Convention, and that within the Convention Article 3 did not give rise to a rule in the sense proposed by the Umpire in the *Gentini* case or by Professor Dworkin. It is far from clear, however, that the plain meaning of Article 3 supports the UK's understanding, particularly when the text is compared to Article 3 of the Climate Change Convention, and in particular the introductory 'chapeau' which seeks to limit the effect of the principles identified thereunder.

The international community has not adopted a binding international instrument of global application which purports to set out the general rights and obligations of the international community on environmental matters. No equivalent to the Universal Declaration of Human Rights, the International Covenant on Civil and Political Rights or the International Covenant on Economic, Social and Cultural Rights has yet been adopted, and none appears imminent. Any effort to identify general principles and rules of international environmental law must necessarily be based on a considered assessment of state practice, including the adoption and implementation of treaties and other international legal acts, as well as the growing number of decisions of international courts and tribunals.[8] The efforts of governmental and nongovernmental lawyers in assessing the evidence which supports the existence of principles and rules has provided some guidance, and has influenced subsequent international law-making. The 1978 UNEP Draft Principles and the 1986 WCED Legal Principles have supplemented the 1972 Stockholm Declaration and influenced the 1992 Rio Declaration, which continues to reflect 'to the extent any international instrument can do so, the current consensus of values and priorities in environment and development'.[9] Since UNCED, further guidance may be obtained from the International Law Commission's Draft Articles on Prevention of Transboundary Harm from Hazardous Activities (2001), and the International Law Association's New Delhi Declaration of Principles of International Law Relating to Sustainable Development (2002).[10]

---

[8] On sources of state practice, see chapter 4, pp. 123–52 above (especially, pp. 143–7).

[9] I. Porras, 'The Rio Declaration: A New Basis for International Co-operation', 1 RECIEL 245 (1992).

[10] Rather less assistance is to be derived from the Institut de Droit Internationale's Resolution on the Environment (1997), www.idi-ii/.org/idiE/resolutions/E1997_str_02_en.pdf; see

Sovereignty over natural resources and the responsibility not to cause damage to the environment of other states or to areas beyond national jurisdiction

B. Bramsen, 'Transnational Pollution and International Law', 42 *Nordisk tidsskrift for International Ret* 153 (1972); L. K. Caldwell, 'Concepts in Development of International Environmental Policies', 13 Natural Resources Journal 190 (1973); M. S. McDougal and J. Schneider, 'The Protection of the Environment and World Public Order: Some Recent Developments', 45 *Mississippi Law Journal* 1085 (1974); G. Handl, 'Territorial Sovereignty and the Problem of Transnational Pollution', 69 AJIL 50 (1975); A. Adede, 'United Nations Efforts Toward the Development of an Environmental Code of Conduct for States Concerning Harmonious Utilisation of Shared Natural Resources', 43 *Albany Law Review* 448 (1979); OECD, *Legal Aspects of Transfrontier Pollution* (1977). A. L. Springer, *The International Law of Pollution: Protecting the Global Environment in a World of Sovereign States* (1983); 'Corpus of Principles and Rules Relative to the Protection of the Environment Against Transfrontier Pollution Established by the French Speaking Section' in Centre for Studies and Research in International Law and International Relations, Hague Academy of International Law, *La Pollution Transfrontière et le Droit International* (1985), 27; World Commission on Environment and Development, *Our Common Future* (1987); R. D. Munro and J. Lammers, *Environmental Protection and Sustainable Development: Legal Principles and Recommendations* (1987); Shimizu, 'Legal Principles and Recommendations on Environmental Protection and Sustainable Development', 14 *Nippon Seikyo Kenkyusho-Kiyo* 13 (1990); F. Perez, 'The Relationship Between Permanent Sovereignty and the Obligation Not to Cause Transboundary Environmental Damage', 26 *Environmental Law* 1187 (1996); N. Schrijver, *Sovereignty Over Natural Resources* (1997); F. Perez, *Co-operative Sovereignty: From Independence to Interdependence in International Environmental Law* (2000).

The rules of international environmental law have developed within the context of two fundamental objectives pulling in opposing directions: that states have sovereign rights over their natural resources; and that states must not cause damage to the environment. These objectives are set out in Principle 21 of the Stockholm Declaration, which provides that:

> States have, in accordance with the Charter of the United Nations and the principles of international law, the sovereign right to exploit their own resources pursuant to their own environmental policies, and the

P. Sands, 'The New "Architecture of International Environmental Law" (or "The Law Professor and the Strange Case of the Missing Green Glasses")' RBDI 512 (1997). See also the IUCN Covenant on Environment and Development (2000).

responsibility to ensure that activities within their jurisdiction or control do not cause damage to the environment of other States or of areas beyond the limits of national jurisdiction.

Principle 21 remains the cornerstone of international environmental law; twenty years after its adoption, states negotiating the Rio Declaration were unable to improve significantly upon, develop, scale back or otherwise alter the language in adopting Principle 2. At UNCED, two words were added to recognise that states have the right to pursue 'their own environmental *and developmental* policies'. Principle 21 and Principle 2 each comprise two elements which cannot be separated without fundamentally changing their sense and effect: the sovereign right of states to exploit their own natural resources; and the responsibility, or obligation, not to cause damage to the environment of other states or of areas beyond the limits of national jurisdiction. Taken together (state practice since 1972 has assiduously avoided their de-coupling), they establish the basic obligation underlying international environmental law and the source of its further elaboration in rules of greater specificity. That Principle 21 reflects customary law is now confirmed by the ICJ's 1996 Advisory Opinion on *The Legality of the Threat or Use of Nuclear Weapons*.

Sovereign rights over natural resources

The principle of state sovereignty allows states within limits established by international law to conduct or authorise such activities as they choose within their territories, including activities which may have adverse effects on their own environment. This fundamental principle underlies the first part of Principle 21/Principle 2. The extension of the sovereignty principle into environmental affairs pre-dates the Stockholm Declaration and is rooted in the principle of permanent sovereignty over natural resources as formulated in various resolutions of the UN General Assembly regularly adopted after 1952.[11] These resolutions were closely related to arrangements between states and foreign private companies for the exploitation of natural resources, particularly oil and minerals, in developing countries. They addressed the need to balance the rights of the sovereign state over its resources with the desire of foreign companies to ensure legal certainty in the stability of its investment.[12] A landmark resolution was adopted by the UN General Assembly in 1962, when it resolved that the 'rights of peoples and nations to permanent sovereignty over their natural wealth and resources must be exercised in the interest of their national development of the well-being of the people of the state concerned'.[13] The resolution reflects the right to permanent sovereignty over national resources as an international

---

[11] See e.g. UNGA Res. 523 (VI) (1950); Res. 626 (VII) (1952); Res. 837 (IX) (1954); Res. 1314 (XIII) (1958); Res. 1515 (XV) (1960).
[12] See chapter 19 below.   [13] UNGA Res. 1803 (XVII) (1962).

legal right, and has been accepted by some international tribunals as reflecting customary international law.[14]

By the 1970s, limits to the application of the principle of state sovereignty over natural resources were emerging as the international community recognised a need to co-operate to protect the environment. In 1972, before the Stockholm Conference, the UN General Assembly declared that 'each country has the right to formulate, in accordance with its own particular situation and in full enjoyment of its national sovereignty, its own national policies on the human environment'.[15] The relationship between permanent sovereignty over natural resources and responsibilities for the environment was formally recognised by Principle 21.

The importance placed by states on the principle of permanent sovereignty over natural resources is also reflected by its frequent invocation, in various forms, in international environmental agreements and during their negotiation. The 1933 London Convention affirmed that all animal trophies were 'the property of the Government of the territory concerned'.[16] The 1971 Ramsar Convention emphasised that the inclusion of national wetland sites in its List of Wetlands did 'not prejudice the exclusive sovereign rights of . . . the party in whose territory the wetland is situated'.[17] The 1983 International Tropical Timber Agreement recalled 'the sovereignty of producing members over their natural resources'.[18] Recent treaties also refer to the sovereign rights of states over natural resources in their territory: the Preamble to the 1989 Basel Convention recognised that 'all states have the sovereign right to ban the entry or disposal of foreign hazardous wastes and other wastes in their territory'. The Preamble to the 1992 Climate Change Convention reaffirmed 'the principle of sovereignty of states in international co-operation to address climate change'. The 1992 Biodiversity Convention more specifically reaffirmed that states have 'sovereign rights . . . over their natural resources', and that 'the authority to determine access to genetic resources rests with the national governments and is subject to national legislation'.[19]

Sovereignty and extra-territoriality

The sovereign right to exploit natural resources includes the right to be free from external interference over their exploitation. This aspect of Principle 21/Principle 2 is brought into question in disputes over the extra-territorial application of environmental laws of one state to activities taking place in areas beyond its

---

[14] *Texaco Overseas Petroleum Co. and California Asiatic Oil Co.* v. *Libya*, 53 ILR 389 (1977), para. 87; *Kuwait* v. *American Independent Oil Co.*, 21 ILM 976 (1982).

[15] UNGA Res. 2849 (XXVI) (1971).   [16] Art. 9(6).   [17] Art. 2(3).

[18] Art. 1. See now 1994 International Tropical Timber Agreement, Art. 1.

[19] Art. 15(1). Cf. the 1983 FAO Undertaking on Plant Genetic Resources and the 1989 Agreed Interpretation, recognising that plant genetic resources are a 'common heritage of mankind': chapter 11, p. 551 below.

national jurisdiction, either within the jurisdiction of another state or in activities beyond national jurisdiction. In 1893, the arbitral tribunal in the *Fur Seals Arbitration* rejected a claim by the US to be entitled to protect fur seals in areas beyond the three-mile limit of the territorial sea and the right to interfere in the internal affairs of other states to secure the enjoyment of their share in the 'common property of mankind'.[20] Nearly one hundred years later, the US banned the import of yellow-fin tuna caught by Mexican vessels, in Mexico's exclusive economic zone and on the high seas, with purse-seine nets the compliance of which with US environmental protection standards could not be proved. This 'extra-jurisdictional' application of US environmental standards was rejected by a GATT panel as being contrary to the GATT, holding that a country 'can effectively control the production or consumption of an exhaustible natural resource only to the extent that the production or consumption is under its jurisdiction' and that to allow the 'extra-jurisdictional' application of its environmental law would allow the US to 'unilaterally determine the conservation policies' of Mexico.[21] More recently, however, the WTO's Appellate Body has taken a broader approach, and recognised the existence of a 'sufficient nexus' between migratory and endangered populations of sea-turtles located in Asian waters and the United States to allow the latter to claim an interest in their conservation.[22] The traditional and absolute prohibition on extra-territorial (or extra-jurisdictional) application of national environmental laws recognised by the earlier decisions is consistent with the principle of absolute sovereignty over natural resources. Those decisions do not rest easily, however, with a more modern conception of an ecologically interdependent world in which limits are placed on the exercise of sovereignty or sovereign rights, an approach with which the Appellate Body seemed sympathetic.

In the absence of generally accepted international standards of environmental protection and conservation, states with strict national environmental standards may seek to extend their application to activities carried out in areas beyond their territory, particularly where they believe that such activities cause significant environmental damage to shared resources (such as migratory species, transboundary watercourses, or air quality and the climate system) or affect vital economic interests. For 'shared natural resources' such as the high seas and atmosphere it will often be difficult, if not impossible, to draw a clear line between natural resources over which a state does and does not have sovereignty or exercise sovereign rights. In such circumstances, it is unlikely that the principle of territorial sovereignty, or permanent sovereignty over natural

---

[20] Chapter 11, pp. 561–6 below.   [21] Chapter 19, p. 956 below.

[22] *Shrimp/Turtle* case, para. 133 (the decision is difficult to square with the Appellate Body's claim that it was not 'pass[ing] upon the question of whether there is an implied jurisdictional limitation in Article XX(g), and, if so, the nature or extent of that limitation'). See further chapter 19, pp. 961–73 below.

resources, can provide much assistance in allocating rights and responsibilities of states over environmental policy.

The permissibility of the extra-territorial application of national laws remains an open question in international law. The PCIJ has stated that 'the first and foremost restriction imposed by international law upon a state is that – failing the existence of a permissive rule to the contrary – it may not exercise its power in any form in the territory of another state outside its territory except by virtue of a permissive rule derived from international custom or from a convention'.[23] However, in the same case the PCIJ went on to state that 'international law as it stands at present' does not contain 'a general prohibition to states to extend the application of their laws and the jurisdiction of their courts to persons, property and acts outside their territory' and that the territoriality of criminal law was 'not an absolute principle of international law and by no means coincides with territorial sovereignty'.[24] Subsequent state practice, as well as decisions of international tribunals, has not determined precisely the circumstances in which a state may take measures over activities outside its territory in relation to the conservation of shared resources. In the *Fisheries Jurisdiction* case, Spain challenged the application and enforcement by Canada of its fisheries conservation legislation in areas beyond its exclusive economic zone, but the ICJ declined jurisdiction, and the case did not reach the merits phase.[25] The right of states to exercise jurisdiction, either by legislation or adjudication, over activities in other states, or in areas beyond national jurisdiction, which are harmful to the environment at the global, regional or local level, could be justified on several grounds. First, corporations carrying on activities abroad might be subject to the environmental laws of their state of registration or incorporation, by application of the 'nationality' principle of jurisdiction. International law does not, according to Oppenheim, prevent a state from exercising jurisdiction within its own territory over its nationals (including corporations) who reside in a foreign state, although the power to enforce such laws depends upon the nationals being in the territorial jurisdiction or having assets therein against which judgment can be enforced.[26] The application of the 'nationality' principle is likely to cause difficulty, however, since the foreigner abroad might be subject to the concurrent jurisdiction of the home state of registration or incorporation and the host state in which it carries out its activities, with the home state having more stringent rules of environmental

---

[23] *Lotus* case (*France* v. *Turkey*), PCIJ Ser. A, No. 10, 19–20   [24] *Ibid.*

[25] Chapter 5, p. 201 above; chapter 11, pp. 567–8 below.

[26] Oppenheim, vol. I, Part 1, 462. In application of this approach, see *Dow Chemical Co.* v. *Alfaro*, 768 SW 2d 674 at 681 (Texas 1990), where a Texan court held that Costa Rican farm workers were entitled to bring a claim for injuries caused by a pesticide manufactured in the United States and exported to Costa Rica. On enforcement jurisdiction generally, see chapter 5, pp. 182–91 below.

protection.[27] This will lead to jurisdictional disputes where some states use lower standards of environmental protection perhaps to gain economic advantage and attract foreign investment, and other states apply the nationality principle and require their companies to apply national environmental protection rules wherever they carry out their activities. In such circumstances, it has been suggested that the home state must not require compliance with its laws at the expense of its duty to respect the territorial sovereignty of the host state. When faced with such a conflict a court would be likely to balance the public policy of the home state, the interests of the host state, and the damage to international comity if it gave precedence to the laws of the home state, and only accord priority to those laws 'where the balance of interest clearly lies in that direction'.[28] The factors applied by a court will also need to be applied by reference to the environment which is being affected or damaged. It would be difficult to justify a home state's taking measures where only the environment of the host state was being damaged. But if the damage was being caused to the environment of the home state or to areas beyond national jurisdiction (global commons) then the home state might have a stronger basis for asserting jurisdiction extra-territorially.

This latter situation creates a second possible basis for allowing the extra-territorial application of national laws: where activities carried out in one state have, or are likely to have, 'effects' in another state, recourse might be had to the 'objective' application of the territorial principle, otherwise known as the 'effects' doctrine. However, the application of the 'effects' principle is said to have 'doubtful consistency' with international law: the justification for assertions of jurisdiction on the basis of an alleged 'effects' principle of jurisdiction has not been generally accepted, and the matter is still one of controversy.[29]

The extra-territorial application of national environmental laws has been particularly controversial in relation to trade issues. Principle 12 of the Rio Declaration declares that unilateral actions addressing environmental challenges 'outside the jurisdiction of the importing country should be avoided' and that 'environmental measures should, as far as possible, be based on an international consensus'. The Rio Declaration and Agenda 21 do not, however, prohibit *per se* all unilateral environmental measures, an approach which now appears to have been endorsed by the WTO Appellate Body, subject to certain conditions being satisfied. The same approach has been taken in the WSSD Plan of Implementation.[30] The challenge for the international community in

---

[27] On this point, see the OECD Guidelines on Multinationals, chapter 3, p. 105, n. 224 above.

[28] Oppenheim, vol. I, Part 1, 464–6, citing, *inter alia*, *Timberlane Lumber Co.* v. *Bank of America*, 66 ILR, 270 (1976–7); *Laker Airways* v. *Pan American World Airways* 23 ILM 748 at 751 (1984).

[29] Oppenheim, vol. I, Part 1, 475. That said, the decision in *Shrimp Turtles* may be seen to be connected to the application of the 'effects' doctrine: see n. 22 above.

[30] Para. 95 (restating the language of the Rio Declaration and Agenda 21).

coming years will be to determine the circumstances in which, in the absence of international consensus on agreed environmental standards, a state will be permitted, under the general rules of international law and specific WTO rules, to adopt unilateral environmental measures and apply them extra-territorially.[31]

Responsibility not to cause environmental damage

The second element of Principle 21/Principle 2 reflects the view of states that they are subject to environmental limits in the exercise of their rights under the principle of permanent sovereignty over natural resources. In the form presented by Principle 21/Principle 2, the responsibility not to cause damage to the environment of other states or of areas beyond national jurisdiction has been accepted as an obligation by all states;[32] without prejudice to its applications on a case-by-case basis, following the ICJ's 1996 Advisory Opinion on *The Legality of the Threat or Use of Nuclear Weapons* there can be no question but that Principle 21 reflects a rule of customary international law, placing international legal constraints on the rights of states in respect of activities carried out within their territory or under their jurisdiction.

Saying that Principle 21/Principle 2 reflect customary international law is not, however, decisive, and will be of only partial assistance in support of an international claim. In the context of activity which causes pollution and environmental degradation, Principle 21/Principle 2 indicate the need to address other questions: what is environmental damage? What environmental damage is prohibited (any damage, or just damage which is serious or significant)? What is the standard of care applicable to the obligation (absolute, strict or fault)? What are the consequences of a violation (including appropriate reparation)? And what is the extent of any liability (including measure of damages)? These and related questions are considered in chapter 18 below.

The responsibility of states not to cause environmental damage in areas outside their jurisdiction pre-dates the Stockholm Conference, and is related to the obligation of all states 'to protect within the territory the rights of other states, in particular their right to integrity and inviolability in peace and war'.[33] This obligation was subsequently relied upon, and elaborated, by the arbitral tribunal in the much-cited *Trail Smelter* case, which stated that:

---

[31] On the trade/environment issue, see chapter 19, pp. 940–1009 below; Agenda 21, para. 39.3(d) includes a number of factors applicable to trade-related environmental measures which may also provide guidance on the permissibility of other extra-territorial environmental measures: see chapter 19, p. 1008 below.

[32] For an excellent account of the negotiating history of Principle 21, which tends to support this view, see L. Sohn, 'The Stockholm Declaration on the Human Environment', 14 *Harvard International Law Journal* 423 at 485–93 (1972).

[33] PCA, *Palmas* Case, 2 HCR (1928) 84 at 93.

> Under the principles of international law . . . no state has the right to use
> or permit the use of territory in such a manner as to cause injury by fumes
> in or to the territory of another of the properties or persons therein, when
> the case is of serious consequence and the injury is established by clear and
> convincing evidence.[34]

Most writers accepted this formulation as a rule of customary international
law and it was cited, with apparent approval, by Judge de Castro in his dissent
in the *Nuclear Tests* case.[35] In that case, Australia had asked the ICJ to adjudge
and declare that the carrying out of further atmospheric nuclear tests was
inconsistent with applicable rules of international law and would be unlawful
'in so far as it involves the modification of the physical conditions of and over
Australian territory [and] pollution of the atmosphere and of the resources
of the seas'.[36] The Rapporteur to the ILA Committee on Legal Aspects of the
Environment concluded from an examination that state practice was founded
upon the rule in the *Trail Smelter* case.[37]

In fact, consistent state practice is not readily discernible. As will be seen in
chapter 18, there are relatively few claims which have been brought by states
relying upon the rule reflected in Principle 21/Principle 2, and one is left to
rely upon state practice as evidenced in particular by participation in and
support for treaties and other international acts, as well as their statements
as to what they consider to be the extent of their obligations. Following the
Chernobyl accident in 1986, a discussion under the auspices of the IAEA threw
some light on the views of states, although the record on this discussion alone
cannot be considered as representing a comprehensive view.[38] The general
rule relied upon in the *Trail Smelter* case derives from an extension of the
principle of good-neighbourliness. Although the UN Charter does not expressly
address environmental issues, Article 74 of the Charter reflects the agreement
of the UN members that 'their policy in their metropolitan areas must be based
on the general principle of good neighbourliness' and must take account of
'the interests and well-being of the rest of the world, in social, economic and
commercial matters'. The principle of good-neighbourliness underlies the *dicta*
of the ICJ that the principle of sovereignty embodies 'the obligation of every

---

[34] *United States* v. *Canada,* 3 RIAA 1907 (1941); citing Eagleton, *Responsibility of States*
(1928), 80; see chapter 7, p. 318 below; and chapter 18, pp. 885–6 below.

[35] *Australia* v. *France* (1974) ICJ Reports 253 at 389. He stated: 'If it is admitted as a general rule
that there is a right to demand prohibition of the emission by neighbouring properties of
noxious fumes, the consequences must be drawn, by an obvious analogy, that the Applicant
is entitled to ask the Court to uphold its claim that France should put an end to the deposit
of radio-active fall-out on its territory.'

[36] ICJ Pleadings, *Nuclear Tests* cases, vol. I, 27. see further chapter 8, pp. 319–21 below.

[37] International Law Association, Report of the Committee on Legal Aspects of the Environment, 60th Conference Report, 157 at 163.

[38] Chapter 18, pp. 887–9 below.

state not to allow its territory to be used for acts contrary to the rights of other states'.[39] In the *Lac Lanoux Arbitration*, involving the proposed diversion of an international river by an upstream state, the arbitral tribunal affirmed that a state has an obligation not to exercise its rights to the extent of ignoring the rights of another:

> France [the upstream state] is entitled to exercise her rights; she cannot ignore the Spanish interests. Spain [the downstream state] is entitled to demand that her rights be respected and that her interests be taken into consideration.[40]

The thread was further developed in 1961 when the UN General Assembly declared, specifically in relation to radioactive fallout, that:

> The fundamental principles of international law impose a responsibility on all states concerning actions which might have harmful biological conse-quences for the existing and future generations of peoples of other states, by increasing the levels of radioactive fallout.[41]

By 1972, shortly before the Stockholm Conference, the General Assembly was able to direct that the Conference must 'respect fully the exercise of permanent sovereignty over natural resources, as well as the right of each country to exploit its own resources in accordance with its own priorities and needs and in such a manner as to avoid producing harmful effects on other countries'.[42]

The development of the second element of Principle 21/Principle 2 can also be traced to earlier environmental treaties. The 1951 International Plant Pro-tection Convention expressed the need to prevent the spread of plant pests and diseases across national boundaries.[43] The 1963 Nuclear Test Ban Treaty prohibits nuclear tests if the explosion would cause radioactive debris 'to be present outside the territorial limits of the state under whose jurisdiction or control such explosion is conducted';[44] and the 1968 African Conservation Convention requires consultation and co-operation between parties where de-velopment plans are 'likely to affect the natural resources of any other state'.[45] Under the 1972 World Heritage Convention, the parties agreed that they would not take deliberate measures which could directly or indirectly damage heritage which is 'situated on the territory' of other parties.[46]

Principle 21 thus developed earlier state practice. It has been affirmed in many General Assembly resolutions and acts of other international organisa-tions. Shortly after the Stockholm Conference, Principle 21, with Principle 22, was expressly stated by UN General Assembly Resolution 2996 to lay down the 'basic rules' governing the international responsibility of states in regard to the

---

[39] *Corfu Channel* case (*UK* v. *Albania*) (1949) ICJ Reports 4 at 22.
[40] *Spain* v. *France*, 12 RIAA 285.   [41] UNGA Res. 1629 (XVI) (1961).
[42] UNGA Res. 2849 (XXVI) (1972), para. 4(a).   [43] Preamble.
[44] Art. I(1)(b).   [45] Art. XVI(1)(b).   [46] Art. 6(3).

environment. It was also the basis of Article 30 of the Charter of Economic Rights and Duties of States, which provides that:

> All states have the responsibility to ensure that activities within their juris-
> diction or control do not cause damage to the environment of other states
> or of areas beyond the limits of national jurisdiction.[47]

It is endorsed by the 1975 Final Act of the Helsinki Conference on Security and Co-operation in Europe,[48] Principle 3 of the 1978 UNEP Draft Principles, which requires states to ensure that 'activities within their jurisdiction or control do not cause damage to the natural systems located within other states or in areas beyond the limits of national jurisdiction', and the 1982 World Charter for Nature, which declares the need to 'safeguard and conserve nature in areas beyond national jurisdiction'.[49] Perhaps more compelling is the reference to Principle 21 in treaties. It has long been referred to,[50] or wholly incorporated,[51] in the preamble to several treaties, and was fully reproduced in the operational part of a treaty, for the first time, as Article 3 of the 1992 Biodiversity Convention without express limitation to matters within the scope of the Convention.[52] Principle 2 of the Rio Declaration is incorporated into the Preamble to the 1992 Climate Change Convention.

Similar language to the second element of Principle 21 also appears in treaties. The 1978 Amazonian Treaty fudges the issue of the legal status of Principle 21, declaring that 'the exclusive use and utilisation of natural resources within their respective territories is a right inherent in the sovereignty of each state and that the exercise of this right shall not be subject to any restrictions other than those arising from International Law'.[53] The 1981 Lima Convention goes a little further by requiring activities to be conducted so that 'they do not cause damage by pollution to others or to their environment, and that pollution arising from incidents or activities under their jurisdiction or control does not, as far as possible, spread beyond the areas where [they] exercise sovereignty and jurisdiction'.[54] The 1982 UNCLOS transforms the 'responsibility' into a 'duty', although it is unclear what was intended by the change. Under Article 193 of UNCLOS, states have the sovereign right to exploit their natural resources pursuant to their environmental policies and in accordance with their duty to protect and preserve the marine environment. UNCLOS shifts the emphasis from a negative obligation to prevent harm to a positive commitment to preserve and protect the environment. To that end, however, Article 194(2) does provide that states:

---

[47] UNGA Res. 3281 (XXVII) (1974).   [48] 14 ILM 1292 (1975); 1 August 1975.
[49] Para. 21(e).   [50] 1992 Baltic Convention.
[51] 1972 London Convention; 1979 LRTAP Convention; 1985 Vienna Convention.
[52] Cf. UK Declaration, chapter 4, p. 135, n. 50 above.
[53] Art. IV.   [54] Art. 3(5); 1983 Quito LBS Protocol, Art. XL.

shall take all measures necessary to ensure that activities under their jurisdiction or control are so conducted as not to cause damage by pollution
to other states and their environment, and that pollution arising from incidents or activities under their jurisdiction or control does not spread
beyond the areas where they exercise sovereign rights in accordance with
[the] Convention.[55]

The 1985 ASEAN Convention goes further, by recognising the second element
of Principle 21 as a 'generally accepted principle of international law'.[56]

Against this background, the time was plainly ripe for confirmation of the
customary status of the obligation not to cause transboundary environmental
harm. France's 1995 announcement of its resumption of underground nuclear
tests provided the unlikely catalyst. In its Order rejecting New Zealand's request,
the ICJ stated, somewhat cryptically, that its Order was 'without prejudice to
obligations of States to respect and protect the natural environment, obligations
to which both New Zealand and France have in the present instance reaffirmed
their commitment'.[57] A review of the pleadings indicates that New Zealand's
affirmation that Principle 21/Principle 2 reflected a 'well established proposition of customary international law' was not opposed by France.[58] It was also
endorsed by Judge Weeramantry in his dissenting opinion.[59]

Within two months of the ICJ's Order, oral arguments opened at the ICJ in the
Legality of the Threat or Use of Nuclear Weapons Advisory Opinion proceedings.
Several states argued that Principle 21/Principle 2 reflected customary law, and
none challenged that view (although some argued that they did not consider
the principles to be of relevance to the case).[60] In its Advisory Opinion, the ICJ
stated that:

> The existence of the general obligation of States to ensure that activities
> within their jurisdiction and control respect the environment of other States
> or of areas beyond national control is now part of the corpus of international
> law relating to the environment.[61]

It is interesting that the ICJ did not merely restate the language of Principle 21
and Principle 2, and it is unclear whether the ICJ intended to effect substantive

---

[55] 1986 South Pacific Natural Resources Convention, Art. 4(6).
[56] Art. 20.   [57] (1995) ICJ Reports 288, para. 64.
[58] New Zealand Request, para. 98, also CR/95/20, 10–12; and CR/95/20, 91. See also *Yearbook of International Environmental Law* 531 at 533 (1995); and P. Sands, 'Pleadings and the Pursuit of International Law: Nuclear Tests II (New Zealand v. France)', in A. Anghie and G. Sturgess (eds.), *Legal Visions of the 21st Century: Essays in Honour of Judge Weeramantry* (1998), 601.
[59] (1995) ICJ Reports 347. See also Judges Koroma (*ibid.*, 378) and Ad Hoc Judge Palmer (*ibid.*, 408, para. 80).
[60] For a summary of the arguments, see *Yearbook of International Environmental Law* 542 (1995). On war and the environment, see chapter 7, pp. 307–15 below.
[61] (1996) ICJ Reports 241, para. 29.

changes by its reformulation. That does not, however, appear to have been the intention, since (arguably) the formulation adopted by the ICJ may be broader than that of Principle 21/Principle 2.[62]

Conclusion

The support given to the rule reflected in Principle 21 (and now Principle 2) by states, by the ICJ and by other international actors over the past three decades indicates the central role now played by the rule. The rule has been developed through the adoption of environmental agreements which establish specific and more detailed obligations giving effect to the basic objectives, as well as national environmental laws. The scope and application of the rule, in particular to the difficult question of what constitutes 'environmental harm' (or damage) for the purposes of triggering liability and allowing international claims to be brought, are considered in chapter 17 below. At the very least, Principle 21 and Principle 2 confirm that the rights of states over their natural resources in the exercise of permanent sovereignty are not unlimited,[63] and are subject to significant constraints of an environmental character. Beyond that, the rule may provide a legal basis for bringing claims under customary law asserting liability for environmental damage. The specific application of the rule will turn on the facts and circumstances of each particular case or situation.

Principle of preventive action

Closely related to the Principle 21 obligation is the obligation requiring the prevention of damage to the environment, and otherwise to reduce, limit or control activities which might cause or risk such damage. This obligation, sometimes referred to as the 'principle of preventive action' or the 'preventive principle', is distinguishable from Principle 21/Principle 2 in two ways. First, the latter arise from the application of respect for the principle of sovereignty, whereas the preventive principle seeks to minimise environmental damage as an objective in itself. This difference of underlying rationale relates to the second distinction: under the preventive principle, a state may be under an obligation to prevent damage to the environment within its own jurisdiction,[64] including by means of appropriate regulatory, administrative and other measures.

---

[62] The word 'respect' could be seen as encompassing consequences where no 'harm' has arisen.

[63] See the ILC's 2001 draft Articles on Prevention of Transboundary Harm from Hazardous Activities, preamble. See also Art. 4 (Prevention).

[64] See Judge N. Singh, 'Foreword', in R. D. Munro and J. G. Lammers (eds.), *Environmental Protection and Sustainable Development: Legal Principles and Recommendations* (1986), xi–xii; in this regard, see also the principle of sustainable development, pp. 252–6 below; and chapter 5, p. 184 above.

The preventive principle requires action to be taken at an early stage and, if possible, before damage has actually occurred.[65] The principle is reflected in state practice in regard to a broad range of environmental objectives. Broadly stated, it prohibits activity which causes or may cause damage to the environment in violation of the standards established under the rules of international law. It has been described as being of 'overriding importance in every effective environmental policy, since it allows action to be taken to protect the environment at an earlier stage. It is no longer primarily a question of repairing damage after it has occurred.'[66] The preventive principle is supported by an extensive body of domestic environmental protection legislation which establishes authorisation procedures, as well as the adoption of international and national commitments on environmental standards, access to environmental information, and the need to carry out environmental impact assessments in relation to the conduct of certain proposed activities. The preventive principle may, therefore, take a number of forms, including the use of penalties and the application of liability rules.

The preventive approach has been endorsed, directly or indirectly, by the 1972 Stockholm Declaration,[67] the 1978 UNEP Draft Principles[68] and the 1982 World Charter for Nature. Principle 11 of the 1992 Rio Declaration requires states to enact 'effective environmental legislation'.[69] More significantly for its development as an international legal principle is the fact that the principle has been relied upon or endorsed in a large number of treaties dealing with particular environmental media or activities.[70] The preventive principle has also been specifically incorporated into treaties of more general application, including those in the field of international economic law, such as the EC Treaty,[71] the 1989 Lomé Convention[72] and the 2001 Treaty establishing the East African Community.[73]

The preventive principle is implicitly supported in relation to transboundary resources by the awards in the *Trail Smelter* case and the *Lac Lanoux Arbitration*.

---

[65] In the *Gabcikovo-Nagymaros* case, the ICJ noted that it was 'mindful that, in the field of environmental protection, vigilance and prevention are required on account of the often irreversible character of damage to the environment and of the limitations inherent in the very mechanism of reparation of this type of damage': (1997) ICJ Reports 7 at 78, para. 140.

[66] L. Krämer, *EEC Treaty and Environmental Protection* (1990), 61.

[67] Principles 6, 7, 15, 18 and 24. [68] Principle 1.

[69] Other relevant provisions include Principle 14 (calling on states to prevent the relocation and transfer to other states of hazardous activities or substances) and Principle 15 (precautionary approach).

[70] 1991 Alpine Convention, Art. 2(c).

[71] Formerly Art. 130r(2) ('preventive action should be taken'), replaced by Art. 174(2).

[72] Art. 35 (parties agree to a 'preventive approach aimed at avoiding harmful effects on the environment as a result of any programme or operation') (the provision is not repeated in the successor 2000 Cotonou Agreement, at Art. 32).

[73] Art. 111.

It was supported in the pleadings of Australia in the *Nuclear Tests* case and in the claim by Nauru that Australia had breached its legal obligation to administer the territory of Nauru in such a way as to not bring about changes in the territory which would cause irreparable damage to, or substantially prejudice, Nauru's legal interests in respect of that territory.[74] The principle of prevention may also be discerned in Hungary's Original Application to the ICJ in the case concerning the Gabcikovo-Nagymaros Project. The preventive approach is endorsed by the large number of international environmental treaties, aiming to prevent *inter alia*:

- the extinction of species of flora and fauna;[75]
- the spread of occupational disease, including radioactive contamination of workers;[76]
- the introduction and spread of pests and diseases;[77]
- pollution of the seas by oil,[78] radioactive waste,[79] hazardous waste and substances,[80] from land-based sources,[81] or from any source;[82]
- river pollution;[83]
- radioactive pollution of the atmosphere;[84]
- hostile environmental modification;[85]
- adverse effects of activities that prevent the migration of species;[86]
- air pollution;[87]
- modification of the ozone layer;[88]
- degradation of the natural environment;[89]
- all pollution;[90]
- significant adverse environmental impacts;[91]
- transboundary impacts generally;[92]
- dangerous anthropogenic interference with the climate system;[93]

---

[74] *Case Concerning Certain Phosphate Lands in Nauru (Nauru v. Australia)* (1992) ICJ Reports 240 at 244.

[75] 1933 London Convention, Art. 12(2), and Protocol, para. 1.

[76] 1949 Agreement for the Establishment of a General Fisheries Council for the Mediterranean, Art. IV(h); 1960 Ionising Radiation Convention, Art. 3(1).

[77] 1951 Plant Protection Convention, Art. 1(1).

[78] 1954 Oil Pollution Prevention Convention, Preamble; 1969 CLC, Art. 1(7).

[79] 1958 High Seas Convention, Art. 25.

[80] 1972 Oslo Convention, Art. 1; 1972 London Convention, Art. 1; MARPOL 73/78, Art. 1(1).

[81] 1974 Paris LBS Convention, Art. 1.

[82] 1982 UNCLOS, Art. 194(1).   [83] 1958 Danube Fishing Convention, Art. 7.

[84] 1963 Test Ban Treaty, Art. 1(1).   [85] 1977 ENMOD Convention, Art. 1(1).

[86] 1979 Bonn Convention, Art. III(4)(b).   [87] 1979 LRTAP Convention, Art. 2.

[88] 1985 Vienna Convention, Art. 2(2)(b); 1987 Montreal Protocol, Preamble.

[89] 1985 ASEAN Convention, Art. 11.   [90] 1986 Noumea Convention, Art. 5(1).

[91] 1991 Espoo Convention, Preamble and Art. 2(1).

[92] 1992 UNECE Transboundary Waters Convention, Art. 2(1) and (2).

[93] 1992 Climate Change Convention, Art. 2.

- loss of fisheries[94] and other biodiversity,[95] including as a result of the release of genetically modified organisms;[96] and
- damage to health and the environment from chemicals[97] and persistent organic pollutants.[98]

Taken together, this extensive body of international commitments provides compelling evidence of: the wide support for the principle of preventive action; the different environmental media for which general preventive measures are required; the types of activities which should be regulated; and the basis upon which states should carry out their commitment to enact effective national environmental legislation pursuant to the general requirement of Principle 11 of the Rio Declaration.

Co-operation

The principle of 'good-neighbourliness' enunciated in Article 74 of the UN Charter in relation to social, economic and commercial matters has been translated into the development and application of rules promoting international environmental co-operation. This is traditionally considered by reference to the application of the maxim *sic utere tuo et alienum non laedas*. The principle is reflected in many treaties and other international acts, and is supported also by state practice, particularly in relation to hazardous activities and emergencies.[99] Principle 24 of the Stockholm Declaration reflects a general political commitment to international co-operation in matters concerning the protection of the environment, and Principle 27 of the Rio Declaration states rather more succinctly that 'States and people shall co-operate in good faith and in a spirit of partnership in the fulfilment of the principles embodied in this Declaration and in the further development of international law in the field of sustainable development'. The importance attached to the principle of co-operation, and its practical significance, is reflected in many international instruments, such as the Preamble to the 1992 Industrial Accident Convention, which underlined (in support of the Convention's specific commitments) 'the principles of international law and custom, in particular the principles of

---

[94] 1995 Straddling Stocks Agreement; see also ITLOS, *Southern Bluefin Tuna* cases, chapter 11, pp. 580–1 below.

[95] 1992 Biodiversity Convention, Preamble and Art. 1.

[96] 2000 Biosafety Protocol, Art. 1.

[97] 1998 Chemicals Convention, Art. 1.   [98] 2001 POPs Convention, Art. 1.

[99] The maxim was invoked, for example, as a 'fundamental rule' by Hungary in its Original Application in the *Gabcikovo-Nagymaros Project* case, para. 32 (citing in support of the maxim the *Corfu Channel* case (1949), the *Trail Smelter* case (1941), the Stockholm Declaration (1972), the World Charter for Nature (1982), the ILC Draft Articles on International Liability (1990) and the Rio Declaration (1992)).

good-neighbourliness, reciprocity, non-discrimination and good faith', and the procedural rules reflected in the 1997 Watercourses Convention.[100]

The obligation to co-operate is affirmed in virtually all international environmental agreements of bilateral and regional application,[101] and global instruments.[102] It also underscores the ICJ's reminder of the need to establish suitable common regimes.[103] The obligation may be in general terms, relating to the implementation of the treaty's objectives[104] or relating to specific commitments under a treaty.[105] The general obligation to co-operate has also been translated into more specific commitments through techniques designed to ensure information sharing and participation in decision-making. These specific commitments, which are considered in more detail in subsequent chapters, include: rules on environmental impact assessment (see chapter 16); rules ensuring that neighbouring states receive necessary information (requiring information exchange, consultation and notification) (see chapter 17); the provision of emergency information (see chapter 12); and transboundary enforcement of environmental standards (see chapter 5). The extent to which these commitments are interrelated is reflected in Principle 7 of the 1978 UNEP Draft Principles, which states that:

> Exchange of information, notification, consultation and other forms of co-operation regarding shared natural resources are carried out on the basis of the principle of good faith and in the spirit of good neighbourliness.

A similar commitment is expressed in Article 4 of the ILC's draft Articles on Prevention of Transboundary Harm (2001). State practice supporting good-neighbourliness and international co-operation is reflected in decisions and awards of international courts and tribunals discussed in subsequent chapters, including the *Lac Lanoux* case.[106] The nature and extent of the obligation to co-operate is being invoked in international disputes. It was a central issue in the dispute between Hungary and Slovakia in the *Gabcikovo-Nagymaros Project* case, at least as originally formulated by Hungary (claiming that Czechoslovakia and then Slovakia had not co-operated in good faith in the implementation

---

[100] Chapter 10, pp. 482–5 below.

[101] Early examples include the 1933 London Convention, Art. 12(2); 1940 Western Hemisphere Convention, Art. VI; 1991 Alpine Convention, Art. 2(1).

[102] 1982 UNCLOS, Arts. 123 and 197; 1985 Vienna Convention, Art. 2(2); 1992 Biodiversity Convention, Art. 5.

[103] See *Case Concerning the Kasiliki/Sedudu Island (Botswana/Namibia)* (1999) ICJ Reports 1045, para. 102.

[104] 1968 African Conservation Convention, Art. XVI(1); 1992 Biodiversity Convention, Art. 5.

[105] 1989 Lomé Convention, Art. 14 (co-operation 'shall [assume] special importance [in relation] to environmental protection and the preservation and restoration of natural equilibria in the ACP States'); 1992 Climate Change Convention, Art. 4(1)(e) (co-operation on preparation for adaptation to the impacts of climate change).

[106] See p. 243 above.

of principles affecting transboundary resources, including the obligation to negotiate in good faith and in a spirit of co-operation, to prevent disputes, to provide timely notification of plans to carry out or permit activities which may entail a transboundary interference or a significant risk thereof and to engage in good faith consultations to arrive at an equitable resolution of the situation).[107] The ICJ did not address in any detail what the obligation to co-operate entailed, beyond recalling what it had said earlier in the *North Sea Continental Shelf* cases, as well as the principle of good faith which obliged the parties to apply their 1977 treaty 'in a reasonable way and in such a manner that its purpose can be realized'.[108]

The requirements of the obligation to co-operate are at the heart of the *MOX* case. In its application instituting arbitration proceedings under the 1982 UNCLOS, Ireland claimed that the United Kingdom had failed to co-operate as required by Articles 123 and 197 of UNCLOS, for example by failing to reply to communications and requests for information in a timely manner or at all, by withholding environmental information requested by Ireland, and by refusing to prepare a supplementary environmental statement.[109] In its Provisional Measures Order, the ITLOS affirmed that:

> the duty to co-operate is a fundamental principle in the prevention of pollution of the marine environment under Part XII of the Convention and general international law and that rights arise therefrom which the Tribunal may consider appropriate to preserve under article 290 of the Convention.

The Tribunal ordered the parties to co-operate and, for that purpose, to enter into consultations forthwith to '(a) exchange further information with regard to possible consequences for the Irish Sea arising out of the commissioning of the MOX plant; (b) monitor risks or the effects of the operation of the MOX plant for the Irish Sea; (c) devise, as appropriate, measures to prevent pollution of the marine environment which might result from the operation of the MOX plant'.[110]

---

[107] Chapter 10, pp. 469–77 below; Hungary's Original Application, 22 October 1992, paras. 27, 29 and 30.

[108] (1997) ICJ Reports 78–9, paras. 141–2. In the *North Sea Continental Shelf* cases, the ICJ said: '[The Parties] are under an obligation so to conduct themselves that the negotiations are meaningful, which will not be the case when either of them insists upon its own position without contemplating any modification of it': (1969) ICJ Reports 47 para. 85.

[109] Application, 25 October 2001, para. 33.

[110] Provisional Measures Order, 3 December 2001, para. 83. At the time of writing, the case on the merits – including the issue of co-operation – is pending before the Annex VII arbitration tribunal. The ITLOS order was affirmed by the Annex VII Tribunal by its Order of 24 June 2003, with a recommendation to establish further arrangements to address the Tribunals concern that 'co-operation and consultation may not always have been as timely or effective as it could have been': paras. 66–7.

Sustainable development

W. Clark and R. Munn (eds.), *Sustainable Development of the Biosphere* (1986); B. Conable, 'Development and the Environment: A Global Balance', 5 *American University Journal of International Law and Policy* 217 (1990); P. S. Elder, 'Sustainability', 36 *McGill Law Journal* 831 (1991); R. Lipschutz, 'Wasn't the Future Wonderful? Resources, Environment, and the Emerging Myth of Global Sustainable Development', 2 *Colorado Journal of International Environmental Law and Policy* 35 (1991); R. D. Munro and M. Holdgate (eds.), *Caring for the Earth: A Strategy for Sustainable Development* (1991); P. Sands, 'International Law in the Field of Sustainable Development', 65 BYIL 303 (1994); W. Lang (ed.), *Sustainable Development and International Law* (1995); United Nations, Department for Policy Co-ordination and Sustainable Development, *Report of the Expert Group Meeting on Identification of Principles of International Law for Sustainable Development* (UN, 26–28 September 1995); A. Boyle and D. Freestone (eds.), *International Law and Sustainable Development* (1999); EC Commission, *The Law of Sustainable Development: General Principles* (2000).

Introduction

The general principle that states should ensure the development and use of their natural resources in a manner which is sustainable emerged in the run-up to UNCED. Although the ideas underlying the concept of sustainable development have a long history in international legal instruments, and the term itself began to appear in treaties in the 1980s, the general 'principle of sustainable development' appears to have been first referred to in a treaty in the Preamble to the 1992 EEA Agreement.[111] The term now appears with great regularity in international instruments of an environmental, economic and social character and has been invoked by various international courts and tribunals, and is now established as an international legal concept.[112]

The term 'sustainable development' is generally considered to have been coined by the 1987 Brundtland Report, which defined it as 'development that meets the needs of the present without compromising the ability of future generations to meet their own needs'. It contains within it two concepts:

---

[111] See also the Preamble to the EC Fifth Environmental Action Programme, referring to the call in the June 1990 EC Declaration of Heads of State and Government for an action programme to be elaborated 'on the basis of the principles of sustainable development, preventive and precautionary action and shared responsibility': see chapter 15, p. 747 below.

[112] See generally the International Law Association's New Delhi Declaration of Principles of International Law Relating to Sustainable Development (2002).

1. the concept of 'needs', in particular the essential needs of the world's poor, to which overriding priority should be given; and
2. the idea of limitations imposed, by the state of technology and social organisation, on the environment's ability to meet present and future needs.[113]

State practice, however, suggests that the idea of 'sustainability' has been a feature in international legal relations since at least 1893, when the United States asserted a right to ensure the legitimate and proper use of seals and to protect them, for the benefit of mankind, from wanton destruction.[114] Since then, many treaties and other international instruments, as well as decisions of international courts, have supported, directly or indirectly, the concept of sustainable development and the principle that states have the responsibility to ensure the sustainable use of natural resources. Its application has been recognised in relation to all parts of the world.[115]

Four recurring elements appear to comprise the legal elements of the concept of 'sustainable development', as reflected in international agreements:

1. the need to preserve natural resources for the benefit of future generations (the principle of intergenerational equity);
2. the aim of exploiting natural resources in a manner which is 'sustainable', or 'prudent', or 'rational', or 'wise' or 'appropriate' (the principle of sustainable use);
3. the 'equitable' use of natural resources, which implies that use by one state must take account of the needs of other states (the principle of equitable use, or intragenerational equity); and
4. the need to ensure that environmental considerations are integrated into economic and other development plans, programmes and projects, and that development needs are taken into account in applying environmental objectives (the principle of integration).

---

[113] Report of the World Commission on Environment and Development (the Brundtland Report), *Our Common Future* (1987), 43.

[114] *Pacific Fur Seals Arbitration*, chapter 10, pp. 561–6 below. Although the arbitral tribunal rejected the argument, it did adopt regulations for the conduct of sealing which incorporated some of the elements of what is now recognised as a 'sustainable' approach to the use of natural resources.

[115] See e.g. Declaration on Establishment of the Arctic Council, 35 ILM 1382 (1996); Yaoundé Declaration on the Conservation and Sustainable Management of Forests, 38 ILM 783 (1999); Agreements on Co-operation for the Sustainable Development of the Mekong River Basin, 34 ILM 864 (1995); Revised Protocol on Shared Watercourses in the Southern African Development Community, 40 ILM 321 (2001); Partnership for Prosperity and Security in the Caribbean, 36 ILM 792 (1997); OECD Guidelines for Multinational Enterprises, Part V, 40 ILM 237 (2001); South East Europe Compact for Reform, Investment, Integrity and Growth, 39 ILM 962 (2000).

These four elements are closely related and often used in combination (and frequently interchangeably), which suggests that they do not yet have a well-established, or agreed, legal definition or status. The 1989 Lomé Convention indicated how some of the elements of the concept of sustainable development can be brought together in a single legal text. Article 33 of the Convention provides that:

> In the framework of this Convention, the protection and the enhancement of the environment and natural resources, the halting of the deterioration of land and forests, the restoration of ecological balances, the preservation of natural resources and their rational exploitation are basic objectives that the [states parties] concerned shall strive to achieve with Community support with a view to bringing an immediate improvement in the living conditions of their populations and to safeguarding those of future generations.

Without referring directly to 'sustainable development', the text introduced into a legal framework the elements identified by the Brundtland Report.[116] There can be little doubt that the concept of 'sustainable development' has entered the corpus of international customary law, requiring different streams of international law to be treated in an integrated manner.[117] In the *Gabcikovo-Nagymaros* case, the ICJ invoked the concept in relation to the future regime to be established by the parties. The ICJ said:

> Throughout the ages, mankind has, for economic and other reasons, constantly interfered with nature. In the past this was often done without consideration of the effects upon the environment. Owing to new scientific insights and to a growing awareness of the risks for mankind – for present and future generations – of pursuit of such interventions at an unconsidered and unabated pace, new norms and standards have been developed [and], set forth in a great number of instruments during the last two decades. Such new norms have to be taken into consideration, and such new standards given proper weight, not only when States contemplate new activities, but also when continuing with activities begun in the past. This need to reconcile economic development with protection of the environment is aptly expressed in the concept of sustainable development. For the purposes of the present case, this means that the Parties together should look afresh at the effects on the environment of the operation of the Gabcikovo power

---

[116] See also 2002 Cotonou Agreement, Art. 32 ('1. Co-operation on environmental protection and sustainable utilisation and management of natural resources shall aim at: (a) mainstreaming environmental sustainability into all aspects of development co-operation and support programmes and projects implemented by the various actors').

[117] See more generally P. Sands, 'International Courts and the Application of the Concept of "Sustainable Development"', 3 *Yearbook of UN Law* 389 (1999); P. Sands, 'Treaty, Custom and the Cross-Fertilisation of International Law', 1 *Yale Human Rights and Development Law Journal* 1 (1998), at http://diana.law.yale.edu/yhrdlj/vol01iss01/sands_philippe_article.htm.

plant. In particular they must find a satisfactory solution for the volume of
water to be released into the old bed of the Danube and into the side-arms
on both sides of the river.[118]

By invoking the concept of sustainable development, the ICJ indicates that the
term has a legal function and both a procedural/temporal aspect (obliging the
parties to 'look afresh' at the environmental consequences of the operation
of the plant) and a substantive aspect (the obligation of result to ensure that
a 'satisfactory volume of water' be released from the by-pass canal into the
main river and its original side arms). The ICJ does not provide further detail
as to the practical consequences, although some assistance may be obtained
from the Separate Opinion of Judge Weeramantry, who joined in the majority
judgment and whose hand may have guided the drafting of paragraph 140
quoted above.[119]

In the *Shrimp/Turtle* case, the WTO Appellate Body noted that the Preamble to the WTO Agreement explicitly acknowledges 'the objective of sustainable development', and characterises it as a concept which 'has been generally
accepted as integrating economic and social development and environmental protection'.[120] The concept appears to have informed the conclusion that
sea turtles are an 'exhaustible natural resource' (within the meaning of Article
XX(g) of the GATT) and that they have a sufficient nexus with the United States
to justify the latter state's conservation measures, at least in principle. The

---

[118] (1997) ICJ Reports 78, para. 140. The concept was invoked by both parties. Slovakia stated
that: 'It is clear from both the letter and the spirit of these principles that the overarching
policy of the international community is that environmental concerns are not directed
to frustrate efforts to achieve social and economic development, but that development
should proceed in a way that is environmentally sustainable. Slovakia submits that these
have been, and are today, the very policies on which the Gabcikovo-Nagymaros Project
is based' (Counter-Memorial, para. 9.56). In reply, Hungary took an opposite view to
support its argument that the Project is unlawful: 'Well-established . . . operational concepts like "sustainable development" . . . help define, in particular cases, the basis upon
which to assess the legality of actions such as the unilateral diversion of the Danube by
Czechoslovakia and its continuation by Slovakia' (Hungarian Reply, para. 3.51).

[119] (1997) ICJ Reports 92 ('It is thus the correct formulation of the right to development
that that right does not exist in the absolute sense, but is relative always to its tolerance
by the environment. The right to development as thus refined is clearly part of modern
international law. It is compendiously referred to as sustainable development.')

[120] 38 ILM 121 (1999), para. 129, at n. 107 and the accompanying text. The view is supported
by reference to numerous international conventions: para. 130, citing Art. 56(1)(a) of the
1982 UNCLOS. See also the Opinion of Advocate General Léger in Case C-371/98, *R. v.
Secretary of State for the Environment, Transport and the Regions, ex parte First Corporate
Shipping Ltd.* [2000] ECR I-9235, who notes that sustainable development 'emphasises
the necessary balance between various interests which sometimes clash, but which must
be reconciled' (relying upon the Preamble to the 1992 Habitats Directive, which refers
to sustainable development: (discussed in D. McGillivray and J. Holder, 'Locating EC
Environmental Law', 20 *Yearbook of European Law* 139 at 151 (2001)).

Appellate Body also invokes 'sustainable development' in assessing whether those measures have been applied in a discriminatory fashion – as it concludes they have – and in this regard refers to 'sustainable development' in the preamble to the WTO Agreement as adding:

> color, texture and shading to our interpretation of the agreements annexed to the WTO Agreement, in this case the GATT 1994. We have already observed that Article XX(g) of the GATT 1994 is appropriately read with the perspective embodied in the above preamble.[121]

Future generations

E. Brown Weiss, *In Fairness to Future Generations: International Law, Common Patrimony and Intergenerational Equity* (1989); A. D'Amato, 'Do We Owe a Duty to Future Generations to Preserve the Global Environment?', 84 AJIL 190 (1990); E. Brown Weiss, 'Our Rights and Obligations to Future Generations for the Environment', 84 AJIL 198 (1990); L. Gundling, 'Our Responsibility to Future Generations,' 84 AJIL 207 (1990); G. Supanich, 'The Legal Basis of Intergenerational Responsibility: An Alternative View – The Sense of Intergenerational Identity', 3 *Yearbook of International Environmental Law* 94 (1992); R. Westin, 'Intergenerational Equity and Third World Mining', 13 *University of Pennsylvania Journal of International Business Law* 181 (1992); E. Agius and S. Busuttil, *Future Generations and International Law* (1998).

The idea that as 'members of the present generation, we hold the earth in trust for future generations'[122] is well known to international law, having been relied upon as early as 1893 by the United States in the *Pacific Fur Seals Arbitration*. It is also expressly or implicitly referred to in many of the early environmental treaties, including the 1946 International Whaling Convention,[123] the 1968 African Conservation Convention[124] and the 1972 World Heritage Convention.[125] Other, more recent treaties have sought to preserve particular natural resources and other environmental assets for the benefit of present and future generations. These include wild flora and fauna;[126] the marine environment;[127]

---

[121] *Ibid.*, para. 153

[122] E. Brown Weiss, 'Our Rights and Obligations to Future Generations for the Environment', 84 AJIL 198 at 199 (1990).

[123] The Preamble recognises the 'interest of the nations of the world in safeguarding for future generations the great nature resources represented by the whale stocks'.

[124] The Preamble provides that natural resources should be conserved, utilised and developed 'by establishing and maintaining their rational utilisation for the present and future welfare of mankind'.

[125] Under Art. 4, the parties agree to protect, conserve, present and transmit cultural and natural heritage to 'future generations'.

[126] 1973 CITES, Preamble.

[127] 1978 Kuwait Convention, Preamble; 1983 Cartagena de Indias Protocol, Preamble; 1982 Jeddah Convention, Art. 1(1).

essential renewable natural resources;[128] the environment generally;[129] the resources of the earth;[130] natural heritage;[131] natural resources;[132] water resources;[133] biological diversity;[134] and the climate system.[135]

International declarations often make reference to intergenerational equity as an important aspect of the concept of sustainable development. According to Principle 1 of the 1972 Stockholm Declaration, man bears 'a solemn responsibility to protect and improve the environment for present and future generations', and UN General Assembly Resolution 35/8, adopted in 1980, affirmed that the responsibility to present and future generations is a historic one for the 'preservation of nature'. The Rio Declaration associates intergenerational equity with the right to development, providing in Principle 4 that the 'right to development must be fulfilled so as to equitably meet developmental and environmental needs of present and future generations'.

In its Advisory Opinion on *The Legality of the Threat or Use of Nuclear Weapons*, the ICJ recognized that 'the environment is not an abstraction but represents the living space, the quality of life and the very health of human beings, including generations unborn'.[136] The purpose of the ICJ's reliance on the concept is not immediately apparent, and it is sometimes said that the undertakings in favour of future generations have limited practical legal consequences. They are considered by some to be closely associated with the civil and political aspects of the relationship between environmental protection and human rights protection.[137] According to this view, the rights of future generations might be used to enhance the legal standing of members of the present generation to bring claims, in cases relying upon substantive rules of environmental treaties where doubt exists as to whether a particular treaty creates rights and obligations enforceable by individuals.[138]

Sustainable use of natural resources

A second approach, reflected in treaties adopting a 'sustainable' approach, is to focus on the adoption of standards governing the rate of use or exploitation of specific natural resources rather than on their preservation for future generations. Particularly for marine living resources, a standard approach has emerged requiring exploitation to be conducted at levels which are 'sustainable'

---

[128] 1976 South Pacific Nature Convention, Preamble.
[129] 1977 ENMOD Convention, Preamble.   [130] 1979 Bonn Convention, Preamble.
[131] 1985 Nairobi Convention, Preamble.   [132] 1985 ASEAN Convention, Preamble.
[133] 1992 Transboundary Waters Convention, Art. 2(5)(c).
[134] 1992 Biodiversity Convention, Preamble.
[135] 1992 Climate Change Convention, Art. 3(1).
[136] (1996) ICJ Reports, 226. See also *Gabcikovo-Nagymaros* case (1997) ICJ Reports 7, para. 53.
[137] See chapter 7, pp. 305–17 below.
[138] See chapter 5, pp. 195–8 above, on the standing issue.

or 'optimal'.[139] The failure of the 1946 International Whaling Convention to prevent the depletion of many whale species can be measured by reference to its stated objective of achieving 'the optimum level of whale stocks' and confining whaling operations 'to those species best able to sustain exploitation in order to give an interval for recovery to certain species of whales now depleted in numbers'.[140] Similar commitments to limit catches or productivity to 'maximum sustained' levels have been agreed for other marine species, such as tuna,[141] North Pacific fish,[142] Pacific fur seals,[143] and living resources in the EEZ.[144] Other treaties limit catches to 'optimum sustainable yields', or subject them to a required standard of 'optimum utilisation'; this applies, for example, in relation to Antarctic seals,[145] high seas fisheries,[146] and some highly migratory species.[147]

Sustainable use is a concept also applicable to non-marine resources. The 1968 African Nature Convention provides that the utilisation of all natural resources 'must aim at satisfying the needs of man according to the carrying capacity of the environment',[148] and the 1983 International Tropical Timber Agreement encouraged 'sustainable utilisation and conservation of tropical forests and their genetic resources'.[149] The 1985 ASEAN Agreement was one of the first treaties to require parties to adopt a standard of 'sustainable utilisation of harvested natural resources . . . with a view to attaining the goal of sustainable development'.[150] Further support for sustainable use or management as a legal term may be found in the 1987 Zambezi Action Plan Agreement,[151] the 1992 Climate Change Convention,[152] the 1992 Biodiversity Convention[153] and its 2000 Biosafety Protocol,[154] and the 1992 OSPAR Convention.[155] The fact that

---

[139] 1995 Straddling Stocks Agreement, Art. 2   [140] Preamble; see also Art. V(2).

[141] 1949 Tuna Convention, Preamble; 1966 Atlantic Tuna Convention, Art. IV(2)(b).

[142] 1952 North Pacific Fisheries Convention, Preamble and Art. IV(1)(b)(ii).

[143] 1976 Pacific Fur Seals Convention, Preamble and Arts. II(1)(a), V(2)(d) and XI.

[144] 1982 UNCLOS, Art. 61(3). See also 1995 Straddling Stocks Agreement.

[145] 1972 Antarctic Seals Convention, Preamble.

[146] 1958 High Seas Fishing and Conservation Convention, which defines conservation as 'the aggregate of the measures rendering possible the optimum sustainable yield from those resources so as to secure a maximum supply of food and other marine products' (Art. 2).

[147] 1982 UNCLOS, Art. 64(1).   [148] Preamble.   [149] Art. 1(h).

[150] Art. 1(1); see also Art. 9 on the protection of air quality, and Art. 12(1) in respect of land use, which is to be based 'as far as possible on the ecological capacity of the land'.

[151] Preamble.   [152] Art. 3(4).

[153] Preamble and Arts. 1, 8, 11, 12, 16, 17 and 18. The Convention defines 'sustainable use' as 'the use of components of biological diversity in a way and at a rate that does not lead to the long-term decline of biological diversity, thereby maintaining its potential to meet the needs and aspirations of present and future generations': Art. 2.

[154] Art. 1.

[155] Preamble. The Convention defines 'sustainable management' as the 'management of human activities in such a manner that the marine ecosystem will continue to sustain the legitimate uses of the sea and will continue to meet the needs of present and future generations': Art. 1.

so many species and natural resources are in fact not sustainably managed illustrates the difficulty in translating the concept of sustainable development into a practical conservation tool.

The term also now appears frequently in instruments relating to international economic law and policy. Under its Articles of Agreement, the European Bank for Reconstruction and Development must 'promote in the full range of its activities environmentally sound and sustainable development'.[156] Under the 1989 Lomé Convention, the development of the sixty-six ACP countries as supported by the EC and its member states was to 'be based on a sustainable balance between its economic objectives, the rational management of the environment and the enhancement of natural and human resources'.[157] The 1992 Maastricht Treaty, which made changes to the EC Treaty, introduced new objectives for the EC, including the promotion of 'sustainable and non-inflationary growth respecting the environment'.[158] The Preamble to the 1994 WTO Agreement commits parties to 'the optimal use of the world's resources in accordance with the objective of sustainable development'.[159]

Other acts of the international community have also relied upon the concept of 'sustainable development', or the spirit which underlies it, without specifying what, precisely, it means. Although the 1972 Stockholm Declaration did not endorse 'sustainable development', it did call for the non-exhaustion of renewable natural resources and the maintenance and improvement of 'the capacity of the earth to produce vital renewable resources'.[160] The 1982 World Charter for Nature stated that resources which are utilised are to be managed so as to 'achieve and maintain optimum sustainable productivity', and provided that living resources must not be utilised 'in excess of their natural capacity for regeneration'.[161] The 1992 Rio Declaration goes further than most instruments by expressly defining the content of the concept of sustainable development, and actively calls for the 'further development of international law in the field of sustainable development', which suggests that international law in this field already existed.[162] Apart from the environmental component of 'sustainable development', the Rio Declaration links environmental issues to matters which might previously be more properly considered as belonging to the realm of economic and development law. These issues, increasingly considered for their environmental implications, include the eradication of poverty, the special responsibility of developed countries, the reduction and elimination of unsustainable patterns of production and consumption, the promotion

[156] Art. 2(1)(vii).
[157] Art. 4. See now Art. 32 of the 2000 Cotonou Agreement: see n. 72 above and the accompanying text.
[158] 1992 Maastricht Treaty, Art. G(2); see chapter 15, pp. 745–6 below.
[159] On the *Shrimp/Turtle* case, see p. 238 above.
[160] Principles 3 and 5.   [161] Paras. 4 and 10(a).   [162] Principle 27.

of appropriate population policies, and a supportive and open international economic system.[163]

Treaties and other international acts have also supported the development of the concept of 'sustainable use' through the use of terms which are closely related; international legal instruments have aimed for conservation measures and programmes which are 'rational', or 'wise', or 'sound', or 'appropriate', or a combination of the above. In some instruments, the preferred objective is the 'conservation' of natural resources, which has been subsequently defined by reference to one or more of the terms identified above. Moreover, the term 'conservation' itself includes elements similar to 'sustainable development'. The Legal Experts Group of the World Commission on Environment and Development defined 'conservation' in terms which recall the principle of sustainable development as:

> [the] management of human use of a natural resource or the environment in such a manner that it may yield the greatest sustainable benefit to present generations while maintaining its potential to meet the needs and aspirations of future generations. It embraces preservation, maintenance, sustainable utilisation, restoration and enhancement of a natural resource or the environment.[164]

'Rational', 'wise', 'sound' and 'appropriate' use are usually used without definition and often interchangeably, and accordingly the meaning of each term will depend upon its application in each instrument. Although attempts at definition have been made, no generally accepted definitions exist, and it is unlikely that distinguishable legal definitions could be agreed. The use of various terms in a single instrument is illustrated by the 1982 UNCLOS: it requires conservation at 'maximum sustainable yield' for the living resources of the territorial and high seas, the 'optimum utilisation' of the living resources found in the EEZ, and the 'rational management' of the resources in the 'Area' in accordance with 'sound principles of conservation'.[165]

'Rational' utilisation and management are the governing standard for migratory birds,[166] fisheries,[167] salmon,[168] all natural resources,[169] seals[170]

---

[163] Principles 5, 7, 8 and 12.   [164] 1986 WCED Legal Principles, para. (i).

[165] Preamble and Arts. 61(3), 62(1), 119(1)(a) and 150(b).

[166] 1940 Western Hemisphere Convention, Art. VII.

[167] 1958 Danube Fishing Convention, Preamble and Art. VIII; 1959 North-East Atlantic Fisheries Convention, Preamble and Art. V(1)(b); 1959 Black Sea Fishing Convention, Preamble and Arts. 1 and 7; 1969 Southeast Atlantic Fisheries Convention, Preamble; 1973 Baltic Fishing Convention, Arts. I and X(h); 1978 Northwest Atlantic Fisheries Convention, Art. II(1).

[168] 1982 North Atlantic Salmon Convention, Preamble.

[169] 1968 African Conservation Convention, Art. II; 1978 Amazonian Treaty, Arts. I and VII.

[170] 1972 Antarctic Seals Convention, Art. 3(1); 1976 North Pacific Fur Seals Convention, Art. II(2)(g).

and hydro resources.[171] They are the required standard called for by Principles 13 and 14 of the Stockholm Declaration, and the 1980 CCAMLR defines 'conservation' objectives as including 'rational use',[172] as does the 1982 Jeddah Regional Seas Convention.[173]

'Proper' utilisation and management has been adopted as a governing standard for fisheries[174] and forests.[175] 'Wise use' has been endorsed for flora and fauna,[176] wetlands[177] and natural resources generally.[178] Other standards introduced by international agreements include: 'judicious exploitation';[179] 'sound environmental management';[180] 'appropriate environmental management';[181] and 'ecologically sound and rational' use of natural resources.[182]

The significance of these terms is that each recognises limits placed by international law on the rate of use or manner of exploitation of natural resources, including those which are shared or are in areas beyond national jurisdiction. These standards cannot have an absolute meaning. Rather, their interpretation is, or should be, implemented by states acting co-operatively, or by decisions of international organisations, or, ultimately, by international judicial bodies in the event that a dispute arises.

Equitable use of natural resources

G. Handl, 'The Principle of Equitable Use as Applied to Internationally Shared Natural Resources: Its Role in Resolving Potential International Disputes Over Transfrontier Pollution', 14 RBDI 40 (1977–8); L. F. E. Goldie, 'Reconciling

---

[171] 1978 Amazonian Treaty, Art. V.

[172] Art. II(1) and (2). 'Principles of conservation' are defined as (a) the 'prevention of decrease in the size of any harvested population to levels below those which ensure its stable recruitment', and (b) the 'maintenance of ecological relationships between harvested, dependent and related populations of Antarctic marine living resources and the restoration of depleted populations to levels' above (a), and the 'prevention of changes or minimisation of the risk of changes in the marine ecosystem which are not potentially reversible over two or three decades . . . with the aim of making possible the sustained conservation of Antarctic marine living resources': Art. II(3).

[173] Art. 1(1), including reference to present and future generations, optimum benefit, and conservation, protection, maintenance, sustainable and renewable utilisation, and enhancement of the environment.

[174] 1949 Agreement for the General Fisheries Council for Mediterranean, Preamble and Art. IV(a).

[175] 1959 Agreement for the Latin American Forest Institute, Art. III(1)(a).

[176] 1968 African Conservation Convention, Art. VII(1); 1972 Stockholm Declaration, Principle 4; 1976 South Pacific Nature Convention, Art. V(1).

[177] 1971 Ramsar Wetlands Convention, Arts. 2(6) and 6(2)(d).

[178] 1979 Bonn Convention, Preamble.   [179] 1963 Niger Basin Act, Preamble.

[180] 1981 Abidjan Convention, Arts. 4(1) and 14(3); 1983 Cartagena de Indias Convention, Art. 4(1); 1985 Nairobi Convention, Art. 4(1).

[181] 1981 Lima Convention, Art. 3(1).

[182] 1992 UNECE Transboundary Waters Convention, Art. 2(2)(b).

Values of Distributive Equity and Management Efficiency in the International Commons', in P. M. Dupuy (ed.), *The Settlement of Disputes on the New Natural Resources* (1983), 335; L. F. E. Goldie, 'Equity and the International Management of Transboundary Resources', 25 *Natural Resources Journal* 665 (1985); J. Lammers, '"Balancing the Equities" in International Environmental Law', in R. J. Dupuy (ed.), *L'Avenir du droit International de l'environnement* (1985), 153; P. Thacher, 'Equity under Change', 81 *Proceedings of the American Society of International Law* 133 (1987); B. Cheng-Kang, 'Equity, Special Considerations and the Third World', 1 *Colorado Journal of International Environmental Law and Policy* 57 (1990).

Equity and equitable principles are terms which are frequently relied upon in international environmental texts. In the absence of detailed rules, equity can provide a conveniently flexible means of leaving the extent of rights and obligations to be decided at a subsequent date, which may explain its frequent usage at UNCED. In many respects, UNCED was about equity: how to allocate future responsibilities for environmental protection between states which are at different levels of economic development, which have contributed in different degrees to particular problems, and which have different environmental and developmental needs and priorities. This is reflected in each UNCED instrument, which reflects efforts to apply equity to particular issues. Principle 3 of the Rio Declaration invokes the 'right of development' as a means of 'equitably' meeting the developmental and environmental needs of future generations. Under the Climate Change Convention, all the parties undertake to be guided on 'the basis of equity' in their actions to achieve the objective of the Convention, and Annex 1 parties agree to take into account the need for 'equitable and appropriate contributions' by each of them to the global effort regarding the achievement of the objective of the Convention.[183] The objectives of the 1992 Biodiversity Convention include the 'fair and equitable' sharing of the benefits arising out of the use of genetic resources.[184]

The application of equity in international environmental affairs pre-dates UNCED, having been associated with the protection of the environment for the benefit of future generations (intergenerational equity);[185] the principle of common but differentiated responsibility which takes into account the needs and capabilities of different countries and their historic contribution to particular problems;[186] and the allocation of shared natural resources,[187] shared fisheries stocks,[188] or shared freshwater resources.[189] Equity has also been relied upon in relation to the participation of states in environmental organisations,[190]

---

[183] Arts. 3(1) and 4(2)(a).
[184] Arts. 1 and 15(7). See chapter 20, pp. 1051–2 below.   [185] See pp. 256–7 above.
[186] See pp. 285–9 below.   [187] See the 1978 UNEP Draft Principles, Principle 1.
[188] *Icelandic Fisheries* case, chapter 11, pp. 567–8 below.   [189] Chapter 10, pp. 461–3 below.
[190] 1992 Oil Pollution Fund Convention, Art. 22(2)(a) (equitable geographic distribution of membership on Executive Committee); 1972 World Heritage Convention, Art 8(2)

financial and other contributions to activities,[191] and the equitable distribution of the benefits of development.[192]

It is, however, in relation to the allocation of shared natural resources that equity is likely to play an important role in coming years, as underscored by the ICJ's ruling in the *Gabcikovo-Nagymaros* case that Czechoslovakia had violated international law by unilaterally assuming control of a shared resource and depriving Hungary of its right to an equitable and reasonable share of the natural resources of the Danube.[193] The Preamble to the 1987 Montreal Protocol reflects the aim of controlling 'equitably total global emissions of substances that deplete the ozone layer', an aim usually translated into specific obligations through the process of intergovernmental negotiations (as reflected in the 1990 and 1992 Adjustments and Amendments to the 1987 Montreal Protocol). The 1992 Climate Change Convention requires the equitable allocation of emission rights, and the Biodiversity Convention requires the determination of what constitutes an equitable sharing of the benefits arising out of the use of genetic resources. In each of these cases, the factors to be taken into account in establishing specific rights and obligations must be determined in the circumstances of each instrument, including its provisions, the context of its negotiation and adoption, and subsequent practice by the organs it establishes and by parties.

Integration of environment and development

A fourth element of 'sustainable development' is the commitment to integrate environmental considerations into economic and other development, and to take into account the needs of economic and other social development in crafting, applying and interpreting environmental obligations. In many ways, this element is the most important and the most legalistic: its formal application requires the collection and dissemination of environmental information, and the conduct of environmental impact assessments.[194] The integration approach may also serve as the basis for allowing, or requiring, 'green conditionality' in bilateral and multilateral development assistance,[195] and the adoption of differentiated legal commitments on the basis of the historic responsibility of states (including the resulting economic benefits) and their capacity to respond to environmental requirements.[196]

('equitable representation of the different regions and cultures of the world' on the World Heritage Committee); 1982 UNCLOS, Art. 161(1)(e) (equitable geographic distribution of membership of the Council of the International Seabed Authority).

[191] 1973 Baltic Sea Fishing Convention, Art. I.   [192] 1978 Amazonian Treaty, Preamble.

[193] (1997) ICJ Reports 7 at 56; chapter 10, pp. 469–77 below.

[194] See e.g. its application by the ICJ in the *Gabcikovo-Nagymaros* case, p. 254 above. See generally chapters 16 and 17 below.

[195] Chapter 20, pp. 1022–9 below.   [196] See pp. 287–9 below.

For many years, the international regulation of environmental issues has taken place in international fora, such as UNEP and the conferences of the parties to environmental treaties, which are not directly connected to international economic organisations, particularly the World Bank and the GATT. One consequence has been a divergence in approaches. This is a constitutional problem, which appears also in the organisation of national governments. The constituent instruments which originally created the UN and its specialised agencies, and in particular the GATT, the World Bank, the multilateral development banks, and regional economic integration organisations such as the European Community, did not address environmental protection requirements or the need to ensure that development was environmentally sustainable. Environmental concerns had historically been addressed on the margins of international economic concerns, and it is only since UNCED that the relationship between environmental protection and economic development has been more fully recognised by the international community. The UNCED process and the instruments reflect the need to integrate environment and development, and it is unlikely that the two objectives could now be easily separated.

Principle 4 of the Rio Declaration provides that: 'In order to achieve sustainable development, environmental protection shall constitute an integral part of the development process and cannot be considered in isolation from it.' An integrated approach to environment and development has significant practical consequences, most notably that environmental considerations will increasingly be a feature of international economic policy and law (and that lawyers working in the area of environmental protection will need to familiarise themselves with economic law and concepts). This is borne out by the changes which have taken place since the late 1980s. Examples include: the various amendments to the EC Treaty to include and then develop specific language on the environment;[197] the establishment of an Environment Department at the World Bank and the adoption of environmental assessment and related requirements; the convergence of trade with environment at the GATT and then the WTO; the elaboration of language on sustainable development in the Articles of Agreement of the EBRD and the WTO; and the development of environmental jurisprudence in competition, subsidy, foreign investment and intellectual property law.[198]

The integration of environment and development began prior to the 1972 Stockholm Conference. Linkage between conservation and development was made at the first UN Conference on conservation and utilisation of resources in

---

[197] See EC Commission Report, 'Integrating Environmental Concerns and Sustainable Development into Community Policies', SEC (1999) 1941 final.
[198] See further chapter 19, pp. 1010–15 below; chapter 20, pp. 1043–53 below; and chapter 21, pp. 1056–61 below.

1949.[199] In 1971, the General Assembly expressed its conviction that 'development plans should be compatible with a sound ecology and that adequate environmental conditions can best be ensured by the promotion of development, both at the national and international levels'.[200] Principle 13 of the Stockholm Declaration called on states to adopt 'an integrated and co-ordinated approach to their development planning so as to ensure that their development is compatible with the need to protect and improve the human environment'. The 1982 World Charter for Nature provided that the conservation of nature was to be taken into account in the planning and implementation of economic and social development activities and that due account was to be taken of the long-term capacity of natural systems in formulating plans for economic development.[201]

Numerous regional treaties support an approach which integrates environment and development. Examples include: the 1974 Paris Convention, which calls for an 'integrated planning policy consistent with the requirement of environmental protection';[202] the 1978 Kuwait Convention, which supports an 'integrated management approach . . . which will allow the achievement of environmental and development goals in a harmonious manner';[203] the 1978 Amazonian Treaty, which affirms the need to 'maintain a balance between economic growth and conservation of the environment';[204] the 1985 ASEAN Convention, which seeks to ensure that 'conservation and management of natural resources are treated as an integral part of development planning at all stages and at all levels';[205] and the 1989 Fourth Lomé Convention, which provided that the development of ACP states 'shall be based on a sustainable balance between its economic objectives, the rational management of the environment and the enhancement of natural . . . resources', and requires the 'preparation and implementation of coherent modes of development that have due regard for ecological balances'.[206] The global treaties at UNCED – and those adopted subsequently – include similar provisions.[207]

The integration of environment and development has re-opened debate over the 'right to development', after efforts to establish a New International Economic Order in the mid-1970s met with opposition from some of the larger industrialised countries. Principle 3 of the Rio Declaration implicitly accepts the 'right to development', although the United States declared that it did not, by joining consensus on the Rio Declaration, change its long-standing opposition to the 'so-called "right to development"'; for the United States, development 'is not a right . . . [it] is a goal we all hold', and the US disassociated itself from any

---

[199] Chapter 2, p. 31 above.   [200] UNGA Res. 2849 (XXVI) (1971).
[201] Paras. 7 and 8.   [202] Art. 6(2)(d).   [203] Preamble.
[204] Preamble.   [205] Art. 2(1).   [206] Arts. 4 and 34.
[207] 1992 Biodiversity Convention, Art. 6(b); 1992 Climate Change Convention, Preamble; 2000 Cotonou Agreement, Art. 32 (requiring the 'mainstreaming' of environmental sustainability throughout development co-operation).

interpretation of Principle 3 that accepted a 'right to development'.[208] Developing countries have, in this context, been careful to introduce language into treaties to safeguard their future development and limit the extent to which international environmental regulation might limit such development. Both UNCED treaties include language to the effect that the overriding priority needs of developing countries are the achievement of economic growth and the eradication of poverty,[209] an objective given more concrete expression by making the effective implementation by developing countries of their commitments dependent upon the effective implementation by developed countries of their financial obligations.[210] Despite the US language, Principle 3 of the Rio Declaration, with which Principle 4 must be read to be fully understood, is part of the bargain struck between developed and developing countries, which is also evident in the convoluted language of Article 3(4) of the Climate Change Convention. This provides that the parties 'have a right to and should, promote sustainable development', which reflects a compromise text between those states which sought an express recognition of a 'right to development' and those states which sought to dilute such a right by recognising only a 'right to promote sustainable development'.

Conclusion

International law recognises a principle (or concept) of 'sustainable development'. The term needs to be taken in the context of its historic evolution as reflecting a range of procedural and substantive commitments and obligations. These are primarily, but not exclusively, recognition of:

- the need to take into consideration the needs of present and future generations;
- the acceptance, on environmental protection grounds, of limits placed upon the use and exploitation of natural resources;
- the role of equitable principles in the allocation of rights and obligations;
- the need to integrate all aspects of environment and development; and
- the need to interpret and apply rules of international law in an integrated and systemic manner.

Precautionary principle

L. Gundling, 'The Status in International Law of the Principle of Precautionary Action', 5 *International Journal of Estuarine and Coastal Law* 23 (1990); D. Bodansky, 'Scientific Uncertainty and the Precautionary Principle', 33 *Environment*

---

[208] UNCED Report, vol. II, 17; UN Doc. A/CONF.151/26/Rev.1 (vol. II) (1993).
[209] 1992 Climate Change Convention, Preamble; 1992 Biodiversity Convention, Preamble.
[210] 1992 Climate Change Convention, Art. 4(7); 1992 Biodiversity Convention, Art. 20(4); see further chapter 20, pp. 1032–4 below.

4 (1991); J. Cameron and J. Abouchar, 'The Precautionary Principle: A Fundamental Principle of Law and Policy for the Protection of the Global Environment',
14 BCICLR 1 (1991); D. Freestone, 'The Precautionary Principle', in R. Churchill
and D. Freestone (eds.), *International Law and Global Climate Change* (1991), 21;
C. Boyden Gray and D. Rivkin, 'A "No Regrets" Environmental Policy', 83 *Foreign
Policy* 47 (1991); R. Rehbinder, *Das Vorsorgeprinzip in Internationalen Rechtsver-
gleich* (1991); E. Hey, 'The Precautionary Concept in Environmental Policy and
Law: Institutionalising Caution', 4 *Georgetown International Environmental Law
Review* 303 (1992); H. Hohmann, *Precautionary Legal Duties and Principles of
Modern International Environmental Law* (1994); T. O'Riordan and J. Cameron
(eds.), *Interpreting the Precautionary Principle* (1994); D. Freestone and E. Hey,
The Precautionary Principle and International Law (1995); A. Fabra, 'The LOSC
and the Implementation of the Precautionary Principle', 10 *Yearbook of Interna-
tional Environmental Law* 15 (1999); D. Freestone, 'Caution or Precaution: "A Rose
by Any Other Name..."?' 10 *Yearbook of International Environmental Law* 25 (1999);
N. de Sadeleer, 'Refléxions sur le statut juridique du principe de précaution', in E.
Zaccai and J.-N. Missa, *Le principe de précaution* (2000); A. Trouwborst, *Evolution and Status of the Precautionary Principle in International Law* (2002); N. de
Sadeleer, *Environmental Principles in an Age of Risk* (2003); S. Marr, *The Precau-
tionary Principle in the Law of the Sea – Modern Decision-Making in International
Law* (2003).

Whereas the preventive principle can be traced back to international environmental treaties and other international acts since at least the 1930s, the precautionary principle only began to appear in international legal instruments
in the mid-1980s, although prior to then it had featured as a principle in domestic legal systems, most notably that of West Germany.[211] The precautionary
principle aims to provide guidance in the development and application of international environmental law where there is scientific uncertainty. It continues
to generate disagreement as to its meaning and effect, as reflected in particular
in the views of states and international judicial practice. On the one hand, some
consider that it provides the basis for early international legal action to address
highly threatening environmental issues such as ozone depletion and climate
change.[212] On the other hand, its opponents have decried the potential which

---

[211] K. von Moltke, 'The Vorsorgeprinzip in West German Environmental Policy', in Twelfth
Report (Royal Commission on Environmental Pollution, UK, HMSO, CM 310, 1988),
57.

[212] See e.g. the support for the precautionary principle by low-lying AOSIS countries in the
climate change negotiations, which is put as follows: 'For us the precautionary principle
is much more than a semantic or theoretical exercise. It is an ecological and moral imperative. We trust the world understands our concerns by now. We do not have the luxury
of waiting for conclusive proof, as some have suggested in the past. The proof, we fear,
will kill us.' Ambassador Robert van Lierop, Permanent Representative of Vanuatu to the
UN and Co-Chairman of Working Group 1 of the INC/FCCC, Statement to the Plenary
Session of the INC/FCCC, 5 February 1991, at 3.

the principle has for over-regulation and limiting human activity. The core of the principle, which is still evolving, is reflected in Principle 15 of the Rio Declaration, which provides that:

> Where there are threats of serious or irreversible damage, lack of full scientific certainty shall not be used as a reason for postponing cost-effective measures to prevent environmental degradation.[213]

Principle 15 also provides that 'the precautionary approach shall be widely applied by states according to their capabilities'.

The precautionary principle (or precautionary approach, as the US and some others prefer to call it) has been adopted in many international environmental treaties since 1989. Although its precise formulation is not identical in each instrument, the language of Principle 15 of the Rio Declaration now attracts broad support. The principle finds its roots in the more traditional environmental agreements which call on parties to such agreements, and the institutions they create, to act and to adopt decisions which are based upon 'scientific findings' or methods,[214] or 'in the light of knowledge available at the time'.[215] These standards suggest that action shall only be taken where there is scientific evidence that significant environmental damage is occurring, and that in the absence of such evidence no action would be required. Examples of a traditional approach include the 1974 Paris Convention, which allows parties to take additional measures 'if scientific evidence has established that a serious hazard may be created in the maritime area by that substance and if urgent action is necessary':[216] this requires the party wishing to adopt measures to 'prove' a case for action based upon the existence of sufficient scientific evidence, which may be difficult to obtain.

The 1969 Intervention Convention was one of the earliest treaties to recognise the limitations of the traditional approach, concerning the environmental consequences of a failure to act. It allows proportionate measures to be taken to prevent, mitigate or eliminate grave and imminent danger to coastlines from threat of oil pollution, taking account of 'the extent and probability of imminent damage if those measures are not taken'.[217] Developments in the mid-1980s to address ozone depletion reflected growing support for precautionary action. The first treaty which refers to the term is the 1985 Vienna Convention, which reflected the parties' recognition of the 'precautionary measures' taken at the national and international levels.[218] By 1987, the parties to the Montreal

---

[213] WSSD Plan of Implementation, paras. 22 and 103.

[214] 1946 International Whaling Convention, Art. V(2); 1972 Antarctic Seals Convention, Annex, para. 7(b); 1972 World Heritage Convention, Preamble; 1972 London Convention, Art. XV(2); 1979 Bonn Convention, Arts. III(2) and XI(3) (action on the basis of 'reliable evidence, including the best scientific evidence available').

[215] 1960 Radiation Convention, Art. 3(1).   [216] Art. 4(4).

[217] Arts. I and V(3)(a).   [218] Preamble.

Protocol noted the 'precautionary measures' to control emission from certain CFCs which had already been taken at the national and regional (EEC) levels and stated their determination to 'protect the ozone layer by taking precautionary measures to control equitably total global emissions of substances that deplete it'.[219]

The precautionary approach has been relied upon in relation to measures to protect other environmental media, especially the marine environment. The Preamble to the 1984 Ministerial Declaration of the International Conference on the Protection of the North Sea reflected a consciousness that states 'must not wait for proof of harmful effects before taking action', since damage to the marine environment can be irreversible or remediable only at considerable expense and over a long period.[220] This introduces the idea that precautionary action may be justified on economic grounds. The Ministerial Declaration of the Second North Sea Conference (1987) accepted that 'in order to protect the North Sea from possibly damaging effects of the most dangerous substances, a precautionary approach is necessary'.[221] At the Third North Sea Conference (1990), Ministers pledged to continue to apply the precautionary principle.[222] The 1990 Bergen Ministerial Declaration on Sustainable Development in the ECE Region was the first international instrument to treat the principle as one of general application and linked to sustainable development. The Declaration provides that:

> In order to achieve sustainable development, policies must be based on the precautionary principle. Environmental measures must anticipate, prevent and attack the causes of environmental degradation. Where there are threats of serious or irreversible damage, lack of full scientific certainty should not be used as a reason for postponing measures to prevent environmental degradation.[223]

Central to this text is the element of anticipation, reflecting a need for effective environmental measures to be based upon actions which take a longer-term approach and which might predict changes in the basis of our scientific knowledge. Moreover, for the precautionary principle to apply, the threat of environmental damage must be 'serious' or 'irreversible', although there is not yet any limitation on grounds of cost-effectiveness as to the measures which should not be postponed. While the amendments to the Montreal Protocol were being prepared, the UNEP Governing Council recognised that 'waiting for scientific proof regarding the impact of pollutants discharged into the marine environment could result in irreversible damage to the marine environment and in human suffering', and recommended that all governments adopt the 'principle

---

[219] Preamble.   [220] Bremen, 1 November 1984.
[221] London, 25 November 1987; also PARCOM Recommendation 89/1 (1989) (supporting the 'principle of precautionary action').
[222] The Hague, 8 March 1990.   [223] Bergen, 16 May 1990, para. 7; IPE (I/B/16_05_90).

of precautionary action' as the basis of their policy with regard to the prevention and elimination of marine pollution.[224]

Since that time, numerous environmental treaties, including some which are of global application on environmental matters of broad concern and applicable to almost all human activities, have adopted the precautionary principle or its underlying rationale. Among the earliest was the 1991 Bamako Convention, which requires parties to strive to adopt and implement

> the preventive, precautionary approach to pollution which entails, *inter alia*, preventing the release into the environment of substances which may cause harm to humans or the environment without waiting for scientific proof regarding such harm. The parties shall co-operate with each other in taking the appropriate measures to implement the precautionary principle to pollution prevention through the application of clean production methods.[225]

This formulation is one of the most far-reaching. It links the preventive and precautionary approaches, does not require damage to be 'serious' or 'irreversible', and lowers the threshold at which scientific evidence might require action. The parties to the 1992 Watercourses Convention agreed to be guided by the precautionary principle

> by virtue of which action to avoid the potential transboundary impact of the release of hazardous substances shall not be postponed on the ground that scientific research has not fully proved a causal link between those substances, on the one hand, and the potential transboundary impact, on the other hand.[226]

This formulation limits the application of the principle to transboundary effects alone, although the level of environmental damage is raised above that required by the Bamako Convention to 'significant adverse effect'. The 1992 Biodiversity Convention does not specifically refer to the precautionary principle, although the Preamble notes that 'where there is a threat of significant reduction or loss of biological diversity, lack of full scientific certainty should not be used as a reason for postponing measures to avoid or minimise such a threat'.[227] The level of environmental damage here is well below the 'serious' or 'irreversible' level required by the 1990 Bergen Declaration. The 2000 Biosafety Protocol relies extensively on the precautionary approach. The objective of the Protocol is, however, stated to be 'in accordance' with Principle 15 of the Rio Declaration, and, to that end, the Protocol affirms that 'lack of scientific certainty due to insufficient relevant scientific information and knowledge regarding the extent of the potential adverse effects of a living modified organism on the conservation and sustainable use of biological diversity' shall

---

[224] Governing Council Decision 15/27 (1989).   [225] Art. 4(3)(f).
[226] Art. 2(5)(a). See also the 1994 Danube Convention, Art. 2(4).   [227] Preamble.

not prevent a party from prohibiting imports.[228] The reference to precaution in the 1992 Climate Change Convention was a controversial matter, and the text as finally adopted established limits on the application of the precautionary principle by requiring a threat of 'serious or irreversible damage' and by linking the commitment to an encouragement to take measures which are 'cost effective'.[229]

Beyond these two conventions, many others now commit their parties to apply the precautionary principle or approach. The 1992 OSPAR Convention links prevention and precaution: preventive measures are to be taken when there are 'reasonable grounds for concern . . . even when there is no conclusive evidence of a causal relationship between the inputs and the effects'.[230] The threshold here is quite low. The standard applied by the 1992 Baltic Sea Convention introduces yet another variation: preventive measures are to be taken 'when there is reason to assume' that harm might be caused 'even when there is no conclusive evidence of a causal relationship between inputs and their alleged effects'.[231] The 1995 Straddling Stocks Agreement commits coastal states and states fishing on the high seas to apply the precautionary approach widely, and sets out in detail the modalities for its application.[232] A growing number of other conventions – both regional and global – also give effect to a precautionary approach in relation to a range of different subject matters.[233] The 1992 Maastricht Treaty amended Article 130r(2) of the EC Treaty so that EC action on the environment 'shall be based on the precautionary principle', and the 1997 Amsterdam Treaty further amended the EC Treaty to apply the principle to Community policy on the environment (Article 174(2)). The European Commission has published a Communication on the precautionary principle which outlines the Commission's approach to the use of the principle, establishes guidelines for applying it, and aims to develop understanding on the assessment, appraisal and management of risk in the face of scientific uncertainty.[234] The Communication considers that the principle has been 'progressively consolidated in international environmental law, and so it has since become a full-fledged and general principle of international law'.[235] The

---

[228] Art. 10(6). See also Art. 11(8) and, in relation to risk assessment, Art. 15 and Annex 3.

[229] Art. 3(3).   [230] Art. 2(2)(a).   [231] Art. 3(2).

[232] Arts. 5(c) and 6 and Annex II (Guidelines for the Application of Precautionary Reference Points in Conservation and Management of Straddling Fish Stocks and Highly Migratory Fish Stocks).

[233] E.g. 1973 CITES, Res. Conf. 9.24 (1994), chapter 11, pp. 505–15 below; 1994 Energy Charter Treaty, Art. 18; 1996 Protocol to the 1972 London Convention, Art. 3; 2000 Biosafety Protocol, Art. 1; 2001 POPs Convention ('Precaution underlies the concerns of all parties and is embedded within this convention', Preamble, also Art. 1); 2002 North-East Pacific Convention, Art. 5(6)(a).

[234] COM 2000 (1), 2 February 2000 (http://europa.eu.int/comm/dgs/ health_consumer/ library/pub/pub07_en.pdf).

[235] *Ibid.*, 11.

principle has been applied by the ECJ[236] and by the EEA Court, which has
ruled that, in cases relating to the effects on human health of certain products,
and where there may be a great measure of scientific and practical uncertainty
linked to the issue under consideration, the application of the precautionary
principle is justified and 'presupposes, firstly, an identification of potentially
negative health consequences arising, in the present case, from a proposed for-
tification, and, secondly, a comprehensive evaluation of the risk to health based
on the most recent scientific information'. The Court went on:

> When the insufficiency, or the inconclusiveness, or the imprecise nature
> of the conclusions to be drawn from those considerations make it impos-
> sible to determine with certainty the risk or hazard, but the likelihood of
> considerable harm still persists were the negative eventuality to occur, the
> precautionary principle would justify the taking of restrictive measures.[237]

The precautionary principle or approach has now received widespread support by the international community in relation to a broad range of subject
areas. What does the principle mean, and what status does it have in international law? There is no clear and uniform understanding of the meaning of the
precautionary principle among states and other members of the international
community. At the most general level, it means that states agree to act carefully and with foresight when taking decisions which concern activities that
may have an adverse impact on the environment. A more focused interpretation provides that the principle requires activities and substances which may be
harmful to the environment to be regulated, and possibly prohibited, even if no
conclusive or overwhelming evidence is available as to the harm or likely harm
they may cause to the environment. As the Bergen Ministerial Declaration put
it, 'lack of full scientific certainty should not be used as a reason for postponing
measures to prevent environmental degradation'. Under the Rio Declaration,

---

[236] See e.g. Case C-180/96, *United Kingdom* v. *EC Commission* [1998] ECR I-2265 ('the institutions may take protective measures without having to wait until the reality and seriousness
of those risks become fully apparent', at paras. 99 and 100); see also Case T-70/99, *Alpharma Inc.* v. *Council of the European Union*, Order of 30 June 1999 (Interim Measures)
[1999] ECR II-2027, the President of the Court of First Instance referring to the principle
and affirming that 'requirements linked to the protection of public health should undoubtedly be given greater weight than economic considerations'). See also Case C-6/99,
Association Greenpeace France and Others v. *Ministere de l'Agriculture et de la Peche and
Others* [2000] ECR I-1651 (French edition) (in relation to Directive 90/220, observance of
the precautionary principle is reflected in the notifier's obligation immediately to notify
the competent authority of new information regarding the risks of the product to human
health or the environment and the competent authority's obligation immediately to inform the Commission and the other member states about this information and, secondly,
in the right of any member state, provisionally to restrict or prohibit the use and/or sale
on its territory of a product which has received consent where it has justifiable reasons to
consider that it constitutes a risk to human health or the environment: para. 44).

[237] Case E-3/00, *EFTA Surveillance Authority* v. *Norway* [2001] 2 CMLR 47.

the requirement is stated to be mandatory: lack of full scientific certainty 'shall not be used' to prevent action. What remains open is the level at which scientific evidence is sufficient to override arguments for postponing measures, or at which measures might even be required as a matter of international law.

A more fundamental change would be adopted by an interpretation of the precautionary principle, one increasingly widely held, which would shift the burden of proof. According to traditional approaches, the burden of proof currently lies with the person opposing an activity to prove that it does or is likely to cause environmental damage. A new approach, supported by the precautionary principle, would tend to shift the burden of proof and require the person who wishes to carry out an activity to prove that it will not cause harm to the environment. This interpretation would require polluters, and polluting states, to establish that their activities and the discharge of certain substances would not adversely or significantly affect the environment before they were granted the right to release the potentially polluting substances or carry out the proposed activity. This interpretation may also require national or international regulatory action where the scientific evidence suggests that lack of action may result in serious or irreversible harm to the environment, or where there are divergent views on the risks of action.

There is growing evidence to suggest that this interpretation is beginning to be supported by state practice, even if it still falls short of having sufficient support to allow it to be considered a rule of general application. Examples include the EC's 1991 Urban Waste Water Directive, which allows certain urban waste water discharges to be subjected to less stringent treatment than that generally required by the Directive providing that 'comprehensive studies indicate that such discharges will not adversely affect the environment'.[238] Under the 1992 OSPAR Convention, parties (France and the United Kingdom) which originally wanted to retain the option of dumping low- and intermediate-level radioactive wastes at sea were required to report to the OSPAR Commission on 'the results of scientific studies which show that any potential dumping operations would not result in hazards to human health, harm to living resources or marine ecosystems, damage to amenities or interference with other legitimate uses of the sea'.[239]

The practice of international courts and tribunals, and of states appearing before them, sheds some light on the meaning and effect of the precautionary principle. Before the ICJ the principle appears to have first been raised in New Zealand's 1995 request concerning French nuclear testing.[240] New Zealand relied extensively on the principle, which it described as 'a very widely accepted and operative principle of international law' and which shifted the burden onto France to prove that the proposed tests would not give rise to

---

[238] EC Directive 91/271, Art. 6(2); chapter 15, pp. 776–8 below.
[239] Annex II, Art. 3(3)(c).   [240] Chapter 8, pp. 319–21 below.

environmental damage.[241] Five 'intervening' states (Australia, Micronesia, the Marshall Islands, Samoa and the Solomon Islands) also invoked the principle. France responded that the status of the principle in international law was 'tout à fait incertain', but that in any event it had been complied with, and that evidentiary burdens were no different in the environmental field than any other area of international law.[242] The ICJ's order did not refer to these arguments, although Judge Weeramantry's dissent noted that the principle had 'evolved to meet [the] evidentiary difficulty caused by the fact [that] information required to prove a proposition' may be 'in the hands of the party causing or threatening the damage', and that it was 'gaining increasing support as part of the international law of the environment'.[243] In the *Gabcikovo-Nagymaros* case, Hungary and Slovakia also invoked the precautionary principle.[244] Again, the ICJ did not feel the need to address the principle, limiting itself to a passing reference to Hungary's claim that the principle justified the termination of the 1977 treaty and its recognition of the parties' agreement on the need to take environmental concerns seriously and to take the required precautionary measures.[245] Of particular note was the failure of the ICJ to refer to or apply the principle in its consideration of the conditions under which Hungary could invoke the concept of ecological necessity to preclude the wrongfulness of its suspension of works on the two barrages in 1989.[246] Having acknowledged without difficulty 'that the concerns expressed by Hungary for its natural environment in the region affected by the Gabcíkovo-Nagymaros Project related to an "essential interest" of that State', the ICJ nevertheless found that Hungary had not proved that 'a real, "grave" and "imminent" "peril" existed in 1989 and that the measures taken by Hungary were the only possible response to it.'[247] The ICJ found that there were serious uncertainties concerning future harm to freshwater supplies and biodiversity, but that these:

---

[241] New Zealand Request, para.105; see also ICJ CR/95/20, at 20–1 and 36–8.

[242] ICJ CR/95/20, at 71–2 and 75.

[243] (1995) ICJ Reports 342; see also Ad Hoc Judge Palmer ('the norm involved in the precautionary principle ha[d] developed rapidly and m[ight] now be a principle of customary international law relating to the environment': *ibid.*, 412). See also Judge Weeramantry's Dissenting Opinion in *The Legality of the Threat or Use of Nuclear Weapons* (1996) ICJ Reports 502.

[244] Chapter 10, pp. 463–4 below.

[245] (1997) ICJ Reports 62, para. 97, and 68, para. 113. See also chapter 10, pp. 463–4 below. But see the Separate Opinion of Judge Koroma, that the precautionary principle was incorporated in the 1977 treaty but 'had not been proved to have been violated to an extent sufficient to have warranted the unilateral termination of the Treaty': *ibid.*, 152.

[246] The ICJ found that a state of necessity was, on an exceptional basis, a ground recognised by customary international law for precluding the wrongfulness of an act not in conformity with an international obligation, and relied on the formulation of draft Article 33 of the ILC's draft Articles on State Responsibility: (1997) ICJ Reports 7 paras. 50–2.

[247] *Ibid.*, para. 54.

could not, alone, establish the objective existence of a 'peril' in the sense of a component element of a state of necessity. The word 'peril' certainly evokes the idea of 'risk'; that is precisely what distinguishes 'peril' from material damage. But a state of necessity could not exist without a 'peril' duly established at the relevant point in time; the mere apprehension of a possible 'peril' could not suffice in that respect. It could moreover hardly be otherwise, when the 'peril' constituting the state of necessity has at the same time to be 'grave' and 'imminent'. 'Imminence' is synonymous with 'immediacy' or 'proximity' and goes far beyond the concept of 'possibility' . . . That does not exclude, in the view of the Court, that a 'peril' appearing in the long term might be held to be 'imminent' as soon as it is established, at the relevant point in time, that the realization of that peril, however far off it might be, is not thereby any less certain and inevitable.[248]

This is not precautionary language, premised as it is on the need to establish the certainty and inevitability of serious harm. However, it must be recognised that the ICJ was concerned here with the application of the law as it stood in 1989, when Hungary had wrongfully (in the view of the ICJ) suspended work on the project. At that time, the precautionary principle had not yet emerged and could not realistically be applied as general international law. It may be that the ICJ also had this in mind when it indicated later in the judgment that '[w]hat might have been a correct application of the law in 1989 or 1992, if the case had been before the Court then, could be a miscarriage of justice if prescribed in 1997'.[249]

The International Tribunal for the Law of the Sea has also been presented with arguments invoking precaution, and has shown itself to be notably more open to the application of the principle, albeit without express reliance. In 1999, in the *Southern Bluefin Tuna* cases, Australia and New Zealand requested the Tribunal to order 'that the parties act consistently with the precautionary principle in fishing for Southern Bluefin Tuna pending a final settlement of the dispute'.[250] Japan, the respondent state, did not address the question of the status or effect of the principle. In its Order the Tribunal expressed the view that the parties should 'act with prudence and caution to ensure that effective conservation measures are taken to prevent serious harm to the stock of southern bluefin tuna' (para. 77), that there was 'scientific uncertainty regarding measures to be taken to conserve the stock of southern bluefin tuna' (para. 79), and that, although it could not conclusively assess the scientific evidence presented by the parties, measures should be taken as a matter of urgency to preserve the rights of the parties and to avert further deterioration of the southern bluefin tuna stock (para. 80). In ordering the parties to refrain from conducting experimental fishing programmes, the Tribunal was plainly

---

[248] *Ibid.*   [249] *Ibid.*, para. 134.   [250] Chapter 11, pp. 580–1 below.

taking a precautionary approach, as Judge Treves recognised in his Separate Opinion.[251]

In 2001, in the *MOX* case, Ireland claimed that the United Kingdom had failed to apply a precautionary approach to the protection of the Irish Sea in the exercise of its decision-making authority in relation to the direct and indirect consequences of the operation of the MOX plant and international movements of radioactive materials associated with the operation of the MOX plant.[252] The principle was invoked by Ireland at the provisional measures phase to support its claim that the United Kingdom had the burden of demonstrating that no harm would arise from discharges and other consequences of the operation of the MOX plant, and to inform the assessment by the Tribunal of the urgency of the measures it is required to take in respect of the operation of the MOX plant.[253] For its part, and while accepting that in assessing the level of risk in any given case considerations of prudence and caution may be relevant, the United Kingdom argued that in the absence of evidence showing a real risk of harm precaution could not warrant a restraint of the rights of the United Kingdom to operate the plant.[254] The Tribunal did not order the suspension of the operation of the plant, as Ireland had requested, but instead ordered the parties to co-operate and enter into consultations to exchange further information on possible consequences for the Irish Sea arising out of the commissioning of the MOX plant and to devise, as appropriate, measures to prevent pollution of the marine environment which might result from the operation of the MOX plant.[255] That Order, which has a certain precautionary character, was premised on considerations of 'prudence and caution'.[256]

---

[251] 'In the present case, it would seem to me that the requirement of urgency is satisfied only in the light of such precautionary approach. I regret that this is not stated explicitly in the Order': Separate Opinion of Judge Treves, para. 8. See also Separate Opinion of Judge Lang ('Nevertheless, it is not possible, on the basis of the materials available and arguments presented on this application for provisional measures, to determine whether, as the Applicants contend, customary international law recognizes a precautionary principle': at para. 15), and Ad Hoc Judge Shearer ('The Tribunal has not found it necessary to enter into a discussion of the precautionary principle/approach. However, I believe that the measures ordered by the Tribunal are rightly based upon considerations deriving from a precautionary approach.').

[252] Chapter 9, p. 436 below; see Ireland's Statement of Claim, 25 October 2001, para. 34 ('the precautionary principle is a rule of customary international law which is binding upon the United Kingdom and relevant to the assessment of the United Kingdom's actions by reference to [UNCLOS]').

[253] Order of 3 December 2001, para. 71.

[254] UK Response, 15 November 2001, para. 150.

[255] Order of 3 December 2001, para. 89(1).

[256] *Ibid.*, para. 84. Cf. the Separate Opinion of Ad Hoc Judge Szekely (the Tribunal 'should have been responsive, in the face of such uncertainty, to the Irish demands regarding the application of the precautionary principle (see paragraphs 96 to 101 of the Request, pp. 43–46). It is regrettable that it did not do so, since acting otherwise would have led

The principle has also been addressed by the WTO Appellate Body.[257] In 1998, in the *Beef Hormones* case, the European Community invoked the principle to justify its claim that it was entitled to prohibit imports of beef produced in the United States and Canada with artificial hormones, where the impacts on human health were uncertain. The Community argued that the principle was already 'a general customary rule of international law or at least a general principle of law', that it applied to both the assessment and management of a risk, and that it informed the meaning and effect of Articles 5.1 and 5.2 of the WTO's Agreement on Sanitary and Phytosanitary Measures (the 'SPS Agreement').[258] The United States denied that the principle represented a principle of customary international law, and preferred to characterise it as an 'approach' the content of which may vary from context to context.[259] Canada referred to a precautionary approach as 'an emerging principle of international law, which may in the future crystallize into one of the "general principles of law recognized by civilized nations", within the meaning of Article 38(1)(c) of the ICJ Statute'.[260] The WTO Appellate Body agreed with the United States and Canada that the precautionary principle did not override Articles 5.1 and 5.2 of the SPS Agreement, although it considered that it was reflected in the preamble to and Articles 3.3 and 5.7 of the SPS Agreement, which did not exhaust the relevance of the principle.[261] Recognising that the status of the principle in international law was the subject of continued debate, and that it was regarded

---

to granting the provisional measure requested by Ireland regarding the suspension of the commissioning of the plant.').

[257] See generally T. Christoforou, 'Science, Law and Precaution in Dispute Resolution on Health and Environmental Protection: What Role for Scientific Experts?', in J. Bourrinet and S. Maljean-Dubois (eds.), *Le Commerce international des organismes génétiquement modifiés* (2002).

[258] Chapter 19, pp. 979–81 below; see Report of the Appellate Body, 16 January 1998, WT/DS48/AB/R, at para. 16.

[259] *Ibid.*, para. 43. The United States stated that the SPS Agreement recognised a precautionary approach (in its Article 5.7) so there was no need to invoke a 'precautionary principle' to be risk-averse.

[260] *Ibid.*, para. 60.

[261] *Ibid.*, para. 124 ('a panel charged with determining . . . whether "sufficient scientific evidence" exists to warrant the maintenance by a Member of a particular SPS measure may, of course, and should, bear in mind that responsible, representative governments commonly act from perspectives of prudence and precaution where risks of irreversible, e.g. life-terminating, damage to human health are concerned'). The Appellate Body went on to state that 'responsible and representative governments may act in good faith on the basis of what, at a given time, may be a divergent opinion coming from qualified and respected sources' (para. 194), a view endorsed in *EC – Asbestos* (Appellate Body Report, 12 March 2001, at para. 178), and adding '[i]n justifying a measure under Article XX(b) of the GATT 1994, a Member may also rely, in good faith, on scientific sources which, at that time, may represent a divergent, but qualified and respected, opinion. A Member is not obliged, in setting health policy, automatically to follow what, at a given time, may constitute a majority scientific opinion.'

by some as having crystallised into a general principle of customary international environmental law, the Appellate Body said:

> Whether it has been widely accepted by Members as a principle of general or customary international law appears less than clear. We consider, however, that it is unnecessary, and probably imprudent, for the Appellate Body in this appeal to take a position on this important, but abstract, question. We note that the Panel itself did not make any definitive finding with regard to the status of the precautionary principle in international law and that the precautionary principle, at least outside the field of international environmental law, still awaits authoritative formulation.[262]

The principle has also been raised before other courts, such as the European Court of Human Rights. In *Balmer-Schafroth* v. *Switzerland*, the applicants claimed that the failure of Switzerland to provide for administrative review of a decision extending the operation of a nuclear facility violated Article 6 of the European Convention on Human Rights.[263] The claim was rejected by the majority, because the connection between the government's decision and the applicants' right was too remote and tenuous. The Court ruled that they had failed to

> establish a direct link between the operating conditions of the power station . . . and their right to protection of their physical integrity, as they failed to show that the operation of Mühleberg power station exposed them personally to a danger that was not only serious but also specific and, above all, imminent. In the absence of such a finding, the effects on the population of the measures which the Federal Council could have ordered to be taken in the instant case therefore remained hypothetical. Consequently, neither the dangers nor the remedies were established with a degree of probability that made the outcome of the proceedings directly decisive.[264]

A dissenting opinion by seven judges, however, criticised this finding, on the grounds that it 'ignored the whole trend of international institutions and public international law towards protecting persons and heritage, as evident [*inter alia*] in . . . the development of the precautionary principle'.[265] At the national level, there have also been several decisions addressing the status of the precautionary

---

[262] *Ibid.*, para. 123. The Appellate Body noted that in the *Gabcikovo-Nagymaros* case, the ICJ had not identified the precautionary principle as a recently developed norm in the field of environmental protection, and had declined to declare that such principle could override the obligations of the 1977 Treaty: *ibid.*, n. 93.

[263] Judgment of 26 July 1987, *European Court of Human Rights Reports*-IV. Art. 6 of the Convention provides that: 'In the determination of his civil rights and obligations . . . everyone is entitled to a fair . . . hearing . . . by [a] . . . tribunal . . .'

[264] *Ibid.*, para. 40.

[265] Dissenting Opinion of Judge Pettiti, joined by Judges Golcukul, Walsh, Russo, Valticos, Lopes Rocha and Jambrek.

principle in international law. In *Vellore*, for example, the Indian Supreme Court ruled that the precautionary principle was an essential feature of 'sustainable development' and as such part of customary international law.[266] By contrast, a United States federal court appears more restrained in its approach, holding that the principle was not yet established in customary international law so as to give rise to a cause of action under the Alien Tort Claims Statute.[267]

The legal status of the precautionary principle is evolving. There is certainly sufficient evidence of state practice to support the conclusion that the principle, as elaborated in Principle 15 of the Rio Declaration and various international conventions, has now received sufficiently broad support to allow a strong argument to be made that it reflects a principle of customary law, and that within the context of the European Union it has now achieved customary status, without prejudice to the precise consequences of its application in any given case. Nevertheless, it must be recognised that international courts and tribunals have been reluctant to accept explicitly that the principle has a customary international law status, notwithstanding the preponderance of support in favour of that view, and diminishing opposition to it. The reluctance may be understandable, in view of its inherently commonsensical approach, even if the practical consequences of its application fall to be determined on a case-by-case basis.[268]

Polluter-pays principle

OECD, *The Polluter-Pays Principle* (1975); H. Smets, 'A Propos d'un ventuel principe pollueur-payeur en matière de pollution transfrontière', 8 *Environmental Policy and Law* 40 (1982); S. E. Gaines, 'The Polluter-Pays Principle: From Economic Equity to Environmental Ethos', 26 *Texas International Law Journal* 463 (1991); R. Romi, 'Le Principe pollueur-payeur, ses implications et ses applications', 8 *Droit de l'environnement* 46 (1991); H. J. Kim, 'Subsidy, Polluter-Pays Principle and Financial Assistance Among Countries', 34 JWTL 115 (2000).

The polluter-pays principle establishes the requirement that the costs of pollution should be borne by the person responsible for causing the pollution. The

---

[266] *Vellore Citizens' Welfare Forum* v. *Union of India and Others*, Writ Petition (C) No. 914 of 1991 (Kuldip Singh and Faizanuddin JJ), Judgment of 28 August 1996, paras. 10, 11 and 15. Cf. *Narmada Bachao Andolan* v. *Union of India and Others*, Supreme Court of India, Judgment of 18 October 2000 (www.narmada.org/sardarsarovar/sc.ruling/majority.judgment.doc).

[267] *Beanal* v. *Freeport-Mcmoran*, 969 F Supp 362 at 384 (US District Court for Eastern District of Louisiana, 9 April 1997) ('the principle does not constitute [an] international tort for which there is universal consensus in the international community as to [its] binding status and [its] content'); affirmed 197 F 3d 161 (US Court of Appeals for the Fifth Circuit, 29 November 1999).

[268] In this sense, see Separate Opinion of Judge Treves, n. 251 above para. 9.

meaning of the principle, and its application to particular cases and situations, remains open to interpretation, particularly in relation to the nature and extent of the costs included and the circumstances in which the principle will, perhaps exceptionally, not apply. The principle has nevertheless attracted broad support, and is closely related to the rules governing civil and state liability for environmental damage (as described in chapter 18 below), the permissibility of certain forms of state subsidies, and the recent acknowledgment in various instruments by developed countries of the 'responsibility that they bear in the international pursuit of sustainable development in view of the pressures their societies place on the global environment', as well as the financial and other consequences that flow from this acknowledgment.[269] The practical implications of the polluter-pays principle are in its allocation of economic obligations in relation to environmentally damaging activities, particularly in relation to liability,[270] the use of economic instruments, and the application of rules relating to competition and subsidy.[271]

The polluter-pays principle has not received the same degree of support or attention accorded over the years to the principle of preventive action, or the attention more recently accorded to the precautionary principle, although its use is now being taken up in other regional agreements.[272] It is doubtful whether it has achieved the status of a generally applicable rule of customary international law, except perhaps in relation to states in the EC, the UNECE and the OECD. The strong objections of some countries to the further development of the polluter-pays principle, particularly for international relations, is evident from the compromise language adopted by Principle 16 of the Rio Declaration, which provides that:

> National authorities should endeavour to promote the internalisation of environmental costs and the use of economic instruments, taking into account the approach that the polluter should, in principle, bear the costs of pollution, with due regard to the public interests and, without distorting international trade and investment.

This text, which falls short of the more specific language of EC, OECD and UNECE instruments, includes language which limits the extent of any obligation which might apply to states.[273] This derives, at least in part, from the view held by a number of states, both developed and developing, that the

---

[269] 1992 Rio Declaration, Principle 7.

[270] See Institut de Droit International, Resolution on Responsibility and Liability under International Law for Environmental Damage, Art. 13, 37 ILM 1473 (1998).

[271] See respectively chapters 18, pp. 904–38 below; chapter 4, pp. 158–67 above; and chapter 19, pp. 1010–17 below.

[272] See e.g. 2002 North-East Pacific Convention, Art. 5(6)(b).

[273] See WSSD Plan of Implementation, para. 14(b).

polluter-pays principle is applicable at the domestic level but does not govern relations or responsibilities between states at the international level.

The polluter-pays principle in treaty law can be traced back to some of the first instruments establishing minimum rules on civil liability for damage resulting from hazardous activities. The conventions on civil liability for nuclear damage, the 1960 Paris Convention and the 1963 IAEA Liability Convention,[274] were influenced by the desire to channel compensation from those responsible for the activity causing damage to the victims. Under the 1969 CLC, however, the shipowner is precluded from relying on the limitation of liability if the incident occurred as a result of his actual fault or privity.[275] Similarly, the Preamble to the 1971 Oil Fund Convention reflects the consideration that the economic consequences of oil pollution damage should be borne by the shipping industry and oil cargo interests.[276]

OECD

The first international instrument to refer expressly to the polluter-pays principle was the 1972 OECD Council Recommendation on Guiding Principles Concerning the International Economic Aspects of Environmental Policies, which endorsed the polluter-pays principle to allocate costs of pollution prevention and control measures to encourage rational use of environmental resources and avoid distortions in international trade and investment.[277] The Recommendation defined the principle in a limited sense to mean that the polluter should bear the expenses of carrying out the measures deemed necessary by public authorities to protect the environment:

> In other words, the cost of these measures should be reflected in the cost of goods and services which cause pollution in production and/or consumption. Such measures should not be accompanied by subsidies that would create significant distortions in international trade and investment.[278]

The 1972 Recommendation does not, on the face of it, apply to the costs of environmental damage. In 1974, the OECD Council adopted a further Recommendation on the Implementation of the Polluter-Pays Principle which reaffirmed that the principle constituted a 'fundamental principle' for member countries, that aid given for new pollution control technologies and the

---

[274] Chapter 18, pp. 905–12 below.

[275] Art V(2), chapter 18, pp. 913–15 below; see also 1977 Civil Liability for Oil Pollution Convention, Art. 6(4).

[276] Chapter 18, pp. 915–22 below.

[277] OECD Council Recommendation C(72)128 (1972), 14 ILM 236 (1975).

[278] *Ibid.*, Annex, para. A.4. The Council further recommended that 'as a general rule, Member countries should not assist the polluters in bearing the costs of pollution control whether by means of subsidies, tax advantages or other measures'.

development of new pollution abatement equipment was not necessarily incompatible with the principle, and that member countries should strive for
uniform observance of the principle.[279] The 1989 OECD Council Recommendation on the Application of the Polluter-Pays Principle to Accidental Pollution
extends the principle to imply that the operator of a hazardous installation
should bear the cost of reasonable measures to prevent and control accidental
pollution from that installation which are introduced by public authorities in
conformity with domestic law prior to the occurrence of an accident.[280] According to the Recommendation, however, this does not necessarily require that 'the
costs of reasonable measures to control accidental pollution after an accident
should be collected as expeditiously as possible from the legal or natural person
who is at the origin of the accident'. Such a domestic legal requirement is merely
'consistent with', rather than implied by, the principle.[281] Examples of specific
applications of the polluter-pays principle cited by the 1989 Recommendation
include adjusting fees or taxes payable by hazardous installations to cover more
fully the cost of certain exceptional measures taken by public authorities to
prevent and control accidental pollution, and charging to the polluter the cost
of reasonable pollution control measures decided on by public authorities following an accident to avoid the spread of environmental damage and limit the
release of hazardous substances (by ceasing emissions at the plant), the pollution as such (by cleaning or decontamination), or its ecological effects (by
rehabilitating the polluted environment).[282] The Recommendation also provides guidance on 'reasonable' measures: they depend on 'the circumstances
under which they are implemented, the nature and extent of the measures, the
threats and hazard existing when the decision is taken, the laws and regulations
in force, and the interests which must be protected'.[283] The Recommendation
cites certain exceptions to the principle, including the need for rapid implementation of stringent measures for accident prevention (provided this does
not lead to significant distortions in international trade and investment), or if
strict and prompt implementation of the principle would lead to severe socio-
economic consequences.[284] The application of the principle does not affect
the possibility under domestic law of requiring the operator to pay other costs

---

[279] C(74)223 (1974), paras. I(1), II(3) and III(1), 14 ILM 234 (1975).
[280] C(89)88 (Final), 28 ILM 1320 (1989); Appendix Guiding Principles Relating to Accidental
Pollution, para. 4; these are measures taken to prevent accidents in specific installations
and to limit their consequences for human health and the environment, including safety
measures, emergency plans, carrying out clean-up operations and minimising ecological
effects, but not including humanitarian measures or measures to compensate victims for
economic consequences: para. 8.
[281] Para. 5.
[282] Paras. 10 and 11; pooling by operators of certain financial risks is considered to be
'consistent' with the Principle: para. 13.
[283] Para. 12.   [284] Paras. 14 and 15.

connected with the public authorities' response to an accident, or compensation for future costs of the accident.[285]

European Community

The polluter-pays principle is also established under EC law. The EC adopted the principle in its first programme of action on the environment in 1973.[286] Two years later, the EC Council adopted a Recommendation regarding cost allocation and action by public authorities on environmental matters which recommended that the EC at Community level and the member states in their national environmental legislation must apply the polluter-pays principle, according to which

> natural or legal persons governed by public or private law who are responsible for pollution must pay the costs of such measures as are necessary to eliminate that pollution or to reduce it so as to comply with the standards or equivalent measures laid down by the public authorities.[287]

This formulation is broader than early OECD recommendations in respect of the costs which might be covered by the principle. The EC Council Recommendation, which is not legally binding, identifies standards and charges as the major instruments of action available to public authorities for the avoidance of pollution, allows certain exceptions to the principle, and says which acts will not be considered to be contrary to the principle.[288] In 1986, the EEC Treaty was amended to provide that EC action relating to the environment shall be based on the principle that 'the polluter should pay'.[289] In 1992, the EC member states and EFTA member countries agreed that action by the parties was to be based on the principle that 'the polluter should pay'.[290] A number of acts of EC secondary legislation also refer to, or incorporate, the principle,[291] and the ECJ

---

[285] Para. 16. [286] OJ C112, 20 December 1973, 1.

[287] Council Recommendation 75/436/EURATOM, ECSC, EEC of 3 March 1975, Annex, para. 2; OJ L169, 29 June 1987, 1.

[288] Paras. 5–7.

[289] 1957 EEC Treaty (as amended) (formerly Art. 130r(2)); see also former Art. 130(s)(5) of the EEC Treaty as amended by the 1992 Maastricht Treaty, allowing for temporary derogations and/or financial support 'without prejudice to the principle that the polluter should pay'. See now Arts. 174(2) and 175(5) of the EC Treaty as amended by the 1997 Amsterdam Treaty.

[290] 1992 EEA Agreement, Art. 73(2).

[291] See e.g. Directive 75/442, Art. 15 (waste); Directive 94/67, Preamble (incineration of hazardous waste); Directive 2000/59, Preamble (port reception facilities for ship-generated waste and cargo residues); Directive 2000/60, Art. 9 (water framework); Decision 2850/2000, Preamble (co-operation in the field of accidental or deliberate marine pollution); the new regulations on Structural Funds, the revised Cohesion Fund and the pre-accession instrument (ISPA) include provisions to apply the principle to the

has occasionally considered its practical implications.[292] The principle has also been applied by the European Commission in relation to state aid.[293]

The polluter-pays principle, or variations thereof, as stated in the OECD and EC instruments, has also been referred to or adopted in other environmental treaties, including the 1985 ASEAN Convention,[294] the 1991 Alps Convention.[295] the 1992 UNECE Transboundary Waters Convention,[296] the 1992 OSPAR Convention,[297] the 1992 Baltic Sea Convention,[298] the 1994 Danube Convention,[299] the 1994 Energy Charter Treaty[300] and certain EC Directives.[301] The 1990 Oil Pollution Preparedness Convention and the 1992 Industrial Accidents Convention describe the polluter-pays principle as 'a general principle of international environmental law'.[302] The increased attention being paid to the polluter-pays principle results, in part, from the greater consideration being given to the relationship between environmental protection and economic development, as well as recent efforts to develop the use of economic instruments in environmental protection law and policy.[303] This is likely to lead to clarification and further definitions of the polluter-pays principle, particularly in relation to two issues.

operations of the funds (see Arts. 26 and 29(1)(c) of Council Regulation (EC) 1260/1999 laying down general provisions on the Structural Funds; Art. 7(1) of Council Regulation (EC) 1264/1999 amending Regulation (EC) 1164/94 establishing a Cohesion Fund; Art. 6(2)(c) of Council Regulation (EC) 1267/1999 establishing an Instrument for Structural Policies for Pre-Accession). See generally EC Commission, Application of the Polluter Pays Principle, 6 December 1999.

[292] See e.g. Case C-293/97, *R. v. Secretary of State for the Environment and Ministry of Agriculture, Fisheries and Food, ex parte H.A. Standley and Others and D.G.D. Metson and Others* [1999] ECR I-2603, paras. 51–2 (the polluter-pays principle reflects a principle of proportionality, and does not mean that farmers must take on burdens for the elimination of pollution to which they have not contributed).

[293] See European Commission, Community Guidelines on State Aid for Environmental Protection, 2001 OJ C37; chapter 20, p. 1029 below. For its application, see e.g. Commission Decision 1999/272, 1999 OJ L109 ('it is clearly not compatible with the "polluter pays" principle enshrined in Article 130r of the EC Treaty that a polluter should sell his contaminated land to one of his firms in order to avoid the clean-up costs, that the firm responsible for the contamination should file for bankruptcy and that the business activity should be carried on by the newly established firm').

[294] Art. 10(d).   [295] Art. 2(1) (the parties respect the polluter-pays principle).

[296] Art. 2(5)(b) (the parties shall be guided by the polluter-pays principle 'by virtue of which costs of pollution prevention, control and reduction measures shall be borne by the polluter').

[297] Art. 2(2)(b) (the parties 'shall apply . . . the polluter-pays principle').

[298] Art. 3(4) (the parties 'shall apply the polluter-pays principle'). See also 1993 Lugano Convention, Preamble; 1994 Agreement on the Protection of the River Meuse, Art. 3(2)(d), 34 ILM 851 (1995); 1996 Protocol to the 1972 London Convention, Art. 3(2).

[299] Art. 2(4).   [300] Art. 19(1).

[301] See e.g. Council Directive 1999/31/EC on the landfill of waste, Art. 10; chapter 13, p. 687 below.

[302] Preamble.   [303] Chapter 4, pp. 158–67 above.

The first concerns the extent of the pollution control costs which should be paid by the polluter. Although it seems clear that the principle includes costs of measures required by public authorities to prevent and control pollution, it is less clear whether the costs of decontamination, clean-up and reinstatement would be included. State practice does not support the view that all the costs of pollution should be borne by the polluter, particularly in inter-state relations.[304] The second issue concerns exceptions to the principle, particularly in relation to rules governing the granting of subsidies. In this regard, consideration should be given to the practice of the EC and account taken of the potential role of the WTO in determining the impact of the polluter-pays principle on its subsidies rules.[305]

Principle of common but differentiated responsibility

C. Kiss, 'La Notion de patrimoine commun de l'humanité', 175 RdC 99 (1982); B. Larschan and B. C. Brennan, 'Common Heritage of Mankind Principle in International Law', 21 *Columbia Journal of Transnational Law* 305 (1983); D. Magraw, 'Legal Treatment of Developing Countries: Differential Contextual and Absolute Norms', 1 *Colorado Journal of International Environmental Law and Policy* 69 (1990); D. Attard, *Proceedings of the Meeting of the Group of Legal Experts to Examine the Concept of the Common Concern of Mankind in Relation to Global Environmental Issues* (UNEP, 1991); F. Biermann, 'Common Concern of Humankind: The Emergence of a New Concept of International Environmental Law', 34 *Archiv der Volkerrechts* 426 (1996); D. French, 'Developing States and International Environmental Law: The Importance of Differentiated Responsibilities', 49 ICLQ 35 (2000).

The principle of common but differentiated responsibility has developed from the application of equity in general international law, and the recognition that the special needs of developing countries must be taken into account in the development, application and interpretation of rules of international environmental law. Principle 7 of the Rio Declaration states the principle thus:

> States shall co-operate in a spirit of global partnership to conserve, protect and restore the health and integrity of the Earth's ecosystem. In view of the different contributions to global environmental degradation, states have common but differentiated responsibilities. The developed countries

---

[304] See generally chapter 18, pp. 890–4 below; examples include the Chernobyl accident and the 1976 Rhine Chloride Convention, which allocates the costs of pollution abatement between the polluters (66 per cent) and the victim (34 per cent): see chapter 10, pp. 478–82 below.

[305] GATT Dispute Settlement Panel, *US – Chemicals Tax* case (1987), holding that GATT rules on tax adjustment allow contracting parties to apply the polluter-pays principle but do not require it: chapter 19, p. 953 below.

acknowledge the responsibility that they bear in the international pursuit of sustainable development in view of the pressures their societies place on the global environment and of the technologies and financial resources they command.

Similar language exists in the 1992 Climate Change Convention, which provides that the parties should act to protect the climate system 'on the basis of equity and in accordance with their common but differentiated responsibilities and respective capabilities'.[306]

The principle of common but differentiated responsibility includes two elements. The first concerns the common responsibility of states for the protection of the environment, or parts of it, at the national, regional and global levels. The second concerns the need to take account of differing circumstances, particularly in relation to each state's *contribution* to the creation of a particular environmental problem and its *ability* to prevent, reduce and control the threat. In practical terms, the application of the principle of common but differentiated responsibility has at least two consequences. First, it entitles, or may require, all concerned states to participate in international response measures aimed at addressing environmental problems. Secondly, it leads to environmental standards which impose differing obligations on states. Despite its recent emergence in the current formulation, the principle of common but differentiated responsibility finds its roots prior to UNCED and is supported by state practice at the regional and global levels.

Common responsibility

Common responsibility describes the shared obligations of two or more states towards the protection of a particular environmental resource, taking into account its relevant characteristics and nature, physical location, and historic usage associated with it. Natural resources can be the 'property' of a single state, or a 'shared natural resource', or subject to a common legal interest, or the property of no state. Common responsibility is likely to apply where the resource is not the property of, or under the exclusive jurisdiction of, a single state.

As early as 1949, tuna and other fish were 'of common concern' to the parties to the relevant treaties by reason of their continued exploitation by those parties.[307] Outer space and the moon, on the other hand, are the 'province of all mankind';[308] waterfowl are 'an international resource';[309] natural and cultural heritage is 'part of the world heritage of mankind as a whole';[310] the

---

[306] Art. 3(1).   [307] 1949 Inter-American Tropical Tuna Convention, Preamble.
[308] 1967 Outer Space Treaty, Art. 1.   [309] 1971 Wetlands Convention, Preamble.
[310] 1972 World Heritage Convention, Preamble.

conservation of wild animals is 'for the good of mankind';[311] the resources of the seabed, ocean floor and subsoil are 'the common heritage of mankind';[312] and plant genetic resources have been defined as 'a heritage of mankind'.[313] Recent state practice supports the emergence of the concept of 'common concern', as reflected in the 1992 Climate Change Convention, which acknowledges that 'change in the Earth's climate and its adverse effects are a common concern of humankind',[314] and the 1992 Biodiversity Convention, which affirms that 'biological diversity is a common concern of humankind'.[315]

While each of these formulations differs, and must be understood and applied in the context of the circumstances in which they were adopted, these attributions of 'commonality' do share common consequences. Although state practice is inconclusive as to the precise legal nature and consequence of each formulation, certain legal responsibilities are attributable to all states in respect of these environmental media and natural resources in accordance with the attribution by treaty (or custom) of a particular legal characteristic. The legal interest includes a legal responsibility to prevent damage to it. While the extent and legal nature of that responsibility will differ for each resource and instrument, the responsibility of each state to prevent harm to them, in particular by the adoption of national environmental standards and international environmental obligations, can also differ.

Differentiated responsibility

The differentiated responsibility of states for the protection of the environment is widely accepted in treaty and other practice of states. It translates into differentiated environmental standards set on the basis of a range of factors, including special needs and circumstances, future economic development of developing countries, and historic contributions to causing an environmental problem.

The 1972 Stockholm Declaration emphasised the need to consider 'the applicability of standards which are valid for the most advanced countries but which may be inappropriate and of unwarranted social cost for the developing countries'.[316] The 1974 Charter of Economic Rights and Duties of States makes the same point in more precise terms: 'The environmental policies of all states

---

[311] 1979 Bonn Convention, Preamble.
[312] UNGA Res. 2749 (XXV) of 17 December 1970; 1982 UNCLOS, Preamble (and now the 1994 Agreement Relating to the Implementation of Part XI of UNCLOS).
[313] 1983 FAO Plant Genetics Undertaking, Art. 1; see chapter 11, p. 552 below.
[314] Preamble. See also UNGA Res. 43/53 (1988), 44/207 (1989) and 45/212 (1990), acknowledging that climate change is a 'common concern of mankind' and rejecting the original proposal in the draft prepared by Malta which described the global climate as the 'common heritage of mankind'.
[315] Preamble.   [316] Principle 23.

should enhance and not adversely affect the present and future development potential of developing countries.'[317] In the Rio Declaration, the international community agreed that '[e]nvironmental standards. management objectives and priorities should reflect the environmental and developmental context to which they apply', and that 'the special situation of developing countries, particularly the least developed and those most environmentally vulnerable, shall be given special priority'.[318] The distinction is often made between the capacities of developing countries and their needs.

The differentiated approach is reflected in many treaties. Under the 1972 London Convention, the measures required are to be adopted by parties 'according to their scientific, technical and economic capabilities'.[319] Other treaties identify the need to take account of states' 'capabilities',[320] or their 'economic capacity' and the 'need for economic development';[321] or the 'means at their disposal and their capabilities'.[322] The principle of differentiated responsibility has also been applied to treaties and other legal instruments applying to developed countries. Examples include the 1988 EC Large Combustion Directive, which sets different levels of emission reductions for each member state;[323] the 1991 VOC Protocol, which allows parties to specify one of three different ways to achieve reduction;[324] and the EC Treaty (as amended by the Maastricht Treaty), which provides that:

> Without prejudice to the principle that the polluter should pay, if a measure . . . involves costs deemed disproportionate for the public authorities of a member state, the Council shall, in the act adopting that measure, lay down appropriate provisions in the form of
>
> – temporary derogations; and/or
> – financial support from the Cohesion Fund . . .[325]

The special *needs* of developing countries are expressly recognised in other instruments.[326] Account is to be taken of their 'circumstances and particular requirements',[327] or of their 'specific needs and special circumstances',[328] or of their 'special conditions' and 'the fact that economic and social

---

[317] Art. 30; UNGA Res. 3201 (1974).
[318] Principles 11 and 6; see also the 1992 Climate Change Convention, Preamble.
[319] Art. 11.
[320] 1981 Abidjan Convention, Art. 4(1).   [321] 1982 UNCLOS, Art. 207.
[322] 1985 Vienna Convention, Art. 2(2).   [323] Chapter 8, pp. 336–9 below.
[324] Chapter 8, pp. 329–32 below.   [325] Article 175(5), and former Article130s(5).
[326] 1976 Barcelona Convention, Art. 11(3); 1982 UNCLOS, Preamble.
[327] 1985 Vienna Convention, Preamble.
[328] 1992 Climate Change Convention, Art. 3(2) (policies and measures 'should be appropriate for the specific conditions of each Party and should be integrated with national development programmes': Art. 3(4)). See now the 1997 Kyoto Protocol, chapter 8, pp. 368–81 below.

development and eradication of poverty are the first and overriding priorities of the developing country parties'.[329]

In practical terms, differentiated responsibility results in different legal obligations. The different techniques available to apply it include 'grace' periods delaying implementation, and less stringent commitments. Under the 1987 Montreal Protocol, the special situation of developing countries entitles them, provided that they meet certain conditions, to delay their compliance with control measures.[330] Under the 1992 Climate Change Convention, the principle of 'common but differentiated responsibilities' requires specific commitments only for developed country parties and other developed parties, and allows differentials in reporting requirements.[331] The 1997 Kyoto Protocol applies the principle of 'differentiated responsibility' to OECD countries, setting a range of different targets depending upon states' historic contribution and capabilities.[332] The special needs of developing countries, the capacities of all countries, and the principle of 'common but differentiated' responsibilities has also resulted in the establishment of special institutional mechanisms to provide financial, technological and other technical assistance to developing countries to help them implement the obligations of particular treaties.[333]

Conclusions

This chapter illustrates the extent to which the practice of states, international organisations and other members of the international community has given rise to a body of discrete principles and rules which may be of general application. Their legal status, their meaning and the consequences of their application to the facts of a particular case or activity remain open. There are several reasons for this. First, they have emerged over a relatively short period of time, some only within the past fifteen years. Secondly, each has emerged in the context of sharp differences of view as to what they mean in practice, and what they should mean. And, thirdly, the extent to which state practice interprets and applies these principles and rules is still evolving, and requires further consideration by reference to what states do both at the national level and in their international affairs. Nevertheless, rational arguments can be made in favour of each having significant legal consequences, and, as has been seen in the chapter, states and international courts and tribunals have increasingly been prepared to rely upon some of these principles and rules to justify their actions and to enable them to reach conclusions in their application of substantive legal obligations to

---

[329] 1992 Biodiversity Convention, Preamble and Art. 20(4); see also 1992 Climate Change Convention, Art. 4(7).

[330] Art. 5(1); see also e.g. 1990 Amendments, Art. 1P.

[331] Arts. 4 and 12; see further the 1997 Kyoto Protocol, chapter 8, pp. 368–81 below.

[332] Chapter 8, pp. 368–81 below.   [333] Chapter 20, pp. 1021–37 below.

particular sets of facts. In some cases, such application has had far-reaching consequences, for example in the *Southern Bluefin Tuna* cases at the provisional measures phase.

The principles and rules of general application which have been described in this chapter provide a framework to shape the future development of international environmental law. Each is important and has its own particular role. Two principles currently seem particularly relevant, and are likely to play a critical role in determining whether international environmental obligations play a marginal or a central role in international affairs. The first is that element of the principle of sustainable development which requires environmental protection to be treated as 'an integral part of the development process and cannot be considered in isolation from it'. If any single provision of the Rio Declaration can contribute to the normative development of international environmental law, this is likely to be it. On the one hand, it can be considered to require all development decisions throughout the range of human economic activity to be subjected to critical environmental scrutiny. If applied in this way, the principle of sustainable development could extend the use of the substantive international environmental norms which have been established over the past three decades to inform decision-making by all states and international organisations, and result in a further reappraisal of the activities of organisations such as the WTO which increasingly, in the interpretation and application of their rules, have regard to legal developments beyond their own legal systems. The *Shrimp/Turtle* case indicates the potential for this approach. On the other hand, this aspect of the principle of sustainable development also requires economic and other development considerations to be taken into account in developing and applying those international environmental norms, providing the underlying basis for the emergence of the principle of differentiated responsibility.

The second critical principle is the precautionary principle, and its impact over time should not be understated. It has already been relied upon, as has been seen in this chapter, to require a shift in the burden of proof in cases concerning the conduct of certain especially hazardous activities. The extent to which it is applied at the international level will serve as a barometer to measure future developments in international environmental law. Some international courts have now been willing to apply the precautionary principle, and others have been willing to do so with stealth. It is surely only a matter of time before other courts follow suit.

7

Human rights and armed conflict

International human rights

C. Stone, *Should Trees Have Standing? Towards Legal Rights for Natural Objects* (1974); M. Uibopuu, 'The Internationally Guaranteed Right of an Individual to a Clean Environment', 1 *Comparative Law Yearbook* 101 (1977); W. Gormley, *Human Rights and the Environment: The Need for International Co-operation* (1976); J. Bryden, 'Environmental Rights in Theory and Practice', 62 *Minnesota Law Review* 163 (1978); P. Kromarek (ed.), *Environnement et droits de l'homme* (1987); W. Gormley, 'The Legal Obligation of the International Community to Guarantee a Pure and Decent Environment: The Expansion of Human Rights Norms', 3 *Georgetown International Environmental Law Review* 85 (1991); G. Alfredsson and A. Ovsiouk, 'Human Rights and the Environment', 60 *Nordic Journal of International Law* 19 (1991); I. Hodkova, 'Is There a Right to a Healthy Environment in the International Legal Order?', 7 *Connecticut Journal of International Law* 65 (1991); D. Shelton, 'Human Rights, Environmental Rights, and the Right to the Environment', 28 *Stanford Journal of International Law* 103 (1991); D. Shelton, 'What Happened in Rio to Human Rights?', 3 *Yearbook of International Environmental Law* 75 (1992); Human Rights Watch and National Resources Defense Council, *Defending the Earth: Abuses of Human Rights and the Environment* (1992); Sierra Club Legal Defense Fund, *Human Rights and the Environment: The Legal Basis for a Human Right to the Environment* (1992); A. Trindade (ed.), *Human Rights, Sustainable Development and the Environment* (1992); R. Desgagne, 'Integrating Environmental Values into the European Convention on Human Rights', 89 AJIL 263 (1995); A. Boyle and M. Anderson (eds.), *Human Rights Approaches to Environmental Protection* (1996); Earthjustice Legal Defense Fund, *Human Rights and the Environment* (2001).

Introduction

As it develops, international environmental law raises many issues already familiar to international human rights lawyers. In the environmental context, questions related to the existence and application of minimum international standards and the proper role of individuals and other non-governmental organisations in the international legal process have raised analogous issues to those arising in international human rights law. The international legal issues are closely related, as is now reflected in the developing activities of human rights bodies.[1] Allegations of civil rights breaches continue to abound in the environmental field, and have focused on: the suppression of environmental discussion and debate and of environmental campaigners; restrictions on the right of association and assembly; the mistreatment of 'whistleblowers'; press censorship; and restrictions on rights of access to environmental information. Human rights issues are equally being raised in relation to 'environmental' refugees forced to flee areas because of drought or desertification, and humanitarian issues involving the use of force and the environmental impacts of war, which are considered in the second part of this chapter. Human rights issues related to environmental protection became the subject of increasing attention following a number of well-known cases, including the 1988 murder of the Brazilian union organiser Chico Mendes, restrictions on the provision of information to citizens of the USSR following the accident at the Chernobyl nuclear power plant, and the limited availability of remedies for breaches of environmental standards and obligations under national legal systems. Against this background, there have been important developments in the past decade, including in particular a growing body of jurisprudence and commentary recognising the existence (and importance) of the linkages between human rights and environmental matters. Of particular note is the 1998 Aarhus Convention, which establishes formal participation and informational rights and affirms, in its Preamble, that 'every person has the right to live in an environment adequate to his or her health or well-being'.[2]

The development of international human rights law pre-dates international environmental law and provides a rich source of experience. Since the 1960s, the two subjects have developed in parallel, intersecting with increasing

---

[1] See most recently the Conclusions of Experts (2002) following the joint Seminar of the Office of the High Commissioner for Human Rights (OHCHR) and UNEP, pursuant to Decision 2001/111 of the UN Commission on Human Rights, on promoting and protecting human rights in relation to environmental questions. The Conclusions (together with six background papers) are available at www.unhchr.ch/environment/; see in particular D. Shelton, *Human Rights and Environment Issues in Multilateral Treaties Adopted Between 1991 and 2001* (2002); D. Shelton, *Human Rights and the Environment: Jurisprudence of Human Rights Bodies* (2002); A. Fabra, *The Intersection of Human Rights and Environmental Issues: A Review of Institutional Developments at the International Level* (2002). The OHCHR/UNEP seminar was, apparently, the first formal effort by UN bodies in the human rights and environment fields to jointly address the connections.

[2] See also Art. 1, chapter 17, p. 858 below; and J. Ebbeson, 'The Notion of Public Participation in International Environmental Law', 8 *Yearbook of International Environmental Law* 51 (1997). Upon signature, the United Kingdom declared that this right was merely 'aspirational' in character.

frequency. The extent to which international environmental law should adopt an anthropocentric approach, based on the view that environmental protection is primarily justified as a means of protecting humans rather than as an end in itself, was an important issue at UNCED. The Rio Declaration supports an anthropocentric approach: Principle 1 states that: 'Human beings are at the centre of concerns for sustainable development. They are entitled to a healthy and productive life in harmony with nature.'[3] Legal developments in other fora and contexts, however, reflect a greater environmental consciousness and suggest that the protection of the environment is increasingly an objective justified in its own terms, and not simply a means of protecting humans.[4]

Development of international human rights law

The UN Charter marked the beginnings of modern international human rights law; in the same way, it established the international framework within which the international community would, some twenty-five years later, address many international environmental issues. The Charter reaffirmed the faith of the 'Peoples of the United Nations' in fundamental human rights and provided that one of the UN's purposes was to promote and encourage 'respect for human rights and for fundamental freedoms for all without distinction as to race, sex, language or religion'.[5] The UN Charter does not identify the human rights and fundamental freedoms which would contribute to the economic and social advancement of all peoples; nor does it provide any support for the idea that a clean or healthy environment should or did form a part of those rights and freedoms.

The first international instrument to elaborate detailed human rights standards applicable globally was the Universal Declaration of Human Rights (UDHR), adopted by the UN General Assembly in 1948.[6] The Declaration was subsequently supplemented in 1966 by two treaties open to all states: the International Covenant on Economic, Social and Cultural Rights (ICESCR)[7] and the International Covenant on Civil and Political Rights (ICCPR).[8] These instruments have since been supplemented by four regional human rights treaties:[9]

---

[3] Principle 1. Cf. Principle 1 of the 1972 Stockholm Declaration; see p. 306 below.

[4] See in particular recent developments concerning the protection of biodiversity (chapter 11, pp. 517–19 below); the inclusion of a new heading of environmental damage in recent civil liability conventions (chapter 18, pp. 896–901 below); and the proposal that environmental degradation should be considered a crime against the peace and security of mankind (chapter 18, pp. 894–6 below).

[5] Preamble and Arts. 1(3) and 55.   [6] UNGA Res. 217 (III) (1948).

[7] Annex to UNGA Res. 2200 (XXI) (1966); 993 UNTS 3, in force 3 January 1976.

[8] Annex to UNGA Res. 2200 (XXI) (1966), 999 UNTS 717, in force 23 March 1976.

[9] See also the Draft Charter on Human and Peoples' Rights in the Arab World, 1987.

the 1950 European Convention for the Protection of Human Rights and Fundamental Freedoms (ECHR);[10] the 1961 European Social Charter (ESC);[11] the 1969 American Convention on Human Rights (ACHR);[12] and the 1981 African Charter of Human and Peoples' Rights (1981 African Charter).[13] Three of these instruments (the ICESCR, the African Charter and the ACHR) recognise a link between the environment and human rights. None of the three identifies environmental rights as being subject to specific rules of protection, although they do allow a conceptual framework and approach for introducing environmental concerns and for the subsequent introduction of express environmental language.

Environmental protection and human rights

In 1968, the UN General Assembly first recognised the relationship between the quality of the human environment and the enjoyment of basic rights.[14] The 1972 Stockholm Declaration proclaimed that man's natural and man-made environment 'are essential to his well-being and to the enjoyment of basic human rights – even the right to life itself'[15] and declared in Principle 1 that:

> Man has the fundamental right to freedom, equality and adequate conditions of life, in an environment of a quality that permits a life of dignity and well-being, and he bears a solemn responsibility to protect and improve the environment for present and future generations.

The international community has not, however, defined in practical terms the threshold below which the level of environmental quality must fall before a breach of a person's human rights will have occurred. Nevertheless, some non-binding and widely accepted declarations supporting the individual's right to a clean environment have been adopted. Although the 1982 World Charter for Nature does not expressly provide for the individual's right to a clean

---

[10] Rome, 4 November 1950, in force 3 September 1953, 213 UNTS 222. The ECHR has been supplemented by twelve Protocols. Protocol 11, which entered into force in November 1998, replaced the European Commission and Court with a single Court: see chapter 5, pp. 193–5 above.

[11] Turin, 18 October 1961, in force 26 February 1965, ETS No. 35.

[12] San José, 22 November 1969, in force 18 July 1978, 9 ILM 673 (1970). The ACHR has been supplemented by the San Salvador Additional Protocol on Economic, Social and Cultural Rights, 14 November 1988, in force 16 November 1999, 28 ILM 161 (1989).

[13] Banjul, 27 June 1981, in force 21 October 1986, 21 ILM 59 (1982).

[14] UNGA Res. 2398 (XXII) (1968). See also the Proclamation of Tehran, UN Doc. A/CONF.32/41, para. 18, recognising the dangers posed by scientific discoveries and technological advances for the rights and freedoms of individuals.

[15] Preambular para. 1.

environment, it was one of the first instruments to recognise the right of individuals to participate in decision-making and have access to means of redress when their environment has suffered damage or degradation. The 1989 Declaration of the Hague on the Environment recognised 'the fundamental duty to preserve the ecosystem' and 'the right to live in dignity in a viable global environment, and the consequent duty of the community of nations vis-à-vis present and future generations to do all that can be done to preserve the quality of the environment'.[16] The UN General Assembly has declared that 'all individuals are entitled to live in an environment adequate for their health and well-being';[17] and the UN Commission on Human Rights has affirmed the relationship between the preservation of the environment and the promotion of human rights.[18] More specifically, the Sub-Commission on Prevention of Discrimination and Protection of Minorities has considered the relationship between human rights and the movement and dumping of toxic and dangerous products and wastes,[19] supported further study,[20] and considered the relationship between the environment and human rights in the context of chemical weapons.[21] The Sub-Commission has also received reports on 'Human Rights and the Environment' which analyse many of the key concepts and provide information on decisions of international bodies.[22] More specifically, the UN Commission on Human Rights has declared that the movement and dumping of toxic and dangerous products endanger basic human rights such as 'the right to the highest standard of health, including its environmental aspects'.[23] Efforts to further develop language on environmental rights continues under the auspices of several international institutions including the Council of Europe and

---

[16] Declaration of the Hague on the Environment, 11 March 1989, 28 ILM 1308 (1989).

[17] UNGA Res. 45/94 (1990).   [18] See e.g. Res. 1990/41 (1990).

[19] Res. 1988/26 (1988); see also Res. 1989/12 (1989) on the movement and dumping of toxic and dangerous products and waste, declaring in draft terms that 'the movement and dumping of toxic and dangerous products endanger basic human rights such as the right to life, the right to live in a sound and healthy environment and consequently the right to health'.

[20] Decision 1989/108 (1989). A note was subsequently prepared on 'Human Rights and Scientific and Technological Developments: Proposals for a Study of the Problem of the Environment and Its Relation to Human Rights', UN Doc. E/CN.4/Sub.2/1990/12, 3 August 1990.

[21] Sub-Commission on Prevention of Discrimination and Protection of Minorities, Res. 1989/39, UN Doc. E/CN.4/1990/2, 1 September 1989.

[22] See Final Report by Special Rapporteur, Ms Fatma Zohra Ksentini, UN Doc. E/CN.4/Sub.2/1994/9 (including a Draft Declaration on Principles of Human Rights and the Environment). See also 'Human Rights and the Environment: Preliminary Report', UN Doc. E/CN.4/Sub.2/1991/8, 2 August 1991; 'Human Rights and the Environment', UN Doc. E/CN.4/Sub.2/1992/7, 2 July 1992; 'Human Rights and the Environment', UN Doc.E/CN.4/Sub.2/1993/7.

[23] Res. 1990/43, UN Doc. E/CN.4/1990/94, 104 (1990); see also the reports by the Special Rapporteur, UN Doc. E/CN.4/2001/55 (19 January 2001).

the UN Economic Commission for Europe.[24] Other efforts include the IUCN's draft International Covenant on Environment and Development prepared by the IUCN's Commission on Environmental Law.[25]

Many states have adopted national measures linking the environment and individual rights.[26] The constitutions of about 100 states now expressly recognise the right to a clean environment.[27] These constitutional provisions vary in their approach: they provide for a state duty to protect and preserve the environment;[28] or declare the duty to be the responsibility of the state and citizens;[29] or declare that the duty is imposed only upon citizens;[30] or declare that the individual has a substantive right in relation to the environment;[31] or provide for an individual right together with the individual or collective duty of citizens to safeguard the environment;[32] or provide for a combination of various state and citizen duties together with an individual right.[33]

What are the practical consequences of recognising the link between international human rights law and the protection of the environment? The question may be addressed in the context of the distinction which has been drawn in international human rights law between economic and social rights, and civil and political rights. The nature and extent of economic and social rights

[24] Recommendation of the Parliamentary Assembly of the Council of Europe on the Formulation of a European Charter and a European Convention on Environmental Protection, Eur. Parl. Ass., 42nd Sess. Recommendation 1130 (1990); and the Draft UNECE Charter on Environmental Rights and Obligations, UN Doc. ENWA/R.38, December 1990.

[25] Second edition, 2000; the preamble recognises that 'respect for human rights and fundamental freedoms contributes to sustainable development'; see also Art. 4. The draft provided that 'all persons have the fundamental right to an environment adequate for the dignity, health and well-being' (Art. 2(1)), and that 'states have the obligation to protect the environment' (Art. 3(1)).

[26] Note in this regard that the Charter of Fundamental Rights of the European Union, OJ C364 (18 December 2000), 1, does not frame environmental concerns in terms of rights ('A high level of environmental protection and the improvement of the quality of the environment must be integrated into the policies of the Union and ensured in accordance with the principle of sustainable development': Art. 37). See also Art. 111 of the Treaty establishing the East African Community ('a clean and healthy environment is a prerequisite for sustainable development').

[27] See 'Human Rights and the Environment: The Legal Basis for a Human Right to the Environment', Report to the UN Sub-Commission on the Prevention of Discrimination and the Protection of Minorities, Sierra Club Legal Defense Fund, April 1992; and Earthjustice Legal Defense Fund, 'Human Rights and the Environment' (Issue Paper) (December 2001).

[28] *Ibid.*, 21, including China, Equatorial Guinea, Germany, Greece, Honduras, Mexico, Mozambique, Namibia, the Netherlands, Nigeria, Panama, Paraguay, the Philippines, Romania, Taiwan, Thailand and the United Arab Emirates.

[29] *Ibid.*, including Albania, Bahrain, Bulgaria, Ethiopia, Guatemala, Guyana, India, Iran, Papua New Guinea, Sri Lanka, Sweden and Tanzania.

[30] *Ibid.*, including Algeria, Bolivia, Haiti, the Russian Federation and Vanuatu.

[31] *Ibid.*, including Burkina Faso and Hungary.

[32] *Ibid.*, including South Korea, Poland, Portugal, Spain and the former Yugoslavia.

[33] *Ibid.*, including Brazil, Chile, Colombia, Ecuador, Nicaragua, Peru, Turkey and Vietnam.

determines the substantive rights to which individuals are entitled, including in particular the level below which environmental standards (for example, in relation to pollution) must not fall if they are to be lawful. Civil and political rights, which are also substantive in nature and sometimes referred to as 'due process' rights, determine procedural and institutional rights (such as the right to information or access to judicial or administrative remedies). International environmental law has progressed considerably in building upon existing civil and political rights and developing important new obligations, most notably in the 1998 Aarhus Convention which provides for rights of access to infor-mation, to participation in decision-making, and to access to justice.[34] While economic and social rights have traditionally been less well developed in prac-tice, recent judicial decisions indicate that international courts and tribunals are increasingly willing to find violations of substantive environmental rights.

Economic and social rights

Although the existence of economic and social rights under international law has been less widely accepted by elements of the international community, it is these rights which promise to allow human rights bodies to consider whether substantive environmental standards and conditions are being maintained at satisfactory levels. Translating general economic and social rights into specific environmental standards will never be an easy task, although it is one which some international bodies are willing to take on. Each of the major human rights instruments identified above recognises the existence of at least some such rights. In the context of environmental issues, those which appear to be most relevant include: the entitlement to the realisation of economic, social and cultural rights indispensable for dignity;[35] the right to a standard of living adequate for health and well-being;[36] the right to the highest attainable standard of health (including improvement of all aspects of environmental and industrial hygiene);[37] the right of all peoples to freely dispose of their natural wealth and resources;[38] safe and healthy working conditions;[39] the protection of children against social exploitation;[40] the right to enjoy the benefits of scientific progress and its applications;[41] and the right of peoples to self-determination and the pursuit of economic and social development.[42]

Environmental degradation could be linked to the violation of each of these rights. Lack of access to drinking water which is free from toxic or other

[34] See Chapter 17, p. 858, and chapter 5, pp. 209–10 above.
[35] 1948 UDHR, Art. 22; 1969 ACHR, Art. 26; 1981 African Charter, Art. 22.
[36] 1948 UDHR, Art. 25; 1966 ICESCR, Art. 11(1).
[37] 1966 ICESCR, Art. 12(1) and (2)(b); 1961 ESC, Art. 11; 1981 African Charter, Art. 16(1); on the activities of the ESC Committee of Independent Experts, see p. 304 below.
[38] 1966 ICESCR, Art. 1(2); 1966 ICCPR, Art. 1(2); 1981 African Charter, Art. 21.
[39] 1966 ICESCR, Art. 7(b); 1961 ESC, Art. 3.
[40] 1966 ICESCR, Art. 10(3); 1961 ESC, Art. 17.
[41] 1966 ICESCR, Art. 15(1)(b).   [42] 1981 African Charter, Art. 20(1).

contaminants, pollution of the atmosphere by heavy metals and radioactive materials, the dumping of hazardous and toxic wastes in the vicinity of people's homes can all be viewed and treated as violations of fundamental economic and social rights. This is now reflected in General Comment No. 15 (Right to Water) of the UN Committee on Economic, Social and Cultural Rights, affirming that everyone is entitled to safe and acceptable water for personal and domestic use.[43] In the United States, the environmental degradation in areas predominantly populated by poor communities and ethnic minorities has come to be known as 'environmental discrimination' or 'environmental racism', terms emphasising the linkage between environmental rights and human rights.

However, only two regional human rights treaties expressly recognise environmental rights. Under the 1981 African Charter, 'all peoples shall have the right to a general satisfactory environment favourable to their development'.[44] The 1988 San Salvador Protocol to the 1969 ACHR provides in its Article 11 that:

> 1. Everyone shall have the right to live in a healthy environment and to have access to basic public services.
> 2. The state parties shall promote the protection, preservation and improvement of the environment.

The San Salvador Protocol distinguishes between the *right* of individuals to 'live in a healthy environment' and the *positive obligation* of states to protect, preserve and improve the environment. The failure of a state to carry out that obligation can therefore give rise to an enforceable right of action. The efforts by the Council of Europe in the 1970s to draft a protocol on environmental rights failed due to a lack of political support by states,[45] and Article 37 of the

---

[43] E/C.12/2002/11, 26 November 2002.   [44] 1981 African Charter, Art. 24.
[45] The draft Protocol stated:

Article 1
   1. No one should be exposed to intolerable damage or threats to his health or to intolerable impairment of his well-being as a result of adverse changes in the natural conditions of life.
   2. An impairment of well-being may, however, be deemed to be tolerable if it is necessary for the maintenance and development of the economic conditions of the community and if there is no alternative way of making it possible to avoid this impairment.
Article 2
   1. If adverse changes in the natural conditions are likely to occur in his vital sphere as a result of the actions of other parties, any individual is entitled to demand that the competent agencies examine the situation in all cases where Article 1 applies.
   2. Any individual acting under paragraph 1 shall, within a reasonable time, receive detailed information stating what measures – if any – have been taken to prevent those adverse changes.

Reprinted in A. Rosas *et al.* (eds.), *Human Rights in a Changing East–West Perspective* (1990).

EU Charter of Fundamental Rights falls well short of declaring the existence of a substantive right.[46]

The relationship between environmental protection and economic and social rights is recognised in other treaties. The 1989 Convention on the Rights of the Child, for example, requires education for '[t]he development of respect for the natural environment'.[47] The 1989 Convention Concerning Indigenous and Tribal Peoples in Independent Countries requires governments to protect the human rights and fundamental freedoms of indigenous and tribal peoples and to guarantee respect for their integrity,[48] including special measures to be adopted to protect and preserve the environment of indigenous and tribal peoples.[49] It also states that the rights of these peoples to the natural resources of their lands must be specially safeguarded.[50]

The practical application of economic and social rights requires international and national courts and tribunals to determine the circumstances in which environmental standards have fallen below acceptable international levels. These standards are being developed, particularly at the regional level. They establish minimum standards of water and air quality which might provide a basis for arguing that standards have fallen below minimum acceptable levels and that an individual right of action to enforce these minimum standards might arise. However, in the absence of specific, binding international standards, it may be more difficult for such claims to succeed, unless the environmental conditions are so poor that blatant abuses will be considered to have occurred. An emerging practice on appropriate standards is reflected in recent international decisions, indicating a growing willingness to identify violations of 'environmental' rights.

The change which is occurring is particularly apparent in respect of the 1950 ECHR, which does not include express provisions on the environment. A 1976 decision of the European Commission on Human Rights illustrated the difficulty in making environmental claims. In *X. and Y.* v. *Federal Republic of Germany* the applicants were members of an environmental organisation which owned 2.5 acres of land for nature observation. They complained on environmental grounds about the use of adjacent marshlands for military purposes. The Commission rejected the application as incompatible *rationae materiae* with the ECHR on the ground that 'no right to nature preservation is as such included among the rights and freedoms guaranteed by the Convention and in particular by Articles 2, 3 or 5 as invoked by the applicant'.[51]

---

[46] See n. 26 above.

[47] 28 November 1989, in force 2 September 1990, 29 ILM 1340 (1990), Art. 29(e); see M. Fitzmaurice and A. Fijalkowski (eds.), *Right of the Child to Clean Environment* (2000).

[48] Geneva, 27 June 1989, in force 5 September 1991, 28 ILM 1382 (1989), Arts. 2 and 3; see also the Draft Universal Declaration on the Rights of Indigenous Peoples, UN Doc. E/CN.4/Sub.2/1991/40/Rev.1.

[49] Arts. 4(1) and 7(4).   [50] Arts. 4(1) and 7(4).

[51] Application No. 7407/76, Decision of 13 May 1976 on the admissibility of the application, 15 DR 161.

An alternative approach has emerged, in the absence of rights being granted in relation to the environment, whereby victims bring claims on the basis that personal or property rights have been violated. A series of judgments by the European Court of Human Rights illustrates how such a claim might now be made, although it is apparent that each case must be taken on its own merits. In *Arrondelle* v. *United Kingdom*, Article 8 of the 1950 ECHR and Article 1 of the First Protocol to the ECHR provided the basis for a 'friendly settlement' between the parties in a complaint alleging nuisance due to the development of an airport and construction of a motorway adjacent to the applicant's home.[52]

In *Powell and Rayner* v. *United Kingdom*, the applicants alleged that the United Kingdom had violated the 1950 ECHR by allowing the operation of Heathrow Airport, under whose flight path they lived, to generate excessive levels of aircraft noise. The relevant parts of the case were based on Article 8 of the ECHR, which provides that, *inter alia*, 'everyone has the right to respect for his private . . . life [and] his home . . . and there shall be no interference by a public authority with the exercise of this right except such as is in accordance with the law and is necessary in a democratic society in the interests of the economic well-being of the country . . .'.[53] The applicants maintained that excessive noise forced them to endure, without legal redress, unreasonable disturbance caused by aircraft flying in accordance with governmental regulations, in breach of Article 8 and the Article 13 right to an effective remedy under domestic law for alleged breaches of the Convention. The Court rejected their argument, noting that its task was to strike 'a fair balance . . . between the competing interests of the individual and the community as a whole'. In this case, that balance had not been upset. While the quality of life of the applicants had been adversely affected, the Court recognised that large international airports, even in densely populated areas, and the increased use of jets, were necessary in the interests of a country's economic well-being. Heathrow was a major artery for international trade and communication which employed several thousand people and generated substantial revenues. The United Kingdom government had taken significant measures to abate noise pollution, taking account of international standards, and had compensated nearby residents for disturbances resulting from aircraft noise. Moreover, the government had, since 1949, proceeded on the basis that aircraft noise was better addressed by taking and enforcing specific regulatory measures than by applying the common law of nuisance. In the context of these considerations, the Court concluded that it could not 'substitute for the assessment of the national authorities any other assessment of what might be the best policy in this difficult social and technical sphere. This is an area where the contracting states are to be recognised as enjoying a wide margin of appreciation.'[54] The judgment reflects a reluctance to allow

[52] Application No. 7889/77, Report of 13 May 1983, 26 DR 5.

[53] *Powell and Rayner* v. *United Kingdom*, Judgment of 21 February 1990, ECHR Ser. A, No. 172, 17, para. 37.

[54] *Ibid.*, para. 44.

environmental concerns of a private person to take precedence over the broader economic concerns of the wider community, particularly where, as in this case, the government was able to point to its compliance with international standards concerning noise from aircraft.

Since *Powell and Rayner*, however, the European Court has shown itself to be more open to environmental claims, particularly in cases involving Article 8 claims to the effect that a correct balance has not been struck between individual and community interests. The leading decision is *Lopez-Ostra* v. *Spain*.[55] Mrs Lopez-Ostra lived twelve metres from a plant treating liquid and solid wastes, which had been built on municipal land with the support of a state subsidy and had operated without a relevant licence. The plant gave off fumes which caused a nuisance to Mrs Lopez-Ostra and her daughter and caused them to temporarily leave their home. Having failed in proceedings in Spain, she brought ECHR proceedings on the grounds that she was the victim of a violation of the right to respect for her home that made her private and family life impossible (Article 8), and the victim also of degrading treatment. The European Court found that the situation which resulted was the result of the inaction of the state, having been prolonged by the municipality's and the relevant authorities' failure to act (para. 40). The Court said:

> Naturally, severe environmental pollution may affect individuals' well-being and prevent them from enjoying their homes in such a way as to affect their private and family life adversely, without, however, seriously endangering their health. Whether the question is analysed in terms of a positive duty on the State – to take reasonable and appropriate measures to secure the applicant's rights . . . – . . . or in terms of an 'interference by a public authority' to be justified . . . the applicable principles are broadly similar. In both contexts regard must be had to the fair balance that has to be struck between the competing interests of the individual and of the community as a whole, and in any case the State enjoys a certain margin of appreciation. (para. 51)

The Court found that the plant caused nuisance and serious health problems to numerous local people, and that, even if the local municipality had fulfilled its functions under Spanish law, it had not taken the measures necessary for protecting the applicant's right to respect for her home and for her private and family life under Article 8 and had not offered redress for the nuisance suffered. In the circumstances, Spain had not succeeded in striking a fair balance between the interest of the town's economic well-being – that of having a waste-treatment plant – and the applicant's effective enjoyment of her right to respect for her home and her private and family life.[56]

The judgment has opened the door to further cases. In *Guerra and others* v. *Italy*, the applicants were citizens living near to a factory which produced

---

[55] Judgment of 9 December 1994.
[56] *Ibid.*, paras. 51–8. The Court awarded damages of 4 million pesetas plus costs.

fertilisers, released large quantities of inflammable gas and other toxic substances into the atmosphere, and (in 1976) had been the source of an explosion
releasing arsenic trioxide and causing 150 people to be hospitalised with acute
arsenic poisoning. The applicants wanted information on the activities of the
plant, and this was not made available to them until after production of fertilisers had ceased. The Court ruled that the 'direct effect of the toxic emissions on
the applicants' right to respect for their private and family life made Article 8
applicable' (para. 57), that Article 8 imposed 'positive obligations' on the state
to ensure 'effective respect for private or family life' (para. 58), and that by allowing the applicants to wait for essential information that would have enabled
them to assess the risks they and their families might run if they continued
to live near the factory, Italy had not fulfilled its obligations under Article 8
(para. 60).[57]

In *Hatton and others* v. *United Kingdom*, the European Court revisited the
issues raised in *Powell and Rayner*, although this time in the context of noise
levels at Heathrow Airport arising from night flights between 4 am and 7 am.
The Court found that the earlier decisions were not on point because the present
case related to an increase in night noise.[58] Invoking the 'positive obligations'
of the United Kingdom, the Court recognised the existence of a 'certain margin
of appreciation' (as opposed to the 'wide margin' it had previously applied)
(para. 96) and signalled a new approach taking into account the particular
needs of environmental protection:

> [I]n striking the required balance, States must have regard to the whole
> range of material considerations. Further, in the particularly sensitive field
> of environmental protection, mere reference to the economic well-being of
> the country is not sufficient to outweigh the rights of others . . . It considers
> that States are required to minimise, as far as possible, the interference with
> these rights, by trying to find alternative solutions and by generally seeking
> to achieve their aims in the least onerous way as regards human rights. In
> order to do that, a proper and complete investigation and study with the
> aim of finding the best possible solution which will, in reality, strike the
> right balance should precede the relevant project.[59]

The Court noted that levels of noise during the relevant period had increased
with the new scheme established in 1993, but that the government did not
appear to have carried out any research of its own as to the reality or extent
of the economic interest in increasing night flights and there had been no
attempt to quantify the aviation and economic benefits in monetary terms.[60]

---

[57] Judgment of 19 February 1998, at paras. 57–8 and 60. The Court awarded 10 million lire
to each applicant in damages. The Court found, however, that there was no violation of
Article 10: see chapter 17, pp. 852–3 below.
[58] Judgment of 2 October 2001, para. 94.
[59] *Ibid.*, para. 97.   [60] *Ibid.*, paras. 98 and 100–1.

It also noted that, while it was likely that night flights contribute to a certain extent to the national economy, their importance had never been assessed critically and only limited research had been carried out into the nature of sleep disturbance and prevention when the 1993 scheme was put in place.[61] The Court concluded that there had been a violation of Article 8 because, in the absence of any serious attempt to evaluate the extent or impact of the interferences with the applicants' sleep patterns, and generally in the absence of a prior specific and complete study with the aim of finding the least onerous solution as regards human rights, the government had not struck the right balance in weighing the interferences of the rights of the individuals against the unquantified economic interest of the country.[62] The judgment, which has been appealed to the Grand Chamber of the European Court, suggests the need to carry out a prior assessment of the human rights impact of economically beneficial measures, where environmental interests are concerned.

The Court has also been willing to recognise the need for environmental protection measures even where they might limit the enjoyment of private property rights.[63] In *Fredin* v. *Sweden*, the Court recognised 'that in today's society the protection of the environment is an increasingly important consideration', and held that on the facts the interference with a private property right to achieve environmental objectives was not inappropriate or disproportionate in the context of Article 1 of the First Protocol to the ECHR.[64] In *Pine Valley Development Ltd and Others* v. *Ireland*, the Court recognised that an interference with the right to peaceful enjoyment of property which was in conformity with planning legislation and was 'designed to protect the environment' was clearly a legitimate aim 'in accordance with the general interest' for the purposes of the second paragraph of Article 1 of the First Protocol to the ECHR.[65]

---

[61] *Ibid.*, paras. 102–3.

[62] *Ibid.*, para. 106. See also the Separate Opinion of Judge Costa: '[H]aving regard to the Court's case law on the right to a healthy environment . . . maintaining night flights at that level meant that the applicants had to pay too high a price for an economic well-being, of which the real benefit, moreover, is not apparent from the facts of the case. Unless, of course, it is felt that the case law goes too far and overprotects a person's right to a sound environment. I do not think so. Since the beginning of the 1970s, the world has become increasingly aware of the importance of environmental issues and of their influence on people's lives. Our Court's case law has, moreover, not been alone in developing along those lines. For example, Article 37 of the Charter of Fundamental Rights of the European Union of 18 December 2000 is devoted to the protection of the environment. I would find it regrettable if the constructive efforts made by our Court were to suffer a setback.'

[63] Cf. the approach taken by various ICSID and NAFTA arbitral tribunals in relation to expropriation cases: chapter 21, pp. 1064–71 below.

[64] Judgment of 18 February 1991, ECHR Ser. A, No. 192, 14, para. 48; see also *Oerlemans* v. *Netherlands*, judgment of 27 November 1991, ECHR Ser. A, No. 219.

[65] Judgment of 29 November 1991, ECHR Ser. A, No. 222, paras. 54 and 57. Cf. *Matos y Silva* v. *Portugal*, Judgment of 16 September 1996 (finding a violation of Article 1 of Protocol 1 where there had been no formal or *de facto* expropriation, since the measures to create a

Moreover, the interference, in the form of a decision by the Irish Supreme Court, which was intended to prevent building in an area zoned for further agricultural development so as to preserve a green belt, had to be regarded as 'a proper way – if not the only way – of achieving that aim' and could not be considered as a disproportionate measure giving rise to a violation of Article 1 of the First Protocol.[66]

The Inter-American Commission on Human Rights has shown itself equally willing to find a violation of 'environmental' rights, but predating the European Court in its approach. In the *Yanomami* case, the Commission concluded that the ecological destruction of Yanomami lands in Brazil had caused violations of the right to life, health and food under the American Declaration of the Rights and Duties of Man.[67] In *Mayagna (Sumo) Awas Tingni Community* v. *Nicaragua*, the Inter-American Court of Human Rights found that the grant of a logging concession violated the property rights (Article 21 of the ACHR) of an indigenous community, adopting an approach analogous to that taken by the European Court.[68]

The Committee of Independent Experts established under the 1961 European Social Chapter (ESC), which considers national reports under the Charter, has also recognised the relationship between the state of the environment and the safeguarding of rights guaranteed under the Charter. The Committee has taken into account national measures to prevent, limit or control pollution in considering compliance with the obligation to ensure the right to the highest attainable standard of health under Article 11 of the ESC.[69] Examples of earlier Committee actions include:

- noting the intention of the French authorities to achieve a 50 per cent reduction in atmospheric sulphur dioxide emissions in the period 1980–90;[70]
- noting measures taken by Denmark to reduce air pollution, including reductions of nitrogen oxide emissions by 50 per cent before 2005 and sulphur dioxide emissions by 40 per cent before 1995;[71]

nature reserve for animals had serious and harmful effects that hindered the applicants' enjoyment of their property right for more than thirteen years, creating uncertainty as to what would become of the possessions and as to the question of compensation, and upsetting the balance between the requirements of the general interest and the protection of property rights).

[66] Para. 59.
[67] Case No. 7615 of 5 March 1985, Annual Report of the Inter-American Commission on Human Rights, OAS Doc. OEA/Ser.L/V/II.66, Doc. 10 rev.1, 24 (1985), cited in Earthjustice Legal Defense Fund, 'Human Rights and the Environment'.
[68] Judgment of 31 August 2001.
[69] 'Human Rights and the Environment: Progress Report', UN Doc. E/CN.4/Sub.2/1992, 2 July 1992, paras. 73 and 74. See also R. J. Dupuy (ed.), *The Right to Health as Human Right* (1979).
[70] 'Human Rights and the Environment: Progress Report', note 69 above, citing Council of Europe/ESC, Committee of Independent Experts – Conclusions IX-2 (1986), 71–2.
[71] *Ibid.*, citing Conclusions XI-I (1989), 118.

- expressing the desire that national reports should contain information on measures taken to reduce atmospheric releases of sulphur dioxide and other acid gases;[72]
- calling for broader measures to control environmental pollution;[73] and
- expressing the view that states should be considered as fulfilling their obligations under Article 11 of the ESC if they provide evidence of the existence of a medical and health system comprising 'general measures aimed in particular at the prevention of air and water pollution, protection from radioactive substances, noise abatement . . . [and] environmental hygiene'.[74]

A similar approach has been taken by the Committee on the Elimination of Discrimination Against Women[75] and by the Committee on the Rights of the Child.[76]

Civil and political rights

Civil and political rights are equally capable of creating practical and enforceable obligations in relation to environmental and related matters. Civil and political rights and obligations are established by several environmental treaties and other international instruments at the global and regional levels. Civil and political rights which are relevant to environmental protection include: the right to life;[77] the prohibition of cruel, inhuman or degrading treatment;[78] the right to equal protection against discrimination;[79] the right to an effective remedy by competent national tribunals for acts violating fundamental rights;[80] freedom

---

[72] *Ibid.*, citing Council of Europe/ESC, *Case Law on the European Social Charter*, Supp. (1986), 37.

[73] 'Human Rights and the Environment: Progress Report', note 69 above, citing Council of Europe/ESC, *Case Law on the European Social Charter* (1982), 105.

[74] *Ibid.*, 104.

[75] See e.g. Concluding Observations on Romania, UN Doc. CEDAW/C/2000/II/Add.7, para. 38 (2000) ('[t]he Committee expresses its concern about the situation of the environment, including industrial accidents, and their impact on women's health').

[76] See e.g. Concluding Observations on South Africa, UN Doc. CRC/C/15/Add.122, para. 30 (2000) ('Le Comité fait part de son inquiétude devant l'aggravation de la dégradation écologique, en particulier en ce qui concerne la pollution atmosphérique. Le Comité recommande à l'État partie d'intensifier ses efforts pour favoriser la mise en oeuvre de programmes de développement durable afin de prévenir la dégradation écologique, en particulier la pollution atmosphérique.').

[77] 1966 ICCPR, Art. 6(1); 1950 ECHR, Art. 2(1); 1969 ACHR, Art. 4(1); 1981 African Charter, Art. 4.

[78] 1966 ICCPR, Art. 7; 1950 ECHR, Art. 3; 1969 ACHR, Art. 5; 1981 African Charter, Art. 5.

[79] 1948 UDHR, Art. 7; 1966 ICCPR, Art. 3; 1969 ACHR, Art. 24; 1981 African Charter, Art. 3(2); see H. Smets, 'Le Principe de non discrimination en matière de protection de l'environnement', 2 *Revue européenne de droit de l'environnement* 1 (2000).

[80] 1948 UDHR, Art. 8; 1950 ECHR, Art. 13; 1969 ACHR, Art. 25; 1981 African Charter, Arts. 7(1) and 26.

of expression[81] and the right to receive information;[82] the right to a fair and public hearing by an independent and impartial tribunal in the determination of rights and obligations;[83] the right to protection against arbitrary interference with privacy and the home;[84] the prohibition of arbitrary deprivation of property;[85] and the right to take part in the conduct of public affairs.[86]

The 1989 Indigenous Peoples Convention illustrates the relationship between civil and political rights and environmental issues in that context.[87] Among the numerous obligations established or recognised by the Convention for indigenous and tribal peoples are environmental and other impact assessment and the right of such peoples to determine their own economic, social and cultural development, the right to be consulted and to participate in decision-making and to take legal proceedings to safeguard against the abuse of their rights.[88] The 1989 Indigenous Peoples Convention illustrates the limitations of the traditional approach of other instruments such as the ECHR. In *X* v. *Federal Republic of Germany*, the European Commission on Human Rights rejected as 'manifestly ill-founded' a claim by an environmental association that Article 11 of the ECHR entitled it to have *locus standi* in administrative court actions to challenge a decision to construct a nuclear power plant; the Commission held that the ECHR does not require that associations be granted the right to institute legal proceedings pursuant to their statutory aims without having to show a legal interest of their own in the matter.[89] Many of the principles set out in the 1992 Rio Declaration and the 1972 Stockholm Declaration, which reflect state practice at the global and regional levels, will be familiar to human rights lawyers who have worked on civil and political rights. One of the central themes at UNCED was the recognition that individuals will need to

---

[81] See e.g. *Bladet Tromso and Stensaas* v. *Norway* (2000) 29 EHRR 125 (newspapers' freedom under Art. 10 of the 1950 ECHR to publish environmental information (regarding the consequences of seal-hunting) of local, national and international interest).

[82] 1981 African Charter, Art. 9(1); see further chapter 17 below, especially pp. 852–9. Note that in *Guerra and others* v. *Italy*, the European Court did not find a violation of Art. 10 of the ECHR: see n. 57 above and the accompanying text.

[83] 1948 UDHR, Art. 10; 1966 ICCPR, Art. 14(1); 1950 ECHR, Art. 6(1); see further chapter 6 above.

[84] 1948 UDHR, Art. 12; 1966 ICCPR, Art. 17; 1950 ECHR, Art. 8(1) (see *Powell and Rayner/*, ECHR (1990) Ser. A, No. 172; 1969 ACHR, Art. 11.

[85] 1948 UDHR, Art. 17; 1950 ECHR, First Protocol, Art. 1; 1969 ACHR, Art. 21; 1981 African Charter, Art. 14.

[86] 1966 ICCPR, Art. 25; 1969 ACHR, Art. 23; 1981 African Charter, Art. 13.

[87] See generally W. Shutkin, 'International Human Rights Law and the Earth: The Protection of Indigenous Peoples and the Environment', 31 *Virginia Journal of International Law* 479 (1991); A. Meyer, 'International Environmental Law and Human Rights: Towards the Explicit Recognition of Traditional Knowledge', 10 RECIEL 37 (2001).

[88] Arts. 6, 7 and 11.

[89] Application No. 9234/81, Decisions of 14 July 1981, 26 DR 270. See also *Balmer-Schafroth* v. *Switzerland* (1998) 25 EHRR 598.

participate fully to ensure the implementation of UNCED and Agenda 21. In supporting the participation of all concerned citizens at the relevant level, the Rio Declaration supports: the right of access to environmental information;[90] the right to participate in decisions which affect their environment;[91] the right of effective access to judicial and administrative proceedings, including redress and remedy;[92] a right to development to meet environmental needs;[93] and the rights flowing from the recognition of the need to ensure the full participation of women, youth and indigenous peoples and other communities.[94] The case law of the European Court and the adoption of instruments such as the 1998 Aarhus Convention indicate that this approach is likely to become increasingly important in the coming years, particularly as efforts to focus on the enforcement of environmental standards are stepped up.[95]

War and armed conflict

J. Goldblat, *The Prohibition of Environmental Warfare* (1975); L. Juda, 'Negotiating a Treaty on Environmental Modification Warfare: The Convention on Environmental Warfare and its Impact on the Arms Control Negotiations', 32 *International Organization* 975 (1978); M. Bothe, 'War and Environment', in R. Bernhardt (ed.), *Encyclopaedia of Public International Law* (1982); D. Momtaz, 'Les Règles rélatives à la protection de l'environnement au cours des conflicts armés à l'épreuve du conflict entre l'Irak et le Koweit', 37 AFDI 203 (1991); B. Oxman, 'Environmental Warfare', 22 *Ocean Development and International Law* 433 (1991); C. Joyner and J. Kirkhope, 'The Persian Gulf War Oil Spill: Reassessing the Law of Environmental Protection and the Law of Armed Conflict', 24 *Case Western Reserve Journal of International Law* 29 (1992); G. Plant (ed.), *Environmental Protection and the Law of War* (1992); E. J. Wallach, 'The Use of Crude Oil by an Occupying Belligerent State as a Munition de Guerre', 41 ICLQ 287 (1992); R. Tarasofsky, 'Legal Protection of the Environment During International Armed Conflict', 24 NYIL 17 (1993); L. Low and D. Hodgkinson, 'Compensation for Wartime Environmental Damage', 35 *Virginia Journal of International Law* 405 (1995); R. Grunawalt, J. King and R. McClain (eds.), *Protection of the Environment During Armed Conflict* (1996); Symposium on Armed Conflict, Security and Environment, 9 RECIEL 1 (2000); D. Momtaz, 'The Use of Nuclear Weapons and the Protection of the Environment: The Contribution of the ICJ', in P. Sands and L. Boisson de Chazournes, *International Law, the ICJ and Nuclear Weapons* (1999), 354.

[90] Principle 10; chapter 17, p. 827 below.   [91] Principle 10, see chapter 18, p. 870 below.

[92] *Ibid.*, chapter 5, pp. 225–6 above.   [93] Principle 3.

[94] Principles 20, 21 and 22; on participation of women, under UNGA Res. 47/191 (1992), representation on the High-Level Advisory Board requires that 'due account should . . . be given to gender balance' (para. 29).

[95] On the 1998 Aarhus Convention, see chapter 5, pp. 209–10 above (access to justice) and chapter 17, pp. 858–9 below (environmental information).

Introduction

Military activities may have significant impacts upon the environment. Preparations, including the testing, development, production and maintenance of conventional, chemical, biological and nuclear weapons, have generated large quantities of hazardous, toxic, and radioactive substances. These, together with their wastes, have contributed on a large scale to the depletion of natural resources and degradation of the environment.[96] The environmental impacts of military activities are well documented, and recent conflicts in Vietnam, Afghanistan, the Persian Gulf and the Balkans have refocused attention on the need to limit these adverse consequences. In another sense, the protection of the environment has even been used as a justification for the use of force: in August 2000 the UN Interim Administration Mission in Kosovo (UNMIK) (assisted by the NATO-led Kosovo Force (KFOR)) took over control of the Zvecan Smelter Plant in Kosovo 'until air pollution control mechanisms are installed and the affected population tested'.[97]

International law recognises and aims to address the link between military activities and environmental protection. Treaties to protect humans and their property from the effects of military activities also aim to protect the environment, albeit indirectly. More recently, treaties have addressed environmental protection as an end in itself. Three separate, but related, questions are worth considering. First, do the rules of international environmental law operate during times of war and armed conflict? Secondly, what indirect protection for the environment is afforded by the rules of international law governing war and armed conflict? And, thirdly, to what extent does the international law of war and armed conflict address environmental protection as an end in itself?

International environmental law during war and armed conflict

The first issue which arises concerns the applicability of the various rules of international environmental law to military activities, including preparatory activities. The general rules of public international law provide little guidance as to the legal validity and consequences of those treaties following the outbreak of military hostilities.[98] The validity and effect of a particular treaty during war

---

[96] A. H. Westing, *Warfare in a Fragile World: Military Impact on the Human Environment* (1980); J. P. Robinson, *The Effects of Weapons on Ecosystems* (1991). See also A. Westing (ed.), *Environmental Warfare: A Technical, Legal and Policy Appraisal* (1984); A. Westing (ed.), *Cultural Norms, War and the Environment* (1988).

[97] UNMIK Press Release, 14 August 2000, UNMIK/PR/312 ('Recent tests indicate that current levels of lead exposure are approaching the most extreme in decades. Levels of atmospheric lead measured last month were around 200 times the World Health Organization's acceptable standards.'). See also NATO/KFOR Press Release, 14 August 2000.

[98] Art. 73 of the 1969 Vienna Convention: '[T]he present Convention shall not prejudice any question that may arise in regard to a treaty from . . . the outbreak of hostilities between States.'

and/or armed conflict will often turn on the terms of the treaty itself. The general instruments of international environmental law and policy also fail to provide any guidance on this question. The 1972 Stockholm Declaration focuses exclusively on nuclear weapons. Principle 26 provides that:

> Man and his environment must be spared the effects of nuclear weapons and all other means of mass destruction. States must strive to reach prompt agreement, in the relevant international organs, on the elimination and complete destruction of such weapons.

The 1982 World Charter for Nature adopts a more general approach, stating the 'general principle' that '[n]ature shall be secured against degradation caused by warfare or other hostile activities', and declaring that 'military activities damaging to nature shall be avoided'.[99] The wording of the 1992 Rio Declaration gets closer to the point but is still ambiguous, stating in Principle 24 that:

> Warfare is inherently destructive of sustainable development. States shall therefore respect international law providing protection for the environment in time of armed conflict and co-operate in its further development, as necessary.

Although not legally binding, the wording of Principle 24 could either be interpreted as requiring states to respect those rules of international law which provide protection for the environment in times of armed conflict, or as requiring states to respect international law by protecting the environment in times of armed conflict.

Most environmental treaties are silent on the issue of their applicability following the outbreak of military hostilities. Some, including those on civil liability for damage, include provisions excluding their applicability when damage occurs as a result of war and armed conflict.[100] Others include provisions allowing for total or partial suspension at the instigation of one of the parties,[101] while yet others require the consequences of hostilities to influence decision-making in the application of the treaty by its institutions.[102] Some treaties do

---

[99] Paras. 5 and 20.

[100] 1960 Paris Convention, Art. 9; 1963 Vienna Convention, Art. IV(3)(a); 1969 CLC, Art. III(2)(a); 1971 Oil Pollution Fund Convention, Art. 4(2)(a) (no liability attached to the Fund for damage from oil from warships used on non-commercial service); 1977 Civil Liability Convention, Art. 3(3); 1988 CRAMRA, Art. 8(4)(b) (if no reasonable precautionary measures could have been taken).

[101] 1954 Oil Pollution Convention, Art. XIX(1), allowing parties to suspend operation of whole or part of the Convention in case of war or other hostilities if they consider themselves affected as a belligerent or as a neutral, upon notification to the Convention's Bureau.

[102] 1952 North Pacific Fisheries Convention, which provides that Commission decisions should make allowance for, *inter alia*, wars which may introduce temporary declines in fish stocks (Art. IV(2)).

not apply to military activities even during peacetime operations,[103] while others are specifically applicable to certain activities which may be associated with hostilities.[104] Finally, the terms and overall purpose of some treaties make it abundantly clear that they are designed to ensure environmental protection at all times.[105] The 1997 Watercourses Convention adopts a different approach, making a renvoi to international humanitarian law: its Article 29 provides that: 'International watercourses and related installations, facilities and other works shall enjoy the protection accorded by the principles and rules of international law applicable in international and non-international armed conflict and shall not be used in violation of those principles and rules.'

The relevance of customary and conventional rules of international environmental law during armed conflict was addressed in the proceedings relating to the ICJ's Advisory Opinion on *The Legality of the Threat or Use of Nuclear Weapons*. A number of non-nuclear weapons states argued that multilateral environmental agreements and the rule reflected in Principle 21 of the Stockholm Declaration and Principle 2 of the Rio Declaration applied in times of armed conflict and governed the use of nuclear weapons.[106] Without addressing the general question of the applicability of multilateral environmental agreements during conflict, some nuclear weapons states argued that such agreements (as well as Principle 21/Principle 2) could not be construed as prohibiting the threat or use of nuclear weapons because they did not address nuclear weapons *per se* and could not be construed as containing an implied prohibition on their use.[107] With regard to treaties, the ICJ side-stepped the differences of view, stating that the issue was not whether they 'are or are not applicable during armed conflict, but rather whether the obligations stemming from these treaties were intended to be obligations of total restraint during military conflict', and concluding that the treaties in question could not have been 'intended to deprive a State of the exercise of its right of self-defence under international law because of its obligations to protect the environment'.[108] With regard to the customary norm relating to the protection of the environment, the ICJ indicates that the environmental obligations it referred to in the second New Zealand *Nuclear Tests*

---

[103] 1972 London Convention, Art. VII(4) (non-applicability of the Convention to vessels and aircraft entitled to sovereign immunity under international law).

[104] 1976 Barcelona Protocol, which generally prohibits the dumping of materials produced for biological and chemical warfare (Annex 1, Section A, para. 9); and 1986 Noumea Protocol, which prohibits special dumping permits from being granted in respect of materials produced for biological and chemical warfare (Art. 10(1) and (2) and Annex I, Section A, para. 6).

[105] 1959 Antarctic Treaty, Art. I(1); 1988 CRAMRA, Art. 2.

[106] See 5 *Yearbook of International Environmental Law* 540–2 (1995) (Solomon Islands, Mexico, North Korea, Egypt, Iran and Qatar).

[107] *Ibid.* (United Kingdom, United States and France).

[108] (1996) ICJ Reports 242, para. 30. It is to be noted that the Court, perhaps deliberately, conflates the distinct concepts of the *jus in bello* and the *jus ad bellum*.

case 'also appl[y] to the actual use of nuclear weapons in armed conflict'.[109] In this way, the ICJ concludes that, although 'existing international law relating to the protection and safeguarding of the environment does not specifically prohibit the use of nuclear weapons it indicates important environmental factors that are properly to be taken into account in the context of the implementation of the principles and rules of the law applicable in armed conflict'.[110]

International law of war and armed conflict: general rules of environmental protection

The international law of war and armed conflict limits the methods and means of warfare available to states. These rules of treaty and customary law were developed to protect humans and their property, and may only be indirectly protective of an environment which is not intended to be the direct beneficiary of these acts. The 'Martens Clause' provides that, until the adoption of specific regulations, inhabitants and belligerents are 'under the protection and the rule of the principles of the law of nations as they result from the usages established among civilised peoples, from the laws of humanity, and the dictates of public conscience'.[111] In modern international law, there is no reason why these should not encompass environmental protection.

It is now a well-accepted general rule of international law that the methods and means of warfare are not unlimited. Methods and means are limited to activities necessary to achieve military objectives; which prevent unnecessary suffering and superfluous injury; which are proportionate; and which respect the rules of international law on neutrality. As early as 1899, states accepted that the 'right of the belligerent to adopt means of injuring the enemy is not unlimited'.[112] The 1977 Additional Protocol I provides that: 'In any armed conflict, the right of the parties to the conflict to choose methods or means of warfare is not unlimited.'[113] As a general rule, the destruction of property is

---

[109] *Ibid.*, 243, para. 32; and see pp. 319–21 below.

[110] *Ibid.*, para. 33. See also para. 30 ('States must take environmental considerations into account when assessing what is necessary and proportionate in the pursuit of legitimate military objectives. Respect for the environment is one of the elements that go to assessing whether an action is in conformity with the principles of necessity and proportionality.').

[111] 1907 Hague Convention IV Respecting the Laws and Customs of War on Land, 3 Martens (3rd) 461, Preamble. The 'Martens Clause' may be helpful in extending customary international law obligations to environmental protection objectives, particularly in the context of current efforts to establish the environment as a civilian objective.

[112] 1899 Hague Regulations to the International Convention with Respect to the Laws and Customs of War by Land (Hague II), 26 Martens (2nd) 949; and 1907 Hague Convention IV, n. 111 above.

[113] Protocol I (Additional to the 1949 Geneva Conventions), Geneva, 8 June 1977, in force 7 December 1978, 16 ILM 1391 (1977).

prohibited unless it is rendered absolutely necessary by military operations,[114] as is the use of mines causing long-lasting threats.[115]

These general obligations limiting the methods and means of warfare have been supplemented by specific treaty obligations prohibiting certain forms of weaponry and warfare which are particularly harmful to the environment. Although these rules are invariably designed to protect people, rather than the environment, their application could also provide protection to the environment. Under the 1977 Additional Protocol I, parties must assess new weapons and means or methods of warfare to determine whether, in their employment, they would be prohibited by the Protocol or by any other applicable rule of international law.[116] Other treaties prohibit the use of conventional weapons causing excessive injuries or indiscriminate effects,[117] including incendiary weapons,[118] chemical and biological weapons,[119] and nuclear weapons.[120] Cultural property is also subject to a regime of special protection.[121] The limited role which such instruments or equivalent rules of customary international law might be able to play was illustrated by the graphic images of the bombardment of Dubrovnik in 1992 which were broadcast around the world.[122]

More specific to environmental protection is the prohibition of attacks on works and installations containing dangerous forces, even when they are military objects, if such attacks might cause the release of dangerous forces and consequent severe losses among the civilian population.[123] Dams, dykes and nuclear power plants are specifically identified, although the effectiveness of this provision is limited by the exceptions provided if these types of works and installations are used in regular, significant and direct support of military operations, and if such an attack is the only feasible way to terminate such

---

[114] 1899 Hague Regulations, n. 112 above, Arts. 23(g) and 55; 1949 Geneva Convention IV, Art. 53.

[115] 1907 Hague Convention VIII on the Laying of Automatic Contact Mines; 19 ILM 1529 (1980); UNGA Res. 37/215 (1982).

[116] Art. 36.

[117] 1980 Inhumane Weapons Convention; the Preamble identifies one of the aims as environmental protection.

[118] See Protocol III (Incendiary Weapons) to the 1980 Inhumane Weapons Convention, which prohibits making forest or other plant cover the object of attack unless used to cover, conceal or camouflage military objectives: Art. 2(4).

[119] 1925 Geneva Protocol; 1972 Biological and Toxic Weapons Convention. See also the draft Convention on the Prohibition of the Development, Production and Stockpiling and Use of Chemical Weapons and on their Destruction, September 1992, GAOR Supp. 47th Sess., Supp. No. 27 (A/47/27), Appendix I.

[120] Chapter 18, pp. 905–12 below.

[121] Hague Convention for the Protection of Cultural Property in the Event of Armed Conflict, 14 May 1954, 249 UNTS 215.

[122] The Old City of Dubrovnik is listed under the 1972 World Heritage Convention as a World Heritage Site.

[123] 1977 Additional Protocol I, Art. 56(1); 1977 Additional Protocol II, Art. 15.

support.[124] Attacks against such works or installations launched in the knowledge that they will cause excessive loss of life, injury to civilians or damage to civilian objects are regarded as war crimes.[125] The IAEA has called for a prohibition of attacks on nuclear facilities, since they 'could result in radioactive releases with grave consequences',[126] and the International Law Association has declared that international law prohibits the destruction of water installations which 'may involve . . . substantial damage to the basic ecological balance'.[127] The increased importance attached by the international community to the protection of the environment in times of armed conflict has also been reflected in the work of the International Law Commission. The first reading of the draft Code of Crimes Against the Peace and Security of Mankind defines an 'exceptionally serious war crime' as, *inter alia*, 'employing methods or means of warfare which are intended or may be expected to cause widespread, long-term and severe damage to the natural environment'.[128] Any lingering doubts about the status of certain acts against the environment will have been laid to rest by the Statute of the International Criminal Court, which expressly characterises as a war crime an attack which is launched 'in the knowledge that [it] will cause . . . widespread, long-term and severe damage to the natural environment which would be clearly excessive in relation to the concrete and direct overall military advantage anticipated'.[129]

International law of war and armed conflict: special rules of environmental protection

The first treaty to establish rules specifically protecting the environment from the consequences of military activities was the 1977 Convention on the Prohibition of Military or Any Other Hostile Use of Environmental Modification Techniques (1977 ENMOD Convention). It prohibits parties from engaging in 'military or any other hostile use of environmental modification techniques

---

[124] 1977 Additional Protocol I, Art. 56(2).

[125] 1977 Additional Protocol I, Art. 85(3) and (5); 1998 Statute of the International Criminal Court, Art. 8(2).

[126] See resolutions of the General Conference of the IAEA, GC(XXVII)/Res. 407 (1983), GC(XXVIII)/Res. 425 (1984), GC(XXIX)/Res. 444 (1985), GC(XXXI)/Res. 475 (1987), and GC(XXXIV)/Res. 533 (1990).

[127] 1976 ILA Madrid Resolution on the Protection of Water Resources and Water Installations in Times of Armed Conflict, resolution of 4 September 1976, Report of the Fifty-Seventh Conference of the International Law Association (1976), 234.

[128] Report of the ILC, 43rd Session, 46 GAOR Supp. 1 No. 10 (A/46/10), Chap. IV. D.1, 30 ILM 1584 (1991), Art. 22(2)(d). See also Art. 26 of the Draft Code: an individual who 'wilfully causes or orders the causing of widespread long-term and severe damage to the natural environment' is liable to be convicted of a crime against the peace and security of mankind.

[129] Art. 8(2)(b)(iv).

having widespread, long-lasting or severe effects as the means of destruction, damage or injury' to any other party.[130] The Convention defines 'environmental modification techniques' as 'any technique for changing – through the deliberate manipulation of natural processes – the dynamics, composition or structure of the Earth, including its biota, lithosphere, hydrosphere and atmosphere, or of outer space'.[131] No definitions are provided of the terms 'widespread', 'long-lasting' and 'severe', although the Conference of the Committee on Disarmament, under whose auspices the Convention was negotiated, did attach 'Understandings' to the text of the Convention which were submitted to the General Assembly.[132] The terms of Article II are sufficiently opaque to leave open the question of whether the act must be deliberately intended to manipulate natural processes, or whether it is sufficient to show that natural processes have been manipulated as the result of an act which was intended to manipulate non-natural processes, as may have been the case with the destruction by Iraq of Kuwaiti oil fields. The former, and far narrower, approach would undoubtedly limit the scope of the Convention's application and its effectiveness.[133]

Several months after the ENMOD Convention was concluded, the 1977 Additional Protocol I to the 1949 Geneva Conventions Relating to the Victims of Armed Conflict was adopted. The 1977 Additional Protocol I contains two explicit obligations designed to protect the environment which, given the large number of parties and views expressed by states, may now reflect a rule of customary international law.[134] Under Article 35, it is 'prohibited to employ methods and means of warfare which are intended, or may be expected, to

---

[130] New York, 10 December 1976, in force 5 October 1978, 1108 UNTS 151. The Convention is not intended to hinder environmental modification techniques for peaceful purposes and is stated to be 'without prejudice to the generally recognised principles and applicable rules of international law concerning such use': Art. III(1).

[131] Art. II.

[132] The Understanding on Art. I provides that the terms should be interpreted in the following way:

1. 'widespread': encompassing an area on the scale of several hundred square kilometres;
2. 'long-lasting': lasting for a period of months, or approximately a season;
3. 'severe': involving serious or significant disruption or harm to human life, natural and economic resources or other assets.

See Understanding Relating to Article I of ENMOD, 31 GAOR Supp. No. 27 (A/31/27), Annex I.

[133] In the ICJ proceedings on the Advisory Opinion on nuclear weapons, some states argued that its provisions reflected customary law, whereas some nuclear weapon states argued that it would not be applicable to most cases in which nuclear weapons might be used because the effect on the environment would be a side effect and not a result of deliberate manipulation: 6 *Yearbook of International Environmental Law* 540 (1995).

[134] Although the UK and US are not parties to the Protocol, they have expressed support for the protection of the environment in similar terms.

cause widespread, long-term and severe damage to the natural environment'.[135] Article 55, entitled 'Protection of the natural environment', provides that:

> Care shall be taken in warfare to protect the natural environment against widespread, long-term and severe damage. This protection includes a prohibition of the use of methods or means of warfare which are intended or may be expected to cause such damage to the natural environment and thereby to prejudice the health or survival of the population.[136]

The Protocol also prohibits attacks against the natural environment by way of reprisals.[137] In its Advisory Opinion on nuclear weapons, the ICJ noted that these provisions of Additional Protocol I provide additional protection for the environment, and impose 'powerful constraints for all the States having subscribed to these provisions'.[138] The implication that the 'powerful constraints' of the Protocol did not – at least in 1996 – reflect customary law, may no longer hold true with the adoption of the 1998 Statute of the International Criminal Court and France's accession, on 11 April 2001, to the Protocol.[139]

Iraq's invasion of Kuwait in August 1990 led the Security Council to consider, for the first time, the responsibility of states for the adverse environmental consequences of unlawful military acts. Security Council Resolution 687 reaffirmed that Iraq was liable under international law for, *inter alia*, 'environmental damage and the depletion of natural resources' resulting from the unlawful invasion and occupation of Kuwait.[140] The Iraqi invasion of Kuwait led to further consideration of the environmental effects of war and armed conflict, including an examination of the adequacy of the existing and rather limited treaty rules. Agenda 21 reflected limited progress. It called on the international community to consider measures in accordance with international law 'to address, in times of armed conflict, large-scale destruction of the environment that cannot be justified under international law', and identified the General Assembly and its Sixth Committee as the appropriate fora to deal with the issue, taking into account the competence and role of the International Committee of the Red

---

[135] Art. 35(3).   [136] Art. 55(1).   [137] Art. 55(2).

[138] (1996) ICJ Reports p. 242, para. 31. On the arguments presented by states, see 6 *Yearbook of International Environmental Law* 538–40 (1995). Only France expressed the view that these Articles of the Protocol did not reflect customary law (CR 95/24, at 23 and 25–6).

[139] See also the Application by the Federal Republic of Yugoslavia instituting proceedings against the United Kingdom, 28 April 1999 ('by taking part in the bombing of oil refineries and chemical plants, the United Kingdom of Great Britain and Northern Ireland has acted against the Federal Republic of Yugoslavia in breach of its obligation not to cause considerable environmental damage') and Request for Provisional Measures, 28 April 1999. Similar claims are made in the applications against nine other NATO members.

[140] Security Council Res. 687/1991, 30 ILM 847 (1991). On the Iraq Compensation Commission and the assessment of 'environmental damage', see chapter 18, pp. 890–4 below. On the arguments of states as to the implications of Resolution 687 for environmental protection in times of armed conflict, see 6 *Yearbook of International Environmental Law* 539–40 (1995).

Cross.[141] In December 1992, the General Assembly adopted a resolution stressing that destruction of the environment not justified by military necessity and carried out wantonly was 'clearly contrary to international law', and noted that existing provisions of international law prohibited the destruction of oil well heads and the release and waste of crude oil into the sea.[142] The General Assembly urged states to 'take all measures to ensure compliance with the existing international law applicable to the protection of the environment in times of armed conflict'. Since then, however, no new treaties have been negotiated or adopted, and it has been left to the ICJ (in its Advisory Opinion on nuclear weapons) and the states negotiating the Statute of the International Criminal Court to mark the modest developments which have occurred.

Conclusions

Over the past decade, environmental considerations have been integrated into human rights discourse and, to a lesser extent, into the definition and application of international humanitarian rules governing methods and means of armed conflict.

In relation to human rights, notwithstanding the fact that most human rights treaties do not expressly refer to environmental considerations, practice under those conventions recognises that a failure to adequately protect the environment may give rise to individual human rights, particularly in relation to rights associated with the enjoyment of a person's home and property. Equally, practice recognises that the collective interest of a community in taking steps to protect the environment may justify reasonable interference with property or other rights. In both aspects, the principal need is to ensure that a balance is found between individual and collective rights. In the very recent past, human rights procedures may also have begun to define the content of participatory rights in the environmental domain: the non-compliance mechanism established under the 1998 Aarhus Convention represents an innovative step.

In relation to armed conflict, it is ironic that proceedings before the ICJ concerning the legality of the use of nuclear weapons catalysed an important debate on the relationship between methods and means of warfare and the protection of the environment. The Court's advisory opinion has recognised, for the first time, the existence of norms of international environmental law as custom, and that they are applicable equally in times of armed conflict.

---

[141] Agenda 21, para. 39.6(a).   [142] UNGA Res. 47/591 (1992).

8

Atmosphere

H. Taubenfeld, 'International Environmental Law: Air and Outer Space', 13 *Natural Resources Journal* 315 (1973); D. Gelsom, *Atmospheric Pollution: A Global Problem* (1992); G. Wetstone and A. Rosencrantz, 'Transboundary Air Pollution: The Search for an International Response', 8 *Harvard Environmental Law Review* 89 (1984); C. Flinterman *et al.* (eds.), *Transboundary Air Pollution: International Legal Aspects of the Co-operation of States* (1986); J. Brunnee, *Acid Rain and Ozone Layer Depletion: International Law and Regulation* (1988); P. Okowa, *State Responsibility for Transboundary Air Pollution in International Law* (2000)

Introduction

The protection of the atmosphere was a relative latecomer to international environment regulation but is now well established. With limited exceptions, until 1979 no treaty sought, as its primary purpose, to place limits on the right of states to allow atmospheric emissions which caused environmental damage. Some treaties had, however, called for general preventive strategies.[1] Since 1979, numerous treaties and other international acts have addressed the protection of the atmosphere. Although there is no atmospheric equivalent to the 1982 UN Convention on the Law of the Sea, international legal instruments have been adopted at the regional and global level which address a range of issues, including: transboundary pollution by sulphur dioxide, nitrogen oxide and volatile organic compounds; the protection of the ozone layer; the prevention of climate change; and the protection of the environment of outer space. The precedents set by treaties relating to the protection of other environmental media, in particular the marine environment, have contributed to the development of these rules.

Landmarks in the development of international law in this area include: the 1938 and 1941 decisions in the *Trail Smelter* case; the applications brought to the ICJ by Australia and New Zealand against France with respect to French atmospheric nuclear tests in the Pacific Ocean region; growing evidence in Europe

---

[1] See chapter 6, pp. 246–9 above.

317

and North America in the 1970s of acid rain damage from atmospheric emissions of sulphur compounds; the 1986 Chernobyl accident; growing evidence in the 1980s of depletion of the ozone layer; and, most recently, evidence that increased atmospheric concentrations of carbon dioxide and other greenhouse gases are likely to cause temperatures to increase worldwide with consequential adverse effects.[2] Since the first edition of this book, the international community has also become aware of the threat posed by forest fires with transnational effects, such as those in Indonesia in 1997 which caused widespread regional problems.[3]

Trail Smelter Case

The award of the arbitral tribunal in the *Trail Smelter* case is frequently cited to support the view that general principles of international law impose obligations on states to prevent transboundary air pollution.[4] This dispute arose out of damage done to crops, pasture land, trees and agriculture in the United States from sulphur dioxide emissions from a smelting plant at the Consolidated Mining and Smelting Company of Canada at Trail, in British Columbia. Emissions and damage had increased significantly after 1906, and again after 1925 and 1927, leading to the submission of the issue to the US–Canada International Joint Commission established, under the 1909 Boundary Waters Treaty. In February 1931, the Commission adopted a unanimous report awarding the United States US$350,000 to compensate for damage suffered in the period up to January 1932. The Commission also made recommendations concerning damages arising after January 1932 and the use of equipment to reduce further sulphur emissions. In February 1933, the US complained that further damage was occurring, and in April 1935 the two countries signed a convention submitting the dispute to an arbitral tribunal composed of three arbitrators, assisted by two scientists designated, respectively, by the two countries.[5] At the heart of the award is the holding of the tribunal that:

> Under the principles of international law . . . no state has the right to use or permit the use of territory in such a manner as to cause injury by fumes in or to the territory of another or the properties or persons therein, when the case is of serious consequence and the injury is established by clear and convincing evidence.[6]

[2] See IPCC, *Third Assessment Report: Climate Change 2001* (2001).
[3] See www.unep.org/unep/per/for_fire/fire.htm.
[4] *Trail Smelter* case, 16 April 1938, 11 March 1941; 3 RIAA 1907 (1941); on damages, see chapter 18, pp. 885–6 below.
[5] Convention of the Final Settlement of the Difficulties Arising Through the Complaints of Damage Done in the State of Washington by Fumes Discharged from the Smelter of the Consolidated Mining and Smelting Company, Trail, British Columbia, 15 April 1935, United States–Canada, 162 LNTS 73.
[6] 3 RIAA 1907 at 1965 (1941).

This much-cited passage has been relied upon to justify a range of views concerning the permissibility of certain atmospheric emissions. It is important to remember that the principle cited was applicable *a priori* by virtue of the arbitral *compromis* between the United States and Canada, and that the case is probably of greater significance for that agreement and for its findings on the assessment and measure of the quantum of recoverable damage.

Nuclear testing

Atmospheric nuclear testing was one of the first environmental issues to be addressed by the UN General Assembly in the 1950s.[7] This resulted in the adoption of the 1963 Treaty Banning Nuclear Weapon Tests in the Atmosphere, in Outer Space and Under Water (1963 Test Ban Treaty), which banned nuclear weapons explosions in those places.[8] By 1973, the Treaty had more than 110 parties, including all the major states which possessed nuclear weapons (China, the former USSR, the United Kingdom and the United States) with the exception of France. Between 1966 and 1972, France conducted atmospheric nuclear tests on Mururoa atoll, off their New Caledonian territory in the South Pacific region, and were preparing to conduct a further series of tests commencing in May 1973.[9] Australia and New Zealand commenced proceedings against France before the International Court of Justice (ICJ) to stop those and other nuclear tests in the Pacific. Australia asked the ICJ to declare that the carrying out of further atmospheric nuclear weapon tests was not consistent with applicable rules of international law and to order France not to carry out any further such tests. Australia claimed that the tests would:

1. violate its right to be free from atmospheric nuclear weapon tests by any country;
2. allow the deposit of radioactive fallout on its territory and airspace without its consent;
3. allow interference with ships and aircraft on the high seas and in the superjacent airspace, and the pollution of the high seas by radioactive fallout, thereby infringing the freedom of the high seas.[10]

New Zealand's claim was slightly different: it argued that French nuclear tests violated rules and principles of international law for similar reasons, but framed the application in terms of the violation of 'the rights of all members of the international community' to be free from nuclear tests which gave rise to radioactive

---

[7] See chapter 2, p. 33 above.
[8] Moscow, 5 August 1963, in force 10 October 1963, 480 UNTS 43.
[9] On subsequent developments declaring the region a nuclear-free zone, see chapter 12, pp. 649–51 below.
[10] *Nuclear Tests* case (*Australia* v. *France*) (Interim Measures) (1973) ICJ Reports 99 at 103.

fallout and the right to be preserved from 'unjustified artificial radioactive contamination of the terrestrial. maritime and aerial environment'.[11] Australia and New Zealand also sought interim measures of protection requiring the French Government to avoid nuclear tests causing the deposit of radioactive fallout on their territory, pending the ICJ's judgments.[12]

France chose not to appear in the case. In June 1973, by eight votes to six the ICJ indicated interim measures of protection which asked France to take no action which might aggravate the dispute or prejudice the rights of the other parties in carrying out whatever decision the ICJ might render.[13] The ICJ did not have an opportunity to address the merits of the case. Following the unilateral declaration by France that it would cease to carry out atmospheric tests, the ICJ held in December 1974 that the declaration made it unnecessary for the case to proceed, since the claims of Australia and New Zealand no longer had any object, and the ICJ therefore was not called upon to give a decision.[14]

The pleadings put forward in the case by Australia and New Zealand, the oral exchanges between some of the judges and counsel for the two applicant states, and the various opinions set forth by the judges, provide a useful source of evidence as to the relevant international law. Australia argued that the 1963 Test Ban Treaty 'embodied and crystallised an emergent rule of customary international law' prohibiting atmospheric nuclear tests which might have assumed the status of a rule of *jus cogens*.[15] During the oral hearings, Australia was asked by the President of the ICJ, Sir Humphrey Waldock, whether it took the view that 'every transmission by natural causes of chemical or other matter from one state into another state's territory, air space or territorial sea automatically created a legal cause of action in international law without the need to establish anything more'. Australia responded that:

> where, as a result of a normal and natural use by one state of its territory, a deposit occurs in the territory of another, the latter has no cause of complaint unless it suffers more than merely nominal harm or damage. The use by a state of its territory for the conduct of atmospheric nuclear tests is

---

[11] *Nuclear Tests* case (*New Zealand* v. *France*) (Interim Measures) (1973) ICJ Reports 135 at 139.

[12] See p. 319 above.

[13] *Nuclear Tests* cases (*Australia* v. *France*) (Interim Measures) (1973) ICJ Reports 99; (*New Zealand* v. *France*) (Interim Measures) (1973) ICJ Reports 135; on interim measures, see chapter 5, p. 218 above.

[14] *Nuclear Tests* cases (*Australia* v. *France*) (Jurisdiction) (1974) ICJ Reports 253; (*New Zealand* v. *France*) (Jurisdiction) (1974) ICJ Reports 457; L. Goldie, 'Nuclear Test Cases: Restraints on Environmental Harm', *Journal of Maritime Law and Commerce* 491 (1974); on the French unilateral declaration, see chapter 4, pp. 151–2 above. In 1995, New Zealand requested the ICJ to consider France's resumption of underground nuclear testing, but the ICJ declined jursidiction: see chapter 5, p. 218 above.

[15] *Nuclear Tests* cases (*Australia* v. *France*) (Interim Measures) (1973) ICJ Reports 99; (*New Zealand* v. *France*) (Interim Measures) (1973) ICJ Reports 135.

not a normal or natural use of its territory. The Australian government also contends that the radioactive deposit from the French tests gives rise to more than merely nominal harm or damage to Australia . . . [T]he basic principle is that intrusion of any sort into foreign territory is an infringement of sovereignty. Needless to say, the government of Australia does not deny that the practice of states has modified the application of this principle in respect of the interdependence of territories. It has already referred to the instance of smoke drifting across national boundaries. It concedes that there may be no illegality in respect of certain types of chemical fumes in the absence of special types of harm. What it does emphasise is that the legality thus sanctioned by the practice of states is the outcome of the toleration extended to certain activities which produce these emissions, which activities are generally regarded as natural uses of territory in modern industrial society and are tolerated because, while perhaps producing some inconvenience, they have a community benefit.[16]

The exchange illustrates the challenge of striking a balance between the community benefit of 'nominal harm or damage' and the individual right not to be subject to significant harm or damage.[17] In relation to atmospheric pollution, the difficulty in striking that balance may be acute, and the ICJ avoided the issue following the unilateral decision by France to stop carrying out atmospheric nuclear tests. One of the ICJ judges, Judge de Castro, nevertheless took the opportunity, in his dissent, to cite the award in the *Trail Smelter* case, with apparent approval.[18]

Customary law

The issues underlying the *Trail Smelter* and *Nuclear Tests* cases raise the question of whether rules of customary law exist specifically in relation to transboundary or other air pollution. This matter has been considered by the International Law Association (ILA) and the Institut de Droit International (IDI), both of which have adopted resolutions on the subject. Article 3(1) of the ILA's 1982 Montreal Draft Rules on Transboundary Pollution restate customary international law as requiring states 'to prevent . . . transfrontier air pollution to such an extent that no substantial injury is caused in the territory of another state'.[19] The

---

[16] *Nuclear Tests* cases (*Australia* v. *France*) (Interim Measures) (1973) ICJ Reports 99; (*New Zealand* v. *France*) (Interim Measures) (1973) ICJ Reports 135.

[17] See more generally chapter 6, pp. 235–46 above; and chapter 18, pp. 904–38 below.

[18] *Nuclear Tests* case (*Australia* v. *France*) (1974) ICJ Reports 253 at 389. He stated: 'If it is admitted as a general rule that there is a right to demand prohibition of the emissions by neighbouring properties of noxious fumes, the consequence must be drawn, by an obvious analogy, that the applicant is entitled to ask the Court to uphold its claim that France should put an end to the deposit of radioactive fall-out on its territory.'

[19] ILA 60th Report (1982), Art. 3(1). The ILA, founded in 1873, is a private organisation of lawyers whose objects include 'the study, elucidation and advancement of international law, public and private'. (Art. 2 of the ILA Constitution).

general obligation to refrain from causing pollution which might result in substantial injury is reinforced by Article 4, which provides, *inter alia*, that 'states shall refrain from causing transfrontier pollution by discharging into the environment substances generally considered as being highly dangerous to human health'.

The rule adopted by the IDI in its 1987 Resolution on Transboundary Air Pollution, which does not purport to restate custom, is less strict. Article 2 provides that:

> In the exercise of their sovereign right to exploit their resources pursuant to their own environmental policies, states shall be under a duty to take all appropriate and effective measures to ensure that their activities or those conducted within their jurisdiction or under their control cause no transboundary air pollution.[20]

With the ICJ's 1996 Advisory Opinion on nuclear weapons it is now clear that customary international law – as reflected in state practice, treaties and other international instruments – prohibits states from causing significant environmental damage from transboundary pollution, including atmospheric pollution.[21] The point is confirmed by the ILC's 2001 draft Articles on Prevention of Transboundary Harm.[22] One of the key issues which remains is the identification of the threshold at which significant, and therefore unlawful, damage has occurred. To a certain extent this aspect has been clarified by some of the treaties discussed in the following sections: those which set limits on the individual or collective emissions of certain substances also provide a basis for determining the level at which damage will be more than nominal and in respect of which an action lies under international law. More generally, the opportunity to further develop this issue, through state practice, following the accident at the Chernobyl plant, was lost as a result of the decision by affected states not to press any claim for damages, although several reserved their right to do so.[23]

Urban and transboundary air pollution

I. H. Van Lier, *Acid Rain and International Law* (1981); C. R. Bath, 'US–Mexico Experience in Managing Transboundary Air Resources: Problems, Prospects and Recommendations for the Future', 22 *Natural Resources Journal* 1197 (1982);

---

[20] 62 AIDI (1987-II), Art. 10 requires states to 'prohibit, prevent and refrain from carrying out any nuclear explosion likely to cause transboundary air pollution of a radioactive nature'. The Institut de Droit International, founded in 1873, is a private association of scholars of public and private international law which aims to facilitate the progress of international law (Art. 1(2) of the IDI Statute).

[21] Chapter 6, pp. 241–6 above.   [22] At draft Art. 3; see chapter 6, p. 234 above.

[23] Chapter 18, p. 890 below.

G. Wetstone and A. Rosencrantz, *Acid Rain in Europe and North America: National Responses to an International Problem* (1983); N. D. Bankes and J. Saunders, 'Acid Rain: Multilateral and Bilateral Approaches to Transboundary Pollution Under International Law', 33 *University of New Brunswick Law Journal* 155 (1984); J. Carroll, *Trans-boundary Air Quality Relations* (1990); S. Hajost, 'International Legal Implications of United States Policy on Acid Rain', in D. Magraw (ed.), *International Law and Pollution* (1991), 344; J. Lammers, 'The European Approach to Acid Rain', in D. Magraw (ed.), *International Law and Pollution* (1991), 265; P. Mercure, 'Principes de droit international applicables au phénomènes des pluies acides', 21 *Revue de Droit de l'Université de Sherbrooke* 373 (1991)

Anthropogenic emissions of gases that are prevalent worldwide, both as urban air pollutants and transboundary atmospheric depositions, include oxides of sulphur (SO_x), nitrogen oxides (NO_x), carbon monoxide (CO), ozone (O_3), trace organics (aldehydes, benzene and polyaromatic hydrocarbons), selected trace metals (most notably lead (Pb)) and suspended particulates,[24] as well as air pollution from ships.[25] Sulphur dioxide (SO_2), which is caused by the combustion of high-sulphur-content fossil fuels (coal and oil), contributes to acid rain and is harmful to human health as a potent respiratory tract irritant. Combustion of fossil fuels, particularly from motor vehicles and power stations, also produces two oxides of nitrogen (nitric oxide (NO) and nitrogen dioxide (NO_2), collectively known as NO_x). Ambient concentrations of NO_2 are generally considered to be too low to pose a significant threat to human health, but NO_x, together with hydrocarbons, are important precursors to the formation of tropospheric O_3 and other photochemical oxidants. Sulphur and nitrogen oxides are transported by prevailing winds for distances up to 1,000 km from their original source before returning to the surface of the earth as wet or dry deposits. Monitoring has established that North America and Europe receive fluxes of sulphur and nitrogen of up to ten times the estimated natural flux, and that adverse effects flowing from deposits include the acidification of fresh waters and terrestrial ecosystems. Although these problems have so far been limited to developed countries, there are indications that certain tropical regions in developing countries, including southern China, south-western India, south-eastern Brazil and northern Venezuela, may soon experience significant problems with acidification, in large part due to rapid industrialisation. The urban and transboundary air pollutants are subject to a number of regional arrangements, although outside Europe and North America there are few specific international arrangements.

---

[24] See UNEP, *Environmental Data Report* (1991), 10, 12 and 37–40.
[25] Chapter 9, p. 444 below.

ECE Regulations Concerning Gaseous Pollutant Emissions from Motor Vehicles

The ECE Regulations Concerning Gaseous Pollutant Emissions from Motor Vehicles have been adopted under the 1958 Agreement Concerning the Adoption of Uniform Technical Prescriptions for Wheeled Vehicles, Equipment and Parts Which Can Be Fitted and/or Be Used on Wheeled Vehicles and the Conditions for Reciprocal Recognition of Approvals Granted on the Basis of These Prescriptions.[26] The Regulations establish uniform conditions for the licensing of motor vehicles and parts as well as the standardisation of environmental specifications for cars. Regulations have been adopted for gasoline engines,[27] motorcycles and mopeds,[28] diesel engines,[29] and passenger cars equipped with internal combustion engines.[30] Compliance with the standards established under the Regulations ensures type approval for importation into many states.

The 1979 ECE Convention on Long Range Transboundary Air Pollution and its Protocols

R. Churchill, G. Kutting and L. Warren, 'The 1994 UNECE Sulphur Protocol', 7 *Journal of Environmental Law* 169 (1995); J. Wettestad, 'Science, Politics and Institutional Design: Some Initial Notes on the Long Range Transboundary Air Pollution Regime', 4 *Journal of Environment and Development* 165 (1995); J. Wettestad, *Acid Lessons? Assessing and Explaining LRTAP Implementation and Effectiveness* (IIASA Working Paper, 1996)

Introduction

The 1979 ECE Convention on Long-Range Transboundary Air Pollution (1979 LRTAP Convention)[31] addresses the growing problem of acid rain and was developed following the Stockholm Declaration, in particular Principle 21, and

---

[26] Geneva, 20 March 1958, in force 20 June 1959; 335 UNTS 211. The Convention was formerly called the Agreement Concerning the Adoption of Uniform Conditions of Approval and Reciprocal Recognition of Approval for Motor Vehicle Equipment and Parts.

[27] Regulation 83/1989, 1078 UNTS 351, as revised.

[28] Regulation 40/1979, 1144 UNTS 308; Regulation 47/1981, 1255 UNTS 158.

[29] Regulation 49/1982–90, UN Doc. E/ECE/324/Rev.1/Add.48/Rev.3; Regulation 96/1995, UN Doc. E/ECE/324/Rev.1/Add.95.

[30] Regulation 101/1997, UN Doc. E/ECE/324/Rev.2/Add.100.

[31] Geneva, 13 November 1979, in force 16 March 1983, 18 ILM 1442 (1979); www.unece.org/env/lrtap/. [000] states are parties to the Convention. See generally A. Rosencrantz, 'ECE Convention of 1979 on Long-Range Transboundary Air Pollution', 75 AJIL 975 (1981); A. Fraenkel, 'The Convention on Long-Range Transboundary Air Pollution: Meeting the Challenge of International Co-operation', 30 *Harvard International Law Journal* 447 (1989); Jackson, 'A Tenth Anniversary Review of the ECE Convention on Long-Range Transboundary Air Pollution', 2 *International Environmental Affairs* 217 (1990).

the environmental chapter of the Final Act of the 1975 Conference on Security and Co-operation in Europe (CSCE). The 1979 LRTAP Convention is supplemented by eight Protocols (on the financing of the monitoring programme, on the emissions of sulphur, nitrogen oxides, volatile organic compounds, heavy metals and persistent organic pollutants (POPs), and on abatement of acidification, eutrophication and ground-level ozone). It was one of the first treaties to recognise the adverse effects of air pollution over the short and long term.

1979 LRTAP Convention

The 1979 LRTAP Convention established a regional framework to protect man and the environment against air pollution, and includes a general obligation on parties to 'endeavour to limit and, as far as possible, gradually reduce and prevent air pollution including long-range transboundary air pollution'.[32] This soft commitment, which is without target or timetable, nevertheless establishes a general limitation on the right to emit atmospheric pollutants. The definitions set out in the Convention have been relied upon in other instruments. The definition of 'air pollution' is broad enough to include atmospheric emissions of greenhouse gases and ozone-depleting substances as 'air pollutants', although the use of the word 'resulting' suggests that actual deleterious effects must have occurred and that gases subject to precautionary measures of regulatory action in the absence of actual deleterious effects may not be considered to be pollutants.[33] 'Long-range transboundary air pollution' is defined as:

> air pollution whose physical origin is situated wholly or in part within the area under the national jurisdiction of one state and which has adverse effects in the area under the jurisdiction of another state at such a distance that it is not generally possible to distinguish the contribution of individual emission sources or groups of sources.[34]

The 1979 LRTAP Convention includes general commitments on policies and strategies to combat the discharge of air pollutants, the exchange of relevant information and review of policies, scientific activities and technical measures, and co-operation in research.[35] Consultations are to be held between parties actually affected by, or exposed to, a significant risk of long-range transboundary air pollution, and parties within which and subject to whose jurisdiction a significant contribution originates or could originate from activities carried on or contemplated.[36] While the requirement to consult may appear rather obvious now, it was, at the time, a notable development which influenced subsequent practice in related areas.[37]

Without being bound by any specific commitments for air quality management, the parties nevertheless must develop the best policies and strategies,

---

[32] Art. 2.   [33] Art. 1(a), chapter 1, pp. 6–8 above.   [34] Art. 1(b).
[35] Arts. 3, 4 and 7.   [36] Art. 5.   [37] Chapter 17, pp. 838–40 below.

including air quality management and control measures, in particular by using best available technology which is economically feasible, as well as low- and non-waste technology.[38] Information is to be exchanged on: the emission data of agreed air pollutants; major changes in policies and industrial development and their potential impact; control technologies; the costs of emission control; physico-chemical and biological data relating to the effects of long-range transboundary air pollution and the extent of the resulting damage; and policies and strategies for the control of sulphur compounds and other major oil pollutants.[39]

The LRTAP Convention also establishes a 'Co-operative Programme for the Monitoring and Evaluation of the Long-range Transmission of Air Pollutants in Europe' (EMEP), to monitor sulphur dioxide and related substances and to develop and use comparable or standardised monitoring procedures, and establish monitoring stations as part of an international programme.[40] Institutional arrangements comprise an Executive Body, composed of representatives of the parties to review implementation of the Convention, utilising EMEP's Steering Body, and assisted by the Executive Secretary of the UNECE which carries out secretariat functions.[41]

The 1979 LRTAP Convention has subsequently provided the forum for the adoption of eight protocols establishing more detailed commitments in relation to particular substances. It has also served as a model for subsequent treaties adopted at the global level to address climate change and ozone depletion, and provides a precedent for other regions in their efforts to address acid rain and related transboundary atmospheric problems.

1984 Monitoring and Evaluation Protocol

The first Protocol to the LRTAP Convention provides for 'Long-Term Financing of the Co-operative Programme for Monitoring and Evaluation of the Long-Range Transmission of Air Pollutants in Europe'.[42] It seeks to ensure the availability of adequate financial resources to implement EMEP beyond the amounts provided by UNEP and voluntary contributions. The 1984 Protocol provides for financing the costs of the international centres co-operating within EMEP

---

[38] Art. 6.

[39] Art. 8; this Article includes a footnote which states that '[t]he present Convention does not contain a rule on State Liability as to damage'.

[40] Art. 9.   [41] Arts. 10 and 11.

[42] Geneva, 28 September 1984, in force 28 January 1988, 2 SMTE 285; thirty-nine states are parties to the Protocol. Related international monitoring systems include WMO's Background Air Pollution Monitoring Network. The ECE has also established five International Co-operative Programmes on Assessment and Monitoring of Air Pollution Effects on Forests (1985); on Assessment and Monitoring of Acidification in Rivers and Lakes (1986); on Effects on Materials, Including Historic and Cultural Monuments (1986); on Research on Evaluating Effects of Air Pollution and Other Stresses on Agricultural Crops (1987); and on Integrated Monitoring (1988).

on the basis of mandatory contributions covering the annual costs of the EMEP work programme, supplemented by voluntary contributions.[43] The basis of annual contributions is set out in an Annex.[44]

1985 Sulphur Protocol

The second Protocol to the LRTAP Convention concerns the 'Reduction of Sulphur Emissions or Their Transboundary Fluxes by at Least 30 Per Cent' (1985 Sulphur Protocol).[45] It was adopted in response to evidence of widespread damage in parts of Europe and North America to natural resources, and to historical monuments and human health, caused by acidification of the environment from sulphur dioxide, nitrogen oxides and other pollutants from the combustion of fossil fuels. The 1985 Protocol establishes a 'Thirty Per Cent Club' by committing all parties to

> reduce their national annual sulphur emissions or their transboundary fluxes by at least thirty per cent as soon as possible and at the latest by 1993, using 1980 levels as the basis for calculation of reductions.[46]

This inflexible approach to standard-setting has not been adopted in the subsequent Protocols to the 1979 LRTAP Convention because it fails to take account of current and historic emissions and other differentials existing between states. The 1985 Sulphur Protocol envisages further reductions, and revisions were adopted in the 1994 Protocol on Further Reduction of Sulphur Emissions.[47] The 1985 Protocol requires parties to report annually to the Executive Body of the LRTAP Convention on their national, annual sulphur emissions, including the method of calculation, the progress made towards achieving targets (without specifying a particular timeframe), and the national programmes, policies and strategies adopted for reaching targets.[48] EMEP provides the Executive Body with information on annual sulphur budgets and transboundary fluxes and deposits of sulphur compounds.[49] The Protocol provides for the use of the institutional organs established under the 1979 LRTAP Convention. For EC member states, the Protocol has been superseded by the 1988 Large Combustion Directive.[50]

---

[43] Arts. 2 and 3(1), (2) and (4).   [44] Art. 4 and Annex.

[45] Helsinki, 8 July 1985, in force 2 September 1987; twenty-two states are parties to the Protocol; 27 ILM 707 (1988).

[46] Art. 2. To this end, parties agree to develop national programmes, policies and strategies: Art. 6.

[47] Oslo, 14 June 1994, in force 5 August 1998, 33 ILM 1540 (1994); twenty-eight states are parties to the Protocol.

[48] Arts. 4 and 6. On compliance with this reporting requirement, see chapter 5, pp. 180–2 above.

[49] Art. 5.   [50] See pp. 336–9 below.

1988 NO$_x$ Protocol

The third Protocol to the LRTAP Convention concerns the 'Control of Emissions of Nitrogen Oxides or Their Transboundary Fluxes' (1988 NO$_x$ Protocol).[51] It is more comprehensive and flexible than the 1985 Sulphur Protocol. It requires the reduction of 'total annual emissions', introducing into international law the concepts of 'national emission standards' and an approach based on 'critical loads aimed at the establishment of an effect-oriented scientific basis'. It also recognises the need to 'create more favourable conditions for exchange of technology'.[52] The 1988 NO$_x$ Protocol specifically requires all parties,

> as soon as possible and as a first step, [to] take effective measures to control and/or reduce their national annual emissions of nitrogen oxides or their transboundary fluxes so that these, at the latest by 31 December 1994, do not exceed their national annual emissions of nitrogen oxides or transboundary fluxes of such emissions for the calendar year 1987 or any previous year to be specified upon signature of, or accession to, the Protocol, provided that in addition, with respect to any party specifying such a previous year, its national average annual transboundary fluxes or national average annual emissions of nitrogen oxides for the period from 1 January 1987 to 1 January 1996 do not exceed its transboundary fluxes or national emissions for the calendar year 1987.[53]

All parties must apply national emission standards to new mobile sources in all major source categories, and introduce pollution control measures for major existing stationary sources.[54] National standards must be based on 'best available technologies which are economically feasible' and take into consideration (without being specifically bound by), *inter alia*, the Technical Annex to the Protocol.[55] The Technical Annex forms an integral part of the Protocol but is only recommendatory.[56] It provides guidance to the parties on identifying 'economically feasible technologies for giving effect to the obligations of the Protocol',[57] and on control technologies for nitrogen oxide emissions from stationary sources (combustion plants, gas turbines and internal combustion engines, industrial process furnaces, and non-combustion processes), as well as from cars.[58]

The parties to the 1988 NO$_x$ Protocol are required to take additional measures. Within six months of the entry into force of the Protocol they must

---

[51] Sofia, 31 October 1988, in force 14 February 1991; twenty-eight states are parties to the Protocol; 28 ILM 214 (1989).

[52] Preambular paras. 3, 6, 8 and 9.   [53] Art. 2(1).   [54] Art. 2(2)(a), (b) and (c).

[55] *Ibid.*   [56] Art. 10.   [57] Technical Annex, para. 2.

[58] The Technical Annex also provides Tables on Performance Standards that can be achieved by Combustion Modifications, Definition of Emission Standards, and Petrol Engine Technologies, Emission Performance, Costs and Fuel Consumption for Emission Standard Levels.

commence negotiations on further steps to reduce national annual emissions, taking into account the best available scientific and technological developments, internationally accepted critical loads, and other elements resulting from work programmes.[59] Parties must also co-operate to establish critical loads, reductions based on critical loads, and measures and a timetable commencing no later than 1 January 1996 for achieving such reductions.[60] Parties are free to adopt more stringent measures than those required by Article 2.[61]

The 1988 NO_x Protocol provides for the exchange of technology to reduce emissions, consistent with national laws, regulations and practices, and requires that unleaded fuel be made sufficiently available to facilitate the international circulation of vehicles equipped with catalytic converters.[62] The Protocol requires parties: to give high priority to research and monitoring through national research programmes and the work plan of the Executive Body; to develop national programmes, policies and strategies to control and reduce emissions under the Protocol; to participate in information exchange; and to report annually to the Executive Body on obligations under the Protocol (including, in particular, levels of national annual emissions, progress in applying national emission standards and on introducing pollution control measures, in making unleaded fuel available, and in establishing critical loads).[63] EMEP provides the Executive Body with calculations of nitrogen budgets, transboundary fluxes, and deposits of nitrogen oxides.[64] The Protocol is implemented under the authority of the institutions of the LRTAP Convention.

1991 Volatile Organic Compounds Protocol

The fourth Protocol addresses the 'Control of Emissions of Volatile Organic Compounds and Their Transboundary Fluxes' (1991 VOC Protocol).[65] Volatile organic compounds (VOCs) are mainly emitted through incomplete combustion of fossil fuels in the engines of motor vehicles,[66] and are released into the atmosphere due to evaporation during refining, distribution and use of petrol and during the use of products containing solvents like paints, glues and inks. In keeping with the developing complexity and sophistication of the earlier Protocols, the 1991 VOC Protocol builds significantly on the base provided by its earlier siblings, and establishes specific targets and timetables committing parties to control and reduce their emissions of VOCs. Unlike the earlier

---

[59] Art. 2(3)(a). 'Critical load' is defined as 'a quantitative estimate of the exposure to one or more pollutants below which significant harmful effects on specified sensitive elements of the environment do not occur according to present knowledge': Art. 1(7).

[60] Art. 2(3)(b).   [61] Art. 2(4).   [62] Arts. 3 and 4.

[63] Arts. 6, 7 and 8.   [64] Art. 9.

[65] Geneva, 18 November 1991, in force 29 September 1997; 31 ILM 568 (1992); twenty-one states are parties to the Protocol.

[66] VOCs are defined, unless otherwise specified, as 'all organic compounds of anthropogenic nature, other than methane, that are capable of producing photochemical oxidants by reactions with nitrogen oxides in the presence of sunlight': Art. 1(9).

LRTAP Protocols the parties have a choice of at least three ways to meet this requirement, to be specified upon signature. This reflects the need to adopt differentiated commitments based on a party's emissions and particular geographic and demographic circumstances. The first option is for a party simply to

> take effective measures to reduce its national annual emissions of VOCs by at least thirty per cent by the year 1999, using 1988 levels as a basis or any other annual level during the period 1984 to 1990, which it may specify upon signature of or accession to the present Protocol.[67]

The second option is only available to a party whose annual emissions contribute to tropospheric ozone concentrations in areas under the jurisdiction of one or more other parties, and where such emissions originate only from areas under its jurisdiction that are specified as tropospheric ozone management areas (TOMA) under Annex 1 to the Protocol.[68] A party which chooses this option is required to:

1. reduce its annual emissions of VOCs from the areas so specified by at least 30 per cent by the year 1999, using 1988 levels as a basis or any other annual level during the period 1984–90, which it may specify upon signature of or accession to the present Protocol; and
2. ensure that its total national annual emissions of VOCs by the year 1999 do not exceed the 1988 levels.[69]

The third option is only available to a party whose annual emissions of VOCs in 1988 were lower than 500,000 tonnes and 20 kilogrammes per inhabitant and 5 tonnes per square kilometre. Such a party may opt as soon as possible, and as a first step, to 'take effective measures to ensure at least that at the latest by the year 1999 its annual emissions of VOCs do not exceed the 1988 levels'.[70] Of the states which have signed the Protocol, three chose the option under Article 2(2)(c),[71] three chose the option under Article 2(2)(b)[72] and sixteen chose the option under Article 2(2)(a).[73] One state apparently failed to make the choice.

No later than two years after the Protocol entered into force, each party was required to apply appropriate national or international emissions standards to new stationary sources based on the 'best available technologies which are economically feasible' (BATEF), to apply national or international

---

[67] Art. 2(2)(a).

[68] Art. 2(2)(b). Currently, Canada has designated two TOMAs within its territory, and Norway has designated the whole of its mainland and parts of its exclusive economic zone as TOMAs: Annex I.

[69] *Ibid.*   [70] Art. 2(2)(c).   [71] Bulgaria, Greece and Hungary.

[72] Canada (1988 base year), Norway (1989 base year) and Ukraine.

[73] Two taking 1990 as a base year, ten taking 1988 as a base year, one taking 1985 as a base year, and three taking 1984 as a base year.

measures to products that contain solvents and to promote the use of labelling of products specifying their VOC content, taking into consideration Annex II. Within the same timeframe the parties were required to 'apply appropriate national or international emission standards to new mobile sources based on best available technologies which are economically feasible, taking into consideration Annex II,[74] and encourage further public participation in emission control programmes, as well as the best use of all modes of transport and the promotion of traffic management schemes.[75]

No later than five years after the provision entered into force, in areas where international tropospheric ozone standards are exceeded or where transboundary fluxes originate or are expected to originate, each party must apply BATEF to existing stationary sources in major source categories, taking into consideration Annex II; each party must also apply techniques to reduce VOC emissions from petrol distribution sources and motor vehicle refuelling operations, and to reduce the volatility of petrol, taking into consideration Annexes II and III.[76] The Protocol requires that high priority be given to reducing and controlling emissions of substances with the greatest photochemical ozone creation potential, taking into consideration Annex IV, and that states ensure that in product-substitution measures they do not substitute toxic and carcinogenic VOCs and those that harm the stratospheric ozone layer for other VOCs.[77] This last requirement amounts to a requirement that an environmental and health assessment of substitute products be carried out; this is an innovative provision that may influence future international agreements.

Within six months of the Protocol entering into force, the parties were required to commence negotiations on further steps to reduce national annual emissions of VOCs or transboundary fluxes of such emissions and the resulting secondary photochemical oxidant products. They must also co-operate to develop, *inter alia*, control strategies; ensure cost-effectiveness, possibly through the use of economic instruments; and adopt measures and a timetable commencing no later than 1 January 2000 for achieving such reductions.[78] Parties are free to take more stringent measures, and are not relieved by the Protocol from obligations to reduce emissions that may contribute significantly to climate change, the formation of tropospheric background ozone or the depletion of stratospheric ozone, or that are toxic or carcinogenic.[79] The Protocol provides for the exchange of technology, research and monitoring, regular

---

[74] Art. 2(3)(a)(i) and (ii). Annex II establishes Control Measures for Emissions of VOCs from Stationary Sources.

[75] Art. 2(3)(a)(iii) and (iv). Annex III establishes control measures for Emissions of VOCs from on-road motor vehicles.

[76] Art. 2(3)(b).

[77] Art. 2(4) and (5). Annex IV provides classification of VOCs based on their 'motorchemical ozone creation potential'.

[78] Art. 2(6) and (7).   [79] Art. 3(1) and (2).

review and the establishment of national programmes, policies and strategies.[80] Implementation of the Protocol will be verified by the exchange of information and annual reporting requirements; alternatively, the parties undertake to establish a 'mechanism for monitoring compliance' with the Protocol.[81] Once again, the Protocol makes use of the institutions established under the 1979 LRTAP Convention.

1994 Sulphur Protocol

Negotiations under the auspices of the 1985 Sulphur Protocol resulted in the conclusion of the 1994 Oslo Protocol on Further Reduction of Sulphur Emissions, which entered into force on 5 August 1998. Like its predecessor, the 1994 Protocol contemplates future negotiations on further obligations to reduce sulphur emissions.[82] The 1994 Protocol applies and develops the concepts of 'critical loads' and the 'effects-based approach' introduced in the 1988 NO_x Protocol. The basic obligation to which the Parties commit is to

> control and reduce their sulphur emissions in order to protect human health and the environment from adverse effects, in particular acidifying effects, and to ensure, as far as possible, without entailing excessive costs, that depositions of oxidised sulphur compounds in the long term do not exceed critical loads for sulphur given, in annex I, as critical sulphur depositions, in accordance with present scientific knowledge.[83]

The 'critical loads' for sulphur are intended as long-term targets for reductions in sulphur emissions and it is recognised that they will not be reached in a single step. Instead, as a first step, parties are required to meet the targets and timetable for reductions of sulphur emissions specified in Annex II.[84] In line with an effects-based approach, the emission reduction obligations of parties are differentiated, with greater emissions reductions allocated to those countries where the overall benefit would be the greatest.

The Protocol requires the parties to make use of the 'most effective measures for the reduction of sulphur emissions' from new and existing sources, including controlling the sulphur content of fuel, energy efficient measures, promotion of renewable energy and the application of best available control technologies using the guidance provided in Annex IV to the Protocol.[85] The Protocol also permits the parties to apply economic instruments to encourage the adoption of cost-effective approaches to the reduction of sulphur emissions, and to enter into agreements for the joint implementation of the Protocol with other parties.[86]

All parties (other than the United States and Canada) must apply national emissions limits to major new stationary sources, and introduce pollution

---

[80] Arts. 4 to 7.   [81] Arts. 3(3) and 8.   [82] Art. 2(8).   [83] Art. 2(1).
[84] Art. 2(2) and (3).   [85] Art. 2(4).   [86] Art. 2(6) and (7).

control measures for major existing stationary sources by 1 July 2004.[87] Parties were also required to apply national standards for the sulphur content of gas oil no later than two years after the Protocol entered into force.[88]

Parties are required to implement their basic obligations under Article 2 through the adoption of national strategies, policies and programmes and by taking and applying national measures to control and reduce sulphur emissions.[89] Each party must collect and maintain information on actual levels of sulphur emissions, and of ambient concentrations and depositions of oxidised sulphur and other acidifying compounds; and on the effects of depositions of oxidised sulphur and other acidifying compounds.[90] The Protocol requires periodic reporting to the Executive Body on national implementation measures and the levels of national annual sulphur emissions.[91]

The Protocol requires parties to facilitate the exchange of technologies and techniques for reducing sulphur emissions. The Protocol also encourages research, development, monitoring and co-operation in respect of various matters relating to: the harmonisation of methods for the establishment of critical loads; the improvement of monitoring techniques and modelling systems; the development of strategies for the further reduction of sulphur emissions; the understanding of the wider effects of sulphur emissions on human health and the environment; emission abatement and energy efficiency technologies; and the economic evaluation of benefits for the environment and human health resulting from the reduction of sulphur emissions.[92]

Like the other Protocols, the 1994 Protocol makes use of the institutions established under the 1979 LRTAP Convention. Article 7 contemplates the establishment of a new body, an Implementation Committee, to oversee compliance.[93] In 1998, the parties to the 1994 Protocol decided that the structure, functions and procedures of the Implementation Committee should be those set out Decision 1997/2 of the Executive Body.[94] The Implementation Committee now oversees compliance with all of the Protocols to the LRTAP Convention.

1998 Aarhus Protocol on Heavy Metals

The 1998 Heavy Metals Protocol was adopted in Aarhus on 24 June 1998.[95] It targets three particularly harmful heavy metals – lead, cadmium and mercury – and requires parties to reduce their emissions of these metals below the levels in a selected reference year (between 1985 and 1995).[96] The Protocol aims to reduce

---

[87] Art. 2(5)(a) and (b); emissions limits are specified in Annex V.
[88] Art. 2(5)(c).   [89] Art. 4(1).   [90] Art. 4(2).
[91] Art. 5.   [92] Arts. 3 and 6.   [93] Chapter 5, p. 178 above.
[94] Decision 1998/6, The Application of the Compliance Procedure to the Oslo Protocol (ECE/EB.AIR/59, Annex II).
[95] Aarhus, 24 June 1998, not in force; thirty-six signatories and thirteen ratifications.
[96] Art. 3(1) and Annex I.

emissions of heavy metals from industrial sources, combustion processes and waste incineration. Parties are required to implement emission standards for these pollutants for stationary sources, based on the best available technologies suggested in the Protocol.[97] In addition, parties undertake to phase out the use of leaded petrol and to introduce measures designed to lower heavy metal emissions from other products.[98] A number of other product management measures are proposed for products containing mercury.[99]

Parties are to develop strategies, policies and programmes, without undue delay, to discharge their obligations under the Protocol. A range of measures are suggested for this purpose, including economic instruments, government/industry covenants and voluntary agreements, more efficient use of resources, use of less polluting sources, development of a less polluting transport system, phasing out certain polluting industrial processes and developing cleaner processes. Parties are free to adopt more stringent measures than those required by the Protocol.[100] As for the other Protocols, the Heavy Metals Protocol promotes technology exchange and other forms of co-operation between the parties.[101] Parties must report periodically to the Executive Body on measures taken to implement the Protocol, with compliance overseen by the Implementation Committee.[102]

1998 Aarhus Protocol on Persistent Organic Pollutants

The Protocol on Persistent Organic Pollutants (POPs) was adopted by the Executive Body at the same time as the Heavy Metals Protocol.[103] Its ultimate objective is to eliminate discharges, emissions and losses of POPs to the atmosphere. The Protocol focuses on a list of sixteen substances (including pesticides, industrial chemicals and contaminants) singled out according to agreed risk criteria. Parties to the Protocol undertake to eliminate the production and use of certain POPs listed in Annex I and to restrict the use of other substances listed in Annex II.[104] For a third group of POPs listed in Annex III, parties are required to reduce their emissions of these substances from the level of emissions in a given reference year (between 1985 and 1995).[105] For emissions of dioxins and furans, parties are required to apply emissions limits, based on best available technologies, for new and existing stationary sources, and must take effective measures to control emissions of POPs from mobile sources.[106]

The Protocol includes provisions dealing with the disposal of wastes containing or generated from listed substances.[107] Parties are to ensure the

---

[97] Art. 3(2) and Annex III.   [98] Art. 3(3) and Annex VI.   [99] Art. 3(4) and Annex VII.
[100] Art. 5.   [101] Arts. 4 and 6.   [102] Arts. 7 and 9.
[103] Aarhus, 24 June 1998, not yet in force; thirty-six signatories and thirteen ratifications.
[104] Art. 3(1). Parties may grant exemptions from these requirements for research purposes or in the event of a public health emergency: see Art. 4.
[105] Art. 3(5)(a).   [106] Art. 3(5)(b) and Annexes IV and V.   [107] Art. 3(1) and (3).

environmentally sound destruction and disposal of these wastes. For Annex I substances, domestic disposal should take place where possible, and any transboundary movement of these wastes should be in accordance with applicable subregional, regional and global regimes governing the transboundary movement of hazardous wastes, in particular the 1989 Basel Convention. Parties are to: develop strategies, policies and programmes to discharge their obligations under the Protocol; promote the provision of information to the general public, including individuals who are direct users of POPs; facilitate the exchange of technology and information; and engage in co-operative research, development and monitoring in relation to POPs.[108] Parties must report periodically to the Executive Body on measures taken to implement the Protocol, with compliance overseen by the Implementation Committee.[109]

1999 Gothenburg Protocol to Abate Acidification, Eutrophication and Ground-Level Ozone

The most recent Protocol to the LRTAP Convention is the 1999 Gothenburg Protocol to Abate Acidification, Eutrophication and Ground-Level Ozone, adopted by the Executive Body on 30 November 1999.[110] The Protocol's objective is to control and reduce anthropogenic emissions of four pollutants – sulphur, NO_x, ammonia and VOCs – which are likely to cause adverse effects on human health, natural ecosystems, materials and crops due to acidification, eutrophication or ground-level ozone.[111] Following full implementation of the Protocol, it is estimated that the area in Europe with excessive levels of acidification will shrink from 93 million hectares (measured in 1990) to 15 million hectares. Similarly excessive levels of eutrophication are expected to fall from 165 million hectares (in 1990) to 108 million hectares and the number of days with excessive ozone levels to be halved.

The Protocol builds on the previous sulphur, NO_x and VOC Protocols, employing a range of mechanisms to reduce atmospheric emissions of the four types of pollutants. On a long-term step-wise basis, the parties commit to ensuring that atmospheric depositions or concentrations of the pollutants do not exceed the critical loads of acidity, nutrient nitrogen and ozone specified in Annex I to the Protocol.[112] Annex II sets emissions ceilings for sulphur, NO_x, VOCs and ammonia which parties are required to attain by 2010. Required emissions reductions are differentiated between the parties on the basis that parties whose emissions have more severe environmental or health impacts and which are relatively inexpensive to reduce will be required to make the largest cuts. In addition, the Protocol sets tight limit values for

---

[108] Arts. 5–8.   [109] Arts. 9 and 11.
[110] Gothenburg (Sweden), 30 November 1999 (not yet in force); thirty-one signatories and four ratifications.
[111] Art. 2.   [112] *Ibid.*

specific emission sources, fuels and new mobile sources, and requires the best available technologies to be used to minimise emissions.[113] Guidance documents adopted together with the Protocol provide details of a wide range of abatement techniques and economic instruments for the reduction of emissions in relevant sectors, including the transport sector.[114]

The Protocol is the first agreement under the Convention to deal specifically with emissions of reduced nitrogen compounds (ammonia), which are particularly associated with farming activities. Parties will be required to: apply ammonia control measures including developing advisory codes of good agricultural practice to control ammonia emissions; take such steps as are feasible to limit ammonia emissions from the use of solid fertilisers based on urea; and implement control measures with respect to manure application and storage, and animal housing.[115]

Once again, parties are required: to develop strategies, policies and programmes to discharge their obligations under the Protocol; to promote the provision of information to the general public; to facilitate the exchange of technology and information; and to engage in co-operative research, development and monitoring.[116] Parties must report periodically to the Executive Body on measures taken to implement the Protocol, with compliance overseen by the Implementation Committee.[117]

1988/2001 EC Large Combustion Directive

The EC has adopted a significant body of secondary legislation aimed at limiting and reducing atmospheric emissions.[118] Of particular note was the 1988 EC Large Combustion Directive, which allocated anthropogenic emissions rights to each of the member states for sulphur dioxide, nitrogen oxides and dust particles from large combustion plants.[119] From 1994, the Directive also applied to six EFTA member countries under the 1992 EEA Agreement.[120] With effect from 27 November 2002, Directive 88/609/EEC was repealed by Directive 2001/80/EC, which is intended to 'recast' Directive 88/609 'in the interests of clarity'.[121]

---

[113] Art. 3(2)–(6).
[114] Decision 1999/1, The Guidance Documents for the Protocol to Abate Acidification, Eutrophication and Ground-Level Ozone (ECE/EB.AIR/68, Annex I).
[115] Art. 3(8) and Annex IX.   [116] Arts. 4–6 and 8.
[117] Arts. 7 and 9.   [118] Chapter 15, pp. 755–68 below.
[119] Council Directive 88/609/EEC of 24 November 1988 on the limitation of emissions of certain pollutants into the air from large combustion plants, as amended, OJ L336, 7 December 1988, 1. A 'large' combustion plant is one with a rated thermal input equal to or greater than 50 MW: Art. 1.
[120] Chapter 15, p. 747 below.
[121] Directive 2001/80/EC on the limitation of emissions of certain pollutants into the air from large combustion plants, OJ L309, 27 November 2001, 1.

Like its predecessor, the new Directive distinguishes between existing and new plants, but excludes a smaller category of plants.[122]

Existing plant emissions of sulphur dioxide and nitrogen oxides

In accordance with Directive 88/609, member states determined their total annual emissions and drew up programmes for the reduction of such emissions from existing plants. Directive 88/609 set emissions ceilings and percentage reductions on the basis of 1980 emissions levels, which each member state was required to meet by 1993, 1998 and 2003 for sulphur dioxide, and by 1993 and 1998 for nitrogen oxides.[123] These target figures were reviewed by the EC Commission after 1994,[124] which involved lengthy negotiations which raised many of the issues faced by the rest of the international community in applying the principle of 'common but differentiated responsibility' under the 1992 Climate Change Convention and its 1997 Kyoto Protocol. The targets took into account the different capabilities of states. For sulphur dioxide, four of the economically wealthier member states (Belgium, Germany, France and the Netherlands) had to reduce their emissions of sulphur dioxide from existing plants by 70 per cent of 1980 levels by 2003, while three of the economically poorer southern member states (Greece, Ireland and Portugal) were allowed to increase their emissions over the same period by 6 per cent, 25 per cent and 79 per cent respectively. The other five member states were to reduce emissions by between 37 per cent and 67 per cent by 2003. For nitrogen oxides, the requirements ranged from a reduction of 40 per cent of 1980 levels by 1998, to permitted increases of up to 178 per cent.

Directive 2001/80 retains the emission ceilings, percentage reductions and targets for existing plants set by the 1988 Directive.[125] For sulphur dioxide, seven states now have to reduce their emissions from existing plants by 70 per cent of 1980 levels by 2003, with Austria, Finland and Sweden added to this group. Sulphur dioxide emission reduction targets for 2003 for the other member states have not been altered. The targets in the 1988 Directive for nitrous oxides also remain unchanged.

Directive 2001/80 introduces a new requirement for member states to achieve 'significant emission reductions' from existing plants. This obligation may be met either by the member state taking appropriate measures to ensure that licences for the operation of existing plants contain conditions requiring

---

[122] Art. 2(7) (for example, gas turbines licensed after 27 November 2002). An 'existing plant' is one for which the original construction licence or original operating licence was granted before 1 July 1987, and a 'new plant' is one for which such licences were granted after 1 July 1987: Art. 2(9) and (10).

[123] Directive 88/609, Art. 3(1), (2) and (3), Annex I and Annex IX.C. See also the emissions reductions set by the 1992 EEA Agreement for the EFTA member countries; see chapter 15, p. 747 below; Annex XX, para. 19.

[124] Art. 3(4).   [125] Directive 2001/80, Art. 3(2).

compliance with the same emission limit values as apply to new plants for which a licence application was lodged prior to 27 November 2002 and which were put into operation by 27 November 2003, or by ensuring that existing plants are subject to a national emission reduction plan.[126] If a member state chooses the latter option, it must design and implement a national emission reduction plan which will reduce the total annual emissions of nitrogen oxides, sulphur dioxide and dust from existing plants to the levels that would have been achieved by applying to the existing plants in operation in the year 2000 the emission limit values for new plants for which a licence application was lodged prior to 27 November 2002 and which were put into operation by 27 November 2003. The closure of a plant included in the national emissions reduction plan cannot result in an increase in the total annual emissions from the remaining plants covered by the plan. The national emissions reduction plans must comprise: objectives and related targets; measures and timetables for reaching the objectives and targets; and a monitoring mechanism. Member states are to communicate their national emission reduction plans to the EC Commission by no later than 27 November 2003.[127]

New plant emissions of sulphur dioxide, nitrogen oxides and dust

In respect of new plants, Directive 88/609 required member states to ensure that licences for their construction or operation included conditions giving effect to the emissions limit values fixed in Annexes III to VII to the Directive for sulphur dioxide, nitrogen oxides and dust.[128] The applicable emissions limit values depended upon the type of fuel used (solid, liquid or gaseous) and the output of the plant. Member states were free to impose more stringent requirements, including the addition of other pollutants.[129]

Directive 2001/80 distinguishes two categories of new plants. For new plants for which a full request for a licence was made prior to 27 November 2002, and which are put into operation no later than 27 November 2003, member states in licensing such plants are to impose conditions relating to compliance with the emissions limit values laid down in Part A of Annexes III to VII to the Directive.[130] Like the emissions limit values under the 1988 Directive, the values under the 2001 Directive depend upon the type of fuel used and the output of the plant. For all other new plants, member states must take appropriate measures to ensure that the relevant licences contain conditions requiring compliance with the more stringent emissions limit values laid down in Part B of Annexes III to VII.[131] Where a combustion plant is extended by at least 50MW, the more stringent emissions limit values apply to the new part of the plant and must be fixed in relation to the thermal capacity of the entire plant.[132] Once again, member states are free to impose more stringent requirements on new

---

[126] Art. 4(3).   [127] Art. 4(6).   [128] Directive 88/609, Art. 4(1).
[129] Art. 4(2) and (3).   [130] Directive 2001/80, Art. 4(1).   [131] Art. 4(2).   [132] Art. 10.

plants, including the addition of other pollutants, additional requirements or adaptation of the plant to technical progress.[133] In the case of construction of a combustion plant which is likely to have significant effects on the environment in another member state, the authorising member state is under an obligation to ensure that all appropriate information and consultation takes place in accordance with Council Directive 85/337/EEC on environmental impact assessment.[134]

Like the previous Directive, Directive 2001/80 provides for derogations, the occurrence of malfunction or breakdown of pollution abatement equipment, the establishment of emissions limits for multi-firing plants using two or more fuels, and the use of emission stacks.[135] National authorities are responsible for ensuring that the monitoring of emissions is carried out by operators, and that the EC Commission receives regular reports on the implementation of the Directive.[136] By 31 December 2004 at the latest, the Commission must submit a report to the European Parliament and the Council assessing the need for further emissions reduction measures, taking into account factors such as the cost-effectiveness of further reductions, their technical and economic feasibility and the effects on the environment and the internal market.[137] The 1988 and 2001 Directives have had important consequences for the choice of fuel supply used by electricity generating utilities. In the United Kingdom, for example, the costs associated with implementing the Directives, and in particular the cost of fitting flue gas desulphurisation (FGD) equipment on coal-fired plants, has contributed to the move away from coal-fired power plants to natural-gas-fired plants, and a consequential decline in the UK coal industry.

1991 Canada–US Air Quality Agreement

E. G. Lee, 'International Law and the Canada–United States Acid Rain Dispute', in D. Magraw (ed.), *International Law and Pollution* (1991), 322.

The 1991 Agreement Between the United States of America and Canada on Air Quality (1991 Canada–US Air Quality Agreement)[138] is designed to control transboundary air pollution between the two countries and provide a framework for addressing shared concerns.[139] The Agreement followed disputes over responsibility for causing acid rain, an issue which dates back at least to the 1930s and the differences over the sulphur emissions from the Trail Smelter.[140] At the heart of the Agreement are air quality objectives to limit and reduce

---

[133] Art. 4(5).   [134] Art. 11.   [135] Arts. 5, 7, 8 and 9.
[136] Arts. 12, 13 and 15.   [137] Art. 4(7).
[138] Ottawa, 13 March 1991, in force 13 March 1991, 30 ILM 676 (1991).
[139] Arts. II and III(1). 'Air pollution' is defined in similar terms to the definition in the 1979 LRTAP Agreement except for the exclusion of 'energy': Art. I(1).
[140] See below.

emissions of sulphur dioxide and nitrogen oxides and to prevent air quality deterioration and visibility protection.[141] The 1991 Agreement also requires compliance monitoring by continuous emissions monitoring systems or their equivalent for certain utilities and comparably effective methods of emissions estimation from other major stationary sources.[142] Since February 2000, the parties have been negotiating an Ozone Annex to the Agreement designed to reduce transboundary flows of ground-level ozone, one of the main contributors to smog.[143]

Sulphur dioxide

The United States is obliged to reduce its annual sulphur dioxide emissions by approximately 10 million tons from 1980 levels by the year 2000, in accordance with its own national legislation (1990 Clean Air Act), to achieve a permanent national emissions cap of 8.95 million tons of sulphur dioxide per year for electric utilities by 2010. It must also adopt new or revised standards as the Administrator of the Environmental Protection Agency deems appropriate, aimed at limiting sulphur dioxide emissions from industrial sources in the event that they may be expected to exceed 5.6 million tons per year.[144] For its part, Canada agrees to reduce sulphur dioxide emissions in its seven easternmost provinces to 2.3 million tonnes per year by 1994 and to establish a cap on emissions from those provinces of 2.3 million tonnes per year from 1995 to 31 December 1999, and a permanent national emissions cap of 3.2 million tonnes per year by 2000.[145]

Nitrogen oxides

The United States must reduce the total annual emissions of nitrogen oxides by approximately 2 million tons from 1980 emission levels by 2000. This is to be achieved through controls on stationary sources (establishing emissions standards for electric utility boilers) and mobile sources (emissions standards from old and new light duty trucks, light duty vehicles and heavy duty trucks).[146] Canada agrees as an interim requirement to reduce by the year 2000 annual national emissions from stationary sources by 100,000 tonnes below its forecast level of 970,000 tonnes for the year 2000, to develop by 1 January 1995 further national annual emissions reduction requirements from stationary sources to be achieved by 2000 and/or 2005, and to limit emissions from mobile sources by adopting specified emissions standards (for light, medium and heavy duty vehicles).[147]

---

[141] Art. IV(2) and Annex 1, Section 4.   [142] Annex I, Section 3.
[143] For details of the parties' negotiations, see www.can-am.gc.ca/menu-e.asp?mid= 1&cat=11#air/.
[144] Annex I, Section 1A.   [145] Annex I, Section 1B. 1 ton – 0.91 tonnes (metric tons).
[146] Annex I, Section 2A.   [147] Annex I, Section 2B.

Assessment, information and institutions

The 1991 Agreement requires assessment of proposed activities likely to cause significant transboundary air pollution, notification and consultation, and measures must be taken to avoid or mitigate the risks posed by actions likely to cause significant transboundary air pollution.[148] It also provides for research, the exchange of information, and other consultations.[149] A bilateral Air Quality Committee is established to prepare progress reports, and the International Joint Commission assists the parties in implementation, by receiving public comments and dealing with other requests from the parties.[150] The Agreement envisages a role for the public and interested organisations in assessing reports and implementing the Agreement.[151]

Aircraft emissions: ICAO Convention

Aircraft emissions are now known to be making a significant contribution to global atmospheric problems.[152] Annex 16 to the 1944 Convention on International Civil Aviation establishes rules on 'Environmental Protection Relating to Aircraft Noise[153] and Aircraft Engine Emissions' (1980 ICAO Aircraft Emissions Standards and Recommended Practices).[154] The Standards were adopted by the ICAO Council in 1980, following proposals to develop Standards and Recommended Practices to achieve 'maximum compatibility between the safe and orderly development of civil aviation and the quality of human environment'.[155]

The 1980 ICAO Aircraft Emissions Standards and Recommended Practices were adopted under Article 37 of the ICAO Convention, which requires contracting states

---

[148] Art. V.   [149] Arts. VI, VII and XI and Annex 2.

[150] Arts. VIII and IX.   [151] Art. XIV(3).

[152] For a recent assessment, see the *Special Report on Aviation and the Global Atmosphere* (1999) prepared at ICAO's request by the IPCC in collaboration with the Scientific Assessment Panel to the Montreal Protocol (available at www.grida.no/climate/ipcc/aviation/index.htm). See also ICAO Resolution A33-7 (2001), 'Consolidated Statement of Continuing ICAO Policies and Practices Related to Environmental Protection', at Annex H.

[153] ICAO, International Standards and Recommended Practices, Environmental Protection, Annex 16 to the 1944 ICAO Convention, vol. I (1988, 2nd edn), as amended.

[154] ICAO, International Standards and Recommended Practices, Environmental Protection, Annex 16 to the 1944 ICAO Convention, vol. II (1980, 1st edn), as amended. A 'Consolidated Statement of Continuing Policies and Practices Related to Environmental Protection' is revised and updated by the ICAO Council every three years for adoption by the ICAO Assembly. The present version, Assembly Resolution A32-8, was adopted in October 1998.

[155] ICAO Assembly Resolution A18-11, para. 2.

> to collaborate in securing the highest practicable degree of uniformity in regulations, standards, procedures and organisation . . . in all matters in which such uniformity will facilitate and improve air navigation.

Where a state finds it 'impracticable' to comply with an international standard, it must, under Article 38, immediately notify the ICAO of the differences between its own practices and those established by the international standard. For the Emission Standards, eleven of the 187 contracting states to the ICAO had notified differences. The Emissions Standards establish rules for vented fuel (Part II) and emission centrification (Part III), including emissions limits for smoke, hydrocarbons, carbon monoxide and oxides of nitrogens for subsonic and supersonic aircraft,[156] and standard techniques for measurement and evaluation, and compliance procedures.[157] In recent years, the ICAO has begun to address the impacts of the aviation industry on climate change.[158]

Ozone depletion

J. Temple Lang, 'The Ozone Layer Convention: A New Solution to the Question of Community Participation in "Mixed" International Agreements', 23 *Common Market Law Review* 157 (1986); J. Lammers, 'Efforts to Develop a Protocol on Chlorofluorocarbons to the Vienna Convention for the Protection of the Ozone Layer', 1 *Hague Yearbook of International Law* 255 (1988); J. Tripp, 'The UNEP Montreal Protocol: Industrialised and Developing Countries Sharing the Responsibility for Protecting the Stratospheric Ozone Layer', 20 *New York University Journal of International Law and Policy* 733 (1988); J. Kindt and S. Menefee, 'The Vexing Problem of Ozone Depletion in International Environmental Law and Policy', 24 *Texas International Law Journal* 261 (1989); C. Granda, 'The Montreal Protocol on Substances that Deplete the Ozone Layer', in L. Susskind and J. W. Breslin (eds.), *Nine Case Studies in International Environmental Negotiation* (1990); D. Caron, 'La Protection de la couche d'ozone stratosphérique et la structure de l'activité normative internationale en matière d'environnement', AFDI 704 (1990); D. Caron, 'Protection of Stratospheric Ozone Layer and the Structure of International Environmental Law-Making', 14 *Hastings International and Comparative Law Review* 755 (1991); Mintz, 'Progress Towards a Healthy Sky: An Assessment of the London Amendments to the Montreal Protocol on Substances that Deplete the Ozone Layer', 16 *Yale Journal of International Law* 571 (1991); P. Haas, 'Banning Chlorofluorocarbons: Epistemic Community Efforts to Protect Stratospheric Ozone', 46 *International*

---

[156] Sections 2.2, 2.3, 3.2 and 3.3.   [157] Appendix 6.

[158] See IPCC, *Special Report on Aviation and the Global Atmosphere* (1999); see also ICAO Assembly Resolution A33-7, resolving to promote scientific research aimed at addressing uncertainties and requesting the ICAO Council to continue to co-operate closely with the IPCC and other organizations involved in the definition of aviation's contribution to environmental problems in the atmosphere.

Organization 187 (1992); D. Brack, *International Trade and the Montreal Protocol* (1996); R. E. Benedick, *Ozone Diplomacy* (1998, 2nd edn); UNEP, *Handbook for the Montreal Protocol on Substances that Deplete the Ozone Layer* (2000, 5th edn); F. S. Rowland, 'Atmospheric Changes Caused by Human Activities: From Science to Regulation', 27 *Ecology Law Quarterly* 1261 (2001); O. Yoshida, *The International Legal Regime for the Protection of the Stratospheric Ozone Layer* (2001). Website: www.unep.org/ozone/index.shtml

The ozone layer comprises a sheet of O_3 molecules (ozone) that are found in the earth. Ninety per cent of atmospheric O_3 is found in the stratosphere, with maximum concentrations occurring at altitudes of 25 kms over the equator and 15 kms over the poles. The ozone layer is thought to provide a shield against harmful exposure to ultraviolet radiation from the sun and control the temperature structure of the stratosphere. O_3 also acts as a greenhouse gas at lower altitude, is a respiratory irritant, and can adversely affect plant growth.[159] Since the 1960s, there have been losses in the ozone layer over the Antarctic during the southern hemisphere spring (September–October), and more recently a hole has appeared in the ozone layer above the Arctic. Since then, significant thinning has also been discovered in the northern hemisphere and ozone depletion has become progressively greater over the course of the 1990s. Serious levels of UVB radiation have been observed over Antarctica, Australia and mountainous regions of Europe, and damage to phytoplankton has been discovered in Antarctica.[160]

The depletion of the ozone layer is caused by the anthropogenic emission of certain inert gases, particularly chlorofluorocarbons (CFCs) and halons. When these gases reach the ozone layer, they are exposed to ultraviolet rays and break down, releasing free chlorine (from CFCs) and bromine (from halons), which break up the ozone molecules and deplete the ozone layer. Increased levels of ultraviolet rays are thought to cause harm to human health and the environment, including organisms in the marine environment. CFCs are used extensively as refrigerants, air conditioner coolants, aerosol spray-can ingredients and in the manufacture of styrofoam.

The protection of the ozone layer from these destructive elements is the subject of a complex legal regime comprising the 1985 Vienna Convention for the Protection of the Ozone Layer (the 1985 Vienna Convention),[161] and the 1987 Montreal Protocol on Substances that Deplete the Ozone Layer (the 1987

---

[159] UNEP, *Environmental Data Report* (1991), 9.

[160] Statement from the Co-Chair of the Ozone Scientific Assessment Panel and Chair of the Assessment Panels, Report of the Fourth Meeting of the Parties to the Montreal Protocol, UNEP/OzL.Pro.4/15, 25 November 1992, 5–6. For the latest assessment of ozone depletion, see WMO/UNEP, *Scientific Assessment of Ozone Depletion* (November 1998).

[161] Vienna, 22 March 1985, in force 22 September 1988, 26 ILM 1529 (1987); 185 states are parties to the Convention.

Montreal Protocol).[162] Since 1990, there have been various adjustments to the production and consumption of controlled substances listed in the Annexes to the Protocol[163] and four amendments to the Protocol, adopted in London (1990),[164] Copenhagen (1992),[165] Montreal (1997)[166] and Beijing (1999).[167] Since the 1960s, monitoring functions have been carried out by states individually and jointly, as well as under the World Meteorological Organization (WMO) Global Ozone Observing System. In 2002, evidence began to emerge to suggest that the global regime was limiting the rate of increase in the degradation of the ozone layer, and that within five years the size of the hole in the ozone layer over the Antarctic might begin to decrease in magnitude, following a decrease in the levels of ozone-depleting gases in the stratosphere and of ozone-depleting chemicals in the troposphere.[168]

1985 Vienna Convention

The Vienna Convention was negotiated over five years under the auspices of UNEP. It was the first treaty to address a global atmospheric issue and is open to participation by all states. It has attracted widespread support from all industrialised nations and a very large number of developing countries. It established a framework for the adoption of measures 'to protect human health and the environment against adverse effects resulting or likely to result from human activities which modify or are likely to modify the ozone layer'.[169] The Vienna Convention does not set targets or timetables for action but requires four categories of 'appropriate measures' to be taken by parties in accordance with means at their disposal and their capabilities, and on the basis of relevant scientific and

---

[162] Montreal, 16 September 1987, in force 1 January 1989, 26 ILM 1550 (1987); 184 states are parties to the Protocol.

[163] Adjustments to the Protocol were adopted, in accordance with the procedure laid down in Art. 2(9), at the Second, Fourth, Seventh, Ninth and Eleventh Meetings of the Parties to the Protocol and came into force for all parties on 7 March 1991, 23 September 1993, 5 August 1996, 4 June 1998 and 28 July 2000, respectively.

[164] London, 29 June 1990, in force 10 August 1992, 30 ILM 537 (1991); 164 states are parties to the 1990 Amendments.

[165] Copenhagen, 25 November 1992, 14 June 1994, 32 ILM 874 (1993); 144 states are parties to the 1992 Amendments; see Report of the Fourth Meeting of the Parties to the Montreal Protocol, UNEP/OzL.Pro.4/15, 25 November 1992, Annexes I, II and III.

[166] Montreal, 25 September 1997, in force 10 November 1999; eighty-nine states are parties to the 1997 Amendments; Annex IV of the Report of the Ninth Meeting of the Parties to the Montreal Protocol, UNEP/OzL.Pro.9/12.

[167] Beijing, 17 December 1999, in force 25 February 2002; forty-five states have accepted the 1999 Amendments. Annex V of the Report of the Eleventh Meeting of the Parties to the Montreal Protocol, UNEP/OzL.Pro.11/10.

[168] UNEP Press Release, 16 September 2002.

[169] Art. 2(1); the 'ozone layer' is defined as 'the layer of atmospheric ozone above the planetary boundary layer': Art. 1(1).

technical considerations.[170] These obligations are: co-operation on systematic observations, research and information exchange; the adoption of appropriate legislative or administrative measures and co-operation on policies to control, limit, reduce or prevent activities that are likely to have adverse effects resulting from modifications to the ozone layer; and co-operation in the formulation of measures, procedures and standards to implement the Convention as well as with competent international bodies.[171] Parties are free to adopt additional domestic measures, in accordance with international law, and maintain in force compatible measures already taken.[172]

Article 3 and Annexes I and II elaborate upon the type of research and systematic observations which are to be carried out directly or through international bodies.[173] Article 4 and Annex II require co-operation in legal, scientific and technical fields, including the exchange of scientific, technical, socio-economic and legal information relevant to the Convention, subject to rules of confidentiality, and the development and transfer of technology and knowledge, taking into account the particular needs of developing countries.

The parties transmit information to the conference of the parties on their implementation measures. That body is entrusted with the implementation of the Convention, assisted by a Secretariat whose services are provided by UNEP.[174] The conference of the parties has other functions, including the adoption of protocols, additional annexes and amendments to protocols and annexes, and the right to take 'any additional action that may be required for the achievement of the purposes of the Convention'.[175] Annexes to the Convention or to any protocols are restricted to scientific, technical and administrative matters, and are to be considered an integral part of the Convention or of such protocols,[176] and only parties to the Convention may become parties to any protocol.[177]

The 1987 Montreal Protocol and the Adjustments and Amendments

Introduction

The first, and to date the only, Protocol to the Vienna Convention is the 1987 Montreal Protocol. It is a landmark international environmental agreement, providing a precedent for new regulatory techniques and institutional

---

[170] Art. 2(1), (2) and (4).   [171] Art. 2(2)(a) to (d).   [172] Art. 2(3).

[173] Annex I identifies three main areas of research need (the physics and chemistry of the atmosphere; health, biological and photodegradation effects; effects on climate) and systematic observations on designated matters. Annex I also identifies substances thought at the time to have the potential to modify the ozone layer: carbon substances (carbon monoxide, carbon dioxide, methane, non-methane hydrocarbon species); nitrogen substances (nitrous oxide, nitrogen oxides); chlorine substances (fully halogenated alkanes, partially halogenated alkanes); bromide substances; and hydrogen substances (hydrogen, water).

[174] Arts. 5 to 7.   [175] Arts. 6(4), 8, 9 and 10.   [176] Art. 10(1).   [177] Art. 16(1).

arrangements, and the adoption and implementation of innovative financial mechanisms. With hindsight, the Montreal Protocol appears to be a relatively straightforward instrument, and the fact that its approach has subsequently been relied upon extensively in other international environmental negotiations belies the controversy and complexity surrounding it at the time of its negotiations. According to one commentator, most observers in and out of government believed at the time that an agreement on international regulation of CFCs would be impossible to reach. The issues were complex, involving interconnected scientific, economic, technological and political variables. The science was still speculative, resting on projections from evolving computer models of imperfectly understood stratospheric processes – models that yielded varying, sometimes contradictory, predictions of potential future ozone losses each time they were further refined. Moreover, existing measurements of the ozone layer showed no depletion, nor was there any evidence of the postulated harmful effects.[178]

The Montreal Protocol sets forth specific legal obligations, including limitations and reductions on the calculated levels of consumption and production of certain controlled ozone-depleting substances.[179] Its negotiation and conclusion, shortly after the 1985 Vienna Convention, were prompted by new scientific evidence indicating that emissions of certain substances were significantly depleting and modifying the ozone layer and would have potential climatic effects.[180] The absence of scientific evidence that actual harm was occurring required the international community to take 'precautionary measures to control equitably total global emissions' of substances that deplete the ozone layer.[181] Like the Vienna Convention, the Montreal Protocol and its amendments have attracted widespread support.[182] In 1990, the Second Meeting of the Parties to the Montreal Protocol adopted the first Adjustment and Amendments to the Montreal Protocol. Those Amendments were ratified by 164 states, including a significant number of developing countries. In 1992, the Fourth Meeting of the Parties to the Montreal Protocol adopted a second round of Adjustment and Amendments. The 1992 changes were adopted within four months of the entry into force of the 1990 Amendments and have been ratified by 144 states. Since 1992, there have been three further rounds of Adjustments in 1995, 1997 and 1999 and two Amendments have been adopted, the first at the Ninth Meeting of the Parties in 1997 (in force 10 November 1999, with eighty-nine ratifications)

---

[178] R. Benedick, *Ozone Diplomacy* (1991), xii, an insider's account of the negotiations of the Montreal Protocol (see also the second edition 1998).

[179] 1987 Montreal Protocol, Art. 3 provides for the method of calculating control levels.

[180] *Ibid.*, preambular paras. 3 and 4.   [181] Preambular para. 6.

[182] On the procedure for the adoption of adjustments and amendments, see chapter 4, pp. 138–40 above.

and the second at the Eleventh Meeting of the Parties in 1999 (in force 25 February 2002, with forty-five ratifications).

The 1990 Amendments introduced important changes to the Montreal Protocol. The Preamble was amended to include a reference to the need to take into account the 'developmental needs of developing countries', the provision of 'additional financial resources and access to relevant technologies', and the 'transfer of alternative technologies'.[183] The definitions of 'controlled substances' and 'production' were amended,[184] and a definition of 'transitional substances' was introduced.[185] The amended definition of 'production' excludes 'recycled' and 'reused' amounts.[186] Article 2(5) was amended to establish new rules concerning transfers of calculated levels of production between parties and, as described below, changes were introduced to all the important operational provisions, particularly those requiring the reduction and, ultimately, the prohibition of the use of controlled substances which were subject to control measures relating to consumption, production and trade. New rules were also adopted relating to the financial arrangements and technology transfer.

The 1992 Adjustments: introduced changes to the timetable for phasing out substances under Articles 2A to 2E of the amended Protocol; listed three new controlled substances and further trade restrictions; adopted new reporting requirements; enlarged the Implementation Committee; and adopted an indicative list of measures to be taken against parties which were not in compliance; it also established the Multilateral Fund on a permanent basis.

The 1997 Montreal Amendment established a new timetable for phasing out the use of methyl bromide and adopted a new licensing system for controlling trade based on licences issued by the parties for each export and import of controlled substances. The licensing system will enable customs and police officials to track trade in CFCs and to detect unlicensed trade. The 1999 Amendment provides for new production controls on Group I, Annex C substances, lists bromochloromethane as a controlled substance and institutes new reporting obligations for quarantine and pre-shipment uses of methyl bromide.

---

[183] 1990 Amendments, sixth, seventh and ninth preambular paragraphs.

[184] *Ibid.*, Art. 1(4) and (5); see also Decision IV/12 of the Fourth Meeting of the Parties to the Montreal Protocol excluding 'insignificant quantities' from the definition: see Report of the Fourth Meeting of the Parties to the Montreal Protocol, UNEP/OzL.Pro.4/15, 25 November 1992.

[185] 1990 Amendments, Art. 1(9). 'Transitional substances' are those in Annex C to the Protocol.

[186] *Ibid.*, Art. 1(5), Decision IV/24 of the Meeting of the Parties adopted 'clarifications' of the terms 'recovery' ('collection and storage of controlled substances . . . during servicing or prior to disposal'), 'recycling' (by re-use of a recovered controlled substance following a basic cleaning process) and 'reclamation' ('re-processing' and upgrading of a recovered controlled substance): Report of the Fourth Meeting of the Parties to the Montreal Protocol, UNEP/OzL.Pro.4/15, 25 November 1992.

Controlled substances

Article 2 and Annex A of the 1987 Montreal Protocol established control measures which were relatively complex and sophisticated as compared to the existing international environmental rules. Annex A established two groups of 'controlled substances' and an estimate of the ozone-depleting potential of each substance in the two groups. Group I listed certain chlorine substances,[187] and Group II listed certain halon substances.[188] The 1987 Protocol allows the parties to make adjustments to the ozone-depleting potentials specified in Annex A, as well as further adjustments and reductions of production and consumption from 1986 levels.[189]

The 1990 Amendments added controlled substances in two new Annexes to the Protocol. Annex B added three new groups of controlled substances (Group I (additional CFCs), Group II (carbon tetrachloride) and Group III (methyl chloroform)), and Annex C added a list of transitional substances (HCFCs).[190] In 1991, the parties to the Montreal Protocol added an Annex D to the Protocol.[191] The 1992 Amendments added methyl bromide as a controlled substance in a new Annex E. The 1999 Amendments added bromochloromethane as a controlled substance in a new Group III in Annex C.

Control measures: consumption and production

Article 2 of the 1987 Montreal Protocol adopted limitation and reduction requirements on the consumption and production of all Annex A substances. By Article 6, as amended by the 1992 and 1999 Amendments, the parties are to assess with the assistance of panels of experts all the Article 2 control measures on the basis of available scientific, environmental, technical and economic information.[192] More stringent control measures in respect of those substances, including an accelerated timetable for phase-out, were imposed by the various Adjustments and Amendments to the Protocol.

---

[187] CFC-11, CFC-12, CFC-113, CFC-114 and CFC-115.

[188] Halon-1211, halon-1301 and halon-2402.

[189] 1987 Montreal Protocol, Art. 2(9). Such adjustments are subject to a simplified decision-making procedure whereby decisions binding on all parties may, as a last resort and consensus having failed, be taken by two-thirds of parties present and voting and representing 50 per cent of total consumption. By Art. 2(1), the parties may also decide to add or remove substances from Annex A and what control measures should apply to those substances, subject to a two-thirds majority vote of parties present and voting.

[190] The 1992 Amendment replaced Annex C with a new section.

[191] Report of the Third Meeting of the Parties to the Montreal Protocol, UNEP/OzL.Pro.3/11, 21 June 1991, Decision III/15.

[192] 1987 Montreal Protocol, Art. 6. Under the Protocol, the control measures are to be assessed at least every four years on the basis of available scientific, environmental, technical and economic information; by Art. 2(11) of the 1987 Montreal Protocol, parties remain free to take more stringent measures than those required by Art. 2.

CFCs Under the 1987 Montreal Protocol as adjusted and amended, each party must limit its calculated level of consumption of Annex A, Group I substances to 1986 levels within nineteen months of the entry into force of the Protocol.[193] Thereafter, annual consumption is to be reduced to 25 per cent of 1986 levels by 1 June 1994, with a complete phase-out by 1 January 1996.[194] Each party is also to reduce calculated levels of production of Annex A substances by the same amounts and by the same dates, except that for each amount the level may be increased by up to 10 per cent based on the 1986 level, provided that such increase is only to satisfy the 'basic domestic needs' of developing country parties operating under Article 5.[195] The 1999 limit of production may be increased, in the same circumstances, by an amount equal to the average annual production for basic domestic needs for the period 1995–7 unless the parties decide otherwise.[196]

The 1999 Amendments introduced new reductions for production for basic domestic needs by Article 5 parties. These parties are required to phase out production of Group I, Annex A CFCs by 1 January 2010, with intermediate reductions of 20 per cent by 2003, 50 per cent by 2005 and 85 per cent by 2007, based on their average annual production for basic domestic needs for the period 1995–7.[197]

Halons For the halons listed in Group II of Annex A, each party was required to freeze its calculated level of consumption at 1986 levels by 1 January 1992, with a complete phase-out by 1 January 1994.[198] Thereafter, production was to be limited to 1986 levels, with a 15 per cent permitted increase until 1 January 2002 to satisfy the 'basic domestic needs' of parties operating under Article 5.[199] Since 1 January 2002, developing country parties operating under Article 5 are required to phase out production for basic domestic needs by 1 January 2010, with a 50 per cent reduction by 1 January 2005, based on a 1995–7 baseline.[200]

Additional CFCs Under the 1990 Amendments, a new Article 2C required each party to ensure that its calculated levels of consumption and production of controlled substances in Annex B, Group I (additional CFCs) for the twelve-month period commencing 1 January 1993 and each twelve-month period thereafter did not exceed 80 per cent of consumption and production levels of those substances in 1989.[201] Annual consumption and production of these controlled substances was not to exceed 25 per cent of 1989 levels in the twelve-month period commencing 1 January 1994 and in each twelve-month period

---

[193] *Ibid.*, Art. 2A(3).   [194] *Ibid.*, Art. 2A(3) and (4).   [195] *Ibid.*, Art. 2A(3).
[196] *Ibid.*, Art. 2A(4).   [197] *Ibid.*, Art. 2A(5)–(8).   [198] *Ibid.*, Art. 2B(1) and (2).
[199] *Ibid.*, Art. 2(2).   [200] *Ibid.*, Art. 2B(3) and (4).   [201] 1990 Amendment, Art. 2C(1).

thereafter, and the consumption and production of these additional CFCs were totally prohibited as from 1 January 1996.[202]

Carbon tetrachloride   Under the 1990 Amendments, each party's calculated annual levels of consumption and production of Annex B, Group II controlled substances (carbon tetrachloride) for the twelve-month period commencing 1 January 1995 and each twelve-month period thereafter must not exceed 15 per cent of 1989 levels for those substances,[203] and the production and consumption of carbon tetrachloride are totally prohibited as from 1 January 1996.[204]

Methylchloroform   Under the 1990 Amendments, each party's calculated annual levels of consumption and production of Annex B, Group III controlled substances (methylchloroform) for the twelve-month period commencing 1 January 1993 and each twelve-month period thereafter was not to exceed its consumption and production levels of those substances in 1989.[205] Thereafter, consumption and production were to be reduced to 50 per cent of 1989 levels by 1 January 1994 and in each twelve-month period thereafter, with a total prohibition on the consumption and production of methylchloroform as from 1 January 1996.[206]

HCFCs, hydrobromofluorocarbons and methyl bromide   The 1992 Amendments added three new Articles to the Montreal Protocol to phase out the use of the three controlled substances listed in Annex C of the Protocol. Article 2F was introduced to require parties to limit their annual consumption of Annex C, Group I substances (HCFCs) to no more than 3.1 per cent[207] of their level of consumption of Annex A, Group I substances in 1989 *and* their total level of consumption of Annex C, Group I substances in 1989.[208] Article 2F then

---

[202] *Ibid.*, Art. 2C(1), (2) and (3). In order to satisfy 'basic domestic needs' a party operating under Art. 5(1) may exceed that level of production by 15 per cent of its 1989 levels up to 1 January 2003. By 1 January 2003, production for basic domestic needs is to be reduced by 20 per cent, with a cut of 85 per cent by 1 January 2007 before a total phase-out by 1 January 2010; *ibid.*, Art. 2C(3)–(5).

[203] 1990 Amendments, Art. 2D(1).

[204] 1992 Amendments, Art. 2D(1) and (2). In order to satisfy 'basic domestic needs' a party operating under Art. 5(1) may exceed that level of production by 15 per cent of its 1998–2000 levels until 1 January 2005 but must achieve a phase-out by 2010; *ibid.*, Arts. 2D(2) and 5(8*bis*).

[205] 1990 Amendments, Art. 2E(1).

[206] *Ibid.*, Art. 2E(1)–(4). Parties operating under Art. 5(1) are required to freeze production for 'basic domestic needs' at 1998–2000 levels by 1 January 2003. Reductions in production must be achieved by 2005 (30 per cent) and 2010 (70 per cent) with a total phase-out by 1 January 2015; *ibid.*, Arts. 2E(3) and 5 (8*bis*).

[207] This level was changed to 2.8 per cent by the 1995 Amendments.

[208] 1992 Amendments, Art. 2F(1).

requires a gradual thirty-five-year phase-out of consumption of HCFCs to levels of 65 per cent (1 January 2004), 35 per cent (1 January 2010), 10 per cent (1 January 2015), 0.5 per cent (1 January 2020) and zero (1 January 2030).[209] Article 2F also commits parties to 'endeavour' to ensure that the use of HCFCs is limited to applications where alternatives are not available, that such use is not outside the areas of application currently met by substances in Annexes A, B and C (except in some cases for the protection of human life and/or human health), and that they are used in a manner that minimises ozone depletion.[210]

Amendments to Article 2F agreed in the 1999 Amendments commit the parties to new control measures for the production of HCFCs. Developed countries are required to limit their annual production of HCFCs to a level calculated as an average of (1) the sum in 1989 of HCFC consumption and 2.8 per cent of the level of consumption of Annex A, Group I substances *and* (2) the sum in 1989 of HCFC production and 2.8 per cent of the level of consumption of Annex A, Group I substances. Developing countries will be subject to a freeze on HCFC production starting in 2016 based on average production and consumption in 2015.

Article 2G introduced a prohibition on the consumption of Annex C, Group II substances (hydrobromofluorocarbons) after 1 January 1996, except for 'essential uses'.

Article 2H was introduced to limit the annual production and consumption of Annex E substances (methyl bromide) to 1991 levels from 1995. A new phase-out programme for methyl bromide was introduced by the 1997 Amendments. Parties are required gradually to reduce the production and consumption of methyl bromide from 1991 levels by 25 per cent (1 January 1999), 50 per cent (1 January 2001), 70 per cent (1 January 2003) and 100 per cent (1 January 2005). Developing county parties operating under Article 5 must freeze production of methyl bromide for basic domestic needs at 1995–8 levels by 1 January 2002, with a total phase-out by 2015.

Transfer of production   The 1987 Montreal Protocol also provides for transfer of production and the rules regarding facilities under construction. For the purpose of industrial rationalisation, Article 2(5) sets out the conditions under which parties whose 1986 production level of Annex A, Group I substances was less than 25 kilotonnes could transfer to or receive from any other party production which exceeded the limits in Article 2(1), (3) and (4). The 1992 Amendments introduced a new Article 2(5)*bis* allowing any party not operating under Article 5(1) to transfer to another such party any portion of its calculated level of consumption set out in Article 2F provided that certain conditions are fulfilled. Article 2(6) allows a party not operating under Article 5 to complete facilities for production under construction or contracted for prior

---

[209] *Ibid.*, Art. 2F(2)–(6).   [210] *Ibid.*, Art. 2F(7).

to 16 September 1987, provided that facilities are completed by 31 December 1990 and the party's level of consumption remains below 0.5 kilograms per capita.

By Article 2(8) of the 1987 Montreal Protocol, parties which are member states of a regional economic integration organisation (such as the EC) may 'jointly fulfil' their obligations provided that their total combined level of consumption does not exceed levels set by the Protocol, and that certain procedural obligations are fulfilled (the parties to any such agreement must inform the Secretariat and all member states of the regional organisation, and the organisation itself).

Control measures: trade in controlled substances

Article 4 of the 1987 Montreal Protocol established innovative trade provisions to achieve its environmental objectives. Although initially somewhat controversial, they are now widely recognised for their effectiveness in creating incentives for states to become party to the Protocol. These measures address: the trade in controlled substances by parties with states which are not parties to the Protocol; the trade in products containing controlled substances; and the trade in products produced with but not containing controlled substances. Article 4 represents the first occasion on which the international community adopted trade measures for environmental protection outside the field of flora and fauna, although the trade prohibition will not apply to a non-party which is found by the parties to be in full compliance with Articles 2, 2A to 2I, 4 and 7 of the Protocol.[211] Imports of controlled substances from non-parties are banned, and from 1 January 1993 developing country parties were prohibited from exporting to non-parties.[212] Article 4(3) provides for the ban on imports of certain products containing controlled substances into certain parties from non-party states. Parties are also required to determine the feasibility of banning or restricting imports of products produced with, but not containing, controlled substances, and if feasible adopt the necessary bans or restrictions.[213]

The 1987 Montreal Protocol also requires parties to discourage exports of technology for producing and using controlled substances,[214] and to refrain from providing new subsidies, aid, credits, guarantees or insurance for the export to non-party states of products, equipment, plants or technology which would facilitate the production of controlled substances.[215] Exceptions are allowed for products, equipment, plants or technology that improve containment, recovery, recycling or destruction of controlled substances, promote the development of alternative substances, or otherwise contribute to reductions of controlled substances.[216]

---

[211] 1987 Montreal Protocol, Art. 4(8).   [212] *Ibid.*, Art. 4(2).   [213] *Ibid.*, Art. 4(4).
[214] *Ibid.*, Art. 4(5).   [215] *Ibid.*, Art. 4(6).   [216] *Ibid.*, Art. 4(7).

The 1990 Amendments introduced significant changes to Article 4 of the Protocol. The import of controlled substances in Annex A from any state not party to the Protocol was banned from 1 January 1990, and those in Annex B from any state not party to the Protocol[217] within one year of the date of entry into force of amended Article 4.[218] The 1992 Amendments introduced a ban on the import of Group II, Annex C substances from non-parties within one year of the entry into force of the Amendments.[219] The 1997 Amendments introduced a ban on the import of Annex E substances from non-parties within one year of the entry into force of the Amendments.[220] Exports to non-parties of Annex A substances are banned from 1 January 1993, and of Annex B substances commencing one year after entry into force of the Amendments.[221] The 1992 Amendments introduced a ban on the export of Annex C, Group II substances to non-parties within one year of the entry into force of the Amendments.[222]

The 1997 Amendments introduced a ban on the export of Annex E substances to non-parties within one year of the entry into force of the Amendments.[223] New timetables were also established for bans of imports from non-parties of products containing controlled substances in Annexes A and B, and for determining the feasibility of banning or restricting imports from non-parties of products produced with, but not containing, controlled substances in Annexes A and B.[224] The 1992 Amendments introduced provisions for banning the import of products containing Annex C, Group II substances, and to determine the feasibility of banning the import of products produced with but not containing Annex C, Group II substances.[225] The 1997 Amendments required parties, by February 2000, to implement a system for licensing the import and export of new, used, recycled and reclaimed controlled substances.[226] Parties are also required, 'to the fullest practicable extent', to discourage exports to non-parties of technology for producing and utilising controlled substances.[227]

---

[217] Such a state includes 'a state or regional economic integration organization that has not agreed to be bound by the control measures in effect for that substance': *ibid.*, Art. 4(9) of the 1990 Amendments.

[218] 1990 Amendments, Art. 4(1) and (1*bis*).   [219] 1992 Amendments, Art. 4(1*ter*).

[220] 1997 Amendments, Art. 4(1*qua*). As of 1 January 2004, parties will be required to ban the import of Group I, Annex C controlled substances from non-parties: Art. 4(1*quin*). Within one year of the entry into force of the 1999 Amendment, parties will be required to ban the import of bromochloromethane from non-parties: Art. 4(1*sex*).

[221] 1990 Amendments, Art. 4(2) and (2*bis*).   [222] 1992 Amendments, Art. 4(2*ter*).

[223] 1997 Amendments, Art. 4(2*qua*). As of 1 January 2004, parties will be required to ban the export of Group I, Annex C controlled substances to non-parties: Art. 4(2*quin*). Within one year of the entry into force of the 1999 Amendments, parties will be required to ban the export of bromochloromethane to non-parties: Art. 4(2*sex*).

[224] 1990 Amendments, Art. 4(3), (3*bis*), (4) and (4*bis*).

[225] 1992 Amendments, Art. 4(3*ter*) and (4*ter*).   [226] 1997 Amendments, Art. 4B.

[227] 1990 Amendments, Art. 4(5). The 1992 Amendment extended this provision only to Annexes A and B and Group II of Annex C substances: 1992 Amendments, Art. 4(5).

Developing countries

The 1987 Montreal Protocol included provisions to take account of the special needs of developing countries, including large users of CFCs such as India and China, who were unwilling to become parties to the Protocol because of the economic and developmental implications of the Protocol. Article 5(1) of the Protocol allowed developing country parties whose calculated level of consumption was less than 0.3 kilograms per capita a grace period of ten years beyond the dates set for phase-out in Article 2(1) to (4) of the Protocol. In addition, but without specifying how it was to be achieved, the parties agreed to facilitate access to 'environmentally safe alternative substances' and to provide developing countries with subsidies, aid, credits, guarantees or insurance programmes for alternative and substitute products.[228]

The original provisions of the Montreal Protocol were insufficiently attractive to encourage the participation of many developing countries, and further incentives were adopted by the 1990 Amendments. These developed the rules concerning the special situation of developing countries by replacing Article 5 in full and establishing, under a new Article 10, a mechanism to provide financial resources. The amended Article 5 created an incentive for developing countries to become parties to the Protocol before 1 January 1999 by fixing that date as the final point at which states would be able to benefit from the commencement of the ten-year period of delay for compliance with the control measures in Articles 2A to 2E as amended.[229] Significantly, Article 5(5) of the 1990 Amendments recognised that the capacity of developing country parties to fulfil their obligations and their implementation would depend upon 'the effective implementation of the financial co-operation as provided by Article 10 and transfer of technology as provided by Article 10A'. This marked the first time that an international environmental agreement linked implementation to the receipt of financial resources and the transfer of technology. The 1992 Amendments created the possibility that the period of grace would also apply to the 1992 Amendments substances after the 1995 review required under Article 5(8) of the 1990 Amendments.[230] The 1992 Amendments also introduced a new Article 5(1 *bis*) requiring the parties to decide by 1 January 1996 on phase-out and/or consumption and production timetable for Annex C, Groups I and II, and Annex E substances for parties operating under Article 5(1). Other changes provided by the new Article 5 include limiting parties operating under Article 5(1) to those with annual levels of consumption of 0.2 kilograms per capita of Annex B substances and providing for the situation in which a party operating under Article 5(1) finds itself unable to obtain an adequate supply of controlled substances or unable to implement any or all of its obligations in

---

[228] 1987 Montreal Protocol, Art. 5(2) and (3).
[229] 1990 Amendments, Art. 5(1).   [230] 1992 Amendments, Art. 5(1).

Articles 2A or 2E due to the inadequate implementation of the new pro-visions on financial co-operation and transfer of technology.[231] The really significant change, however, was the amendment to Article 10, which set a precedent followed in subsequent agreements addressing global environmental problems.

Technical, financial and other assistance

The original Article 10 of the Montreal Protocol contained rather innocu-ous and traditional environmental treaty provisions on technical assistance, particularly for developing countries, to facilitate participation in and imple-mentation of the Protocol, including through the preparation of workplans. The 1990 Amendments introduced a radical and innovative change which has had profound consequences on the negotiation of subsequent global environ-mental treaties, particularly the Climate Change and Biodiversity Conventions. The innovation was to introduce financial incentives, almost of a compensatory nature, to entice hesitant developing countries to join the Montreal Protocol regime.

The new Article 10 established a 'Financial Mechanism' to provide financial and technical co-operation, including the transfer of technologies, to parties operating under Article 5(1) of the Protocol to enable their compliance with Articles 2A to 2E of the amended Protocol.[232] The mechanism, which is to meet 'all agreed incremental costs' of such parties, includes a Multilateral Fund to meet, on a grant or concessional basis, the agreed incremental costs; to finance certain clearing house functions related to, *inter alia*, identifying needs for and facilitating co-operation; and to finance the secretariat services of the Fund.[233] The Fund operates under the authority of the parties, who decide on its overall policies, and is operated by an Executive Committee which discharges its tasks and responsibilities with the co-operation of the World Bank, UNEP, UNDP and (more latterly) UNIDO.[234] The Multilateral Fund is financed by contributions from parties not operating under Article 5(1) on the basis of the UN scale of

---

[231] 1990 Amendments, Art. 5(2), (4) and (6).

[232] 1990 Amendments, Art. 10(1); for further details, see chapter 20, pp. 1031–2 below. The 1992 Amendments extend the application of the Financial Mechanism to control measures under Arts. 2F to 2H that are decided pursuant to Art. 5(1*bis*) of the 1992 Amendments. Since the establishment of the Multilateral Fund in 1990, the Executive Committee has approved the expenditure of more than US$1.2 billion, to support over 3,850 projects and activities in 124 developing countries (see www.unmfs.org/general.htm).

[233] 1990 Amendment, Art. 10(2) and (3); see Annex VIII of the Report of the Fourth Meeting of the Parties to the Montreal Protocol for an 'Indicative List of Categories of Incremental Cost', UNEP/OzL.Pro.4/15, 25 November 1992.

[234] 1990 Amendments, Art. 10(4) and (5); on financial resources, see chapter 20, pp. 1021–37 below.

assessments, in convertible currency, in kind, and/or in national currencies.[235] The Protocol as amended in 1990 also allows bilateral and regional co-operation in financing in certain specified circumstances.[236] Resources are to be disbursed with the concurrence of the beneficiary party.[237] Under Article 10A, introduced by the 1990 Amendments, each party agrees to take every practicable step to ensure that the best available environmentally safe substitutes and technologies are expeditiously transferred, under fair and most favourable conditions, to parties operating under Article 5(1).

Reporting

The principal technique for ensuring compliance with the Protocol and its amendments, apart from the non-compliance procedure and trade sanctions, are the reporting requirements, which are more detailed than most environmental treaties.[238] Article 7 requires all parties to report data on production, imports and exports of each controlled substance for 1986 and for the year during which it became a party and each year thereafter. Article 9 provides for research, development, public awareness and exchange of information. The 1990 Amendments introduced changes to Article 7 concerning the provision of data on production, imports and exports of controlled substances in Annexes A and B and Group 1 of Annex C, and separate data on amounts used for feedstocks, amounts destroyed by approved technologies, and imports and exports to parties and non-parties.[239]

Institutional arrangements

The Protocol is operated under the auspices of regular meetings of the parties whose functions include: reviewing implementation of the Protocol; deciding on any adjustments or reductions under Article 2(9) and on the addition or removal of substances from any Annex under Article 2(10); assessing the Article 2 control measures; and considering and adopting proposals for amendment of the Protocol or any Annex and for any new Annex.[240] Fourteen meetings of the parties have been held to date. At their first meeting, the parties approved procedures and mechanisms for determining non-compliance and the consequences

---

[235] 1990 Amendments, Art. 10(6). The Fund has been replenished four times: US$240 million (1991–3), US$455 million (1994–6), US$466 million (1997–9) and US$440 million (2000–2). As at 20 July 2001, the contributions made to the Multilateral Fund by some thirty-two industrialised countries amounted to US$1.3 billion.

[236] *Ibid.*   [237] *Ibid.*, Art. 10(8).

[238] On the Implementation Committee and the Non-Compliance Procedure established by the Meeting of the Parties of the Montreal Protocol, see chapter 5, pp. 205–7 above.

[239] Art. 7(1), (2) and (3) of the 1990 Amended Montreal Protocol. See also Art. 7(2) and (3) as amended by 1992 Amendments; Art. 7(3*bis*) of the 1992 Amendments introduces a reporting requirement on imports and exports of certain substances that have been recycled.

[240] 1987 Montreal Protocol, Art. 11(1) and (3).

thereof.[241] The Protocol also establishes specific tasks for the Secretariat, which is provided by UNEP.[242]

Climate change

V. Nanda (ed.), *World Climate Change: The Role of International Law and Institutions* (1983); C. Tickell, *Climatic Change and World Affairs* (1986); M. Grubb, *The Greenhouse Effect: Negotiating Targets* (1989); R. Benedick, 'The Montreal Ozone Treaty: Implications for Global Warming', 5 *American University Journal of International Law and Policy* 217 (1990); D. Zaelke and J. Cameron, 'Global Warming and Climate Change: An Overview of International Legal Process', 5 *American University Journal of International Law and Policy* 248 (1990); C. Stone, 'The Global Warming Crisis, If There Is One, and the Law', 5 *American University Journal of International Law and Policy* 497 (1990); US National Academy of Sciences, *Policy Implications of Greenhouse Warming* (1991); R. Benedick, A. Chayes *et al.*, *Greenhouse Warming: Negotiating a Global Regime* (1991); D. Caron, 'When Law Makes Climate Change Worse: Rethinking the Law of Baselines in Light of a Rising Sea Level', 17 *Ecology Law Quarterly* 621 (1991); R. Churchill and D. Freestone (eds.), *International Law and Global Climate Change* (1991); T. Iwama (ed.), *Policies and Laws on Global Warming: International and Comparative Analysis* (1991); P. Roderick, 'A Charter for Global Warming', 1 RECIEL 158 (1992); P. Sands, 'The United Nations Framework Convention on Climate Change', 1 RECIEL 270 (1992); C. Stone, 'Beyond Rio: "Insuring" Against Global Warming', 86 AJIL 445 (1992); E. Barratt-Brown *et al.*, 'A Forum for Action on Global Warming: The UN Framework Convention on Climate Change', 4 *Colorado Journal of International Law and Policy* 103 (1993); D. Bodansky, 'The United Nations Framework Climate Change Convention: A Commentary', 18 *Yale Journal of International Law* 451 (1993); I. Mintzer and J. Leonard (eds.), *Negotiating Climate Change: The Inside Story of the Rio Convention* (1994); L. Boisson de Chazournes, 'De Kyoto à la Haye, en passant par Buenos Aires et Bonn: La régulation de l'effet de serre aux forceps', AFDI 709 (2000); Symposium on Climate Change, 11 RECIEL (2002)
Website: http://unfccc.int.

Introduction

The earth's climate is determined in large part by the presence in the atmosphere of naturally occurring greenhouse gases, including in particular water vapour, carbon dioxide (CO_2), methane (CH_4), CFCs, nitrous oxide (N_2O) and tropospheric ozone (O_3). These are transparent to incoming shortwave solar radiation but absorb and trap longwave radiation emitted by the earth's surface. Their presence exerts a warming influence on the earth. Scientific evidence

---

[241] *Ibid.*, Art. 8; see chapter 5, pp. 205–7 above.   [242] *Ibid.*, Art.

suggests that continued increases in atmospheric concentrations of selected greenhouse gases due to human activities will lead to an enhanced 'greenhouse effect' and global climatic change.[243] Carbon dioxide from emissions from the combustion of fossil fuels, the production of cement, and agricultural and other land use (including deforestation) is widely considered to be the most significant contribution to the threat of climate change, but global emissions of CFC-11 and 12, methane and nitrous oxide also pose a significant threat. In 1988, UNEP and the WMO established the Intergovernmental Panel on Climate Change (IPCC) to provide the scientific guidance necessary to take further action. The first IPCC report, published in August 1990, predicted that, on a 'business-as-usual' emissions scenario, global mean temperatures could rise by an average rate of about 0.3°C per decade (with an uncertainty range of 0.2–0.5°C) during the next century.[244] This could lead to an increase in global mean temperature of about 2°C above that occurring in pre-industrial times by the year 2025, and about 4°C by 2100. Such a rate of increase would be expected to lead to increased global average of rainfall by a few per cent by 2030, to diminution of areas of sea ice and snow cover, and to a rise in global mean sea level of 20 cm by 2030 and 65 cm by the end of the next century.[245] In February 1992, the IPCC produced its second report, which concluded that findings of scientific research since 1990 did not affect the Working Group's understanding of the science of the greenhouse effect and either confirmed or did not justify altering the major conclusions of the 1990 report.[246] In its latest report, published in 2001, the IPCC predicted that anthropogenic warming is likely to lie in the range of 0.1–0.2°C per decade over the next few decades, leading to a likelihood of increased precipitation and a greater risk of extreme weather conditions such as floods and droughts.[247] The environmental, economic and social consequences of such rates of warming are described by the IPCC Working Group on Impacts.

The negotiation of a treaty to address climate change and its effects was formally set in motion by the UN General Assembly and the specialised agencies. In 1988 and 1989, the General Assembly determined that 'climate change is a common concern of mankind' and urged governments and intergovernmental

---

[243] See IPCC, WG I, 'Climate Change 2001: The Scientific Basis', in *Third Assessment Report: Climate Change 2001* (2001); see also Hadley Centre for Climate Change, *Climate Change: An Update of Recent Research* (2000). The 1992 Climate Change Convention defines 'greenhouse gases' as 'those gaseous constituents of the atmosphere, both natural and anthropogenic, that absorb and re-emit infra-red radiation': Art. 1(5).

[244] IPCC, *Climate Change: The IPCC Scientific Assessment* (1990).

[245] The 'business-as-usual' scenario assumed a continued reliance on coal and oil, modest improvements in energy efficiency, limited controls on emissions of carbon dioxide, continued deforestation, uncontrolled emissions of methane and nitrous oxide from agricultural sources, and a reduction of CFCs in line with the 1987 Montreal Protocol.

[246] IPCC, *1992 Supplement* (1992), Section II, para. 2.

[247] IPCC, WG I, 'Climate Change 2001: The Scientific Basis', in *Third Assessment Report: Climate Change 2001* (2001).

and non-governmental organisations to collaborate in a concerted effort to prepare, as a matter of urgency, a framework convention on climate change.[248] The political process leading to the negotiation of a legal instrument was given further impetus by the 1990 Ministerial Declaration of the Second World Climate Conference,[249] which called for negotiations on an effective framework convention on climate change containing appropriate commitments to begin without delay. In December 1990, the UN General Assembly established a single intergovernmental negotiating process under the auspices of the General Assembly, supported by UNEP and WMO, for the preparation by an Intergovernmental Negotiating Committee for a Framework Convention on Climate Change (INC/FCCC).[250] The INC/FCCC held five sessions and the Convention was adopted at the close of the resumed fifth session in May 1992. The UN Framework Convention on Climate Change (1992 Climate Change Convention) was signed by 155 states and the EC in June 1992 at UNCED and comprises a package which contains elements for almost all the negotiating states but left none entirely satisfied.[251] It reflected a compromise between those states which were seeking specific targets and timetables for emissions reductions, and those which wanted only a 'bare-bone' skeleton Convention which could serve as the basis for future Protocols, like the 1985 Vienna Convention. In 1997, the Kyoto Protocol was adopted, establishing more detailed commitments for developed parties.

The Convention went beyond the scope of the 1985 Vienna Convention, which took nearly three times as long to negotiate among a smaller group of states. The word 'Framework' in the title is something of a misnomer, since the 1992 Convention established:

1. commitments to stabilise greenhouse gas concentrations in the atmosphere at a safe level, over the long term, and to limit emissions of greenhouse gases by developed countries in accordance with soft targets and timetables;
2. a financial mechanism and a commitment by certain developed country parties to provide financial resources for meeting certain incremental costs and adaptation measures;
3. two subsidiary bodies to the conference of the parties;
4. a number of important guiding 'Principles'; and
5. potentially innovative implementation and dispute settlement mechanisms.

The Convention was the first international environmental agreement to be negotiated by virtually the whole of the international community, with 143 states participating in the final session of the INC/FCCC, and is potentially unique in the scope of its direct and indirect consequences: it is difficult to

---

[248] UNGA Res. 43/53 (1988); UNGA Res. 44/207 (1989).
[249] UN Doc. A/45/696/Add.1, Annex III (1990).   [250] UNGA Res. 45/221 (1990).
[251] New York, 9 May 1992, in force 24 March 1994, 31 ILM 849 (1992), Art. 23(1). The Convention attracted twenty-six ratifications within a year of its adoption, and by June 2001 186 states were parties.

identify any type of human activity which will, over time, fall outside its scope. Affecting the vital economic interests of almost all states, it attempted to adopt a comprehensive approach to integrating environmental considerations into economic development and defined, in legal terms, rights and obligations of different members of the international community in the quest for 'sustainable development' and the protection of the global climate.

The relationship between the Climate Change Convention and vital national economic, social and environmental interests was evident from the different interest groups of states which emerged during the negotiation. On the key issues, the 'Commitments' section, this was not simply a North–South negotiation, as was clear from the failure of both the OECD and the Group of 77 countries to reach common positions. Developed countries were far from united, with the United States alone in publicly opposing the adoption of specific targets and timetables and seeking to ensure a 'comprehensive' approach which dealt with all greenhouse gas emissions, not just carbon dioxide. The economic implications of the Convention played a significant role in defining country positions, with Germany and Japan at the forefront of those developed countries viewing the Convention also as an instrument for gaining longer term competitive advantage by requiring the further development, production, use and dissemination of innovative new technologies. The differing economic capacities of developed countries, and in particular the problems faced by the former socialist countries of central and eastern Europe, led to a novel distinction being drawn in the Convention: for the purposes of differentiating those specific commitments relating to sources and sinks,[252] and those relating to finance, a distinction was drawn between all developed country parties and developed parties (included in Annex 1)[253] and those developed country parties and developed parties not 'undergoing the process of transition to a market economy' (listed in Annex II).[254] Developing countries were also divided. The oil producing countries, led by Saudi Arabia, strongly opposed any substantive obligations in the Convention, and plainly would not have been unhappy to see

[252] Under the Convention, a 'source' is 'any process or activity which releases a greenhouse gas, aerosol or precursor of a greenhouse gas into the atmosphere': Art. 1(9); a 'sink' is 'any process, activity or mechanisms which removes a greenhouse gas or a precursor of a greenhouse gas from the atmosphere': Art. 1(8).

[253] Annex I lists all the OECD countries and the EC (for which the term 'developed party' was used, apparently for the first time in international law), as listed in Annex II, plus eleven former socialist countries: Belarus, Bulgaria, Czechoslovakia, Estonia, Hungary, Latvia, Lithuania, Poland, Romania, Russia and Ukraine. Albania, Yugoslavia and certain members of the Commonwealth of Independent States appear in neither Annex and must therefore be deemed to be developing countries within the meaning of the Convention.

[254] Annex II lists all OECD member countries (Australia, Austria, Belgium, Canada, Denmark, Finland, France, Germany, Greece, Iceland, Ireland, Italy, Japan, Luxembourg, the Netherlands, New Zealand, Norway, Portugal, Spain, Sweden, Switzerland, Turkey, the United Kingdom and the United States) and the EC. Decision 26 at the seventh conference of the parties (2001) removed Turkey from Annex II.

the negotiations fail altogether. The large industrialising developing countries, such as India and China, were understandably concerned to ensure that their economic development, including use of large coal reserves, should not in any way be limited. Developing countries with extensive forests, such as Brazil and Malaysia, were concerned to ensure that the primary emphasis of the Convention should be on limiting developed country emissions and not on protecting or enhancing developing countries' sinks (forests). And developing countries particularly vulnerable to the effects of climate change, such as the forty-two member Alliance of Small Island States (AOSIS), sought a Convention with strong and enforceable commitments and an emphasis on the adverse effects of climate change. The fragmentation of countries into special interest groups created alliances between unlikely partners. On specific commitments relating to emissions, the interests of the US, Saudi Arabia and China were broadly similar, as were those of the EC and EFTA countries and AOSIS and certain African countries suffering from drought and desertification at the other end of the spectrum. It is in the context of these complex economic and environmental interests that the emergence of a package Convention must be understood.

Preamble, definition, objective and principles

The Convention's Preamble reflects a wide range of interests. It includes matters jettisoned from the 'Principles', and expressly recognises, *inter alia*, 'the principle of sovereignty', that the largest share of historical and current global emissions has originated in developed countries, and includes (for the first time in a treaty) Principle 2 of the Rio Declaration (rather than Principle 21 of the Stockholm Declaration). The Preamble also refers to the concepts of 'per capita emissions' and 'energy efficiency', matters which did not receive sufficient support to be included in the operational part of the Convention. Of note in the definitions Article is the omission of the concept of 'net emissions' (sources minus sinks, but no agreement was possible on whether to include natural sinks such as oceans), and a footnote to the first title ('Definitions', Article 1) which states that: 'Titles of articles are included solely to assist the reader.'[255]

The ultimate objective of the Climate Change Convention is to stabilise greenhouse gas concentrations in the atmosphere 'at a level that would prevent dangerous anthropogenic interference with the climate system', emphasising that prevention of climate change is the primary objective.[256] However, the Convention implicitly recognises that some climate change is inevitable, since the objective is to be achieved within a timeframe sufficient to allow

---

[255] On the possible legal consequences of this footnote, see chapter 6, p. 233 above

[256] Art. 2. The 'climate system' is defined as 'the totality of the atmosphere, hydrosphere, biosphere and geosphere and their interactions': Art. 1(3); 'climate change' is 'a change of climate which is attributed directly or indirectly to human activity that alters the composition of the global atmosphere and which is in addition to natural climate variability observed over comparable time periods': Art. 1(2).

'ecosystems to adapt naturally to climate change, to ensure that food production is not threatened and to enable economic development to proceed in a sustainable manner'.[257] Moreover, the Convention includes numerous references to the 'effects' and 'adverse effects' of climate change (twenty-two times), and to 'vulnerability' and 'impacts' (seven times), suggesting that it also has the additional, but unstated, objective of establishing an instrument to address the adverse effects of climate change and ensure that countries, particularly those most vulnerable, are able to prepare adequately for adaptation to the adverse effects of climate change.[258]

Article 3 of the Convention sets out a number of 'Principles' to guide the parties in achieving the objective and implementing the provisions. The obligation of parties to protect the climate system is 'on the basis of equity' and 'in accordance with their common but differentiated responsibilities and respective capabilities', in accordance with which developed country parties should take the lead.[259] Parties should adopt measures and policies which are 'precautionary', 'cost-effective' and 'comprehensive', and which take into account different 'socio-economic contexts'.[260] Climate change policies should also be integrated with national development programmes, and measures to combat climate change 'should not constitute a means of arbitrary or unjustifiable discrimination or a disguised restriction on international trade.[261] Finally, throughout the 'Principles' section, and elsewhere in the Convention, reference is made to the need to ensure 'sustainable economic growth' in order to address the problems of climate change.

General commitments

To achieve the objectives of the Convention, all parties are committed under Article 4(1) to take certain measures, taking into account their common but differentiated responsibilities and priorities, objectives and circumstances. These general commitments include the development of national inventories of anthropogenic emissions by sources and removals by sinks of all greenhouse gases not controlled by the Montreal Protocol,[262] and the formulation and implementation of national and, where appropriate, regional programmes containing measures to mitigate climate change by addressing emissions and removals of these gases and by facilitation of adequate adaptation to climate change.[263] All parties are required: to promote, and co-operate in the diffusion of, technologies, practices and processes that control, reduce or prevent anthropogenic emissions of greenhouse gases not controlled by the Montreal Protocol;

---

[257] *Ibid.*

[258] 'Adverse effects of climate change' means 'changes in the physical environment or biota resulting from climate change which have significant deleterious effects on the composition, resilience or productivity of natural and managed ecosystems or on the operation of socio-economic systems or on human health and welfare': Art. 1(1).

[259] Art. 3(1).   [260] Art. 3(3).   [261] Art. 3(5).   [262] Art. 4(1)(a).   [263] Art. 4(1)(b).

to promote sustainable management, conservation and enhancement of sinks and reservoirs of these greenhouse gases; and to co-operate in preparing for adaptation to the impacts of climate change.[264] All parties are also required to take climate change into account, to the extent feasible, in their social, economic and environmental policies; to promote and co-operate in research, systematic observation and development of data archives to the further understanding of climate change and response strategies; to promote and co-operate in full, open and prompt exchange of relevant information, and to promote and co-operate in education, training and public awareness.[265]

Reporting

The Convention establishes broad reporting requirements for the communication of certain information, with specific provision for financial resources to be made available to developed country parties. All parties are required to communicate, to the conference of the parties: information on implementation; a national inventory of anthropogenic emissions by sources and removals by sinks of all greenhouse gases not controlled by the Montreal Protocol; a general description of steps taken or envisaged to implement the Convention; and any other relevant information including that relevant for calculating global emission trends.[266] The effective implementation by developing country parties of their communication commitments is linked to the effective implementation by developed country parties of their financial commitments, including the need for adequacy and predictability in the flow of funds.[267] Annex I parties are to include information relating to measures and policies to fulfil commitments under Article 4(2)(a) and (b), and a specific estimate of the effects those policies and measures would have on emissions and removals by the year 2000.[268] Annex II parties must include details of measures taken in accordance with Article 4(3), (4) and (5).[269]

Initial communications for each Annex I party were required within six months of the entry into force of the Convention for that party, and most have now reported three times. For all other parties, reports were to be made within three years of entry into force for that party, or upon the availability of financial resources under Article 4(3), and least-developed country parties could make their initial communications at their discretion, and the timetable for subsequent communications is set by the conference of the parties.[270] Article 12 also

---

[264] Art. 4(1)(c)–(e); a 'reservoir' is defined as 'a component or components of the climate system where a greenhouse gas or a precursor of a greenhouse gas is stored': Art. 1(7).

[265] Art. 4(1)(f)–(i).   [266] Arts. 4(1)(j) and 12(1).   [267] Art. 4(3) and (7).

[268] Art. 12(2).   [269] Art. 12(3).

[270] Art. 12(5). Decisions 9/CP.2 and 10/CP.2 of the second conference of the parties established guidelines, a schedule and process for consideration of communications from Annex I and non-Annex I parties (see Report of the Conference of the Parties on its Second Session, Geneva, 8–19 July 1996, FCCC/CP/1996/15/Add.1, 29 October 1996). The reporting

provides for joint communication by a group of parties, for the protection of confidential information, and for making communications public.[271]

Specific commitments: sources and sinks

At the heart of the Convention are the specific commitments relating to sources and sinks of greenhouse gases binding on all developed country parties and the EC under Article 4(2). The extent of these commitments is unclear as a result of the convoluted language agreed to by way of compromise between various OECD members, and the different interests in and between developed and developing countries. The relevant provisions of the opaque language of Article 4(2) provide:

> (a) Each [Annex I party] shall adopt national policies and take correspond-
> ing measures on the mitigation of climate change, by limiting its anthro-
> pogenic emissions of greenhouse gases and protecting and enhancing
> its greenhouse gas sinks and reservoirs. These policies and measures
> will demonstrate that developed countries are taking the lead in mod-
> ifying longer-term trends in anthropogenic emissions consistent with
> the objective of this Convention, recognising that the return by the end
> of the present decade to earlier levels of anthropogenic emissions of
> carbon dioxide and other greenhouse gases not controlled by the Mon-
> treal Protocol would contribute to such modification; and taking into
> account the differences in these parties' starting points and approaches,
> economic structures and resource bases, the need to maintain strong
> and sustainable economic growth, available technologies and other
> individual circumstances, as well as the need for equitable and ap-
> propriate contributions by each of these parties to the global effort
> regarding that objective. These parties may implement such policies
> and measures jointly with other parties and may assist other parties in
> contributing to the achievement of the Convention and, in particular,
> that of this sub-paragraph;
>
> (b) In order to promote progress to this end, each [Annex I party] shall
> communicate, within six months of the entry into force of the Conven-
> tion for it and periodically thereafter, and in accordance with Article
> 12, detailed information on its policies and measures referred to in sub-
> paragraph (a) above, as well as on its resulting projected anthropogenic
> emissions by sources and removals by sinks of greenhouse gases not
> controlled by the Montreal Protocol for the period referred to in sub-
> paragraph (a), with the aim of returning individually or jointly to their
> 1990 levels of these anthropogenic emissions of carbon dioxide and
> other greenhouse gases not controlled by the Montreal Protocol . . .

guidelines were substantially revised by the fifth conference of the parties (see Decisions 3/CP.5 and 4/CP.5, Report of the Conference of the Parties on its Fifth Session, Bonn, 25 October–5 November 1999, FCCC/CP/1999/6/Add.1, 17 January 2000). Most developing country parties have now reported at least once.

[271] Art. 12(8)–(10).

Even when read together, these two paragraphs do not reflect a clear commitment to stabilise carbon dioxide and other greenhouse gas emissions by the year 2000 at 1990 levels, as advocated by the EC and others during the negotiations. Article 4(2)(a) requires only the 'limitation' by each developed country party of its anthropogenic emissions of greenhouse gases, as opposed to stabilisation at a particular level or reduction. It also recognises, in an especially unattractive 117-word sentence, that the return to 'earlier levels' by the year 2000 'would' contribute to the modification of longer term trends in emissions consistent with the objective of the Convention. This is clearly something other than a provision requiring a mandatory return to a specified earlier level by a specified date. Also noteworthy is the absence of any express commitment to keep emissions no higher than 1990 levels after 2000 (although it is not readily apparent that increases or unchecked emissions after 2000 would be compatible with the Convention's object and purpose). Further, each party's contribution is dependent on a series of factors, including its economic structure, resource base, starting point, and approach, as well as the application of 'equity'. Article 4(2)(b) is perhaps a little less opaque. It requires information to be provided on projected anthropogenic emissions for the period up to 2000, and establishes only the 'aim' of returning to 1990 levels without providing a date by when such a return should be achieved. The most that can reasonably be said of these provisions is that they establish soft targets and timetables with many loopholes; the adequacy of Articles 4(2)(a) and (b) was reviewed at the first conference of the parties. The parties agreed 'to begin a process to enable [the conference of the parties] to take appropriate action for the period beyond 2000, including the strengthening of the commitments of the Parties included in Annex I to the Convention (Annex I Parties) in Article 4, paragraph 2(a) and (b), through the adoption of a protocol or another legal instrument'.[272] This process led to the adoption of a protocol to the Convention at the third conference of the parties in Kyoto in 1997. The Kyoto Protocol set quantified targets and a timetable for the reduction of greenhouse gas emissions by developed country parties.[273] The second review of adequacy mandated by Article 4(2)(d) remains subject to competing views as to whether the review extends to the commitments of developing countries or is limited to those of Annex I parties.

The Convention provides for 'joint implementation' by Annex I parties of their policies and measures, subject to further decisions to be taken by the conference of the parties regarding criteria for such 'joint implementation'.[274]

---

[272] In accordance with Art. 2(4)(d), a second review of the adequacy of Art. 4(2)(a) and (b) took place during the fourth conference of the parties at Buenos Aires in 1998. The parties failed to reach a decision on the review and subsequent consideration of the matter at the fifth and sixth conferences of the parties has similarly produced no agreed result.

[273] See the Decision 1/CP.3, Report of the Conference of the Parties on its Third Session, Kyoto, 1–11 December 1997, FCCC/CP/1997/7/Add.1.

[274] Art. 4(2)(a) and (d). At its first session, the conference of the parties launched a 'pilot phase of activities implemented jointly' (AIJ) (see Decision 5/CP.1, Report of the Conference of

This will provide the foundation for the efforts of those states which sought to ensure that emissions reductions should be carried out in the most 'cost-effective' way possible. The Convention additionally requires that 'a certain degree of flexibility' should be allowed to developed country parties 'undergoing the process of transition to a market economy'.[275] Parties are also to take into consideration in the implementation of commitments the situation of parties, particularly developing country parties, with economies vulnerable to the adverse effects of implementation of response measures.[276]

The calculation of emissions by sources and removal by sinks will take into account the best available scientific knowledge, pending agreement by the conference of the parties on common methodologies.[277] Each developed country party is also required to co-ordinate relevant economic and administrative instruments and identify and periodically review its own policies and practices which encourage activities that lead to greater levels of anthropogenic emissions.[278]

Commitments: financial resources and technology transfer

Annex II parties undertake specific financial commitments. They agree to provide 'new and additional' financial resources to meet the 'agreed full costs' incurred by developing country parties in fulfilling their commitment to communicate information relating to implementation (Article 12), and to provide such financial resources needed by developing country parties 'to meet the agreed full incremental costs of implementing measures' relating to their general commitments under Article 4(1) and which are agreed between the developing country party and the entity responsible for the financial mechanism.[279] Annex II parties also undertake to assist developing country parties that are 'particularly vulnerable to the adverse effects' of climate change in meeting the costs of adaptation to those adverse effects.[280] In what amounts to an implicit acceptance by developed country parties of responsibility for causing climate change, Article 4(4) may ultimately emerge as one of the more unusual, contentious, and perhaps costly, commitments in the Convention.

In the implementation of Article 4, the parties must give full consideration to the actions necessary to meet the specific needs and concerns of developing country parties arising from the adverse effects of climate change, and/or the

---

the Parties on its First Session, Berlin, 28 March–7 April 1995, FCCC/CP/1995/7/Add.1). Under the pilot phase, parties may implement projects that reduce greenhouse gas emissions, or enhance removals of greenhouse gases by 'sinks', in the territories of other parties, although no credits may accrue to any party for greenhouse gas emission reductions or removals.

[275] Art. 4(6).   [276] Art. 4(10).

[277] Art. 4(2)(c). See also Decision 4/CP.1 on Methodological Issues, Report of the Conference of the Parties on its First Session, Berlin, 28 March–7 April 1995, FCCC/CP/1995/7/Add.1.

[278] Art. 4(2)(e).   [279] Art. 4(3).   [280] Art. 4(4).

impact of implementing response measures, including actions related to funding, insurance and the transfer of technology.[281] Certain categories of countries are identified, including small island countries, countries with low-lying coastal areas, countries with areas liable to drought and desertification, and countries whose economies are highly dependent on income generated from, or the consumption of, fossil fuels.

Annex II parties are required to take all practicable steps to promote, facilitate and finance the transfer of, or access to, environmentally sound technologies and know-how, and support the development of endogenous capacities and technologies of developing country parties.[282] In the short term, the financial mechanism is likely to devote a significant proportion of the available financial resources to technology transfer.

Institutional arrangements

The Climate Change Convention establishes a conference of the parties, a secretariat, two subsidiary bodies and a financial mechanism.[283] The conference of the parties is the supreme body of the Convention, entrusted with keeping the implementation of the Convention under regular review and making decisions to promote its effective implementation.[284] It met for the first time in 1995 and has subsequently met annually.[285] It has several functions, including:

- to examine periodically the obligations of the parties;
- to facilitate the co-ordination of measures;
- to promote and guide comparable methodologies for preparing inventories of greenhouse gas emissions;
- to assess the implementation of the Convention by all parties and the overall effect of measures; and
- to adopt regular reports on the implementation of the Convention.

A multidisciplinary Subsidiary Body for Scientific and Technological Advice was established to provide information on scientific and technological matters to the conference of the parties.[286] A Subsidiary Body for Implementation was established to assist the conference of the parties in the assessment and review of the implementation of the Convention.[287] Although some states wanted to limit participation, both subsidiary bodies are open to participation by all parties.

The Convention defines a financial mechanism for the provision of financial resources on a grant or concessional basis, including for the transfer of technology.[288] After specific commitments this was the most disputed aspect of the Convention. The mechanism functions under the guidance of, and is accountable to, the conference of the parties, which is responsible for its policies, programme priorities and eligibility criteria, and its operation was to

---

[281] Art. 4(8) and (9).   [282] Art. 4(5).   [283] Arts. 7 to 11.
[284] Art. 7(2).   [285] Art. 7(4).   [286] Art. 9(1).   [287] Art. 10(1).   [288] Art. 11(1).

be entrusted to one or more existing international entities.[289] The mechanism is required to have an equitable and balanced representation of all parties within a transparent system of governance. The Global Environment Facility (GEF) of the UNDP, UNEP and IBRD was initially entrusted with the operation of the financial mechanism on an interim basis, and, in 1996, the second conference of the parties adopted a memorandum of understanding with the GEF on their respective roles and responsibilities.[290] In 1998, the fourth conference of the parties entrusted the GEF with the operation of the financial mechanism on a long-term basis, subject to review every four years.[291]

Implementation and dispute settlement

Apart from the role of the conference of the parties and the Subsidiary Body for Implementation, the Convention provides for the possibility of establishing a 'multilateral consultative process' for the resolution of implementation questions, which will be available to parties on their request.[292] This whittles down two more ambitious original proposals. Additionally, a dispute settlement Article provides for possible compulsory recourse to arbitration or the International Court of Justice with the consent of the relevant parties to a dispute, as well as the possibility for the compulsory establishment of a conciliation commission, with the power to make a recommendatory award, at the request of one of the parties to a dispute twelve months after notification of the dispute.[293] The Convention provides for amendment, the adoption and amendment of Annexes, and the adoption of Protocols.[294] No reservations are permitted.[295] Prior to its entry into force, Article 21 of the Convention established interim arrangements concerning the designation of an interim secretariat, co-operation with the IPCC and other scientific bodies.[296]

The 1997 Kyoto Protocol

P. Davies, 'Global Warming and the Kyoto Protocol', 47 ICLQ 446 (1998); F. Yamin, 'The Kyoto Protocol', 7 RECIEL 113 (1998); D. French, '1997 Kyoto Protocol to the 1992 UN Framework on Climate Change', 10 JEL 227 (1998); M. Grubb, C. Vrolijk

---

[289] Art. 11(1)–(3).

[290] See Decision 13/CP.2, Memorandum of Understanding Between the Conference of the Parties and the Council of the Global Environment Facility, Report of the Conference of the Parties on its Second Session, Geneva, 8–19 July 1996, FCCC/CP/1996/15/Add.1.

[291] See Decision 3/CP.4, Report of the Conference of the Parties on its Fourth Session, Buenos Aires, 2–14 November 1998, FCCC/CP/1998/16/Add.1.

[292] Art. 13.   [293] Art. 14.   [294] Art. 24.   [295] Art. 24.

[296] Art. 21(1) and (2). The Secretariat of the INC, established by UN General Assembly Resolution 45/212, acted as interim secretariat until the completion of the first session of the conference of the parties. UNGA Res. 47/195 of 22 December 1992 decided that the INC will continue to function in order to prepare for the first conference of the parties.

and D. Brack, *The Kyoto Protocol: A Guide and Assessment* (1999); S. Oberthur and H. Ott, *The Kyoto Protocol* (1999); F. Depledge, 'Tracing the Origins of the Kyoto Protocol: An Article by Article History', UN Doc. FCCC/TP/2000/2 (2000); K. Nowrot, 'Saving the International Legal Regime on Climate Change? The 2001 Conferences of Bonn and Marrakech', 44 *German Yearbook of International Law* 396 (2001).

The Kyoto Protocol to the Framework Convention on Climate Change was adopted by the third conference of the parties in December 1997.[297] Negotiations for a Protocol to the Convention commenced in 1995 after the first conference of the parties, meeting in Berlin, determined that the commitments provided for in Article 4(2)(a) and (b) of the Convention were 'not adequate' and decided to launch a process to strengthen the commitments of Annex I parties through the adoption of a protocol or another legal instrument.[298] The 'Berlin Mandate' was to

> [a]im, as the priority in the process of strengthening the commitments in Article 4.2(a) and (b) of the Convention, for developed country/other Parties included in Annex I, both to elaborate policies and measures, as well as to set quantified limitation and reduction objectives within specified timeframes, such as 2005, 2010 and 2020, for their anthropogenic emissions by sources and removals by sinks of greenhouse gases not controlled by the Montreal Protocol.[299]

The process was not intended to introduce any new commitments for non-Annex I parties, but merely to 'reaffirm existing commitments in Article 4.1 and continue to advance the implementation of these commitments'.[300] Negotiations were to be conducted as a matter of urgency with a view to adopting the results at the third conference of the parties in 1997.[301] At the second conference of the parties at Geneva in 1996, a Ministerial Declaration was adopted by which Ministers urged their representatives to accelerate negotiations on a legally binding protocol or another legal instrument, and stated that:

> [the] outcome should fully encompass the remit of the Berlin Mandate, in particular:
>
> – commitments for Annex I Parties regarding:
>   • policies and measures including, as appropriate, regarding energy, transport, industry, agriculture, forestry, waste management, economic instruments, institutions and mechanisms;

---

[297] Kyoto, 10 December 1997, not yet in force; reprinted at 37 ILM 22 (1998).

[298] See Decision 1/CP.3, Report of the Conference of the Parties on its Third Session, Kyoto, 1–11 December 1997, FCCC/CP/1997/7/Add.1.

[299] Decision 1/CP.1, Report of the Conference of the Parties on its First Session, Berlin, 28 March–7 April 1995, FCCC/CP/1995/7/Add.1, para. 2(a).

[300] *Ibid.*, para. 2(b).   [301] *Ibid.*, para. 6.

- quantified legally-binding objectives for emission limitations and significant overall reductions within specified timeframes, such as 2005, 2010, 2020, with respect to their anthropogenic emissions by sources and removals by sinks of greenhouse gases not controlled by the Montreal Protocol;
  - commitments for all Parties on continuing to advance the implementation of existing commitments in Article 4.1.[302]

The Geneva Ministerial Declaration clarified the scope of the Berlin Mandate in the final push of preparatory meetings leading up to the third conference of the parties in 1997. The Kyoto Protocol was adopted at the third conference of the parties and opened for signature on 16 March 1998.

Given the economic and developmental implications, it is not surprising that the Kyoto Protocol negotiations were among the most difficult and complex ever conducted for a multilateral environmental agreement. Deep divisions between the parties emerged in relation to a range of key issues, such as emissions reduction targets, sinks, emissions trading, joint implementation and the treatment of developing countries. Although consensus was reached at Kyoto, subsequent negotiations on the detailed rules, guidelines and methodologies needed to implement the Protocol have proved equally contentious as the original negotiations for the Protocol. In early 2001, the future of the Protocol was thrown into doubt with the announcement by President George W. Bush that the United States (responsible for about a quarter of 1990 global greenhouse gas emissions) would not ratify the Protocol.[303] Nevertheless, at the resumed session of the sixth conference of the parties, held in Bonn in July 2001, the remaining states parties reached agreement on mechanisms for implementing commitments under the Protocol. The 'Bonn Agreements' were not drafted as a legal text, but, at a political level, reflected an important breakthrough on many of the critical negotiating issues, and a clear signal that the world community was prepared to go ahead with the Kyoto Protocol, even without United States support.[304] It remained for the political agreement in Bonn to be converted into a legal text, which was the task of the seventh conference of the parties held in November 2001. The parties were able to incorporate almost all of the deals made in Bonn into the legal text of the 'Marrakesh Accords', a series of decisions concerning the implementation of the Kyoto Protocol which pave the way for its entry into force.[305] With the announcement by Japan and Russia at

---

[302] Geneva Ministerial Declaration, Annex, Report of the Conference of the Parties on its Second Session, Geneva, 8–19 July 1996, FCCC/CP/1996/15/Add.1.

[303] See Transcript, Bush Press Conference at White House, 29 March 2001, available at http://usinfo.state.gov/topical/global/environ/climate/01032904.htm.

[304] 'The Bonn Agreements on the Implementation of the Buenos Aires Plan of Action', Decision 5/CP.6, Report of the Conference of the Parties on the Second Part of its Sixth Session, Bonn, 16–24 July 2001, FCCC/CP/2001/5, 36–49.

[305] See Report of the Conference of the Parties on its Seventh Session, Marrakesh, 29 October–10 November 2001, FCCC/CP/2001/13. The decisions of the seventh conference of the parties which make up the Accords are in four volumes: FCCC/CP/2001/13/Add.1–Add.4.

the WSSD in September 2002 that they would ratify the Protocol, its entry into force during 2003 or 2004 seemed likely.

Emissions reduction targets and timetable

The major achievement of the Kyoto Protocol was the commitment of Annex I parties to quantified emissions reduction targets and a timetable for their achievement. The basic obligation accepted by the Annex I parties is set out in Article 3(1). It provides that Annex I parties 'shall, individually or jointly, ensure that their aggregate anthropogenic carbon dioxide equivalent emissions of the greenhouse gases listed in Annex A do not exceed their assigned amounts'.[306] The 'assigned amounts' are calculated pursuant to each party's quantified emissions limitation and reduction commitment set out in Annex B. Annex I parties must implement their obligation under Article 3(1) 'with a view to reducing their overall emissions of [Annex A] gases by at least 5 per cent below 1990 levels in the commitment period 2008 to 2012'. This is estimated to represent an actual reduction of about 30 per cent over 'business as usual' emissions levels.

By 2005, each Annex I party is required to 'have made demonstrable progress in achieving its commitments under [the] Protocol'.[307] The first commitment period commences in 2008 and continues until 2012. Annex I parties with economies in transition can use a base year other than 1990, calculated in accordance with Article 3(5). Commitments for subsequent periods will be established by amendments to Annex B adopted in accordance with the provisions of Article 21(7). The Meeting of the Parties to the Protocol is required to initiate reconsideration of the commitments in Annex B by 2005.[308] Banking of assigned amounts for future commitment periods is permitted as any Annex I party with emissions in a commitment period which are less than its assigned amount can request the difference be added to its assigned amount for subsequent commitment periods.[309]

The determination of emissions targets for the Annex I parties was a difficult issue. Annex B lists differentiated targets for individual countries and regional economic organisations. For example, the European Community and its member states agreed to an emissions limitation of 92 per cent of the 1990 base year, or an 8 per cent reduction in the first commitment period of 2008–12. The United States agreed to a 7 per cent reduction. Japan and Canada each accepted a 6 per cent reduction, while Australia and Iceland were permitted to make increases of respectively 8 per cent and 10 per cent. Russia, the largest emitter of the Eastern bloc countries, agreed to stabilise its emissions at 100 per cent of 1990 levels.

---

[306] The gases covered by the Protocol are carbon dioxide, methane, nitrous oxide, hydrofluorocarbons, perfluorocarbons and sulphur hexafluoride.

[307] Art. 3(2).   [308] Art. 3(9).

[309] Art. 13(3). However, borrowing assigned amounts from future commitment periods is not permitted.

Six gases are covered by the emissions reduction commitments of the Annex I parties: carbon dioxide, methane, nitrous oxide, hydrofluorocarbons, perfluorocarbons and sulphur hexafluoride.[310] The number of gases covered by the Protocol was also a controversial issue with strong disagreement during the negotiations as to whether only three (carbon dioxide, methane and nitrous oxide) or six (adding hydrofluorocarbons, perfluorocarbons and sulphur hexafluoride) gases should be covered. In the end, all six gases were listed in Annex A. However, Article 3(8) provides that any Annex I party may use 1995 as its base year for the latter three gases.

Policies and measures

Article 2 of the Protocol contains a list of policies and measures which parties may implement in order to achieve their quantified limitation and emissions reduction targets. During negotiations for the Protocol, the European Union pushed for the adoption of mandatory and co-ordinated 'policies and measures' but this was resisted by the United States, Canada, Australia and some other Annex I parties who sought a more flexible approach, with policies and measures to be determined principally by each individual party. This latter approach was largely adopted in Article 2, which provides that each Annex I party, in achieving its emissions limitation and reduction commitments under Article 3, shall implement policies and measures 'in accordance with its national circumstances'. A list of indicative measures follows, which includes enhancement of energy efficiency, the protection and enhancement of sinks, the promotion of sustainable forms of agriculture, increased research on and use of new and renewable forms of energy, measures to limit or reduce emissions in the transport sector and the limitation or reduction of methane emissions.[311] Parties are required to co-operate 'to enhance the individual and combined effectiveness of their policies and measures' through taking steps to share relevant experience and information, including developing ways of improving the compatibility, transparency and effectiveness of policies and measures.[312] Parties must pursue limitation and reduction of emissions from aviation and bunker fuels, which remain outside the scope of the Protocol, by working through the ICAO and IMO respectively.

Emissions trading, joint implementation and the CDM

By far the most innovative (and controversial) aspect of the Kyoto Protocol negotiations was the proposal to enable Annex I parties to meet their commitments under the Protocol by purchasing or acquiring credits representing greenhouse gas reductions in other countries. Emissions trading permits an Annex B party to 'buy' emissions reduction credits, in the form of assigned amounts units or AAUs, from another Annex B party where it would be more

---

[310] Annex A.   [311] Art. 2(1)(a).   [312] Art. 2(1)(b).

cost-effective for it to do so rather than to undertake the reduction domestically. The inclusion of emissions trading in the Protocol was strongly supported by the United States, which has domestic experience with similar schemes (although in more discrete areas such as sulphur dioxide emissions)[313] and advocated their adoption internationally as cost-effective means of achieving reductions of emissions in greenhouse gases. However, emissions trading was strongly opposed by many parties, particularly China and the Group of 77 developing countries.

An eleventh-hour compromise text was included in the Protocol as Article 17. This allows Annex B parties to 'participate in emissions trading for the purposes of fulfilling their commitments under Article 3', but provides that any such trading must be 'supplemental' to domestic actions taken to achieve emissions reductions. Article 17 left to the conference of the parties the task of defining 'relevant principles, modalities, rules and guidelines, in particular for verification, reporting and accountability for emissions trading.'[314]

A further economic incentive mechanism included in the Protocol is the possibility for joint implementation by Annex I parties of their emissions reduction commitments. Article 6 provides that, for the purpose of meeting its commitments under Article 3, any Annex I party may transfer to, or acquire from, any other Annex I party 'emission reduction credits resulting from projects aimed at reducing anthropogenic emissions by sources or enhancing anthropogenic removals by sinks of greenhouse gases in any sector of the economy'.[315] An Annex I party may authorise private legal entities, under its responsibility, to participate in actions leading to the generation, transfer or acquisition of emissions reduction units (ERUs) from joint implementation.[316] However, any such joint implementation must result in a reduction in emissions by sources, or an enhancement of removals by sinks, that is additional to any that would otherwise occur and should be supplemental to domestic actions.[317]

The Clean Development Mechanism (CDM) defined by Article 12 provides a further innovation, establishing a means for Annex I parties to gain emission reductions credits to assist them in achieving compliance with their quantified emissions limitation and reduction commitments under Article 3. As part of the CDM, Annex I parties can invest in emissions reductions projects in non-Annex I parties and use the certified emissions reductions (CERs) accruing from such project activities 'to contribute to compliance with part of their quantified emission limitation and reduction commitments under

---

[313] For example, its sulphur dioxide emissions trading scheme under Title IV of the Clean Air Act, 42 USC 7651.

[314] In December 2002, the EC adopted a regional emissions trading arrangement, designed to be implemented in accordance with the scheme to be established under the Kyoto Protocol. It will begin to operate in January 2005: chapter 4, p. 163 above.

[315] Art. 6(1).   [316] Art. 6(3).   [317] Art. 6(1)(b) and (d).

Article 3'.[318] Certified emissions reductions obtained between 2000 and 2005 can be used to assist in achieving compliance in the first commitment period.[319] A share of the proceeds from certified project activities must be used to cover administrative expenses 'as well as to assist developing country Parties that are particularly vulnerable to the adverse effects of climate change to meet the costs of adaptation'.[320]

The CDM is subject to the authority and guidance of the Conference of the Parties serving as the Meeting of the Parties to the Protocol and is to be supervised by an Executive Board.[321] Emissions reductions resulting from project activities require certification by operational entities to be designated by the Conference of the Parties serving as the Meeting of the Parties to the Protocol on the basis of various factors, including that the reductions in emissions are additional to any that would occur in the absence of the certified project activity and that there are real, measurable and long-term benefits related to the mitigation of climate change.[322] As with joint implementation, participation in the CDM may involve private and/or public entities, subject to the guidance of the Executive Board.[323] Article 12 leaves the 'modalities and procedures with the objective of ensuring transparency, efficiency and accountability through independent auditing and verification of project activities' to be elaborated by the Meeting of the Parties to the Protocol.[324]

Sinks

The inclusion of carbon sinks within the Protocol remained controversial up to the final stages of the negotiations. Some countries, particularly the United States and Australia, were strongly in favour of allowing activities which resulted in carbon sequestration (e.g. afforestation, reafforestation and land-use changes) to count towards their quantified commitments. The inclusion of carbon sinks was strongly opposed by other countries, particularly the members of the European Union. The final text adopted in Article 3(3) allowed for commitments to be met by 'net changes in greenhouse gas emissions by sources and removals by sinks resulting from direct human-induced land-use change and forestry activities, limited to afforestation, reforestation and deforestation since 1990, measured as verifiable changes in carbon stocks in each commitment period'. A last-minute proposal to include additional sinks resulted in the inclusion of Article 3(4) which provides that the Conference of the Parties serving as the Meeting of the Parties to the Protocol shall at its first session or as soon as practicable thereafter 'decide upon modalities, rules and guidelines as to how, and which, additional human-induced activities related to changes in greenhouse gas emissions by sources and removals by sinks in the agricultural soils and land-use change and forestry categories shall be added to, or

---

[318] Art. 12(3)(b).   [319] Art. 12(10).   [320] Art. 12(8).   [321] Art. 12(4).
[322] Art. 12(5).   [323] Art. 12(9).   [324] Art. 12(7).

subtracted from, the assigned amounts for parties included in Annex I'. Any such decision would apply in the second and subsequent commitment periods, although a party may choose to have it apply for the first commitment period, provided that the 'additional human-induced activities' have taken place since 1990.

Developing countries

Article 10 deals with that part of the 'Berlin Mandate' which called for the advancement of the implementation of commitments by all parties, including developing country parties. The Preamble to Article 10 affirms that the provision is not 'introducing any new commitments for Parties not included in Annex I' but is merely reaffirming existing commitments under Article 4(1) of the Convention, and 'continuing to advance the implementation of these commitments in order to achieve sustainable development'. A number of measures are listed in Article 10 which cover areas such as the formulation of 'cost-effective national, and where appropriate regional programmes to improve the quality of local emission factors, activity data and/or models which reflect the socioeconomic conditions of each Party for the preparation and periodic updating of national inventories' of emissions of greenhouse gases and the formulation, implementation, publication and updating of 'national and, where appropiate, regional programmes containing measures to mitigate climate change and measures to facilitate adequate adaption to climate change'. Other measures include the provision of information on programmes which contain measures addressing climate change and its adverse impacts, and the promotion of effective modalities relating to the transfer of environmentally sound technologies pertinent to climate change.

Reporting and compliance

Detailed reporting obligations for Annex I parties are established by Articles 5, 7 and 8 of the Protocol. These build upon the reporting and review procedures developed under the Convention, particularly the in-depth review process. Article 5(1) provides that each Annex I party is required to have in place, no later than 2007, a national system for the estimation of anthropogenic emissions by sources and removals by sinks of greenhouse gases. Guidelines for such national systems are to be decided upon by the Conference of the Parties serving as the Meeting of the Parties to the Protocol at its first session. Under Article 7(1), each Annex I party is required to incorporate in its annual inventory of anthropogenic emissions by sources and removals by sinks, 'the necessary supplementary information for the purposes of ensuring compliance with Article 3'. Annex I parties are also required to include supplementary information to demonstrate compliance with commitments under the Protocol.[325]

---

[325] Art. 7(2).

The information submitted under Article 7 by Annex I parties will be reviewed by 'expert review teams' in accordance with guidelines to be adopted by the Meeting of the Parties at its first session.[326] The review process is to provide 'a thorough and comprehensive technical assessment of all aspects of the implementation by a Party' of the Protocol.[327] The expert review teams report to the Meeting of the Parties on the implementation of commitments by the party, identifying any potential problems in, and factors influencing, the fulfilment of commitments.[328] The reports of the expert review teams are circulated to all parties to the Convention, and the Conference of the Parties will consider the information submitted under Article 7 and the expert review reports and 'take decisions on any matter required for the implementation of [the] Protocol'.[329]

Apart from the review of information submitted by parties, the Protocol contemplates a further mechanism for ensuring compliance with commitments under the Protocol. Article 18 provides that the Meeting of the Parties at its first session shall 'approve appropriate and effective procedures and mechanisms to determine and to address cases of non-compliance with the provisions of this Protocol, including through the development of an indicative list of consequences, taking into account the cause, type, degree and frequency of non-compliance'. However, any such procedures and mechanisms entailing 'binding consequences' would require an amendment to the Protocol.

Entry into force and amendments

In order to enter into force, the Protocol requires the ratification, acceptance, approval or accession of at least fifty-five parties to the Convention, which must include Annex I parties which accounted for at least 55 per cent of the total carbon dioxide emissions of Annex I parties in 1990. The refusal of the world's largest greenhouse gas emitter, the United States, to ratify the Protocol made the participation by other Annex I parties with significant emissions, such as Japan, the European Community and Russia, essential for the Protocol to come into force. Japan, the European Community and Canada recently ratified the Protocol, bringing the number of parties to 100. In September 2002, at the World Summit on Sustainable Development held in Johannesburg, Russia pledged that it would ratify the Protocol in the near future, making likely its entry into force in 2003 or 2004.

Amendments to the Protocol can be adopted by a three-fourths majority vote of the parties present and voting at the meeting at which it is proposed for adoption, followed by its ratification or acceptance by at least three-fourths of the parties to the Protocol.

---

[326] Art. 8(1).   [327] Art. 8(3).   [328] *Ibid.*   [329] Art. 8(5) and (6).

Subsequent developments: the Marrakesh Accords

Following the adoption of the Protocol, negotiations continued on the sub-sidiary rules, guidelines and methodologies called for by the Protocol text. A number of issues reflected divisions between states. Some of these covered matters relating to the implementation of commitments under the Conven-tion, particularly those relating to financing, capacity-building, adaptation and transfer of technology. Other matters related to the Protocol, such as carbon sinks, rules for emissions trading and penalties for non-compliance with com-mitments. These are addressed in the 'Marrakesh Accords' agreed at the seventh conference of the parties in November 2001.[330] The 218-page Marrakesh Ac-cords translate the Bonn Agreements into a legal text of some complexity, sug-gesting 'more possibilities for hidden meanings, ambiguities and "agreements to disagree" than the almost 30 pages of the Kyoto Protocol'.[331]

The sections of the Marrakesh Accords dealing with Protocol issues will be presented to the first meeting of the Conference of the Parties serving as the Meeting of the Parties to the Protocol for adoption. A major compo-nent of the Marrakesh Accords relates to the rules for implementation of the Kyoto Protocol's 'flexibility mechanisms', the establishment of a compliance mechanism (potentially one of the most important aspects of the Marrakesh Accords[332]) and the elaboration of permissible land-use, land-use change and forestry (LULUCF) activities. Building on the Bonn Agreements, the Accords also consolidate matters under the Convention relating to funding arrange-ments[333] and capacity-building provisions for developing countries,[334] and provide guidelines for the preparation of National Adaptation Programmes for Action (NAPAs).[335] The Accords also provide guidelines on national systems for the estimation of anthropogenic sources of greenhouse gas emissions, the

---

[330] The Marrakesh Accords are reproduced in four volumes of the Report of the seventh conference of the parties, FCCC/CP/2001/13/Add.1–Add.4. A useful summary of the Kyoto Protocol provisions as supplemented by the Marrakesh Accords has been produced by the Climate Change Secretariat, *A Guide to the Climate Change Convention and its Kyoto Protocol* (2002), at http://unfccc.int/resource/guideconvkp-p.pdf.

[331] *Ibid.*   [332] Decision 24/CP.7; see chapter 4, p. 162 above.

[333] Three new funds are established, two under the UNFCCC and one under the Protocol. The new Convention funds are a 'special climate change' fund to finance activities, pro-grammes and measures related to climate change and a fund for least developed countries: Marrakesh Accords, Decision 7/CP.7. Under the Protocol an 'adaptation fund' is estab-lished to finance concrete adaptation programmes and projects in developing countries. The fund will be financed by voluntary contributions (the EU, together with Canada, Iceland, New Zealand, Norway and Switzerland made a commitment at the Bonn meet-ing to contribute collectively 450 million euros annually by 2005) and 2 per cent of the proceeds generated by CDM projects: Decision 10/CP.7.

[334] *Ibid.*, Decision 2/CP.7. Decision 3/CP.7 deals with capacity-building for parties with economies in transition.

[335] *Ibid.*, Decision 28/CP.7.

preparation of information required for fulfilment of the reporting obligations under the Protocol, and performance of reviews by expert review teams under Article 8.[336]

In relation to the flexibility mechanisms as a whole, the Marrakesh Accords do not place a numerical cap on their use to fulfil emissions reduction commitments, as was urged by the EU, developing countries and many environmental NGOs; instead the Accords provide that the use of these mechanisms is to be 'supplemental to domestic action' and that domestic action must constitute a 'significant element' of the effort made by Annex I parties in meeting their commitments under Article 3(1) of the Protocol.[337] While there is thus no quantitative limit on *acquiring* credits to use towards fulfilling emissions reduction commitments, the parties did agree to adopt a safeguard against *overselling* of emission reduction credits by participating countries. All Annex I parties are required to keep a 'Commitment Period Reserve' (CPR) at all times which consists of either 90 per cent of their originally assigned AAUs, or five times the emissions of the most recently reviewed emissions inventory, whichever is the lower.[338]

Emissions reduction credits, in the form of AAUs, ERUs and CERs, gained through use of the flexibility mechanisms, as well as 'removal units' (RMUs) generated by sink activities, may be used to meet the emissions reduction commitments of Annex I parties under Article 3(1).[339] Transfers and acquisitions of credits may take place between national registries under the responsibility of the parties, and each national registry will maintain electronic accounts of a party's AAUs, ERUs, CERs and RMUs, as well as accounts for holdings of any legal entities authorised by the party to engage in the acquisition and transfer of credits.[340]

Eligibility to participate in the flexibility mechanisms is limited to Annex I parties which have ratified the Protocol and complied with their methodological and reporting requirements under Articles 5 and 7.[341] Japanese and Russian resistance prevented agreement on a strict link between acceptance of the arrangements for dealing with non-compliance under the Protocol (discussed below) and eligibility to participate in the Protocol's flexibility mechanisms.[342]

---

[336] *Ibid.*, Decisions 20/CP.7, 22/CP.7 and 23/CP.7.   [337] *Ibid.*, Decision 15/CP.7, para. 1.

[338] *Ibid.*, Decision 18/CP.7, Annex, para. 6. The commitment period reserve may consist of holdings of ERUs, CERs, AAUs and/or RMUs for the relevant commitment period which have not been acquired by an Annex I party.

[339] Marrakesh Accords, Decision 15/CP.7, para. 6.

[340] Decision 19/CP.7, paras. 17 and 19. The Climate Change Secretariat will establish a transaction log to verify transactions of credits as they are proposed and to halt any transactions where a discrepancy is detected: paras. 38–43.

[341] Decision 15/CP.7, para. 5.

[342] Decision 15/CP.7, para. 5 requires the enforcement branch of the compliance committee to provide oversight of eligibility to participate in the flexibility mechanisms. See also

The Marrakesh Accords adopt detailed modalities and guidelines for each of the flexibility mechanisms.[343] In relation to the Clean Development Mechanism (CDM), the Marrakesh Accords affirm that it is the host party's prerogative to confirm whether a CDM project activity assists it in achieving sustainable development, although Annex I parties must 'refrain from using certified emission reductions generated from nuclear facilities' to meet their commitments under Article 3(1).[344] Afforestation and reafforestation are the only eligible land-use and forestry projects allowed under the CDM in the first commitment period,[345] and for the first commitment period the total additions to a party's assigned amount resulting from such activities may not exceed 1 per cent of the base year emissions of the party multiplied by five.

The parties have agreed to a 'prompt start' for the CDM, so that project activities starting from 2000 may register to accrue CERs, to be certified by the newly established Executive Board elected at the seventh conference of the parties.[346] They have also agreed upon the composition and functioning of the Executive Board of the CDM.[347] Two initial tasks for the Executive Board include the development of a simplified procedure for small-scale projects under the CDM, and the accreditation of independent organisations, known as operational entities, which play a central role in the validation of proposed CDM project activities and the verification and certification of emission reductions.[348] To be validated by an operational entity, a project must result in emissions reductions which are 'additional' to any that would have occurred in the absence of the project.[349] The issue of a certification report by a designated

the decisions relating to each of the flexibility mechanisms: Decision 16/CP.7, Annex, para. 22(b) (joint implementation); Decision 17/CP.7, Annex, para. 32(b) (CDM); Decision 18/CP.7, Annex, para. 3(b) (emissions trading).

[343] See Decision 16/CP.7 (joint implementation); Decision 17/CP.7 (CDM); and Decision 18/CP.7 (emissions trading).

[344] Decision 17/CP.7, Preamble.

[345] The Subsidiary Body for Scientific and Technical Advice has been requested by the conference of the parties to develop definitions and modalities for including afforestation and reafforestation project activities under the CDM with the aim of adopting a decision on this matter at the ninth conference of the parties: *ibid.*, paras. 7 and 10.

[346] *Ibid.*, paras. 1 and 13.   [347] *Ibid.*, Annex, paras. 7, 12 and 13.

[348] *Ibid.*, Annex, para. 27. 'Validation' involves the independent evaluation of a project activity by a designated operational entity against the requirements of the CDM set out in Decision 17/CP.7 and other relevant decisions of the COP/MOP. A validated project then becomes 'registered' when it is formally accepted by the Executive Board as a CDM project activity. 'Verification' involves the periodic independent review and *ex post* determination by the designated operational entity of the monitored reductions in anthropogenic emissions by sources that have occurred as a result of the registered CDM project activity. 'Certification' is the written assurance by the operational entity that the project activity achieved the verified reductions within a specified period of time.

[349] *Ibid.*, Annex, para. 43. Additionality is determined by reference to project-specific baselines and monitoring plans devised according to methodologies specified in the Marrakesh Accords.

operational entity is the basis for the Executive Board's issuing CERs equal to the verified amount of emissions reductions.[350] The Accords also provide that public funding for CDM project activities must not result in a diversion in official development assistance and is separate from and not counted towards the financial obligations of Annex I parties under the Protocol. The parties agree that 2 per cent of the certified emission reductions issued for CDM project activities would go towards assisting developing country parties that are particularly vulnerable to the adverse effects of climate change to meet the costs of adaptation.[351]

The Marrakesh Accords' guidelines for implementation of Article 6 (joint implementation) are less elaborate than those for the CDM. An Article 6 supervisory committee is established to supervise the verification of ERUs from joint implementation activities, and its composition and functioning are provided for.[352] A two-track procedure is established for verification of ERUs from joint implementation activities. Where a host party meets the eligibility requirements for participation in the flexibility mechanisms, it may itself certify ERUs generated by activities within its territory as being additional to reductions that would otherwise be made. If the host party does not meet the eligibility requirements it may still host joint implementation projects; however, any resulting ERUs have to be verified by the Article 6 supervisory committee under a procedure comparable to the CDM procedure.[353] Projects starting from 2000 may qualify as joint implementation activities, but the resulting ERUs may only be issued for a crediting period starting after 2008.[354]

At Marrakesh, the parties agreed on a number of new provisions regarding land-use, land-use change and forestry (LULUCF) activities eligible to be credited against the assigned amounts for Annex I parties in accordance with Article 3(4) of the Protocol. Various governing principles for the inclusion of LULUCF activities were articulated:

- the treatment of such activities is to be based on 'sound science';
- consistent methodologies are to be used for estimation and reporting of these activities;
- the mere presence of carbon stocks is to be excluded from accounting, as is increased removals due to faster growth caused by increasing concentrations of atmospheric carbon dioxide and indirect nitrogen deposition associated with climate change;

---

[350] *Ibid.*, Annex, para. 64. CERs are issued automatically by the Executive Board unless a party involved in the project activity or at least three members of the Executive Board request a review of the proposed issuance; any review of proposed issues of CERs is limited to matters of fraud, malfeasance or incompetence of the designated operational entity: para. 65.

[351] *Ibid.*, para. 15.   [352] Decision 16/CP.7, para. 3; and Annex, paras. 4 and 15.

[353] Annex, paras. 23 and 24.   [354] *Ibid.*, para. 5.

- any reversals of LULUCF removals are to be accounted for at the appropriate time; and
- the implementation of LULUCF activities must contribute to biodiversity conservation and sustainable use of natural resources.[355]

Forest management, cropland management, grazing land management and revegetation were designated as additional eligible LULUCF activities under Article 3(4) of the Protocol.[356] A party may choose to apply these activities during the first commitment period provided it makes its choice of eligible activities prior to the start of that period.[357] To include such activities, the party must be able to demonstrate that the activities occurred since 1990 and are human-induced.[358]

Removal by sinks generated a new category of emissions reduction credits known as removal units (RMUs). To be available for credit against an Annex I party's emissions reduction commitment under Article 3(1), RMUs must be verified by the expert review teams established by the Protocol. Use of RMUs to meet emission reduction targets during the first commitment period is subject to conditions. First, as a general rule, any emissions from eligible LULUCF activities must be offset by emissions cuts or removals elsewhere.[359] Secondly, if a party's afforestation, reafforestation and deforestation activities result in emissions which are greater than the amount of removals, the party can offset these emissions against removals from forest management activities up to a total of nine megatonnes of carbon (MtC) per year.[360] Thirdly, the extent to which removals from forest management activities can be accounted for beyond 9 MtC per year is subject to country-specific numerical caps.[361] Finally, emissions and removals from cropland management, grazing management and revegetation can only be used to help meet emissions targets on a net-net basis, i.e. the net change in carbon stocks from LULUCF emissions and removals during 1990, multiplied by five, will be subtracted from the net change in LULUCF carbon stocks during the first commitment period for land where such activities took place.[362]

---

[355] Decision 11/CP.7, para. 1.

[356] *Ibid.*, Annex, para. 6. Definitions are in Decision 11/CP.7, Annex, para. 1.

[357] *Ibid.*, Annex, para. 7.

[358] *Ibid.*, Annex, para. 8. Activities credited under Art. 3.4 cannot also be credited under Art. 3.3.

[359] *Ibid.*, Annex, para. 4.   [360] *Ibid.*, Annex, para. 10.

[361] *Ibid.*, para. 11 and Appendix. At Bonn, Russia agreed to a figure of 17.63 megatonnes of carbon (MtC) per year from forest management. However, it subsequently questioned the validity of this figure, asserting that carbon-absorbing activities from forest management accounted for 33 MtC annually. To prevent the Accords unravelling, Decision 12/CP.7 was agreed upon, authorising a figure of 33 MtC per year for credits from forest management for Russia.

[362] Decision 11/CP.7, para. 9.

Outer space

C. Christol, *The Modern Law of Outer Space* (1982); B. Schafer, 'Solid, Hazardous and Radioactive Wastes in Outer Space, Present Control and Suggested Changes', 19 *California Western International Law Journal* 1 (1988); K. H. Bockstiegel, *Environmental Aspects of Activities in Outer Space* (Proceedings of the 1988 Cologne Colloquium, 1990); H. Baker, *Space Debris: Legal and Policy Implications* (1989); L. D. Roberts, 'Addressing the Problem of Orbital Space Debris: Combining International Regulatory and Liability Regimes', 15 BCICLR 51 (1992); R. I. R. Abeyratme, 'The Use of Nuclear Power Sources in Outer Space and Its Effect on Environmental Protection', 25 *Journal of Space Law* 17 (1997); I. H. P. Diederiks-Verschoor, *An Introduction to Space Law* ((1999, 2nd edn); D. Tan, 'Towards a New Regime for the Protection of Outer Space as the "Province of All Mankind"', 25 *Yale Journal of International Law* 145 (2000); website: www.oosa.unvienna.org/index.html.

Environmental problems in outer space are of three types: orbital space debris; environmental damage caused on or to other planets as a result of human exploratory activity; and environmental damage caused on earth as a result of man-made objects falling from space. The international legal regime regulating environmental aspects of outer space includes three treaties and two sets of principles: the Treaty on Principles Governing the Activities of States in the Exploration and Use of Outer Space Including the Moon and Other Celestial Bodies (1967 Outer Space Treaty);[363] the Convention on Registration of Objects Launched into Outer Space (1975 Space Registration Convention);[364] the Agreement Governing the Activities of States on the Moon and Other Celestial Bodies (1979 Moon Treaty);[365] and the Principles Relevant to the Use of Nuclear Power Sources in Outer Space (1992 Outer Space Principles).[366] The 1972 Space Liability Convention is considered in chapter 18 below.

Four of these agreements were adopted before environmental considerations had become an important international legal issue, and do not reflect some of the legal innovations which have occurred in the past decade. In the meantime, increased human activity in outer space has contributed to greater

---

[363] London, Moscow, Washington, 27 January 1967, in force 10 October 1967, 610 UNTS 205.
[364] 14 January 1975, in force 15 September 1976, 28 UST 695.
[365] New York, 5 December 1979, in force 11 July 1984, 18 ILM 1434 (1979).
[366] UNGA Res. 47/68, 32 ILM 917 (1993). See also the Declaration on International Cooperation in the Exploration and Use of Outer Space for the Benefit and in the Interest of All States, Taking into Particular Account the Needs of Developing Countries, UNGA Res. 51/122.

environmental threats. It has been estimated that space debris now comprises some 7,000 pieces of debris larger than ten centimetres; 17,500 pieces of between one and ten centimetres; and 3,500,000 pieces of less than one centimetre.[367] Space debris constitutes an environmental hazard as it increases the risk of collision and consequential damage; because of the high speed at which they travel, objects as small as one centimetre can penetrate the crew compartments of spacecraft, and debris one-half millimetre in size can kill an astronaut protected only by a spacesuit.[368]

1967 Outer Space Treaty

The 1967 Outer Space Treaty states that the exploration and use of outer space (including the moon and other celestial bodies) is to be carried out for the benefit and interests of all countries, and shall be 'the province of all mankind'.[369] Outer space is not subject to national claims of sovereignty and all activities are to be carried out in the interest of maintaining international peace and security.[370] The Treaty includes provisions with important implications for environmental protection. In particular, nuclear weapons and other weapons of mass destruction may not be placed in orbit around the earth, installed on celestial bodies, or stationed in outer space, and the moon and other celestial bodies may only be used for 'peaceful purposes'.[371]

Article IX sets out some fundamental obligations:[372] exploration and use of outer space is to be guided by the principle of co-operation and mutual assistance, and all activities are to be conducted 'with due regard to the corresponding interests' of all other parties to the Treaty. Moreover, studies and exploration of outer space must avoid 'the harmful contamination and adverse changes in the environment of the earth resulting from the introduction of extra-territorial matter'. Parties are also under an obligation to undertake 'appropriate international consultations' before proceeding with activities or experiments which may cause 'potentially harmful interference' with activities of other state parties. It is evident that the approach of Article IX is directed towards the protection of human beings, rather than the protection of the environment as an end in itself.

---

[367] Figures cited in L. D. Roberts, 'Addressing the Problem of Orbital Space Debris: Combining International Regulatory and Liability Regimes', 15 BCICLR 53 (1992); the sources of debris include fragments caused by explosion, hyper-velocity impact or deterioration of the surfaces of payloads, as well as inactive payloads, spent rocket thrusters and other material produced by spacecraft operations: *ibid.*, 54–5.

[368] *Ibid.*, 55.   [369] Art. I.   [370] Arts. II and III.   [371] Art. IV.

[372] The 1967 Treaty also includes provisions on international responsibility and liability (Arts. VI and VIII): see chapter 18, pp. 896–8 below.

1979 Moon Treaty

The 1979 Moon Treaty, which applies to the moon and celestial bodies other than the earth, provides that the moon and its natural resources are the 'common heritage of mankind' and are to be used exclusively for peaceful purposes.[373] Exploration and use of the moon is the province of all mankind, and due regard is to be paid in activities relating to it, and to the interests of present and future generations.[374] Article 7 sets out provisions on the protection of the environment of celestial bodies going beyond that established in the 1967 Outer Space Treaty. In their exploration and use of the moon, the parties are required to:

> take measures to prevent the disruption of the existing balance of its environment whether by introducing adverse changes in that environment, by its harmful contamination through the introduction of extra-environmental matter or otherwise. States parties shall also take measures to avoid harmfully affecting the environment of the earth through the introduction of extra-territorial matter or otherwise.[375]

The 1979 Treaty does not prohibit the placement of radioactive materials on the moon but does require the UN Secretary General to be notified in advance of all such placements. The Treaty also provides for the possible designation of international scientific preserves.[376] The exploitation of the natural resources of the moon is not prohibited by the Treaty. Instead, the parties agree to establish an international regime to govern such exploitation when it is about to become feasible, and to include in such a regime provisions for the orderly and safe development and rational management of the moon's natural resources.[377] Although the provisions on the exploitation of the moon's natural resources do not expressly refer to the need to establish rules on environmental protection, they should be read as being subject to the environmental protection requirements established by Article 7. The 1979 Moon Treaty includes provisions on international responsibility and recognises the need to develop arrangements on liability.[378]

Outer Space Principles

The eleven Principles Relevant to the Use of Nuclear Power Sources in Outer Space, which were adopted by the UN General Assembly in December 1992, were prepared by the Committee on the Peaceful Uses of Outer Space.[379] In

---

[373] Arts. 1(1), 3(1) and 11(1).   [374] Art. 4(1).

[375] Art. 7(1). Parties are also required to take all practicable measures to safeguard the life and health of persons on the moon: Art. 10(1).

[376] Art. 7(2) and (3).   [377] Art. 11(5) and (7)(a) and (b).

[378] Art. 14.   [379] UNGA Res. 47/68 (1992).

order to minimise the quantity of radioactive material in space, Principle 3 provides that the use of nuclear power sources in space is to be restricted to those missions which cannot be operated by non-nuclear energy sources in a reasonable way. To that end, the Principles establish general goals for radioactive protection and safety, including the requirement that hazards in foreseeable operational or accidental circumstances are kept within acceptable levels and that radioactive material does not cause a 'significant contamination' of outer space.[380] The use of nuclear reactors in space is limited to interplanetary missions, in sufficiently high orbits and to low-earth orbits if they are subsequently stored in sufficiently high orbits,[381] and only highly enriched uranium-235 may be used as fuel. Radio-isotope generators may only be used for interplanetary missions and other missions leaving earth's gravity.[382] The Principles also include rules on safety assessment, the notification of re-entry, consultation and assistance to states, and on responsibility and liability.[383]

UNCED

Chapter 9 of Agenda 21, on 'Protection of the Atmosphere', was among the most difficult subjects addressed at UNCED – evidence of the potential impacts of international environmental regulation on the fundamental economic interests of many states. A number of OPEC states, led by Saudi Arabia, Libya and Kuwait, opposed the Chapter in its entirety. The political sensitivity of Chapter 9 is clear from its introduction, which states that 'the recommendations contained in this chapter do not oblige any Government to take measures which exceed the provisions' of the 1985 Vienna Convention, the 1987 Montreal Protocol as amended, the 1992 Climate Change Convention, and any other international, including regional, instruments.[384] On the other hand, to achieve a balance and with an eye to possible future trade disputes over unilateral national atmospheric protection and energy standards, it is also stated that 'within the framework of this chapter, Governments are free to carry out additional measures which are consistent with those legal instruments'.[385] The Chapter establishes four programme areas which emphasise the priorities of the international community in the coming years: addressing uncertainties; promoting sustainable development; preventing stratospheric ozone depletion; and transboundary air pollution.

---

[380] Principle 3(1)(a). Acceptable levels are defined in Principle 3(1)(b) and (c), including recommendations of the ICRP, generally accepted international radiological protection guidelines and specified numerical values.
[381] Principle 3(2).   [382] Principle 3(3).
[383] Principles 4 to 7; see chapter 18, pp. 896–8 below.
[384] Para. 9.2.   [385] Ibid.

*Addressing uncertainties: improving the scientific basis
for decision-making*

The basic objective of this programme area is to improve the understanding of the processes that influence and are influenced by the earth's atmosphere on a global, regional and local scale, to enhance international co-operation, and to improve understanding of the economic and social consequences of atmospheric changes and mitigation and response measures.[386] To those ends, the programme area proposes, *inter alia*, a more balanced geographical coverage of the Global Climate Observing System and its components, including Global Atmosphere Watch, co-operation in early detection systems, developing methodologies, and identifying threshold levels of atmospheric pollutants and greenhouse gas concentrations.[387]

Promoting sustainable development

This programme head contains sections on energy development efficiency and consumption, transportation, industrial development, and resource development and land use. With regard to the energy sector, the programme recognises that:

> the need to control atmospheric emissions of greenhouse and other gases and substances will increasingly need to be based on efficiency in energy production, transmission, distribution and consumption, and on growing reliance on environmentally sound energy systems, particularly new and renewable sources of energy.[388]

The objective of the programme area is:

> to reduce adverse effects on the atmosphere from the energy sector by promoting policies or programmes, as appropriate, to increase the contribution of environmentally safe and sound and cost-effective energy systems, particularly new and renewable ones, through less polluting and more efficient energy production, transmission, distribution and use. The objective should reflect the need for equity, adequate energy supplies and increasing energy consumption in developing countries as well as the needs of certain vulnerable countries.[389]

---

[386] Para. 9.7.   [387] Para. 9.8.

[388] Para. 9.9. New and renewable sources of energy are defined as 'solar thermal, solar photovoltaic, wind, hydro, biomass, geothermal ocean, animal and human power, as referred to in the reports of the Committee on the Development and Utilisation of New and Renewable Sources of Energy', prepared specifically for UNCED: see A/CONF.151/PC/119 and A/AC.218/1992/5.

[389] Para. 9.11.

The programme area identifies activities to be carried out by governments which could serve as a possible basis for future international legislation, and is important as the first occasion on which the whole of the international community has come together to propose the basis for future international energy policy. The programme area seeks: to promote research into, and the development, transfer and use of, improved energy efficient technologies and practices and sound energy systems; to promote the development of capacities to develop, produce and use increasingly efficient and less polluting forms of energy; to review current energy supply mixes; to co-ordinate energy plans regionally and sub-regionally; to promote cost-effective policies or programmes (including administrative, social and economic measures) to improve energy efficiency; to promote energy efficiency and emissions standards at the national level; to encourage education and public awareness about energy efficiency and environmentally sound energy systems; and to establish energy efficiency labelling programmes.[390]

Apart from the rules established by the ICAO in respect of aircraft emissions, the UNECE rules for motor vehicles, and the rules of EC law, international legislation on pollution from the transport sector is minimal. In the UN system, no single institution or body has responsibility for transport in general, and the regulation of its environmental protection standards in particular. The Agenda 21 programme area on transportation is therefore an indicator of possible future international legal developments. The overall objective of the programme area on transportation is to develop cost-effective policies and programmes to limit, reduce or control harmful atmospheric emissions and other adverse environmental effects of the transport sector, taking into account development priorities, safety and national circumstances.[391] The programme area on industrial development seeks to encourage industrial development in ways that minimise adverse impacts on the atmosphere by increasing industry's efficiency in consumption and production, improving pollution-abatement technologies, and developing new environmentally sound technologies.[392] Both programme areas are to be achieved through measures taken by governments, intergovernmental and non-governmental organisations and the private sector, *inter alia*, to develop cost-effective, more efficient and less polluting transport systems, particularly rural and urban mass transit; to encourage the transfer of resource-efficient and less polluting transport and other industrial technologies, particularly to developing countries; to develop technologies, products and processes which are less polluting and more efficient in their use of natural resources; and to promote administrative, social and economic measures to encourage transport modes and industrial practices which minimise adverse impacts on the atmosphere.[393] The programme area on terrestrial and marine resource development and land use is designed to reduce atmospheric pollution

---

[390] Para. 9.12.   [391] Para. 9.14.   [392] Para. 9.17.   [393] Paras. 9.15 and 9.18.

and limit anthropogenic emissions of greenhouse gases; to conserve, sustainably manage and enhance greenhouse gas sinks and natural and environmental resources; and to ensure that atmospheric changes are fully taken into account in planning and implementing policies and programmes.[394]

Preventing stratospheric ozone depletion

The objective of this programme area does little more than call for further international support of the Vienna Convention and Montreal Protocol.[395] It does call for further expansion of the Global Ozone Observing System and the replacement of CFCs and other ozone-depleting substances with substances the suitability of which 'should be evaluated holistically and not simply based on its contribution to solving one atmospheric or environmental problem'.[396]

Transboundary atmospheric pollution

Central to this programme area is the objective of establishing new regional agreements for limiting transboundary air pollution, based upon the experience of the 1979 LRTAP Convention and its Protocols, and ensuring the implementation of that agreement.[397] The programme also calls for the strengthening of systematic observation and monitoring, the development and exchange of emissions control technologies from mobile and stationary sources, and the establishment and strengthening of early warning systems and response mechanisms for transboundary air pollution from industrial and nuclear accidents and natural disasters.[398]

World Summit on Sustainable Development

The Implementation Plan of the WSSD identifies the 1992 Climate Change Convention as the key instrument for addressing climate change, and affirms the commitment to meet its objective, and includes a call by all states which have ratified the Kyoto Protocol to those which have not, to do so 'in a timely manner'.[399] It also aims to promote the sustainable use of biomass and other renewable energies, to support the 'transition to the cleaner use of liquid and gaseous fossil fuels', and to promote environmentally sound energy services.[400] On other issues addressed in this chapter, it calls for: strengthening the capacity of developing countries and economies in transition to assess and reduce the impacts of transboundary air pollution; ensuring replenishment of the Montreal

---

[394] Para. 9.20.   [395] Paras. 9.23 and 9.24(a).   [396] Paras. 9.24(b) and (e).
[397] Paras. 9.26, 9.27(e) and 9.28(a).   [398] Paras. 9.27 and 9.28.   [399] Para. 36.
[400] Para. 8(a)–(g). No targets or timetables are set for the use of renewable energy supplies.

Protocol fund and supporting the Protocol's compliance mechanism; and addressing the illegal traffic in ozone-depleting substances.[401]

Conclusions

Despite its slow start, the rules of international law governing the protection of the atmosphere and outer space are now among the most detailed and complex in international environmental law. As described in this chapter, regional and global developments have taken place which establish significant limitations on the right of states to allow emissions of gases which cause urban and transboundary air pollution, depletion of the ozone layer, and increased atmospheric concentrations of greenhouse gases. In so doing, a broad range of regulatory techniques has been deployed, including the total phase-out of the production and consumption of certain ozone-depleting substances, the use of a 'target-and-timetable' approach, differentiated commitments for developed and developing countries, and innovative new instruments addressing the attainment of the objectives of the ozone depletion and climate change regimes. Supplementing these substantive commitments and techniques are a number of innovative institutional arrangements (to provide technical assistance and address non-compliance), as well as new procedural obligations, recognition of the primary responsibility of industrialised nations, and the establishment of financial arrangements to encourage the participation of developing countries in new global rules.

The new international rules governing the protection of the atmosphere are at the cutting edge of international environmental law. They have attracted interest from states, scientists, business and environmental organisations largely because of the significance of the threat they seek to address and the broad scope of the activities they embrace, including in particular the transport and energy sectors. These are far-reaching and relatively speedy developments. Nevertheless, major gaps remain to be addressed. First, in relation to urban and transboundary air pollution the rules are almost entirely applicable to developed countries in the OECD/ECE/EC context; as rapid industrialisation takes place in other regions, there is a need to develop rules to address these related problems, perhaps through the development of a regional approach modelled upon UNEP's Regional Seas Programme. This is even more the case today than in the mid-1990s when the first edition of this book appeared. Secondly, the recently adopted agreements such as the 1999 Amendments to the Montreal Protocol and the 1997 Kyoto Protocol to the Climate Change Convention need to be brought into force promptly, and the financial arrangements necessary to encourage the participation of, in particular, the largest developing countries, should be assured. Thirdly, greater attention needs to be given to the

---

[401] Para. 37.

enforcement of these agreements, including in respect of meeting reporting requirements and providing independent verification that targets and timetables
have been and are being complied with. And, fourthly, international lawyers
will need to address a new range of legal issues thrown up by the development
of innovative international mechanisms and techniques to assist in compliance:
tradeable permits, 'joint implementation' and the Clean Development Mechanism are among the new approaches which raise political, economic and legal
questions which have not been fully addressed or understood and will challenge the skills of public international lawyers, who will increasingly have to
intersect with the work of commercial and private sector lawyers involved in
the practical implementation of these arrangements.

9

Oceans and seas

W. Douglas, 'Environmental Problems of the Oceans: The Need for International Controls', 1 *Environment Law* 149 (1971); L. Caflisch, 'International Law and Ocean Pollution: The Present and the Future', 8 RBDI 7 (1972); J. Schneider, 'Something Old, Something New: Some Thoughts on Grotius and the Marine Environment', 18 *Virginia Journal of International Law* 147 (1974); J. L. Hargrove (ed.), *Who Protects the Ocean?: Environment and the Development of the Law of the Sea* (1975); E. Mann Borgese and D. Krieger (eds.), *The Tides of Change: Peace, Pollution, and Potential of the Oceans* (1975); R. Johnson (ed.), *Marine Pollution* (1976); A. Kiss, 'La Pollution du milieu marin', 38 ZaöRV 902 (1978); G. J. Timagenis, *International Control of Marine Pollution* (1980); K. Hakapaa, *Marine Pollution in International Law* (1981); D. M. Johnston (ed.), *The Environmental Law of the Sea* (IUCN, Environmental Policy Paper No. 18, 1981); E. Gold, *Handbook on Marine Pollution* (1985); R. Soni, *Control of Marine Pollution in International Law* (1985); J. van Dyke, D. Zaelke and G. Hewison (eds.), *Freedom of the Seas in the 21st Century: Ocean Governance and Environmental Harmony* (1993); A. Couper and E. Gold (eds.), *The Marine Environment and Sustainable Development* (1993); K. Gjerde and D. Freestone, 'Particularly Sensitive Sea Areas', 9 IJMCL 431 (1994) (special issue); L. Lucchini and M. Voelckel, *Le Droit de la mer* (1996); H. Ringbom (ed.), *Competing Norms in the Law of Marine Environmental Protection* (1997); UN, *Oceans and Law of the Sea: Report of the Secretary General* (1998); R. Churchill and A. Lowe, *The Law of the Sea* (1999, 3rd edn); J.-P. Beurier, A. Kiss and S. Mahmoudi, *New Technologies and Law of the Marine Environment* (2000); M. Nordquist and J. Norton Moore, *Current Marine Environmental Issues and the International Tribunal for the Law of the Sea* (2001); S. Marr, *The Precautionary Principle in the Law of the Sea – Modern Decision-Making in International Law* (2003).

Introduction

General rules concerning the protection of the marine environment from pollution are well developed at the regional and global levels, largely as a result of the treaties and other international acts adopted by states since 1972.[1] More

---

[1] Marine living resources are addressed in chapter 11, pp. 558–600 below.

detailed and specific obligations govern dumping at sea and pollution from vessels, and the rules on enforcement are now also relatively well developed.[2] The general and specific rules have not, however, halted the continued degradation of the marine environment as a result of pollution from the principal sources, namely, land-based sources (including pollution through the atmosphere); dumping by vessels at sea; offshore vessels; and seabed activities.

In 1990, the Joint Group of Experts on the Scientific Aspects of the Marine Environment (GESAMP) reported that coastal pollution was increasing and more widespread globally than in 1982. Moreover, although the open ocean was relatively clean, the margins of the seas were affected by human activity, primarily from land-based activities including intensive human settlement of coastal zones.[3] GESAMP reported that 'if unchecked, these trends will lead to global deterioration in the quality and productivity of the marine environment'.[4] The major causes of concern include coastal development, destruction of habitats, eutrophication from nutrients and sewage, overfishing and changes in sediment flows due to hydrological changes. Urban, industrial and recreational developments have resulted in large-scale destruction of coastal habitats, especially wetlands, mangroves, salt marshes and seagrasses:[5] by way of example, Italy had lost more than 95 per cent of its historic wetlands by 1972;[6] the United States has lost over 50 per cent of its coastal wetlands;[7] and a group of thirty-one tropical developing countries in Africa, Central America and Asia are estimated to have lost more than 50 per cent of their mangroves since pre-agricultural times.[8] Overall it is estimated that nearly 30 per cent of the land area in the world's coastal ecosystems has been extensively altered or destroyed by growing demands for housing, industry and recreation.[9]

---

[2] See chapter 5, on enforcement generally.

[3] GESAMP Reports and Studies No. 39 (1990), jointly sponsored by IMO, FAO, UNESCO, WMO, WHO, IAEA, UNEP and the UN. Susbequent studies have found a similar pattern of pollution: see GESAMP, 'A Sea of Troubles', GESAMP Report No. 70 (2001).

[4] *Ibid.*, 1.

[5] The degradation continues despite the fact that by 1989 states had established 977 marine and coastal protected areas over more than 211 million hectares: World Resources Institute, *World Resources 1992–3*, 298–9, Table 20.1.

[6] IBRD and EIB, *The Environmental Programme for the Mediterranean: Preserving a Shared Heritage and Managing a Common Resource (1990)*, 23 in World Resources Institute, *World Resources 1992–3*, 177.

[7] R. W. Tiner, *Wetlands of the United States: Current Status and Recent Trends* (US Fish and Wildlife Service, 1984), 36, in World Resources Institute, *World Resources 1992–3*, 177.

[8] World Resources Institute, *World Resources 1990–1*, 306–7, Table 20.4. In many cases, extensive losses have occurred in the last fifty years. For example, much of the estimated 84 per cent of original mangroves lost to Thailand were lost since 1975. Panama lost 67 per cent of its mangroves during the 1990s: World Resources Institute, *World Resources 2000–2001*, 72.

[9] Lauretta Burke *et al.*, *Pilot Analysis of Global Ecosystems: Coastal Ecosystems* (2001), 3.

The situation has not generally improved in the past decade. In its most recent report, published in 2001, GESAMP has confirmed that the situation is not improving: coastal activity is increasing the amounts of nitrogen and phosphorous entering the marine environment of coastal areas by between 50 and 200 per cent;[10] other sources of pollution include microbial contamination of seafood and beaches from the discharge of untreated human sewage, the fouling of the seas by plastic litter, the progressive build-up of chlorinated hydrocarbons, and the accumulation of tar on beaches from oil spills; and longer term issues, such as climate change and ozone depletion, are identified.[11] Another phenomenon which may be a symptom of environmental change is 'coral bleaching', which takes place when coral dies and loses its colour due to the loss of symbiotic algae; it is caused by the water at the sea surface getting warmer.[12]

Development of standards of international law[13]

International rules for the protection of the marine environment are established under regional and global treaties, and other international acts, and the rules of customary law are reflected in these acts and non-binding soft law obligations. Early international efforts addressed discharges of oil, and can be traced back to the 1926 Preliminary Conference on Oil Pollution of Navigable Waters, held in Washington.[14] The first treaty to address oil pollution of the sea was the 1954 International Convention for the Prevention of Pollution of the Sea by Oil (1954 Oil Pollution Convention), based on a draft text from the 1926 Washington Conference.[15] The 1954 Oil Pollution Convention was followed by environmental protection provisions in the 1958 High Seas Fishing and Conservation Convention,[16] the 1958 Convention on the Continental Shelf,[17] and the 1958 Convention on the High Seas.[18]

In 1959, the IMCO (now IMO) Assembly assumed responsibility for the 1954 Oil Pollution Convention and many of the UN's functions in relation

---

[10] GESAMP, 'A Sea of Troubles', GESAMP Report No. 70 (2001), 15.

[11] *Ibid.*

[12] National Science Foundation, US EPA, NOAA, *Workshop on Coral Bleaching, Coral Reef Ecosystems and Global Change: Report of Proceedings* (1991), 1–7; cited in World Resources Institute, *World Resources 1992–3*, 178.

[13] As to the competence of states to prescribe and enforce rules for the protection of the marine environment, see chapter 1, pp. 13–14, and chapter 5, p. 175 above.

[14] Report of the Preliminary Conference on Oil Pollution of Navigable Waters, 1926 June 8–16 (US Government Printing Office, 1926).

[15] London, 12 May 1954, in force 26 July 1958, 327 UNTS 3, as amended in 1962, 1969 and 1971.

[16] Geneva, 29 April 1958, in force 20 March 1966; 559 UNTS 285.

[17] Geneva, 29 April 1958, in force 10 June 1964; 499 UNTS 311.

[18] Geneva, 29 April 1958, in force 30 September 1962; 450 UNTS 82.

to oil pollution.[19] Subsequent international efforts were often triggered by a major oil spill such as the accidents involving the *Torrey Canyon* in 1967, the *Amoco Cadiz* in 1978, the *Exxon Valdez* in 1989 and the *Prestige* in 2002. These and other incidents led to the adoption under IMO auspices of the 1969 Intervention Convention, the 1969 (now 1992) CLC, the 1971 (now 1992) Oil Pollution Fund Convention, and the various amendments to MARPOL 73/78 requiring double hulls on new oil tankers,[20] and, more recently, first indications that certain states could act unilaterally to limit rights of passage even within their EEZs.[21] Following the *Torrey Canyon* accident, the UN General Assembly gave increased attention to the protection of the marine environment,[22] and in 1969 it adopted a resolution 'Promoting Effective Measures for the Prevention and Control of Marine Pollution'.[23] This called on the UN to: prepare reports for the 1972 Stockholm Conference; review harmful substances and wastes which might affect human health and activities in the marine environment and coastal area, and national and international activities for prevention and control of marine pollution; and make suggestions for comprehensive action and improved international co-ordination. Marine pollution was an important issue at the Stockholm Conference, and Principle 8 of the 1972 Stockholm Declaration called on states to 'take all possible steps to prevent pollution of the seas by substances that are liable to create hazards to human health, to harm living resources and marine life, to damage amenities or to interfere with other legitimate uses of the sea'.[24] The Stockholm Conference did not adopt a proposed global convention on ocean dumping as the text had not been completed. The United States had introduced a text in 1971 at the IMO Intergovernmental Working Group on Marine Pollution,[25] but it was not until December 1972 that the global Convention on the Prevention of Marine Pollution by Dumping of Wastes and Other Matter (1972 London Convention) was actually adopted.[26] This followed by several months the adoption of the regional Convention for the Prevention of Marine Pollution by Dumping from Ships and Aircraft (1972 Oslo Dumping Convention).[27]

---

[19] ECOSOC Res. 537A (XVIII) (1959).   [20] See p. 440 below.

[21] In November 2002, France, Spain and Portugal indicated that they would undertake unilateral actions to prevent passage through their EEZs of certain old ships without double hulls, following the accident involving the Prestige, and France apparently excluded some such ships. The actions have been condemned by shipping bodies as contravening UNCLOS: see 'Shipping Bodies Condemn European Tanker Expulsions', 13 December 2002, www.planetark.org.

[22] See e.g. UNGA Res. 2414 (XXII) (1968).   [23] UNGA Res. 2566 (XXIV) (1969).

[24] See generally P. S. Thacher, 'Assessment and Control of Marine Pollution: The Stockholm Recommendations and Their Efficacy', 8 *Stanford Journal of International Studies* 79 (1973).

[25] 10 ILM 1021 (1971).

[26] London, Mexico City, Moscow, Washington, 29 December 1972, in force 30 August 1975, 1046 UNTS 120; see pp. 416–23 below.

[27] Oslo, 15 February 1972, in force 7 April 1974, 932 UNTS 3; see pp. 423–5 below.

In 1973, the International Convention for the Prevention of Pollution from Ships (MARPOL 73) was adopted under IMO auspices,[28] and in 1976 UNEP established its Regional Seas Programme, which has led to over thirty regional treaties.[29] In 1982, the international community finally adopted the United Nations Convention on the Law of Sea (UNCLOS), addressing pollution of the marine environment comprehensively with a view to establishing rules and standards of global application. Further efforts have taken place within the framework of the treaty institutions and the IMO which, together with the IOC, GESAMP and UNEP, continue to play a leading role in efforts to develop international law for the protection of the marine environment. During 1992, a 'second generation' of regional environmental treaties was introduced with the adoption of the 1992 Convention on the Protection of the Baltic (1992 Baltic Sea Convention)[30] (to supersede the 1974 Baltic Convention) and the 1992 Convention for the Protection of the Marine Environment of the North-East Atlantic (1992 OSPAR Convention) (to supersede the 1972 Oslo Dumping Convention and the 1974 Paris Convention). Both of the 1992 instruments adopt a more comprehensive approach by addressing marine pollution from all sources, and introduce new principles, substantive rules and institutional arrangements. The approach is now reflected in other regional instruments, identified below.

The treaty regime

Marine environment protection rules fit into two broad categories: global rules (of which the 1982 UNCLOS is the most comprehensive, and the 1972 London Convention and MARPOL 73/78 the most specific); and regional rules. The second category includes treaties under the UNEP Regional Seas Programme, and those which are *ad hoc* regional and sub-regional arrangements establishing special rules in Europe and the Antarctic.[31]

UNCLOS

D. P. O'Connell, *The International Law of the Sea* (ed. I. Shearer, 2 vols., 1982 and 1984); P. Allott, 'Power Sharing in the Law of the Sea', 77 AJIL 1 (1983); B. Boczek, 'Global and Regional Approaches to the Protection and Preservation of the Marine Environment', 16 *Case Western Reserve Journal of International Law* 39 (1984);

---

[28] P. 440 below.   [29] Pp. 399–405 below.

[30] Helsinki, 9 April 1992, in force 17 January 2000; IMO Doc. LDC.2/Circ.303, 10 August 1992.

[31] See chapter 13 below; for a helpful assessment, see T. Treves, 'Regional Approaches to the Protection of the Marine Environment', in J. Norton Moore and M. Nordquist (eds.), *The Stockholm Declaration and Law of the Marine Environment* (2003).

K. Ramakrishna, 'Environmental Concerns and the New Law of the Sea', 16 *Journal of Maritime Law and Commerce* 1 (1985); A. E. Boyle, 'Marine Pollution under the Law of the Sea Convention', 79 AJIL 347 (1985); R. Platzoder, *Third United Nations Conference on the Law of the Sea: Documents* (15 vols., 1982–); J. Sebenius, *Negotiating the Law of the Sea* (1984); M. H. Nordquist, S. Rosenne, A. Yancov and N. Grandy (eds.), *United Nations Convention on the Law of the Sea 1982: A Commentary*, vol. IV, *Articles 192 to 278, Final Act, Annex VI* (1991); UN Office for Ocean Affairs and the Law of the Sea, *The Law of the Sea: Protection and Preservation of the Marine Environment: Repertory of International Agreements Relating to Section 5 and 6 of Part XII of the United Nations Convention on the Law of the Sea* (1990); O. Schachter, 'The Value of the 1982 UN Convention on the Law of the Sea: Preserving Our Freedoms and Protecting the Environment', 23 *Ocean Development and International Law* 55 (1992); R. Churchill and A. V. Lowe, *The Law of the Sea* (1999, 3rd edn); J. Charney, 'The Marine Environment and the 1982 UNCLOS', 28 *International Lawyer* 879 (1994).

The 1982 UNCLOS aims to establish 'a legal order for the seas and oceans which will facilitate international communication, and will promote the peaceful uses of the seas and oceans, the equitable and efficient utilisation of their resources, the conservation of their living resources, and the study, protection and preservation of the marine environment'.[32] It is one of the most far-reaching and influential of global environmental agreements, and is now widely supported, with 142 parties. Although UNCLOS only entered into force in 1994, more than ten years after it was signed, it has influenced the development of regional rules for the protection of the marine environment, as well as broader international environmental law. Its provisions on the protection and preservation of the marine environment are considered by many states to reflect generally applicable principles or rules of customary law, as evidenced by the reference in the Preamble to the 1992 OSPAR Convention which recalls the relevant provisions of customary law reflected in Part XII of the UNCLOS. Agenda 21 endorsed the view that the provisions of UNCLOS on protection and preservation of the marine environment reflect international law.[33] The legal force of the principles established in UNCLOS as customary obligations is further supported by the widespread state practice pursuant to treaty and national rules which address particular sources of marine pollution as set out in Part XII.

UNCLOS requires states to pursue two main environmental objectives: to prevent, reduce and control marine pollution; and to conserve and manage marine living resources. For both objectives, UNCLOS establishes rules on

[32] Preamble.
[33] Agenda 21, paras. 17.1 and 17.22; this view was stated to be without prejudice to the position 'of any state with respect to signature, ratification or accession to the Convention' or the 'position of states which view the Convention as having a unified character': *ibid.*, at nn. 1 and 2.

information, scientific research, monitoring, environmental assessment, enforcement (including developing rules in relation to enforcement by coastal states and port states)[34] and liability.[35] Part XII of UNCLOS addresses the 'protection and preservation of the marine environment', although principles and rules on environmental protection and the conservation of marine living resources may also be found throughout the Convention: among the various provisions, UNCLOS authorises coastal states to adopt certain laws relating to innocent and transit passage through territorial seas, straits and archipelagic sea lanes for the preservation of the environment of the coastal state and the prevention, reduction and control of pollution,[36] and it provides for coastal state jurisdiction (in accordance with the Convention) with regard to protection and preservation of the marine environment of the EEZ.[37] Part XII comprises forty-six Articles, divided into eleven Sections, which elaborate upon the general provisions of Section 1, which includes the primary obligation of all states 'to protect and preserve the marine environment'.[38] Drawing upon the language of Principle 21 of the Stockholm Declaration, UNCLOS declares that 'states have the sovereign right to exploit their natural resources pursuant to their environmental policies and in accordance with their duty to protect and preserve the marine environment'.[39]

This general obligation is further elaborated, and a distinction is drawn between the duty to protect the environment and the responsibility not to cause damage by pollution to other states and their environment. Under Article 194(1), the duty to protect the environment requires states to take all the measures consistent with UNCLOS which are necessary to prevent, reduce and control pollution of the marine environment from any source, using the best practicable means at their disposal and in accordance with their capabilities. This introduces the element of differentiated responsibility based upon

---

[34] Chapter 5, pp. 175–6 above, and the literature there cited.
[35] Chapter 18, pp. 923–4 below.   [36] Arts. 21(1)(f), 42(1)(b) and 54.
[37] Art. 56(1)(b)(iii); in exercising their rights, coastal states are to 'have due regard to the rights and duties of other States and shall act in a manner compatible with the provisions of the Convention': Art. 56(2). The rights of other states include freedoms of navigation in the EEZ (Art. 58(1)). Following the sinking of the *Prestige* involving an oil spill off the west coast of Spain on 19 November 2002, it was reported that Spain, France and Portugal were proposing to ask all single-hull tankers over fifteen years of age and laden with crude or fuel oil to sail outside their EEZs (see Lloydslist.com, 'Spain, France and Portugal Ban Single Hull Tankers', 3 December 2002), raising an issue as to whether this apparent exercise of jursidiction in relation to the prevention of pollution was compatible with freedoms of navigation under the 1982 Convention (see Lloydslist.com, 'Spain Single Hull Ban Flies in Face of Law of the Sea', 4 December 2002, referring to Art. 211 of UNCLOS; and see pp. 440–4 below on MARPOL regulations concerning double hulls). On 13 December 2002, the EC Commission proposed an immediate ban on the transport of heavy grades of oil to or from EU ports by all single-hull tankers (and to speed up the phase-out of single-hull tankers): Press Release IP/02/1953, 20 December 2002.
[38] Art. 192.   [39] Art. 193.

economic and other resources available which subsequently emerged as a major theme at UNCED. Article 1(4) of UNCLOS defines pollution of the marine environment, on the basis of an earlier GESAMP definition, as:

> the introduction by man, directly or indirectly, of substances or energy into the marine environment, including estuaries, which results or is likely to result in such deleterious effects as harm to living resources and marine life, hazards to human health, hindrance to marine activities, including fishing and other legitimate use of the sea, impairment of quality for uses of sea water and reduction of amenities.[40]

The definition has since been relied upon in other agreements. It includes both acts which result in, and those which are 'likely to' result in, harmful effects.[41] UNCLOS thus distinguishes between 'pollution' and 'damage'. Under Article 194(2), states are required not to cause damage by pollution, being directed to:

> take all measures necessary to ensure that activities under their jurisdiction or control are so conducted as not to cause damage by pollution to other states and their environment, and that pollution arising from incidents or activities under their jurisdiction or control does not spread beyond the areas where they exercise sovereign rights in accordance with the Convention.

Article 194(3) further elaborates the obligation to prevent pollution damage by addressing particular sources of pollution: from land-based activities; from seabed activities; from activities in the 'Area'; from dumping; from vessels; and from or through the atmosphere.[42] Article 194(5) requires special protection for rare or fragile ecosystems as well as the habitat of depleted, threatened or endangered species and other forms of marine life. States must not transfer damage or hazards, or transform one type of pollution into another, and must limit the use of technologies or the introduction of alien or new species which may cause significant and harmful changes to the marine environment.[43]

   These general obligations serve as the basis for more detailed standards. They are supplemented by procedural obligations to give effect to the requirements of global and regional co-operation set forth in Article 197 and, in respect of semi-enclosed seas, Article 123. Techniques for implementing the substantive rules and standards include: notifying imminent or actual damage; developing pollution contingency plans and scientific research;[44] providing technical assistance, particularly to developing countries;[45] and the monitoring and carrying out of environmental assessments of certain activities.[46] UNCLOS also

---

[40] Art. 1(4); see generally M. Tomczak, 'The Definition of Marine Pollution: A Comparison of Definitions Used by International Conventions', 8 *Marine Policy* 311 (1984).
[41] See p. 406 below.   [42] Arts. 194(3) and 207–12.   [43] Arts. 195–6.
[44] Arts. 198–200.   [45] Arts. 202 and 203.
[46] Arts. 204–6. On 'environmental impact assessment', see generally chapter 16 below.

establishes new rules on enforcement,[47] ice-covered areas,[48] responsibility and liability,[49] and sovereign immunity,[50] and provides for the relationship between UNCLOS and other conventions for the protection and preservation of the marine environment.[51]

The contribution of UNCLOS to the progressive development of international environmental law at the general level cannot be overstated. The freedom of states to pollute the marine environment is no longer unconstrained and the obligation to develop specific rules to give effect to the general obligations of UNCLOS is reinforced. By bringing together elements which had previously been scattered among different agreements, these general provisions of UNCLOS establish a framework for the further development of rules on substantive matters at the global and regional levels.

UNEP Regional Seas Programme[52]

L. M. Alexander, 'Regional Arrangements in the Oceans', 71 AJIL 84 (1977); C. Okidi, *Regional Control of Ocean Pollution: Legal and Institutional Problems and Prospects* (1978); J. De Yturriaga, 'Regional Conventions on the Protection of the Marine Environment', 162 RdC 319 (1979); D. Alhéritière, 'Marine Pollution Control Regulation: Regional Approaches', 6 *Marine Policy* 162 (1982); P. Hayward, 'Environmental Protection: Regional Approaches', 8 *Marine Policy* 106 (1984); A. Boyle, 'Regional Pollution Agreements and the Law of the Sea Convention', in W. E. Butler (ed.), *The Law of the Sea and International Shipping*, (1985) 315; P. Sand, *Marine Environment Law in the United Nations Environment Programme* (1988); P. Verlaan and A. Khan, 'Paying to Protect the Commons: Lessons from the Regional Seas Programme', 31 *Ocean and Coastal Management* 83 (1996); E. Franckx, 'Regional Marine Environment Protection Regimes in the Context of UNCLOS', 13 IJMCL 307 (1998).

UNCLOS was preceded by the emergence of the UNEP Regional Seas Programme, an ambitious attempt at developing treaties and soft rules and standards at the regional level, taking account of the different needs and capabilities of the various regions. The Regional Seas Programme followed the 1972 Stockholm Conference and the creation of UNEP. In 1974, the FAO General Fisheries Council for the Mediterranean had sponsored guidelines for a framework convention on the protection of the marine environment against pollution in the Mediterranean.[53] This led to the adoption in February 1975, under the

---

[47] Arts. 213–33; chapter 5, pp. 175–80 above.   [48] Art. 234; see chapter 14, p. 712 below.
[49] Art. 235; chapter 18, pp. 923–4 below.   [50] Art. 236.
[51] Art. 237; on the relationship between UNCLOS and other conventions, see chapter 3, pp. 136–8 above.
[52] www.unep.ch/seas/.
[53] Protection of the Marine Environment Against Pollution in the Mediterranean, FAO Fisheries Report No. 148 (1974), Annex I.

auspices of UNEP, of the Mediterranean Action Plan,[54] which has since become a model for other regions. The Plan comprised five basic components:
environmental assessment, environmental management, institutional arrangements, financial arrangements, and regional legal instruments. It was followed
by the 1976 Barcelona Convention for the Protection of the Mediterranean Sea
Against Pollution (1976 Barcelona Convention) and two Protocols: a Protocol
for the Prevention of Pollution of the Mediterranean Sea by Dumping from
Ships and Aircraft (1976 Barcelona Dumping Protocol), and a Protocol for
Co-operation in Combating Pollution of the Mediterranean Sea by Oil and
Other Harmful Substances in Cases of Emergency (1976 Barcelona Emergency
Protocol). In November 1976, UNEP convened its first 'Task Force on Legal
Instruments for Regional Seas';[55] and in 1978 the UNEP Governing Council
endorsed a Regional Seas Programme,[56] which is now a part of the broader
UNEP Programme Activity Centre for Oceans and Coastal Areas.

The UNEP Regional Seas Programme extends to fourteen regional areas:[57]
of these, thirteen regions now have their own Action Plans,[58] and an Action
Plan for the Upper South-West Atlantic is in development. Ten regions are the
subject of binding international agreements: the Mediterranean, the Arabian
Gulf, the Gulf of Guinea, the South-East Pacific, the Red Sea and Gulf of Aden,
the Caribbean, the Indian Ocean and East Africa, the South Pacific, the Black
Sea and the North-East Pacific. The UNEP Regional Seas Programme now
comprises a total of thirty-two framework Conventions and Protocols; others
are under negotiation.

Mediterranean

D. De Hoyos, 'The United Nations Environment Programme: the Mediterranean
Conferences', 17 *Harvard International Law Journal* 639 (1976); B. Boxer, 'Mediter-
ranean Pollution: Problem and Response', 10 *Ocean Development and International
Law* 315 (1982); P. Haas, *Saving the Mediterranean: The Politics of International
Environmental Co-operation* (1990); E. Raftopoulos, *The Barcelona Convention and
its Protocols* (1993); A. Vallega, 'Geographical Coverage and Effectiveness of the
UNEP Convention on the Mediterranean', 31 *Ocean and Coastal Management* 199

---

[54] UNEP/WG.2/5INF.3, reprinted in 14 ILM 481 (1975).
[55] See P. H. Sand, 'Drafting of Regional Legal Instruments for Marine Environment Protection: The Case of the Mediterranean', UNEP/Doc. TFLIRS /Inf.4 Nairobi (1976).
[56] UNEP Governing Council Decision 6/2 (1978) and Programme Doc. UNEP/GC.6/7
(1978), 139–66.
[57] The term 'region' has no precise meaning, and as used in the Regional Seas Programme has
been applied to different types of region including those comprising stretches of coastal
waters, archipelagos and semi-enclosed seas.
[58] Mediterranean (1975), Kuwaiti (1978), Wider Caribbean (1981), East Asian (1981), South-
East Pacific (1981), Red Sea and Gulf of Aden (1982), South Pacific (1982), West and Central
African (1982), Eastern African (1985), North-West Pacific (1994), South Asian (1995),
Black Sea (1996) and North-East Pacific (2001).

(1996); S.-Y. Chung, 'Is the Mediterranean Regional Co-operation Model Applicable to Northeast Asia?', 11 *Georgetown International Environmental Law Review* 363 (1999); T. Scovazzi (ed.), *Marine Specially Protected Areas: The General Aspects of the Mediterranean Regional System* (1999); T. Scovazzi, 'The Transboundary Movement of Hazardous Waste in the Mediterranean Regional Context', 19 *UCLA Journal of Environmental Law and Policy* 231 (2001).

The Mediterranean region was the first Programme region and is now the most advanced. It comprises the 1976 Barcelona Convention[59] and six Protocols: the 1976 Barcelona Dumping Protocol,[60] the 1976 Barcelona Emergency Protocol,[61] the 1980 Athens Protocol for the Protection of the Mediterranean Sea Against Pollution from Land-Based Sources (1980 Athens LBS Protocol),[62] the 1982 Geneva Protocol Concerning Mediterranean Specially Protected Areas (1982 Geneva SPA Protocol),[63] the Protocol for the Protection of the Mediterranean Sea Against Pollution Resulting from Exploration and Exploitation of the Continental Shelf and the Seabed and its Subsoil (1994 Madrid Offshore Protocol),[64] and the Protocol on the Prevention of Pollution of the Mediterranean Sea by Transboundary Movements of Hazardous Wastes and their Disposal (1996 Izmir Hazardous Wastes Protocol).[65] The meetings of the parties to these instruments have also adopted assessments and common measures since 1985 which further develop the treaty rules.[66] Secretariat functions are provided

---

[59] Barcelona, 16 February 1976, in force 12 February 1978, 15 ILM 290 (1976); twenty-one states and the EC are party. Revised in Barcelona, 9–10 June 1995 as the Convention for the Protection of the Marine Environment and the Coastal Region of the Mediterranean (not yet in force).

[60] Barcelona, 16 February 1976, in force 12 February 1978, 15 ILM 300 (1976); twenty-one states and the EC are party. Revised in Barcelona, 9–10 June 1995 as the Protocol for the Prevention and Elimination of Pollution of the Mediterranean Sea by Dumping from Ships and Aircraft or Incineration at Sea.

[61] Barcelona, 16 February 1976, in force 12 February 1978, 15 ILM 306 (1976); twenty-one states and the EC are party.

[62] Athens, 17 May 1980, in force 17 June 1983, 19 ILM 869 (1980); twenty-one states and the EC are party. Amended in Syracusa, Italy, 6–7 March 1996 as the Protocol for the Protection of the Mediterranean Sea Against Pollution from Land-Based Sources and Activities not in force.

[63] Geneva, 3 April 1982, in force 23 March 1986, IELMT 982:26; twenty-one states and the EC are party. Revised in Barcelona on 9–10 June 1995 as the Protocol Concerning Specially Protected Areas and Biological Diversity in the Mediterranean (SPA and Biodiversity Protocol) not in force.

[64] Madrid, 14 October 1994, not yet in force.   [65] Izmir, 1 October 1996, not yet in force.

[66] See Interim Environmental Quality Criteria Concerning Mercury Content of Seafood (1985); Interim Environmental Quality Criteria Concerning Microbial Concentrations of Bathing Waters (1985); Maximum Concentration of Mercury in Effluent Discharges (1987); Interim Environmental Quality Criteria Concerning Microbial Concentrations of Shellfish Waters (1987); Control of Pollution by Used Lubricating Oils (1989); Control of Pollution by Cadmium and Cadmium Compounds (1989); Control of Pollution by Organotin Compounds (1989); Control of Pollution by Organohalogen Compounds

by UNEP and are carried out by the Co-ordinating Unit for the Mediterranean Action Plan (MEDU-UNEP) in Athens.

Arabian Gulf

S. S. Saqat, 'The Kuwait Convention for Co-operation on the Protection from Pollution of the Marine Environment of the Arabian Gulf Area', 34 REDI 149 (1978); S. Amin, 'The Gulf States and the Control of Marine Pollution: Regional Arrangements and National Legislation', *Lloyd's Maritime and Commercial Law Quarterly* 104 (February 1982); M. A. Mekouar, 'La Convention de Jeddah du 14 février 1982 pour la protection de l'environnement de la Mer Rouge et du Golfe d'Aden', 8 RJE 81 (1983); S. Amin, *Marine Pollution in International and Middle Eastern Law* (1986).

The next Regional Seas Programme was developed in the Arabian Gulf region. It comprises a framework Convention, the 1978 Kuwait Regional Convention for Co-operation on Protection of the Marine Environment from Pollution (1978 Kuwait Convention),[67] and four Protocols: a 1978 Kuwait Protocol Concerning Co-operation in Combating Pollution by Oil and other Harmful Substances in Cases of Emergency (1978 Kuwait Emergency Protocol),[68] a 1989 Kuwait Protocol Concerning Marine Pollution Resulting from Exploration and Exploitation of the Continental Shelf (1989 Kuwait Exploration Protocol),[69] the 1990 Kuwait Protocol Concerning Pollution from Land-Based Sources (1990 Kuwait LBS Protocol),[70] and the 1998 Protocol on the Control of Marine Transboundary Movements and Disposal of Hazardous Wastes (1998 Hazardous Wastes Protocol).[71] During the early 1990s, the secretariat had to cope with the severe damage which resulted from the release of oil from Kuwaiti terminals in January 1991 by Iraqi forces in unlawful occupation. The estimated release, of about 950,000 cubic metres of oil, was nearly twice the previous record spill at Ixtoc in the Gulf of Mexico and twenty times the size of the spill from the *Exxon Valdez*.

Gulf of Guinea

D. Alhéritière, 'Convention Sur le Milieu Marin de l'Afrique de l'Ouest et du Centre', 7 *Environmental Policy and Law* 61 (1981)

(1989) (all reprinted in 'Common Measures Adopted by the Contracting Parties to the Convention for the Protection of the Mediterranean Sea Against Pollution' (MAP Technical Report Series No. 38, UNEP, 1990). See also Common Measures on Control of Pollution by Organophosphorus Compounds (1991); Pollution by Persistent Synthetic Materials (1991); Pollution by Radioactive Substances (1991); Pollution by Pathogenic Microorganisms (1991), reprinted in Report of the Seventh Meeting of the Contracting Parties to the 1976 Barcelona Convention.

[67] Kuwait, 24 April 1978, in force 1 July 1979, 1140 UNTS 133; eight states are party.
[68] Kuwait, 24 April 1978, in force 1 July 1979, 17 ILM 526 (1978); eight states are party.
[69] Kuwait, 29 March 1989, in force 17 February 1990; eight states are party.
[70] Kuwait, 20 February 1990, not in force.
[71] Kuwait, adopted in 1998, not yet in force.

The protection of the marine environment of the Gulf of Guinea is addressed by the 1981 Abidjan Convention for Co-operation in the Protection and Development of the Marine and Coastal Environment of the West and Central African Region (1981 Abidjan Convention),[72] and one Protocol, the 1981 Abidjan Protocol Concerning Co-operation in Combating Pollution in Cases of Emergency (1981 Abidjan Emergency Protocol).[73]

South-East Pacific

E. Ferrero Costa, 'Pacific Resources and Ocean Law: A Latin American Perspective', 16 *Ecology Law Quarterly* 245 (1989).

The protection of the marine environment of the South-East Pacific is addressed by the 1981 Lima Convention for the Protection of the Marine Environment and Coastal Areas of the South-East Pacific (1981 Lima Convention)[74] and five Protocols: the 1981 Lima Agreement on Regional Co-operation in Combating Pollution of the South-East Pacific by Hydrocarbons or Other Harmful Substances in Cases of Emergency (1981 Lima Emergency Agreement)[75] (as supplemented by the 1983 Quito Supplementary Protocol to the 1981 Lima Agreement (1983 Quito Protocol)),[76] the 1983 Quito Protocol for the Protection of the South-East Pacific Against Pollution from Land-Based Sources (1983 Quito LBS Protocol),[77] the 1989 Paipa Protocol for the Conservation and Management of Protected Marine and Coastal Areas of the South-East Pacific (1989 Paipa SPA Protocol),[78] the 1989 Paipa Protocol for the Protection of the South-East Pacific Against Radioactive Contamination (1989 Paipa Radioactive Contamination Protocol),[79] and the 1992 Protocol on the Programme for the Regional Study on the El Niño Phenomenon (ERFEN) in the South-East Pacific (1992 El Niño Protocol).[80]

Red Sea and Gulf of Aden

The Red Sea and Gulf of Aden are addressed by the 1982 Jeddah Regional Convention for the Conservation of the Red Sea and Gulf of Aden Environment (1982 Jeddah Convention)[81] and a single Protocol, the 1982 Jeddah Protocol

---

[72] Abidjan, 23 March 1981, in force 5 August 1984, 20 ILM 746 (1981); ten states are party.
[73] Abidjan, 23 March 1981, in force 5 August 1984, 20 ILM 756 (1981); ten states are party. A Protocol on land-based sources of pollution is in the early stages of preparation.
[74] Lima, 12 November 1981, in force 19 May 1986; five states are party; IELMT 981:85.
[75] Lima, 12 November 1981, in force 14 July 1986; five states are party; IELMT 981:85.
[76] Quito, 22 July 1983, in force 20 May 1987; five states are party; IELMT 983:55.
[77] Quito, 22 July 1983, in force 23 September 1986, IELMT 983:54; five states are party.
[78] Paipa, 21 September 1989, in force 1994, IELMT 989:71.
[79] Paipa, 21 September 1989, in force 1995, IELMT 989:70.
[80] Adopted in 1992, not yet in force.
[81] Jeddah, 14 February 1982, in force 20 August 1985, 9 *Environmental Policy and Law* 56 (1982); six states and Patestine are party.

Concerning Regional Co-operation in Combating Pollution by Oil and Other Harmful Substances in Cases of Emergency (1982 Jeddah Emergency Protocol).[82]

Caribbean

G. Bundschuh, 'Transfrontier Pollution: Convention for the Protection and Development of the Marine Environment of the Wider Caribbean: Agreement Involving Collective Response to Marine Pollution Incidents and Long Range Environmental Planning', 14 *Georgetown Journal of International and Comparative Law* 201 (1984); W. Anderson, *The Law of Caribbean Marine Pollution* (1997).

The protection of the Caribbean environment is the subject of the 1983 Cartagena Convention for the Protection and Development of the Marine Environment of the Wider Caribbean Region (1983 Cartagena Convention),[83] and three Protocols: the 1983 Cartagena Protocol Concerning Co-operation in Combating Oil Spills (1983 Cartagena Oil Spills Protocol),[84] the 1990 Kingston Protocol Concerning Specially Protected Areas and Wildlife in the Wider Caribbean Region (1990 Kingston SPA Protocol),[85] and the 1999 Protocol on the Prevention, Reduction and Control of Land-Based Sources and Activities (1999 LBS Protocol).[86]

Indian Ocean and East Africa

C. Okidi, 'Nairobi Convention: Conservation and Development Imperatives', 15 *Environmental Policy and Law* 43 (1985); M. Pathmarajah and N. Meith, 'A Regional Approach to Marine Environmental Problems in East Africa and the Indian Ocean', 5 *Ocean Yearbook* 162 (1985).

The protection of the marine environment of the Indian Ocean and East Africa is the object of the 1985 Nairobi Convention for the Protection, Management and Development of the Marine and Coastal Environment of the Eastern African Region (1985 Nairobi Convention),[87] and two Protocols: the 1985 Nairobi Protocol Concerning Protected Areas and Wild Fauna and Flora (1985 Nairobi

---

[82] Jeddah, 14 February 1982, in force 20 August 1985, IELMT 982:14; six states and Palestine are party.

[83] Cartagena, 24 March 1983, in force 11 October 1986, 22 ILM 221 (1983); twenty-one states are party.

[84] Cartagena, 24 March 1983, in force 11 October 1986, 22 ILM 240 (1983); twenty-two states are party.

[85] Kingston, 18 January 1990, in force 18 June 2000, 1 *Yearbook of International Environmental Law* 441 (1990); nine states are party.

[86] Oranjestad, Aruba, 6 October 1999, Annex to Final Act of the Conference of Plenipotentiaries to Adopt the Protocol Concerning Pollution from Land-Based Sources and Activities to the Convention for the Protection and Development of the Marine Environment of the Wider Caribbean Region, not yet in force.

[87] Nairobi, 21 June 1985, in force 1996, IELMT 985:46; four states are party.

Fauna and Flora Protocol),[88] and the 1985 Nairobi Protocol Concerning Co-operation in Combating Marine Pollution in Cases of Emergency (1985 Nairobi Emergency Protocol).[89]

South Pacific

B. Cicin-Sain and R. Knecht, 'The Emergence of a Regional Ocean Regime in the South Pacific', 16 *Ecology Law Quarterly* 171 (1989); S. Riesenfeld, 'Pacific Ocean Resources: The New Regionalism and the Global System', 16 *Ecology Law Quarterly* 355 (1989); L. Osmundsen, 'Paradise Preserved? The Contribution of the SPREP Convention to the Environmental Welfare of the South Pacific', 19 *Ecology Law Quarterly* 727 (1992).

The protection of the marine environment of the South Pacific under the UNEP Regional Seas Programme is the subject of the 1986 Noumea Convention for the Protection of the Natural Resources and Environment of the South Pacific Region (1986 Noumea Convention),[90] and two Protocols: the 1986 Noumea Protocol concerning Co-operation in Combating Pollution Emergencies (1986 Noumea Pollution Emergencies Protocol),[91] and the 1986 Noumea Protocol for the Prevention of Pollution of the South Pacific Region by Dumping (1986 Noumea Dumping Protocol).[92]

Black Sea and North-East Pacific

In 1992 the six Black Sea states, with the assistance of UNEP, adopted a Convention on the Protection of the Black Sea Against Pollution, together with Protocols on land-based sources of marine pollution, emergency situations for oil pollution and other harmful substances, and dumping.[93] A further Protocol on transboundary movements of hazardous wastes will be negotiated.

Finally, in 2002, a Convention on the Protection and Sustainable Development of the Marine and Coastal Environment of the North-East Pacific was adopted.[94]

---

[88] Nairobi, 21 June 1985, not in force, IELMT 985:47. See chapter 11 below.

[89] Nairobi, 21 June 1985, not in force, IELMT 985:48.

[90] Noumea, 25 November 1986, in force 18 August 1990, 26 ILM 38 (1987); twelve states are party. This Convention was relied upon by New Zealand in its 1995 application to the ICJ on the legality of French nuclear testing; see below.

[91] Noumea, 25 November 1986, in force 18 August 1990; IELMT 986:878; twelve states are party.

[92] Noumea, 25 November 1986, in force, 18 August 1990; IELMT 986:87A; eleven states are party.

[93] Bucharest, 21 April 1992, in force 15 January 1994; 32 ILM 1101 (1993); six states are party.

[94] Antigua (Guatemala), 18 February 2002, not yet in force.

The framework conventions

The nine regional seas framework conventions follow a similar approach for co-operation between parties. They include basic substantive and procedural obligations, institutional arrangements, and mechanisms for the adoption of protocols and annexes. Each convention defines its geographic scope of application, and provides for its relationship with other international conventions and rules of international law. Except for the 1983 Cartagena Convention, which includes no definition, each Convention defines 'pollution' similarly to Article 2(a) of the 1976 Barcelona Convention, according to which pollution is:

> the introduction by man, directly or indirectly, of substances or energy into the marine environment, including estuaries, which results, or is likely to result, in such deleterious effects as harm to living resources and marine life, hazards to human health, hindrance to marine activities, including fishing and other legitimate uses of the sea, impairment of quality for use of seawater and reduction of amenities.[95]

General obligations   Each framework convention includes general obligations to take, individually or jointly, appropriate measures to prevent, abate and combat pollution to protect and enhance the marine environment, and to formulate and adopt protocols on agreed measures, procedures and standards. These commitments are general in nature, and it is doubtful whether they could create enforceable obligations in specific situations except in the most egregious cases. The framework conventions establish further obligations to conserve biological diversity, to combat pollution from different sources, including dumping from ships and aircraft, from vessels, from exploration and exploitation of the territorial sea and/or continental shelf and/or seabed, from land-based sources, from transboundary movement of hazardous wastes and their disposal, and from the atmosphere, as well as to co-operate in dealing with pollution emergencies.[96] Other provisions to be found in some of the framework conventions include: action to prevent coastal erosion;[97] the sound

---

[95] 1976 Barcelona Convention, Art. 2(a) (as revised in 1995); 1978 Kuwait Convention, Art. I(a); 1981 Abidjan Convention, Art. 2(1) (adding 'coastal zones, and related inland waters' to the 'marine environment'); 1981 Lima Convention, Art. 2(a); 1982 Jeddah Convention, Art. 1(3); 1985 Nairobi Convention, Art. 2(b); 1986 Noumea Convention, Art. 2(f).

[96] 1976 Barcelona Convention (as revised in 1995), Arts. 4–11; 1978 Kuwait Convention, Arts. III to IX; 1981 Abidjan Convention, Arts. 4–9 and 12; 1981 Lima Convention, Arts. 3–6; 1982 Jeddah Convention, Arts. III to IX; 1983 Cartagena Convention, Arts. 3–11; 1985 Nairobi Convention, Arts. 3–12; 1986 Noumea Convention, Arts. 4–9 and 15.

[97] 1981 Abidjan Convention, Art. 10; 1981 Lima Convention, Art. 5; 1986 Noumea Convention, Art. 13.

environmental management of natural resources;[98] specially protected areas;[99] and prevention of environmental damage from engineering activities.[100] The 1986 Noumea Convention includes detailed obligations on the disposal of wastes, environmental assessment, storage of toxic and hazardous wastes, and contamination from nuclear tests.[101]

Procedural obligations   Apart from the general commitments, the eight framework conventions establish procedural obligations to implement substantive obligations. Legal techniques which find support in the framework conventions include: monitoring; scientific and technological co-operation; technical assistance; exchange of information; public access to information and participation; environmental impact assessment; and reporting requirements.[102] Although the obligations are general, they provide a starting point for co-operation and the elaboration of more detailed commitments in subsequent protocols or other treaties.

Institutional arrangements   Each framework convention also creates basic institutional structures for the administration of the Convention and Plan for each region. The importance of these arrangements should not be understated since they establish, often for the first time, regional institutions for environmental protection. The institutions usually comprise regular meetings of the parties and a secretariat. The meetings are charged with reviewing implementation and may usually adopt, review and amend Annexes to the Convention and Protocols, make recommendations, and undertake any additional action that may be required for the achievement of the purposes of the Convention and Protocols.[103] Secretariat functions are carried out by UNEP[104] or by regional intergovernmental organisations.[105] The 1978 Kuwait Convention establishes

---

[98] 1981 Abidjan Convention, Art. 4(1).

[99] 1981 Abidjan Convention, Art. 11; 1985 Nairobi Convention, Art. 10; 1986 Noumea Convention, Art. 14.

[100] 1985 Nairobi Convention, Art. 12.   [101] Arts. 10–12.

[102] 1976 Barcelona Convention (as revised in 1995), Arts. 12, 13 and 15; 1978 Kuwait Convention, Arts. X to XII and XXIII; 1981 Abidjan Convention, Arts. 13, 14 and 22; 1981 Lima Convention, Arts. 7–10 and 14; 1982 Jeddah Convention, Arts. X to XII and XXII; 1983 Cartagena Convention, Arts. 12, 13 and 22; 1985 Nairobi Convention, Arts. 13, 14 and 23; 1986 Noumea Convention, Arts. 16–19.

[103] 1976 Barcelona Convention (revised in 1995), Art. 17; 1981 Abidjan Convention, Arts. 16 and 17; 1981 Lima Convention, Arts. 12 and 13; 1983 Cartagena Convention, Arts. 15 and 16; 1985 Nairobi Convention, Arts. 16 and 17; 1986 Noumea Convention, Arts. 21 and 22.

[104] 1976 Barcelona Convention (revised in 1995), Art. 17; 1981 Abidjan Convention, Art. 16(1).

[105] 1981 Lima Convention, Art. 13 (Permanent Commission of the South Pacific); the 1986 Noumea Convention, Arts. 2(g) and 21 (the South Pacific Commission; in 1991 the

a Regional Organisation for the Protection of the Marine Environment (comprising a Council, a Secretariat and a Judicial Commission for the Settlement of Disputes),[106] and the 1982 Jeddah Convention establishes a Regional Organisation for the Conservation of the Red Sea and the Gulf of Aden Environment (comprising a Council, a General Secretariat, and a Committee for the Settlement of Disputes).[107]

Other regional arrangements

Other agreements outside the UNEP Regional Seas Programme establish regional rules for protection of the marine environment. Apart from treaties specifically addressing particular sources of pollution, the most developed arrangements address the North-East Atlantic and the North Sea,[108] the Baltic region,[109] the Arctic,[110] the Caspian Sea[111] and Scandinavia.[112] EC rules are considered in chapter 15,[113] and those for the Antarctic region in chapter 14.[114] A number of regional and global conventions addressing the protection of natural resources include provisions on the protection of the marine environment.[115] Significant obligations have also been adopted by regional intergovernmental conferences; although not formally binding as a matter of international law, such declarations or recommendations have influenced the subsequent development of international law by treaty or resolution of international organisation. Examples include measures for the protection of the North Sea environment adopted by four international conferences.[116]

---

secretariat functions were delegated on a temporary basis to the South Pacific Regional Environment Programme).
[106] Arts. XVI to XVIII.   [107] Arts. XVI to XX.
[108] 1969 Bonn Agreement; 1983 Bonn Agreement; 1972 Oslo Dumping Convention; 1974 Paris LBS Convention; 1992 OSPAR Marine Environment Convention; Ministerial Declarations on the Protection of the North Sea (1984, 1987, 1990, 1995 and 2002).
[109] 1974 Baltic Convention; 1992 Baltic Convention.
[110] Chapter 14; G. Nelson and R. D. Needham, 'The Arctic as a Regional Sea', 12 *Environmental Conservation* 7 (1985); A. Roginko and M. LaMourie, 'Emerging Marine Environmental Protection Strategies for the Arctic', 16 *Marine Policy* 259 (1992).
[111] C. Romano, 'The Caspian and International Law: Like Oil and Water?', in W. Ascher and N. Mirovitskaya (eds.), *The Caspian Sea: A Quest for Environmental Security* (2000), 145.
[112] 1971 Agreement Between Denmark, Finland, Norway and Sweden Concerning Cooperation in Measures to Deal with Pollution of the Sea by Oil; see also 1976 Agreement Concerning Protection of the Waters of the Mediterranean Shores, Monaco, 10 May 1976, in force 1 January 1981.
[113] Chapter 15, pp. 781–3 below.   [114] Chapter 14, p. 712 below.
[115] 1985 ASEAN Agreement, Arts. 11 and 13.
[116] First International Conference on the Protection of the North Sea; Declaration, Bremen, 1 November 1984; Second International Conference on the Protection of the North Sea; Ministerial Declaration, London, 24–5 November 1987; Third International Conference on the Protection of the North Sea; Final Declaration, The Hague, 8 March 1990; Fourth

North-East Atlantic and the North Sea

S. Saetevik, *Environmental Co-operation Between North Sea States: Success or Failure?* (1988); D. Freestone and T. Ijlstra (eds.), 'The North Sea: Perspectives on Regional Environmental Co-operation', 5 IJECL (1990) (special issue); D. Freestone and T. Ijlstra (eds.), *The North Sea: Basic Legal Documents on Regional Environmental Co-operation* (1991); E. Hey, 'The Precautionary Approach: Implications of the Revision of the Oslo and Paris Conventions', 15 Marine Policy 1441 (1991); M. Pallemaerts, 'The North Sea Ministerial Declarations from Bremen to the Hague: Does the Process Generate any Substance?', 7 IJECL 1 (1992); E. Hey, T. Ijlstra and A. Nollkaemper, 'The 1992 Paris Convention for the Protection of the Marine Environment of the North-East Atlantic: A Critical Analysis', 8 IJMCL 1 (1993); J. Hilf, 'The Convention for the Protection of the Marine Environment of the North-East Atlantic: New Approaches to an Old Problem', 55 ZaöRV 580 (1995); C. Plasman, 'The State of the Marine Environment of the North Sea', 13 IJMCL 325 (1998); A. Nollkaemper, 'The Distinction Between Non-Legal Norms and Legal Norms in International Affairs: An Analysis with Reference to the North Sea', 13 IJMCL 355 (1998); L. de la Fayette, 'The OSPAR Convention Comes into Force: Continuity and Progress' 14 IJMCL 247 (1999).

The principal instruments regulating the North Sea and the North-East Atlantic are the Convention for the Protection of the Marine Environment of the North-East Atlantic (1992 OSPAR Convention) (replacing the 1972 Oslo Dumping Convention[117] and the 1974 Paris Convention)[118] and the 1983 Agreement for Co-operation in Dealing with Pollution of the North Sea by Oil and other Harmful Substances. The 1992 OSPAR Convention adopts a more comprehensive and integrated approach to the protection of the North Sea and the north-east Atlantic than its predecessor conventions.

OSPAR Convention The 1992 OSPAR Convention represents a new approach to the protection of the marine environment by seeking to regulate all sources of marine pollution in a single instrument.[119] From its entry into force in March 1998, it replaced the two earlier conventions, providing a 'comprehensive and simplified' approach. Its provisions reflect many of the principles which emerged during the UNCED process, and it transformed many of the

International Conference on the Protection of the North Sea; Declaration, Esbjerg, 8–9 June 1995; Bergen North Sea Minsterial Declaration, 22 March 2002.

[117] Oslo, 15 February 1972, in force 7 April 1974, 932 UNTS 3; amended by Protocol of 2 March 1983, in force 1 September 1989.

[118] Paris, 4 June 1974, in force 5 October 1976.

[119] www.ospar.org; Paris, 22 September 1992, in force 25 March 1998; 32 ILM 1228 (1993). The Convention's contracting parties are Belgium, Denmark, the EU, Finland, France, Germany, Iceland, Ireland, Luxembourg, the Netherlands, Norway, Portugal, Spain, Sweden, Switzerland and the United Kingdom.

Oslo and Paris Commissions' recommendations into treaty obligations. The significant legal developments adopted by the Convention include the following: an expanded use of Annexes; a commitment to 'sustainable management' (rather than sustainable development); the incorporation of the precautionary principle and the polluter-pays principle, and the concepts of best available techniques, best available practice and clean technology; a commitment to increased public participation through the right of access to information and participation of non-governmental organisations; and the creation of a new Commission with powers to take legally binding decisions and participate in compliance. The Convention applies to the maritime area of the North-East Atlantic and Arctic Oceans, including the North Sea, comprising internal waters and territorial seas, as well as applying to high seas and the seabed and subsoil.[120]

The Preamble to the Convention emphasises environmental protection as an end in itself, signalling a move away from anthropocentrism and a recognition of the importance of the marine environment and the flora and fauna it supports. The Preamble recalls the relevant provisions of customary international law which are reflected in Part XII of the 1982 UNCLOS and in particular in Article 197. In defining the 'sustainable management' of the maritime area, it endorses 'sustainability' as an emerging international legal concept.[121]

The Convention adopts a comprehensive 'ecosystem' approach to the control and prevention of pollution. Pollution is to be eliminated (rather than 'prevented, reduced and controlled'), and degraded areas should be restored. Under Article 2(1)(a), parties must:

> take all possible steps to prevent and eliminate pollution and . . . take the necessary measures to protect the maritime area against the adverse effects of human activities so as to safeguard human health and to conserve marine ecosystems and, when practicable, restore marine areas which have been adversely affected.

The parties commit themselves to adopt programmes and measures and harmonise policies and strategies which will contain time-limits and take full account of the latest technological developments and practices designed to 'prevent and eliminate pollution fully', although each may adopt more stringent measures.[122] In accordance with the criteria in Appendix 1 to the Convention they must define and apply the 'best available techniques' and 'best

---

[120] It does not apply to the Baltic or Mediterranean Seas.

[121] Chapter 6, pp. 252–66 above. 'Sustainable management' is defined in the Convention as 'the management of human activities in such a manner that the marine ecosystem will continue to sustain the legitimate uses of the sea and will continue to meet the needs of present and future generations': Preamble.

[122] Art. 2(1)(b), (3)(a) and (5).

environmental practice', including the use of 'clean technology'.[123] The Convention also requires parties to apply the precautionary and polluter-pays principles.[124]

The five OSPAR Convention Annexes adopt commitments on pollution from land-based sources, dumping or incineration, offshore sources, and other sources, on the assessment of the quality of the marine environment and on the protection and conservation of the ecosystems and biological diversity of the maritime area.[125] The Convention promotes scientific and technical research, settlement of disputes and, for the first time in an international treaty, rules on the right of access to environmental information.[126] A Commission (the OSPAR Commission) comprising a representative from each party is established to supervise the implementation of the Convention; review the condition of the maritime area and the effectiveness of measures adopted and priorities; and draw up programmes and measures, including economic instruments.[127] Unlike its predecessors, the OSPAR Commission may adopt legally binding decisions as well as non-binding recommendations: to establish flexibility these rules and recommendations may apply different timetables 'having regard to the differences between ecological and economic conditions' in the various regions and sub-regions covered by the Convention.[128] Apart from receiving reports from the parties, the Commission may, at the request of a party, consider transboundary pollution which is likely to prejudice the interests of a party and make recommendations to reach a solution.[129] It will also be required to assess compliance and call for steps to bring about full compliance, including measures to assist a party to carry out its obligations.[130] These new powers imply extended functions for the permanent secretariat.[131] Parties undertake and publish regular joint assessments of the quality of the marine environment, including the effectiveness of measures taken and planned on the basis of monitoring, modelling, remote sensing and progressive risk assessment strategies.[132] The role

---

[123] Art. 2(3)(b). 'Clean technology' is not defined; but see the 1991 Bamako Convention, at chapter 13, pp. 695–6 below.

[124] Art. 2(2)(a) and (b); chapter 6 above.   [125] Arts. 3–7.

[126] Arts. 8, 9 and 32; chapter 17, p. 849 below; on the *Ireland* v. *United Kingdom*, OSPAR arbitral tribunal, award pending, see chapter 16, pp. 806–7 below.

[127] Art. 10.

[128] Arts. 10(3), 13 and 24. Decisions and recommendations are adopted by unanimous vote unless unanimity is not attainable, in which case a three-quarters majority vote of parties will suffice: Art. 13(2).

[129] Arts. 21(2) and 22.   [130] Art. 23.   [131] Art. 12.

[132] Art. 6 and Annex IV, Art. 2. 'Monitoring' is defined as 'the repeated measurement of: (a) the quality of the marine environment and each of its compartments, that is, water, sediments and biota; (b) activities or natural and anthropogenic inputs which may affect the quality of the marine environment; (c) the effects of such activities and inputs': Annex IV, Art. 1(1).

of the OSPAR Commission includes implementing collaborative monitoring programmes and carrying out assessments.[133]

The Ministerial Meeting which adopted the 1992 OSPAR Convention endorsed an Action Plan for the Paris and Oslo Commissions,[134] which included examples of 'best available techniques' and/or 'best environmental practice' for particular industrial activities,[135] and the reduction of pollutants from diffuse sources with specific targets and timetables.[136] The 1998 Ministerial Meeting of the OSPAR Commission adopted strategies to direct its future work in four main areas: protection and conservation of ecosystems and biological diversity; hazardous substances; radioactive substances; and eutrophication. The relationship between the 1982 UNCLOS and the 1992 OSPAR Convention is currently the subject of litigation between Ireland and the UK, in the *MOX* case.[137]

Baltic Sea

B. Johnson, 'The Baltic Conventions', 25 ICLQ 1 (1976); B. Boczek, 'International Protection of the Baltic Sea Environment Against Pollution: A Study in Marine Regionalism', 72 AJIL 782 (1978); M. Fitzmaurice, *The International Legal Aspects of the Environmental Protection of the Baltic Sea* (1992); M. Fitzmaurice, 'The 1992 Convention on the Baltic Sea Environment', 2 RECIEL 24 (1993); U. K. Jenisch, 'The Baltic Sea: The Legal Regime and Instruments for Co-operation', 11 IJMCL 47 (1996); R. Platzoder and P. Verlaan, *The Baltic Sea: New Developments in National Policies and International Co-operation* (1997); M. Fitzmaurice, 'The Helsinki Conventions 1974 and 1992', 13 IJMCL 379 (1998); J. Ebbesson, 'A Critical Assessment of the 1992 Baltic Sea Convention', 43 GYIL 38 (2000).

The geography and marine ecology of the Baltic Sea has contributed to the environmental degradation resulting from unchecked industrialisation. It is a relatively closed sea with only limited inflows of water past the Danish and Swedish coasts, further aggravated by the fact that much of it is covered by ice in the winter months. Although some of the Baltic Sea coastal states have stringent environmental standards (Denmark, Sweden, Finland and Germany), others have only recently begun to tighten their standards but are hampered by the limited availability of funds (Estonia, Latvia, Lithuania, Russia and Poland). Pollution from the wider catchment area, including the Czech Republic and

---

[133] Annex IV, Art. 3.

[134] See Final Declaration of the Ministerial Meeting of the Oslo and Paris Commissions, 22 September 1992, LDC 15/INF.11, Annex 2, 2 October 1992, Part III.

[135] Action Plan, Appendix A lists the following industries: energy production from fossil fuel, fertiliser production, foundries, mining, non-ferrous metal industry, pharmaceuticals, other organic chemicals, primary aluminium, primary iron and steel, pesticides and biocides, pulp and paper, refineries, secondary iron and steel, shipyards, surface treatment of metals, tanneries, textiles and waste incineration.

[136] Appendix B.   [137] P. 436 below.

Slovakia, has exacerbated environmental problems. In this context, the original 1974 Convention failed to fulfil its aims. The objective of the 1974 Convention on the Protection of the Marine Environment of the Baltic Sea Area (1974 Baltic Convention), which has now been superseded by the 1992 Baltic Convention, was to 'prevent and abate pollution and to protect and enhance the marine environment of the Baltic Sea Area' while seeking to prevent an increase in pollution outside that area.[138] The 1974 Baltic Convention included general commitments to prevent pollution from land-based sources, ships, dumping and exploration and exploitation of the seabed and its subsoil.[139] Additionally, the parties undertook 'to counteract the introduction, waterborne or other-wise' into the Baltic Sea of hazardous substances specified in Annex I,[140] and to 'strictly limit pollution by noxious substances and materials in accordance with Annex II by requiring the discharge of significant quantities to be subject to a prior special permit.[141] The parties were also to control pollution from other harmful substances by attaining the Annex II goals and criteria for the prevention of land-based pollution, particularly from municipal sewage, industrial wastes, and discharge of cooling water from nuclear power plants.[142] Three further Annexes addressed substances carried on ships (Annex IV), exceptions to the general provision on dumping of waste and other matters (Annex V), and co-operation in combating marine pollution (Annex VI).

The administering body for the 1974 (and now the 1992) Convention is the Baltic Marine Environment Protection Commission (HELCOM), which has met annually (twenty-one times) since the 1974 Convention entered into force. HELCOM's functions include observing the implementation of the Convention, making recommendations on measures, including amendments to the Convention and its Annexes, and defining pollution control criteria and objectives for the reduction of pollution, and objectives concerning measures.[143] Decisions of the Commission, including recommendations, are taken by unanimity unless provided otherwise in the Convention.[144]

The inadequacies of the 1974 Convention, which did not prevent massive pollution of the Baltic Sea leading to more than 100,000 square kilometres being described as 'totally dead',[145] led to the adoption of a new Convention in

---

[138] www.helcom.fi; Helsinki, 22 March 1974, in force 3 May 1980; 13 ILM 546 (1974), Art. 3(1) and (2). For the text as amended by the amendments adopted by the Helsinki Commission in 1983, 1987, 1989 and 1990 see OJ C222, 18 August 1993, 15 (appended to the text of an EC Commission proposal for EC accession to the Convention).

[139] Arts. 6–10.

[140] Art. 5; HELCOM Recommendation 4/1 added one additional substance (PCTs) to Annex I, 18 February 1983.

[141] Art. 6(2) and (3).   [142] Art. 6(6).

[143] 1992 Baltic Convention, Art. 20.   [144] 1992 Baltic Convention, Art. 19(5).

[145] *Financial Times*, 14 July 1993, 14: dangerous concentrations include nitrogen and phosphorus, sewage effluents, toxic substances (PCBs, DDT, chlorine, mercury, lead and cadmium) and chemical weapons dumped after the Second World War.

1992. The 1992 Convention on the Protection of the Marine Environment of the Baltic Sea Area (1992 Baltic Sea Convention)[146] replaces the 1974 Convention and enlarges the Convention area by including internal waters. The 1992 Convention includes new definitions and provisions on: fundamental principles and obligations; notification and consultation; environmental impact assessment; nature conservation and biodiversity; reporting and exchange of information; and public information.

The 1992 Convention amends the six Annexes to the 1974 Convention and adds a new Annex VII on the prevention of pollution from offshore activities. Parties must, individually or jointly, take measures to 'prevent and eliminate pollution in order to promote the ecological restoration of the Baltic Sea Area and the preservation of its ecological balance'.[147] They must apply the precautionary principle and the polluter-pays principle, promote the use of best environmental practice and best available technology, and use best endeavours to ensure that implementation of the Convention does not cause transboundary pollution in areas beyond the Baltic Sea or lead to other 'unacceptable environmental strains'.[148] The Convention applies to the water-body and the seabed, including each party's territorial sea and internal waters, but not to ships and aircraft used for the time being only on governmental, non-commercial service.[149]

These general commitments and principles are supplemented by specific obligations. The parties are required to prevent and eliminate pollution by harmful substances from all sources under Annex I, which sets out general principles, and identifies banned substances and pesticides.[150] Pollution from land-based sources is to be prevented and eliminated in accordance with Annex III,[151] and pollution from ships is subject to the measures required by Annex IV.[152] Incineration is prohibited, as is dumping, subject to exemptions for dredged material and safety.[153] The exploration and exploitation of the seabed and its subsoil are also regulated.[154]

Implementation of these commitments is assisted by a range of techniques. The Convention requires notification to the Commission, and consultations

---

[146] Helsinki, 9 April 1992, in force 17 January 2000; LDC.2/Circ.303, 10 August 1992; 10 states are party.

[147] Art. 3(1).

[148] Art. 3(2) to (4) and (6). Annex II establishes Criteria for the Use of Best Environmental Practice and Best Available Technology.

[149] Art. 4.   [150] Art. 5; Annex I.

[151] Art. 6. Annex III contains three Regulations relating to: general provisions; specific requirements governing, *inter alia*, municipal water sewage, industrial plant water management, industrial waters; and principles for issuing permits.

[152] Art. 8. Annex IV contains Regulations on co-operation, assistance in investigations, and definitions, and requires parties to apply the provisions of the Annexes of MARPOL 73/78, subject to the Regulation on sewage.

[153] Arts. 10 and 11 and Annex V.   [154] Art. 12 and Annex VI.

between parties, whenever an environmental impact assessment of a proposed activity that is likely to cause a significant adverse impact on the marine environment is required by international law or supra-national regulations.[155] The Convention contains provisions on pleasure craft, notification and consultation on pollution incidents, co-operation in combating marine pollution, reporting requirements, and public information on the condition of the Baltic Sea, measures taken or planned, permits issued, sampling results, and water quality objectives.[156] It requires the parties to 'conserve natural habitats and biological diversity and to protect ecological processes' to ensure the sustainable use of natural resources.[157]

Pollution by dumping

R. N. Duncan, 'The 1972 Convention on the Prevention of Marine Pollution by Dumping of Wastes at Sea', 5 *Journal of Maritime Law and Commerce* 299 (1974); J. A. Rogers, 'Ocean Dumping', 7 *Environmental Law* 1 (1976); K. W. Goering, 'Mediterranean Protocol on Land-Based Sources: Regional Response to a Pressing Transnational Problem', 13 *Cornell International Law Journal* 269 (1980); G. Winter, 'The Implementation of the Oslo Convention for the Prevention of Marine Pollution by Dumping from Ships and Aircraft', 3 *Zeitschrift fur Umweltpolitik* 707 (1980); P. Bliss-Guest, 'The Protocol Against Pollution from Land-Based Sources: A Turning Point in the Rising Tide of Pollution', 17 *Stanford Journal of International Law* 261 (1981); C. E. Curtis, 'Legality of Seabed Disposal of High-Level Radioactive Waste under the London Dumping Convention', 14 *Ocean Development and International Law* 383 (1985); M. A. Zeppetello, 'National and International Regulation of Ocean Dumping: The Mandate to Terminate Marine Disposal of Contaminated Sewage Sludge', 12 *Ecology Law Quarterly* 619 (1985); L. Kramer, 'Le Déversement des déchêts en mers et le droit Communautaire', 318 *Revue de Marché Commun* 36 (1988); E. McCann, 'Terminating Ocean Dumping of Municipal Sewage Sludge: a Political Solution to an Environmental Problem', 9 *Temple Environmental Law and Technology Journal* 69 (1990); D. Susman, 'Regulation of Ocean Dumping by the European Economic Community', 18 *Ecology Law Quarterly* 559 (1991); E. Hey, 'Hard Law, Soft Law, Emerging International Law and Ocean Disposal Options for Nuclear Waste', 40 *Netherlands International Law Review* 405 (1993); R. J. Baird, 'Ocean Dumping – An Overview of the International and Domestic Regulatory System', 15 *Environmental and Planning Law Journal* 174 (June 1998); L. de la Fayette, 'The London Convention 1972: Preparing for the Future', 13 IJMCL 515 (1998); E. A. Kirk, 'OSPAR Decision 98/3 and the Dumping of Offshore Installations', 48 ICLQ 458 (1999).

Pollution by dumping, which accounts for approximately 10 per cent of pollution of the marine environment, is addressed by two international agreements

---

[155] Art. 7(1) and (2).   [156] Arts. 9, 13, 14 and 16–18.   [157] Art. 15.

of global application and at least six regional agreements. Of these instruments, the 1982 UNCLOS establishes broad principles, and detailed regulations are set out at the global level by the 1972 London Convention.

UNCLOS

UNCLOS requires states to adopt laws and regulations to prevent, reduce and control dumping, which laws may not be less effective than global rules and standards, and to establish global and regional rules, standards and recommended practices and procedures.[158] In general, dumping in accordance with such laws and regulations must not be carried out without the permission of the relevant state authority, and dumping within the territorial sea and the EEZ or on the continental shelf must not be carried out without the express prior approval of the coastal state after due consideration of the matter with states which may be adversely affected.[159]

1972 London Convention

The 1972 London Convention (known as the London Dumping Convention until 1992) is an instrument of global application to all marine waters other than internal waters, which has attracted the support of seventy-eight parties including forty-three developing countries.[160] The objective is to 'prevent the pollution of the sea by the dumping of waste and other matter that is liable to create hazards to human health, to harm living resources and marine life, to damage amenities or to interfere with other legitimate uses of the sea', and to encourage the development of regional agreements.[161] Dumping is defined by Article III of the Convention as

1. any deliberate disposal at sea of wastes or other matter from vessels, aircraft, platforms or other man-made structures at sea; or
2. any deliberate disposal at sea of vessels, aircraft, platforms or other man-made structures at sea.

This does not include 'the disposal at sea of wastes or other matter incidental to, or derived from, the normal operations of' man-made structures and their equipment at sea, other than wastes or other matter transported by or to man-made structures at sea operating for the purpose of disposal of such matter or related to offshore activities arising from the exploitation, exploration or

---

[158] Art. 210(1), (4) and (6). 'Dumping' is defined similarly to the 1972 London Convention: Art. 1(1)(5).
[159] Art. 210(3) and (5).   [160] www.londonconvention.org; Art. III(3).
[161] Arts. I and VIII. On regional agreements, see below.

processing of seabed mineral resources.[162] Under Article III, 'wastes or other matters' are broadly defined as 'material and substance of any kind, form or description'.

Central to the 1972 London Convention are the rules which prohibit or regulate the dumping of waste. Three categories of wastes are established, each of which is subject to specific obligations. The dumping of highly hazardous waste substances listed in Annex I (the 'black list') is prohibited, except in emergency situations and after consultation with countries likely to be affected, and with the IMO.[163] The prohibition does not apply to Annex I substances which are rapidly rendered harmless by physical, chemical or biological processes in the sea, provided that they do not make edible marine organisms unpalatable or endanger human health or that of domestic animals.[164] Nor does the prohibition apply to the dumping of trace contaminants.[165] The dumping of Annex II 'special care' substances and wastes (the 'grey list') requires a prior 'special' permit.[166] The dumping of all other wastes requires a prior 'general' permit.[167] Exceptions to the rules of the London Convention concerning dumping are provided for in relation to the safety of human life and vessels, and emergency situations where unacceptable risk is posed to human health and no other solution is possible.[168] The Convention does not apply to vessels and aircraft entitled to sovereign immunity under international law, although each party must ensure that they act consistently with the Convention.[169]

---

[162] Art. III(1)(a) and (b). Cf. the definitions in the 1972 Oslo Dumping Convention, p. 423 below; and the 1992 OSPAR Convention, p. 425 below. On the issues arising in relation to the disposal of the *Brent Spar* oil platform in 1995, see S. Mankabady, 'Decommissioning of Offshore Oil Installations', 28 *Journal of Maritime Law and Commerce* 603 (1997).

[163] Art. IV(1)(a). Annex I, as amended in 1978, 1980 and 1993, includes organohalogen compounds, mercury and its compounds, cadmium and its compounds, persistent plastics and other persistent synthetic materials, crude oil and its waste and petroleum products, high-level radioactive wastes or matter, and materials produced for biological and chemical warfare. See also Guidelines for Allocation of Substances to the Annexes to the London Convention, Resolution LDC.31(11) (LDC 11/14, Annex 3).

[164] Annex I, para. 8 (see Resolution LDC 24(10), Guidelines for the Implementation of Paragraphs 8 and 9 of Annex I to the London Dumping Convention (LDC 10/15, Annex 3)).

[165] Annex I, para. 10. See Regulations for the Control of the Incineration of Wastes and other Matter at Sea, Addendum to Annex I. Para. 10 and the Addendum were adopted as amendments by the third consultative meeting of the contracting parties in 1978.

[166] Art IV(1)(b). Annex II, as amended in 1978 and 1980, includes wastes containing significant amounts of hazardous substances (e.g. arsenic, lead, copper, fluorides, pesticides not covered by Annex I, etc.), large quantities of acids and alkalis, bulky wastes, radioactive wastes not in Annex I, and certain other non-toxic substances.

[167] Art. IV(1)(c).

[168] Art. V. See Interim Procedures and Criteria for Determining Emergency Situations (LDC V/12, Annex 5).

[169] Art. VII(4).

'Special' and 'general' permits are granted by national authorities, for matter intended for dumping which is loaded in its territory, or loaded by a vessel
or aircraft registered in its territory, or flying its flag when the loading occurs
in the territory of a non-party.[170] The grant of 'special' and 'general' permits
must comply with Annex III, which requires criteria to be taken into account in
deciding whether a permit should be granted (the characteristics and composition of the matter and of the dumping site and method of deposit, and other
general considerations and conditions including possible effects on amenities,
marine life and other uses of the sea, and the practical availability of alternative
methods of treatment, disposal or elimination).[171] National authorities must
keep detailed records of all matter permitted to be dumped, and monitor the
condition of the seas, and parties must report this and other information to
the IMO.[172] In theory, this should allow the international community to determine what is being dumped. In practice, reporting requirements are not fully
complied with, and there is considerable evidence of large-scale unauthorised
dumping by nationals of parties in violation of the London Convention.

The 1972 London Convention also requires collaboration between parties
on training, research and monitoring and methods for disposal and treatment of waste, to develop procedures to assess liability and the settlement of
disputes, and the promotion of measures to protect the marine environment
against pollution from specific sources (such as hydrocarbons and radioactive
pollutants).[173] The Convention is administered by consultative meetings of
the parties, which are responsible for keeping under review the implementation of the Convention, amending it and the Annexes, ensuring the availability
of relevant scientific and technical information, receiving the parties' reports,
and developing and adopting procedures and criteria for determining exceptional and emergency situations.[174] Consultative Meetings are held annually in
London at the IMO, and secretariat functions are provided by the IMO, which
was designated in 1975 as the competent organisation.[175] Amendments to the
Convention are adopted by a two-thirds majority of those parties present, and
they enter into force for parties accepting them sixty days after two-thirds of
them have done so.[176] Amendments to Annexes are also adopted by two-thirds
majority of those present, and enter into force for all parties except those which

---

[170] Art. VI(1)(a) and (b) and (2).
[171] Art. VI(3) and Annex III, as amended in 1989. Resolution LDC 32(11), Amendments to
the Guidelines for the Application of Annex III (LDC 11/14, Annex 4).
[172] Art. VI(1)(c) and (d). On notification of permits, see Procedure for the notification of
permits issued for the dumping of wastes and other matter at sea (LDC 12/16, Annex 2).
[173] Arts. IX, X, XI and XII.
[174] Art. XIV. See Resolution LDC 10(v), Procedures for Preparation and Consideration of
Amendments to Annexes to the London Dumping Convention (LDC V/12, Annex 3).
[175] Art. XIV(2).
[176] Art. XV(1)(a). The only amendments so far adopted are the 1978 Amendments on Dispute
Settlement, which have not yet entered into force; Resolution LDC 6(III).

declare they are unable to accept an amendment within 100 days of the approval of the amendment.[177] Other resolutions adopted by the Consultative Meetings are not formally binding.

Twenty-three Consultative Meetings of the parties have been held so far, adopting resolutions on a wide range of matters. Consultative Meetings agreed to a moratorium on the dumping of radioactive wastes at sea,[178] and to limit, regulate or prohibit *inter alia*:

- the export of wastes for disposal at sea;[179]
- the disposal of persistent plastics and other persistent synthetic materials;[180]
- the disposal of dredged materials;[181]
- waste incineration at sea;[182]
- the disposal of radioactive wastes into the seabed;[183]
- the disposal at sea of industrial wastes;[184] and
- the application of the precautionary principle.[185]

The Consultative Meetings have established several subsidiary bodies, including a Scientific Group on Dumping and an Ad Hoc Legal Group of Experts, which discussed issues including: the relationship between the London Convention and the Antarctic Treaty regime; the control of dumping by ships flying the flag of a party in the waters of a non-party; the development of a liability regime; and a further interpretation of the definition of dumping.[186] The parties to the London Convention established a Steering Group to identify future directions under the Convention, and at the fourteenth and fifteenth meetings the parties discussed the possible amendment of the London Convention to incorporate new trends and thinking, including the formal incorporation of several past resolutions. Areas identified as subjects for amendment included the extension of the Convention to include the sub-seabed and internal waters, a ban on the

---

[177] Art. XV(2).

[178] Resolution LDC 21(9) (1985); the parties agreed to a suspension of all dumping at sea of radioactive waste until the completion of studies and assessments required by the resolution (see also the earlier Resolution LDC 14(7) (1983)). Following completion of these studies, the parties agreed in 1993 to amend Annexes I and II to the Convention to ban the dumping of all radioactive wastes (Res. LDC 51(16)). The prohibition entered into force on 20 February 1994.

[179] Res. LDC 29(10) (1986).   [180] Res. LDC 22(9) (1985).

[181] Res. LDC 23(10) (1986). The eighteenth consultative meeting adopted a 'Dredged Material Assessment Framework' by Res. LC 52(18) (1995).

[182] Res. LDC 5(111) (1981), Addendum to Annex I to the LDC. IMO, Revised Interim Technical Guidelines on the Control of Incineration of Wastes and Other Matter at Sea, Res. LDC 33(11) (1988); and Res. LDC 35(11) (1988). In early 1991, incineration at sea operations came to a halt, ahead of the agreed global deadline of 31 December 1992.

[183] Res. LDC 41(13) (1990).

[184] Res. LDC 43(13) (1990); under the resolution, the parties agree to cease dumping industrial waste by 31 December 1995 at the latest.

[185] Res. LDC 44(14) (1991).

[186] 2 *Yearbook of International Environmental Law* 148–9 (1991), LDC 14/INF.34.

dumping of radioactive and industrial wastes, and the formal adoption of the precautionary principle.

In 1993, the parties commenced a detailed review of the London Convention, leading initially to the adoption of a number of amendments to Annexes I and II. These amendments incorporated previous resolutions concerning prohibitions on dumping industrial wastes, radioactive wastes and other radioactive matter, as well as the prohibition on incineration at sea of industrial wastes and of sewage sludge. In 1996, this review was completed with the adoption of the 1996 Protocol to the London Convention,[187] which is expected to enter into force in late 2003 and will then replace the London Convention. Two issues were particularly controversial in negotiations for the 1996 Protocol: the dumping of radioactive waste at sea, and the sub-seabed disposal of radioactive wastes.

Radioactive waste dumping[188]

As adopted in 1972, the London Convention included high-level radioactive wastes (HLW) in Annex I, but intermediate-level radioactive wastes (ILW) and low-level radioactive wastes (LLW) were listed in Annex II and therefore could be dumped at sea by 'special' permit. Its subsequent transformation is illustrative of law-making in the international environmental field. In 1983, three proposals were put forward at the seventh Consultative Meeting. Nauru and Kiribati proposed an amendment to the London Convention to include all radioactive wastes in Annex I. Five Nordic countries put forward an alternative proposal whereby the dumping of all radioactive wastes at sea would be phased out by 1990. Spain proposed an immediate moratorium on all radioactive waste dumping at sea. Resolution 14(7) adopted the Spanish proposal by nineteen votes in favour, with six against and five abstentions. Two years later, in 1985, the Consultative Meeting adopted Resolution 21(9), which provided for an indefinite moratorium to 'permit time for . . . a broader basis for an informed judgment on proposals' and to allow additional studies to be made of the wider political, legal, economic and social aspects of radioactive waste dumping at sea. That resolution was adopted by twenty-six votes in favour, with five against and seven abstentions, and since 1985 no state has formally permitted the dumping of radioactive wastes at sea, although unlawful dumping may have occurred. Following the 1985 moratorium, the parties to the London Convention established an Intergovernmental Panel of Experts on Radioactive Wastes (IGPRAD) to address some of these issues, and IGPRAD produced its final report in November 1993.[189] IGPRAD identified seven options which were presented to the consultative parties at their sixteenth meeting:

[187] London, 7 November 1996, not yet in force; 36 ILM 1 (1997).
[188] See C. Curtis, 'The London Convention and Radioactive Waste Dumping at Sea: A Global Treaty Regime in Transition' conference paper delivered at Woods Hole Oceanographic Institute, Massachusetts, US, 7–9 June 1993.
[189] Res. LDC 28(10), Studies and Assessments Pursuant to Resolution LDC 21(9).

1. to lift the moratorium and allow the disposal at sea of LLW under IAEA and London Convention rules;
2. to lift the moratorium and allow the disposal at sea in accordance with amended and strengthened international rules;
3. to link action on radioactive waste to the phase-out of industrial waste dumping by 1995 as provided for by Resolution 43(13);
4. to continue a limited or indefinite moratorium;
5. to develop a new consultative procedure to govern the disposal at sea of radioactive wastes;
6. to amend the London Convention to prohibit disposal of all radioactive wastes; and
7. to prohibit the disposal of radioactive waste by amending the London Convention, while allowing certain countries to opt out of the prohibition after an agreed period of time has passed (following the approach of the 1991 Antarctic Environment Protocol and the 1992 OSPAR Convention).[190]

In the meantime, Agenda 21 called on all states to encourage

> the London Convention to expedite work to complete studies on replacing the current voluntary moratorium on disposal of low-level radioactive wastes at sea by a ban, taking into account the precautionary approach...[191]

In November 1993, the sixteenth Consultative Meeting adopted amendments to Annex I prohibiting the disposal of all radioactive wastes at sea.[192]

Sub-seabed disposal of radioactive wastes

In 1983, the issue of sub-seabed disposal of radioactive wastes was raised for the first time at a consultative meeting. This form of disposal, which remains under consideration by several states, would allow HLW to be injected under the seabed from a platform or vessel to a great enough depth to stop radioactive material from being released into the marine environment. The relevant issue is whether such disposal is covered by the London Convention. A special legal experts meeting was unable to reach consensus on the point, although the eighth Consultative Meeting, in 1984, apparently agreed that the London Convention was the appropriate international forum to address the matter, and that:

> No such disposal should take place unless and until it is proven to be technically feasible and environmentally acceptable, including a determination that such waste can be effectively isolated from the marine environment,

---

[190] See pp. 425–6 below, and chapter 14, pp. 721–6 below.   [191] Agenda 21, para. 22.5(b).
[192] Res. LDC 51(16) Concerning Disposal at Sea of Radioactive Wastes and other Radioactive Matter. The amendment was adopted with thirty-seven votes in favour, none against, and seven abstentions, and entered into force in 1994 (not for the Russian Federation, which on 18 February 1994 submitted a declaration of non-acceptance of these amendments).

and a regulatory mechanism is elaborated in accordance with the provisions of the London Convention to govern disposal into the seabed of such radioactive wastes.[193]

A minority of parties remain opposed to sub-seabed disposal being interpreted as a form of 'disposal at sea'. In 1990, the thirteenth Consultative Meeting adopted a resolution which stated that sub-seabed disposal of LLW into repositories accessed from the sea would be covered by the 1983–5 moratorium.[194] Agenda 21 called on states to:

> [n]ot promote or allow the storage or disposal of high-level, intermediate-level or low-level radioactive wastes near the marine environment unless they determine that the scientific evidence, consistent with the applicable internationally agreed principles and guidelines, shows that such storage or disposal poses no unacceptable risk to people and the marine environment or does not interfere with other legitimate uses of the sea, making, in the process of consideration, appropriate use of the concept of the precautionary principle.[195]

1996 Protocol

Upon its entry into force, the 1996 Protocol will replace the 1972 London Convention. Twenty-six ratifications or other expressions of consent by states are required before the Protocol will enter into force; and at least fifteen of these must come from contracting parties to the London Convention.[196] At present, fifteen states have ratified the Protocol. The objective of the 1996 Protocol is to 'protect and preserve the marine environment from all sources of pollution' and, to this end, contracting parties are required to take effective measures to prevent, reduce and where practicable eliminate marine pollution caused by dumping or incineration at sea.[197] In respect of internal waters, each contracting party has a discretion either to apply the provisions of

[193] *Report of the 8th Consultative Meeting of the LC* (1984), 31, cited in Curtis, *The London Convention*.

[194] Res. LDC 41(13), adopted with twenty-nine votes in favour, four against and four abstentions.

[195] Agenda 21, para. 22.5(c). In April 1997, the United Kingdom Government rejected an application by a UK company (NIREX) for permission to construct a 'rock characterisation facility' to explore the feasibility of establishing a long-term storage facility for radioactive waste in proximity to, and possibly under, the Irish Sea (Letter from the Director of Infrastructure and Planning, Government Office for North West, UK, to UK Nirex, 17 March 1997). In reaching his decision, the United Kingdom Secretary of State for the Environment noted and agreed with the planning inspector's conclusions, which had noted, *inter alia*, para. 22.5(c) of Agenda 21, and stated that he was 'acutely aware of the Government's obligations to other states which are set out in various international obligations in respect of the sea and the environment more generally'.

[196] 1996 Protocol, Art. 25(1).   [197] *Ibid.*, Art. 2.

the Protocol or to adopt 'other effective permitting and regulatory measures to control the deliberate disposal of wastes or other matter' where such disposal would be 'dumping' or 'incineration at sea' within the meaning of the Protocol.[198]

The purpose of the Protocol is similar to that of the Convention, but the Protocol is more restrictive: application of a 'precautionary approach' to environmental protection from dumping of wastes or other matter is included as a general obligation;[199] a 'reverse list' approach is adopted whereby contracting parties are required to prohibit the dumping of 'any wastes or other matter' with the exception of those listed in Annex 1, which require a permit;[200] incineration of wastes at sea is prohibited;[201] and the export of wastes or other matter to other countries for dumping or incineration at sea is banned.[202] The Protocol includes extended technical co-operation and assistance provisions,[203] as well as a commitment to develop procedures for assessing and promoting compliance with the Protocol within two years of its entry into force.[204] Article 26 of the Protocol makes provision for a transitional period to allow new contracting parties to phase in compliance with the Protocol over a period of five years, provided certain conditions are met.

1972 Oslo Convention

The first regional agreement to regulate and prohibit dumping at sea, pre-dating by several months the London Convention, was the 1972 Convention for the Prevention of Marine Pollution by Dumping from Ships and Aircraft (1972 Oslo Dumping Convention).[205] The Oslo Convention applied to the north-east Atlantic Ocean, including the North Sea, but not the Baltic and Mediterranean Seas.[206] As amended, the definition of 'dumping' was broader than UNCLOS and the 1972 London Convention and included:

> any deliberate disposal into the sea, including through the medium of incineration at sea, of substances and materials by or from ships or aircraft other than:
> (a) any discharge or incineration incidental to or derived from the normal operation of ships and aircraft and their equipment;
> (b) the placing of substances and materials for a purpose other than mere disposal thereof, if not contrary to the aim of the Convention.[207]

---

[198] *Ibid.*, Art. 7(2).   [199] *Ibid.*, Art. 3(1).   [200] *Ibid.*, Art. 4(1) and (2).

[201] *Ibid.*, Art. 5.   [202] *Ibid.*, Art. 6.   [203] *Ibid.*, Art. 13.   [204] *Ibid.*, Art. 11.

[205] Oslo, 15 February 1972, in force 7 April 1974, 932 UNTS 3; amended by Protocol of 2 March 1983, in force 1 September 1989; the Oslo Dumping Convention was replaced by the 1992 OSPAR Convention upon the latter's entry into force in 1998.

[206] Art. 2.

[207] Art. 19(1), as amended. 'Incineration' was defined as 'any deliberate combustion of substances and materials at sea for the purpose of their thermal destruction': Art. 19(2).

A 1983 amendment introduced incineration into the definition. Subject to certain exceptions, the dumping of Annex I substances was prohibited, and the dumping of waste containing substances and materials listed in Annex II was required to be authorised by national authorities with a specific permit in accordance with the provisions of Annexes II and III. No substance or material could be dumped without the approval of national authorities, which approval had to apply the conditions set out in Annex III.[208] Annex IV, adopted in 1983, established Rules of Incineration at Sea: the incineration of substances for which 'practical alternative land-based methods of treatment, disposal or elimination are available' was prohibited, and guidance was provided as to which substances and materials could be the subject of an incineration permit.[209] Annex IV also required approval of incineration systems, permits and operational requirements, the recording of data, and a prohibition on the disposal of wastes from the facility except by means of the incinerator during naval operation.[210] The Annex required a prior consultation procedure and established criteria for the selection of incineration sites.[211] Annex III included permit conditions which were required to take into account the waste's characteristics and the dumping site and method of deposit, interference with legitimate uses of the sea, and the practical availability of alternative means of disposal and elimination. National authorities were required to ascertain the waste's composition in accordance with Annex III before permits or approval were granted, and to keep and transmit to the Commission established under the Convention detailed records relating to permits or approvals.[212] Other measures provided for scientific and technical co-operation, monitoring, and additional measures for specific pollutants.[213]

The Convention was administered by a Commission (OSCOM), which exercised overall supervision over its implementation, received and considered reports from parties, and kept under review the Annexes. The Commission could also recommend amendments, additions or deletions, which were adopted by unanimous vote and entered into force after unanimous approval by the parties.[214] OSCOM met annually between 1974 and 1998 and adopted a large

---

[208] Arts. 5, 6 and 7. Exceptions under Arts. 8 and 9 included cases of *force majeure* threatening the safety of human life or of a ship or aircraft, where substances occur as trace contaminants not added for the purposes of dumping, and emergencies. Arts. 5, 6 and 7 did not apply to disposal by incineration at sea, which was generally prohibited and could only be allowed with a specific permit granted by national authorities in accordance with Annexes III and IV: Art. 8(3). See OSCOM Decision 85/1 (1985) concerning Annexes I and II to the Convention.

[209] Annex IV, Rule 2(1) and (4). Permissible substances were organohalogen compounds, pesticides and certain of their by-products, substances and materials not listed in Annexes I and II which could be incinerated without damage to the marine environment, and certain wastes containing these substances.

[210] Annex IV, Rules 3–7.   [211] Annex IV, Rules 8 and 9.   [212] Arts. 10 and 11.
[213] Arts. 12. 13 and 14.   [214] Arts. 16, 17 and 18(2).

number of resolutions and recommendations. Of particular note are those re-lating to the export of wastes for disposal at sea[215] and establishing guidelines for the disposal of offshore installation.[216] In 1989, OSCOM agreed to cease dumping of industrial wastes in the North Sea by 31 December 1989 and in other Convention waters by 31 December 1995, except for inert materials of natural origin and industrial wastes for which there were 'no practical alternatives on land' and where 'the materials cause no harm in the marine environment'.[217] In 1990, the parties agreed to phase out the dumping of sewage sludge by the end of 1998,[218] and to terminate all incineration at sea by 31 December 1991.[219]

1992 OSPAR Convention

The 1972 Oslo Convention was replaced by the 1992 OSPAR Convention, which came into force on 25 March 1998. The 1992 OSPAR Convention incorporates many of the earlier treaty's resolutions and decisions into treaty obligations. Under Annex II to the 1992 Convention, the parties must prevent and eliminate pollution by dumping or incineration of wastes or other matter,[220] and pollu-tion from the abandonment of vessels or aircraft as a result of accidents.[221] The OSPAR Convention adopts an expanded definition of dumping as:

(i) any deliberate disposal in the maritime area of wastes or other matter
    (1) from vessels or aircraft;
    (2) from offshore installations;
(ii) any deliberate disposal in the maritime area of
    (1) vessels or aircraft;
    (2) offshore installations and offshore pipelines.[222]

The 1992 OSPAR Convention reverses the traditional approach to defining waste: 'wastes or other matter' includes everything except human remains, off-shore installations, offshore pipelines and unprocessed fish and offal discarded from vessels.[223]

---

[215] OSCOM Recommendation 88/1 (1988).

[216] OSCOM, Guidelines for the Disposal of Offshore Installations at Sea, The Hague, 12 June 1991.

[217] OSCOM Decision 89/1 (1989); and Report on Justification for the Issue of Permits for the Dumping of Industrial Wastes at Sea (OSCOM, 1989).

[218] OSCOM Decision 90/1 (1990). [219] OSCOM Decision 90/2 (1990).

[220] Art. 4 and Annex II. [221] Annex II, Art. 8.

[222] Art. 1(f). See also the exclusions from the definition, including disposal under MARPOL 73/78 or other applicable international law, placement of matter for a purpose other than mere disposal, and for the purposes of Annex III the 'leaving wholly or partly in place of a disused offshore installation or disused offshore pipeline, provided that any such operation takes place in accordance with any relevant provision of the Convention and with other relevant international law': Art. 1(g).

[223] Art. 1(o).

Annex II prohibits the incineration and dumping of all wastes or other matter, except for those expressly excluded by the Annex.[224] The Annex permits, subject to authorisation or regulation, the dumping of dredged material, certain inert material of natural origin, sewage sludge (until 31 December 1998), fish waste from industrial fish processing operations, and vessels or aircraft (until 31 December 2004).[225] However, authorisation will not be granted for the dumping of vessels or aircraft containing substances which result or are likely to result in harm or interference with other legitimate uses of the sea.[226] The OSPAR Convention further prohibits the 'placement' of matter in the maritime area for a purpose other than that for which it was originally designed without authorisation or regulation.[227]

Annex II also prohibits the dumping of low- and intermediate-level radioactive substances, including wastes.[228] However, the United Kingdom and France, desiring to retain the option of dumping these radioactive substances, negotiated an exception to the rule which left the way open for them to resume dumping after 1 January 2008.[229] However, before 2008, the OSPAR Commission could decide unanimously not to continue the exception granted to the United Kingdom and France.[230] On 9 February 1999, the OSPAR Commission adopted Decision 98/2 on Dumping of Radioactive Waste, as a result of which the exceptions granted to the United Kingdom and France have ceased to have effect.

UNEP Regional Seas Protocols

Three UNEP Regional Seas Protocols require parties to prevent dumping from ships and aircraft: the 1976 Barcelona Dumping Protocol, the 1986 Noumea Dumping Protocol, and the 1989 Paipa Dumping Protocol, each of which applies to the same geographic area as defined by their respective framework Conventions.[231] They use the same definitions as the 1972 London Convention[232] and similarly provide for three categories of substances: except in emergency

---

[224] Annex II, Arts. 2 and 3(1). The Annex does not apply to the deliberate disposal of wastes or other matter from offshore installations or the disposal of offshore installations and offshore pipelines: Art. 1. Art. 7 provides further exceptions on the grounds of, *inter alia*, *force majeure*, stress and safety. Art. 10(3) provides that the Annex does not 'abridge the sovereign immunity to which certain vessels are entitled under international law'.

[225] Annex II, Arts. 3(2) and 4(1). Authorisations and regulation must be in accordance with the criteria, guidelines and procedures adopted by the Commission under Art. 6 of Annex II: *ibid.*, Art. 4(1)(b).

[226] Annex II, Art. 4(2).   [227] Annex II, Art. 5.

[228] Annex II, Art. 3(3)(a).   [229] Annex II, Art. 3(3)(b).   [230] Art. 3(3)(c).

[231] 1976 Barcelona Convention, Art. 2; 1986 Noumea Dumping Convention, Art. 2; 1989 Paipa Dumping Convention, Art. 1.

[232] 1976 Barcelona Convention, Art. 3(2), (3) and (4); 1986 Noumea Convention, Art. 2(b) and (c).

or exceptional cases those listed in Annex I cannot be dumped; Annex II substances can only be dumped after a 'special' permit has been granted by the competent national authorities; and the dumping of all other wastes requires a prior 'general' permit from the competent national authorities.[233] The Protocols require the reporting of incidents or conditions giving rise to suspicions that dumping is taking place.[234] Special and general permits must be issued for wastes loaded in the territory of the party or by a ship or aircraft registered in its territory or flying its flag when the loading occurs in the territory of a non-party, after taking account of the factors set out in Annex III.[235] Meetings of the parties to the Protocols ensure review of the implementation of the Protocols, the review and amendment of the Annexes, and the consideration of the records of permits issued.[236] Amendments to the Annexes to the Protocols require a three-fourths majority vote of the parties.[237]

Other regional agreements

Prohibitions on dumping have also been adopted by the EC[238] and in relation to the Antarctic region.[239] The 1985 Rarotonga South Pacific Nuclear Free Zone Treaty prohibits the dumping of radioactive waste and radioactive matter at sea anywhere within the South Pacific Nuclear Free Zone.[240]

Pollution from land-based sources including through the atmosphere

R. Busby, 'The Convention for the Prevention of Marine Pollution from Land-Based Sources: An Effective Method for Arbitrating International Effluent Pollution Disputes', 5 *California Western International Law Journal* 350 (1975); S. Burchi, 'International Legal Aspects of Pollution of the Sea from Rivers', 3 *Italian Yearbook of International Law* 115 (1977); J. E. Hickey, 'Custom and Land-Based Pollution of the High Seas', 15 *San Diego Law Review* 409 (1978); B. Kwiatowska, 'Marine Pollution from Land-Based Sources: Current Problems and Prospects', 14 *Ocean Development and International Law* 315 (1984); P. S. Passman, 'Japanese

---

[233] 1976 Barcelona Protocol, Arts. 4, 5, 6, 8 and 9; 1986 Noumea Dumping Protocol, Arts. 4, 5, 6, 9 and 10 (radioactive waste dumping is prohibited by the 1986 Noumea Convention).

[234] 1976 Barcelona Protocol, Art. 12; 1986 Noumea Dumping Protocol, Art. 14.

[235] 1976 Barcelona Protocol, Arts. 7 and 10(2); 1986 Noumea Dumping Protocol, Arts. 7 and 11(2) (in addition, Art. 8 and Annex IV provide for specific criteria for the allocation of substances to the Annexes).

[236] 1976 Barcelona Protocol, Art. 14; 1986 Noumea Dumping Protocol, Art. 16.

[237] 1976 Barcelona Protocol, Art. 14(3); 1986 Noumea Dumping Protocol, Art. 16(3).

[238] Chapter 15, pp. 768–78 below.   [239] Chapter 14, p. 725 below.

[240] Rarotonga, 6 August 1985, in force 11 December 1986, 24 ILM 1142 (1985), twelve states are party.

Hazardous Waste Policy: Signalling the Need for Global and Regional Measures to Control Land-Based Sources of Pollution', 26 *Virginia Journal of International Law* 921 (1986); P. Szell, 'The Montreal Guidelines for the Protection of the Marine Environment Against Pollution from Land-Based Sources', 37 *International Digest of Health Legislation* 391 (1986); D. Baur and S. Iudicello, 'Stemming the Tide of Marine Debris Pollution: Putting Domestic and International Control Authorities to Work', 17 *Ecology Law Quarterly* 71 (1990); R. M. M'Gonigle, '"Developing Sustainability" and the Emerging Norms of International Environmental Law: The Case of Land-Based Marine Pollution', 128 *Canadian Yearbook of International Law* 169 (1990); M. Berman, 'Protection of the Marine Environment from Land-Based Activities', in UNEP, *UNEP's New Way Forward: Environmental Law and Sustainable Development* (1995); A. Nollkaemper, 'Balancing the Protection of Marine Ecosystems with Economic Benefits from Land-Based Activities', 27 *Ocean Development and International Law* 153 (1996); D. A. Ring, 'Sustainability Dynamics: Land-Based Marine Pollution and Development Priorities in the Island States of the Commonwealth Caribbean', 22 *Columbia Journal of Environmental Law* 65 (1997); M. Pallemaerts, 'The North Sea and Baltic Sea Land-Based Sources Regimes: Reducing Toxics or Rehashing Rhetoric?', 13 IJMCL 421 (1998); T. Mensah, 'The International Legal Regime for the Protection and Preservation of the Marine Environment from Land Based Sources', in A. Boyle and D. Freestone (eds.), *International Law and Sustainable Development* (1999), 297.

Pollution of the marine environment from land-based sources is the principal source of ocean pollution, which arises from two general sources. First, it arises from substances and energy entering the marine environment by run-off from land, rivers, pipelines and other outfall structures, which accounts for some 44 per cent of all marine pollution.[241] Secondly, it arises from or through the atmosphere, generated principally from land-based activities but also from ships and aircraft, which accounts for some 33 per cent of marine pollution. The importance of land-based sources is emphasised in Agenda 21.[242] Rules are to be found in the 1982 UNCLOS (establishing one of the causes of action for Ireland's claim against the United Kingdom in respect of the MOX plant),[243] the 1974 Paris Convention and the 1992 OSPAR Convention; three UNEP Regional Seas Protocols;[244] the 1974 and 1992 Baltic Conventions; numerous non-binding international instruments; and EC Directives.[245] The 1995 Global Programme of Action for the Protection of the Marine Environment from Land-Based

---

[241] On the relationship between watercourse laws and the protection of oceans, see A. E. Boyle, 'The Law of the Sea and International Watercourses: An Emerging Cycle', 14 *Marine Policy* 151 (1990).

[242] See p. 456 below.   [243] See p. 455 below.

[244] Two further Protocols dealing with land-based sources of pollution have been concluded for the Caribbean (1999) and Black Sea regions but are not yet in force.

[245] Chapter 15, pp. 768–78 below.

Activities (GPA) also provides for the development of national measures, and facilitates a comprehensive, multi-sectoral approach to the issue of pollution from land-based sources. Other treaties and international agreements to limit atmospheric pollution, as identified in chapter 8 above, also indirectly protect the marine environment.

UNCLOS

Article 207 of UNCLOS requires states to 'prevent, reduce and control pollution of the marine environment from land-based sources, including rivers, estuaries, pipelines and outfall structures'. States must take into account: internationally agreed rules, standards and recommended practices and procedures; characteristic regional features; the economic capacity of developing countries and their need for economic development; and the need 'to minimise, to the fullest extent possible, the release of toxic, harmful or noxious substances, especially those which are persistent, into the marine environment'.[246] In the context of the wide support for these principles in regional and global agreements and instruments, as set out below, the principles of Article 207 now reflect rules of customary international law. It should be recalled that these provisions are general in character, their detailed obligations being informed by the content of applicable and relevant international rules, whether global or regional.

1995 Global Programme of Action (GPA)

The GPA, and an accompanying Declaration,[247] were adopted by 108 states and the EC at a conference held in Washington from 23 October to 3 November 1995. The GPA drew upon relevant provisions of Chapters 17, 33 and 34 of Agenda 21 and the Rio Declaration on Environment and Development, as well

---

[246] Art. 207(1), (4) and (5).

[247] Washington, DC, 1 November 1995. In the Declaration, participating states declared their commitment to protect and preserve the marine environment from the impacts of land-based activities – specifically those resulting from sewage, persistent organic pollutants, radioactive substances, heavy metals, oils, nutrients, sediment mobilisation, litter, and physical alteration and destruction of habitat. The states pledged to undertake various activities to further this common goal including: the development or review of national action programmes; taking forward action to implement national programmes; co-operating to build capacities and mobilise resources for the development and implementation of such programmes; taking immediate preventive and remedial action, wherever possible; promoting access to cleaner technologies, knowledge and expertise; co-operating on a regional basis to co-ordinate efforts for maximum efficiency and to facilitate action at the national level; encouraging and/or making available external financing; giving priority to the treatment and management of waste water and industrial effluents; and acting to develop a global, legally binding instrument dealing with persistent organic pollutants.

as the 1985 Montreal Guidelines on the Protection of the Environment Against Pollution from Land-Based Sources (1985 Montreal LBS Guidelines).[248]

The GPA, which is administered by a UNEP-led GPA Co-ordination Office, provides the framework for the realisation of the commitments agreed to by states in the Washington Declaration. It aims at 'preventing the degradation of the marine environment from land-based activities by facilitating the realization of the duty of States to preserve and protect the marine environment', and is designed to assist states 'in taking actions individually or jointly within their respective policies, priorities and resources, which will lead to the prevention, reduction, control and/or elimination of the degradation of the marine environment, as well as to its recovery from the impacts of land-based activities'.[249] The GPA recommends actions at the state, regional and international level to address the problem of marine pollution from land-based activities. At the national level, these recommendations relate to the identification and assessment of problems, the establishment of priorities for action, setting management objectives for priority problems, identifying, evaluating and selecting strategies and measures to achieve objectives and developing criteria to assess the effectiveness of strategies and measures.[250] At the regional level, states are encouraged to strengthen, and where necessary create, regional co-operative arrangements and joint actions to support effective national action, strategies and programmes.[251] Internationally, the GPA seeks to develop institutional arrangements, and facilitate capacity-building and the mobilisation of financial resources.[252] The GPA also calls upon the Executive Director of UNEP, in close partnership with other international organisations, to prepare a proposal setting forth a specific plan for addressing the global nature of the problems related to the inadequate management and treatment of waste water. The GPA also records agreement on the need for international action to develop a global, legally binding instrument dealing with persistent organic pollutants.[253] The final chapter of the GPA provides specific guidance to states and regional organisations concerning recommended objectives and actions for addressing particular sources of land-based pollution, namely, sewage, persistent organic pollutants, radioactive substances, heavy metals, oils (hydrocarbons), nutrients, sediment, litter, and habitat destruction and alteration.[254]

1974 Paris Convention

The first treaty to establish detailed rules on land-based sources of marine pollution was the 1974 Paris Convention, agreed on to protect the marine

---

[248] 24 May 1985, UNEP/GC/DEC/13/1811.
[249] 5 December 1995, UNEP(OCA)/LBA/IG.2/7, 7.
[250] *Ibid.*, Chapter II.   [251] *Ibid.*, Chapter III.
[252] *Ibid.*, Chapter IV.   [253] *Ibid.*, paras. 86 and 88.   [254] *Ibid.*, Chapter V.

environment of the North East Atlantic by supplementing the 1972 Oslo Convention.[255] The Convention has now been replaced by the 1992 OSPAR Convention. The Paris Convention defined marine pollution from land-based sources as pollution of the maritime area:

1. through watercourses;
2. from the coast, including introduction through underwater or other pipelines; and
3. from man-made structures placed under the jurisdiction of a contracting party within the limits of the area to which the Convention applies.[256]

The 1986 amendment added to this definition a fourth source: emissions 'into the atmosphere from land or from man-made structures as defined in [paragraph 3] above'.[257] Parties were required to adopt programmes and measures to eliminate pollution of the maritime area from land-based sources by substances listed in Part I of Annex A,[258] and to limit strictly pollution by substances listed in Part II of Annex A, which were to be discharged only after approval by national authorities.[259] These programmes and measures were to 'take into account the latest technical developments', within time limits, and to allow for measures to reduce unlisted substances if scientific evidence 'established that a serious hazard may be created in the maritime area by that substance and if urgent action is necessary'.[260]

The parties were also required to 'adopt measures to forestall and, as appropriate, eliminate pollution of the maritime area' by radioactive substances listed in Part III of Annex A, taking into account the recommendations of international organisations and agencies and their monitoring procedures.[261] These relatively specific commitments were supplemented by general obligations: to

---

[255] Paris, 4 June 1974, in force 5 October 1976; Preamble; amended 26 March 1986 to allow the EC to become a party; OJ L24, 27 January 1987, 49.

[256] Art. 3(c). The Paris Convention covered the North-East Atlantic excluding the Baltic Sea and the Mediterranean Sea: Art. 2.

[257] 1986 Amendment, Art. I.

[258] Art. 4(1)(a) and 4(2)(a). Part I substances were included because they are not readily degradable or naturally rendered harmless, and are dangerous to the food chain, the marine ecosystem or legitimate uses of the sea, and necessitate urgent action. Listed substances included organohalogen compounds and substances, mercury and mercury compounds, cadmium and cadmium compounds, certain persistent synthetic materials, and persistent oils and hydrocarbons: Annex A, Part I.

[259] Art. 4(1)(b) and 4(2)(b); substances listed in Part II were those which had similar characteristics to those listed in Part I but which were less noxious or more readily rendered harmless by natural processes, and included certain organic compounds of phosphorus, silicon and tin, elemental phosphorus, non-persistent oils and hydrocarbons, arsenic, chromium, copper, lead, nickel and zinc, and other substances agreed by PARCOM to have a deleterious effect on the taste or smell of marine products for human consumption: Annex A, Part II.

[260] Art. 4(3) and (4).   [261] Art. 5.

reduce existing pollution from land-based sources and forestall new pollution from such sources; to avoid increasing pollution elsewhere through implementation of the Convention; to allow parties to take more stringent measures; to consult, establish scientific research programmes and exchange information; to establish a permanent monitoring system; and to co-operate to prevent incidents leading to pollution from land-based sources.[262]

The Paris Convention was administered by PARCOM, comprising representatives of each party, which met annually to supervise implementation; examine the feasibility of, and draw up, programmes and measures under Article 4; and make recommendations to amend the substances listed in Annex A.[263] PARCOM was competent to adopt certain *binding* programmes, measures and decisions by unanimity. Where unanimity was unattainable, any decision had to be adopted by three-quarters majority vote of its members, in which case the programme, measure or decision was only binding for those members voting for it or subsequently deciding expressly to accept the programme or measure, which they were free to do at any time.[264] PARCOM's recommendations for amendments to Annex A, adopted by a three-quarters majority vote of its members, entered into force for all parties unless one of them notified the depositary government in writing within 200 days of its adoption that it could not approve an amendment.[265]

Between 1978 and 1998, PARCOM met annually and adopted a large number of recommendations and decisions, some of which were very detailed and specific. In 1988, the parties agreed not to construct new nuclear reprocessing installations, or substantially to increase the capacity of existing installations, unless they could ascertain, following an environmental impact assessment, that such facilities did not cause radioactive pollution.[266] The parties also agreed to respect the recommendations of international organisations and apply 'best available technology' to minimise and eliminate pollution from radioactive discharges into the marine environment.[267] Other PARCOM recommendations addressed: the principle of precautionary action;[268] the use of best available technology;[269] and the phasing-out and destruction of all identifiable polychlorinated biphenyls (PCBs) by 1995 and the end of 1999 at the latest for Iceland and for North Sea parties, and by 2005 and by the end of 2010 at the latest for the other parties.[270] In 1991, PARCOM agreed that the disposal of

---

[262] Arts. 6–11, 13 and 17.   [263] Arts. 15 and 16.   [264] Art. 18(3).   [265] Art. 18(4).

[266] PARCOM Recommendation 88/4 (1988).

[267] PARCOM Recommendation 88/5 (1988); and PARCOM Recommendation 90/2 (1990) on Reporting on Progress in Applying the Best Available Technology on Radioactive Discharges from All Nuclear Industries. PARCOM Recommendation 91/4 (1991) consolidated Recommendations 88/5 and 90/3 into a single Recommendation and establishes guidelines.

[268] PARCOM Recommendation 89/1 (1989).

[269] PARCOM Recommendation 89/2 (1989); PARCOM Recommendation 90/1 (1990).

[270] PARCOM Decision 90/4 (1990).

radioactive wastes in repositories constructed in bedrock under the seabed and accessed from land 'constituted a potential land-based source of marine pollution' and that PARCOM had competence to consider such developments.[271]

In 1987, PARCOM decided that the Convention did not need to be amended to provide expressly for environmental impact assessment, and that PARCOM had the authority to agree to measures on environmental impact assessment regarding projects involving the discharge of substances, but that the legal basis for agreeing on legally binding decisions regarding assessments for projects with impacts of a physical nature was unclear. PARCOM concluded that it should consider the implementation of the 1985 EC Directive on Environmental Impact Assessment, but that there was no need at the present time to formally include environmental impact assessments in the framework of the Paris Convention.[272] Nevertheless, the subject of environmental impact assessment, and related issues, continued to be controversial. PARCOM Recommendation 93/5, adopted at the fifteenth joint meeting of the Oslo and Paris Commissions in June 1993, illustrated the extent to which international organisations now address specific issues such as the authorisation of individual plants. PARCOM Recommendation 93/5 was adopted in the context of the proposed authorisation by the United Kingdom of a spent nuclear fuel reprocessing facility (THORP) on the north-west coast of England at Sellafield. No environmental impact assessment had been carried out because the plant had been subject to a planning enquiry in 1977 and subsequent authorisation before the adoption of the EC Environmental Impact Assessment Directive.[273] Concerned about the apparent unwillingness of the United Kingdom to require an environmental assessment, certain countries, including neighbouring Ireland and non-neighbouring Denmark, raised the matter at PARCOM. Recommendation 93/5 was adopted with the support of nine parties, representing the necessary three-quarters majority, since only three parties (Belgium, France and the United Kingdom) entered reservations against it. The parties to PARCOM agreed:

1. to adopt further measures, including the application of best available techniques for the reduction or elimination of inputs of radioactive substances to the maritime area;
2. that a new or revised discharge authorisation for radioactive discharges from nuclear reprocessing installations should only be issued by national authorities if special consideration is given to:

---

[271] PARCOM Recommendation 91/5 (1991). The Recommendation rejected the idea that such disposal constituted 'dumping'; cf. the discussion concerning seabed disposal under the 1972 London Convention, at pp. 416–21 above.

[272] Paris Commission, *Procedures and Decisions Manual*, D3/87, Environmental Impact Assessment; reprinted in D. Freestone and T. Ijlstra (eds.), *The North Sea: Basic Legal Documents on Regional Environmental Co-operation (1991)*, 148; on the EC Directive and environmental impact assessment in general, see chapter 16 below.

[273] Chapter 16, pp. 807–11 below.

(a) information on the need for spent fuel reprocessing and on other options;
(b) a full environmental impact assessment;
(c) the demonstration that the planned discharges are based upon the use of the best available techniques and observe the precautionary principle; and
(d) a consultation with the Paris Commission on the basis of (a), (b) and (c) above.

Recommendation 93/5 is not binding, although this does not preclude the possibility that it might reflect existing obligations under the Paris Convention. The United Kingdom gave precise reasons for not supporting the Recommendation:

> the United Kingdom reservation made was because the first limb of the recommendation made no progress beyond the commitment in the 1992 action plan, while the second limb both was too vague to provide a proper basis for a PARCOM recommendation and, insofar as it provided for a role for the Paris Commission in the decision process, was inappropriate.[274]

These reasons themselves raised further questions, both of a substantive nature (was PARCOM precluded from adopting recommendations on matters previously dealt with in a similar manner?) and of an institutional nature (was PARCOM precluded from participating in decision-making processes of this type?).

1992 OSPAR Convention

Under the terms of the 1992 OSPAR Convention, the parties are required to prevent and eliminate pollution from land-based sources, including accidents.[275] The definition of 'land-based sources' includes point and diffuse sources on land from which substances or energy reach the maritime area by water, through the air or from the coast; moreover, it specifically includes:

> sources associated with any deliberate disposal under the sea-bed made accessible from land by tunnel, pipeline or other means and sources associated with man-made structures placed, in the maritime area under the jurisdiction of a contracting party, other than for the purpose of offshore activities.[276]

Programmes and measures require the use of best available techniques for point sources and best environmental practice for point and diffuse sources, using the

---

[274] Minister for the Environment and Countryside, *Hansard*, 30 June 1993, Written Answers, col. 524. On the 1992 Action Plan, see above.
[275] Art. 3; and Annex I, Art. 1(3).   [276] Art. 1(e); cf. pp. 421–2 above.

criteria in Appendix 2 to the Convention.[277] The adoption of such programmes and measures is mandatory for certain substances,[278] and measures for radioactive substances, including waste, must take account of the recommendations of other international organisations.[279] Under Annex I, all discharges into the maritime area, and releases into water or air which reach and may affect the maritime area, must be authorised or regulated and be subject to a system of regular monitoring to assess compliance.[280]

The parties to the OSPAR Convention subsequently agreed to more stringent commitments, particularly in relation to the disposal of radioactive wastes. By a 1998 Ministerial Declaration, the parties agreed:

> to prevent pollution of the maritime area from ionising radiation through progressive and substantial reductions of discharges, emissions and losses of radioactive substances, with the ultimate aim of concentrations in the environment near background values for naturally occurring radioactive substances and close to zero for artificial radioactive substances.[281]

They further agreed to ensure that:

> discharges, emissions and losses of radioactive substances are reduced by the year 2020 to levels where the additional concentrations in the marine environment above historic levels, resulting from such discharges, emissions and losses, are close to zero.

At the same meeting, the contracting parties adopted a strategy for the purposes of directing the future work of the OSPAR Commission with regard to radioactive substances, to put into effect the requirements of the 1998 OSPAR

[277] Annex I, Art. 1(1) and (2). The criteria listed in Appendix 2 include persistency, toxicity, bioaccumulation, radioactivity, the effect of concentrations, the risk of eutrophication, transboundary significance, the risk of undesirable change in the marine ecosystem and irreversibility or durability of effects, interference with legitimate uses of the sea, effects on the taste and/or smell of products for human consumption from the sea, or effects on smell, colour, transparency or other characteristics of the water in the marine environment, distribution patterns, and non-fulfilment of environmental quality objectives: Appendix 2, para. 1.

[278] Substances which shall be the subject of programmes include heavy metals, organohalogen compounds, organic compounds of phosphorus and silicon, biocides, oils, nitrogen and phosphorus compounds, radioactive substances including wastes, and persistent synthetic materials: Appendix 2, para. 3.

[279] Annex I, Art. 1(4).

[280] Annex I, Art. 2. The OSPAR Commission is required to draw up plans to reduce and phase out certain hazardous substances and to reduce inputs of nutrients from urban, municipal, industrial, agricultural and other sources: Art. 3.

[281] In achieving this objective, the following issues would, *inter alia*, be taken into account: legitimate uses of the sea; technical feasibility; and radiological impacts on man and biota.

Ministerial Declaration.[282] In 2000, the OSPAR Commission adopted a Decision requiring parties to review (as a matter of priority) current authorisations for discharges or releases of radioactive substances from nuclear reprocessing facilities, with a view to implementing the non-reprocessing option (for example, dry storage) for spent nuclear fuel management at appropriate facilities, and taking preventive measures to minimise the risk of pollution by accidents.[283] These commitments are the subject of litigation in the *MOX* case between Ireland and the UK.[284]

UNEP Regional Seas Protocols

Four UNEP Regional Seas Protocols address land-based pollution: the 1980 Athens LBS Protocol, the 1983 Quito LBS Protocol, the 1990 Kuwait LBS Protocol and the 1992 Black Sea LBS Protocol.[285] The four Protocols follow the same general approach and structure as the 1974 Paris Convention, obliging parties to eliminate pollution through the development of programmes and measures, including common emission standards and standards for use.[286]

Parties must prohibit the discharge of 'black list' substances listed in Annex I, based on their high level of toxicity, persistence and bioaccumulation, and strictly limit the less noxious substances listed in Annex II ('grey list' substances). The discharge of grey list substances must be authorised, taking account of the characteristics and composition of waste, the discharge site and the receiving marine environment, the availability of waste technologies, and the potential impairment of marine ecosystems and sea-water uses.[287]

---

[282] Strategies were also adopted on hazardous substances, to combat eutrophication, on the protection and conservation of the ecosystems and biological diversity of the maritime area, and on environmental goals and management mechanisms for offshore activities.

[283] Decision 2000/1 on Substantial Reductions and Elimination of Discharges, Emissions and Losses of Radioactive Substances, with Special Emphasis on Nuclear Reprocessing, in force 16 January 2001 (France and the United Kingdom abstained from the vote); see also OSPAR Decision 2001/1 on the Review of Authorisations for Discharges or Releases of Radioactive Substances from Nuclear Reprocessing Activities.

[284] Chapter 17, p. 807 below.

[285] A further LBS Protocol (1999) has been concluded under the 1983 Cartagena Convention, but is yet to come into force.

[286] 1980 Athens LBS Protocol, Arts. 5 and 6; 1983 Quito LBS Protocol, Arts. IV and V (the obligation being slightly less onerous by requiring parties, respectively, to 'endeavour to prevent, reduce, control and eliminate' and to 'endeavour progressively to reduce').

[287] 1980 Athens LBS Protocol, Art. 6(3) and Annex III; 1983 Quito LBS Protocol, Arts. IV and V and Annex III.

Each Protocol adopts a similar definition of land-based pollution,[288] and provides for: co-operation on guidelines and standards; the systematic assessment of pollution levels and evaluation of the effectiveness of measures; the exchange of scientific and other information and co-ordination of research; technical assistance for developing countries; co-operation where watercourses flow through the territories of two or more countries; and consultations where land-based pollution originating in the territory of one party is prejudicing the interests of another.[289] Reviewing the implementation of the Protocols, revision and amendments of Annexes, and other functions are performed by meetings of the parties to the Protocols.[290] Under the 1980 Athens LBS Protocol, decisions on programmes and measures are adopted by two-thirds majority vote, and parties unable to accept a programme or measure must inform the meeting of the parties about the action they intend to take.[291] The 1983 Quito LBS Protocol, however, merely grants the parties the power to 'examine' the need to amend or revise the Protocol and its Annexes and formulate programmes and measures.[292]

Atmospheric pollution

A significant proportion of pollution from or through the atmosphere generally originates from land-based sources. Under Article 212 of UNCLOS, all states must 'prevent, reduce and control pollution of the marine environment, from or through the atmosphere, applicable to the air space under their sovereignty and to vessels flying their flag or vessels or aircraft of their registry'. The 1992 OSPAR Convention, the 1992 Baltic Convention, the 1980 Athens LBS Protocol, the 1983 Quito LBS Protocol and the 1990 Kuwait LBS Protocol include pollution through the atmosphere as a land-based source.[293] In 1991, the parties to the 1980 Athens LBS Protocol adopted a new Annex IV to the Protocol which defines the application of the Protocol to land-based sources of pollution transported through the atmosphere, including the compilation of data on sources, on effects and on the effectiveness of existing measures.[294] None of these provisions establishes its own programmes or standards; instead, they incorporate by reference 'internationally agreed rules, standards and recommended practices

---

[288] 1980 Athens LBS Protocol, Art. 4(1) (includes direct and indirect land-based sources, atmospheric sources, and fixed man-made offshore structures other than for exploration and exploitation of the seabed); 1983 Quito LBS Protocol, Art. II (not including fixed man-made offshore structures).

[289] 1980 Athens LBS Protocol, Arts. 7–13; 1983 Quito LBS Protocol, Arts. VI to XII.

[290] 1980 Athens LBS Protocol, Art. 14.

[291] 1980 Athens LBS Protocol, Art. 15.   [292] Art. XV.

[293] 1992 OSPAR Convention, Art. 1(e); 1992 Baltic Convention, Art. 2(2); 1980 Athens LBS Protocol, Art. 4(1)(b); 1983 Quito LBS Protocol, Art. II(c).

[294] 2 Yearbook of International Environmental Law 128 at 136 (1991).

and procedures'.[295] Prior to UNCLOS, the only international instrument of significance was the 1963 Test Ban Treaty, which has protected the marine environment from atmospheric nuclear tests.[296]

Pollution from vessels

Y. Dinstein, 'Oil Pollution from Ships and Freedom of the High Seas', 3 *Journal of Maritime Law and Commerce* 363 (1971–2); A. W. Anderson, 'National and International Efforts to Prevent Traumatic Vessel Source Pollution', 30 *University of Miami Law Review* 985 (1976); R. M. M'Gonigle and M. W. Zacher, *Pollution, Politics and International Law: Tankers at Sea* (1979); P. S. Dempsey and L. L. Hellings, 'Oil Pollution by Vessels – An Environmental Tragedy: The Legal Regime of Flags of Convenience, Multilateral Conventions and Coastal States', 10 *Denver Journal of International Law and Policy* 37 (1980); J. Kindt, 'Vessel Source Pollution and the Law of the Sea', 17 *Vanderbilt Journal of Transnational Law* 287 (1984); D. W. Abecassis and R. L. Jarashow, *Oil Pollution from Ships* (1985, 2nd edn); P. Hagen, 'The International Community Confronts Plastics Pollution from Ships: MARPOL Annex V and the Problem that Won't Go Away', 5 *American University Journal of International Law and Policy* 425 (1990); D. Bodansky, 'Protecting the Marine Environment from Vessel-Source Pollution: UNCLOS III and Beyond', 18 *Ecology Law Quarterly* 719 (1991); T. Alcock, 'Ecology Tankers and the Oil Pollution Act of 1990: A History of Efforts to Require Double Hulls on Oil Tankers', 19 *Ecology Law Quarterly* 97 (1992); Y. Sasamura, 'Prevention and Control of Marine Pollution from Ships,' 25 *Proceedings of the Law of the Sea Institute* 306 (1993); R. Mitchell, *International Oil Pollution at Sea* (1994); W. Chao, *Pollution from the Carriage of Oil by Sea: Liability and Compensation* (1996); G. F. Little, 'The Hazardous and Noxious Substances Convention: A New Horizon in the Regulation of Marine Pollution', *Lloyd's Maritime and Commercial Law Quarterly* 554 (November 1998); C. de la Rue and C. Anderson, *Shipping and the Environment* (1998); G. Gauci, 'Protection of the Marine Environment Through the International Ship-Source Oil Pollution Compensation Regimes', 8 RECIEL 29 (1999).

Pollution from vessels is caused by operational discharges from ships, such as cleaning of tanks or de-ballasting, or from discharges following accidents. This source is estimated to account for about 12 per cent of the total, but has a high public profile due to the visibility and obvious environmental consequences of incidents, particularly involving oil spills, in the past twenty-five years, and most recently the oil spill following the *Prestige* accident.[297] The prevention

---

[295] 1982 UNCLOS, Art. 212(1); on regional and global rules, see pp. 395–9 above.
[296] See chapter 12, pp. 649–51 below.   [297] See n. 21 above.

of pollution from vessels is an objective addressed mainly by UNCLOS and MARPOL 73/78.

UNCLOS

Under Article 211 of UNCLOS, states must establish international rules and standards to prevent, reduce and control pollution of the marine environment from vessels, and adopt routing systems to minimise the threat of accidents which might cause such pollution. They must also adopt national laws for vessels flying their flag or of their registry which 'at least have the same effect as that of generally accepted international rules and standards'.[298] This commits all states to ensuring that their national law complies with, at a minimum, standards generally accepted under international law. Without prejudice to the right of innocent passage, states can establish, individually or as part of co-operative arrangements, special rules for the prevention, reduction and control of vessel pollution as a condition for entry into ports or internal waters of foreign vessels, provided they are given 'due publicity' and are communicated to international organisations.[299] States may also adopt laws to combat vessel pollution from passage of foreign vessels in their territorial seas, including those exercising the right of innocent passage.[300] With respect to their EEZ, states may for the purposes of enforcement adopt laws and regulations which conform to and give effect to generally accepted international rules and standards.[301] Additionally, for a defined area of the EEZ, states may, with the agreement of the competent international organisation, adopt 'special mandatory measures for the prevention of pollution from vessels' which implement international rules, standards or navigational practices made applicable by that organisation for special areas; this right is limited to a defined area of the EEZ as 'required for recognised technical reasons in relation to its oceanographical and ecological conditions, as well as its utilisation or the protection of its resources and the particular character of its traffic'.[302] Additional laws and regulations for the same area relating to discharges or navigational practices (but not design, construction, manning or equipment standards other than generally accepted international rules and standards) may be adopted by states with the agreement of a competent international organisation.[303]

---

[298] Art. 211(1) and (2).
[299] Art. 211(3); see e.g. EC Council Directive 95/21/EC establishing a system of port state control based on uniform inspection and detention procedures, OJ L157, 7 July 1995, 1; and amendments by Council Directive 2001/106/EC, OJ L19, 22 January 2002, 17.
[300] Art. 211(4).   [301] Art. 211(5).
[302] Art. 211(6)(a); see generally IMO, Guidelines for the Designation of Special Areas and the Identification of Particularly Sensitive Sea Areas, Res. A.720(17), 6 November 1991.
[303] Art. 211(6)(c).

MARPOL 73/78

The main international convention regulating pollution from vessels is MARPOL 73/78, which was first adopted at the International Conference on Marine Pollution convened by the IMO in 1973 to replace the 1954 Oil Pollution Convention. MARPOL 1973, the original treaty,[304] was modified by the 1978 Protocol (MARPOL 1978).[305] The modified convention is known as the International Convention for the Prevention of Pollution from Ships, as modified by the Protocol of 1978 relating thereto, and is usually referred to as MARPOL 73/78. The detailed rules on pollution from ships are set out in six Annexes to the Convention. Further clarifications to various provisions of MARPOL 73/78 have been adopted by the IMO Marine Environment Protection Committee (MEPC) in the form of resolutions setting out unified and authoritative interpretations or amendments to the Convention. MARPOL 73/78 has attracted widespread support, although the Annexes have received less support and two have not yet entered into force.

MARPOL 73/78 establishes specific international regulations to implement the objective of completely eliminating intentional pollution of the marine environment by oil and other harmful substances and minimising accidental discharges. Needless to say, that objective has not yet been accomplished, even though the substantive obligations are among the most precise and comprehensive in any international environmental agreement. The parties agree to give effect to the provisions of the Convention which includes, unless expressly provided otherwise, the Protocols and Annexes.[306] MARPOL 73/78 establishes a framework for the adoption of the regulations in the Annexes, and sets out basic definitions. 'Harmful substances' include:

> any substance which, if introduced into the sea, is likely to create hazards to human health, to harm living resources and marine life, to damage amenities or to interfere with other legitimate uses of the sea.[307]

---

[304] International Convention for the Prevention of Pollution from Ships, London, 2 November 1973, 12 ILM 1319 at 1434 (1973); 125 states are parties to MARPOL 73/78 or its Annexes I and II; 107 states are parties to Annex III; 91 states are parties to Annex IV; 112 states are parties to Annex V.

[305] Protocol Relating to the 1973 International Convention for the Prevention of Pollution from Ships, London, 17 February 1978, in force 2 October 1983, 17 ILM 546 (1978). Before MARPOL 1973 entered into force, it was recognised that the provisions of Annex II would be difficult for even the most economically advanced states to comply with. MARPOL 1978 was therefore negotiated and adopted to establish a new instrument which provided that the new convention comprised the 1978 Protocol and its Annex *and* MARPOL 1973 as amended by MARPOL 1978, and that the provisions of MARPOL 1973 and MARPOL 1978 should be 'read and interpreted together as one single instrument': MARPOL 1978, Art. 1. MARPOL 1978 delayed the implementation of Annex II and amended one of the provisions concerning the communication of information: MARPOL 1978, Arts. II and III.

[306] MARPOL 73/78, Art. 1.   [307] Art. 2(2).

The definition of 'discharge' is similarly broad, and covers intentional and unintentional releases from a ship, including 'any escape, disposal, spilling, leaking, pumping, emitting or emptying'; however, it does not include dumping within the meaning of the 1972 London Convention, releases directly arising from exploration and exploitation of seabed mineral resources, or releases for certain scientific research.[308] MARPOL 73/78 applies to ships which are entitled to fly the flag of a party or operate under the authority of a party, but it does not apply to warships or other state-owned ships operated by a state and used only on governmental non-commercial service.[309] The parties must prohibit and sanction violations and accept certificates required by the regulations which are prepared by other parties as having the same validity as their own certificates.[310] A ship which is in the port or offshore terminal of a party may be subject to an inspection to verify the existence of a valid certificate unless there are 'clear grounds for believing that the condition of the ship or its equipment does not correspond substantially with the particulars of that certificate'.[311] Where that is the case or where no certificate exists, the inspecting party must ensure that the ship does not sail 'until it can proceed to sea without presenting an unreasonable threat of harm to the marine environment'. MARPOL 73/78 requires parties to apply the Convention to ships of non-parties so as to ensure that 'no more favourable treatment is given to such ships'.[312] MARPOL 73/78 also provides for the detection of violations and enforcement, such as in-port inspections to verify whether ships have discharged harmful substances, reporting requirements on incidents involving harmful substances, the communication of information to the IMO, and technical co-operation.[313] Disputes are to be settled by negotiation or arbitration.[314] MARPOL 73/78 includes six annexes. Annexes I and II bind all parties, whereas Annexes III, IV, V and VI are options which a state may declare it does not accept when first becoming a party to the Convention or may subsequently accede to.[315]

Annex I

Annex I of MARPOL 73/78 comprises twenty-six Regulations for the Prevention of Pollution by Oil and six Appendices. It entered into force on 2 October

---

[308] Art. 2(3).
[309] Art. 3(1) and (3); warships and other state-owned ships must, however, act in a manner which is consistent, so far as is reasonable and practicable, with the Convention: *ibid.*
[310] Art. 5(1) and (2).   [311] Art. 5(2).   [312] Art. 5(4).
[313] Arts. 6, 8, 11 and 17. Protocol I sets out detailed Provisions Concerning Reports on Incidents Involving Harmful Substances. See also IMO Assembly Res. A.648(16) on general principles for ship reporting systems and ship reporting requirements, including guidelines for reporting incidents involving dangerous goods, harmful substances and/or marine pollutants, 19 October 1989.
[314] Art. 10 and Protocol II.   [315] Art. 14.

1983, and has been amended in 1984, 1987, 1990, 1991, 1992, 1994, 1997, 1999 and 2001. Annex I is divided into four Chapters. Chapter I establishes 'General' provisions including definitions and scope of application, rules concerning surveys and inspections of oil tankers, and rules concerning the issue form, and duration of certificates.[316] Chapter II concerns Requirements for Control of Operational Pollution. It prohibits, subject to certain exceptions, any discharge of oil or oily mixtures into the sea.[317] Eight areas are designated as 'special areas' for which the prohibition on discharges is even stricter: the Mediterranean Sea, the Baltic Sea, the Black Sea, the Red Sea, the 'Gulf area', the Gulf of Aden, the Antarctic and the 'North West European Waters'.[318] Specific regulations are adopted for reception facilities, ballast tanks and crude oil washing, retention of oil on board, discharge monitoring and control system and oily water separating equipment, sludge tanks, pumping and piping arrangements, and specific requirements for drilling rigs and other platforms.[319] At its thirty-second session, the MEPC adopted further amendments to this chapter of Annex I including the adoption of rules requiring 'double hulls' for certain new and existing tankers, a requirement introduced at the urging of the United States following the *Exxon Valdez* accident.[320] Further amendments were adopted in 2001 to bring in a new global timetable for accelerating the phase-out of single-hull oil tankers. The timetable will see most single-hull oil tankers eliminated by 2015 or earlier.[321] Chapter III establishes provisions on 'Requirements for minimising oil pollution from oil tankers due to side and bottom damages', and includes Regulations on tank size limitation and damage stability.[322] Chapter IV, on the 'Prevention of pollution arising from an oil pollution incident', provides for shipboard oil pollution emergency plans.[323]

Annex II

Annex II, which establishes Regulations for the Control of Pollution by Noxious Liquid Substances in Bulk, entered into force on 6 April 1987, as amended by the MEPC.[324] It was further amended in 1989,[325] and 1994, and comprises fourteen Regulations and five Appendices. Regulations deal with definitions, application and categorisation of substances; the discharge of residues inside and outside 'special areas'; pumping, piping and unloading arrangements;

---

[316] Annex I, Regulations 1, 2 and 4–8.   [317] Annex I, Regulations 9 and 11.
[318] Annex I, Regulation 10.   [319] Annex I, Regulations 12–21.
[320] Res. MEPC.52(32) introducing new Regulations 13F and 13G to Annex I which entered into force on 6 July 1993.
[321] The amendments were adopted on 27 April 2001 and will enter into force on 1 September 2002; in the EU they are implemented by Regulation (EC) No. 417/2002 on the accelerated phasing-in of double hull or equivalent design requirements for single-hull oil tankers, OJ L64, 7 March 2002, 1.
[322] Annex I, Regulations 22–25A.   [323] Annex I, Regulation 26, in force 4 April 1993.
[324] Res. MEPC.17(22) (1985).   [325] Res. MEPC.34(27) (1989).

reception facilities and cargo record books; surveys and certification; requirements for minimising accidental pollution; and the carriage and discharge of
oil-like substances.[326]

Annex III

The Regulations for the Prevention of Pollution by Harmful Substances in Packaged Form set out in the draft revised Annex III of MARPOL 73/78 entered
into force on 1 July 1992. Annex III, which is implemented through the IMO
International Maritime Dangerous Goods Code,[327] includes Regulations on
packing, marking and labelling, documentation, stowage, and quantity limitations.[328] It also prohibits the jettisoning of harmful substances except for safety
reasons.[329]

Annex IV

The Regulations for the Prevention of Pollution by Sewage, set out in Annex
IV of MARPOL 73/78, have not yet entered into force, due to the existing
construction of ships. The Regulations address such matters as surveys and
certification[330] and reception facilities.[331] When they enter into force, they will,
with some exceptions, prohibit the discharge of sewage into the sea, unless the
sewage complies with disinfection requirements or the ship has an approved
sewage treatment plant, or is situated in the waters of a state imposing less
stringent requirements.[332]

Annex V

The Regulations for the Prevention of Pollution by Garbage from Ships, set out
in Annex V to MARPOL 73/78, entered into force on 31 December 1988. The
Regulations apply to all ships and regulate different types of garbage, subject
to rules of special application, special areas and exceptions.[333] The disposal
from ships into the sea of all plastics is prohibited;[334] dunnage, lining and
packing materials which float cannot be disposed of within twenty-five nautical
miles of land; disposal of food waste and all other garbage is prohibited within
twelve nautical miles of land, unless it has passed through a comminuter or
grinder in which case it may not be disposed of within three nautical miles of
land.[335] Except for food wastes, no garbage may be disposed of from any fixed

---

[326] Annex II, Regulations 1–14.
[327] See IMO Assembly Res. A.81(IV); see chapter 12, pp. 638–41 below.
[328] Annex III, Regulations 2–6.   [329] Annex III, Regulation 7.
[330] Annex IV, Regulations 3–7.   [331] Annex IV, Regulations 10 and 11.
[332] Annex IV, Regulation 8.
[333] Annex V was amended in 1989, 1990, 1991 and 1995. The exceptions are set out in
  Regulation 6. See also the Guidelines for the Implementation of Annex V of MARPOL
  73/78.
[334] Annex V, Regulation 3(1)(a).   [335] Annex V, Regulation 3(1)(b) and (c).

or floating platforms for the exploration, exploitation and associated offshore processing of seabed mineral resources, and from all ships when alongside or within 500 metres.[336] For special areas, more stringent requirements apply, such as a prohibition on the disposal of all plastics and all other garbage and rules on reception facilities located in such areas.[337]

Annex VI

The Regulations for the Prevention of Air Pollution from Ships, set out in Annex VI to MARPOL 73/78, were adopted on 26 September 1997. The Annex will enter into force twelve months after being ratified by fifteen states whose combined fleets of merchant shipping constitute at least 50 per cent of the world fleet.[338] When the Regulations come into force, they will set limits on sulphur oxide (SO_x) and nitrogen oxide (NO_x) emissions from ship exhausts and prohibit deliberate emissions of ozone-depleting substances. A global cap of 4.5 per cent m/m on the sulphur content of fuel oil is included, with the IMO expected to monitor the worldwide average sulphur content of fuel once the Protocol comes into force. The Annex makes provision for the establishment of special 'SO_x Emission Control Areas' with more stringent standards for sulphur emissions by ships in these areas.[339] The Annex also prohibits the incineration on board ship of certain products, such as contaminated packaging materials and polychlorinated biphenyls (PCBs).

Safety agreements

International standards on the safety of shipping have been adopted for load lines,[340] the prevention of collisions at sea,[341] the safety of life at sea[342] and

---

[336] Annex V, Regulation 4(1). Food wastes may be disposed of provided they have passed through a comminuter or grinder and the location is more than twelve nautical miles from land: Regulation 4(2).

[337] Annex V, Regulation 5(2) to (4). The special areas are the Mediterranean Sea, the Baltic Sea, the Black Sea, the Red Sea and the Gulf. Regulation 5(1). The North Sea area was added with effect from 18 April 1991, the Antarctic area with effect from 17 March 1992, and the wider Caribbean region with effect from 4 April 1993.

[338] Currently, only three states have ratified, representing 8.42 per cent of world tonnage.

[339] The Baltic Sea is designated as a SO_x Emission Control area under the Protocol.

[340] International Convention on Load Lines, as amended, London, 5 April 1966, in force 21 July 1968, 604 UKTS 133; Protocol, London 11 November 1988, in force 3 February 2000.

[341] Convention on the International Regulations for Preventing Collisions at Sea, London, 20 October 1972, in force 15 July 1977, UKTS 77 (1977) Cmnd 6962; amended in 1981, Misc. 8 (1982), Cmnd 8500, in force 1 June 1983. Further amendments were made in 1987, 1989 and 1993.

[342] International Convention for the Safety of Life at Sea, London, 1 November 1974, in force 25 May 1980, 1184 UNTS 2; see Protocol of 1978, London, 17 February 1978, in force 1 May 1981, UKTS 40 (1981) Cmnd 8277; Protocol of 1988, London, 11 November 1988, in force 3 February 2000.

the training of seafarers and fishing vessel personnel.[343] These address matters relating to safety at sea, rather than operational or accidental discharge, and have attracted broad support from states. As a body of binding rules they establish detailed commitments on the design and construction of ships, as well as equipping, manning, operations and matters related to the training of the crew.

Pollution from seabed activities

T. Treves, 'La Pollution résultant de l'exploration et de l'exploitation des fonds marins en droit international', 24 AFDI 827 (1978); A. L. C. De Mestral, 'The Prevention of Pollution of the Marine Environment Arising from Offshore Mining and Drilling', 20 *Harvard International Law Journal* 469 (1979); J. Kindt, 'The Law of the Sea: Offshore Installations and Marine Pollution', 12 *Pepperdine Law Review* 381 (1984); S. M. Evans, 'Control of Marine Pollution Generated by Offshore Oil and Gas Exploration and Exploitation', 10 *Marine Policy* 82 (1986); J. Kindt, 'The Environmental Aspects of Deep Seabed Mining', 8 *UCLA Journal of Environmental Law and Policy* 125 (1989); B. Barrett and R. Howells, 'The Offshore Petroleum Industry and Protection of the Marine Environment', 2 JEL 53 (1990); A. Nollka-emper, 'Deep Sea-Bed Mining and the Protection of the Environment', 15 *Marine Policy* 55 (1991); M. Gavouneli, *Pollution from Offshore Installations* (1995); Z. Gao (ed.), *Environment Regulation of Oil and Gas* (1998); E. Kirk, 'OSPAR Decision 98/3 and the Dumping of Offshore Installations', 48 ICLQ 458 (1999).

Pollution from seabed activities is caused by the release of harmful substances arising directly from the exploration, exploitation and processing of sea-bed materials. It accounts for only 1 per cent of pollution of the marine environment, although in certain regions, such as the Gulf, the proportion is considerably higher due to oil exploration activities. International legislation on pollution from this source is undeveloped. UNCLOS establishes a basic framework of general commitments, which have so far been supplemented by regional rules in the north-east Atlantic, the North Sea, the Arabian Gulf and the Mediterranean.

UNCLOS

For seabed activities within areas of national jurisdiction, Article 208 of UNCLOS requires coastal states to prevent, reduce and control pollution of the marine environment 'arising from or in connection with seabed activities subject to their jurisdiction and from artificial islands, installations and structures

---

[343] International Convention on Standards of Training, Certification and Watchkeeping for Seafarers, London, 7 July 1978, in force 28 April 1984, UKTS 50 (1984) Cmnd 9266. Amendments in 1995, which completely revised the Convention, entered into force on 1 February 1997. The amended Convention is reprinted in F. Wiswall (ed.), *Benedict on Admiralty* (1998, 7th edn), Doc. 14-6 at 14-483.

under their jurisdiction', which should not be less effective than international rules, standards and recommended practices and procedures. States should also establish detailed global and regional rules, standards and recommended practices.[344]

For seabed activities outside areas of national jurisdiction, under Article 145 of UNCLOS the International Seabed Authority will adopt rules, regulations and procedures for the seabed and ocean floor and subsoil beyond the limits of national jurisdiction (known as 'the Area') for

1. the prevention, reduction and control of pollution and other hazards to the marine environment, including the coastline, and of interference with the ecological balance of the marine environment, particular attention being paid to the need for protection from harmful effects of such activities as drilling, dredging, excavation, disposal of waste, construction and operation or maintenance of installations, pipelines and other devices related to such activities; and
2. the protection and conservation of the natural resources of the Area and the prevention of damage to the flora and fauna of the marine environment.[345]

Rules for the protection of the marine environment are adopted by the institutions comprising the Authority, namely, the Assembly, following provisional adoption by the Council, and in accordance with the recommendations of the Legal and Technical Commission. The Council must refuse to approve areas for exploitation 'where substantial evidence indicates the risk of serious harm to the marine environment'.[346] Under Article 162, the Council can ensure compliance with the provisions on the protection of the marine environment from activities in the international seabed area, including emergency orders to prevent serious harm, and an inspectorate.[347] In 2000, the International Seabed Authority adopted Regulations on Prospecting and Exploration of Polymetallic Nodules in the Area, Part V of which address the 'Protection and Preservation of the Marine Environment'.[348] These require the Authority to establish and keep under review environmental rules, regulations and procedures to ensure effective protection for the marine environment from harmful effects which may arise from activities in the Area, applying (with sponsoring states) a precautionary approach to activities in the Area. The Regulations impose a duty on each contractor to 'take necessary measures to prevent, reduce and control

---

[344] Art. 208(5).

[345] Art. 145. See also UNCLOS, Annex III, Art. 17(1)(b)(xii), enabling the Authority to adopt minimum standards and practices, including those relating to conservation of the resources and protection of the marine environment; and Section 1, para. 5(g) of the Annex to the 1994 Agreement on Part XI of UNCLOS (requiring the Authority to concentrate on the adoption of rules, regulation and procedures incorprating applicable standards for the protection and preservation of the marine environment).

[346] Art. 162(2)(x).   [347] Art. 162(2)(iv) and (3).   [348] Regulation 31.

pollution and other hazards to the marine environment arising from its activities in the Area as far as reasonably possible using the best technology available to it'. The duty is elaborated in the Regulations, contractual clauses and recommendations adopted by the Legal and Technical Commission in 2001. The contractor is required to gather environmental data as exploration activities progress and to establish environmental baselines against which to assess the likely effects of its activities on the marine environment. The contractor is also required to establish and implement a programme to monitor and report on such effects. The Regulations also contain procedures for the exercise by the Council, pursuant to Article 162(2)(w) of the Convention, of its power to issue emergency orders to prevent serious harm to the marine environment arising out of activities in the Area.

OSPAR Convention

Under the 1992 OSPAR Convention, the parties are required to prevent and eliminate pollution from offshore sources, including accidents, and comply with the rules set out in Annex III.[349] Dumping of wastes or other matter from offshore installations is prohibited.[350] Discharges or emissions from offshore sources are not included in the prohibition, but they, together with the use of substances which may reach and affect the maritime area, are strictly subject to authorisation or regulation, and monitoring.[351] Disused offshore installations or pipelines must not be dumped, and no disused offshore installation can be left wholly or partly in place without a permit issued on a case-by-case basis granted in accordance with applicable decisions, recommendations and other agreements adopted under the Convention.[352] Permits will not be granted if the disused installation or pipeline contains substances which result or are likely to result in hazards, harms or interference with other legitimate uses of the sea.[353] The Annex includes rules on placement, compliance, sovereign immunity and the role of the OSPAR Commission.[354]

Other treaties

Dumping from offshore installations placed on the continental shelf is regulated by the 1972 London Convention and the 1976 Mediterranean Convention, although they do not apply to disposals which occur in the course of normal operations. In 1982, UNEP adopted Guidelines on Offshore Mining

---

[349] Art. 5 and Annex III. 'Offshore sources' are defined as 'offshore installations and offshore pipelines from which substances or energy reach the maritime area': Art. 1(k). Exceptions are provided for in Annex III, Arts. 1 and 6.

[350] Annex III, Art. 3. [351] Annex III, Art. 4. [352] Annex III, Art. 5(1).

[353] Annex III, Art. 5(2). [354] Arts. 8–10.

and Drilling,[355] but to date the only international agreements which address this issue are the 1989 Kuwait Protocol Concerning Marine Pollution Resulting from Exploration and Exploitation of the Continental Shelf (1989 Kuwait Exploration Protocol) and the 1994 Mediterranean Protocol Concerning the Protection of the Mediterranean Sea Against Pollution Resulting from Exploration and Exploitation of the Continental Shelf and the Seabed and its Subsoil (1994 Madrid Offshore Protocol). The 1992 Black Sea Convention commits parties to adopt laws and regulations to prevent, reduce or control pollution of the Black Sea from continental shelf activities.[356] The 1992 Baltic Sea Convention goes further, committing parties to take 'all measures in order to prevent pollution . . . resulting from exploration or exploitation of its part of the seabed and the subsoil thereof'.[357] More detailed obligations are set out in Annex VI, including a commitment to use best available technology and best environmental practice; to carry out an environmental impact assessment before offshore activity can start; to apply discharge limits during exploration and exploitation; and to comply with international reporting and information exchange requirements.[358] Moreover, all abandoned, disused or accidentally wrecked offshore units must be 'entirely removed and brought ashore under the responsibility of the owner' and disused drill wells must be plugged.[359]

Environmental emergencies

Fourteen international conventions and protocols provide a framework for international co-operation to combat emergency situations threatening the marine environment.[360] They were developed in response to individual oil pollution incidents, beginning in 1969 with the *Torrey Canyon* accident which resulted in the escape of 117,000 tons of crude oil in the western approaches to the United Kingdom, causing extensive damage to the British coast and to the coast of France.[361] The ship was registered under the flag of Liberia and the accident occurred outside the territorial sea of the United Kingdom, raising the question of whether the coastal state could intervene to address a pollution incident occurring in areas beyond national jurisdiction. This led to the Brussels Conference of 1969 and the adoption of the 1969 Intervention Convention. Of these international instruments, three are global and eleven are regional; of the latter, eight are Protocols to UNEP Regional Seas Conventions.

---

[355] UNEP, Environmental Law Guidelines and Principles No. 4, Offshore Mining and Drilling (1982) (Conclusions of the study of legal aspects concerning the environment related to offshore mining and drilling within the limits of national jurisdiction; Decision 10/14/VI of the Governing Council of UNEP, 31 May 1982).

[356] Art. XI(1).   [357] Art. 12(1).

[358] Annex VI, Regulations 2–6 and 9.   [359] Annex VI, Regulation 8.

[360] See also 1986 IAEA Notification Convention and 1986 IAEA Assistance Convention, chapter 16 below.

[361] Report of the Home Office, *The Torrey Canyon*, Cmnd 3246 (1967).

1969 Intervention Convention

The 1969 International Convention Relating to Intervention on the High Seas in Cases of Oil Pollution Casualties (1969 Intervention Convention) was adopted under the auspices of IMCO (now IMO).[362] It allows action by coastal states in an area of the global commons without affecting the high seas freedoms or other rights and duties.[363] It allows parties to

> take such measures on the high seas as may be necessary to prevent, mitigate or eliminate grave and imminent danger to their coastline or related interests from pollution or threat of pollution of the sea by oil, following upon a maritime casualty or acts related to such a casualty, which may reasonably be expected to result in major harmful consequences.[364]

Before such action is taken, unless extreme urgency requires otherwise, prior notification or consultation must take place between the coastal state and other affected states, particularly the flag state, and independent experts chosen from an IMO list.[365] The measures taken by the coastal state must satisfy certain principles and conditions: they must be proportionate to the actual or threatened damage, must not go beyond what is reasonably necessary to achieve the purpose of Article I, and must cease as soon as that purpose has been achieved.[366] A party which goes beyond what is permitted by the Convention and causes damage to others will be liable to pay compensation for such damage.[367]

1973 Intervention Protocol

The 1969 Convention was supplemented in 1973 by a Protocol on Intervention on the High Seas in Cases of Marine Pollution by Substances Other Than Oil (1973 Intervention Protocol).[368] The 1973 Protocol allows parties to take similar action to that permitted under the 1969 Convention in relation to substances listed by the IMO and annexed to the Intervention Protocol, as well as other substances 'which are liable to create hazards to human health, to harm living resources and marine life, to damage amenities or to interfere with other legitimate uses of the sea'.[369] In the case of the latter, the party taking

---

[362] Brussels, 29 November 1969, in force 6 May 1975, 9 ILM 25 (1970).

[363] Preamble and Art. VII.

[364] Art. I(1). 'Maritime casualty' includes ship collisions, stranding or navigation incident or other occurrence resulting in material damage to a ship: Art. II(1). The Convention does not apply to warships or state-owned or -operated ships on non-commercial service: Art. I(2).

[365] Arts. III and IV.   [366] Art. V.   [367] Art. VI.

[368] 2 November 1973, in force 30 March 1983, UKTS 27 (1983), Cmnd 8924.

[369] Art. I(1) and (2). The IMO list annexed is subject to an amendment procedure requiring adoption with the support of two-thirds of parties to the Protocol present and voting. Arts. I(2) and II to VIII of and the Annex to the 1969 Intervention Convention apply to substances in Art. I. Amendments to the list of substances were made in 1991 (in force 30 March 1993) and 1996 (in force 19 December 1997).

action will have the burden of establishing that the substance could reasonably pose a grave and imminent danger which is analogous to that posed by listed substances.[370]

1989 Salvage Convention

The 1989 International Convention on Salvage has the dual purpose of encouraging salvage and measures to protect the marine environment from the consequences of accidents.[371] It was adopted largely as a consequence of the accident in 1978 involving the *Amoco Cadiz*, which resulted in massive pollution of the Brittany coast of France. This highlighted the inadequacy of existing instruments, in particular the 1910 Convention for the Unification of Certain Rules of Law Respecting Assistance and Salvage at Sea,[372] and the need to provide for rules governing the remuneration of efforts by salvors to prevent or mitigate pollution. The 1989 Salvage Convention addresses this point by creating an incentive for salvors to take measures to protect the environment, even if those measures may have no useful result. The Convention also protects the legal position of coastal states with respect to pollution. Article 9 provides:

> Nothing in this Convention shall affect the right of the Coastal state concerned to take measures in accordance with generally recognised principles of international law to protect its coastline or related interests from pollution or the threat of pollution following upon a maritime casualty or acts relating to such a casualty which may reasonably be expected to result in major harmful consequences, including the right of the Coastal state to give directions in relation to salvage operations.

The heart of the Convention is set out in Articles 12 to 14. Under Article 12, salvage operations entitle the salvor to a reward only if the operations have had a useful result, except as otherwise provided. Article 13 recognises that preventing environmental damage can contribute a useful result: the reward is to be fixed to encourage salvage operations and is to take into account, *inter alia*, 'the skill and efforts of the salvors in preventing or minimising damage to the environment'.[373] Moreover, under Article 14, a 'safety net' is established to provide 'special compensation' from the owner of the vessel, equivalent to his expenses, for salvage operations for a vessel which threatened damage to the environment and for which the salvor has not earned a reward under Article 13 which is at least equivalent to the special compensation formula

---

[370] Art. I(3).
[371] London, 28 April 1989, not yet in force, IMO Leg/Conf.7/27, 2 May 1989.
[372] Brussels, 23 September 1910, UKTS 4 (1913) Cmnd 6677; as amended by Protocol, Brussels, 27 May 1967, UNTS 22 (1978), Cmnd 7095.
[373] Art. 13(1)(b).

provided by Article 14.[374] According to Article 14(2), the special compensation payable by the owner to the salvor under Article 14(1) may be increased by up to 30 per cent of the expenses incurred by the salvor if the salvor has 'prevented or minimised damage to the environment. By way of incentive, the competent tribunal may increase the special compensation up to 100 per cent if it is 'fair and just' to do so and bearing in mind the criteria set out in Article 13. The salvor is also subject to a negative incentive: negligence and the failure to prevent or minimise environmental damage may result in the salvor being deprived of the whole or part of any special compensation due.[375]

1990 OPRC Convention

The 1990 London International Convention on Oil Pollution Preparedness, Response and Co-operation Convention (1990 OPRC Convention)[376] promotes international co-operation in the event of a major oil pollution threat. Its provisions are applicable to ships, offshore units, sea ports and oil handling facilities. Even before it came into force in 1995, the Convention was being implemented by many states pursuant to the resolution of the conference which adopted it,[377] and it has been relied upon on numerous occasions, including to help Saudi Arabia and other countries cope with a major oil spill in the Gulf in 1991.

The Preamble to the 1990 OPRC Convention includes a number of provisions of relevance to general rules of international environmental law, noting the 'importance of precautionary measures and prevention in avoiding oil pollution in the first instance', and taking 'account of the polluter-pays principle as a general principle of international environmental law'. The Convention commits parties to take all appropriate measures in accordance with its provisions to prepare for and respond to an oil pollution incident.[378] These measures include: oil pollution emergency plans on ships, offshore units and sea ports and oil handling facilities; oil pollution reporting procedures; and national and regional systems for preparedness and response.[379] The Convention sets out the action to be taken on receiving an oil pollution report and provides for international co-operation in pollution response.[380] An Annex establishes principles governing reimbursement for costs of assistance, which are without prejudice

---

[374] Art. 14(1).   [375] Art. 14(5).

[376] London, 30 November 1990, in force 13 May 1995, 30 ILM 735 (1991).

[377] Conf.Res.2 (Implementation Pending Entry Into Force), 30 ILM 753 (1991).

[378] Art. 1(1). 'Oil pollution incident' is defined as 'an occurrence or series of occurrences having the same origin, which results or may result in a discharge of oil and which poses or may pose a threat to the marine environment, or to the coastline or related interests of one or more States, and which requires emergency action or other immediate response': Art. 2(2).

[379] Arts. 3, 4 and 6.   [380] Arts. 5 and 7.

to the rights of parties to recover from third parties under other applicable provisions of national and international law.[381]

2000 HNS Protocol

The 2000 Protocol to the OPRC Convention on Preparedness, Response and Co-operation to Pollution Incidents by Hazardous and Noxious Substances (2000 HNS Protocol) was adopted at a conference held at IMO headquarters in London in March 2000.[382] The hazardous and noxious substances covered by the Protocol are defined by reference to lists of substances included in other IMO Conventions and Codes and include: oils; other liquid substances defined as noxious or dangerous; liquefied gases; liquid substances with a flashpoint not exceeding 60°C; dangerous, hazardous and harmful materials and substances carried in packaged form; and solid bulk materials defined as possessing chemical hazards. As with the 1992 Convention, the 2000 HNS Protocol seeks to provide a global framework for international co-operation in combating major pollution incidents involving hazardous and noxious substances. Parties to the 2000 HNS Protocol will be required to establish measures for dealing with pollution incidents, either nationally or in co-operation with other countries. Ships will be required to carry a shipboard pollution emergency plan to deal specifically with incidents involving hazardous and noxious substances.

1969 and 1983 Bonn Agreements

The first regional agreement in this area was the 1969 Bonn Agreement for Co-operation in Dealing with Pollution of the North Sea by Oil (1969 Bonn Agreement),[383] which established a model followed by the other agreements. Limited to pollution by oil which 'presents a grave and imminent danger to the coast or related interests' of one or more parties,[384] the Agreement required parties to share information on relevant national organisations and techniques for avoiding and dealing with oil pollution, to inform other parties without delay of a casualty or the presence of oil slicks which present a serious threat, and to require their ships and aircraft to report such casualties and oil

---

[381] Annex; it also provides that 'special attention' shall be paid to the 1969 CLC and the 1971 Oil Pollution Fund Convention and any subsequent amendments (see also Art. 11).

[382] London, 15 March 2000, not yet in force.

[383] Bonn, 9 June 1969, in force 9 August 1969, 704 UNTS 3. See also the 1971 Agreement Between Denmark, Finland, Norway and Sweden Concerning Co-operation in Measures to Deal with Pollution of the Sea by Oil, and the 1990 Accord of Co-operation for the Protection of the Coasts and Waters of the Northeast Atlantic Against Pollution Due to Hydrocarbons or Other Harmful Substances, Lisbon, 17 October 1990, 30 ILM 1231 (1991).

[384] Art. 1.

slicks.[385] The 1969 Bonn Agreement divides the North Sea into zones for which parties are responsible for assessing the nature, extent and movement of the spillage, keeping it under observation, and providing information to other parties.[386] Parties are not specifically required to clean up the spillage, but if they engage in disposal, they may seek assistance from other parties likely to be affected, in which case other parties called upon to help must 'use their best endeavours to bring such assistance as is within their power'.[387]

In 1983, the North Sea coastal states adopted the 1983 Agreement for Co-operation in Dealing with Pollution of the North Sea by Oil and Other Harmful Substances (1983 Bonn Agreement) which superseded the 1969 Bonn Agreement.[388] The 1983 Agreement extends the co-operative framework to oil and other harmful substances and includes threatened as well as actual pollution.[389] It goes beyond the 1969 Agreement by requiring parties: to jointly develop and establish guidelines for joint action; to provide information on pollution incidents of this kind which they have dealt with; to establish a standard form for the reporting of pollution; to provide for rules concerning the costs of action covered by the 1983 Agreement in the absence of an agreement concerning financial arrangements; and to have regular meetings of the parties and to designate a secretariat.[390]

UNEP Regional Seas Protocols

Eight of the UNEP Regional Seas Conventions have emergency Protocols: the 1976 Barcelona Emergency Protocol; the 1978 Kuwait Emergency Protocol; the 1981 Abidjan Pollution Emergency Protocol; the 1981 Lima Emergency Agreement (with its 1983 Quito Protocol); the 1982 Jeddah Pollution Emergency Protocol; the 1983 Cartagena Oil Spills Protocol; the 1985 Nairobi Emergency Pollution Protocol; and the 1986 Noumea Pollution Emergencies Protocol. These include similar provisions which establish frameworks for co-operation in cases of grave and imminent danger to the marine environment, the coast or related interests due to the presence of massive quantities of oil or other harmful substances (not those in the 1983 Cartagena Oil Spills Protocol) resulting from accidental causes or an accumulation of small discharges which are polluting or threatening to pollute.[391] Each Protocol reflects variations on

---

[385] Arts. 4 and 5.   [386] Art. 6.   [387] Art. 7.
[388] Bonn, 13 September 1983, in force 1 September 1989; IELMT 983:68, Art. 19(2).
[389] Art. 1.   [390] Arts. 3(2), 4(e), 5(3) and 9–15.
[391] 1976 Barcelona Emergency Protocol, Art. 1; 1978 Kuwait Emergency Protocol, Art. 1(2) and (5); 1981 Abidjan Pollution Emergency Protocol, Art. I(2) and (5); 1981 Lima Emergency Agreement, Arts. I and III; 1982 Jeddah Pollution Emergency Protocol, Art. I(2) and (5); 1983 Cartagena Oil Spills Protocol, Arts. I(3) and (4) and II; 1985 Nairobi Emergency Pollution Protocol, Arts. 1(d) to (g) and 2; and 1986 Noumea Pollution Emergencies Protocol, Arts. 1(c) and (d) and 2.

a theme which generally provides for co-operation based upon obligations: to maintain contingency plans for combating pollution; to develop and apply monitoring activities; to salvage and recover harmful substances which have been released or lost overboard; to exchange information; to co-ordinate the means of communication; to ensure the reporting by their ships and aircraft of specified accidents; to take certain actions (including assessment and measures to avert or reduce the effects of pollution) in the event of a threat; to call for assistance first from other parties likely to be affected; and to establish regional or sub-regional co-ordination centres.[392] In each case ensuring implementation of the Protocol is a matter for meetings of the parties to the Protocol[393] or the organ established under the relevant framework convention.[394]

Liability and compensation

Rules of liability and compensation for damage to the marine environment establish an incentive to prevent harm and also may require restoration; several instruments have been adopted to establish rules of liability in relation to pollution or damage to the marine environment, and they are considered in chapter 17 below. At the global level, the principal treaties are the 1992 International Convention on Civil Liability for Oil Pollution Damage (1992 CLC), the 1992 International Convention on the Establishment of an International Fund for Compensation for Oil Pollution Damage (1992 Oil Pollution Fund Convention, which establishes mechanisms for compensation), the 1996 International Convention on Liability and Compensation for Damage in Connection with the Carriage of Hazardous and Noxious Substances by Sea (1996 HNS Convention) and the 2001 International Convention on Civil Liability for Bunker Oil Pollution Damage (2001 Bunker Oil Convention).[395] UNCLOS establishes basic rules on state responsibility and liability,[396] and the 1972 London Convention and some of the UNEP Regional Seas framework conventions also call

---

[392] 1976 Barcelona Emergency Protocol, Arts. 3–11 and Annex A; 1978 Kuwait Emergency Protocol, Arts. II to XII (establishing a Marine Emergency Mutual Aid Centre), and Appendix A; 1981 Abidjan Pollution Emergency Protocol, Arts. 4–10; 1981 Lima Emergency Agreement, Arts. IV to XI; and the 1983 Quito Protocol, Arts. I to III (establishing detailed co-operation mechanism for massive oil spills); 1982 Jeddah Pollution Emergency Protocol, Arts. II to XI (establishing a Marine Emergency Mutual Aid Centre); 1983 Cartagena Oil Spills Protocol, Arts. 3–9; 1985 Nairobi Emergency Pollution Protocol, Arts. 3–9; and 1986 Noumea Pollution Emergencies Protocol, Arts. 3–9.

[393] 1976 Barcelona Emergency Protocol, Art. 12; 1981 Abidjan Pollution Emergency Protocol, Art. 11; 1981 Lima Emergency Agreement, Art. XII; 1983 Cartagena Oil Spills Protocol, Art. 10; 1985 Nairobi Emergency Pollution Protocol, Art. 10; and 1986 Noumea Pollution Emergencies Protocol, Art. 10.

[394] 1978 Kuwait Emergency Protocol, Art. XIII; 1982 Jeddah Pollution Emergency Protocol, Art. XIII.

[395] See chapter 18, pp. 912–31 below.   [396] See chapter 18, pp. 922–4 below.

for the development of rules on liability and compensation. However, to date, no such rules have been adopted, although they are being prepared as a Protocol to the 1976 Barcelona Convention.[397]

UNCED

B. Cicin-Sain and R. W. Knecht, 'Implications of the Earth Summit for Ocean and Coastal Governance', 24 *Ocean Development and International Law* 323 (1993); A. Nollkaemper, 'Agenda 21 and the Prevention of Sea-Based Marine Pollution: A Spurious Relationship?', 17 *Marine Policy* 537 (1993); U. Beyerlin, 'New Developments in the Protection of the Marine Environment: Potential Effects of the Rio Process', 55 ZaöRV 544 (1995); A. Yankov, 'The Law of the Sea Convention and Agenda 21: Marine Environmental Implications', in A. Boyle and D. Freestone (eds.), *International Law and Sustainable Development* (1999), 271.

One of the most recent efforts by the international community to develop rules for the protection of the marine environment is Chapter 17 of Agenda 21, which recognises that international law, as reflected in the provisions of UNCLOS, 'provides the international basis upon which to pursue the protection and sustainable development of the marine and coastal environment and its resources'.[398] Chapter 17 of Agenda 21 establishes seven programme areas for the protection of oceans and seas, of which two are particularly relevant: the programme to provide for integrated management and sustainable development of coastal areas (including the EEZ), and the programme on marine environmental protection.[399] Recognising that coastal resources and the coastal environment are being rapidly degraded and eroded in many parts of the world, Chapter 17 of Agenda 21 outlines proposals to guide future international legislation, including: the establishment of national co-ordinating mechanisms to develop land and water use and siting policies; integrated coastal and marine management; the preparation of coastal profiles; prior environmental impact assessment and systematic observation; disaster contingency plans; the

---

[397] 1972 London Dumping Convention, Art. X; 1976 Barcelona Convention, Art. 12; 1978 Kuwait Convention, Art. XIII; 1981 Abidjan Convention, Art. 15; 1981 Lima Convention, Art. 11; 1982 Jeddah Convention, Art. XIII; 1983 Cartagena de Indias Convention, Art. 14; 1985 Nairobi Convention, Art. 15; 1986 Noumea Convention, Art. 20.

[398] Agenda 21, Chapter 17, 'Protection of the oceans, all kinds of seas, including enclosed and semi-enclosed seas, and coastal areas and the protection, rational use and development of their living resources', para. 17.1. The WSSD Plan of Implementation aims to promote Chapter 17 of Agenda 21, in particular by advancing implementation of the 1995 Global Programme of Action.

[399] The other five programme areas are: sustainable use and conservation of marine living resources of the high seas; sustainable use and conservation of marine living resources under national jurisdiction; addressing critical uncertainties for the management of the marine environment and climate change; strengthening international (including regional) co-operation and co-ordination; and sustainable development of small islands.

improvement of coastal human settlements (especially by the treatment and disposal of sewage, solid wastes and industrial effluents); and the conservation and restoration of altered critical habitats.[400]

For protection of the marine environment, the emphasis is on preventing marine pollution from land-based sources, for which 'there is currently no global scheme' in the form of an international convention, and on pollution from maritime transport and 'dumping-at-sea activities'.[401] Agenda 21 supports a 'precautionary and anticipatory rather than a reactive approach', requiring: precautionary measures; environmental impact assessments; clean production techniques; recycling; waste audits and minimisation; sewage treatment facilities; quality management criteria for the handling of hazardous substances; and a comprehensive approach to deal with the damaging impacts from air, land and water.[402] More specifically, Chapter 17 calls on states to take account of the 1985 Montreal Guidelines, which should be strengthened and extended, and to co-operate on assessing the effectiveness of the existing regional agreements, developing new regional agreements, providing guidance on technologies, and developing policy guidance for relevant global funding mechanisms.[403] Sewage is a matter for priority action; Agenda 21 calls for the building and maintenance of sewage treatment facilities (locating coastal outfalls so as to avoid exposing shell fisheries, water intakes and bathing areas); promoting environmentally sound co-treatments of domestic and compatible industrial effluents and primary treatment of municipal sewage discharged to rivers, estuaries and seas.[404] Priority issues for other sources of pollution include establishing regulatory and monitoring programmes to control effluent discharges and emission, promoting risk and environmental impact assessment, eliminating discharges of organohalogen compounds, reducing discharges of other synthetic organic compounds, controlling anthropogenic inputs of nitrogen and phosphorus, establishing environmentally-sound, land-based waste disposal alternatives to sea dumping, using environmentally less harmful pesticides and fertilisers and controlling the input of non-point source pollutants.[405]

Agenda 21 calls for additional measures to address degradation of the marine environment from shipping, dumping, offshore oil and gas platforms, and ports.[406] Specific actions promoted include: the development of existing international rules and the creation of new rules for the protection of rare and fragile

[400] Agenda 21, para. 17.6.
[401] Agenda 21, para. 17.19. Agenda 21 estimates that 600,000 tons of oil enter the oceans each year as a result of 'normal shipping operations, accidents and illegal discharges': *ibid.*, para. 17.20.
[402] Agenda 21, para. 17.21.
[403] Agenda 21, para. 17.25; UNEP is invited to convene an intergovernmental meeting on the protection of the marine environment from land-based sources: Agenda 21, para. 17.26. These efforts are now being progressed under the Global Programme of Action for the Protection of the Marine Environment from Land-Based Activities (GPA).
[404] Agenda 21, para. 17.27.   [405] Agenda 21, para. 17.28.   [406] Agenda 21, para. 17.30.

ecosystems; a more rigorous enforcement of MARPOL; preventing the spread of non-indigenous organisms from ballast water discharges; risk reduction of accidents and pollution from cargo ships; the carriage of irradiated nuclear fuel in flasks; an IMO Code of Safety for Nuclear Merchant Ships; reducing air pollution from ships; the possible development of compensation funds for pollution damage caused by substances other than oil; stopping the dumping and incineration of hazardous substances in oceans; reducing inputs of organotin compounds from anti-fouling paints; and strengthening oil and chemical spill response centres.[407] Finally, Agenda 21 calls for strengthening international co-operation and co-ordination, including provision by the General Assembly for regular consideration of general marine issues within the UN system, developing a centralised system to provide information on legislation and advice on implementation of legal agreements, and extending intergovernmental regional co-operation and the UNEP Regional Seas Programme.[408]

Conclusions

The rules for the protection of the marine environment are among the most highly developed in the field of international environmental law. As this chapter shows, a range of regulatory techniques are applied to tackle pollution from different sources, with pollution from ships (in particular oil) and by dumping at sea often addressed by rules of considerable specificity. Moreover, a network of regional institutions has been established since 1972 which provides for a under whose auspices international co-operation might flourish and supplement global arrangements created earlier. Some evidence suggests that conventions such as MARPOL 73/78, the oil pollution liability conventions and the dumping conventions have contributed positively to the protection of the marine environment. However, there is more evidence to suggest that these sources do not pose the greatest threat, and that so long as the oceans remain a dumping ground for land-based sources of pollution from industrial and domestic activities the benefits arising from the modest successes which have been achieved will be of limited consequence over the long term. In this regard, the UNCLOS Annex VII arbitral tribunal established to resolve the MOX dispute between Ireland and the UK may clarify and make a singular contribution to the interpretation of the rules.

The great majority of marine pollution originates from land-based sources and these are subject to regulation which is, according to GESAMP, of only limited effectiveness. At best, existing regulation of land-based sources might marginally limit the rate of increase; it has not resulted in real decreases in the total amount of pollutants entering the oceans and seas from this source. The fact that the regional and global rules described in this chapter have attracted

[407] Agenda 21, paras. 17.31 to 17.35.   [408] Agenda 21, paras. 17.118 to 17.120.

widespread support suggests either that they are not being applied or that they are inadequate. Clearly there exists an urgent need for regulatory measures which go beyond calling on states to adopt unspecified measures to 'prevent, reduce and control pollution'. Experience in this and other sectors indicates that targets and timetable for regulated phase-out will provide a more effective regulatory tool, and in this regard the soft targets and timetables set out in the Action Plan endorsed by Ministers when they signed the 1992 OSPAR Convention identify a likely new trend. Whatever regulatory techniques are deployed, there is additionally a clear need for a more stringent application of existing rules, the development of new techniques and instruments to address pollution from land-based and other sources, and more effective enforcement mechanisms, including independent monitoring and surveillance. The entry into force of UNCLOS has created some momentum by speeding up the extension of port state control, and also by bringing a range of new institutional arrangements into operation which may, in time, contribute positively to the prevention of marine pollution. The emphasis in Agenda 21 on improving coastal zone management and regulating human habitats recognises that the protection of the oceans and seas will ultimately be achieved only by integrating considerations requiring the protection of the marine environment into activities which are carried out on land. This suggests the need for a cradle-to-grave regulatory approach which would also require greater use of environmental impact assessment procedures and the integration into those procedures of a consideration of the consequences on the marine environment. Regulating the oceans currently targets the rubbish dump; it will be more effective when it targets the sources.

10

Freshwater resources

R. Baxter, *The Law of International Waterways* (1964); C. B. Bourne, 'International Law and Pollution of International Rivers and Lakes', 21 *University of Toronto Law Journal* 193 (1971); A. Utton, 'International Water Quality Law', 13 *Natural Resources Journal* 282 (1973); F. Florio, 'Water Pollution and Related Principles of International Law', 17 *Canadian Yearbook of International Law* 134 (1979); J. Lammers, *Pollution of International Watercourses: A Search for Substantive Rules and Principles* (1984); J. Sette-Camara, 'Pollution of International Rivers', 186 RdC 117 (1984); H. Ruiz Fabri, 'Règles coutumières générales et droit international fluvial', AFDI 818 (1990); D. Caponera, *Principles of Water Law and Administration, National and International* (1992); A. Nollkaemper, *The Legal Regime for Transboundary Water Pollution: Between Discretion and Constraint* (1993); G. Hafner, 'The Optimum Utilization Principle and the Non-Navigational Uses of Drainage Basins', 45 *Austrian Journal of Public International Law* 45 (1993); E. Benvenisti, 'Collective Action in the Utilization of Shared Freshwater: The Challenges of International Water Resources Law' 90 AJIL 384 (1996); S. Toope and J. Brunee, 'Environmental Security and Freshwater Resources: Ecosystem Regime Building' 91 AJIL 26 (1997); C. Graffy, 'Water, Water Everywhere, Nor Any Drop to Drink: The Urgency of Transnational Solutions to International Riparian Disputes', 10 *Georgetown International Environmental Law Review* 399 (1998); S. Salman and L. Boission de Chazournes (eds.), *International Watercourses: Enhancing Co-operation and Managing Conflict* (World Bank Technical Paper No. 414, 1998); X. Fuentes, 'Sustainable Development and the Equitable Utilization of International Watercourses', 69 BYIL 119 (1998); H. Elver, *Peaceful Uses of Transboundary Watercourses in International Law and Politics* (2000); D. Tarlock, 'Safeguarding International River Ecosystems in Times of Scarcity' 3 *University of Denver Water Law Review* 231 (2000); S. McCaffrey, 'The Harmon Doctrine One Hundred Years Later: Buried, Not Praised', 36 *Natural Resources Journal* 659 (1996); S. McCaffrey, *The Law of International Watercourses: Non-Navigational Uses* (2002).

Introduction

A well-developed body of international rules to prevent pollution of freshwater resources (including rivers, lakes, groundwaters and reservoirs) is set forth in bilateral and regional treaties, as well as the guidelines in non-binding instruments adopted by UNEP, OECD, ECE and other international organisations, including those in the non-governmental sector, such as the ILA and the IDI. In 1997, under the auspices of the UN, and building on the work of the ILC, a global framework Convention on the Law of Non-Navigational Uses of International Watercourses (1997 Watercourses Convention) was adopted, elements of which are broadly recognised to reflect customary law.[1]

These agreements have emerged for geographical and political reasons: nearly one-half of the world's river basins are shared by two or more countries, and, although they comprise only about 3 per cent of the volume of water on the planet, they provide the vast majority of the supply used in human activity. Nearly 90 per cent of the total is locked into ice caps or glaciers, in the atmosphere or soil, or is deep underground.[2] Thus, the primary source of the planet's supply of freshwater is in rivers, lakes and reservoirs. Rainfall patterns have important implications for the quality of water. Scientists have estimated that the average amount of global runoff (the amount of water that is available for human use after evaporation and infiltration takes place) is between 39,500 km^3 and 42,700 km^3 a year, of which only around 9,000 km^3 is readily accessible to humans, with an additional 3,500 km^3 stored in reservoirs.[3] Rainfall varies widely. Heavy rainfall in the Amazon Basin and south and south-east Asia compares with lower rainfall in arid and semi-arid states, which receive only 2 per cent of the world's runoff.[4] Currently, more than 40 per cent of the world's population lives in conditions of water stress and this percentage is estimated to grow to almost 50 per cent by 2025.[5] Current threats to freshwater resources are two-fold: increased use, and declining quality as a result of anthropogenic sources of pollution. Future threats include climate change,[6] and population growth increasing the worldwide demand for water. Between 1990 and 1995, for example, water use increased at a rate significantly greater than the rate of population growth.[7] Of this use, it is estimated that approximately 70 per cent is for agriculture, 23 per cent for industry and the remainder for domestic use.

Industrial and agricultural activities and population growth are increasing the demand for water, requiring new management techniques. Options

---

[1] Adopted on 21 May 1997, by General Assembly Resolution 51/229; 36 ILM 700 (1997); not yet in force. See also Committee on Economic, Social and Cultural Rights, General Comment No. 15 (Right to Water), 26 November 2002; chapter 7, p. 298 above.

[2] World Resources Institute, *World Resources 1992–3*, 160.

[3] Revenga *et al.*, *Pilot Analysis of Global Ecosystems: Freshwater Systems* (World Resources Institute, 2000), 25.

[4] *Ibid.*

[5] *Ibid.*, 8. See also chapter 11, pp. 555–8 below, on international efforts to combat drought and desertification.

[6] G. Goldenman, 'Adapting to Climate Change: A Study of International Rivers and Their Legal Arrangements', 17 *Ecology Law Quarterly* 741 (1990).

[7] WMO, *Comprehensive Assessment of the Freshwater Resources of the World* (1997), 9.

include improved efficiency in use; greater re-use; reallocation of water; and limiting pollution of supplies. For pollution, the direct discharge of municipal and industrial waste into rivers and lakes has been reduced in many developed countries, but pollution from diffuse sources (non-point source pollution) has proved to be more difficult to control. Non-point source pollution includes agricultural, industrial and urban runoff, which transports pesticides, nitrates, phosphates and other pollutants into the water supply. This source of pollution of freshwater can be divided into three main types: excess nutrients from sewage and soil erosion; pathogens from sewage; and heavy metals and synthetic organic compounds from industry, mining and agriculture.[8]

Customary law

The rules of international environmental law to protect freshwater resources, including international watercourses, from pollution and over-use, are mainly reflected in piecemeal and *ad hoc* responses to problems with particular rivers, lakes and freshwater ecosystems. The most important of these are described in this chapter, although the contents should not be treated as exhaustive. State practice is reflected in this body of treaty law, in decisions of the ICJ and international arbitral tribunals, in the work of the ILC and private organisations, such as the ILA and the IDI, and in national legislation. These generally address the *use* of freshwater and its contamination by *pollution*. Notwithstanding such practice, as recently as the mid-1980s it was authoritatively claimed that 'there are no rules of global application and, in particular, there is no rule of customary international law prohibiting pollution of international rivers'.[9] If the view was accurate when it was expressed, it certainly no longer holds good today. Activities which may be harmful to international rivers and other freshwaters are subject to the general principles and rules identified in chapter 6, including Principle 21 of the Stockholm Declaration and Principle 2 of the Rio Declaration, as well as the procedural requirements associated with the duty to co-operate, which reflect customary law.[10]

As early as 1929, the PCIJ had held that the utilisation of international rivers, including their flow, was subject to international law: the Court identified the 'community of interests in a navigable river [which] becomes the basis of a common legal right, the essential features of which are the perfect equality of all riparian states in the use of the whole course of the river and the exclusion

---

[8] Revenga *et al.*, *Pilot Analysis of Global Ecosystems: Freshwater Systems* (World Resources Institute, 2000), 33 (the pollutants include sediments, nutrients, organic materials, disease-causing agents, heavy metals, toxic chemicals, acids, chlorides and increased temperatures).

[9] J. Sette-Camara, 'Pollution of International Rivers', 186 *Receuil des Cours* 117–218 at 198 (1984).

[10] See chapter 6, pp. 235–46 and 248 above; relied upon by Hungary in the *Gabcikovo-Nagymaros Project* case at the ICJ; see p. 471 below.

of any preferential privilege of any one riparian in relation to others'.[11] Some seventy years later, the ICJ revisited the paragraph and extended its application to non-navigational uses:

> Modern development of international law has strengthened this principle for non-navigational uses of international watercourses as well, as evidenced by the adoption of the Convention of 21 May 1997 on the Law of the Non-Navigational Uses of International Watercourses by the United Nations General Assembly. The Court considers that Czechoslovakia, by unilaterally assuming control of a shared resource, and thereby depriving Hungary of its right to an equitable and reasonable share of the natural resources of the Danube – with the continuing effects of the diversion of these waters on the ecology of the riparian area of the Szigetköz – failed to respect the proportionality which is required by international law.[12]

The extended principle reflects an approach that has received wide support from states. It indicates that water resources which are the subject of a 'common legal right', including rivers or lakes or groundwaters, may not be used by states in such a manner as to prevent or otherwise limit other 'riparian' states from making full use of their equitable and reasonable entitlements in relation to that shared resource. Although international law does not necessarily prohibit all pollution, it is clear that the quality of freshwaters should not be altered in such a way as to result in significant or substantial damage to the point that the resource may no longer be used, or that its potential for use is materially diminished.[13] The view that the rights of states in the use of shared rivers are not unlimited is now well established. As early as 1933, the Conference of American States declared that the exploitation of international rivers should not injure the rights of the neighbouring states and should be subject to a process of notification and agreement, stating that 'no state may, without the consent of the other riparian state, introduce into water courses of an international character, for the industrial or agricultural exploitation of their waters, any alteration which may prove injurious to the margin of the other interested state'.[14] States are subject to a customary obligation to negotiate, consult and co-operate to reach an equitable solution to the problems posed by activities which may

---

[11] *Case Concerning the Territorial Jurisdiction of the International Commission of the River Oder*, Judgment No. 16 (1929) PCIJ Ser. A, No. 23, 27. The language is similar to that of the ICJ in the *Fisheries Jurisdiction* case, nearly fifty years later: see chapter 11, pp. 567–8 below.

[12] (1997) ICJ Reports 7, at para. 85. See also Separate Opinion of Judge Kooijmans in the *Kasikili/Sedudu Island* case (*Botswana* v. *Namibia*) (1999) ICJ Reports 1045, paras. 31–7.

[13] On the level of pollution which may be permitted, see Australia's answer to a question from Sir Humphrey Waldock in the *Nuclear Tests* cases, chapter 8, pp. 319–21 above.

[14] Declaration on the Industrial and Agricultural Use of the International Rivers, Adopted by the Seventh International Conference of American States, Montevideo, 1933, Whiteman, 3 *Digest of International Law* 936.

affect international rivers providing a shared natural resource, including water pollution and excessive use. This view is reflected in treaties, including some very early ones,[15] and non-binding instruments.[16] It is also reflected in the World Bank's Operational Policy 7.50 on Projects on International Waterways, which reflects the Bank's recognition that 'the co-operation and goodwill of riparians is essential for the efficient use and protection of the waterway'. To that end, the Bank seeks to ensure that international aspects of a project on an international waterway are dealt with at the earliest possible opportunity, and requires the state receiving financial support formally 'to notify the other riparians of the proposed project and its Project Details'.[17] The Bank will not lend if the borrower does not notify or allow the Bank to notify.

Lac Lanoux arbitration

The 'community of interests' approach invoked by the PCIJ in 1929 is reflected in the arbitral award in the *Lac Lanoux* case between France and Spain.[18] This concerned a proposal by the French Government to authorise the construction of a barrage to channel water through a hydro-electric power plant, diverting approximately 25 per cent of the flow of the Carol River before returning the same amount of water to the river at a point prior to its use by farmers in Spain. The arbitral tribunal held that the proposed French works did not constitute an infringement of Spain's rights under earlier treaties, although the tribunal did suggest that the Spanish claim to an infringement of rights might have been stronger if it could have shown, which it had not, that the proposed works would pollute the waters of the River Carol or change the chemical composition, temperature or other characteristics of the waters in such a way as to injure its interests.[19] The award considered whether riparian states have any obligation to notify and consult with others who may be potentially affected prior to engaging in activities which may harm a shared river resource. The tribunal held that:

> France is entitled to exercise her rights; she cannot ignore Spanish interests. Spain is entitled to demand that her rights be respected and that her interests be taken into consideration.[20]

---

[15] See e.g. Convention Relative to the Development of Hydraulic Power Affecting More than One State, Geneva, 9 December 1923, 36 LNTS 76; and the 1997 Watercourses Convention, pp. 466–8 below.

[16] See p. 465 below; and generally chapter 6, p. 250 above.

[17] OP 7.50, June 2001, para. 4. The Bank will ascertain whether the riparians have entered into agreements or arrangements for the international waterway and, following notification, if another riparian raises objections to the proposed project, the Bank may appoint an independent expert to examine the issues (paras. 5 and 6). Para. 7 permits certain limited exceptions.

[18] 24 ILR 101 (1957). [19] *Ibid.*, 123. [20] *Ibid.*, 140.

However, in finding that France was not in breach of her obligation to take into account Spain's interests in the course of negotiations, the tribunal stated that 'the rule that states may utilise the hydraulic power of international watercourses only on condition of a *prior* agreement between the interested states cannot be established as a custom, even less as a general principle of law'.[21]

The award indicates the limits imposed by international law on the use of shared natural resources, and on procedural obligations linked to the substantive aspects of environmental protection and conservation. The award heralds the provisions now set forth in the regional 1992 UNECE Convention on Watercourses and the potentially global 1997 Watercourses Convention, as well as non-binding rules. It also reflected, however, the limited state of customary law in 1957.

Helsinki Rules

The adoption in 1966 of the ILA's non-binding Helsinki Rules on the Uses of the Waters of International Rivers marked an important further stage in international efforts to manage and protect freshwaters.[22] In this case, the effort addressed rivers and international drainage basins. The Helsinki Rules were not the first attempt by international lawyers to consider this question,[23] but reflected a committed effort to identify, in a comprehensive manner, the rights and obligations of states. The Rules govern the use of the waters of an international drainage basin except as otherwise provided by applicable treaty or custom,[24] and provide that each basin state is entitled to 'a reasonable and equitable share in the beneficial use' of the waters, in accordance with the relevant factors in each case.[25] States are obliged to prevent new forms of water pollution or any increase in the degree of existing pollution which would cause 'substantial injury' in the territory of other basin states, and to take all reasonable measures to abate existing pollution.[26] Violation of these obligations

---

[21] *Ibid.*, 130.

[22] 20 August 1966, Fifty-Second Report of the International Law Association (1967), 484; 2 IPE 5741. See also ILA, Helsinki Rules on Private Law Remedies for Transboundary Damage in International Watercourses (1996).

[23] See e.g. Institut de Droit International, Resolution on International Regulations Regarding the Use of International Watercourses for Purposes other than Navigation (Preamble), Madrid, 19 April 1911, 11 IPE 5702.

[24] Art. I. 'International drainage basin' is described as 'a geographical area extending over two or more States determined by the watershed limits of the system of waters, including surface and underground waters, flowing into a common terminus': Art. II.

[25] Arts. III, IV and V(1).

[26] Art. X(1). 'Water pollution' is defined as 'any detrimental change resulting from human conduct in the natural composition, content or quality' of waters: Art. IX.

creates a responsibility for the injury caused, or requires negotiations to reach an equitable settlement.[27] The approach of the Helsinki Rules is generally followed by the subsequent work of the IDI on pollution of rivers and lakes.[28]

Subsequent developments

Since the Helsinki Rules, the ILA has also adopted non-binding Rules on Water Pollution in an International Drainage Basin[29] and Rules on International Groundwaters.[30] The Groundwaters Rules call on states to prevent or abate the pollution of international groundwaters 'in accordance with international law applicable to existing, new, increased and highly dangerous pollution'.[31] International groundwaters are the 'waters of an aquifer that is intersected by the boundary between two or more states', which are basin states within the meaning of the 1966 Helsinki Rules.[32] These non-governmental efforts have been followed by non-binding instruments adopted under the auspices of international organisations, including recommendations and guidelines developed by the UN[33] and UNEP,[34] the OECD[35] and the UNECE, as well as a large number of conventions and the EC framework Directive, which have, increasingly, sought to take a drainage basin approach.[36]

[27] Art. XI.
[28] Resolution on Pollution of Rivers and Lakes and International Law, Athens, 1979, 58-1 AIDI 193 (1979).
[29] Montreal, 4 September 1982, Sixtieth Report of the International Law Association (1983), 535.
[30] Seoul, 30 August 1986, 62 ILA 251 (1987); on the background, see D. Caponera and D. Alhéritière, 'Principles for International Groundwater Law', 18 *Natural Resources Journal* 589 (1978); L. Teclaff and E. Teclaff, 'Transboundary Groundwater Pollution: Survey and Trends in Treaty Law', 19 *Natural Resources Journal* 629 (1979); L. Teclaff and A. Utton, *International Groundwater Law* (1981).
[31] Art. 3(1).
[32] Art. 1. The Rules use the term 'aquifer' to include 'all underground water bearing strata capable of yielding water on a practicable basis, whether these are in other instruments or contexts called by another name such as "groundwater reservoir", "groundwater catchment area" etc. including the waters in fissured or fractured rock formations and the structures containing deep, so-called "fossil waters"': *ibid.*
[33] UN Water Conference, Recommendation on Environment and Health, Mar Del Plata, 25 March 1977, 26 IPE 166, E/CONF.70/29.
[34] UNEP, Environmental Guidelines for Watershed Development, UNEP EMG #3 (1982).
[35] See OECD Council Recommendation, Control of Eutrophication of Waters, 14 November 1974, OECD C(74)220; OECD Council Recommendation, Strategies for Specific Water Pollutants Control, 14 November 1974, OECD C(74)221; OECD Council Recommendation, Water Management Policies and Instruments, 5 April 1978, OECD C(78)4 (Final).
[36] L. Teclaff and E. Teclaff, 'Transboundary Toxic Pollution and the Drainage Basin Concept', 25 *Natural Resources Journal* 589 (1985); 'The International Law of the Hydrologic Cycle', 31 *Natural Resources Journal* 213 (1991) (special issue) (1991).

1997 Watercourses Convention

L. Caflisch, 'La Convenbtion du 27 mai 1997 sur l'utilisation des cours d'eau internationaux à des fins autre que la navigation', 43 AFDI 751 (1997); C. Bourne, 'The Primacy of the Principle of Equitable Utilization in the 1997 Watercourses Convention', 35 CYIL 222 (1997); E. Hey, 'The Watercourses Convention: To What Extent Does it Provide a Basis for Regulating International Uses of Watercourses?', 7 RECIEL 291 (1998); S. McCaffrey, C. Stephen and M. Sinjela, 'The 1997 United Nations Convention on International Watercourses', 92 AJIL 97 (1998); P. Wouters, 'The Legal Response to International Water Conflicts: the UN Water Convention and Beyond', 42 *German Yearbook of International Law* 293 (1999); S. McCaffrey and M. Sinjela, 'The 1997 UN Convention on International Watercourses', 92 AJIL 97 (1998); A. Tanzi and M. Arcari, *The UN Convention on the Law of International Watercourses* (2000).

This body of instruments, together with the treaties identified and described subsequently in this chapter, provided the background for the negotiation and adoption of the 1997 Watercourses Convention, which was based on the codification efforts of the ILC as reflected in the draft Articles on the Law of Non-Navigational Uses of International Watercourses.[37] The 1997 Convention applies to uses of international watercourses and their waters for purposes other than navigation, and encourages watercourse states to enter into watercourse agreements.[38] It establishes a framework of general principles to guide the behaviour of states, and its general approach has been noted with apparent approval by the ICJ.[39]

The Convention comprises an introductory section, and five operational parts. Part II proposes general principles. The Convention is without prejudice to rights and obligations arising from agreements already in force (Article 3(1)), and permits states to enter into new agreements which 'apply and adjust' its provisions 'to the characteristics and uses of a particular international watercourse' (Article 3(3)). Article 5 of the Convention is of central importance: it provides that watercourse states 'shall . . . utilise an international watercourse in an equitable and reasonable manner', which requires the optimal and sustainable utilisation of the watercourse and its benefits 'consistent with adequate

---

[37] 30 ILM 1575 (1991). The ILC's work began in 1971, following a request from the UN General Assembly. A first reading of a full set of draft Articles was adopted at the ILC's forty-third session in 1991, and a revised set of draft Articles was adopted in 1994. The tension between the interests of upstream and downstream states was tangible during the course of the ILC's efforts, and in the diplomatic negotiations leading to the adoption of the 1997 Convention.

[38] Arts. 1(1), 3 and 4. 'Watercourse' is defined as a 'system of surface and ground waters constituting by virtue of their physical relationship a unitary whole and normally flowing into a common terminus': Art. 2(a). 'International watercourse' means 'a watercourse, parts of which are situated in different States': Art. 2(b).

[39] See n. 58 below.

protection of the watercourse.[40] The right to equitable utilisation is balanced by the requirement of Article 7 (together with the obligation to prevent pollution, as required by Article 21), which commits watercourse states to 'take all appropriate measures to prevent the causing of significant harm to other watercourse States'. Where significant harm is nevertheless caused, the responsible state must take all appropriate measures, in consultation with the affected state, to eliminate or mitigate the harm and 'where appropriate, to discuss the question of compensation'.[41]

Other principles require states to co-operate and regularly exchange data and information,[42] and deal with the relationship between different kinds of uses of a watercourse.[43] Part III is concerned with planned measures that may have an effect on an international watercourse. It establishes a phased procedure comprising information exchange and consultation, notification, and a waiting period of six months to allow for a reply to the notification, during which time the notifying state 'shall not implement or permit the implementation of the planned measures without the consent of the notified state'.[44] The Convention envisages a reply to notification, consultations and negotiations, and procedures to be followed in the absence of a notification or a reply, or where urgent implementation of a particular measure is required.[45]

Part IV deals specifically with the protection, preservation and management of ecosystems, which watercourse states are under an obligation to jointly or individually protect and preserve.[46] Article 21 provides that pollution which may cause 'significant' harm to other watercourse states or their environment is to be prevented, reduced and controlled, and states should consult among themselves to establish lists of substances which should be prohibited, limited, investigated or monitored.[47] New or alien species which may have detrimental effects on the ecosystem resulting in significant harm to other watercourse states should not be introduced,[48] and watercourse states are required to take all measures necessary to protect and preserve the marine environment, taking into

---

[40] Art. 5. Art. 6 identifies a non-exhaustive list of factors and circumstances which are to be taken into account to ensure an equitable and reasonable utilisation, including: (a) geographic and other factors of a natural character; (b) social and economic needs; (c) population; (d) effects on uses in another watercourse state; (e) existing and potential uses; (f) conservation of water resources; and (g) availability of alternatives. On its customary status, see Separate Opinion of Judge Kooijmans in the *Kasikili/Sedudu* case, n. 12 above.

[41] Art. 7(1) and (2).   [42] Art. 9.

[43] Art. 10. It is stated that, in the absence of agreement or custom to the contrary, 'no use of an international watercourse enjoys inherent priority over other uses': Art. 10(1).

[44] Arts. 11–14.   [45] Arts. 15–19.   [46] Art. 20.

[47] Art. 21(2) and (3). 'Pollution' is defined broadly as 'any detrimental alteration in the composition or quality of the waters of an international watercourse which results directly or indirectly from human conduct': *ibid.*, Art. 21(1).

[48] Art. 22.

account generally accepted international rules and standards.[49] Watercourse states are required, at the request of any of them, to enter into consultations concerning the management of an international watercourse, which may include the establishment of a joint management mechanism.[50] They must also co-operate, where appropriate, in 'response to needs and opportunities for regulation of the flow of the waters of an international watercourse' through the use of hydraulic works, and within their own territories, and must employ their best efforts to maintain and protect installations, facilities and other works related to an international watercourse.[51] Part V deals with harmful conditions and emergency situations, and Part VI establishes miscellaneous provisions on, *inter alia*, armed conflict, indirect contacts between watercourse states, confidentiality of certain data, and non-discrimination.[52] Part VI also contains a dispute settlement provision which directs parties to seek settlement of any dispute concerning the Convention initially by way of negotiation, mediation, conciliation or submission of the dispute to arbitration or to the ICJ with the agreement of both parties.[53] Under Article 33(10), parties may elect, when ratifying, accepting, approving or acceding to the Convention, or at any time thereafter, to submit a written declaration recognising the jurisdiction of the ICJ or an arbitral tribunal constituted in accordance with the Convention's Annex as 'compulsory ipso facto and without special agreement in relation to any party accepting the same obligation'.[54] Alternatively, if the conditions in Article 33(10) are not met and the dispute is not resolved within six months of the initial request for negotiations, the dispute can be submitted, at the option of either of the parties, to an impartial fact-finding commission.[55] The parties are to provide the Commission with such information as it may require and must permit members of the commission to have access to the state's territory for the purpose of inspecting facilities, plant or equipment, construction works or any natural feature relevant for the purpose of the commission's inquiry.[56] The commission reports back to the parties and may make recommendations designed to secure 'an equitable solution of the dispute', which the parties are required to consider in good faith.[57]

The Convention marks an important development by stating rules of general application which are capable of global application. It provides an important starting point, and reflects minimum international standards below which states may not fall, indicating the basis upon which states can further their efforts to achieve co-operative arrangements with their neighbours in the use of shared freshwater resources. It remains to be seen how practice and jurisprudence establishes the balance between the right to equitable utilisation and the obligation not to cause significant harm, which will necessarily turn on a case-by-case approach.

---

[49] Art. 23.   [50] Art. 24.   [51] Arts. 25 and 26.   [52] Arts. 29–32.   [53] Art. 33(2).
[54] Art. 33(10).   [55] Art. 33(4)–(6).   [56] Art. 33(7).   [57] Art. 33(8).

Case Concerning the Gabcikovo-Nagymaros Project[58]

S. Stec and G. Eckstein, 'Of Solemn Oaths and Obligations: The Environmental Impact of the ICJ's Decision in the Case Concerning the Gabcíkovo-Nagymaros Project', 8 *Yearbook of International Environmental Law* 41 (1997); C. Bourne, 'The Case Concerning the Gabcikovo-Nagymaros Project: An Important Milestone in International Water Law', 8 *Yearbook of International Environmental Law* 3 (1997); P. Canelas de Castro, 'The Judgment in the Case Concerning the Gabcikovo-Nagymaros Project: Positive Signs for the Evolution of International Water Law', 8 *Yearbook of International Environmental Law* 21 (1997); A. E. Boyle, 'The Gabcikovo-Nagymaros Case: New Law in Old Bottles', 8 *Yearbook of International Environmental Law* 13 (1997); J. Klabbers, 'The Substance of Form: The Case Concerning the Gabcikovo-Nagymaros Project, Environmental Law, and the Law of Treaties', 8 *Yearbook of International Environmental Law* 32 (1997); A. A. Khavari and D. R. Rothwell, 'The ICJ and the Danube Dam Case: A Missed Opportunity for International Environmental Law?', 22 *Melbourne University Law Review* 507 (1998).

Notwithstanding the fact that the ICJ did not apparently have jurisdiction, in October 1992 Hungary filed an application to the ICJ to submit its dispute with Czechoslovakia over the construction of the Gabcikovo and Nagymaros barrages and the diversion of the Danube River in Slovakia.[59] In July 1993, following further negotiations, Hungary and Slovakia signed a Special Agreement submitting the matter to the ICJ.

The dispute arose over the 1977 Treaty Providing for the Construction and Joint Operation of the Gabcikovo-Nagymaros Barrage System, according to which Hungary and Czechoslovakia agreed to build the Dunakiliti dam and reservoir, a barrage system including two hydro-electric power stations (one on Czechoslovak territory at Gabcikovo, and one on Hungarian territory at Nagymaros), and a 25 km by-pass canal for diverting the Danube from its original course through a system of locks and then back to its original course.[60] The power generators were originally due to begin operation between 1986 and 1990 but the deadline was subsequently put back to 1994. In 1988, as a result of public pressure, the Hungarian Parliament resolved that ecological interests should take priority over economic considerations and prompted the government to order a re-evaluation of the project. This led to a decision by the

---

[58] *Case Concerning the Gabcikovo-Nagymaros Project* (1997) ICJ Reports 7.

[59] See Declaration of Hungary on the Termination of the 1977 Treaty on the Construction and Operation of the Gabcikovo-Nagymaros Barrage System, 16 May 1992, 32 ILM 1260 (1993); Special Agreement Between Hungary and the Slovak Republic for Submission to the ICJ of the Differences Between Them, 32 ILM 1294 (1993). Although Hungary's Original Application was superseded by the 1993 Special Agreement, it provides interesting historical evidence of Hungary's views on the rules of customary law concerning the diversion of an international river.

[60] Budapest, 16 September 1977, 32 ILM 1247 (1993).

Hungarian Government in May 1989 to suspend construction on its part of the Gabcikovo barrage, and work on the Nagymaros barrage.[61] Following diplomatic exchanges and unsuccessful negotiations between experts appointed by both sides, the Czechoslovak Government decided to continue with a 'provisional solution' to limit construction works and the unilateral diversion of the Danube to the Slovak territory.[62] In February 1992, Hungary formally protested against the 'provisional solution' and the unilateral diversion. In April 1992, the EC Commission accepted a request by the two governments to play a conciliation role and to chair a trilateral committee of experts to find a technically feasible solution. The EC Commission asked both sides to refrain from taking steps during the investigation that would prejudice the committee's findings.[63] On 19 May 1992, Hungary sought unilaterally to terminate the 1977 Treaty with effect from 25 May 1992.[64] In October 1992, following the failure to settle the dispute, Hungary filed its Original Application with the ICJ, and later that month Czechoslovakia diverted a significant proportion of the Danube into a by-pass canal.

In July 1993, by Special Agreement the two sides asked the ICJ to consider the legality of certain acts of each state. The Agreement, which asked the ICJ to decide, on the basis of the 1977 Treaty and 'rules and principles of general international law', three questions: (1) whether Hungary was entitled to suspend and subsequently abandon the works on the project; (2) whether the Czech and Slovak Federal Republic was entitled to proceed to and put in operation the 'provisional solution'; and (3) what were the legal effects of the notification on 19 May 1992 of the termination of the 1977 Treaty?[65] Additionally, the ICJ was asked to determine the legal consequences arising from its judgment on these matters. Under the Special Agreement, the parties also agreed to establish and implement a temporary water management regime, and to request immediate consultation if one party believed that the other party's conduct was endangering its rights, and not to seek protection by asking the ICJ to indicate provisional measures.[66] Although the Special Agreement did not expressly refer to environmental aspects, arguments put forward by Hungary in the case were largely based on perceived environmental consequences.

Hungary's Original Application stated that the 'provisional solution' would cause irreversible damage to the ecology and environmental resources of the region, threaten drinking water reserves, and endanger vegetation and fauna. In its Original Application, Hungary had asked the ICJ to declare: (1) that the 'provisional solution' violated general rules of international law and bilateral and multilateral treaties and agreements; (2) that Czechoslovakia should cancel the 'provisional solution'; (3) that the main course of the Danube should

---

[61] Paras. 3 and 4.   [62] Paras. 5–8.   [63] Para. 12.   [64] Para. 13.

[65] See *Case Concerning the Gabcikovo-Nagymaros Project* (1997) ICJ Reports 7, para. 2.

[66] 1993 Special Agreement, Art. 4; on provisional measures under Art. 41 of the Statute of the ICJ, see chapter 5, p. 218 above.

remain unaltered; and (4) that the 'provisional works' should be immediately suspended. In its legal arguments in the Original Application, Hungary relied on the violation of its territorial sovereignty and nine principles and rules of customary law on the utilisation of transboundary environmental resources of an international river. The legal arguments were based on the view that the 'provisional solution' would deprive Hungary of its due share of water quantity, water quality and power potential, and would impair the quality and quantity of other natural resources, including forests, groundwater reserves and genetic diversity. The rules of customary international law upon which Hungary relied in its Original Application included the following claimed obligations of states: to maintain ecosystems and related ecological processes; to conserve flora and fauna; to participate in good faith negotiation; to prevent transnational environmental interference; not to cause significant harm to other watercourse states; to make reasonable and equitable use of transboundary resources; to give prior notification of activities which might cause significant transboundary adverse effects; to engage in good faith consultations; and to take precautionary measures to anticipate, prevent or minimise damage to transboundary resources and mitigate adverse effects.[67] Hungary also relied on several regional treaties.

These arguments were refined in the proceedings before the ICJ; Hungary sought to rely on a number of grounds under the law of treaties and general rules of state responsibility to justify its suspension of works and subsequent termination of the 1977 Treaty. To justify its conduct, Hungary relied primarily on a 'state of ecological necessity', contending that the various installations in the Gabcikovo-Nagymaros system of locks had been designed to enable the Gabcikovo power plant to operate in peak mode. Water would only have come through the plant twice each day, at times of peak power demand. Operation in peak mode required the vast expanse (60 km^2) of the planned reservoir at Dunakiliti, as well as the Nagymaros dam, which was to alleviate the tidal effects and reduce the variation in the water level downstream of Gabcikovo. Hungary argued that such a system, considered to be more economically profitable than using run-of-the-river plants, carried ecological risks which it considered to be unacceptable. These included the danger of silting up of the side-arms of the Danube, thereby impairing water quality; the risk of eutrophication of surface waters; the reduction of water flow in the Danube itself; and the resulting loss of fluvial fauna and flora.[68]

---

[67] Hungarian Application, paras. 24–33. In support of its Application, Hungary relied on a variety of sources, including the 1982 World Charter for Nature; the Legal Principles of the WCED Legal Experts Group; the IUCN Draft Covenant on Environmental Conservation and Sustainable Use of Natural Resources; the *Lac Lanoux Arbitration*; the *River Oder* case; the ILC Draft Articles on International Watercourses; the 1992 UNECE Watercourses Convention; the 1991 Espoo Convention; the *Corfu Channel* case; the *Trail Smelter* award; Principle 21 of the Stockholm Declaration; and Principle 15 of the Rio Declaration.

[68] (1997) ICJ Reports 7, para. 40

As for the dam at Nagymaros, Hungary argued that, if it had been built, the bed of the Danube upstream would have silted up causing deterioration of water quality in this sector. Moreover, the operation of the Gabcikovo power plant in peak mode would have occasioned significant daily variations in the water level in the reservoir upstream, threatening aquatic habitats. Hungary also contended that the construction and operation of the Nagymaros dam would have caused the erosion of the riverbed downstream, lowering the water level in this section of the river and appreciably diminishing the yield of the bank-filtered wells providing two-thirds of the water supply of the city of Budapest. The filter layer would also have shrunk or perhaps even disappeared, and fine sediments would have been deposited in certain pockets in the river, further contributing to the deterioration of water quality.[69]

The ICJ considered the question of the existence of a 'state of ecological necessity' in the light of the criteria laid down by the ILC in Article 33 of the draft Articles on the International Responsibility of States adopted on first reading, which the parties had agreed were applicable.[70] Article 33 at the time of the Court's decision was worded as follows:

> 1. A state of necessity may not be invoked by a State as a ground for precluding the wrongfulness of an act of that State not in conformity with an international obligation of the State unless:
> (a) the act was the only means of safeguarding an essential interest of the State against a grave and imminent peril; and
> (b) the act did not seriously impair an essential interest of the State towards which the obligation existed.
> 2. In any case, a state of necessity may not be invoked by a State as a ground for precluding wrongfulness:
> (a) if the international obligation with which the act of the State is not in conformity arises out of a peremptory norm of general international law; or
> (b) if the international obligation with which the act of the State is not in conformity is laid down by a treaty which, explicitly or implicitly, excludes the possibility of invoking the state of necessity with respect to that obligation; or
> (c) if the State in question has contributed to the occurrence of the state of necessity.

In the ICJ's view, draft Article 33 established five basic conditions for the existence of a state of necessity, which reflected customary international law.

---

[69] *Ibid.*

[70] For the text of the Draft Articles adopted on first reading, see ILC, *Yearbook of the International Law Commission 1996*, vol. II (Part 2), 58–65. In 2001, the ILC adopted a final text of the Articles; see chapter 18, p. 873 below.

1. the breach of an international obligation must have been occasioned by an 'essential interest' of the state which was the author of the wrongful act;
2. that interest must be threatened by a 'grave and imminent peril';
3. the act being challenged should be the 'only means' of safeguarding that interest;
4. that act should not have 'seriously impaired an essential interest' of the State towards which the obligation existed; and
5. the state which was the author of that act should not have 'contributed to the occurrence of the state of necessity'.[71]

The ICJ stated that it had 'no difficulty in acknowledging that the concerns expressed by Hungary for its natural environment in the region affected by the Gabcikovo-Nagymaros Project related to an "essential interest" of that state, within the meaning given to that expression in [draft] Article 33'.[72] However, the ICJ did not consider that the objective existence of a 'peril' had been established, notwithstanding the 'serious uncertainties' raised by Hungary as to the ecological impact of putting in place the Gabcikovo-Nagymaros barrage system. The ICJ stated that:

> The word 'peril' certainly evokes the idea of 'risk'; that is precisely what distinguishes 'peril' from material damage. But a state of necessity could not exist without a 'peril' duly established at the relevant point in time; the mere apprehension of a possible 'peril' could not suffice in that respect. It could moreover hardly be otherwise, when the 'peril' constituting the state of necessity has at the same time to be 'grave' and 'imminent'. 'Imminence' is synonymous with 'immediacy' or 'proximity' and goes far beyond the concept of 'possibility'. As the International Law Commission emphasized in its commentary, the 'extremely grave and imminent' peril must 'have been a threat to the interest at the actual time' (Yearbook of the International Law Commission, 1980, vol. II, Part 2, p. 49, para. 33). That does not exclude, in the view of the Court, that a 'peril' appearing in the long term might be held to be 'imminent' as soon as it is established, at the relevant point in time, that the realization of that peril, however far off it might be, is not thereby any less certain and inevitable.[73]

The ICJ's approach to the issue of the existence of an environmental 'peril' seemingly does not apply.[74] Without ruling on the merits of the parties' differing views as to the likelihood of environmental damage (advanced in an 'impressive amount of scientific material'), the ICJ found that the perils invoked by Hungary were not sufficiently established in 1989, nor were they 'imminent' since

---

[71] *Case Concerning the Gabcikovo-Nagymaros Project* (1997) ICJ Reports 7, para. 52.
[72] *Ibid.*, para. 53.   [73] *Ibid.*, para. 54.
[74] Principle 15 of the Rio Declaration; see chapter 6, p. 268 above.

they were long-term in nature and uncertain.[75] As a consequence of these findings, the ICJ concluded that Hungary's ecological concerns over the project were not sufficient to justify a suspension of works in 1989 on the basis of necessity.[76]

The ICJ then turned to the question of whether the Czech and Slovak Federal Republic was entitled to proceed to the 'provisional solution' following Hungary's suspension of works on the project. Czechoslovakia had submitted that the 'provisional solution' was essentially no more than what Hungary had already agreed to and that the only modifications made were those which had become necessary by virtue of Hungary's decision not to implement its treaty obligations. While the ICJ agreed that Hungary, in concluding the 1977 Treaty, had consented to the damming of the Danube and the diversion of its waters into the by-pass canal, it had done so 'only in the context of a joint operation and a sharing of its benefits'. Thus, although Hungary's refusal to continue with the joint operation constituted a violation of its legal obligations, that did not mean that Hungary forfeited its basic right to an equitable and reasonable sharing of the resources of an international watercourse.[77] Accordingly, the ICJ concluded that Czechoslovakia had committed an internationally wrongful act by putting the provisional solution into operation. Significantly, the ICJ distinguished between preparatory actions and the wrongful act itself in determining the point of time at which the internationally wrongful act crystallised. The ICJ noted that:

> between November 1991 and October 1992, Czechoslovakia confined itself to the execution, on its own territory, of the works which were necessary for the implementation of Variant C, but which could have been abandoned if an agreement had been reached between the parties and did not therefore predetermine the final decision to be taken. For as long as the Danube had not been unilaterally dammed, Variant C had not in fact been applied.[78]

The ICJ went on to consider whether the wrongfulness of Czechoslovakia's actions might be precluded on the ground that it was a lawful countermeasure, adopted in response to Hungary's prior failure to comply with its obligations under the 1977 Treaty. While the ICJ concluded that Czechoslovakia's actions met some of the conditions for lawful countermeasures, they did not satisfy the 'important consideration' that the 'effects of a countermeasure must be commensurate with the injury suffered, taking into account the rights in question'.[79] Referring to the decision of the PCIJ in the *River Oder Case*[80] and modern

---

[75] *Case Concerning the Gabcikovo-Nagymaros Project* (1997) ICJ Reports 7, paras. 56 and 57.

[76] *Ibid.*, para. 57.   [77] *Ibid.*, para. 78.   [78] *Ibid.*, para. 79.   [79] *Ibid.*, para. 85.

[80] *Case Concerning the Territorial Jurisdiction of the International Commission of the River Oder*, Judgment No. 16 (1929) PCIJ Ser. A, No. 23, 27.

developments evidenced by the recent adoption of the Watercourses Convention, the ICJ stated that:

> Czechoslovakia, by unilaterally assuming control of a shared resource, and thereby depriving Hungary of its right to an equitable and reasonable share of the natural resources of the Danube – with the continuing effects of the diversion of these waters on the ecology of the riparian area of the Szigetkoz – failed to respect the proportionality which is required by international law.[81]

Consequently, the ICJ held that the diversion of the Danube carried out by Czechoslovakia was not a lawful countermeasure because it was not proportionate.

To justify its termination of the 1977 Treaty, Hungary again raised an argument of necessity, together with arguments based on: the impossibility of performance of the Treaty; the occurrence of a fundamental change of circumstances; the material breach of the Treaty by Czechoslovakia; and the development of new norms of international environmental law. These arguments were dismissed by the ICJ, which found that Hungary's purported notification of termination in 1992 did not have the legal effect of terminating the 1977 Treaty and related instruments.[82] However, the ICJ pointed out that newly developed norms of environmental law were relevant for the implementation of the Treaty and that the Treaty itself made provision for their incorporation, with the agreement of the parties, through various Articles 'requiring the parties, in carrying out their obligations to ensure that the quality of the water in the Danube is not impaired and that nature is protected, to take new environmental norms into consideration when agreeing upon the means to be specified in the Joint Contractual Plan'.[83] The ICJ remarked that the 'awareness of the vulnerability of the environment and the recognition that environmental risks have to be assessed on a continuous basis have become much stronger in the years since the Treaty's conclusion'.[84] The ICJ recognised that both parties agreed on the need to take environmental concerns seriously and to take the required precautionary measures, but fundamentally disagreed over the consequences this had for the joint project.[85] However, the ICJ itself provided no resolution of this issue, instead recommending that 'third-party involvement may be helpful and instrumental in finding a solution, provided each of the parties is flexible in its position'.[86]

The ICJ took a similar approach in deciding the appropriate future conduct of the parties in respect of the project. It noted that it was of 'cardinal importance' that it had found that the 1977 Treaty was still in force and governed the relationship between the parties, although it acknowledged that it could not

---

[81] *Case Concerning the Gabcikovo-Nagymaros Project* (1997) ICJ Reports 7, para. 85.
[82] *Ibid.*, para. 115.   [83] *Ibid.*, para. 112.   [84] *Ibid.*   [85] *Ibid.*, para. 113.   [86] *Ibid.*

overlook the factual situation – or the practical possibilities or impossibilities to which it gave rise – in deciding on the legal requirements for the future conduct of the parties.[87] In light of the course of events, the ICJ considered that decisions on the future implementation of the Gabcikovo-Nagymaros project were, first and foremost, for the parties themselves.[88] The ICJ stressed that in future negotiations between the parties the project's impact upon, and implications for, the environment, should be a key issue. Evaluation of the environmental risks would need to be undertaken, taking into account current standards.[89] The ICJ was also mindful of the need for vigilance and prevention in the field of environmental protection 'on account of the often irreversible character of damage to the environment and of the limitations inherent in the very mechanism of reparation of this type of damage'.[90] The ICJ referred to the concept of 'sustainable development', remarking that, for the purposes of the present case, this meant that:

> the Parties should look afresh at the effects on the environment of the operation of the Gabcikovo power plant. In particular they must find a satisfactory solution for the volume of water to be released into the old bed of the Danube and into the side-arms on both sides of the river.[91]

The ICJ considered that it was not for it to determine the final result of the negotiations between the parties. Instead, the ICJ instructed the parties 'to find an agreed solution that takes account of the objectives of the Treaty, which must be pursued in a joint and integrated way, as well as the norms of international environmental law and the principles of the law of international watercourses'.[92]

On the final issue of reparation for the internationally wrongful acts committed by both parties, the ICJ noted that both Hungary and Slovakia were under an obligation to pay compensation to the other.[93] However, the ICJ declined to indicate the quantum of damages payable, instead resolving the issue as follows:

> Slovakia is . . . entitled to compensation for the damage suffered by Czechoslovakia as well as by itself as a result of Hungary's decision to suspend and subsequently abandon the works at Nagymaros and Dunakiliti, as those actions caused the postponement of the putting into operation of the Gabcikovo power plant, and changes in its mode of operation once in service.
>
> Hungary is entitled to compensation for the damage sustained as a result of the diversion of the Danube, since Czechoslovakia, by putting into operation Variant C, and Slovakia, in maintaining it in service, deprived Hungary of its rightful part in the shared water resources, and exploited those resources essentially for their own benefit.

---

[87] *Ibid.*, para. 132.   [88] *Ibid.*, paras. 133–7.   [89] *Ibid.*, para. 140.
[90] *Ibid.*   [91] *Ibid.*   [92] *Ibid.*, para. 141.   [93] *Ibid.*, para. 152.

> Given the fact, however, that there have been intersecting wrongs by both Parties, the Court wishes to observe that the issue of compensation could satisfactorily be resolved in the framework of an overall settlement if each of the Parties were to renounce or cancel all financial claims and counter-claims.[94]

Overall, the ICJ's judgment affirms the importance of environmental considerations in addressing the rights and obligations of riparian states in an international watercourse. In assessing the implications of the judgment it must be borne in mind that the ICJ was largely concerned with the application of the law as it was in 1989 and in 1992, when the relevant acts occurred. It is perhaps for this reason that the ICJ was reluctant to go too far, for example in recognising or applying a precautionary approach. But the ICJ has made an important contribution to the development of international environmental law in this area, recognising the concept of 'ecological necessity' and the need for environmental risks associated with a project to be assessed on a continuous basis, in light of current environmental standards. That said, the ICJ shied away from offering more detailed guidance on broader questions, such as the relationship between equitable utilisation and the obligation to prevent environmental damage, and the principles to be applied in valuing environmental damage.

Regional rules

Apart from the obligations of general and global application, many bilateral regional agreements establish binding obligations for states.

Europe

The EC has adopted rules on various aspects of water quality (groundwater, drinking water, bathing water),[95] and in 2000 adopted a far-reaching and innovative framework Directive on the protection of inland surface waters, transitional waters, coastal waters and groundwater.[96] Additionally, more than forty bilateral treaties are in force between European states which protect the quality and use of freshwaters.[97] These include pollution prevention or

---

[94] *Ibid.*, paras. 152–3.

[95] Chapter 15, pp. 771–5 below; see generally J. Lammers, 'International and European Community Law Aspects of Pollution of International Watercourses', in W. Lang, H. Neuhold and K. Zemanek (eds.), *Environmental Protection and International Law* (1991), 115; R. Macrory, 'European Community Water Law', 20 *Ecology Law Quarterly* 119 (1993).

[96] Chapter 15, p. 775 below.

[97] For a partial list, see E. Brown Weiss, P. C. Szasz and D. B. Magraw, *International Environmental Law: Basic Documents and References* (1992), 47–50.

environmental protection agreements for Lake Constance,[98] Lake Geneva,[99] the River Danube,[100] the River Elbe,[101] the Mosel,[102] the Scheldt,[103] the Meuse,[104] Luso-Spanish River Basins,[105] and for the Benelux countries generally.[106] Other regional agreements not directly dealing with freshwater resources also have indirect benefits. The EC's 1988/2001 Large Combustion Directive and the SO_2 Protocols to the 1979 LRTAP Convention, as well as the more recent Protocol to Abate Acidification, Eutrophication and Ground-Level Ozone, were also, to a large extent, the result of efforts to combat acidification of lakes and other freshwater resources in Europe.[107]

Rhine

A well-developed regime exists for the River Rhine, which flows through France, Switzerland, the Netherlands and Germany, and its basin which covers 225,000 square kilometres and includes eight countries. The Rhine has been the subject

---

[98] Convention on the Protection of Lake Constance Against Pollution, Steckborn, 27 October 1960, in force 10 November 1961, 620 UNTS 191.

[99] Convention Concerning the Protection of the Waters of Lake Geneva Against Pollution, Paris, 16 November 1962, in force 1 November 1963, 922 UNTS 49.

[100] See Convention on Co-operation for the Protection and Sustainable Use of the Danube River, Sofia, 29 June 1994, in force 22 October 1998. See also Declaration on Co-operation by the Danube States in Matters of Water Management of the Danube, in particular for the Protection of the Waters of the Danube Against Pollution, Bucharest, 13 December 1985, 37 ÖZRV 430 (1987); Agreement on Co-operation on Management of Water Resources in the Danube Basin, Regensburg, 1 December 1987, not yet in force; OJ L90 5 April 1990, 20.

[101] Convention for the International Commission for the Protection of the Elbe, Magdeburg, 8 October 1990, IELMT 990:75.

[102] Protocol Concerning the Constitution of an International Commission for the Protection of the Mosel Against Pollution, Paris, 20 December 1961, in force 1 July 1962, 940 UNTS 211.

[103] Agreement on the Protection of the River Scheldt, 26 April 1994, in force 1 March 1995, 34 ILM 859 (1995).

[104] Agreement on the Protection of the River Meuse, 26 April 1994, in force 1 March 1995, 34 ILM 854 (1995); see Jan M. van Dunné, *Non-Point Source River Pollution: The Case of the River Meuse* (1996).

[105] Convention on Co-operation for the Protection and Sustainable Use of the Waters of the Luso-Spanish River Basins, 30 November 1998, in force 17 January 2000; see 'La Convención Luso-Española sobre las Aguas de las Cuencas Hidrográficas Compartidas: Un marco de cooperación para la protección de las aguas y para el desarrollo sostenible', in A. Fabra and A. Barreira (eds.), *La aplicación de la Directiva Marco del Agua en España: Retos y Oportunidades* (2000); see also 10 *Yearbook of International Environmental Law* 236–8 (1999); A. Barreira, 'Monitoring and Evaluation of the Portuguese–Spanish Convention Appliance: Public Involvement and Participation', in Luso-American Foundation for Development, *Implementing Transboundary River Conventions* (2002).

[106] Protocol to Establish a Tripartite Standing Committee on Polluted Waters, Brussels, 8 April 1950, in force 8 April 1950, 66 UNTS 285.

[107] Chapter 8, pp. 327–33 and 335–9 above; and chapter 15, pp. 762–7 below.

of five environmental protection treaties, apart from earlier agreements on fishing and navigation.[108] The 1963 Berne Agreement on the International Commission for the Protection of the Rhine Against Pollution (1963 Berne Pollution Agreements) established an international commission (the Rhine Commission) to research and propose measures to protect the Rhine from pollution, and prepare arrangements for its protection.[109] It was one of the first international institutions to be granted an environmental mandate.

The 1963 Berne Pollution Agreement was amended in 1976 and two new treaties were adopted. The 1976 Convention for the Protection of the River Rhine Against Chemical Pollution (1976 Rhine Chemical Pollution Convention) requires parties to eliminate pollution of the surface waters of the Rhine basin by those dangerous substances listed in Annex I and to reduce pollution by those dangerous substances listed in Annex II.[110] Parties are required, for their own use, to establish national inventories of discharges and to communicate their contents to the Rhine Commission.[111] The Convention also establishes a scheme of prior authorisation for the discharge of Annex I substances, emissions standards for maximum permissible concentrations and quantities of discharges, and national programmes for the discharge of Annex II substances.[112] Limit values are proposed by the Rhine Commission, which may also propose measures for the protection of underground waters, on the basis of toxicity, persistence and bioaccumulation, taking into account the 'best technical facilities available'.[113] The Convention also provides for information exchange, monitoring, and emergency situations.[114] This mechanism failed in November 1986 to ensure that the Swiss authorities notified other parties of the discharge of large quantities of toxic chemicals into the Rhine following a fire at a facility owned by the Sandoz company in Basel, Switzerland. These destroyed living resources in the river ecosystem, including eels, fish and waterfowl, and the consequences of the pollution were felt in France, Germany, the Netherlands and at the point of discharge into the North Sea. Groundwater resources were contaminated, and other damage was caused to the fishing industry, to agriculture as a result of contaminated water supplies, and to tourism. In September 1987, Sandoz agreed to pay an indemnity of just under

---

[108] Berne Convention Establishing Uniform Regulations Concerning Fishing in the Rhine Between Constance and Basel, 9 December 1869, 9 IPE 4695.

[109] Berne, 29 April 1963, in force 1 May 1965, 994 UNTS 3; amended Bonn, 3 December 1976, IELMT 976:91, Art. 2.

[110] Bonn, 3 December 1976, in force 1 February 1979, 1124 UNTS 375, Art. 1(1). The Rhine is defined in Annex A. See generally A. Kiss, 'The Protection of the Rhine Against Pollution', 25 *Natural Resources Journal* 613 (1985); I. Romy, *Les pollutions transfrontières des eaux: l'exemple du Rhin* (1990).

[111] Art. 2 and Annex III.   [112] Arts. 3, 4 and 6(1)–(3).

[113] Arts. 5(1), (2) and (5) and 7(2). Once limit values have been adopted, they are included in Annex IV.

[114] Arts. 10–12.

US$10 million to cover reimbursement of the French Government's costs, compensation to individuals and groups, and a programme of analysis, monitoring, restoration and emergency information.[115]

The 1976 Convention for the Protection of the Rhine River Against Pollution by Chlorides (1976 Rhine Chlorides Convention) has more specific objectives, aiming to reduce the discharge of chloride ions, and requiring France to construct a plant to reduce discharges from the Alsace potassium mines.[116] The Convention is one of the earliest to address the economic aspects of international environmental obligations, by providing for the costs of the works to be borne primarily by France, and by stating that Germany, the Netherlands and Switzerland should contribute a total of FFr132 million between them. The Convention also provides for the circumstances in which the work should be halted and in which the parties might compensate France for damage which cannot be fully compensated by the constructors of the works or by third parties.[117] Each party must take measures to prevent increases in the quantity of chloride ions discharged into the Rhine basin, in accordance with national concentration figures set out in Annex II to the Convention, and control all discharges of chloride ions greater than one kilogram per second in the Rhine basin.[118] The Rhine Commission receives annual reports from the parties, provides opinions on increases in concentrations, and may request parties to take steps to halt increases in concentration levels.[119] The Convention also provides for the installation and operation of measuring equipment and action to be taken where sudden and sizeable increases of concentrations occur.[120]

In September 1991, the five parties adopted a Protocol to the 1976 Rhine Chlorides Convention to further reduce chlorides in the river and to ensure that the water was restored to a drinkable quality.[121] The Protocol requires France to take additional measures to those required by Article 2(2) of the 1976 Convention to reduce the inputs of chlorides where the level of chlorides exceeds 200 milligrams per litre in the Rhine at the Netherlands–Germany border, and to provisionally store the chlorides on land.[122] The stored chlorides may subsequently be discharged into the Rhine after the Mine de Potasse d'Alsace has reduced its output, and in accordance with criteria fixed by the parties on the basis of a proposal by the Rhine Commission, and taking account of ecological requirements and the different uses of the waters.[123] In addition the Netherlands is required to take measures to limit discharges of chlorides

---

[115] See A. Kiss and D. Shelton, *International Environmental Law* (1991), 220.

[116] Bonn, 3 December 1976, in force 5 July 1985, 16 ILM 265 (1977); Art. 2(1) and (2) and Annex 1.

[117] Arts. 4, 5 and 7(1) and (2).

[118] Art. 3(1) and (4). Art. 3 and Annex II have been replaced by the provisions of the 1991 Protocol: see n. 121 below.

[119] Arts. 3(3) and (5) and 9.   [120] Arts. 11 and 12.

[121] Brussels, 25 September 1991.   [122] Art. 1(1) and Annex I.   [123] Art. 2.

into the Ijsselmeer and discharges of salt water into the Wadden Sea.[124] The Protocol established new obligations in respect of the discharge of chloride ions and replaced Annex II to the 1976 Convention with a new Annex IV.[125] The Protocol also allocates the costs incurred by the parties in fulfilment of these obligations.[126]

More recently, the parties have concluded a new 1999 Convention on the Protection of the Rhine.[127] On its entry into force, the 1963 Berne Pollution Agreement and the 1976 Rhine Chlorides Convention will be repealed, and replaced with an updated approach.[128] The parties undertake to pursue a number of aims, including the sustainable development of the Rhine ecosystem, the production of drinking waters from the Rhine, the improvement of sediment quality, general flood prevention, and the protection and restoration of the North Sea in conjunction with other actions taken to protect it.[129] Article 4 sets out a number of guiding principles to be observed in pursuing these aims, including the precautionary principle, the polluter-pays principle and the principle of sustainable development. The contracting parties also agree on various specific measures to protect the Rhine, including: prior authorisation of waste water discharges or general rules laying down emission limits; gradual reduction of discharges of hazardous substances, with a view to their complete elimination; monitoring of compliance with authorisations, discharges and general rules; periodical examination and adjustment (when substantial improvements in the state of the art permit or when the state of the receiving medium so necessitates) of authorisations and general rules; reduction of risk of pollution from incidents or accidents; and prior authorisation of technical measures liable to have a serious effect on the ecosystem.[130] The Rhine Commission's powers are strengthened by the Convention, including the power to take binding decisions on measures to be implemented by the contracting parties.[131]

In 1986, following the Sandoz accident, the Rhine states adopted the Rhine Action Programme, which was intended to produce potable water from the river and to improve it sufficiently to allow the return of indigenous aquatic life. This was to be achieved on the basis of a 50 per cent reduction of discharges of thirty priority substances to 1985 levels by 1995. The Action Programme has now been succeeded by the 2001 Programme on the Sustainable Development of the Rhine, to implement the general aims and principles set forth in Articles 3 and 4 of the 1999 Convention.[132] The Programme defines general protection targets for the next twenty years including restoration of the main stream,

---

[124] Art. 3 and Annex II.   [125] Arts. 5 and 6 and Annex IV.   [126] Art. 4 and Annex III.

[127] Convention on the Protection of the Rhine, Berne, 12 April 1999, OJ L289, 16 November 2000, 30.

[128] Art. 19.   [129] Art. 3.   [130] Art. 5(4).   [131] Arts. 8 and 10.

[132] Conference of the Rhine Ministers, 'Rhine 2020: Programme on the Sustainable Development of the Rhine', Strasbourg, 29 January 2001.

permanent compliance with the target values of all substances relevant for
the Rhine in water, suspended matter, sediments and organisms, protection
of groundwater against infiltration of polluted Rhine water and protection of
Rhine water against polluted groundwater.[133]

1992 Convention on the Protection and Use of Transboundary Watercourses and International Lakes

The 1992 Convention on the Protection and Use of Transboundary Watercourses and International Lakes (1992 Watercourses Convention), adopted
under the auspices of the UNECE,[134] reflected a move towards rules of general applicability to all transboundary waters in the territories of the parties,
as well as transboundary waters between parties and non-parties.[135] The 1992
Watercourses Convention draws heavily on the 1980 UNECE Declaration of
Policy on Prevention and Control of Water Pollution (Including Transboundary Pollution), which called for a range of new approaches to the protective
regulation of watercourses, including standardisation of water quality, the use
of legal and administrative measures and suitable economic incentives, and the
adoption as far as possible of the general principle that 'the direct or indirect
costs attributable to pollution should be borne by the polluter'.[136] Under the
1992 Convention, the parties accept a general obligation to take all appropriate measures to prevent, control and reduce any transboundary impact. They
commit to preventing pollution of waters which causes or is likely to cause
transboundary impact, to use transboundary waters in an ecologically sound
and rational, and reasonable and equitable way, and to ensure conservation
and restoration of ecosystems.[137] The Convention encourages the adoption
of preventive measures at source, prohibits the transfer of pollution to other

---

[133] *Ibid.*, Part 2.

[134] Helsinki, 17 March 1992, in force 6 October 1996; 31 ILM 1312 (1992); states are
party. See also the earlier related instruments adopted by the UNECE: Declaration
of Policy on Water Pollution Control, 29 April 1966, ECE/RES/10(XXI); Decision
on Body on Water Resources and Water Pollution Control Problems, 2 May 1968, ECE/
DEC/E(XXIII); Decision on International Co-operation on Shared Water Resources,
2 April 1982, ECE/DEC/D(XXXVII); Declaration of Policy on the Rational Use of Water,
14 April 1984, ECE/DEC/C(XXXIX); Decision on Co-operation in the Field of Transboundary Waters, 26 April 1986, ECE/DEC/B(41); Decision on Principles on Co-
operation in the Field of Transboundary Waters, 10 April 1987, ECE/DEC/I(42); Charter
on Groundwater Management, 21 April 1989, ECE/DEC/E(44). See generally A. Tanzi,
'Regional Integration and the Protection of the Environment: The UNECE Process on
Water Law as a Model for the Global Dimesnion', in T. Scovazzi, *The Protection of the
Environment in a Context of Regional Economic Integration* (2001), 347.

[135] 'Transboundary waters' are defined as 'any surface or ground waters which mark, cross
or are located on boundaries between two or more States': Art. 1(1).

[136] ECE/DEC/B(XXXV), E/1980/28, 23 April 1980, paras. 4, 5 and 11.

[137] Art. 2(1) and (2). 'Transboundary impact' is defined as 'any significant adverse effect
on the environment resulting from a change in the conditions of transboundary waters
caused by human activity': Art. 1(2).

parts of the environment, and calls for measures to be guided by the application of the precautionary and polluter-pays principles.[138] The Convention does not preclude other bilateral and multilateral agreements and allows parties to adopt and implement more stringent measures than those set out in the Convention.[139]

In requiring measures for the prevention, control and reduction of transboundary impact, the Convention identifies a range of options including: the use of low- and non-waste technologies; biological or equivalent treatment of municipal waste water; and a reduction of nutrient inputs and hazardous substances from industrial, municipal and other sources.[140] These approaches may be elaborated in amendments or protocols to the 1992 Convention.[141] The Convention supports a standard based upon 'best environmental practices', guidelines for which are set out in Annex II to the Convention.[142] The Convention calls for: the prior licensing and subsequent monitoring of waste water discharges (with limits to be based on best available technology for discharges of hazardous substances); stricter requirements (including prohibition) when the ecosystem so requires; environmental impact assessment; and sustainable water resources management including an ecosystems approach.[143]

The Convention signals efforts to regulate directly particular industries and activities, requiring each party to set limits for discharges for specific industries from which hazardous substances derive, based on 'best available technology'.[144] The Guidelines in Annex III require parties to develop general water-quality objectives and criteria,[145] and to provide for monitoring, research and development, the exchange of information,[146] and international efforts to elaborate rules on responsibility and liability.[147]

---

[138] Art. 2(3)–2(5).   [139] Art. 2(6) and (8).

[140] Art. 3(1)(a), (e), (f) and (g).   [141] See p. 484 below.

[142] Under Annex II, the measures to be considered in developing 'best environmental practices' include: the provision of information to the public and users; codes of practice covering the whole of the product's life; product labels; recycling, recovery and re-use; economic instruments; and licensing. The choice of particular measures should take into account the environmental hazard of the product (including production, use and disposal), substitute processes or substances, and scale of use.

[143] Art. 3(1)(b), (c), (d), (h) and (i). Annex I defines 'best available technology' as 'the latest stage of development of processes, facilities or methods of operation which indicate the practical suitability of a particular measure for limiting discharges, emissions and waste'. The Annex identifies a range of factors which should be given special consideration, and states that the 'best available technology' for a particular process will change with time in the light of technological advances, economic and social factors, and changes in scientific knowledge and understanding.

[144] Art. 3(2). 'Hazardous substances' means substances which are toxic, carcinogenic, mutagenic, teratogenic or bioaccumulative, especially when they are persistent: Art. 1(6).

[145] Art. 3(3).   [146] Arts. 4, 5, 6 and 8.

[147] Arts. 4–8. Research and development is to include 'the physical and financial assessment of damage resulting from transboundary impact': Art. 5(h).

Part II of the Convention includes provisions for riparian parties, and goes some way towards codifying on a regional basis the rules as established by the treaties and arbitral awards identified earlier. Bilateral and multilateral co-operation is to focus on the development or adaptation of treaties in conformity with the basic principles of the convention, including the establishment of joint bodies to deal with specified catchment areas.[148] Riparian parties are also encouraged to co-operate through consultations, joint monitoring and assessment, and common research and development.[149] Exchange of information includes facilitating the exchange of best available technology and, in the event of a critical situation that may have a transboundary impact, riparian parties must inform each other 'without delay'.[150] The Convention also requires warning and alarm systems and the provision of mutual assistance between parties.[151] According to the provisions on public information, the parties must make available to the public, at all times and at reasonable cost, relevant information including water-quality objectives, permits and their conditions, and the results of monitoring and assessment.[152] The implementation of the Convention will be reviewed by meetings of the parties to be held at least every three years, with the assistance of a secretariat provided by UNECE.[153]

The parties to the 1992 Convention have taken further steps to give effect to its general objectives. In 1999, they adopted a Protocol on Water and Health,[154] whose objective is to promote the protection of human health and well-being by improving water management, including protection of water ecosystems.[155] The Protocol commits parties to ensure adequate supplies of wholesome drinking water, adequate sanitation (thorough collective systems), effective protection of drinking water supplies, safeguards for human health against water-related diseases, and effective monitoring.[156] These measures are to be based on an assessment of any proposed measure in respect of all its implications for human health, water resources and sustainable development, and are to be guided by the precautionary and polluter-pays principles.[157] In taking their actions, parties are also to be guided by other principles and approaches, including the need to take preventive action, to ensure intergenerational equity, to adopt actions at the lowest appropriate administrative level, to make use of economic instruments, to ensure access to information and public participation, and to manage water resources in an integrated manner.[158] The Protocol also requires each party to establish and publish national and/or local targets to achieve or maintain a high level of protection against water-related diseases, and to that end to establish appropriate legal and institutional

---

[148] Art. 9(1) and (2). The tasks of the joint bodies relate to data collection and assessment, monitoring, inventories, emissions limits, water-quality objectives, action programmes, warning and alarm procedures, exchange of information and environmental impact assessments: Art. 9(2).

[149] Arts. 10–12.   [150] Arts. 13 and 14.   [151] Arts. 14 and 15.   [152] Art. 16.

[153] Arts. 17 and 19.   [154] London, 17 June 1999, not yet in force.   [155] Art. 1.

[156] Art. 2(2).   [157] Art. 4(4) and 5(a) and (b).   [158] Art. 5.

frameworks.[159] The Protocol includes provisions on the review and assessment of progress, response systems and public awareness and information,[160] and provisions on international co-operation (including on transboundary waters) and joint and co-ordinated international action.[161] As with other recent international agreements, provision is also made for reviewing compliance by means of 'non-confrontational, non-judicial and consultative' means.[162] In July 2001, the parties to the 1992 Convention (and the 1992 Industrial Accidents Convention) established an intergovernmental negotiation process aimed at adopting a legally binding instrument on civil liability for transboundary damage caused by hazardous activities.[163]

Americas

Since the early part of the twentieth century, the states of North and South America have adopted several bilateral agreements for the protection of freshwater resources. The most comprehensive rules are found in the agreements between Canada and the United States which relate to the protection and use of the Great Lakes, although important instruments are also in force between the United States and Mexico[164] and between Central and South American countries.[165]

1909 Washington Treaty Relating to Boundary Waters and Questions Arising Along the Boundary Between the US and Canada

The 1909 Boundary Waters Treaty between the United States and Canada was a pioneering treaty which was adopted to protect water levels and the navigability of the Great Lakes and other boundary waters. It includes one of the earliest

---

[159] Art. 6. Targets are to include, *inter alia*, quality of drinking water, reduction of diseases, areas to be covered by collective systems, the occurrence of discharges of untreated waters, and the disposal or re-use of sludge.

[160] Arts. 7–10.   [161] Arts. 11–13.

[162] Art. 15. Art. 20 includes traditional dispute settlement provisions.

[163] See ECE/MP.WAT/7-ECE/CP.TEIA/5; chapter 18, p. 937 below.

[164] Washington Treaty Relating to the Utilization of the Waters of the Colorado and Tijuana Rivers and of the Rio Grande, 3 February 1944, 3 UNTS 314; Agreement Concerning the Permanent and Definitive Solution to the International Problems of the Salinity of the Colorado River, 30 August 1973, 915 UNTS 203; see P. Mumme, 'Innovation and Reform in Transboundary Resource Management: A Critical Look at the International Boundary Water Commission, US and Mexico', 33 *Natural Resources Journal* 93 (1993); 'Symposium: Water Issues in the US–Mexico Borderlands', 40, *Natural Resources Journal* 199 (1999).

[165] Treaty on the River Plate Basin, Brasilia, 23 April 1969, in force 14 August 1970, 875 UNTS 3; Treaty Concerning the Rio de la Plata and the Corresponding Maritime Boundary, 19 November 1973, Brasilia, 23 April 1969, in force 14 August 1970, 875 UNTS 3; see J. Trevin and J. Day, 'Risk Perception in International River Basin Management: The Plata Basin Example', 30 *Natural Resources Journal* 87 (1990); L. de Castillo Laborde, 'Legal Regime of the Rio de la Plata', 36 *Natural Resources Journal* 251 (1996).

treaty provisions on the prevention of pollution, and was the first instrument to establish an international institution with competence for pollution matters.[166] Article IV of the 1909 Treaty provides that 'boundary waters and waters flowing across the boundary shall not be polluted on either side to the injury of health or property of the other'; the Treaty does not define the terms 'pollution' or 'injury'. The Treaty established a permanent International Joint Commission comprising six commissioners with three appointed by each party.[167] Its functions include approval of governmental applications for works which may affect the level or flows of boundary and other waters, surveillance and monitoring, and dispute settlement provisions (which have not yet been invoked).[168] Under Article IX, the parties can refer to the Commission any question involving the rights or interests of either party along the common frontier, following which the Commission can adopt reports and make recommendations which are advisory. The Commission has considered a number of pollution problems, following references from the parties, resulting in the adoption of publications such as the 1970 report on phosphate and other pollution, which led directly to the 1972 Agreement between the United States and Canada.[169]

Gut Dam arbitration

The use of the waters of the Great Lakes by Canada and the US has been the subject of numerous disputes between the two states, and led to the establishment of the Lake Ontario Claims Tribunal in 1965 to adjudicate claims by US nationals against Canada for damage caused to property owned by US nationals by the construction and operation of the Gut Dam[170] on the St Lawrence River between Adams Island in Canadian territory and Les Galops Island in US territory.[171] The dam was intended to stop the flow of water through the channel between the two islands. Between 1904 and 1951, the water level of the St Lawrence River and Lake Ontario increased, principally as a result of the diversion by Canada of water into the Great Lakes to increase hydro-electric power generation, and also because of a reduction in the rate at which the US withdrew water at Chicago. In 1951 and 1952, the water in the St Lawrence

---

[166] 11 January 1909, in force 5 May 1910, TS No. 548, 10 IPE 5158. See S. Toope and J. Brunnée, 'Freshwater Regimes: The Mandate of the International Joint Commission', 15 *Arizona Journal of International and Comparative Law* 273 (1998).

[167] Art. VII.   [168] Arts. VIII to X.

[169] International Joint Commission, *Pollution of Lake Erie, Lake Ontario and the International Section of the St Lawrence River* (1970). See also International Joint Commission, 'Risks of Oil Pollution in Lake Erie', 27 October 1969, 8 ILM 1363 (1969).

[170] The details concerning the dispute are set out in the Report of the Agent of the United States, 8 ILM 118 (1968); see also the Agreement establishing the Tribunal, 4 ILM 468 (1965).

[171] The US gave permission for the construction, subject to the condition that Canada would pay compensation if the dam caused damage or detriment to US property owners: Report of the US Agent, 120.

River reached unprecedented levels which, after severe storms, caused extensive flooding and erosion damage to the north and south shores of all the Great
Lakes, including Lake Ontario. The damage which was caused to US property
was argued by the owners to be the result of the construction of the Gut Dam.
In 1953, Canada removed the Gut Dam, and following the failure of efforts to
reach a friendly settlement the Tribunal was established in 1965.

The US claimed a total of US$653,386.02 from Canada. In 1968, the US and
Canada settled the case for US$350,000 as full and final satisfaction of all claims
of US nationals 'for damage allegedly caused by Gut Dam'.[172] The settlement
followed the earlier findings by the Tribunal that Canada was potentially liable
to any citizen of the US whose property suffered damage or who suffered
detriment caused by the construction and operation of Gut Dam (not only
property owners on Les Galops Island, as Canada had argued), and that Canada
had in diplomatic correspondence, prior to the establishment of the Tribunal,
recognised its obligation to pay compensation for damage attributable to the
Gut Dam.[173] Canada agreed to settle after the Tribunal had concluded that its
only task was to determine whether the dam had caused the damage for which
claims were filed and the quantum of such damages. Although the settlement
was stated to be without prejudice to the legal and factual positions maintained
by the parties, it is not unreasonable to infer that the episode supports the
conclusion that states are subject to limitations on their use of international
waters, and that they may be subject to an international claim if such use leads
to damage to foreign private property. The case does not provide support either
way on the question of whether states are liable for pure environmental damage,
since all the claims related to property damage resulting from changes to the
environment.

1978 Great Lakes Water Quality Agreement

In 1978, the United States and Canada signed an Agreement on Great Lakes
Water Quality (1978 Great Lakes Water Quality Agreement)[174] which has been
amended by Protocols in 1983[175] and 1987[176] and supersedes the earlier 1972
Agreement.[177] The 1978 Agreement is designed to 'restore and maintain the
chemical, physical, and biological integrity of the waters of the Great Lakes

---

[172] *Ibid.*, 141.   [173] *Ibid.*, 138–9.

[174] Ottawa, 22 November 1978, in force 22 November 1978, 30 UST 1383; see T. Vigod,
'Global Environmental Problems: A Legal Perspective on Great Lakes Toxic Pollution',
12 *Syracuse Journal of International Law and Commerce* 185 (1985); G. Francis, 'Bina-
tional Co-operation for Great Lakes Water Quality: A Framework for the Groundwater
Connection', 65 *Chicago-Kent Law Review* 359 (1989).

[175] 16 October 1983, in force 16 October 1983, TIAS No. 10798.

[176] 18 November 1987, not yet in force.

[177] See 1972 Agreement Between the United States and Canada Concerning Great Lakes
Water Quality, Ottawa, 15 April 1972, in force 15 April 1972; 11 ILM 694 (1972).

Basin Ecosystem', including by the elimination or reduction to the maximum extent practicable of the discharge of pollutants into the Great Lakes system.[178] The 1978 Agreement records that it is the policy of the parties to prohibit or 'virtually eliminate' the discharge of toxic or persistent toxic substances, to provide public financial assistance to construct publicly owned waste treatment works, and to co-ordinate planning processes and best management practices.[179] The 'General Objectives' of the 1978 Agreement are to keep the Great Lakes system unpolluted by a specified range of substances, including those which will form sludge deposits or adversely affect aquatic life or waterfowl, floating materials, and toxic or otherwise harmful materials, as well as nutrients that contribute to aquatic life.[180] 'More Specific Objectives' are adopted under Article IV and Annex 1: they establish maximum water concentration levels for specific chemicals which are persistent and non-persistent toxic substances, as well as other substances, and objectives for physical material and microbiological and radiological matter. Other specific objectives include the elimination of 'Areas of Concern, Critical Pollutants and Point Source Impact Zones' identified in Annex 2. The 1978 Agreement makes it clear that these objectives represent minimum levels of water quality and do not preclude the parties from adopting more stringent requirements.

The 1978 Agreement requires the parties to adopt water quality standards and other regulatory requirements which are consistent with the 'General and Specific Objectives', and to develop and implement programmes and other measures to fulfil the objectives of the Agreement.[181] To that end, the programmes and measures are to be developed for pollution from municipal and industrial sources, for an inventory of pollution abatement requirements, for eutrophication, and for pollution from agricultural and other land use, from shipping and dredging activities, and from onshore and offshore facilities.[182] Measures and programmes are also to be developed for contingency plans, for surveillance and monitoring, and for elaborating lists of hazardous substances, the control of persistent toxic substances, and airborne pollution.[183] The parties also agree to exchange information between themselves, to consult as appropriate,[184] and to meet twice a year to co-ordinate work plans and evaluate progress.

The International Joint Commission assists in implementation of the 1978 Agreement by collating, analysing and disseminating data and information, by tendering advice and recommendations, by providing assistance, and by investigating such matters as the parties may refer to it.[185] The powers of the Commission are broad, and include a competence to conduct public hearings

---

[178] Art. II. The system includes all streams, rivers, lakes and other bodies of water within the drainage basin of the St Lawrence River: *ibid.*, Art. I(h).
[179] *Ibid.*   [180] Art. III.   [181] Arts. V and VI.
[182] Art. VI(1)(a)–(h), and Annexes 3–8.   [183] Art. VI(1)(i)–(m) and Annexes 9–12.
[184] Arts. IX and X.   [185] Art. VII(1).

and to compel testimony and the production of documents,[186] to publish reports at its discretion, to verify data provided to it, and to request the provision of information relating to water quality.[187] A Great Lakes Water Quality Board and a Science Advisory Board assist the Commission.[188]

Africa

African states have also adopted a number of important bilateral and regional treaties to protect and manage freshwater resources. Of particular note, because of their comprehensive approach, are the regimes established by treaty for the Niger basin and the Zambezi River system.[189] Other arrangements, for example in relation to the Nile, are under discussion.[190]

Niger basin

Under the 1963 Act Regarding Navigation and Economic Co-operation Between the States of the Niger Basin, the parties undertake to co-operate closely on projects likely to have an appreciable effect on the conditions of the waters and biological characteristics of the fauna and flora of the River Niger and its tributaries, under the auspices of an 'Intergovernmental Organisation Concerned with the Exploitation of the River'.[191] This organisation was subsequently renamed the River Niger Commission, under which the riparian states agree to inform the Commission of certain works which they propose to undertake and to abstain from carrying out any works likely to pollute the waters or modify the flora and fauna without adequate notice to and prior consultation with the Commission.[192] The Convention Creating the Niger Basin Authority replaced the River Niger Commission with the Niger Basin Authority, which was designed to ensure the integrated development of the Niger Basin.[193] The responsibilities of the Authority extend to environmental control and preservation, including the establishment of norms and measures in the alternative

---

[186] Art. VII(2), under legislation passed pursuant to the Boundary Waters Treaty.

[187] Arts. VII(2) and (4), (5) and IX(1).   [188] Art. VIII.

[189] See also treaties for the Lake Chad Basin, the Senegal River and the River Gambia.

[190] C. Mallat, 'Law and the Nile River: Emerging International Rules and the Shari'a', in P. Howell and J. A. Allen (eds.), *The Nile: Sharing a Scarce Resource* (1994), 365; J. Brunnée and S. Toope, 'The Changing Nile Basin Regime: Does Law Matter?', 43 *Harvard International Law Journal* 105 (2002).

[191] Niamey Act Regarding the Navigation and Economic Co-operation Between the States of the Niger Basin, Niamey, 26 October 1963, in force 1 February 1966, 587 UNTS 9, Arts. 4 and 5.

[192] Agreement Concerning the Niger River Commission and the Navigation and Transport on the River Niger, Niamey, 25 November 1964, in force 3 December 1982, 587 UNTS 21, Art. 12.

[193] Faranah Convention Creating the Niger Basin Authority, Faranah, 21 November 1980, IELMT 980:86, Art. 3(1).

uses of the waters, prevention and reduction of pollution, and preservation of human health and genetic resources.[194]

Southern Africa, including the Zambezi River

The 1987 Agreement on the Action Plan for the Environmentally Sound Management of the Common Zambezi River System establishes an ambitious programme for environmentally sound water resources management to strengthen regional co-operation for sustainable development in eight African countries, under the auspices of the Southern African Development Community (SADC) (formerly the Southern African Development Co-ordination Conference or SADCC).[195] The Agreement adopts the Action Plan for the Environmental Management of the Common Zambezi River System (ZACPLAN) set out in Annex I to the Agreement, in the context of the Mar del Plata Action Plan and UNEP's programme on the environmentally sound management of inland water (EMINWA). The ZACPLAN, which is designed to deal with water resource and environmental management problems of the river system in a co-ordinated manner to avoid possible future conflicts, is divided into four component elements comprising environmental assessment, environmental management, environmental legislation, and supporting measures.[196] While setting a broad framework for co-operation, the ZACPLAN also identifies programme categories and specific programmes, establishes a workplan and timetable, and institutional and financial arrangements, including the establishment of a Trust Fund.[197] The Zambezi Action Plan is implemented by the SADC, an Intergovernmental Monitoring and Co-ordinating Committee, a Co-ordinating Unit, and national focal points.[198]

In 1995, the SADC states concluded a Protocol on Shared Watercourses in the SADC region, which was revised in August 2000.[199] The Protocol's objective is to 'foster closer co-operation for judicious, sustainable and co-ordinated management, protection and utilisation of shared watercourses and advance the SADC agenda of regional integration and poverty alleviation'.[200] The states parties recognise the unity and coherence of shared watercourses and

---

[194] Art. 4(2)(d).
[195] Harare Agreement, 28 May 1987, in force 28 May 1987, 27 ILM 1109 (1988).
[196] Annex I, paras. 28–39.
[197] Annex II, paras. 25–7 and Appendix II.   [198] Arts. 2 and 3.
[199] Protocol on Shared Watercourses in the Southern African Development Community (SADC) Region, Maseru, 16 May 1995, in force 29 September 1998; K. K. Lebotse, 'Southern African Community Protocol on Shared Watercourses: Challenges of Implementation', 12 *Leiden Journal of International Law* 173 (1999), S. Salman, 'Legal Regime for the Use and Protection of International Watercourses in the Southern African Region: Evolution and Context', 41 *Natural Resources Journal* 981 (2001). The Heads of State or Government of the SADC agreed to a Revised Protocol in August 2000 which will repeal and replace the 1995 Protocol once it enters into force.
[200] Art. 2.

that their utilisation should be open to each watercourse state on an equitable and reasonable basis.[201] The states parties also undertake to respect existing rules of 'customary or general' international law relating to shared watercourse utilisation and management.[202]

Under the Protocol, parties are required, individually or jointly, to protect and preserve shared watercourse ecosystems.[203] States parties must notify other watercourse states of planned measures which may have a 'significant adverse effect' and, if necessary, to negotiate the possible effects of planned measures on the condition of a shared watercourse.[204] States parties using a shared watercourse must take all appropriate measures to prevent causing significant harm to other watercourse states, but, if harm is nevertheless caused, the state causing the harm shall take 'all appropriate measures' to eliminate or mitigate the harm; and, where appropriate, discuss the question of compensation.[205] The Protocol establishes several organs responsible for implementation of the Protocol, including a Committee of Water Ministers and a Water Sector Co-ordinating Unit.[206]

Asia

Since the first edition of this book, there have been a number of significant developments in Asia, to supplement the limited number of earlier river treaties.[207]

Mekong River Basin

Of particular note – as a regional effort – is the 1995 Agreement on Co-operation for the Sustainable Development of the Mekong River Basin. This commits Thailand, Vietnam, Laos and Cambodia to co-operate 'in all fields of sustainable development, utilization, management and conservation of the water and related resources of the Mekong River Basin', including irrigation, hydro-power, navigation, flood control, fisheries, timber floating, recreation and tourism, with a view to minimising harmful effects that might result from natural occurrences and man-made activities.[208] The Agreement commits parties to the protection of the environment, the application of the principles of reasonable and equitable utilisation and the prevention and cessation of harmful effects, as well as the application of state responsibility for harmful effects which cause 'substantial damage'.[209] The Agreement establishes a Mekong River Commission, now based in Phnom Penh.[210]

---

[201] Art. 3.1, 3.2 and 3.7.   [202] Art. 3.3.   [203] Art. 4.2(a).
[204] Art. 4.1.   [205] Art. 3.10.   [206] Art. 5.1.
[207] I. Kasto, *Water Management and Environmental Protection in Asia and the Pacific* (1983).
[208] Chiang Rai (Thailand), 5 April 1995, in force 5 April 1995 34 ILM 864 (1995), Art. 1; G. Bowder and L. Ortolano, 'The Evolution of an International Water Resources Management Regime in the Mekong River Basin', 40 *Natural Resources Journal* 499 (2000).
[209] Arts. 3, 5, 7 and 8.   [210] Arts. 11–33.

India/Bangladesh and India/Nepal

India became a party to two important bilateral treaties in 1996, notable for their differing approaches. The Bangladesh–India Treaty on sharing the waters of the Ganges River[211] and the India–Nepal Treaty on sharing the waters of the Mahakali River[212] are intended to bring to an end long-running differences between India and her neighbours over the entitlement to water flows following the construction by India of barrages on the Ganges and Mahakali Rivers.[213] The treaties aim to establish long-term water discharge regimes of thirty and seventy-five years respectively, focusing on the utilisation of waters rather than their conservation. These instruments take only limited account of recent developments in the international law of watercourses and efforts to promote sustainable development. The two treaties adopt similar approaches, but differ in their scope of application, the extent of their reliance upon general principles governing rights over shared watercourses, and dispute settlement arrangements.

The Bangladesh–India Treaty has as its principal objective the determination of the amount of water to be released by India to Bangladesh at the Farraka Barrage on the Ganges for a period of thirty years (Articles I and XII). It entered into force upon signature and fills the gap left when a 1977 Agreement lapsed.[214] The difficulty of that task will not be apparent from the text of the Treaty, which makes only implicit reference to the long-running dispute between the two countries following the construction and operation by India of the Farraka Barrage.[215] The 1996 Treaty establishes a new formula for sharing the Ganges waters at Farraka in the dry season (1 January to 31 May), and also provides that below Farraka the waters are not to be reduced further except for 'reasonable use' in a limited amount (Article III). Further provision is made for the situation where the flow falls below 50,000 cusecs (Article II(iii)). The sharing arrangements are to be reviewed every five years and if no agreement can be reached on adjustments India is to release at least 90 per cent of Bangladesh's share as provided by Article II. The Treaty makes reference to a number of guiding principles. It aims to achieve 'optimum utilisation' of the waters of the

---

[211] New Delhi, 12 December 1996, 36 ILM 519 (1997).

[212] New Delhi, 12 February 1996, 36 ILM 531 (1997).

[213] B. Desai, 'Sharing of International Water Resources: The Ganga and Mahakali River Treaties', 3 *Asia Pacific Journal of Environmental Law* 172 (1998); S. Salman and K. Uprety, 'Hydro-Politics in South Asia: A Comparative Analysis of the Mahakali and the Ganges Treaties', 39 *Natural Resources Journal* 295 (1999); S. Subedi, 'Hydro-Diplomacy in South Asia: The Conclusion of the Mahakali and Ganges River Treaties', 93 AJIL 953 (1999).

[214] Bangladesh–India, Agreement on Sharing of the Ganges' Waters, Dacca, 5 November 1977, 17 ILM 103 (1978).

[215] See Nazrul Islam, 'International Watercourses Law and the Farraka Barrage Dispute' (unpublished PhD thesis, London University, 2000).

region, bringing a 'fair and just' solution to the Farraka waters problem but without establishing 'any general principles of law or precedent' (Preamble). It provides for application of the principles of 'equity, fair play and no harm to either party' to emergency situations, future adjustments of the Treaty, and the conclusion of agreements for other rivers (Articles II(iii), X and IX). The Treaty establishes an Indo-Bangladesh Joint Rivers Commission with the more limited mandate of monitoring daily flows, submitting data, and implementing arrangements under the Treaty (Articles IV, VI and VII). The Treaty refers disputes to the Indo-Bangladesh Joint Rivers Commission and then the two governments (Article VII).

The Mahakali River (known as the Sharda River in India) has formed the border between Nepal and India since 1816, and has been the subject of tension between the two countries since India's occupation of some 50 square kilometres of land at its source following the India–China conflict of 1961. The 1996 Treaty replaces a 1992 agreement which Nepal had rejected as providing inadequate amounts of water and electricity. The new Treaty has four objectives. First, it settles Nepal's entitlement to waters from the existing Sarada Barrage (Article 1). Secondly, it authorises (without prejudice to Nepal's sovereign rights over that land) India's prior construction of the part of the recently constructed Tanakpur Barrage which occurred on 2.9 hectares of Nepalese territory; in return Nepal will receive an agreed supply of water, a guaranteed amount of electricity annually, the construction by India of a new electricity transmission line, and additional water and electricity in the event that the flow of the Mahakali River is subsequently augmented by new works (Article 2). Thirdly, it provides framework rules for the construction of an integrated Pancheshwar Multipurpose Project on the boundary along the Mahakali River where the two states have equal rights in the water (to be the largest dam in Asia, with two power stations of equal capacity, the costs and total energy output of which are to be shared, although Nepal agrees to sell some of its electricity to India (Article 3). Fourthly, it commits India to supply irrigation water to Nepal (Article 4). The Treaty also requires all other projects in the Mahakali River – where it is a boundary river – to be designed and implemented on the basis of the 'principles' set forth in the Treaty (Article 6). The Treaty provides for 'equal partnership' in the context of the Project's objective of producing 'maximum total net benefit' (Article 3(1)), and makes only limited reference to underlying principles of 'equality, mutual benefit and no harm to either party' (Article 9(1)). Nepal's water requirements are to be given 'prime consideration' (Article 5(1)), and the parties agree not to obstruct or divert the waters so as to adversely affect its natural flow and level except by agreement, provided that local users may take a limited amount (Article 7). The Treaty establishes the Mahakali River Commission, to make recommendations for the conservation and utilisation of the river, evaluation of projects, and examination of differences between the parties concerning interpretation and application of the Treaty (Article 9(3)).

Disputes are to go to a tribunal of three arbitrators, the decisions of which are to be final, definitive and binding (Article 11).

Israel–Jordan Peace Treaty

The 1994 Israel–Jordan Peace Treaty is of singular importance for the development of water law in the Middle East.[216] Its Article 6 is intended to contribute to a 'comprehensive and lasting settlement of all the water problems' between the two countries. It commits the parties to agree mutually to recognise the rightful allocations of both of them in Jordan River and Yarmouk River waters and in certain ground waters 'in accordance with agreed acceptable principles, quantity and quality' as provided for in Annex II to the Treaty (Article 6(1)). By Article 6(2), the parties,

> recognising the necessity to find a practical, just and agreed solution to their water problems . . . jointly undertake to ensure that the management and development of their water resources do not, in any way, harm the water resources of the other Party.[217]

The parties agree to co-operate on alleviating water shortages, recognising that water issues must be dealt with 'in their totality', and commit to develop existing and new water resources, prevent contamination, assist in alleviation, share information and conduct joint research and development.[218] Annex II to the Treaty provides for detailed allocations of water quantities, for storage arrangements and the maintenance of water quality and protection against 'any pollution, contamination, harm or unauthorized withdrawals of each other's allocations'. It also makes provision for the disposal of wastewaters, for the protection and use of groundwaters, and for co-operation, including through the establishment of a Joint Water Committee.

UNCED and WSSD

Agenda 21 set out seven programme areas to protect the quality and supply of freshwater resources.[219] While short on detailed commitments or restatements of any existing obligations, it set out the basis of the measures to be adopted

---

[216] 34 ILM 46 (1995); see R. Fathallah, 'Water Disputes in the Middle East: An International Law Analysis of the Israel–Jordan Peace Accord', 12 *Journal of Land Use and Environmental Law* 119 (1996), and, more generally, J. A. Allan and C. Mallat (eds.), *Water in the Middle East: Legal, Political and Commercial Implications* (1995). See also Israel–Jordan–PLO Declaration on Co-operation on Water-Related Matters, 13 February 1996, 36 ILM 761 (1997).

[217] Art. 6(2).   [218] Art. 6(3).

[219] Agenda 21, Chapter 18, 'Protection of the quality and supply of freshwater resources: application of integrated approaches to the development, management and use of water resources'.

in future international legal instruments. The sensitivities associated with legal issues relating to these resources is evident throughout Chapter 18 of Agenda 21; even the introduction is limited to noting that co-operation among riparian states 'may' be desirable 'in conformity with existing agreements and/or other relevant arrangements, taking into account the interests of all riparian states concerned'.[220] The two programme areas most relevant to the development of international law relate to integrated water resources development and management, and protection of water resources, water quality and aquatic ecosystems.[221]

The programme on integrated development and management of water resources established a soft target for all states, according to their capacity and available resources, to put in place national action plans, institutional structures and legal instruments, and to establish efficient water use programmes, by the year 2000.[222] For transboundary water resources, the programme recognises the need for riparian states to formulate water resource strategies and to consider the harmonisation of strategies and action programmes.[223] The programme does not call for any international legal action at the global level, limiting itself to calling for improved delineation of responsibilities and co-ordination of international organisations and programmes.[224]

The programme area for the protection of water resources is more specific. It supports the 'holistic management of resources and a recognition of the interconnectedness of the elements related to freshwater and freshwater quality', taking a 'catchment management approach'.[225] The protection of groundwater is identified as an essential element of water resource management, and aquatic ecosystems are to be preserved from 'any form of degradation on a drainage basin basis'.[226] This is to be achieved through, *inter alia*, identification of, and preparation of, 'outlines' for, the protection, conservation and rational use of all potential sources of water supply; water pollution prevention and control programmes (based on pollution reduction-at-source strategies, environmental impact assessment and enforceable standards for major point source discharges and high risk non-point sources); and international water quality monitoring and management programmes.[227] The programme also envisages the following activities to protect water resources and to prevent pollution: rehabilitation of degraded catchment areas; application of the polluter-pays principle; treatment facilities for domestic and industrial effluent; the establishment of effluent discharge standards;

---

[220] *Ibid.*, para. 18.4.
[221] The other programme areas relate to: assessment of water resources; drinking water supply and sanitation; water and sustainable urban development; water and sustainable food production; and the impact of climate change on water resources.
[222] Agenda 21, para. 18.11.   [223] *Ibid.*, para. 18.10.   [224] *Ibid.*, para. 18.12(o)(iv).
[225] *Ibid.*, paras. 18.35–18.36.   [226] *Ibid.*, paras. 18.37–18.38.
[227] *Ibid.*, paras. 18.39(a), (c) and (d).

the introduction of the precautionary approach; the mandatory environmental impact assessment of all major projects potentially impairing water quality and aquatic ecosystems; and the use of risk assessment and risk management.[228]

The protection of groundwater focuses on non-degrading agricultural practices; mitigation of saline intrusion; regulation of toxic substances and establishment of protection zones in groundwater recharge and abstraction areas; and design and management of landfills based upon sound hydrogeological information and impact assessment, using the best practicable and best available technology.[229] Measures envisaged to protect aquatic ecosystems include: rehabilitation of polluted and degraded water bodies and agricultural lands; conservation and protection of wetlands; and control of noxious aquatic species.[230] This programme area also identifies the development of the necessary international legal instruments. These are for: monitoring and control of pollution and its effects on national and transboundary waters; control of long-range atmospheric transport of pollutants; control of spills in national or transboundary water bodies; and environmental impact assessment.[231]

In 2002, the World Summit on Sustainable Development (WSSD) adopted a number of specific goals, to give effect to UNCED commitments. Among the commitments adopted were the goals of:

- halving, by the year 2015, the proportion of people who are unable to reach or to afford safe drinking water, and the proportion of people without access to basic sanitation;
- intensifying water pollution prevention to reduce health hazards and protect ecosystems by introducing appropriate technologies and mitigating the effects of groundwater contamination, and establishing at the national level monitoring systems and effective legal frameworks;
- adopting prevention and protection measures to promote sustainable water use and to address water shortages;
- developing integrated water resource management and water efficiency plans by 2005; and
- developing and implementing national and regional strategies, plans and programmes on integrated river basin, watershed and groundwater management.[232]

---

[228] *Ibid.*, para. 18.40(a) and (b).   [229] *Ibid.*, para. 18.40(d).   [230] *Ibid.*, para. 18.40(e).
[231] *Ibid.*, para. 18.40(h). Whether by coincidence or design, the four areas mirror the four ECE conventions adopted since 1979 without specifically identifying them by name (1979 LRTAP Convention and Protocols; 1991 Espoo Convention; 1992 Watercourses Convention; and 1992 Industrial Accidents Convention).
[232] WSSD Plan of Implementation, paras. 24–8.

Conclusions

Many consider the management of fresh water to be the single greatest environmental challenge facing the international community, in large part because pollution and overuse have contributed to the unsanitary conditions leading to the world's most serious health problems. It is also, clearly, a major human rights issue. According to the World Bank, one billion people in developing countries do not have access to clean water and nearly two billion have no access to sanitation, resulting in the deaths of more than three million children every year.[233] In the face of statistics such as these, international law cannot, in the absence of strong political will and adequate financial resources, be expected to produce immediate results.

What international law can do is to set the framework according to which minimum international standards can be developed and effective, practical measures applied. Apart from the principles and rules of international law to which they are subject, freshwater resources are now the subject of a global framework convention, together with a range of bilateral and regional agreements which specifically address the use of freshwater resources, and their protection from contamination by pollution. These provide the first steps on which further developments might be constructed. Although the main emphasis in the past has been on developing co-operative international arrangements to govern use, in recent years the attention given to conservation has increased markedly, and recent treaties such as the 1992 Watercourses Convention and the 1997 Watercourses Convention reflect the widely held view that states are no longer entitled, as a matter of international law, to allow activities to take place which cause significant pollution to shared freshwater resources.

This conclusion nevertheless should not obscure the significant amount of work which remains to be done if international law is to contribute to halting overuse of freshwater and its pollution. There continue to be three priority areas. First, it is clear that rules establishing general standards and obligations, including those established by customary law, will be wholly inadequate. There is a need to develop specific international water quality standards, at the regional or global level, which may be of general application and which take account of particular regional or local circumstances. On the basis of these standards, targets and timetables can be adopted for the elimination of harmful substances, or the conduct of certain activities, for particular rivers, or lakes or groundwater resources, or on the basis of a regional approach.

Secondly, and in a similar fashion to that needed for the protection of oceans and seas, it is evident both from this chapter and from the rest of this book that protecting freshwater resources from pollution and overuse cannot be

---

[233] World Bank, *World Development Report* (1992), 5.

achieved otherwise than by addressing the root causes of the problem (basically, agricultural practices and industrial activities). Without effective environmental assessment on a broad scale of these practices and activities, both before and after their authorisation, it is unlikely that freshwater resources can benefit from anything other than cosmetic protection. In this regard, it will be equally important that the findings of such assessments are fully integrated into decision-making processes.

Thirdly, the protection of freshwater resources will not be achieved without effective enforcement mechanisms available to public and private entities which allow cases of non-compliance to be challenged.

11

Biological diversity

Introduction

The role of law in the conservation of biological diversity (biodiversity), which includes flora and fauna and the variety among living organisms and the ecological communities they inhabit, dates back to the creation of the Yosemite National Park in California as the world's first protected area.[1] Since then, legal rules have been adopted at the local, national, bilateral, regional and, relatively recently, the global levels to halt what is now considered by some members of the scientific community to be a crisis that leaves biodiversity more threatened than at any time in the past sixty-five million years.[2]

Biodiversity can be considered in relation to three hierarchical categories which describe different aspects of living systems measured in different ways: genetic diversity (the variation of genes within a species); species diversity (the variety of species within a region); and ecosystem diversity (the variety of ecosystems within a region). Other expressions of biodiversity include the relative abundance of species, the age structure of populations, the pattern of communities in a region, and changes in community composition and structure over time.

Threats to biodiversity come from several sources. Tropical deforestation is readily cited as the main issue, but serious threats are also posed by the destruction of temperate forests, wetland and coral reefs. Human activity contributes to the destruction of nature and the loss of biodiversity through direct activities (hunting, collection and persecution) and indirect activities (habitat destruction and modification from industrial, agricultural and other activities). The destruction and loss of habitats and species bring with them known and unknown ecological consequences: what is ultimately threatened is the ability of ecosystems to purify water, regenerate soil, protect watersheds, regulate temperature, recycle nutrients and waste, and maintain the atmosphere. The costs are not purely ecological, and extend to economic, medical and agricultural losses, and have profound moral and aesthetic implications. The reasons for conserving nature and biodiversity are essentially threefold. First, biodiversity

---

[1] World Resources Institute, *World Resources (1992–3)*, 127 at 136.
[2] *Ibid.*, 127.

provides an actual and potential source of biological resources (including food, pharmaceutical, and other material values which support fisheries, soil conditions, and parks). Secondly, biodiversity contributes to the maintenance of the biosphere in a condition which supports human and other life. Thirdly, biodiversity is worth maintaining for non-scientific reasons of ethical and aesthetic value.

The rate of species and habitat loss has not been precisely quantified. It has been estimated that continued loss at the current rate would destroy up to 15 per cent of the earth's species over the next twenty-five years, with twenty to seventy-five species per day being condemned by 2040.[3] The loss of habitat to farm land, rangelands and human and industrial settlement since pre-agricultural times appears to be equally dramatic. The United States has lost all of its grasslands and savannah, and New Zealand has lost more than 90 per cent.[4] In many developing countries, the picture is not markedly better: Madagascar has lost nearly 80 per cent of grasslands and savannah, and Botswana has lost more than 50 per cent. It has been estimated that most habitats have been reduced to less than half their pre-agricultural extent, and even the past two or three decades have led to serious loss: for example, 56 per cent of Europe's forest has already been lost.[5] Habitat loss is not the only threat to biodiversity. Other threats include: over-exploitation of plant and animal species; water, soil and air pollution; and industrial agriculture and forestry. Ozone depletion and climate change are expected to bring additional threats.

World Resources (1992–3) identified seven types of habitat which are particularly rich in species and highly threatened: tropical forests, temperate forests, coral reefs, Mediterranean climate areas, islands, freshwater lakes, and areas of high crop diversity. It also identified the root causes of biodiversity loss in these and other habitats as: (1) population growth and increasing resource consumption; (2) ignorance about species and ecosystems; (3) poorly conceived policies; (4) the effects of global trading systems; (5) inequity of resource distribution; and (6) failure to account fully for the value of biodiversity.[6] Legal efforts to address loss of biodiversity will therefore have to focus not only on the species and habitats which might be considered as requiring priority action, but also on these root causes if they are to have any long-term effects. Underlying these root causes are defective rules of national and international law, including modern land laws which are 'generally incompatible with the few remaining community property systems'; environmentally destructive subsidies; an international

---

[3] For an account of species loss, see World Conservation Monitoring Centre, *Global Biodiversity: Earth's Living Resources in the 21st Century* (2000), 91–5 and 117–25.

[4] World Resources Institute, *World Resources (1990–1)*, Table 20.4, 306–7.

[5] World Conservation Monitoring Centre, 'European Forests and Protected Areas: Gap Analysis 2000', www.unep-wcmc.org/forest/eu_gap/index.htm.

[6] World Resources Institute, *World Resources (1992–3)*, 134–5.

trading system which creates pressures to build national economies based on comparative advantage; and inadequate property rights which fail to provide incentives for conservation.[7] The international legal order does not lend itself to an approach which allows the totality of the earth's resources to be managed and used in a manner which is sustainable over the long term.[8]

International law

S. Hayden, *The International Protection of Wildlife* (1942); C. de Klemm, 'Conservation of Species: The Need for a New Approach', 9 *Environmental Policy and Law* 117 (1982); S. Lyster, *International Wildlife Law* (1985); M. Bowman, 'The Protection of Animals under International Law', 4 *Connecticut Journal of International Law* 487 (1989); C. de Klemm, *Wild Plant Conservation and the Law* (1990); S. Bilderbeek (ed.), *Biodiversity and International Law: The Effectiveness of International Environmental Law* (1992); J. Doremus, 'Patching the Ark: Improving Legal Protection of Biological Diversity', 18 *Ecology Law Quarterly* 265 (1991); M. Maffei, *La Protezione Internazionale delle Specie Animali Minacciate* (1992); F. Burhenne-Guilmin and S. Casey-Lefkowitz, 'The New Law of Biodiversity', 3 *Yearbook of International Environmental Law* 43 (1992); C. de Klemm and C. Shine, *Biological Diversity Conservation and the Law* (1993); C. Joyner, 'Biodiversity in the Marine Environment: Resource Implications for the Law of the Sea', 28 *Vandefloilt Journal of Transnational Law* 635 (1995); M. Bowman and C. Redgwell (eds.), *International Law and the Conservation of Biological Diversity* (1996); T. Swanson, *Global Action for Biodiversity* (1997); P. Van Heijnsbergen, *International Legal Protection of Wild Fauna and Flora* (1997); L. Juda, 'Considerations in Developing a Functional Approach to the Governance of Large Marine Ecosystems', 30 *Ocean Development and International Law* 89 (1999); M. Austen and T. Richards (eds.), *International Animal Welfare Law* (2000).

International law for the conservation of biodiversity is relatively well developed.[9] There are now in place a large number of bilateral and regional treaties, incorporating new approaches recently reflected in the EC's 1992 Habitats Directive, the 1992 Biodiversity Convention and the 1995 Straddling Stocks Agreement. International biodiversity conservation policy has emerged from a variety of sources. The 1972 Stockholm Declaration called for flora and fauna to be safeguarded for the benefit of present and future generations through careful planning or management; for the maintenance of the earth's capacity to produce vital renewable resources; and for states to prevent pollution liable to harm living resources and marine life.[10] Principle 4 declared:

---

[7] *Ibid.*   [8] See chapter 1, pp. 11–15 above.
[9] See chapter 2, pp. 26–30 above.   [10] Principles 2, 3 and 7.

> Man has a special responsibility to safeguard and wisely manage the heritage of wildlife and its habitat, which are now gravely imperilled by a combination of adverse factors. Nature conservation, including wildlife, must therefore receive importance in planning for economic development.

The 1982 World Charter for Nature affirmed: that the genetic viability on earth shall not be compromised; that population levels of all life forms 'must be at least sufficient for their survival, and to this end necessary habitats shall be safeguarded'; and that special protection shall be given to unique areas, to representative samples of all different types of ecosystem, and to the habitats of rare or endangered species.[11] Chapter 15 of Agenda 21 addresses the conservation of biological diversity,[12] and has been reaffirmed by the 2002 WSSD Plan of Implementation.[13] Other initiatives contributing to the development of international law include the IUCN World Conservation Strategy (1980)[14] and the Action Plan for Biosphere Reserves (1984).[15]

Classifying and arranging biodiversity conservation agreements into a coherent structure provides something of a challenge, since species and habitats have an interdependent existence. Moreover, efforts at classification might suggest the existence of an ordered and structured legal approach to the conservation of biodiversity. The reality is otherwise: the rules of international law have developed in a piecemeal and *ad hoc* way, and their limited success is reflected in the continued loss of biodiversity. The interdependence of species, habitats and ecosystems necessarily means that each of the instruments addressed in this chapter and the rest of the book will have consequences for any particular habitat or species. Measures to protect the atmosphere, the marine environment and freshwater resources may also benefit biodiversity, as will those adopted to address hazardous substances and waste.

International law for the conservation of biodiversity may usefully be arranged in three categories.

1. The first category includes treaties which are potentially applicable to all species and habitats on the planet: there are only two such treaties, the 1973 Convention on International Trade in Endangered Species (CITES) and the 1992 Biodiversity Convention.
2. The second category includes obligations which are applicable to all species and habitats within a particular region.
3. The third category includes treaties and other international agreements which are applicable at the regional or global level but which have as their objective the conservation of particular habitat or species types; this third category thus includes: international regulatory efforts which promote conservation of the following species or habitats: wetlands; forests; plants; soil

---

[11] Paras. 2 and 3.   [12] See below.   [13] See below.
[14] Chapter 2, pp. 47–8 above.   [15] UNEP/GC.13/L.6.

and land; marine living resources (which include whales and cetaceans, tuna, seals and other fisheries); birds; polar bears; and migratory species. Included in this category are the results of international efforts to address the protection of cultural and natural heritage, which can include certain natural resources as well as those which are man-made.

Regulatory techniques

Across these three categories, different regulatory techniques have been used to promote conservation. The maintenance of biological diversity, that is to say, viable populations of species, can be carried out on-site (*in situ*) or off-site (*ex situ*),[16] and on a habitat or ecosystem basis, or on a species basis; it is only in respect of the latter that *ex situ* efforts are applicable. Comprehensive inventories of the global conservation status of plant and animal species are set out in the IUCN Red Lists, which use a set of criteria to evaluate the extinction risk of thousands of species and sub-species.[17] The Lists are compiled by the IUCN's Species Survival Commission, which is a network of some 7,000 species experts and partner organisations around the world. International regulatory techniques which are applied to support these efforts include:

1. the establishment of protected areas;
2. prohibitions and/or regulations on the taking of particular species;
3. the establishment of seasons or other periods in which the taking of species is permitted;
4. regulated taking or exploitation subject to compliance with general standards limiting utilisation to that which is 'rational', or 'optimal' or 'maximal';
5. prohibitions and/or regulation of international trade in species;
6. the establishment of quotas for the taking of species;
7. management of habitats;
8. management of ecosystems;
9. prohibition on methods or means of taking; and
10. prohibition on the introduction of new or alien species.

Of these, the most widely and long-used is the establishment of protected areas,[18] together with *ex situ* conservation in zoos, botanic gardens, gene banks and scientific aquaria. Between 1950 and 1994 the total number and extent of

[16] World Conservation Monitoring Centre, *Global Biodiversity* (2000), 220–2.
[17] The 2000 IUCN Red List contains assessments of more than 18,000 species of plants and animals, 11,000 of which are threatened. The Red List is now too large to publish as a book as was done in the past. Instead, it is available in electronic format at www.redlist.org.
[18] The definition of a protected area adopted by IUCN is: 'An area of land and/or sea especially dedicated to the protection and maintenance of biological diversity, and of natural and associated cultural resources, and managed through legal or other effective means.'

protected areas increased by a factor of more than five, and by 1997 there were 30,350 protected areas around the planet, extending over a total of more than 13 million square kilometres.[19] Of this total, nearly 6 million square kilometres were *totally protected areas* which are maintained in a natural state and closed to all extractive uses according to Categories Ia, Ib, II and III of the IUCN management categories.[20] The remainder, some 7 million square kilometres, are *partially protected areas* which fall within IUCN Categories IV, V and VI and may be managed for specific uses, such as recreation or tourism, and for which some extractive use is allowed.[21] These protected areas were usually established to preserve species, vistas or geological formations, and historical or recreational sites, and to protect watersheds or reserve timber supplies. Only recently have they begun to be established expressly to preserve biodiversity generally.

Traditional efforts at custodial management have generally not been success-ful and the average rate of species extinction has continued to increase. Reasons cited for the lack of success include the fact that the boundaries of protected areas often follow a political rather than ecological course; that many such areas are too small to be effective; and that conflicts frequently arise with local com-munities who see the establishment of such areas as a limitation on their right to economic and other development. Other factors limiting the effectiveness of protected areas include the effects of activities taking place outside the protected areas, ineffective management and insufficient funding. The reasons may vary from region to region. For certain protected areas which are World Heritage Sites, one report suggested that in North America, Europe and Oceania the

---

[19] 17,892 (59 per cent) protected areas are less than 1,000 hectares in size and they account for a total area of 28,713 km², which is only 0.2 per cent of the global protected areas network. World Conservation Monitoring Centre, 'State of the World's Protected Areas at the End of the Twentieth Century', paper presented at IUCN World Commission on Protected Areas Symposium on 'Protected Areas in the 21st Century: From Islands to Networks', Albany, Australia, 24–29 November 1997, section 2.1.

[20] *Ibid.*, Table 3. Category Ia comprises scientific reserves and strict nature reserves with outstanding representative ecosystems with limited public access and used only for scien-tific and educational purposes. Category Ib comprises wilderness areas of unmodified or slightly modified land and/or sea, retaining their natural character and influence, without permanent or significant habitation, which are protected and managed so as to preserve their natural condition. Category II comprises national parks and provincial parks of national or international significance used by visitors for recreation and study. Category III comprises natural monuments and landmarks containing unique formations, special animals or plants, or unusual habitats: IUCN, *Guidelines for Protected Areas Management Categories* (1994).

[21] *Ibid.* Category IV comprises managed nature reserves and wildlife sanctuaries which are protected for specific purposes. Category V includes protected landscapes and seascapes which may be entirely natural or might include cultural landscapes. Category VI comprises managed resource protected areas managed mainly for the sustainable use of natural ecosystems: IUCN, *Guidelines for Protected Areas Management Categories* (1994).

greatest threat is industrial development; in Asia it is inadequate management; in Africa it is poaching; and in South America it is fire and natural threats.[22] The relative failure of international efforts is spurring new approaches to conservation techniques. These include the use of 'buffer zones' and 'biosphere reserves', first designated in 1976 by the Man and the Biosphere Programme of UNESCO and of which there are now 411,[23] and 'bio-regional management' which seeks to integrate economic, ecological, cultural and managerial considerations at the regional level. Examples of the latter include the Great Barrier Reef Marine Park in Australia and the Adirondack regional park in New York state.

Although some progress has been made, the rules of international law have a considerable way to go before these changes might be considered to have been fully, or even significantly, integrated.

General instruments of global application

The 1973 CITES and the 1992 Biodiversity Convention are the only two conventions which are potentially applicable to all species in any habitat in the world. The conference of the parties of both Conventions have become important international fora for addressing conservation issues, and developing new regulations and instruments, such as the 2000 Biosafety Protocol.

Convention on International Trade in Endangered Species

L. H. Kosloff and M. C. Trexler, 'The Convention on International Trade in Endangered Species: No Carrot, But Where's the Stick?', 17 *Environmental Law Review* 10,222 (1987); D. S. Favre, *International Trade in Endangered Species* (1989); P. Sands and A. Bedecarré, 'Convention on International Trade in Endangered Species: The Role of Public Interest Non-Governmental Organisations in Ensuring the Effective Enforcement of the Ivory Trade Ban', 17 *Boston College Environmental Affairs Law Review* 799 (1990); K. D. Hill, 'The Convention on International Trade in Endangered Species: Fifteen Years Later', 13 *Loyola of Los Angeles International and Comparative Law Journal* 231 (1990); V. Karno, 'Protection of Endangered Gorillas and Chimpanzees in International Trade: Can CITES Help?' 14 *Hastings International and Comparative Law Review* 989 (1991); W. Wijnstekers, *The Evolution of CITES* (1995, 4th edn); P. Sand, 'Whither CITES? The Evolution of a Treaty Regime on the Borderland of Trade and Environment', 8 JEL 29 (1997);

---

[22] World Resources Institute, *World Resources (1992–3)*, Table 20.3, 302–3. Other factors cited as limiting the effectiveness of protected areas include tourism, pollution and the introduction of plant and animal species.

[23] UNESCO, 'World Network of Biosphere Reserves: 411 Reserves in 94 Countries', Man and Biosphere Secretariat, SC/ECO/September 2001.

D. M. Ong, 'CITES: Implications of Recent Developments in International and EC Environmental Law', 10 JEL 291 (1998); M. Bowman, 'Conflict or Compatibility? The Trade, Conservation and Animal Welfare Dimension of CITES', 1 JIWLP 9 (1998); J. Baker, 'A Substantive Theory of the Relative Efficiency of Environmental Treaty Compliance: The Case of CITES', 2 JIWLP 9 (1999); S. M. Dansky, 'The CITES "Objective" Listing Criteria: Are They "Objective" Enough to Protect the African Elephant?' 73 *Tulane Law Review* 961 (1999); M. Bowman, 'CITES: Trade Conservation and Animal Welfare', 2 JIWLP 9 (1999).

In 1973, twenty-one countries signed the Convention on International Trade in Endangered Species (CITES), ten years after IUCN first called for an international convention to regulate trade in threatened species.[24] Tens of thousands of species of plants and animals are subject to its regulations, which are designed to protect endangered species of flora and fauna from over-exploitation by regulating or prohibiting their international trade and reducing their economic value. The adoption of CITES was the culmination of a process which began in 1960 at the Seventh General Assembly of the IUCN, a 1963 IUCN General Assembly resolution calling for an international convention, and a first draft of a treaty in 1964. In 1972, the Stockholm Conference adopted Recommendation 99.3 which led to the convening of a plenipotentiary conference in Washington DC in February and March 1973 and the adoption of the Convention.[25]

Institutions

A permanent Secretariat located in Lausanne, Switzerland, oversees the application of the CITES system, although the day-to-day operation is a matter for the national authorities of the parties.[26] In addition to its general regulatory duties, the Secretariat convenes regular and extraordinary meetings of the conference of the parties.[27] The conference of the parties meets at least every two years to consider and adopt amendments to Appendices I and II, to review the progress of restoration and conservation of listed species, and to make recommendations for improving the effectiveness of the Convention.[28] To date, the conference of the parties has met twelve times, most recently in Santiago in November 2002. The conference of the parties has established committees, subcommittees and working groups and in 2000 consolidated arrangements into a Standing Committee of the conference of the parties, an Animals Committee, a Plants Committee, and a Nomenclature Committee.[29] The conference of the

---

[24] Washington, 3 March 1973, in force 1 July 1975, 993 UNTS 243; CITES has 162 parties. Amending Protocols were adopted in Bonn on 22 June 1979 (in force 13 April 1987) and in Gaborone on 30 April 1983 (not yet in force). For a detailed guide to the Convention and its history, see W. Wijnstekers, *The Evolution of CITES* (1995, 4th edn).

[25] *Ibid.*, 1.   [26] Art. XII.   [27] Arts. XI(2) and XII(2)(a) to (i).

[28] Art. XI(3)(b) to (c) and (e). The Conference also approves the CITES Secretariat's budget and considers any reports presented by the Secretariat or any party. Art. XI(3)(a) and (d).

[29] Res. Conf. 11.1 (2000, Establishment of Committees).

parties may establish additional committees and working groups as needed: a Panel of Experts on the African Elephant was established in 1989,[30] and the Working Group on Transport of Live Specimens is now a permanent working group.[31]

At the discretion of the CITES Secretary General, the Secretariat may seek assistance from 'suitable inter-governmental or non-governmental international or national agencies and bodies technically qualified in protection, conservation and management of wild fauna and flora'.[32] The IUCN Environmental Law Programme has been asked by the conference of the parties to prepare legal opinions on matters arising under CITES, and non-governmental organisations participate as observers in its meetings, although they cannot vote.[33]

Preamble and definitions

The preamble recognises that 'wild fauna and flora in their many beautiful and varied forms are an irreplaceable part of the natural systems of the earth which must be protected for this and the generations to come', and indicates the primary purpose of the Convention as international co-operation to protect wild fauna and flora against over-exploitation through international trade. CITES operates by listing endangered species on one of its three Appendices, an approach drawn from some of the earliest environmental treaties.[34] A 'species' is any 'species, sub-species, or geographically separate population thereof';[35] a specimen is defined as:

> (i) any animal or plant, whether alive or dead;
> (ii) in the case of an animal: for species included in Appendices I and II, any readily recognisable part or derivative thereof; and for species included in Appendix III, any readily recognisable part or derivative thereof specified in Appendix III in relation to the species; and
> (iii) in the case of a plant: for species included in Appendix I, any readily recognisable part or derivative thereof; and for species included in Appendices II and III, any readily recognisable part or derivative thereof specified in Appendices II and III in relation to the species.[36]

---

[30] Res. Conf. 7.9 (1989). See also Res. Conf. 10.9 (1997, Consideration of Proposals for the Transfer of African Elephant Populations from Appendix I to Appendix II).

[31] Res. Conf. 7.13 (1989, Shipment of Live Animals).   [32] Art. XII(1).

[33] Art. XI(7) (NGOs may be refused admittance, however, upon the objection of at least one-third of the parties present).

[34] Chapter 2, pp. 26–30 above.

[35] Art. I(a); see Res. Conf. 2.20 (1979, Use of the Subspecies as a Taxonomic Unit in the Appendices).

[36] Art. I(b); see Res. Conf. 2.18 (1979, Parts and Derivatives of Animal Species Listed on Appendix III and of Plant Species Listed on Appendix II or III); Res. Conf. 4.24 (1983, Parts and Derivatives of Appendix II or III Plants and Appendix III Animals); Res. Conf. 4.8 (1983, Treatment of Export of Parts and Derivatives Without Permit from a Party to Another Which Deems Them Readily Recognisable); Res. Conf. 5.9 (1985, Control of

Appendices I, II and III and international trade

The level of protection afforded to the species depends upon which Appendix, if any, a species is listed on. Parties are free to introduce stricter domestic measures.[37] Appendix 1 includes 'all species threatened with extinction which are or may be affected by trade'.[38] Except in very limited circumstances, CITES prohibits all trade in Appendix I species;[39] any trade must not be 'detrimental to the survival of the species', must not be for 'primarily commercial purposes', and cannot be in relation to a species obtained in contravention of the laws of the export state.[40] Dependent upon these and other inquiries, CITES requires the exporting and importing parties to issue permits for proposed trade in Appendix I specimens.[41] Certificates are also required for re-export of specimens and for any specimen introduced from the sea.[42]

Appendix II lists 'all species which although not necessarily threatened with extinction may become so unless trade in specimens is subject to strict regulation in order to avoid utilisation incompatible with their survival'.[43] Commercial trade in Appendix II specimens is allowed if it is not 'detrimental to the survival of that species' and the specimen was not obtained in contravention of the law of the exporting state.[44] No import permit is required, but the importer must present an export permit or re-export certificate before entry is allowed.[45] Otherwise, the conditions on trade in Appendix II specimens are similar to those for Appendix I specimens.

Appendix III includes 'all species which any party identifies as being subject to regulation within its jurisdiction for the purpose of preventing or restricting exploitation, and as needing the co-operation of other parties in the control

---

Readily Recognisable Parts and Derivatives); Res. Conf. 6.16(a) (1987, Trade in Worked Ivory from African Elephants); Res. Conf. 6.18 (1989, Additional Considerations for Plant Parts and Derivatives); Res. Conf. 8.17 (1992, Improving the Regulation of Trade in Plants); Res. Conf. 9.6 (Rev.) (1994, Trade in Readily Recognisable Parts and Derivatives).

[37] Art. XIV(1). Art. XIV(2)–(4) includes provisions on the relationship with other treaties or international agreements, including those relating to marine species.

[38] Art. II(1).

[39] Art. II(1). 'Trade' is defined as 'export, re-export, import and introduction from the sea': Art. I(c). For a detailed account of the rules governing trade in specimens of species in Appendix I, see Wijnstekers, *The Evolution of CITES*, 25–41.

[40] Art. III(2)(a) and (b) and (3)(c). The determination of these factors is made by a scientific authority in the state of export: *ibid.* According to Art. IX of CITES, each party must designate one or more 'Scientific Authorities' to determine the consequences of import/export transactions and one or more 'Management Authorities' to grant trade permits: Art. III(3)(c) (determination is made by the scientific or management authority of the importing state).

[41] Art. III(2) and (3).   [42] Art. III(4) and (5).

[43] Art. II(2). Art. II(2)(b) provides that other species also must be subject to regulation if necessary to effectively regulate an Appendix II species.

[44] Art. IV(2)(a) and (b). For a detailed account of the rules regulating trade in specimens of species in Appendix II, see Wijnstekers, *The Evolution of CITES*, 43–50.

[45] Art. IV(4).

of trade'.[46] Appendix III allows parties to assist each other in enforcing their domestic wildlife legislation, and species originally listed in Appendix III often make their way into Appendix II.[47] The management authority of the exporting state must issue an export permit for Appendix III specimens based upon somewhat less stringent standards than those for Appendices I and II species.[48]

Amendments

The most important task of the conference of the parties is to consider and adopt amendments to Appendices I and II.[49] Article XV sets out the basic principles and procedures for amending Appendices to include or remove species and to move species from one Appendix to another. Amendments at conferences of the parties are adopted by two-thirds majority of those present and voting and enter into force ninety days after that meeting for all parties which have not entered a reservation.[50] Amendments may also be adopted between meetings.[51] The first meeting of the conference of the parties adopted more detailed criteria for listing and de-listing species, known as the 'Berne criteria'.[52] These criteria were the source of some controversy, in part because of their perceived protectionist requirements for removing or downlisting species. For example, in the context of the attempts to uplist the African elephant to Appendix I in 1989, the opponents of such an amendment argued that the African elephant did not meet the Berne criteria for threatened extinction 'at the species level',[53] and the issue of elephants and ivory has continued to challenge the conference of the parties and the CITES system.[54]

---

[46] Art. II(3).   [47] Art. V.

[48] Art. V(2). For an account of the rules regulating trade in specimens of species in Appendix III, see Wijnstekers, *The Evolution of CITES* (1992, 3rd edn), 51–3.

[49] Art. XI(3).   [50] Art. XV(1).   [51] Art. XV(2).

[52] Res. Conf. 1.1 (1976, Criteria for the Addition of Species and Other Taxa to Appendices I and II and for the Transfer of Species and Other Taxa from Appendix II to Appendix I).

[53] CITES Secretariat, 'Views of the CITES Secretariat on Potential Problems Raised by the Inclusion of the African Elephant on Appendix I', in *Proceedings of the Seventh Meeting of the Conference of the Parties* (1989). This argument relied on the existence of large, well-managed stocks of elephants in several southern African nations. Given that healthy herds of elephants exist in some places, so the argument went, it did not matter that the species might be extinguished elsewhere. The conference of the parties rejected this argument and voted to move the African elephant from Appendix II to Appendix I by a vote of seventy-six to eleven, with four abstentions; Doc. Plen. 7.4, in *Proceedings of the Seventh Meeting of the Conference of the Parties* (1989) (for subsequent events concerning reservations, see chapter 5, pp. 215–18 above).

[54] R. Martin, *African Elephants, CITES, and the Ivory Trade* (1986); E. Barbier, J. Burgess, T. Swanson and D. Pearce, *Elephants, Ivory and Economics* (1990); M. J. Glennon, 'Has International Law Failed the Elephant?', 84 AJIL 1 (1990); D. J. Harland, *Killing Game: International Law and the African Elephant* (1994); S. Hitch, 'Losing the Elephant Wars: CITES and the "Ivory Ban"', 27 *Georgia Journal of International and Comparative Law* 167 (1998); J. Anderson, 'Recent Events Affecting the International Ivory Trade', 11 *Colorado Journal of International Environmental Law and Policy* 71 (2000).

In 1992, the conference of the parties directed the Standing Committee to undertake a revision of the Berne criteria for consideration at the ninth meeting.[55] Revised criteria were adopted at the ninth meeting: these set forth new standards for judging amendment proposals, and require that when considering any proposal to amend Appendix I or II the parties 'shall apply the precautionary principle so that scientific uncertainty should not be used as a reason for failing to act in the best interest of the conservation of the species'.[56] Under the revised criteria, to qualify for Appendix I a species must be currently threatened with extinction, in the sense that it meets at least one of certain specified biological criteria. These include: species with a small population in the wild or one which has a restricted area or distribution; species which have experienced a decline in the number of individuals in the wild; or species whose status is such that they are likely to become threatened species within a period of five years.[57] Proposals to amend Appendix I should be based on the best information available, giving details of the species distribution, habitat availability, population status, population trends, geographic trends, ecosystem role and specific threats.[58] With regard to its trade status, a species which meets the biological criteria should be listed in Appendix I if it 'is or may be affected by trade'; this is defined broadly to include species probably in trade but for which conclusive evidence is lacking.

For Appendix II listing, the criteria provide that species need not currently be threatened with extinction but it is known, inferred or projected that they might become so. Other species which must be included in Appendix II are species which closely resemble listed species and any species which is a member of a taxon of which most of the species are included in Appendix II.[59]

Any species included in Appendix I for which sufficient data are available to demonstrate that it does not meet the biological criteria should be transferred to Appendix II only in accordance with certain precautionary measures listed in Annex 4. Similar precautionary measures must be observed in respect of any proposal to delete a species from Appendix II that does not meet the criteria for listing in that appendix.[60]

---

[55] Res. Conf. 8.20 (1992, Development of New Criteria for the Amendment of the Appendices).

[56] Res. Conf. 9.24 (1994, Criteria for Amendment of Appendices I and II); B. Dickinson, 'The Precautionary Principle in CITES: A Critical Assessment', 39 *Natural Resources Journal* 211 (1999).

[57] *Ibid.*, Annex 1.   [58] *Ibid.*, Annex 6.   [59] *Ibid.*, Annex 2a and 2b.

[60] Annex 4 precautionary measures, applicable in the case of uncertainty over the status of a species or the impact of trade, include the following: no species listed in Appendix I shall be removed from the Appendices unless it has been first transferred to Appendix II, with monitoring of any impact of trade on the species for at least two intervals between meetings of the conference of the parties; species which do not meet the biological criteria for Appendix I should be retained in that Appendix unless the species is not in demand for international trade, is subject to satisfactory management or an export quota or is the subject of a ranching proposal.

Exemptions

CITES incorporates several provisions that allow parties to bypass the regulations applicable to particular species listed in the Appendices. First, the trade provisions do not apply to the transit or transhipment of species.[61] Secondly, subject to certain exceptions, the trade provisions do not apply to specimens that are personal or household effects.[62] Thirdly, Article VII(2) provides that, when the management authority of a state of export or re-export determines that a specimen was acquired before the provisions of CITES applied to that specimen, the restrictions of Articles III, IV and V do not apply; in these circumstances, the exporting state's Management Authority issues a 'pre-Convention specimen' certificate so that the specimen may be traded. This section exempts 'pre-Convention specimens' from the restrictions relating to a listing on Appendix I, II or III, notably regarding permits, and it has caused certain difficulties requiring consideration by the conference of the parties.[63] One of the objectives of Article VII(2) was to allow stockholders to trade their existing stocks before the Convention originally entered into force, and to trade in old or antique specimens other than personal effects. In practice, traders have abused this provision by stockpiling large quantities of specimens that are likely to be listed in the appendices or uplisted to a higher level of protection.

A fourth exemption applies to non-commercial trade between scientists or scientific institutions in certain specimens.[64] A fifth exemption may be applied in respect of certain specimens forming part of a travelling zoo, circus or other travelling exhibition.[65] Special provisions apply to trade in captive bred animals and artificially propagated plants.[66] Finally, CITES permits parties to make reservations to the Convention in respect of any species listed in Appendix I, II or III or any parts or derivatives specified in relation to an Appendix III species either at the time at which it becomes a party[67] or upon amendment to an

---

[61] Art. VII(1); see also recommendations of Res. Conf. 9.7 (1994).

[62] Art. VII(3). This has been one of the more complicated provisions to apply: see Wijnsteker, *The Evolution of CITES*, 79–83 and Res. Conf. 10.6 (1997, Control of Trade in Tourist Souvenir Specimens); Res. Conf. 6.8 (1987, Implementation with Regard to Personal and Household Effects); and Res. Conf. 10.20 (1997, Frequent Cross-Border Movements of Personally Owned Live Animals).

[63] See Res. Conf. 4.11 (1983, Interpretation of 'Pre-Convention Acquisition'), which was replaced by Res. Conf. 5.11 (1985, Definition of the Term 'Pre-Convention Specimen').

[64] Art. VII(6); Res. Conf. 11.15 (2000, Non-Commercial Loan, Donation or Exchange of Museum and Herbarium Specimens).

[65] Art. VII(7); Res. Conf. 8.16 (1992, Travelling Live Animal Exhibitions).

[66] Art. VII(4) and (5); see Wijnsteker, *The Evolution of CITES*, 89–90 and Res. Conf. 10.16 (Rev.) (1997, Specimens of Animal Species Bred in Captivity) and Res. Conf. 9.19 (1994, Guidelines for the Registration of Nurseries Exporting Artificially Propagated Specimens of Appendix I Species).

[67] Art. XXIII(2); see Res. Conf. 5.9 (1985, Control of Readily Recognisable Parts and Derivatives).

Appendix.[68] In the case of additions to Appendices I and II, a reserving party has ninety days after the amendment to register its reservation with Switzerland, the depository government,[69] whereas reservations to Appendix III listings may be taken at any time.[70] Reserving parties are treated as non-parties with regard to trade in the designated species or its parts or derivatives,[71] which allows them to trade with actual non-parties and other parties taking matching reservations unfettered by CITES requirements.[72]

The reservation clauses seem contradictory to the general goals of CITES, and there is little doubt that their operation has detrimental effects on listed endangered species. While noting that the drafters of CITES probably included the reservation clauses to encourage greater state participation, one commentator has suggested that the drafters envisioned that the reservations would be used infrequently. Neither the number of parties utilising the clauses nor the quantity of reservations taken have fulfilled that expectation.[73] Determining the effect of a reservation to an amendment uplisting a species from Appendix II to Appendix I has presented a persistent problem in CITES enforcement. On a literal reading of the Convention, a reserving party that was following the strict requirements applicable to trade in Appendix II specimens prior to an uplisting becomes almost completely unregulated after amendment. France embraced this interpretation in 1979 when it took reservations to the uplisting of most populations of saltwater crocodiles and stated that its trade in such specimens thereafter would be outside the scope of the Convention.[74] In response to this flaw in CITES regulation, the fourth meeting of the conference of the parties

---

[68] Arts. XV(3) (Appendix I and II species); Art. XVI(2) (Appendix III species); see Res. Conf. 4.25 (1983, Effect of Reservations) and Res. Conf. 6.3 (1987, Implementation of CITES, mentioning that reservations made by importing countries allow loopholes through which specimens illegally acquired in the countries of origin can find legal markets without any control).

[69] Art. XV(3).   [70] Art. XVI(2).   [71] Arts. XV(3), XVI(2) and XXIII(3).

[72] Art. X imposes requirements on trade between parties and non-parties such as 'comparable documentation issued by the competent authorities' in the non-party state, which 'substantially conforms' with CITES requirements. This provision also applies to trade between reserving parties and non-reserving parties for trade in Appendices II and III specimens; see also Res. Conf. 5.4 (1985, Periodic Reports); Res. Conf. 5.12(h) (1985, Trade in Ivory from African Elephants); Res. Conf. 5.16(j) (1985, Trade in Ranched Specimens); Res. Conf. 7.11 (1989, Trade in Ranched Specimens Between Parties, Non-Parties and Reserving Parties); and Res. Conf. 9.5 (1994, Trade with States Not Party to the Convention).

[73] S. Lyster, *International Wildlife Law* (1985), 262–4 (discussing French, Italian, Japanese and Indonesian reservations).

[74] S. Lyster, *International Wildlife Law* (1985), 264, pointing out that less-endangered crocodiles remained on Appendix II and France continued to follow those procedures. The 'absurd' result was that the more endangered crocodiles were not protected while the less endangered were; however, with effect from 1 January 1984, all EC member states were required to withdraw all CITES reservations pursuant to Commission Regulation (EEC) 3626/82, OJ L384, 12 December 1982, 1 (as amended).

recommended that parties taking reservations on transfers from Appendix II to Appendix I should continue to follow the requirements for trade in Appendix II specimens.[75]

Marking, ranching and quotas

CITES includes provisions concerning the adoption of rules on the marking of specimens.[76] Other rules have emerged as practice under the Convention has developed. Thus, although the Convention does not mention ranching, which is defined as 'the rearing in a controlled environment of specimens taken from the wild',[77] rules have developed to allow ranching and trade in ranching products without the Convention having been amended. The rules take account of the fact that Article VII(4) of the Convention excludes commercial trade in any specimens of Appendix I species taken from the wild, including 'captive bred' specimens. Accordingly, in 1981 the conference of the parties adopted Resolution 3.15, which allowed parties to transfer a population of an Appendix I species to Appendix II for ranching, provided that certain conditions are fulfilled. Under the resolution, criteria are established which must be fulfilled before the ranching operations may be carried out.[78]

Similarly, although CITES does not contain express provisions on the establishment of quota systems, the conference of the parties has used its powers to adopt four quota systems.[79] The first governs trade in leopard skins. This was permitted according to a quota approved by the conference of the parties in 1983, and is now regulated by Resolution 10.14 adopted by the conference of the parties in 1997. It creates a quota of 2,085 leopard skins, divided between eleven African parties, and subject to certain conditions.[80] The second quota system

---

[75] Res. Conf. 4.25 (1983, Effects of Reservations). The 1983 Conference also requested that all types of reserving parties keep and report trading statistics for species under reservations so that the monitoring function of CITES at least could be maintained.

[76] Art. VI(7); see Wijnsteker, *The Evolution of CITES*, 65–74.

[77] Res. Conf. 3.15 (1981, Ranching); Res. Conf. 11.16 (2000, Ranching and Trade in Ranched Specimens of Species Transferred from Appendix I to Appendix II).

[78] The criteria are set out in Wijnsteker, *The Evolution of CITES*, 194–204; see also Res. Conf. 5.16 (1985, Trade in Ranched Specimens); Res. Conf. 6.22 (1987, Monitoring and Reporting Procedures for Ranching Operations); Res. Conf. 6.23 (1987, Guidelines for Evaluating Marine Turtle Ranching Proposals); Res. Conf. 7.11 (1989, Trade in Ranched Specimens Between Parties, Non-Parties and Reserving Parties); Res. Conf. 8.11 (1992, Stocks of Hair and Cloth of Vicuna); Res. Conf. 8.15 (1992, Guidelines for a Procedure to Register and Monitor Operations Breeding Appendix I Animal Species for Commercial Purposes); Res. Conf. 8.22 (1992, Additional Criteria for the Establishment of Captive-Breeding Operations and for the Assessment of Ranching Proposals for Crocodilians); Res. Conf. 11.16 (2000, Ranching and Trade in Ranched Specimens of Species Transferred from Appendix I to Appendix II).

[79] See Res. Conf. 9.21 (1994, The Interpretation and Application of Quotas for Species Included in Appendix I).

[80] Res. Conf. 10.14 (1997, Quotas for Leopard Hunting Trophies and Skins for Personal Use).

governs trade in markhor hunting trophies. Resolution 10.15 allows an export quota of six hunting trophies of markhor (*Capra falconeri*) from Pakistan per calendar year.

Two further quota systems are specified in the Appendices themselves: trade in ivory from African elephants, which does not currently apply following the listing of the African elephant on Appendix I at the 1989 conference of the parties,[81] and trade in the African spurred tortoise (*Geochelone sulcata*). The final type of quota system will be applicable in accordance with Resolution 9.24 of the conference of the parties. This states that in certain circumstances the transfer of taxa from Appendix I to Appendix II may be allowed even where there is uncertainty over the status or impact of trade on a species if an integral part of the amendment proposal is an export quota approved by the conference of the parties based on management measures described in the amendment proposal, and provided effective enforcement controls are in place. The resolution additionally makes provision for review procedures which, in the event of non-compliance with a quota, may result in a recommendation by the Standing Committee for all parties to suspend trade with the party concerned in specimens of the species.[82]

Export quotas may also be set by each party individually provided that the Scientific Authority of the state has advised that the proposed export would not be detrimental to the survival of the species. A party setting its own national export quotas for CITES species should inform the Secretariat,[83] which in turn informs the other parties through notifications, and by listing the quotas on the Secretariat's website.[84]

Enforcement

The enforcement provisions of CITES are relatively detailed compared to many other environmental treaties. All parties must take appropriate measures to enforce the Convention and prohibit trade in specimens in violation of its provisions, including by penalising trade and possession, and providing for confiscation or return to the state of export.[85] The conference of the parties has adopted various resolutions aimed at improving compliance.[86] In 2000, the conference of the parties urged the parties, intergovernmental organisations and NGOs to provide additional financial support for the enforcement of the Convention, and directed the Secretariat to utilise such funds towards the following priorities:

---

[81] Wijnsteker, *The Evolution of CITES*, 208–25.   [82] Res. Conf. 9.24 (1994), Annex 4.

[83] Res. Conf. 10.2 (1997, Permits and Certificates).

[84] See the list of national export quotas maintained on the CITES Secretariat website at www.cites.org.

[85] Art. VIII(1).

[86] Res. Conf. 3.9 (1981, International Compliance Control); Res. Conf. 6.3 (1987, Implementation of CITES); Res. Conf. 8.4 (1992, National Laws for Implementation of the Convention).

1. the appointment of additional officers to the Secretariat to work on enforcement-related matters;
2. assistance in the development and implementation of regional law-enforcement agreements; and
3. training and technical assistance to the parties.

The Secretariat was also directed to pursue closer international liaison between the Convention's institutions, national enforcement agencies, and existing intergovernmental bodies, particularly the World Customs Organization and ICPO-Interpol.[87] Resolutions have also been adopted to improve enforcement and compliance by targeted countries and regions.[88] CITES also provides for the communication of information on the adverse effects of trade on species or the non-implementation of the Convention, which envisages a role for the Secretariat.[89]

1992 Convention on Biological Diversity

M. A. Hermitte, 'La Convention sur la Diversité Biologique', AFDI 844 (1992); C. Shine and P. T. B. Kohona, 'The Convention on Biological Diversity: Bridging the Gap Between Conservation and Development', 1 RECIEL 307 (1992); F. Burhenne-Guilmin and S. Casey-Lefkowitz, 'The Convention on Biological Diversity: A Hard Won Global Achievement', 3 *Yearbook of International Environmental Law* 43 (1992); M. Chandler, 'The Biodiversity Convention: Selected Issues of Interest to the International Lawyer', 4 *Colorado Journal of International Law and Policy* 141 (1993); M. Coughlin, 'Using the Merck-INBio Agreement to Clarify the Convention on Biological Diversity', 31 *Columbia Journal of Transnational Law* 337 (1993); F. McConnell, *The Biodiversity Convention: A Negotiating History* (1996); V. Koester, 'The Biodiversity Convention Negotiating Process and Some Comments on the Outcome', 27 *Environmental Policy and Law* 175 (1997); A. Ansari and J. Parveen, 'The Convention on Biological Diversity: A Critical Appraisal with Special Reference to Malaysia', 40 *Indiana Journal of International Law* 14 (2000); Secretariat of the Convention on Biological Diversity, *Handbook of the Convention on Biological Diversity* (2001); 'International Biodiversity Law', 11 RECIEL Issue 1 (2002) (special issue).

The 1992 Convention on Biological Diversity (1992 Biodiversity Convention) was negotiated under the auspices of UNEP and signed by 153 states and the EC at UNCED in June 1992.[90] It goes beyond CITES by establishing objectives for

---

[87] Res. Conf. 11.3 (2000, Compliance and Enforcement).
[88] Res. Conf. 6.4 (1987, Implementation of the Convention in Bolivia); Res. Conf. 11.9 (2000, Conservation of and Trade in Freshwater Turtles and Tortoises in Asia and Other Regions).
[89] Art. XIII.
[90] Rio de Janeiro, 5 June 1992, in force 29 December 1993, 31 ILM 822 (1992). As at 1 April 2003, the Convention had 187 parties; (www.biodiv.org).

the comprehensive preservation of biological diversity, reflecting objectives of the 1980 World Conservation Strategy. In 1984, IUCN prepared principles for the conservation of wild genetic resources. Three years later, IUCN submitted draft legal articles on a proposed convention to a UNEP Ad Hoc Working Group of Experts on Biological Diversity, and the following year, in 1988, the seventeenth General Assembly of the IUCN endorsed the proposal for a convention on biological diversity. At this early stage, the IUCN draft had been concerned solely with conservation and financing mechanisms, and it was the UNEP Governing Council decision to press ahead with a convention, and establish a Working Group of Legal and Technical Experts which led to a broadening of the Convention's scope. The Working Group was renamed the Intergovernmental Negotiating Committee and, as such, it met seven times in 1991 and 1992 when the text of the Convention was finalised. The Convention has three objectives:

> the conservation of biological diversity, the sustainable use of its components and the fair and equitable sharing of the benefits arising out of the utilisation of genetic resources, including by appropriate access to genetic resources and by appropriate transfer of relevant technologies, taking into account all rights over those resources and to technologies, and by appropriate funding.[91]

It establishes basic rules and provides a framework for the adoption of Protocols and Annexes, and does not allow reservations.[92] For some developed countries, the Convention's provisions are problematic because they go beyond conservation and provide rules on the sustainable use of genetic resources and on the use of biotechnology. It is the latter two issues, together with the rules on financial resources, which led the United States, alone among the industrialised nations, to decide against signing the Convention at UNCED.[93]

Preamble and jurisdictional scope

The Preamble to the Biodiversity Convention affirms that the conservation of biological diversity is 'a common concern of humankind', that states have 'sovereign rights over their own biological resources', and that they are 'responsible for conserving their biological diversity and for using their

---

[91] Art. 1; on the potential application of this provision, see Case C-377/98, *Netherlands* v. *European Parliament and EU Council* [2001] ECR I-7079, paras. 57–8; and chapter 20, p. 1034 below. 'Biological diversity' is defined in Art. 2 as 'the variability among living organisms from all sources including, *inter alia*, terrestrial, marine and other aquatic ecosystems and the ecological complexes of which they are part; this includes diversity within species, between species and of ecosystems'.

[92] Arts. 28–30 and 37.

[93] US Declaration made at the UNEP Conference for the Adoption of the Agreed Text of the Convention on Biological Diversity, 22 May 1992, 21 ILM 848 (1992). On 4 June 1993, the US signed the Convention but is yet to ratify it.

biological resources in a sustainable manner'. Without expressly endorsing the precautionary approach, the Preamble provides that measures should not be avoided or postponed where there is a lack of full scientific certainty, and that biodiversity should be conserved and sustainably used for the benefit of present and future generations. The Convention is the first to incorporate Principle 21 of the Stockholm Declaration into the operational part of its text rather than merely the preambular section.[94]

With regard to components of biodiversity, the Convention applies within the limits of national jurisdiction.[95] For processes and activities carried out under the jurisdiction or control of a party, however, the Convention applies within areas of national jurisdiction or beyond the limits of national jurisdiction, regardless of where the effects of such processes and activities occur.[96]

Conservation and sustainable use

The Convention includes several commitments of a general nature. Under Article 5, all parties must co-operate for the conservation and sustainable use of biodiversity, in respect of areas beyond national jurisdiction and on other matters of mutual interest.[97] Parties must develop national strategies, plans or programmes for the conservation and sustainable use of biodiversity, or adapt existing strategies, plans or programmes, and integrate, wherever possible and appropriate, the conservation and sustainable use of biodiversity into relevant sectoral or cross-sectoral plans, programmes and policies.[98]

Each party is required, as far as possible, to adopt the following more specific measures: to identify components of biodiversity important for conservation and sustainable use; to monitor these components while paying particular attention to those requiring urgent conservation measures and those which offer the greatest potential for sustainable use; and to identify, and monitor the effects, processes and categories of activities which have or are likely to have significant adverse impacts on the conservation and sustainable use of biodiversity.[99] Where a significant adverse effect has been determined, the processes or activities must be regulated or managed. For these purposes, Annex I sets forth the following indicative list of categories of ecosystems or habitats for identification and monitoring:

- those containing high diversity, large numbers of endemic or threatened species, or wilderness;
- those required by migratory species;
- those of social, economic, cultural or scientific importance; and
- those which are representative, unique or associated with key evolutionary or other biological processes.

---

[94] Art. 3; see further chapter 6 above.   [95] Art. 4(a).   [96] Art. 4(b).
[97] Art. 5. For the definition of 'substainable use' in Art. 2, see chapter 6, pp. 257–61 above.
[98] Art. 6.   [99] Art. 7.

Species and communities to be identified and monitored are:

- threatened, wild relatives of domesticated or cultivated species;
- those of medicinal, agricultural or other economic value, or of social, scientific or cultural importance; and
- those of importance for research into the conservation and sustainable use of biological diversity.

Annex I requires described genome and genes of social, scientific or economic importance to be identified and monitored. The Convention also includes general obligations on research and training, public education and awareness, the exchange of information, and technical and scientific co-operation.[100]

More detailed rules exist for *in situ* and *ex situ* conservation. *In situ* conservation envisages a range of measures.[101] First, each party undertakes, as far as possible and as appropriate, to establish a system of protected areas or areas where special measures are needed, and to develop guidelines for the selection, establishment and management of such areas.[102] Secondly, biological resources important for the conservation of biological diversity must be regulated or managed, and the protection of ecosystems, natural habitats and the maintenance of viable populations must be promoted.[103] Thirdly, parties must establish or maintain the means to regulate, manage or control risks associated with the use and release of living modified organisms resulting from biotechnology which are likely to have adverse environmental impacts, and to prevent the introduction of or to control or eradicate alien species which threaten ecosystems, habitats or species.[104] Subject to national legislation, each party undertakes to respect, preserve and maintain knowledge, innovations and practices of indigenous and local communities embodying traditional lifestyles.[105]

Ex situ conservation is predominantly complementary to *in situ* conservation.[106] Each party must take measures which will conserve components of biological diversity; establish and maintain facilities for conservation of and research on plants, animals and micro-organisms; and ensure the recovery and rehabilitation of threatened species and their reintroduction into natural

---

[100] Arts. 12, 13, 17 and 18.

[101] '*In situ* conservation' is defined in Art. 2 as 'the conservation of ecosystems and natural habitats and the maintenance and recovery of viable populations of species in their natural surroundings and, in the case of domesticated or cultivated species, in the surroundings where they have developed their distinctive properties'.

[102] Art. 8(a) and (b).   [103] Art. 8(c) and (d).   [104] Art. 8(g) and (h).

[105] Art. 8(j). In May 1998, the Fourth Conference of the Parties established an *ad hoc* working group on Art. 8(j) to provide advice on forms of protection for traditional knowledge and to develop a programme of work for implementation at the national and international level (see Decision IV/9, para. 1). The working group held its first meeting in Seville, Spain, on 27–31 March 2000.

[106] '*Ex situ* conservation' is defined in Art. 2 as 'the conservation of components of biological diversity outside their natural habitats'.

habitats under appropriate conditions.[107] The earlier proposal to include a global list of species important for conservation and sustainable use was dropped following opposition from developing countries.

The Convention requires components of biodiversity to be used sustainably, the carrying out of environment impact assessment of proposed projects likely to have significant adverse effects, and ensuring the minimisation of adverse impacts.[108] The Convention provides for notification, exchange of information and consultation on activities likely to have a significant adverse effect on the biological diversity of other states or areas beyond national jurisdiction. Notification is required in cases of imminent or grave danger or damage, and emergency responses must be promoted for activities or events which present a grave and imminent danger to biodiversity.[109] Under Article 14(2), the conference of the parties will examine the development of rules on liability and redress, for damage to biological diversity, including restoration and compensation.

Access to genetic resources and transfer of technology

The Convention includes new international rules on access to genetic resources, access to and transfer of technology, and the handling of biotechnology and the distribution of its benefits. These are controversial to the extent that they are perceived by some countries to threaten the stability of existing intellectual and other property rights. Article 15 seeks to ensure access to genetic resources which have been provided by parties that are the countries of origin or by parties that have acquired the genetic resources in accordance with the Convention,[110] although the Convention states that the authority to determine such access rests with national governments and is subject to national legislation.[111] Each party is to facilitate such access for environmentally sound uses by other parties, and must not impose restrictions which run counter to the Convention's objectives.[112] Where access is granted, it will be on mutually agreed terms and subject to Article 15, the party seeking access having received the prior informed consent of the party providing the resources unless otherwise determined by that party.[113] Moreover, each party is to carry out scientific research based on genetic resources provided by another party with the full participation of, and where possible in the territory of, such party.[114] Finally, and to the dismay of

---

[107] Art. 9(a), (b) and (c).   [108] Arts. 10 and 14.   [109] Art. 14(1)(c) to (e).
[110] Art. 15, especially paras. (1) and (3). 'Genetic resources' means 'genetic material of actual or potential value', and 'genetic material' means 'any material of plant, animal, microbial or other origin containing functional units of heredity': Art. 2. 'Country of origin of genetic resources' means 'the country which possesses those genetic resources in *in situ* conditions', and 'country providing genetic resources' means 'the country supplying genetic resources collected from *in situ* sources, including populations of both wild and domesticated species, or taken from *ex situ* sources, which may or may not have originated in that country': *ibid.*
[111] Art. 15(1).   [112] Art. 15(2).   [113] Art. 15(4) and (5).   [114] Art. 15(6).

the United States and other developed countries, each party is to take measures, as appropriate,

> with the aim of sharing in a fair and equitable way the results of research and development and the benefits arising from the commercial and other utilisation of genetic resources with the contracting party providing such resources. Such sharing shall be upon mutually agreed terms.[115]

These provisions are seen to allow possible claims being made on the financial profits arising from the exploitation and development of resources by companies based in developed country parties. The Director of the International Board for Plant Genetic Resources has expressed the concern clearly: 'One interpretation of the Convention is that a research centre would have to get permission from the countries of origin before it distributes materials.' Some crop varieties may have twenty or more different 'parents' in plants from twenty or more different countries, which would require the permission of all the countries of origin before the materials could be distributed.[116] In 2002, the sixth conference of the parties adopted the 'Bonn Guidelines on Access to Genetic Resources and Fair and Equitable Sharing of the Benefits Arising out of their Utilization, Access and Benefit Sharing', which are intended to assist parties in developing an overall access and benefit-sharing strategy, which may be part of their national biodiversity strategy and action plan, and in identifying the steps involved in the process of obtaining access to genetic resources and sharing benefits.[117] To that end, the Bonn Guidelines address the following elements as relevant to access to genetic resources and benefit-sharing:

- roles and responsibilities in access and benefit-sharing (paras. 13–16);
- participation of stakeholders (paras. 17–21);
- steps in the access and benefit-sharing process, including in relation to prior informed consent and mutually agreed terms (including in relation to benefit-sharing) (paras. 22–50);[118] and
- other provisions, including in relation to incentives, accountability, monitoring, verification and settlement of disputes (paras. 51–61).

Article 16 establishes rules on access for and transfer between parties of technologies, including biotechnologies, relevant to the conservation and sustainable use of biodiversity or which make use of genetic resources and do not cause significant damage to the environment, in accordance with the financial mechanism where necessary. Access and transfer of technology is to be on 'fair

---

[115] Art. 15(7).
[116] J. Madeley, 'Summit Hitch for Plant Breeders', *Financial Times*, 30 June 1992, 58.
[117] Decision VI/24, para. 12.
[118] The Guidelines include Appendices on Suggested Elements for Material Transfer Agreements (Appendix 1) and Monetary and Non-Monetary Benefits (Appendix 2).

and most favourable terms': where technology is subject to patent and other intellectual property rights, access and transfer are to be provided on terms which recognise and are consistent with the adequate and effective protection of intellectual property rights.[119] Under Article 16(3), parties are required to take measures to give those parties which provide genetic resources, particularly developing countries, access to technology (including technologies protected by patent and other intellectual property rights) which makes use of those resources, on mutually agreed terms and in accordance with international law. Additional measures will be required to ensure that parties' private sectors facilitate access to, joint development of, and transfer of these technologies for the benefit of governmental institutions and the private sectors of developing countries.[120] They must co-operate, subject to national legislation and international law, to ensure that patents and other intellectual property rights 'are supportive of and do not run counter to' the objectives of the Convention.[121] Regarding the relationship between the Convention and other international conventions, including those relating to patents and other intellectual property rights, the Convention

> shall not affect the rights and obligations of any contracting party deriving from any existing international agreement, except where the exercise of those rights and obligations would cause a serious damage or threat to biological diversity.[122]

The language used is sufficiently broad to allow an interpretation that the Convention could, in certain circumstances, prevail over patent and intellectual property rights protected by other international agreements.[123]

The Convention additionally provides for the exchange of information between parties, including repatriation of information, technical and scientific co-operation, personnel training and exchange, joint research programmes and joint ventures, and a clearing-house mechanism to promote co-operation.[124]

Biotechnology

Among the 1992 Biodiversity Convention's most controversial provisions were those of Article 19 on the handling of biotechnology and the distribution of its benefits. This was the first attempt by the international community to legislate international rules on biotechnology at the global level.[125] Each party must provide for the effective participation in biotechnological research activities by parties which provide the genetic resources, especially developing countries.[126] Each party must

---

[119] Art. 16(2).   [120] Art. 16(4).   [121] Art. 16(5).   [122] Art. 22(1).
[123] Chapter 20, pp. 1045–6 below.   [124] Arts. 16(3), 17 and 18.
[125] Chapter 12, pp. 625–37 below.   [126] Art. 19(1).

take all practicable measures to promote and advance priority access on a fair and equitable basis by contracting parties, especially developing countries, to the results and benefits arising from biotechnologies based upon genetic resources provided by those contracting parties. Such access shall be on mutually agreed terms.[127]

The Convention did not include detailed rules on genetically modified organisms, other than the requirement for each party to provide, to the party 'into which' such organisms are to be introduced, any available information on the use and safety regulations it requires in handling such organisms, and on the potential adverse impact of the specific organism concerned.[128] However, Article 19(3) committed the parties to

> consider the need for and modalities of a protocol setting out appropriate procedures, including, in particular, advance informed agreement, in the field of the safe transfer, handling and use of any living modified organism resulting from biotechnology that may have adverse effect on the conservation and sustainable use of biological diversity.

At its second meeting in November 1995, the conference of the parties to the Convention decided to establish an Open-Ended Ad Hoc Working Group on Biosafety (BSWG) to draft a protocol on biosafety, focusing specifically on the transboundary movement of living modified organisms resulting from modern biotechnology with potentially adverse effects on the conservation and sustainable use of biological diversity.[129] The BSWG held six meetings between July 1996 and February 1999 before submitting a draft negotiating text to the conference of the parties.[130] The draft text formed the basis for negotiations at the first extraordinary conference of the parties (ExCOP), convened for the purpose of adopting a protocol on biosafety, and held in Cartagena, Colombia, in February 1999. However, a number of aspects of the draft text proved controversial – notably the scope of application of the protocol, the inclusion of the precautionary principle, risk assessment and risk management procedures, requirements for documentation and labelling, the effect of the protocol on parties' trade obligations under the GATT/WTO and provision for liability and redress. As a result, the ExCOP was unable to finalise the text of a protocol at its Cartagena session but agreed to suspend negotiations and reconvene no later than the fifth conference of the parties.[131] The resumed ExCOP was held in Montreal on 24–29 January 2000. After a week of intense negotiations which saw the parties split into a series of negotiating groups,[132] the ExCOP adopted

---

[127] Art. 19(2).   [128] Art. 19(4).   [129] Decision II/5.

[130] Open-Ended Working Group on Biosafety, Draft Negotiating Text, UNEP/CBD/BSWG/6/2, 18 November 1998.

[131] Decision EM-I/1.

[132] The negotiating groups included the Miami group of agricultural nations with a large investment in biotechnology led by the United States, the European Union, and the Like-Minded Group of Developing Countries.

a final text of the Cartagena Protocol on Biosafety on 29 January 2000.[133] An Intergovernmental Committee for the Cartagena Protocol on Biosafety (ICCP) was established at the same time, with a mandate to undertake the necessary preparations prior to the first meeting of the parties to the Protocol. To date, the ICCP has held two meetings, in December 2000 and October 2001.

Financial resources and mechanism

Articles 20 and 21 provide for the allocation of financial resources and establish a financial mechanism to provide new and additional financial resources to enable developing country parties to meet the agreed full incremental costs to them of implementing the Convention.[134]

Institutions and other mechanisms

The institutional arrangements to oversee implementation of the Convention comprise the conference of the parties, which keeps the implementation of the Convention under review;[135] a Subsidiary Body on Scientific, Technical and Technological Advice, to provide scientific, technical and technological advice to the conference of the parties;[136] various working groups established on an *ad hoc* basis; and a secretariat.[137] The Convention provides for settlement of disputes concerning the interpretation or application of the Convention according to traditional means, including negotiation, the use of good offices, mediation and an Annex on submission to the International Court of Justice or arbitration and conciliation.[138]

The Convention is the principal framework within which the development and implementation of rules on biodiversity conservation now occurs. The relationship of the Biodiversity Convention to other global instruments, including in particular CITES, as well as regional instruments, remains unclear.

General instruments of regional and sub-regional application

The second category of biodiversity conservation rules are those adopted at the regional level which are, broadly speaking, of potential application to all species in the given region. The regional approach has been justified as allowing the environmental needs and concerns of different regions to be addressed. It also seeks to ensure that the powers attached to the responsibility for managing international environmental affairs are devolved to the most appropriate level of governance, whether at the regional, sub-regional or bilateral level.

The earliest regional agreement was the 1900 London Convention and the most recent the 1999 SADC Protocol on Wildlife Conservation and Law

---

[133] 39 ILM 1027 (2000); see chapter 12, pp. 653–8 below.
[134] Chapter 20, pp. 1032–6 below.   [135] Art. 23.   [136] Art. 25.
[137] Art. 24. Between entry into force of the Convention and the first meeting of the conference of the parties, the secretariat was provided by the Executive Director of UNEP: Art. 40.
[138] Art. 27 and Annex II.

Enforcement. In the intervening period, regional arrangements (in roughly chronological order) have been adopted for parts of Africa, the Americas and the Caribbean, the South Pacific, Europe, and south-east Asia. The agreements governing the Antarctic region, and the emerging principles applicable to the Arctic, are considered in chapter 14 below.

Africa[139]

Flora and fauna on the African continent were the subject of the earliest nature conservation agreements, adopted by colonial powers in the first part of the twentieth century. The first treaty was the 1900 London Convention for the Protection of Wild Animals, Birds and Fish in Africa,[140] which was adopted by the colonial powers of the region (Great Britain, Italy, Portugal, Spain and France) to 'prevent the uncontrolled massacre and to ensure the conservation of diverse wild animal species in their African possessions which are useful to man or inoffensive'.[141] The 1900 Convention was replaced by the 1933 London Convention Relative to the Preservation of Flora and Fauna in Their Natural State.[142] Both agreements included provisions and techniques for international conservation that are still found in modern treaties, including a system of annexes to list protected species, and the use of trade regulations as an instrument of environmental protection. The 1933 Convention required parties to take all necessary measures within their power to ensure 'a sufficient degree of forest country and the preservation of the best native indigenous forest species',[143] and recognised a link between conservation and economic development, although the emphasis was on encouraging 'the domestication of wild animals susceptible of economic utilisation'.[144]

1968 African Nature Convention

The 1933 Convention was superseded in 1968 with the adoption of the African Convention on the Conservation of Nature and Natural Resources (1968 African Nature Convention), which was negotiated under the auspices of the Organization of African Unity (OAU) by the governments of newly independent African states.[145] The Convention includes broad objectives; except for atmospheric protection, the Convention applies to all environmental media, committing parties to a comprehensive approach including research,

---

[139] See also Agreement on Joint Regulations on Fauna and Flora (Enugu, 3 December 1977) (Lake Chad); Protocol Agreement on the Conservation of Coma Natural Resources (Khartoum, 24 January 1982) (Sudan, Uganda, Zaire).

[140] London, 19 May 1900, 4 IPE 1607.

[141] Preamble; cited in S. Lyster, *International Wildlife Law* (1985), 112.

[142] London, 8 November 1933, in force 14 January 1936, 172 LNTS 241.

[143] Art. 7(4).   [144] Art. 7(4) and (8).

[145] Algiers, 15 September 1968, in force 16 June 1969, 1001 UNTS 3.

conservation education, development plans, and national conservation services.[146] It requires parties to take measures which are reconcilable with customary rights 'to ensure conservation, utilisation and development of soil, water, flora and faunal resources in accordance with scientific principles and with due regard to the best interests of the people'.[147]

The 1968 Convention is one of the few environmental treaties with provisions for the protection of soil from erosion and misuse through the development of land-use plans, and agricultural practices and agrarian reforms which ensure long-term productivity.[148] It promotes water conservation policies and protection of flora by scientifically-based conservation measures which take into account social and economic needs.[149] The Convention subjects fauna to 'conservation, wise use and development . . . within the framework of land-use planning and of economic and social development', and to that end wildlife populations must be managed in designated areas with the aim of achieving an 'optimum sustainable yield'.[150] Hunting, capture and fishing are subject to the grant of properly regulated permits, and certain methods are prohibited.[151]

The 1968 Convention, like its predecessor, makes use of an annex system to protect endangered species. Class A species are totally protected throughout the territory of the party, while Class B species may be hunted, killed, captured or collected under special authorisation granted by the competent national authority.[152] Parties may add additional species to Class A or B according to their own specific requirements.[153] Like its predecessor, the 1968 Convention regulates trade in listed and unlisted species, in particular by making export of the former subject to authorisation, and import and transit subject to presentation of the export authorisation.[154] The Convention lacks any institutional arrangements for its implementation, a feature which has contributed to its limited effectiveness. In 1985, the OAU convened a meeting to discuss possible revision of the Convention, and, although draft amendments were prepared with the assistance of IUCN, they were never formally adopted.

At a ministerial meeting in September 1994, the governments of seven African states adopted the Lusaka Agreement on Co-operative Enforcement Operations Directed at Illegal Trade in Wild Fauna and Flora.[155] The objective of the Agreement is to reduce and ultimately eliminate illegal trade in wild fauna and flora within the territories of the states parties.[156] Article 5 of the Agreement provides for the establishment of a Task Force for Co-operative

---

[146] Arts. XII to XV.

[147] Arts. II and XI. Art. XVII allows certain exceptions to the Convention, including the 'paramount interest of the state', *force majeure* and defence of human life.

[148] Art. IV.   [149] Arts. V and VI.   [150] Art. VII(1).   [151] Art. VII(2).

[152] Art. VIII(1) and Annex.   [153] Art. VIII(2).   [154] Art. IX.

[155] Lusaka, 8 September 1994, in force 10 December 1996, UNEP Doc. No. 94/7929; six states are party.

[156] Art. 2.

Enforcement Operations Directed at Illegal Trade in Wild Fauna and Flora, which is composed of a Director, Field Officers and an Intelligence Officer. The Director and Field Officers are drawn from national law enforcement authorities and liaise with 'National Bureaus' in each of the member states to co-ordinate enforcement operations directed at illegal wildlife trade.[157] The functions of the Task Force include facilitating co-operative activities among the National Bureaus in carrying out investigations pertaining to illegal trade; investigating violations of national laws pertaining to illegal trade at the request of the National Bureaus or with the consent of the parties concerned; collecting, processing and disseminating information on activities that pertain to illegal trade, including establishing and maintaining databases; and providing, upon request of the parties concerned, information related to the return to the country of original export, or country of re-export, of confiscated wild fauna and flora.[158] The Task Force (or 'regional Interpol' as it is sometimes referred to) was officially launched and commenced operational activities on 1 June 1999. The operations of the Task Force are overseen by a Governing Council composed of representatives from each of the parties.[159]

1985 Nairobi SPA Protocol

In 1985, the Protocol Concerning Protected Areas and Wild Fauna and Flora in the Eastern African Region (1985 Nairobi SPA Protocol) was adopted as a Protocol to the 1985 Nairobi Convention.[160] It establishes sub-regional arrangements for the conservation of flora and fauna in Eastern Africa and commits parties to 'take all appropriate measures to maintain essential ecological processes and life support systems, to preserve genetic diversity, and to ensure the sustainable utilisation of harvested natural resources under their jurisdiction'.[161]

The 1985 Nairobi SPA Protocol goes beyond the 1968 African Nature Convention. It requires parties to protect and preserve rare or fragile ecosystems, and to develop national conservation strategies within the framework of regional conservation activities, while taking into account the traditional activities of local populations.[162] The Protocol has four Annexes establishing more detailed commitments. Parties undertake to 'take all appropriate measures' to ensure the protection of the wild flora species listed in Annex I, to ensure 'the strictest protection' of the endangered wild fauna species listed in Annex II, to ensure the protection of the depleted or threatened wild fauna species listed in Annex III, and to co-ordinate their efforts for the protection of migratory species listed in Annex IV.[163] The 1985 Protocol also includes: general rules on the introduction of alien or new species; the establishment of protected areas and the adoption

---

[157] Art. 6.   [158] Art. 5(9).   [159] Art. 7.

[160] Nairobi, 21 June 1985, not yet in force, IELMT 985:47; on the 1985 Nairobi Convention, see chapter 9, pp. 404–5 above.

[161] Art. 2(1).   [162] Arts. 2(1) and (2) and 12.   [163] Arts. 3–6.

of measures and common guidelines, standards or criteria for those areas; the establishment of buffer areas to strengthen the protection of protected areas; and rules on consultation for frontier protected areas, publicity and notification, public information and education, and the exchange of information.[164] One aspect of the Protocol is particularly significant. It is the first biodiversity conservation agreement in Africa to create an institutional authority: meetings of the parties to the Protocol, which are mandated to review implementation of the Protocol, examine the need for further measures, and adopt amendments to the Annexes.[165] In practice, these take place bi-annually.

1999 SADC Protocol on Wildlife Conservation and Law Enforcement

More recently, in August 1999, the Wildlife Conservation and Law Enforcement Protocol to the Treaty establishing the Southern African Development Community (SADC) was signed by the Heads of State and Government in Maputo, Mozambique.[166] The Protocol seeks to establish common approaches to the conservation and sustainable use of wildlife resources in the SADC region and makes provision for collaboration between member states to achieve the objectives of international agreements concerning the conservation and sustainable use of wildlife. The Protocol also places an obligation on parties to ensure that activities within their borders do not cause damage to the wildlife resources of other states or areas beyond the limits of national jurisdiction. The Protocol will come into force once it is ratified by two-thirds of the SADC member states.

The Americas and the Caribbean

The region of the Americas and the Caribbean is the subject of three regional and sub-regional agreements: the 1940 Western Hemisphere Convention; the 1978 Amazonian Treaty; and the 1990 Kingston Protocol. Several bilateral agreements have also been adopted which include general provisions on flora and fauna.[167]

1940 Western Hemisphere Convention

The 1940 Convention on Nature Protection and Wildlife Preservation in the Western Hemisphere (1940 Western Hemisphere Convention), negotiated under the auspices of the Pan-American Union (now the Organization

---

[164] Arts. 7–18.   [165] Art. 21.

[166] Maputo, 18 August 1999, not yet in force; see www.sadc.int/english/protocols/ p_wildlife_conservation_and_law_enforcement.html.

[167] See also the Convention for the Conservation of the Biodiversity and the Protection of Wilderness Areas in Central America, Managua, 5 June 1992, not yet in force.

of American States (OAS)), was in many respects a visionary agreement.[168] The primary objectives of the Convention are to:

> protect and preserve in their natural habitat representatives of all species and genera of their native flora and fauna, including migratory birds, in sufficient numbers and over areas extensive enough to assure them from becoming extinct through any agency within man's control . . .[169]

The nineteen parties to the Convention, which is only open to member states of the OAS, agree to explore the possibility of establishing national parks, national reserves, nature monuments and strict wilderness reserves as defined by the Convention.[170] National parks are absolutely protected against exploitation for commercial profit, and there is to be no hunting, killing or capturing of fauna or collecting of flora in national parks except by or under the direction or control of the park authorities, or for authorised scientific investigations.[171] Strict wilderness reserves are to be maintained, as far as practicable, 'inviolate' except for authorised scientific investigations or other uses consistent with the purposes for which the area was established.[172]

The Western Hemisphere Convention also requires parties to protect and preserve all other flora and fauna, to engage in scientific co-operation, to protect migratory birds, and to protect species listed in the single Annex to the Convention 'as completely as possible'.[173] The Convention has general provisions establishing trade restrictions: the import, export and transit of protected fauna and flora is to be controlled and regulated by the issuing of export and transit authorisation certificates.[174] The great weakness of the Convention is the absence of any institutions to oversee and ensure its implementation. In 1979, a group of experts convened by the Secretary General of the OAS considered the possibility of amending the Convention, and proposed the adoption of a new rule requiring other parties to take account of certain fundamental criteria: stability and diversity of ecology, biological productivity, continuous long-term production of renewable natural resources, protection of soil and of hydrographic and marine ecology, integrated rural development, and continuous research and surveillance. The expert group also proposed the establishment of an institutional mechanism and improved procedures to regulate international trade. More recently, the Inter-American Judicial Committee of the OAS has considered using the Convention as the basis for an Inter-American system for nature conservation. In the meantime, the Convention has less practical effect

---

[168] Washington, 12 October 1940, in force 1 May 1942, 161 UNTS 193; nineteen states are party.
[169] Preamble.   [170] Art. II(1).   [171] Art. III.   [172] Art. IV.
[173] Arts. V to VIII. The Annex comprises a compilation of the national lists of the parties, rather than an agreed list of general application, and has not been revised since 1967.
[174] Art. IX.

than ought to be the case, and has been virtually ignored in respect of certain road-building and oil exploration activities recently carried out.

1978 Amazonian Treaty

The conservation of biodiversity is an important secondary, but not primary, objective of the 1978 Treaty for Amazonian Co-operation.[175] Its primary objective is to promote the harmonious development of the parties' Amazonian territories; the secondary objective is to ensure that these joint actions produce equitable and mutually beneficial results 'and achieve also the preservation of the environment, and the conservation and rational utilisation of the natural resources of those territories'.[176] The 1978 Amazonian Treaty is mainly concerned with economic development, as reflected in the language stating that the use of natural resources is 'a right inherent in the sovereignty of each state' which may only be restricted by international law.[177] This provision reflects the concern that evidently existed, even at this early period in the development of international environmental law, about interference from countries outside the region seeking to influence future development in the Amazon forest. The 1978 Treaty is silent as to the limitations which might be established by international law on environmental grounds. Measures of environmental protection required under the Treaty, which are designed to maintain the 'ecological balance' of the region and to preserve species in the context of rationally planned exploitation of flora and fauna, are limited simply to promoting scientific research and exchanging information.[178] The Treaty's institutional arrangements comprise *ad hoc* meetings of the parties' Ministers of Foreign Affairs, annual meetings of the Amazonian Co-operation Council, a secretariat, Permanent National Commissions, and Special Commissions which may be set up to study specific problems or matters.[179] The right of any state to exercise a veto on important questions is guaranteed: decisions taken by the Ministers or the Council are taken by unanimous vote of all parties, although decisions by the Special Commissions are adopted by unanimous vote only of those parties participating.[180]

In 1989, the parties to the Amazonian Treaty adopted the Amazon Declaration which reiterated support for the preservation of Amazonian resources for present and future generations and declared that the defence of the Amazonian environment was one of the essential objectives of the Treaty.[181] It provides little guidance, however, as to how that objective is to be attained, or what it means in practice. The emphasis is rather on linking environmental protection and economic development, especially by denouncing the burden of foreign debts owed by countries of the region. The Amazonian Declaration objects to conditionalities imposed in the allocation of international resources, and

---

[175] Brasilia, 3 July 1978, in force 2 February 1980, 17 ILM 1045 (1978); eight states are party.
[176] Art. I.   [177] Art. IV.   [178] Art. VII.   [179] Arts. XX to XXIV.   [180] Art. XXV.
[181] Manaus, Brazil, 6 May 1989, 28 ILM 1303 (1989).

emphasises the need for the concerns of the north over the Amazon region to be translated into financial and technological support and assistance.

The 1990 Kingston SPA Protocol

The 1990 Kingston Protocol Concerning Specially Protected Areas and Wildlife to the Cartagena de Indias Convention (1990 Kingston SPA Protocol) was adopted by the parties to the 1983 Cartagena Convention, and includes innovative provisions on nature conservation for several countries in the region.[182] It was signed by thirteen parties to the 1983 Convention, representing a range of developed and developing countries, including eight Caribbean islands and Central American states, Mexico, France, the Netherlands, the United Kingdom and the United States. The 1990 Protocol applies to the area included under the 1983 Convention (marine environment) *and* territorial waters and terrestrial areas.[183] It requires parties to protect, preserve and manage in a sustainable way areas requiring special protection and threatened or endangered species of flora and fauna.[184] To that end, the parties must regulate and prohibit activities having adverse effects on these areas, and manage species of flora and fauna so as to prevent them from becoming endangered or threatened.[185] Protected areas must be established to conserve and restore representative coastal and marine ecosystems and maintain long-term viability and biological and genetic diversity, habitats and associated ecosystems critical to the survival of endangered flora or fauna. The Protocol seeks to maintain the productivity of ecosystems and natural resources that provide benefits to local inhabitants, and areas of special value whose ecological and biological processes are essential to the functioning of the wider Caribbean ecosystems.[186] Protected areas will be subject to a range of protection measures and to a planning and management regime, and parties may create buffer zones.[187] Where the protected area or buffer zone is contiguous to an international boundary, there is to be consultation between the relevant states.[188]

The protection of wild flora and fauna requires parties to identify endangered or threatened species (including migratory species) and accord protected status to them by regulating and prohibiting activities having adverse effects on them or their habitats and ecosystems.[189] The 1990 Kingston SPA Protocol establishes varying degrees of protection for species listed in the Annexes, ranging from the absolute protection of flora listed in Annex I and fauna listed in Annex II,[190] to the regulated use of flora and fauna listed in Annex III.[191] The Protocol also regulates or prohibits the introduction of non-indigenous or genetically altered species, and provides for environmental impact assessment,

---

[182] Kingston, 18 January 1990, in force 18 June 2000, 1 *Yearbook of International Environmental Law* 441 (1990); nine states are party.
[183] Arts. 2(1) and 1(c).   [184] Art. 3(1).   [185] Art. 3(2).   [186] Art. 4.   [187] Art. 8.
[188] Art. 9.   [189] Art. 10.   [190] Art. 11(1)(a) and (b).   [191] Art. 11(1)(c).

the exemption of traditional activities, information and public awareness, research and assistance.[192] Implementation is through periodic reports to the meetings of the parties, and the establishment and adoption by the meetings of common guidelines and criteria formulated by a Scientific and Technical Advisory Committee.[193]

In June 1991, the conference of the parties to the Kingston SPA Protocol adopted three Annexes, listing 56 plant species, 116 animal taxa and all cetaceans for full protection. Annex III lists forty plants and thirty animal species, as well as corals.[194]

South Pacific

The states of the South Pacific region have adopted a number of treaties aimed at conserving and protecting their flora and fauna. Apart from the 1985 Rarotonga Treaty, which prohibits nuclear activities in the region,[195] the main regional instruments are the 1976 Convention on the Conservation of Nature in the South Pacific (1976 Apia Convention)[196] and the 1986 Noumea Convention.[197]

The Apia Convention, which has five parties, seeks to contribute to the 'maintenance of the capacity of the earth to produce essential renewable natural resources' and to safeguard 'representative samples of natural ecosystems, and . . . the heritage of wildlife and its habitat', while providing for 'customary use of areas and species in accordance with traditional cultural practices'.[198] Its approach to nature conservation is drawn from the earlier regional agreements for Africa and the Americas. Parties must establish 'protected areas' (national parks and national reserves) and co-operate in research and training and in developing programmes of education and public awareness.[199] The established size of the national parks may only be altered after the 'fullest examination', and they may only be exploited commercially after such examination.[200] Fauna and flora in national parks, including migratory species, are protected from 'unwise exploitation and other threats that may lead to their extinction'.[201] National reserves are, as far as practicable, to be maintained as 'inviolate'.[202] Each party establishes its own list of fauna and flora threatened with extinction, which it is to protect 'as completely as possible as a matter of special urgency and

---

[192] Arts. 12 to 18.   [193] Arts. 19 to 20.

[194] Annex V of the Report of the Meeting of the Ad Hoc Group of Experts for the Development of Annexes to the Protocol Concerning Specially Protected Areas and Wildlife in the Wider Caribbean Region, Martinique, 5–8 November 1990, UNEP(OCA)/CAR WG.4/4.

[195] See chapter 12, pp. 649–51 below.

[196] Apia, 12 June 1976, in force 28 June 1990; IELMT 976:45; five states are party.

[197] This addresses the conservation of living resources in the marine environment; see pp. 558–600 below.

[198] Preamble and Art. VI.   [199] Arts. II(1) and VII.   [200] Art. III(1) and (2).

[201] Arts. III(3) and V(1).   [202] Art. IV.

importance', and to carefully consider the introduction of new species.[203] The Apia Convention does not establish mechanisms for meetings of the parties, and the secretariat functions are now provided by the secretariat of the South Pacific Regional Environment Programme (SPREP).[204]

Overall co-ordination of nature conservation activities in the region now rests with SPREP, which was established as an autonomous regional organisation in 1993 under the Agreement Establishing the South Pacific Regional Environment Programme.[205] The organisation's Action Plan for 2001–4 identifies nature conservation as a 'Key Results Area', critical to achieving sustainable development in the region.[206] It sets out five focus areas for the 2001–4 period:

- conservation areas;
- ecosystem management;
- conservation of endangered species and control of invasive species;
- biosafety, access to genetic resources and intellectual property rights; and
- traditional resource management.[207]

Europe

Under the auspices of the Council of Europe and the EC, a number of treaties and other international agreements addressing the conservation of biological diversity have been adopted and implemented which establish general principles and rules. Treaties and other agreements addressing specific sectors, including migratory species and the expanding body of EC secondary legislation on biodiversity conservation, are considered subsequently in this chapter and in later chapters.[208]

1979 Berne Convention

The Berne Convention on the Conservation of European Wildlife and their Natural Habitats (1979 Berne Convention) was negotiated under the auspices of the Council of Europe.[209] Initially, the Convention had mostly developed

---

[203] Art. V(2) to (4).

[204] Art. VIII. They were originally provided by the South Pacific Commission.

[205] Apia, 16 June 1993, in force 31 August 1995, ATS No. 24, 1995; fourteen states are party.

[206] SPREP, *Action Plan for Managing the Environment of the Pacific Islands Region: 2001–2004* (2000).

[207] *Ibid.*, section 5.1.

[208] On EC rules other than those set out in this chapter, see chapter 15, pp. 779–83 below; on migratory species, see pp. 574–83 below.

[209] Berne, 19 September 1979, in force 1 June 1982, UKTS No. 56 (1982), Cmnd 8738. See generally the Explanatory Report Concerning the Convention on the Conservation of European Wildlife and Natural Habitats (Council of Europe, 1979), www.nature.coe.int/english/cadres/bern.htm. The Convention has forty-five parties.

country parties, including the EC,[210] but membership has since been expanded to Africa and Central and Eastern Europe. The Convention imposes mandatory obligations on parties which are clear and unequivocal and subject to a system of administration which has been created to promote and oversee the implementation of its provisions.[211] It has three objectives: to conserve wild flora and fauna and their habitats; to promote co-operation between states; and to give particular attention to endangered and vulnerable species, including endangered and vulnerable migratory species.[212] It applies to all species and their habitats, regardless of their scarcity, and is applicable to visiting migratory species that are not confined to Europe and to European species of flora and fauna found outside the European continent. To give effect to the objectives, the parties are required to take protective measures

> to maintain the population of wild flora and fauna at, or adapt it to, a level which corresponds in particular to ecological, scientific and cultural requirements while taking account of economic and recreational requirements and the needs of sub-species, varieties or forms at risk locally.[213]

More generally, parties must: promote national conservation policies; have regard to conservation in regional planning policies and pollution abatement; promote education and the dissemination of information; co-ordinate research; and encourage the re-introduction of species while strictly controlling the introduction of non-native species.[214]

The 1979 Berne Convention includes specific obligations. Parties must take special measures to ensure the conservation of habitats of wild flora and fauna species which are listed as strictly protected in Appendices I and II, and give 'special attention' to the protection of areas of importance to migratory species specified in Appendices II and III.[215] The deliberate picking, collecting, cutting or uprooting of species of wild flora listed in Appendix I is prohibited, and their possession or sale is prohibited.[216] The deliberate capture, keeping, killing, damage, destruction or disturbance of wild fauna species listed in Appendix II is also prohibited, as is the possession of and internal trade in these species or their parts.[217] Listed fauna species are to be protected, and their exploitation regulated to keep them out of danger. All indiscriminate means of capture and

---

[210] The Convention has attracted many reservations, which has led the Standing Committee to discourage such reservations (Recommendation No. 4 (1986)).

[211] S. Lyster, *International Wildlife Law* (1985).

[212] Art. 1; 'endangered and vulnerable' is broader than 'threatened' and brings the Convention into line with the 1973 CITES.

[213] Art. 2; this provision is very similar to Art. 2 of the 1979 EC Wild Birds Directive, see pp. 602–5 below.

[214] Arts. 2, 3 and 11.   [215] Arts. 4 and 10.

[216] Art. 5. This provision, which only regulates internal measures, also applies to sale and barter: see Explanatory Report, n. 210 above, para. 26.

[217] Art. 6.

killing, including those listed in Appendix IV, and all means capable of causing local disappearance or serious disturbance to populations are prohibited.[218] The parties are free to adopt stricter conservation measures.[219]

Under Article 9, the Convention permits exceptions to the prohibitions set out in Articles 4–8, although they are subject to the fulfilment of general and specific conditions. The general conditions require that there must be 'no other satisfactory solution' and that 'the exception will not be detrimental to the survival of the population concerned'.[220] The specific conditions only permit exceptions:

- for the protection of flora and fauna;
- to prevent serious damage to crops, livestock, forests, fisheries, water and other forms of property;
- in the interest of public health and safety, air safety or overriding public interests;
- for research and education, of repopulation, of reintroduction and for necessary breeding; and
- to permit, under strictly supervised conditions, on a selective basis and to a limited extent, the taking, keeping or other judicious exploitation of certain wild animals and plants in small numbers.[221]

These provisions include numerous ambiguities. For example, in Article 6(b), does the reference to 'deliberate' damage or destruction exclude damage or destruction caused by activities which do not have such damage or destruction as their primary purpose, or is it sufficient that such damage or destruction should be a reasonably foreseeable consequence of those activities? The former interpretation would exclude activities such as road-building which are not deliberately intended to cause damage or destruction but will often have that effect as a matter of course. With regard to the exceptions, what is meant by 'other overriding public interests', and do such interests include economic interests? The Explanatory Report provides some guidance, suggesting that all construction works would be included within the definition of 'deliberate' damage or destruction, and stating that exceptions may be made for construction works subject to the fulfilment of the conditions in Article 9 and the provisions in Article 3(2) concerning planning and development policies.[222]

Implementation of the 1979 Berne Convention is entrusted to a Standing Committee composed of a representative of each party with a range of functions, including the power to recommend measures and make proposals for improving the effectiveness of the Convention.[223] It reports to the Committee

---

[218] Arts. 7 and 8.   [219] Art. 12.   [220] Art. 9(1).   [221] Art. 9(1).

[222] Explanatory Report, n. 210 above, para. 41; cf. Art. 16(1) of the 1992 EC Habitats Directive, where derogations for imperative reasons of overriding public interest include those of a social or economic nature: see p. 540 below.

[223] Arts. 13 and 14.

of Ministers of the Council of Europe, and may adopt amendments to the Appendices by a two-thirds majority of the parties, which enter into force for all parties which have not notified objections, provided that less than one-third of parties have entered such objections.[224] The Standing Committee meets regularly and has amended the Appendices on several occasions; in December 1991, for example, over 400 species were added to Appendix I; an additional 107 Eastern European species were added to Appendix I in December 1996.[225]

1982 Benelux Convention

The Benelux Convention on Nature Conservation and Natural Resources provides a framework for concerted action and co-operation in the conservation, management and rehabilitation of the natural environment and landscapes.[226] It goes beyond the 1979 Berne Convention by requiring the *harmonisation* of policy principles, instruments, laws and regulations, information exchange, information and education campaigns, and 'co-ordinated implementation of agreements concluded within a wider international framework'. The Convention calls for effective protection activities including, *inter alia*, the development of 'protection and management concepts for transboundary natural areas and landscapes of value' and the establishment of inventories of such areas, as well as reciprocal consultation on development projects which might adversely affect such transboundary areas.[227] It recognises that natural resources and ecosystems do not respect national boundaries, an approach reflected in several instruments subsequently adopted.

1991 Convention on the Protection of the Alps[228]

T. Treves, L. Pineschi and A. Fodella (eds.), *International Law and the Protection of Mountain Areas* (2002).

The 1991 Alps Convention signals a move towards the international regulation of ecosystems which cross national boundaries; it was also the first international legal instrument to address the environmental issues of mountain regions.[229] The Convention establishes a general framework to apply the precautionary principle, the polluter-pays principle, and the principle of co-operation to preserve and protect the Alps, taking into account the equitable

---

[224] Arts. 15 and 17.

[225] 2 *Yearbook of International Environmental Law* 203 (1991); Report of the Standing Committee, 16th Meeting, Strasbourg, 2–6 December 1996, T-PVS (96) 102.

[226] Brussels, 8 June 1982, in force 1 October 1983, 2 SMTE 163; three states are party.

[227] Art. 3.

[228] Salzburg, 7 November 1991, in force 6 March 1995; 31 ILM 767 (1992); eight states and the EC are party.

[229] See also Agenda 21, chapter 13, 'Managing Fragile Ecosystems: Sustainable Mountain Development'.

interests of all Alpine states and ensuring the sustainable use of natural re-sources.[230] The Convention envisages protocols and other measures to address specific issues, including: the promotion of cultural identity; the protection of air, land soil and water; the preservation of flora and fauna and mountain forests; the conservation of energy and reduction of waste; and sustainable tourism and transport.[231] An Alpine conference of the parties meets every two years to adopt measures on research and systematic observation and to adopt Protocols and Amendments.[232] A Permanent Committee of the Alpine Con-ference is established as the executive organ, with support from a permanent secretariat (the Commission Internationale pour la Protection des Alpes).[233]

1992 EC Habitats Directive

L. Krämer, 'The Interdependency of Community and Member State Activity on Nature Protection Within the European Community', 20 *Ecology Law Quarterly* 25 (1993); A. Nollkaemper, 'Habitat Protection in European Community Law: Evolving Conceptions of a Balance of Interest', 9 JEL 271 (1997).

The EC Directive on the Conservation of Natural Habitats and of Wild Fauna and Flora (1992 EC Habitats Directive) is an important regional instrument which incorporates new approaches for 'ensuring biodiversity', implicitly recog-nising the failure of earlier approaches.[234] EC member states were required to implement the Directive by May 1994.[235] The Directive has two objectives: the conservation of natural habitats and habitats of species, and the protection of species.[236] It is the first international instrument to adopt the comprehensive protection of all habitat, in terms of both geographical region and type. It provides a basis for taking into account ecological conditions and the needs of all the territories of the EC member states, and recognises that measures to promote conservation of habitats and species of a Community interest is a

---

[230] Art. 2.
[231] Art. 3. Nine Protocols have been adopted but are not yet in force, dealing with nature conservation and landscape protection (1994), mountain farming (1994), regional man-agement and sustainable development (1994), mountain forests (1996), tourism (1998), energy (1998), soil protection (1998), transport (2000) and dispute settlement (2000).
[232] Arts. 3, 6 and 7.   [233] Arts. 8 and 9.
[234] Council Directive 92/43/EEC of 21 May 1992, OJ L206, 22 July 92, 7, Art. 2(1). Annexes I and II were amended by Council Directive 97/62/EC of 27 October 1997, OJ L305, 8 November 1997, 42.
[235] The Commisison has brought succesful infringement proceedings against several member states (e.g. Greece, [1997] ECR I-3749 and Germany, [1997] ECR I-7191).
[236] 'Natural habitats' are defined as 'terrestrial or aquatic areas distinguished by geographic, abiotic and biotic features, whether entirely natural or semi-natural': Art. 1(b); 'habitat of a species' is defined as 'an environment defined by specific abiotic and biotic factors, in which the species lives at any stage of its biological cycle': Art. 1(f). See also the definition of 'conservation' at Art. 1(a).

matter of 'common responsibility'.[237] It includes procedures for the designation of protected areas in an integrated and holistic manner, including priority habitats and species. It recognises that conservation measures can impose an excessive financial burden on some member states, since habitats and species are unevenly distributed, and that the polluter-pays principle is of limited application in the special case of conservation.[238]

Habitats The Habitats Directive sets forth substantive and procedural rules to establish a 'coherent European ecological network of special areas of conservation' (Natura 2000), including the special protection areas classified under the 1979 Wild Birds Directive.[239] Member states were required to notify to the EC Commission by May 1995 a list of sites indicating the natural habitat types listed in Annex I and the species listed in Annex II that are native to its territory which the site hosts.[240] For animals which range over wide areas, the sites must 'correspond to the places within the natural range of such species which present the physical or biological factors essential to their life and reproduction'; for aquatic species which range over wide areas, sites should only be proposed where 'there is a clearly identifiable area representing the physical and biological factors essential to their life and reproduction'.[241] Annex I lists nine habitat types whose conservation requires designation as a 'special area of conservation': coastal and halophytic habitats; coastal sand dunes and inland dunes; freshwater habitats; temperate heath and scrub; sclerophyllous scrub (matorral); natural and semi-natural grassland formations; raised bogs and mires and fens; rocky habitats and caves; and forests. Annex II lists several hundred animal and plant species of Community interest requiring the designation of special areas. Annex III lists the criteria for selecting sites of Community importance in

[237] Preamble. The English High Court has ruled that the European territory to which the Directive applies includes areas over which member states exercise sovereign rights beyond territorial waters: *R. v. Secretary of State for Trade and Industry, ex parte Greenpeace (No. 2)* [2000] 2 CMLR 94.

[238] *Ibid.* [239] Art. 3(1); on the 1979 Wild Birds Directive, see pp. 602–5 below.

[240] Art. 4(1) (see Commission Decision 97/266/EC concerning a site information format for proposed Natura 2000 sites, OJ L107, 24 April 1997, 1. The lists may subsequently be amended: *ibid.* The Directive establishes a procedure to be followed in the event that the Commission finds that a national list fails to mention a site hosting a priority natural habitat type or priority species: Art. 5. The ECJ has ruled that member states are not entitled to take into account economic, social and cultural requirements or regional and local characteristics (mentioned in Art. 2(3) of Directive 92/43) when selecting and defining the boundaries of sites to be proposed as eligible for identification as sites of Community importance: Case C-371/98, *R. v. Secretary of State for the Environment, Transport and the Regions, ex parte First Corporate Shipping Ltd* [2000] ECR I-9235. On the failure to transmit information within the prescribed period, see e.g. Case C-71/99, *Commission v. Germany* [2001] ECR I-5811; Case C-220/99, *Commission v. France* [2001] ECR I-5831; Case C-67/99, *Commission v. Ireland* [2001] ECR I-5757.

[241] *Ibid.*

accordance with a two-stage process. Stage 1 assesses the relative importance of sites for the habitat types and species in Annexes I and II. Stage 2 assesses the Community importance of the sites included on the national lists.

By June 1998, the EC Commission was to have adopted a list of sites of Community importance drawn from the member states' lists identifying those sites which have lost one or more priority natural habitat types or priority species;[242] however, no Community list could be adopted by that date owing to delays in submission of complete national lists. The Commission list will be drawn up on the basis of the criteria set out under Stage II of Annex III in the framework of five biogeographical regions and the European territory of the member states to which the EC Treaty applies. The Directive allows a degree of flexibility in drawing up the list in respect of member states whose sites host habitats or species which represent more than 5 per cent of their national territory. Once a site of Community importance has been designated, the relevant member state must, as soon as possible and within six years (which originally meant 2004 at the latest), designate the site as a 'special area of conservation', and establish priorities for maintenance or restoration.[243]

Once a 'special conservation area' is placed on the EC Commission list, the member state must take special conservation measures, including management plans, which correspond to the 'ecological requirements' of the site.[244] First, under Article 6(2), they must avoid the deterioration of natural habitats and the habitats of species as well as disturbance of the species. Secondly, under Article 6(3), they must conduct an 'appropriate assessment' of the implications for the site of any plan or project not directly connected with or necessary to the site's management but which is likely to have significant effects for it. Thirdly, if the plan or project goes ahead after the assessment shows 'negative' implications, there are no alternative solutions, and there are 'imperative reasons of overriding public interest, including those of a social or economic nature', the member state must 'take all compensatory measures necessary to show that the overall coherence of Natura 2000 is protected', and inform the EC Commission

---

[242] Arts. 4(2) and (3). 'Priority natural habitat types' are defined as 'natural habitat types in danger of disappearance, which are present on the territory referred to in Article 2 and for the conservation of which the Community has particular responsibility in view of the proportion of their natural range which falls within the territory referred to in Article 2': Art. 1(d); 'priority species' include endangered species: Art. 1(h).

[243] Art. 4(4).

[244] Art. 6(1); these provisions replace obligations under the relevant parts of Art. 4(1) of the 1979 Wild Birds Directive, Art. 7, p. 604 below. See EC, *Managing NATURA 2000 Sites: The Provisions of Article 6 of the 'Habitats' Directive 92/43/ CEE* (2000). On non-compliance with Art. 6, see Case C-117/00, *Commission* v. *Ireland* [2002] ECR I-5335 (failing to take the measures necessary to safeguard a sufficient diversity and area of habitats for the red grouse, and failing to take appropriate steps to avoid, in the Owenduff-Nephin Beg Complex special protection area, the deterioration of the habitats of the species for which the special protection area was designated).

of the compensatory measures adopted.[245] However, if the site hosts a 'priority natural habitat type and/or a priority species', the plan or project may only go ahead if there are considerations relating to human health or public safety, or there are beneficial consequences of primary importance for the environment or, further to an opinion from the Commission, there are other imperative reasons of overriding public interest.

The Habitats Directive recognises that conservation measures can entail significant economic costs. The Directive establishes the basis for the co-financing by the EC of measures which are 'essential for the maintenance or re-establishment at a favourable conservation status of the priority natural habitat types and priority species on the sites concerned'.[246] Provision is also made for the conservation obligations of member states where co-financing is not available. Other obligations under the Directive are more generous in the discretion they accord to the member states. They are, for example, required by Article 10 to endeavour, where they consider it necessary, to encourage the management of landscape features which are of major importance for wild flora and fauna, such as rivers with their banks or traditional systems for marking field boundaries, which are essential for migration, dispersal and genetic exchange. The Directive requires the Commission to review periodically the contribution of Natura 2000 towards the achievement of its objectives, and requires the member states to undertake surveillance of habitats.[247]

Protection of species   The Directive adopts a more traditional approach to the protection of species. Member states must establish a system of strict protection for the animal species listed in Annex IV(a), including prohibitions on all forms of deliberate capture or killing of wild specimens, deliberate disturbance, deliberate destruction or taking of eggs, and deterioration or destruction of breeding sites, as well as keeping, transport and sale or exchange.[248] They must also monitor the incidental capture and killing of these species.[249] Similar prohibitions

---

[245] Art. 6(4). See Commission Opinion 96/15/EC on the intersection of the Peene Valley (Germany) by the planned A20 motorway, OJ L006, 9 January 1996, 14, where the Commission concludes that '[t]aking into account the foreseen compensation and mitigation measures and considering that the least damaging alternative solution has been chosen . . . [the] [a]dverse effects on the protection area "Peenetal vom Kummerower See bis Schadefähre" through the planned A20 motorway east of Jarmen are justified by imperative reasons of overriding public interest'. The Opinion notes that priority habitats 'are not directly affected' and that 'no particularly rare birds, whose presence has been the reason for the designation of the valley as special protection area, will be directly affected'.

[246] Art. 8.   [247] Arts. 9 and 11.

[248] Art. 12(1) and (2). On the failure of member states to comply, see Case C-103/00, *Commission* v. *Greece* [2002] ECR I-1147 (failure to take requisite measures to establish and implement an effective system of strict protection for the sea turtle *Caretta caretta* on Zakinthos so as to avoid any disturbance of the species during its breeding period and any activity which might bring about deterioration or destruction of its breeding sites).

[249] Art. 12(4).

are established in respect of the plant species listed in Annex IV(b).[250] Annex V includes a list of flora and fauna for which measures may be taken under Article 14 to ensure that their taking in the wild and their exploitation is compatible with their being maintained at a favourable conservation status. The Directive also prohibits the use of indiscriminate means which are capable of causing local disappearances of, or serious disturbance to, populations of wild animal species listed in Annex V(a) and animal species listed in Annex IV(a) for which derogations have been granted under Article 16.[251] Prohibited measures include the means of capture and killing listed in Annex VI(a) and the capture and killing from modes of transport listed in Annex VI(b).

These rules are subject to the Article 16 derogations, provided that there is no satisfactory alternative and the derogation is not detrimental to the maintenance of the populations of the species concerned at a favourable conservation status in their natural range.[252] Derogations may be granted to protect wild flora and fauna in their habitat; to prevent serious damage; in the interests of public health and safety; for other imperative reasons of overriding public interest, including those of a social or economic nature and beneficial consequences of primary importance for the environment; for research and education; and to allow the limited taking or keeping of Annex IV species.[253] Member states must report derogations which are applied, including their reasons, circumstances and supervisory measures, and the Commission may give an opinion on the derogations but is not expressly empowered to prevent them or attach conditions to their grant.[254]

Supplementary provisions   The Directive includes reporting requirements on implementation, provisions on research, and procedures for amending the Annexes, and establishes a committee to assist the Commission.[255] Additionally, member states are required to regulate the deliberate introduction into the wild of any species which is not native to their territory, and to promote education and general information.[256]

Asia

The conservation of nature and biodiversity in Asia is addressed at the regional level by just one agreement. Given the large proportion of the world's population which lives in Asia, the size of the countries, their important natural resources, and their growing industrial base, further efforts are clearly needed. The Agreement on the Conservation of Nature and Natural Resources adopted by the Association of South East Asian Nations (1985 ASEAN Agreement)[257]

---

[250] Art. 13.   [251] Art. 15.   [252] Art. 16(1).
[253] *Ibid.*; cf. Art. 9(1) of the 1979 Berne Convention, p. 534 above.
[254] Art. 16(2) and (3).   [255] Arts. 17 to 21.   [256] Art. 22(b) and (c).
[257] Kuala Lumpur, 9 July 1985, not in force, 15 *Environmental Policy and Law* 64 (1985).

has not yet entered into force as it has not attracted the required ratification by six of the ten members of ASEAN (Brunei, Indonesia, Malaysia, the Philippines, Singapore, Cambodia, Laos, Myanmar, Vietnam and Thailand). Nevertheless, it merits consideration since it introduces innovative legal provisions compared with earlier regional biodiversity conservation agreements, including efforts to address conservation and economic development in an integrated manner, based on a 'sustainable use' standard which relies upon an ecosystem approach and the consideration of capacities of the parties.

The 1985 ASEAN Agreement will commit the parties to adopt measures and conservation strategies

> necessary to maintain essential ecological processes and life-support systems, to preserve genetic diversity, and to ensure the sustainable utilisation of harvested natural resources under their jurisdiction in accordance with scientific principles and with a view to attaining the goal of sustainable development [and to] ensure that conservation and management of natural resources are treated as an integral part of development planning at all stages and at all levels.[258]

The substantive part of the Agreement is divided into six Chapters. Chapter II ('Conservation of Species and Ecosystems') commits parties to 'maintain maximum genetic diversity' by acting for the conservation and survival of all species under their jurisdiction and control, to protect endangered species and to protect the habitats of endangered species listed on Appendix I.[259] The sustainable use of harvested species should be ensured by implementing management plans aimed at 'preventing decrease in the size of any harvested population to levels below those which ensure its stable recruitment', by maintaining the 'ecological relationship' between harvested, dependent and related populations, and by restoring depleted populations to levels which ensure 'stable recruitment'.[260] To this end, harvesting activities will be subject to a permit system, a prohibition on indiscriminate taking and use and on harvesting during certain periods, and regulated trade and possession.[261] Conservation of species and ecosystems includes measures to conserve vegetation cover, especially forests, soil conservation, land rehabilitation, the conservation of underground and surface water resources, and air quality management.[262]

The 1985 ASEAN Agreement addresses forest protection by calling for the establishment of forest reserves, reforestation and afforestation plans, and by requiring parties to ensure, to the maximum extent possible, the conservation of their natural forests (particularly mangroves) and to develop forestry management plans which maintain the potential 'for optimum sustained yield and avoiding depletion of the resource capital'.[263]

---

[258] Arts. 1 and 2(1).   [259] Arts. 3 and 5.   [260] Art. 4(1).
[261] Art. 4(2).   [262] Arts. 6 to 9.   [263] Art. 6(2).

Under Chapter III, parties must prevent, control and reduce degradation of the natural environment and polluting discharges and emissions. Again, the provisions on environmental degradation are innovative and progressive in addressing the need to promote environmentally sound agricultural practices and industrial processes and products, including the use of economic and fiscal incentives.[264] Without specifically mentioning the polluter-pays principle, the Agreement reflects its spirit by requiring parties to undertake,

> as far as possible, to consider the originator of the activity which may lead to environmental degradation responsible for its prevention, reduction and control as well as, wherever possible, for rehabilitation and remedial measures required . . .[265]

With regard to pollution prevention, the Agreement requires consideration of the 'cumulative effects' of pollutants, making control measures conditional upon the treatment of emissions, and establishing national environmental quality monitoring programmes.[266] Chapter IV supports land use planning to achieve 'optimum sustainable land use' based on the 'ecological capacity' of the land, the establishment of protected areas, and environmental impact assessment.[267] In relation to protected areas, the Agreement prohibits the use or release of toxic substances or pollutants as well as, to the maximum extent possible, activities outside the protected area which are likely to cause disturbance or damage.[268] Chapter V of the Agreement proposes measures for scientific research, education, public participation, and administrative machinery.[269] Chapter VI envisages international monitoring, research, the exchange of data and information, and the conservation and harmonious utilisation of shared natural resources.[270] The latter includes the following: environmental impact assessments before allowing activities which may create a risk of significantly affecting the environment of another party; notifying other parties of such activities and consulting with related plans; and informing other parties of emergency situations or sudden grave natural events which may have repercussions on their environment.[271] The Agreement is also the first to integrate a large part of Principle 21 of the Stockholm Declaration into the operational part of an international treaty.[272]

The institutional arrangements for implementing the Agreement comprise meetings of the parties, a secretariat, and national focal points for co-ordination and channelling of communications.[273] The meetings of the parties, to be held at least once every three years, will review implementation, amend the Appendix, consider reports submitted by the parties, establish working groups or other bodies, and take any additional action.[274] Amendments to the Agreement and to the Appendix require consensus.[275]

---

[264] Art. 10(a) to (c).   [265] Art. 6(d).   [266] Art. 11(a) to (c).
[267] Arts. 12 to 14.   [268] Art. 13(5)(b) and (c).   [269] Arts. 15 to 17.
[270] Arts. 18 and 19.   [271] Art. 19(2)(c) to (f).   [272] Art. 20(1).
[273] Arts. 21 to 23.   [274] Art. 21.   [275] Arts. 25 and 26.

Regulation of particular habitats or species

Many international environmental agreements regulate specific habitats, species or species types. They fall into eight basic categories which have as their *primary purpose* the conservation and enhancement of: wetlands; forests; plants; soil and land; marine living resources; birds; land animals; and migratory species. In addition, three agreements specifically address cultural and other heritage, including the heritage of nature and natural resources.

Wetlands

A. Timoshenko, 'Protection of Wetlands by International Law', 5 *Pace Environmental Law Review* 463 (1988); IUCN and Synge (eds.), *Legal Aspects of the Conservation of Wetlands* (1991); G. Matthews, *The Ramsar Convention on Wetlands: Its History and Development* (1993); M. Bowman, 'The Ramsar Convention Comes of Age', 42 NYIL 1 (1995); T. Davis, *Le Manuel de la Convention de Ramsar: guide de la convention relative aux zones humides d'importance internationale, particulièrement comme habitats des oiseaux d'eau* (1996); D. Farrier and L. Tucker, 'Wise Use of Wetlands under the Ramsar Convention: A Challenge for Meaningful Implementation of International Law', 12 JEL 21 (2000).

The first global agreement to address the conservation of a particular habitat was the Convention on Wetlands of International Importance Especially as Waterfowl Habitat (1971 Ramsar Convention),[276] which aims to conserve and enhance wetlands. As defined in the Ramsar Convention, wetlands are:

> areas of marsh, fen, peatland, or water, whether natural or artificial, permanent or temporary, with water that is static or flowing, fresh, brackish or salt, including areas of marine water the depth of which at low tide does not exceed six metres.[277]

This definition does not reflect the enormous variety of wetland types or the fact that they are dynamic, capable of changing with the seasons and over longer periods of time, and that accordingly their boundaries are often difficult to define with any degree of precision.[278] Recent estimates suggest that globally

---

[276] Ramsar, 2 February 1971, in force 21 December 1975, 996 UNTS 245 (www.ramsar.org). The Convention has 133 parties, and has been amended twice: first by the Paris Protocol of 3 December 1982, in force 10 October 1986, 22 ILM 698 (1982); and secondly by the Regina Amendments of 28 May 1987, in force 1 May 1994, IELMT 977:9/13. The Paris Protocol inserted a new Art. 10*bis* to provide for amendment of the Convention.

[277] Art. 1(1).

[278] See World Conservation Monitoring Centre, *Global Biodiversity: Earth's Living Resources in the 21st Century* (2000), noting that, according to the broadest grouping of habitat types, there are thirty categories of natural wetlands and nine man-made categories.

there remain between 5.3 and 5.7 million square kilometres of wetlands including bogs, fens, swamps, marshes, floodplain and shallow lakes. They serve a variety of functions, including flood and erosion control, water purification, and shoreline stabilisation.[279] The loss of wetlands has been difficult to quantify, and the only country in which the rate is well documented is the United States, where estimates suggest that the wetlands in ten states fell from 895,000 square kilometres in the 1780s to 422,397 square kilometres in the 1980s.[280] The major threats include pollution, hunting, human settlement, agricultural drainage and fishing. Wood-cutting, degradation of the watershed, soil erosion, siltation and the diversion of water supplies are additional threats.

The Ramsar Convention reflected new international legal efforts aimed at conservation by protecting a habitat type rather than a species, resulting largely from the activities of the non-governmental International Waterfowl Research Bureau. The Ramsar Convention has over 130 parties and now protects 1,109 sites in those countries, comprising a total surface area of 87,254,670 hectares. Without prejudice to their sovereign rights, each party must designate suitable wetlands within its territory for inclusion in the List of Wetlands of International Importance, taking account of their international significance in terms of ecology, botany, zoology, limnology or hydrology.[281] At least one wetland must be designated upon signature or ratification or accession; thereafter the addition of further wetlands, or the extension of listed wetlands, is a matter for each party.[282] The deletion or restriction of listed wetlands is permitted on grounds of 'urgent national interest' but must, as when designating entries, take into consideration the 'international responsibilities for the conservation, management and wise use of migratory stocks of waterfowl' and compensate for any loss of wetland resources, such as the establishment of additional nature reserves.[283] In 1990, the conference of the parties adopted criteria for the designation of wetlands sites which were updated at the sixth and seventh meetings in 1996 and 1999 respectively. The criteria are divided into two groups: Group A criteria for identifying sites containing representative, rare or unique wetland types; and Group B criteria for identifying sites of international importance for conserving biological diversity, including general criteria based on species and ecological communities and specific criteria based on waterbirds and fish.[284]

Each party's basic commitments include formulating and implementing wetlands conservation and its wise use; establishing nature reserves; endeavouring to increase waterfowl populations; and ensuring that it is informed of any actual or likely change in the ecological character of any of its listed

---

[279] *Ibid.*   [280] *Ibid.*   [281] Art. 2(1) to (3).
[282] Art. 2(4) and (5).   [283] Arts. 2(5) and (6) and 4(2).
[284] See Strategic Framework and Guidelines for the Future Development of the List of Wetlands of International Importance of the Convention on Wetlands (Ramsar, Iran, 1971), adopted by Ramsar Res. VII.11 (1999), Part V.

wetlands, which information is to be passed on to the Convention secretariat.[285] The Convention also encourages research, the exchange of data, the training of personnel, and consultation between parties about implementing their obligations.[286] Implementation of the Convention is reviewed by Conferences on the Conservation of Wetlands and Waterfowl held every three years, the latest in 2002. The Conference may consider problems of implementation, additions and changes to the List of Wetlands, and changes in the character of listed wetlands. The Conference may make recommendations to the parties on the conservation, management and wise use of wetlands and their flora and fauna which must be taken into consideration by the parties.[287] Each party has one vote at the Conference, and recommendations are adopted by a simple majority of votes cast, provided that half the parties vote.[288] The Conference has also established a number of working groups, including a wide use of working groups to guide the decisions of the Conference. The Conference is assisted by a secretariat, which maintains the List of Wetlands and informs parties of changes.[289]

Since 1975, eight conferences of the parties have been held and a range of recommendations adopted. To improve implementation, particularly by developing countries and countries with economies in transition, the conference of the parties established a 'Wetland Conservation Fund' in 1990 (subsequently renamed the Ramsar Small Grants Fund for Wetland Conservation and Wise Use), decided to treat amendments as being in force from the time of their adoption, and adopted general measures to improve implementation and monitoring.[290]

Forests

M. Prieur (ed.), *Forêts et environnement en droit comparé et droit international* (1985); M. B. Saunders, 'Valuation and International Regulation of Forestry Ecosystems: Prospects for a Global Forest Agreement', 66 *Washington Law Review* 871 (1991); A. Fabra, *The International Legal Protection of the Forest: A Case Study in Ecuador* (1992); H. Schally, 'Forests: Towards an International Legal Regime?', 4 *Yearbook of International Environmental Law* 30 (1993); Canadian Council of International Law, *Global Forests and International Environmental Law* (1996); R. Tarasofsky, 'The Global Regime for the Conservation and Sustainable Use of Forests', 56 ZaöRV 669 (1996).

---

[285] Arts. 3 and 4(1) and (4); 'waterfowl' are defined as 'birds which are ecologically dependent on wetlands': Art. 1(2).

[286] Arts. 4(3) and (5) and 5.   [287] Art. 6(3).   [288] Art. 7(2).

[289] Art. 8. The secretariat function is fulfilled by IUCN.

[290] Decision in 'Framework for Implementation of the Ramsar Convention', Annex Recommendation 2.3 of the Conference of the Parties, 12 *Environmental Policy and Law* 118 (1984) (Doc. C.4.12) (see also the Kushiro Statement, Res. V.I, Annex 1 (1993)); and Decision on Monitoring (1988); see chapter 20, p. 1031 below.

Forests have three important ecological functions: they provide habitats for the preservation of biodiversity; they act as carbon sinks (for removing carbon from the atmosphere and limiting atmospheric concentrations of carbon dioxide and consequential climate change); and they contribute to maintaining and enhancing the quality of soil. The fact that preserving forests contributes to climate stability and biodiversity goals has provided developing states with extensive forests with significant leverage in response to the efforts by developed states to agree an international forest convention. So far, those efforts have been unsuccessful, resulting in the limited statement of Forest Principles adopted at UNCED and a general commitment in Agenda 21 to 'consider the need for and feasibility of all kinds of appropriately internationally agreed arrangements to promote international co-operation' on forests.[291] There is no consensus on the need for a global forest convention.

It is estimated that, between 1700 and 1980, more than 11 million square kilometres of forest and woodland were lost, amounting to nearly 20 per cent of the total.[292] Temperate and boreal forests have suffered acute deforestation, including the virtual elimination of ecosystem types such as the cedar groves of Lebanon and the old-growth hardwood forests of Europe and North America. Of the estimated original 31 million hectares of non-tropical forests found on earth, 56 per cent are believed to have been logged or cleared.[293] Recent FAO figures suggest a lower rate of net loss of forests worldwide in the 1990s than in the 1980s owing mainly to a higher rate of natural expansion of forest area in industrialised countries.[294] Rates of tropical deforestation remain high with an estimated 15.2 million hectares of forest lost annually in the tropics.[295] Deforestation rates are highest in Africa and South America; the loss of natural forests in Asia is also high but has been significantly offset by forest plantation establishment.[296] The causes of deforestation, as identified at UNCED, include increased human needs, agricultural expansion, and environmental mismanagement, including unsustainable commercial logging, over-grazing, airborne pollutants and economic incentives.[297]

International legal efforts to address forest issues have taken place in the context of the historical loss of the forests of developed countries, and of these states' efforts to ensure that the bulk of remaining forests in developing countries is preserved for their contribution to ecological cycles, particularly in relation to biodiversity and climate issues. Attempts by developed countries to 'internationalise' forest issues have so far been unsuccessful in legal terms, and the tropical forest resources of developing countries are carefully

[291] Agenda 21, para. 11.12(e).

[292] World Resources Monitoring Centre, *Global Biodiversity: Earth's Living Resources in the 21st Century* (2000), 253.

[293] World Watch Institute, *State of the World 1992* (1992), 11.

[294] FAO, *State of the World's Forests 2001* (2001), 46.

[295] *Ibid.*, 45–6.   [296] *Ibid.*   [297] Agenda 21, para. 11.10.

guarded as part of the national patrimony of these countries. Contrary to certain views which have been expressed, tropical and other forests are not the 'common heritage of mankind' under international law, and were not identified as a 'common concern' to mankind in the Forest Principles. Apart from the specific instruments identified below, forests are subject to general protection under the regional agreements identified in the earlier part of this chapter, EC obligations,[298] the 1973 CITES (if a particular forest species has been listed as endangered),[299] the 1992 Biodiversity Convention and the 1992 Climate Change Convention.[300] Agenda 21 does not suggest that new international legal developments are imminent. Chapter 11 of Agenda 21 ('Combating Deforestation') is divided into four programme areas which more or less repeat the content of the statement of Forest Principles. The first programme area is intended to sustain the multiple roles and functions of all types of forests;[301] the second is to enhance the protection, sustainable management and conservation of all forests and 'green' degraded areas through rehabilitation, afforestation and reforestation;[302] the third will promote efficient use and assessment to recover the full value of goods and services provided by forests;[303] and the fourth is to establish and strengthen planning, assessment and systematic observation.[304]

1994 International Tropical Timber Agreement

The objectives of the 1994 International Tropical Timber Agreement (ITTA)[305] include developing 'industrial tropical timber reforestation and forest management activities' and encouraging 'national policies aimed at sustainable utilisation and conservation of timber producing forests and their genetic resources, and at maintaining the ecological balance in the regions concerned'.[306] These are but two of fourteen ITTA objectives, the others including the expansion and diversification of international trade in tropical timber from sustainable sources and promotion of the industrialisation of tropical timber-producing member countries. A major initiative of the ITTA is the 'Year 2000 objective', which aims to ensure that by the year 2000 all tropical timber products traded internationally by member states shall originate from sustainably managed

---

[298] See chapter 15, p. 779 below; see also the Agreement for the Establishment of a Latin-American Forest Research and Training Institute, Rome, 18 November 1959, 1 SMTE 143.

[299] For example, at the conference of the parties in 2002, mahogany was added to Annex II.

[300] See chapter 8, pp. 357–68 above.   [301] Paras. 11.1 to 11.9.

[302] Paras. 11.10 to 11.19.   [303] Paras. 11.20 to 11.28.   [304] Paras. 11.29 to 11.40.

[305] Geneva, 26 January 1994, in force 1 January 1997, 33 ILM 1014 (1994); 36 states and the EC are party. The 1994 Agreement replaced the expired 1983 International Tropical Timber Agreement (Geneva, 18 November 1983, in force 1 April 1985, UN Doc. TD/TIMBER/11/Rev.1 (1984)).

[306] Art. 1(j) and (l).

forests.[307] Article 18 of the ITTA establishes the Bali Partnership Fund to assist producing members to make the investments necessary to enhance their capacity to implement the Year 2000 objective.

The ITTA is administered by the International Tropical Timber Organization (ITTO), which functions through a Council.[308] The permanent committees of the ITTO include a Committee on Reforestation and Forest Management, the functions of which include harmonising international co-operation in reforestation and forest management.[309] The tenth session of the ITTO, held in 1991, established a small working group to develop Guidelines for the Conservation of Biological Diversity in Tropical Production Forests, adopted in December 1993, the principal objective of which is to 'optimise the contribution of [tropical] forests to the conservation of biological diversity that is consistent with their primary objective, namely the sustainable production of timber and other products'.[310]

FAO Tropical Forestry Action Plan

The non-binding Tropical Forestry Action Plan (TFAP) was adopted in 1985 as a non-binding global strategy developed by FAO, with the World Bank, UNDP, UNEP and the non-governmental World Resources Institute, to provide a framework for concerted national and international action to manage, protect and restore forest resources in states in tropical regions. By 1991, seventy-four countries were participating in programmes under the TFAP. Activities carried out in individual countries under the TFAP include a preliminary forest sector review which will then lead to a national Tropical Forestry Action Plan. TFAP exercises are intended to establish national targets on policies and practices to halt deforestation, contribute forest resources to sustainable economic development, conserve forests, and integrate forest-related issues into other sectors. The TFAP was subject to criticism for not addressing the root causes of deforestation, and it has now been subsumed into the FAO's national forest programme and into the work undertaken under the auspices of the UN Commission on Sustainable Development (discussed below).

1992 Forest Principles

The 'Non-Legally Binding Authoritative Statement of Principles for a Global Consensus on the Management, Conservation and Sustainable Development of All Types of Forests' (the 1992 Forest Principles) was adopted at UNCED.[311] Its weakness reflects the absence of international consensus on the subject, and

---

[307] See Poore and Chiew, 'Review of Progress Towards the Year 2000 Objective', November 2000, ITTC(XXVIII)/9/Rev.2.

[308] Art. 3.   [309] Arts. 26(1) and 27(2).

[310] ITTO, *Guidelines on the Conservation of Biological Diversity in Tropical Production Forests*, ITTO Policy Development Series No. 5 (1993).

[311] 13 June 1992, 31 ILM 881 (1992).

it is of limited legal authority and content. The guiding objective of the Forest Principles is to contribute to the management, conservation and sustainable development of forests and to provide for their multiple and complementary functions and uses.[312] It is 'a first global consensus on forests' which may serve as a basis for a future legal instrument. It applies to all types of forests,[313] and provides that forest issues must be dealt with in a 'holistic and balanced' manner. The Principles do not 'internationalise' forest issues, or state that forests are 'a common concern of mankind'. Instead, they note that:

> their sound management and conservation is of concern to *the Governments of the countries to which they belong* and are of value to local communities and to the environment as a whole (emphasis added).[314]

The fifteen Principles do not have titles, are difficult to classify in any logical or coherent way, and are poorly drafted. As a practical guide to the sustainable management of forests, the statement has been of little assistance. Consistently through the statement runs the theme that forest issues are a matter for national, rather than international, policies.[315] Several governing principles to inform the development of national policies are set forth, including 'the right to socio-economic development on a sustainable basis', Principle 21 of the Stockholm Declaration, the needs of present and future generations, an integrated and comprehensive approach, and the rights of indigenous peoples.[316]

The Principles make only limited reference to institutional arrangements and their development,[317] endorse public participation, scientific research, forest inventories and assessments, education and training, the international exchange of information, and the utilisation of indigenous knowledge.[318] Environmental impact assessments should be carried out where actions are likely to have significant adverse impacts on important forest resources, and where such actions are subject to a decision of a competent national authority.[319]

This weak language regarding environmental impact assessments, which obviates the need for an environmental impact assessment where actions do not require a decision of an authority, is further limited by the requirement that decisions on forest resources should benefit from 'a comprehensive assessment of economic and non-economic values of forest goods and services and of the environmental costs and benefits'.[320] Positive and transparent actions are called

---

[312] Preamble, para. (b).
[313] '[N]atural and planted, in all geographic regions and climatic zones, including austral, boreal, subtemperate, temperate, subtropical and tropical': Preamble, para. (e).
[314] Preamble, para. (f).
[315] Principle 2(a). 'National policies' are also referred to, *inter alia*, in Principles 3(a), 5(a), 6(b), 8(d), 8(f), 8(h) and 9(c).
[316] Preamble, para. (a); Principles 1(a), 2(b) and (c), 3(c), 4, 5(a) and (b), 8(d) and 15.
[317] Principle 3(a).   [318] Principles 2(d) and 12.
[319] Principle 8(h).   [320] Principle 6(c).

for, notably in developed countries, by means of reforestation, rehabilitation, afforestation and forest conservation.[321]

To this end, financial incentives for sustainable forest management should be provided. The 'agreed full incremental costs' of forest conservation and sustainable development should be equitably shared by the international community,[322] and specific financial resources should be provided to developing countries 'with significant forest areas which establish programmes for the conservation of forests'.[323] National policies and programmes should be supported by international financial and technical co-operation, and 'new and additional financial resources' should be provided to enable them to manage, conserve and develop their forest resources.[324] The Principles endorse incentives to encourage conservation and sustainable development, such as: the incorporation of environmental costs and benefits into market forces and mechanisms; the redress of external debt; and the avoidance of fiscal, trade, industrial, transportation and other policies and practices which may lead to forest degradation.[325] International trade in forest products should be based on non-discriminatory and multilaterally agreed rules and procedures consistent with international trade law and practices.[326] Moreover, in restrictive language, the Principles provide that:

> [u]nilateral measures, incompatible with international obligations or agreements, to restrict and/or ban the international trade in timber or other forest products should be removed or avoided . . .[327]

Following UNCED, renewed efforts were made to establish institutional arrangements for international forest management, conservation and sustainable development. At its third session, in April 1995, the UN Commission on Sustainable Development (CSD) established an Intergovernmental Panel on Forests (IPF) with a two-year mandate. The IPF's primary responsibility was the implementation of the forest-related decisions taken at UNCED. Its work was supported by an Interagency Taskforce on Forests (ITF) which co-ordinated the inputs of various international organisations into the forest policy process. In July 1997, the IPF was replaced by an *ad hoc* open-ended Intergovernmental Forum on Forests (IFF) with responsibility for promoting and facilitating the implementation of proposals for action developed by the IPF. The IFF was also given a mandate to consider international arrangements and mechanisms to promote forest management, conservation and sustainable development, with the view to developing a legally binding instrument. The IFF's mandate came to an end in 2000, and it was replaced by the United Nations Forum on Forests (UNFF),[328] a subsidiary body of the UN Economic and Social Council, which

---

[321] Principle 8(a) and (b).   [322] Principle 1(b).   [323] Principle 7(b).
[324] Principles 8(c) and 10.   [325] Principles 9(a) and 13(c) and (d).
[326] Principle 13(a) and (b).   [327] Principle 14.
[328] ECOSOC Res. E/2000/35, 18 October 2000.

held its first session in June 2001. UNFF's primary goal is the development of a legal framework dealing with all types of forests. Its work is supported by the Collaborative Partnership on Forests (replacing the ITF) which consists of representatives from relevant United Nations organisations as well as other international and regional organisations in the forestry area.[329]

Plants

S. Johnston, 'Conservation Role of Botanic Gardens and Gene Banks', 2 RECIEL 172 (1993); D. Cooper, 'The International Undertaking on Plant Genetic Resources', 2 RECIEL 158 (1993); R. L. Margulies, 'Protecting Biodiversity: Recognising International Intellectual Property Rights in Plant Genetic Resources', 14 *Michigan Journal of International Law* 322 (1993).

Several international agreements aim to improve co-operation in controlling pests and diseases of plants and plant production and in preventing their introduction and spread across national boundaries. These include the 1951 International Convention for the Establishment of the European and Mediterranean Plant Protection Organization,[330] the 1951 FAO International Plant Protection Convention,[331] the 1954 Phyto-Sanitary Convention for Africa South of the Sahara,[332] the 1956 Plant Protection Agreement for the Asia and Pacific Region,[333] the 1959 Agreement Concerning Co-operation in the Quarantine of Plants and Their Protection Against Pests and Diseases[334] and the 1993 Agreement for the Establishment of the Near East Plant Protection Organization.[335] These treaties provide for a combination of measures, including the development of national standards, restrictions on import and export, and research on phyto-sanitary conditions.

---

[329] The current membership of the CPF includes the Secretariat of the Convention on Biological Diversity; the Centre for International Forestry Research; the UN Department of Economic and Social Affairs; the Food and Agriculture Organization; the International Tropical Timber Organization; the United Nations Development Programme; the United Nations Environment Programme; the World Bank; the UN Convention to Combat Desertification; the Global Environment Facility; and the UN Framework Convention on Climate Change.

[330] Rome, 18 April 1951, in force 1 November 1953, UKTS 44 (1956), as amended by the EPPO Council on 27 April 1955, 9 May 1962, 18 September 1968, 19 September 1973, 23 September 1982, 21 September 1988 and 15 September 1999.

[331] Rome, 6 December 1951, in force 3 April 1952, 150 UNTS 67, as revised by the FAO Conference in 1979. At its twenty-ninth session in November 1997, the FAO Conference adopted a new revised text of the Convention; however, this is not yet in force.

[332] London, 29 July 1954, in force 15 June 1956, 1 SMTE 115.

[333] Rome, 27 February 1956, in force 2 July 1956, 247 UNTS 400.

[334] Sofia, 14 December 1959, in force 19 October 1960, 1 SMTE 153.

[335] Rabat, 18 February 1993, not yet in force.

The need to prevent the spread of plant pests may conflict with the need to protect the diversity of plant genetic resources and ensure the international dissemination of such resources for research purposes. In 1983, the FAO Council adopted a non-binding International Undertaking on Plant Genetic Resource (FAO Undertaking) to preserve plant genetic resources and make them as widely available as possible for plant breeding,[336] which is administered by the Commission on Genetic Resources for Food and Agriculture (CGRFA). It provides for *in situ* and *ex situ* conservation and has been supplemented by an International Fund for Plant Genetic Resources.[337] The FAO Undertaking, which contains elements subsequently reflected in the Biodiversity Convention, is based on 'the universally accepted principle that plant genetic resources are a heritage of mankind' and should be made available without restriction.[338] It supports the identification of potentially valuable plant genetic resources that are in danger of becoming extinct and other plant genetic resources which may be useful for development but whose existence or essential characteristics are unknown.[339] Adhering states undertake to protect and preserve the genetic resources of plants growing in their habitat, and to ensure the collection and safeguarding of material where resources are in danger of becoming extinct because of agricultural or other development.[340] They also undertake to make plant genetic resources under their control available, free of charge, for scientific research, plant breeding, or genetic resource conservation.[341] The Undertaking's objective of furthering international co-operation includes the establishment of an international network of base collections in gene banks.[342] The Undertaking is stated to be without prejudice to any measures taken by governments in accordance with the 1951 Convention, to regulate the entry of plant genetic resources in order to prevent the introduction or spread of plant pests.[343]

In 1989, the FAO Conference adopted an Agreed Interpretation of the International Undertaking (1989 Agreed Interpretation)[344] which recognised that plant genetic resources are 'a common heritage of mankind to be preserved, and to be freely available for use, for the benefit of present and future generations'. It was adopted to attract the participation of states which had not adhered to the Undertaking because of potential conflict with plant breeders' rights and farmers' rights adopted under the International Union for the Protection of New Varieties of Plants (UPOV).[345] The 1989 Agreed Interpretation

---

[336] Rome, 23 November 1983, as supplemented; Res. 8/83 of the twenty-second FAO Conference. The Undertaking is part of the FAO's Global System on Plant Genetic Resources for Food and Agriculture. One hundred and thirteen states have expressed their commitment to the Undertaking.

[337] Arts. 3, 4 and 6(d).   [338] Art. 1.   [339] Art. 3(1).   [340] Art. 4.   [341] Art. 5.

[342] Art. 7(1)(a).   [343] Art. 10.   [344] 29 November 1989, 25 FAO Conf. Res. 5189.

[345] 1961 UPOV Convention, as revised in 1978. The UPOV Convention requires each party to adopt national legislation to give at least twenty-four genera or species legal protection,

declares that plant breeders' rights under the UPOV are not incompatible with the FAO Undertaking, and that an adhering state may impose such minimum restrictions on the free exchange of plant genetic resources as are necessary to conform with national and international obligations.[346] The Interpretation makes it clear that the best way to implement the concept of farmers' rights (allowing farmers to replant seeds developed on the basis of germ plasm from their own native plants) is to ensure the conservation, management and use of plant genetic resources for the benefit of present and future generations of farmers, including making funds available from the International Fund for Plant Genetic Resources.[347]

With the entry into force of the Biodiversity Convention and the concomitant rise of agro-biotechnology in the early 1990s, it became clear that a non-binding undertaking was no longer sufficient to ensure the conservation and sustainable use of plant genetic resources. Thus in November 1993 the FAO Conference called on the CGRFA to open negotiations for the revision of the Undertaking as a legally binding agreement which would operate in harmony with the Biodiversity Convention. After some seven years of negotiation, an Agreed Text of the International Undertaking on Plant Genetic Resources was adopted by the CGRFA on 1 July 2001. The Agreed Text was forwarded to the thirty-first session of the FAO Conference which adopted the International Treaty on Plant Genetic Resources for Food and Agriculture.[348] The objectives of the new treaty are 'the conservation and sustainable use of plant genetic resources for food and agriculture and the fair and equitable sharing of the benefits arising out of their use, in harmony with the Convention on Biological Diversity, for sustainable agriculture and food security'.[349] In furtherance of these objectives, the parties are to promote an integrated approach to the exploration, conservation and sustainable use of plant genetic resources through activities such as: surveying and collecting plant genetic resources; promoting on-farm, *in situ*

in accordance with the Convention, within eight years of signing. A plant variety is subject to protection under the Convention if it is distinct, uniform and stable, and it satisfies the requirement of 'novelty'. Protection granted under the Convention generally lasts for twenty to thirty years, and the grant of plant variety rights confers on the holder the exclusive right, *inter alia*, to sell the reproductive material (e.g. seeds, cuttings or whole plants) but not material for consumption (e.g. fruit). In 1991, the UPOV Convention was revised to give greater protection by requiring parties to apply the Convention to all genera and species, to extend the exclusive right to include harvested materials (e.g. fruit), to allow enforcement against farm-saved seed (where a farmer produces further seed of the protected variety from the previous year's crop), and to allow double protection through the grant of patentability: see World Resources Monitoring Centre, *Global Biodiversity: Earth's Living Resources in the 21st Century* (2000), 496.

[346] 1989 Agreed Interpretation, paras. 1 and 2.   [347] Para. 4.

[348] FAO Conference Res. 3/2001. As at 1 November 2002, nine states were parties to the Treaty, which will enter into force on the nineteenth day following the fortieth ratification, provided that at least twenty of the ratifications are received from FAO members.

[349] Art. 1.

and *ex situ* conservation of such resources; and monitoring the maintenance of the viability, the degree of variation, and the genetic integrity of collections of plant genetic resources for food and agriculture.[350] Parties also commit to develop and maintain policy and legal measures to promote the sustainable use of plant genetic resources, such as the promotion of diverse farming systems and broadening the genetic base of crops.[351] Pursuant to Article 9 of the Treaty, parties are to take measures to protect and promote 'farmer's rights', including traditional knowledge, the right to participate in the equitable sharing of benefits arising from the utilisation of plant genetic resources and the right to participate in national decision-making on matters related to the conservation and sustainable use of plant genetic resources.

Part IV of the Treaty establishes a Multilateral System for access to plant genetic resources for food and agriculture, and the sharing of benefits deriving from their utilisation. The treaty recognises the sovereign rights of parties over their plant genetic resources, including that the authority to determine access to those resources rests with national governments and is subject to national legislation.[352] The Multilateral System covers plant genetic resources in food crops and forages, listed in Annex I, which are under the management and control of parties and in the public domain.[353] Other private entities which hold plant genetic resources are to be encouraged to include those resources within the Multilateral System.[354] The contracting parties undertake to facilitate access by other contracting parties, including natural and legal persons under their jurisdiction, to the plant genetic resources under the Multilateral System.[355] Access is subject to the condition that it is provided solely for the purpose of utilisation and conservation for research, breeding and training for food and agriculture; pharmaceutical and industrial uses are not permitted.[356] Any benefits (including commercial benefits) arising from the use of resources under the Multilateral System are to be shared fairly and equitably through mechanisms such as the exchange of information, access to and transfer of technology, capacity-building and the sharing of any benefits arising from commercialisation.[357] Benefits are to flow primarily, directly or indirectly, to farmers.[358]

The implementation of the Treaty is to be overseen by a Governing Body composed of the contracting parties. The Governing Body has oversight of the Multilateral System, may establish subsidiary bodies as necessary, and may consider amendments to the Treaty or its Annexes.[359] The Governing Body is assisted by a Secretary appointed by the Director General of the FAO.[360]

---

[350] Art. 5.   [351] Art. 6.   [352] Art. 10.   [353] Art. 11.1 and 11.2.
[354] Art. 11.3.   [355] Art. 12.1.   [356] Art. 12.3(a).   [357] Art. 13.
[358] Art. 13.3.   [359] Art. 19.   [360] Art. 20.

Land and soil conservation

A 1992–3 study sponsored by UNEP found that an area of 1.2 billion hectares, nearly 11 per cent of the earth's vegetated surface, suffers from soil degradation. This has been defined as 'a process that describes human-induced phenomena which lower the current and/or future capacity of the soil to support human life', and occurs as: light degradation (good soils that show signs of degradation but can be restored using good conservation practices); moderate degradation (which allows continued agricultural use but with greatly reduced productivity, and restoration requires major changes in land use practices); severe degradation (agricultural use is no longer possible and restoration is possible at a high cost); and extreme degradation (the area is unsuitable for agriculture and is beyond restoration).[361] Apart from wind and water erosion, soil degradation results from chemical deterioration due to salinisation, acidification and pollution, or from physical deterioration due to compaction, waterlogging or subsidence of organic soils. These are caused principally by agricultural activities, deforestation, over-exploitation, industrial and bio-industrial activities, and overgrazing; the rate of soil degradation has intensified significantly over the past forty-five years.[362]

International legal responses to address soil degradation have been limited. Apart from the commitments which establish general obligations,[363] a 1998 Protocol on Soil Protection to the Alpine Convention and a solitary EC Directive,[364] no legally binding instruments have been adopted which have, as their primary aim, specific measures to conserve, improve and rehabilitate soil, and prevent erosion and other forms of degradation.

Some non-binding instruments establish general guidelines. The FAO Council's World Soil Charter adopts agreed principles and guidelines to improve productivity, conservation and rational use of soils, and to promote 'optimum land use', recognising the responsibility of governments to ensure long-term maintenance and improvement of soil productivity.[365] UNEP has subsequently adopted a World Soils Policy,[366] developed environmental guidelines for the formulation of National Soil Policies,[367] and adopted an Action

---

[361] World Resources Institute, *World Resources (1992–3)*, 113. See also the recent joint study by the International Food Policy Research Institute (IFPRI) and World Resources Institute, *Pilot Analysis of Global Ecosystems: Agroecosystems* (November 2000), 45–54.

[362] *Ibid.*, 111–12, citing International Soil Reference and Information Centre (ISRIC) and UNEP, Global Assessment of Soil Degradation (GLASOD).

[363] 1968 African Nature Convention, Art. IV; 1985 ASEAN Agreement, Art. 7.

[364] Council Directive 86/278/EEC, OJ L181, 12 June 1986, 6.

[365] 25 November 1981, 21 FAO Conf. Res. 8/81, 50 *FAO Soils Bulletin* 79.

[366] UNEP GC/DEC/10/14, 31 May 1982; see also Plan of Action for Implementation of the World Soils Policy, UNEP/GC/DEC/12/12, 28 May 1984.

[367] UNEP Environmental Guidelines for the Formulation of National Soil Policies, UNEP Environmental Management Guidelines No. 7 (1983).

Plan on Drought and Desertification.[368] The Revised Montevideo Programme identifies the conservation of soil as a priority legal issue, and will promote the effective implementation of the Plan of Action of the World Soil Charter through the preparation of guidelines for domestic legislation and related institutional arrangements.[369] In 1992, the Committee of Ministers of the Council of Europe adopted a Recommendation on Soil Protection which set out four fundamental principles: soil protection should be declared of general public interest and integrated into development planning; soil should be recognised by states as a common heritage and a natural, non-renewable resource, and its community interest transcends private interests associated with its use; soil should be taken into consideration in all other policies, including agricultural, forestry, industrial, transport and town planning; and the public should have access to information on soil and be permitted to participate in relevant procedures.[370]

Following on from this, the Sixth Environment Action Programme of the European Community for the period 2001–10 contains a commitment by the European Commission to develop a thematic strategy for soil with the ultimate goal of raising the political importance of soil issues at the European Union level.

One aspect of soil degradation which is now more firmly on the international legal agenda after UNCED is drought and desertification, which is a particularly serious form of soil degradation. It is defined by Agenda 21 as 'land degradation in arid, semi-arid and dry sub-humid areas resulting from various factors, including climatic variations and human activities',[371] and encompasses soil degradation and associated changes in vegetation in arid and semi-arid areas. Chapter 12 of Agenda 21 ('Managing Fragile Ecosystems: Combating Desertification and Drought') establishes six programme areas to combat desertification (including soil degradation) and drought. These are intended to combat land degradation through intensified soil conservation, afforestation and reforestation and through developing anti-desertification programmes and drought preparedness and relief schemes, including programmes to cope with environmental refugees.[372]

In December 1992, at the request of UNCED, the UN General Assembly established an intergovernmental negotiating committee to elaborate an international convention to combat desertification in those countries experiencing

---

[368] UNEP/GC.6/11, 24 May 1978.   [369] UNEP/GC.17/5, Annex, Section K (1993).

[370] Rec. 92(8), 18 May 1992, cited in 3 *Yearbook of International Environmental Law* 334 (1992).

[371] Agenda 21, Chapter 12, para. 12.2; desertification is said to affect about one-sixth of the world's population, 70 per cent of all drylands, amounting to 3.6 billion hectares, and one-quarter of the total land area of the world: *ibid.*

[372] Paras. 12.15 to 12.25; 12.35 to 12.44; and 12.45 to 12.54.

serious drought and/or desertification, particularly in Africa.[373] The United Nations Convention to Combat Desertification in Countries Experiencing Serious Drought and/or Desertification, Particularly in Africa (UNCCD) was adopted in June 1994 and entered into force on 26 December 1996.[374] One hundred and seventy-eight states are currently party to the Convention.

The objective of the Convention is:

> to combat desertification and mitigate the effects of drought in countries experiencing serious drought and/or desertification, particularly in Africa, through effective action at all levels, supported by international co-operation and partnership arrangements, in the framework of an integrated approach which is consistent with Agenda 21, with a view to contributing to the achievement of sustainable development in affected areas.[375]

Affected country parties (i.e. countries whose lands include, in whole or in part, arid, semi-arid and/or dry sub-humid areas affected or threatened by desertification) are required to develop national action programmes to combat desertification in accordance with regional criteria set out in four Annexes to the Convention.[376] The purpose of the programmes is to identify factors contributing to desertification and practical measures necessary to combat desertification and to mitigate the effects of drought such as the establishment of early warning systems, the strengthening of drought contingency plans, the establishment of food security systems and the development of sustainable irrigation programmes. National action programmes must specify the respective roles of government, local communities and land users and the resources available and needed.[377] Development of the national programmes should take a 'bottom-up' approach ensuring the participation of populations and local communities and the creation of an 'enabling environment' at higher levels to facilitate action at national and local levels.[378] The programmes should also be integrated with other national policies for sustainable development.[379]

---

[373] UNGA Res. 47/188 (1992).

[374] Paris, 17 June 1994, 33 ILM 1328 (1994); states are party.

[375] Art. 2. 'Desertification' is defined as land degradation in arid, semi-arid and dry sub-humid areas resulting from various factors, including climatic variations and human activities (Art. 1(a)). 'Drought' is defined as the naturally occurring phenomenon that exists when precipitation has been significantly below normal recorded levels, causing serious hydrological imbalances that adversely affect land resource production systems (Art. 1(c)).

[376] Art. 5. Regional Implementation Annexes are provided for Africa, Asia, Latin America and the Caribbean, and the Northern Mediterranean.

[377] Art. 10.1 and 10.2.   [378] Art. 3(a).   [379] Art. 5(b).

Obligations are also placed on developed country parties to provide 'substantial' financial resources and other forms of support to affected developing countries, particularly those in Africa, and to promote and facilitate access by affected country parties, particularly affected developing country parties, to appropriate technology, knowledge and know-how.[380] In implementing the Convention, the parties must give priority to affected African country parties, in the light of the particular situation prevailing in that region, while not neglecting affected developing country parties in other regions.[381]

The primary institution of the Convention is the conference of the parties which is responsible for reviewing the implementation of the Convention, facilitating the exchange of information on implementing measures and adopting amendments to the Convention.[382] It is supported by a Permanent Secretariat[383] and a Committee on Science and Technology, which provides the conference of the parties with information and advice on scientific and technological matters relating to combating desertification and mitigating the effects of drought.[384]

Marine living resources

D. M. Johnston, *The International Law of Fisheries: A Framework for Policy Oriented Enquiries* (1965); D. Caron, 'International Sanctions, Ocean Management, and the Law of the Sea: A Study of Denial of Access to Fisheries', 16 *Ecology Law Quarterly* 311 (1989); W. Herrington, 'In the Realm of Diplomacy and Fish: Some Reflections on the International Convention on High Seas Fisheries in the North Pacific Ocean and the Law of the Sea Negotiations', 16 *Ecology Law Quarterly* 101 (1989); D. Lodge, 'New Approaches to Fisheries Enforcement', 2 RECIEL 277 (1993); W. T. Burke, *The New International Law of Fisheries: UNCLOS 1982 and Beyond* (1994); J. de Yturriaga, *The International Regime of Fisheries: From UNCLOS to the Presencial Sea* (1997); E. Hey (ed.), *Developments in International Fisheries Law* (1999); F. Orrego Vicuna, *The Changing International Law of High Seas Fisheries* (1999); R. Churchill and A. Lowe, *The Law of the Sea* (1999, 3rd edn); OECD, *Towards Sustainable Fisheries: Economic Aspects of the Management of Living Marine Resources* (1999); D. Vidas and W. Ostreng (eds.), *Order for the Oceans at the Turn of the Century* (1999); S. Kaye, *International Fisheries Management* (2000); O. Stokke (ed.), *Governing High Seas Fisheries* (2001).

---

[380] Art. 6.   [381] Art. 7.   [382] Art. 22.
[383] Art. 23. Since January 1999, the permanent Secretariat of the UNCCD has been located in Bonn, Germany.
[384] Art. 24.

Introduction

The marine living resources of the oceans and seas include marine fish,[385] cephalods,[386] crustaceans[387] and marine mammals.[388] Other sea-dependent mammals not usually included in international fisheries and other marine statistics include sea otters and polar bears. FAO statistics show that the annual take of living resources from the oceans is occurring at a rate which goes far beyond the maximum sustainable yield (MSY) and that further international efforts are needed to conserve fisheries and other marine living resources. According to the FAO, the average annual global marine catches of fish, cephalods and crustaceans increased by 35 per cent in the decade up to 1989.[389] In the decade up to 1999, there was a production increase of 20 million tonnes over the previous decade although this was mainly due to aquaculture, as capture fisheries production remained relatively stable.[390] These annual catch data, which relate to the 840 'species items' identified by the FAO and in its nineteen marine statistical areas, suggest that most traditional marine fish stocks have reached full exploitation: any further intensified fishing effort is unlikely to produce an increase in catch, and the use of new fishing methods that increased catches, such as driftnet fishing, would result in overfishing and further declines in fish populations.[391] The FAO's statistics show that in the period 1987–9 four of the seventeen major marine fishing areas were overfished (the Mediterranean and Black Sea, the North-West Pacific Ocean, the South-East Pacific Ocean and the Eastern Indian Ocean) to the extent that catches exceeded the maximum sustainable limit recognised by the FAO, and that the world's total marine catch was within approximately 20 per cent of the estimated total maximum sustainable yield. In the past decade, catches in many of these fisheries have stabilised, but the FAO estimates that some 47–50 per cent of stocks remain fully exploited, with another 15–18 per cent of stocks being overexploited.[392] The development and use of new technologies and fishing practices, such as

---

[385] These include the following nine FAO species groupings: flounders, halibuts, soles, etc.; cods, hakes, haddocks, etc.; redfishes, basses, congers, etc.; jacks, mullets, sauries, etc.; tunas, bonitos, billfishes, etc.; herrings, sardines, anchovies, etc.; mackerels, snoeks, cutlassfishes, etc.; sharks, rays, chimeras, etc.; and miscellaneous marine fishes: World Resources Institute, *World Resources (1992–3)*, 343.

[386] *Ibid.* The FAO grouping includes squids, cuttlefishes, octopuses, etc.

[387] *Ibid.* The FAO grouping includes the following categories: seaspiders, crabs, etc.; lobsters, spinyrock lobsters, etc.; squat lobsters; shrimp, prawns. etc.; krill, planktonic crustaceans, etc.; and miscellaneous marine crustaceans.

[388] *Ibid.*; divided into three main groups: cetaceans, including whales and dolphins; pinnipeds, including seals, sea lions and walruses; and sirenians, including manatees and dugongs.

[389] FAO, *Yearbook of Fishery Statistics* for 1983, 1984, 1986 and 1989; World Resources Institute, *World Resources (1992–3)*, 343 and Table 23.4.

[390] FAO, *The State of World Fisheries and Aquaculture* (2000).   [391] *Ibid.*   [392] *Ibid.*

large-scale driftnet fishing and electronic equipment to identify and track marine living resources, and increased demand for fisheries resources for human consumption and animal feed, are placing an overwhelming strain on the ability of these ocean resources to sustain and replenish themselves. This has led to an increase in the number of international disputes over fisheries, including cases being brought to the ICJ and under the 1982 UNCLOS. According to one commentator, three policy failures at the national and international levels are responsible for the threat to fisheries: the over-capitalisation of fishing fleets and the over-exploitation of fisheries; the environmental deterioration, including the degradation of coastal and estuarine habitats which are frequently the breeding grounds of fisheries; and the increasing use of fisheries for recreational purposes.[393]

The main objective of international law for fisheries conservation has been to establish a framework for international co-operation towards the management and conservation of fisheries and marine living resources which is built upon two related obligations: international research and scientific co-operation, and international regulation. Both are influenced by changes which have taken place over the past century resulting in an extension of the rights of coastal states and a corresponding diminution of the area of high seas on which any state is allowed to fish. Despite the belief that the extension of the coastal states' rights would benefit conservation efforts, reports of landings do not suggest that the new regime has led to a stabilisation of fish stocks at levels which are sustainable. This aspect of the conservation of biological diversity poses particularly complex challenges for international law. Many marine living resources are migratory over medium or long distances and do not remain conveniently within the territorial jurisdiction of any single state.[394] The fact that many marine living resources are found in the high seas area, beyond the national jurisdiction of any state, means that they have been traditionally subject to the right of all states to allow fishing activities and to benefit from the freedom of the high seas. In the absence of effective international management regimes for these areas, there is little incentive for a state to impose conservation measures unilaterally when it knows that its abstention will be replaced by the activities of fishing vessels from other states. Many marine living resources are therefore 'shared' within the meaning of the 1978 UNEP Principles.[395] According to Churchill and Lowe, four consequences of particular note flow from the common property nature of marine living resources:

---

[393] F. W. Bell, *Food from the Sea: The Economics and Politics of Ocean Fisheries* (1978), 339–40, cited in L. K. Caldwell, International Environmental Policy (1990, 2nd edn), 285.

[394] See in this regard the decision of the WTO Appellate Body in the *Shrimp/Turtle* case, chapter 19, pp. 965–73 below.

[395] See chapter 2, p. 43 above.

a tendency for fish stocks to be fished above biologically optimal levels; a tendency for more fishermen to engage in a fishery than is economically justified; a likelihood of competition and conflict between different groups of fishermen; and the necessity for any regulation of marine fisheries to have a substantial international component.[396]

International conservation rules are closely related to the jurisdictional rights of states.[397] Today the main points of reference relating to those jurisdictional rights are the maritime zones established by the 1982 UNCLOS, according to which different rules govern marine living resources in and beyond national territory.[398] This is reflected in the two relevant programme areas of Agenda 21: the first addresses the sustainable use and conservation of marine living resources of the high seas,[399] and the second addresses the sustainable use and conservation of marine living resources under national jurisdiction, including the exclusive economic zone.[400]

This part of chapter 11 is divided into the following five sections: (1) the historical background; (2) the general conservation rules established by the 1982 UNCLOS; (3) the particular conservation rules established under the multilateral fisheries arrangements; (4) driftnet fishing; and (5) the rules for the conservation of whales, tuna and seals.

Historical background

The rules of international law relating to the sustainable use and conservation of marine living resources have a lengthy history, particularly compared to other international environmental issues. The current legal regime reflects developments in state practice and treaty law which extend back to the second half of the eighteenth century. Landmark historical developments include the 1893 award of the arbitral tribunal in the *Pacific Fur Seal Arbitration*, the establishment of the FAO in 1945, the Geneva Conventions adopted by the 1958 United Nations Conference on the Law of the Sea, and the ICJ judgment in the *Fisheries Jurisdiction* case in 1974. These have been joined more recently by the ITLOS provisional measures order in the *Southern Bluefin Tuna* case in 1999, and cases filed at the ICJ (the *Estai* case in 1999) and at ITLOS (the *Swordfish* case in 2000), reflecting efforts by coastal states to take measures to prevent unlawful fishing.[401]

Pacific Fur Seal Arbitration The *Pacific Fur Seal Arbitration* award of 1893 is relevant today for at least three reasons:[402] it reflects the inherent difficulties in

---

[396] R. R. Churchill and A. V. Lowe, *The Law of the Sea* (1988, 2nd edn), 224.
[397] See chapter 1, pp. 13–14 above, and pp. 569–72 below.   [398] Paras. 17.44 and 17.69.
[399] Agenda 21, paras. 17.44 to 17.88.   [400] Agenda 21, paras. 17.69 to 17.95.
[401] See also in this regard the series of 'prompt release' cases at ITLOS, similarly premised on efforts by coastal states to prevent illegal fishing: chapter 5, pp. 218–20 above.
[402] 15 August 1893, 1 *Moore's International Arbitration Awards* 755.

the conservation of natural resources which fall, wholly or partly, outside the jurisdiction of a single state; the Regulations adopted in the award illustrate early international legal techniques for the conservation of shared natural resources; and it indicates the role of international courts and tribunals in the peaceful resolution of disputes and the progressive development of international legal arrangements. The *Pacific Fur Seal Arbitration* concerned the right of states to adopt regulations to conserve fur seals in areas beyond national jurisdiction. It arose out of a dispute between the United States and the United Kingdom following their failure (with France, Germany, Japan, Russia, Sweden and Norway) to agree on international rules to protect fur seal fisheries in the Bering Sea from indiscriminate destruction and extermination by over-exploitation. The United States had previously proposed international arrangements to protect the seals by limiting the annual take based upon provisions of the 1882 North Sea fisheries convention.[403] Negotiations collapsed following the seizures in 1886 and 1889 by the US of British Columbian and British vessels engaged in fur sealing in the Bering Sea beyond the three-mile limit of US territorial sea. An 1892 Treaty of Arbitration between the US and the UK submitted five questions to a tribunal to settle the dispute over jurisdictional rights in the Bering Sea, the preservation of fur seals, and the rights of nationals of each country to take these fur seals.[404] The first four questions concerned the following issues: Russia's historic claims to jurisdiction in the Bering Sea and its assertion of seal fishing rights; the UK's recognition of such rights; and the transfer of those rights to the US by a Treaty of 1867. The fifth question raised an environmental issue, asking whether the US had any right, and if so what right, 'of protection or property in the fur seals frequenting the islands of the United States in the Bering Sea when such seals are found outside the ordinary three-mile limit'.[405]

The award and the Regulations   The arbitrators found by a majority of six to one that Russia had never asserted any exclusive jurisdiction in the Bering Sea or in the seal fisheries beyond territorial waters, and that the UK had not recognised any claim to exclusive jurisdiction over the seal fisheries in the Bering Sea outside territorial waters. The arbitrators unanimously agreed that the Bering Sea was part of the Pacific Ocean as that term was used in the Treaty of 1825, and by a majority of six to one held that Russia held no exclusive rights of jurisdiction in the Bering Sea and no exclusive rights as to its seal fisheries outside of ordinary territorial waters after the Treaty of 1825. The arbitrators also held unanimously that Russia's rights as to jurisdiction and as to the seal

---

[403] The Hague, 6 May 1882, S. Ex. Doc. 106, 50 Cong. 2 Sess. 97.
[404] Treaty Between Great Britain and the United States for Submitting to Arbitration the Questions Relating to the Seal Fisheries in the Bering Sea, Washington, 29 February 1892, 176 CTS 447, 8 IPE 3874. Art. 1. The Tribunal comprised seven arbitrators: two appointed by each of the United States and the UK and one appointed by France, Italy and Sweden.
[405] *Ibid.*

fisheries in the Bering Sea in the 1867 Treaty passed unimpaired to the US under the Treaty.

On the important question of conservation, the arbitrators held by a majority of five to two that the US had no 'right of protection or property in the fur seals frequenting the islands of the United States in the Bering Sea, when such seals are found outside the ordinary three-mile limit'.[406]

Having rejected the United States' argument that the US could apply conservation measures in areas beyond national jurisdiction, the arbitrators adopted Regulations for the protection and preservation of fur seals outside jurisdictional limits. The Regulations included elements recognisable in modern international environment law, including rules establishing closed seasons, and limiting the methods and means of hunting. They prohibited the two countries from allowing the killing, capture or pursuit of fur seals at any time within a zone of sixty miles around the Pribilov Islands, including the territorial waters, and between 1 May and 31 July inclusively on the high seas in certain other parts of the Pacific Ocean.[407] Such fur seal fishing as was permitted could only be carried out with the use of sailing vessels authorised by a special government-issued licence and carrying a distinguishing flag, and the Regulations required information to be kept on the seal captures and the communication of the information between the governments at the end of each season.[408] The Regulations prohibited the use of nets, firearms and explosives, required the governments to control the fitness of men engaged in fur seal fishing, and were not applicable to Indians carrying on fur seal fishing in traditional ways.[409] The arbitrators adopted a Supplementary Declaration on fur-sealing within the territorial limits of each state which recommended that the critical condition of fur seal populations required both governments to come to an understanding to prohibit any killing of fur seals, either on land or at sea, for a period of two or three years, or at least one year, subject to appropriate exceptions.[410] Neither government accepted the recommendation.

The arguments   The legal arguments of the two states are of some interest. The US based its claim on its jurisdiction over the Bering Sea and on a right of protection and property in the fur seals found outside the ordinary three-mile limit 'based upon the established principles of the common and the civil law, upon the practice of nations, upon the laws of natural history, and upon the common interests of mankind'.[411]

The US argued that property rights entitled it to preserve the fur seals from destruction by the use of 'such reasonable force as may be necessary', and that

---

[406] 8 IPE 3877.   [407] Regulations, Arts. 1 and 2.
[408] Regulations, Arts. 3 to 5.   [409] Regulations, Arts. 6 to 8.
[410] Declaration 11, *Pacific Fur Seals Arbitration*, 15 August 1893, 1 *Moore's International Arbitral Awards* 755; the arbitrators adopted a Supplementary Declaration, *ibid.*, 856.
[411] *Ibid.*, 811.

even if it did not have property rights it had an interest in the 'legitimate and proper use of the seal herd on its territory' which it was entitled to protect against wanton destruction. In terms not dissimilar to its position underlying the yellow-fin tuna case nearly one hundred years later, the US argued that no part of the high sea was open to individuals for the purpose of destroying national interests of such a character and importance. Moreover, it argued that it alone possessed the power of preserving the seals and that it was acting as the trustee 'for the benefit of mankind and should be permitted to discharge their trust without hindrance'.[412] The property argument was based upon the belief that the dominion conferred upon particular nations over things of the earth was limited since nations 'are not made the absolute owners; their title is coupled with a trust for the benefit of mankind. The human race is entitled to participate in the enjoyment.'[413] The trust argument was illustrated in the following way:

> The coffee of central America and Arabia is not the exclusive property of those two nations; the tea of China, the rubber of South America, are not the exclusive property of those nations where it is grown; they are, so far as not needed by the nations which enjoy the possession, the common property of mankind; and if nations which have custody of them withdraw them, they are failing in their trust, and other nations have a right to interfere and secure their share.[414]

The UK's defence, which prevailed, was traditional and less elaborate: the Bering Sea was 'an open sea in which all nations of the world have the right to fish and navigate', which rights could 'not be taken away or restricted by the mere declaration or claim of any one or more nations', since they were natural rights which continued to exist to their full extent 'unless specifically modified, controlled or limited by treaty'.[415] Denying the existence of any property right in the US, the UK relied upon 'the law on which depends the freedom of the sea . . . The right to come and go upon the high sea without let or hindrance, and to take therefrom at will and pleasure the produce of the sea.'[416] The UK argued that the US claim of property in and the right to protect the fur seal outside the three-mile limit was without precedent and unsupported even by US practice: the right to protect the seals was limited to the right to prevent ships and persons from entering territorial waters for the purpose of capturing them.[417] The UK successfully argued that this view was 'shorn of all support of international law and of justification from the usage of nations' and based solely on 'a claim of property':[418]

---

[412] *Ibid.*, 813–14.   [413] *Ibid.*, 853.   [414] *Ibid.*, 853.   [415] *Ibid.*, 816.
[416] *Ibid.*, 845–6.   [417] *Ibid.*, 819–20.   [418] *Ibid.*, 845.

the United States takes refuge in a claim for protection where there is no property, under circumstances so novel that its supporters confess with candour that it can be rested on no precedent, but that precedent ought to be established by international law to meet the exigencies of the case. To all this shadowy claim the government of the Queen submit but one answer – the law.[419]

The Regulations adopted by the *Pacific Fur Seal Arbitration* in 1893 were followed by treaties in 1911, 1942 and 1957,[420] which also introduced some innovative principles, including quantitative limits on the number of seals that could be taken and a commitment to transfer, by way of compensation, a number of sealskins between the various parties.

Subsequent developments The principle of absolute freedom to fish on the high seas endorsed by the *Pacific Fur Seal Arbitration* meant that coastal states did not have jurisdiction for that reason alone over the marine living resources of the high seas. Jurisdiction to prescribe legislation for the conservation of these resources and to enforce such legislation was a matter exclusively for the state which has granted to a ship the right to sail under its flag (flag state).[421] Today the advent of new technologies and practices leading to over-exploitation of the marine living resources of the high seas illustrates the limitations of the principle underlying the award of the *Pacific Fur Seal Arbitration*, and is causing the traditional approach to be challenged by coastal states concerned with the effects of high seas fisheries activities, and also by international legislative and judicial efforts which are seeking to place limits on traditional high seas fisheries freedoms, in particular the 1995 Straddling Stocks Agreement. In this context, the *Pacific Fur Seal Arbitration* award shaped the form and content of subsequent agreements to conserve marine living resources, including the International Whaling Conventions of 1931 and 1937,[422] and many bilateral fisheries agreements to conserve individual species or regional stocks.[423] These were *ad hoc* efforts which could not effectively address the global expansion of international fisheries activities in the period after the Second World War.

The establishment of the FAO in 1945 created a forum for the development of a more co-ordinated international approach to fisheries regulation at the

---

[419] *Ibid.*

[420] Treaty for the Preservation and Protection of Fur Seals, 7 July 1911, 104 BFSP 175; Provisional Fur Seals Treaty, 156 UNTS 363; Interim Convention on the Conservation of North Pacific Fur Seals, 9 February 1957, 314 UNTS 105.

[421] UNCLOS, Art. 92.   [422] See p. 592 below.

[423] See e.g. Canada–United States, Convention for the Preservation of the Halibut Fishery of the Northern Pacific Ocean, 2 March 1923, 32 LNTS 93; Canada–United States, Convention for the Preservation of the Halibut Fishery of the Northern Pacific Ocean and the Bering Sea, 9 May 1930, 121 LNTS 209.

regional and global levels. It will be recalled that the FAO was the only UN specialised agency with a mandate to promote the conservation of natural resources, and its competence over agricultural matters included fisheries and other marine products.[424] The Committee on Fisheries (COFI) has served as a focal point for the activities of the organisation, has assisted in developing a number of regional fisheries agreements, and provides advice and assistance to governments and international organisations.[425] After 1945, international efforts addressed the management and conservation of fisheries at the regional level, and instruments were adopted for the European Community, Nordic marine waters, the North Pacific, the South Pacific, the Black Sea, the South-East Atlantic, the North-West Atlantic, the North-East Atlantic and North Atlantic,[426] and the Antarctic.[427] Future developments were also very significantly influenced by adoption at the First UN Conference on the Law of the Sea in 1958.

The First UN Conference on the Law of the Sea (1958)   In 1958, the First United Nations Conference on the Law of the Sea adopted four conventions.[428] Three of the conventions established general rules. The 1958 Convention on the Territorial Sea and the Contiguous Zone recognised the sovereignty of the coastal state and rights over living resources in the territorial sea up to twelve nautical miles from the baseline. Article 2 of the Convention on the High Seas, which includes all parts of the sea that are not included in the territorial sea or in the internal waters of a state, recognised the freedom of the high seas for coastal and non-coastal states under the general principles of international law, including freedom of fishing, which is 'to be exercised by all states with reasonable regard to the interests of other states in the exercise of the freedom'. The 1958 Convention on the Continental Shelf granted sovereign rights to coastal states over the continental shelf for exploration and exploitation of the natural resources without affecting the legal status of superjacent waters as high seas.[429] Under Article 5(1), such exploration or exploitation 'must not result in any unjustifiable interference . . . [with] fishing or the conservation of the living resources of the sea'.

Of the four conventions, the only one which established detailed obligations was the 1958 High Seas Fishing and Conservation Convention which, like the High Seas Convention, recognised the general right of all states to engage in

---

[424] Chapter 3, pp. 95–6 above.   [425] www.fao.org/fi/body/cofi/cofi.asp.
[426] Pp. 585–6 below.   [427] Chapter 14, pp. 714–15 below.   [428] Chapter 9, p. 393 above.
[429] Art. 2(1) and (3). 'Natural resources' include 'living organisms belonging to the sedentary species; that is to say, organisms which, at the harvestable stage, either are immobile on or under the seabed or are unable to move except in constant physical contact with the seabed or subsoil': Art. 2(4). In the *North Sea Continental Shelf* cases, the ICJ found that Arts. 1 and 2 of the Convention represented customary international law: (1969) ICJ Reports 3, para. 72.

fishing on the high seas.[430] The right to fish on the high seas was not, however, unlimited. The Convention required states to adopt such measures for their nationals 'as may be necessary for the conservation of the living resources of the high seas', which co-operation should lead to negotiated agreements for the conservation of living resources.[431] The Convention also recognised the special interests of coastal states in maintaining the productivity of living resources of adjacent areas of high seas, and declared that coastal states could take unilateral measures of conservation for any stock of fish or other resources in any areas of the high seas to maintain the productivity of the living resources of the sea.[432] However, such measures could only be taken if negotiations with other states concerned had not led to a conservation agreement within six months,[433] and limits existed on the right of recourse to unilateral measures: the need for conservation measures should be urgent, based on scientific findings, and should be non-discriminatory against foreign fishermen.[434] In 1960, a Supplementary Conference failed to agree on the extension of the territorial sea beyond the traditional three-mile limit or on the extension of certain exclusive fishing rights for coastal states beyond their territorial seas.[435] Consequently, a number of states, including Iceland, extended their claims to exclusive fishing rights to a twelve-nautical-mile limit and, in some cases, even up to a 200-nautical-mile limit.

Fisheries Jurisdiction Case   In 1972, Iceland extended its exclusive fishing zone to fifty nautical miles, catalysing disputes with the United Kingdom and the Federal Republic of Germany over access to fishing grounds. The disputes were submitted to the ICJ, which was thus presented with an opportunity to consider, *inter alia*, the issue of conservation and its relationship to traditional fisheries freedoms.[436] The Court denied Iceland's right to extend its exclusive fishery zone to fifty nautical miles from the baseline and held that Iceland could not unilaterally exclude vessels of the United Kingdom and the Federal Republic of Germany from the area within the fifty-nautical-mile limit from the baseline. The Court also held, however, that as Iceland was a state which was specially dependent on coastal fisheries it had certain preferential fishing

---

[430] Geneva, 29 April 1958, in force 20 March 1966, 559 UNTS 285.

[431] Arts. 1(2) and 2. The Convention defines 'conservation' as 'the aggregate of the measures rendering possible the optimum sustainable yield from those resources so as to secure a maximum supply of food and other marine products': Art. 2.

[432] Arts. 6 and 7(1).   [433] Art. 7(1).

[434] Art. 7(2). Disputes, including those over unilateral measures, could go before a special commission with the power to take binding decisions: Arts. 9 and 11.

[435] Whiteman, 4 *Digest of International Law* 91–137.

[436] *Fisheries Jurisdiction* cases (*United Kingdom v. Iceland*) (Merits), (1974) ICJ Reports 3; (*Federal Republic of Germany v. Iceland*) (Merits), (1974) ICJ Reports 175; Sands *et al.*, *Basic Documents in International Environmental Law* (1995), vol. IIA, 810.

rights in areas beyond its territorial sea; the United Kingdom and the Federal Republic of Germany had traditional fishing rights in those areas; an 'equitable solution' required these two potentially conflicting rights to be reconciled; and for these reasons and for 'conservation needs' neither right was 'absolute'.[437] Accordingly, the Court held that the states concerned had

> an obligation to take full account of each other's rights and of any fishery conservation measures the necessity of which is shown to exist in those waters. It is one of the advances in maritime international law, resulting from the intensification of fishing, that the former laissez faire treatment of the living resources of the sea in the high seas has been replaced by a recognition of a duty to have due regard to the rights of other states and the needs of conservation for the benefits of all. Consequently, both parties have the obligation to keep under review the fishery resources in the disputed waters and to examine together, in the light of the scientific and other available information, the measures required for the conservation and development, and equitable exploitation, of those resources, taking into account any international agreement in force between them, such as the North-East Atlantic Fisheries Convention of 24 January 1959, as well as such other agreements as may be reached in the matter in the course of further negotiation.[438]

This *dictum* from the Court recognised the duty of states to have 'due regard' to the 'needs of conservation for the benefits of all', and in effect established limits on the right of states to fish on the high seas. The decision of the Court provides a basis for the establishment of further limitations on the traditional rights of states, in respect both of fisheries and of other shared natural resources.

Related developments   In the period prior to and following the judgment in the *Fisheries Jurisdiction* cases, other developments were emphasising the need for international collaboration to address over-exploitation of marine living resources. Apart from the provisions to be found in the 1972 Stockholm Declaration and Action Plan,[439] the 1978 UNEP Draft Principles set forth a range of principles which could be incorporated into legal agreements.[440]

UNCLOS and UNCED

The 1982 UNCLOS is the principal international legal instrument setting forth the general rights and obligations of states and other members of the international community for the conservation and sustainable use of marine living resources. It was negotiated over a period of nearly two decades and the question

---

[437] *Fisheries Jurisdiction* cases (*United Kingdom v. Iceland*) (Merits) (1974) ICJ Reports 3 at 30–1; (*Federal Republic of Germany v. Iceland*) (Merits) (1974) ICJ Reports 174 at 198–9.
[438] *Fisheries Jurisdiction* cases (*United Kingdom v. Iceland*) (Merits) (1974) ICJ Reports 3 at 31; (*Federal Republic of Germany v. Iceland*) (Merits) (1974) ICJ Reports 174 at 199.
[439] See below.   [440] Chapter 2, p. 43 above.

of fisheries rights and obligations, including conservation, was a central issue. Most developing countries and some developed countries, including Australia, Canada and Norway, sought an extension of the jurisdictional rights of coastal states over fisheries; other states, including the United States, proposed a management approach which took into account the migratory characteristics of different species so that highly migratory species would be regulated by the various international fisheries commissions, and other species would be primarily subject to the jurisdiction of coastal states; states whose ships engaged in long-distance fishing, including Japan and the former Soviet Union, generally opposed any extension of coastal states' management rights which might interfere with their long-distance fishing rights.[441] On balance, the provisions of the 1982 UNCLOS extended the rights of coastal states, principally by formalising the legal status of exclusive economic zones. The Convention also recognised the need for special rules to manage and conserve particular types of species.

UNCLOS has exerted a significant influence on the practice of states, particularly since it came into force in 1994. In respect of the provisions on the management and conservation of fisheries, it may be considered to reflect customary international law. UNCLOS provided the basis for the deliberations at UNCED on international legal aspects of conservation, and is described by Agenda 21 as setting forth 'rights and obligations of states with respect to conservation and utilisation' of marine living resources.[442] UNCLOS includes provisions on the conservation and sustainable use of marine living resources in territorial waters, in archipelagic waters, on the continental shelf, in the exclusive economic zone, and on the high seas. UNCLOS also includes special rules for common stocks, for highly migratory species, for marine mammals and for anadromous and catadromous species.

Territorial waters, archipelagic waters and the continental shelf Under UNCLOS, a coastal state has sovereignty over the twelve-nautical-mile territorial sea and the marine living resources found therein.[443] Each coastal state is free to set laws for the conservation and sustainable use of living resources subject to compliance with its international legal obligations. Each coastal state can adopt laws governing innocent passage through its territorial waters in respect of, *inter alia*, the conservation of marine living resources, the prevention of infringement of its fisheries laws, and the preservation of its environment.[444]

---

[441] Churchill and Lowe, *The Law of the Sea* (1988, 2nd edn), 231–2.

[442] Agenda 21, paras. 17.44 and 17.69; see also the Preamble to the 1992 OSPAR Convention, which describes UNCLOS as reflecting customary international law: chapter 9, pp. 425–6 above.

[443] Arts. 2 and 3.

[444] Art. 21(1)(d) to (f). Fishing activities which occur in the territorial seas are inconsistent with innocent passage: Art. 19(2)(i).

Archipelagic states have sovereignty over the waters within archipelagic baselines, including marine living resources found therein, and the rules of innocent passage applicable to territorial waters apply also to archipelagic waters.[445] However, archipelagic states must recognise the traditional fishing rights of neighbouring states which are immediately adjacent to the archipelagic waters, for areas falling within archipelagic waters, subject to these rights being regulated by non-transferable bilateral agreements.[446]

Coastal states continue to have exclusive sovereign rights over their continental shelf to explore and exploit natural resources.[447] These rights do not affect the legal status of superjacent waters and their exercise must not infringe or unjustifiably interfere with navigation and other rights and freedoms of other states.[448]

Exclusive economic zone   UNCLOS established new rules of international law for the exclusive economic zone of coastal states. Under Article 56(1), the coastal state has within the EEZ 'sovereign rights for the purpose of exploring and exploiting, conserving and managing the natural resources, whether living or non-living'.

Subject to its right to determine the total allowable catch (TAC) of living resources in its EEZ, the coastal state must ensure through conservation and management measures that living resources are not endangered by over-exploitation, taking into account the best scientific evidence available to it.[449] This requirement is clarified by the additional obligation of states to ensure that populations of harvested species are restored or maintained

> at levels which can produce the maximum sustainable yield, as qualified by relevant environmental and economic factors, including the economic needs of coastal fishing communities and the special requirements of developing states, and taking into account fishing patterns, the interdependence of stocks, and any generally recommended international minimum standards, whether sub-regional, regional or global.[450]

These measures must also take into consideration the need to keep associate or dependent species above a level at which they would be seriously threatened.[451] Coastal states must promote the 'optimum utilisation' of living resources and determine their capacities to harvest the living resources of their EEZ, and have the right to give other states access to the surplus of the allowable catch.[452] In

---

[445] Arts. 49 and 52(1).   [446] Art. 51(1).

[447] Art. 77(1) and (2). The 'natural resources' include the sedentary species as defined in the 1958 Continental Shelf Convention, p. 566 above.

[448] Art. 78. Cf. the equivalent provision in the 1958 Continental Shelf Convention, p. 566 above.

[449] Art. 61(1) and (2).   [450] Art. 61(3).   [451] Art. 61(4).   [452] Art. 62(1) to (3).

determining whether to give access to other states, the coastal state must take into account all relevant factors including, *inter alia*:

> the significance of the living resources of the area to the economy of the coastal state concerned and its other national interests, the provisions of Articles 69 and 70, the requirements of developing states in the region or subregion in harvesting part of the surplus and the need to minimise economic dislocation in states whose nationals have habitually fished in the zone or which have made substantial efforts in research and identification of stocks.[453]

Nationals of other states fishing in the EEZ must comply with the measures, laws and regulations adopted by the coastal state, including conservation laws. Coastal states must give due notice of such measures and laws.[454] The conservation and development of a stock or stocks of associated species which occur in the EEZ of two or more coastal states, or in the EEZ and in an area beyond and adjacent to the EEZ, often referred to as 'straddling stocks' (and now governed by the 1995 Straddling Stocks Agreement), should be subject to agreed measures by those states which are necessary to co-ordinate and ensure the conservation and development of such stocks without prejudice to other provisions relating to the EEZ.[455]

UNCLOS also includes in relation to the EEZ rules which are applicable to highly migratory species, marine mammals, anadromous stocks, catadromous stocks and sedentary species. Marine mammals, such as whales and seals, are subject to the provisions of Articles 65 and 120.[456] For anadromous species (such as salmon, which spawn in freshwaters but spend most of their time in the sea), the management and conservation is primarily a matter for the states in whose rivers they originate, subject to the rule that fishing for such stocks on the high seas is prohibited in the waters beyond the high seas unless this would result in economic dislocation for a state other than a state of origin.[457] For catadromous stocks (such as eels, which spawn at sea but spend most of their time in freshwaters), management responsibilities rest with the coastal state in whose waters they spend the greater part of their life cycles, and fishing on the high seas of such stocks is prohibited.[458] UNCLOS treats sedentary species as part of the natural resources of the coastal state's continental shelf.[459]

Article 64 of UNCLOS provides that the

> coastal state and other states whose nationals fish in the region for the highly migratory species listed in Annex I shall co-operate directly or through appropriate international organisations with a view to ensuring conservation and promoting the objective of optimum utilisation of such species

---

[453] Art. 62(3); Arts. 69 and 70 relate to the rights of land-locked and geographically disadvantaged states.

[454] Art. 62(4) and (5).   [455] Art. 63.   [456] See p. 591 below.

[457] Art. 66.   [458] Art. 67.   [459] Art. 68.

throughout the region, both within and beyond the exclusive economic
zone. In regions for which no appropriate international organisation exists, the coastal state and other states whose nationals harvest these species
in the region shall co-operate to establish such an organisation and participate in its work.[460]

The over-exploitation of highly migratory species, such as tuna, has given rise
to numerous disputes over appropriate conservation measures and permissible
techniques for fishing, particularly in the Eastern Pacific.[461]

High seas   Part VII of UNCLOS establishes rules for high seas activities.
Article 87 maintains the freedom of all states to fish on the high seas, subject to the limited conditions established by the Convention and by other rules
of international law, and 'with due regard for the interests of other states in
their exercise of the freedom of the high seas, and also with due regard for the
rights under this Convention with respect to activities in the Area'. Article 116
limits in three ways the right of nationals to fish on the high seas. First, treaty
obligations must be complied with.[462] Secondly, the rights, duties and interests
of coastal states must be respected in relation to the provisions on common
stocks, highly migratory species, marine mammals, anadromous stocks and
catadromous stocks (as set out in Articles 63(2) and 64–67 and supplemented
by the 1995 Straddling Stocks Agreement). Thirdly, provisions concerning the
conservation and management of the living resources of the high seas as set out
in Articles 116–120 must be respected.

Under Article 117, states must take such measures for their nationals as
may be necessary for the conservation and management of the living resources
of the high seas, and under Article 118 they must co-operate for the establishment of regional or sub-regional fisheries organisations where nationals
exploit identical living resources, or different living resources in the same area,
and must negotiate to take measures necessary for the conservation of the
living resources concerned. In determining the allowable catch and in establishing other conservation measures for the high seas, Article 119 requires
that measures be based on the best scientific evidence available to produce the
maximum sustainable yield, and that consideration be given to the effects on associated or dependent species. Such measures and their implementation must

---

[460] Art. 64(1). Species listed in Annex 1 include eight species of tuna, and frigate mackerel,
pomfrets, marlins, sail-fishes, swordfish, sauries, dolphins, oceanic sharks and cetaceans.

[461] See chapter 19, pp. 953–61 below.

[462] See in this regard the 1993 Agreement to Promote Compliance with International Conservation and Management Measures by Fishing Vessels on the High Seas, November 1993
(FAO Res. 15/93). Art. VI of the Agreement requires parties to exchange information on
vessels authorised by them to fish on the high seas, and obliges the FAO to facilitate this
information exchange. The Agreement has been accepted by nineteen states and the EC,
and will enter in force when accepted by twenty-five parties.

be non-discriminatory, in form or in fact, against fishermen of any state.[463] Article 65 also applies to the conservation of marine mammals on the high seas.[464]

UNCED UNCLOS has not prevented the over-exploitation of fisheries within the EEZ or on the high seas, and Agenda 21 recognised the inadequacy of many conservation measures.[465] States set themselves several specific objectives, of which four are relatively focused and are likely to be priority areas in the coming years: the maintenance or restoration of species at levels that can produce the maximum sustainable yield as qualified by relevant environmental and economic factors; the use of selective fishing gear and practices that minimise waste in the catch of the target species and minimise by-catch of non-target species; the protection and restoration of endangered marine species; and the preservation of habitats and other ecologically sensitive areas.[466] Other objectives agreed at UNCED include: giving full effect to the provisions of UNCLOS for straddling stocks of fisheries and highly migratory species; minimising incidental catches; deterring reflagging to avoid compliance with conservation rules; prohibiting certain destructive fishing practices such as dynamiting and poisoning; and fully implementing General Assembly Resolution 46/215 on large scale pelagic driftnet fishing.[467]

In the absence of any substantive agreement at UNCED on the issue of straddling fish stocks and highly migratory fish stocks, Agenda 21 called for states to convene an intergovernmental conference to promote the effective implementation of UNCLOS on the issue.[468] At UNCED, states also committed themselves to the conservation and sustainable use of marine living resources under national jurisdiction, adopting similar objectives to those accepted in relation to high seas fisheries. However, this was without prejudice to the need to ensure that coastal states, particularly developing countries and states whose economies are overwhelmingly dependent on the exploitation of the marine living resources of their EEZ, should continue to obtain 'the full social and economic benefits from sustainable utilisation of marine living resources within their exclusive economic zone and other areas under national jurisdiction'.[469] Other general commitments were made to preserve rare or fragile ecosystems, giving priority to coral reefs, estuaries, temperate and tropical wetlands (including mangroves), seagrass beds, and other spawning and nursery areas.[470]

---

[463] Art. 119(3)(a).   [464] Art. 120.   [465] Agenda 21, para. 17.45.
[466] Para. 17.46. This commitment is stated to be without prejudice to the right of a state or the competence of an international organisation to prohibit, limit or regulate the exploitation of marine mammals on the high seas more strictly than para. 17.47.
[467] Paras. 17.49(a) and (b) and 17.50–17.54.
[468] Para. 17.49(e).   [469] Paras. 17.73–17.74.   [470] Paras. 17.74(f) and 17.85.

1995 Straddling Stocks Agreement and the Code of Conduct for Responsible Fisheries

E. Hey, *The Regime for the Exploitation of Transboundary Marine Fisheries Resources: The United Nations Law of the Sea Convention* (1989); E. Meltzer, 'Global Overview of Straddling and Highly Migratory Fish Stocks: The Non-Sustainable Nature of High Seas Fisheries', 25 *Ocean Development and International Law* 255 (1994); M. Hayashi, 'The 1995 Agreement on the Conservation and Management of Straddling and Highly Migratory Fish Stocks: Significance for the Law of the Sea Convention', 29 *Ocean and Coastal Management* 51 (1995); D. Momtaz, 'L'Accord rélatif à la conservation et la gestion des stocks chévauchants et grands migrateurs', AFDI 676 (1995); F. Orrega Vicuna, 'Coastal States Competences over High Seas Fisheries and the Changing Role of International Law', 55 ZaöRV 520 (1995); D. Anderson, 'The Straddling Stocks Agreement of 1995: An Initial Assessment', 45 ICLQ 463 (1996); P. G. Davies and C. Redgwell, 'The International Legal Regulation of Straddling Fish Stocks' 67 BYIL 199 (1996); D. Balton, 'Strengthening the Law of the Sea: The New Agreement on Straddling Fish Stocks and Highly Migratory Fish Stocks', 27 *Ocean Development and International Law* 125 (1996); D. Freestone and Z. Makuch, 'The New International Environmental Law of Fisheries: The 1995 UN Straddling Stocks Convention', 7 *Yearbook of International Environmental Law* 3 (1996); E. de Lone, 'Improving the Management of the Atlantic Tuna: The Duty to Strengthen the ICCAT in Light of the 1995 Straddling Stocks Agreement' 6 NYUELR 657 (1998); A. Boyle, 'Problems of Compulsory Jurisdiction and the Settlement of Disputes Relating to Straddling Fish Stocks', 14 IJMCL 1 (1999).

Following UNCED, the UN General Assembly convened a conference on straddling and highly migratory fish stocks in 1993 to identify and assess existing problems related to the conservation and management of such fish stocks, to consider means of improving fisheries co-operation, and to formulate appropriate recommendations.[471] The resolution reaffirmed that the work and results of the conference

> should be fully consistent with the provisions of the [UNCLOS], in particular the rights and obligations of coastal states and states fishing on the high seas, and that states should give full effect to the high seas fisheries provisions of the [UNCLOS] with regard to fisheries populations whose ranges lie both within and beyond exclusive economic zones (straddling fish stocks) and highly migratory fish stocks.[472]

The UN Agreement for the Implementation of the Provisions of the United Nations Convention on the Law of the Sea of 10 December 1982 Relating to the Conservation and Management of Straddling Fish Stocks and Highly Migratory Fish Stocks (1995 Straddling Stocks Agreement)[473] was adopted on

---

[471] UNGA Res. 47/192 (1992).   [472] Para. 4.

[473] 34 ILM 1542 (1995) in force 11 December 2001. As at 1 April 2003, the Agreement had thirty-four parties.

4 August 1995 and came into force on 11 December 2001, after the deposit of the thirtieth instrument of ratification or accession. The Agreement sets out specific principles to guide the development of conservation and management measures for straddling and highly migratory fish stocks, with a view to addressing the problems identified in Chapter 17 of Agenda 21. By Article 2, the object of the Agreement is

> to ensure the long-term conservation and sustainable use of straddling fish stocks and highly migratory fish stocks through effective implementation of the relevant provisions of the Convention.

The Agreement applies to the conservation and management of straddling fish stocks and highly migratory fish stocks beyond areas under national jurisdiction, except that its Articles 6 and 7 apply also to the conservation and management of such stocks within areas under national jurisdiction, and coastal states must apply the general principles enumerated in Article 5 to stocks within areas under national jurisdiction.[474] No reservations are permitted.[475] Part II addresses management and conservation. Article 5 commits coastal states and states fishing on the high seas to adopt a broad range of measures, which merit restating in full:

(a) adopt measures to ensure long-term sustainability of straddling fish stocks and highly migratory fish stocks and promote the objective of their optimum utilization;

(b) ensure that such measures are based on the best scientific evidence available and are designed to maintain or restore stocks at levels capable of producing maximum sustainable yield, as qualified by relevant environmental and economic factors, including the special requirements of developing States, and taking into account fishing patterns, the interdependence of stocks and any generally recommended international minimum standards, whether subregional, regional or global;

(c) apply the precautionary approach in accordance with article 6;

(d) assess the impacts of fishing, other human activities and environmental factors on target stocks and species belonging to the same ecosystem or associated with or dependent upon the target stocks;

(e) adopt, where necessary, conservation and management measures for species belonging to the same ecosystem or associated with or dependent upon the target stocks, with a view to maintaining or restoring populations of such species above levels at which their reproduction may become seriously threatened;

(f) minimize pollution, waste, discards, catch by lost or abandoned gear, catch of non-target species, both fish and non-fish species (hereinafter referred to as non-target species) and impacts on associated or dependent species, in particular endangered species, through measures including, to the extent practicable, the development and use

[474] Art. 3(1) and (2).   [475] Art. 42.

of selective, environmentally safe and cost-effective fishing gear and techniques;

(g) protect biodiversity in the marine environment;

(h) take measures to prevent or eliminate overfishing and excess fishing capacity and to ensure that levels of fishing effort do not exceed those commensurate with the sustainable use of fishery resources;

(i) take into account the interests of artisanal and subsistence fishers;

(j) collect and share, in a timely manner, complete and accurate data concerning fishing activities on, inter alia, vessel position, catch of target and non-target species and fishing effort, as set out in Annex I, as well as information from national and international research programmes;

(k) promote and conduct scientific research and develop appropriate technologies in support of fishery conservation and management; and

(l) implement and enforce conservation and management measures through effective monitoring, control and surveillance.

In applying a precautionary approach, states must establish stock-specific 'precautionary reference points' of two kinds: limit reference points and target reference points. Limit reference points set boundaries which are intended to constrain harvesting within safe biological limits within which the stocks can produce maximum sustainable yield. Target reference points are intended to meet management objectives. Management strategies are to seek to maintain or restore populations of harvested stocks at levels consistent with previously agreed precautionary reference points. Fishery management strategies should ensure that the risk of exceeding limit reference points is very low and that target reference points are not exceeded on average. If a stock falls below a limit reference point or is at risk of falling below such a reference point, conservation and management action must be initiated to facilitate stock recovery. When information for determining reference points for a fishery is insufficient or absent, provisional reference points may be set by analogy to similar and better-known stocks.[476] In addition to developing measures for target stocks, states are required to take a variety of measures to minimise the impact of fishing for such stocks on the marine environment. These measures include devising conservation and management measures for associated and dependent species, minimising pollution and by-catch, protecting biodiversity, and preventing or eliminating overfishing and excess fishing capacity.[477] Coastal states and states fishing in adjacent high seas areas are required to co-operate in devising conservation and management measures for straddling and highly migratory stocks to ensure the compatibility of national and high seas measures.[478]

Part III of the 1995 Agreement addresses mechanisms for international co-operation, and envisages a significant role for sub-regional and regional fisheries organisations and arrangements in facilitating co-operation by states in the

---

[476] Art. 6 and Annex II.   [477] Art. 5(d)–(h).   [478] Art. 7.

development and enforcement of conservation and management measures for straddling and migratory stocks.[479] Where a regional fisheries organisation is competent to establish conservation and management measures for a particular stock, states fishing for those stocks are required to become members of or participants in the organisation, or agree to apply its measures, in order to be permitted to continue to fish for the stock.[480] This far-reaching provision has the consequence, in effect, of departing from traditional principles reflecting absolute rights of high seas fisheries freedoms, even for those states which are not parties to regional agreements. Where there is no existing regional fisheries organisation or arrangement, the states concerned are to co-operate to establish a suitable organisation or arrangement to ensure the conservation and management of the particular stock.[481] Part III also provides for the conditions for new membership or participation of organisations, transparency in their activities and decision-making and strengthening of existing organisations,[482] as well as rules on enclosed and semi-enclosed seas and certain high seas areas.[483] Part V governs the duties of the flag state, including the obligation to take such measures as may be necessary to ensure that vessels flying its flag comply with regional and sub-regional conservation and management measures.[484] Part VI addresses compliance and enforcement,[485] and Part VII provides for the dispute settlement provisions of UNCLOS to apply also to the 1995 Agreement.[486] While the 1995 Agreement has contributed positively to the development of the law of the sea fisheries, such development is uneven, as one leading commentator has noted:

> If looked upon from the perspective of the traditional freedoms of the sea there is here undoubtedly a departure from those principles; but if the same matter is looked upon from the perspective of the need to ensure effective conservation and management . . . the conclusion is then entirely different since such developments are the necessary corollary to implement effectively these other objectives.[487]

In parallel with the elaboration of the 1995 Agreement, the FAO has sponsored the elaboration of a voluntary Code of Conduct on Responsible Fisheries, which was unanimously adopted by the FAO Conference on 31 October 1995.[488] The Code is intended to be global in scope, and is directed toward members and non-members of FAO, fishing entities, sub-regional, regional and global

---

[479] Arts. 8–10.

[480] Art. 8(4) and Art. 17 (Part IV, 'Non-Members and Non-Participants').

[481] Art. 8(5). Detailed prescriptions of the functions which the new fisheries organisation should perform are provided in Art. 10.

[482] Arts. 11–13. [483] Arts. 15 and 16. [484] Art. 18(1).

[485] Chapter 5, p. 186 above. [486] Chapter 5, p. 186 above.

[487] F. Orrego Vicuña, *The Changing International Law of High Seas Fisheries* (1999), 289.

[488] www.fao.org/fi/agreem/codecond/ficonde.asp.

organisations, whether governmental or non-governmental, and all persons concerned with the conservation of fishery resources and the management and development of fisheries. It provides principles and standards applicable to the conservation, management and development of all fisheries, and covers the capture and processing of and trade in fish and fishery products, fishing operations, aquaculture, fisheries research and the integration of fisheries into coastal area management. The core of the Code is set forth in its section 6 (general principles), section 7 (fisheries management), section 8 (fisheries operations) and section 9 (aquaculture).

International cases   The negotiation and adoption of the 1995 Agreement – and the trend towards a new era of environmental constraint and more limited rights of access to high seas fisheries rights – has coincided with a renewed willingness of certain states to bring international proceedings to enforce fisheries conservation requirements, including in areas beyond national jurisdiction. Beyond the three important cases filed between 1995 and 2000, the International Tribunal for the Law of the Sea (ITLOS) has also had occasion to comment upon (but not act upon) fisheries conservation requirements in a series of 'prompt release' cases.[489]

Estai case (Canada v. Spain)
The dispute between Canada and Spain over fishing for the Greenland halibut in the high seas occurred against the background of the UN negotiations on the 1995 Agreement, and may well have influenced the outcome of those negotiations. On 12 May 1994, Canada adopted legislation on the conservation and management of fish stocks in the North Atlantic Fisheries Organization (NAFO) Regulatory Area, including areas beyond Canada's 200-nautical-mile zone. Canadian regulations on the implementation of the new legislation were adopted on 25 May 1994, specifying the classes of vessels that were considered to pose the most immediate threat to the conservation of straddling stocks: those flying the flags of states with open registries and those with no nationality at all. The regulations also prescribed particular stocks, such as Greenland halibut, as being straddling stocks and subject to prescribed Canadian conservation and management measures. According to the Canadian Government, the legislation

---

[489] Chapter 5, p. 220 above. See in particular the Dissenting Opinion of Judge Anderson in the *Camouco* case (*Panana v. France*), Judgment of 7 February 2000, 39 ILM 666 (2000) ('Article 292 aims to protect certain economic and humanitarian values: ships and crews should be released from detention upon posting "reasonable" security pending trial on fishery or pollution charges. At the same time, Part V of the Convention protects other values, including the conservation of the living resources of the sea and the effective enforcement of national fisheries laws and regulations. In my opinion, greater significance should have been accorded to these latter values in deciding the question of the reasonableness of the security in this case.').

and regulations were intended to enable Canada to take the urgent steps necessary to prevent further destruction of straddling fish stocks on the Grand Banks of Newfoundland, and to permit their rebuilding.

These measures had followed stringent cuts for the Greenland halibut fishery which had been adopted by Canada, for areas within its own jurisdiction. In September 1994, Canada proposed that the NAFO should manage the Greenland halibut stock. NAFO agreed to establish a total allowable catch (TAC) for Greenland halibut of 27,000 tonnes for 1995, 8,000 tonnes less than the amount Spain had caught in 1993. This TAC was for the entire stock in certain NAFO regulatory areas, including the parts of those areas that lay within Canada's 200-nautical-mile zone. The NAFO Commission adopted allocations of Greenland halibut for Canada (16,300 tonnes for 1995) and the European Union (3,400 tonnes for 1995), with the remainder being divided principally between Russia and Japan. On 3 March 1995, the European Union objected to the NAFO quota and set for itself a unilateral quota in excess of the TAC that had been allocated to it by NAFO. On 9 March 1995, the Spanish fishing vessel *Estai* was boarded and inspected, and then charged with offences under Canada's Coastal Fisheries Protection Act, including excessive fishing for Greenland halibut in areas beyond Canada's 200-nautical-mile zone. On 28 March 1995, Spain initiated proceedings with the ICJ, asking:

(A) that the Court declare that the Canadian legislation, insofar as it purports to exercise jurisdiction over vessels flying foreign flags on the high seas, beyond Canada's exclusive economic zone, is unopposable to the Kingdom of Spain;

(B) that the Court adjudge and declare that Canada must refrain from repeating the actions complained of, and make due amends to the Kingdom of Spain in the form of compensation, the amount of which shall cover all damage and injury caused; and

(C) that, consequently, the Court also declare that the boarding of the Spanish flag vessel *Estai* on the high seas on 9 March 1995, as well as the coercive measures and the exercise of jurisdiction over it and its captain, constitutes a concrete violation of the above-indicated principles and norms of international law.

As described in chapter 5 above, the ICJ declined jurisdiction, on the grounds that Canada's acceptance of the Court's jursidiction did not, following a new reservation made by Canada, encompass the matters which were the subject of the dispute, namely, 'disputes arising out of or concerning conservation and management measures taken by Canada with respect to vessels fishing in the NAFO Regulatory Area'.[490] In reaching this conclusion, the Court rejected Spain's argument that Canada's acts were not 'conservation and management' measures:

---

[490] (1998) ICJ Reports 432; chapter 5, p. 216 above.

for a measure to be characterised as a 'conservation and management measure', it is sufficient that its purpose is to conserve and manage living resources and that, to this end, it satisfies various technical requirements.[491] Having regard to various international agreements, including the 1995 Stradddling Stocks Agreement and the 1993 FAO Agreement, a majority of the Court concluded that the measures taken by Canada fell within its reservation.[492]

The view was not supported by all members of the Court, particularly those who saw the object of Canada's reservation as being 'to signal *urbi et orbi* that Canada claims special jurisdiction over the high seas', with consequences for traditional high seas fisheries freedoms.[493]

Southern Bluefin Tuna cases (New Zealand v. Japan, Australia v. Japan)

B. Kwiatkowska, Case Report, 94 AJIL 150 (2000); B. Kwiatkowska, Case Report, 95 AJIL 162 (2001); A. Boyle, 'The Southern Bluefin Tuna Arbitration', 50 ICLQ 337 (2001); S. Marr, 'The Southern Bluefin Tuna Cases: The Precautionary Approach and Conservation and Management of Fish Resources', 11 *European Journal of International Law* 815 (2000); B. Kwiatkowska, 'The Southern Bluefin Tuna Cases', 15 IJMCL 1 (2000); J. Peel, 'The Future for Resolving Fisheries Disputes under UNCLOS in the Aftermath of the Southern Bluefin Tuna Arbitration', 1 *Melbourne Journal of International Law* 53 (2002).

In July 1999, Australia and New Zealand initiated arbitration proceedings under Part XV of and Annex VII to UNCLOS, alleging that Japan had breached its obligations under Articles 64 and 116–119 of UNCLOS in relation to the conservation and management of southern bluefin tuna stock through implementation of a unilateral experimental fishing programme. The three states were parties to the 1993 Convention for the Conservation of Southern Bluefin Tuna, a regional fisheries convention established to 'ensure, through appropriate management, the conservation and optimum utilisation of southern bluefin tuna'.[494] The Convention established a Commission for the Conservation of Southern Bluefin Tuna with power to decide upon a total allowable

---

[491] Para. 70.

[492] Para. 71. The Court went on to reject Spain's argument that Canada's reservation had to be interpreted so as to cover only acts compatible with international law.

[493] Dissenting Opinion of Judge Bedjaoui, (1998) ICJ Reports 519 (the conflation of the merits of the case with the Court's jursidiction appears even more evident in Judge Bedjaoui's expression of regret 'that the Court did not reject, or even hold null and void, a reservation whose object and purpose . . . was to permit encroachment upon an essential freedom of international law, both past and present, without fear of judicial intervention': *ibid.*, 536).

[494] Convention for the Conservation of Southern Bluefin Tuna, adopted 10 May 1993, in force 30 May 1994, 1819 UNTS 360, Art. 3.

catch (TAC) for southern bluefin tuna and its allocation among the parties to the Convention.[495] The parties had been unable to reach agreement through the Commission on a new TAC: Japan had sought an increase in the size of the previous TAC, whereas Australia and New Zealand argued that available scientific information did not indicate that the southern bluefin tuna stock had recovered sufficiently to support a higher TAC. In 1998, Japan initiated a unilateral experimental fishing programme on the basis that this was necessary in order to gather scientific data on the state of the southern bluefin tuna stock. Australia and New Zealand objected to Japan's experimental fishing programme, claiming that its purpose was simply to allow Japan to take more than its allocated portion of the southern bluefin tuna TAC. Australia and New Zealand claimed that Japan had *inter alia*: failed to adopt necessary conservation measures so as to maintain or restore stocks to levels which could produce a maximum sustainable yield; carried out unilateral experimental fishing which would result in southern bluefin tuna being taken by Japan over and above the national allocations previously agreed under the Convention; failed to co-operate with New Zealand and Australia; and otherwise failed in its UNCLOS obligations in respect of conservation and management of southern bluefin tuna, having regard to the precautionary principle.

Two weeks after initiating the Annex VI proceedings, Australia and New Zealand requested the ITLOS to prescribe provisional measures pending the decision of the arbitral tribunal to be set up in accordance with Annex VII to UNCLOS. By its Order of 27 August 1999, the ITLOS ordered the three states to ensure that their annual catches did not exceed national annual allocations at the levels last agreed by the parties, and to

> [r]efrain from conducting an experimental fishing programme involving the taking of a catch of southern bluefin tuna, except with the agreement of the other parties or unless the experimental catch is counted against its annual national allocation.[496]

Of particular note in the Order is the Tribunal's view that, in the face of scientific uncertainty as to the status of the southern bluefin tuna stock, 'the parties should . . . act with prudence and caution to ensure that effective conservation measures are taken to prevent serious harm to the stock of southern bluefin tuna'.[497] The case did not proceed to the merits after the decision of the Annex VII arbitral tribunal, the following year, accepting Japan's argument that the tribunal did not have jurisdiction to receive the claims.[498]

---

[495] Arts. 6 and 8(3)(a).

[496] *Southern Bluefin Tuna* cases (*New Zealand* v. *Japan*; *Australia* v. *Japan*) (Provisional Measures), 38 ILM 1624 (1999), para. 90(c) and (d).

[497] *Ibid.*, para. 77.   [498] Chapter 5, p. 220 above.

Swordfish case (Chile v. EC)

A. Serdy, 'See You in Port: Australia and New Zealand as Third Parties in the Dispute Between Chile and the EC over Chile's Denial of Port Access to Spanish Vessels Fishing for Swordfish on the High Seas', 1 *Melbourne Journal of International Law* 79 (2002).

During much of the 1990s, Chile and the EU were involved in a dispute concerning the conservation of declining stocks of swordfish in the South Pacific. Concerned about the state of stocks, in 1991 Chile implemented a number of conservation measures within its exclusive economic zone and, in relation to its own nationals, in the high seas adjacent to that zone. Thereafter, Chile prohibited the unloading in its ports (for onward transportation) of swordfish caught in waters beyond its jurisdiction. Once again the unilateral act of a coastal state to conserve fisheries led to a dispute, which was eventually brought to two different dispute settlement procedures.

Following unsuccessful negotiations, in April 2000 the EU brought the matter to the WTO Dispute Settlement Body (DSB), claiming that Chile's prohibition was inconsistent with GATT 1994, in particular Article V (providing for freedom of transit for goods through the territory of each contracting party) and Article XI (prohibiting quantitative restrictions on imports or exports). For its part, Chile considered that its measures were covered by Article XX(g), permitting it to adopt and enforce measures relating to the conservation of natural resources in conjunction with restrictions on domestic production or consumption.[499] In December 2000, the WTO DSB established a Panel to resolve the dispute.[500]

Thereafter, by September 2000, Chile had initiated UNCLOS Annex VII arbitration proceedings against the EU, alleging violations of various fisheries provisions of UNCLOS. The parties subsequently agreed that the dispute be submitted to a special chamber of ITLOS composed of five members.[501] The parties requested the special chamber to decide, on the basis of UNCLOS, issues put forward by the parties. The issues put forward by Chile were *inter alia*:

> (a) whether the EC had complied with its obligations under the Convention, especially articles 116 to 119, to ensure conservation of swordfish, in the fishing activities undertaken by vessels flying the flag of any of its member States in the high seas adjacent to Chile's exclusive economic zone;

---

[499] Chapter 19, p. 948 below.

[500] Case DS193: Chile: Measures Affecting the Transit and Importation of Swordfish, WTO Press Release, 12 December 2000.

[501] *Case Concerning the Conservation and Sustainable Exploitation of Swordfish Stocks in the South-Eastern Pacific Ocean (Chile – EC)*, Order 2000/3 of 20 December 2000, 40 ILM 475 (2001). The special chamber comprises Judges Chandrasekhara Rao (President), Caminos, Yankov, Wolfrum and Judge Ad Hoc Orrego Vicuña.

(b) whether the EC had complied with its obligations under the Convention, in particular article 64, to co-operate with Chile as a coastal State for the conservation of swordfish in the high seas adjacent to Chile's exclusive economic zone;

(c) whether the EC had challenged the sovereign right and duty of Chile, as a coastal State, to prescribe measures within its national jurisdiction for the conservation of swordfish and to ensure their implementation in its ports, in a non-discriminatory manner, as well as the measures themselves, and whether such challenge would be compatible with the Convention;

(d) whether the obligations arising under Articles 300 and 297(1)(b) of the Convention had been fulfilled by the EC.

The issues put to ITLOS by the EC were:

(a) whether the Chilean Decree 598 which purported to apply Chile's unilateral conservation measures relating to swordfish on the high seas was in breach of, *inter alia*, articles 87, 89 and 116 to 119 of the Convention;

(b) whether the 'Galapagos Agreement' signed in Santiago de Chile on 14 August 2000 was negotiated in keeping with the provisions of the Convention and whether its substantive provisions were in consonance with, *inter alia*, articles 64 and 116 to 119 of the Convention;

(c) whether Chile's actions concerning the conservation of swordfish were in conformity with article 300 of the Convention and whether Chile and the European Community remained under a duty to negotiate an agreement on co-operation under article 64 of the Convention; and

(d) whether the jurisdiction of the special chamber extended to the issue referred to in paragraph (c) above.

In January 2001, the EU and Chile agreed to suspend (but not terminate) the WTO and ITLOS proceedings,[502] to resume bilateral co-operation, and to put in place a provisional arrangement. The provisional arrangement comprised three elements: a resumption of meetings within the framework of the Bilateral Scientific and Technical Commission on Swordfish Stocks in the South-East Pacific; access for a limited number of EU vessels to Chilean ports, permitting transhipment or landing up to 1,000 tons of swordfish under a joint programme to assist in the joint scientific evaluation of the swordfish stocks; and a commitment to agree on a multilateral framework for the conservation and management of the swordfish in the South East Pacific, with a diplomatic conference to be held in 2002. The provisional arrangement envisaged a more permanent agreement being put in place by 2004.

---

[502] See ITLOS Order, 15 March 2001, www.itlos.org/case_documents/2001/document_en_99.pdf.

Regional rules for the conservation of fisheries

It is in the context of these developments that commissions and other international organisations established by regional and bilateral fisheries conservation treaties have been established and conduct their activities. The 1995 Straddling Stocks Agreement underlines their growing importance. Many were established in the 1940s and 1950s or earlier. In light of the changing rules of fisheries jurisdiction several have been amended or replaced to take account of the development of new fisheries laws. These regional bodies are established by treaty between two or more states and endowed with either or both of two related functions: an informational and research function, to study or obtain information on the conservation status of the fisheries over which they have competence; and a regulatory function, which grants them power to adopt binding or non-binding conservation measures (such as total allowable catches; meshes and net sizes; size limits of fish; seasons and areas; fishing gear and appliances; closed seasons; and total catches by species, group of species or region). As indicated above, the coming into force of the 1995 Straddling Stocks Agreement affirms and strengthens the role of sub-regional and regional fisheries organisations and arrangements in respect of straddling and highly migratory fish stocks.

The International Council for the Exploration of the Sea was among the first informational/research organisations. It is a regional scientific research body established in 1902 and reorganised in 1964 to collect and publish information supplied by its seventeen members.[503] The Council carries out co-operative research on particular species within the Atlantic area and adjacent seas, or parts of it. Although it does not have regulatory functions, it can make recommendations and has played an influential role. In the 1920s, the International Council was asked by the League of Nations to establish a commission of jurists to 'consider whether it is possible to establish by way of international agreement rules regarding the exploitation of the products of the sea', and this led to the adoption of a report prepared by Professor J. L. Suarez which proposed a far-sighted international regulatory regime but which had no immediate consequences in practical terms.[504] The Council has served as a model for international scientific bodies in other regions, which were subsequently rationalised under the auspices of the FAO.

In 1919, the International Commission for the Scientific Exploration of the Mediterranean Sea was established, which was replaced in 1949 by the Agreement which established the General Fisheries Commission for the

---

[503] Copenhagen, 12 September 1964, in force 22 July 1968, superseding the 1902 constituent instrument.
[504] 20 AJIL 230–41 and 752–3 (1926).

Mediterranean under Article 14 of the FAO Constitution.[505] Following the 1976 amendments, the competence of the organisation was expanded to include all matters for the conservation and rational management of fisheries, and its research and development activities were added to by allowing it to adopt recommendations. In 1948, the FAO established the Indo-Pacific Fisheries Commission (now the Asia-Pacific Fisheries Commission) to promote the full and proper utilisation of living aquatic resources.[506]

These scientific and informational bodies are accompanied by a number of other regional organisations which combine a scientific role with a regulatory role. The principal regulatory commissions or organisations are the following:

- International Pacific Halibut Commission (1923);[507]
- North Pacific Anadromous Fish Commission (NPAFC, 1952/1992);[508]
- South Pacific Permanent Commission on the Exploitation of the Marine Resources of the South Pacific (1952);[509]
- South-East Atlantic Fisheries Organization (SEAFO, 1973/2001);[510]
- International Baltic Sea Fishery Commission (1973);[511]
- Northwest Atlantic Fisheries Organization (NAFO, 1978);[512]
- South Pacific Forum Fisheries Agency (SPFFA, 1979);[513]

---

[505] Rome, 24 September 1949, in force 20 February 1952, 126 UNTS 257, amended 1963 and 1976; twenty-four states and the EC are party.

[506] Baguio, 26 February 1948, in force 9 November 1948, 120 UNTS 59, amended 1952, 1955, 1958, 1961, 1977 and 1993; twenty-one states are party.

[507] 32 LNTS 93, amended in 1930 (121 LNTS 45) and 1937 (159 LNTS 209). The new Convention was signed in Ottawa on 2 March 1953 and entered into force on 28 October 1953; the US and Canada are party.

[508] Convention for the Conservation of Anadromous Fish Stocks in the North Pacific Ocean, Moscow, 11 February 1992, in force 16 February 1993; four states are party. The 1992 Convention replaced the International Convention for the High Seas Fisheries of the North Pacific Ocean, Tokyo, 9 May 1952, in force 12 June 1953, 205 UNTS 65.

[509] 201 UNTS 374; four states are party.

[510] Convention on the Conservation and Management of the Fishery Resources in the Southeast Atlantic Ocean, Windhoek, 20 April 2001, not yet in force. The 2001 Convention replacing the 1973 Convention on the Conservation of the Living Resources of the Southeast Atlantic, Rome, 23 October 1969, in force 24 October 1971, 801 UNTS 101.

[511] 1973 Convention on Fishing and Conservation of the Living Resources in the Baltic Sea and the Belts, Gdansk, 13 September 1973, in force 28 July 1974, 12 ILM 1291 (1973); five states and the EC are party; Amendment Protocol, Warsaw, 11 November 1982, in force 10 February 1984, 22 ILM 704 (1982).

[512] Convention on Future Multilateral Co-operation in the Northwest Atlantic Fisheries, Ottawa, 24 October 1978, in force 1 January 1979, 2 SMTE 60 (replacing the North-West Atlantic Fisheries Commission established in 1959); the Convention has fourteen parties.

[513] 1979 South Pacific Forum Fisheries Convention, Honiara, 10 July 1978, in force 9 August 1979, IELMT 979:57; seventeen states are party.

- North-East Atlantic Fisheries Commission (NEAFC, 1980);[514] and
- North Atlantic Salmon Conservation Organization (1982).[515]

Since the adoption of the 1996 Straddling Stocks Agreement, several other regional fisheries conventions have been concluded which will give rise to further regulatory commissions in the future.[516]

In addition to these fisheries organisations, other bodies which regulate marine living resources include those with regional competence (the European Community;[517] the Commission for the Conservation of Antarctic Marine Living Resources[518]) or species competence (the International Whaling Commission;[519] the Inter-American Tropical Tuna Commission; the International Commission for the Conservation of Atlantic Tunas; the Convention for the Conservation of Southern Bluefin Tuna; and the Indian Ocean Tuna Commission[520]).

Each organisation is governed by its own constitutional instrument and rules of procedure, and they have varied records of achievement in respect of fulfilling their objectives. Judging by fisheries catch statistics which continue to show significant over-exploitation even in areas where many of the commissions operate, it is clear that their achievements are, for the most part, limited. According to one commentator, 'most fisheries commissions have proved to be relatively ineffective in the management of fisheries within their competence';[521] according to another, a plausible case could be made that even if none of the international conservation agreements negotiated prior to 1970 had been consummated, the state of fisheries generally (as well as worldwide wildlife) would not have been significantly different.[522] Despite these historic failures and the growing emphasis being placed on coastal states' management rights and

---

[514] Convention on Future Multilateral Co-operation in North-East Atlantic Fisheries, London, 18 November 1980, in force 17 March 1982, 2 SMTE 107 (replacing the North East Atlantic Fisheries Commission established in 1949); the Convention has nine parties.

[515] Convention for the Conservation of Salmon in the North Atlantic Ocean, Reykjavik, 2 March 1982, in force 1 October 1983, 2 SMTE 157; NASCO, *Ten Year Review of the Activities of the North Atlantic Salmon Conservation Organization, 1984–94* (1995). The Convention has nine parties.

[516] See the Convention on the Conservation and Management of Highly Migratory Fish Stocks in the Western and Central Pacific Ocean, 5 September 2000, not yet in force, 40 ILM 277 (2001); Framework Agreement for the Conservation of the Living Marine Resources of the High Seas of the South Pacific (Galapagos Agreement), 14 August 2000, not yet in force (www.oceanlaw.net/texts/galapagos.htm); Convention on the Conservation and Management of Fishery Resources in the South East Atlantic Ocean, 20 April 2001, not yet in force, 41 ILM 257 (2002).

[517] Chapter 15, p. 781 below.   [518] Chapter 14, pp. 714–15 below.   [519] See p. 592 below.

[520] See p. 597 below.   [521] G. Rose, *Global Biodiversity*, 534.

[522] L. K. Caldwell, *International Environmental Policy* (1990, 2nd edn), 40 (citing the now expired North Pacific Fur Seal Convention as an exception).

conservation obligations, the fisheries commissions will continue to play a role, especially for migratory and high seas species.

Several reasons have been put forward to explain the limited success of these legal and institutional arrangements, suggesting the need for a radical overhaul to the law-making and enforcement process which would require further incursions to be made on the extensive right of states to permit high seas fishing.[523] First, the availability of reliable information on the status of stocks needs to be improved to ensure that decisions can be made on the basis of the best available information, including future trends. In particular, there is a need for an independent information-gathering function. Secondly, the manner in which the commissions determine total allowable catches needs to be based upon objective scientific criteria, including biological requirements, and if conservation on a sustainable basis is to be assured economic needs will have to be de-emphasised. Moreover, the decision to set total allowable catches should be separated from the decision on the allocation of quotas to individual parties to ensure that the decision on the former is reached on an objective basis. Thirdly, experience suggests that the allocation of quotas to parties works best when it is carried out by small commissions, suggesting that the institutional arrangements for commissions with more than three or four parties should be restructured. Fourthly, the emphasis on setting quantitative limits may be inefficient in that it applies to a catch after it has been caught, and should be supplemented by increased emphasis upon regulatory measures which are subject to port enforcement, including regulation of gear, area, season and duration requirements, and new techniques for limiting entry to particular areas and the conduct of certain activities. Fifthly, the commissions will increasingly need to take binding decisions on the basis of a majority vote to by-pass the blocking ability of the lone dissenter. Sixthly, there is a need to improve the domestic enforcement of international fisheries obligations, building on efforts which allow some of the commissions (such as the NEAFC and NAFO) to carry out limited surveillance based upon mutual inspection. To that end, consideration needs to be given to finding effective ways to allow the commissions to participate in the enforcement process. Seventhly, the whole question of membership in the commissions needs to be addressed to ensure that all states participating in fisheries activities in areas within their competence can participate in the legislative and enforcement process. Finally, there is a need to extend the use of international licensing and radar surveillance systems to improve upon existing, *ad hoc* monitoring arrangements which are relatively inefficient.[524]

---

[523] See G. Rose, *Global Biodiversity*, 534.

[524] Note, in this regard, that the ITLOS has ruled that the fitting of a surveillance device does not fall within the permissible limits of setting a bond in respect of the release of a vessel alleged to be engaged in illegal fishing: the *Volga* case (2002), see chapter 5, p. 220 above.

Driftnet fishing

D. M. Johnston, 'The Driftnetting Problem in the Pacific Ocean: Legal Considerations and Diplomatic Options', 21 *Ocean Development and International Law* 5
(1990); W. T. Burke, 'Driftnets and Nodules: Where Goes the United States?', 21
Ocean Development and International Law 237 (1990); W. T. Burke, 'Regulation
of Driftnet Fishing on the High Seas and the New International Law of the Sea', 3
Georgetown International Environmental Law Review 265 (1991); M. R. Islam, 'The
Proposed "Driftnet Free Zone" in the South Pacific and the Law of the Sea Conven-
tion', 40 ICLQ 184 (1991); T. Burke, M. Freeburg and E. Miles, 'UN Resolutions on
Driftnet Fishing: An Unsustainable Precedent for High Seas and Coastal Fisheries
Management', 25 *Ocean Development and International Law* 127 (1994).

Apart from the rules designed to protect particular species or habitats of fisheries, international law also regulates methods and means of fishing to conserve stocks. The Regulations established by the tribunal in the *Pacific Fur Seal
Arbitration* prohibited the use of nets, firearms and explosives, and similar provisions are to be found in many other international fisheries agreements. Recent
technological innovations have led to the use of driftnets of a width of up to
thirty miles to sweep the high seas with 'the single most destructive fishing
technology ever devised by man'.[525] Driftnets have been controversial because
of the advantages of scale which they bring to fishing practices and because
they incidentally catch non-target fish, dolphins, turtles and sea birds.

The first agreement to address driftnet fishing directly was the 1989 Convention for the Prohibition of Fishing with Long Driftnets in the South Pacific,
which requires parties to prohibit its nationals and 'vessels documented under
its laws' from engaging in driftnet fishing activities in the area governed by
the 1986 Noumea Convention.[526] The 1989 Convention defines a driftnet as a
'gillnet or other net or a combination of nets which is more than 2.5 kilometres
in length the purpose of which is to enmesh, entrap or entangle fish by drifting
on the surface of or in the water'.[527] Driftnet fishing activities include: the use
of a driftnet to catch, take or harvest fish; attempts to carry out such activities
or engage in activities which can reasonably be expected to have that result;
and any supporting or preparatory activities.[528] Parties must adopt measures
to prevent assistance in the use of driftnets in the Convention's area of application (the 'Area'), to prohibit the use of driftnets within their jurisdiction,
and to prohibit the transhipment of driftnet catches within areas under their
jurisdiction.[529] Further measures which parties are permitted but not required
to adopt (provided that they are consistent with international law) include: prohibiting the landing of driftnet catches within their territories; prohibiting the

---

[525] Cited in C. Stone, *The Gnat is Older than Man* (1993), 7–8.
[526] Wellington, 23 November 1989, in force 17 May 1991, 29 ILM 1454 (1990); thirteen states
are party. On the 1986 Noumea Convention, see p. 531 above.
[527] Art. 1(b).   [528] Art. 1(c).   [529] Art. 3(1).

processing of driftnet catches in their facilities; prohibiting imports of fish or fish products caught using a driftnet; restricting port access for driftnet fishing vessels; and prohibiting the possession of driftnets on board any fishing vessel within their jurisdiction.[530] The South Pacific Forum Fisheries Agencies (FFA) has administrative responsibilities, and the Convention additionally provides for consultation and co-operation with 'distant water fishing nations' and other entities in the conservation of South Pacific albacore tuna.[531] The Convention is only open to signature, ratification and accession by members of the FFA and to certain states or territories who are within or linked to the Convention Area.[532] In 1990, Protocols to the Convention were adopted to allow states outside the Convention Area to associate themselves with the Convention. Protocol I is open to states whose nationals or fishing vessels fish within the Convention Area and requires them, *inter alia*, to prohibit the use of driftnets by their nationals or vessels.[533] Protocol II is open to states which are contiguous with or adjacent to the Convention Area, and also requires them, *inter alia*, to prohibit the use of driftnets by their nationals or vessels.[534]

In 1989, the UN General Assembly took up the issue and in 1991 adopted a resolution calling on all members of the international community to ensure that a global moratorium on all large-scale pelagic driftnet fishing was fully implemented on the high seas, including enclosed seas and semi-enclosed areas, by 31 December 1992.[535] The resolution is addressed to 'all members of the international community', rather than to states or to members of the United Nations, and was adopted despite strong lobbying by commercial interests. The resolution also appears to implement the precautionary principle by shifting the burden of proof in decision-making: its Preamble notes that some members of the international community had reviewed the best available scientific data on the impact of driftnet fishing and failed to conclude that the practice had no adverse impacts on the conservation and sustainable management of marine living resources. The resolution is not itself legally binding, but the fact that it was adopted by consensus, that its terms are clear, and that it has received support from a very large number of states since its adoption, suggests that it may now reflect a rule of customary international law.[536]

---

[530] Art. 3(2). Parties may also take stricter measures: Art. 3(3).

[531] Arts. 5 to 9.   [532] Art. 10.

[533] Noumea, New Caledonia, 20 October 1990, not yet in force, 29 ILM 1462 (1990); Arts. 2 and 7.

[534] *Ibid.*, Arts. 2 and 7.

[535] UNGA Res. 46/215 (1991); also UNGA Res. 44/225 (1989); and UNGA Res. 45/197 (1990).

[536] Agenda 21 declares that 'states should fully implement' Res. 46/215: para. 17.54. The General Assembly has regularly returned to the subject, with a view to ensuring compliance with Res. 46/215 (see Resolutions 49/116 and 118 (1994); 50/25 (1995); 51/36 (1996); 52/29 (1997); 53/33 (1998); and 55/8 (2000). UNGA Res. 50/25, 51/36 and 52/29 all '[reaffirm] the rights and duties of coastal States to ensure proper conservation and

Marine mammals and tuna

R. M. M'Gonigle, 'Economising of Ecology: Why Big, Rare Whales Still Die', 9 *Ecology Law Quarterly* 119 (1980); P. Birnie, *International Regulation of Whaling: From Conservation of Whaling to Conservation of Whales and Regulation of Whale-Watching* (1985); P. Birnie, 'International Legal Issues in the Management and Protection of the Whale: A Review of Four Decades of Experience', 29 *Natural Resources Journal* 903 (1989); N. Doubleday, 'Aboriginal Subsistence Whaling: The Right of Inuit to Hunt Whales and Implications for International Environmental Law', 17 *Denver Journal of International Law and Policy* 373 (1989); A. D'Amato and S. Chopra, 'Whales: Their Emerging Right to Life', 85 AJIL 21 (1991); G. Rose and S. Crane, 'The Evolution of International Whaling' in P. Sands, (ed.), *Greening International Law* (1993), 159; D. Caron, 'The International Whaling Commission and the North Atlantic Marine Mammal Commission: The Institutional Loss of Coercion in Consensual Structures', 89 AJIL 154 (1995); P. Birnie, 'Small Cetaceans and the International Whaling Commission', 10 *Georgetown International Environmental Law Review* 1 (1997); M. Maffei, 'The International Convention for the Regulation of Whaling', 12 IJMCL 287 (1997); P. Birnie, 'Are Twentieth Century Marine Conservation Conventions Adaptable to Twenty First Century Goals and Principles?', 12 IJMCL 488 (1997).

The conservation of marine mammals (cetaceans, pinnipeds, sirenians), including whales, dolphins and seals, is an issue which has received widespread public attention since 1972, when a proposal was put forward at the Stockholm Conference to establish a total moratorium on commercial whaling.[537] Since then, the whale has emerged as a symbol of the world environment movement and has come to represent, perhaps better than any other single issue, the difficulty of reconciling the need to conserve biological diversity, protect cultural and indigenous values, and give effect to economic needs. Thirty years after Stockholm, the issue remains controversial.

Whale species have been hunted on a large scale since the eighteenth and nineteenth centuries for lamp oil, for perfume ingredients, and for the whale-bones used in corset stays.[538] In the second half of the nineteenth century, new technological developments, such as cannon-fired harpoons, allowed whalers

---

management measures with respect to the living resources in areas under their national jurisdiction, in accordance with international law as reflected in [UNCLOS]'. UNGA Res. 53/33 and 55/8 both '[reaffirm] the importance [they attach] to sustainable management and conservation of the marine living resources of the world's oceans and seas, and the obligations of States to co-operate to this end, in accordance with international law, as reflected in the relevant provisions of [UNCLOS], in particular, the provisions on co-operation set out in Part V and Part VII, Section 2, of the Convention regarding straddling stocks, highly migratory species, marine mammals, anadromous stocks and marine living resources of the high seas'.

[537] Chapter 2, p. 37 above.

[538] World Resources Institute, *World Resources (1988–9)*, 155.

to catch the faster species, such as blue, fin, sei, Bryde's and minke whales. By 1988, the grey whale was extinct in the Atlantic and has been nearly extinct in the Western North Pacific; the humpback, bowhead and black right whales were categorised as endangered; and the population of the blue whale, estimated at between 166,000 and 226,400 in pre-whaling times, had dropped to between 7,500 and 15,000 worldwide.[539] Other members of the cetacean family include dolphins, which are not generally endangered but have been adversely affected by modern fishing practices, such as driftnet fishing, in a way which has attracted widespread criticism because of the high rate of incidental taking of dolphins. Of the pinniped species, the Galapagos fur seal, the Juan Fernandez fur seal and the Guadalupe fur seal are thought to be vulnerable as a result of nineteenth- and twentieth-century sealing, tourism and human disturbance. The Japanese sea lion is thought to be extinct as a result of persecution by fishermen and coastal development.[540] For similar reasons the Mediterranean monk seal and the Hawaiian monk seal are endangered, and the Caribbean monk seal is thought to be extinct. Among the sirenian species the West African and the Caribbean manatee and the dugong are thought to be vulnerable species, and the Amazonian manatee is endangered.

Marine mammals are subject to the general rules established by UNCLOS governing the conservation of marine living resources as well as the special provisions of Article 65 of UNCLOS, which provides that nothing in the provisions relating to the exclusive economic zone

> restricts the right of a coastal state or the competence of an international organisation, as appropriate, to prohibit, limit or regulate the exploitation of marine mammals more strictly than provided for in [the provisions of UNCLOS on the EEZ]. States shall co-operate with a view to the conservation of marine mammals and in the case of cetaceans shall in particular work through the appropriate international organisations for their conservation, management and study.

This provision applies to the conservation and management of marine mammals in the high seas.[541] Marine mammals are protected by other treaties, including those which establish general rules, the 1973 CITES,[542] and 1979 Bonn Convention on migratory species. Four agreements are in place which specifically address whaling issues: the 1946 International Convention for the Regulation of Whaling (International Whaling Convention); the 1992 Agreement on the Conservation of Small Cetaceans of the Baltic and North Seas (1992 ASCOBANS); the 1992 Agreement Establishing the North Atlantic Marine Mammals Organization; and the 1996 Agreement on the Conservation of

---

[539] *Ibid.*, 156, Table 9.4.   [540] *Ibid.*   [541] UNCLOS, Art. 120.

[542] By 1983, Appendix I to CITES listed the following whales: sperm, fin, sei, blue, humpback, bowhead, right, Bryde's, grey and bottlenose, as well as several dolphin types, and all cetaceans not listed on Appendix I or II.

Cetaceans of the Black Sea, Mediterranean Sea and Contiguous Atlantic Area (1996 ACCOBAMS).

Whales: the International Whaling Commission   The International Whaling Commission (IWC) was established by the 1946 International Whaling Convention,[543] which replaced the 1937 Agreement.[544] It currently has forty-two parties. The 1946 Convention began as a whaling club, established 'to provide for the proper conservation of whale stocks and thus make possible the orderly development of the whaling industry', while taking into account the need to safeguard whale resources from over-fishing and to achieve optimum levels of whale stocks without causing widespread economic and nutritional distress in the context of an international system of regulation.[545] The Convention, which includes a Schedule establishing the detailed regulations and obligations under the Convention, applies to factory ships, land stations and whale catchers and 'to all waters in which whaling is prosecuted'.[546] The Convention does not, however, define what is meant by a 'whale' and this has led to differences of view as to whether the IWC has competence over dolphins and porpoises, which are all cetaceans and therefore members of the same taxonomic family as whales. The IWC has, however, exercised competence over small cetaceans in the past. For example, in 1980 it adopted a resolution recommending that the Scientific Committee, in part through the Sub-Committee on Small Cetaceans, continue to consider the status of small cetaceans.[547]

The IWC is the principal institutional organ established by the Convention, assisted by a secretariat.[548] Subsidiary organs include a Finance and Administrative Committee, a Scientific Committee and a Technical Committee, and other sub-committees established on an *ad hoc* basis. Decisions of the IWC are taken by simple majority of those members voting, except that a three-fourths majority of those voting is required for action under Article V.[549] The IWC's functions include studies and investigations, collecting and analysing statistical information, and methods of maintaining and increasing populations of whale stocks. More specifically, it has the power under Article V(1) to amend the provisions of the Schedule by adopting 'regulations' for the conservation and utilisation of whale resources, and under Article VI it may make 'recommendations' (which are not binding) on any matter relating to whales or whaling. The powers of the IWC under Article V(1) allow it to fix:

---

[543] Washington, 2 December 1946, in force 10 November 1948, 161 UNTS 72; forty-two states are party; the Convention has been subject to one amending Protocol (19 November 1956, 338 UNTS 366), but is usually subject to an annual amendment of its Schedule.

[544] 8 June 1937, 190 LNTS 79, and amending Protocol (24 June 1938, 196 LNTS 131); the 1937 Convention itself superseded the 1931 Convention for the Regulation of Whaling, Geneva, 24 September 1931, 55 LNTS 349.

[545] Preamble.   [546] Art. I.   [547] IPE III/B/26-07-80.   [548] Art. III.   [549] Art. III(2).

- protected and unprotected species;
- open and closed seasons;
- open and closed waters, including the designation of sanctuary areas;
- size limits for each species;
- time, methods and intensity of whaling (including the maximum catch of whales to be taken in any one season);
- types and specifications of gear and apparatus and appliances which may be used;
- methods of measurement; and
- catch returns and other statistical and biological records.[550]

The IWC has thus taken binding decisions on whaling, although the Convention establishes strict criteria for the adoption of amendments to the Schedule. Amendments must be necessary to carry out the objectives of the Convention; they must be based on scientific findings; and they must take into consideration the interests of the consumers of whale products and the whaling industry.[551] An amendment adopted by the IWC is binding on all parties unless one or more parties object to the amendment, in which case it is binding on all parties except those which object to it within the period of time provided by the Convention.[552]

There are a number of exceptions to the specific obligations established under the Convention and in the Schedule. The main one is scientific: parties may grant a special permit authorising a national to kill, take or treat whales 'for the purposes of scientific research subject to such restrictions as to number . . . and other conditions' as the party thinks fit.[553] The authorising party must report such authorisations to the IWC, as well as scientific information relating to whaling, including the results of the research conducted pursuant to Article VIII(1).[554] Despite these conditions the scientific exception was used by Japan, Norway, Iceland and the former USSR to continue whaling, although in 2001 Japan was the only country to issue such 'special permits'. The Convention also includes enforcement provisions. Each party must ensure the application of the Convention and the prosecution and punishment of infractions, and since 1949 at least two inspectors must be maintained on factory ships, and adequate inspection maintained at land stations.[555] In 1971, the IWC established an international observer scheme which grants the IWC limited powers of observation, intended to provide some international oversight.

The Schedule is subject to amendment at the annual sessions of the IWC and sets forth detailed rules which contain binding legal obligations for the parties. The six sections of the Schedule contain provisions interpreting key terms (in particular whale types); establishing seasons; limiting capture; providing for the treatment, supervision and control of whales; and setting out

---

[550] Art. V(1).   [551] Art. V(2).   [552] Art. V(3).
[553] Art. VIII(1).   [554] Art. VIII(1) and (3).   [555] Art. IX.

information requirements in relation to whaling.[556] In recent years, the Convention has been reoriented. Originally intended to be an instrument for the 'orderly development of the whaling industry', it has been transformed into the primary international instrument prohibiting commercial whaling. Events leading up to the moratorium on commercial whaling adopted in 1986 can be divided into phases. The first, which lasted until 1972, regulated the total amount of whales that could be taken in any year by setting 'blue whale units', (one blue whale was equal to two fin whales, or two and a half humpbacks, or six sei whales) but did not set individual species limits.[557] From 1972 to 1976, the IWC operated a quota on a species-by-species basis. In 1976, a 'New Management Procedure' (NMP) was put in place which divided each species into stocks and established a quota for each stock (Initial Management Stocks; Sustained Management Stocks; and Protection Stocks). In the meantime, by the early 1980s, the membership of the IWC had grown significantly, and for the first time composed a majority of anti-whaling nations. In 1982, the requisite three-fourths majority existed, and the IWC adopted a prohibition on commercial whaling by amending the Schedule to provide that

> catch limits for the killing for commercial purposes of whales from all stocks for the 1986 coastal and the 1985/86 pelagic seasons and thereafter shall be zero. This provision will be kept under review, based upon the best scientific advice, and by 1990 the Commission will undertake a comprehensive assessment of the effects of this decision on whale stocks and consider modification of this provision and the establishment of other catch limits.[558]

The Schedule was not amended at the May 2002 meeting of the IWC to allow a limited resumption of commercial whaling, despite strong lobbying efforts in support of lifting the moratorium. The ban on commercial whaling has led a number of countries, in particular Japan and Iceland, to make use of the Article VIII 'scientific whaling' exception, leading to further controversy and dispute over the meaning of 'scientific research', which is undefined by the Convention or Schedule.[559] The IWC has also adopted other exceptions including

---

[556] 1999 Schedule to the 1946 International Whaling Convention.

[557] S. Lyster, *International Wildlife Law (1985)*, 25.

[558] 1992 IWC Schedule, para. 10(e). The amendment came into force on 3 February 1983 except for the Governments of Japan, Norway, Peru and the USSR, which lodged objections. Peru withdrew its objection on 22 July 1983. Japan withdrew its objections with effect from 1 May 1987 for commercial pelagic whaling, from 1 October 1987 for commercial coastal whaling for minke and Bryde's whales, and from 1 April 1988 for commercial coastal sperm whaling. As Norway and the Russian Federation have not withdrawn their objections, the paragraph is not binding on them.

[559] In 1987, the IWC mandated the Scientific Committee to review annually all research programmes involving the killing of whales under special permits and report on whether the programmes satisfy the criteria on special permits for scientific research: see

catch limits for aboriginal subsistence whaling to satisfy aboriginal subsistence needs.[560] Other issues concern the competence of the IWC over whales in the exclusive economic zone, and countries such as Mexico and Brazil have taken the view that they remain free to take whales in their exclusive economic zones if they wish; whether to establish an Antarctic whaling sanctuary (in 1979, a sanctuary was established for the Indian Ocean, which was extended by ten years in 1992, and in 1994 a Southern Ocean Sanctuary was established to be reviewed after ten years[561]); and whether to replace the NMP with a Revised Management Procedure which would establish a new system for 'sustainable' commercial whaling based upon a new 'catch limit algorithm' formulated by the Scientific Committee in 1992.[562] The IWC has decided that the operation of any such procedure would require the establishment of a 'fully effective' inspection and observation scheme, comprising two elements: population assessment and monitoring; and an international inspection and observer scheme. The tensions in the organisation are reflected by developments in 1991 and 1992 which led to the creation of two new instruments, following the departure of Canada and Iceland from the IWC, and doubts expressed by Norway and Japan about their future participation.

Whales: other developments In March 1992, the Agreement on the Conservation of Small Cetaceans of the Baltic and North Seas (1992 ASCOBANS) was signed, and adopted as an agreement under the 1979 Bonn Agreement.[563] The Convention was negotiated in the context of drastic decreases in the population of harbour porpoises of the Baltic Sea and the adverse effects of by-catches, habitat deterioration and disturbance on populations of small cetaceans, in the Baltic and North Seas. It establishes a framework for co-operative action to

---

Resolution on Scientific Research Programme (1987). The Resolution establishes the following criteria:

- whether the research addresses questions which need to be answered to aid candid comprehensive assessment or meet other critically important research needs;
- whether the research adversely affects the overall status and trends of stock or the success of the comprehensive assessment;
- whether the research addresses questions which cannot be answered by analysis of existing data and/or the use of non-lethal research; and
- whether the research is likely to yield results leading to reliable answers.

See also Res. IWC 38/28 on Special Permits for Scientific Research.

[560] See para. 13(a) of the 1999 Schedule, which was adopted in 1982.

[561] 1999 IWC Schedule, paras. 7(a) and (b). In 2002, proposals for sanctuaries in the South Pacific and the South Atlantic failed to gain the necessary three-quarters majorities to be adopted.

[562] The Scientific Committee has unanimously recommended the Revised Management Procedures to the Commission.

[563] New York, 17 March 1992, in force 29 March 1994; eight states are party.

maintain a 'favourable conservation status' for small cetaceans, and commits parties to apply the conservation, research and management measures set out in the Annex within the limits of their jurisdiction and in accordance with their international obligations.[564] Its provisions do not affect the rights and obligations of a party arising under any other existing treaty, convention or agreement.[565] The Annex establishes a Conservation and Management Plan which establishes general obligations in relation to: habitat conservation and management; surveys and research; the use of by-catches and strandings; legislation; and information and education. The habitat and conservation measures commit parties to 'work towards' the prevention of release of hazardous substances, the development of modifications to fishing gear and practice to reduce by-catches, the effective regulation of activities which affect their food resources, and the prevention of other significant disturbance. Additional measures are required to establish an efficient system for reporting and retrieving by-catches and stranded specimens, and further obligations to 'endeavour to establish' the prohibition under national law of the intentional killing and taking of small cetaceans and the obligation to release any animals caught alive and in good health. The Convention is administered by meetings of the parties, assisted by an Advisory Committee and a secretariat. A second Agreement on the Conservation of the Cetaceans of the Black Sea, Mediterranean Sea and Contiguous Atlantic Area (1996 ACCOBAMS) was adopted in 1996 and came into force in June 2001.[566]

In April 1992, the Faroe Islands, Greenland, Iceland and Norway adopted an Agreement on the North Atlantic Marine Mammals Conservation Organization (NAMMCO)[567] as a counterbalance to the IWC which was seen by these countries as having been hijacked by non-whaling interests. The aims of NAMMCO include the conservation of marine mammals in the North Atlantic, although its powers are limited to those of an advisory and scientific nature. Participation in NAMMCO is open to other states provided that they are approved by all parties, a stringent requirement which reflects the desire to prevent entry by states which do not share a similar desire to allow the resumption of at least some commercial whaling and for increased cultural exceptions to the existing moratorium. It remains to be seen whether NAMMCO is an 'appropriate international organisation' within the meaning of Article 65 of UNCLOS.

More recently, France, Italy and Monaco concluded an Agreement Concerning the Creation of a Marine Mammal Santuary in the Mediterranean.

---

[564] Art. 2(1) and (2); 'small cetacean' is defined as 'any species, subspecies or population of toothed whales *Odontocet*, except the sperm whale *Physter macrocephalus*': Art. 1(2)(a).
[565] Art. 8.2.
[566] Monaco, 24 November 1996, in force 1 June 2001, 36 ILM 777 (1997); twelve states are party.
[567] Nuuk, Greenland, 9 April 1992, in force 7 July 1992; four states are party.

The 1999 Agreement establishes a sanctuary for whales and dolphins in the Mediterranean Sea off the coasts of the signatory states which is the largest marine protected area in the Mediterranean.[568]

Agenda 21 recognised the role of the IWC and its responsibility for the conservation and management of whale stocks and the regulation of whaling, as well as the work of its Scientific Committee in carrying out studies of large whales and other cetaceans.[569] This left open the question of the competence of the IWC to regulate cetaceans other than whales; Agenda 21 limited itself to calling on states to co-operate for the conservation, management and study of cetaceans.[570]

Tuna

A. Szekely, 'Yellow-Fin Tuna: A Transboundary Resource of the Eastern Pacific, 29 *Natural Resources Journal* 1051 (1989); J. F. Pulvenis, 'Vers une emprise des etats riverains sur la haute mer au titre des grands migrateurs? Le Régime international de la pêche au thon dans le Pacifique oriental', AFDI 774 (1989).

A number of international agreements specifically regulate tuna fishing: the 1949 Convention for the Establishment of an Inter-American Tropical Tuna Commission (1949 Tropical Tuna Convention),[571] the 1966 International Convention for the Conservation of Atlantic Tuna (1966 Atlantic Tuna Convention),[572] the 1989 Convention Establishing the Eastern Pacific Tuna Organization,[573] the 1991 Western Indian Ocean Tuna Organization Convention,[574] the 1993 Agreement for the Establishment of the Indian Ocean Tuna Commission[575] and the 1993 Convention for the Conservation of Southern Bluefin Tuna.[576] Outside these areas, no binding international management regime exists, which has led to disputes concerning fishing stocks and

---

[568] Rome, 25 November 1999.

[569] Agenda 21, paras. 17.61(a) and (b) and 17.89(a) and (b).   [570] Para. 17.62.

[571] Washington, 30 May 1949, in force 3 March 1950, 80 UNTS 3; thirteen states are party. In June 1998, a working group was established to review the IATTC Convention in light of the significant changes in international law relating to the conservation and management of marine resources since the Convention was adopted in 1949.

[572] Rio de Janeiro, 14 May 1966, in force 21 March 1969, 637 UNTS 63; the Convention was amended in 1984 and 1992; thirty-four states and the EC are party.

[573] Agreement Creating the Eastern Pacific Tuna Fishing Organization, Lima, 21 July 1989, not yet in force, www.oceanlaw.net/texts/oapo.htm.

[574] 1991 Western Indian Ocean Tuna Organization Convention, Seychelles, 19 June 1991, in force December 1992, www.oceanlaw.net/texts/wioto.htm.

[575] 1993 Agreement for the Establishment of the Indian Ocean Tuna Commission, Rome, 25 November 1993, in force 27 March 1996, www.oceanlaw.net/texts/iotc.htm.

[576] 1993 Convention for the Conservation of Southern Bluefin Tuna, Canberra, 10 May 1993, in force 20 May 1994, 1819 UNTS 360.

techniques, particularly concerning yellow-fin tuna in the Eastern Pacific area between the United States and Mexico.[577]

The 1949 Tropical Tuna Convention establishes a Commission to maintain populations of yellow-fin and skipjack tuna and other kinds of fish in the Eastern Pacific Ocean.[578] Its functions are to gather and interpret information necessary to maintain the populations of these fish, and to recommend on the basis of scientific investigations 'proposals for joint action by the . . . parties designed to keep the populations of fishes covered by [the] Convention at those levels of abundance which will permit the maximum sustained catch'.[579] In 1962, the Commission established a Yellow-fin Regulatory Area covering over five million square nautical miles, within which there were established annual maximum permissible global catch quotas.[580] The establishment of EEZs in the mid-1970s during the negotiation of UNCLOS led to more extensive claims by coastal states, and the exclusion of foreign vessels, in particular those of the US, from previously accessible waters. The 1989 Eastern Pacific Convention, which has not yet entered into force, was negotiated by Ecuador, El Salvador, Mexico, Nicaragua and Peru to limit the access of foreign fleets to surpluses left by coastal fleets. Each party is represented on the Commission and has one vote, and 'decisions, resolutions, recommendations, and publications' are taken by unanimous vote.[581] The Commission meets annually, and since 1949 has adopted resolutions and recommendations on a wide range of issues.

The objective of the 1966 Atlantic Tuna Convention is to maintain populations of tuna and 'tuna-like fishes' in the Atlantic Ocean and adjacent seas (including the Mediterranean) at levels 'which will permit' the maximum sustainable catch for food and other purposes.[582] The Convention establishes an International Commission for the Conservation of Atlantic Tunas composed of delegates from the parties, which meets once every two years, a Council with a smaller but representative membership which gives due consideration to the 'geographic, tuna fishing and tuna processing interests' of the parties, and an Executive Secretary.[583] In the Commission, each party has one vote, and, except as provided otherwise, decisions are taken by simple majority of the parties.[584] The Commission studies populations and may establish panels to review species, groups of species or geographic areas, and propose recommendations for joint action by the parties and studies and investigations.[585]

The Commission may, on the basis of scientific evidence, make recommendations 'designed to maintain the populations of tuna and tuna-like fishes that may be taken in the Convention area at levels which will permit the maximum

---

[577] Canberra, 10 May 1993, in force 20 May 1994, 1819 UNTS 360.
[578] Preamble and Art. I(1).   [579] Art. II(1) to (5).
[580] See P. Sand (ed.), *The Effectiveness of International Environmental Agreements* (1992), 265–5.
[581] Art. I(1) and (8).   [582] Preamble and Art. I.
[583] Arts. III(1), (2) and (4), IV(1) and VII.   [584] Art. I(3).   [585] Arts. IV and VI.

sustainable catch'.[586] Such recommendations become 'effective' for all parties six months after the date of notification, subject to a process of objections, depending on whether fewer than one-fourth, more than one-fourth or a majority of the parties object. This system essentially imposes an 'opt-out' process for parties objecting to a recommendation.[587]

Since 1966, the Commission has held annual regular meetings and special meetings every alternate year, during which it has adopted a range of resolutions designed to conserve tuna.[588] Of particular note are the quotas imposed on bluefin tuna harvests in the western North Atlantic, which has resulted in fisheries operations being moved to the North Pacific Ocean where no international management programme has yet been developed. Other regulations have been adopted on minimum size for yellow-fin tuna, bigeye tuna, bluefin tuna and swordfish; and limits on fishing mortality for bluefin tuna. In 1992, in the face of evidence suggesting the rapid and serious depletion of stocks of bluefin tuna, an attempt was made at the eighth CITES conference of the parties to list the bluefin tuna as an Appendix II endangered species. This led to a dispute over which treaty, CITES or the 1966 Convention, had jurisdiction. Without adequate support, no decision was taken at CITES and the matter was held over until the next meeting of the Atlantic Tuna Commission. However, a resolution was adopted under the 1966 Atlantic Tuna Convention which required the compulsory presentation of a statistical document when bluefin tuna are imported into the territory of a party, signalling a move by that treaty organisation towards a regulatory approach based upon trade information.[589]

The objective of the 1993 Agreement for the Establishment of the Indian Ocean Tuna Commission is to promote co-operation among its members with a view to ensuring the conservation and optimum utilisation of tuna and tuna-like stocks in the Indian Ocean and adjacent seas.[590] The Agreement establishes the Indian Ocean Tuna Commission (IOTC) with membership open to FAO members that are situated within the Agreement's area of competence, or whose nationals fish for tuna stocks within the area. Non-FAO members situated in the Indian Ocean or fishing in that area may also be admitted as members with the approval of a two-thirds majority of the IOTC.[591] In the Commission, each party has one vote and, except as provided otherwise, decisions are taken by a simple majority of the parties.[592] The Commission is assisted by a permanent Scientific Committee and may establish sub-commissions to deal with

---

[586] Art. VIII(1)(a).   [587] Art. VIII(2) to (4).

[588] See Compendium of Management Recommendations and Resolutions Adopted by ICCAT for the Conservation of Atlantic Tunas and Tuna Like Species, COM-SCRS/01/10, October 2001.

[589] Recommendation 92-1 by ICCAT Concerning the ICCAT Bluefin Tuna Statistical Document Programme, in force 25 July 1993.

[590] Art. V(1).   [591] Art. IV.   [592] Art. VI(2).

particular stocks covered by the Agreement.[593] The IOTC may, on the basis of scientific evidence, adopt conservation and management measures for covered stocks.[594] If adopted by a two-thirds majority of the Commission, the measures are binding though parties may 'opt-out' of particular measures by registering an objection within a 120-day period.[595] Since 1996, the IOTC has held six regular sessions and two special sessions adopting a range of resolutions concerning tuna conservation, including mandatory statistical requirements for IOTC members and a recommendation to establish a bigeye statistical document programme.[596]

The 1993 Convention for the Conservation of Southern Bluefin Tuna (CCSBT) establishes a special regime for the conservation and management of southern bluefin tuna, a highly migratory species. The Convention has four parties – Australia, New Zealand, Japan and South Korea – which are required to encourage accession to the Convention by other states whose nationals harvest southern bluefin tuna or coastal states with EEZs or fishery zones through which southern bluefin tuna migrate.[597] The Convention establishes a Commission for the Conservation of Southern Bluefin Tuna with competence to decide on a total allowable catch for the species which is allocated among the three parties.[598] The Commission's decisions are based on advice from a Scientific Committee composed of representatives from the parties.[599] Disputes over the setting of the TAC and Japan's implementation of a unilateral 'experimental fishing programme' to increase its catch of southern bluefin tuna in 1998 and 1999 led to invocation of the UNCLOS compulsory dispute settlement procedures by Australia and New Zealand in the *Southern Bluefin Tuna* cases.[600]

WSSD Plan of Implementation

One of the few areas in which the WSSD made a reasonable concrete commitment was in relation to fisheries, with a commitment to 'maintain or restore stocks to levels that can produce the maximum sustainable yield with the aim of achieving these goals for depleted stocks on an urgent basis and where possible not later than 2015'.[601] The Plan of Implementation also calls for states to become parties to the 1995 Straddling Stocks Agreement, to implement the 1995 Code of Conduct for Responsible Fisheries, and to develop and implement national and regional plans to put into effect the FAO's international plan of action to prevent, deter and eliminate illegal, unreported and unregulated fishing by 2004.[602]

---

[593] Art. XII.   [594] Art. V(2)(c).   [595] Art. IX.
[596] Resolutions 01/04 and 01/05.   [597] Art. 13.   [598] Arts. 6 and 7(3)(a).
[599] Art. 9.   [600] See p. 580 above.   [601] Para. 30(a).
[602] Para. 30(b)–(d). The Implementation Plan also calls for the elimination of subsidies that contribute to illegal, unreported and unregulated fishing: para. 30(f).

Birds

M. Bowman, 'International Treaties and the Global Protection of Birds', 11 JEL 87 and 281 (1999); D. Owen, 'The Application of the Wild Birds Directive Beyond the Territorial Sea of EC Member States', 13 JEL 39 (2001).

The international legal protection of birds is the express objective of three specific agreements: the 1950 Birds Convention, the 1970 Benelux Convention, and the regional EC 1979 Wild Birds Directive. Birds are also protected by the 1973 CITES, the 1971 Ramsar Convention, the 1979 Berne Convention, and agreements under the 1979 Bonn Convention, as well as many treaties of general application to flora and fauna adopted at the regional level. Several important bilateral treaties have also been adopted.[603]

1950 Birds Convention   The only global instrument specifically designed to protect birds is the 1950 International Convention for the Protection of Birds (1950 Birds Convention),[604] which superseded the 1902 Convention.[605] The absence of any institutional or financial arrangements to ensure that the Convention is implemented has limited its effectiveness. The 1950 Birds Convention, which has attracted limited participation, is intended to protect birds in the wild by granting protection to all birds during their breeding season, to migratory birds during their return flight to nesting grounds between March and July, and to species in danger of extinction or of scientific interest throughout the year.[606] Subject to certain exceptions, the Convention prohibits the import, export, sale, offer for sale, giving or possession of any live or dead bird, or part, or eggs or their shells or broods killed or captured in breach of the Convention.[607] The Convention also outlaws certain methods likely to result in the mass killing or capture of birds or cause them unnecessary suffering.[608] Articles 6 and 7 set forth a number of exceptions, subject to certain administrative obligations including the grant of individual permits. Each party must

---

[603] See e.g. Convention for the Protection of Migratory Birds in the United States and Canada, Washington, 16 August 1916, 4 IPE 1638; Convention for the Protection of Migratory Birds and Game Mammals (Mexico–United States), 7 February 1936, 178 LNTS 309; and Convention for the Protection of Birds and Birds in Danger of Extinction, and Their Environment (Japan–US), Tokyo, 4 March 1972, 25 UST 3329. Other bilateral agreements include US/USSR (1976); US/Japan (1972); Japan/USSR (1973); and Australia/Japan (1974); Japan/China (1981); India/USSR (1985); and Australia/China (1986).

[604] Paris, 18 October 1950, in force 17 January 1963, 638 UNTS 185. The Convention has ten parties.

[605] Paris, 19 March 1902, IELMT 902:22.

[606] Arts. 1 and 2. In *Count Lippens* v. *Etat Belge, Ministre d'Agriculture,* 13 March 1964, 47 ILR 336, the Belgian Conseil d'Etat held that Art. 2 did not lay down a positive rule of law, but constituted 'an undertaking on the part of the contracting parties that each one of them will take such steps by way of legislation or regulation as may be necessary to implement it', and it created neither rights nor duties for the individual: *ibid.,* 339.

[607] Arts. 3 and 4.   [608] Art. 5.

prepare a list of birds which may be captured or killed in its territory and a list of species of indigenous or migratory birds which may be kept in captivity, for the purpose of regulating trade in birds, to prevent their destruction, and to promote the creation of undisturbed water or land reserves.[609] In one of the earliest international provisions of this kind, parties are called upon to educate the public on the need to preserve and protect birds.[610]

1970 Benelux Convention   The 1970 Benelux Convention on the Hunting and Protection of Birds[611] further provides for the harmonisation of dates for the opening and closing of hunting seasons, procedures and methods permitted for hunting, and the adoption of additional measures for the protection of particular species of birds.[612]

1979 EC Wild Birds Directive   The 1979 EC Wild Birds Directive establishes a complex regulatory scheme for the protection of all species of birds and their eggs, nests and habitats in the European territories of the member states.[613] Member states must maintain the population of wild birds 'at a level which corresponds in particular to ecological, scientific and cultural requirements, while taking account of economic and recreational requirements, or to adapt the population of these species to that level'.[614] To this end, they must preserve, maintain or re-establish a sufficient diversity and habitat area for wild birds, including protected areas, re-establishment of destroyed biotopes and creation of biotopes.[615]

The Directive uses an Annex system to establish different levels of protection for various species. The 181 species listed in Annex I are subject to special habitat conservation measures to ensure their survival and reproduction, account being taken of species in danger of extinction, species vulnerable to habitat changes, species rarity, and any other reasons requiring particular attention.[616] For these species, the member states must classify the most suitable territories as special protection areas, taking into account protection requirements in their geographical sea and land area where the Directive applies.[617] In the *Santona*

---

[609] Arts. 8 to 11.   [610] Art. 10.

[611] Brussels, 10 June 1970, in force 1 July 1972, 847 UNTS 255.

[612] Arts. 1, 2, 4, 7 and 8.

[613] Council Directive 79/409/EEC of 2 April 1979 on the Conservation of Wild Birds, OJ L103, 25 April 1979, 1 (as amended), Art. 1; see Case 247/85, *EC Commission* v. *Belgium* [1987] ECR 3029, on the scope of application of the Directive.

[614] Art. 2.   [615] Art. 3.   [616] Art. 4(1).

[617] Art. 4(1). The ECJ has ruled that Art. 4(1) or (2) of the Directive does not allow a member state, when designating a Special Protection Area and defining its boundaries, to (1) take account of the economic requirements mentioned in Art. 2 of the Directive, (2) take account of economic requirements as constituting a general interest superior to that represented by the ecological objective of that directive, and (3) take account of economic requirements which may constitute imperative reasons of overriding public

Marshes case, the ECJ ruled that in giving effect to its obligation to designate under Article 4(1) and (2) a member state was not entitled to subordinate ecological interests to other interests, such as economic and social interests, and that although Member States have

> a certain margin of discretion with regard to the choice of special protection areas, the classification of those areas is nevertheless subject to certain ornithological criteria determined by the directive, such as the presence of birds listed in Annex I, on the one hand, and the designation of a habitat as a wetland area, on the other.[618]

The Court noted:

> In this connection, it is common ground that the Santona marshes are one of the most important ecosystems in the Iberian peninsula for many aquatic birds. The marshes serve as a wintering area or staging post for many birds on their migrations from European countries to the southern latitudes of Africa and the Iberian peninsula itself. The birds observed in the area include various species that are becoming extinct, in particular the spoonbill, which feeds and rests in the Santona marshes in the course of its migrations. Moreover, it emerged from the case file and at the hearing before the Court that the area in question is regularly visited by 19 of the species listed in Annex I to the directive and at least 14 species of migratory birds.[619]

Similar measures must also be taken for the breeding, moulting and wintering areas of regularly occurring migratory species including wetlands of international importance.[620] These provisions so far as they relate to protection areas have been superseded by the coming into force of the 1992 Habitats Directive. Member states are additionally required to take steps to avoid pollution, deterioration of habitat or any disturbance affecting the birds in these special protection areas.[621]

Wild birds are protected from deliberate killing, capture, destruction of or damage to nests and eggs, taking of eggs, deliberate disturbance, and keeping of species of which hunting and capture are prohibited.[622] The sale and transport of wild birds or their parts is prohibited, except subject to certain exceptions for the twenty-six species listed in Annex III.[623] The Directive allows the hunting of

---

interest of the kind referred to in Art. 6(4) of the 1992 Habitats Directive: Case C-44/95, *R. v. Secretary of State for the Environment, ex parte Royal Society for the Protection of Birds* [1996] ECR I-3805.

[618] Case C-355/90, *Commission* v. *Spain* [1993] ECR I-4221, paras. 10 and 26.

[619] *Ibid.*, para. 27. The ECJ went on to find that Spain had also failed to take appropriate steps to avoid pollution or deterioration of habitats in the area of the Santona marshes, contrary to the requirements of Art. 4 of the Directive: *ibid.*, para. 58.

[620] Art. 4(2).

[621] Art. 4(4). On the Habitats Directive, see pp. 536–40 above.   [622] Art. 5.   [623] Art. 6.

the seventy-seven species listed in Annex II in accordance with its provisions,[624] provided that it is carried out in accordance with national measures in force, complies with the principles of wise use and ecologically balanced control of the species, and is compatible with the maintenance of regulation levels.[625] The Directive also limits the methods and means of capture and killing in accordance with Annex IV.[626]

The Directive allows limited rights of derogation, which have been strictly construed by the ECJ.[627] In *Commission* v. *Germany*, the Court held that a derogation must be based on at least one of the reasons listed exhaustively in Article 9(1) and must meet the criteria laid down in Article 9(2), the purpose of which was to limit derogations to what were strictly necessary and to enable the Commission to supervise them.[628] The Court has also made clear that the need to faithfully transpose Article 9 into national law 'becomes particularly important in a case where the management of the common heritage is entrusted to the member states in their respective territories'.[629] The Directive encourages research, and requires member states to ensure that the introduction of species of birds which are not wild does not prejudice local flora and fauna.[630] Member states must provide the EC Commission with a triennial report on implementation, and may introduce more stringent requirements.[631]

The Directive has been the subject of a significant body of case law before the ECJ, almost invariably involving cases brought by the EC Commission against individual member states for non-compliance with the provisions of the Directive, although frequently the Commission will have acted on the basis of information provided by environmental groups. The Court has held Germany, France, Belgium, Italy, the Netherlands and Ireland to be in violation.[632] Since some of the important substantive provisions of the Directive are similar, if not

---

[624] Art. 7.   [625] Art. 7(4).   [626] Art. 8.

[627] Art. 9. One of the grounds for derogation is 'serious damage' to crops, livestock, forests, fisheries and water: Art. 9(1)(a). In Case 247/85, *EC Commission* v. *Belgium* [1987] ECR 3029, the ECJ stressed that damage should be 'serious' to justify derogations.

[628] [1987] ECR 3503.

[629] Case C-339/87, *EC Commission* v. *Netherlands* [1993] 2 CMLR 360 at 386.

[630] Arts. 10 and 11.

[631] Arts. 12 and 14. On the introduction of measures which do not relate to an endangered species, see Case 169/89, *Re Gourmetterie Van den Burg* [1990] ECR 2143; see chapter 19, p. 990 below.

[632] See e.g. Case 236/85, *EC Commission* v. *Netherlands* [1987] ECR 3989; Case 247/85, *EC Commission* v. *Belgium* [1987] ECR 3029; Case 252/85, *EC Commission* v. *France* [1988] ECR 2243; Case 262/85, *EC Commission* v. *Italy* [1987] ECR 3073; Case 412/85, *EC Commission* v. *Germany* [1987] ECR 3503; Case C-288/88, *EC Commission* v. *Germany* [1990] ECR I-2721; Case C-3/96, *EC Commission* v. *Netherlands* [1998] ECR I-3031; Case C-166/97, *EC Commission* v. *France* [1999] ECR I-1719; Case C-96/98, *EC Commission* v. *France* [1999] ECR I-8531; Case C-38/99, *EC Commission* v. *France* [2000] ECR I-10941; Case C-374/98, *EC Commission* v. *France* [2000] ECR I-10799; and Case C-159/99, *EC Commission* v. *Italy* [2001] ECR I-4007.

identical, to those of the 1979 Berne Convention and the 1992 Habitats Directive, the Court's jurisprudence is of broader significance, particularly in respect of derogations and exceptions. In a later *Commission* v. *Germany* case, the EC Commission sought an injunction to stop works and a declaration from the Court that Germany was in breach of Article 4 of the Directive by planning or undertaking dyke-building works which were detrimental to the habitat of protected birds in a special protection area, and which would lead to a reduction of that special protection area.[633] The Commission argued that the first sentence of Article 4(4) of the Directive (Annex I species 'shall be the subject of special conservation measures') required member states to take positive steps to avoid deterioration or pollution of habitats as part of the management of special protection areas, without exception and without economic interests being taken into consideration. The Court accepted that member states could only reduce the extent of a special protection area on exceptional grounds corresponding to a general interest which was superior to the interest represented by the ecological objective of the Directive. The Court made it clear that the interests referred to in Article 2 (economic and recreational requirements) were not relevant to the establishment of such a general interest. However, the Court relied upon a superior general interest, the need to prevent flooding and to ensure coastal protection, and held the dyke works, which included the protection of a fishing port and the strengthening of coastal structures, to be sufficiently important to override the conservation provisions of the Directive. This finding was subject to the limitation, based upon the principle of proportionality, that the measures should be confined to the strict minimum necessary and should result in the smallest possible reduction of special protection areas. In reaching its conclusion, the Court was evidently influenced by the fact that the dyke would also have some positive consequences for the habitat of the birds, by allowing the formation of meadows of ecological importance.

Other land animals[634]

1973 Polar Bear Agreement   The 1973 Agreement on Conservation of Polar Bears[635] prohibits the taking of polar bears in the Arctic except for *bona fide* scientific or conservation purposes, and to prevent serious disturbance of the management of other living resources.[636] Taking is also permitted by local

---

[633] [1991] ECR I-883.

[634] See also Agreement on Conservation of Seals in the Wadden Sea Area, Bonn, 16 October 1990, in force 1 October 1991, www.wcmc.org.uk/cms/sea_text.htm.

[635] Oslo, 15 November 1973, in force 26 May 1976, 13 ILM 13 (1973); [000] states are party. The Convention replaces the interim Convention adopted at Washington on 9 February 1957, amended by Protocol adopted at Washington on 8 October 1963, by exchange of notes entering into force on 3 September 1969, and by a second Protocol adopted at Washington on 7 May 1976, a third Protocol in 1980 and a fourth Protocol on 12 October 1984.

[636] Arts. I and III(1)(a)–(c); 'taking' includes hunting, killing and capturing: Art. I(2).

people using traditional methods in the exercise of their traditional rights and wherever polar bears have or might have been subject to taking by traditional means by nationals.[637] Parties must protect the ecosystems of polar bears, including habitat components such as denning and feeding sites and migration patterns, and must manage populations in accordance with sound conservation practices on the basis of the best available scientific data.[638] Trade in polar bears or their parts is prohibited under the Convention, which also encourages research, actions for compliance by nationals of non-parties, and consultation.[639] The Convention establishes no institutions, but consultation meetings for the parties are held every four years, most recently in 1991.

1979 Vicuna Convention[640]   The 1979 Convention for the Conservation and Management of the Vicuna,[641] which is premised in part upon the potential economic benefits of the vicuna, prohibits hunting and illegal trade in the vicuna and its products and derivatives in the territories of all parties, and provides for co-operation on research, technical assistance and training.[642] Internal and external trade was prohibited until 31 December 1989, but any party may allow trade under strict state control if the population of the vicuna 'would allow the production of meat, viscera and bones, as well as the processing of skins and wool into cloth', and in accordance with internationally recognised marks and in co-ordination with CITES.[643] Fertile vicunas and their semen or other reproductive material may only be exported to other parties for the purpose of research or repopulation.[644]

Migratory species

N. D. Bankes, 'Migratory Caribou Convention', 18 *Canadian Yearbook of International Law* 285 (1980); C. de Klemm, 'Migratory Species in International Law', 29 *Natural Resources Journal* 935 (1989); S. Lyster, 'The Convention on the Conservation of Migratory Species of Wild Animals', 29 *Natural Resources Journal* 979 (1989); D. Navid, 'The International Law of Migratory Species: The Ramsar Convention', 29 *Natural Resources Journal* 1001 (1989); G. R. Munro, 'Extended Jurisdiction and the Management of Pacific Highly Migratory Species', 21 *Ocean Development and*

---

[637] Art. III(1)(d) and (c).   [638] Art. II.   [639] Arts. V, VII and VIII.

[640] See also Agreement for the Protection and Conservation of the Vicuna, Buenos Aires, 2 February 1981.

[641] Lima, 20 December 1979, in force 19 March 1982, IELMT 979:94; 2 SMTE 74 (unofficial translation), replacing the 1969 Convention for the Conservation of the Vicuna, La Paz, 16 August 1969.

[642] Arts. 2, 7 and 8. 'Illegal trade' is defined as 'any form of transaction relating to vicuna and/or its products (sale, barter, import, export, transport, etc.) without control or authorisation from the competent State authority': Art. 9.

[643] Art. 3.   [644] Art. 4.

International Law 289 (1990); L. Glowka, 'Complementarities Between the CMS and CITES', 3 JIWLP 205 (2000).

Migratory species can be classified into four general categories: (1) marine species which breed on the shores of coastal states but migrate to sea during adult life (e.g. seals, sea turtles, anadromous fish); (2) highly migratory marine species which travel between adjacent areas on the EEZ and high seas (e.g. tuna, whales); (3) territorial species with a well-established migration pattern (e.g. ducks and geese); and (4) territorial or marine species which live in border areas and regularly cross jurisdictional boundaries (e.g. gorillas, elephants).[645] Since these migratory species do not respect national boundaries, they pose a particular challenge to an international legal order premised upon the territorial state. In order to apply conservation measures effectively, the only effective approach is by international legal regulation to apply 'concerted action of all states within the national jurisdictional boundaries of which such species spend any part of their life cycle'.[646] Several of the agreements described earlier apply to migratory species,[647] and the *raison d'être* for a host of others is the migratory nature of the species which is being conserved.[648] To date, the only treaty which has as its main objective the conservation of migratory species is the 1979 Bonn Convention.

1979 Bonn Convention The origins of the 1979 Convention on the Conservation of Migratory Species of Wild Animals (1979 Bonn Convention)[649] can be traced to Recommendation 32 of the 1972 Stockholm Action Plan and an initiative by the West German Government to prepare a draft migratory species convention which would remedy the lack of uniformity and limited application of the agreements in force at the time.[650] The 1979 Bonn Convention is potentially of global application and has seventy-nine parties. It is, according to Lyster, a particularly interesting agreement for three reasons: it covers an unusually broad range of threats to listed species; its provisions are 'unusually rigorous in their restrictions'; and it establishes a precedent in international wildlife law for providing subsidiary agreements which focus attention and efforts on particular species.[651]

The 1979 Bonn Convention has as its objective the conservation and effective management of migratory species, which are defined as:

---

[645] C. de Klemm, 'Migratory Species: A Review of Existing International Instruments', 15 *Environmental Policy and Law* 81 (1985).

[646] 1979 Bonn Convention, Preamble.

[647] 1971 Ramsar Convention, Preamble; 1979 Wild Birds Directive; 1992 EC Habitats Directive.

[648] E.g. the fisheries agreements; 1946 International Whaling Convention; 1966 Atlantic Tuna Convention.

[649] Bonn, 23 June 1979, in force 1 November 1983, 19 ILM 15 (1979); eighty states and the EC are party.

[650] S. Lyster, *International Wildlife Law* (2000), 278–9.   [651] *Ibid.*, 297.

the entire population or any geographically separate part of the population of any species or lower taxon of wild animals, a significant proportion of whose members cyclically and predictably cross one or more national jurisdictional boundaries.[652]

Article III provides for the listing in Appendix 1 of migratory species where there is reliable evidence that the species is endangered.[653] 'Endangered' means that a migratory species is 'in danger of extinction throughout all or a significant portion of its range'.[654] Parties that are range states of Appendix I migratory species must then endeavour: to conserve and restore habitats; to prevent or minimise adverse effects of activities which seriously impede or prevent the migration of species; and to prevent, reduce or control factors that are endangering or are likely to further endanger the species.[655] Range state parties must also prohibit the taking of Appendix I migratory species, unless the taking is for scientific purposes, or to enhance the propagation or survival of a species, or to accommodate the needs of subsistence users, or where extraordinary circumstances require, and subject to notification of the secretariat of any such taking.[656]

Articles IV and V provide for the listing in Appendix II of migratory species (which could also be listed in Appendix I) which

> have an unfavourable conservation status and which require international agreements for their conservation and management, as well as those which have a conservation status which would significantly benefit from the international co-operation that could be achieved by an international agreement.[657]

An 'unfavourable conservation status' exists where:

1. the migratory species is not maintaining itself on a long-term basis as a viable component of its ecosystems; or
2. the range of the migratory species is either being reduced or likely to be reduced on a long-term basis; or
3. there is not, and will not be in the foreseeable future, a sufficient habitat to maintain the population of the migratory species on a long-term basis; or
4. the distribution and abundance of the migratory species do not approach historic coverage and levels to the extent that potentially suitable ecosystems exist and to the extent consistent with wise wildlife management.[658]

---

[652] Preamble and Arts. I(1)(a) and II(1).   [653] Art. III(1) and (2).   [654] Art. I(1)(e).

[655] Art. III(4). A 'range state' is one which 'exercises jurisdiction over any part of the range of that migratory species, or a state, flag vessels of which are engaged outside national jurisdictional limits in taking that migratory species': Art. I(1)(h). 'Range' means 'all the areas of land or water that a migratory species inhabits, stays in temporarily, crosses or overflies at any time on its normal migration route': Art. I(1)(f).

[656] Art. III(5) and (7).   [657] Art. IV(1).   [658] Art. I(1)(c) and (d).

In such circumstances, range states are required to endeavour to conclude agreements to benefit these species, with a view to restoring the migratory species concerned to a favourable conservation status or to maintain such a status.[659] The agreements should cover the whole of the range of the migratory species concerned, deal with more than one migratory species, and be open to accession to all range states even if they are not parties to the 1979 Bonn Convention.[660] Article V(4) sets out the basic characteristics of these agreements. So far, eleven such agreements have been adopted under the Appendix II procedure:

- the 1990 Agreement on the Conservation of Seals in the Wadden Sea Area;[661]
- the 1991 Agreement on Conservation of Bats in Europe;[662]
- the 1992 Agreement on Small Cetaceans in the North Sea and the Baltic;[663]
- the 1994 Memorandum of Understanding Concerning Conservation Measures for the Slender-Billed Curlew;[664]
- the 1995 African-Eurasian Migratory Waterbird Agreement;[665]
- the 1996 Agreement on the Conservation of Cetaceans of the Black Sea, Mediterranean Sea and Contiguous Atlantic Area;[666]
- the 1998 Memorandum of Understanding Concerning Conservation Measures for the Siberian Crane;[667]
- the 1999 Memorandum of Understanding Concerning Conservation Measures for Marine Turtles of the Atlantic Coast of Africa;[668]

[659] Arts. IV(3) and (4) and V(1).   [660] Art. V(2) and (3).

[661] Bonn, 16 October 1990, in force 1 October 1991, www.wcmc.org.uk/cms/sea_text.htm. The Agreement seeks to prohibit the taking of seals from the Wadden Sea, to preserve habitats, and to limit pollution (Arts. VI to VIII).

[662] 1991 Agreement on the Conservation of Populations of European Bats, London, 4 December 1991, in force 16 January 1994, www.wcmc.org.uk/cms/bat_text.htm. The Agreement, which is open to range states which are not parties to the 1979 Bonn Convention, establishes rules of special protection for bats and their habitats (Art. III). The Agreement allows specific reservations for particular species of bat (Art. VIII).

[663] See below.

[664] 1991 Memorandum of Understanding Concerning Conservation Measures for the Slender-Billed Curlew, in force 10 September 1994, www.wcmc.org.uk/cms/sbc_text.htm. Parties to the MOU agree to provide strict protection for the slender-billed curlew and identify and conserve the wetlands and other habitats essential for its survival. States are also required to implement the provisions of an Action Plan annexed to the MOU.

[665] 1995 Agreement on the Conservation of African-Eurasian Migratory Waterbirds, The Hague, 16 June 1995, in force 1 November 1999, 6 *Yearbook of International Environmental Law* 306 (1995). Parties are required to undertake conservation activities in accordance with an Action Plan to protect 172 species of waterbirds dependent on wetlands.

[666] See below.

[667] 1998 Memorandum of Understanding Concerning Conservation Measures for the Siberian Crane, Ramsar, 13 December 1998, in force 1 January 1999, www.wcmc.org.uk/cms/sib_text.htm. The MOU seeks to ensure the survival of the West and Central Asian populations of the Siberian crane which are on the brink of extinction.

[668] 1999 Memorandum of Understanding Concerning Conservation Measures for Marine Turtles of the Atlantic Coast of Africa, Abidjan, 29 May 1999, in force 1 July 1999,

- the 2000 Memorandum of Understanding on the Conservation and Management of the Middle-European Population of the Great Bustard;[669]
- the 2001 Memorandum of Understanding on the Conservation and Management of Marine Turtles and Their Habitats of the Indian Ocean and South-East Asia;[670] and
- the 2001 Agreement on the Conservation of Albatrosses and Petrels.[671]

Further agreements are expected to be adopted on waterbirds of the Americas and Asia-Pacific, and for Sahelo-Sahahan mammals.

Range state parties must provide the secretariat with regular information on the migratory species listed in Appendices I and II for which they consider themselves to be range states, and on the implementing of measures.[672] Institutional arrangements comprise the conference of the parties, a Scientific Council and a secretariat.[673] The conference is the principal 'decision-making organ' of the Convention and has responsibility for reviewing implementation of the Convention, including reviewing and assessing the conservation status of migratory species, and making recommendations to the parties for improving the conservation status of migratory species and improving the effectiveness of the Convention.[674] Amendments to Appendices I and II are adopted at meetings of the conference of the parties by a two-thirds majority of parties present and voting, and they enter into force ninety days after the conference of the parties at which they were adopted for all parties, except for those which make a reservation within that ninety-day period.[675] The conference of the parties meets every three years and has met seven times, most recently in 2002, and added numerous species to Appendices I and II. The conference of the parties

---

39 ILM 1 (2000). The MOU signatories agree to work closely to improve the conservation of marine turtles and the habitats upon which they depend. States must endeavour to put in place measures to conserve and protect marine turtles at all stages of their life-cycle.

[669] 2000 Memorandum of Understanding Conservation and Management of the Middle-European Population of the Great Bustard, 5 October 2000, in force 1 June 2001, www.wcmc.org.uk/cms/Otis%20tarda_MoU.htm. The MOU seeks to improve the conservation status of the great bustard throughout its breeding, migratory and wintering range.

[670] 2001 Memorandum of Understanding on the Conservation of Marine Turtles and Their Habitats of the Indian Ocean and South-East Asia, Manila, 23 June 2001, in force 1 September 2001, www.oceanlaw.net/texts/turtles_mou2.htm. The objective of the MOU 'is to protect, conserve, replenish and recover marine turtles and their habitats, based on the best scientific evidence, taking into account the environmental, socio-economic and cultural characteristics of the signatory States'.

[671] 2001 Agreement on the Conservation of Albatrosses and Petrels, Canberra, 19 June 2001, www.wcmc.org.uk/cms/albatross_MoU.htm. The objective of the Agreement 'is to achieve and maintain a favourable conservation status for albatrosses and petrels' (Art. II(1)). This objective is to be implemented having regard to the 'precautionary approach' (Art. II(3)).

[672] Art. VI.   [673] Arts. VII, VIII and IX.
[674] Art. VII.   [675] Art. XI(1) and (4)–(6).

has also established a formal review process for selected Appendix I species with a view to recommending specific conservation action.

Cultural and natural heritage and landscape

Five international agreements establish rules for the conservation of cultural and natural heritage and landscape. Although these are not primarily aimed at the conservation of biodiversity, nature or natural resources, their provisions are generally broad enough to allow them to contribute towards conservation efforts of that type.[676] The primary instrument is the 1972 World Heritage Convention, which was supplemented in 2001 by the Convention on Underwater Heritage,[677] and regional heritage treaties have also been adopted for Europe[678] and the Americas.[679] In 2000, the Council of Europe adopted the European Landscape Convention.[680]

1972 World Heritage Convention The 1972 Convention for the Protection of the World Cultural and Natural Heritage (1972 World Heritage Convention), adopted under the auspices of UNESCO, establishes a 'system of collective protection of the cultural and natural heritage of outstanding universal value, organised on a permanent basis and in accordance with modern scientific methods'.[681] Natural heritage' is defined to include: (1) natural features 'of outstanding universal value from the aesthetic or scientific point of view';

---

[676] On the relationship between cultural heritage and the environment, see chapter 1, pp. 17–18 above, and chapter 18, pp. 876–7 below (relationship with liability for environmental damage).

[677] 2001 Convention on Underwater Heritage, Paris, 2 November 2001, not yet in force, 41 ILM 40 (2002). The Convention's objectives are to ensure and strengthen the protection of underwater cultural heritage and to preserve underwater cultural heritage for the benefit of humanity (Art. 2). It does not apply to natural heritage (Art. 1(1)).

[678] 1969 European Convention on the Protection of Archaeological Heritage, London, 6 May 1969, in force 20 November 1970, 788 UNTS 227. A revised convention was adopted in Valetta on 16 January 1992, ETS No. 143. See also European Cultural Convention, Paris, 19 December 1954, in force 5 May 1955, 218 UNTS 139.

[679] Convention on the Protection of the Archaeological, Historical and Artistic Heritage of the American Nations, Santiago, 16 June 1976, in force 30 June 1978, 15 ILM 1350 (1976); see also 1935 Treaty on the Protection of Artistic and Scientific Institutions and Historic Monuments, in force 26 August 1935, 167 LNTS 289.

[680] 2000 European Landscape Convention, Florence, 20 October 2000, not yet in force, http://conventions.coe.int/Treaty/en/Treaties/Html/176.htm. The aims of the Convention are 'to promote landscape protection, management and planning, and to organise European co-operation on landscape issues' (Art. 3), and to that end it provides for national measures (Arts. 4–6) and European cooperation (Arts. 7–11), including in relation to 'transfrontier landscapes' (Art. 9). Landscape is defined as 'an area, as perceived by people, whose character is the result of the action and interaction of natural and/or human factors' (Art. 1(a)).

[681] Paris, 16 November 1972, in force 17 December 1975, 1037 UNTS 151, Preamble; 176 states are party.

(2) geological and physiological formations and areas 'which constitute the habitat of threatened species of animals and plants of outstanding universal value from the point of view of science or conservation'; and (3) natural sites or areas 'of outstanding universal value from the point of view of science, conservation or natural beauty'.[682]

Each party identifies and delineates its own cultural and natural heritage sites, which constitute a world heritage for whose protection it is the duty of the international community as a whole to co-operate, but for whom the duty of protection, conservation, presentation and transmission to future generations belongs primarily to the individual party.[683] To that end, each party must adopt a general policy to integrate such protection into comprehensive planning programmes, to set up appropriate services, to foster training, to take necessary legal and other measures, and to submit reports to the general Conference of UNESCO on measures they have taken.[684] More specifically, each party is 'not to take any deliberate measures which might damage directly or indirectly the cultural and natural heritage' of the territory of other parties.[685]

In *Commonwealth of Australia and Another* v. *State of Tasmania and Others*,[686] the Australian High Court was required to interpret Articles 4 and 5 of the 1972 Convention, and by a narrow majority held that the provisions imposed an international obligation on Australia to take appropriate measures for the preservation of the world heritage area. The case arose following the nomination by the Commonwealth of Australia in November 1991, at the request of the Premier of the State of Tasmania, of three parks in south-west Tasmania for inclusion on the World Heritage List. Australia maintained the nomination despite the request for its withdrawal by the next Premier of Tasmania who took over following an election. In December 1982, the World Heritage Committee included the three parks in the World Heritage List under Article 11(2) of the Convention. The Government of Tasmania nevertheless authorised and commenced work on the construction of a hydro-electric dam which would have flooded a large part of the nominated area. In entering the parks on the List, the World Heritage Committee expressed its concern at the likely effect of the construction of the dam and recommended that 'the Australian authorities take all possible measures to protect the integrity of the property'. The Australian Government then adopted the World Heritage Properties Conservation Act 1983 and Regulations under the National Parks and Wildlife Conservation Act 1975 (Commonwealth) which would make the construction of the dam unlawful on

---

[682] Art. 2. 'Cultural heritage' includes monuments, groups of buildings and sites of outstanding universal value from the point of view of, *inter alia*, history, art, science, aesthetics, ethnology or anthropology: Art. 1.

[683] Art. 4.   [684] Arts. 5 and 29.   [685] Art. 6(3).

[686] Judgment of 1 July 1983, 68 ILR 266; T. Atherton and T. Atherton, 'The Power and the Glory: National Sovereignty and the World Heritage Convention', 69 *Australian Law Journal* 631 (1995).

the basis, *inter alia*, that it was necessary to give effect to the provisions of the 1972 Convention.

The case turned on the validity of the 1983 Act and the Regulations, and in particular whether they were within the constitutional power of the Commonwealth. Central to the case was the question of whether Articles 4 and 5 of the World Heritage Convention imposed any legal obligation upon Australia to protect the area entered on the List and, if so, what kind of obligation. A four-judge majority of the High Court held that Articles 4 and 5 imposed an international obligation on Australia to take appropriate measures for the preservation of the world heritage area; two dissenting judges took the view that Articles 4 and 5 imposed no obligation on a country with respect to its own heritage area; and one judge did not decide the point. The individual judgments bear careful consideration, not only because they throw some light on the provisions under scrutiny but also because they illustrate the different approaches to interpretation of treaty language and their consequences which are also relevant in respect of the provisions found in other international environmental agreements. The language used in the 1972 Convention is similar to that in many other environmental agreements, in particular for couching obligations in terms which are neither particularly clear nor framed so as to impose what might be considered to be mandatory and inflexible requirements.

Justice Mason, with the majority, considered that Articles 4 and 5 imposed binding obligations on Australia, and that Article 5 imposed a series of obligations, including the taking of legal measures, as

> an element in a general framework which has as its foundation (a) the responsibility of each state under Art. 3 to identify and delineate the different properties situated in its territory which answer the descriptions of 'cultural heritage' in Art. 1 and 'natural heritage' in Art. 2; and (b) the first sentence in Art. 4 which amounts to a recognition of the general or universal responsibility for the protection, preservation, etc. of the heritage and a declaration that it 'belongs primarily to' the state in which the heritage is situated. The sentence which follows is a strong and positive declaration of what each state will do in the discharge of the responsibility affirmed by the first sentence.[687]

Justice Mason held that Article 5 imposed obligations on each state which 'could not be read as a mere statement of intention: it was 'expressed in the form of a command requiring each party to endeavour to bring about the matters dealt with' in the subparagraphs.[688] For Judge Murphy, the Convention, in particular Article 5, imposed a real obligation, even taking into account the imprecise standards of obligation under international law.[689] Judge Brennan held that Articles 4 and 5 created a clear obligation upon Australia to act 'though the extent of that obligation may be affected by decisions taken by Australia in good

---

[687] 68 ILR 266 at 340.   [688] *Ibid.*   [689] *Ibid.*, 379.

faith'.[690] For Judge Deane, the absence of precision in Articles 4 and 5 did not prevent Australia from binding itself under the terms of the Convention and assuming real and substantive obligations in respect of the three parks.[691]

The minority included the Chief Justice, who concluded that, on 'the proper construction of the articles, the questions what a state party can do, how far its resources extend, what is possible and what is appropriate are clearly left to the state party itself to decide. [Articles 4 and 5] do not impose on any state Party an obligation to take any specific action.'[692] For Judge Wilson, Article 4 was at most a promise by each party to do what it can to advance the objectives of the Convention with 'no resort to the language of obligation',[693] and the purpose and functions of Article 5 were aspirational to set goals in order to encourage and guide the parties.[694]

Judge Dawson remained on the fence. He was prepared to 'assume for the purposes of the argument that [the provisions of the Convention] are oblig- atory', but that the terms of the Convention fell short of 'demonstrating the degree of international concern over its subject matter . . . sufficient to stamp it with the characteristics necessary to make it part of [Australia's] external affairs'.[695] Judge Dawson considered that the Convention reflected

> the extreme care which has been taken to affirm the right of individual par- ties to determine not only what constitutes the cultural and natural heritage situated upon its territory which is deserving of international attention, but also the right to determine whether it is possible or appropriate to en- deavour to take measures suggested by the Convention for the protection, conservation and presentation of that heritage. The Convention recognises plainly that in this field of endeavour there can be no absolute imperatives and that difficult decisions must be made which involve the compromise of environmental, social and economic values. Those decisions are left to the individual parties to the Convention with the exhortation that they should endeavour, in so far as possible, and as appropriate for each country, to identify and conserve their heritage.[696]

The Convention is administered by the World Heritage Committee (Intergov- ernmental Committee for the Protection of the Cultural and Natural Heritage of Outstanding Universal Value), which comprises twenty-one parties repre- senting an 'equitable representation of the different regions and cultures of the world', and a secretariat at UNESCO, and the General Assembly of state parties to the Convention.[697] Parties submit inventories of their properties to the World Heritage Committee, from which the Committee maintains a World Heritage List of sites, which now amounts to 721 sites, of which 554 are cultural, 144 are

---

[690] *Ibid.*, 423.   [691] *Ibid.*, 454–5.   [692] *Ibid.*, 301–2.   [693] *Ibid.*, 390.
[694] *Ibid.*, 391: according to Judge Wilson, the use of the word 'endeavour' in Art. 5 fell short of creating an obligation: *ibid.*
[695] *Ibid.*, 497.   [696] *Ibid.*, 497.   [697] Arts. 8(1) and (2), 14 and 16(1).

natural, and 23 are cultural and natural.[698] Inclusion on the List requires the consent of the party or parties concerned.[699] From the World Heritage List the Committee establishes a subsidiary 'List of World Heritage in Danger', comprising sites threatened by 'serious and specific dangers' and for the conservation of which 'major operations' are necessary and for which assistance under the Convention is requested.[700] The Committee has established criteria for both lists. Properties included or potentially suitable for inclusion in the lists can receive international assistance to secure their protection, conservation, presentation or rehabilitation.[701]

The Convention establishes a World Heritage Fund as a trust fund of compulsory and voluntary contributions and other resources, the use of which is to be decided by the Committee.[702] Any party may request international assistance for cultural or natural heritage property identified on the List or the Danger List which has outstanding universal value situated within its territory.[703]

Conclusions

The conservation of biodiversity probably presents greater regulatory challenges to international law than any other environmental issue. The threats to biodiversity come from a multitude of sources, requiring a comprehensive approach to regulation of a broad range of human activities. Moreover, the conservation of biodiversity illustrates clearly the range of difficulties which exist in developing and applying rules of international law to resources which frequently do not respect national boundaries or are found in areas beyond national jurisdiction, and which require full consideration to be given to the social, cultural, ecological and economic values which different people place on different species. The conservation of biodiversity has, for many environmentalists and for citizens, a particularly important symbolic value which also raises issues about the balance to be struck between the conservation of nature and the conduct of human behaviour; the role of law must, ultimately, be limited to reflecting the values which humans ascribe to other forms of life.

International rules to address the conservation of biodiversity have been developed over a long period and reflect a consistent effort to rein in the human impulse for economic and industrial development even if it results in the loss of species. The roots of international environmental law date back to nineteenth-century efforts to ensure the conservation of biodiversity for economic, environmental, aesthetic and recreational reasons, and, from the

---

[698] Art. 11(1) and (2).   [699] Art. 11(3).

[700] Art. 11(4). These dangers include the threat of disappearance from accelerated deterioration, development projects, armed conflict, and natural disasters including changes in water level, floods and tidal waves: *ibid.*

[701] Art. 13(1).   [702] Arts. 13(6) and 15 to 18; chapter 20, p. 1030 below.

[703] Arts. 19 and 20.

cumulative experience which has been built up at all levels, it is now possible to obtain a sense of the effectiveness of various approaches. Many of the lessons learned about governance and the conservation of biodiversity apply equally to other areas of international environmental law. Three lessons merit particular attention.

The first relates to the observation that international law can be most effective where it is applied to address clear objectives: a lack of precision in legal language is invariably seized upon to justify a permissive interpretation of text, and its application becomes more difficult to oppose on political or legal grounds than would be the case if the legal instruments were clear. At one end of the scale it is hard to be clearer than language which completely prohibits an activity, and the experience following the adoption of the moratorium on commercial whaling suggests that, so long as they are supported by the necessary political will, absolute prohibitions can work. Similar considerations apply where legal instruments adopt targets and timetables, setting forth, for example, permissible catches of a particular species over a given timeframe, although the effectiveness of this approach depends in large part on the existence and operation of effective monitoring and enforcement arrangements. At the other end of the scale, it seems clear that the use of general language which calls on states to 'encourage' certain practices, or to use their 'best endeavours' to protect biodiversity, is unlikely to achieve any tangible conservation benefits. Lying between these two opposites is the more usual language which might, for example, require a general prohibition on deliberate damage, destruction or disturbance but allow exceptions on the basis of, for example, overriding public interest (see, for example, the 1979 Berne Convention, Articles 6 and 9; and the 1992 EC Habitats Directive, Articles 12 and 16). Exceptions are frequently used to justify activities harmful to biodiversity which would otherwise be prohibited. If international law is to be effective, a far more rigorous approach needs to be applied to the interpretation and application of exceptions of this sort, and the burden of justifying an exception should be subjected to a higher threshold of proof.

The second important lesson relates to the need to adopt a comprehensive approach and to plug gaps. Recent moves towards adopting an ecosystem approach suggest that the limited effectiveness of regulating particular species or types of species is recognised, and a broader approach to the conservation of biodiversity is now underway. Nevertheless, there are still important gaps which need to be filled. In 1985, Simon Lyster wrote that there were no migratory bird treaties covering South America, Africa, or Asia beyond the former USSR, and that there were no Asian wildlife treaties;[704] these gaps still exist some twenty years later. On the other hand, the 1992 Biodiversity Convention does promise to fill the other important gap he identified, namely, the absence of a

---

[704] S. Lyster, *International Wildlife Law* (2002) n. 130, 303.

worldwide treaty for the protection of habitats and ecosystems. This Convention is particularly important because it is global, adopts an ecosystem approach, and introduces on a broad basis the linkage between conservation and financial resources, by allowing the implementation by developing countries of their obligations dependent upon the receipt of adequate financial resources.

The third lesson relates to implementation and enforcement. It is clear that the adoption of regulations and the application of innovative regulatory techniques will not in themselves conserve biodiversity: international obligations need to be implemented and enforced, locally, regionally and globally, through the joint efforts of citizens, governments and international organisations. This will ultimately require the vesting of greater authority in international organisations to allow them to set standards and quotas, monitor activities, and enforce obligations. Additionally, there is a need to strengthen existing enforcement mechanisms and, if necessary, develop new arrangements which could be modelled on the conciliatory schemes established under the Montreal Protocol in respect of ozone depletion and under consideration for the climate change regime. The limited success of many existing legal arrangements derives from the lack of appropriate arrangements to address non-compliance, and the inability to adopt sanctions which can be enforced. In this regard, there is also much to be said for making greater use of the sanctions available under national legal systems, drawing from the experience (at least in some countries) of using national law to apply international legal commitments devolved downwards from CITES conference decisions. The belated recognition that implementation requires the availability of dedicated financial resources marks a new and significant development; the creation of a biodiversity 'account' at the Global Environment Facility is an important step, building upon the use of trade measures in instruments such as CITES which have proved to be reasonably effective in achieving their objectives.

12

Hazardous substances and activities

Introduction

International environmental law has tended to regulate specific environmental media and/or resources rather than particular activities or products. There is, however, a significant emerging body of rules which regulate those activities or products considered by the international community, within a region or globally, to be hazardous or dangerous and to merit specific attention. This chapter describes those rules by reference to international regulation of five areas, namely: (a) accident prevention, preparedness and response; (b) the classification, international trade, and transportation of hazardous chemicals and pesticides; (c) the working environment; (d) radioactive materials; and (e) biotechnology. This chapter also identifies and outlines the main international regulations which address activities considered to be particularly damaging to the environment, such as energy, mining, transport and agriculture. It will be apparent that the past few years have seen significant developments, in particular the adoption of legally binding instruments on international trade in chemicals and pesticides (1998), on trade and marketing of living modified organisms (2000) and on the production and use of persistent organic pollutants (2001).

To develop a comprehensive understanding of the extent to which international law regulates hazardous activities and substances, it is necessary also to consider the disposal of and international trade in hazardous wastes (chapter 13); the disposal of hazardous wastes at sea or in freshwater (chapters 9 and 10); the environmental impact assessment of hazardous activities (including lists and annexes indicating categories of activities which require prior environmental assessment) (chapter 16); information on hazardous activities and substances (including activities in respect of which information must be made available to the public or for which environmental auditing or accounting is recommended) (chapter 17); the regional rules of the Antarctic and the EC (chapters 14 and 15); and the rules on international liability for environmental damage caused by hazardous activities and substances (chapter 18). The first hazardous substances the production of which was prohibited by international law – certain ozone-depleting substances – are subject to the global regime described in chapter 8 in relation to the protection of the atmosphere.

This chapter describes particular aspects of the management of hazardous substances over their life cycle. It is clear that these rules have not been developed or applied in the framework of a co-ordinated regulatory strategy. The result is a patchwork of international regulations the applicability of which depends upon the nature and characteristics of a particular substance and the location of the activity which is manufacturing them or using them. Agenda 21 noted that globally harmonised hazard classification and labelling systems are not yet available, and the same is true of the rules governing manufacture and use. For hazardous substances and activities the absence of global rules is a real problem, since they may be easily transportable and do not, as a general matter, distinguish in their damaging effects between different peoples or environments. Harmonised rules establishing high standards of human and environmental protection are necessary but do not yet exist generally. Industrialised countries have put in place an extensive and complex body of binding legal obligations under regional agreements, EC law and OECD acts. The extent to which many of these rules apply to the activities of their registered corporations in developing countries is not clear; Agenda 21 recommended that companies should demonstrate a commitment, in respect of toxic chemicals, 'to adopt standards of operation equivalent to or not less stringent than those existing in the country of origin'.[1] In the 1990s, the increased concern of developing countries about hazardous substances was directed principally towards adopting national and international laws to stop the 'dumping' of hazardous wastes in their territories, although the 1991 Bamako Convention applies also to hazardous substances banned in the country of export. More recently, international efforts have been directed towards the adoption of binding international rules on trade in hazardous chemicals and pesticides (other than waste) and the production and use of 'persistent organic pollutants', as reflected in the 1998 Chemicals Convention and the 2001 POPs Convention.

As will be seen, hazardous substances and activities are not regulated by any single international organisation or treaty which establishes principles and rules of general application to all such substances or activities. The international community has, however, adopted broad policy guidelines. Principle 6 of the 1972 Stockholm Declaration declared that the 'discharge of toxic substances or of other substances and the release of heat, in such quantities or concentrations as to exceed the capacity of the environment to render them harmless, must be halted in order to ensure that serious or irreversible damage is not inflicted upon ecosystems'. According to Principle 14 of the Rio Declaration, 'states should effectively co-operate to discourage or prevent the relocation and

---

[1] See below. On the OECD's guidelines for multinationals, see chapter 3, pp. 102–4 above.

transfer to other states of any activities and substances that cause severe environmental degradation or are found to be harmful to human health'. As set out in the concluding section of this chapter, Agenda 21 and the WSSD Plan of Implementation have elaborated upon this general objective.

Rules developed after the 1972 Stockholm Conference arise from a range of international acts with differing legal qualities, with competence devolved to different international organisations. This has contributed to a certain lack of coherence, and reactive and fragmented rules which may be difficult to identify or interpret. Moreover, there is no general definition under international law as to what constitutes a hazardous or dangerous activity or substance, and many industrial and other activities which may, over time, pose significant long-term environmental threats are not subject to specific international environmental regulation. Examples include transport, mining, agriculture and energy, for which dedicated international rules are virtually non-existent.

Numerous international agreements internationalise the definition of hazardous or dangerous substances and activities and at least four approaches are discernible. The most common approach defines hazardous substances and activities by reference to their inherent characteristics, including their toxicity, flammability, explosiveness and oxidisation.[2] A second approach characterises activities as hazardous by reference to a listing system which identifies certain activities or projects on the basis that they are, *per se*, likely to have significant effects on the environment.[3] A third approach defines hazardous substances by reference to national laws. Finally, a fourth approach (which is increasingly utilised) is reflected in those efforts which do not seek to establish definitions of general application but instead regulate specific substances.[4]

Accident prevention, preparedness and response

Several international agreements promote international co-operation on accident prevention, preparedness and response in relation to hazardous activities or substances. These may relate to the provision of information in certain emergency situations[5] or might have been adopted to address particular hazards,

---

[2] 1996 EC Seveso Directive, pp. 622–3 below; 1992 Industrial Accidents Convention, pp. 623–5 below; EC Council Directive 67/548, as amended, chapter 15, pp. 784–6 below; and the various instruments relating to transport, p. 637 below; 1993 Lugano Convention, chapter 18, pp. 933–7 below, Art. 2(1) and (2) and Annex I; 1993 ILO Accidents Convention, Art. 3(a).

[3] 1985 EC EIA Directive (as amended), chapter 16, pp. 807–13 below; 1991 Espoo Convention, pp. 814–17 below; World Bank Operational Directive 4.01, pp. 821–2 below.

[4] 1985 Vienna Convention and 1987 Montreal Protocol, chapter 8, pp. 344–57 above; 1986 Asbestos Convention, pp. 639–40 below; 1998 Chemicals Convention, pp. 635–6 below; 2000 Biosafety Protocol, pp. 653–8 below; 2001 POPs Convention, pp. 628–30 below.

[5] OECD Council Decision on Exchange of Information Concerning Accidents Capable of Causing Transfrontier Damage (Preamble, Appendices I–III), 8 July 1988, 28 ILM 247

such as radioactive substances[6] or oil pollution at sea.[7] A large number of bilateral treaties also address transboundary accident preparedness and prevention, such as the Agreement between the United States and Mexico on the discharge of hazardous substances along the international boundary. This establishes a joint contingency plan to deal with polluting incidents, consultation, and joint responses to polluting incidents, and establishes a 'Joint Response Team' to, *inter alia*, advise on measures needed to respond to the incident and to take measures to co-ordinate resources.[8] The International Labor Organization (ILO) has adopted a Code of Conduct on Major Industrial Accidents[9] and a Convention on the Prevention of Major Industrial Accidents which draws on regional arrangements, and establishes responsibilities for the employer and public authorities, in relation to the conduct of activities and the preparation of emergency preparedness arrangements.[10] UNEP runs a programme on Awareness and Preparedness for Emergencies at the Local Level (APELL),[11] and in 1991 established, on an experimental basis, a UN Centre for Urgent Environmental Assistance to address the assessment of and responses to man-made environmental emergencies, including industrial accidents.[12] The Centre co-ordinates information and refers matters to existing emergency response mechanisms in the UN system and in other organisations. Its main focus has been on sudden events requiring immediate and urgent action, including industrial, transport, oil spill and other technological emergencies.[13]

The two most important instruments adopted to date are regional agreements, which aim to establish rules applicable to a wide range of hazardous and dangerous activities. These are the EC Seveso Directive (first enacted in 1982 and now replaced by a 1996 Directive), and the 1992 UNECE Convention on Industrial Accidents, which draws heavily on the Seveso Directive.

(1989); OECD Council Decision/Recommendation on Provision of Information to Public and Public Participation in Decision Making Processes Related to the Prevention of, and Responses to, Accidents Involving Hazardous Substances, 8 July 1988, OECD C(88)85, 28 ILM 277 (1989).

[6] See pp. 641–51 below.   [7] Chapter 9, pp. 440–54 above.

[8] Agreement of Co-operation Between the United States of America and the United Mexican States Regarding Pollution of the Environment Along the Inland International Boundary by Discharges of Hazardous Substances (Annex II to the US–Mexico Environment Co-operation Agreement), 18 July 1985, in force 29 November 1985, 26 ILM 19 (1987); Arts. II, III, V and VI and Appendices I and II.

[9] Prevention of Major Industrial Accidents: An ILO Code of Practice (1991).

[10] Convention No. 174 on the Prevention of Major Industrial Accidents, Geneva, 22 June 1993, in force 3 January 1996, www.ilo.org/ilolex/cgi-lex/convde.pl?C174.

[11] See UNEP Governing Council Decision 21/17, Further improvement of environmental emergency prevention, preparedness, assessment, response and mitigation (2001).

[12] UNEP Governing Council Decision 16/9 (1991); UNGA res. 44/224 (1989).

[13] See now the Joint UNEP/Office for the Co-ordination of Humanitarian Affairs (OCHA) Environment Unit to provide international assistance to countries facing environmental emergencies (www.reliefweb.int/ochaunep/).

1996 EC 'Seveso' Directive

EC rules are now to be found in a 1996 Directive, which has replaced the 1982 Directive adopted following a major industrial accident at Seveso, Italy.[14] The 1996 Directive has a more extensive application, by reason of the lower thresholds it applies, and provides more detailed obligations in relation to the prevention of accidents and the provision of information after they have occurred. The 1996 Directive is aimed at preventing major accidents which involve dangerous substances, and the limitation of their consequences for man and the environment, and is applicable to establishments where dangerous substances are present in quantities exceeding limits as listed in its Annex I.[15] A major accident is defined as:

> an occurrence such as a major emission, fire, or explosion resulting from uncontrolled developments in the course of the operation of any establishment covered by this Directive, and leading to serious danger to human health and/or the environment, immediate or delayed, inside or outside the establishment, and involving one or more dangerous substances.[16]

Dangerous substances are substances, mixtures or preparations listed in Annex 1, Part 1 (named substances) or fulfilling the criteria laid down in Annex 1, Part 2 (substances classified as hazardous under certain EC Directives (including Directive 67/548) or on account of their characteristics), and which are present as a raw material, product, by-product, residue or intermediate, including substances which may be generated in the event of accident.[17] The Directive does not apply to certain installations, including nuclear and military installations, transports (including in pipelines), extractive industries and waste landfill sites.[18]

Member states must ensure that operators take all measures necessary to prevent major accidents and to limit their consequences for man and the environment, to notify certain activities, prepare a document setting out the major-accident prevention policy (and ensure that it is properly implemented) and prepare a safety policy.[19] The Directive also requires national authorities to identify (on the basis of notifications received) establishments where 'the likelihood and the possibility or consequences of a major accident may be increased because of the location and the proximity of such establishments, and their inventories of dangerous substances' (referred to as the 'domino effect').[20]

---

[14] Council Directive 96/82/EC on the control of major-accident hazards involving dangerous substances, OJ L10, 14 January 1997, 13 (repealing and replacing Council Directive 82/501/EEC, OJ L230, 5 August 1982, 1, as amended).

[15] Arts. 1 and 2(1).   [16] Art. 3(5).   [17] Art. 3(4).   [18] Art. 4.

[19] Arts. 5 to 7 and 9, and Annex III (setting out the principles to be followed in establishing the policy).

[20] Art. 8 and Annex II.

Member states are required to ensure that operators responsible for the establishments to which Article 9 applies draw up emergency plans (in accordance with Annex IV), that the objectives of preventing major accidents and limiting consequences are taken into account in land-use and other relevant policies, and that any establishment, installation or storage facility where the measures taken by the operator for the prevention and mitigation of major accidents are seriously deficient is not used.[21] Safety plans are to be made available to persons liable to be affected by a major accident originating in an establishment covered by Article 9, and provision is made for inspections, for the information which is to be provided in the event of an accident (including to the EC Commission) and for information systems and the exchange of information.[22]

1992 Industrial Accidents Convention

The 1992 Convention on the Transboundary Effects of Industrial Accidents (1992 Industrial Accidents Convention) was adopted under the auspices of the UNECE and follows the approach of the original 1982 Seveso Directive. Its objectives include the prevention of, preparedness for, and response to industrial accidents, including those caused by natural disasters.[23] The Convention does not prejudice 'any obligations of the parties under international law with regard to industrial accidents and hazardous activities'.[24] The Convention applies to industrial accidents from activities involving hazardous substances, including categories of substances and preparations and named substances which are set out in Annex I.[25] It does not apply to nuclear accidents or accidents at military installations, dam failures, certain land-based transport accidents, accidental releases of genetically modified organisms, activities in the marine environment, and spills of oil and other harmful substances at sea.[26]

Parties must identify hazardous activities within their jurisdiction and ensure that affected parties are notified, holding any necessary discussions on the identification of hazardous activities that are reasonably capable of causing transboundary effects.[27] Annex III establishes procedures for consultations between parties of origin and potentially affected parties.[28] The Convention promotes international co-operation and the implementation of policies and

---

[21] Arts. 11, 12 and 17.   [22] Arts. 14, 15, 18 and 19.

[23] 17 March 1992, in force 19 April 2000, 31 ILM 1330 (1992), Art. 2(1); twenty-six states and the EC are party.

[24] Art. 3(5).

[25] Art. 1(a) and (b) and Annex I. The Convention follows the same categories as the original Seveso Directive and adds a new category of 'dangerous for the environment'.

[26] Art. 2(2).

[27] Art. 4(1) and (2). Disagreement on whether an activity is hazardous may be submitted by any affected party to an inquiry commission in accordance with Annex II for advice: *ibid.*

[28] Art. 4(3) and Annex III.

strategies towards measures of prevention, preparedness and response, including restoration, and requires parties to ensure that operators take 'all measures necessary' for the safe performance of hazardous activities and for the prevention of industrial accidents.[29] Annex IV details the preventive measures to be taken including: the setting of safety objectives; the adoption of legislative provisions or guidelines concerning safety measures and standards; the identification of activities requiring licensing or authorisation; risk evaluation for hazardous activities; information provision to authorities; application of the 'most appropriate technology'; appropriate education and training; the establishment of managerial structures and practices; and the monitoring and auditing of hazardous activities.[30] Operators are required to demonstrate the safe performance of the hazardous activity.[31]

Parties must develop policies on the siting of activities to minimise risk to the population and environment of all affected parties,[32] and establish and maintain adequate emergency preparedness, including on-site and off-site contingency plans.[33] In areas capable of being affected by an industrial accident arising out of a hazardous activity, the public must be given adequate information and an opportunity to participate in the relevant procedures on the development of prevention and preparedness measures.[34] The Convention goes beyond the Espoo Convention, by also providing that:

> Parties shall, in accordance with their legal systems and, if desired, on a reciprocal basis provide natural or legal persons who are being or are capable of being adversely affected by the transboundary effects of an industrial accident in the territory of a party, with access to, and treatment in, the relevant administrative and judicial proceedings, including the possibilities of starting a legal action and appealing a decision affecting their rights, equivalent to those available to persons within their own jurisdiction.[35]

The Convention establishes an industrial accident notification system, and requires parties to ensure that adequate response measures are taken as soon as possible, using the most efficient methods to contain and minimise effects.[36] The Convention establishes a framework for mutual assistance, requires parties to support appropriate international efforts to elaborate rules on responsibility

---

[29] Art. 3(1) to (3).   [30] Art. 6(1) and Annex IV.   [31] Art. 6(2) and Annex V.

[32] Art. 7 and Annex V, para. 2(1) to (8), and Annex VI.

[33] Art. 8 and Annex V, para. 2(1) to (5), and Annex VII.

[34] Art. 9(1) and (2) and Annex V, para. 2(1) to (4) and (9), and Annex VIII.

[35] Art. 9(3); on the 1991 Espoo Convention, see chapter 16, pp. 814–17 below.

[36] Art. 10 and Annex IX, and Art. 11. The first conference of the parties (November 2000) accepted a more detailed UNECE Industrial Accident Notification System, based on three reports (early warning, information, request for assistance): www.unece.org/env/teia/system.htm.

and liability, and supports research and development and exchange of information and technology.[37] The Convention is administered by the competent authorities of each party, annual meetings of the conference of the parties, and a secretariat provided by the UNECE.[38] Negotiations are currently underway to establish a civil liability regime.[39]

Chemicals, pesticides and other dangerous substances

R. Lutz, V. Nanda, D. Wirth, D. Magraw and G. Handl, 'International Transfer of Hazardous Technology and Substances: Caveat Emptor or State Responsibility? The Case of Bhopal, India', 79 *Proceedings of the American Society of International Law* 303 (1985); R. Brickman *et al.*, *Controlling Chemicals: The Politics of Regulation in Europe and the United States* (1985); F. B. Cross and B. S. Winslett, '"Export Death": Ethical Issues and the International Trade in Hazardous Products', 25 *American Business Law Journal* 487 (1987); 'The Regulation of Hazardous Exports: A Symposium', 12 *Columbia Journal of Environmental Law* 1 (1987); D. A. Bagwell, 'Hazardous and Noxious Substances', 62 *Tulane Law Review* 433 (1988); G. Handl and R. Lutz, 'An International Policy Perspective on the Trade of Hazardous Materials and Technologies', 30 *Harvard International Law Journal* 351 (1989); M. Baender, 'Pesticides and Precaution: The Bamako Convention as a Model for an International Convention on Pesticide Regulation', 24 NYUJILP 557 (1991); OECD, *Guiding Principles for Chemical Accident Prevention, Preparedness and Response* (1992); G. Rose, 'Prior Informed Consent: Hazardous Chemicals', 1 RECIEL 64 (1992); W. Howarth, 'Poisonous, Noxious, or Polluting: Contrasting Approaches to Environmental Regulation', 56 MLR 171 (1993)

According to Agenda 21 there are approximately 100,000 chemical substances in commerce, many of which appear as pollutants and contaminants in food, commercial products and the various environmental media, but for a great number of which there is insufficient scientific information for the assessment of risks.[40] Many aspects of pesticide regulation fall within the general regulatory framework for chemicals, and are often categorised within the sub-group of hazardous chemicals but not necessarily named as pesticides. However, pesticides must be distinguished from hazardous chemicals because they are often highly toxic, produced and used in large quantities, and widely applied over large areas of land directly to the environment and over foodstuffs in such a way as to limit individual control over them. Studies have shown that fertiliser use worldwide increased by almost 250 per cent in the twenty years between 1966–8

---

[37] Arts. 12 to 16 and Annexes X and XI. Information is to be subject to rules of confidentiality: Art. 22.

[38] Arts. 17 to 20. Annex XII sets out tasks for mutual assistance to be subject to the conference of the parties' programme of work.

[39] Chapter 18, p. 937 below.   [40] Agenda 21, paras. 19.1 and 19.11.

and 1986–8 and that worldwide pesticide use increased by 13 per cent in the period 1975 to 1984. Moreover, declines reported in some countries were offset by the increased potency of pesticides used.[41] Treaties and other international acts which have as their objective the international regulation of chemicals,[42] pesticides[43] and other hazardous substances have addressed four related issues: registration and classification (including labelling and packaging); production and use; international trade; and transport.

Registration and classification (including labelling and packaging)

International rules and practices for the registration and classification of hazardous substances are extensive as a result of the activities of the ILO, UNEP, the WHO, the FAO, the OECD and the EC. Space limitations foreclose the possibility of a detailed assessment of the numerous instruments which have been developed, most of which are not legally binding but nevertheless provide evidence of widely accepted international standards and practices.

The main registration and classification schemes are those applied: by UNEP, the ILO and the WHO, under the International Programme in Chemical Safety (IPCS);[44] by UNEP under the International Register of Potentially Toxic Chemicals (IRPTC);[45] by the WHO;[46] under the auspices of the EC;[47] and by the UN ECOSOC.[48] In addition, the 1990 Convention Concerning Safety in the Use of Chemicals at Work requires states to establish systems and criteria for the classification of chemicals according to the type of hazards they present, in accordance with national or international systems.[49] With regard to production,

---

[41] See UNEP, *Environmental Data Report* (1991), 142.

[42] For a definition of chemicals, see n. 102, p. 633, and n. 118, p. 635 below.

[43] For a definition of pesticides, see n. 86, p. 632 below.

[44] Established in 1980 to establish the scientific health and environmental risk assessment basis for safe use of chemicals (normative functions) and to strengthen national capabilities for chemical safety (technical co-operation) (www.who.int/pcs/).

[45] UNEP Governing Council Decisions, Revised Objectives and Strategies of the International Register of Potentially Toxic Chemicals, UNEP/GC/DEC/15/28 (1989). The Register includes details of more than 500 substances, including information on their physical and chemical characteristics, methods of use, and effects on man and the environment.

[46] WHO, *Recommended Classification of Pesticides by Hazard: Guidelines to Classification* (2000–2).

[47] Council Directive 67/548/EEC (as amended), which requires the EC Commission to draw up an inventory of substances available on the EC market: chapter 14, pp. 784–6 below, Art. 1(3). The list is known as the European Inventory of Existing Commercial Chemical Substances (EINECS).

[48] Recommendations on Tests and Criteria for the Classification of Dangerous Goods, ST/SG/AC.10/11/Rev.1 (1991).

[49] Convention Concerning Safety in the use of Chemicals at Work (ILO Convention No. 170), Geneva, 25 June 1990, Art. 6.

UNEP and the FAO have developed a range of guidelines on various aspects of pesticide production and use, including on crops;[50] registration and control;[51] packaging and storage;[52] labelling;[53] retail distribution;[54] national legislation;[55] prior informed consent;[56] and obsolete stocks.[57] The OECD Council has also adopted a wide range of binding and non-binding Acts.[58]

Other schemes which apply include that developed by the *Codex Alimentarius* Commission, which was established in 1962 to implement the joint FAO/WHO Food Standards Programme. The purposes of the Programme include protecting the health of consumers; promoting co-ordination of food standards work undertaken by international governmental and non-governmental organisations; and preparing and finalising regional or global standards. The Commission now has more than 130 members, and amongst the various standards it has developed are those setting maximum limits for pesticide residues.[59] The *Codex Alimentarius* has since been supplemented by the Consolidated List of Products whose consumption and/or sale has been banned, withdrawn, severely restricted or, in the case of pharmaceuticals, not approved by governments, which has been prepared by the UN Secretary General at the request of the General Assembly in 1982.[60]

---

[50] UNEP Environmental Guidelines for Pesticide Use on Industrial Crops, 1982, UNEP EMG#1.

[51] FAO Guidelines on Environmental Criteria for the Registration of Pesticides, 1985; FAO Guidelines for the Registration and Control of Pesticides, 1985, Addenda, 1988.

[52] FAO Guidelines for the Packaging and Storage of Pesticides, 1985.

[53] FAO Guidelines on Good Labelling Practices for Pesticides, 1995 (revised).

[54] FAO Guidelines for Retail Distribution of Pesticides with Particular Reference to Storage and Handling at the Point of Supply to Users in Developing Countries, 1988.

[55] FAO Guidelines for Legislation on the Control of Pesticides, 1989.

[56] FAO Guidelines on the Operation of Prior Informed Consent, 1990.

[57] FAO Guidelines on the Prevention of Accumulation of Obsolete Pesticide Stocks, 1995.

[58] These include: 1981 and 1989 OECD Council Recommendations on Mutual Acceptance of Data in the Assessment of Chemicals and Good Laboratory Practices (OECD C(81)30); 1973 OECD Decision/Recommendation on Protection of the Environment by Control of Polychlorinated Biphenyls (OECD C(73)1); 1982 OECD Council Decision on Minimum Pre-Marketing Set of Data in Assessment of Chemicals (OECD C(82)196); 1987 OECD Decision/Recommendation on Further Measures for the Protection of the Environment by Control of Polychlorinated Biphenyls; the 1987 Decision/Recommendation on the Systematic Investigation of Existing Chemicals; 1991 Decision/Recommendation on the Co-operative Investigation and Risk Reduction of Existing Chemicals; 1992 Recommendation Concerning Chemical Accident Prevention, Preparedness and Response (OECD C(92)1); 1996 Recommendation on Implementing Pollutant Release and Transfer Registers (OECD C(96)41).

[59] Chapter 3, pp. 95–6 above; see FAO/WHO, *Procedural Manual of the Codex Alimentarius Commission* (2000, 11th edn).

[60] UNGA res. 37/137 (1982); see also Res. 38/149 (1983) and Res. 39/229 (1984).

Production and use

Although international law has long prohibited the production and use of certain weapons,[61] it has only recently moved to prohibit, on environmental grounds, the production and use of certain industrial substances and products.[62] In 1998, the parties to the 1979 LRTAP Convention adopted a Protocol on Persistent Organic Pollutants, which aims to eliminate the production and use of certain POPs within the ECE region.[63] The 2001 Stockholm Convention on Persistent Organic Pollutants (2001 POPs Convention) globalises that objective, aiming to protect human health and the environment from persistent organic pollutants, and to that end it imposes measures to reduce or eliminate releases from the production and use of certain POPs.[64] The Convention is precautionary in approach, and initially targets twelve POPs: Annex A lists those which are targeted for elimination, and Annex B lists those which are to be restricted.[65]

Article 3(1) requires parties to eliminate the production and use of all the chemicals listed in Annex A, in accordance with that Annex, and to restrict production and use of chemicals listed in Annex B. Annexes A and B identify 'specific exemptions' in relation to the production and/or use of some but not all of the chemicals, and Annex B additionally identifies certain 'acceptable purposes'.[66] Article 3(2) requires parties to permit imports of chemicals listed on Annex A or Annex B for the purposes of environmentally sound disposal (in accordance with Article 6(1)(d)) or for a use which is permitted for the importing party under Annex A or B.[67] It also requires parties to allow exports only for environmentally sound disposal, or to a party which is permitted to

---

[61] E.g. the Convention on the Prohibition of the Development, Production, Stockpiling and Use of Chemical Weapons, 13 January 1993, in force 29 April 1997.

[62] 1987 Montreal Protocol, in respect of certain ozone-depleting substances; chapter 8, pp. 345–57 above.

[63] Chapter 8, pp. 334–5 above.

[64] Stockholm, 22 May 2001, not yet in force, 40 ILM 532 (2001) (www.pops.int). The Convention will enter into force with fifty ratifications (currently twenty-three). POPs are considered to be especially hazardous because of their toxicity, persistence, mobility (they evaporate and can travel long distances) and propensity to accumulate in fatty tissue. See generally P. L. Lallas, 'The Stockholm Convention on Persistent Organic Pollutants', 95 AJIL 692 (2001); J. A. Mintz, 'Two Cheers for Global POPs: A Summary and Assessment of the Stockholm Convention on Persistant Organic Pollutants', 14 *Georgetown International Environmental Law Review* 319 (2001).

[65] Annex A lists: aldrin, chlordane, dieldrin, endrin, heptachlor, hexachlorobenzene, mirex, toxaphene, and polychlorinated biphenyls (PCBs). Annex B lists DDT.

[66] Production or use pursuant to a 'specific exemption' or 'acceptable purpose' must be carried out in a manner that minimises human exposure or releases into the environment: Art. 3(6). Pursuant to Art. 4, a register is established to list 'specific exemptions' under Annexes A and B, except those that may be exercised by all parties.

[67] Art. 3(2)(a).

use that chemical under Annex A or B, or to a state which is not a party to the Convention but which has provided an annual certification to the exporting party.[68] Finally, Article 3(2) also provides that a party may only export an Annex A chemical for which production and use exemptions are no longer in effect for it for the purpose of environmentally sound disposal.[69] Parties must take measures to regulate the prevention of production and use of new industrial chemicals which exhibit the characteristics of persistent organic pollutants, taking into account the criteria set forth in Annex D.[70] These criteria are also to be taken into account when assessing other pesticides or industrial chemicals already in use but not listed in Annexes A or B.[71]

With regard to unintentional production, Article 5 requires parties to take certain measures to reduce releases from anthropogenic sources of the chemicals listed in Annex C, including action plans to identify and address releases, the use of substitutes, and the use of 'best available techniques' and 'best environmental practices'. The Convention also commits parties to develop implementation plans and provides for information exchange, public awareness and information, research and monitoring, and the provision of technical assistance to developing countries and economies in transition.[72] Developed countries undertake to provide new and additional financial resources to enable developing countries and economies in transition to meet the 'agreed full incremental costs' of implementing measures, and to that end a financial mechanism is 'defined'.[73] As with earlier conventions relating to climate change and biodiversity, it is recognised that the extent to which developing countries will effectively implement their commitments will depend on the effective implementation by developed country parties of their commitments relating to financial resources, technical assistance and technology transfer.[74] The Convention also sets forth reporting requirements and commits the conference of the parties to establish a non-compliance mechanism as soon as practicable.[75] The conference of the parties is entrusted with implementation of the Convention (and must evaluate the effectiveness of the Convention four years after its entry into force), and

---

[68] Art. 3(2)(b). The certificate must specify the intended use of the chemical and state that the importing state is committed to protecting human health and the environment and complying with Art. 6(1) and (where appropriate) Annex B, Part II, para. 2. Art. 6(1) defines measures to reduce or eliminate releases from stockpiles or wastes, and Art. 6(2) calls for co-operation with the 1989 Basel Convention.

[69] Art. 3(2)(c).

[70] Art. 3(3). The criteria relate to: chemical identity; persistence; bioaccumulation; potential for long-range environmental transports; and adverse effects.

[71] Art. 3(4).   [72] Arts. 7 and 9–12.

[73] Art. 13(2) and (6). The GEF is designated on an interim basis: Art. 14; see chapter 20, pp. 1032–4 below.

[74] Art. 13(4).   [75] Arts. 15 and 17.

is assisted by a secretariat (UNEP).[76] Provision is also made for adoption and amendment of the Convention and, in particular, its Annexes.[77]

International trade

International trade in chemicals, pesticides and banned or severely restricted products and substances has been a legally and politically complex subject. It has also been a source of tension between developed and developing countries as substances banned from consumption or sale in developed countries have found their way on to the markets of some developing countries. Initially, some international organisations addressed this by means of non-binding guidelines. These were followed by regional commitments established by the OECD and the EC and the commitments reflected in the 1991 Bamako Convention. In 1998, under the auspices of the FAO and UNEP, a convention of potentially globally application was adopted.

By way of background, the UN has frequently considered the issue of the regulation of products harmful to health and the environment, usually by placing the emphasis on the need to regulate their international traffic. In 1983, the General Assembly adopted a resolution which provided the basis for the principle of 'prior informed consent', declaring that:

> products that have been banned from domestic consumption and/or sale because they have been judged to endanger health and the environment should be sold abroad by companies, corporations or individuals only when a request for such products is received from an importing country or when the consumption of such products is officially permitted in the importing country.[78]

The principle of 'prior informed consent' has subsequently been defined as 'the principle that international shipment of a chemical that is banned or severely restricted in order to protect human health or the environment should not proceed without the agreement, where such agreement exists, or contrary to the decision, of the designated national authority in the importing country'.[79]

---

[76] Arts. 16 and 19–20.

[77] Arts. 21 and 22. By Art. 8, a party may propose a chemical for listing in Annexes A, B and/or C, which is reviewed by a POPs Review Committee, which may prepare a risk profile in accordance with the criteria set forth in Annex E and, as appropriate, a risk management evaluation (on the basis of information provided by parties and observers relating to the considerations specified in Annex F). In deciding whether to list the chemical in Annex A, B and/or C, the conference of parties must take due account of the recommendations of the POPs Review Committee, including any scientific uncertainty, and act in a precautionary manner.

[78] UNGA Res. 37/137 (1983), para. 1.

[79] Adopted by UNEP Governing Council Decision 14/27 of 27 June 1987, amended by UNEP Governing Council Decision 15/30 of 25 May 1989, para. 1(g).

The prior informed consent procedure, which requires the formal obtaining and disseminating of the decisions of importing countries on whether they wish to receive further shipments of chemicals which have been banned or severely restricted, has been used in UNEP and FAO non-binding instruments, and integrated into the legally binding arrangements for international trade in hazardous waste established by, for example, the 1989 Basel Convention,[80] the 1991 Bamako Convention[81] and the 1993 EC Regulation.[82] The 1983 UN General Assembly resolution also resolved that:

> all countries that have severely restricted or have not approved domestic consumption and/or sale of specific products, in particular pharmaceuticals and pesticides, should make available full information on these products with a view to safeguarding the health and environment of the importing country, including clear labelling in a language acceptable to the importing country.[83]

In 1990, the General Assembly endorsed the utilisation and implementation of the 'prior informed consent schemes for chemicals and pesticides in international trade', and requested the UN Regional Economic Commissions to contribute to the prevention of illegal traffic in toxic and dangerous products and wastes by monitoring and ensuring regional assessment of illegal traffic and its environmental and health consequences.[84] The resolution also called on the Secretary General to disseminate the UN Consolidated List, ensure the more effective involvement of non-governmental organisations in its utilisation, and study sustainable alternatives to banned and severely restricted products and unregistered pesticides. This was followed by the 1985 FAO Code of Conduct and the 1987 UNEP Guidelines, which now adopt the approach taken in, and will be replaced by, the 1998 Chemicals Convention once it has entered into force.

1985 FAO Code of Conduct

The most widely used 'soft' instrument, which applies only to pesticides, has been the voluntary International Code of Conduct on the Distribution and Use of Pesticides adopted by the FAO Conference in 1985 (1985 FAO Code).[85] The Code defines and clarifies the responsibilities of all public and private entities involved in the distribution and use of pesticides, including conditions

---

[80] Chapter 13, pp. 691–5 below.   [81] Chapter 13, pp. 695–6 below.
[82] Chapter 13, pp. 699–703 below.   [83] Note 78 above, para. 2.
[84] UNGA Res. 44/226 (1990); see also the Report of the UN Secretary General on 'Products Harmful to Health and the Environment', A/44/276 (1989).
[85] 23 FAO Conference Res. 10/85 (1985) (www.chem.unep.ch/pic/). The Code was amended in 1989 to include the principle of prior informed consent in Art. 9: FAO Conference Res. 6/89 (1989).

for international trade.[86] The Code establishes basic rules on pesticide management, testing, reducing health hazards, and adoption of regulatory and technical requirements, including registration and recording of import data and use.[87] It recommends that the availability and use of pesticides should be subject to national rules and regulations, and restricted as necessary.[88] It recommends that industry should test all pesticide products to evaluate safety for human health and the environment, and submit the test results to independent evaluation before the product can be traded.[89] Governments and national authorities should prohibit repackaging, decanting or dispensing in food or beverage containers and should establish a legal basis for the acceptance of pesticide residues in accordance with recommendations of the *Codex Alimentarius* Commission.[90] The FAO Code also includes provisions on labelling, packaging, storage and advertising.[91]

Central to the FAO Code are the provisions on information exchange and prior informed consent, adopted by the 1989 amendments. As amended, the FAO Code recommends that governments should notify the FAO as soon as possible of actions taken to ban or severely restrict the use or handling of a pesticide and should provide information on its identity, control action taken and its reasons, and any additional information available.[92] The FAO will then notify the designated national authorities of other countries.[93] Exporting countries must ensure that the national authorities of importing countries are provided with relevant information about banned or severely restricted pesticides at the time of first export following the control action (including the information provided to the FAO at the time of notification of control action), and an indication that an export of the chemical concerned is expected or about to occur. This information should be provided prior to export.[94] The prior informed consent procedure ('PIC procedure') applies to pesticides that are banned or

---

[86] Pesticides are defined as 'any substance or mixture of substances intended for preventing, destroying or controlling any pest, including vectors of human or animal disease, unwanted species of plants or animals causing harm during or otherwise interfering with the production, processing, storage, transport, or marketing of food, agricultural commodities, wood and wood products or animal feedstuffs, or which may be administered to animals for the control of insects, arachnids or other pests in or on other bodies. The term includes substances intended for use as a plant growth regulator, defoliant, desiccant, or agent for thinning fruit or preventing the premature fall of fruit, and substances applied to crops either before or after harvest to protect the commodity from deterioration during storage and transport': Art. 2.

[87] Arts. 3 to 6.   [88] Art. 7.   [89] Art. 8(1).   [90] Art. 8(2) and (3).

[91] Arts. 10 and 11.   [92] Art. 9(1) and (2).   [93] Art. 9(1).

[94] Art. 9(3)–(5). The Code defines a banned pesticide as one 'for which all registered uses have been prohibited by final government regulatory action, or for which all requests for registration or equivalent action for all uses have, for health or environmental reasons, not been granted', and severely restricted is identified as 'a limited ban' for which 'virtually all registered uses have been prohibited by final government regulatory action but certain specific registered use or uses remain authorised': Art. 2.

severely restricted for reasons of health or the environment. It provides that
no pesticide in these categories should be exported to an importing country
participating in the PIC procedure contrary to that country's decision made in
accordance with the FAO's procedures for PIC.[95] The PIC procedure is implemented by the FAO and governments of importing and exporting countries.
The FAO ensures that control actions are taken in conformity with the Code
definitions, maintains a database (with UNEP) of control actions and decisions
taken by all member governments, and informs national authorities and relevant international organisations of notifications received under the Code and
decisions communicated to it regarding the use and importation of a pesticide
included in the PIC procedure.[96] Importing countries participating in the PIC
procedure must decide on the acceptability of a pesticide subject to control
action and advise the FAO on the decision, ensure that their measures are not
discriminatory against imported pesticides, and ensure that the decision is not
inconsistent with WTO rules.[97] Exporting countries must advise pesticide exporters and industry of the decisions of participating importing countries and
take measures 'to ensure that exports do not occur contrary to the decision
of participating importing countries'.[98] The Code does not establish any new
institutional arrangements to apply the provisions on information exchange
and prior informed consent: the FAO and other international organisations are
called upon to give full support to the observance of the Code, and governments
must monitor its observance.[99]

1987 UNEP London Guidelines

The UNEP London Guidelines for the Exchange of Information on Chemicals
in International Trade (1987 UNEP London Guidelines) apply to all chemicals, including pesticides.[100] The Guidelines are complementary to the UN
and WHO instruments and the FAO Code of Conduct, and the latter remains
(until the entry into force of the 1998 Convention) the primary guidance for
the management of pesticides internationally.[101] The Guidelines are designed
to assist governments to increase chemical safety and to protect human health
and the environment against potential harm by calling on importing and exporting states to exchange information on chemicals in international trade.[102]

---

[95] Art. 9(7).　[96] Art. 9(8).
[97] Art. 9(10); on the GATT, see chapter 19, pp. 946–85 below.
[98] Art. 9(11).　[99] Art. 12(5) and (6).
[100] Adopted by UNEP Governing Council Decision 14/27 of 27 June 1987, amended by UNEP Governing Council Decision 15/30 of 25 May 1989.
[101] London Guidelines, Introduction, para. 7.
[102] Guideline 2(a). 'Chemical' is defined as 'a chemical substance whether by itself or in a mixture or preparation, whether manufactured or obtained from nature and includes such substances used as industrial chemicals and pesticides': para. 1(a). The Guidelines are not intended to apply to pharmaceutical or radioactive materials, small quantities of research chemicals, personal or household effects, and food additives: para. 3.

General principles adopted by the London Guidelines include the requirement that regulations and standards should not create unnecessary obstacles to international trade, should be non-discriminatory, and should develop legislative and regulatory structures, creating national registers of toxic chemicals, and improving information collection and dissemination.[103]

Part II of the Guidelines addresses notification of and information on banned and severely restricted chemicals and the operation of the PIC procedure. Participation in the PIC procedure, which is voluntary, is effected by communication to the IRPTC, which maintains a list of participating countries, those which do not participate, and those which have not responded, as well as a list of chemicals included in the PIC procedure.[104] All exporting countries are expected to participate in the PIC procedure.[105] Under the PIC procedure, each participating country designates a national authority as a point of contact for information exchange, with the IRPTC acting as a centre for the channelling of notifications and information.[106] States must notify the IRPTC of actions to ban or severely restrict chemicals as soon as practicable after such action is taken, whereupon the IRPTC will notify participating states.[107] On the basis of the notifications received, the IRPTC identifies all chemicals banned or severely restricted by five or more countries, which will be introduced immediately into the PIC procedure if banned or severely restricted by ten or more countries.[108] Chemicals banned or severely restricted by five to ten countries are introduced into the PIC procedure only if found by an expeditious informal consultation procedure to have met the definitions of chemicals which have been banned and severely restricted for human health or environmental reasons.[109]

A Decision Guidance Document is prepared for each chemical placed into the PIC procedure, comprising a summary of the control action, summary information on the chemical, and a response form to allow participating countries to register their decision with the IRPTC.[110] If a chemical which is banned or severely restricted in the country of export is to be exported, information concerning the export should be provided to the importing country, including an estimate of the amount to be exported annually and any other shipment-specific information which is available.[111] Additional Guidelines are provided on channels of notification and information, feedback and confidential data, as well as on the role of national authorities.[112]

By 1998, 155 countries had designated national authorities for the implementation of the PIC procedure. Its implementation, however, proved to be more complicated than had been expected, due to difficulties in the collection and interpretation of data on national regulatory decisions, and by mid-1998

---

[103] Guideline 2(c), (d) and (f).   [104] Guideline 7.1(e) and (f).   [105] Guideline 7.1(b).
[106] Guidelines 9 and 12.   [107] Guideline 6.   [108] Annex II, para. 1(b).
[109] Annex II, para. 1(b)(ii).   [110] Annex III.   [111] Guideline 8.
[112] Guidelines 9 to 12; see also Annex II (Procedure for Initial Identification of Chemicals for Inclusion in the Prior Informed Consent Procedure) and Annex III (Information to be Included in the PIC Decisions Guidance Document).

little more than a couple of dozen chemicals had been identified for which the procedure would apply.

1998 Chemicals Convention

The objective of the 1998 Rotterdam Convention on the Prior Informed Consent Procedure for Certain Hazardous Chemicals and Pesticides in International Trade (1998 Chemicals Convention) is:

> to promote shared responsibility and co-operative efforts among Parties in the international trade of certain hazardous chemicals in order to protect human health and the environment from potential harm and to contribute to their environmentally sound use, by facilitating information exchange about their characteristics, by providing for a national decision-making process on their import and export and by disseminating these decisions to Parties.[113]

The Convention is not expected to enter into force until late 2003 or 2004. In the meantime, the Conference of Plenipotentiaries adopting the Convention decided to change – with immediate effect – the voluntary FAO and UNEP PIC procedures into line with the procedure established by the Convention and to operate it as an 'interim PIC procedure'.[114] The Convention draws upon the FAO and UNEP voluntary schemes in applying a prior informed consent procedure (PIC procedure) for chemicals listed in Annex III to the Convention, which is applicable to banned or severely restricted chemicals and severely hazardous pesticide formulations,[115] subject to certain exceptions.[116] Each party is to designate a national authority.[117] With regard to chemicals,[118] a party which has banned or severely restricted a chemical (taken a 'final regulatory

---

[113] Rotterdam, 10 September 1998, not yet in force (thirty-six out of fifty required ratifications), Art. 1.

[114] Final Act, UNEP.FAO/PIC/CONF/5, 17 September 1998, Annex I, para. 2.

[115] Art. 3(1). A 'banned chemical' is 'a chemical all uses of which within one or more categories have been prohibited by final regulatory action, in order to protect human health or the environment': Art. 2(b). A 'severely restricted chemical' is a chemical virtually all use of which within one or more categories has been prohibited by final regulatory action in order to protect human health or the environment, but for which certain specific uses remain allowed': Art. 2(c). A 'severely hazardous pesticide formulation' means a chemical formulated for pesticidal use that produces severe health or environmental effects observable within a short period of time after single or multiple exposure, under conditions of use': Art. 2(d).

[116] By Art. 3(2), the Convention does not apply to: narcotic drugs and psychotropic substances; radioactive materials; wastes; chemical weapons; pharmaceuticals, including human and veterinary drugs; chemicals used as food additives; food; and chemicals in quantities not likely to affect human health or the environment provided they are imported.

[117] Art. 4.

[118] A 'chemical' is 'a substance whether by itself or in a mixture or preparation and whether manufactured or obtained from nature, but does not include any living organism':

action') is to notify the secretariat, which will then forward the information to all parties.[119] With regard to pesticides, any party that is a developing country or a country with an economy in transition and that is experiencing problems caused by a severely hazardous pesticide formulation under conditions of use in its territory, may propose to the secretariat the listing in Annex III of the severely hazardous pesticide formulation.[120] The secretariat will then forward the proposal to the Chemical Review Committee, which will review the information and recommend to the conference of the parties whether the formulation should be subject to the PIC procedure and, accordingly, listed in Annex III.[121] The Convention already lists twenty-five chemicals (or categories of chemicals). It will be for the conference of the parties to add further chemicals to Annex III (chemicals not listed but included in the voluntary PIC procedure shall be included).[122] Articles 10 and 11 establish the PIC procedure in respect of imports and exports of chemicals listed in Annex III.[123] The export of banned or severely restricted chemicals which are not so listed is governed by a separate notification procedure.[124] Without prejudice to the requirements of the importing party, exported chemicals which are listed in Annex III or which are banned or severely restricted must be labelled to ensure 'adequate availability of information with regard to risks and/or hazards to human health or the environment, taking into account relevant international standards'.[125]

The Convention makes provision for general information exchange and technical assistance, as well as implementation of the Convention.[126] A conference of the parties is responsible for reviewing and evaluating implementation of the Convention, assisted by a secretariat (FAO and UNEP), and will appoint the Chemical Review Committee and establish a non-compliance mechanism.[127] Provision is also made for adoption and amendment of the Convention and its Annexes.[128]

Art. 2(a). It consists of two categories: pesticide (including severely hazardous pesticide formulations) and industrial.

[119] Art. 5(1) and (2). Notifications under the amended London Guidelines or the Code of Conduct need not be submitted: Art. 5(2). Annex I identifies information requirements for Art. 5 notifications.

[120] Art. 6(1).   [121] Art. 6(3)–(5).

[122] Arts. 7 and 8. Amendments to Annex III are to be adopted by consensus: Art. 22(5)(b). Provision is also made for removal of chemicals from the list: Art. 9. The criteria for listing (and removing) chemicals and pesticides is set forth in Annexes II and IV.

[123] Chapter 17, p. 841 below.

[124] Art. 12. The notification must include the information set out in Annex V.

[125] Art. 13(2). A party may also require that chemicals subject to environmental or health labelling requirements in its territory are, when exported, subject to labelling requirements that ensure adequate availability of information with regard to risks and/or hazards to human health or the environment, taking into account relevant international standards: Art. 13(3).

[126] Arts. 14–16.   [127] Arts. 17–19.   [128] Arts. 21–22.

Other regional developments

EC law has established a system of notification and information for imports from and export to third countries of certain chemicals which are banned or severely restricted on health or environmental grounds, applying the PIC procedure.[129] The EC also requires the export of certain items and technologies having dual uses, including for use in chemical and other prohibited weapons.[130] The 1991 Bamako Convention takes a more draconian approach, rejecting the regulated trade approach of the FAO Code and the London Guidelines: it bans all imports from non-parties into Africa of 'hazardous substances which have been banned, cancelled or refused registration by government regulatory action, or voluntarily withdrawn from registration in the country of manufacture, for human health or environmental reasons'.[131]

Transport

International regulations for the transport of hazardous substances and goods establish standards and guidelines to govern the conditions under which such transport is to take place. These conditions relate to labelling, packaging, shipping and marking, and different standards and rules have been put in place to cover different modes of transport. Apart from the general Recommendations adopted by ECOSOC,[132] rules have been adopted to govern the transportation of hazardous goods and substances by road,[133] by rail,[134] by sea,[135] by air[136] and by inland waterways.[137] Special rules have been promulgated by the IAEA to govern the transport of radioactive materials.[138]

---

[129] Council Regulation (EC) No. 2455/92 concerning the export and import of certain dangerous chemicals, OJ L251, 29 August 1992, 13 (as amended most recently by Commission Regulation (EC) No. 300/2002, OJ L52, 22 February 2002, 1).

[130] Council Regulation (EC) No. 1334/2000 setting up a Community regime for the control of exports of dual-use items and technology, OJ L159, 30 June 2000, 1 (as amended).

[131] 1991 Bamako Convention, Arts. 2(1)(d) and 4(1); chapter 13, p. 696 below.

[132] ECOSOC Recommendations on the Transport of Dangerous Goods, Geneva, 26 April 1957, 12th edition, 2001, ECOSOC Res. 645/G/XXIII, ST/SG/AC.10/1/Rev.7 (1991).

[133] See e.g. European Agreement Concerning the International Carriage of Goods by Road (1957 ADR), Geneva, 30 September 1957 (619 UNTS 77, as amended (1297 UNTS 406) and restructured with effect from 1 July 2001).

[134] Regulations Concerning the International Carriage of Dangerous Goods by Rail (RID), www.unece.org/trans/danger/publi/adr/adragree_e.pdf.

[135] International Maritime Dangerous Goods Code (IMDG Code), as amended, IMO (mandatory – with effect from 1 January 2004 – following May 2002 amendments to SOLAS Convention).

[136] ICAO Technical Instruction for the Safe Transport of Dangerous Goods by Air, DOC.9284-AN/905 (ICAO TI); Convention Concerning the Safe Transport of Dangerous Goods by Air (Annex 18 to the 1944 ICAO Convention) (updated 1999).

[137] See e.g. Agreement on International Carriage of Dangerous Goods by Inland Waterways (2000 ADN), 25 May 2000.

[138] IAEA, Regulations for the Safe Transport of Radioactive Material (2000).

The working environment

The principal international organisation in the development of international rules to protect the working environment has been the ILO, under whose auspices at least nine international agreements have been negotiated, adopted and implemented, and all but one of which are in force. These relate to: nuclear hazards; benzene; carcinogenic substances; hazards due to air pollution and noise; occupational health services; asbestos; construction safety; chemicals generally; and the prevention of industrial accidents.[139] Although these agreements are primarily intended to protect humans rather than the environment, their application contributes to the protection of the environment, and many contain innovative provisions which have been incorporated into other environmental agreements.

The ILO's first Convention addressed nuclear hazards,[140] and was followed in 1971 by the Convention Concerning Protection Against Hazards of Poisoning Arising from Benzene (1971 Benzene Convention), which now has twenty-eight parties.[141] The 1971 Benzene Convention applies to all activities exposing workers to benzene and products containing benzene, and requires harmless or less harmful substances to be used instead of benzene or products containing benzene whenever they are available, and a prohibition on their use as a solvent or diluent in most situations.[142] The Convention fixes maximum benzene concentration in the air; requires occupational hygiene and technical measures, regular medical examinations, and labelling requirements; and requires pregnant women and children under eighteen not to be exposed to benzene and benzene products.[143]

The 1974 Convention Concerning Prevention and Control of Occupational Hazards Caused by Carcinogenic Substances and Agents commits its twenty-five parties to determine the carcinogenic substances and agents in respect of which occupational exposure is to be prohibited or subjected to authorisation or other control and to protect workers against the risk of exposure to such substances and agents.[144]

The 1977 Convention Concerning the Protection of Workers Against Occupational Hazards in the Working Environment Due to Air Pollution, Noise and Vibration (1977 Working Environment Convention), which has twenty-five parties, applies to all economic activities and requires parties to adopt national laws or regulations to protect against hazards in the working environment from air pollution, noise and vibration.[145] The Convention does not set individual

---

[139] See p. 621 above.   [140] See p. 646 below.
[141] Geneva, 23 June 1971, in force 27 July 1973, 2 UNTS 45.
[142] Arts. 1, 2 and 4(2).   [143] Arts. 6(2), 9(1), 11 and 12.
[144] Geneva, 26 June 1974, in force 10 June 1976, 1010 UNTS 5.
[145] Geneva, 20 June 1977, in force 11 July 1979, 1 SMTE 482 (ILO Convention No. 148), Arts. 1(1) and 4(1).

standards of general application, but requires national authorities to specify exposure limits on the basis of criteria established and regularly revised in the light of national and international knowledge and data, with a general objective of keeping the working environment 'as far as possible' free from these hazards.[146]

The 1985 Convention Concerning Occupational Health Services, which has fifteen parties, requires the parties to formulate, implement and regularly review a coherent national policy, and to provide occupational health services for workers in all areas of economic activity.[147] Occupational health services must identify and assess health risk, ensure surveillance of factors affecting health, advise on the planning and organisation of work and on health, safety and hygiene, provide surveillance of workers' health, organise first aid and emergency treatment, and analyse accidents and occupational diseases.[148] Personnel providing occupational health services must be professionally independent from employers and workers, and all workers are entitled to be informed of health hazards.[149]

The 1986 Convention Concerning Safety in the Use of Asbestos, which has ten parties, applies to all activities exposing workers to asbestos, and requires parties to adopt laws or regulations to protect workers' health.[150] The Convention gets very close to a complete ban on asbestos and products containing asbestos, requiring where necessary and whenever possible the replacement of asbestos or products containing asbestos by other materials which have been scientifically evaluated as harmless or less harmful, and the total or partial prohibition of the use of asbestos and products containing asbestos in certain work processes.[151] The Convention prohibits the use of crocidolite and products containing the fibre, and the spraying, of all forms of asbestos,[152] requires labelling of containers containing asbestos and products containing asbestos, and the prescription of exposure limits fixed in the light of technological progress and technological and scientific knowledge.[153] Removal of asbestos may only be carried out by qualified employers or contractors, subject to the drawing up of a work plan, and disposal of waste containing asbestos must not pose a health risk to workers or the population in the vicinity.[154]

The 1988 Convention Concerning Safety and Health in Construction applies to all construction activity, and establishes a general obligation to ensure that

---

[146] Arts. 8 and 9.

[147] Geneva, 26 June 1985, in force 17 February 1988, 2 SMTE 126 (ILO Convention No. 155), Arts. 2 and 3.

[148] Art. 5.   [149] Arts. 10 and 13.

[150] Geneva, 24 June 1986, in force 16 June 1989, 2 SMTE 359 (ILO Convention No. 162), Art. 3(1). See also EC Council Directive 83/477/EEC (OJ L263, 24 September 1983, 25) and EC Council Directive 87/217/EEC of 19 March 1987 on the prevention and reduction of environmental pollution by asbestos (OJ L85, 28 March 1987, 40).

[151] Art. 10.   [152] Arts. 11 and 12.   [153] Arts. 14 and 15.   [154] Arts. 17 and 19.

all work places are safe and without risk of injury to the safety and health of workers.[155] Of particular relevance to broader environmental concerns are the provisions on health hazards requiring preventive measures to be taken to prevent exposure of workers to chemical, physical or biological hazards which are liable to be dangerous to health.[156] To that end, hazardous substances must be replaced by harmless or less harmful substances wherever possible, or technical measures are to be applied to the plant, machinery, equipment or process, or other effective measures such as the use of personal protective equipment and clothing are to be used.[157] Adequate measures must also be provided where workers enter areas in which a toxic or harmful substances may be present, and waste should not be destroyed on a construction site in a manner liable to injure health.[158]

The 1990 Convention Concerning Safety in the Use of Chemicals at Work establishes rules for all economic activity on the classification of chemicals according to the inherent hazards they pose for health and physical safety, as well as rules designed to protect workers from these hazards, including marking and labelling, and the maintenance of chemical safety data sheets by employers.[159] Under the Convention, all chemicals must be marked, and hazardous chemicals must be marked in a way easily understandable to workers to provide essential information regarding their classification, the hazards they present and the safety precautions to be taken.[160] Employers must be provided with chemical safety data sheets for hazardous chemicals, and suppliers have particular responsibilities for the classification, marking and labelling of chemicals and hazardous chemicals, as well as the preparation of the safety sheets.[161] The responsibilities of employers include the obligation to ensure that chemicals which are not classified, identified and assessed or labelled and marked in accordance with the Convention are not used, and to ensure that workers are not exposed to chemicals 'to an extent which exceeds exposure limits or other exposure criteria for the evaluation and control of the working environment' established by the national authority in accordance with national or international standards.[162] The employer must also assess, monitor and record the exposure of workers to hazardous chemicals, and assess the risks arising from the use of chemicals at work and protect workers against such risks by choosing chemicals or technologies that eliminate or minimise risk as mentioned previously.[163] Other obligations relate to the disposal of hazardous chemicals and containers which may contain residues in a manner which eliminates or

---

[155] Geneva, 18 June 1988, not yet in force, 2 SMTE 440, Art. 13.   [156] Art. 28(1).
[157] Art. 28(2).   [158] Art. 28(3) and (4).
[159] Geneva, 24 June 1990, not yet in force (ILO Convention No. 170). The Convention defines 'chemicals' as 'chemical elements and compounds, and mixtures thereof, whether natural or synthetic': Art. 2(a).
[160] Art. 7(1) and (2).   [161] Arts. 8 and 9.   [162] Arts. 10 and 12(a).
[163] Arts. 12(b) and (c) and 13.

minimises risk in accordance with national law and practice, and to provide information and training.[164] The Convention also requires exporting states which have banned or restricted the use of certain hazardous chemicals to communicate the fact and the reasons underlying it to the national authorities of any importing country.[165]

Radioactive substances

V. Lamm, *The Utilization of Nuclear Energy and International Law* (1984); A. O. Adede, *The IAEA Notification and Assistance Conventions in Case of a Nuclear Accident: Landmarks in the History of the Multilateral Treaty-Making Process* (1987); P. Cameron, L. Hancher and W. Kuhn, *Nuclear Energy After Chernobyl* (1988); A. Boyle, 'Chernobyl and the Development of International Environmental Law', in W. Butler (ed.), *Perestroika and International Law* (1990), 203; G. Handl, 'Transboundary Nuclear Accidents: The Post-Chernobyl Multilateral Legislative Agenda', 15 *Ecology Law Quarterly* 203 (1988); P. Sands, *Chernobyl: Law and Communication: Transboundary Nuclear Air Pollution* (1988); L. de la Fayette, 'International Environmental Law and the Problem of Nuclear Safety', 5 JEL 31 (1993); J. Goldblat, 'The Nuclear Non-Proliferation Regime: Assessment and Prospects', 256 *Recueil des Cours* 9 (1995); L. Boisson de Chazournes and P. Sands (eds.), *International Law, the International Court of Justice and Nuclear Weapons* (1999). See also the *Nuclear Law Bulletin* (published by the OECD).

The international regulation of radioactive substances commenced with the establishment in 1955 by the UN General Assembly of the Scientific Committee on the Effects of Atomic Radiation (UNSCEAR),[166] followed by the creation of the International Atomic Energy Agency.[167] The other principal international institutions exercising competence in the field of radioactive substances are the European Atomic Energy Agency (EURATOM), established in 1957,[168] and the Nuclear Energy Agency of the OECD, also established in 1957.[169]

Specialised international treaty obligations concerning nuclear materials commenced with the adoption of treaties on liability for nuclear damage[170] and the protection of workers. Subsequent agreements have been adopted on atmospheric nuclear testing;[171] the use and proliferation of nuclear weapons;[172]

---

[164] Arts. 14 and 15.   [165] Art. 19; see above.

[166] UNGA Res. 913 (X), 3 December 1955.

[167] 23 October 1956, in force 29 July 1957, 276 UNTS 3, subsequently amended; see chapter 3, p. 100 above.

[168] Chapter 15, p. 734 below.   [169] Chapter 3, p. 102 above.

[170] Chapter 18, pp. 905–12 below.   [171] Chapter 8, pp. 319–21 above.

[172] Treaty on the Non-Proliferation of Nuclear Weapons, 1 July 1968, in force 5 March 1970, 729 UNTS 161 ('nuclear weapon parties' agree not to transfer to 'non-nuclear weapon

border area co-operation; co-operation on nuclear safety and research; the protection of nuclear material; and nuclear emergencies. Disposal of radioactive waste is also regulated,[173] and some regions have been designated by states as nuclear-free zones. Under the auspices of the IAEA, two international conventions have been adopted, on Nuclear Safety (1994) and on the Safety of Spent Fuel Management and on the Safety of Radioactive Waste Management (1997).

Nuclear safety

The IAEA is required by its Statute to 'establish or adopt . . . standards of safety for protection of health and minimisation of danger to life and property' (including such standards for labour conditions).[174] It has adopted, with the assistance of the International Commission on Radiological Protection (ICRP) and other organisations, instruments on nuclear safety which are binding upon itself and must be applied in respect of its own research operations, but which are not binding upon its member states or third parties. This compares unfavourably with EURATOM[175] and the OECD's Nuclear Energy Agency, which have the power to adopt binding acts. In practice, however, many IAEA standards are relied upon by states in developing and implementing national legislation and standards. The instruments which the IAEA may adopt include Safety Fundamentals, Safety Standards, Safety Guides, Safety Practices, and Safety Reports.[176] Five Codes of Practice and more than sixty volumes of Nuclear Safety Standards (NUSS) have been adopted, relating to government organisation, siting, design, operation and quality assurance. Significant instruments include the Basic Safety Standards which have been adopted for Radiation Protection,[177] the Regulations for Safe Transport of Radioactive Material,[178] the Radioactive Waste Safety Standards,[179] and the Safety Standards Governing Radiological Emergency.[180] In September 1991, the General Conference of the IAEA invited

parties' any nuclear weapons or devices, or to assist the latter to manufacture, acquire or control such weapons or devices, and 'non-nuclear weapon parties' undertake to submit themselves to verification safeguards under the auspices of and in agreement with the IAEA). In 1995, the Treaty's application was extended indefinitely: 1995 Review and Extension Conference of Parties to NPT, Annex, Decision 3, 34 ILM 959 (1995).

[173] Chapter 13, pp. 684–6 below.   [174] IAEA Statute, Art. III(A)(6).
[175] Chapter 15, pp. 793–4 below.
[176] P. Szasz, 'The IAEA and Nuclear Safety', 1 RECIEL 165 at 168 (1992).
[177] International Basic Safety Standards for Protection Against Ionizing Radiation and for the Safety of Radiation Sources (1996) (supersedes IAEA Safety Series No. 9, 1982).
[178] TS-R-1 (2000) (supersedes ST-1 (1996) and Safety Series No. 6 (1985) and No. 80); see n. 204, p. 646 below.
[179] See WS-R-2, Predisposal Management of Radioactive Waste, Including Decommissioning (2000); WS-R-1, Near Surface Disposal of Radioactive Waste (1999); on radioactive waste, see chapter 13, pp. 681, 697–9 and 707–8 below.
[180] GS-R-2, Preparedness and Response for a Nuclear or Radiological Emergency (2002).

its Director General to prepare an outline of the possible elements of a nuclear safety convention.[181] An Expert Group subsequently identified a tentative list of obligations to be included in a nuclear safety convention, including a legislative framework for the regulation of civil nuclear facilities and activities of the nuclear fuel cycle; education and training of employees; emergency plans; safety (including siting, design, construction, commissioning and decommissioning); safe operation and maintenance; continuous safety surveillance; safe management and disposal of waste; and the sharing of information.[182]

In June 1994, the Convention on Nuclear Safety was adopted under the auspices of the IAEA.[183] The Convention has three objectives: to achieve and maintain a high level of nuclear safety worldwide: to establish and maintain effective defences in nuclear installations against potential radiological hazards to protect individuals, society and the environment from harmful effects of ionising radiation; and to prevent accidents with radiological consequences and to mitigate such consequences should they occur.[184] Parties are required to establish a national regulatory body and to establish and maintain a legislative and regulatory framework to govern the safety of nuclear installations, providing, *inter alia*, for the establishment of applicable national safety requirements and regulations, a system of licensing, a system of regulatory inspection and assessments, and the enforcement of applicable regulations and of the terms of licences, including suspension, modification or revocation.[185] Parties must give effect to 'general safety considerations' by prioritising safety, and must ensure adequate financial and human resources; implement quality assurance programmes; carry out comprehensive and systematic safety assessments; ensure that radiation exposure to workers and the public is kept as low as reasonably achievable (and that no individual shall be exposed to radiation doses which exceed prescribed national dose limits); and establish on-site and off-site emergency preparedness plans.[186] In relation to safety, siting should be evaluated by reference to factors likely to affect safety for the projected lifetime of the installation and for impacts on individuals, society and the environment; design and construction should provide for 'several reliable levels and methods of protection' against the release of radioactive materials, technologies incorporated

---

[181] IAEA GC(XXXV)/res./553 (1991).

[182] Report of the Expert Group on Outline of the Possible Elements for an International Convention on Nuclear Safety, 13 December 1991, reprinted in Report by the Director General on Implementation of General Conference Resolution GC(XXXV)/res./553, GOV/2567 (1992).

[183] Vienna, 17 June 1994, in force 24 October 1996; fifty-three states and Euratom are party; M. Kamminga, 'The IAEA Convention on Nuclear Safety', 44 ICLQ 872 (1995).

[184] Art. 1. A 'nuclear installation' is 'any land-based civil nuclear power plant under its jurisdiction including such storage, handling and treatment facilities for radioactive materials as are on the same site and are directly related to the operation of the nuclear power plant': Art. 2(i).

[185] Arts. 7 and 8.   [186] Arts. 10–16.

in the design and construction should be proven by experience or qualified by testing or analysis, and the design should allow for reliable, stable and easily manageable operation. Minimum standards are to be applied with regard to operation, including the principle that the generation of radioactive waste resulting from the operation of a nuclear installation should be kept to the minimum practicable for the process concerned, in terms of activity and volume.[187] These obligations are characterised by their generality, by the failure to make reference to any of the IAEA's own international standards, and by the absence of any commitment to established and broadly accepted environmental requirements, such as environmental impact assessment.

Three years later, also under IAEA auspices, the Joint Convention on the Safety of Spent Fuel Management and on the Safety of Radioactive Waste Management (1997 Joint Safety Convention) was adopted. Its objectives are to achieve and maintain a high level of safety worldwide in spent fuel and radioactive waste management, to ensure that during all stages of spent fuel and radioactive waste management there are effective defences against potential hazards to protect against harmful effects of ionising radiation, and to prevent accidents.[188] The Convention applies to spent fuel management when the spent fuel results from the operation of civilian nuclear reactors, including certain discharges: it does not cover spent fuel held at reprocessing facilities as part of a reprocessing activity, or waste that contains only naturally occurring radioactive materials and that does not originate from the nuclear fuel cycle, or the safety of management of spent fuel or radioactive waste within military or defence programmes (unless the contracting party declares otherwise).[189] The 1997 Convention addresses the safety of spent fuel management[190] and of radioactive waste management[191] (addressing general requirements, existing facilities, siting, design and construction, safety assessment, operation, disposal of spent fuel and institutional measures after closure). With regard to general safety provisions, it includes similar provisions to the 1994 Convention in relation to the adoption of a legislative and regulatory framework, a regulatory body and responsibilities of the licence holder, as well as requirements in relation to human and financial resources, quality assurance and operational radiation procedure, emergency preparedness and decommissioning.[192]

It is noteworthy that, unlike the 1994 Convention, the 1997 Convention refers to international standards: in relation to radiation protection, for example, it requires each party to ensure that 'no individual shall be exposed, in normal situations, to radiation doses which exceed national prescriptions for dose

---

[187] Art. 17–19.
[188] Vienna, 5 September 1997, in force 18 June 2001, 36 ILM 1431 (1997), Art. 1; thirty-one states are party.
[189] Art. 3.   [190] Arts. 4–10.   [191] Arts. 11–17.   [192] Arts. 18–26.

limitation which have due regard to internationally endorsed standards on radiation protection'.[193] In this regard, the 1997 Convention also requires a party involved in transboundary movement to 'take the appropriate steps to ensure that such movement is undertaken in a manner consistent with the provisions of this Convention and relevant binding international instruments', and commits parties to a system of prior notification and consent.[194]

Transport

Beyond the requirements of the 1997 Joint Safety Convention governing transboundary movements of spent fuel and radioactive waste, the provisions of the 1980 Convention on the Physical Protection of Nuclear Material apply to nuclear material used for peaceful purposes when being transported internationally and, to a more limited extent, the domestic use, storage and transport of nuclear material used for peaceful purposes.[195] The Convention requires parties to ensure as far as practicable that nuclear material in international transport is protected in accordance with the requirements set forth in Annex I, and that nuclear material shall not be exported, imported or permitted transit through the territory unless assurances have been received that the nuclear material will be protected at Annex I levels.[196] The party responsible for receiving such assurances must identify and inform in advance transit states, as well as states whose airports or seaports the nuclear material is expected to enter.[197] Parties must identify and share information on their central authority having responsibility for the physical protection of nuclear material, co-operate in the event of theft, robbery or other unlawful taking, and co-operate and consult on the design, maintenance and improvement of physical protection systems.[198] The Convention establishes a range of offences to be made punishable by each state, including theft or robbery or threats to use nuclear material to cause death or injury or property damage (but not environmental damage), and provides for jurisdiction over offences, and rules on detention, prosecution and extradition, as well as assistance between parties in criminal proceedings.[199] Interestingly, and rarely, the Convention has a dispute settlement clause providing for the compulsory jurisdiction of the ICJ.[200]

In 1993, the IMO Assembly adopted a Code for the Safe Carriage of Irradiated Nuclear Fuel, Plutonium and High-Level Radioactive Wastes in Flasks On Board

---

[193] Art. 24(1)(ii) and (2)(ii).   [194] Art. 27; chapter 13, pp. 697–9 below.

[195] Vienna and New York, 3 March 1980, in force 8 February 1987, IELMT 980:18, Art. 2(1) and (2); eighty-six states and Euratom are party.

[196] Arts. 3 and 4(1) to (3). These provisions do not apply to domestic activities. Annex I sets out 'Levels of Physical Protection to be Applied in International Transport of Nuclear Materials as Categorised in Annex II'.

[197] Art. 4(5).   [198] Art. 5.   [199] Arts. 7 to 14.   [200] Art. 17.

Ships (INF Code).[201] The INF Code recommends how certain materials should be carried, including specifications for ships. The material covered by the Code includes irradiated nuclear fuel, plutonium and high-level radioactive wastes, and the Code applies to all ships carrying INF cargo except warships, naval auxiliary ships or other ships used only on government non-commercial service. The Code became legally binding with effect from 1 January 2001.[202] Non-binding instruments adopting guidelines and recommendations for maritime aspects of radioactive substances have also been adopted by the IMO[203] and the IAEA.[204]

Protection of workers and the public

Beyond the IAEA Safety Standards,[205] the 1960 ILO Convention (No. 115) Concerning the Protection of Workers Against Ionising Radiations aims to ensure effective protection of workers against ionising radiations.[206] Their exposure must be restricted to the lowest practicable level, and parties must fix maximum permissible doses of radiation which may be received and maximum permissible amounts which can be taken into the body for workers directly engaged in radiation work, as well as others who may be exposed.[207] The Convention provides for warnings to be used to indicate radiation hazards, the instruction of workers on precautions, the monitoring of workers and workplaces, and regular medical examinations.[208]

Border area co-operation

Several bilateral and other treaties promote consultations and other information sharing on the construction of nuclear power plants in border areas.[209] A typical example is the 1980 Agreement Between Spain and Portugal on Co-operation in Matters Affecting the Safety of Nuclear Installations in the Vicinity

---

[201] IMO Res. A.748(18) (1993). The Code's regulations address, *inter alia*, damage stability, fire protection, structural consideration, cargo securing arrangements, radiological protection equipment and management, training and shipboard emergency plans.

[202] IMO Res. MSC.88(71) (27 May 1999).

[203] IMO Code of Safety for Nuclear Merchant Ships, IMO Res. A.491(XII), Part A (19 November 1981).

[204] Regulations for the Safer Transport of Radioactive Material (2000).

[205] See p. 642 above.

[206] Geneva, 22 June 1960, in force 17 June 1962, 431 UNTS 41, Art. 3(1). On EC rules adopted under EURATOM, see chapter 15, pp. 793–4 below.

[207] Arts. 5, 6(1), 7 and 8.   [208] Arts. 9 to 12.

[209] See e.g. France–Belgium Agreement on Radiological Protection Concerning the Installations of the Nuclear Power Station of the Ardennes, 7 March 1967, 588 UNTS 227; Guidelines for Nordic Co-operation Concerning Nuclear Installations in the Border Areas, 15 November 1976; Denmark–Federal Republic of Germany, Agreement Relating to Exchange of Information on Construction of Nuclear Installations Along the Border, 4 July 1977, 17 ILM 274 (1978).

of the Frontier, which provides that 'the competent authorities of the constructor country shall notify the neighbouring country of applications for licences for the siting, construction or operation of nuclear installations in the vicinity of the frontier which are submitted to them'.[210] More generally, Article 17 of the 1994 Nuclear Safety Convention and Article 13 of the 1997 Joint Safety Convention commit parties to consult with other parties in the vicinity of a proposed nuclear installation or facility, insofar as they are likely to be affected by that installation or facility. Together with the general requirements of international law relating to prevention and notification, as well as environmental assessment, there is now sufficient treaty and other state practice to indicate that customary international law requires states that are planning nuclear activities which might entail a significant risk of transfrontier pollution to give early advice to any state affected and to enter into good faith consultations at the request of such a state.[211]

Emergencies

Following the Chernobyl accident, treaties on emergency notification and assistance were negotiated at the IAEA. The 1986 IAEA Convention on Early Notification of a Nuclear Accident (1986 Notification Convention)[212] was modelled on existing IAEA guidelines[213] and supplemented the bilateral and other treaties already adopted.[214] The 1986 Notification Convention has been followed by numerous bilateral and regional arrangements, including EC rules. The 1986 IAEA Convention on Assistance in the Case of a Nuclear Accident or Radiological Emergency (1986 Assistance Convention)[215] was also modelled on

[210] Agreement Between Portugal and Spain on Co-operation in Matters Affecting the Safety of Nuclear Installations in the Vicinity of the Border, Lisbon, 31 March 1980, in force 13 July 1981, Art. 2.

[211] See e.g. 1982 ILA Montreal Rules, Arts. 6 and 7; 1987 IDI Resolution, Art. 8(1); on the principle of good-neighbourliness, see chapter 6, pp. 249–51 above; on the provision of information see chapter 17, pp. 838–40 below.

[212] 26 September 1986, in force 27 October 1986, 25 ILM 1370 (1986); see chapter 17, pp. 845–7 below.

[213] IAEA Guidelines on Reportable Events, Integrated Planning and Information Exchange in a Transboundary Release of Radioactive Material, IAEA Doc. INFCIRC/321 (January 1985).

[214] See e.g. Federal Republic of Germany–Luxembourg, Agreement on the Exchange of Information in Case of Accidents Which Could Have Radiological Consequences, 2 March 1978, 29 IPE 251; France–Switzerland, Agreement on the Exchange of Information in Case of Accidents Which Could Have Radiological Consequences, 18 October 1979, 27 IPE 382; Finland–USSR, Agreement on Early Notification of a Nuclear Accident and on Exchange of Information Relating to Nuclear Facilities, 7 January 1987, IAEA LegSer No. 15, 187; Sweden–USSR, Agreement on Early Notification of a Nuclear Accident and on Exchange of Information Relating to Nuclear Facilities, 1 January 1988, IAEA LegSer No. 15, 407; see generally the list cited in E. Brown Weiss, P. C. Szasz and D. B. Magraw, *International Environmental Law: Basic Instruments and References* (1992).

[215] Vienna, 26 September 1986, in force 26 February 1987, 25 ILM 1377 (1986).

existing IAEA guidelines[216] and bilateral and other regional arrangements.[217] It is intended to 'facilitate prompt assistance in the event of a nuclear accident or radiological emergency to minimise its consequences and to protect life, property and the environment from the effects of radioactive releases'.[218] The 1986 Assistance Convention applies whether or not the accident occurred within the requesting state's territory or jurisdiction, and requires requesting states to specify the scope and type of assistance they require and to provide any information.[219] Once a state has received a request for information, it must promptly decide and notify the requesting state whether it is in a position to render the assistance requested and the scope and terms of assistance it might provide, and to identify and notify the IAEA of experts, equipment and material which could be made available, and the terms on which it will provide assistance.[220] The IAEA's responsibilities include making available appropriate resources for emergency purposes, transmitting information about resources, and if requested co-ordinating available assistance at the national level.[221] The 1986 Assistance Convention also includes administrative provisions on the direction and control of assistance, competent national authorities, reimbursement of costs, confidentiality of information, and rules on privileges, immunities, claims and compensation relating to persons or property injured or damaged in the course of providing assistance.[222] The 1986 Assistance Convention clearly marks a step in the right direction, and should remove many of the administrative barriers which frequently limit the effectiveness of international assistance in emergency situations. Nevertheless, it has been criticised for emphasising the protection of the assisting state: Argentina, for example, noted that under Article 10(2) the state receiving assistance is to be held responsible for all damage suffered by the assisting state, but the assisting state apparently assumes no responsibility for any damage which it might cause.[223] Furthermore, Article 7, on the reimbursement of costs, has the result that a state which caused a nuclear accident and which agrees to provide assistance to another affected state has the right to require reimbursement of assistance costs. This seems to be unsatisfactory, and led the representative of Luxembourg to conclude that the fundamental question of responsibility had not been properly resolved.[224]

---

[216] Guidelines for Mutual Emergency Assistance Arrangements in Connection with a Nuclear Accident or Radiological Emergency, IAEA Doc. INFCIRC/310 (January 1984).

[217] See e.g. Nordic Mutual Emergency Assistance Agreement in Connection with Radiation Accidents, 17 October 1963, 525 UNTS 75.

[218] Art. 1(1).   [219] Arts. 1(1) and 2(2).   [220] Art. 2(3) and (4).

[221] Art. 2(6).   [222] Arts. 3, 4, 6, 7, 8 and 10.

[223] See comment of the representative of Argentina at the Final Plenary Meeting of Governmental Experts, 15 August 1986, IAEA Doc. GC(SPL.I)/2, Annex V, 18 (1986).

[224] *Ibid.*, 28.

Nuclear weapons and testing, and nuclear-free zones

The acquisition, use and testing of nuclear weapons has been addressed by a number of international conventions. They have also been the subject of various proceedings before the ICJ which, ironically perhaps, have made a rather significant contribution to the development of international environmental law.[225]

Aside from the 1968 Treaty on the Non-Proliferation of Nuclear Weapons,[226] the objectives of the 1963 Treaty Banning Nuclear Weapon Tests in the Atmosphere, in Outer Space and Under Water include the desire to 'put an end to the contamination of man's environment by radioactive substances'.[227] To that end, the parties have undertaken to prohibit, and not to participate in or encourage, any nuclear weapon test or other nuclear explosion at any place under their jurisdiction or control in the atmosphere, outer space, or under water or in any other environment if it causes radioactive debris to be present outside the territorial limit of the state under whose jurisdiction or control it is conducted.[228] The 1963 Treaty allows underground nuclear tests, and does not establish institutional arrangements or mechanisms for verification and compliance. In 1991, an amendment conference was convened to widen the scope of the treaty to include underground testing and establish compliance controls as part of a comprehensive test ban treaty, but no amendments were adopted.[229] The 1996 Comprehensive Nuclear Test Ban Treaty (1996 CTBT) commits parties 'not to carry out any nuclear weapon test explosion or any other nuclear explosion, and to prohibit and prevent any such nuclear explosion at any place under its jurisdiction or control', and to refrain from 'causing, encouraging, or in any way participating in the carrying out of any nuclear weapon test explosion or any other nuclear explosion'.[230] The 1996 Treaty establishes a comprehensive verification and inspection system.

The 1971 Treaty on the Prohibition of the Emplacement of Nuclear Weapons and other Weapons of Mass Destruction on the Sea-Bed and the Ocean Floor and in the Sub-Soil Thereof prohibits the placing of nuclear weapons or any other types of weapons of mass destruction, as well as related structures and facilities, on the seabed and ocean floor and in the subsoil beyond the outer limit of the seabed zone.[231] The Treaty establishes a verification procedure leading ultimately to the reference of disputes to the UN Security Council.[232] The UN

---

[225] *Australia* v. *France, New Zealand* v. *France* (1974), chapter 6, p. 242 above, and chapter 18, pp. 879–81 below; *New Zealand* v. *France* (1995), chapter 6, p. 245 above, and chapter 16, p. 800 below; Advisory Opinion on *The Legality of the Threat or Use of Nuclear Weapons* (1996), chapter 6, pp. 245–6 above.

[226] See p. 641 above.

[227] 5 August 1963, in force 10 October 1963, 480 UNTS 43, Preamble.

[228] Art. I(1).   [229] PTBT/CONF.13/Rev.1 (1991).

[230] New York, 24 September 1996, not yet in force, 35 ILM 1439 (1996).

[231] 11 February 1971, in force 18 May 1972, UKTS 13 (1973), Art. 1(1).   [232] Art. III.

General Assembly has called on the UN Conference on Disarmament to agree on an international convention prohibiting the use or threat of use of nuclear weapons under any circumstances.[233]

The 1967 Treaty for the Prohibition of Nuclear Weapons in Latin America prohibits the testing, use, manufacture, production, acquisition, receipt, storage, installation, deployment or possession of any nuclear weapons by the parties in their territories.[234] The Treaty does not prejudice the right of parties to use nuclear energy for peaceful purposes and to carry out, subject to certain conditions, explosions of nuclear devices for peaceful purposes.[235] Compliance with the Treaty is to be ensured by the Agency for the Prohibition of Nuclear Weapons in Latin America (OPANAL) and by a control system, including IAEA safeguards, to verify that devices and facilities intended for peaceful uses of nuclear energy are not being used in the testing or manufacture of weapons, that the prohibited activities are not being carried out, and that explosions for peaceful purposes are compatible with the Treaty.[236]

The 1985 South Pacific Nuclear Free Zone Treaty is designed to keep the South Pacific region 'free of environmental pollution by radioactive wastes and other radioactive matter'.[237] Under the Treaty, each party agrees not to manufacture, acquire, possess or control any nuclear explosive device anywhere inside or outside the South Pacific Nuclear Free Zone; to prevent the stationing of nuclear explosive devices in their territory; to prevent the testing of nuclear explosive devices; and to prevent the dumping of radioactive wastes or matter in the Zone.[238] Parties may only provide source or special fissionable material or related equipment or material to non-nuclear weapon states which are subject to safeguards under Article III(1) of the 1968 NPT or to nuclear weapon states subject to safeguard agreements with the IAEA.[239] The Treaty establishes a control system which includes the application of IAEA safeguards to verify the non-diversion of nuclear material from peaceful nuclear activities to nuclear explosive devices.[240] Protocol 1 to the Treaty allows France, the United Kingdom and the United States to undertake to apply the prohibitions under Articles 3, 5 and 6 of the Treaty which relate to manufacture, stationing and testing to territories for which they are internationally responsible situated within the Zone.[241] Parties to Protocol 2 to the Treaty, which is open to signature by France, the People's Republic of China, the United Kingdom, the former USSR and the United States, undertake not to use or threaten to use any nuclear

---

[233] UNGA Res. 43/76 (1988).

[234] 14 February 1967, in force 22 April 1968, 6 ILM 521 (1967), Arts. 1(1) and 4.

[235] Arts. 17 and 18.   [236] Arts. 7 to 16.

[237] Rarotonga, 6 August 1985, in force 11 December 1986, 24 ILM 142 (1988), Preamble.

[238] Arts. 3 and 5 to 7. Parties are free to decide whether to allow visits by ships or aircraft and transit of airspace and navigation by ships in their territorial sea or archipelagic waters: Art. 5(2).

[239] Art. 4(a).   [240] Art. 8(2)(c) and Annex 2.   [241] Protocol 1, Art. 1.

explosive device against parties to the Treaty or any territory for which a state that has become a party to Protocol 1 is internationally responsible.[242] Parties to Protocol 3, which is open to signature to the same five states, agree not to test any nuclear explosive device anywhere within the zone.[243]

The 1996 Treaty on the Nuclear-Weapon-Free Zone in Africa (1996 Pelindaba Treaty) establishes an African nuclear-weapon-free zone and commits parties to renounce research on, or to develop, manufacture, stockpile or otherwise acquire, possess or have control over, any nuclear explosive device by any means anywhere, to prevent the stationing of nuclear explosive devices in its territory, and to prohibit the testing of nuclear explosive devices.[244] Parties also commit to declare, dismantle, destroy or convert nuclear explosive devices and the facilities for their manufacture.[245] Going beyond other regional arrangements, the 1996 Pelindaba Treaty also commits parties to give effect to the 1991 Bamako Convention, to prohibit the dumping of radioactive wastes and other radioactive matter anywhere within the African nuclear-weapon-free zone, and to apply measures of physical protection equivalent to those provided for in the 1980 Convention on Physical Protection of Nuclear Material and in IAEA recommendations and guidelines.[246] Three Protocols address the non-use of nuclear weapons, the prohibition on weapons testing, and the application of IAEA safeguards.

The 1996 Pelindaba Treaty was adopted following a call by the UN General Assembly on all states not to test, manufacture, use or deploy nuclear weapons in Africa, and to refrain from transferring such weapons, scientific data or technical assistance, either directly or indirectly, in any way which could assist in the manufacturing or use of nuclear weapons.[247] The UN General Assembly has also endorsed, in principle, the concept of a nuclear-weapons-free zone in South Asia and urged the states of South Asia to continue to make all efforts to establish a nuclear-weapons-free zone in their region.[248]

Biotechnology

P.-T. Stoll, 'Controlling the Risks of GMOs: The Cartagena Protocol on Biosafety and the SPS Agreement', 10 *Yearbook of International Environmental Law* 82 (1999); B. Eggers and R. Mackenzie, 'The Cartagena Protocol on Biosafety', 3 *Journal of International Economic Law* 525 (2000); R. Pomerance, 'The Biosafety Protocol: Cartagena and Beyond', 8 NYUELJ 3 (2000); M. Scheyli, 'Das Cartagena-Protokoll über biologisches Sicherheit zur Biodiversitätskonvention', 60 ZaöRV 771 (2000); L. Boisson de Chazournes and U. Thomas, 'The Biosafety Protocol:

---

[242] Protocol 2, Art. 2. China and the USSR have ratified this Protocol.
[243] Protocol 3, Art. 1. China and the USSR have ratified this Protocol.
[244] Cairo, 1 April 1996, not yet in force, Arts. 1 and 3–5.   [245] Art. 6.
[246] Arts. 7 and 10.   [247] UNGA Res. 2033 (XX) (1965).   [248] UNGA Res. 45/53 (1990).

Regulatory Innovation and Emerging Trends', *Revue suisse de droit international*
513 (2000); A. H. Qureshi, 'The Cartagena Protocol on Biosafety and the WTO:
Coexistence or Incoherence?', 49 ICLQ 835 (2000); V. Köster, 'A New Hot Spot
in the Trade–Environment Conflict', 31 *Environmental Policy and Law* 82 (2001);
D. Katz, 'The Mismatch Between the Biosafety Protocol and the Precautionary Principle', 13 *Georgetown International Environmental Law Review* 949 (2001); C. Bail,
R. Falkner and H. Marquard (eds.), *The Cartagena Protocol on Biosafety* (2002); J.
Bourrinet and S. Maljean-Dubois (eds.), *Le Commerce international des organismes
génétiquement modifiés* (2002).

The regulation of genetically modified organisms and biotechnology is among
the most contentious issues currently subject to international regulation.
Biotechnology is described by Agenda 21 as 'a set of enabling techniques for
bringing about specific man-made changes in di-oxyribonucleic acid (DNA),
or genetic material in plants, animals and microbial systems'.[249] The subject
caused considerable difficulties during the negotiation of the 1992 Biodiversity
Convention and in the preparations for UNCED.[250] The main issue was the
appropriate balance to be struck between the objectives of ensuring, on the
one hand, that developments in the field of biotechnology do not cause adverse
effects for human health and the environment and, on the other hand, that
new international regulatory arrangements do not place undue limits on the
development, dissemination and use of biotechnology. The concern expressed
about excessive regulation was reflected in the written statement submitted by
the United States at UNCED, specifically in reference to Chapter 16 of Agenda
21, which set out its understanding that 'biotechnology is in no way an intrinsically unsafe process'.[251]

Biodiversity Convention

Prior to the adoption of Article 19 of the 1992 Biodiversity Convention, international law was, essentially, limited to laws regulating the introduction of alien
species into regions.[252] The Biodiversity Convention was the first international
legal instrument outside the EC to indicate that biotechnology was a matter
of concern for the international community and that consideration should be
given to adopting regulations.[253] The Biodiversity Convention merely provides
a basis upon which more detailed regulations might subsequently be adopted
in a protocol setting out 'appropriate procedures, including, in particular, advance informed agreement, in the field of the safe transfer, handling and use

---

[249] Agenda 21, para. 16.1.   [250] Chapter 11, p. 521 above.
[251] Report of UNCED, A/CONF.151/26/Rev.1 (vol. II), 19 (1993).
[252] Chapter 11, pp. 521–3 above.
[253] 'Biotechnology' is defined as 'any technological application that uses biological systems,
living organisms, or derivatives thereof, to make or modify products or processes for
specific uses': Art. 2.

of any living modified organism resulting from biotechnology that may have adverse effect on the conservation and sustainable use of biological diversity'.[254] It also requires each party to provide to a party into whose territory genetically modified organisms are to be introduced any available information on the use and safety regulations it requires in handling living modified organisms, and on the potential adverse impact of the specific organisms concerned.[255]

2000 Biosafety Protocol

The Cartagena Protocol on Biosafety was adopted on 29 January 2000 and is expected to enter into force in 2003.[256] Article 1 sets forth its objective:

> In accordance with the precautionary approach contained in Principle 15 of the Rio Declaration on Environment and Development, the objective of this Protocol is to contribute to ensuring an adequate level of protection in the field of the safe transfer, handling and use of living modified organisms resulting from modern biotechnology that may have adverse effects on the conservation and sustainable use of biological diversity, taking also into account risks to human health, and specifically focusing on transboundary movements.

Parties must ensure that the development, handling, transport, use, transfer and release of any living modified organisms are undertaken in a manner that prevents or reduces the risks to biological diversity, taking also into account risks to human health.[257] They are free to take action that is more protective of biological diversity provided that such action 'is consistent with the objective and the provisions of [the] Protocol and is in accordance with [the] Party's other obligations under international law'.[258]

The scope of the Protocol is limited to the transboundary movement, transit, handling and use of 'living modified organism' (LMO) that may have adverse effects on the conservation and sustainable use of biological diversity, taking also into account risks to human health.[259] LMOs which are pharmaceuticals for humans that are addressed by other relevant international agreements or organisations, or LMOs in transit through a state's territory or destined for contained use, are not subject to the Protocol.[260] The Preamble reaffirms the

---

[254] Art. 19(3).   [255] Art. 19(4).

[256] 39 ILM 1027 (2000); in force 11 September 2003 (thirty-seven ratifications, fifty needed: Art. 37). On the background, see chapter 11, p. 523 above.

[257] Art. 2(1) and (2).   [258] Art. 2(4).

[259] Art. 4. An LMO is 'any living organism that possesses a novel combination of genetic material obtained through the use of modern biotechnology': Art. 3.

[260] Arts. 5 and 6. 'Contained use' is defined in Art. 3 to mean 'any operation, undertaken within a facility, installation or other physical structure, which involves living modified organisms that are controlled by specific measures that effectively limit their contact with, and their impact on, the external environment'.

parties' commitment to the 'precautionary approach' contained in Principle 15 of the Rio Declaration, expresses their awareness of growing public concern over potential adverse effects on biological diversity and human health, and recognises the 'great potential' of biotechnology. As to the relationship with trade agreements, the Preamble cryptically states:

> *Recognizing* that trade and environment agreements should be mutually supportive with a view to achieving sustainable development,
>
> *Emphasizing* that this Protocol shall not be interpreted as implying a change in the rights and obligations of a Party under any existing international agreements,
>
> *Understanding* that the above recital is not intended to subordinate this Protocol to other international agreements . . .

The principal mechanism for regulating LMOs is the advance informed agreement (AIA) procedure, to govern transboundary movement of LMOs for intentional introduction into the environment of the party of import.[261] This category of LMO does not include LMOs intended for direct use as food or feed, or for processing (LMO-FFPs) or to LMOs which the meeting of the parties to the Protocol decides are not likely to have adverse effects on biological diversity and human health.[262] Prior to the first intentional transboundary movement of an LMO, the party of export or the exporter must notify the national authority of the importing party.[263] The party of export must ensure that there is a legal requirement for the accuracy of information provided by the exporter.[264] On receipt of the notification, the importing party must provide a written acknowledgment to the notifier within ninety days, informing the notifier whether to proceed in accordance with the domestic regulatory framework of the importing party (which must be consistent with the Protocol) or with the decision procedure specified in Article 10.[265] If the importing party proceeds in accordance with Article 10, it must inform the notifier, in writing, within ninety days of the receipt of the initial notification, whether the intentional transboundary movement may proceed: (a) only after the importing party has given its written consent; or (b) after no less than ninety days

---

[261] Art. 7(1). Importing parties may opt to apply a simplified procedure to LMO imports instead of the 'advance informed agreement' procedure, 'provided that adequate measures are applied to ensure the safe intentional transboundary movement of living modified organisms in accordance with the objective of [the] Protocol': Art. 13.

[262] Art. 7(2) and (4).

[263] Pursuant to Art. 19(1), each party must designate one or more competent national authorities. The information includes, *inter alia*, contact details for the exporter and importer, the name and identity of the LMO and its genetic characteristics, a description of the modification, details of the intended use of the LMO and suggested methods for safe handling, storage, transport and use of the LMO.

[264] Art. 8.

[265] Art. 9(1)–(3). This recognises that many developing countries lack a regulatory framework for LMO imports.

without a subsequent written consent.[266] If the importing party informs the notifier that import can only proceed with the importing party's consent, the importing party has a period of 270 days from the initial notification in which to make a decision on import. The decision must be notified to the exporter and to the Biosafety Clearing-House established as part of the clearing-house mechanism under Article 18(3) of the Protocol.[267] Before making a decision on import of an LMO, the importing party must perform a risk assessment 'in a scientifically sound manner, in accordance with Annex III and taking into account recognised risk assessment techniques'.[268] Following the risk assessment, the importing party may approve or prohibit the import. Approval may be subject to conditions. The importing party may also request additional relevant information in accordance with its domestic regulatory framework or Annex I, or extend the decision-making period by a defined period of time.[269] Provision is made for the application of a precautionary approach by the importing party in Article 10(6), which provides:

> Lack of scientific certainty due to insufficient relevant scientific information and knowledge regarding the extent of the potential adverse effects of a living modified organism on the conservation and sustainable use of biological diversity in the Party of import, taking also into account risks to human health, shall not prevent that Party from taking a decision, as appropriate, with regard to the import of the living modified organism in question . . . in order to avoid or minimize such potential adverse effects.

The provision does not appear to preclude the possibility that an importing party could prohibit the import of an LMO even where there was no convincing scientific evidence demonstrating the potential for adverse effects to biological diversity or human health as a result of the import. An alternative decision-making procedure applies in respect of LMO-FFPs. Under Article 11, parties taking a final decision regarding domestic use, including placing on the market, of an LMO that may be subject to transboundary movement for direct use as food or feed, or for processing, are simply required to inform other parties through the Biosafety Clearing-House within fifteen days of making the decision. A party may take decisions on the import of LMO-FFPs in accordance with its domestic regulatory framework, provided this framework is consistent with the objective of the Protocol.[270] Alternatively, developing country parties, or parties with economies in transition, which lack a domestic regulatory framework, may declare through the Biosafety Clearing-House that decisions prior

---

[266] Art. 10(2).   [267] Art. 10(3).

[268] Art. 15(1). Annex III details general principles of risk assessment, the methodology to be used and points to consider in the assessment. The risk assessment may be undertaken by the importing party, or the exporter can be required to carry out the risk assessment: Art. 15(2) and (3).

[269] Art. 10(3).   [270] Art. 11(4).

to the first import of an LMO-FFP will be taken following a risk assessment undertaken in accordance with Annex III and within a predictable timeframe, not exceeding 270 days.[271] Again, lack of scientific certainty will not prevent a party from taking a decision designed to avoid or minimise the potential adverse effects of the LMO-FFP on the environment or human health.[272]

Where risks to biological diversity or human health are identified in the risk assessment process under the Protocol, the parties agree to establish and maintain appropriate mechanisms, measures and strategies to regulate, manage and control those risks.[273] Measures based on risk assessment must be imposed 'to the extent necessary to prevent adverse effects of the living modified organism on the conservation and sustainable use of biological diversity, taking also into account risks to human health, within the territory of the Party of import'.[274] Parties must also take appropriate measures to prevent unintentional transboundary movements of LMOs, including requiring a risk assessment to be carried out prior to the first release of an LMO.[275] New scientific evidence permits an importing party to review a previous decision regarding an intentional transboundary movement. The revised decision and accompanying reasons must be notified to any exporters that have previously notified movements of the LMO referred to in the decision, as well as to the Biosafety Clearing-House.[276] A party of export or a notifier may also seek a review of an importing party's decision in respect of an LMO import if it considers that a change in circumstances has occurred that may influence the outcome of the risk assessment upon which the decision was based or if additional relevant scientific or technical information has become available.[277]

Article 14 of the Protocol permits parties to enter into bilateral, regional and multilateral agreements and arrangements regarding intentional transboundary movements of LMOs which are consistent with the objective of the Protocol and do not result in a lower level of protection than that provided for by the Protocol. Parties may also enter into bilateral, regional and multilateral agreements and arrangements with non-parties to permit transboundary movements of LMOs which are consistent with the objective of the Protocol.[278] Intentional transboundary movements that take place pursuant to such agreements and arrangements are exempted from the provisions of the Protocol.[279] These provisions were included despite opposition from the European Union and developing countries, which saw them as a way for non-parties, such as the United States,[280] to circumvent the protective provisions of the Protocol. Parties entering into bilateral agreements with non-parties are required, however, to 'encourage' non-parties to adhere to the Protocol and to contribute

---

[271] Art. 11(6).   [272] Art. 11(8).   [273] Art. 16(1).   [274] Art. 16(2).   [275] Art. 16(3).
[276] Art. 12(1).   [277] Art. 12(2).   [278] Art. 24(1).   [279] Art. 14(3).
[280] As the United States is not a party to the Convention on Biological Diversity, it cannot become a party to the Protocol: Art. 37(1). The United States participated in the negotiations for the Biosafety Protocol as an observer.

appropriate information to the Biosafety Clearing-House on LMOs released in, or moved into or out of, areas within their national jurisdictions.[281]

Article 18 requires parties to take the necessary measures to require that LMOs that are subject to intentional transboundary movement within the scope of the Protocol are handled, packaged and transported under conditions of safety, taking into consideration relevant international rules and standards.[282] During the negotiations for the Protocol, the most controversial aspect of Article 18 was its provisions relating to documentation requirements for exports of various types of LMOs, particularly LMO-FFPs. The compromise agreed upon provides for parties to require that documentation accompanying LMO-FFPs clearly identifies that they 'may contain' living modified organisms.[283]

Article 20 establishes a Biosafety Clearing-House. Its functions are to facilitate the exchange of scientific, technical, environmental and legal information on, and experience with, LMOs, and to assist parties (especially developing countries, countries with economies in transition and countries that are centres of origin and centres of genetic diversity) in implementing the Protocol. Subject to commercial confidentiality requirements (under Article 21), parties must provide the Biosafety Clearing-House with specified information, which is publicly accessible.[284]

Under Article 17, parties must take appropriate measures to notify affected or potentially affected states, the Biosafety Clearing-House and international organisations of a release that leads, or may lead, to an unintentional transboundary movement of an LMO that is likely to affect biological diversity or human health.[285] Under Article 25, transboundary movements of LMOs carried out in contravention of a party's domestic measures implementing the Protocol are deemed to be illegal, and the affected party may request the party of origin to dispose of the LMO in question by repatriation or destruction, as appropriate.[286]

The limited capabilities of developing countries with respect to known and potential risks associated with LMOs was a factor in the adoption of the Protocol. Article 22 requires parties to co-operate in the development and/or strengthening of human resources and institutional capacities in biosafety within developing countries. Financial assistance may be provided for capacity-building through the financial mechanism established under Article 21 of the Convention, and the needs of parties with economies in transition are also to be

---

[281] Art. 24(2).

[282] Art. 18(1).   [283] Art. 18(2)(a); on labelling, see chapter 17, p. 861 below.

[284] Art. 20(3). A pilot phase of the Biosafety Clearing-House has been initiated prior to entry into force of the Protocol: http://bch.biodiv.org/pilot/Home.asp; on information exchange, see chapter 17, p. 832 below.

[285] Art. 17(1).

[286] Art. 25(1) and (2). The Protocol includes an enabling provision for the adoption of detailed rules on liability: see chapter 18, p. 938 below.

taken into account for capacity-building.[287] Further, Article 26 allows parties, in making decisions on the import of LMOs, to take into account 'socio-economic considerations' arising from the impact of LMOs on the conservation and sustainable use of biological diversity, provided such consideration is consistent with the party's international obligations.

The Protocol will utilise the institutional arrangements established under the Convention, with the conference of the parties serving as the meeting of the parties to the Protocol.[288] The meeting of the parties is to keep the implementation of the Protocol under regular review and may consider and adopt, as required, amendments to the Protocol and its Annexes, as well as any additional Annexes, that are deemed necessary for the implementation of the Protocol.[289] Parties must report on implementing measures.[290] The meeting of the parties is directed to establish a non-compliance mechanism, and to evaluate the effectiveness of the Protocol, after five years.[291]

EC law

The first international legal acts regulating biotechnology were adopted by the EC in the form of two 1990 Directives, which identify many of the issues and approaches addressed in the Biosafety Protocol. Council Directive 90/219/EEC addresses the contained use of genetically modified micro-organisms,[292] and Council Directive 2001/18/EC (replacing Directive 90/220/EEC) addresses the deliberate release into the environment of genetically modified organisms.[293] Both were adopted following the determination by the EC that, having regard to the environment, the adoption of measures for the evaluation and best use of biotechnology was a priority.[294] Their adoption reflected EC concern that biotechnology might pose certain threats to the environment or to human health which require its regulated development.

Directive 90/219 established common measures for the contained use of genetically modified micro-organisms (GMMs) with a view to protecting human health and the environment.[295] The Directive required member states to ensure that 'all appropriate measures are taken to avoid adverse effects on

---

[287] Art. 22(2) (the financial mechanism established in Art. 21 of the Convention is designated as the financial mechanism for the Protocol: Art. 28(2)); see chapter 20, p. 1035 below.

[288] Arts. 29–31.   [289] Art. 29(4).   [290] Art. 33.   [291] Arts. 34 and 35.

[292] Council Directive 90/219/EEC of 23 April 1990, OJ L117, 8 May 1990, 1 (amended by Directive 94/51/EC (OJ L297, 18 November 1994) and Directive 98/81/EC (OJ L330, 5 December 1998)).

[293] Directive 2001/18/EC, OJ L106, 17 April 2001, 1 (repealing Council Directive 90/220/EEC of 23 April 1990, OJ L117, 8 May 1990, 15 (as amended)).

[294] Fourth Environmental Action Programme, OJ C328, 7 December 1987, 1.

[295] Art. 1. 'Micro-organism' is defined as 'any microbiological entity, cellular or non-cellular, capable of replication or of transferring genetic material, including viruses, viroids, animal and plant cells in culture'; 'genetically modified micro-organism' (GMM) is defined as

human health and the environment which might arise from the contained use of GMMs' and to that end require the user to carry out an assessment of the contained uses as regards the risks to human health and the environment that these contained uses may incur.[296] The assessment is to result in the classification of the contained uses in one of four classes, applying the procedure set out in Annex III.[297] The user is generally then to apply the principles of containment and other protective measures set out in Annex IV, corresponding to the class of the contained use, in order to keep workplace and environmental exposure to any GMMs to 'the lowest reasonably practicable level, and so that a high level of safety is ensured'.[298] The Directive provides for notification of first and subsequent uses depending on the class.[299] Each member state designates a competent authority which is charged with fulfilling certain functions, including in relation to emergency plans and notification in the event of an accident.[300] A member state may, where appropriate, provide that the public shall be consulted on aspects of the proposed contained use, subject to certain requirements as to confidentiality.[301]

Directive 2001/18 updates and 'strengthens' the risk assessment and decision-making process established by Directive 90/220 on the release of genetically modified organisms (GMOs) into the environment, in particular, requiring information to be made available to the public and by introducing rules on mandatory labelling and traceability. Under Directive 90/220, the commercial releases of eighteen GMOs had been authorised in the EU by Commission decision (usually by a qualified majority vote in the Regulatory Committee), although in two cases the member state concerned did not implement the decision. The Commission granted no authorisations after October 1998 and, as at December 2002, fourteen applications were pending. Moreover, in eight cases (involving Austria, Luxembourg, France, Greece and Germany), member states invoked the Article 16 'safeguard clause' (under Directive 90/220) to temporarily ban the placing on the market of genetically modified maize and oilseed rape products.[302] Against this background, Directive 2001/18 has as its objective, in

---

'a micro-organism in which the genetic material has been altered in a way that does not occur naturally by mating and/or natural recombination': Art. 2(a) and (b). The Directive does not apply to certain categories of activity: Arts. 3 and 4.

[296] Art. 5(1) and (2). The user is to use, as a minimum, the elements of assessment and the procedure set out in Annex III, Sections A and B: Art. 5(2).

[297] Art. 5(3).   [298] Art. 6(1).   [299] Arts. 7–10 and Annex V.

[300] Arts. 11–12 and 14–15. Provision is also made for: consultation with other member states likely to be affected in the event of an accident; for notification to the EC Commission; and for information exchange: Art. 16.

[301] Arts. 13 and 19.

[302] In each case, the Scientific Committee on Plants determined that the information submitted by the member states did not justify the ban. See also Case C-6/99, *Association Greenpeace France and Others* v. *Ministère de l'Agriculture et de la Pêche and Others* [2000] ECR I-1651, in which the ECJ decided that, if, after an application for placing a GMO

accordance with the precautionary principle, the protection of human health and the environment when:

- carrying out the deliberate release into the environment of genetically modified organisms for any other purposes than placing on the market within the Community;
- placing on the market GMOs as or in products within the Community.[303]

Member states have a general obligation, in accordance with the precautionary principle, to ensure that all appropriate measures are taken to avoid adverse effects on human health and on the environment which might arise from the deliberate release or the placing on the market of GMOs, and that GMOs may only be deliberately released or placed on the market in conformity with the Directive.[304] The Directive distinguishes between deliberate release of a GMO for a purpose other than placing on the market (Part B) and placing on the market as or in GMOs (Part C). In respect of both, there must be a notification, which before being submitted must be subject to an environmental risk assessment.[305] The assessment will assess the potential adverse effects on human health and on the environment, which may occur directly or indirectly through gene transfer from GMOs to other organisms, on a case-by-case basis and in accordance with the criteria set forth in Annex II, taking into account the environmental impact according to the nature of the organism introduced and the receiving environment.[306] Member states designate the competent authority for complying with the requirements of this Directive, including for the examination of notifications, inspections and other control measures to ensure compliance with this Directive (including termination, remediation and the

---

on the market has been forwarded to the Commission, no member state has raised an objection or if the Commission has taken a favourable decision, the competent authority which forwarded the application, with a favourable opinion, to the Commission must issue the consent in writing, allowing the product to be placed on the market. However, if in the meantime the member state concerned has new information which leads it to consider that the product for which notification has been received may constitute a risk to human health and the environment, it will not be obliged to give its consent, provided that it immediately informs the Commission and the other member states about the new information in order that a decision may be taken in the matter.

[303] Art. 1. An 'organism' means 'any biological entity capable of replication or of transferring genetic material' and a 'genetically modified organism' (GMO) means an 'organism, with the exception of human beings, in which the genetic material has been altered in a way that does not occur naturally by mating and/or natural recombination': Art. 2(a) and (b). The Directive does not apply to certain organisms or to carriage by rail, road, inland waterway, sea or air: Art. 3.

[304] Art. 4(1).

[305] Art. 4(2), and including the information set forth in Annex III. This provision also aims to phase out antibiotic resistance markers in GMOs which may have adverse effects on human health and the environment, by December 2008 at the latest.

[306] Art. 4(3).

provision of information in respect of any unauthorised release or placing on the market, to initiate remedial action if necessary).[307]

Articles 5 to 11 (Part B) deal with deliberate release for a purpose other than placing on the market, distinguishing between standard and differentiated procedures.[308] The standard procedure comprises a system of notification (including the results of the environmental risk assessment) to the competent authority and a decision as to consent by the national authority, after having considered any observations by other member states in accordance with Article 11. The differentiated procedure may be applied where there has been 'sufficient experience . . . of releases of certain GMOs in certain ecosystems and the GMOs concerned meet the criteria set out in Annex V', and involves a decision by the commission assisted by relevant committees.[309] Part B also provides for modifications and new information, consultation with the public, and the reporting of releases.[310]

Articles 12 to 24 (Part C) impose more onerous obligations for placing on the market as or in a GMO. The system comprises a procedure for notification to the competent authority of the member state where the GMO is to be placed on the market for the first time.[311] The competent authority then examines the notification for compliance with the Directive and prepares an assessment report as to whether the GMO should be placed on the market and if so under what conditions.[312] The assessment report is sent to the notifier and the EC Commission, which circulates it to the other member states for comment. Under the standard procedure, the national authority may then grant a consent of up to ten years (where there has been no objection from a member state or the Commission) or it may refuse consent.[313] Where an objection is raised and maintained by a competent authority or the Commission (under Articles 15, 17 and 20), it will then be for the Commission to adopt the decision, which is communicated to the requesting national authority, which then puts it into effect.[314] If the decision is positive then the GMO may be placed on the market,

---

[307] Art. 4(4) and (5). Member states must also ensure traceability in accordance with Annex IV.

[308] Arts. 6 and 7 (not applicable under certain conditions for medicinal substances and compounds for human use consisting of, or containing, a GMO or combination of GMOs).

[309] Art. 7.   [310] Arts. 8–10.

[311] Art. 13(1). The procedure does not apply to certain GMOs as or in products as far as they are authorised by Community legislation: Art. 12(1). The notification must include the information required by Annexes III and IV and the environmental risk assessment: Art. 13(2).

[312] Art. 14(1)–(3)

[313] Art. 15 (the consent may be renewed under certain conditions: Art. 17). Art. 16 provides for criteria and information for specified GMOs.

[314] Art. 18(1). The decision is to be adopted and published within 120 days in accordance with the procedure laid down in Art. 30. The Commission is assisted by a Scientific Committee and a Committee on Ethics: Arts. 28 and 29.

and may then circulate freely within all member states.[315] GMOs placed on the market as or in products must be labelled and packaged in accordance with the Directive; however, where adventitious or technically unavoidable traces of authorised GMOs cannot be excluded, a minimum threshold may be established by the Commission below which such products will not have to be labelled.[316] Without prejudice to confidentiality requirements, the Directive also requires the Commission to make certain information publicly available, including some assessment reports, and the public is entitled to make comments to the Commission, which are to be forwarded to the competent authorities.[317]

As with Article 16 of the previous Directive, Article 23 establishes a 'safeguard clause', whereby a member state may provisionally restrict or prohibit the use and/or sale of the GMO as or in a product on its territory if it has 'detailed grounds for considering that a GMO as or in a product which has been properly notified and has received written consent . . . constitutes a risk to human health or the environment', provided that those grounds arise 'as a result of new or additional information made available since the date of the consent and affecting the environmental risk assessment or reassessment of existing information on the basis of new or additional scientific knowledge'.[318]

The Directive also requires member states to establish effective, proportionate and dissuasive penalties applicable to breaches of their laws giving effect to the Directive.

Other hazardous activities

States and other members of the international community have accepted that the activities and substances identified in the preceding sections of this chapter pose sufficient risks to the environment and to human health to warrant the development and adoption of particularised international rules. Certain other activities are increasingly recognised as posing sufficient threats to the environment at the local, national, regional and global levels to warrant their special consideration by international organisations with a view to the

---

[315] Art. 22.

[316] Art. 21 (also Art. 26). On 25 July 2001, the Commission presented a proposal for a regulation on traceability and labelling (COM (2001) 182 final), on which political agreement was reached on 10 December 2002. The Regulation is expected to be adopted in early 2003, and may be challenged by the United States and other states as being incompatible with WTO rules on free movement of goods. See chapter 19, pp. 985–7 below.

[317] Arts. 24 and 25.

[318] The member state must inform the Commission and other member states, and a decision will be taken within 60 days, under Art. 30(2). A member state must also take emergency measures, such as suspension or termination of the placing on the market, in the event of severe risk: Art. 23(1).

development of international rules. Apart from rules on noise pollution,[319] new international environmental norms are increasingly likely to be developed at the regional and global levels to address energy, mining, agriculture, transport and tourism. These may follow the approach taken by existing rules and guidelines adopted under the auspices of UNEP, the OECD and the EC.

Energy

Energy generation other than by nuclear sources has been the subject of limited attention, and even less action, by international organisations. Apart from the ECOSOC Committee on New and Renewable Sources of Energy (which has a limited mandate and no power to make binding or other acts),[320] no UN body has responsibility for non-nuclear energy sources. The environmental risks posed by energy use from fossil fuel sources (including coal, gas and oil), as well as non-renewable sources such as hydro-power, remain essentially unregulated at the international level and beyond the scope of a concerted or coherent international regulatory regime. To the extent that fossil fuel use in energy generation is 'regulated' by international law, it is as an incidental aspect of the rules governing mainly atmospheric pollution (in particular SO_2, NO_x and greenhouse gas obligations), waste, and the use of environmental impact assessments (and even then only in respect of very large plants and not overall energy policy).

There is, however, a growing recognition that the significant impact which energy policy and use has on the environment requires it to be the subject of its own institutional arrangements and substantive rules, which would be designed to develop national energy strategies, reduce the use of fossil fuel and wastage in energy distribution, develop renewable and other non-fossil fuel sources, and use energy more efficiently in homes and industry.[321] Energy was one of the most controversial issues addressed at UNCED. Despite the opposition of some states, the majority of states managed to ensure that some energy-related topics, including energy efficiency and the development and application of new and renewable sources of energy, were addressed in Agenda 21.[322] At the WSSD, no agreement was reached on fixing a specified

---

[319] See e.g. OECD Council Recommendation on Noise Prevention and Abatement, OECD C(74)217, 14 November 1974; OECD Council Recommendation on Noise Abatement Policies, OECD C(78)73 (Final), 3 July 1978; and OECD Council Recommendation on Strengthening Noise Abatement Policies, OECD C(85)103, 20 June 1985. See also the rules adopted by the EC (chapter 15, pp. 783–4 below), the ILO (pp. 638–9 above) and the ICAO (chapter 3, p. 99 above).

[320] See chapter 3, pp. 91–3 above.

[321] See IUCN, UNEP and WWF, *Caring for the Earth* (1991), 89–95.

[322] Chapter 8 above.

target for the use of renewable sources of energy.[323] In the meantime, the main global forum for addressing energy issues has, in effect, been the conference of the parties to the Climate Change Convention and the 1997 Kyoto Protocol, which is charged with keeping under review the commitments adopted under the Convention and developing new commitments on limiting emissions of greenhouse gases from fossil fuel sources.[324] Guidance on the content of more specific future international energy-related legislation may be found in non-binding Recommendations adopted by the OECD on various aspects of energy's impact upon the environment[325] and on the reduction of sulphur emissions from fuel plants,[326] and acts of the EC, which has adopted a range of measures on energy efficiency and conservation.[327]

The 1994 Energy Charter Treaty establishes a legal framework to promote long-term co-operation in the energy field.[328] Recognising that state sovereignty and sovereign rights over energy resources must be exercised in accordance with and subject to the rules of international law, it commits parties to 'strive to minimize in an economically efficient manner harmful Environmental Impacts occurring either within or outside its Area from all operations within the Energy Cycle in its Area', in pursuit of sustainable development and taking into account parties' obligations under those international agreements concerning the environment to which they are party.[329] It commits parties to strive to take precautionary measures 'to prevent or minimize environmental degradation', and recognises that the polluter should, in principle, bear the cost of pollution, including transboundary pollution.[330] To those ends, it requires parties, *inter alia*, to: take account of environmental considerations throughout the formulation and implementation of their energy policies; more fully reflect environmental costs and benefits; encourage co-operation in international environmental standards; develop and use renewable energy sources; promote public awareness of the environmental impacts of energy systems;

---

[323] Para. 19(c) of the Plan of Implementation merely commits states to give 'a greater share of the energy mix to renewable energies'; and para. 19(e) calls on states to 'with a sense of urgency, substantially increase the global share of renewable energy sources'.

[324] Chapter 8, pp. 366–77 above.

[325] OECD Council Recommendation on Energy and the Environment, OECD C(74)222, 14 November 1974; OECD Council Recommendation on Reduction of Environmental Impacts from Energy Production and Use, OECD C(76)162 (Final), 12 October 1976; OECD Council Recommendations on Reduction of Environmental Impacts from Energy Use in the Household and Commercial Sectors. OECD C(77)109 (Final), 21 September 1977; and OECD Council Recommendation on Environmentally Favourable Energy Options and their Implementation, OECD C(85)102, 20 June 1985.

[326] OECD Council Recommendation, Guidelines for Action to Reduce Emissions of Sulphur Oxides and Particulate Matter from Fuel Combustion in Stationary Sources, OECD C(74)16 Final, 15 IPE 7627; see chapter 8, pp. 327 and 336–8 above.

[327] See chapter 15, pp. 767–8 below.

[328] Energy Charter Protocol on Energy Efficient and Related Environmental Aspects, Lisbon, 17 December 1994, in force 8 April 1998, 33 ILM 446 (1995), Art. 1.

[329] Arts. 18 and 19(1).   [330] *Ibid.*

promote energy-efficient and environmentally sound technologies, practices and processes; and promote the transparent assessment at an early stage and prior to decision, and subsequent monitoring, of environmental impacts of environmentally significant energy investment projects. The Charter also has a Protocol on Energy Efficiency and Related Environmental Aspects which aims to promote energy efficiency policies consistent with sustainable development, to create conditions which induce producers and consumers to use energy as economically, efficiently and environmentally soundly as possible, and to foster co-operation in the field of energy efficiency.[331] It commits parties to establish energy-efficiency policies, to create a legal and regulatory framework which promotes energy efficiency, to develop, implement and update programmes, and to co-operate internationally.[332]

Mining

Despite its significant adverse environmental effects, mining has been the subject of few international rules (beyond environmental impact assessment and human rights requirements[333]), with the significant exception of obligations imposed in the Antarctic region[334] and in relation to deep seabed mining.[335] The impact of mining begins to be felt at the exploration stage, but becomes more significant during the extraction and metallurgical phases, where significant effects may occur for flora and fauna, sedimentation of rivers, acid and toxic drainage from tailings dumps and accidental overflow of waters, and in the pollution and toxic waste generated by the smelting process.[336] Like energy, mining is regulated by international law only to the extent that it is incidentally addressed by rules developed more specifically to address the protection of flora and fauna, the disposal of wastes, air pollution and environmental impact assessments. Future international legislation on mining might be guided by the principles developed under non-binding guidelines such as those adopted by UNEP.[337]

---

[331] Lisbon, 17 December 1994, in force x April 1998, 33 ILM 446 (1995), Art. 1.

[332] Arts. 3(2) and 8(1).

[333] See M. Orellana, *Indigenous Peoples, Mining and International Law* (International Institute for Environment and Development, Mining, Minerals and Sustainable Development Project, 2002).

[334] See 1988 CRAMRA and 1991 Antarctic Environment Protocol, chapter 14, pp. 716–26 below.

[335] Chapter 9, p. 446 above.

[336] See T. Wilde, 'Environmental Policies Towards Mining in Developing Countries', 10 JENRL 327 at 329–30 (1992).

[337] UNEP, 'Conclusions of the Study of Legal Aspects Concerning the Environment Related to Offshore Mining and Drilling Within the Limits of National Jurisdiction', UNEP/GC/Dec./10/14VI, 31 May 1982, 7 *Environmental Policy and Law* 50; UNEP Environmental Guidelines: Restoration and Rehabilitation of Land and Soils After Mining Activities, UNEP EMG No. 8, 1983.

In 1989, the ICJ was presented with an opportunity to consider some of the environmental aspects of mining in the *Case Concerning Certain Phosphate Lands in Nauru*,[338] brought by Nauru against Australia. The issues raised by the case, which was settled by agreement between the parties in September 1993, included the extent of certain legal obligations on the use of natural resources, including the obligation to rehabilitate mined lands, and the land rights of indigenous inhabitants. Nauru is a central Pacific island with a land mass of twenty-one square kilometres and a population of approximately 6,000 which achieved independence in 1968. Despite its small size, it is rich in phosphate, which was discovered there in 1900, and subsequently the island became an important source of the substance for phosphate-poor countries like Australia and New Zealand.

From 1947 until 1968, Nauru had been a territory administered under a UN General Assembly-approved Trusteeship Agreement between Australia, New Zealand and the United Kingdom. By the time it reached independence in 1968, large amounts of the phosphate had been mined and large parts of the island had been rendered uninhabitable. In May 1989, Nauru submitted an application to the ICJ asking it to declare Australia's responsibilities for breaches of international legal obligations relating to its phosphate mining activities in Nauru. Nauru claimed, *inter alia*, that Australia had violated the 1947 Trusteeship Agreement and Article 76 of the UN Charter by contributing to the physical destruction of the island as a unit of self-determination accompanied by a failure to rehabilitate the land; had violated the principle of self-determination, occasioned by the literal disposal of the territorial foundation of the unit of self-determination accompanied by a failure to provide an adequate sinking fund to cover the costs of rehabilitating the mined lands; and had breached the obligation to respect the right of the Nauruan people to permanent sovereignty over natural resources, because a major resource was being depleted on grossly inequitable terms and the extraction of phosphate involved a physical reduction of the homeland of the people of Nauru. Nauru asked the Court to declare that Australia had incurred an international legal responsibility for breach of these and other obligations, and requested primarily a declaration of Australia's liability. Included among the five forms of loss identified as the basis of relief was the cost of rehabilitation of the phosphate lands worked out before 1 July 1967.

In June 1992, the Court found by nine votes to four that it had jurisdiction over the application and that the application was admissible, with the exception of one claim.[339] Some of the grounds raised by Australia, and the findings by the Court in respect thereof, are of some relevance to broader issues of international environmental law, including the waiver of environmental claims,

---

[338] *Case Concerning Nauru v. Australia* (Preliminary Objections) (1992) ICJ Reports 240.
[339] *Ibid.*

the time period within which such claims should be brought, the conditions in which good faith principles will have been violated, and the issue of joint and several liability. Each merits consideration. Australia's second objection to admissibility, that Nauru had waived all claims relating to rehabilitation of the lands before various organs of the UN and before the Trusteeship Council, was rejected on the facts.[340] The Court also rejected Australia's objection of inadmissibility on the grounds that termination of the Trusteeship by General Assembly Resolution 2347 (XXII) of 19 December 1967 precluded allegations of breaches of the Trusteeship Agreement being examined by the Court. While the resolution had 'definitive legal effect' and did not expressly reserve any rights which Nauru might have with regard to rehabilitation of the phosphate lands, the Court did not view Resolution 2347 as discharging the administrative authority in respect of Nauru's rights. The Court took this view because 'everyone was aware of subsisting differences of opinion between the Nauru local government council and the administering authority with regard to rehabilitation of the phosphate lands worked out before 1 July 1967 as evidenced by statements made by France, Liberia, the USSR and India in the Trusteeship Council and elsewhere.[341] Australia's fourth objection, that Nauru's claim was inadmissible on the ground that it had not been submitted within a reasonable time, was also rejected by the Court. The Court recognised that 'even in the absence of any applicable treaty provision, delay on the part of the claimant state may render an application inadmissible', but held that 'international law does not lay down any specific time-limit in that regard'.[342] The Court rejected Australia's fifth objection, namely, that Nauru had failed to act consistently and in good faith in relation to rehabilitation, or that Nauru's conduct amounted to an abuse of process.[343]

The major issue raised in the Preliminary Objections phase concerned Australia's sixth objection, and it is of some relevance to international environmental law in that in many environmental claims it may not be possible to identify all the defendants in a particular case, or to find a court which has jurisdiction over each of them, or to be able to determine with any certainty the extent to which each state might have contributed to a particular form of environmental damage. Australia argued that the application was inadmissible as the Nauru claim was in substance against the administering authority and any judgment on the question of breach of the Trusteeship Agreement would involve the responsibility of third states (the United Kingdom and New Zealand) which had not consented to the Court's jurisdiction in the case. By nine votes to four, the

---

[340] *Ibid.*, 247–50.   [341] *Ibid.*, 252–3.

[342] *Ibid.*, 253–4; the Court found that it would have 'to ensure that Nauru's delay in seising it will in no way cause prejudice to Australia with regard to both the establishment of the facts and the determination of the content of the applicable law': *ibid.*, 255.

[343] *Ibid.*, 255.

Court rejected this argument.[344] It found that Australia, New Zealand and the United Kingdom constituted the administering authority, that the authority did not have international legal personality distinct from the three states, and that of those states Australia had played 'a very special role' established by the various Agreements and by practice.[345] The Court distinguished between the question of whether the liability of the states would be 'joint and several',[346] which was a matter for the Merits phase, and the question of whether Australia could be sued alone: nothing in the character of the Trusteeship Agreement debarred the Court from considering a claim of a breach of Australia's obligations.[347] As to the lack of consent granted by New Zealand and the United Kingdom, the Court held that a finding

> regarding the existence or the content of the responsibility attributed to Australia by Nauru might well have implications for the legal situation of the two other states concerned, but no finding in respect of that legal situation will be needed as a basis for the Court's decision against Australia. Accordingly the Court cannot decline to exercise its jurisdiction.[348]

In August 1993, Australia offered Nauru A\$107 million in full and final settlement of the claim, which sum was accepted by Nauru with an undertaking to discontinue proceedings and bring no further claims.[349] The Court did not have the opportunity to consider the merits, including the possibility of assessing the costs of rehabilitation. Nevertheless, it set out certain principles of some significance for the development of international environmental law. First, for the waiver of any claim, including an environmental claim, to be effective it will need to be made in a clear and express form. Secondly, acts of international institutions (in this case, a General Assembly resolution) which have definitive legal effects will not discharge rights which might exist in regard to environmental and other claims in the face of clearly expressed differences of opinion which exist between states supporting such an act. Thirdly, provided

---

[344] *Ibid.*, 1256–62. President Sir Robert Jennings, Vice President Oda, and Judges Ago and Schwebel entered strongly dissenting opinions on this issue: *ibid.*, 301–2, 302–25, 326–8 and 329–43. See also the Separate Opinion of Judge Shahabuddeen: *ibid.*, 270–300. While also dissenting on Australia's second, third, fourth and fifth objections, Judge Oda nevertheless stated that he was 'not denying the importance of the preservation of an environment from any damage that may be caused by the development or exploitation of resources, particularly in the developing regions of the world': *ibid.*, 325.

[345] *Ibid.*, 258.

[346] According to which 'any one of the three would be liable to make full reparation for damage flowing from any breach of obligations of the Administering Authority, and not merely a one-third or some other proportionate share': *ibid.*, 258.

[347] *Ibid.*, 258–9.

[348] *Ibid.*, 1261–2. This finding 'does not settle the question whether reparation would be due from Australia, if found responsible, for the whole or only part of the damage Nauru alleges it has suffered': *ibid.*, 262.

[349] 32 ILM 1471 (1993).

that certain minimum steps are taken to maintain a legal position and promote a legal claim, the passage of time will not necessarily render a claim inadmissible. Fourthly, and particularly of significance in the environmental field, the question of whether states have 'joint and several liability' is to be distinguished from the question of whether one of those states may be sued alone in respect of a claim of a breach of an international legal obligation, and the possibility that attributing responsibility to one state might have implications for the legal situation of other states concerned does not establish a bar to proceedings being brought against that one state.

Agriculture

The impact of agriculture on the environment is well documented. Threats which are incidentally subject to international legal regulation include expanding farms which destroy forests and wetlands; soil erosion; the use of pesticides which damage flora and fauna; and chemical run-off and consequential contamination of freshwater resources from excessive fertiliser use.[350] Agricultural practices are significantly influenced and affected by the rules of international law addressing the use of pesticides, the protection of watercourses, environmental assessment, and the conservation of biodiversity, including forests. Nevertheless, agriculture is not subject to a co-ordinated regime of legal obligations which apply specific rules at the regional or global level, and which might prepare and implement strategies to use agricultural land optimally, control the use of fertilisers and pesticides, and promote proper land husbandry. While specific agreements address drought and desertification[351] and the humane treatment of animals,[352] only non-binding instruments on the regulation of agricultural practices have been adopted by UNEP and the FAO. These address the use of environmental impact assessment on agricultural activities,[353] and other environmental aspects of agricultural practices.[354] EC legislation is also

---

[350] World Resources Institute and International Institute for Environment and Development, *World Resources 1988–9* (1989), 135–7.

[351] Chapter 11, pp. 524–7 above.

[352] See European Convention for the Protection of Animals During International Transport, Paris, 30 December 1986, ETS No. 65, and Additional Protocol, Strasbourg, 10 May 1979, ETS No. 103; European Convention for the Protection of Animals Kept for Farming Purposes, Strasbourg, 10 March 1976, ETS No. 102.

[353] FAO, Comparative Legal Study on Environmental Impact Assessment and Agricultural Development, FAO Paper 2 (1982).

[354] Environmental Guidelines for the Formulation of National Soil Policies, UNEP EMG No. 7 (1983); Environmental Guidelines for Agricultural Mechanization, UNEP EMG No. 10 (1986); Environmental Guidelines for Agroforestry Projects, UNEP EMG No. 11 (1986); UNEP Environmental Guidelines for Farming Systems Research, UNEP EMG, No. 12 (1986).

limited,[355] and it remains to be seen how the WTO Agreement on Agriculture's exemption of environmental programmes from rules limiting governmental subsidies will be applied.[356]

Transportation

Transportation is a major contributor to fossil fuel use and a significant source of urban air pollution, sulphur dioxide emissions and greenhouse gas emissions. Roads and railways also make use of land in ways which can be particularly damaging to biodiversity. The regulation of environmental aspects of air and sea transport is a matter for the ICAO and the IMO respectively, but transportation by road and rail is not addressed by any UN body, or subject to a body of international rules which would allow the development of an integrated transport policy which takes account of the environmental consequences of the different modes of transport and the elaboration and implementation of fuel efficiency standards, emission standards, and waste-minimisation standards. In this regard, only the UNECE and the EC[357] have adopted binding standards which may provide a basis for the adoption of minimum standards in other regions and globally.

Tourism

Finally, in recent years, tourism has begun to be the subject of a new body of rules aimed at addressing environmental degradation from this source. The adverse environmental effects of tourism and related recreational activities have led to the adoption of national environmental standards, and at the international level restrictions have been imposed on tourism in the Antarctic region,[358] and non-binding guidelines adopted by UNEP and the OECD.[359]

UNCED and WSSD

Agenda 21 includes two chapters on toxic and dangerous products: Chapter 19 on 'Environmentally Sound Management of Toxic Chemicals, Including Prevention of Illegal International Traffic in Toxic and Dangerous Products'; and Chapter 16 on 'Environmentally Sound Management of Biotechnology'.

---

[355] EC Council Directive 86/278/EEC, OJ L181, 4 July 1986, 6 (use of sewage sludge in agriculture).

[356] 1994 Agreement, Annex 2.

[357] See respectively chapter 8, p. 324 above, and chapter 15, pp. 758–9 below.

[358] Chapter 14, p. 723 below.

[359] OECD Council Recommendation: Environment and Tourism, OECD C(79)115, 8 May 1979; 1982 UNEP Environmental Guidelines for Coastal Tourism, UNEP EMG No. 6.

The WSSD addresses both subjects and also addresses the need to develop sustainable agriculture,[360] promote eco-tourism,[361] and foster sustainable mining practices (in accordance with national regulations and taking into account significant transboundary impacts).[362]

Toxic and dangerous products

Chapter 19 of Agenda 21 proposed six programme areas on: (1) the international assessment of chemical risks; (2) the harmonisation and classification of labelling of chemicals; (3) information exchange on toxic chemicals and chemical risk; (4) risk reduction programmes; (5) the management of chemicals; and (6) the prevention of illegal international traffic in toxic and dangerous products.

The first programme area sought to expand and accelerate international assessment of chemical risks by assessing several hundred priority chemicals or groups, including major pollutants and contaminants of global significance, and producing guidelines for acceptable exposure to a greater number of toxic chemicals.[363] Agenda 21 called also for a strengthening of the programmes within the Integrated Programme on Chemical Safety (IPCS) of the UN and FAO in collaboration with the OECD, based on the precautionary approach, and the development of criteria for setting priorities for chemicals of global concern.[364] The second programme area called for the harmonisation of systems for the classification and labelling of chemicals by the year 2000, including material safety data sheets and easily understandable symbols.[365] The objective of the third programme area was the exchange of information on chemical safety, use and emissions standards to achieve, by the year 2000, full implementation of the 'prior informed consent procedure' of the UNEP London Guidelines and the FAO Code of Conduct, including possible 'mandatory applications through legally binding instruments'.[366]

The objectives of the fourth programme area were to eliminate unacceptable or unreasonable risks and to reduce the risks posed by toxic chemicals by employing a wide range of risk reduction options, taking precautionary measures derived from a life cycle analysis which covers manufacturing, trade, transport, use and disposal.[367] Mechanisms include the use of cleaner products and technologies; emission inventories; product labelling; use limitations; economic incentives; phasing out or banning of certain toxic chemicals; identifying national needs for standard-setting in the context of the *Codex Alimentarius*; policies on accident prevention, preparedness and response; reducing over-dependence

---

[360] Plan of Implementation, para. 38; see also para. 39 (land degradation).
[361] Para. 41.   [362] Para. 44(b).   [363] Para. 19.13.
[364] Paras. 19.14(a) and 19.17(a).   [365] Paras. 19.27 and 19.29.
[366] Para. 19.38.   [367] Paras. 19.48 and 19.49(a).

on the use of agricultural chemicals; and preparation of on-site and off-site emergency response plans.[368] General measures of international co-operation include support for large industrial enterprises (including transnational corporations) to introduce policies which demonstrate a commitment to 'adopt standards of operation equivalent to or not less stringent than those existing in the country of origin'.[369]

The fifth programme proposed to strengthen national capabilities by further developing the basic elements for sound management of chemicals. These were identified as: (1) adequate legislation; (2) information gathering and dissemination; (3) capacity for risk assessment and interpretation; (4) establishment of risk management policy; (5) capacity for implementation and enforcement; (6) capacity for rehabilitation of contaminated sites and poisoned persons; (7) effective education; and (8) a capacity to respond to emergencies.[370] To that end, the programme proposed the preparation of guidelines; support for developing national legislation and implementation; the adoption of right-to-know programmes, including toxic emissions inventories; the implementation of UNEP's programme on Awareness and Preparedness for Emergencies at the Local Level (APELL); and the preparation by UNEP of principles for accident prevention, preparedness and response, building on ILO, OECD and UNECE work.[371] Finally, the sixth programme called for the strengthening of international co-operation to prevent illegal transboundary movement of toxic and dangerous products, building on General Assembly Resolutions 42/183 and 44/226. The programme does not call for the development of a binding international agreement or the strengthening of the UNEP and OECD non-binding instruments.[372]

The WSSD Plan of Implementation renews these Agenda 21 commitments, aiming to ensure by 2020 that 'chemicals are used and produced in ways that lead to the minimization of significant adverse effects on human health and the environment, using transparent science-based risk assessment and management procedures, taking into account the precautionary approach'. To that end, the Plan calls for ratification and implementation of the 1998 Chemicals Convention and the 2001 POPs Convention, the implementation of a new globally harmonised system for classification and labelling (by 2008) and the development of national pollutant release and transfer registers.[373]

Management of biotechnology

Chapter 16 of Agenda 21 has a general objective of fostering internationally agreed principles to ensure environmentally sound management of

---

[368] Para. 19.49.   [369] Para. 19.52(d).
[370] Para. 19.56.   [371] Para. 19.61.   [372] Paras. 19.66 to 19.76.
[373] Para. 22. The Plan also focuses on heavy metals, in particular mercury and its compounds.

biotechnologies through six programme areas to enhance protection of the environment and to develop international co-operation. From the international legal perspective, the most notable programme area is the fourth, which seeks to enhance safety and to develop co-operation through internationally agreed principles on risk assessment and management of all aspects of biotechnology. The final text of this programme reflected the sharp divisions between states on the desirability of international measures, and the concern of the United States that UNCED should not suggest that biotechnology was inherently unsafe. The programme contained little of substance to guide future efforts on developing internationally agreed principles, calling simply for 'consideration of the need for and feasibility of an international agreement', now reflected in the 2000 Biosafety Protocol, which the WSSD Plan of Implementation calls on all states to ratify and implement.[374]

Conclusions

The rules of international law relating specifically to hazardous substances and activities are set out in a multitude of sources which are often inaccessible and difficult to comprehend easily. Since the first edition of this book appeared, there have been a number of significant developments, reflected in particular in the consolidation and development of existing instruments and the adoption of new international conventions relating to chemicals and pesticides (1998), biosafety (2000) and persistent organic pollutants (2001). These instruments reflect a commitment to establish and implement global minimum standards which are legally binding and (relatively) accessible, and which give effect to a more precautionary approach to international regulation. They also reflect a commitment to make use of a mix of regulatory approaches, including trade mechanisms, prohibitions and information requirements (labelling in particular), but not the more innovative economic instruments adverted to in the UNCED proceedings. In the medium term, it is plain that efforts will focus on encouraging broad support for these instruments and their implementation, including through the new non-compliance mechanisms which will shortly emerge. Notwithstanding these important developments, much remains to be done. There has been some progress in consolidating arrangements so as to remove disparities in, for example, legal obligations relating to transport. But the proliferation of classification and registration schemes has not been addressed, and there has been no easing of the task of collecting and disseminating information and ensuring ease of use by those who need it most, citizens and workers. As the WSSD Plan of Implementation recognises, the absence of a comprehensive scheme of classification and registration needs to be addressed as a matter of urgency; and international minimum standards in respect of each,

---

[374] Para. 16.35(c); Plan of Implementation, para. 42(t).

as well as labelling and packaging, need to be developed and applied. Other gaps also exist. In most regions of the world there are no international rules of general application on emergency preparedness and response, and the ILO's Convention on Emergency Preparedness should be accorded high priority as an instrument to be applied in the various regions.

Finally, notwithstanding certain claims as to the similarity of their hazard characteristics, in certain respects the international regulation of radioactive substances and biotechnology have followed different paths. It remains to be seen whether the 2000 Biosafety Protocol will provide the effective environmental regulation which ensures that the limitations of international nuclear regulation are not repeated, in particular the need to ensure that the international organisation (or organisations) given primary competence over biotechnology is not endowed with a dual promotional and regulatory function. These are fundamentally incompatible objectives which national agencies are not normally granted, and they have served to undermine the effective functioning of the IAEA.

13

Waste

Introduction

This chapter describes the rules of international law relating to the management of waste, including: prevention and treatment; disposal; recycling and re-use; and international movement (including trade). Liability for environmental damage caused by wastes is addressed in chapter 18, and there is an emerging case law at the European Court of Human Rights linking waste with the protection of fundamental human rights.[1] Except for rules on international trade in wastes, this is not a well-developed area of international law, which law has to date played a limited role in preventing the generation of waste. Other than the special rules which are applicable in the Antarctic[2] and the EC,[3] there is no regional or global legal framework for waste management strategy. Rather, waste has traditionally been regulated incidentally to the attainment of other objectives. Among the relevant international legal measures are those regulating the disposal of wastes at sea;[4] limiting atmospheric emissions of gaseous wastes;[5] and preventing the disposal of wastes in rivers and other freshwaters.[6] This approach does not address the source of the problem by preventing waste generation; it merely shifts the disposal problem to another environmental medium.

In the context of the massive increase in the generation of all types of waste resulting from industrialisation, this is a major shortcoming in the rules of international environmental law. Part of the problem is institutional: at the global level, no UN or other body has overall responsibility for waste, which has led to a fragmented, *ad hoc* and piecemeal international response. The Stockholm Conference did not focus on the issue of waste as such. Without specifically mentioning waste, Principle 6 of the 1972 Stockholm Declaration called for the discharge of toxic or other substances to be halted. The 1982 World Charter for Nature called for 'special precautions' to be taken to prevent

---

[1] E.g. *Lopez Ostra* v. *Spain* (1995) 20 EHRR 277 (Judgment 41/1993/436/515 of 9 December 1994); and *Guerra and Others* v. *Italy* (1998) 26 EHRR 357 (Judgment 116/1996/735/932 of 19 February 1998); see chapter 7, pp. 301–2 above.
[2] Chapter 14, pp. 716–18 below.   [3] Chapter 15, pp. 786–93 below.
[4] See pp. 684–5 below.   [5] See pp. 686–7 below.   [6] See pp. 685–6 below.

discharge of radioactive or toxic wastes, but did not encourage minimisation of the generation of such wastes. At UNCED, the issue of waste was addressed in some detail in Agenda 21 with the development of proposals, including targets and timetables, for the management of hazardous and other wastes and radioactive wastes.[7] Principle 14 of the Rio Declaration limited itself to calling for effective co-operation to 'discourage or prevent the relocation or transfer to other states of any activities and substances that cause severe environmental degradation or are found to be harmful to human health'.

One of the first serious attempts to establish the basis for a more comprehensive international approach to waste management was the 1976 OECD Council Recommendation on a Comprehensive Waste Management Policy. This recommended that member countries implement waste policies to protect the environment and ensure rational use of energy and resources while taking account of economic constraints.[8] Recommended principles included the need to take environmental protection into account; to encourage waste prevention; to promote recycling; to use policy instruments; and to ensure access to information.[9] The Recommendation also endorsed administrative arrangements, including inventories of wastes to be disposed; the organisation of waste collection; the establishment of disposal centres; the promotion of research and development on disposal methods and low-waste technology; and encouraging markets for recycled products.[10]

Ten years later, the UNEP Governing Council endorsed the 1987 Cairo Guidelines and Principles for the Environmentally Sound Management of Hazardous Wastes, which assist governments to develop policies for environmentally sound management of hazardous wastes from generation to final disposal.[11] The Guidelines include general principles to protect human health and the environment from damage from hazardous waste, including its transfrontier movement, and the requirement that 'all practicable steps' should be taken to ensure that management of hazardous waste is conducted in accordance with applicable international law in matters of environmental protection.[12] Further principles address non-discrimination, international co-operation, transfer of technology, and a recognition that the protection of the environment 'is not achieved by the mere transformation of one form of pollution into another, nor by the mere transfer of the effects of pollution from one location to another, but only by the use of the waste treatment option . . . which minimises the environmental impact'.[13] Subsequent principles address generation and management (Principles 7 and 8); disposal (Principles 9 to 18); monitoring, remedial action and record-keeping (Principles 19 and 20); safety and contingency planning (Principles 21 to 23); transport (Principles 24 to 28);

---

[7] See pp. 705–8 below.   [8] OECD C(76) 155 Final (1976).
[9] Annex, paras. 2 to 6.   [10] Para. 7.
[11] UNEP/GC.14/17 (1987), Annex II, UNEP GC/dec./14/30, UNEP ELPG No. 8.
[12] Principle 2.   [13] Principles 3 to 6.

and liability and compensation (Principle 29). In 1990, the EC adopted a framework, the Community Strategy for Waste Management,[14] to guide waste management policy for member states. Following a Commission review of the Strategy, in 1997 the EC Council adopted a revised Community Strategy for Waste Management.[15]

Defining and treating waste

International legal regulation of waste began in the early 1970s with the adoption of two treaties which prohibited the disposal at sea of certain types of waste. This raised the difficulty of defining waste, a matter which continues to cause legal difficulties today. Human activity generates waste in solid, liquid or gaseous form, and these wastes have tended to be categorised by regulatory instruments at the national and international level according to two characteristics: their source (municipal or industrial, including agricultural and mining); and/or their hazardous qualities (non-hazardous, hazardous and ultra-hazardous). Within these categorisations, international legal instruments adopt a range of different definitions, as the following examples illustrate. One approach, adopted by the Cairo Guidelines, is to define waste by reference to national law, although this approach has not been widely followed. Other efforts establish internationally agreed definitions. Under the 1972 London Convention, wastes or other matters are defined broadly to include 'material and substance of any kind, form or description'.[16] The 1989 Basel Convention, on the other hand, defines wastes by reference to their end use: they are 'substances or objects which are disposed of or are intended to be disposed of or are required to be disposed of by the provisions of national law'.[17] Under this definition, a substance which is not to be disposed of (perhaps to be recycled) may not be waste. A similar definition exists under EC law, which originally (in 1975) defined waste as 'any substance or object which the holder disposes of or is required to dispose of pursuant to the rules of national law'.[18] This definition caused practical problems because it allowed many substances to be excluded if the holder treated the substances other than by disposal. In 1990, the ECJ broadened the definition of waste under Directive 75/442/EEC by interpreting Article 1(a) as not 'excluding substances and objects which are capable of economic re-utilisation'.[19] The following year the definition was further amended to mean 'any substance or

[14] Chapter 15, pp. 786–7 below.
[15] Council Resolution of 24 February 1997 on a Community strategy for waste management, OJ C076, 11 March 1997, 1.
[16] Art. III(4). The 1976 Barcelona Dumping Protocol adopted the same definition: Art. 3(2).
[17] Art. 2(1). The 1991 Bamako Convention adopts a similar definition: Art. I(1).
[18] Council Directive 75/442/EEC, Art. 1(a).
[19] Joined Cases C-206 and C-207/88, *Vessoso and Zanetti* [1990] ECR I-1461; see also Case C-359/88, *Zanetti and Others* [1990] ECR I-1509, holding that national legislation defining waste as excluding substances or objects which are capable of economic re-utilisation was incompatible with Directives 75/442 and 78/319.

object . . . which the holder discards or intends or is required to discard'
and which falls into one of the categories set out in Annex 1 to the amended
Directive.[20] The Directive does not, however, apply to atmospheric emissions of
gases and certain wastes covered by other legislation.[21] More recently, the 1992
OSPAR Convention has reversed the traditional approach by defining waste by
reference to what it was not, rather than what it was,[22] and the 1996 Protocol
to the 1972 London Convention defines wastes and other matters as 'material
and substance of any kind, form or description'.[23] It remains to be seen whether
this approach will clear up the matter and permit more effective international
regulation by limiting the scope for definitional disagreements.

Municipal waste

Municipal waste, which is not deemed to be hazardous, generally includes
that generated by households, shops, offices and other commercial units, and
includes paper and cardboard, glass, plastics, metals, organic matters and pu-
trescible materials. The generation of municipal wastes is closely related to
levels of industrialisation and income: by the early 1990s, in industrialised
countries each person generated between 2.75 and 4 kg of waste per day, but
in least-developed countries each person generated on average only 0.5 kg per
day.[24] Rapid industrialisation has resulted in large increases in the generation
of waste paper and plastic.[25] The two main techniques for disposal of municipal
waste are landfill (accounting for over 70 per cent in most OECD countries)
and incineration.[26] The main environmental problems related to landfill are

---

[20] Council Directive 75/442/EEC, as amended by Council Directive 91/156/EEC, OJ L78, 26
March 1991, 32, Art. 1(a). On the meaning of 'discard', the ECJ has tended to take an expansive approach: see Cases C-206/88 and C-207/88, *Vessaso and Zanetti* [1990] ECR
I-1461; Joined Cases C-242/94, C-304/94, C-330/94, C-224/95, *Criminal Proceedings
Against Tombesi and Others* [1997] ECR I-3561 (the concept of 'waste' is not to be understood as excluding substances and objects which are capable of economic re-utilisation,
even if the materials in question may be the subject of a transaction or quoted on public
or private commercial lists); Case C-129/96, *Inter-Environnement Wallonie ASBL* v. *Region
Wallonne* [1997] ECR I-7411; and Case C-9/00, *Palin Granit Oy and Vehmassalon Kansan-
terveystyon Kuntayhtyman Hallitus* [2002] ECR I-3533 (the holder of leftover stone resulting from stone quarrying which is stored for an indefinite length of time to await possible
use discards or intends to discard that leftover stone, which is accordingly to be classified as
waste within the meaning of Council Directive 75/442/EEC; the place of storage of leftover
stone, its composition and the fact, even if proven, that the stone does not pose any real
risk to human health or the environment are not relevant criteria for determining whether
the stone is to be regarded as waste).
[21] Art. 2(1). Annex I lists sixteen categories of waste.
[22] Art. 1(o); waste does not include human remains, offshore installations, offshore pipelines,
and unprocessed fish and fish offal.
[23] Art. 1(8).   [24] UNEP, *Environmental Data Report* (1991, 3rd edn), 334.
[25] *Ibid.*, and Table 8.2.   [26] *Ibid.*, 336–7 and Table 8.6.

the generation of methane (a greenhouse gas), and the production of leachates which may contaminate surface or groundwaters. Incineration contributes to air pollution by generating dust, acidic and greenhouse gases, vaporised metals, metal salts, and dioxins and furans.[27]

Hazardous and toxic wastes (industrial, agricultural and mining waste and sewage sludge)[28]

Non-municipal waste tends to be categorised by reference to its source (industrial, mining or agricultural) and, in relation to the applicable rules, its characteristics (non-hazardous, hazardous, toxic, radioactive). Industrial wastes include general factory rubbish, packaging materials, organic wastes, acids, alkalis and metalliferous sludges. Mining wastes are a by-product of the extraction process and include topsoil, rock and dirt, which may be contaminated by metals and coal. Agricultural wastes comprise animal slurries, silage effluents, tank washings following pesticide use, and empty plastic packaging. Non-municipal wastes also include sewage sludges, which is produced by the treatment of industrial and domestic wastes and is often contaminated with heavy metals, organic chemicals, greases and oils. Many industrial and mining wastes are hazardous and require special treatment in their disposal. The options for hazardous waste include physical or chemical treatment, incineration, landfill, sea disposal, storage or containment, and recycling.[29] Large quantities of organic waste, including sewage sludge, animal slurries and silage effluents, are applied to agricultural land.[30]

The international legal regimes governing the transboundary movement of wastes apply different definitions of hazardous wastes. The 1989 Basel Convention defines hazardous wastes as those belonging to any category of waste set out in Annex I to the Convention, unless they do not possess any of the characteristics contained in Annex III, as well as wastes defined as or considered to be hazardous wastes under the legislation of export, import or transit parties.[31] 'Other wastes', also subject to certain requirements under the 1989 Basel Convention, are those which belong to any category contained in Annex II.[32] The 1989 Basel Convention does not apply to radioactive wastes which 'are

---

[27] *Ibid.* [28] *Ibid.*, 335–6. [29] *Ibid.*, 348 and Table 8.7. [30] *Ibid.*, 338–9.

[31] Art. 1(1). Parties must inform the secretariat of wastes defined as hazardous under their national legislation: Art. 3. Annex I lists categories of wastes to be controlled by reference to eighteen waste streams and twenty-six constituents. A similar definition is found in the Convention to Ban the Importation into Forum Island Countries of Hazardous and Radioactive Wastes and to Control the Transboundary Movement and Management of Hazardous Wastes Within the South Pacific, Waigani, 16 September 1995, in force 21 October 2001, www.basel.int/misclinks/waigani.html, Art. 2.

[32] Art. 1(2); Annex II lists household wastes and residues from the incineration of household wastes.

subject to other international control systems, including, international instruments, applying specifically to radioactive materials', or to wastes which 'derive from the normal operations of a ship, the discharge of which is covered by another international instrument'.[33] Under this approach, it is possible that certain radioactive wastes would not be subject to an 'international control system' within the meaning of the Convention, and could therefore be included as hazardous waste and subject to the Convention.

Under the 1991 Bamako Convention, 'hazardous wastes' are defined more broadly in four categories. These are: wastes belonging to the categories identified in Annex I, which combines Annexes I and II to the Basel Convention; wastes so defined or considered by national legislation of the party of import, export or transit; wastes which possess any of the characteristics contained in Annex II; and 'hazardous substances which have been banned, cancelled or refused registration by government regulatory action, or voluntarily withdrawn from registration in the country of manufacture, for human health or environmental reasons'.[34] The Convention applies to radioactive wastes which are subject to any international control systems applying to radioactive materials, but does not apply to ship wastes.[35]

The defunct 1989 Lomé Convention defined hazardous wastes as those categories of products listed in Annexes I and II to the 1989 Basel Convention but expressly included radioactive wastes.[36] The 1986 Mexico–United States Hazardous Waste Agreement defines hazardous wastes as 'any waste, as designated or defined by the applicable designated authority pursuant to national policies, laws or regulations, which, if improperly dealt with in activities associated with them, may result in health or environmental damage'.[37] Under EC law, hazardous wastes are redefined by Directive 91/689/EEC as non-domestic wastes which: (a) feature on a list to be drawn up on the basis of Annexes I and II to the Directive, which wastes must also have one or more of the properties listed in Annex III;[38] and (b) any other waste which is considered by a

---

[33] Art. 1(3) and (4).

[34] Art. 2(1)(a) to (c). Similar definitions are found in the Protocol on the Prevention of Pollution of the Mediterranean Sea by Transboundary Movements of Hazardous Wastes and their Disposal, Izmir, 1 October 1996, not yet in force, www.unepmap.gr/pdf/hazardous.pdf, Art. 3; and the Central America Regional Agreement on the Transboundary Movement of Hazardous Waste, 11 December 1992, in force 17 November 1995, UN Doc. UNEP/CHW/C.1/INF.2 (October 1993), Art. 1(1).

[35] Art. 2(2) and (3).   [36] Art. 39(3).

[37] Art. 1(2). But cf. the 1986 Canada–US Hazardous Waste Agreement, Ottawa, 28 October 1986, in force 8 November 1986, TIAS 11099: Art. 1(b).

[38] Council Directive 91/689/EEC, OJ L377, 31 December 1991, 20, Art. 1(4) and (5) (amended by Commission Decision 2000/532/EC, OJ L 226, September 2000, 3); the list must also take into account the origin and composition of the waste and limit values of concentrations. On the Directive, see chapter 15, pp. 789–91 below.

member state to display any of the properties listed in Annex III and notified to the EC Commission.[39] Annex I lists categories or generic types of hazardous waste listed according to their nature or the activity which generated them; Annex II lists the constituents of some of the wastes in Annex I which render them hazardous; and Annex III identifies properties which render wastes hazardous.[40]

Radioactive waste

C. A. Mawson, *Management of Radioactive Wastes* (1985); E. Moisé, *International Regulations on Radioactive and Toxic Wastes: Similarities and Differences* (1991).

Radioactive wastes, which are generally subject to special rules, are the product of nuclear power generation, military sources, and medical, industrial and university establishments. Low-level radioactive wastes include contaminated laboratory debris, biological materials, building materials and uranium mine tailings. High-level radioactive wastes include spent fuel from nuclear power reactors and liquid and solid residues from reprocessing of spent nuclear fuels. The disposal of radioactive wastes is generally through storage on land, although it has been estimated that between 1949 and 1982 at least 46 Pbq of radioactive wastes were disposed of at sea.[41] Radioactive wastes have been defined by the IAEA Code and by EC law.[42]

Prevention and treatment

Few binding international obligations establish targets and timetables, quantitative restrictions or other limits on the generation of municipal and industrial waste, including hazardous and radioactive wastes. Insofar as certain polluting gases, such as sulphur dioxide, nitrogen oxide, volatile organic compounds, and carbon dioxide are waste products, treaties establishing quantitative limits on atmospheric emissions of such gases in effect limit the generation of certain wastes.[43] These treaties, however, are exceptional, and are characterised by the few industrial countries, in regional terms, which are bound by their substantive provisions. The EC has, however, recently adopted legislation

[39] *Ibid.*
[40] These properties include whether the wastes are explosive; oxidising; highly flammable; flammable; irritant; harmful; toxic; carcinogenic; corrosive; infectious; teratogenic; mutagenic; and ecotoxic; as well as substances and preparations which release toxic or very toxic gases, capable of yielding a leachate.
[41] UNEP, *Environmental Data Report* (1991, 3rd edn), 338 and Table 8.11.
[42] See p. 697 and n. 220. p. 704 below.
[43] See generally chapter 8 above, nn. 92–6 below.

establishing quantitative restrictions on the generation of certain categories of waste.[44]

Recent acts of international organisations and international agreements have set forth general commitments to limit and prevent waste generation. They usually do not provide specific details as to how this is to be achieved. Resolutions of the Consultative Meetings of the 1972 London Convention have recognised that parties should give priority to no-waste and low-waste technology.[45] The EC Treaty requires EC environmental action to be based upon objectives and principles which ensure a 'prudent and rational utilisation of natural resources' based on 'preventive action'.[46] The 1989 Basel Convention requires parties to take measures to '[e]nsure that the generation of hazardous wastes and other wastes within it is reduced to a minimum, taking into account social, technological and economic aspects', and to prevent, or minimise the consequences of, pollution due to management of hazardous and other wastes.[47] The 1989 Basel Convention also requires parties to ensure the availability of 'adequate disposal facilities, for the environmentally sound management of hazardous wastes and other wastes, that shall be located, to the extent possible, within it [the state], whatever the place of their disposal'.[48] Co-operation is needed to develop new environmentally sound low-waste technologies and improve existing technologies to eliminate, as far as practicable, the generation of wastes and ensure their environmentally sound management.[49] The 1999 conference of the parties to the Basel Convention determined a number of priority goals for future action, including 'the prevention, minimisation, recycling, recovery and disposal of hazardous wastes . . . taking into account social, technological and economic concerns', and 'the active promotion and use of clear technologies'.[50]

---

[44] See Council Directive 94/62/EC on packaging and packaging waste, OJ L365, 31 December 1994, 10; and Council Directive 2000/76/EC on the incineration of waste, OJ L322, 28 December 2000, 91. See further, chapter 15, pp. 791–2 below.

[45] Res. LDC.39(13) on the status of incineration of noxious liquid wastes at sea, Preamble; and Res. LDC.51(16) banning ocean dumping of radioactive waste.

[46] Art. 174(1) and (2) (formerly Art. 130r(1) and (2)); see also Council Directive 75/442/EEC, as amended by Council Directive 91/156/EEC and 96/350/EC, chapter 15, pp. 786–9 below; Council Directive 91/689/EEC, as amended by Council Directive 94/31/EC, chapter 15, p. 792 below; Council Directive 94/62/EC, chapter 15, pp. 790–1 below; Council Directive 99/31/EC, chapter 15, p. 792 below; and Council Directive 2000/76/EC, chapter 15, p. 765 below.

[47] Art. 4(2)(a) and (c).

[48] Art. 4(2)(b). 'Environmentally sound management' means 'taking all practicable steps to ensure that hazardous wastes or other wastes are managed in a manner which will protect human health and the environment against the adverse effects which may result from such wastes': Art. 2(8).

[49] Art. 10(2)(c).

[50] Decision V/33 on Environmentally Sound Management, Report of the Fifth Meeting of the Conference of the Parties to the Basel Convention, UNEP/CHW.5/29, 10 December 1999.

The 1991 Bamako Convention is marginally more ambitious in limiting and preventing hazardous waste generation in Africa. Each party must ensure that hazardous waste generators submit reports to allow the secretariat to produce a hazardous waste audit, and that the hazardous waste generation is 'reduced to a minimum taking into account social, technological and economic aspects'.[51] The parties must also impose strict and unlimited liability on generators, and ensure that persons involved in hazardous waste management take necessary steps to prevent pollution from such waste and minimise the consequence of any such pollution.[52] Each party must implement the 'preventive, precautionary approach' and promote 'clean production' methods applicable to the entire product life cycle, including raw material, production, transportation, usage, and the 'reintroduction of the product into industrial systems or nature when it no longer serves a useful function'.[53] 'Clean production' excludes 'end-of-pipe' pollution controls such as filters or scrubbers or chemical, physical or biological treatment, or measures which reduce the volume of waste by incineration or concentration, mask the hazard by dilution, or transfer pollutants from one medium to another.[54]

The 2001 Stockholm Convention on Persistent Organic Pollutants (2001 POPs Convention) regulates the production, use and transboundary movement of hazardous chemicals known as Persistent Organic Pollutants (POPs).[55] These are chemicals that remain intact in the environment for long periods, become widely distributed geographically, accumulate in the fatty tissue of living organisms and are toxic to humans and wildlife. When it comes into force, the 2001 POPs Convention will require states parties to prohibit and/or take the necessary legal and administrative measures to eliminate the production and use of chemicals listed in Annex A to the Convention.[56] States parties will also be required to restrict the use of other harmful chemicals, such as DDT, listed in Annex B.[57]

Apart from EC developments and the 2001 POPs Convention discussed above, international commitments establishing binding rules of general application remain limited. In order to become effective, these introductory measures on the prevention and management of waste will have to be supplemented, over time, by clear targets and timetables establishing quantitative

---

[51] Art. 4(3)(a) and (c). A 'generator' is 'any person whose activity produces hazardous wastes, or, if that person is not known, the person who is in possession and/or control of those wastes': Art. 1(20).

[52] Art. 4(3)(b) and (e).

[53] Art. 4(3)(f) and (g). 'Clean production methods' means 'production or industrial systems which avoid or eliminate the generation of hazardous wastes and hazardous products': Art. 1(5).

[54] *Ibid.*

[55] Convention on Persistent Organic Pollutants, Stockholm, 22 May 2001, not yet in force, 40 ILM 532(2001); chapter 12, p. 628 above.

[56] Art. 3(1)(a)(i).   [57] Art. 3(1)(b).

limits for waste generation. The basis upon which such targets and timetables are established will raise similar issues to those addressed in other regional and global negotiations, including in particular those relating to ozone depletion and climate change.

Disposal

International environmental law is more developed in limiting or prohibiting certain methods of disposal of particular waste types, although no single instrument comprehensively and globally regulates waste disposal. Treaties now regulate the disposal of waste into the sea, rivers and lakes, by incineration, and into the atmosphere as a by-product of other activities. The General Assembly has called on all states 'to ensure that no nuclear-waste dumping practices occur that would infringe upon the sovereignty of states'.[58] Other treaties promote safe disposal of asbestos;[59] 'appropriate' disposal of wastes during the demolition of buildings or structures;[60] and appropriate disposal of chemicals.[61] Even the use of certain wastes as packing materials is to be avoided.[62] With the exception of the EC rules, international regulation of landfill is non-existent.[63]

Disposal at sea[64]

The disposal at sea of different wastes is an increasingly limited option in most regions. Extensive state practice, as reflected in treaties and acts of international organisations, supports the view that the unregulated disposal at sea of any wastes would now violate rules of customary international law, and that the authorised disposal at sea of certain hazardous wastes would also violate customary law.[65] As described in chapter 9 above, the disposal of hazardous wastes at sea is subject to regulation by six regional or global instruments; and specific prohibitions on the disposal of radioactive, hazardous, industrial, sewage sludge and other wastes have been adopted under several of the treaties identified above.

The disposal of radioactive waste at sea has long been discouraged,[66] and has been addressed by international organisations for many years.[67] It is prohibited

---

[58] UNGA Res. 43/75 (1988).   [59] 1986 Asbestos Convention, Art. 19.

[60] 1988 Convention Concerning Safety and Health in Construction, Art. 24.

[61] 1990 ILO Chemicals Convention, Art. 14.

[62] 1959 Plant Protection Agreement, Art. VI.

[63] See Council Directive 99/31/EC on the landfill of waste, p. 792 below.

[64] See generally chapter 9, pp. 415–27 above.

[65] See e.g. UNEP Council Decision, Precautionary Approach to Marine Pollution, including Waste Dumping at Sea, 25 May 1989, UNEP/GC/dec./15/27.

[66] 1958 Convention on the High Seas, Art. 25(1).

[67] See e.g. UNGA Res., Prohibition of Dumping of Radioactive Wastes for Hostile Purposes, 7 December 1988, A/RES./43/75Q; UNGA Res., Dumping of Radioactive Wastes, 7 December 1988, A/RES./43/75T, 10 December 1996, A/RES./51/45J, 4 December 1998, A/RES./53/77C, 1 December 1999, A/RES./54/54C.

by treaty in the South Pacific[68] and in Africa,[69] and states have prohibited the dumping of radioactive wastes at sea in the North-East Atlantic.[70] The 1972 London Convention now prohibits the dumping of all radioactive wastes or matter, following a 1985 non-binding moratorium.[71]

Additionally, the disposal of industrial waste at sea has been prohibited in the North Sea since 31 December 1989,[72] and the other waters of the former 1974 Oslo Convention area after 31 December 1995,[73] and in Africa.[74] Since December 1998, the disposal of sewage sludge has been prohibited in the North Sea[75] and in the former 1974 Oslo Convention area.[76] The disposal of dredged materials at sea is also now a matter of international concern and is likely to be the subject of international regulatory action.[77] Moreover, the disposal at sea of oily wastes from ships is also prohibited by numerous treaties.

Disposal into rivers and lakes by other land-based sources[78]

The disposal of wastes into rivers and lakes is prohibited or regulated by many bilateral and multilateral treaties. Such prohibition and regulation is either intended to protect the environmental quality of freshwater resources or to protect the quality of seas and oceans by limiting the transportation of waste pollutants by rivers and estuaries into the seas and oceans and other land-based

---

[68] 1985 Rarotonga Treaty, Art. 7; 1986 Noumea Convention, Art. 10(1).

[69] 1991 Bamako Convention, Art. 4(2), which also prohibits disposal in the seabed and subseabed. See also OAU Council of Ministers Resolution, Dumping of Nuclear and Industrial Waste in Africa, 23 May 1988, 28 ILM 567 (1989).

[70] Chapter 9, pp. 425–6 above.   [71] Chapter 9, pp. 420–1 above.

[72] Ministerial Declaration of the Second International Conference on the Protection of the North Sea, 25 November 1987, para. 22(a); OSCOM Decision 89/1, June 1989. The UK agreed to end such dumping by the end of 1992 with an extension to 1993 'only if absolutely necessary on technical grounds and excluding new dumping licences': Third North Sea Ministerial Declaration, para. 18 (1990).

[73] OSCOM Decision 89/1 on the Reduction and Cessation of Dumping Industrial Wastes at Sea (1989). The Decision creates exceptions for inert materials of natural origin and industrial wastes for which it can be shown that there are no practical alternatives on land, and that the materials cause no harm in the marine environment: para. 1.

[74] OAU Council of Ministers Resolution, Dumping of Nuclear and Industrial Waste in Africa, 23 May 1988, 28 ILM 567 (1989).

[75] Third North Sea Ministerial Declaration, paras. 14 and 15 (1990). See also Brussels Agreement on the Implementation of a European Project on Pollution, on the Topic 'Sewage Sludge Processing', 23 November 1971, 12 ILM 9 (1973).

[76] OSPAR Convention, Art. 3(2)(c).

[77] Third North Sea Ministerial Declaration, paras. 19–22 (1990); see also the Dredged Material Assessment Framework adopted in 1995 under the London Convention (Res. LC52.18) and the 1998 OSPAR Guidelines for the Management of Dredged Material (Agreement 1998-20).

[78] Chapter 10, pp. 460–5 above.

sources of pollution.[79] The EC has adopted specific legislation on the treatment and disposal of urban waste water and municipal waste.[80]

Incineration

The incineration of wastes is limited by treaty and acts of international institutions in several regions and, in the case of the EC, subject to conformity with stringent technical standards. Incineration of marine waste at sea has been banned in the North Sea since 31 December 1991,[81] and in the former 1974 Oslo Convention area by the same date.[82] The 1992 OSPAR Convention prohibits incineration at sea.[83] In November 1990, parties to the 1972 London Convention agreed to 're-evaluate incineration at sea of noxious liquid wastes as early in 1992 as possible with a view to proceeding towards the termination of this practice by 31 December 1994'.[84] The re-evaluation was to take into account the practical availability of safer and environmentally more acceptable land-based alternatives, and in the meantime parties were not to export such wastes intended for incineration at sea or allow their disposal in other ways harmful to the environment.[85] In fact the incineration at sea of such wastes ceased at the end of 1990 with the decommissioning of the last incineration vessel. The *de facto* situation was formally confirmed by amendments to the 1972 London Convention in February 1994 prohibiting the incineration of industrial wastes and sewage sludge at sea, and requiring special permits for the incineration of other types of wastes.[86] The 1996 Protocol to the 1972 London Convention prohibits the incineration of wastes at sea, though this agreement is yet to come into force. The 1991 Bamako Convention prohibits the incineration of hazardous waste at sea.[87]

Land-based incineration of waste is currently dealt with only by EC legislation,[88] although it is considered to be a sufficiently hazardous activity to warrant mandatory environmental impact assessment under the relevant

---

[79] Chapter 9, pp. 427–38 above.

[80] Chapter 15, pp. 776–8 below; see also UNEP Environmental Guidelines for Domestic Wastewater Management, 1988 UNEP EMG No. 14.

[81] See Third North Sea Ministerial Declaration, para. 23 (1990).

[82] See chapter 9, pp. 423–5 above; OSCOM Decision 90/2 on the Termination of Incineration at Sea, 23 June 1990, para. 1. The Decision repealed Decision 88/1 on the Termination of Incineration at Sea by 31 December 1994.

[83] Chapter 9, pp. 425–6 above.

[84] Res. LDC.39(13), Status of Incineration of Noxious Liquid Wastes at Sea, para. 1. See also Res. LDC.35(11) on the Status of Incineration of Noxious Liquid Wastes at Sea, and Res. LDC.33(11) on Revised Interim Technical Guidelines on Incineration of Wastes and Other Matter at Sea. See also 1972 London Convention, 1978 London Amendments on Incineration of Wastes and Other Matter at Sea, 12 October 1978, not yet in force.

[85] Para. 2.   [86] Annex I, para. 10.   [87] Art. 4(2).

[88] Directive 2000/76/EC on the incineration of waste, chapter 15, pp. 765–6 below.

regional arrangements.[89] The 1991 Antarctic Environment Protocol has banned the open burning of wastes since the end of the 1998/9 season, and allows the burning of certain non-hazardous combustible wastes in incinerators which 'to the maximum extent practicable reduce harmful emissions'.[90] The EC's recent legislation on the limitation of air pollution from new and existing waste incineration plants provides a model which could be followed by other regions.[91]

The incineration of fossil fuels, with its by-product of waste gases, has been the subject of a number of treaties and acts of international institutions. Emissions of waste gases of sulphur dioxide,[92] nitrogen oxide,[93] volatile organic compounds,[94] and carbon dioxide and other greenhouse gases,[95] are regulated. Limits have also been placed on the generation of waste gases by combustion from motor vehicles and aircraft.[96]

Landfill and other land disposal and storage

There is no international regulation of standards for domestic landfill, other than the recent EC Council Directive 99/31/EC establishing minimum standards for the design and management of landfill waste.[97] This Directive, which was to be implemented by 16 July 2001, details stringent rules on the landfill of solid waste with the dual aims of improving the sound environmental management of landfills and reducing the amount of landfill waste.[98] The Directive incorporates the 'polluter-pays principle' requiring member states to ensure that all of the set-up and operating costs of landfills are covered by the price charged by operators.[99] Member states are also required to establish a national strategy providing for the reduction of the landfill of biodegradable waste.[100] The strategy must ensure that the amount of biodegradable municipal waste going to landfill is reduced progressively across fifteen years compared to a 1995 baseline. A reduction to 75 per cent of the 1995 baseline must be achieved within five years of implementation; 50 per cent within eight years; and 35 per cent within fifteen years.[101] Under the 1985 EC Environmental Impact Assessment Directive, all landfill of toxic and dangerous wastes must be subjected to an environmental impact assessment,[102] and the 1991 Espoo Convention requires landfill of toxic and dangerous wastes likely to cause a significant adverse transboundary impact to be subjected to environmental impact assessment and notified to potentially affected parties to ensure adequate and

---

[89] 1985 EC EIA Directive, Annex I, para. 9; 1991 Espoo Convention, Appendix 1, para. 10.
[90] Annex III, Art. 3.
[91] Chapter 15, pp. 764–6 below.   [92] Chapter 8, p. 327 above.
[93] Chapter 8, pp. 328–9 above.   [94] Chapter 8, pp. 329–32 above.
[95] Chapter 8, pp. 357–81 above.   [96] Chapter 8, pp. 324 and 341–2 above.
[97] Council Directive 99/31/EC on the landfill of waste, OJ L182, 16 July 1999, 1.
[98] Art. 1.   [99] Art. 10.   [100] Art. 5(1).   [101] Art. 5(2).
[102] Chapter 16, pp. 807–13 below; Art. 4(1) and Annex I, para. 9.

effective consultation.[103] The Antarctic area is subject to more detailed rules. Here, the disposal of radioactive waste has been prohibited since 1959.[104] The 1991 Environmental Protection Protocol prohibits disposal of wastes on to ice-free areas and establishes rules for the disposal of sewage, domestic and other liquid wastes and wastes generated at field camps, which should generally be removed by the generator.[105] Wastes to be removed from the Antarctic Treaty area should also be stored to prevent their dispersal into the atmosphere.[106] Elsewhere, the 1986 Noumea Convention is one of the few treaties to establish detailed rules on storage, requiring the storage of toxic and hazardous wastes to be subject to measures to prevent pollution, and prohibiting storage of radioactive wastes or matter.[107] When it comes into force, the 2001 POPs Convention will require states parties to take appropriate measures to dispose of wastes consisting of, containing or contaminated with POPs in such a way that the POP content is destroyed or irreversibly transformed.[108] Where destruction or irreversible transformation does not represent the environmentally preferable option or the persistent organic pollutant content is low, states parties must ensure that the wastes are disposed of in an environmentally sound manner, taking into account international rules, standards, guidelines and relevant global and regional regimes governing the management of hazardous wastes.[109] States parties are to ensure that POPs wastes are not permitted to be subjected to disposal operations that may lead to recovery, recycling, reclamation, direct reuse or alternative uses of POPs.[110]

Recycling and re-use

Political efforts to encourage recycling, recovery and re-use of materials and products have not yet led to international legal commitments. The OECD's International Energy Agency is committed to research and development on waste heat utilisation and municipal and industrial waste utilisation for energy conservation,[111] and the OECD has adopted recommendations on re-use and recycling of beverage containers and on recovery of waste

---

[103] Chapter 16, pp. 814–17 below; Arts. 2(2), 3(1) and 5, and Appendix I, para. 10.
[104] Antarctic Treaty 1959, Art. V(1).   [105] Annex III, Art. 4.
[106] Annex III, Art. 6.   [107] Art. 11.   [108] Art. 6(d)(ii).
[109] *Ibid.* The conference of the parties of the 2001 POPs Convention is required to co-operate closely with the appropriate bodies of the 1989 Basel Convention to: (a) establish levels of destruction and irreversible transformation necessary to remove the hazardous characteristics of POPs; (b) determine what they consider to be methods that constitute environmentally sound disposal; and (c) work to establish, as appropriate, the concentration levels of the chemicals which can be defined as 'low persistent organic pollutant content': Art. 6(2).
[110] Art. 6(d)(iii).
[111] 1974 Agreement on an International Energy Programme, Art. 42(c).

paper.[112] The 1987 Montreal Protocol calls for research and development and the exchange of information on the best technologies for improving the recovery and recycling of certain controlled and transitional ozone-depleting substances,[113] but does not establish targets for recovery or recycling.[114] The 1989 Basel Convention may provide a basis for future international legislation by identifying disposal operations which may lead to recovery, recycling and re-use.[115] It does not, however, identify recycling, re-use and recovery as a matter for international co-operation or call for any specific international action or measures.[116]

EC law requires member states to encourage the recovery of wastes, including hazardous and toxic wastes, by means of recycling, re-use or reclamation or other processes to extract secondary raw materials and to use waste as a source of energy.[117] EC law also permits national recycling legislation to limit, in certain circumstances, the free movement of goods between member states,[118] and the grant of government subsidies to encourage recycling and re-use.[119] In 1994, the European Parliament and Council adopted a Directive on packaging and packaging waste which established national targets for waste recovery of certain substances (including cardboard, plastic and glass), thereby creating a strong incentive for manufacturers to re-use packaging.[120]

---

[112] OECD Council Recommendation, Re-Use and Recycling of Beverage Containers, OECD C(78)8 Final, 3 February 1978; OECD Council Recommendation, Waste Paper Recovery, OECD C(79)218 Final, 30 January 1980. See also Decision of the Council Concerning the Control of Transfrontier Movements of Wastes Destined for Recovery Operations, OECD C(92)39 Final, 6 April 1002.

[113] Art. 9(1)(a), as amended by the 1990 amendments.

[114] As amended in 1990, the Montreal Protocol encourages recycling of certain ozone-depleting substances by excluding recycled substances from the definition of 'production': see chapter 8, pp. 345–57 above.

[115] Annex IV(B). These operations include use as a fuel (other than in direct incineration) to generate energy, reclamation or regeneration of solvents and non-solvents, recycling or reclamation of metals and metal compounds and other inorganic materials, regeneration of acids, recovery of pollution abatement and catalyst components, refining of used oil, land treatment, and uses of residue materials. The Bamako Convention identifies the same list but does not distinguish these operations from other disposal operations: Annex III.

[116] Art. 10(2). See also the 1991 Bamako Convention, Art. 10.

[117] Council Directive 75/442/EEC, as amended by Council Directive 91/156/EEC, Art. 3(1), Council Directive 91/692/EEC and Commission Decision 96/350/EC; Council Directive 91/689/EEC, Art. 4, as amended by Council Directive 94/31/EC and Commission Decisions 2000/532/EC and 2001/118/EC.

[118] *Danish Bottles* Case, chapter 19, pp. 987–90 below.   [119] Chapter 19, pp. 1011–15 below.

[120] European Parliament and Council Directive 94/62/EC of 20 December 1994 on packaging and packaging waste, OJ L365, 31 December 1994, 10. The Directive required states to meet quantified targets for recovery and recycling of packaging wastes by mid-2001 with a view to increasing these targets significantly in a second phase to be achieved by mid-2006. See chapter 15, p. 792 below.

International movement (including trade) in waste

M. Forster, 'Hazardous Waste: Towards International Agreement', 12 *Environmental Policy and Law* 64 (1984); H. Smets, 'Transfrontier Movements of Hazardous Wastes: An Examination of the Council Decision and Recommendation', 14 *Environmental Policy and Law* 16 (1985); E. Moisé, 'La Convention de Bâle sur les Mouvements Transfrontières de Déchets Dangereux', 93 RGDIP 899 (1989); V. Sebek (ed.), 'Marine Transport, Control and Disposal of Hazardous Waste', 14 *Marine Policy* (1990) (special issue); W. L. Long, 'Economic Aspects of Transport and Disposal of Hazardous Wastes', 14 *Marine Policy* 199 (1990); L. Gilmore, 'The Export of Nonhazardous Waste', 19 *Environmental Law* 879 (1989); A. Kiss, 'The International Control of Transboundary Movement of Hazardous Waste', 26 *Texas International Law Journal* 521 (1991); H. Smets, 'Quelques problèmes rélatifs aux mouvements transfrontières de déchets dangereux', 21 *Environmental Policy and Law* 141 (1991); N. Van Aelstyn, 'North–South Controversy Mounts Around the International Movement of Hazardous Waste', 1 RECIEL 340 (1992); B. Kwiatowska and A. Soons (eds.), *Transboundary Movements and Disposals of Hazardous Wastes in International Law: Basic Documents* (1993); E. Louka, *Overcoming National Barriers to International Waste Trade: A New Perspective on the Transnational Movements of Hazardous and Radioactive Wastes* (1994); J. Kitt, 'Waste Exports to the Developing World: A Global Response', 7 *Georgetown International Environmental Law Review* 485 (1995); B. Desai, 'Regulating Transboundary Movement of Hazardous Waste', 37 *Indian Journal of International Law* 43 (1997); F. Bitar, *Les Mouvements transfrontieres de dechets dangereux selon la Convention de Bale* (1997); J. L. Gudofsky, 'Transboundary Shipments of Hazardous Waste for Recycling and Recovery Operations', 34 *Stanford Journal of International Law* 219 (1998); T. Scovazzi, 'The Transboundary Movement of Hazardous Waste in the Mediterranean Regional Context', 19 *UCLA Journal of Environmental Law and Policy* 231 (2001).

International law on waste has focused primarily on the permissibility of international movement and trade in waste. This follows several notorious incidents which occurred in the mid-1980s involving the unlawful dumping in developing countries of hazardous wastes produced in industrialised countries.[121] Among the tensions between different members of the international community one stood out in particular: the desire of many developing countries, particularly in Africa, to ban international trade in wastes, and the opposition to such an approach by many industrialised countries wanting to keep open their waste disposal options. As a result, various international legal arrangements were adopted in a two-year period, each of which established different rules and definitions. Prior to the adoption of these agreements, the issue had

---

[121] *The International Trade in Wastes: A Greenpeace Inventory* (1988, 3rd edn); Illegal Traffic in Toxic and Dangerous Products and Wastes: Report of the Secretary General to the UN General Assembly, UN Doc. A/44/362 (1989).

been addressed by binding and non-binding acts of various international organisations, including the EC, the OECD[122] and the UN.[123] International trade
in waste has also been addressed by UN bodies as a human rights issue.[124]
Transboundary movements of hazardous and other wastes are now regulated
by three regional or global treaties, each of which establishes different rules:
the 1989 Basel Convention, the 1990 Lomé Convention and the 1991 Bamako
Convention.[125] Other instruments include the 2001 POPs Convention, bilateral treaties such as the 1986 Canada–US Hazardous Waste Agreement and
the 1986 Canada–Mexico Hazardous Waste Agreement, as well as OECD Acts
and the increasingly complex EC rules established by legislation and by the
jurisprudence of the ECJ.

The 1989 Basel Convention

D. P. Hackett, 'An Assessment of the Basel Convention on the Control of Transboundary Movements of Hazardous Wastes and Their Disposal', 5 *American University Journal of International Law and Policy* 295 (1990); C. Shearer, 'Comparative
Analysis of the Basel and Bamako Conventions on Hazardous Waste', 23 *Environmental Law* 141 (1993); K. Kummer, *International Management of Hazardous
Wastes: The Basel Convention and Related Legal Rules* (1995); A. Sanders and
P. Bowal, 'International Trade in Hazardous Wastes and the Basel Convention',
11 *Journal of Environmental Law and Practice* 143 (2001).

---

[122] See e.g. OECD Council Decision/Recommendation, Transfrontier Movements of
Hazardous Waste, OECD C(83)180 Final, 1 February 1984; OECD Council Resolution,
International Co-operation Concerning Transfrontier Moments of Hazardous Wastes,
OECD C(85)100, 20 June 1985; OECD Council Decision/Recommendation, Exports of
Hazardous Wastes from the OECD Area, OECD C(86)64 Final, 5 June 1986; OECD
Council Decision, Transfrontier Movements of Hazardous Wastes OECD C(88)90 Final,
27 May 1988; OECD Council Decision, the Control of Transfrontier Movements of Wastes
Destined for Recovery Operation, OECD C(92)39 Final, 30 March 1992; OECD Council
Decision, Document for Tranfrontier Movements of Waste, OECD C(94)154 Final, 28
July 1994.

[123] UNGA Res. 42/183 (1987); UNGA Res. 44/226 (1989).

[124] See Commission on Human Rights Res. E/CN.4/RES/1999/23 on the adverse effects of
the illicit movement and dumping of toxic and dangerous products and wastes on the
enjoyment of human rights, chapter 7, pp. 294–7 above.

[125] Several other regional agreements have been adopted but are not yet in force: 1995
Waigani Convention to Ban the Importation into Forum Island Countries of Hazardous Radioactive Wastes and to Control Transboundary Movement and Management
of Hazardous Wastes Within the South Pacific Region, Waigani, 16 September 1995,
in force 21 October 2001, www.basel.int/misclinks/waigani.html; the 1996 Izmir Protocol on the Prevention of Pollution of the Mediterranean Sea by Transboundary Movements of Hazardous Wastes and Their Disposal, Izmir, 1 October 1996, not yet in force,
www.unepmap.gr/pdf/hazardous.pdf; and the 1998 Protocol on the Control of Marine
Transboundary Movements and Disposal of Hazardous Wastes and Other Wastes to the
Kuwait Regional Convention for Co-operation on the Protection of the Marine Environment from Pollution, Kuwait, not yet in force.

The 1989 Convention on the Control of Transboundary Movements of Hazardous Wastes and their Disposal (1989 Basel Convention) is intended to establish a global regime for the control of international trade in hazardous and other wastes.[126] It was negotiated under the auspices of UNEP on the basis of texts produced by a working group which had drawn on the Cairo Guidelines. The Convention, which entered into force on 5 May 1992, establishes rules designed to regulate trade in these wastes rather than prohibit it. The Convention sets forth general obligations requiring all parties to ensure that transboundary movements of wastes are reduced to the minimum consistent with environmentally sound and efficient management, and it reflects an approach premised upon the view that wastes should, as far as possible, be disposed of in the state where they were generated (this has come to be known as the 'proximity principle'). The Convention has attracted broad support, although there is a consensus among commentators that, although 'far from providing a perfect solution to the problem of transboundary movements of hazardous wastes, it does address most of the relevant issues and is therefore a step in the right direction'.[127]

Article 4 sets forth general obligations designed to minimise waste generation and its transboundary movement, and ensure its environmentally sound management. The parties must not allow exports to parties which have prohibited by legislation all imports, or where they have reason to believe that the wastes will not be managed in an environmentally sound manner, and are obliged to co-operate to improve and achieve environmentally sound management of such wastes.[128] Parties may prohibit the import of such wastes and must consent in writing to any specific imports which they have not prohibited.[129] Parties must provide information on proposed transboundary movements of hazardous and other wastes to the states concerned, and prevent imports if they have reason to believe that the imports will not be managed in an environmentally sound manner.[130] In order to encourage states to become parties to the Convention, wastes may not be exported to or imported from a non-party, and they cannot be exported for disposal to the Antarctic area.[131] Traffic which contravenes notification or consent requirements, or fails to conform with its documentation, or results in deliberate disposal in contravention of the Convention and general principles of international law, will be illegal and considered to be criminal.'[132]

---

[126] Basel, 22 March 1989, in force 24 May 1989, 28 ILM 657 (1989); 155 states and the EC are party. On the definition of hazardous and other wastes under the Basel Convention, see pp. 677–8 above.

[127] K. Kummer, 'The International Regulation of Transboundary Traffic in Hazardous Wastes: The 1989 Basel Convention', 41 ICLQ 530 at 560 (1992).

[128] Arts. 4(2)(d), (e) and (h) and 10. The criteria for environmentally sound management are to be decided by the first conference of the parties: Art. 4(8).

[129] Art. 4(1)(a) and (c).   [130] Art. 4(2)(f) and (g).

[131] Art. 4(5) and (6).   [132] Arts. 4(3) and 9.

The Convention discourages exports of hazardous and other wastes, which should only be allowed if the exporting state does not have the capacity, facilities or suitable sites to dispose of them in an environmentally sound or efficient manner, or if the wastes are required as a raw material for recycling or recovery in the importing state, or in accordance with other criteria decided by the parties.[133] Moreover, parties may not transfer to importing or transit states their obligation under the Convention to carry out environmentally sound management, and can impose additional requirements consistent with the Convention to better protect human health and the environment.[134] The transport and disposal of hazardous and other wastes may only be carried out by authorised persons, and transboundary movements must conform with generally accepted and recognised international rules and standards of packaging, labelling and transport, and take account of relevant internationally recognised practices, and be accompanied by a movement document until disposal.[135]

The Convention sets forth detailed conditions for the international regulation of transboundary movements of hazardous and other wastes between parties based upon a system of 'prior informed consent'. The exporting state, generator or exporter must notify the states concerned of any proposed transboundary movement, including the information specified in Annex V(A).[136] The importing state responds by giving its consent with or without conditions, denying permission, or requiring additional information, and no transboundary movement may commence until the exporting state has received the written consent of the importing state and confirmation from that state of the existence of a contract between the exporter and the disposer specifying environmentally sound management of the wastes.[137] Transit states can prohibit transit passage, and the exporting state must not allow transboundary movement to commence until it has the written consent of the transit state.[138] The Convention allows for general notifications and consents to cover a twelve-month period where wastes having the same characteristics are shipped regularly to the same disposer via the same exit office of the exporting state, entry office of the importing state, and customs office of the transit state.[139] Importing states and transit states which are parties may require the wastes to be covered by insurance or other guarantee.[140] When a transboundary movement cannot be completed in accordance with the terms of the contract, the exporting state must take back the wastes if alternative arrangements cannot be made for their disposal in an environmentally sound manner.[141]

---

[133] Art. 4(9).   [134] Art. 4(10) and (11).   [135] Art. 4(7).

[136] Art. 6(1). 'States concerned' are 'parties which are states of export or import, or transit states whether or not parties': Art. 2(13). Art. 6(1) also applies to transboundary movements from a party through a state or states which are not parties: Art. 7.

[137] Art. 6(2) and (3).   [138] Art. 6(4).   [139] Art. 6(6) to (8).

[140] Art. 6(11).   [141] Art. 8.

Parties can enter into bilateral, multilateral or regional agreements or arrangements regarding transboundary movements of wastes provided that they do not derogate from the requirements of the Convention and provided they stipulate provisions which are no less environmentally sound than the Convention.[142] The Convention will not affect transboundary movements taking place entirely among the parties to such agreements, which must be notified to the secretariat, provided that they are compatible with the requirements of the Convention.[143] The parties are subject to detailed reporting requirements, and the Convention provides for consultations on liability to be held as soon as possible.[144]

The Convention is kept under review by a conference of the parties and a secretariat.[145] At the fifth conference of the parties, held in December 1999, the parties adopted a Protocol on Liability and Compensation.[146] Compared to many other environmental agreements, the Convention sets out relatively detailed tasks for the Secretariat, including gathering and sharing information, and examination of notifications and other aspects of transboundary movements.[147] Until the first conference of the parties, which was held in November 1992, UNEP carried out the secretariat functions on an interim basis.

The second conference of the parties, held in March 1994, approved an immediate ban on the export from OECD countries to non-OECD countries of hazardous wastes intended for final disposal and also agreed to ban the export of wastes intended for recovery and recycling by 31 December 1997.[148] The 'Basel Ban', as it became known, was not formally incorporated into the Convention by the second conference of the parties, and disputes arose as to whether it was legally binding on the parties. To resolve the dispute, it was proposed at the third conference of the parties, in September 1995, that the Basel Ban be formally incorporated in the Basel Convention as an amendment.[149] The Basel Ban amendment adopted by the third conference of the parties does not refer to OECD and non-OECD countries, but rather bans hazardous waste exports for final disposal and recycling from Annex VII parties (members of the EU,

---

[142] Art. 11(1). Two such regional agreements or arrangements may fall within this provision: the 1991 Bamako Convection, and the 1993 EC Regulation. See generally J. Crawford and P. Sands, *The Availability of Article 11 Agreements in the Context of the Basel Convention's Export Ban on Recyclables* (International Council on Metals and the Environment, 1997).

[143] Art. 11(2).   [144] Arts. 12 and 13; on liability, see chapter 18, pp. 924–6 below.

[145] Arts. 15 and 16. Five meetings of the conference of the parties have been held to date with a sixth meeting scheduled for 9–13 December 2002 in Geneva.

[146] Chapter 18, p. 924 below.   [147] Art. 16.

[148] Decision II/12, Report of COP-2, UNEP/CHW.2/30, 25 March 1994.

[149] Decision III/1, Report of COP-3, Part 2, UNEP/CHW.3/34, 17 October 1995; L. de la Fayette, 'Legal and Practical Implications of the Ban Amendment to the Basel Convention', 6 *Yearbook of International Environmental Law* 703 (1995); J. Crawford and P. Sands, *The Availability of Article 11 Agreements in the Context of the Basel Convention's Export Ban on Recyclables* (International Council on Metals and the Environment, 1997).

OECD and Liechtenstein) to non-Annex VII parties.[150] The Basel Ban has not yet entered into force as only twenty-nine of the required sixty-two ratifications have so far been received.[151]

1989 Lomé Convention

The 1989 Lomé Convention is now of historical interest only, since it has been replaced by the 2000 Cotonou Agreement between ACP countries and the EC. However, it is still noteworthy as reflecting a different approach from the regulated waste trade rules established by the 1989 Basel Convention: the EC was subject to a blanket prohibition on all direct or indirect exports of hazardous waste and radioactive waste from the EC to the ACP states, and ACP states must prohibit the direct or indirect import of such waste from the EC or from any other country.[152] These obligations were stated to be 'without prejudice to specific international undertakings to which the contracting parties have subscribed or may subscribe in the future in these two areas within the competent international fora', and they did not prevent processed waste being returned from the EC to the ACP state of origin.[153]

1991 Bamako Convention

S. W. Donald, 'The Bamako Convention as a Solution to the Problem of Hazardous Waste Exports to Less Developed Countries', 17 *Columbia Journal of Environmental Law* 419 (1992); F. Ouguergouz, 'La Convention de Bamako sur l'Interdiction d'Importer en Afrique des Déchets Dangereux et Sur le Contrôle des Mouvements Transfrontières et la Gestion des Déchets Dangereux Produits en Afrique', AFDI 871 (1992).

The Convention on the Ban of Imports into Africa and the Control of Transboundary Movement and Management of Hazardous Wastes within Africa

---

[150] Art. 4A and Annex VII, Basel Ban Amendment. The amendment will also insert a new preambular para. 7*bis* into the Convention in the following terms: 'Recognizing that transboundary movements of hazardous wastes, especially to developing countries, have a high risk of not constituting an environmentally sound management of hazardous wastes as required by this Convention . . .'.

[151] The Basel Ban Amendment has to be ratified by three-quarters of the parties present at the time of the adoption of the amendment in order to enter into force: Art. 17.

[152] Lomé, 15 December 1989, in force 1 September 1991; 29 ILM 783 (1990), Art. 39(1). 'Hazardous waste' covers categories of products listed in Annexes I and II to the 1989 Basel Convention, and the definitions and thresholds of 'radioactive waste' are to be 'those laid down in the framework of the IAEA', and, pending that, the definitions and thresholds specified in the declaration in Annex VIII to the 1989 Lomé Convention: Art. 39(3).

[153] 1989 Lomé Convention, Art. 39(1).

(1991 Bamako Convention) was adopted by African governments following negotiations under the auspices of the Organization of African Unity.[154] It establishes a regional regime to prohibit trade in waste, giving effect to the positions many African governments had adopted in the negotiations on the 1989 Basel Convention.[155] To a large extent, the 1991 Bamako Convention follows the approach taken in the 1989 Basel Convention, but departs from it in a number of important respects. First, and most notably, like the former 1989 Lomé Convention, the Bamako Convention prohibits trade in hazardous waste: parties must prohibit the import of all hazardous wastes into Africa from non-contracting parties and deem such imports illegal and criminal.[156] A second difference is that parties must ensure that hazardous wastes to be exported are managed in an environmentally sound way in the state of import and transit, and only authorised persons may store such wastes.[157] Thirdly, the definition of hazardous waste adopted by the Bamako Convention is broader than that in the Basel Convention.[158] The Bamako Convention includes several other subtle but significant differences. Wastes to be used as raw materials for recycling and recovery may not be exported, and parties must appoint a national body to act as a 'Dumpwatch' to co-ordinate governmental and non-governmental bodies.[159] Moreover, parties may not decide not to require prior written consent; parties must not allow use of general notifications;[160] the rule requiring notification of the transit state applies to transboundary movements from a party through a state or states which is or are not parties,[161] and illegal traffic may be returned only to the exporter.[162] The Bamako Convention is administered by its own conference of the parties and secretariat, the functions of which are carried out on an interim basis by the OAU and the UN Economic Commission for Africa.[163] Significantly, the secretariat of the Bamako Convention is granted greater powers than the secretariat of the Basel Convention since it may verify the substance of allegations of breach of the Convention and submit a report to all parties.[164] Moreover, it provides for the apparently compulsory jurisdiction of an *ad hoc* dispute settlement organ, or the ICJ.[165]

---

[154] Bamako, 29 January 1991, in force April 1998, 30 ILM 775 (1991); eighteen states are party.

[155] See UNEP, *Proposals and Positions of the African States During the Negotiations on the Basel Convention on the Control of Transboundary Movements of Hazardous Wastes and Their Disposal and the Status of Their Incorporation into the Basel Convention* (1989).

[156] Art. 4(1); since only member states of the OAU may become parties to the Convention (Arts. 22 and 23), it effectively prohibits imports from outside Africa.

[157] Art. 4(3)(i) and (m)(i).   [158] See above.   [159] Art. 5(4).

[160] Art. 6(6); cf. Art. 6(6) of 1989 Basel Convention.

[161] Art. 7; cf. Art. 7 of the 1989 Basel Convention.

[162] Art. 9(3) and (4); cf. Art. 9(3) and (4) of the 1989 Basel Convention.

[163] Arts. 15 and 16.   [164] Art. 19   [165] Art. 20.

North America

The 1986 Mexico–US Hazardous Waste Agreement requires the exporting country to notify the importing country of individual shipments or a series of shipments over a twelve-month period, which the importing country must respond to within forty-five days indicating its consent, with or without conditions, or its objection.[166] The exporting country must re-admit any shipment that may be returned for any reason by the country of import.[167] The Agreement Between the United States and Canada Concerning the Transboundary Movement of Hazardous Waste requires the exporting country to notify the importing country of proposed transboundary shipments of hazardous waste, and states that if no response is received within thirty days the country of import will be deemed to have granted its consent.[168]

1990 IAEA Code of Conduct on Radioactive Waste and 1997 Joint Convention on Spent Fuel and Radioactive Waste

The IAEA Code of Practice on the International Transboundary Movement of Radioactive Waste establishes a set of non-binding principles designed to serve as guidelines.[169] Whether the Code of Practice constitutes an 'international control system' within the meaning of Article 1(3) of the Basel Convention is open to interpretation, but certainly the scheme it applies is less stringent than even the Basel Convention. The Code defines radioactive waste as 'any material that contains or is contaminated with radionuclides at concentrations or radioactivity levels greater than the "exempt quantities" established by the competent authorities and for which no use is foreseen'.[170] Exempt quantities are levels below which the regulatory requirements do not apply because the individual and collective dose equivalents received from such levels are not significant for the purposes of radiation protection. These should be agreed by the authorities in the countries concerned with the international

---

[166] Washington, 12 November 1986, in force 29 January 1987, 26 ILM 25 (1987), Art. III(1), (2) and (4); see E. C. Rose, 'Transboundary Harm: Hazardous Waste Management Problems and Mexico's Maquiladoras', 23 *International Law* 223 (1989); A. Moskonite, 'Criminal Environmental Law: Stopping the Flow of Hazardous Waste to Mexico', 22 *California Western International Law Journal* 159 (1991/2); V. L. Engfer, G. A. Partida, T. C. Vernon, A. Toulet and D. A. Renas, 'By-Products of Prosperity: Transboundary Hazardous Waste Issues Confronting the Maquiladora Industry', 28 *San Diego Law Review* 819 (1991).

[167] Art. IV.   [168] Ottawa, 28 October 1986, in force 8 November 1986, TIAS 11099.

[169] IAEA Doc. GC(XXXIV)/920, 21 September 1990, Annex 1; D. Currie and J. van Dyke, 'The Shipment of Ultrahazardous Nuclear Materials in International Law', 8 RECIEL 113 (1999).

[170] Section II. A 'competent authority' is 'an authority designated or recognised by a government for specific purposes in connection with radiation protection and/or nuclear safety': *ibid.*

transboundary movement.[171] Spent nuclear fuel is not, for the purposes of the Code, considered to be radioactive waste.[172] Instead, this is dealt with by the recently adopted Joint Convention on the Safety of Spent Fuel Management and on the Safety of Radioactive Waste Management (1997 Joint Convention).[173]

Despite its non-binding legal character, the Code is more limited in scope than the more stringent approaches set out in the Basel and Bamako Conventions. Its 'obligations' are so soft that it is questionable whether they provide any enforceable guidance: states should minimise the amount of radioactive waste and take appropriate steps to ensure that radioactive waste within its territory, jurisdiction or control is safely managed and disposed of.[174] The Code recognises the sovereign right of a state to prohibit the movement of radioactive waste into, from or through its territory, and calls on states to ensure that movements are taken in a manner consistent with international safety standards.[175] Under the Code, transboundary movements should only take place 'with the prior notification and consent of the sending, receiving and transit states in accordance with their respective laws and regulations'. States should have a relevant regulatory authority and appropriate procedures, and should not permit the receipt or sending of radioactive waste unless they have the capacity and regulatory structure to manage and dispose of the waste consistently with international safety standards.[176] Finally, states are called upon to adopt national laws and regulations giving effect to the requirements of the Code, and to establish provisions for liability, compensation or other remedies arising from international transboundary movements of radioactive waste.[177]

In contrast to the Code, the 1997 Joint Convention contains more stringent regulation of the transboundary movement of spent nuclear fuel or radioactive waste. Article 27 of the Joint Convention is modelled on the Basel Convention and requires exporting parties to take appropriate steps to ensure that transboundary movement is authorised and takes place only with the prior notification and consent of the state of destination.[178] An originating state may only authorise exports of waste if it can satisfy itself that the destination state has the administrative and technical capacity, as well as the regulatory structure, needed to manage the spent fuel or the radioactive waste in a manner consistent with the Joint Convention.[179] Where a transboundary movement cannot be completed in conformity with the requirements of Article 27, and

[171] Ibid.   [172] Ibid.

[173] See the Joint Convention on the Safety of Spent Fuel Management and on the Safety of Radioactive Waste Management, 5 September 1997, in force 18 June 2001, 36 ILM 1436 (1997), Art. 27.

[174] Section III, paras. 1 and 2.   [175] Section III, paras. 3 and 4.

[176] Section III, paras. 5 to 7.   [177] Section III, paras. 8 and 9.

[178] Art. 27(1)(i).   [179] Art. 27(1)(iii) and (iv).

no alternative safe arrangement can be made, the originating state must take appropriate steps to allow the re-entry of the waste into its territory.[180]

EC Law

In their efforts to update the 1984 EC legislation on the supervision and control of shipments of hazardous waste, the EC member states had a difficult balancing act to perform. The EC had to establish rules governing the movement of waste within individual member states, between member states, and between member states and third countries. For the latter, the rules had to be sufficiently flexible to allow implementation of the 1989 Lomé Convention rules and the 1989 Basel Convention, to which the EC became a party in 1994. In February 1992, the EC adopted Directive 92/3/EURATOM on the supervision and control of shipments of radioactive waste between member states and into and out of the EC,[181] and in February 1993 the EC Council adopted Regulation (EC) No. 259/93 on the supervision and control of shipments of waste within, into and out of the EC.[182]

Regulation (EC) No. 259/93: waste shipment

Apart from the international agreements to which the EC was a party or intended to become a party, the Regulation also sought to integrate the provisions of an OECD Council Decision on the control of transfrontier movements of wastes designed for recovery operations,[183] and to take account of the ruling of the ECJ in the *Wallonian Waste* case, which had defined waste as a 'good' within the meaning of the EC rules on free movement of goods and permitted restrictions on its free movement partly in application of the 'proximity principle' and the environmental rules of the EC Treaty.[184]

Regulation (EC) No. 259/93 applies to shipments of waste within, into and out of the EC.[185] Five categories of waste are excluded from the application of

---

[180] Art. 27(1)(v).   [181] Directive 92/3/EURATOM, OJ L35, 12 February 1992, 24.

[182] Council Regulation (EC) No. 93/259, OJ L30, 6 February 1993, 1, as amended by Commission Regulation (EC) No. 120/97, OJ L22, 24 January 1997, 14; Commission Decision 816/99/EC, OJ L316, 10 December 1999, 45; and Commission Regulation (EC) No. 2557/2001, OJ L349, 31 December 2001, 1. The Regulation replaces Directive 84/631/EEC, OJ L326, 13 December 1984, 31.

[183] The Regulation, as amended, integrates the provisions of the latest OECD Council Decision on the control of transfrontier movements of wastes designed for recovery operations, Decision C(2001)107 of the OECD Council on the Revision of Decision C(92)39 Final.

[184] Chapter 19, pp. 990–2 below. The ECJ has, however, ruled that the principles of self-sufficiency and proximity are not applicable to shipments of waste for recovery: Case C-203/96, *Chemische Afvalstoffen Dusseldorp BV and Others* v. *Minister van Volkshuisvesting* [1998] ECR I-4075.

[185] Art. 1. The definition of waste is that in Directive 75/442; see chapter 15, n, 398, p. 788 below.

the Regulation,[186] as are certain wastes destined for recovery only and listed in Annex II to the Regulation.[187] The Regulation establishes rules of control to govern four different situations: (1) shipments of wastes between member states; (2) shipment of wastes within member states; (3) export of wastes; and (4) imports of wastes. Additional rules are established for transit and in respect of provisions common to each of the four types of shipment.

Shipments of waste between member states   The Regulation distinguishes between waste for disposal and waste for recovery.[188] As a general rule, waste may be shipped between member states for disposal subject to the rules governing prior notification and authorisation by competent national authorities, including any conditions applied.[189] There are, however, three general grounds on which a shipment may be stopped. First, to implement the principles of proximity, priority for recovery, and self-sufficiency at Community and national levels in accordance with Directive 75/442/EEC, member states may object to the shipment of waste and may prohibit generally or partially, or object systematically to, shipments of waste.[190] Secondly, reasoned objections may be raised to planned shipments by competent authorities of dispatch and destination if either the shipments are not in accordance with the principle of self-sufficiency, or where the installation has to dispose of priority waste from a nearer source or in order to ensure that shipments are in accordance with waste management plans.[191] Thirdly, reasoned objections may be raised to the planned shipment by competent authorities of dispatch, destination and transit if either the shipment is not in accordance with national laws relating to environmental protection, public order, public safety or health protection, or the notifier or consignee was guilty of illegal trafficking or the shipment conflicts with obligations resulting from international conventions.[192]

The shipment of waste for recovery listed in Annex III ('amber waste') is subject to a system of prior notification and authorisation, including possible conditions.[193] The competent authorities of dispatch and destination may raise reasoned objections to the planned shipment under Directive 75/442; either if it is not in accordance with national laws relating to environmental

---

[186] Art. 1(2)(a) (certain ship and offshore platform waste; civil aviation waste; radioactive waste as defined in Art. 2 of Directive 92/3/EURATOM; wastes mentioned in Art. 2(1)(b) of Directive 75/442; and waste under the 1991 Antarctic Environment Protocol).

[187] Art. 1(3).

[188] 'Disposal' and 'recovery' are defined by Art. 1(e) and (f) of Directive 75/442.

[189] Arts. 3 to 5.

[190] Art. 4(3)(a)(i). This provision will not apply, however, in the case of hazardous waste produced in a member state of dispatch 'in such a small quantity overall per year that the provision of new specialised disposal installations within that state would be uneconomic': Art. 4(3)(a)(ii).

[191] Art. 4(3)(b).   [192] Art. 4(3)(c).   [193] Arts. 6 to 8.

protection, public order, public safety or health protection, or if the notifier or consignee was guilty of illegal trafficking, or if the shipment conflicts with obligations resulting from international conventions, or if the ratio of the re- coverable and non-recoverable waste, the estimated value of the materials to be finally recovered, or the cost of the recovery and the cost of the disposal of the non-recoverable fraction, do not justify the recovery under economic and environmental considerations.[194] The Regulation allows competent authorities to object to shipments of certain types of waste to a specific recovery facility.[195] Shipments of waste for recovery listed in Annex IV ('red list') are generally subject to the same procedures as for the amber list.[196] Finally, with regard to shipments between member states, the Regulation also provides for certain information requirements and for transit via non-member states.[197]

Shipment of wastes within member states   The provisions on shipment between member states (Title II of the Regulation), on common provisions (Title VII), and on other provisions (Title VIII) do not apply to shipments within a member state, although member states may decide, and are free, to apply those provisions.[198] At a minimum, member states must establish an 'appropriate system' for the supervision and control of shipments of waste within their jurisdiction.[199]

Export of wastes   All exports to ACP countries are prohibited, except that a member state may return to an ACP state waste which that state has cho- sen to have processed in the EC.[200] For all states other than ACP states, the Regulation distinguishes between wastes for disposal and waste for recovery. With regard to waste for disposal, the Regulation bans all exports of waste ex- cept to EFTA countries which are also parties to the 1989 Basel Convention.[201] Exports to EFTA countries are allowed, subject to the notification and autho- risation provisions,[202] or may be banned where the EFTA country prohibits imports of wastes or has not given its written consent to the specific import, or the authorities of the dispatch state in the EC believe that the waste will not be managed in accordance with environmentally sound methods.[203] The Regulation sets forth the conditions for exports of waste for recovery in respect of wastes under Annex II ('green list'), Annex III ('amber list') and Annex IV ('red list').[204]

Article 16(1) of the Regulation deals with exports of waste for recovery. This provision was substantially amended in 1997 to bring it into line with

---

[194] Art. 7(4)(a). The competent authorities of transit may also raise certain reasoned objec- tions: Art. 7(4)(b).

[195] Art. 9.   [196] Art. 10.   [197] Arts. 11 and 12.

[198] Art. 13(1) and (4).   [199] Art. 13(2).   [200] Art. 18.

[201] Art. 14(1).   [202] Art. 15.   [203] Art. 14(2).   [204] Art. 17.

the export bans agreed under the Basel Convention.[205] In its amended form, Article 16(1) prohibits all exports of waste for recovery listed in a new Annex V except those to countries to which the OECD Decision applies and to other countries which are parties to the Basel Convention and/or parties to agreements under Article 11(2) of the Basel Convention, or with which individual EC member states have concluded bilateral agreements and arrangements prior to the Regulation and which are compatible with EC legislation and in accordance with Article 11(2) of the Basel Convention.[206] Such exports, however, were banned completely from 1 January 1998.[207] The EC Commission must keep Annex V under review and amend it as required to take into full consideration the lists of wastes adopted under Directive 91/689/EEC and any lists of wastes characterised as hazardous for the purposes of the Basel Convention. Annex V was reviewed and substantially amended in 1999 and again in 2001.[208] In its current form, Annex V consists of three parts, with the latter two parts applying only where Part 1 is not applicable. Part 1 is itself divided into two subsections: List A, which enumerates wastes classified as hazardous for the purposes of the Basel Convention and covered by the Article 16(1) export ban (this list corresponds to that under Annex VIII to the Basel Convention), and List B, which sets out wastes not covered by the export ban (this list corresponds to Annex IX to the Basel Convention). Wastes not listed in Part 1 but which are included in Parts 2 or 3 to Annex V are also covered by the export ban. Part 2 lists wastes classified as hazardous under Directive 91/689/EEC whereas Part 3 corresponds to the list of amber wastes under the OECD Decision.

Imports of wastes   The Regulation distinguishes between waste for disposal and waste for recovery. With regard to waste for disposal, the Regulation bans all imports of waste except from EFTA countries which are also parties to the 1989 Basel Convention and from other countries which are parties to the Basel Convention or with which certain bilateral agreements or arrangements are concluded with the EC or the EC and its member states.[209] For those countries, the Regulation establishes a system of prior notification and authorisation.[210]

With regard to waste for recovery, the Regulation prohibits all such imports except those from countries to which the OECD Decision applies and other countries which are parties to the Basel Convention and/or parties to agreements under Article 11(2) of the 1989 Basel Convention or with which individual EC member states have concluded bilateral agreements and arrangements

---

[205] See Commission Regulation (EC) No. 120/97, OJ L22, 24 January 1997, 14.
[206] Art. 16(1) and (2).   [207] Art. 16(3).
[208] See Commission Decision 816/99/EC, OJ L316, 10 December 1999, 45; and Commission Regulation (EC) No. 2557/2001, OJ L349, 31 December 2001, 1.
[209] Art. 19(1).   [210] Art. 20.

prior to the Regulation and which are compatible with EC legislation and in accordance with Article 11(2) of the Basel Convention, or with which individual member states have concluded authorised bilateral agreements or arrangements.[211] The Regulation applies different control procedures for the import of wastes for recovery from countries to which the OECD Decision applies and those to which the Decision does not apply.[212]

Other provisions   The Regulation establishes rules on the transit of waste from outside and through the EC for disposal or recovery outside the EC.[213] It also contains other provisions which are common to all shipments of waste relating to: non-completion of shipments in accordance with consignment notes or contracts and their return; the conditions in which traffic will be deemed to be illegal and the consequences of such illegality; the requirement that all shipments of waste must be subject to a financial guarantee; the circumstances and conditions for a general notification procedure; the obligation not to mix wastes which are subject to different notifications; measures to ensure compliance with the Regulation, including inspections; and the appropriate form for consignment notes.[214]

Finally, the Regulation sets out a number of subsidiary provisions. These include: the express requirement that certain international transport conventions be complied with where they apply to the waste;[215] a provision on charging for administrative costs;[216] the obligation of the producer of waste to take all necessary steps to dispose of or recover the waste so as to protect the quality of the environment in accordance with Directives 75/442 and 91/689;[217] and the obligation to keep all documents in the EC for three years.[218] Given the complexity of the Regulation, it also requires each member state to designate a correspondent responsible for information or advising anyone who makes enquiries.[219]

Directive 92/3/EURATOM: radioactive waste shipment

The regulation of movements of radioactive waste in the EC is governed by EURATOM Directive 92/3, which applies to shipments of radioactive waste between member states and into and out of the EC whenever the quantities

---

[211] Art. 21(1) and (2).   [212] Art. 22.   [213] Arts. 23 and 24.   [214] Arts. 25 to 31.

[215] Art. 32 and Annex I; the conventions are the 1957 ADR (road); 1985 COTIF and 1985 RID (rail); 1966 SOLAS (sea); IMDG Code (sea; incorporated in SOLAS since 1985); 1944 Chicago Convention (air); MARPOL 73/78 (sea); 1970 ADNR (Rhine river).

[216] Art. 33.

[217] Art. 34; this obligation is stated to be without prejudice to, *inter alia*, EC and national provisions concerning civil liability.

[218] Art. 35.

[219] Art. 37. At the time of writing, no correspondent had yet been designated in the United Kingdom.

and concentrations exceed the levels set by Directive 80/836.[220] The Directive distinguishes between three types of shipment: those between member states; those involving imports into and out of the EC; and reshipment operations. In respect of each, the Directive requires transport operations necessary for shipment to comply with EC and national provisions and international agreements on the transport of radioactive material.[221] The drafting of the Directive is less clear than the 1993 Regulation and is likely to require careful scrutiny in respect of the application of its provisions to the shipment of, for example, radioactive waste for processing and irradiated nuclear fuel for reprocessing.

With regard to shipments between member states the basic rule is that the shipment must be authorised by the country of origin and the country of destination, as well as any country of transit,[222] although the authorisation does not in any way affect the responsibility of the holder, the transporter, the owner, the consignee or anyone else involved in the shipment.[223] Applications may be made in respect of more than one shipment over a period of up to three years.[224] With regard to imports into the EC from third countries, the consignee must obtain authorisation from the authorities of the destination member state using standard documentation.[225] The Directive also establishes rules governing the situation where an EC member state is a transit state.[226]

With regard to exports out of the EC, the member states' authorities cannot authorise shipments to the Antarctic region or to a party to the 1989 Lomé Convention (unless, in respect of the latter, the waste is being returned after having been reprocessed), or to a third country which does not have the technical, legal or administrative resources to manage radioactive waste safely.[227] If radioactive waste is to be exported to a third country, the authorities of the EC member state are required to 'contact the authorities of the country of destination regarding such a shipment', and may authorise the shipment '[i]f all the conditions for shipment are fulfilled', whereupon they must inform the authorities of the country of destination about the shipment.[228] The holder of the radioactive waste must notify the competent authorities of the country of origin that the waste has reached its destination, and the notification must be accompanied by a declaration or certification of the consignee to that effect.[229]

---

[220] Art. 1(1); 'radioactive waste' is defined as 'any material which contains or is contaminated by radionuclides and for which no use is foreseen': Art. 2. On Directive 80/836/EEC and its successor, see chapter 15, pp. 793–4 below.

[221] Art. 3.

[222] Arts. 4, 6 and 7; see also Art. 20 for the standard documents. See also Council Regulation (EURATOM) No. 1493/93 of 8 June 1993 on shipments of radioactive substances between member states, establishing a system of prior declaration for all movements of radioactive substances, including wastes: OJ L148, 19 June 1993, 1.

[223] Art. 7.   [224] Art. 5.   [225] Art. 10(1).   [226] Art. 10(2).

[227] Arts. 11 and 14.   [228] Art. 12(1) and (2).   [229] Art. 12(5) and (6).

With regard to reshipment operations, sealed sources containing non-fissile material do not fall within the scope of the Directive.[230] The Directive does not affect the right of a member state or a company in the member state to (a) return radioactive waste after processing to the country of origin, and (b) to return to the country of origin waste and/or other products of the reprocessing of irradiated nuclear fuel.[231] Where a shipment of radioactive waste cannot be completed, or if the conditions of shipment are not complied with, the member state is to ensure that the radioactive waste will be returned to the holder of the waste.[232]

In respect of imports and exports from third countries, the operational part of the Directive does not expressly require the prior informed consent of third countries before authorising the shipment. However, the Preamble makes it clear that this is required, stating that to protect human health and the environment account must be taken of risks occurring outside the EC and that accordingly in the case of radioactive waste entering and/or leaving the EC 'the third country of destination or origin and any third country or countries of transit must be consulted and informed and must have given their consent'.

UNCED

Agenda 21 signalled a more concerted effort to regulate waste internationally. It distinguishes between hazardous wastes, solid wastes (including sewage) and radioactive wastes.[233]

Hazardous wastes

Chapter 20 of Agenda 21 identifies the overall objective in relation to hazardous waste as being 'to prevent to the extent possible, and minimise, the generation of hazardous wastes, as well as to manage those wastes in such a way that they do not cause harm to health and the environment'.[234] To that end,

---

[230] Art. 13.   [231] Art. 14.   [232] Art. 15.

[233] The WSSD Plan of Implementation calls in the most general terms on the need to '[p]revent and minimize waste and maximize reuse, recycling and use of environmentally friendly alternative materials', including actions to '(a) [d]evelop waste management systems, with highest priorities placed on waste prevention and minimization, reuse and recycling, and environmentally sound disposal facilities, including technology to recapture the energy contained in waste, and encourage small-scale waste-recycling initiatives that support urban and rural waste management and provide income-generating opportunities, with international support for developing countries; (b) [p]romote waste prevention and minimization by encouraging production of reusable consumer goods and biodegradable products and developing the infrastructure required'.

[234] Agenda 21, Chapter 20 ('Environmentally Sound Management of Hazardous Wastes, Including Prevention of Illegal International Traffic in Hazardous Wastes'), para. 20.6.

the overall objectives include: developing an integrated cleaner production approach; eliminating or reducing to a minimum transboundary movements; and implementing the 'self-sufficiency principle' to ensure that management should as far as possible take place in the country of origin.[235] Chapter 20 includes four programme areas: promoting the prevention and minimisation of waste; strengthening institutional capacities for management; strengthening international co-operation in management of transboundary movements; and preventing illegal traffic.

These programme areas are likely to form the basis for future international measures, including treaties and other international acts. Objectives include establishing intermediate goals to stabilise the quantity of hazardous waste generated, establishing long-term programmes and policies including targets for reducing the amount of hazardous waste produced per unit of manufacture, and qualitative improvement of waste streams.[236] Chapter 20 also calls for: an end to discrimination against environmentally sound recycled materials; the adoption of economic or regulatory incentives to support cleaner production, preventive or recycling technologies and waste minimisation; and recycling, re-use and disposal of waste at the source of generation or as close as possible to it (the 'proximity principle').[237] It supports ratification of the 1989 Basel Convention and the 1991 Bamako Convention, and calls for the expeditious elaboration of protocols on liability and compensation, and the elimination of exports to countries which prohibit them, including parties to the 1989 Basel Convention and the 1989 Lomé Convention.[238]

Other non-radioactive wastes

Chapter 21 of Agenda 21 identifies four interrelated programme areas for solid wastes and sewage. These are intended to create a framework for minimising wastes, maximising environmentally sound waste re-use and recycling, promoting environmentally sound waste disposal and treatment, and extending waste service coverage.[239] The specific waste minimisation objectives include goals based on waste weight, volume and composition for stabilising or reducing waste production over an agreed timeframe and inducing separation to facilitate recycling and re-use.[240] A soft target is established which calls upon

---

[235] Para. 20.7(a).   [236] Para. 20.12(c)–(e).
[237] Para. 20.13(a), (b) and (f).   [238] Para. 20.7(b)–(d).
[239] Chapter 21 ('Environmentally Sound Management of Solid Wastes and Sewage-Related Issues'), paras. 21.5 and 21.6. 'Solid wastes' are defined as 'domestic refuse and non-hazardous wastes such as commercial and institutional wastes, street sweepings and construction debris': para. 21.3. Human wastes, ash from incinerators, septic tank sludge and other sludge should be treated as hazardous wastes if they manifest 'hazardous characteristics': *ibid.*
[240] Para. 21.8(a).

industrialised countries to have put in place, by the year 2000, programmes to stabilise or reduce waste production destined for final disposal, including per capita waste production, at the levels which exist on that date.[241] Re-use and recycling objectives include national plans and the possible establishment by the year 2000 in industrialised countries of programmes with recycling and re-use targets.[242] Specific incentives which are encouraged include technical assistance, economic and regulatory incentives to support the principle that generators should pay for disposal, deposit/refunds systems, and developing markets.[243]

With regard to environmentally sound waste disposal and treatment, Agenda 21 calls for the establishment of waste treatment and disposal quality criteria and capacity in order to: undertake water-related pollution impact monitoring by the year 2000; ensure that at least 50 per cent of all sewage, waste waters and solid wastes are treated or disposed of in conformity with national or international guidelines by the year 1995 in industrialised countries and by the year 2005 for developing countries; and dispose of all sewage, waste waters and solid wastes in conformity with national or international guidelines by the year 2025.[244] The programme area to extend waste service coverage aims to provide all urban populations with adequate waste services by the year 2025, and to apply the polluter-pays principle by setting waste management charges at rates that reflect the cost of the service and ensure that those who generate the wastes pay the full cost of disposal.[245]

Radioactive wastes

Chapter 22 of Agenda 21, which has only one programme area, addresses the management of radioactive wastes, and takes as its basis for action the radiological and safety risk resulting from the 200,000 m^3 of low-level and intermediate-level radioactive waste and 10,000 m^3 of high-level radioactive waste which is produced annually.[246] The chapter on radioactive waste was among the most contentious of the forty chapters in Agenda 21, and, although it is the shortest, it includes provisions which are relatively precise. Four activities are called for: promoting policies and practical measures to minimise and limit the generation of radioactive wastes and to provide for their safe processing, conditioning, transportation and disposal; supporting efforts within the IAEA to develop and apply radioactive waste safety standards or guidelines and codes of practice; promoting safe storage, transportation and disposal; and promoting proper planning of safe and environmentally sound management,

---

[241] Para. 21.9(b).   [242] Paras. 21.19(c) and 21.18(b).
[243] Para. 21.24.   [244] Para. 21.29.   [245] Paras. 21.39(b) and 21.40(b).
[246] Chapter 22 ('Safe and Environmentally Sound Management of Radioactive Wastes'), para. 22.1.

including environmental impact assessment where appropriate.[247] Specific international co-operation is called for: to implement the 1990 IAEA Code and keep under review a possible legally binding instrument; to encourage the 1972 London Convention to complete studies on replacing the voluntary moratorium on low-level radioactive waste disposal at sea by a ban, taking into account the precautionary approach;[248] not to promote or allow the storage or disposal of high-, intermediate- or low-level radioactive wastes near the marine environment;[249] and not to export radioactive wastes to countries that prohibit the import of such wastes, such as the parties to the 1991 Bamako Convention and the 1989 Lomé Convention; and to respect, in accordance with international law, the decisions taken by parties to other relevant regional environmental conventions dealing with other aspects of radioactive wastes.[250]

Conclusions

The rules of international law relating to waste are, with a few exceptions, aimed at regulating the disposal of waste rather than addressing and preventing its generation. There is now extensive international law regulating or prohibiting the transboundary movement of hazardous and radioactive wastes and the disposal of such wastes into the marine environment. These obligations are supported, or supplemented, by emerging concepts such as the 'self-sufficiency principle' and the 'proximity principle', which also encourage communities to limit the amount of waste they generate by requiring them to dispose of the waste they themselves produce. There is considerably less international law on other methods of disposal, such as landfill and incineration on land, although in both the EC and the Antarctic rules have recently been adopted on these forms of disposal, which may well serve as models for other regions. The gaps which plainly exist should be filled in order to complete the range of disposal options which are subject to international regulation.

Regulating disposal has a certain logic: there is some evidence to suggest that a tightening of the international and national disposal regulations will increase costs and that this might act as an incentive to encourage people to generate less waste. On the other hand, it seems clear that limiting the avalanche of waste which is now threatening to engulf industrialised countries (and will presumably follow the same path over time for developing countries) requires the development of strategies and legal rules which address the waste problem at source by preventing its generation. There is some suggestion that the rules of international law might be encouraged to move in that direction: the

[247] Para. 22.4.   [248] Para. 22.5(a) and (b).
[249] Para. 22.5(c); see chapter 9, pp. 429–37 above.   [250] Para. 22.5(d) and (e).

establishment of quantitative targets and timetables for the recovery and re-use of hazardous and non-hazardous wastes is now on the international agenda, as is the emerging effort to encourage the use of cleaner technologies which aim at waste minimisation. Agenda 21 endorsed both approaches, and provides a useful framework against which future international waste management and prevention policies can be judged.

14

The polar regions: Antarctica and the Arctic

R. D. Hayton, 'The Antarctic Settlement of 1959', 54 AJIL 349 (1960); B. Boczek, 'The Protection of the Antarctic Ecosystem: A Study in International Environmental Law', 13 *Ocean Development and International Law* 347 (1983); J. E. Carroll, 'Of Icebergs, Oil Wells, and Treaties: Hydrocarbon Exploitation Offshore Antarctica', 19 *Stanford Journal of International Law* 207 (1983); S. Lyster, *International Wildlife Law* (1985), 156–177; C. C. Joyner, 'Protection of the Antarctic Environment: Rethinking the Problems and Prospects', 19 *Cornell International Law Journal* 259 (1986); G. Triggs (ed.), *The Antarctic Treaty Regime: Law, Environment, and Resources* (1987); W. Bush, *Antarctica and International Law* (3 vols., 1982–8); J. Verhoeven, P. Sands and M. Bruce (eds.), *The Antarctic Environment and International Law* (1992); A. Watts, *International Law and the Antarctic Treaty System* (1992); L. A. Kimball, 'Environmental Law and Policy in Antarctica', in P. Sands (ed.), *Greening International Law* (1993), 122; J. Heap, *Handbook of the Antarctic Treaty System* (1994, 8th edn); F. Francioni and T. Scovazzi (eds.), *International Law for Antarctica* (1996, 2nd edn); D. Rothwell, *The Polar Regions and the Development of International Law* (1996); O. S. Stokke and D. Vidas (eds.), *Governing the Antarctic: The Effectiveness and Legitimacy of the Antarctic Treaty System* (1996); J. M. Spectar, 'Saving the Ice Princess: NGOs, Antarctica and International Law in the New Millennium', 23 *Suffolk Transnational Law Review* 57 (1999); D. Vidas (ed.), *Implementing the Environmental Protection Regime for the Antarctic* (2000); D. Vidas (ed.), *Protecting the Polar Marine Environment* (2000).

The Antarctic and the Arctic polar regions are subject to special regional rules of environmental protection. These rules reflect the unique physical conditions of these areas and the important role they play in maintaining regional and global environmental conditions. They also provide useful models for the development of international environmental law in other regions and globally. For the Antarctic, the environmental rules have developed in the context of complex legal issues arising from claims made by some states to sovereign rights over Antarctic territory, and the opposing view of most other states that the Antarctic is part of the global commons and not subject to the exclusive jurisdiction of any state. These differences have not prevented the adoption of innovative and potentially far-reaching rules for the protection of the Antarctic

environment and its ecosystem. The Arctic region, on the other hand, is subject
to the undisputed jurisdiction of certain states, and for the most part environmental protection in that area is based on national environment laws, although
these may implement international environmental obligations. In 1991, Arctic
states recognised the need for international co-operation to address threats to
the Arctic environment and its ecosystem in the knowledge that it too plays an
important role in maintaining the global environmental balance. In 1996, they
established the Arctic Council, a high-level intergovernmental forum designed
to provide a mechanism to address the common concerns and challenges faced
by the Arctic governments and the peoples of the Arctic.

Introduction

The Antarctic continental region extends over 14 million square kilometres
and comprises 26 per cent of the world's wilderness area, representing 90 per
cent of all terrestrial ice and 70 per cent of planetary fresh water. The Antarctic
also extends to a further 36 million square kilometres of ocean. It has a limited
terrestrial life and a highly productive marine ecosystem, comprising a few
plants (e.g. microscopic algae, fungi and lichen), marine mammals, fish and
hordes of birds adapted to the harsh conditions, as well as the krill, which is
central to the marine food chain and upon which other animals are dependent.
The Antarctic plays an important role in maintaining climatic equilibrium, and
deep ice cores provide an important source of information about greenhouse
gas concentrations and atmospheric temperatures of hundreds and thousands
of years ago. Since 1959, activities in the area have been limited to scientific
research, fishing and tourism. Even these limited activities have not prevented
parts of the region from being degraded by waste as a result of oil spills (such as
the *Bahia Paraiso* in 1989), by the incidental destruction of flora and fauna and
the adverse effects of tourism, and by economic pressures to exploit resources
such as the Patagonian toothfish.

The Antarctic region is subject to a regime comprising five treaties: the 1959
Antarctic Treaty;[1] the 1972 Convention for the Conservation of Antarctic Seals
(1972 Antarctic Seals Convention);[2] the 1980 Convention on the Conservation
of Antarctic Marine Living Resources (1980 CCAMLR);[3] the 1988 Convention
on the Regulation of Antarctic Mineral Resource Activities (1988 CRAMRA);[4]
and the 1991 Protocol on Environmental Protection to the Antarctic Treaty

---

[1] Washington, 1 December 1959, in force 23 June 1961, 402 UNTS 71; forty-three states are
party.
[2] London, 1 June 1972, in force 11 March 1978; 11 ILM 251 and 417 (1972); sixteen states
are party.
[3] Canberra, 20 May 1980, in force 7 April 1982; 19 ILM 841 (1980); www.ccamlr.org; twenty-
eight states and the EC are party.
[4] Wellington, 2 June 1988, not in force; Misc. 6 (1989), Cmnd 634; 27 ILM 868 (1988).

(1991 Antarctic Environment Protocol).[5] In addition, under the 1959 Antarctic Treaty, numerous recommendations have been adopted, and under the 1980 CCAMLR a series of conservation measures have been adopted. Several other treaties, such as the 1982 UNCLOS, marine protection treaties, the 1989 Basel Convention and the 1997 Joint Safety Convention (IAEA), also include provisions applicable to the Antarctic region. Since the regime was initiated with the Antarctic Treaty in 1959, the international rules applicable to the region have increasingly addressed environmental concerns, and the area is now subject to a large body of environmental regulation. Apart from the substantive norms establishing environmental standards, including activities which are prohibited or regulated, the Antarctic treaty regime has contributed significantly to the development of institutional and procedural techniques which have been applied in other areas of international environmental law. In many ways, the Antarctic region has played a catalytic and innovative role, contributing to the progressive development of rules and techniques relating to information exchange, scientific advisory processes, environmental impact assessment, observation and inspection, the management of waste streams, liability for environmental damage, enforcement procedures, and institutional arrangements.

From time to time, the issue of a UN role in Antarctica has been raised at the UN General Assembly. Early UN efforts began in the late 1950s, and continued again in 1983 as a result of growing interest in mineral exploitation in the region. In 1994, the General Assembly welcomed the designation of Antarctica as a nature reserve in the 1991 Environmental Protocol and commended the prohibition on mineral resource activities contained in that treaty.[6] However, the earlier idea proposed by Malaysia and other states which are not parties to the 1959 Antarctic Treaty, as well as non-governmental organisations, to turn the Antarctic region into a 'world park', prohibiting any human activity, has not met with universal approval.

The Antarctic Treaty regime

1959 Antarctic Treaty

The 1959 Antarctic Treaty, which 'freezes' national claims to sovereignty in the continent,[7] was not primarily intended to establish rules of environmental

---

[5] Madrid, 4 October 1991, in force 14 January 1998; 30 ILM 1461 (1991); twenty-nine states are party.

[6] UNGA Res. 49/80 (1994). See also UNGA Res. 51/56 (1996) and UNGA Res. 54/45 (1999).

[7] Seven states claim sovereign rights over parts of Antarctic territory: Argentina, Australia, Chile, France, New Zealand, Norway and the United Kingdom. To the extent that sovereign claims are maintained by these states the Antarctic area would not, at least in their eyes, be considered as part of the 'global commons'. Nevertheless, the area is often referred to as an example of the 'global commons' or of 'areas beyond the limits of national jurisdiction' within the meaning of Art. 21 of the Stockholm Declaration and Art. 2 of the Rio Declaration.

protection.[8] Nevertheless, a number of its provisions contribute incidentally to environmental protection in the region. Under Articles I and II, Antarctica is to be used for peaceful purposes only, including scientific investigation, and military activities are prohibited. Article V prohibits nuclear explosions and the disposal of radioactive waste material in Antarctica. Article IX allows parties having consultative status to take additional measures regarding, *inter alia*, the 'preservation and conservation of living resources in Antarctica'.[9]

The 1959 Antarctic Treaty did not establish a permanent secretariat (although in 2001 the twenty-fourth Antarctic Treaty Consultative Meeting agreed to establish such a body in Buenos Aires). Rather, regular consultative meetings of the parties are held to ensure consultation on matters of common interest, exchange information, and recommend measures to the parties. Twenty-seven parties have consultative status under the Treaty, which allows them to vote, while eighteen do not have such status.[10] The meetings of the consultative parties to the Antarctic Treaty led to the first dedicated environmental measures for the area with the adoption in 1964 of the Brussels Agreed Measures for the Conservation of Antarctic Fauna and Flora.[11] The 1964 Agreed Measures designate the Antarctic region a 'Special Conservation Area'; the Measures apply to the continent and to ice shelves and do not prejudice high seas rights in which the parties must prohibit interference with native mammals or birds without prior authorisation, such authorisation to be granted only in specified circumstances, including scientific and educational research.[12] The 1964 Agreed Measures also create 'Specially Protected Areas' with even stricter authorisation requirements.[13]

1972 Antarctic Seals Convention

The 1972 Antarctic Seals Convention applies to the sea area regulated by the 1959 Treaty. It requires parties to limit annually the number of seals which can be killed or captured, and grants complete protection to certain species.[14] For those seals which can be taken, the hunting season is limited to a specified

---

[8] The Antarctic Treaty applies to the area south of 60° South latitude, including all ice shelves: Art. VI.

[9] Art. IX(1)(f).

[10] Art. IX. Parties achieve consultative status by 'conducting substantial scientific research activity' in the region: Art. IX(2).

[11] Brussels, 13 June 1964, 17 UST 992; TIAS 6058. See also the London Arrangements for the Regulation of Antarctic Pelagic Whaling, 6 June 1962, 486 UNTS 263; C. C. Joyner, 'Recommended Measures under the Antarctic Treaty: Hardening Compliance with Soft International Law', 19 *Michigan Journal of International Law* 401 (1998).

[12] Preamble.

[13] Arts. VI(3) and VIII. By 1991, twenty Specially Protected Areas had been designated; the system was replaced with the entry into force in 1998 of the 1991 Protocol: see p. 725 below.

[14] Arts. 3 and 4 and Annex.

period in defined zones; the method of hunting is regulated; and scientific and breeding reserves are established. The Convention establishes more detailed obligations on exchange of information, according to which each party must provide annual reports to the contracting parties and to the non-governmental Scientific Committee for Antarctic Research (SCAR).[15] The reports require fairly comprehensive information on the number of seals killed or taken, their sex and age, and details about the ships used in the hunt. No institutions are created, although meetings of the contracting parties are envisaged at least every five years and may be convened more regularly.[16]

1980 CCAMLR

D. Vignes, 'La Convention sur la Conservation de la Faune et de la Flore Marines de l'Antarctique', 26 AFDI 741 (1980).

The objective of the 1980 CCAMLR is the conservation (including 'rational use') of the marine living resources in the Antarctic Treaty area and in the surrounding area which forms part of the Antarctic marine ecosystem. Harvesting and associated activities are to be carried out in accordance with three principles of conservation adopted under the Convention:

1. preventing decreases in the size of any harvested population to a level below that which ensures its stable recruitment;
2. maintaining the ecological relationships between harvested, dependent and related populations of Antarctic marine living resources and the restoration of depleted populations to the levels defined in paragraph (1) above; and
3. preventing changes or minimising risk of changes in the marine ecosystem which are not potentially reversible over two or three decades with the aim of making possible the sustained conservation of Antarctic marine living resources.[17]

These principles go some way towards establishing criteria for 'rational use', and provide a legal basis for approaching 'sustainable development'. The ecosystem approach is an early example of a novel concept subsequently relied upon in other environmental agreements. The 1980 CCAMLR approach combines prevention (even 'precaution'), sustainability and restoration. The overall effort is similar to that adopted in subsequent agreements addressing other global environmental concerns, such as ozone depletion, climate change and biological diversity.

The 1980 CCAMLR provides that for the Antarctic Treaty area all parties are bound by Articles IV and VI of the 1959 Antarctic Treaty, irrespective of whether they are parties to that Treaty.[18] It also requires parties to observe, as

---

[15] Art. 5(1) and (2).   [16] Arts. 6 and 7.   [17] Art. II(3).   [18] Art. IV(1).

and when appropriate, the 1964 Agreed Measures and such other environmental measures as recommended by the Antarctic Treaty consultative parties in the fulfilment of their 'special obligations and responsibilities . . . for the protection and preservation of the environment of the Antarctic Treaty area'.[19] Under the 1980 CCAMLR, no derogation is intended from the rights and obligations of parties to the 1946 International Whaling Convention or the 1972 Antarctic Seals Convention.[20]

The 1980 CCAMLR is mainly administered by a Commission for the Conservation of Antarctic Marine Living Resources, membership of which is open to parties with full decision-making rights. The function of the Commission is to give effect to the objective and principles of the Convention, including the formulation, adoption and revision of conservation measures on the basis of the best scientific evidence available.[21] The Commission has legal personality and wide-ranging powers, particularly to acquire and disseminate information and notify parties of activities which are contrary to the Convention. The Commission compiles data on Antarctic marine living resources, gathers statistics on catches of harvested populations, and analyses and publishes this information.[22] The Commission has a limited compliance role: it can draw the attention of all parties to any activity which, in its opinion, affects the implementation by a party of obligations, as well as activities undertaken by nationals or vessels of non-parties.[23] The Commission is assisted by a consultative Scientific Committee for the Conservation of Antarctic Marine Living Resources.[24]

Provisions on environmental impact assessment are also included for the first time in a multilateral international treaty, albeit in embryonic form: the Scientific Committee must 'assess the effects of proposed changes in the methods or levels of harvesting and proposed conservation measures'.[25] The Convention also establishes a system of observation and inspection to ensure compliance with the Convention, including procedures for boarding and inspection by designated observers and inspectors.[26]

---

[19] Art. V(1).   [20] Art. VI. On the 1946 Convention, see chapter 10, pp. 592–5 above.

[21] Arts. VII to XIII, at Art IX(1)(f). The Commission has adopted a significant body of conservation measures, relating, *inter alia*, to mesh sizes, fisheries, precautionary catches, scientific research, compliance, inspection, driftnet fishing and catch documentation schemes (those currently in force are available on the CCAMLR website, www.ccamlr.org).

[22] Art. IX(1)(b), (c) and (d). Its catch documentation scheme for toothfish (Conservation Measure 170/XIX) came into force on 7 May 2000.

[23] Art. X(1) and (2). The Commission has also adopted a number of conservation measures dealing with the enforcement of fisheries regulations in the CCAMLR area, including Conservation Measure 147/XIX, Provisions to Ensure Compliance with CCAMLR Conservation Measures by Vessels, Including Co-operation Between Contracting Parties; and Conservation Measure 118/XX, Scheme to Promote Compliance by Non-Contracting Party Vessels with CCAMLR Conservation Measures.

[24] Arts. XIV to XVI.   [25] Art. XV(2)(d).   [26] Art. XXIV.

1988 CRAMRA

J. Barnes, *The Emerging Convention on the Conservation of Antarctic Marine Living Resources: An Attempt to Meet the New Realities of Resource Exploitation in the Southern Ocean* (1982); C. C. Joyner, 'The Antarctic Minerals Negotiating Process', 81 AJIL 888 (1987); L. A. Kimball, 'The Antarctic Minerals Convention' (Special Report for the World Resources Institute (1988); F. Orrega Vicuña, *Antarctic Mineral Exploitation* (1988); M. P. Jacobsen, 'Convention on the Regulation of Antarctic Mineral Resources', 30 *Harvard International Law Journal* 237 (1989); A. Watts, 'The Convention on the Regulation of Antarctic Mineral Resource Activities', 39 ICLQ 169 (1990); R. Wolfrum, *The Convention on the Regulation of Antarctic Mineral Resource Activities* (1991).

The 1988 CRAMRA marked a further stage in the development of international law for the protection of the Antarctic environment and the adoption of rules, procedures and institutions which go significantly beyond anything previously adopted in international law.[27] By the time of its adoption, however, CRAMRA was widely considered not to go far enough in protecting the Antarctic environment. The decision by France and Australia in the autumn of 1989 not to ratify CRAMRA makes it unlikely that it will ever be brought into force.[28] The adoption in October 1991 of the Protocol on Environmental Protection leaves CRAMRA on ice, but the possibility of it re-emerging cannot, in theory at least, be excluded. In the meantime, many of its innovative provisions have influenced developments in relation to other international environmental treaties, and it remains an important model for the further development of international environmental law concerning rules on liability for environmental damage, environmental impact assessment, international supervision, institutional arrangements and dispute settlement.

CRAMRA was intended to be an integral part of the Antarctic Treaty system to establish the framework for determining whether Antarctic mineral resource[29] activities were acceptable and, if so, under what conditions they could be carried out.[30] Antarctic mineral resource activities comprised

---

[27] See also the Antarctic Treaty Consultative Meeting Recommendation XI-I on Antarctic Mineral Resources, which led to negotiation of a legal regime for Antarctic mineral resources, 7 July 1981, 20 ILM 1265 (1981).

[28] CRAMRA will only enter into force after ratification by sixteen of the Antarctic Treaty consultative parties which participated in the final session of the fourth Special Antarctic Treaty consultative meeting provided that number includes all the states necessary to establish all of the institutions of the Convention in respect of every area of the Antarctica, including five developing countries and eleven developed countries: Art. 62(1).

[29] 'Mineral resources' are defined as 'all non-living natural non-renewable resources, including fossil fuels, metallic and non-metallic minerals': Art. 1(6).

[30] Arts. 2(1) and 5. The CRAMRA area is generally the same as that for the 1959 Antarctic Treaty, and CRAMRA expressly applies to impacts from activities conducted within

prospecting, exploration and development,[31] but did not include scientific research. CRAMRA recognised the dangers posed by mineral resource activities for the environment, and elaborated a range of measures designed to ensure environmental protection. CRAMRA also reflected an acknowledgment of the special responsibility of the Antarctic Treaty consultative parties to protect the Antarctic environment and dependent and associated ecosystems; to respect Antarctica's significance for the global environment and its scientific value and aesthetic and wilderness qualities; and to take into account the interests of the international community as a whole.[32] To that end, decisions on Antarctic mineral resource activities were to be based upon the availability of adequate information and a precautionary approach: no such activities would be allowed to take place until it was judged, based upon assessment of possible impacts on the Antarctic environment and on dependent and associated ecosystems, that the activity in question would not cause environmental harm.[33] CRAMRA also established, for the first time in a treaty, a comprehensive environmental impact assessment process, which was stated to be an objective and a principle of the Convention.[34] The operation of the assessment process is set out in some detail,[35] and applications for permits were to be accompanied by an assessment.[36]

CRAMRA would also have prohibited activities until it could be judged that they would 'not cause significant adverse effects on global or regional climate or weather patterns', that safe technologies and procedures were available, and that there was a capacity to monitor key environmental parameters and to respond to accidents.[37] This would have established a high burden of proof on the person wishing to engage in such activities.

Under CRAMRA, Antarctic mineral resource activities would be prohibited outright in an area designated as a 'Specially Protected Area' or a 'Site of Special Scientific Interest' under Article IX of the Antarctic Treaty, or in any other area designated by the Commission as a protected area, and may be prohibited or restricted in adjacent areas.[38] Mineral resource activities would be required to respect other established uses of Antarctica, including the operation of stations, scientific research, conservation and rational use of marine

---

that area which are felt outside the area, including impacts on dependent or associated ecosystems: Art. 5(1) and (4). CRAMRA is also without prejudice to high seas rights, but it governs mineral activities on the continent's islands and ice shelves, and activities taking place in the seabed and subsoil of adjacent offshore areas up to the deep seabed, which could extend north of the 60° South line (Art. 5(3)).

[31] See pp. 718–20 below.   [32] Art. 2(3)(a), (b), (d) and (g).

[33] Art. 4(1) and (2). Assessment is to include the possible effects on air and water quality, changes in atmospheric, terrestrial or marine environments, significant changes to flora and fauna, jeopardy to endangered species, and other degradation: Art. 4(2).

[34] Arts. 2(1)(a) and 4(1) to (5).   [35] Art. 26(2), (3) and (4).

[36] Arts. 37(7)(d), 39(2)(e), 44(2)(b) and 53(2)(b).   [37] Art. 4(3) and (4).   [38] Art. 13.

living resources, tourism, preservation of historic monuments, and navigation and aviation.[39]

Institutions

CRAMRA would have established several new institutions. Primary among them would have been the Antarctic Minerals Resource Commission, which would be granted broad powers: to facilitate and promote information; to designate areas in which mineral activities are prohibited; to determine maximum drilling depths; and to adopt other measures relating to information, exploration and development.[40] Membership in the Commission would be open to decision-making states[41] and its powers would include monitoring and the adoption of measures for the protection of the environment and dependent and associated ecosystems.[42]

CRAMRA would also have established Antarctic Mineral Resources Regulatory Committees for geographic areas identified by the Commission, and a Scientific, Technical and Environmental Advisory Committee.[43] The primary functions of the Regulatory Committees would have included the grant and monitoring of exploration and development activities; each Regulatory Committee would have comprised ten members determined by the Commission, including members which assert rights or claims in the identified area.[44] The Advisory Committee would have advised the Commission and Regulatory Committees on the scientific, technical and environmental aspects of Antarctic mineral resource activities; the role would be advisory, and participation in the Committee would be open to all parties.[45] CRAMRA would also require special meetings of the parties,[46] and establish a single secretariat to serve the Commission, the Regulatory Committees, the Advisory Committee, the special meeting of the parties, and any subsidiary bodies established.[47]

Resource activities

CRAMRA would divide mineral resource activities into three categories: prospecting, exploration and development. Prospecting would be governed by Articles 37 and 38, and be conducted in compliance with CRAMRA but without a requirement of authorisation by any CRAMRA institution.[48] The sponsoring state would be subject to obligations to ensure the compliance by the operator with all provisions of the Convention, such as environmental

---

[39] Art. 15.   [40] Arts. 18 to 22.   [41] Art. 18(2).
[42] Art. 21(1)(a) and (c).   [43] Arts. 23 to 27 and 29 to 32.
[44] Art. 29(2).   [45] Art. 23(2).   [46] Art. 28.   [47] Art. 33.
[48] Art. 37(2). 'Prospecting' is defined as, *inter alia*, 'activities, including logistical support, aimed at identifying areas of mineral resource potential for possible exploration and development, including geological, geochemical and geophysical investigations and field observations, the use of remote sensing techniques and collection of surface, seafloor and sub-ice samples': Art. 1(8).

impact assessment, monitoring, emergency response and liability. Additional obligations upon the sponsoring state would include notification to the Commission of planned prospecting at least nine months in advance, notification of the cessation of prospecting, and the provision of a general annual report.[49] Each operator would be responsible for the removal of all installations and equipment and site rehabilitation.[50] The Commission could be convened to consider whether prospecting was consistent with the CRAMRA, and would be able to take appropriate action.[51]

Exploration would be governed by Articles 39 to 52 (Chapter IV).[52] Although not in force the procedure establishes a useful model illustrating the potential relationship between the private sector, a state, and an international organisation.The process for identification of areas for exploration would go through several stages. After having established its desire to engage in exploration, any party would submit to the Executive Secretary a notification requesting the Commission to identify areas for exploration (and development). The notification would be referred to all parties, and circulated to observers attending a meeting of the Commission which would have to be held within two months of the receipt of the notification.[53] The Commission would receive advice from the Advisory Committee on the notification, and a special meeting of the parties, comprising all parties (unlike the Commission) would consider whether the identification of an area by the Commission was compatible with CRAMRA, and adopt a report setting out its conclusions.[54] The Commission would then decide whether to identify an area for exploration and development as requested, taking full account of, and giving special weight to, the conclusions of the special meeting of parties, and taking full account also of the conclusions of the Advisory Committee.[55] The Commission may decide only by consensus that identification of an area was consistent with CRAMRA.[56]

If an area was identified, the Regulatory Committee would carry out the preparatory work for exploration, including the division of the area into blocks, and establish procedures for making applications for exploration and

---

[49] Art. 37(3), (7) and (8). The sponsoring state would be required to ensure that its operations maintain financial capacity 'commensurate with the nature and level of the activity undertaken and the risks involved' to comply with the strict liability provisions under Art. 8(2): Art. 37(3)(b).

[50] Art. 37(6).   [51] Art. 38(1).

[52] 'Exploration' is defined as 'activities, including logistical support, aimed at identifying and evaluating specific mineral resource occurrences or deposits, including exploratory drilling, dredging and other surface or subsurface excavations required to determine the nature and size of mineral resource deposits and the feasibility of their development, but excluding pilot projects or commercial production': Art. 1(9).

[53] Arts. 19(2)(a) and 39(3).   [54] Art. 40.

[55] Art. 41(1); the Commission may consider whether there are any areas in which exploration or development should be prohibited or restricted: Art. 41(1)(b).

[56] Art. 41(2).

development.[57] Applications would be lodged with the Regulatory Committee by any party on behalf of an operator for which it was the sponsoring state.[58] The Regulatory Committee would elaborate a Management Scheme setting out specific terms and conditions for exploration and development including: measures to minimise environmental risks and damage; provision for the restoration to the *status quo ante*; contingency plans; performance requirements; technical and safety specifications; monitoring and inspection; liability; resource conservation requirements; financial obligations; financial guarantees and insurance; applicable law; enforcement of the Scheme; and dispute settlement.[59] Once the Management Scheme had been approved, exclusive exploration (and development) permits could be issued by the Regulatory Committee.[60] The Commission could review the decision by the Regulatory Committee to approve a Management Scheme or issue a development permit at the request of any member of the Commission or Regulatory Committee, and could request the Regulatory Committee to reconsider its decision.[61] The Regulatory Committee would monitor compliance by operators and could under certain circumstances suspend, modify or cancel the Management Scheme and permits.[62]

Articles 53 and 54 (Chapter V) would establish procedures for applications to proceed from exploration to development in the area. Once a Management Scheme and an exploration permit were in force for an operator, the sponsoring state could apply for a development permit, on behalf of the operator, to the Regulatory Committee, which in turn could issue a development permit after taking full account of the views of the Advisory Committee.[63] The specific terms and conditions for exploration and development would be set out in the Management Scheme and could be modified at this stage.

Compliance

CRAMRA significantly develops the provisions included in the earlier treaties for compliance with international environmental obligations. Apart from the obligations of any sponsoring state, independent compliance is provided for, including additional inspection powers and rights of aerial inspection.[64] Data and information would be made freely available, subject to rules on confidentiality of commercial information.[65] The Commission and an Advisory Committee would have powers to gather information, and both the Commission and the Advisory Committee would themselves be subject to the obligation

---

[57] Art. 43.   [58] Art. 44.   [59] Art. 47.
[60] Art. 48.   [61] Art. 49.   [62] Arts. 51 and 52.
[63] Arts. 53 and 54. 'Development' is defined as 'activities, including logistical support, which takes place following exploration and are aimed at or associated with exploitation of specific mineral resource deposits, including pilot projects, processing, storage and transport activities': Art. 1(10).
[64] Art. 12.   [65] Art. 16.

to give advance public notice of matters on which advice from the Advisory Committee had been requested.[66] The Commission would be required to co-operate with relevant international organisations including non-governmental organisations having a scientific, technical or environmental interest in the Antarctic.[67] Finally, activities relating to prospecting, exploration and exploitation would be subject to additional information requirements.[68]

Liability and dispute settlement

The 1988 CRAMRA also includes new approaches to liability for environmental damage, and a link between civil and state liability. These are considered in more detail in chapter 17 below.[69] Significant advances are envisaged for dispute settlement under CRAMRA, including detailed provisions on arbitration and the role of the ICJ.[70] Of particular note is the express role to be given to national courts, recourse to which is envisaged, and to which the Commission would have access.[71] Additionally, management schemes relating to terms and conditions of exploration and development would also be required to make express provision for the settlement of disputes.[72]

1991 Environment Protocol

J. P. Puissochet, 'Le Protocole au Traité sur l'Antarctique relatif à la Protection de l'Environnement', AFDI 755 (1991); C. C. Joyner, 'The 1991 Madrid Environmental Protocol: Rethinking the World Park Status for Antarctica', 1 RECIEL 328 (1992); F. Francioni, 'The Madrid Protocol on the Protection of the Antarctic Environment', 28 *Texas International Law Journal* 47 (1993); C. Redgwell, 'Environmental Protection in Antarctica: The 1991 Protocol', 43 ICLQ 599 (1994); L. Cordonnery, 'Area Protection and Management in Antarctica: A Proposed Strategy for the Implementation of Annex V of the Madrid Protocol Based on Information Management', 14 *Environmental and Planning Law Journal* 38 (1997); D. French, 'Sustainable Development and the 1991 Madrid Protocol to the 1959 Antarctic Treaty: The Primacy of Protection of the Particularly Sensitive Environment', 2 JIWLP 291 (1999).

On 4 October 1991, twenty-three of the then twenty-six Antarctic Treaty consultative parties and eight non-consultative parties signed the 1991 Antarctic Environmental Protocol, including its then four Annexes, which established a fifty-year moratorium on Antarctic mineral resource activities from its entry into force on 14 January 1998. A fifth Annex was adopted shortly thereafter. The Protocol and Annexes, to which no reservations are permitted,[73] comprise

---

[66] Arts. 21(1) and 25(3).   [67] Art. 34.
[68] Arts. 37, 47 and 53.   [69] Chapter 18, pp. 896–901 below.
[70] Arts. 55 to 59, and Annex.   [71] Art. 8(10).   [72] Art. 47.   [73] Art. 24.

the most comprehensive and stringent regime of environmental protection rules ever established under the rules of public international law anywhere in the world. The Protocol was negotiated following the decision by France and Australia not to ratify CRAMRA on the ground that it failed to provide adequate protection to the Antarctic environment.

At the heart of the Protocol is Article 7, which provides in unambiguous terms that '[a]ny activity relating to mineral resources, other than scientific research, shall be prohibited'.[74] The Protocol adopts a fifty-year moratorium on any mineral resource activities in the Antarctic area. However, the Protocol permits modifications and amendments to be made at any time in accordance with the relevant provisions of the Antarctic Treaty, which require the agreement of all the Antarctic Treaty consultative parties.[75] To overcome the unanimity problem, the Protocol allows a review conference to be called at the request of any of the Antarctic Treaty consultative parties fifty years after its entry into force. The review conference will be able to adopt modifications or amendments to the Protocol, but only under strict conditions. They must be supported by a majority of the parties, including three-fourths of the Antarctic Treaty consultative parties at the time of the adoption of the Protocol.[76] They will only enter into force after ratification by three-fourths of the Antarctic Treaty consultative parties, including all states which were consultative parties at the time of the adoption of the Protocol.[77] Moreover, any modification or amendment to Article 7 must be accompanied by a binding legal regime on 'Antarctic mineral resource activities that includes an agreed means for determining whether, and if so, under which conditions, any such activities would be acceptable', and must fully safeguard the interests of states referred to in Article IV of the Antarctic Treaty and apply the principles of the Antarctic Treaty.[78] Recognising the real possibility that the modification and amendment procedure will make it virtually impossible to adopt changes to Article 7, any party may give notice of its withdrawal from the Protocol if a modification or amendment has not entered into force within three years of the date of its communication to the parties.[79]

The objective of the Protocol, which supplements the Antarctic Treaty without modifying or amending its provisions or derogating from rights and obligations of parties under other international instruments in force within the Antarctic Treaty system, is the comprehensive protection of the Antarctic environment and dependent and associated ecosystems, based upon the conviction

[74] The Final Act of the eleventh Antarctic Treaty special consultative meeting notes that 'the harvesting of ice was not considered to be an Antarctic mineral resource activity': cited in J. Verhoeven, P. Sands and M. Bruce (eds.), *The Antarctic Environment and International Law* (1992), 218.
[75] Art. 25(1). The relevant procedures in the Antarctic Treaty are set out in Art. XII(1)(a) and (b).
[76] Art. 25(2) and (3).   [77] Art. 25(4).   [78] Art. 25(5).
[79] Art. 25(6); withdrawal will take effect two years after the receipt of notice of withdrawal.

that such a goal is 'in the interest of mankind as a whole'.[80] Antarctica is designated as a 'natural reserve, devoted to peace and science', but is not formally called a 'world park', as some states had wished.[81] The Protocol includes guiding principles to support environmental protection in the planning and conduct of the non-mineral resource activities which are permitted, principally scientific research and tourism, including research which is essential to the understanding of the global environment.[82] These principles include: the obligation to plan and conduct activities so as to limit adverse environmental impacts; to ensure the prior assessment of, and informed judgments about, possible impacts; and to carry out regular and effective monitoring to allow assessment of impacts and early detection of possible unforeseen effects.[83]

Apart from Article 7, the Protocol requires co-operation, and includes provisions on environmental impact assessment,[84] together with four other Annexes which form an integral part of the Protocol.[85] Annex II, on 'Conservation of Fauna and Flora', prohibits the taking of or harmful interference with flora and fauna except in accordance with a permit, which may only be granted in relation to scientific or educational activities.[86] Permits may be granted only in exceptional circumstances for the Specially Protected Species designated in Appendix A to Annex II.[87] Species of animal or plant which are not native to the Antarctic Treaty area may only be introduced by permit, and then only if they are listed in Appendix B.[88] Dogs are prohibited in the Antarctic Treaty area,[89] and precautions are to be taken to prevent the introduction of non-native micro-organisms.[90]

Annex III, on 'Waste Disposal and Waste Management', represents an advanced attempt by the international community to develop treaty obligations giving effect to a comprehensive waste prevention and minimisation strategy. It applies to all activities in the Antarctic Treaty area, and requires wastes produced or disposed of in the area to be reduced to minimise the impact on the Antarctic environment or interference with the natural conditions of Antarctica.[91] Waste

---

[80] Preamble and Arts. 2 and 4. Under Art. 5, the parties to the Protocol undertake to avoid any inconsistency with other instruments of the Antarctic Treaty system.

[81] Art. 2.   [82] Art. 3(1) and (3).

[83] Art. 3(1) and (2). The Protocol specifically requires activities to avoid: adverse effects on climate or weather patterns; air or water quality; changes in atmospheric, terrestrial, glacial or marine environments; changes in fauna and flora; further jeopardy to endangered species; and degradation of or substantial risk to areas of biological, scientific, historic, aesthetic or wilderness significance: Art. 3(2)(b).

[84] Art. 8 and Annex I; on environmental impact, assessment, see chapter 16, pp. 818–19 below.

[85] Art. 9(1). The Annexes have their own rules on, *inter alia*, emergency situations, review and amendment.

[86] Annex II, Art. 3(1) and (2). This revises and updates the 1964 Agreed Measures.

[87] Annex II, Art. 3(4) and (5).   [88] Annex II, Art. 4(1) and (3).

[89] Annex II, Art. 4(2).   [90] Annex II, Art. 4(6) and Appendix C.

[91] Annex III, Art. 1(1) and (2).

storage, disposal and removal, as well as recycling and source reduction, are essential for all activities, and wastes should be returned to the country from which the activities generating the waste were organised or to any other country in accordance with international agreements.[92] Past and present waste disposal sites on land, and abandoned work sites, are to be cleaned up by the generator of such wastes and the user of the sites.[93] Annex III requires the removal by the generator of eight categories of waste generated after entry into force of the Annex and for certain other wastes to be removed to the maximum extent practicable.[94] Disposal by incineration of certain combustible wastes will be permitted in accordance with certain conditions, but open burning of waste was to be phased out by the 1998/9 season.[95] The Annex limits disposal of other wastes on land and in the sea, requires all wastes to be stored to prevent their dispersal in the environment, and prohibits the introduction of certain products into the Antarctic treaty area.[96] Finally, each party must establish a waste disposal classification system and prepare waste management plans and an inventory of locations of past activities.[97]

Annex IV, on 'Prevention of Marine Pollution', applies to ships of parties which are used to support their operations while operating in the Antarctic treaty area.[98] The Annex prohibits or regulates the discharge of oil and oily and other mixtures into the sea, and prohibits the discharge of noxious liquid substances, certain garbage and certain sewage.[99] Annex IV also establishes rules on ship retention capacity and retention facilities, design, construction and manning of ships, and preventive measures and emergency preparedness and response.[100] The Annex is consistent with MARPOL 73/78 provisions on special areas and does not derogate from the rights and obligations of parties to MARPOL 73/78.[101]

Annex V, on 'Area Protection and Management',[102] provides for the designation of Antarctic Specially Protected Areas and Antarctic Specially Managed Areas in which activities must be prohibited, restricted or managed in accordance with Management Plans adopted under the Annex.[103] Antarctic Specially Protected Areas are designated to protect outstanding environmental, scientific, historic, aesthetic or wilderness values or scientific research, and entry to these

---

[92] Annex III, Art. 1(3) and (4).   [93] Annex III, Art. 1(5).

[94] Annex III, Art. 2.   [95] Annex III, Art. 3.

[96] Annex III, Arts. 4 to 7. Prohibited products include PCBs, non-sterile soil, polystyrene or similar packaging, or pesticides other than those required for scientific, medical or hygiene purposes: Art. 7.

[97] Annex III, Art. 8. These are all subject to review by the Environment Committee: Art. 9.

[98] Annex IV, Art. 2.   [99] Annex IV, Arts. 3 to 6.   [100] Annex IV, Arts. 9 to 12.

[101] Annex IV, Art. 14; on MARPOL 73/78, see chapter 9, pp. 440–4 above.

[102] Annex V was adopted at the sixteenth Antarctic Treaty consultative meeting, Bonn, 18 October 1991.

[103] Annex V, Art. 2.

areas is prohibited except by permit.[104] Annex V redesignates Specially Protected Areas and Sites of Special Scientific Interests designated by Antarctic Treaty Consultative Meetings as Antarctic Specially Protected Areas.[105] Antarctic Specially Managed Areas are established to assist in the planning and co-ordination of activities, to avoid conflicts and to improve co-operation, and entry is not permitted without a permit.[106] Antarctic Specially Managed Areas may contain Antarctic Specially Protected Areas.[107] The Annex envisages Management Plans, designation procedures, the issuing of permits, the listing of historic sites and monuments, and information exchange and publicity.[108]

At the seventeenth Antarctic Treaty consultative meeting, in November 1992, five parties proposed a sixth Annex to cover tourism and other non-governmental activities, which would require advance approval for tourist visas, limiting the areas which tourists could visit, and limiting the overall number of tourists and visits by NGOs. No agreement was then reached.

Institutional arrangements

The operation of the Protocol is placed under the supervision of the Antarctic Treaty consultative meetings and a newly created Committee for Environmental Protection. The meetings define general policy for the comprehensive protection of the Antarctic environment and dependent and associated ecosystems and adopt measures under Article IX of the Antarctic Treaty to implement the Protocol.[109] The Committee, subject to review by the meetings, provides advice and recommendations on implementation including: on the effectiveness of measures taken under the Protocol, and the need for improvements or additional measures; the application of EIA procedures; the means of minimising environmental impacts; the procedures for urgent actions including environmental emergencies; the operation and elaboration of the Protected Area system; inspection procedures; environmental information; the state of the Antarctic environment; and the need for scientific research.[110] Each party is a member of the Committee, and observer status is open to any contracting party, to the President of SCAR and the Chair of the Scientific Committee of the CCAMLR, as well as other relevant scientific, environmental and technical organisations who have received the approval of the Antarctic Treaty consultative meeting.[111]

---

[104] Annex V, Art. 3(1) and (4).

[105] Annex V, Art. 3(3). There are currently fifty-nine Specially Protected Areas: www.era.gs/resources/apa/aspa/index.html.

[106] Annex V, Art. 4(1) and (3).   [107] Annex V, Art. 4(4).   [108] Annex V, Arts. 5 to 10.

[109] Art. 10(1). The meetings are to draw upon the advice and recommendations of the Committee. and the advice of SCAR: Art. 10(2).

[110] Art. 12(1). The Committee may consult with SCAR and the Scientific Committee for the Conservation of Antarctic Marine Living Resources, as well as other relevant organisations: Art. 12(2).

[111] Art. 11(3) and (4).

Compliance and related matters

The Committee does not have a formal role in the compliance process. Rather, each party must take 'appropriate measures within its competence' to ensure compliance with the Protocol.[112] Additionally each party must exert appropriate efforts consistent with the UN Charter to ensure that no one engages in any activity contrary to the Protocol, and to draw to the attention of all other parties any activity which affects implementation.[113] The Antarctic Treaty consultative meeting must draw to the attention of non-parties activities by it or those under its control, on any activity which affects implementation.[114] The Protocol also provides for inspections by observers in accordance with Article VII of the Antarctic Treaty, and for the formulation, establishment and implementation of contingency plans for response to emergencies and incidents with potential adverse effects on the environment, as well as procedures for the immediate notification of and co-operative response to environmental emergencies.[115] The parties will elaborate procedures relating to liability which are consistent with the objectives of the Protocol for the 'comprehensive protection of the Antarctic environment and dependent and associated ecosystems'.[116] The Protocol provides for mandatory dispute settlement in respect of certain provisions, including Articles 7, 8, 15, the provisions of any Annex (except to the extent that the Annex provides otherwise) and Article 13 (insofar as it relates to these particular Articles or the Annexes).[117]

Other treaty provisions

There are also a number of other international legal instruments of global application which have important provisions of great relevance to the Antarctic. Particularly significant among these are the 1982 UNCLOS, the provisions of which apply to the Antarctic marine environment,[118] and the 1989 Basel Convention which prohibits the export of hazardous wastes or other wastes for disposal within the Antarctic region.[119] Other treaties whose provisions apply to the Antarctic marine environment include the 1972 London Convention and MARPOL 73/78.

---

[112] Art. 13(1). Each party is to provide an annual report on its implementation: Art. 17.
[113] Art. 13(2) and (4).   [114] Art. 13(5).   [115] Art. 15.
[116] Art. 16. The seventeenth Antarctic Treaty consultative meeting, in November 1992, agreed to create a legal working group to consider this subject. Discussion of liability rules commenced in 1993, but the complexity of the issue and the differences of view has led to slow progress: see chapter 18, p. 932 below.
[117] Arts. 18 to 20; a Schedule to the Protocol defines an Arbitral Tribunal.
[118] Part XII, Protection and Preservation of the Marine Environment, Arts. 192 to 237; M. Peterson, 'Antarctic Implications of the New Law of the Sea', 16 *Ocean Development and International Law* 137 (1986).
[119] Art. 4(6).

The Arctic

R. M'Gonigle, 'Unilateralism and International Law: The Arctic Waters Pollution Prevention Act', 34 *University of Toronto Faculty Law Review* 180 (1976); B. Feder, 'Legal Regime for the Arctic', 6 *Ecology Law Quarterly* 785 (1978); D. McRae and D. Goundrey, 'Environmental Jurisdiction in Arctic Waters: The Extent of Article 234', 16 *University of British Columbia Law Review* 197 (1982); D. J. Bederman, 'High Stakes in the High Arctic: Jurisdiction and Compensation for Oil Pollution from Offshore Operations in the Beaufort Sea', 4 *Alaska Law Review* 37 (1987); D. Rothwell, 'The Arctic Environmental Protection Strategy and International Environmental Co-operation in the Far North', 6 *Yearbook of International Environmental Law* 65 (1995); R. J. Ansson, 'The North American Agreement on Environmental Protection and the Arctic Council Agreement: Will These Multinational Agreements Adequately Protect the Environment?', 29 *California Western International Law Journal* 101 (1998); O. R. Young, *Creating Regimes: Arctic Accords and International Governance* (1998); E. T. Bloom, 'Establishment of the Arctic Council', 93 AJIL 712 (1999).

Unlike the Antarctic area, the Arctic area is part of the sovereign land or marine territory of eight states: Canada, Denmark, Finland, Iceland, Norway, Sweden, Russia and the United States. Respective parts of the Arctic area which are under the jurisdiction of these states are subject to their international legal obligations, including those relating to environmental protection. Nevertheless, beginning in September 1989, on the initiative of Finland, these eight states began co-operation on measures to combat threats to the Arctic ecosystem which could not effectively be addressed by each acting alone. This resulted in the adoption of the Arctic Environmental Protection Strategy (AEPS) 'to ensure the protection of the Arctic environment and its sustainable and equitable development, while protecting the cultures of indigenous peoples'. Although not legally binding, the AEPS contains detailed commitments relating to objectives and principles, identifies problems and priorities for which actions are to be taken, and adopts measures for monitoring and assessment, the protection of the marine environment, emergency preparedness, and conservation of flora and fauna.

In 1996, the Arctic states established a high-level intergovernmental forum, the Arctic Council, to provide a mechanism for co-ordinating their activities in the region and to oversee and co-ordinate the programmes established under the AEPS.[120] Membership of the Council is restricted to the eight Arctic states. In addition, the Association of Indigenous Minorities of the North, Siberia and the Far East of the Russian Federation, the Inuit Circumpolar Conference, the Saami Council, the Aleutian International Association, the

---

[120] Declaration on the Establishment of the Arctic Council, Ottawa, 19 September 1996, reprinted in 35 ILM 1382 (1996).

Arctic Athabaskan Council and the Gwich'in Council International are granted status as 'permanent participants' in the Council.[121] There is also provision for non-Arctic states, global and regional intergovernmental and interparliamentary organisations and non-governmental organisations to be granted observer status.[122] The Council normally meets at the ministerial level biennially. The Chair and Secretariat of the Council rotates every two years among the members, beginning with Canada in 1996.[123]

AEPS

The objectives of the AEPS include: protection of the Arctic ecosystem; protection, enhancement and restoration of the environmental quality and sustainable utilisation of natural resources; recognition and accommodation of the needs, values and practices of indigenous peoples; reviewing the state of the Arctic environment; and identifying, reducing and, as a final goal, eliminating pollution.[124] Guiding principles to implement the AEPS include:

- conservation, sustainable utilisation and protection for the benefit of and enjoyment of present and future generations;
- consideration for the value and interdependent nature of ecosystem components;
- informed assessment of the possible impacts of activities on the environment, including cumulative impacts;
- maintaining ecological systems and biodiversity;
- respecting the relationship with global climate;
- taking into account scientific investigations and traditional knowledge;
- developing and sharing information and knowledge;
- developing a network of protected areas;
- promoting international co-operation; and
- ensuring mutual co-operation in fulfilling national and international responsibilities, including the use and transfer of and trade in effective and appropriate technology.[125]

An Arctic Plan, with specific commitments, has been adopted to address six serious environmental issues. With respect to persistent organic contaminants, the Arctic countries agree to: undertake co-operative monitoring and research; consider the feasibility of developing national inventories on production, use and emissions; develop proposals for international action under the 1979 LRTAP Convention, the 1974 Paris Convention and the 1974 Helsinki Convention; reduce or control the use of chlordane, DDT, toxaphene and PCBs; and establish priorities and timetables for a programme of emissions elimination.[126] To

---

[121] Para. 2.   [122] Para. 3.   [123] Paras. 4 and 5.
[124] AEPS, para. 2.1.   [125] Para. 2.2.   [126] Para 5.1.

prevent oil pollution, the Arctic countries agree to: co-operate in monitoring; consider establishing a reporting system on discharges and spills; take measures as soon as possible to adhere to 'the strictest relevant international standards within the conventions, to which the countries are parties, regarding discharges irrespective of origin'; and undertake joint action to strengthen recognition of the particularly sensitive character of ice-covered parts of the Arctic Ocean.[127] With regard to heavy metals, it is agreed to undertake a programme of co-ordinated monitoring and research and to implement measures to control conditions that allow the release of heavy metals, including the implementation of best available technology.[128] For noise, the Arctic countries agree to implement measures to avoid or mitigate the impact of noise on marine mammals, to improve their knowledge of the auditory function, communication and behaviour of marine mammals, and to determine the exposure of migrating stocks to noise.[129] With respect to radioactivity, the commitments are more general, and include little more than the development of common standards and techniques for monitoring and analysis, considering the development of more specific measures of co-operation to deal with emergencies, and the collation and exchange of data and information.[130] In the context of the radiation damage caused by the Chernobyl accident in 1986, and the evidence of illegal dumping in Arctic waters of nuclear-powered submarines and other radioactive material by the former USSR, these measures of the Strategy appear to be inadequate. Finally, in respect of oxidification, the AEPS calls for: research on the current loadings and potential effects of acid deposition; consideration to be given to expanding deposition monitoring programmes; defining critical loads and setting and meeting target loads for sensitive ecosystems; and reducing emissions of sulphur and nitrogen by the use of 'best available technology'.[131]

Programmes of general application are also established. The Arctic countries agreed: to develop an Arctic Monitoring and Assessment Programme (AMAP) to measure levels of anthropogenic pollutants and assess their effects;[132] to take preventive measures regarding marine pollution in the Arctic, including by applying the principles reflected in the 1982 UNCLOS, by taking measures as soon as possible to adhere to the strictest relevant international standards within the conventions to which they are parties, and by jointly supporting the development of mandatory standards to improve protection from accidental pollution;[133] and to adopt measures for emergency prevention, preparedness and response.[134] The measures envisaged for the protection of Arctic flora and fauna are more specific, recognising that the 1973 Polar Bears Agreement is the only agreement specifically adopted for the Arctic region. Apart from general

---

[127] Para. 5.2. The AEPS refers to the 1969 CLC, the 1969 Intervention Convention, the 1971 Oil Pollution Fund Convention, the 1972 London Convention, the 1974 Paris Convention, MARPOL 73/78, the 1982 UNCLOS and the 1990 Oil Pollution Preparedness Convention.

[128] Para. 5.3.   [129] Para 5.4.   [130] Para. 5.5.   [131] Para. 5.6.

[132] Para. 6.   [133] Para. 7.   [134] Para. 8.

co-operation the Arctic countries agree to: exchange information and experts; develop more effective laws, regulations and practices for the conservation of flora, fauna, diversity and their habitat; and propose strategies for enhanced conservation.[135]

In June 1997, following the submission of a report by AMAP on Arctic pollution issues, the Arctic Council agreed to a number of measures designed to increase efforts to limit and reduce the emissions of pollutants into the Arctic environment, and to promote international co-operation in order to reduce the identified pollution risks. In September 1998, the Arctic Council gave instructions for the development of an overall plan identifying actions to address the pollution sources identified by AMAP. The resulting Arctic Council Action Plan to Eliminate Pollution of the Arctic (ACAP) establishes a framework for co-operation and an accompanying Action Plan which is intended to evolve dynamically in response to changing priorities for action in the region.[136] During the first phase of the ACAP, priority is to be given to addressing the following sources of pollution: persistent organic pollutants; heavy metals; radioactivity; and depletion of the ozone layer.[137]

Conclusions

The Antarctic Treaty system has served 'as a microcosm for the evolution of international environmental law and policy', with environmental policies being put in place before there were 'environmentalists', and rules of a substantive, procedural and institutional nature being developed and put in place, on which other international agreements have frequently drawn.[138] The various treaties adopted under the Antarctic system have provided important precedents which have internationalised domestic techniques and have significantly expanded upon existing international techniques. The Antarctic regime reflects an incremental approach to environmental protection for a region which forms part of the global commons, although its precedential value extends also to areas which are indisputably subject to national jurisdiction. Examples of the significant contribution made by the Antarctic system relate to: decision-making by international organisations, including the broad range of conservation measures adopted under CCAMLR; expanded use of techniques for environmental impact assessment, monitoring and access to information; the participation of

---

[135] Para. 9.1.

[136] Arctic Council Action Plan to Eliminate Pollution of the Arctic, Barrow, October 2000.

[137] The Action Plan gives priority to actions that are complementary to existing action plans and actions under the Arctic Council such as the Regional Programme of Action for the Protection of the Arctic Marine Environment from Land-Based Activities, established in September 1998.

[138] L. Kimball, 'Environmental Law and Policy in Antarctica', in P. Sands (ed.), *Greening International Law* (1993), 122 at 138–9.

non-governmental organisations in the legal process; and the development of new approaches to liability, including for environmental damage, which link civil and state liability approaches. Many of the provisions on the enforcement of rules also introduce novel elements to international law. The challenge over the coming few years will be to increase the number of states which are party to the 1991 Antarctic Environment Protocol, and to develop the rules to make it work effectively, efficiently and equitably to protect the Antarctic environment. Since the Protocol does not incorporate all of the procedural and institutional innovations of the 1988 CRAMRA, further work is needed to develop such rules, including those on liability, information and enforcement. In the meantime, the challenges facing the regime will include, increasingly, its decision-making authority and its relationship with other regimes, such as CITES and fisheries.

The adoption of the Arctic Environmental Protection Strategy and the establishment of the Arctic Council provide a useful opportunity to develop new legal arrangements and institutions to govern an ecosystem which transcends national boundaries and requires international co-operation for its adequate protection to be assured. The soft law approach currently envisaged provides a first step; ultimately, it will be necessary to establish appropriate institutional arrangements and substantive rules, perhaps similar to those applied in the Antarctic, to ensure that agreed obligations are respected and enforced.

15

European Community environmental law

Introduction

E. Rehbinder and R. Stewart, *Environmental Protection Policy* (1985); J. Charpentier (ed.), *La Protection de l'environnement par les Communautés Européennes* (1988); S. P. Johnson and G. Corcelle, *The Environmental Policy of the European Communities* (1989); E. Haagsma, 'The European Community's Environmental Policy: A Case Study in Federalism', 12 *Fordham International Law Journal* 311 (1989); R. B. Stewart, 'Environmental Law in the United States and the European Community: Spillovers, Co-operation, Rivalry, Institutions', 1992 *University of Chicago Legal Forum* 41; R. Wagenbaur, 'Regulating the European Environment: The EC Experience', 1992 *University of Chicago Legal Forum* 17; M. Wheeler, 'Greening the EEC Treaty', in P. Sands (ed.), *Greening International Law* (1993), 85; G. Bennett, *Conserving Europe's Natural Heritage* (1994); S. Johnson and G. Corcelle, *The Environmental Policy of the European Communities* (1995); S. Ercmann, *Pollution Control in the European Community* (1996); J. Holder (ed.), *The Impact of EC Environmental Law in the United Kingdom* (1997); A. Kiss and D. Shelton, *Manual of European Environmental Law* (1997, 2nd edn); J. Scott, *EC Environmental Law* (1998); R. Revesz, 'Environmental Regulation in Federal Systems', 1 *Yearbook of European Environmental Law* 1 (2000); J. Jans, *European Environmental Law* (2000, 2nd edn); L. Krämer, *EC Environmental Law* (2000, 4th edn); L. Krämer, *Casebook on EU Environmental Law* (2002).

On EC law generally see T. C. Hartley, *Foundations of European Community Law* (1998, 4th edn); *Wyatt and Dashwood's European Union Law* (2000, 4th edn); P. Craig and G. de Burca, *EU Law: Text, Cases and Materials* (2002, 2nd edn).

The EC has the most extensive developed body of regional rules of international environmental law, with practical experience of developing and applying principles and rules which set standards, implement procedures and operate institutional arrangements. The experience includes the integration of environmental considerations into economic obligations, particularly in relation to the rules governing trade, competition, subsidies and intellectual property rights. EC environmental law is currently applicable to the fifteen member states. The 1992 European Economic Area (EEA) Agreement extends EC environmental rules to the three EFTA countries that are not EC members.[1] The Europe Agreements between the EC and central and eastern European states and the Association Agreements with Cyprus and Malta have led to the transposition of EC environmental rules into domestic law in preparation for membership of the EC which is due to take place from 1 May 2004.

In this context, it is appropriate to consider the relevance for international environmental law of developments in the EC. The rules of EC environmental law constitute a regional regime of international environmental law: they currently bind fifteen states, and after 1 May 2004 they will apply directly to twenty-five European states. EC rules also provide a possible model for other regions, including those which are establishing free trade arrangements (such as the NAFTA, the African Economic Community and the Free Trade Agreement of the Americas) as well as the Caribbean and the South Pacific regions which are committed to developing their regional environmental laws. Although the EC member states are relatively homogenous, many of the problems faced by the international community as a whole also exist in the EC, such as economic disparities (the North–South issue) and legal and political differences on the adoption, implementation and interpretation of international rules. Moreover, the EC is itself an actor in international environmental law-making, and is party to more than thirty regional and global environmental agreements.[2] The active role played by the EC in the negotiations leading to the adoption of these instruments, within the framework of its competence, has required changes to the processes of international law-making and enforcement that may enable other regional groupings to participate more effectively in international fora.[3] Finally, the integration of EC environmental law into economic arrangements

---

[1] See p. 747 below.

[2] On early developments, see J. Temple Lang, 'The Ozone Layer Convention: A New Solution to the Question of Community Participation in "Mixed" International Agreements', 23 *Common Market Law Review* 157 (1986); A. Nollkaemper, 'The European Community and International Environmental Co-operation: The Legal Aspects of External Community Powers', 2 *Legal Issues of European Integration* 55 (1987); A. Kiss and M. Brusasco-MacKenzie, 'Les Relations exterieures des Communautés Européennes en matière du protection de l'environnement', 35 AFDI 702 (1989); P. Demaret, 'Trade-Related Environmental Measures (TREMs) in the External Relations of the European Community', in M. Marescea (ed.), *The European Community's Commercial Policy after 1992* (1992), 285; N. Haigh, 'The European Community and International Environmental Policy', in A. Hurrell and B. Kingsbury (eds.), *The International Politics of the Environment: Actors, Institutions and Interests* (1992), 228.

[3] See e.g. the 1991 Espoo Convention (chapter 16, pp. 814–17 below), which expressly provides for: the participation of regional economic integration organisations (Arts. 16 and 17(1)); the allocation of responsibilities between each organisation and its respective member states (Art. 17(4)); and special voting rules for those occasions in which regional integration organisations participate at the same time as some, or all, of their members (Art. 18(2)).

illustrates many of the legal difficulties which arise in the integration of environmental and economic concerns.

Like international environmental law, the rules of EC environmental law fall to be considered in the context of the EC's overall legal and political structure. Although EC law is a part of the old order of public international law from which it grew,[4] it is also a specialised legal order of international law, rather like the European Convention on Human Rights' regional human rights law,[5] and similar to the special order of rules of international law applied by international administrative tribunals.[6]

The EC legal order is innovative and has shifted the 'goalposts' of traditional international law. It has changed perceptions of how international law can work as a dynamic and effective force: by expanding the formal membership of the legal community to which it applies directly beyond states to include companies, environmental groups and associations, granting to them rights that they can enforce before national courts as well as the ECJ;[7] by applying the doctrines of direct effect, supremacy and implied powers; by creating mechanisms for international enforcement; and by instituting a decision-making process based on qualified majority, rather than unanimous, voting. While each of these doctrines existed under traditional international law, the EC legal system has expanded their application.

Sources and institutions

The European Communities were established by three separate treaties. The European Coal and Steel Community (ECSC) was originally established by representatives of France, Germany, Italy, Belgium, Holland and Luxembourg,[8] with the primary objective of creating a common market for coal and steel. In 1957, the same six states signed two further treaties establishing the European Community of Atomic Energy (EURATOM),[9] to develop and distribute nuclear energy within the Community, and the European Economic Community (EEC).[10]

---

[4] The ECJ has called the Community 'a new legal order of international law': Case 26/62, *Van Gend and Loos* [1963] ECR 3.

[5] Chapter 7, pp. 291–4 above.

[6] See *De Merode* v. *World Bank*, WBAT Rep., Decision No. 1, at 12–13 (1981) ('the Tribunal, which is an international tribunal, considers that its task is to decide internal disputes between the Bank and its staff within the organised legal system of the World Bank and that it must apply the internal law of the Bank as the law governing the conditions of employment').

[7] Chapter 5, pp. 222–5 above; and chapter 18, pp. 926–30 below.

[8] Treaty Establishing the European Coal and Steel Community, 18 April 1951, 261 UNTS 140.

[9] Treaty Establishing the European Atomic Energy Community, 25 March 1957, in force 1 January 1958, 298 UNTS 167; see below.

[10] Treaty Establishing the European Economic Community, Rome, 25 March 1957, in force 1 January 1958 298 UNTS 267.

Currently, the EEC and the other two communities have fifteen members: the original six, and the United Kingdom, Denmark, Ireland,[11] Greece,[12] Spain, Portugal[13] and most recently Sweden, Austria and Finland.[14] Besides Turkey (which has been accepted as a candidate country but has not been accepted into negotiations), accession negotiations commenced with Hungary, Poland, Estonia, the Czech Republic, Slovenia and Cyprus in March 1998. In October 1999, the Commission recommended member states to open negotiations with Romania, the Slovak Republic, Latvia, Lithuania, Bulgaria and Malta. In 2002, the EC members agreed that all these states (except Bulgaria and Romania) could join from 1 May 2004, as reflected in the Nice Treaty, thus bringing EC membership to twenty-five states.[15]

The EEC's original objectives were the establishment of a common market and the progressive approximation of the economic policies of the member states, to be achieved by adherence to four fundamental principles, which remain applicable:[16] (1) the free movement of goods between the member states;[17] (2) a common agricultural policy;[18] (3) the free movement of persons,[19] services[20] and capital based on the right of establishment and the principle of non-discrimination;[21] and (4) a common transport policy.[22] These foundations were supplemented by a number of policies (which did not originally include an environmental policy) including in relation to competition[23] and state aids granted by member states which distort or threaten to distort competition.[24] While the EC does not at present have the objective of creating a uniform system of taxation among the member states, it prohibits the imposition

---

[11] Acceded to membership on 1 January 1973.

[12] Acceded to membership on 1 January 1981.

[13] Acceded to membership on 1 January 1986.

[14] Acceded to membership on 1 January 1995. A referendum in Norway resulted in a vote against membership.

[15] Conclusions of the EU Council, 12–13 December 2002; Treaty of Nice, OJ C80, 10 March 2001, 1. Negotiations with Bulgaria and Romania will continue, and accession negotiations with Turkey could begin after December 2004.

[16] The EC Treaty has been amended, and the 1997 Treaty of Amsterdam (2 October 1997) renumbered the Articles of the 1957 EEC Treaty; old Article numbers are indicated in brackets after the new ones. A consolidated version of the Treaty on European Union is at OJ C340, 10 November 1997, 145–72; a consolidated version of the EC Treaty is at OJ C340, 10 November 1997, 173–308.

[17] EC Treaty, as amended, Arts. 23–31 (formerly Arts. 9–37); see further chapter 19, pp. 985–7 below.

[18] Arts. 32–38 (formerly Arts. 38–47).   [19] Arts. 39–42 (formerly Arts. 48–51).

[20] Arts. 49–55 (formerly Arts. 59–66).

[21] Arts. 43–48 and 56–69 (formerly Arts. 52–58 and 67–73).

[22] Arts. 70–80 (formerly Arts. 74–84).

[23] Arts. 3(8) and 81–86 (formerly Arts. 3(f) and 85–90); chapter 19, pp. 985–97 below.

[24] Arts. 87–89 (formerly Arts. 92–94); chapter 19, pp. 985–97 below.

of taxes which might prevent the free movement of goods.[25] The 1957 Treaty left to each member state the direction of its national economic policy, subject to an obligation to pursue policies which would ensure an equilibrium of over-all balance of payments and the maintenance of confidence in the currency, high levels of employment and stable prices. Such economic policies are stated, however, to be of common concern.[26] The EEC also had a common commercial policy, on the basis of uniform principles in tariff rates, the conclusion of tariff and trade agreements, export policy, and the protection of trade.[27] By a 1965 Merger Treaty, the separate institutions of the ECSC, EURATOM and the EEC were merged.[28]

The principal EC institutions are the Commission, the Council, the Parliament (formerly known as the Assembly), the European Court of Justice (ECJ) (including the Court of First Instance (CFI)) and the Court of Auditors.[29] The Commission, based in Brussels, is composed of twenty Commissioners 'chosen on the grounds of their general competence and whose independence is beyond doubt'.[30] The Commissioners hold office for five years, having been chosen by mutual agreement between the members,[31] and they have under their direction some thirty Directorates, encompassing the executive arms of the EC. The Commission is the EC's civil service, the body which represents the interests of the EC. It has been described as 'an initiator and co-ordinator of Community policy; it is the executive agency of the Communities; it is the guardian of the Community Treaties'.[32] The Commission's functions include proposing environmental and other legislation and ensuring that the environmental and other provisions of the EC Treaty and secondary legislation are applied,[33] including where necessary taking cases to the ECJ. The Environment Directorate General (formerly known as Directorate General XI) of the EC Commission is responsible for the environment.

The Council is composed of one representative from each member state. The particular minister attending from each member state will vary depending on the subject matter to be discussed and the decisions to be made. Meetings of the Council of Ministers occur periodically in one of the member states.

---

[25] Arts. 90–92 (formerly Arts. 95–98).   [26] Arts. 99–111 (formerly Arts. 103–109).

[27] Arts. 131–135 (formerly Arts. 110–116).

[28] Treaty Establishing a Single Council and a Single Commission of the European Communities, 8 April 1965, 4 ILM 776 (1965).

[29] 1997 Amsterdam Treaty, Art. 7 (formerly Art. 4).

[30] 1965 EC Merger Treaty, Art. 10. By the Treaty of Nice, from 2005 the Commission will be composed of one commissioner per member state; and once the EU Reaches twenty-seven member states there will be fewer Commissioners than there are member states.

[31] The Treaty of Nice also provides for changes to the procedure to nominate the members of the Commission. From 2004, the nomination will be voted by a qualified majority.

[32] D. Lasok and J. Bridge, *An Introduction to the Law and Institutions of the European Economic Communities* (1976, 2nd edn), 112.

[33] Art. 211 (formerly Art. 155).

The actual powers of the Council vary with each Treaty, 'but in effect the Council expresses the political will of the members and exercises a legislative or regulatory function'.[34] Environmental issues are generally addressed by the Environment Council (ministers responsible in each member state for the environment portfolio), although increasingly environmental issues are also addressed by ministers for trade, finance and energy. Environment ministers meet at least twice a year.

The European Parliament is the parliamentary organ for the three Communities. It comprises 626 members elected by direct universal suffrage and meets in Brussels or Strasbourg.[35] After the reforms adopted in 1997, the Parliament has three main roles: it exercises democratic control over all the Community institutions, in particular the Commission; it shares legislative power with the Council; and it plays a decisive role in the adoption of the budget.

The ECJ and the CFI sit in Luxembourg. Each has fifteen judges and, in the case of the ECJ, eight Advocates General.[36] The ECJ's primary function is to ensure respect for the rule of law in the application and interpretation of the Treaties and of acts made by the EC institutions.

The sources of EC law comprise the Treaties, general principles of law, international obligations binding upon the EC, and secondary legislation. Secondary legislation is adopted under the EC Treaty, which provides in Article 249 (formerly Article 189) that:

> in order to carry out their task and in accordance with the provisions of this Treaty, the European Parliament acting jointly with the Council, the Council and the Commission shall make regulations and issue directives, take decisions, make recommendations or deliver opinions.

While recommendations and opinions have no binding force *per se*, much of the secondary legislation (Regulations, Directives and Decisions) creates rights and obligations which can, in certain circumstances, be relied upon by legal and natural persons before the courts of the member states, known as 'direct effect'.[37] Moreover, in the event of a conflict between a rule of EC law and

---

[34] P. Sands and P. Klein, *Bowett's Law of International Institutions* (2001, 5th edn), 180.

[35] By the Treaty of Nice, the maximum number of European Members of Parliament will be set at 732 (currently 700), and the number of seats allocated to the existing fifteen members will be reduced from 626 to 535.

[36] See chapter 5, p. 224 above. With the Treaty of Nice, the ECJ will continue to be composed of one judge from each member state, and the CFI will have at least one judge from each member state.

[37] See e.g. Case 26/62, *Van Gend and Loos*. In Case C-72/95, *Kraaijeveld* [1996] ECR I-5403, the Court held that, where a Directive has no direct effect and entails discretionary action by the national authority, national courts can act only *ex post* by evaluating the action and its conformity with the procedural rules imposed by the relevant Directives. See also Case C-236/92, *Comitato di Difesa della cava* [1994] ECR I-483, and Case C-168/95, *Arcaro* [1996] ECR I-4705, where the ECJ refused to apply the doctrine of direct effect in favour of a state in a criminal procedure against a polluter.

a rule of national law, EC law will prevail.[38] The failure of member states to implement all their EC environmental obligations has led the Commission to exercise its enforcement with great regularity, and since 1985 the ECJ has heard a large number of cases concerning the non-implementation by member states of their environmental obligations.[39]

The ECJ derives its jurisdiction from each of the Treaties. Cases reach the ECJ in a variety of ways. The ECJ is empowered to give preliminary rulings on references from national courts of the member states on the interpretation of the EC Treaty, and on the validity and interpretation of environmental and other acts of the institutions.[40] The CFI and the ECJ may also review the legality of the acts adopted jointly by the Parliament and Council, the Council and Commission's binding acts, or failures to act, in actions brought by member states, the Council and the Commission and, subject to the rules on standing, by legal or natural persons.[41] The ECJ may also decide matters brought by the Commission or a member state against a member state which is alleged to be failing to fulfil an obligation under the Treaty[42] and hear matters alleging the non-contractual liability of the EC.[43] The ECJ's jurisprudence has contributed greatly to the development of a coherent and effective legal system, and has extended the powers of the Community and the influence of EC law into the legal systems of the member states.[44] As this chapter indicates, the ECJ and

---

[38] On the supremacy of Community law, see Case 106/77, *Simmenthal* [1978] ECR 629, paras. 17 and 18. In two recent decisions, the ECJ has extended the effect of Directives beyond the limit of direct effect. See Case C-287/98, *Luxembourg* v. *Berthe Linster EA* [2000] ECR I-6917, and Case C-443/98, *Unilever* [2000] ECR I-7535, where the Court held that national courts may take under consideration Directives imposing procedural requirements on state authorities or otherwise imposing vague, undefined obligations which need to be specified by regulatory actions of state authorities. Those procedural or undefined provisions can be taken under consideration for the limited purpose of assessing the action of the national administrative bodies and their consistency with the Directives. Pursuant to the principle of supremacy of EU law, where found inconsistent with a Directive lacking direct effect, the national measures/regulations will be disapplied by the national courts. However, in Case C-129/96, *Inter-Environment Wallonie* [1997] ECR I-7411, the Court stated that, where the member state has failed to transpose the Directive or has issued conflicting national rules before the expiration date for transposing the Directive, national courts cannot apply the Directive, either as directly effective, or as a parameter for assessing the acts of national authorities.

[39] On enforcement and the role of the ECJ, see chapter 5, pp. 222–4 above.

[40] 1997 Amsterdam Treaty, Art. 234 (formerly Art. 177).

[41] Arts. 230–232 (formerly Arts. 173–175).

[42] Arts. 226–227 (formerly Arts. 169–170); see further chapter 5, pp. 222–4 above.

[43] Arts. 235 and 288 (formerly Arts. 178 and 215).

[44] P. Sands, 'European Community Environmental Law: Legislation, the European Court of Justice and Common-Interest Groups', 53 MLR 685 (1990); R. Wagenbaur, 'The European Community's Policy on Implementation of Environmental Directives', 14 *Fordham International Law Journal* 455 (1990); L. Krämer, 'The Implementation of Environmental Laws by the European Economic Communities', 34 *German Yearbook of International Law* 9 (1991); R. Macrory, 'The Enforcement of Community Environmental Law: Some Critical

CFI have also contributed materially to the development of environmental jurisprudence.

In 1986, the EEC Treaty was amended by the Single European Act (1986 SEA) which committed the Community to 'concrete progress towards European unity' by taking measures to establish an 'internal market' by 31 December 1992 which would remove the remaining physical, technical and fiscal barriers to trade.[45] The SEA introduced important institutional changes, including the creation of a Court of First Instance and a 'co-operation' procedure giving the European Parliament greater influence in the legislative process.[46] The SEA also introduced qualified majority voting under the then new Article 100a for internal market measures, removing the power of the veto, and making use of the new co-operation procedure. It also added, for the first time, express provisions on environmental protection. In 1992, the Maastricht Treaty on European Union adopted further institutional and environmental amendments.[47] For the first time, the term 'environment' was referred to in Articles 2 and 3 of the Treaty among the objectives and activities of the European Union. This was followed by the adoption of the Treaty of Amsterdam in 1997 which enshrines the principle of sustainable development as one of the European Communities' aims, together with integrating environmental requirements into community policies and activities. The 2001 Nice Treaty, which came into force on 1 February 2003, introduces institutional and procedural reforms, but does not amend the susbtantive environmental rules of the EC.[48]

European Environment Agency

In 1990, the EC created the European Environment Agency,[49] and it became operational in 1994. The Agency provides the EC and the member states with information at the European level to enable environmental protection measures to be taken, to assess the results of such measures, and to ensure that the public

Remarks', 20 *Common Market Law Review* 347 (1992); European Commission, Communication on Implementing Community Environmental Law, COM (96) 0500; R. Macrory and R. Purdy, 'Enforcement of EC Environmental Law Against Member States', in J. Holder (ed.), *Impact of EC Environmental Law in the UK* (1997); L. Borzsak, 'Punishing Member States or Influencing Their Behaviour or Iudex (Non) Calculate?', 13 JEL 244 (2001).

[45] Single European Act, 17 February 1986, in force 1 July 1987, 25 ILM 503 (1986), Arts. 1(1) and 13.

[46] *Ibid.*, Arts. 6, 8 and 11.   [47] See pp. 745–6 below.

[48] Treaty of Nice Amending the Treaty on European Union, the Treaties Establishing the European Communities and Certain Related Acts, Nice, 26 February 2001, OJ C80, 10 March 2001, 12. On the amendments to the political institutions of the EU made by the Treaty of Nice, see René Barents, 'Some Observations on the Treaty of Nice', 8 *Maastricht Journal of European and Comparative Law* 121 at 124 (2001).

[49] Council Regulation (EEC) No. 1210/90, OJ L120, 11 May 1990, 1, amended by Council Regulation (EC) No. 933/1999, OJ L117, 5 May 1999, 1; D. A. Westbrook, 'Environmental Policy in the European Community: Observations on the European Environment Agency', 15 *Harvard Environmental Law Review* 257 (1991).

is properly informed.[50] The Agency is an autonomous entity having separate legal personality, and is run by a management board, an Executive Director and a scientific committee.[51]

The Agency's principal task is to monitor, gather information, establish the European environment information and observation network,[52] provide the EC and member states with objective information, and record, collate and assess data on the state of the environment.[53] Additionally, the Agency seeks to: ensure that environmental data at the European level are comparable; provide European environmental information to international bodies; ensure broad dissemination of reliable information (including a tri-annual report on the state of the environment); and stimulate the development of environmental forecasting techniques and methods for assessing environmental costs.[54] The Agency's assessment functions relate to the pressures on and quality and sensitivity of the environment including placing these in the context of sustainable development, and address priority areas, including 'transfrontier, plurinational and global phenomena' and the socio-economic dimension.[55] Subject to certain conditions, the Agency may publish information and make it available to the public.[56] It is open to countries which are not members of the EC,[57] and may be a model for international environmental monitoring arrangements in other regions and globally.[58]

Historical development[59]

EC environmental law has developed over five distinct periods: the first is from 1957 to 1972, prior to the Stockholm Conference. The second runs from 1973 to 1986, prior to the SEA amendments to the 1957 EEC Treaty. The third period

---

[50] Art. 1.   [51] Arts. 7 to 10.

[52] The European environment information and observation network comprises the main component elements of national information networks, national focal points and topic centres: Art. 4(1).

[53] Art. 2(i)–(iii).   [54] Art. 2(iv)–(viii).

[55] Art. 3(1) and (2). The priority areas are air and water quality, soil, fauna and flora, biotopes, land use and natural resources, waste management, noise emissions, hazardous chemicals and coastal protection.

[56] Art. 6.

[57] In June 2001, Hungary, Poland, Estonia, the Czech Republic, Slovenia, Cyprus, Romania, the Slovak Republic, Latvia, Lithuania, Bulgaria, Turkey and Malta concluded Agreements with the EC concerning their participation in the European Environment Agency and the European environment information and observation network.

[58] Art. 19.

[59] P. Sands, 'European Community Environmental Law: The Emergence of a Regional Regime of International Environmental Protection', 100 *Yale Law Journal* 2511 (1991); D. McGillivray and J. Holder, 'Locating EC Environmental Law', 20 *Yearbook of European Law* 139 (2001); L. Krämer, '30 Years of European Environmental Law', 2 *Yearbook of European Environmental Law* 155 (2002).

covers 1987 to 31 October 1993. A fourth period began with the entry into force on 1 November 1993 of the amendments introduced by the 1992 Maastricht Treaty until May 1999. The fifth and current phase began with the entry into force of the 1997 Treaty of Amsterdam, in May 1999.

Until 1986, the EEC Treaty had no express provisions on environmental protection, although this did not prevent the EC from adopting legislation on environmental matters. During the first two periods, until 1986, two EEC Treaty provisions were utilised: Article 100 (now Article 94), which empowers the EC Council to issue Directives to harmonise such laws, regulations or administrative actions in member states 'as directly affect the establishment or functioning of the common market'; and Article 235 (now Article 308) which empowers the EC Council to adopt measures which are necessary to attain 'one of the objectives of the Community' and for which the Treaty has not provided the necessary powers. In 1967, with the adoption of a Directive on the classification, packaging and labelling of dangerous substances,[60] the EC began to address environmental issues. In 1970, the EC Commission declared the necessity of drawing up a Community Action Programme on the Environment, and the following year adopted a formal communication on the matter.[61] The 1972 Stockholm Conference was a major catalyst for the development of EC environmental law, which is one of the most tangible outcomes of the Stockholm Conference. A Declaration on the Environment was adopted by the heads of state and governments of the then nine EC member states in October 1972. The following year, the first EC Action Programme on the Environment was adopted, and three further Action Programmes on the Environment were adopted in the period to 1987.[62]

By July 1987, when the SEA amendments to the EEC Treaty came into effect, the EC had adopted more than 150 Regulations, Directives and Decisions on the environment, and had prepared its fourth Action Programme on the Environment. Between 1973 and 1987, an extensive body of substantive environmental rules had been adopted on water, air, noise, the management of waste and hazardous substances, and the protection of flora, fauna and the countryside. The EC had also introduced a number of important environmental protection procedures, including the first example of international legislation on environmental impact assessment. Four environmental research programmes had been adopted, together with scientific and technical co-operation agreements with third countries, a fund for EC environmental action, and a Recommendation

---

[60] Council Directive 67/548/EEC, OJ L196, 16 August 1967, 1, as amended; chapter 12, pp. 620 and 626 above.

[61] Commission SEC (71) 2616 final (22 July 1971).

[62] First Programme (1973–6), OJ C112, 20 December 1973, 1; Second Programme (1977–81), OJ C399, 13 June 1977, 1; Third Programme (1982–6), OJ C46, 17 February 1983, 1; Fourth Programme (1987–92), OJ C328, 7 December 1987, 1.

on the polluter-pays principle.[63] The EC had also become a party to a number of environmental treaties during this period,[64] and its approach to the development of regional rules of environmental protection began to attract attention in other regions. In 1980, the ECJ confirmed the legality of using Article 100 (now Article 94) to legislate on environmental matters.[65]

EC environmental law during this period was legally premised on the justification that it removed non-tariff barriers to intra-Community trade by harmonising the national environmental laws of the member states.[66] It was therefore based on the original intent of the EEC Treaty to regulate trade and competition, and did not develop from the desire to regulate environmental protection as an end in itself. By 1985, however, with a large body of EC environmental rules already adopted, the ECJ ruled that, even in the absence of express reference in the EEC Treaty, the protection of the environment was one of the Community's 'essential objectives' and that it justified certain limitations on the principle of free movement of goods, although the ECJ stressed that these limitations must not 'go beyond the inevitable restrictions which are justified by the pursuit of the objective of environmental protection'.[67] The 1986 SEA amendments formalised environmental protection as an EC objective.

Single European Act (1986)[68]

The changes introduced by the SEA added to the momentum of an area of EC law and policy which was still relatively discrete and self-contained. The SEA transformed an extensive but marginal body of environmental policy and law into one of central and growing importance, bringing environmental considerations to bear on areas which were previously beyond the bounds of environmental legislation, including corporations, tax, financial services, broadcasting and civil procedure. Article 25 of the 1986 SEA added a new Title VII on 'Environment' to the EEC Treaty, consisting of Articles 130r, 130s and 130t

---

[63] Chapter 6, pp. 279–85 above.

[64] The first environmental treaty to which the EC became a party was the 1974 Paris Convention (see chapter 9, pp. 430–4 above): Council Decision 75/437/EEC, OJ L194, 25 July 1975, 5.

[65] Cases 91 and 92/79, *Commission of the European Communities* v. *Italian Republic* [1980] ECR 1099 and 1115.

[66] Council Directive 80/778/EEC, OJ L229, 30 August 1980, 11 (relating to quality of water intended for human consumption) which provides in the Preamble that a 'disparity between provisions . . . in the various Member States relating to the quality of water for human consumption may create differences in the conditions of competition and, as a result, directly affect the operation of the common market'.

[67] Case 240/83, *Procureur de la République* v. *Association de Défense des Bruleurs d'Huiles Usagées* [1985] ECR 531 at 549.

[68] L. Krämer, 'The Single European Act and Environment Protection: Reflections on Several New Provisions in Community Law', 24 *Common Market Law Review* 659 (1987); D. Vandermeersch, 'The Single European Act and the Environmental Policy of the European Economic Community', 12 *European Law Review* (1987).

(now Articles 174–176). It went beyond the codification of existing environmental law, and established a firm legal basis for its future development, in effect bringing the whole of the EC's economic activities within the potential scope of environmental law-making. Article 130r(1) (now Article 174(1)) provided that EC action related to the environment must have the following objectives:

1. to preserve, protect and improve the quality of the environment;
2. to contribute towards protecting human health; and
3. to ensure a prudent and rational utilisation of natural resources.

As amended, the EEC Treaty also provided that EC action was to be preventive, that environmental damage should as a priority be rectified at source, that the polluter should pay for damage, and that environmental protection should be a component of other EC policies.[69] The EEC Treaty now expressly provided that the EC could participate in international environmental agreements.[70] Under Article 130r(3) (now Article 174(3)), environmental action had to take account of: available scientific and technical data; environmental conditions in the Community as a whole; potential benefits and costs of action or lack of action; and the economic and sound development of the Community as a whole and the balanced development of its regions. Former Article 130r(4) (now Article 174(4)) established the principle of 'subsidiarity', requiring action to be taken at the Community level only when objectives could be better obtained than at the level of individual member states. Environmental actions taken under Article 130r (now Article 174) were to be taken by the EC Council acting unanimously, unless otherwise agreed by the Council.[71] Significantly, where measures are taken under Title VII (now Title XIX), member states could maintain or introduce 'more stringent protective measures compatible with this Treaty'.[72]

On the basis of these amendments, since 1987 environmental legislation in the EC has become increasingly broad in its scope and ambitious in its intent: the EC adopted legislation prohibiting television advertisements which encouraged behaviour prejudicial to the protection of the environment,[73] on eco-labelling[74] and on environmental audits.[75] New legislation was proposed on, *inter alia*, civil liability for damage caused by waste,[76] and on an energy/carbon tax.[77]

---

[69] Art. 174(2) (formerly Art. 130r(2)).   [70] Art. 174(4)(ii) (formerly Art. 130r(5)).

[71] Art. 175 (formerly Art. 130s); see W. Wils, 'Subsidiarity and EC Environmental Policy: Taking People's Concerns Seriously', 6 JEL 85 (1994).

[72] Art. 176 (formerly Art. 130t). This formulation left open the question of which measures would be compatible with the EEC Treaty, leaving the matter to be decided in the event of a dispute by the ECJ.

[73] Council Directive 89/552/EEC, OJ L298, 17 October 1989, 23, at Art. 12(e).

[74] Chapter 17, pp. 860–2 below.   [75] Chapter 17, pp. 865–6 below.

[76] Proposal for a Council Directive on Civil Liability for Damage Caused by Waste, COM (89) 282 final, OJ C251, 4 October 1989, 3; Amended Proposal, COM (91) 219 final, OJ C192, 23 July 1991, 6; see chapter 18, pp. 926–30 below.

[77] Chapter 4, p. 161 above.

Under the SEA, the EC adopted legislation creating the European Environment Agency and adopted a Directive on access to information on the environment.[78] It also began work to study the harmonisation of citizen suit provisions in member states' environmental laws. Under Article 130s (now Article 175), the EC established its first financial instrument dedicated to environmental matters (LIFE).[79]

However, even after the SEA came into force, environmental law-making under Title VII required the unanimous support of all member states, resulting in protracted negotiations and watered-down provisions. As the Commission, with the support of the Parliament, proposed increasingly ambitious legislation, particularly in relation to enforcement measures, the legislative process slowed down as certain member states sought to limit or prevent the adoption of new rules. The SEA's new Article 100a (now Article 95) in the EEC Treaty provided a means to overcome this institutional foot-dragging. For measures 'which have as their object the establishment and functioning of the internal market', Article 100a(1) allowed qualified majority voting, rather than unanimous voting. Furthermore, it required environmental measures to take as a base a high level of environmental protection.[80] These two provisions in Article 100a created the opportunity for environmental legislation to be adopted by qualified majority voting, by-passing the requirement of unanimity.[81] In the context of the right of states to exercise the veto under Article 130s (now Article 175), it was not surprising that the EC Commission proposed environmental legislation on the basis of Article 100a, which is primarily concerned with removing barriers to trade, rather than Article 130.

In 1989, the EC Commission commenced a legal action against the EC Council, challenging its use of Article 130s (now Article 175) of the EEC Treaty as the legal basis for the adoption of a Directive on titanium dioxide waste, rather than Article 100a (now Article 95) as originally proposed by the Commission and supported by the Parliament.[82] The ECJ found in favour of the Commission and declared the Directive to be void.[83] The Court considered that the goal and content of the Directive pursued the double objective of environmental protection and improvement of competition, but that reliance on the double legal

---

[78] Chapter 17, pp. 854–6 below.   [79] Chapter 20, pp. 1036–7 below.

[80] Art. 100a(3) (now Art. 95(3)).

[81] Art. 100a also allows a member state to adopt national provisions for environmental protection which are more stringent than the Community's harmonisation measures as long as the member state can demonstrate a major need referred to in Art. 36: Art. 100a(4). Art. 100a(5) allows harmonisation measures to include a safeguard clause authorising the member states to take provisional measures for one or more of the non-economic reasons referred to in Art. 36, subject to a Community control procedure.

[82] Council Directive 89/428/EEC, OJ L201, 14 July 1989, 56.

[83] Case C-300/89, *EC Commission* v. *Council* [1991] ECR I-2687.

base of Articles 100a and 130s was excluded because it would defeat the purpose of ensuring the use of the co-operation procedure to strengthen the participation of the European Parliament in the legislative process. The Court justified reliance on Article 100a rather than on Article 130s on three grounds: first, Article 130r(2) provided that environmental protection was to be a component of the Community's other policies, which implied that a Community measure did not have to be based on Article 130s solely because it pursued environmental aims; secondly, that this environmental protection measure affected conditions of production in a given industry with the aim of eliminating distortions of competition and came within Article 100a; and, thirdly, the requirements under Article 100a(3) that proposals take as a base a high level of environmental protection indicated that the objectives of environmental protection of Article 130r could be effectively pursued by means of a harmonisation measure adopted under Article 100a. The judgment opened the door to the Commission's increased use of Article 100a. However, in March 1993 the ECJ appeared to reverse itself, holding that the Council had been justified in basing Directive 91/156 on waste on Article 130s, and rejecting the Commission's arguments favouring the use of Article 100a.[84] By then, however, the Maastricht Treaty had introduced qualified majority voting for many environmental matters.

Maastricht Treaty on European Union (1992)[85]

In February 1992, the then twelve EC member states signed the Treaty on European Union (1992 Maastricht Treaty) which introduced further amendments to the EEC Treaty, including the provisions on environment, with the objective of establishing European Monetary and Political Union.[86] The Maastricht Treaty establishes a *European Community*, which had as its objectives, by establishing a common market and monetary union and by implementing common policies and activities:

> to promote throughout the Community a harmonious and balanced development of economic activities, sustainable and non-inflationary growth respecting the environment, a high degree of convergence of economic performance, a high level of employment and of social protection, the raising of

---

[84] Case C-155/91, *EC Commission* v. *Council* [1993] ECR I-939.

[85] D. Wilkinson, 'Maastricht and the Environment: The Implications for the EC's Environment Policy of the Treaty on European Union', 4 JEL 222 (1992); M. Hession and R. Macrory, 'Maastricht and the Environmental Policy of the Community: Legal Issues of a New Environment Policy', in D. O'Keeffe and P. Twomey, *Legal Issues of the Maastricht Treaty* (1994), 151–70.

[86] 7 February 1992, in force 1 November 1993, 31 ILM 247 (1992).

the standard of living and quality of life, and economic and social cohesion and solidarity among member states.[87]

The Maastricht Treaty thus elevated environmental protection to one of the fundamental objectives of the Community.

The environmental provisions of the EEC Treaty (introduced by the 1986 SEA) were amended by the Maastricht Treaty. Under the old Article 130r(1), Community policy was to promote international measures to deal with regional or worldwide environmental problems, and under the old Article 130r(2) environmental policy was to aim at 'a high level of protection taking into account the diversity of situations in the various regions of the Community'.[88] The precautionary principle was added to the list of guiding principles, and environmental protection requirements were henceforth to be 'integrated into the definition and implementation of other Community policies', rather than simply being a 'component', as required by the SEA.[89] Further provision was made for the inclusion, where appropriate, of a 'safeguard clause' in EC harmonisation measures to allow member states to take 'provisional measures, for non-economic environmental reasons, subject to a Community inspection procedure'.[90] The amendments also introduced qualified majority voting as the norm for measures under Article 130r (now Article 174).[91] Unanimity voting remained the rule, however, for provisions which were primarily of a fiscal nature, measures concerning town and country planning, land use (not waste management or general measures) and management of water resources, as well as measures which significantly affect choice between different energy sources and the general structure of a member state's energy supply.[92] These amendments also laid the groundwork for a distinction to be drawn between measures of a Community nature and those which might be considered to be more specific to the member states, with the latter being financed and implemented by the member states.[93] Recognising that certain measures could impose disproportionate costs on public authorities, provision was also made for temporary derogations by member states and for financial support from the proposed new Cohesion Fund.[94] The principle of 'subsidiarity', previously limited to environmental measures, was extended by the Maastricht Treaty to all EC action.[95] The Maastricht Treaty therefore set the basis for the further extension and development of environmental policy and law in the EC.

---

[87] Amended Art. 2; see Art. 3, requiring the EC to adopt 'a policy in the sphere of the environment'.

[88] See 1997 Amsterdam Treaty, Art. 174.   [89] Amended Art. 130r(2) as it then was.

[90] *Ibid.*

[91] Amended Art. 130s(1) and (3) as they then were. Now see Art. 175 of the 1997 Amsterdam Treaty.

[92] Amended Art. 130s(2) as it then was.   [93] Amended Art. 130s(4) as it then was.

[94] Amended Art. 130s(5) as it then was. The Cohesion Fund was established under amended Art. 130d (now Art. 161); chapter 20, p. 1037 below.

[95] New Art. 3(b) as it then was.

Agreement on the European Economic Area (1992)

In May 1992, the EC member states and the then seven EFTA states signed the Agreement on the European Economic Area (1992 EEA Agreement) to promote a strengthening of trade and economic relations between the parties with 'equal conditions of competition, and the respect of the same rules, with a view to creating a homogenous' European Economic Area.[96] These objectives are to be achieved by applying rules on the free movement of persons, goods, services and capital, as well as competition rules and closer co-operation on, *inter alia*, environmental matters.[97] The Preamble to the EEA Agreement reflects the determination of the parties to:

> preserve, protect and improve the quality of the environment and to ensure a prudent and rational utilisation of natural resources on the basis, in particular, of the principle of sustainable development, as well as the principle that precautionary and preventive action should be taken and to take a high level of environmental protection as a basis for the further development of rules.

The EEA Agreement includes rules on environmental protection, including provision for the formal incorporation of the most important acts of EC environmental law into the internal law of the EFTA states. Article 73 of the EEA Agreement uses the language of Article 130r(1) and (2) of the EEC Treaty as amended by the 1992 Maastricht Treaty, and its Article 74 and Annex XX identify thirty-two environmental Directives to be applied by the EFTA states, and six further acts of which they and the other parties to the EEA Agreement will 'take note'. For each of the thirty-eight instruments referred to, any reference in the provisions to 'member states' is to be understood as meaning all the parties to the EEA Agreement, and the rights conferred and obligations imposed upon the EC member states or their public entities, undertakings (companies) or individuals in relation to each other 'shall be understood to be conferred or imposed' upon the parties to the EEA Agreement, including their competent authorities, public entities, undertakings or individuals.[98] In effect, the provisions cited will be binding upon and become part of the law of the EFTA states, extending the application of these rules of EC environmental law to eighteen states.[99]

---

[96] OJ L1, 3 January 1994, 3; and Protocol Adjusting the EEA Agreement, Brussels, OJ L1, 3 January 1994, 572, Art. 1(1). The seven EFTA members were Austria, Finland, Iceland, Liechtenstein, Norway, Sweden and Switzerland (Switzerland did not become a party to the EEA Agreement following a majority vote against ratification by referendum in December 1992); Austria, Finland and Sweden became EC members in 1995.

[97] Art. 1(2).   [98] Protocol 1 (Horizontal Adaptations), point 7, and Annex XX.

[99] Art. 7; the Treaty provides that Regulations shall as such become part of the internal legal order, and Directives shall leave to the authorities the choice of form and method of implementation.

Amsterdam Treaty (1997)[100]

In October 1997, the fifteen EC members adopted the Amsterdam Treaty, which introduced further amendments with its entry into force on 1 May 1999. The Amsterdam Treaty sought to simplify the decision-making procedures that applied to environment policy, and remove the conflict of legal basis between the 'environment procedure' (Article 175, formerly Article 130s) and the 'approximation of laws' procedure for the internal market (Article 95, formerly Article 100a). The co-operation procedure in environmental matters (Article 175, formerly Article 130s) is replaced with the co-decision procedure which already applied in relation to measures taken to approximate laws in connection with the internal market (Article 95, formerly Article 100a).

The Amsterdam Treaty enshrines the principle of 'sustainable development' in the Preamble and in the objectives of the Maastricht Treaty, and in Article 2 of the EC Treaty, laying down the tasks of the Community. A new Article 6 of the EC Treaty includes a provision calling for environmental protection requirements to be integrated into the definition and implementation of other policies (this was previously contained in Article 174 (formerly Article 130r)). The new Article 6 also cites such integration as one means of promoting sustainable development, and is to be seen in conjunction with the Declaration on environmental impact assessments, annexed to the Final Act of the Intergovernmental Conference which drafted the Treaty of Amsterdam, by which the Conference noted the Commission's undertaking to prepare environmental impact assessment studies when making proposals which may have significant environmental implications.

The Treaty of Amsterdam also strengthened the framework created by the 1986 SEA for free movement, reflecting the need to take account of issues of vital importance for society such as the environment, public health or consumer protection (Article 95(3), formerly Article 100a(3)). The EC Treaty now requires all proposals by the Commission to be based on a high level of environmental protection. Previously, after a harmonisation measure had been adopted by the Council, any member state could still apply different national provisions if warranted by major environmental protection requirements. The member state in question had to notify the Commission, which then verified that the provisions involved were not a means of arbitrary discrimination or a disguised restriction on trade between the member states. This approach has now been extended, drawing a distinction between two separate situations (Article 95, formerly Article 100a). After a Community harmonisation measure has been adopted, member states may either maintain existing national

---

[100] R. Macrory, 'The Amsterdam Treaty – An Environmental Perspective', in D. O'Keeffe and P. Twomey, *Legal Issues of the Amsterdam Treaty* (1999), 171–84; H. Sevenster, 'The Environmental Guarantee after Amsterdam: Does the Emperor Have New Clothes?', 1 *Yearbook of European Environmental Law* 291 (2000).

provisions to protect the environment, or introduce new national provisions to protect the environment. In the first case, the member state must notify the Commission and give its reasons for maintaining those national provisions. In the second case, the member state must again notify the Commission of the new national provisions and explain its reasons for introducing them. Moreover, those measures must be based on new scientific evidence and must be in response to a problem that specifically affects the member state in question and that arose after the harmonisation measure was adopted. In both cases, it is for the Commission to check whether or not the national measures involved are a means of arbitrary discrimination, a disguised restriction on trade between member states, or an obstacle to the functioning of the internal market. The Commission has six months to decide whether to approve or reject the measure. This may be extended by a further six months in certain circumstances. In the absence of a decision, the national provisions are deemed to have been approved.

Principles and rules

EC environmental law now comprises the general principles and rules set forth in the EC Treaty (and the EURATOM Treaty), as amended in 1986, 1992, 1997 and 2001, together with hundreds of Directives, Regulations and Decisions addressing environmental issues which have been adopted since 1967, and the obligations arising for the EC under the many international environmental agreements to which it is a party. The following sections identify the main provisions which have been adopted in relation to general policy, air quality, water quality, biodiversity and nature, noise, chemicals and other hazardous substances, waste, and radioactive substances (given the number of instruments the account which follows is intended to be illustrative of the approach taken by the Community, and is not intended to be comprehensive). Other chapters in this book consider EC provisions on environmental impact assessment,[101] environmental information (including eco-labelling and eco-audits),[102] the use of economic instruments (including the carbon tax),[103] trade and competition,[104] compliance[105] and liability.[106]

General policy and principles

The general objectives and principles of EC environmental law are set out in the EC Treaty, now contained in Articles 174 and 175 of the EC Treaty. Following the various amendments to the EC Treaty, Article 174 provides, in relevant part:

[101] Chapter 16, pp. 807–10 below.   [102] Chapter 17, pp. 860–6 below.
[103] Chapter 4, pp. 158–61 above.   [104] Chapter 19, pp. 985–7 below.
[105] Chapter 5, pp. 222–5 above.   [106] Chapter 18, pp. 878–81 below.

1. Community policy on the environment shall contribute to pursuit of the following objectives:
– preserving, protecting and improving the quality of the environment;
– protecting human health;
– prudent and rational utilisation of natural resources;
– promoting measures at international level to deal with regional or world-wide environmental problems.

2. Community policy on the environment shall aim at a high level of protection taking into account the diversity of situations in the various regions of the Community. It shall be based on the precautionary principle and on the principles that preventive action should be taken, that environmental damage should as a priority be rectified at source and that the polluter should pay . . .

3. In preparing its policy on the environment, the Community shall take account of:
– available scientific and technical data;
– environmental conditions in the various regions of the Community;
– the potential benefits and costs of action or lack of action;
– the economic and social development of the Community as a whole and the balanced development of its regions.

Community policy on the environment, including programmes for future legislation and action, has been progressively developed in six Action Programmes on the Environment proposed by the Commission and approved by the Council, of which the most recent are the Fifth Action Programme (covering the period 1993–7[107] and subsequently extended) and the Sixth Action Programme (for the period 2001–10).[108]

The Fifth Action Programme identified six issues that were to be addressed because of their seriousness, their Community-wide dimension, and because they were considered to have a crucial bearing on environmental quality and conditions in almost all regions of the Community. These were: climate change; acidification and air pollution; depletion and pollution of water resources; deterioration of the urban environment; deterioration of coastal zones; and waste.[109] Action on these issues was to emphasise the following priority fields of action:

• sustainable management of natural resources;
• integrated pollution control and prevention of waste;
• reduction in consumption of non-renewable energy;

---

[107] Fifth Environmental Action Programme, 'Towards Sustainability': A European Community Programme of Policy and Action in Relation to the Environment and Sustainable Development, OJ C138, 17 May 1993, 1.

[108] Sixth Environment Action Programme, 'Environment 2010: Our Future, Our Choice, COM (2001) 31, OJ C154 E, 29 May 2001, 218.

[109] Fifth Environmental Action Programme, 13, para. 16.

- improved mobility management;
- environmental quality in urban areas; and
- improvement of public health and safety.[110]

The five target sectors to be specifically addressed were industry, energy, transport, agriculture and tourism, and were to be regulated by a broader range of instruments and techniques, including legislative instruments (to set fundamental levels of protection), market-based instruments (to 'sensitise' producers and consumers and to internalise environmental costs), horizontal supporting instruments (relating to baseline and statistical data, public and consumer information, and education and training) and financial support mechanisms.[111] The Programme applied the principle of subsidiarity, as provided by Article 3(b) of the Maastricht Treaty, which provided that the EC 'will take action only if and insofar as the objectives of the proposed action cannot be sufficiently achieved by the member states and can therefore, by reason of the scale or effects of proposed action, be better achieved by the [EC]'.[112] The Programme set forth for each of the main issues a combination of long-term objectives and performance targets for the period up to the year 2000, together with a representative selection of actions to achieve those targets. The Programme envisaged further EC measures to allow individuals and public interest groups to have practicable access to the courts to ensure that their legitimate interests were protected and that prescribed environmental measures were enforced and illegal practices stopped.[113] The Commission also committed itself, as soon as practicable, to establish a mechanism whereby damage to the environment was restored by the person or body responsible for the damage incurred.[114] In 1995, the Commission reported on, and evaluated the implementation of the Programme.[115] The approach adopted in the Fifth Environmental Action Programme was confirmed in the Commission's 1998 strategy for integrating the environment into European Union policies.[116] The Council also called on the Commission to put forward a strategy for implementing the new Article 6 of the EC Treaty. A communication on the European strategy for sustainable development was approved in May 2001 prior to the 2002 World Summit on

---

[110] *Ibid.*, para. 17.   [111] *Ibid.*, paras. 18 to 31.

[112] *Ibid.*, para. 32; the principle of subsidiarity was first introduced into EC law when the Title on environment was adopted by the 1986 SEA: see pp. 745–6 above.

[113] *Ibid.*, see chapter 9 above.   [114] *Ibid.*

[115] Progress Report from the Commission on the Implementation of the EC Program of Policy and Action in Relation to the Environment and Sustainable Development, COM (95) 624 final. See Decision No. 2179/98/EC, OJ L275, 10 October 1998, 1, reviewing the Fifth Environmental Action Programme.

[116] Communication from the Commission to the European Council of 27 May 1998 on a partnership for integration: a strategy for integrating the environment into EU policies (Cardiff, June 1998), COM (98) 333 final.

Sustainable Development in Johannesburg, setting out the Community's long-term objectives for sustainable development.[117]

The Sixth Environmental Action Programme was approved by the European Parliament and Council in July 2002.[118] The Programme addresses 'the key environmental objectives and priorities based on an assessment of the state of the environment and prevailing trends including emerging issues that require a lead from the Community'.[119] It focuses on four priority areas for action:

- climate change (in particular reducing greenhouse gas emissions by 8 per cent by 2008–12 compared to 1990 levels);
- nature and biodiversity (with the object of halting biodiversity decline by 2010);
- environment and health and quality of life (including the objective of aiming to achieve within one generation (i.e. by 2020) that chemicals are produced and used only in ways that do not lead to a significant negative impact on health and the environment); and
- natural resources management (including the objective that by 2010 22 per cent of electricity be produced from renewable sources).

The Programme proposes five priority avenues of strategic action:

- improving the implementation of existing legislation;
- integrating environmental concerns into other policies;
- working closer with the market;
- empowering people as private citizens and helping them to change behaviour; and
- taking account of the environment in land-use planning and management decisions.

The Programme also sets out specific actions which are to be taken in relation to each of these avenues.

It is apparent that the integration of environmental concerns into all aspects of the European Union's activities – including in the field of external relations – is the fundamental objective of the Sixth Environmental Action Programme.[120] This objective takes account of the prospect of European Union enlargement and indicates close co-operation with the administrations in the candidate member countries on sustainable development, as well as establishing closer

---

[117] Communication from the Commission of 15 May 2001, A Sustainable Europe for a Better World: A European Union Strategy for Sustainable Development (Commission's Proposal to the Gothenburg European Council), COM (2001) 264 final.

[118] Decision No. 1600/2002/EC, OJ L242, 10 September 2002, 1.   [119] Ibid., Art. 1(1).

[120] See also European Commission, Partnership for Integration: A Strategy for Integrating the Environment into EU Policies, COM (98) 333; D. Wilkinson, 'Steps Towards Integrating the Environment into other EU Policies', in T. O'Riordan and H. Voisey, The Transition to Sustainability: The Politics of Agenda 21 in Europe (1998).

cooperation with NGOs and businesses in these countries. The programme will be increasingly based on scientific and economic analyses and on environmental indicators, and to this end it is proposed that the Commission should work in closer co-operation with the European Environment Agency. The Programme identifies a number of priority areas for action on international issues, including:

- integrating environmental protection requirements into all the Community's external policies;
- strengthening international environmental governance by the reinforcement of multilateral co-operation and the institutional framework;
- aiming for swift ratification and effective compliance and enforcement of international conventions where the Community is a party;
- promoting sustainable environmental practices in foreign investments and export credits;
- intensifying efforts to arrive at a consensus on methods for the evaluation of risks to health and the environment, as well as approaches of risk management including the precautionary principle;
- achieving mutual supportiveness between trade and environmental needs, including by 'sustainability impact assessments' of multilateral trade agreements;
- promoting a world trade system that fully recognises multilateral and regional environmental agreements and the precautionary principle; and
- promoting cross-border environmental co-operation with neighbouring countries and regions.

The Community's Environmental Action Programmes and many of the instruments that it has adopted since the late 1960s, together with various regulatory techniques which are now commonplace in general international environmental law, were often first adopted internationally at the EC level. These included legislation on environmental impact assessment, the right of access to environmental information, and eco-labelling, environmental management and auditing, integrated pollution control, and financial instruments (such as the LIFE programme). While EC environmental legislation has generally followed a traditional 'command-and-control' approach to regulation, the EC is moving towards greater use of economic instruments and market-based techniques, for which the eco-labelling Directive and the recently adopted tradeable permits scheme, as well as the earlier carbon/energy tax proposal are examples.[121] The EC has also contributed to the development of general rules of international environmental law in international development assistance agreements, in particular the 1989 Lomé Convention[122] and its successor, the 2000 Cotonou

---

[121] Chapter 17, p. 861 below.
[122] See p. 792 below; and chapter 20, pp. 1022–3 below.

Agreement.[123] In relation to the prevention of pollution, the EC now has a comprehensive legal structure.

Integrated pollution prevention and control

After nearly three decades of seeking to prevent pollution of distinct environmental media, in 1996 the EC adopted Council Directive 96/61/EC on integrated pollution prevention and control (IPPC Directive) with a view to achieving a more integrated and horizontal approach.[124] The Directive is premised on the view that 'different approaches to controlling emissions into the air, water or soil separately may encourage the shifting of pollution between the various environmental media rather than protecting the environment as a whole' (Preamble), and aims to:

> achieve integrated prevention and control of pollution arising from the activities listed in Annex I. It lays down measures designed to prevent or, where that is not practicable, to reduce emissions in the air, water and land from the abovementioned activities, including measures concerning waste, in order to achieve a high level of protection of the environment taken as a whole.[125]

The integrated approach imposes basic obligations on the operator, in particular the obligation to ensure that: installations are operated so as to ensure that all appropriate preventive measures are taken against pollution (in particular through application of the best available techniques); no significant pollution is caused; waste production is avoided (in accordance with Council Directive 75/442/EEC) and waste which is produced is recovered or disposed of while avoiding or reducing any impact on the environment; energy is used efficiently; measures are taken to prevent accidents and limit their consequences; and measures are taken upon definitive cessation of activities to avoid pollution risk and return the site of operation to a satisfactory state.[126] The Directive establishes a detailed procedure for applying for, issuing and amending operating permits for industrial installations, and requires member states to ensure that the grant of permits and the conditions applying thereto guarantee 'an effective integrated approach' by national authorities.[127] In particular, all permits granted, and modified permits, must include details of the arrangements made for achieving a high level of protection for air, water and land, and must include emissions

---

[123] Cotonou, Benin, 23 June 2000, not yet in force.

[124] OJ L257, 10 October 1996, 26. The Directive will be amended by the passage of the proposed framework Directive for greenhouse gas emissions trading within the European Community (COM (2001) 581 final, OJ C75E, 26 March 2002, 33).

[125] Art. 1. Annex 1 lists categories of activities to which the Directive applies: energy industries, production and processing of metals, mineral industry, chemical industry, and waste management.

[126] Art. 3.   [127] Arts. 6, 7, 12 and 13.

limit values for pollutants to air and water (in particular pollutants listed in Annex III), monitoring of discharges, and minimisation of long-distance or transboundary pollution.[128] Emissions limit values are to be based on best available techniques, taking into account the technical characteristics of the installation concerned, its geographical location and local environmental conditions.[129] The Directive requires member states to 'periodically reconsider and, where necessary, update permit conditions',[130] and includes provisions on compliance, access to and exchange of information, transboundary effects and transitional provisions governing entry into force.[131]

Air quality[132]

The EC has a range of legislative instruments aimed at the protection and improvement of air quality. Five regulatory techniques have been adopted in pursuance of this objective: equipment standards for certain activities and processes (cars, industrial plant, waste incinerators); standards relating to fuel content (diesel and other fuels); limits on atmospheric concentrations (lead); limits on the total emissions of member states of certain pollutants (nitrogen dioxide, sulphur dioxide); and reductions and prohibitions on the production and consumption of certain harmful substances (CFCs). More recently, the EC

[128] Arts. 8 and 9. Where the need for Community action has been identified, the Council will set emissions limit values for activities listed in Annex I (except landfills) and the polluting substances referred to in Annex III: Art. 18(1). Where no such emissions limit values are defined 'the relevant emission limit values contained in the Directives referred to in Annex II and in other Community legislation shall be applied as minimum emission limit values': Art. 18(2).

[129] Art. 9(4). This is without prejudice to Art. 10, which provides that '[W]here an environmental quality standard requires stricter conditions than those achievable by the use of the best available techniques, additional measures shall in particular be required in the permit, without prejudice to other measures which might be taken to comply with environmental quality standards'.

[130] Art. 13(1). Reconsideration is to be undertaken where: the pollution caused by the installation is of such significance that the existing emissions limit values of the permit need to be revised or new such values need to be included in the permit; substantial changes in the best available techniques make it possible to reduce emissions significantly without imposing excessive costs; the operational safety of the process or activity requires other techniques to be used; and new provisions of Community or national legislation so dictate: Art. 13(2).

[131] Arts. 14–17 and 20–21. On failure to transpose the Directive, see Case C-29/01, *Commission* v. *Spain* [2002] ECR I-2503; Case C-39/01, *Commission* v. *United Kingdom* [2002] ECR I-2513; and Case C-64/01, *Commission* v. *Greece* [2002] ECR I-2523.

[132] Fifth Environmental Action Plan, n. 107 above, 42–4 and Tables 7 to 9 (addressing climate change, acidification and air quality). The Sixth Environment Action Programme, n. 108 above, in its target area on environment and health, aims to achieve levels of air quality that do not give rise to unacceptable impacts on, and risks to, human health and the environment.

has adopted new Directives on air pollution, a new clean air strategy[133] and an integrated pollution prevention and control Directive.[134] In 2001, it adopted a 'Clean Air for Europe (CAFE) Programme' as the first of the thematic strategies announced in the Sixth Environmental Action Programme. The objectives of the CAFE Programme are, *inter alia*: to develop and collect scientific information on the effects of air pollution; to support the implementation and review the effectiveness of existing legislation and to develop new proposals; and to determine an integrated strategy (by 2004 at the latest) to include appropriate objectives and cost-effective measures. The objectives of the first programme phase include, tropospheric ozone, acidification and eutrophication.[135] The Commission has also signalled its intention to make greater use of economic instruments: its proposal in 1995 to establish a carbon/energy tax marked the first effort by a group of countries to consider the use of taxation policy as an international instrument of environmental protection.[136] More recently the Community has adopted a scheme for greenhouse gas emissions allowance trading in the Community.[137] The Community is a party to the 1992 Climate Change Convention and to its 1997 Kyoto Protocol,[138] and the EC has a new package of proposed legislation for implementing the Kyoto Protocol. There are also Programmes for energy conservation and energy technology, including a commitment to increase the use of renewable energies from its present 6 per cent to 12 per cent by 2010.[139]

Air framework

The Fifth Environmental Action Programme recommended the adoption of a long-term programme on air quality. This led to the adoption of Directive 96/62/EC on ambient air quality assessment and management, laying the foundations for common objectives on ambient air quality to prevent harmful effects

---

[133] Commission Communication 'The Clean Air for Europe (CAFE) Programme: Towards a Thematic Strategy for Air Quality', COM (2001) 245 final, 4 May 2001.

[134] Directive 96/61/EC, OJ L257, 10 October 1996, 26.

[135] Commission Communication, 'The Clean Air for Europe (CAFE) Programme: Towards a Thematic Strategy for Air Quality', COM (2001) 245 final, 4 May 2001.

[136] See COM (95) 172 final, 10 May 1995; chapter 4, pp. 158–67 above.

[137] Chapter 8, p. 371 above. For background, see COM (2001) 581 final, OJ C75E, 26 March 2002, 33. See also Commission Green Paper on Greenhouse Gas Emissions Trading Within the European Union, COM (2000) 87 final; and Final Report: Designing Options for Implementing an Emissions Trading Regime for Greenhouse Gases in the EC, 22 February 2000.

[138] The Kyoto Protocol was signed by the European Community on 10 December 1997. See COM (2001) 579 final, OJ C75E, 26 March 2002, 17; COM (2001) 580 final; COM (2001) 581 final, OJ C75E, 26 March 2002, 33.

[139] This intention was confirmed in Council Resolution of 8 June 1998 on renewable sources of energy, OJ C198, 24 June 1998, 1.

on human health and the environment.[140] The Directive covers the revision of existing legislation and the introduction of new air quality standards for previously unregulated air pollution. It has been followed by proposals for 'daughter Directives' establishing limit values for certain specified air pollutants.[141] Directive 96/62 does not itself set limit values, but its Article 4 provides that the Commission shall submit to the Council proposals for the setting of limit values and, as appropriate, alert thresholds.[142] Directive 96/62 defines terms like 'ambient air', 'pollutant', 'limit value' and 'alert threshold',[143] and directs member states to take any action needed to prevent concentrations of nitrogen dioxide and lead in the ambient air, as assessed in accordance with the rules under the Directive.[144]

In order to maintain and improve air quality within the Community, the Directive also defines basic principles which make it possible to: establish quality objectives for ambient air (outdoor air in the troposphere); draw up common methods and criteria for assessing air quality; and obtain and disseminate information on air quality.[145] Member states are required to monitor ambient air quality throughout their territories to draw up a list of areas and conurbations where pollution levels exceed the limit values.[146]

In addition to the framework Directive and the daughter Directives, a Directive on national emissions ceilings for certain atmospheric pollutants was adopted in 2001.[147] The Directive aims to set a strategy to combat acidification, eutrophication and photochemical air pollutants. It provides for the introduction, by the end of 2010 at the latest, of national emissions ceilings for sulphur dioxide (SO_2), nitrogen oxides (NO_x), volatile organic compounds (VOCs) and ammonia (NH_3).[148] The Directive includes a review clause which requires the Commission to report in 2004 and 2008 on the progress being

---

[140] Council Directive 96/62/EC, OJ L296, 21 November 1996, 55.

[141] See e.g. Directive 2000/69/EC, OJ L313, 13 December 2000, 12, introducing specific limit values for two pollutants (benzene and carbon monoxide) in ambient air; Directive 2002/3/EC, OJ L67, 9 March 2002, 14, relating to ozone in ambient air, (see n. 220 below); and Directive 99/30/EC of 22 April 1999, OJ L163, 29 June 1999, 41 (see n. 192 below).

[142] See Art. 4 and Annex 1.   [143] Art. 2.

[144] On failure to designate a competent authority and bodies responsible for implementing the Directive, see Case C-417/99, *Commission* v. *Spain* [2001] ECR I-6015.

[145] Art. 1   [146] Arts. 5 and 6. See also Arts. 8 to 10.

[147] Directive 2001/81/EC, OJ L309, 27 November 2001, 22. See also Directive 2001/80/EC, OJ L309, 27 November 2001, 1, on the limitation of emissions of certain pollutants into the air from large combustion plants, chapter 8, p. 337 above. In light of these new Directives, the Commission has recently made a proposal to accede to the 1999 Protocol to the 1979 LRTAP Convention, chapter 8, p. 325 above; see COM (2002) 44 final, OJ C151E, 25 June 2002, 74.

[148] See Art. 4 and Annex I. Member states are required to draw up national programmes for the progressive reduction of national emissions of the four pollutants by 1 October 2002: Art. 6.

made in meeting the targets, and requires examination of air pollution caused by aviation and shipping.

Motor cars

The first EC Directive designed to protect air quality and human health was adopted in 1970 to establish mandatory technical standards for emissions of carbon monoxide, unburnt hydrocarbons, nitrogen oxides and particulates from certain vehicles with petrol engines,[149] based on technical requirements adopted by the UNECE. The Council has since been empowered to adopt legislation to stabilise and reduce emissions of carbon dioxide and other greenhouse gases from motor cars and introduce certain tax incentives for vehicles covered by the Directive.[150] The EC Council is also committed to limiting carbon dioxide emissions from motor vehicles, adopting emission standards for all commercial vehicles, and implementing a research and development programme to encourage the marketing of clean vehicles and fuels.[151]

Subsequent amending Directives cover motor vehicles with spark-ignition and compression-ignition engines and apply to tailpipe emissions, evaporative emissions, emissions of crankcase gases and the durability of anti-pollution devices for specified motor vehicles.[152] The Directives lay down differing limit values for emissions (by petrol and diesel cars) of: carbon monoxide; unburnt hydrocarbons; nitrogen oxides; and, specifically for diesel engines, limit values for particulate pollutants. The most stringent values, laid down by Directive 98/69/EC, have become applicable from 2000 onwards, according to the type of vehicle.[153]

Measures to reduce air emissions from cars have also been prepared within the first Auto/Oil Programme[154] and the Auto/Oil II Programme, which aim for significant improvements in urban air quality by 2010.[155] The Commission has also entered into environmental agreements with motor manufacturers

---

[149] Council Directive 70/220/EEC, OJ L76, 6 April 1970, 1, as amended, Annex I, paras. 5.3.1.4 and 7.1.1.1.

[150] Council Directive 89/458/EEC, amending Council Directive 70/220/EEC, OJ L226, 3 August 1989, 1, as amended, Arts. 3 and 6.

[151] Council Directive 91/441/EEC, amending Council Directive 70/220/EEC, OJ L242, 30 August 1991, 1 (Preamble).

[152] Council Directive 70/220/EEC, OJ L76, 6 April 1970, 1, has been amended by, *inter alia*, the following: Council Directive 93/59/EC of 28 June 1993, OJ L186, 28 July 1993, 21; Council Directive 94/12/EC of 23 March 1994, OJ L100, 19 April 1994, 42. Commission Directive 96/44/EC of 1 July 1996, OJ L210, 20 August 1996, 25; Directive 98/69/EC of 13 October 1998, OJ L350, 28 December 1998, 1; Commission Directive 99/102/EC of 15 December 1999, OJ L334, 28 December 1999, 43; and Directive 2001/1/EC of 22 January 2001, OJ L35, 6 February 2001, 34.

[153] OJ L350, 28 December 1998, 1.

[154] See COM (96) 248 final, 18 June 1996, OJ C77, 11 March 1997, 8.

[155] See COM (2000) 626 final.

to reduce CO_2 emissions from cars. These include agreements with ACEA (Association des constructeurs européens d'automobiles)[156] and the Japanese and Korean Automobile Manufacturers Association.[157]

Diesel engines

Council Directive 72/306/EEC establishes limits on emissions of soot from all vehicles with diesel engines except those run on rails, agricultural tractors and machines and public works vehicles.[158] It was supplemented in 1988 by a Directive establishing emissions limits for carbon monoxide, hydrocarbons and nitrogen oxides for new models and existing models of vehicles with diesel engines.[159]

Directive 99/96/EC amends the 1988 Directive by introducing provisions on polluting emissions from new heavy-duty engines fuelled by natural gas (NG) and liquefied petroleum gas (LPG). The Directive also introduces measures on the introduction of a new concept of Enhanced Environmentally Friendly Vehicles and actions likely to facilitate the type-approval of engines and vehicles using ethanol as a substitute fuel.[160] Another amending Directive grants to small diesel engines for use in commercial vehicles a derogation from the limit value applicable from 1 October 1995, as prescribed by Directive 91/542/EEC. It also authorises member states to provide for tax incentives encouraging the placing on the market of vehicles which satisfy the provisions of the EC Treaty and to introduce a new statistical method of monitoring production.[161] There has also been a proposal for a Directive to reduce the atmospheric pollution caused by agricultural or forestry tractor engines by laying down, at Community level, standards for acceptable emissions that apply to those engines.[162]

Non-road mobile machinery

Directive 97/68/EC sets out air emissions limit values for machinery other than passenger and commercial vehicles, airplanes and ships; it covers machinery

---

[156] See COM (98) 495 final, 29 July 1998, announcing the agreement and the Recommendation addressed by the European Commission to ACEA, Commission Recommendation 1999/125/EC, OJ L40, 13 February 1999, 49.

[157] See Commission Recommendation 2000/304/EC, OJ L100, 20 April 2000, 57, and Commission Recommendation 2000/303/EC, OJ L100, 20 April 2000, 55.

[158] Council Directive 72/306/EEC, OJ L190, 20 August 1972, 1, as amended, Art. 2 and Annexes I and VI as amended.

[159] Council Directive 88/77/EEC, OJ L36, 9 February 1988, 33, Art. 2 and Annex I, as amended. Directive 2001/27/EC, OJ L107, 18 April 2001, 10, adapts to technical progress Council Directive 2001/27/EC, OJ L107, 18 April 2001, 10.

[160] Directive 99/96/EC, OJ L44, 16 February 2000, 1.

[161] Directive 96/1/EC, OJ L40, 17 February 1996, 1.

[162] Commission Proposal, COM (98) 472 final, OJ C303, 2 October 1998, 9.

such as compressors, forestry equipment, snowplough equipment, aerial lifts and mobile cranes.[163]

Fuels and lead

The Community has long regulated the content of fuels. Directive 75/716/EEC established limits on the concentration of certain substances in gas oils marketed in the EC.[164] It was followed by a Directive establishing limits on the permitted lead-compound content of leaded petrol and the benzene content of leaded and unleaded petrol on their markets, which required member states to ensure the availability and balanced distribution within their territories of unleaded petrol.[165] An alternative approach to the maintenance of air quality is provided by Council Directive 82/884/EEC, which fixes a limit value (concentration levels which must not be exceeded) for lead in the air.[166]

Council Directive 93/12/EC[167] introduced a gradual reduction in the sulphur content of gas oil to reach the emission limit values fixed in other Community provisions. Another Directive relating to the quality of petrol and diesel fuels meets the commitment given in Directive 93/12/EC that target values would be adopted involving a substantial reduction in pollutant emissions from motor vehicles after 2000; it sets the environmental specifications to apply successively (with effect from 1 January 2000 and 1 January 2005) to fuels for vehicles equipped with petrol and diesel engines.[168] The Directive banned leaded petrol from the market from 2000 and provides for progressive improvements in the environmental quality of unleaded petrol and diesel fuel. Notwithstanding the general rules of the Directive, member states may in certain specific cases allow petrol or diesel fuels which fail to comply with the Directive to remain on the market. They may also impose more stringent standards on fuels marketed on their territory in order to protect the environment or public health in a specific ecologically sensitive area, provided the measures are restricted to those areas.

---

[163] Directive 97/68/EC, OJ L59, 27 February 1998, 1, as amended by Directive 2001/63/EC, OJ L227, 23 August 2001, 41. The amending Directive relates to measures to counter the emission of gaseous and particulate pollutants from internal combustion engines to be installed in non-road mobile machinery. See Case C-320/99, *Commission* v. *France* [2000] ECR I-10453, on non-compliance.

[164] Council Directive 75/716/EEC, OJ L307, 27 November 1975, 22, as amended; see Case 92/79, *EC Commission* v. *Italy* [1980] ECR 1115, (non-implementation).

[165] Council Directive 85/210/EEC, OJ L96, 3 April 1985, 25, as amended, Arts. 2, 3 and 4. See Case-162/89, *EC Commission* v. *Belgium* [1990] ECR I-2391, (non-implementation by failure to provide reports to the Commission). This Directive is now repealed by Directive 98/70/EC, OJ L350, 28 December 1998, 58.

[166] Council Directive 82/884/EEC, OJ L378, 31 December 1982, 15, as amended, Arts. 1 and 2, now repealed (see n. 194 below).

[167] Directive 93/12/EC, OJ L74, 27 March 1993, 81, as amended.

[168] Directive 98/70/EC, OJ L350, 28 December 1998, 58, as amended. This repeals Directives 85/210/EEC, OJ L96, 3 April 1985, 25, 85/536/EEC, OJ L334, 12 December 1985, 20, and 87/441/EEC, OJ L238, 21 August 1987, 40, as from 1 January 2000.

Ozone layer

Despite initial misgivings about the need for action, the EC has been an active participant in the 1985 Vienna Convention and the 1987 Montreal Protocol. In 1980, the EC required member states to stop increases in the 'production capacity' of certain chlorofluorocarbons and to ensure that industries situated in their territories reduced the use of these chlorofluorocarbons in the filling of aerosol cans by 30 per cent compared with 1976 levels by 31 December 1981.[169] Council Decision 82/795 defined 'production capacity' for purposes of the application of Decision 80/372 and provided for the regular collection by the EC Commission of statistical information on production and use of certain chlorofluorocarbons.[170]

In 1988, the EC became a party to the 1985 Vienna Convention and the 1987 Montreal Protocol,[171] and in 1991 it implemented the 1990 Amendments and Adjustments and introduced control measures for phase-out which were more stringent than those under the amended Montreal Protocol.[172] The 1991 Regulation established quantitative restrictions on imports of substances from third countries and of controlled substances from non-parties, as well as for imports from non-parties of products which contain or are produced with controlled substances, and exports to non-parties.[173] The Regulation also implemented a new phase-out schedule for the production and consumption of certain substances, as well as specific EC management, reporting and inspection requirements.[174]

The current Community law in respect of the protection of the ozone layer is laid down in Council Regulation (EC) No. 2037/2000.[175] It replaced Council Regulation (EC) No. 3093/94 on substances that deplete the ozone layer, so as to adapt Community rules in the light of the technical developments which had occurred since the earlier Regulation was adopted, and in line with the changes made, in 1995 and 1997, to the 1990 Montreal Protocol.[176] In laying down stricter provisions, the new Regulation takes into account the increasing availability of products that can replace those which deplete the ozone layer, such as hydrochlorofluorocarbons (HCFCs) and methyl bromide. The Regulation includes controls on production, importation, exportation, supply, use, leakage and recovery of controlled substances. It also establishes a licensing procedure for all imports of ozone-depleting substances.[177] In the landmark decision in

---

[169] Council Decision 80/372/EEC, OJ L90, 3 April 1980, 45, as amended, Art. 1.

[170] Council Decision 82/795/EEC, OJ L329, 25 November 1982, 29, Arts. 1 and 2 and Annex.

[171] Council Decision 88/540/EEC, OJ L297, 31 October 1988, 8; chapter 8, pp. 344–57 above.

[172] Council Regulation (EEC) No. 91/594, OJ L67, 14 March 1991, 1; chapter 8, pp. 345–57 above.

[173] Part I, Arts. 3 to 9, and Annex II.

[174] Part II, Arts. 10 and 11; and Part III, Arts. 13 to 15.

[175] OJ L244, 29 September 2000, 1, as amended.   [176] OJ L333, 22 December 1994, 1.

[177] Arts. 6–8. See Case T-336/94, *Efisol* [1996] ECR II-1343.

Gianni Bettati, the ECJ held that provisions on the production, supply and use in the Community of certain ozone-depleting substances did not impinge on other provisions of Community law.[178] Notably, the Court stated that:

> [I]t is settled law that Community legislation must, so far as possible, be interpreted in a manner that is consistent with international law, in particular where its provisions are intended specifically to give effect to an international agreement concluded by the Community (see to that effect Case C-61/94, *Commission* v. *Germany* [1996] ECR I-3989, paragraph 52).[179]

Sulphur dioxide and nitrogen dioxide

The EC has adopted far-reaching legislation aimed at curbing emissions of sulphur dioxide and nitrogen dioxide. The first legislative act, in 1980, fixed limit values and guide values for sulphur dioxide and suspended particulates in the atmosphere.[180] Subject to the exceptions laid down in the Directive, member states were required to ensure that atmospheric concentrations were not greater than the limit values fixed in Annex I to the Directive by 1 April 1983, and to endeavour to move towards the guide values in Annex II wherever measured concentrations were higher than those values.[181] The Directive also established reference methods for sampling and analysis.[182] In 1981, the EC became a party to the 1979 LRTAP Convention;[183] in 1993, it acceded to the 1988 NO_x Protocol;[184] and in 2001 it approved the Heavy Metals Protocol.[185] The Commission plans to accede to the 1999 Protocol to Abate Acidification, Eutrophication and Ground-Level Ozone.[186]

Limit value and guide values have also been fixed for concentrations of nitrogen dioxide in the atmosphere other than at work or inside buildings.[187] Subject to the exceptions laid down in the Directive, member states have been required to ensure that atmospheric concentrations of nitrogen oxide are limited to the values set out in Annex I to the Directive by 1 July 1987.[188] Lower values may be fixed for zones in which member states consider it necessary

---

[178] See Case C-341/95, *Gianni Bettati* v. *Safety Hi-Tech Srl* [1998] ECR I-4355, paras. 31 *et seq.*

[179] *Ibid.*, para 20.

[180] Council Directive 80/779/EEC, OJ L229, 30 August 1980, 30, Art. 1 and Annexes I and II now repealed; see n. 193 below.

[181] Arts. 3 and 5.   [182] Art. 10 and Annexes III and IV.

[183] Council Decision 81/462/EEC, OJ L171, 27 June 1981, 11, see chapter 8, pp. 324–36 above. See also Council Decision 86/277/EEC, OJ L181, 4 July 1986, 1.

[184] Council Decision 93/361/EEC, OJ L149, 21 June 1993, 14; chapter 8, pp. 328–9 above.

[185] Commission Decision 2001/379/EC of 4 April 2001, OJ L134, 17 May 2001, 40; chapter 8, pp. 333–4 above.

[186] See COM (2002) 44 final, OJ C151E, 25 June 2002, 74; chapter 8, pp. 335–6 above.

[187] Council Directive 85/203/EEC, OJ L87, 27 March 1985, 1, as amended, Art. 1 and Annexes I and II, now repealed; see n. 195 below.

[188] Art. 3.

to limit or prevent a foreseeable increase in pollution by nitrogen dioxide in the wake of urban or industrial development, as well as lower values than the Annex II guide values for zones for which special environmental protection is required.[189] Member states are free to fix more stringent values.[190] The Directive also establishes measuring and reporting requirements, reference methods of analysis and institutional arrangements.[191]

These Directives have been superseded by a 1999 'daughter Directive' relating to limit values for sulphur dioxide, nitrogen dioxide and oxides of nitrogen, and particulates and lead in the ambient air.[192] This Directive repeals: Council Directive 80/779/EEC on air quality limit values and guide values for sulphur dioxide and suspended particulates;[193] Council Directive 82/884/EEC on a limit value for lead in the air;[194] and Council Directive 85/203/EEC on air quality standards for nitrogen dioxide,[195] and fixes binding limit values for the different pollutants.

Industrial plants

Industrial plants are also subject to specific legislation. Council Directive 84/360/EEC established general measures and procedures to prevent or reduce air pollution from industrial plants in the EC.[196] It required member states to ensure the prior authorisation of operation of plants in relation to industrial activities listed in Annex I, except those which serve national defence purposes.[197] Authorisation was only to be granted where the national authority was satisfied that certain environmental conditions had been fulfilled, including the application of 'best available technology, provided that the application of such measures does not entail excessive cost' (BATNEEC), that the operation of the plant will not cause significant air pollution, that applicable emissions limit

---

[189] Art. 4(1) and (2). Where this applies in a border region, the member state is required to hold prior consultations with the other member states concerned: Art. 11(1). Belgium has been held to be in violation of the Directive by reason of its failure to implement the provisions relating to the consultation procedures: see Case C-186/91, *EC Commission* v. *Belgium* [1993] ECR I-851.

[190] Art. 5.   [191] Arts. 6 to 14.

[192] Directive 99/30/EC of 22 April 1999, OJ L163, 29 June 1999, 41.

[193] The Directive was repealed with effect from 19 July 2001, apart from Arts. 1, 2(1), 3(1), 9, 15 and 16, together with Annexes I, III(B) and IV which will be repealed with effect from 1 January 2005.

[194] The Directive was repealed with effect from 19 July 2001, apart from Arts. 1, 2, 3(1), 7, 12 and 13, which are repealed with effect from 1 January 2005.

[195] The Directive was repealed with effect from 19 July 2001, apart from Art. 1(1), first indent, and (2), Art. 2, first indent, Arts. 3(1), 5, 9, 15 and 16 and Annex I, which are repealed with effect from 1 January 2010.

[196] Council Directive 84/360/EEC, OJ L188, 16 July 1984, 20, Art. 1 and Annex I, as amended.

[197] Arts. 3 and 15. Annex I categories of plants include energy, production and processing of metals, manufacture of non-metallic mineral products, the chemical industry, waste disposal, and some paper pulp manufacturing plants.

values will not be exceeded, and that all air quality limit values will be taken into account.[198] Member states are additionally required to implement policies and strategies to gradually adapt plants which were in operation before 1 July 1987, or built or authorised before that date, to 'best available technology'.[199] The Directive allows more stringent requirements, provides for public information and confidentiality, and enables the Council, if necessary, to fix emissions limit values.[200] Limit values were fixed in 1988 – by Directive 88/609/EEC – and then updated in 2001.[201]

The significance of Council Directive 84/360 has been much reduced by the entry into force of the IPPC Directive,[202] which repeals the earlier Directive eleven years after the latter's entry into force, from 30 October 1996. Its provisions will continue to apply to existing installations until Article 5 of the IPPC Directive has been complied with.[203]

Waste incineration plants

In 1989, the EC focused its legislative efforts on regulating both new and existing waste incineration plants. Council Directive 89/369/EEC establishes air pollution standards for the prior authorisation of municipal waste incineration plants for which authorisation to operate is granted from 1 December 1990.[204] Subject to certain exceptions and derogation rights, the Directive establishes emissions limit values for specific pollutants, including dust, heavy metals, hydrochloric and hydrofluoric acids, and sulphur dioxide.[205] Member states may lay down emissions limit values for other pollutants, including dioxins and furans, because of the composition of the waste to be incinerated and the characteristics of the plant, the values for which must take account of the potential harmful effects of the pollutants and of BATNEEC.[206] The Directive establishes further environmental conditions which must be fulfilled prior to authorisation. These relate to the temperature of gases burned, oxygen content, concentrations of carbon monoxide and organic compounds in the combustion gases, measurement requirements, public information and commercial secrecy, and verification.[207]

A 1994 Directive on the incineration of hazardous wastes established uniform and integrated criteria for all hazardous waste facilities.[208] It requires

---

[198] Art. 4. Annex II lists polluting substances which are considered to be particularly relevant.
[199] Art. 13.
[200] Arts. 5 to 10. For its failure to fulfil its obligations under Arts. 3, 4, 9 and 10 of the Directive, see Case C-230/00, *Commission* v. *Belgium* [2001] ECR I-4591.
[201] Chapter 8, p. 336 above.   [202] Art. 20(3) of the IPPC Directive.
[203] See p. 774 below.
[204] OJ L163, 14 June 1989, 32, Arts. 3 and 12(1). Existing waste incineration plants were regulated by Directive 89/429/EEC, OJ L203, 15 July 1989, 50.
[205] Art. 3.   [206] Art. 3(4).   [207] Arts. 4, 6, 9 and 11.
[208] Directive 94/67/EC, OJ L365, 31 December 1994, 34.

the setting up and maintaining of appropriate operating conditions and sets emissions limit values for hazardous wastes incineration plants. Plants are to be operated in order to achieve a level of incineration that is as complete as possible, and designed in such a way that specified emissions values are not exceeded.[209] Installations for the incineration of municipal waste and for the disposal or recovery of hazardous waste beyond a specified capacity are subject to the provisions of the IPPC Directive. Directive 94/67/EC sets out the licensing procedure to be followed before an incineration plant can become operational. 'Best available technologies' are to be employed in new and existing plants, and licences are to be reviewed every five years. In the event of threshold values being exceeded, the plant must cease operation until the situation has been rectified and the plant complies once more with the requirements laid down in the Directive.[210]

With the adoption in 2000 of a new Directive on the incineration of waste, Directives 89/369/EEC and 89/429/EEC on municipal waste and Directive 94/67/EC on hazardous waste plants will be repealed with effect from 28 December 2005.[211] The aim of the new Directive is to prevent or limit as far as practicable the negative effects on the environment caused by the incineration and co-incineration of waste. In particular, it aims to reduce pollution and harm to human health caused by emissions into the air, soil, surface water and groundwater. This is to be achieved through stringent operational conditions and technical requirements and by setting up emissions limit values for waste incineration and co-incineration plants within the Community.[212] It sets emissions limit values for air (in particular for dust, SO_2, NO_x and heavy metals), and introduces dioxins as a new parameter for discharges into water. It stipulates that residues from the combustion process must be minimised in their amount and harmfulness and recycled where appropriate, and, if not possible, disposed of only under certain conditions.[213] Controls on releases to water aim to reduce the pollution impact of incineration on marine and freshwater ecosystems. The Directive excludes from its scope certain plants like those treating bio-mass and experimental plants.[214] It distinguishes between incineration plants (which may or may not recover heat generated by combustion) and co-incineration plants (such as cement kilns, steel or power plants whose main purpose is energy generation or the production of material products), and envisages procedures for the application and granting of operating permits.[215] It sets up a series of operating conditions including the recovery, as far as practical, of heat generated during the incineration process, and provides for public consultation, access to information and participation in the permit procedure.[216] The Directive

---

[209] Arts. 6(1) and 7.   [210] Art. 12.
[211] Council Directive 2000/76/EC, OJ L332, 28 December 2000, 91, Art. 18.   [212] Art. 1
[213] Art. 9   [214] Art. 2   [215] Arts. 3(4) and (5) and 4.   [216] Arts. 6 and 12.

will apply to existing plants as from 28 December 2005 and to new plants as from 28 December 2002.

Air pollution by ozone and other substances

Council Directive 92/72/EEC establishes harmonised procedures for monitoring, exchanging information on and warning the population about air pollution by ozone.[217] The Directive requires member states to designate or establish measuring stations and provides for specified reference methods or their equivalent.[218] Member states must inform the public (by radio, television and press) when thresholds for ozone concentration in the atmosphere are exceeded, and must also provide regular information to the Commission.[219] This Directive will be repealed by Directive 2002/3/EC relating to ozone in ambient air with effect from 9 September 2003.[220]

Directive 91/441/EEC and other Directives on emissions from motor vehicles had earlier introduced measures to reduce volatile organic compounds (VOCs) emissions from motor vehicles.[221] A 1994 Directive follows the line of those Directives and applies to the operations, installations, vehicles and vessels used for storage, loading and transporting petrol from one terminal to another or from a terminal to a service station.[222] It applies to road trucks and stationary sources and allows states to fix more stringent conditions.[223] It does not set emissions level values. In 1999, the Council adopted another Directive on emissions of VOCs from solvent-using industries.[224] This Directive describes the activity and not the installations that are covered. It sets threshold and emissions limit values for different activities, and member states are required to ensure compliance either by incorporating the Directives requirements or by general emissions regulations. Other Community measures to prevent air pollution include Directive 87/217/EEC on the prevention and reduction of environmental pollution from asbestos, legislation for the protection of forests,[225] and a Directive requiring member states to establish and

---

[217] Council Directive 92/72/EC, OJ L297, 13 October 1992, 1, Art. 1(1).

[218] Arts. 3 and 4(1) and Annexes II and V.

[219] Art. 5 and Annexes I and IV, and Arts. 4(2) and 6.

[220] Directive 2002/3/EC, OJ L67, 9 March 2002, 14, relating to ozone in ambient air.

[221] See n. 151 above. See also Directive 91/542/EEC, OJ L295, 25 October 1991, 1; Directive 93/59/EC, OJ L186, 28 July 1993, 21; and Directive 94/12/EC, OJ L100, 19 April 1994, 42.

[222] Directive 94/63/EC, OJ L365, 31 December 1994, 24, on the control of volatile organic compound emissions resulting from the storage of petrol and its distribution from terminals to service stations.

[223] Arts. 3(3) and 4(3).

[224] Council Directive 99/13/EC, OJ L85, 29 March 1999, 1, on the limitation of emissions of volatile organic compounds due to the use of organic solvents in certain activities and installations.

[225] Council Regulation (EEC) No. 3528/86, OJ L326, 21 November 1986, 2; and Regulation (EC) No. 2158/92, OJ L217, 31 July 1992, 3, on the protection of the Community forests against fire.

implement programmes to limit CO_2 emissions by improving energy efficiency (SAVE).[226]

Monitoring

The EC has also adopted legislation establishing a system for the reciprocal exchange of information and data from networks and individual stations which measure air pollution.[227] It provides for the transmission by member states to the EC Commission of annual measurements of emissions of certain pollutants, to the extent that they are measured, on the basis of which the EC Commission prepares an annual report.[228]

A 1993 Council Decision establishes a monitoring mechanism for CO_2 and other greenhouse gas emissions,[229] and will be employed to determine the total quantity of allowances to allocate within the scope of the new Directive on greenhouse gas emissions trading. A 1997 Decision establishes arrangements for the reciprocal exchange of information and data collected from networks and individual stations measuring ambient air pollution within the member states.[230] The exchange of information and data relates to the networks and stations set up in the member states to measure air pollution and the air quality measurements taken by those stations.[231] All data is to be sent by the member states to the Commission, which will in turn make available to the member states (by 1 July 1997 at the latest) its database, containing information on the networks and stations and on air quality. The data is to be accessible to the public through an information system set up by the European Environment Agency.

Climate change and energy efficiency

The Commission participated actively in the negotiation of the 1992 Climate Change Convention, which it signed in June 1992 at UNCED.[232] Since then, the EU has been at the forefront of the international community's efforts to

---

[226] Directive 93/76/EC, OJ L237, 22 September 1993, 28.

[227] Council Decision 82/459/EEC, OJ L210, 19 July 1982, 1. The Decision repeals the earlier Decision 75/441/EEC, OJ L194, 25 July 1975, 32, Art. 8.

[228] Arts. 2 to 7.

[229] Council Decision 93/389/EC, OJ L167, 9 July 1993, 31, as amended by Decision 99/296/EC, OJ L117, 5 May 1999, 35.

[230] Council Decision 97/101/EC, OJ L35, 5 February1997, 14, as amended. The information exchange relates to the pollutants listed in Directive 96/62/EC, OJ L296, 21 November 1996, 55, and to other polluting substances (Annex I).

[231] The stations included in the exchange programme are the stations set up as part of the implementation of Directive 96/62/EC, OJ L296, 21 November 1996, 55, and stations not covered by the Directive, but which can monitor the pollutants listed above at local and regional levels and other stations which took part in the reciprocal exchange introduced by Decision 82/459/EEC, OJ L210, 19 July 1982, 1.

[232] See Decision 94/69/EC, OJ L33, 7 February 1994, 11.

combat climate change. The data suggests that the EU fulfilled its obligation under the 1992 Climate Change Convention to ensure that its greenhouse gas emissions in 2000 were no greater than in 1990. In 1998, the EC signed the 1997 Kyoto Protocol,[233] and it became a party in May 2002. It has sought to achieve a consensus on ways to comply with the Kyoto commitments.[234] In October 2001, the European Commission adopted a package of initiatives aimed at combating climate change and meeting the Community's obligations under the Kyoto Protocol,[235] including a Communication on the implementation of the first phase of the European Climate Change Programme[236] and a draft Directive on greenhouse gas emissions trading (which was adopted, in codified form, in December 2002).[237] Other measures address the availability of consumer information on fuel conomy and CO_2 emissions from cars and a scheme to monitor CO_2 emissions from cars.[238]

Water quality[239]

EC legislation to protect water quality originated in 1973 with the adoption of a Directive prohibiting the sale and use of certain detergents with a low level of biodegradability.[240] Subsequent legislation has addressed the quality and protection of drinking water, bathing water, groundwater, fish, and urban

---

[233] Council Decision of 23 March 1998 concerning the signature by the European Community of a Protocol to the United Nations Framework Convention on Climate Change, COM (98) 96 final.

[234] See e.g. Communication of 3 June 1998 from the Commission, 'Climate Change – Towards an EU Post-Kyoto Strategy', COM (98) 353 final; Communication of 19 May 1999 from the Commission, 'Preparing for Implementation of the Kyoto Protocol', COM (99) 230 final.

[235] See COM (2001) 579 final, OJ C 75E, 26 March 2002, 17.

[236] In March 2000, the Commission launched the European Climate Change Programme (ECCP) to prepare additional policies and measures, as well as an emissions trading scheme, to ensure that the EU achieves the 8 per cent cut in emissions by 2008–12 to which it is committed under the Kyoto Protocol.

[237] See n. 124 above; on the greenhouse gases trading Directive, see chapter 4, p. 163 above.

[238] Directive 99/94/EC, OJ L12, 18 January 2000, 16; and Decision 1753/2000/EC, OJ L202, 10 August 2000, 1.

[239] See Fifth Environmental Action Programme, n. 107 above, 50–2 and Table 11 (setting overall quantitative and qualitative targets up to 2000); and Sixth Environmental Action Programme, n. 108 above and the accompanying text. See also R. Macrory, 'European Community Water Law', 20 *Ecology Law Quarterly* 119 (1993); D. Grimeaud, 'Reforming EU Water Law: Towards Sustainability?', 10 RECIEL 41 (2001).

[240] Council Directive 73/404/EEC, OJ L347, 17 December 1973, 51. The Directive was amended by Council Directive 82/242/EEC, OJ L109, 22 April 1982, 1, and Council Directive 86/94/EEC, OJ L80, 25 March 1986, 51. The Commission has brought several successful prosecutions for failure to implement Directive 82/242/EEC, OJ L109, 22 April 1982, 1: see Case 309/86, *EC Commission* v. *Italy* [1988] ECR 1237; Case 134/86, *EC Commission* v. *Belgium* [1988] ECR 2415.

waste water, and regulated discharges of certain dangerous substances. In the mid-1990s, the Community decided to refashion its approach and adopt an overall Community framework on water pollution leading to the adoption, in 2000, of the Water Framework Directive.

Water Framework Directive

The framework Directive for the protection of inland surface waters, transitional waters, coastal waters and groundwater was adopted in 2000, with the purposes of providing a sufficient supply of good quality surface water and groundwater as needed for sustainable, balanced and equitable water use, by: preventing further deterioration and protecting and enhancing the status of aquatic ecosystems; promoting sustainable water use based on the long-term protection of available water resources; enhancing the protection and improvement of the aquatic environment (by progressive reduction of discharges, emissions and losses of priority substances and the cessation or phasing-out of discharges, emissions and losses of the priority hazardous substances); and ensuring the progressive reduction of pollution of groundwater.[241] It adopts an innovative and modern ecosystem approach, premised on the view that 'water is not a commercial product like any other but, rather, a heritage which must be protected, defended and treated as such'.[242]

The Directive embodies the concept of integrated river basin management, and aims to rationalise and update current water legislation and replace – over time – seven existing Directives.[243] Member states must identify their river basins and assign them to individual river basin districts.[244] Within four years of entry into force member states must complete an analysis of the characteristics of each river basin district, a review of the impact of human activity on the water, and an economic analysis of water use, and compile a register of areas requiring special protection.[245] Within nine years of entry into force member states must devise a management plan for each district lying entirely

---

[241] Directive 2000/60/EC, OJ L327, 22 December 2000, 1, Arts. 1 and 2.

[242] Preamble. For critique of the Directive as ambiguous and overly broad, see David Grimeaud, 'Reforming EU Water Law: Towards Sustainability?', 10 RECIEL 41 (2001).

[243] Most 'first wave' Community water instruments will be repealed with effect from seven years after the Directive's entry into force, including: Directives 75/440/EEC and 79/869/EEC on drinking water (see p. 771 below); Directives 78/659/EEC and 79/923/EEC on the quality of waters to support fish life (see p. 775 below); Directive 80/68/EEC on groundwater (see p. 774 below); Directive 76/464/EEC on pollution caused by dangerous substances (partially) and its daughter Directives (see p. 773 below): Art. 22.

[244] Art. 3. A 'river basin' is 'the area of land from which all surface run-off flows through a sequence of streams, rivers and, possibly, lakes into the sea at a single river mouth, estuary or delta': Art. 1(13). A competent authority is to be designated for each of the river basin districts by December 2003 at the latest and river basins covering the territory of more than one member state will be assigned to an international river basin district.

[245] Arts. 5 and 6.

within its territory, taking into account the results of their analyses.[246] For an international river basin district falling entirely within the EC, member states must 'co-ordinate with the aim of producing a single international river basin management plan'.[247] For an international river basin district extending beyond the boundaries of the EC the member states

> shall endeavour to produce a single river basin management plan, and, where this is not possible, the plan shall at least cover the portion of the international river basin district lying within the territory of the member state concerned.
>
> Where such an international river basin management plan is not produced, member states shall produce river basin management plans covering at least those parts of the international river basin district falling within their territory to achieve the objectives of this Directive.[248]

The measures provided for in the river basin management plan are intended to prevent deterioration of surface water and groundwater and preserve protected areas. Article 4(1) sets out the environmental objectives in making operational the programmes of measures specified in the river basin management plans, in respect of surface waters, groundwater and protected areas. Article 4(3) to (9) provides for certain derogations and exemptions, laying down a sustainable water policy which combines both environmental and development goals.[249] These objectives are to be achieved at the latest fifteen years after the Directive's entry into force, although this deadline may be extended under certain conditions. The Directive lists priority substances which are deemed to present a significant risk to the aquatic environment, and sets forth measures to control such substances, as well as quality standards applicable to their concentrations, and the basis for measures to reduce, stop or eliminate discharges, emissions and losses of priority substances.[250] The Directive includes specific provisions (including water quality standards) on waters used for abstraction of drinking water (Article 7) and on monitoring of surface waters and groundwaters and protected areas (Article 8). The Directive requires member states to ensure (within twelve years of the Directive's entry into force or unless otherwise specified) that all discharges into surface waters are subject to emissions controls based on best available techniques, or the relevant emission limit values, or in the case of diffuse impacts the controls including, as appropriate,

---

[246] Art. 13(1); Annex VII includes information to be included in the plan.

[247] Art. 13(2). Where no such plan is produced, each member state must produce plans covering at least those parts of the international river basin district falling within its territory.

[248] Art. 13(3).

[249] Art. 11 requires member states to establish a programme of measures for each river basin district, or for each part of an international river basin district within its territory.

[250] Decision 2455/2001/EC, OJ L331, 15 December 2001, 1, established the list of priority substances. See also Annex X to the Directive.

best environmental practices, set out in various existing EC Directives (96/61 (integrated pollution prevention and control), 91/271 (urban waste water) and 91/76 (nitrates)), as well as Directives adopted under Article 16 or listed in Annex IX to the Water Framework Directive.[251] By 2010, member states are to ensure that water-pricing policies provide adequate incentives for users to use water resources efficiently, and ensure an adequate contribution by the different water uses (disaggregated into at least industry, household and agriculture) to the recovery of the costs of water services.[252] The Directive also includes provisions on public information and reporting, and commits the European Parliament and the Council to adopt specific measures against pollution of water by individual pollutants or groups of pollutants, and specific measures to prevent and control groundwater pollution.[253]

Drinking water

Two principal Directives address drinking water quality standards. Council Directive 75/440/EEC establishes quality standards for drinking water after it has been abstracted from surface freshwater and after it has been treated.[254] The Directive divides surface water into three categories (A1, A2 and A3) in accordance with methods of treatment set out in Annex I and corresponding with the physical, chemical and microbiological characteristics of the waters as set out in forty-six parameters identified in Annex II.[255] Surface waters falling short of the A3 standard may only be used for the abstraction of drinking water in exceptional circumstances and after notification to the EC Commission.[256] Member states are free to fix more stringent values.[257]

Under Directive 80/778/EEC, member states must fix quality values for all waters intended for human consumption (except natural mineral waters and medicinal waters) in accordance with the parameters set out in Annex I.[258] The Directive is designed to promote the free movement of goods within the

---

[251] Art. 10.

[252] Art. 9(1). This is to be based on the economic analysis conducted according to Annex III and taking account of the polluter-pays principle.

[253] Arts. 14–17.

[254] Council Directive 75/440/EEC, OJ L194, 25 July 1975, 26. On non-implementation, see Joined Cases 30 to 34/81, *EC Commission* v. *Italy* [1981] ECR 3379; and Case 73/81, *EC Commission* v. *Belgium* [1982] ECR 189; see also Council Decision 77/795/EEC, OJ L334, 24 December 1977, 29, as amended. This Directive will be repealed in 2007: see n. 243 above.

[255] Art. 2. See Council Directive 79/869/EEC, OJ L271, 29 October 1979, 44, as amended.

[256] Art. 4(3). For failure to fulfil obligations under Arts. 3 and 4 with regard to the quality of surface water intended for the abstraction of drinking water, see Case C-266/99, *Commission* v. *France* [2001] ECR I-1981.

[257] Art. 6.

[258] Council Directive 80/778/EEC, OJ L229, 30 August 1980, 11, as amended, Arts. 1, 2, 4 and 7. See Case C-42/89, *EC Commission* v. *Belgium* [1990] ECR I-2821, holding that the exclusion of private water supplies was incompatible with the Directive. In Case

EC and to protect human health and the environment, and it allows member states to set more stringent levels.[259] Annex I lays down maximum admissible concentration (MAC) levels and guide levels (GL) for sixty-two parameters and minimum required concentrations (MRC) for four parameters, in six categories: organoleptic parameters, physico-chemical parameters, parameters concerning substances undesirable in excessive amounts, toxic substance parameters, microbiological parameters, and MRC for softened water intended for human consumption. The Directive allows derogations, provides for emergency situations, and requires member states to ensure regular monitoring of the quality of drinking water intended for human consumption in accordance with Annexes II and III.[260] Directive 98/83/EC on the quality of water intended for human consumption will replace Directive 80/778/EEC in 2003. The new Directive seeks to improve assessment criteria for, and monitoring of, pollution of drinking water and to speed up the harmonisation of such criteria at the European level.[261]

Bathing water

Council Directive 76/160/EEC, which now applies to more than 14,000 bathing areas in the EC, requires member states to set the values applicable to bathing water for the nineteen imperative (I) and guideline (G) physical, chemical and microbiological parameters set forth in the Annex.[262] Member states had ten years from the notification of the Directive, until December 1985, to ensure that the quality of bathing water conformed to the limit values in the Annex,

---

C-340/96, *Commission v. United Kingdom* [1999] ECR I-2023, the ECJ held that undertakings from water companies, under national legislations, are an insufficient way to ensure that the quality of water complies with the requirements of the Directive if the conditions governing the acceptance of such undertakings are not specified.

[259] Art. 16.

[260] Arts. 9, 10 and 12. The ECJ has upheld several claims by the Commission alleging violations of the Directive: see Case 97/81, *Commission v. Netherlands* [1982] ECR 1819; Case C-42/89, *Commission v. Belgium* [1990] ECR I-2821; Case C-237/90, *Commission v. Germany* [1992] ECR I-5937 (unlawful derogations); Case C-337/89, *Commission v. United Kingdom* [1992] ECR I-6103 (unlawful derogations).

[261] OJ L330, 5 December 1998, 32.

[262] Council Directive 76/160/EEC, OJ L31, 5 February 1976, 1, as amended, Arts. 1, 2 and 3. The Directive applies to all bathing waters except those used for therapeutic purposes and water used in swimming pools: Art. 1(1). Several violations of the Directive have been upheld by the ECJ: see Joined Cases 30 to 34/81, *Commission v. Italy* [1981] ECR 3379 (non-implementation); Case 72/81, *Commission v. Belgium* [1982] ECR 183; Case 96/81, *Commission v. Netherlands* [1982] ECR 1791; Case C-56/90, *Commission v. United Kingdom* [1993] ECR I-4109 (holding that the United Kingdom had failed to take all necessary measures to ensure that the quality of bathing waters in Blackpool and those adjacent to Southport conform to the limit values under Art. 3 of the Directive); Case C-92/96, *Commission v. Spain* [1998] ECR I-505; and Case C-198/97, *Commission v. Germany* [1999] ECR I-3257. In December 2000, the Commission adopted a Communication on the development of a new bathing water policy with a view to revising the twenty-five-year-old Bathing Water Directive: COM (2000) 860 final.

subject to derogations granted by member states and communicated to the EC Commission. within the time limit granted.[263] Member states remain free to fix more stringent values.[264] Riparian member states are to collaborate in setting common quality objectives for 'sea water in the vicinity of frontiers and water crossing frontiers which affect the quality of the bathing water of another member state'.[265] The Directive requires regular sampling by the competent authorities of the member states and may be waived in exceptional circumstances, including exceptional weather or geographical conditions.[266]

Dangerous substances

Council Directive 76/464/EEC on pollution caused by certain dangerous substances discharged into the aquatic environment of the Community was designed to prevent pollution of inland surface water, territorial waters, internal coastal waters and groundwater by eliminating discharges of dangerous substances specified in List 1 of the Annex, and by reducing discharges of substances in List 2 of the Annex.[267] The EC Council is required to lay down limit values and quality objectives which the emissions standards must not exceed for the List 1 substances.[268] To date, the Council has set specific emissions limit values for a number of List 1 substances in five specific Directives, referred to as 'daughter Directives'. These include mercury,[269] cadmium,[270] hexachlorocyclohexane[271] and certain other dangerous substances.[272] Legal action has been taken where national legislation has not been adopted[273] and for failures to

---

[263] Art. 4(1) and (3). For failure of obligations under Art. 4, see Case C-307/98, *Commission v. Belgium* [2000] ECR I-3933; and for inadequate implementation see Case C-368/00, *Commission v. Sweden* [2001] ECR I-4605.

[264] Art. 7(2).   [265] Art. 4(4).

[266] Arts. 6 and 8. On failure to carry out requisite sampling and failure of obligations under Arts. 3, 4, 5 and 6 of the Directive, see Case C-147/00, *Commission v. France* [2001] ECR I-2387.

[267] OJ L129, 18 May 1976, 23, Arts. 1 and 2, as amended. See also Council Directive 91/676/EEC, OJ L375, 31 December 1991, 1. The Directive is repealed with effect from 2013 (see above); however, the Water Framework Directive provides that, for bodies of surface water, environmental objectives established under the first river basin management plan shall, as a minimum, give effect to quality standards at least as stringent as those required by Directive 76/464/EEC: Art. 22(6).

[268] Art. 6. This provision will be repealed in 2007: see n. 243 above.

[269] Council Directive 82/176/EEC, OJ L81, 27 March 1982, 29, as amended; and Council Directive 84/156/EEC, OJ L74, 17 March 1984, 49, as amended.

[270] Council Directive 83/513/EEC, OJ L291, 24 October 1983, 1, as amended.

[271] Council Directive 84/491/EEC, OJ L274, 17 October 1984, 11, as amended.

[272] Council Directive 86/280/EEC, OJ L181, 4 July 1986, 16, as amended by, *inter alia*, Council Directive 88/347/EEC, OJ L158, 25 June 1988, 35, and Council Directive 90/415/EEC, OJ L219, 14 August 1990, 49.

[273] See C-213/97, *Commission v. Portugal* [1998] ECR I-3289, on failure to transpose Directive 86/280/EEC, OJ L181, 4 July 1986, 16, and Directive 88/347/EEC, OJ L158, 25 June 1988, 35; Case C-208/97, *Commission v. Portugal* [1998] ECR I-4017, on failure to transpose the

comply with other obligations under the Directives.[274] The regulation of other 'candidate List 1 substances' was suspended at the beginning of the 1990s due to the preparation of a more comprehensive and integrated permit system for industrial installations. Article 7 requires the establishment of implementation programmes to reduce pollution from List 2 substances[275] and for List 1 substances for which the Council has not yet determined emissions limit values.[276] The Council has not yet adopted any implementing Directives for these substances. Although the IPPC Directive will be applicable to new installations, the provisions of this Directive will remain applicable to existing installations until the measures required pursuant to Article 5 of the IPPC Directive have been taken by the competent authorities.[277]

Groundwater

Council Directive 80/68/EEC is designed to prevent the pollution of groundwater by the substances listed in Lists I or II in the Annex to the Directive, but does not apply to certain discharges of domestic effluents, certain small quantities and concentrations, or radioactive substances.[278] Member states must prevent the introduction into groundwater of substances on List I, by prohibiting direct discharges and taking appropriate measures, including prior investigation and authorisation of activities which might lead to indirect discharge.[279] They must

Mercury Directive; or where the Directive was transposed by an administrative circular rather than binding legislation, as in Case C-262/95, *Commission* v. *Germany* [1996] ECR I-5729.

[274] For failure to comply with the reporting obligations under Directive 76/464/EEC, OJ L129, 18 May 1976, 23, on pollution caused by certain dangerous substances discharged into the aquatic environment and its daughter Directives, see Case C-435/99, *Commission* v. *Portugal* [2000] ECR I-11179.

[275] The first judgment under this Directive was rendered in 1998 in Joined Cases C-232 and 233/95, *Commission* v. *Greece* [1998] ECR I-3343. In 1996 and 1997, the Commission brought actions against Luxembourg, Spain, Italy, Germany, Belgium and Greece essentially for the absence of pollution reduction programmes for List 2 substances. See also Case C-152/98, *Commission* v. *Netherlands* [2001] ECR I-3463.

[276] Those substances are provionally treated as List 2 substances governed by Art. 7. Case C-207/97, *Commission* v. *Belgium* [1999] ECR I-275, paras. 34 and 35; and Case C-184/97, *Commission* v. *Germany* [1999] ECR I-7837, para. 27.

[277] Art. 20 of the IPPC Directive. See also Case C-207/97, *Commission* v. *Belgium* [1999] ECR I-275, para. 36.

[278] Council Directive 80/68/EEC, OJ L20, 26 January 1980, 43, as amended, Arts. 1 and 2. See also Council Resolution of 25 February 1992, OJ C59, 6 March 1992, 2. The Directive wil be repealed in 2007: see n. 243 above.

[279] Arts. 3(a) and 4. 'Direct discharge' is defined as 'the introduction into groundwater of substances in Lists I or II without percolation through ground or subsoil'; 'indirect discharge' is defined as the introduction of such substances into the groundwater 'after percolation through the ground or subsoil': Art. 1(2)(b) and (c). For its failure to fulfil its obligations under Arts. 3–5, 7 and 10, see Case C-230/00, *Commission* v. *Belgium* [2001] ECR I-4591.

also limit the introduction of List II substances by making potential direct or indirect discharges subject to prior investigation and authorisation.[280] Where appropriate, more stringent measures may be taken individually or jointly.[281] Member states must monitor compliance with the conditions of authorisation and the effects of discharges on groundwater, keep an inventory of authorisations, and supply the EC Commission with any relevant information at its request and on a case-by-case basis.[282] The Directive has been the subject of numerous violations.[283] In 1997, the Commission submitted a proposal for a decision on an action programme for integrated groundwater protection and management.[284]

Protection of fish

The protection of the quality of waters to support fish life is the subject of two principal Directives. Under Council Directive 78/659/EEC, member states must designate salmonid waters (supporting salmon, grayling and whitefish) and cyprinid waters (supporting cyprinids, pike, perch and eel) which require protection or improvement, and set in respect of those designated waters guideline values (G) and imperative values (I) in accordance with the parameters set forth in Annex I.[285] The designated waters were required to conform to the standards set out in Annex I within five years of designation, and member states may set more stringent standards.[286] The Directive provides for establishing programmes,[287] sampling, derogations, and the provision of information and reports by the member states to the EC Commission.[288] Where fresh waters cross or form national frontiers between member states, and one of the member states

---

[280] Arts. 3(b) and 5. Arts. 8 to 12 specify the criteria for authorisations.

[281] Art. 18.   [282] Arts. 15 to 17.

[283] See e.g. Case 1/86, *EC Commission* v. *Belgium* [1987] ECR 2797; Case C-174/91, *EC Commission* v. *Belgium* [1993] ECR I-2275; Case 291/84, *EC Commission* v. *Netherlands* [1987] ECR 3483; Case C-360/87, *EC Commission* v. *Italy* [1991] ECR I-791; Case C-131/88, *EC Commission* v. *Germany* [1991] ECR I-825; and Case C-183/97, *Commission* v. *Portugal* [1998] ECR I-4005.

[284] The framework Directive 2000/60/EC, OJ L327, 22 December 2000, 1, on water will repeal Council Directive 80/68/EEC, OJ L20, 26 January 1980, 43, on groundwater.

[285] Council Directive 78/659/EEC, OJ L222, 14 August 1978, 1, as amended, Arts. 1 to 4. This Directive will be repealed in 2013. See also Case 14/86, *Pretore di Salo* v. *Persons Unknown* [1987] ECR 2545, holding that Directive 78/659/EEC cannot of itself and independently of an implementing national law determine or aggravate the liability in criminal law of persons who act in contravention of its provisions.

[286] Arts. 5 and 9.

[287] 'Specific programmes' are required; general water purification programmes are not sufficient: see Case C-298/95, *Commission* v. *Germany* [1996] ECR I-6747, para. 24.

[288] Arts. 6, 7, 11, 15 and 16. On non-implementation of notification and designation, see Case 322/86, *EC Commission* v. *Italy* [1988] ECR 3995; and Case C-291/93, *Commission* v. *Italy* [1994] ECR I-859.

considers designating these waters, consultations are to take place between the states.[289]

Council Directive 79/923/EEC applies a similar approach to the protection of coastal and brackish waters designated by member states as needing protection or improvement to support shellfish life.[290] Member states have six years following designation to ensure that waters conform with the standards set out in the Annex to the Directive.[291] Implementation has not been speedy.[292]

Urban waste water

The objective of Council Directive 91/271/EEC is to protect the environment from the adverse effects of discharges of urban waste water and waste water from certain industrial sectors, both of which are responsible for large quantities of marine pollution.[293] The Directive reflected an early example of the increasingly detailed nature of EC environmental law, and has entailed significant and costly improvements to the treatment of waste waters in many of the member states. Under the terms of the Directive, all agglomerations (urban areas) were to have collecting systems for urban waste water by 31 December 2000 in areas where there is a population equivalent (p.e.) of more than 15,000 people, and by 31 December 2000 where the p.e. is between 2,000 and 15,000.[294] Where urban waste waters are discharged into receiving waters which are 'sensitive areas', collection systems were to be provided by 31 December 1998 for agglomerations of more than 10,000 p.e.[295] Systems achieving the same level of environmental protection may be used instead of a collecting system if the use of a collecting system is not justified on environmental or (excessive) cost grounds.

Urban waste water entering collecting systems is to be subject to 'secondary treatment' or an equivalent treatment before discharge, by 31 December 2000 for all discharges from agglomerations of more than 15,000 p.e., and by 31 December 2005 for all discharges from agglomerations of between 10,000 and 15,000 p.e. and discharges to fresh waters and estuaries from agglomerations of between 2,000 and 10,000 p.e.[296] Discharges from collecting systems to fresh

---

[289] Art. 10.

[290] Council Directive 79/923/EEC, OJ L281, 10 November 1979, 47, as amended, Arts. 1 to 4. This Directive will be repealed in 2013: see n. 243 above.

[291] Art. 5.

[292] See e.g. Case C-225/96, *Commission* v. *Italy* [1997] ECR I-6887.

[293] Council Directive 91/271/EEC, OJ L135, 30 May 1991, 40, as amended, Art. 1. 'Urban waste water' is defined as 'domestic waste water or the mixture of domestic waste water with industrial waste water and/or runoff rain water': Art. 2(1).

[294] Art. 3(1). Basic requirements for 'collecting systems' are set out in Annex I(A).

[295] Art. 3(1); the criteria for 'sensitive areas' are set out in Annex II, Part A.

[296] Art. 4(1). 'Secondary treatment' means 'treatment of urban waste water by a process generally involving biological treatment with a secondary settlement or other process in which the requirements established in Table I of Annex I are respected': Art. 2(8). Discharges to waters situated in high mountain regions may be subject to less stringent

waters and estuaries from agglomerations of less than 2,000 p.e. and to coastal waters from agglomerations of less than 10,000 p.e. were to be subject to appropriate treatment by 31 December 1995.[297] These discharges are to satisfy the requirements set out in Annex IB, including parameters for demand of biochemical oxygen and chemical oxygen, suspended solids, phosphorus and nitrogen.[298]

All discharges from agglomerations of more than 10,000 p.e. into sensitive areas were to be subject to more stringent treatment than that described above by 31 December 1998.[299] Sensitive areas were to be identified by member states by 31 December 1993 in accordance with Annex II, and reviewed at least every four years.[300] Discharges from agglomerations of between 10,000 and 150,000 p.e. to coastal waters and from agglomerations of between 2,000 and 10,000 p.e. to estuaries in less sensitive areas may be subject to less stringent treatment provided that they receive at least primary treatment and comprehensive studies indicate that they will not adversely affect the environment.[301] In exceptional circumstances where it can be demonstrated that advanced treatment will not produce any environmental benefits, discharges into less sensitive areas from agglomerations of more than 150,000 p.e. may also be subject to this less stringent treatment.[302] The Directive also makes provision for the voluntary identification of less sensitive areas which will be subject to less stringent standards.[303]

Since 31 December 1993, the discharge of industrial waste water into collecting systems and urban waste water treatment plants has been subjected to prior regulations and/or specific authorisations, to satisfy the requirements of Annex IC.[304] Biodegradable industrial waste water from plants in the industrial sectors

---

treatment: Art. 4(2). A longer time period may be established in exceptional cases due to technical problems and for geographically defined populations: Art. 8.

[297] Art. 7. 'Appropriate treatment' is defined as 'treatment of urban waste water by any process and/or disposal system which after discharge allows the receiving waters to meet the relevant quality objectives and the relevant provisions of this and other Community Directives': Art. 2(9).

[298] Art. 4(3).

[299] Art. 5(1) and (2). Certain exceptions may be established for individual plants: Art. 5(4).

[300] Art. 5(1) and (6). Sensitive areas do not have to be identified in certain circumstances: Art. 5(8).

[301] Art. 6(2). 'Primary treatment' means treatment by 'a physical and/or chemical process involving settlement of suspended solids, or other processes in which the BOD5 [biochemical oxygen demand for five days] of the incoming waste water is reduced by at least twenty per cent before discharge and total suspended solids of the incoming waste water are reduced by at least fifty per cent': Art. 2(7). On the conditions under which the exemption may be applied, see R. v. *Secretary of State for the Environment, ex parte Kingston upon Hull City Council and ex parte Bristol City Council* [1996] Env LR 248; (1996) 8 Admin LR 509.

[302] Art. 8(5).   [303] Art. 6.   [304] Art. 11.

listed in Annex III is subject to separate rules.[305] The Directive encourages the re-use of treated waste water and sludge and has provided for the conditions of their disposal, and prohibited the disposal of sludge to surface waters by dumping from ships or by other means after 31 December 1998.[306] Finally, the Directive establishes basic requirements concerning the adverse effects of discharges of urban waste waters from one member state on another member state, for the design, construction and operation of treatment plants, and for monitoring and other basic implementation requirements.[307] The Directive was to be transposed into national law by mid-1993. In 1996, Greece, Germany and Italy were taken before the ECJ for non-compliance.[308]

The Directive was amended by Directive 98/15/EC,[309] with the aim of clarifying the rules relating to discharges from urban waste water treatment plants in order to put an end to differences in interpretation by the member states. It specifies, *inter alia*, that:

- the option of using daily averages for the total nitrogen concentration applies both to agglomerations of 10,000–100,000 population equivalent and to those of more than 100,000 p.e.;
- the condition concerning the temperature of the effluent in the biological reactor and the limitation on the time of operation to take account of regional climatic conditions only apply to the 'alternative' method using daily averages;
- use of the 'alternative' method must ensure the same level of environmental protection as the annual mean technique.

A Commission report of November 2001 concluded that most member states had made considerable efforts to comply with the Directive resulting in significant improvements in water quality in Europe.[310]

Marine pollution

The EC is a party to several regional and international conventions concerning the protection of the marine environment, including: the 1974 Paris LBS Convention,[311] the 1974 Baltic Sea Convention,[312] the 1976 Barcelona Convention

---

[305] Art. 13.   [306] Arts. 12 and 14.   [307] Arts. 9, 10 and 15 to 17.

[308] See e.g. Cases C-161/95, *Commission* v. *Greece* [1996] ECR I-1979; C-297/95, *Commission* v. *Germany* [1996] ECR I-6739; and Case C-302/95, *Commission* v. *Italy* [1996] ECR I-6765. See also Case C-236/99, *Commission* v. *Belgium* [2000] ECR I-5657.

[309] OJ L67, 7 March 1998, 29.

[310] Commission Report, COM/2001/685 final, 21 November 2001.

[311] See chapter 9, pp. 430–4 above, Council Decision 75/437/EEC, OJ L194, 25 July 1975, 5, as amended by Council Decision 87/57/EEC, OJ L24, 27 January 1987, 46. See also Council Decision 85/613/EEC, OJ L375, 31 December 1985, 20 (implementing PARCOM Decisions 85/1 and 85/2).

[312] Council Decision 94/156/EC of 21 February 1994, OJ L73, 16 March 1994, 1; and Council Decision 94/157/EC of 21 February 1994, OJ L73, 16 March 1994.

and Protocols,[313] the 1983 Bonn Agreement,[314] the 1992 OSPAR Convention,[315] the 1998 Rhine Convention,[316] the 1992 Watercourses Convention[317] and the 1982 UNCLOS.[318]

In December 2000, the EC Council adopted a Decision setting up a Community framework for co-operation in the field of accidental or deliberate marine pollution.[319] The Commission has also put forward a proposal for a Regulation on the establishment of a fund for compensation for oil pollution damage in European waters and related measures.[320]

Nature and biodiversity[321]

The EC has made a significant contribution to the development of international law for the conservation of biodiversity, most notably by the 1979 Wild Birds Directive and the 1992 Habitats Directive, which are described in chapter 11 above.[322] The EC has also legislated on: the importation of whales and other cetacean products;[323] the importation of skins of seal pups and their products;[324] the importation of raw and worked ivory;[325] the protection of animals used for experimental purposes;[326] the protection of dolphins;[327] and

---

[313] Chapter 9, pp. 400–2 above, Council Decision 77/585/EEC, OJ L240, 19 September 1977, 1. The EC is also a party to the 1976 Barcelona Dumping Protocol (Council Decision 77/585/EEC); the 1976 Barcelona Oil Pollution Protocol (Council Decision 81/420/EEC, OJ L162, 19 June 1981, 4); the 1980 Athens LBS Protocol (Council Decision 83/101/EEC, OJ L67, 12 March 1983, 1); and 1982 Geneva SPA Protocol (Council Decision 84/132/EEC, OJ L68, 10 March 1984, 36).

[314] Chapter 9, pp. 452–3 above. Council Decision 84/358/EEC, OJ L188, 16 July 1984, 7.

[315] Council Decision 98/249/EC of 7 October 1997, OJ L104, 3 April 1998, 1, which entered into force on 25 March 1998 to replace the Oslo (1972) and Paris (1974) Conventions; see chapter 9, pp. 409–12 above.

[316] Council Decision 2000/706/EC of 7 November 2000, OJ L289, 16 November 2000, 30.

[317] Council Decision 95/308/EC of 24 July 1995, OJ L186, 5 August 1995, 42.

[318] Council Decision 98/392/EC of 23 March 1998, OJ L179, 23 June 1998, 1.

[319] Council Decision 2850/2000/EC, OJ L332, 28 December 2000, 1.

[320] Commission Proposal COM (2000) 802 final, OJ C120E, 24 April 2001, 83.

[321] Fifth Environmental Action Programme, n. 107 above, Table 10, setting forth specific targets up to 2000 on maintenance or restoration of natural habitats, the creation of a European network of protected sites, and strict control of abuse and trade of wild species.

[322] Chapters 11, pp. 536–40 and 602–5 above.

[323] Council Regulation (EEC) No. 348/81, OJ L39, 12 February 1981, 1, as amended.

[324] Council Directive 83/129/EEC, OJ L91, 9 April 1983, 30, as amended.

[325] Commission Regulation (EEC) No. 2496/89, OJ L240, 17 August 1989, 5.

[326] Council Directive 86/609, OJ L358, 18 December 1986, 1. On 23 March 1998, the Council adopted Decision 1999/575/EC, OJ L222, 24 August 1999, 29, on the conclusion of the European Convention for the protection of vertebrate animals used for experimental and other scientific purposes.

[327] Council Decision 99/337/EC, OJ L132, 27 May 1999, 1, on the signature by the European Community to the agreement on the International Dolphin Conservation Programme.

the keeping of wild animals in zoos.[328] The EC is a party to various international conventions including: the 1980 CCAMLR;[329] the 1979 Berne Convention;[330] the 1979 Bonn Convention;[331] the 1992 Biodiversity Convention;[332] the 1994 Geneva Convention on tropical wood;[333] and the 1994 Desertification Convention.[334]

The EC is not a party to the 1973 CITES, but has adopted legislation providing for the implementation of that Convention.[335] A 1997 Regulation is now the core of the Community's wildlife trade legislation.[336] Protected species covered by the Regulation are listed in four Annexes, and changes to the list are made by way of new Regulations. The Regulation establishes common conditions for the import, export and sale of the species covered and sets out the conditions and restrictions for the movement of species within the Community. It also sets out various obligations of member states including that of monitoring compliance with the provisions of the Regulation. It introduces a system for the exchange of information between the authorities concerned, and states that stricter measures may be taken by the member states, particularly as regards the keeping of specimens of species listed in Annex A.

Beyond the Habitats Directive and other legislation, in 1998 the Community adopted a Biodiversity Strategy, addressing conservation and the sustainable use of natural resources, research and the exchange of information, the sharing of genetic resources, and education.[337] In March 2001, the Community adopted a Biodiversity Action Plan for the Conservation of Natural Resources. The Community's areas of activity were the conservation of natural resources, agriculture, fisheries and development and economic co-operation.[338] Earlier,

---

[328] Council Directive 99/22/EC, OJ L94, 9 April 1999, 24.

[329] Chapter 14, pp. 714–16 above. Council Decision 81/691/EEC, OJ L252, 5 September 1981, 26, as amended.

[330] Chapter 11, pp. 532–5 above. Council Decision 82/72/EEC, OJ L38, 10 February 1982, 1.

[331] Chapter 11, pp. 607–11 above. Council Decision 82/461/EEC, OJ L210, 19 July 1982, 10.

[332] Council Decision 93/626/EC, OJ L309, 13 December 1993, 1, concerning the conclusion of the Convention on Biological Diversity; chapter 11, pp. 515–23 above.

[333] Council Decision 94/493/EC, OJ L201/1, 1996.

[334] Council Decision 98/216/EC, OJ L83, 19 March 1998, 1.

[335] Chapter 11, pp. 505–15 above; G. A. Vandeputte, 'Why the European Community Should Become a Member of the Convention on International Trade in Endangered Species of Fauna and Flora', 3 *Georgetown International Environmental Law Review* 245 (1991). Council Regulation (EEC) No. 82/3626, OJ L384, 31 December 1982, 1, as amended. In 1997, the old legislation was replaced by Council Regulation (EC) No. 338/97, OJ L61, 3 March 1997, 1, as amended.

[336] Commission Regulation (EC) No. 939/97, OJ L140, 30 May 1997, 9, as amended, sets out detailed rules concerning the implementation of Council Regulation (EC) No. 338/97, OJ L61, 3 March 1997, 1.

[337] COM (98) 42, OJ C341, 9 November 1998, 41.   [338] COM (2001) 162 final.

the Community had adopted several Regulations with regard to forests,[339] and the Community has adopted a Communication regarding coastal zone management.[340]

Fisheries

The EC has also developed an extensive body of secondary legislation for the conservation of fisheries resources, relying principally on Articles 32 to 38 of the EC Treaty (formerly Articles 38 to 46), which provide for a common policy in the field of agriculture.[341] In 1978, the EC Commission published proposals for total allowable catches (TACs) for most states in Community waters. The principal instrument governing conservation was, until 1993, Council Regulation (EEC) No. 83/170, which established a system to protect fishing grounds, the conservation of biological resources of the sea, and their balanced exploitation on a lasting basis and in appropriate economic and social conditions.[342] The Regulation allowed the TAC to be fixed each year and to be distributed between the member states in a manner which assured the relative stability of fishing activities for each of the states concerned.[343] Provided that they gave prior notice to the EC Commission, member states could exchange parts or all of the quotas allocated to them, which in effect established a system of tradeable fisheries rights.[344] The conservation measures were formulated in the light of scientific advice, and included: (1) the establishment of zones where fishing is prohibited or limited to certain periods or vessels or fishing gear; (2) the setting of standards for fishing gear; (3) the setting of minimum fish size, or weight

---

[339] See Regulations to protect forests from fire, Regulation (EEC) No. 2158/92, OJ L217, 31 July 1992, 3, as amended; from atmospheric pollution, Regulation (EEC) No. 2157/92 amending Regulation (EEC) No. 3528/86, OJ L217, 31 July 1992, 1, as amended; Regulation (EC) No. 2494/2000, OJ L288, 15 November 2000, 6, on measures to promote the conservation and sustainable management of tropical forests and other forests in developing countries; and Regulation (EEC) No. 1615/89, OJ L165, 15 June 1989, 12, as amended, establishing a European Forestry Information and Communication System (EFICS).

[340] See Communication on 'Integrated Coastal Zone Management: A Strategy for Europe' and a Proposal for a Recommendation Concerning the Implementation of Integrated Coastal Zone Management in Europe, COM (2000) 547 final, of 17 September 2000 and COM (2000) 545 final of 8 September 2000.

[341] For an account of the history, development and application of this extensive area of law, including the case law of the ECJ, see R. R. Churchill, *EEC Fisheries Law* (1987).

[342] Council Regulation (EEC) No. 170/83, OJ L24, 27 January 1983, 1, Art.1(1). See also Council Regulation (EEC) No. 86/3094, OJ L288, 11 October 1986, 1, on minimum mesh sizes, attachment to nets, minimum fish sizes, prohibitions on fishing for certain species, restrictions on types of vessels and fishing gear, and prohibitions on processing operations.

[343] Arts. 3(1) and 4(1). See e.g. Council Regulation (EEC) No. 3926/90, OJ L 378, 31 December 1990, 1, fixing TACs for 1991.

[344] Art. 5(1).

for a species; and (4) limits on catches.[345] The EC Commission also manages a licensing system to govern certain fishing activities,[346] and has adopted a large number of instruments implementing these fisheries measures as well as measures for conservation and management in respect of fishing vessels of third states.[347]

In December 1992, the EC adopted Regulation (EC) No. 3760/92 which replaced the 1983 Regulation with effect from 1 January 1993. This sought to extend and consolidate the earlier legal regime

> to protect and conserve available and accessible living marine aquatic resources, and to provide for rational and responsible exploitation on a sustainable basis, in appropriate economic and social conditions for the sector, taking account of its implications for the marine ecosystem, and in particular taking account of the needs of both producers and consumers.[348]

The Regulation recognises the need to protect accessible resources, including those in the waters of third countries to which EC fishing vessels have access pursuant to bilateral or other arrangements. The new Regulation relies upon a range of management tools to limit exploitation, including:

1. establishing prohibited fishing zones;
2. limiting exploitation rates;
3. setting quantitative limits on catches;
4. limiting time spent at sea;
5. fixing the number and types of fishing vessels authorised to fish;
6. laying down measures on fishing gear and its use;
7. setting minimum size or weight of catches; and
8. establishing incentives, including those of an economic nature, to promote more selective fishing.[349]

The licensing system established under the 1983 regime has been amended: the EC Council now establishes management objectives for each fishery or group of fisheries in relation to specific resources on a multi-annual or multi-species basis, establishes a management strategy, and sets the total allowable catches and/or total allowable fishing efforts for particular fisheries on the basis of quotas set for each member state in such a way as to ensure the relative stability of fishing patterns in the EC.[350] The licensing system breaks new ground in being

---

[345] Art. 2.   [346] Art. 7(1).

[347] See R. R. Churchill, *EEC Fisheries Law* (1987), 167–202.

[348] Regulation (EEC) No. 92/3760, OJ L389, 31 December 1992, 1, Art. 2(1).

[349] Art. 4(2).

[350] Art. 8 (as amended by Council Regulation (EC) No. 1181/98 of 4 June 1998, OJ L 164, 9 June 1998, 1, to provide for the exercise of powers by the Council as regards allocating catches in Community waters to vessels of third countries authorised to fish in those waters, and to set the technical conditions under which catches must be made). For TACs

applicable to all EC fishing vessels in EC waters, in waters of third countries, or on the high seas; the previous rules applied only for fishing of 'species of special importance' in EC waters. The current licensing system combines a national system with the possibility of the EC Commission imposing further licensing requirements on behalf of the EC where 'species of special importance' require special regulation.[351]

The Regulation required the Council to set, by January 1994, objectives and detailed rules for the restructuring of the control system for enforcing the Regulation by establishing an EC control system for the entire EC fisheries sector, including the state of resources and the economic situation of coastal regions and communities.[352]

Noise

The EC has developed an extensive body of secondary legislation limiting permissible sound levels of various products and activities. Specific legislation has been adopted establishing limits on noise levels from motor vehicles;[353] motorcycles;[354] construction plant and equipment;[355] subsonic aircraft;[356] compressors;[357] tower cranes;[358] welding generators;[359] power generators;[360] hand-held concrete-breakers and picks;[361] lawnmowers;[362] household appliances;[363]

---

in 2002, see Council Regulation (EC) No. 2555/2001 of 18 December 2001, OJ L347, 31 December 2001, 1, fixing for 2002 the fishing opportunities and associated conditions for certain fish stocks and groups of fish stocks, applicable in Community waters and, for Community vessels, in waters where limitations in catch are required.

[351] Arts. 5 and 7. Annex I fixes special arrangements for fishing in coastal waters of each member state; Annex II identifies sensitive regions and fixes the maximum number of vessels with a length of not less than 26 metres authorised to fish for demersal species.

[352] Art. 11.

[353] Council Directive 70/157/EEC, OJ L42, 23 February 1970, 16, as amended.

[354] Council Directive 78/1015/EEC, OJ L349, 13 December 1978, 21, as amended. This Directive is repealed by Directive 97/24/EC, OJ L226, 18 August 1997, 1, on certain components and characteristics of two- or three-wheel motor vehicles.

[355] Council Directive 79/113/EEC, OJ L33, 8 February 1979, 15, as amended.

[356] Council Directive 80/51/EEC, OJ L18, 24 January 1980, 26, as amended; Council Directive 89/629/EEC, OJ L363, 13 December 1989, 27. These comply with standards set by the ICAO. Directive 92/14/EC, OJ L 76, 23 March 1992, 30, provides for a ban as of 1995 of civil subsonic aircraft that do not comply with ICAO requirements. On the reconciling of trade and environment in respect of aircraft, see Case C-389/96, *Aher-Waggon GmbH v. Bundesrepublik Deutschland* [1998] ECR I-4473.

[357] Council Directive 84/533/EEC, OJ L300, 19 November 1984, 123, as amended.

[358] Council Directive 84/534/EEC, OJ L300, 19 November 1984, 130, as amended.

[359] Council Directive 84/535/EEC, OJ L300, 19 November 1984, 142, as amended.

[360] Council Directive 84/536/EEC, OJ L300, 19 November 1984, 149, as amended.

[361] Council Directive 84/537/EEC, OJ L300, 19 November 1984, 156, as amended.

[362] Council Directive 84/538/EEC, OJ L300, 19 November 1984, 171, as amended.

[363] Council Directive 86/594/EEC, OJ L344, 1 December 1986, 24.

and excavators.[364] A new Directive relating to the noise emission in the environment by equipment used outdoors was introduced in July 2000.[365] This Directive repeals several earlier Directives including Directive 79/113/EEC, Directives 84/532/EEC to 84/538/EEC and Directive 86/662/EEC with effect from 3 January 2002.[366] The aim of the Directive is to promote the internal market and to improve the health and well-being of the population by reducing noise emitted by equipment used outdoors.[367] It harmonises noise emissions standards, conformity assessment procedures, noise level marking, and the gathering of data on noise emissions. The Commission envisages the appointment of the European Environment Agency to collect and evaluate these data.

In July 2000, the Commission adopted a Proposal for a general Directive on environmental noise.[368] The Proposal aims at providing a basis for a coherent, integrated EU policy on environmental noise. It introduces measures to classify and understand the problems caused by noise, as a necessary step towards preparing concrete measures to reduce noise pollution. The Commission has proposed the idea of establishing EU-wide 'noise-maps' which should form the basis for the development of action plans and strategies at local, national and EU levels to combat noise pollution.

Chemicals, hazardous substances, industrial risks and biotechnology

The EC has adopted a large body of technical rules regulating hazardous substances. The frequency with which many of the secondary acts are amended often makes it difficult to know the current status of a particular rule or the extent to which a particular substance or activity is regulated. Some of the legislation, such as the 'Seveso Directive', has influenced developments in other regions and at the global level. Legislation on the classification, packaging and labelling of dangerous substances was first adopted in 1967, and has since been amended or adapted to technical progress more than thirty-five times.[369] Currently, there are fifteen classes of danger in Directive 67/548/EEC, such as 'explosive', 'very toxic', 'carcinogenic' or 'dangerous for the environment'. Several member states have been held to be in violation of the 1967 Directive

---

[364] Council Directive 86/662/EEC, OJ L384, 31 December 1986, 1, as amended.
[365] Council Directive 2000/14/EC, OJ L162, 3 July 2000, 1. Annex 1 sets out the definition of equipment.
[366] Art. 21(1).   [367] Art. 1.
[368] Proposal for a Directive of the European Parliament and of the Council Relating to the Assessment and Management of Environmental Noise, COM (2000) 468, OJ C337, 28 November 2000, 251.
[369] Council Directive 67/548/EEC, n. 60 above, OJ L196, 16 August 1967, 1, as amended. See Joined Cases C-218/96, C-219/96, C-220/96, C-221/96 and C-222/96, *Commission* v. *Belgium* [1996] ECR I-6817.

and its amending Directives.[370] The 1967 Directive has been supplemented by legislation requiring the listing of certain chemical substances,[371] as well as measures addressing particular chemicals and substances, including asbestos[372] and batteries.[373] The 1988 legislation to regulate the classification, packaging and labelling of dangerous preparations was comprehensively reviewed in 1999,[374] and rules were developed on the provision of information.[375] The rules on the marketing and use of dangerous substances and preparations have been harmonised,[376] and rules have been developed and applied, partly on the basis of OECD recommendations, on good laboratory practice and testing.[377] The import and export of chemicals is also addressed by a 1988 Regulation,[378] and the following year the export of certain chemical products was also the subject of legislation.[379] The Seveso and Seveso II Directives[380] and the EC legislation on genetically modified organisms[381] are discussed in chapter 12 above. In 1998, the Community signed the 1992 Industrial Accidents Convention,[382] and it became a party to the 2000 Biosafety Protocol in August 2002.[383]

In 1993, the Council adopted the Existing Substances Regulation (ESR), introducing a comprehensive framework for the evaluation and control of 'existing' chemical substances. The Regulation was intended to complement the rules under Council Directive 67/548/EEC for 'new' chemical substances. An 'existing' chemical substance is defined as any chemical substance listed

---

[370] See Case 208/85, *EC Commission* v. *Germany* [1987] ECR 4045; Case 278/85, *EC Commission* v. *Denmark* [1987] ECR 4069. See also Case 187/84, *Criminal Proceedings Against Giacomo Caldana* [1985] ECR 3013, holding that Directive 67/548/EEC, as amended by Directive 79/831/EEC, OJ L259, 15 October 1979, 10, does not require preparations containing one or more of the dangerous substances to be listed. See also Case C-238/95, *Commission* v. *Italy* [1996] ECR I-1451, on the failure to fulfil obligations under Directive 93/67/EEC, OJ L227, 8 September 1993, 9, on assessment of risks to man and the environment posed by dangerous substances; and Case C-79/98, *Commission* v. *Belgium* [1999] ECR I-5187.

[371] Commission Decision 85/71/EEC, OJ L30, 2 February 1985, 33.

[372] Council Directive 87/217/EEC, OJ L85, 28 March 1987, 40.

[373] Council Directive 91/157/EEC, OJ L78, 26 March 1991, 38.

[374] Council Directive 99/45/EC, OJ L200, 30 July 1999, 1, relating to the classification, packaging and labelling of dangerous preparations, replaced the earlier Council Directive 88/379/EEC, OJ L187, 16 July 1988, 14, as amended.

[375] Commission Decision 91/155/EEC, OJ L76, 22 March 1991, 35, as amended.

[376] Council Directive 76/769/EEC, OJ L262, 27 September 1976, 201, as amended.

[377] Council Directive 87/18/EEC, OJ L15, 17 January 1987, 29; see also Council Directive 88/320/EEC, OJ L145, 11 June 1988, 35; Council Decision 86/569/EEC, OJ L315, 28 October 1989, 1.

[378] Council Regulation (EEC) No. 88/1734, OJ L155, 22 June 1988, 2.

[379] Council Regulation (EEC) No. 89/428, OJ L50, 22 Febuary 1989, 1. See also Council Regulation (EC) No. 92/2455, OJ L251, 29 August 1992, 13.

[380] Chapter 12, pp. 622–3 above.   [381] Chapter 12, pp. 658–62 above.

[382] Council Decision 98/685/EC, OJ L326, 3 December 1998, 1.

[383] Council Decision 2002/628/EC, OJ L201, 31 July 2002, 48.

in the European Inventory of Existing Commercial Substances (EINECS), an inventory currently listing more than 100,000 substances.[384]

In 2001, the European Commission adopted a White Paper setting out a strategy for a future Community Policy for Chemicals. The main objective of the new Strategy is to ensure a high level of protection for human health and the environment, while ensuring the efficient functioning of the internal market and stimulating innovation and competitiveness in the chemical industry. It addresses the shortcomings of the current system and relates mainly to the Directive on the classification, packaging and labelling of dangerous substances and dangerous preparations, the Regulation on the evaluation and control of the risks of existing substances and the Directive on restrictions on the marketing and use of certain dangerous substances and preparations.[385]

Important legislation not affected by the White Paper includes a Regulation concerning control of the international trade in certain dangerous chemicals, which implements the provisions of the 1998 Chemicals Convention. Many other linked measures have been adopted, dealing with plant protection products[386] and biocides,[387] and the reduction of industrial emissions, to form a network of environmental legislation concerning chemicals.

Waste

H. Von Lersner, 'Requirements on Waste Disposal in Europe', 20 *Environmental Policy and Law* 211 (1990); A. Schmidt, 'Transboundary Movements of Waste Under EC Law: The Emerging Regulatory Framework', 4 JEL 57 (1992); H. Jans, 'Waste Policy and European Community Law: Does the EEC Treaty Provide a Suitable Framework for Regulating Waste?' 20 *Ecology Law Quarterly* 165 (1993); J.-P. Hannequart, *European Waste Law* (1998); S. Tromans, 'EC Waste Law – A Complete Mess?', 13 JEL 133 (2001); I. Cheyne, 'The Definition of Waste in EC Law', 14 JEL 61 (2002).

Current EC policy on waste is set out in the non-binding 1990 Community Strategy for Waste Management, which proposed the principles, policy objectives and actions which the EC Commission has followed in developing legislative proposals and other action.[388] The Strategy adopted five guidelines to influence EC policy:

---

[384] Council Regulation (EC) No. 793/93 of 23 March 1993, OJ L84, 5 April 1993, 1.

[385] White Paper on the Strategy for a Future Chemicals Policy, COM (2001) 88.

[386] Council Directive 91/414/EEC, OJ L230, 19 August 1991, 1, deals with the authorisation of placing agricultural pesticides on the market. On non-transposition, see Case C-137/96, *Commission* v. *Germany* [1997] ECR I-6749; and Case C-380/95, *Commission* v. *Greece* [1996] ECR I-4837.

[387] Council Directive 98/8/EC, OJ L123, 24 April 1998, 1.

[388] The Strategy has been endorsed by the EC Council: see Council Resolution of 7 May 1990 on waste policy, OJ C122, 18 May 1990, 2.

1. prevention of waste by technologies and products;
2. recycling and re-use of waste;
3. optimisation of final disposal;
4. regulation of transport; and
5. remedial action.[389]

The Strategy also focused on the need to improve the implementation of EC legislation and the movement of waste prior to disposal within the EC and outside the EC. The Fifth Environmental Action Plan reinforced the EU strategy on waste management, and in July 1996 the Commission presented a new strategy continuing and adapting the old strategy.[390]

Apart from the waste legislation dealing with the protection of water quality, which prohibits disposal into the marine environment of certain wastes, and the protection of air quality, which limits atmospheric emissions of certain waste gases, the EC has adopted legislation on waste, toxic and dangerous wastes, and the disposal of particular wastes. In 1993, the EC adopted a new Regulation on the movement of wastes.[391]

Waste framework

Council Directive 75/442/EEC on waste,[392] as amended by Council Directive 91/156/EEC,[393] requires member states to prevent or reduce waste production and recover waste by recycling, re-use, reclamation or any other process, or use waste as a source of energy.[394] Prevention and reduction is to be achieved by the development of clean technologies, products designed to minimise waste, and techniques for final disposal of dangerous substances.[395] The ECJ has construed Directive 75/442 as not giving individuals the right to sell or use plastic bags and other non-biodegradable containers.[396] In the amended Directive, waste is

---

[389] Proposals concerning remedial action include the proposed Directive on Civil Liability for Damage Caused by Waste, OJ C251, 4 October 1989, 3; see chapter 18, pp. 926–30 below.

[390] COM (1996) 399 final.

[391] Council Regulation (EC) No. 259/93, OJ L30, 6 February 1993, 1, chapter 13, pp. 699–703 above. On the relationship between trade and environmental protection in relation to waste, see chapter 19, pp. 990–2 below.

[392] Council Directive 75/442/EEC, OJ L196, 26 July 1975, 39. On non-implementation, see e.g. Joined Cases 30 to 34/81, *Commission* v. *Italy* [1981] ECR 3379; and Case 69/81, *Commission* v. *Belgium* [1982] ECR 163.

[393] Council Directive 91/156/EEC, OJ L78, 26 March 1991, 32, as amended; on the dispute concerning the legal basis of this Directive, see n. 86 above.

[394] Art. 3.   [395] *Ibid.*

[396] Case C-380/87, *Enichem Base and Others* v. *Commune di Cinisello Balsamo* [1989] ECR 2491. The ECJ also held that Art. 3(2) of the 1975 Directive requires member states to inform the EC Commission of any draft rules regarding the sale or use of certain products prior to their final adoption, but that Art. 3(2) does not give individuals enforceable rights before national courts to obtain the suspension or annulment of such rules on the

defined as 'any substance or object in the categories set out in Annex I which the holder discards or intends or is required to discard'. In the *Inter-Environment* case, the ECJ acknowledged that the scope of the term 'waste' depends on the meaning of the word 'discard'.[397] The Directive does not apply to atmospheric emissions of gases and certain categories of waste covered by other legislation.[398]

Member states are encouraged to take the measures necessary to ensure recovery or disposal of waste, including a prohibition on dumping and uncontrolled disposal,[399] and measures to establish an integrated and adequate

    ground that they were adopted without having previously been communicated to the Commission.

[397] Case-129/96, *Inter-Environment Wallonie ASBL* v. *Waals Gewest* [1997] ECR I-7411. The Court found that 'discard' covers both disposal and recovery of a substance or object, and held that a substance or object that forms part of an industrial process may constitute waste within the meaning of the Waste Framework Directive. Therefore, a substance or object is not excluded from the meaning of the term 'waste' by the mere fact that it directly forms an integral part of an industrial process. See also Joined Cases 418/97 and C-419/97, *ARCO Chemie Nederland Ltd* [2000] ECR I-4475, where the ECJ held that substances which are capable of being recovered as fuel without substantial treatment must still be classified as waste. The decision lays down circumstances which must be considered in classifying as waste a substance which is treated under the operations of Annexes IIA and IIB to the Waste Framework Directive.

[398] Arts. 1(a) and 2(1). Annex I lists sixteen categories of waste. 'Waste' was originally defined in Directive 75/442/EEC, OJ L194, 25 July 1975, 39, as 'any substance or object which the holder disposes of or is required to dispose of pursuant to the provisions of national law in force' (Art. 1). In Joined Cases C-206/88 and C-207/88, *Vessaso and Zanetti* [1990] ECR I-1461, the ECJ held that the concept of waste was not to be understood as excluding substances and objects which were capable of economic re-utilisation, and did not presume that the holder disposing of a substance or object intended to exclude all economic re-utilisation of the substance or object by others. See also Case C-359/88, *Zanetti and Others* [1990] ECR I-4747, holding that national legislation defining waste as excluding substances or objects which are capable of economic re-utilisation was incompatible with Directive 75/442/EEC, OJ L194, 25 July 1975, 39, and Directive 78/319/EEC, OJ L84, 31 March 1978, 43. In the *Tombesi* case, the ECJ ruled that its earlier interpretations were not affected by the amendments to Directive 91/156/EEC, OJ L78, 26 March 1991, 32. See Joined Cases C-304/94, C-330/94, C-342/94 and C-224/95, *Tombesi and Others* [1997] ECR I-3561, para. 48. The ECJ ruled that the concept of 'waste' in Art. 1 of Directive 75/442/EEC as referred to in Art. 1(3) of Directive 91/689/EEC, OJ L377, 31 December 1991, 20, on hazardous waste, and Art. 2(a) of Regulation (EEC) No. 259/93, OJ L30, 6 February 1993, 1, on the supervision and control of shipments of waste within, into and out of the European Community, is not to be understood as excluding substances and objects which are capable of economic re-utilisation, even if the materials in question may be the subject of a transaction or quoted on public or private commercial lists. In particular, a de-activation process intended merely to render waste harmless, landfill tipping in hollows or embankments and waste incineration constitute disposal or recovery operations falling within the scope of the above-mentioned Community rules. The fact that a substance is classified as a re-usable residue without its characteristics or purpose being defined is irrelevant in that regard. The same applies to the grinding of a waste substance.

[399] Art. 4. See Case C-387/97, *Commission* v. *Greece* [2000] ECR I-5047, where the ECJ held that failing to take the measures necessary to ensure that waste was disposed of without

network of disposal installations taking account of BATNEEC, designed to enable the EC to become self-sufficient in waste disposal.[400] The network must enable waste to be disposed of in one of the nearest appropriate installations and ensure a high level of protection for the environment and human health.[401] In the *Dusseldorp* case, the ECJ ruled that the principles of self sufficiency and proximity are not to be applied to waste for recovery.[402] The competent national authorities must, as soon as possible, draw up waste management plans and take the measures necessary to prevent the movement of waste not in accordance with those plans.[403] Any company carrying out the disposal operations in Annex IIA or the recovery operations in Annex IIB must obtain a permit from the competent national authorities.[404] Companies which collect or transport waste or dealers or brokers who arrange for disposal require registration.[405] The Directive also provides that in accordance with the polluter-pays principle the cost of waste disposal must be borne by the holder who has waste handled by a waste collector or authorised disposal company, and/or the previous holders or the producer of the product from which the waste came.[406]

Hazardous waste

Council Directive 78/319/EEC requires member states to take appropriate steps to encourage the prevention of toxic and dangerous waste, its processing and

endangering human health and harming the environment in accordance with Art. 4 and by failing to draw up plans for the disposal of waste, pursuant to Arts. 6 and 12 of Directive 78/319/EEC, OJ L84, 31 July 1978, 43, Greece had not implemented all the necessary measures to comply with the ECJ's earlier judgment in Case C-45/91, *Commission v. Greece* [1992] ECR I-2509, and had failed to fulfil its obligations under Art. 171 of the EC Treaty. On 4 July 2000, Greece became the first country to be ordered to pay the Commission a fine of 20,000 euros for each day of delay in fulfilling its obligations for the safe management of waste in the Chania area on Crete. For violations of Arts. 4 and 8, see Case C-365/97, *Commission v. Italy* [1999] ECR I-7773.

[400] Art. 5(1).   [401] Art. 5(2).

[402] Case C-203/96, *Dusseldorp* [1998] ECR I-4075, para. 30. See also Case 209/98, *Sydhavnens Sten and Grus* [2000] ECR I-3743, where the ECJ ruled that member states may impose export restrictions on waste if this is necessary for the protection of the environment, because the concept of environment is to be interpreted in the light of the source principle.

[403] Art. 7.

[404] Arts. 9 and 10. Art. 11 lists certain exceptions, including for companies carrying out their own waste disposal at the place of production. On the grant of permits, see generally Joined Cases 372 to 374/85, *Ministère Public v. Oscar Traen and Others* [1987] ECR 2141, and for its failure to fulfil its obligations under Art. 9, see Case C-230/00, *Commission v. Belgium* [2001] ECR I-4591.

[405] Art. 12.

[406] Art. 15. 'Holder' means 'the producer of the waste or the natural or legal person who is in possession of it': Art. 1(c). 'Producer' means 'anyone whose activities produce waste (original producer) and/or anyone who carries out pre-processing, mixing or other operations resulting in a change in the nature or composition of this waste': Art. 1(b).

recycling, and the use of certain processes for its re-use.[407] The Directive does not apply to radioactive waste, atmospheric emissions, and other specified categories.[408] Member states must take the measures necessary to ensure that toxic and dangerous waste is disposed of safely and that uncontrolled discharges and disposals are prohibited.[409] The Directive requires the designation or establishment of a competent national authority to plan, authorise, and supervise the disposal of toxic and dangerous waste, and to ensure that such waste is kept separate from other matter and residues, is appropriately labelled, and that deposits are recorded.[410] Companies engaged in the storage, treatment or deposit of toxic and dangerous waste must have a permit; carriage is to be controlled by the competent authorities; and any person producing or holding such waste without a permit must as soon as possible have such waste stored by an authorised person.[411] The Directive also provides that, in accordance with the polluter-pays principle, the cost of waste disposal must be borne by the holder who has waste handled by a waste collector or authorised disposal company, and/or the previous holders or the producer of the product from which the waste came.[412] The Directive requires the competent authorities to draw up and keep up to date public plans for the disposal of toxic and dangerous wastes. The Directive provides for derogations in emergency situations, requires detailed records to be kept in relation to production, holding, disposal and transport, and provides for inspection.[413]

Council Directive 91/689/EEC on hazardous waste repealed the earlier 1978 Directive on toxic and dangerous wastes.[414] The 1991 Directive applies to all wastes featuring on a list.[415] The objective of the Directive is to approximate the laws of the member states on the controlled management of hazardous waste, by establishing more stringent rules than for other types of waste, by applying a precise and uniform definition of hazardous wastes, and by ensuring the fullest possible monitoring of the disposal and recovery of hazardous wastes. The 1991 Directive seeks to achieve these objectives by applying most of the provisions of Directive 75/442 to hazardous wastes and then setting out additional obligations which will apply only to hazardous wastes.[416] The 1991 Directive establishes

---

[407] Council Directive 78/319/EEC, OJ L84, 31 March 1978, 43, as amended, Art. 4.

[408] Art. 3.   [409] Art. 5.   [410] Arts. 5 and 6.   [411] Arts. 9 and 10.   [412] Art. 11.

[413] Arts. 12 to 15. See Case 239/85, *Commission v. Belgium* [1986] ECR 3645, establishing a failure to fully implement Art. 14 of Directive 78/319/EEC, OJ L84, 31 July 1978, 43. See also Case C-422/92, *Commission v. Germany* [1995] ECR I-1097, where the Court held that the concept of waste within the meaning of Art. 1 of Directives 75/442/EEC and 78/319/EEC, also includes substances and objects which are capable of economic re-utilisation. A member state which excludes certain categories of recyclable waste from the scope of its legislation has not properly implemented those Directives.

[414] Council Directive 91/689/EEC, OJ L377, 31 December 1991, 20, as amended.

[415] Decision 2000/532/EC, OJ L226, 6 September 2000, 3, establishes a single Community list which integrates earlier lists of dangerous waste and other wastes. The list does not prevent member states from classifying as hazardous wastes other than those featuring on the list.

[416] Art. 1(1) and (2).

a new definition of hazardous wastes by reference to three new Annexes, and does not apply to domestic waste.[417]

The additional requirements to those set out in Directive 75/442 establish basic management rules for hazardous wastes, and include the following rules: all tipping (discharges) on every site must record and identify the waste and there must be no mixing between different categories of hazardous wastes or between hazardous and non-hazardous wastes, except in prescribed circumstances;[418] hazardous wastes must be properly packaged and labelled in accordance with international and EC standards;[419] national authorities must draw up public plans for the management of hazardous wastes;[420] in cases of emergency and grave danger, member states must ensure that hazardous wastes are dealt with so as not to constitute a threat to the population or the environment;[421] and member states must supply the EC Commission with detailed information on every establishment and undertaking which carries out the disposal or recovery of hazardous waste on behalf of third parties.[422] Directive 91/689 excludes the application to hazardous wastes of certain derogations allowed by Directive 75/442, and expressly provides for the application of certain provisions of that Directive to hazardous wastes.[423]

Disposal of particular wastes

Under EC law, certain categories of waste are subject to special disposal rules, including waste oils,[424] polychlorinated biphenyls and terphenyls,[425] waste from

---

[417] Art. 1(3)–(5); for the definition, see chapter 13, pp. 677–81 above. In Case C-318/98, *Fornasar* [2000] ECR I-4785, the ECJ ruled that the decisive criterion, as regards the definition of hazardous waste, is whether the waste displays one or more of the properties listed in Annex III to the Directive.

[418] Art. 2.   [419] Art. 5(1).

[420] Art. 6(1). On the failure to draw up waste management plans, see Case C-35/00, *Commission v. United Kingdom* [2002] ECR I-953, and Case C-466/99, *Commission v. Italy* [2002] ECR I-851.

[421] Art. 7.   [422] Art. 8(3).

[423] Arts. 3, 4, 6 and 8. See Case C-65/00, *Commission v. Italy* [2002] ECR I-1795.

[424] Council Directive 75/439/EEC, OJ L194, 25 July 1975, 23, as amended. See Case 172/82, *Syndicat National des Fabricants Raffineri d'Huiles de Graissage and Others v. Inter-Huiles AG* [1983] ECR 555, holding that Directive 75/439/EEC and the Community rules on free movement of goods do not allow a member state to organise a system for the collection and disposal of waste oils within its territory in such a way as to prohibit exports to an unauthorised disposal or regenerating undertaking in another member state; and Case 295/82, *Groupement d'Interêts Economique 'Rhone Alpes Huiles' and Others v. Syndicat National des Fabricants Raffineri d'Huiles de Graissage and Others* [1984] ECR 575, holding that Directive 75/439/EEC and the EEC Treaty require that waste oils may be delivered by either a holder or an approved collector to a disposal undertaking in another member state which has obtained a permit as provided by Art. 6 of the Directive in that state. On non-implementation, see Joined Cases 30 to 34/81, *Commission v. Italy* [1981] ECR 3379; Case 70/81, *Commission v. Belgium* [1982] ECR 169. See also Case C-102/97, *Commission v. Germany* [1999] ECR I-5051.

[425] Council Directive 96/59/EC, OJ L243, 24 September 1996, 31, on disposal of PCBs and PCTs, which repealed Council Directive 76/403/EEC, OJ L108, 26 April 1976, 41. On

the titanium dioxide industry,[426] certain liquid containers,[427] sewage sludge,[428] and waste from spent batteries and accumulators.[429] The Commission has also adopted legislation on the incineration of hazardous waste,[430] on limiting packaging waste,[431] and on landfills.[432] The priority objective of the Directive on the management of end-of-life vehicles is waste prevention, requiring manufacturers to reduce the use of hazardous substances when designing vehicles, increase the use of recycled materials, and design and produce vehicles which facilitate the dismantling, re-use, recovery and recycling of end-of-life vehicles.[433] The Directive also requires member states to set up collection systems for end-of-life vehicles and used parts, with producers being required to meet all (or a significant part of) the costs of allowing the last holder of an end-of-life vehicle to dispose of it free of charge (referred to as the 'free take-back principle').[434] A similar approach is reflected in the Commission's proposed Directive on waste electrical and electronic equipment.[435]

Treaties

The EC was a party to the 1989 Lomé Convention, which controlled the movement of hazardous wastes to ACP countries (until it was replaced by the 2000 Cotonou Agreement), and to the 1989 Basel Convention on the control of transboundary movements of hazardous wastes and their disposal.[436]

the non-implementation of the earlier Directive, see Case 71/81, *Commission* v. *Belgium* [1982] ECR 175; and Joined Cases 30 to 34/81, *Commission* v. *Italy* [1981] ECR 3379.

[426] Council Directive 78/176/EEC, OJ L54, 25 February 1978, 19, as amended; Council Directive 82/883/EEC, OJ L378, 31 December 1982, 1, as amended; and Council Directive 92/112/EEC, OJ L409, 31 December 1992, 11. On non-implementation, see Case 68/81, *Commission* v. *Belgium* [1982] ECR 153.

[427] Council Directive 85/339/EEC, OJ L176, 6 July 1985, 18.

[428] Council Directive 86/278/EEC, OJ L181, 4 July 1986, 6.

[429] Council Directive 91/157/EEC, OJ L78, 26 March 1991, 38, as amended. See Case C-347/97, *Commission* v. *Belgium* [1999] ECR I-309, on failure to comply with Art. 6 obligations under the Directive.

[430] Council Directive 94/67/EC, OJ L365, 31 December 1994, 34; and Directive 2000/76/EC, OJ L332, 28 December 2000, 91, on the incineration of waste, n. 211 above.

[431] Council Directive 94/62/EC, OJ L 365, 31 December 1994, 10. There is currently a proposal to amend this Directive, COM (2001) 729 final, OJ C103E, 30 April 2002, 17.

[432] Council Directive 99/31/EC, OJ L182, 16 July 1999, 1.

[433] Directive 2000/53/EC on end-of-life vehicles, OJ L269, 21 October 2000, 34.

[434] Art. 5. The Directive aims to increase the recycling of metal content of vehicles from the current 75 per cent to 85 per cent average weight per vehicle by 2006 and to 95 per cent by 2015.

[435] COM (2000) 347 final, OJ C365, 19 December 2000, 195. See also the proposed Directive on restriction of the use of certain hazardous substances in electrical and electronic equipment, COM (2000) 347 final, OJ C365, 19 December 2000.

[436] Chapter 13, pp. 691–5 above.

Radioactive substances[437]

EC law on radioactive substances is generally governed by the EURATOM Treaty, which was adopted in 1957 to raise the standard of living in the member states and to improve the development of commercial exchanges with other countries by creating the conditions necessary for the speedy establishment and growth of nuclear industries.[438] The main provisions of the EURATOM Treaty relating to the environment concern health and safety. The Treaty provides for basic standards to be laid down for the protection of the health of workers and the public arising from ionising radiation.[439] Member states must adopt provisions to ensure compliance with these standards, including measures relating to teaching, education and training.[440] Additional health and safety measures must be taken if a member state allows particularly dangerous experiments, and the opinion of the EC Commission must first be obtained.[441]

Member states must also establish facilities to carry out continuous monitoring of radioactivity levels in the air, water and soil and to ensure compliance with basic standards.[442] The EC Commission has the right of access to these facilities and can verify their operation and efficiency, and national authorities are required to keep the Commission informed about the level of radioactivity to which the public is exposed.[443] Under Article 37(1), member states must provide the Commission with general data relating to plans to dispose of radioactive waste so as to make it possible to determine whether the implementation of the plan is liable to result in contamination of the water, soil or airspace of another member state. The Commission must give its opinion within six months, and the ECJ has held that Article 37 requires the member state to provide the general data of a plan before such disposal is authorised by the competent authorities of the member state, in order to ensure that the Commission's opinion has a genuine chance of receiving detailed consideration and influencing the attitude of the member state.[444] The Commission may also make recommendations to member states concerning levels of radioactivity in the air, water and soil, and can, in situations of urgency, issue a Directive requiring a member state to take all necessary measures to prevent an infringement of the basic standards and to ensure compliance with regulations.[445]

Secondary legislation has been adopted under the EURATOM Treaty which establishes basic safety standards for the protection of the public and workers

---

[437] Chapter 13, especially pp. 703–5 above.   [438] 1957 EURATOM Treaty, Art. 1.

[439] Art. 30. 'Basic standards' are defined as: (a) maximum permissible doses compatible with adequate safety; (b) maximum permissible levels of exposure and contamination; and (c) the principles governing health surveillance of workers: Art. 30(a)–(c).

[440] Art. 30(1).   [441] Art. 34.   [442] Art. 35(1).   [443] Arts. 35(2) and 36.

[444] Art. 37(2); Case C-187/87, *Saarland and Others* v. *Ministry of Industry and Others* [1988] ECR 5013. See now Commission Recommendation of 6 December 1999 on the application of Article 37 of the Euratom Treaty, 1999/829/Euratom, OJ L324, 16 December 1999, 23.

[445] Art. 38.

against radiation;[446] on the management and storage of radioactive waste;[447] on information exchange and informing the public in the event of a radiological emergency;[448] and on shipments of radioactive waste.[449] Non-binding acts have been adopted for other associated activities, such as the storage and reprocessing of irradiated nuclear fuels.[450] Following the Chernobyl accident, the Commission adopted legislation on the radioactive contamination of certain foods.[451]

Conclusions

The extensive body of EC environmental law which has been developed and applied since 1967, together with the jurisprudence of the ECJ and CFI which interprets and applies that law, provides a rich source from which experiences can be drawn and applied to developments in other regions and globally. Although the member states of the EC are a relatively homogenous group with historic links developed over several centuries, many of the conditions which apply in the EC legal, economic and political system are analogous to circumstances which apply elsewhere. And while the specific environmental issues raised in the EC are particular to its geographical and climatic circumstances, the underlying environmental issues and needs are the same as elsewhere. In particular, the fifteen member states have differing legal traditions and systems, are at different stages of economic development, and value the environment in

---

[446] Directive 96/29/EURATOM, OJ L159, 29 June 1996, 1 (the 'Basic Safety Standards Directive'), replacing Directive 80/836/EURATOM, OJ L246, 17 September 1980, 1, and Directive 84/467/EURATOM, OJ L265, 5 October 1984, 4.

[447] Council Decision 75/406/EURATOM, OJ L178, 9 July 1975, 28.

[448] Council Decision 87/600/EURATOM, OJ L371, 30 December 1987, 76; Council Directive 89/618/EURATOM, OJ L357, 7 December 1989, 31. In this context, see also Directive 98/618/EURATOM, OJ C190, 18 June 1998, 7, which directs states to provide information on radiological emergencies so that the population adopts appropriate behaviour. In a normal situation, prior information about emergency response behaviour must be given to the population covered by an emergency plan; immediate information must be given to the population affected in the event of a radiological emergency.

[449] Council Directive 92/3/EURATOM, OJ L35, 12 February 1992, 24; chapter 13, pp. 703–5 above. See also the 1989 ACP–EC Lomé Convention, chapter 13, p. 695 above. See also Council Regulation (Euratom) No. 1493/93, OJ L148, 19 June 1993, 1, on shipments of radioactive substances between member states; Council Regulation (EC) No. 1420/1999, OJ L166, 1 July 1999, 6; and Commission Regulation (EC) No. 1547/99, OJ L185, 17 July 1999, 1, on rules and procedures applying to shipments of certain types of waste to non-OECD countries; chapter 13, p. 705 above.

[450] Commission Recommendation 82/74/EURATOM, OJ L37, 10 February 1982, 36.

[451] Council Regulation 87/3954/EURATOM, OJ L371, 30 December 1987, 11, as amended by Regulation (EURATOM) No. 89/2218, OJ L211, 22 July 1989, 1; Council Regulation (EEC) No. 89/2219, OJ L211, 22 July 1989, 4; Council Regulation (EEC) No. 90/737, OJ L82, 29 March 1990, 1; Commission Regulation (EURATOM) No. 90/770, OJ L83, 30 March 1990, 78.

different ways. Moreover, as the EC has integrated some of the EFTA member countries, and as moves are made to integrate countries in central and eastern Europe and the Mediterranean, the EC will become increasingly diverse, and will place new strains on the development and application of EC environmental law.

EC environmental law thus represents a model of sorts. It reflects the first attempt of any region in the international community to legislate widely on national and transboundary environmental issues. In seising jurisdiction over the internal affairs of member states by regulating environmental matters which do not raise *prima facie* transboundary issues, EC environmental law goes even further. It effectively says that the member states share a single, indivisible environment. The implications of this for our understanding and treatment of sovereignty are significant, providing further support for the view that states are increasingly willing to limit sovereignty and take on board the emerging concept of 'reasonable sovereignty'.[452]

EC environmental law may rightly be criticised for establishing weak standards in certain areas, and views as to its adequacy and effectiveness will depend in large part on national legal perspectives, that is, whether the EC rules might tend to weaken domestic standards (as may arguably be the case for Germany, the Netherlands and Denmark) or whether they impose new, higher standards (as may arguably be the case for Italy, Spain, Portugal, Greece and, to a lesser extent, the United Kingdom). Nevertheless, it is unparalleled as a manifestation of international environmental law in both its substantive and procedural content, for bringing a wide range of actors into the legal process, and for illustrating the tensions which exist where a legal system which was designed to establish international economic arrangements finds itself subject to ecological constraints.

---

[452] A. V. Lowe, 'Reflections on the Water: Changing Conceptions of Property Rights in the Law of the Sea', 1 IJECL 1 (1986), cited by P. Birnie, 'International Environmental Law: Its Adequacy for Present and Future Needs', in A. Hurrell and B. Kingsbury (eds.), *The International Politics of the Environment* (1992), 51 at 84.

PART III

Techniques for implementing international principles and rules

16

Environmental impact assessment

H. A. Becker and A. L. Porter, *Methods and Experiences in Impact Assessment* (1986); W. Kennedy, 'The Directive on Environmental Impact Assessment', 8 *Environmental Policy and Law* 84 (1988); C. Klein-Chesivoir, 'Avoiding Environmental Injury: The Case for Widespread Use of Environmental Impact Assessments in International Development Projects', 30 *Virginia Journal of International Law* 517 (1990); R. Macrory, 'Environmental Assessment: Critical Legal Issues in Implementation', in D. Vaughan (ed.), *EC Environmental and Planning Law* (1990); W. Futrell, 'Environmental Assessment: The Necessary First Step in Successful Environmental Strategies', 10 *UCLA Pacific Basin Law Journal* 234 (1991); P. Sands and D. Alexander, 'Assessing the Impact', 141 *New Law Journal* 1487 (1991); N. Robinson, 'International Trends in Environmental Impact Assessment', 19 *Boston College Environmental Affairs Law Review* 591 (1992); R. Stewart, 'Environmental Risk Assessment: The Divergent Methodologies of Economists, Lawyers and Scientists', 10 *Environment and Planning Law Journal* 10 (1993); M. Yeater and L. Kurukulasuriya, 'Environmental Impact Assessment Legislation in Developing Countries', in Sun Lin and L. Kurukulasuriya (eds.), *UNEP'S New Way Forward: Environmental Law and Sustainable Development* (1995); P. Okowa, 'Procedural Obligations in International Environmental Agreements', 67 BYIL 275 (1996); UNEP, *Environmental Impact Assessment: Issues, Trends and Practise* (1996); J. Glasson, J. Chadwick and R. Therivel, *An Introduction to Environmental Impact Assessment* (1999, 2nd edn); J. Ebbeson, 'Innovative Elements and Expected Effectiveness of the 1991 EIA Convention', 19 *Environmental Impact Assessment Review* 47 (1999); K. Gray, 'International Environmental Impact Assessment: Potential for a Multilateral Environmental Agreement', 11 *Colorado Journal of Environmental Law and Policy* 83 (2000); J. Knox, 'The Myth and Reality of Transboundary Environmental Impact Assessment', 96 AJIL 291 (2002).

Introduction

Environmental impact assessments emerged internationally after the 1972 Stockholm Conference and are now an established international and domestic legal technique for integrating environmental considerations into socio-economic development and decision-making processes. An environmental impact assessment describes a *process* which produces a written *statement* to be used to guide decision-making, with several related functions. First, it should provide decision-makers with information on the environmental consequences of proposed activities and, in some cases, programmes and policies, and their alternatives. Secondly, it requires decisions to be influenced by that information. And, thirdly, it provides a mechanism for ensuring the participation of potentially affected persons in the decision-making process.

Since environmental impact assessments were first established in the domestic law of the United States under the 1972 National Environmental Protection Act, they have been progressively adopted in a very large number of national legal systems. Internationally, environmental impact assessments are required under numerous international conventions and in EC law, in the requirements of various multilateral development banks, and in various non-binding instruments adopted at the regional and global level. Principle 17 of the Rio Declaration states that:

> environmental impact assessment, as a national instrument, shall be undertaken for proposed activities that are likely to have a significant adverse impact on the environment and are subject to a decision of a competent national authority.

The mandatory language of Principle 17 is consistent with the view that environmental impact assessments are now required by general international law, particularly in respect of environmentally harmful activities which may have transboundary consequences, and if only to meet a state's obligation to ensure that activities within its jurisdiction and control 'respect the environment of other States or of areas beyond national control' without first having assessed the transboundary environmental consequences of potentially harmful activities.[1] The language of Principle 17, however, is general, and does not provide the detail as to the minimum requirements which states need to satisfy. To a certain extent the details relating to common approaches are reflected in the instruments described in this chapter and in the international cases which have arisen since Principle 17 was adopted: New Zealand's application to the ICJ concerning the resumption by France of underground nuclear testing (1995), the case concerning the Gabcikovo-Nagymaros project (1997), and the dispute between Ireland and the United Kingdom concerning the MOX plant (2001). These cases indicate an increasing recognition that international law requires the preparation of a prior environmental impact assessment before a state engages in, or permits, an activity which may have serious adverse impacts on the environment. Other developments, described below, reflect the growing role

---

[1] Chapter 6, p. 245 above.

of strategic environmental assessment (of programmes and plans) and risk assessments associated, in particular, with foodstuffs.

Non-binding instruments

The Principles of the 1972 Stockholm Declaration do not expressly identify environmental impact assessment as an instrument of national or international policy. However, the rationale underlying environmental impact assessment can be identified in the principle that 'rational planning constitutes an essential tool' for reconciling development and environment needs, and that planning 'must be applied to human settlements and urbanisation with a view to avoiding adverse effects on the environment and obtaining maximum social, economic and environmental benefits for all'.[2] An earlier draft of the Stockholm Declaration contained a draft Principle 20 which would have provided the elements of a clearer commitment to environmental impact assessment. The proposal set out in draft Principle 20 was not agreed at Stockholm following the objections of several developing countries, which maintained that the obligation to consult, dependent upon a prior determination that activities or developments could lead to significant adverse effects on the environment, might be abused by developed states to impede projects by developing countries. UN General Assembly Resolution 2995 (XXVII) (1972) partially revived draft Principle 20 by providing that technical information on proposed works should be supplied to other states where there is a risk of significant transboundary environmental harm, but that this information should be received in good faith and not used to delay or impede the development of natural resources.

Subsequent non-binding instruments developed the approach underlying draft Principle 20. Principle 5 of the 1978 UNEP draft Principles of Conduct proposed that:

> states should make an environmental impact assessment before engaging in any activity with respect to a shared natural resource which may create a risk of significantly affecting the environment of another state or states sharing that resource.[3]

Whilst Principle 5 was innovative, it did not provide any detail on how the assessment should be carried out, who should participate in it, and to what purpose it should be put. This gap was partly remedied by the 1982 UNEP Conclusions of the Study on the Legal Aspects Concerning the Environment Related to Offshore Mining and Drilling within the Limits of National Jurisdiction, which provided more detailed guidance on the appropriate modalities for carrying out an environmental impact assessment.[4] Support for environmental impact assessment is found in a range of other acts of international

---

[2] Principles 14 and 15.   [3] Principle 5.   [4] UNEP/GC/Dec./10/14VI (1982).

institutions adopted after the Stockholm Conference,[5] including in relation to development assistance.[6] The 1982 World Charter for Nature supports the 'exhaustive examination' and 'assessment' of activities likely to pose a significant risk to nature or which may disturb nature, and requires that activities should not proceed or should minimise potential adverse effects on the basis of the findings of the assessment or examination.[7] By 1986, the Experts Group on Environmental Law of the World Commission on Environment and Development had identified environmental impact assessment as an 'emerging principle of international law', taking the view that states planning to carry out or permit activities which may significantly affect a natural resource or the environment should make or require an assessment of their effects before carrying out or permitting the planned activities.[8] In 1987, UNEP prepared guidelines on the nature and extent of the obligation to carry out an assessment.[9] The UNEP Goals and Principles include three related objectives in ensuring the 'environmentally sound and sustainable development' of planned activities: ensuring that environmental effects should be taken into account before decisions are taken to allow activities to be carried out; providing for the implementation of national environmental impact assessment procedures; and encouraging reciprocal procedures for notification, information, exchange and consultation on activities likely to have significant transboundary effects. The Principles, which propose bilateral, regional or multilateral arrangements, reflect a minimum set of standards which have been broadly endorsed and are reflected in state practice, at the national level and in binding international instruments.

UNCED and the ILC

References to environmental impact assessment abound in Agenda 21. It calls on all countries to 'assess the environmental suitability of infrastructure in human settlements', ensure that 'relevant decisions are preceded by environmental impact assessments and also take into account the costs of any ecological consequences', integrate environmental considerations in decision-making at

---

[5] See e.g. OECD Council Recommendation C(74)216, Analysis of the Environmental Consequences of Significant Public and Private Projects, 14 November 1974; OECD Council Recommendation C(79)116, Assessment of Projects with Significant Impact on the Environment, 8 May 1979; FAO Comparative Legal Strategy on Environmental Impact Assessment and Agricultural Development, 1982, FAO Environmental Paper.

[6] OECD Council Recommendation C(85)104, Environmental Assessment of Development Assistance Projects and Programmes, 20 June 1985.

[7] Paras. 11(b) and (c).

[8] *Environmental Protection and Sustainable Development: Legal Principles and Recommendations* (1986), 58–62.

[9] Goals and Principles of Environmental Impact Assessment, UNEP/GC/Dec./14/25 (1987); see also UNGA Res. 42/184 (1987).

all levels and in all ministries, and ensure the transparency of and account-ability for the environmental implications of economic and other policies.[10] Agenda 21 also endorses 'comprehensive analytical procedures for prior and simultaneous assessment of the impacts of decisions', including their environ-mental impacts and the assessment of 'costs, benefits and risks', and the sys-tematic application of techniques and procedures for assessing environmental impacts.[11] Environmental impact assessment is also encouraged in specific Agenda 21 programmes, including deforestation, atmospheric protection and energy use, fragile mountain ecosystems, conservation of biological diversity, management of biotechnology, protection of oceans and seas, protection of freshwater resources, management of toxic chemicals, solid wastes and sewage, and radioactive wastes.[12] Agenda 21 endorses the need for individuals, groups and organisations to participate in environmental impact assessment proce-dures.[13] The WSSD broadly confirmed UNCED's requirements.[14]

Article 7 of the ILC's draft Articles on the Prevention of Transboundary Harm from Hazardous Activities draws upon the output of UNCED, and in particular Principle 17 of the Rio Declaration. Article 17 provides that:

> Any decision in respect of the authorization of an activity within the scope
> of the present articles shall, in particular, be based on an assessment of
> the possible transboundary harm caused by that activity, including any
> environmental assessment.

The ILC's commentary to its draft Articles notes that the requirement of assess-ment of adverse effects of activities has been incorporated in many international agreements, and that the practice of requiring an environmental impact assess-ment 'has become very prevalent' in order to assess whether a particular activity has the potential to cause significant transboundary harm.[15]

Treaties and other binding instruments

A number of treaties and other binding instruments include provisions re-quiring the performance of an environmental impact assessment in specified circumstances. The 1985 EC Directive on Environmental Impact Assessment[16] led the way in providing international guidance on the nature and extent of an environmental impact assessment and the use to which it should be put, an ap-proach subsequently adopted and extended in the 1991 UNECE Convention on Environmental Impact Assessment in a Transboundary Context (1991 Espoo

---

[10] Paras. 7.41(b) and 8.4.   [11] Paras. 8.5(b) and 10.8(b).
[12] Paras. 9.12(b), 11.24(a), 13.17(a), 15.5(k), 16.45(c), 17.5(d), 18.22(c), 19.21(d), 21.31(a) and 22.4(d).
[13] Para. 23.2.   [14] Plan of Implementation, e.g. paras. 18(e), 34(c) and 36(i).
[15] A/56/10, 402–3 (2001).   [16] Council Directive 85/337/EEC, OJ L175, 5 July 1985, 40.

Convention),[17] and in the 1991 Protocol on Environmental Protection to the Antarctic Treaty. But these were by no means the first instruments supporting, in general terms, the use of environmental assessment. The 1974 Nordic Environmental Protection Convention required an assessment of the effects in the territory of one party of activities carried out in the territory of another party:[18] the Convention allows authorities to require an applicant for a permit to carry out environmentally harmful activities to 'submit such additional particulars, drawings and technical specifications' as are deemed necessary for evaluating the effects in another state. The UNEP Regional Seas Conventions include general language on environmental impact assessment,[19] as does the 1982 UNCLOS (see below).

Article 14(1) of the 1985 ASEAN Agreement similarly limits the extent of the obligation to carry out an environmental impact assessment, requiring that the contracting parties:

> undertake that proposals for any activity which may significantly affect the natural environment shall as far as possible be subjected to an assessment of their consequences before they are adopted, and they shall take into consideration the results of their assessment in their decision-making process.

Many other international agreements addressing specific environmental media or particular activities provide for express or implied general obligations on environmental impact assessment. Such agreements include those governing the Antarctic,[20] atmospheric emissions of nitrogen oxide,[21] occupational health,[22] asbestos use,[23] transboundary movements of waste,[24] transboundary watercourses,[25] industrial accidents,[26] the energy sector,[27] public

---

[17] See pp. 814–17 below.

[18] Stockholm, 19 February 1974, in force 5 October 1976; 13 ILM 511 (1974), Art. 6.

[19] 1976 Barcelona Dumping Protocol, Annex III; 1978 Kuwait Convention, Art. XI; 1981 Abidjan Convention, Art. 13; 1981 Lima Convention, Art. 8; 1982 Jeddah Convention, Art. XI; 1983 Cartagena Convention, Art. 12; 1985 Nairobi Convention, Art. 13; and 1986 Noumea Convention, Art. 16. See also Recommendation 17/3 of the Helsinki Commission (1996), recommending consultations with potentially affected contracting parties 'where an Environmental Impact Assessment is required by either national or international law'.

[20] 1980 CCAMLR, Art. XV(2)(d); 1988 CRAMRA, Arts. 2(1)(a) and 4.

[21] 1988 NO$_x$ Protocol, Art. 6.

[22] 1985 Occupational Health Services Convention, Art. 5.

[23] 1986 Asbestos Convention, Art. 1(2).

[24] 1989 Basel Convention, Art. 4(2)(f) and Annex V(A).

[25] 1992 Watercourses Convention, Arts. 3(1)(h) and 9(2)(j), and its 1999 Protocol on Water and Health, Art. 4(6). See also 1997 Watercourses Convention, Art. 12 (requiring notification of results of any environmental impact assessment).

[26] 1992 Industrial Accidents Convention, Art. 4 and Annex III.

[27] 1994 Energy Charter Treaty, Art. 19 ('each Contracting Party shall strive to minimize in an economically efficient manner harmful Environmental Impacts occurring either within or outside its Area from all operations within the Energy Cycle in its Area'). See also its 1994 Protocol on Energy Efficiency and Related Environmental Aspects, Arts. 3(7) and 9.

participation,[28] and mining on the seabed of the high seas.[29] For some early conventions which did not include provisions on environmental impact assessment, such as the 1971 Ramsar Convention, the parties have subsequently adopted guidelines.[30] The 1985 Vienna Convention and its 1987 Montreal Protocol do not expressly require that the development of replacement technologies for prohibited ozone-depleting substances be subject to an environmental impact assessment; this will limit the effectiveness of those treaties. The convoluted language of the 1992 Climate Change Convention appears to require an impact assessment of the measures taken to mitigate or adapt to climate change on a range of factors including the environment, and requires all parties to:

> take climate change considerations into account, to the extent feasible, in their relevant social, economic and environmental policies and actions, and employ appropriate methods, for example impact assessments, formulated and determined nationally, with a view to minimizing adverse effects on the economy, on public health and on the quality of the environment, of projects or measures undertaken by them to mitigate or adapt to climate change.[31]

1982 UNCLOS

The 1982 UNCLOS requires the prior assessment of the effects of activities on the marine environment. Under Article 206:

> When states have reasonable grounds for believing that planned activities under their jurisdiction or control may cause substantial pollution of or significant and harmful changes to the marine environment, they shall, as far as practicable, assess the potential effects of such activities on the marine environment and shall communicate reports of the results of such assessments at appropriate intervals to the competent international organisations, which should make them available to all states.[32]

---

[28] 1998 Aarhus Convention, Art. 6(2)(e) and Annex I.

[29] Chapter 9, p. 446 above.

[30] Recommendation 6.2 on Environmental Impact Assessment (1996), requested parties and national and international organisations to submit guidelines on EIAs, and called for drafting of EIA guidelines; Resolution VII.16 on Impact Assessment (1999) calls on parties to 'reinforce and strengthen their efforts to ensure that any projects, plans, programmes and policies with the potential to alter the ecological character of wetlands in the Ramsar List, or impact negatively on other wetlands within their territories, are subjected to rigorous impact assessment procedures and to formalise such procedures under policy, legal, institutional and organisational arrangements.

[31] Art. 4(1)(f).

[32] Arts. 205 and 206. The 1994 Agreement relating to the implementation of Part XI of UNCLOS requires applications for approval of exploration on the seabed of the high seas to be accompanied by an assessment of the potential environmental impacts of the proposed activities: Annex, para. 1.7, and chapter 9, p. 446 above.

The authoritative Virginia Commentary describes the obligation as being 'similar to the requirements of some national environmental legislation, for example, the United States National Environmental Policy Act (NEPA) of 1969, to prepare environmental impact statements in respect of actions likely to affect the quality of the environment in a significant way', its purpose being to ensure that such activities may be effectively controlled, and to keep other states informed of the potential risks and effects of such activities.[33] The Virginia Commentary describes prior assessment as 'an essential part of a comprehensive environmental management system, and is a particular application of the obligation on States, enunciated in article 194, paragraph 2, to "take all necessary measures to ensure that activities under their jurisdiction or control are so conducted as not to cause damage by pollution to other States and their environment"'.[34]

Article 206 has been the subject of an international dispute between Ireland and the United Kingdom. In October 2001, Ireland brought proceedings against the United Kingdom under UNCLOS concerning the authorisation by the United Kingdom of a new nuclear plant to manufacture mixed oxide (MOX) fuel. Ireland claimed, *inter alia*, that the United Kingdom had violated the obligation set forth in Article 206 of UNCLOS, in particular for authorising the plant on the basis of a 1993 Environment Impact Statement which failed to assess the potential effects of the operation of the MOX plant on the marine environment of the Irish Sea,[35] including in relation to international movements of radioactive materials to be transported to and from the MOX plant, and which had not been updated to take into account the factual and legal developments which had occurred between 1993 and the plant's authorisation in 2001.[36] In December 2001, ITLOS prescribed provisional measures but declined to suspend the operation of the plant, as Ireland had requested, pending the constitution of the arbitral tribunal which would address the merits. In this regard, Judge Mensah expressed the view that:

> none of the violations of the procedural rights arising from the duty to . . . undertake appropriate environmental assessments are 'irreversible' in the sense that they cannot effectively be enforced against the United Kingdom by decision of the Annex VII arbitral tribunal, if the arbitral tribunal were to conclude that any such violations have in fact occurred.[37]

[33] M. Nordquist *et al.* (eds.), *United Nations Convention on the Law of the Sea 1982, A Commentary* (1990), vol. IV, 122.

[34] *Ibid.*

[35] Ireland, Statement of Claim, 25 October 2000, at paras. 7 and 31 (Ireland's concerns related *inter alia* to the failure of the 1993 Environmental Impact Statement to consider properly or at all: the topography, seismology, geology, demography and meteorology of the site and its relation to the Irish Sea; the relationship with the marine environment of the Irish Sea and the assessment of the environmental impact of radioactive discharges into the sea; the impacts on flora and fauna in the Irish Sea, including commercial fisheries; the impacts of international transports of radioactive materials on the Irish Sea).

[36] ITLOS Order, 3 December 2001, 41 ILM 405 (2002), para. 26; see chapter 9, p. 436 above.

[37] Separate Opinion of Judge Mensah, 7.

A different – but minority – view was expressed by ad hoc Judge Szekely, to the effect that the inadequacy of the 1993 Environmental Impact Statement justified more extensive provisional measures, 'since the environmental impact assessment is a central tool of the international law of prevention'.[38] The merits phase is likely to address, among other issues, the extent of the obligations flowing from Article 206, including the relationship between that provision and other applicable environmental assessment obligations.

EC law

Council Directive 85/337/EEC on the environment was the first international instrument to provide details on the nature and scope of environmental assessment, its use, and participation rights in the process. Despite the limitations which have become apparent since it entered into force in July 1988, the Directive has served as a model for subsequent legal instruments, from which practical experience in implementation can be discerned. The Directive was adopted unanimously by the (then) ten EEC member states and requires them to take 'the measures necessary to comply with [the] Directive by 3 July 1988'.[39] In 1997, the Directive was significantly amended by Council Directive 97/11/EC, which member states were required to bring into force by 14 March 1999.[40] In 1999, the Commission published guidance on the assessment of indirect and cumulative impacts,[41] and two years later on the screening[42] and scoping of projects.[43] Also, in 2001, the EU adopted Directive 2001/42/EC on the assessment of the effects of certain plans and programmes on the environment.[44]

Directive 85/337/EEC (as amended)

The 1985 Directive had a lengthy gestation period. Its origins lay in the EEC's 1973 First Environmental Action Programme, which identified the need to implement procedures to evaluate the environmental effects of certain activities at the earliest possible stage. The EC Commission's first proposal was in 1980, and it required a further five years, including lengthy deliberations at the European Parliament and the Economic and Social Committee, before the European Council adopted the proposal in 1985. Since the EEC Treaty had, at that time, no express provision for the adoption of environmental legislation, the Directive was based upon Articles 100 and 235, and for this reason its primary objective was stated to be economic rather than environmental: to approximate national laws on environmental assessment in order to remove disparities

---

[38] Separate Opinion of Judge Szekely, paras. 12–17.
[39] Art. 13.   [40] OJ L73, 14 March 1997, 5.
[41] http://europa.eu.int/comm/environment/eia/eia-studies-and-reports/guidel.pdf.
[42] http://europa.eu.int/comm/environment/eia/eia-guidelines/g-screening-full-text.pdf.
[43] http://europa.eu.int/comm/environment/eia/eia-guidelines/g-scoping-full-text.pdf.
[44] OJ L197, 21 July 2001, 30.

which could create unfavourable competitive conditions and affect the functioning of the common market. By contrast, the amending Directive 97/11/EC is firmly rooted in attaining environmental objectives, in a precautionary context.[45]

Directive 85/337/EEC requires the environmental assessment 'of public and private projects which are likely to have significant effects on the environment', excluding projects serving national defence purposes or projects whose details are adopted by a specific act of national legislation, since these were expected to undergo an appropriate assessment during the legislative process.[46] Article 2(1) of the Directive provides that:

> member states shall adopt all measures necessary to ensure that, before consent is given, projects likely to have significant effects on the environment by virtue, *inter alia*, of their nature, size or location are made subject to an assessment with regard to their effects.[47]

'Significant effects on the environment' are not defined by the Directive. Member states may, in exceptional cases, exempt a specific project in whole or in part from the Directive, subject to compliance with the obligation to inform the public and the EC Commission of the reasons for the exemption.[48] Article 4 divides projects subject to assessment into two classes: certain projects which are presumed to have 'significant effects on the environment' and for which assessments are mandatory (Annex I projects), and other projects for which assessment is not presumed to be necessary but will be required if they are likely to have 'significant effects on the environment' (Annex II projects).[49] Annex I originally listed nine categories of projects which were subject to a mandatory assessment, including crude-oil refineries, thermal power stations of over 300 megawatts and nuclear power stations, radioactive waste disposal and storage installations, certain iron and steel works, integrated chemical installations, construction of motorways, express roads and long-distance railway lines, trading ports, and waste disposal installations. Directive 97/11/EC has extended the list to twenty-one categories of project, including certain projects previously

---

[45] A. Sifakis, 'Precaution, Prevention and the Environmental Impact Assessment Directive', 1998 *European Environmental Law Review* 349.

[46] Art. 1(1) and (4). On the extent of the exception under Art. 1(5), see Case C-287/98, *Luxembourg* v. *Linster* [2000] ECR I-6917; and Case C-435/97, *WWF and Others* v. *Autonome Provinz Bozen and Others* [1999] ECR I-5613.

[47] Art. 2(1). Directive 97/11/EC amended the final part so as to read 'are made subject to a requirement for development consent and an assessment with regard to their effects. These projects are defined in Article 4.'

[48] Art. 2(3) (amended by Directive 97/11/EC).

[49] Annex I projects must be assessed irrespective of whether they are separate constructions, are added to a pre-existing construction or even have close functional links with a pre-existing construction: Case C-431/92, *Commission* v. *Germany* [1995] ECR I-2189, paras. 34–6.

listed in Annex II (for example, reprocessing of nuclear fuels and certain agricultural projects).

Annex II projects were originally subject to an assessment 'where member states consider that their characteristics so require'.[50] Directive 97/11/EC has revised Article 4 of Directive 85/337/EEC so as to permit a member state to make that determination either by a 'case-by-case examination' or on the basis of thresholds or criteria set by the member state, or by applying both procedures, and the member state must take into account the selection criteria set out in a new Annex III.[51]

The list of illustrative projects in the original Annex II was lengthy, and is now even lengthier. It includes projects as diverse as car racing tracks, theme parks, the construction of ski-lifts, and the rubber industry.[52]

The assessment process is defined in Articles 5 to 10 of Directive 85/337/EEC. The assessment is to include:

1. the supply by the developer of information set out in Annex IV (formerly Annex III), in an appropriate form;[53]
2. consultation with authorities likely to be concerned by the project;[54]
3. provision of information to, and consultation with, the public concerned;[55]
4. provision of information to, and consultation with, other member states likely to be affected;[56]

---

[50] Art. 4(2). It was not clear whether member states had a discretion in determining whether the characteristics of a particular project required an assessment, or whether an objective threshold existed. This lack of clarity, intended to introduce a degree of flexibility, led to differences of opinion between the member states and the EC Commission.

[51] Revised Art. 4(2) and (3). The Annex III criteria relate to the project's characteristics and location, and the characteristics of the potential impact. The determinations are to be made public: Art. 4(4).

[52] Annex II divides Art. 4(2) projects into thirteen categories (formerly twelve): agriculture, silviculture and aquaculture; extractive industry; energy industry; production and processing of metals; mineral industry; chemical industry; food industry; textile, leather, wood and paper industries; rubber industry; infrastructure projects; other projects; tourism and leisure; and any change or extension of projects listed in Annex I or Annex II, already authorised, executed or in the process of being executed, which may have significant adverse effects on the environment, as well as projects in Annex I, undertaken exclusively or mainly for the development and testing of new methods or products and not used for more than two years.

[53] Art. 5 (amended by Directive 97/11/EC).

[54] Art. 6(1) (amended by Directive 97/11/EC).

[55] Art. 6(2) and (3) (amended by Directive 97/11/EC).

[56] Art. 7. As amended by Directive 97/11/EC (which seeks to give effect to the requirements of the 1991 Espoo Convention) the potentially affected member state is entitled to participate in the EIA process, rather than merely be provided with information. This means that all persons affected by potential project impacts may be involved in the project consent process, not only those persons located within the territory of the member state.

5. the obligation that information gathered must be taken into consideration in the development consent procedure;[57] and

6. provision of information by the competent authority to the public when a decision has been taken.[58]

By Article 10 full respect is to be given to the limitations regarding industrial and commercial secrecy and safeguarding of the public interest which are imposed by national regulations, administrative provisions and accepted legal practices. The Annex IV (formerly Annex III) information to be provided in accordance with Article 5 includes a description of the project (including physical characteristics of the whole project, land use requirements, production processes, residues and emissions resulting from the operation of the project), an outline of the main alternatives where appropriate, the aspects of the environment likely to be significantly affected, and measures to limit adverse environmental effects.

Application of the Directive

Differences in the interpretation of the Directive by member states, the Commission and private persons have resulted in many disputes between individual citizens and their governments, and between the EC Commission and the member states.[59] It has been said that the Directive attracts more complaints to the EC Commission than any other environmental Directive.[60] The Commission has published two reports on the implementation of the Directive, in 1991 and 1997.[61] These have addressed a broad range of concerns, relating to matters such as:

- the extent to which the Directive applies to projects which were initiated and for which planning permission was sought, or partially granted, before 3 July 1988 (the date of entry into force);[62]
- the definition of Annex I projects;

---

[57] Art. 8 (amended by Directive 97/11/EC).

[58] Art. 9 (amended by Directive 97/11/EC).

[59] The Commission has brought several cases concerning non-implementation: see e.g. Case C-313/93, *Commission* v. *Luxembourg* [1994] ECR I-1279.

[60] Complaints increased from thirty-four in 1988 to 170 as early as 1990: 221 *ENDS Report* 20 at 24 (June 1993), citing the EC's 1993 annual report.

[61] COM (93) 28 final (13 vols., 1993), as reported in 'Taking Stock of Environmental Assessment', 221 *ENDS Report* 20 (June 1993); and http://europa.eu.int/comm/environment/eia/eia-studies-and-reports/5years.pdf.

[62] The ECJ has held that the Directive does not permit a member state which has transposed the Directive into national law after the deadline for transposition to waive, for projects in respect of which the consent procedure had been initiated before the entry into force of the national law transposing the Directive, but after the date for transposition, the obligations imposed by the directive: Case C-396/92, *Bund Naturschutz in Bayern eV and Others* v. *Freistaat Bayern* [1994] ECR I-3717; Case C-431/92, *Commission* v. *Germany* [1995] ECR I-2189; Case C-150/97, *Commission* v. *Portuguese Republic* [1999] ECR I-259; and Case C-81/96, (the Directive requires an assessment where an application is made after

- the extent to which EC member states have a discretion in determining whether to subject Annex II projects to an environmental assessment; and
- the adequacy of implementation by member states, including the failure to ensure that environmental assessments be recorded in writing.

The resolution of these interpretative issues has to a certain extent been assisted by a developing jurisprudence from the ECJ, although the number of cases is not large. Even before the amendments introduced by Directive 97/11/EC, the ECJ has sought to limit the extent of the discretion which may be exercised in relation to Annex II projects, requiring the discretion to be informed by the principles laid down in Article 2(1).[63] The Court has also ruled that entire classes of projects may not be excluded[64] and that in determining whether an assessment is required pursuant to Article 4(2) it is necessary to have regard to a project's location or nature and the cumulative effect of a series of projects, so that generally applicable *de minimis* thresholds are inadequate.[65] The Court has confirmed that modifications to Annex II projects may be subject to assessment where they may have significant effects on the environment.[66] There has also been considerable national litigation over the Directive, before the courts of various member states, including early support for the view that the obligations set out in the Directive are sufficiently clear to be directly effective.[67]

---

3 July 1988 seeking 'fresh consent' for an Annex I project for which consent was obtained years or even decades previously without any environmental assessment being made in accordance with the requirements of the Directive, and where 'scarcely any progress was made in implementing the project'). Note also the view of Advocate General Mischo in Case C-81/96, *Burgemeester* v. *Holland* [1998] ECR I-3923, para. 32 ('Who cannot call to mind some grandiose project drawn up ten years ago, or even more recently, in the name of economic development (sacrosanct) or simply of progress, unopposed at the time but not implemented for lack of funds, and which no-one would dare to recommend today because of the foreseeable impact on the environment?').

[63] Case C-301/95, *Commission* v. *Germany* [1998] ECR I-6135. For an early decision of a national court highlighting the difficulties caused by the absence of fixed criteria, see *R.* v. *Swale Borough Council, ex parte Royal Society for the Protection of Birds* [1990] 2 Admin LR 790; [1991] JPL 39.

[64] Case C-133/94, *Commission* v. *Belgium* [1996] ECR I-2323; see also Case C-301/95, *Commission* v. *Germany* [1998] ECR I-6135; and Case C-435/97, *WWF and Others* v. *Autonome Provinz Bozen and Others* [1999] ECR I-5613.

[65] Case C-392/96, *Commission* v. *Ireland* [1999] ECR I-5901; see also Case C-72/95 *Kraaijeveld* v. *Holland* [1996] ECR I-5403.

[66] Case C-72/95, *Kraaijeveld* v. *Holland* [1996] ECR I-5403.

[67] See *Twyford Parish Council* v. *Secretary of State for the Environment* [1992] 1 CMLR 276 at 279, where Judge McCullogh stated that 'I have no doubt that the applicants were among those whom the directive was intended to benefit and that its provisions were unconditional and sufficiently precise' (concerning an Annex I project). But see *Kincardine and Deeside District Council* v. *Forestry Commissioners*, 1992 SLT 1180; [1992] 2 CMLR 869; [1993] Env LR 151, holding that the Directive did not have 'direct effect' in respect of Annex II projects.

Directive 2001/42/EC and strategic environmental assessment

In the 1990s it became apparent that the assessment of projects alone did not ensure that potential environmentally harmful activities would necessarily be prevented, and that underlying policies and plans which would give rise to individual projects were not being assessed adequately, if at all, for their environmental effects. EC Directive 2001/42/EC is the first international instrument to impose binding obligations, requiring member states to ensure that 'an environmental assessment is carried out of certain plans and programmes which are likely to have significant effects on the environment', and is to be domestically implemented by 21 July 2004.[68] The Directive is likely to inspire changes elsewhere: a Protocol on strategic environmental assessment is being negotiated under the 1991 Espoo Convention (see below),[69] and the World Bank and other multilateral development banks have been informally making use of, and considering the adoption of an instrument on, strategic environmental assessment.[70]

Under the EC Directive, an assessment is to be carried out for all programmes prepared in specified areas or which require an assessment under Article 6 of the 1992 Habitats Directive, unless they use only small areas at local level and entail minor modifications, in which case an assessment is only required where the member state determines that it is likely to have a 'significant environmental effect'.[71] Plans and programmes relating to national defence, or civil emergency or financial or budget matters are not subject to the Directive.[72]

The assessment is to be carried out during the preparation of a plan or programme and its adoption or submission to a legislative procedure.[73] It requires the preparation of a report which identifies, describes and evaluates the likely significant effects, and must include the information referred to in Annex I, including reasonable alternatives.[74] The Directive provides for consultations involving relevant authorities and the public which may be affected or which have an interest in the plan or programme, as well as transboundary consultations with potentially affected member states and their public.[75] By Article 8,

---

[68] Art. 1. By Art. 2(a), 'plans and programmes' encompasses those 'which are subject to preparation and/or adoption by an authority at national, regional or local level or which are prepared by an authority for adoption, through a legislative procedure by Parliament or Government, and which are required by legislative, regulatory or administrative provisions'.

[69] www.unece.org/env/eia/ad-hocwg.htm.   [70] Chapter 20, p. 1028 below.

[71] Art. 3(3). Such determination is to be on a case-by-case basis or by specifying types of plans and programmes, taking into account the criteria set forth in Annex II. The areas requiring assessment are agriculture, forestry, fisheries, energy, industry, transport, waste management, water management, telecommunications, tourism, town and country planning or land use and those which set the framework for future development consent of projects listed in Annexes I and II to Directive 85/337/EEC: Art. 3(2)(a).

[72] Art. 3(8). Certain co-financed plans are also excluded: Art. 3(9).

[73] Art. 4(1).   [74] Art. 5(1).   [75] Arts. 6 and 7.

the environmental report and opinions resulting from the various consultations are to be taken into account during the preparation of the plan and programme and before its adoption. The Directive also requires that certain specified information be made available to consultees and, innovatively, that the member state monitors the significant environmental effects of the implementation of the plan or programme 'to identify at an early stage unforeseen adverse effects, and to be able to undertake appropriate remedial action'.[76]

1986 Noumea Convention

Article 16 of the 1986 Noumea Convention requires each party to assess, within its capabilities, 'the potential effects of [major projects which might affect the marine environment] so that appropriate measures can be taken to prevent any substantial pollution of, or significant harm within, the Convention Area'.[77] On 21 June 1995, New Zealand filed proceedings at the ICJ challenging France's resumption of underground nuclear tests, on the ground, among others, that the tests violated France's obligation to carry out a prior assessment of their impacts on the environment, in accordance with Article 16.[78] New Zealand also asserted that customary international law required an environmental impact assessment to be carried out 'in relation to any activity which is likely to cause significant damage to the environment, particularly where such effects are likely to be transboundary in nature'.[79] The approach was endorsed by four South Pacific states and Australia, which had sought to intervene in the ICJ proceedings.[80] In response, France did not deny the existence of obligations under the 1986 Noumea Convention or customary law, but rather stated that too much should not be read into the 1986 Convention or customary law, and that environmental assessment requirements permitted a considerable 'margin of appreciation' to states as to the manner in which they sought to avoid causing damage.[81] As the Court found that it did not have jurisdiction to entertain the application, the arguments were not addressed by the majority. Two dissenting opinions, however, reflected an emerging recognition of the potential place of environmental assessment in customary law. Of particular note is Judge Weeramantry's opinion that the requirement to carry out an environmental impact assessment was 'gathering strength and international acceptance, and has reached the level of

---

[76] Arts. 9 and 10.   [77] Art. 16(2).
[78] New Zealand Request, paras. 74–88, and CR/95/20, 10–25.
[79] New Zealand Request, para. 89.
[80] See e.g. Solomon Islands statement, para. 11; Australia statement, para. 33.
[81] CR/95/20, 71–2 ('l'on ne doit pas faire dire au droit coutumier en general, ni à la convention de Nouméa, plus qu'ils ne dissent eux-mêmes . . . [EIA] laisse . . . une marge considerable d'appréciation à chaque Etat concerné quant à la façon de s'assurer préalablement à l'entreprise d'activités qui seraient potentiellement dangeureuse, que leur incidence sur l'environnement ne serait pas dommageable').

general recognition at which [the ICJ] should take notice of it'.[82] As described below, that opinion appears to have informed the Court's decision two years later in the case concerning the Gabcikovo-Nagymaros project.

1991 Espoo Convention

The 1991 Espoo Convention was adopted under the auspices of the UNECE, and in several aspects it imposes more onerous requirements than the 1985 EC Directive on which it is based. It came into force on 10 September 1997, and commits parties to take all appropriate and effective measures to prevent, reduce and control significant adverse transboundary environmental impacts from proposed activities. The Convention requires that parties of origin must notify affected parties of certain proposed activities which are likely to cause a significant adverse transboundary impact, and requires discussions between concerned parties.[83] The Convention defines 'impact' broadly to include:

> any effect caused by a proposed activity on the environment including human health and safety, flora, fauna, soil, air, water, climate, landscape and historical monuments or other physical structures or the interaction among these factors; it also includes effects on cultural heritage or socio-economic conditions resulting from alterations to those factors.[84]

A 'transboundary impact' is defined as:

> any impact, not exclusively of a global nature, within an area under the jurisdiction of a party caused by a proposed activity the physical origin of which is situated wholly or in part within the area under the jurisdiction of another party.[85]

The party of origin is required to ensure that, in accordance with the provisions of the Convention, an environmental impact assessment is undertaken 'prior to a decision to authorise or undertake a proposed activity listed in Appendix I that is likely to cause a significant adverse transboundary impact'.[86] Appendix III

---

[82] (1995) ICJ Reports, 344. See also the Dissenting Opinion of Ad Hoc Judge Palmer that 'customary international law may have developed a norm of requiring [EIA] where activities may have a significant effect on the environment': *ibid.*, 412, para. 91.

[83] Espoo, 25 February 1991; in force 10 September 1997; 30 ILM 802 (1991), Art. 2(1), (4) and (5); thirty-nine states and the EC are party. 'Party of origin' means the party or parties 'under whose jurisdiction a proposed activity is envisaged to take place' (Art. 1(ii)); 'affected party' means the party or parties 'likely to be affected by the transboundary impact of a proposed activity' (Art. 1(iii)); assessment under the Convention may also fulfil requirements under the 1992 Industrial Accidents Convention: see Art. 4(4) of the latter Convention.

[84] Art. 1(vii).   [85] Art. 1(viii).

[86] Art. 2(3). 'Proposed activity' means 'any activity or any major change to an activity subject to a decision of a competent authority in accordance with an applicable national procedure': Art. 1(v). The Convention applies, at a minimum, to the 'project

provides guidance for determining the environmental significance of activities not listed.[87] The assessment procedure must allow public participation in the preparation of the documentation, ensure an opportunity to the public living in areas likely to be affected to participate in procedures, and ensure that the opportunity provided to the public in the affected country is equivalent to that provided to the public of the party of origin.[88]

The Convention requires transboundary co-operation. Under Article 3, the party of origin must notify any of the seventeen proposed activities listed in Appendix I which is likely to cause a significant adverse transboundary impact, as early as possible, to 'any party which it considers may be an affected party' and no later than when informing its own public.[89] The notification must include information on the proposed activity, its possible transboundary impact, and the nature of the possible decision, and should allow a reasonable time for a response as to whether the affected party will participate in the procedure. Where the affected party decides not to participate, the operational provisions of the Convention will not apply, and the party of origin can decide on the basis of its national law and practice whether to carry out an assessment.[90]

Once the affected party decides to participate in the procedure, and after it has received information relevant to the proposed activity and its possible significant transboundary impact, it must promptly provide the party of origin, at its request, with reasonably obtainable information relating to the potentially affected environment under its jurisdiction, where such information is necessary for the preparation of the environmental impact assessment.[91] Where a party considers that it is likely to be affected by a significant adverse transboundary impact of a proposed activity listed in Appendix I, and it has not been notified in accordance with Article 3(1), an exchange of 'sufficient information' must take place at the request of the affected party 'for the purposes of holding

---

level' of the proposed activity, although parties undertake to 'endeavour to apply the principles of environmental impact assessment to policies, plans and programmes': *ibid.*, Art. 2(7).

[87] Factors include: the size of the activity; its proposed location (not in or close to an area of special environmental sensitivity or importance); and its effects (will they be particularly complex and potentially adverse, and will they threaten the existing or potential use of an area, or will they cause additional loading which cannot be sustained by the carrying capacity of the environment?).

[88] Art. 2(2) and (6).

[89] The activities listed in Appendix I include: crude oil and certain other refineries; thermal power stations and other combustion installations with an output of 300 megawatts or more and nuclear installations; nuclear facilities; major cast iron and steel installations; asbestos plants; integrated chemical installations; construction of motorways, express roads, long-distance railway lines and long airport runways; pipelines; large trading ports; toxic and dangerous waste disposal installations; large dams and reservoirs; groundwater abstraction; pulp and paper manufacturing; major mining; offshore hydrocarbon production; major oil and chemical storage facilities; and deforestation of large areas.

[90] Art. 3(4). The operational provisions are Arts. 4–7.   [91] Art. 3(6).

discussions on whether there is likely to be a significant adverse transboundary impact'.[92] If the parties agree that such an impact is likely, the provisions of the Convention are to apply. If there is no such agreement, any such party may submit the question to an inquiry commission established under Appendix IV unless another method of settling the question is agreed.[93] Concerned parties must ensure that the affected party's public is informed about the proposed activity and is provided with an opportunity to make comments or objections to the competent authority of the party of origin.[94]

The documentation to be submitted to the competent authority of the party of origin must contain the information required in Appendix II, which is more comprehensive than that required by the original Annex III to the 1985 Directive. This includes, but is not limited to, descriptions of: the proposed activity and its purpose; reasonable alternatives and the 'no-action alternative'; the environment likely to be significantly affected and its alternatives; the potential environmental impact, its alternatives and an estimation of its significance; and mitigation measures.[95] Indications should also be given of predictive methods, underlying assumptions and relevant environmental data used, gaps in knowledge and uncertainties, an outline for monitoring and management and any plans for post-project analysis, and a non-technical summary with appropriate visual presentations.[96] The documentation must be provided to the affected party and distributed to its authorities and public in areas likely to be affected, and the comments of those authorities and that public are to be submitted to the competent authority of the party of origin 'within a reasonable time before the final decision is taken on the proposed activity'.[97]

Under Article 5, consultations must take place between the party of origin and the affected parties concerning the potential transboundary impact and measures to reduce or eliminate the impact. These may relate to alternatives to the proposed activity (including the 'no-action alternative' and mitigating measures), other forms of mutual assistance, and any other appropriate matters. In taking the final decision on the proposed activity, the parties must take due account of the outcome of the environmental impact assessment, including the documentation, as well as the comments received under Articles 3(8) and 4(2) and consultations under Article 5.[98] The party of origin must inform the affected party of the final decision and the reasons and considerations on which it was based.[99] If new information which could have materially affected

---

[92] Art. 3(7). Decision 1/IV of the meeting of the parties establishes an agreed format for notification.

[93] Appendix IV sets out the rules of procedure for the establishment of a compulsory inquiry commission.

[94] Art. 3(8). See Decision II/3 of the meeting of the parties, on public participation.

[95] Art. 4(1) and Appendix II.   [96] Appendix II.

[97] Art. 4(2).   [98] Art. 6(1).   [99] Art. 6(2).

the decision becomes available to a concerned party after- the decision was made, that party shall inform other concerned parties and, as requested, hold consultations on revision of the decision.[100]

A further innovation of the Convention is the provision of requirements on post-project analysis and follow-up. Concerned parties must decide, at the request of any one of them, whether and to what extent a post-project analysis is to be carried out, including surveillance of the activity and a determination of any adverse transboundary impact.[101] The objectives of a post-project analysis are set out in Appendix V; they include monitoring compliance with authorisation conditions and the effectiveness of mitigation measures; a management review; and verification of past predictions. Where the post-project analysis establishes reasonable grounds for concluding that there is a significant adverse transboundary impact or factors which may result in such an impact, the concerned parties must consult on 'necessary measures' to reduce or eliminate the impact.[102]

The Convention also provides for bilateral and multilateral co-operation to implement its provisions in accordance with the elements set out in Appendix VI, and on the development of research programmes.[103] Institutional arrangements include an annual meeting of the parties, which is charged with keeping the implementation of the Convention under review, with the assistance of the secretariat.[104] In 2001, an Implementation Committee was established,[105] and on 21 May 2003 a Protocol on strategic environmental assessment was adopted in Kiev.

A number of more general provisions of the Convention are also relevant to the further development of international law in relation to environmental assessment, information and co-operation. Concerned parties must enter into discussions, at the request of any such party, on whether a proposed activity not listed in Appendix I is likely to cause a significant adverse transboundary impact, and therefore should be treated as if so listed.[106] Appendix III provides general guidance to assist in the determination of the environmental significance of activities not listed in Appendix I, by virtue of one or more criteria, including its size, location and effects. The Convention does not affect parties' rights under national laws, provisions or practices to protect information the supply of which would be prejudicial to industrial and commercial secrecy or national security, and does not affect the right of a party to implement more stringent measures.[107] Moreover, the Convention does not prejudice 'any obligations of the parties under international law with regard to activities having or likely to have a transboundary impact'.[108]

---

[100] Art. 6(3).   [101] Art. 7(1).   [102] Art. 7(2).   [103] Arts. 8 and 9.   [104] Art. 13.
[105] Decision II/IV (2001); once in force, the Protocol will require parties to evaluate the environmental consequences of their official draft plans and programmes.
[106] Art. 2(5).   [107] Art. 2(8) and (9).   [108] Art. 2(10).

1991 Antarctic Environment Protocol

Article 8 of the 1991 Antarctic Environment Protocol (which supersedes the environmental assessment provisions under the 1988 CRAMRA) requires prior assessment of the impacts of activities on the Antarctic environment or on dependent or associated ecosystems. The detailed obligations take a different approach from the 1985 EC Directive and the 1991 Espoo Convention. They establish a range of procedures, the use of which will be dependent on whether the activity is expected to have (a) less than a minor or transitory impact; or (b) a minor or transitory impact; or (c) more than a minor or transitory impact.[109] This approach is similar to that recommended in paragraph 11 of the 1982 World Charter for Nature. The assessment must be:

> applied in the planning processes leading to decisions about any activi-
> ties undertaken in the Antarctic Treaty area pursuant to scientific research
> programmes, tourism and all other governmental and non-governmental
> activities in the Antarctic Treaty area for which advance notice is required
> under Article VII(5) of the Antarctic Treaty, including associated logistic
> support activities.[110]

Assessments are also required for any change in activity, including an increase or decrease of intensity, the decommissioning of a facility, or otherwise.[111]

Annex I to the Protocol sets out a five-stage procedure for carrying out the assessment.

1. In the preliminary stage, the proposed activity is considered in accordance with national procedures, and, if the activity is determined to have less than a minor or transitory impact, the activity may proceed.[112]
2. If the activity will have a minor or transitory impact or more, an Initial Environmental Evaluation will be prepared, which should contain sufficient information to assess whether the activity will have more than a minor or transitory impact.[113] The information should include a description of the proposed activity, including its purpose, location, duration and intensity, and a consideration of any alternatives and impacts, including cumulative impacts. If this evaluation indicates that a proposed activity is likely to have no more than a minor or transitory impact, the activity may proceed subject to compliance with appropriate procedures, including monitoring of impacts.[114]
3. If this evaluation indicates a likelihood of more than a minor or transitory impact, a Comprehensive Environmental Evaluation must be prepared, and

---

[109] Art. 8(1). Annex I to the Protocol does not apply to emergencies relating to the safety of human life or of ships or aircraft or other high value equipment or facilities, or the protection of the environment: Annex I, Art. 7.
[110] Art. 8(2).   [111] Art. 8(3).   [112] Annex I, Art. 1.
[113] Annex I, Art. 2(1).   [114] Annex I, Art. 2(2).

must include descriptions of the proposed activity, the initial and predicted future environment reference state, and methods and data used to forecast impacts.[115] The Comprehensive Evaluation will also include an estimation of likely and direct impacts; indirect or second order and cumulative impacts; mitigation measures; unavoidable impacts; effects on the conduct of scientific research; gaps in knowledge and uncertainties; a non-technical summary; and a contact person or organisation.[116]

4. The draft Evaluation is to be made publicly available, circulated to all parties and forwarded to the Protocol's Committee on Environmental Protection, with a ninety-day comment period and at least 120 days before the next Antarctic Treaty Consultative Meeting.[117] The proposed activity may not proceed until the draft Evaluation has been considered by the Antarctic Treaty Consultative Meeting on the advice of the Committee, within a maximum period of fifteen months from the date of the draft's circulation.[118]

5. A final Evaluation must address comments received and be circulated to all parties and made publicly available at least sixty days before the commencement of the proposed activity.[119] The decision on whether to proceed with a proposed activity must be based on the Comprehensive Evaluation and other relevant considerations.[120] Procedures will be put in place to assess and verify the impact of activities following the Comprehensive Evaluation, including the monitoring of key environmental indicators.[121]

Biodiversity and risk assessment[122]

The 1992 Biodiversity Convention requires parties to identify 'processes and categories of activities which have or are likely to have significant adverse impacts on the conservation and sustainable use of biological diversity, and monitor their effects through sampling and other techniques' and to require environmental impact assessment of proposed projects that are likely to have 'significant adverse effects on biological diversity'.[123] Article 14 also requires

---

[115] Annex I, Art. 3(1) and (2)(a)–(c).   [116] Annex I, Art. 3(2)(d)–(1).
[117] Annex I, Art. 3(3) and (4). See also Art. 6.
[118] Art. 3(5).   [119] Art. 3(6).   [120] Art. 4.   [121] Annex I, Art. 5.
[122] Risk assessment has also been addressed in the WTO's Agreement on Sanitary and Phytosanitary Measures, chapter 19, p. 977 below; see also chapter 12, p. 655 above.
[123] Arts. 7(c) and 14(1)(a). These requirements are supplemented by decisions of the conference of the parties, including: Decision IV/10 (calling on parties to submit to the secretariat impact assessments, reports on the effectiveness of EIAs, reports relating to national legislation on EIAs, and incentive schemes to encourage participation in EIA programmes); Decision V/18 (calling on parties, *inter alia*, to 'integrate environmental impact assessment into the work programs' in all areas of biological diversity; to use the loss of biological diversity as a factor in determining impact when conducting an EIA; to ensure wide involvement of all impacted when conducting an EIA; to look at the cumulative impact of multiple projects; and to report on national practices and experiences with

parties to promote notification, exchange of information and consultation on activities under their jurisdiction or control which are likely to significantly and adversely affect the biological diversity of other states or areas beyond the limits of national jurisdiction, and to provide for immediate notification in any case of imminent or grave danger or damage.[124] The sixth conference of the parties endorsed draft guidelines for incorporating biodiversity-related issues into environmental impact assessment legislation and processes and in strategic environmental assessment, and urged parties and other governments and organisations to apply the guidelines in the context of their implementation of Article 14(1) of the Convention.[125] The Guidelines provide considerable detail as to the context of an environmental impact assessment (following the approach set forth in other international instruments), and the conditions under which assessments must and should be carried out.

The 2000 Biosafety Protocol to the Convention requires 'risk assessments' to be carried out in respect of import decisions relating to living modified organisms, in order

> to identify and evaluate the possible adverse effects of living modified organisms on the conservation and sustainable use of biological diversity, taking also into account risks to human health.[126]

The risk assessments are to be carried out in a 'scientifically sound manner, in accordance with Annex III and taking into account recognized risk assessment techniques', and may be carried out by the exporter.[127] Annex III identifies the methodology to be applied in carrying out a risk assessment, including:

(a) An identification of any novel genotypic and phenotypic characteristics associated with the living modified organism that may have adverse effects on biological diversity in the likely potential receiving environment, taking also into account risks to human health;

(b) An evaluation of the likelihood of these adverse effects being realized . . . ;

(c) An evaluation of the consequences should these adverse effects be realized;

(d) An estimation of the overall risk posed by the living modified organism based on the evaluation of the likelihood and consequences of the identified adverse effects being realized;

(e) A recommendation as to whether or not the risks are acceptable or manageable . . . ; and

---

EIAs); and Decision VI/7 (endorsing guidelines for incorporating biodiversity-related issues into environmental impact assessment legislation and processes and in strategic environmental assessment contained in the Annex to the Decision).

[124] Art. 14(1)(c) and (d).

[125] Decision VI/7 (identification, monitoring, indicators and assessments) (2002).

[126] Biosafety Protocol, Art. 15(1).

[127] Art. 15(2). See also Art. 16 on 'risk management'.

(f) Where there is uncertainty regarding the level of risk, it may be addressed by requesting further information on the specific issues of concern or by implementing appropriate risk management strategies and/or monitoring the living modified organism in the receiving environment.[128]

World Bank and other multilateral lending institutions[129]

Many international organisations, including multilateral development banks, have developed their own environmental impact assessment procedures, of which the most widely studied is that adopted by the World Bank in 1989.[130] World Bank Operational Directive 4.01 was adopted in 1989, its objective being to ensure that the development options adopted were sound and enduring from an environmental perspective and that environmental consequences were recognised at an early stage in the project cycle and included in the project scheme.[131] The Operational Directive was the subject of significant criticism, including the failure to provide for a 'no-action alternative' whereby the project may be stopped because the environmental risks are too great to allow the project to proceed at all, and its silence as to mandatory requirements concerning the provision of information to local populations and their right to participate in the environmental impact assessment process. In 1999, the policy was converted into a new format, now reflected in Operation Policy (OP) 4.01 and Bank Procedures (BP) 4.01, which have sought to address these and other issues.

By OP 4.01, the World Bank requires environmental assessment (EA) of projects proposed for Bank financing to help ensure that they are environmentally sound and sustainable, thereby improving decision-making.[132] EA is described as a process, which: evaluates a project's potential environmental risks and impacts in its area of influence; examines project alternatives; identifies ways of improving project selection, siting, planning, design and

---

[128] Annex III, para. 8. 'Risk Assessment' is to take into account the relevant technical and scientific details regarding the characteristics of: recipient organism or parental organisms; donor organism or organisms; vector; insert or inserts and/or characteristics of modification; living modified organism: detection and identification of the living modified organism; information relating to the intended use; and the receiving environment.

[129] On environmental assessment of overseas development assistance, see chapter 20, pp. 1022–9 below.

[130] See also International Finance Corporation, OP 4.01; EBRD, Environmental Procedures (1996); ADB, Environmental Assessment Requirements (1998); North American Development Bank, 1993 Agreement, 32 ILM 1545 (1993), Art. II(3)(c), www.nadbank.org, and Border Environment Co-operation Commission Guidelines (in particular Art. VII), 21 September 1995, 60 US Fed. Reg. 48982.

[131] Operational Directive 4.00, Annex A, Environmental Assessment (1989).

[132] See OP 4.01, Annex A (definitions). The Bank's internal procedures are governed by BP 4.01.

implementation; and includes the process of mitigating and managing adverse environmental impacts throughout the implementation of the project. It is premised on the Bank's preference for 'preventive measures over mitigatory or compensatory measures, whenever feasible'.[133] The borrower is responsible for carrying out the EA, which may comprise one or more of an environmental impact assessment (EIA), a regional or sectoral EA, an environmental audit, a hazard or risk assessment, and an environmental management plan (EMP).[134] The Bank is responsible for environmental screening of each proposed project to determine the appropriate extent and type of EA, and classifies the proposed project into one of four categories. A proposed project is classified as Category A if it is 'likely to have significant adverse environmental impacts that are sensitive, diverse, or unprecedented', and will normally require an EIA (or a comprehensive regional or sectoral EA).[135] A proposed project is classified as Category B if its potential adverse environmental impacts are site-specific, if few of the impacts are irreversible, and if mitigatory measures can be designed more readily than for Category A projects. The scope of EA for a Category B project will be narrower than for a Category A project. A proposed project is classified as Category C if it is likely to have minimal or no adverse environmental impacts. A proposed project is classified as Category FI if it involves investment of Bank funds through a financial intermediary, in subprojects that may result in adverse environmental impacts. Environmental assessments are also required for special project types. Category A and B projects must be subject to public consultation.

The adequacy of the application of OP 4.01 is reflected in the fact that thirteen of the twenty-three requests filed at the World Bank Inspection Panel by July 2001 alleged inadequate environmental assessments. In some cases, the Panel found no violations, but in others the Panel found violations which led or contributed to a decision to withdraw financing,[136] or other proposed remedial actions.[137]

Gabcikovo-Nagymaros Case

The developments described in this chapter, which largely took place in the late 1980s and early 1990s, provided the background to one aspect of the dispute between Hungary and Slovakia concerning the construction of two barrages on the

[133] Para. 2.   [134] OP 4.01, Annex C describes the environmental management plan.

[135] OP 4.01, Annex B describes the content of a Category A environmental assessment report (to include executive summary; policy, legal and administrative framework; project description; baseline data; environmental impacts; analysis of alternatives; environmental management plan (EMP)).

[136] *Nepal/Arun* III (25 October 1994); *China/Western Poverty Reduction Project* (18 June 1999); see generally chapter 5, pp. 210–11 above.

[137] *Ecuador/Mining Development and Environmental Control Technical Assistance* (7 May 2000).

River Danube.[138] A central part of Hungary's case was that the two parties to the 1977 Treaty had failed, by 1989, to adequately assess the project's impact on the environment, in particular the impacts on freshwaters and biodiversity.[139] The ICJ considered that Hungary was not entitled (in 1989) to suspend construction on its part of the project, or (in 1992) to terminate the 1977 Treaty, and that the 1977 Treaty therefore remained in force between the parties. However, the Court recognised that the project's impact upon, and its implications for, the environment were a key issue, and that the impact and implications were considerable, and ruled that Articles 15 and 19 of the 1977 Treaty prescribed 'a continuing – and thus necessarily evolving – obligation on the parties to maintain the quality of the water of the Danube and to protect nature'.[140] Noting that 'vigilance and prevention are required on account of the often irreversible character of damage to the environment and of the limitations inherent in the very mechanism of reparation of this type of damage', the Court ruled that:

> the Parties together should look afresh at the effects on the environment of the operation of the Gabcikovo power plant. In particular they must find a satisfactory solution for the volume of water to be released into the old bed of the Danube and into the side-arms on both sides of the river.

The Court has, in effect, read into the two provisions of the 1977 Treaty a requirement that the parties carry out a continuing environmental assessment of the project's impacts on the environment. The rationale behind the Court's approach is reflected in the Separate Opinion of Judge Weeramantry, who was in the majority and a member of the Court's drafting Committee. Developing his Opinion in the 1995 New Zealand nuclear tests case, Judge Weeramantry states:

> In the present case, the incorporation of environmental considerations into the Treaty by Articles 15 and 19 meant that the principle of EIA was also built into the Treaty. These provisions were clearly not restricted to EIA before the project commenced, but also included the concept of monitoring during the continuance of the project . . . Environmental law in its current state of development would read into treaties which may reasonably be considered to have a significant impact upon the environment, a duty of environmental impact assessment and this means also, whether the treaty expressly so provides or not, a duty of monitoring the environmental impacts of any substantial project during the operation of the scheme.[141]

---

[138] (1997) ICJ Reports 7; chapter 10, pp. 469–77 above.   [139] Para. 35.

[140] Para. 140. Art. 15 specified that the contracting parties 'shall ensure, by the means specified in the joint contractual plan, that the quality of the water in the Danube is not impaired as a result of the construction and operation of the System of Locks'; Art. 19 provided that: 'The Contracting Parties shall, through the means specified in the joint contractual plan, ensure compliance with the obligations for the protection of nature arising in connection with the construction and operation of the System of Locks.'

[141] (1997) ICJ Reports 7 at 111.

Moreover, according to Judge Weeramantry, the 'principle of contemporaneity' in the application of environmental norms supplemented his observations regarding continuing assessment and provided the standard by which the continuing assessment is to be made:

> It matters little that an undertaking has been commenced under a treaty of 1950, if in fact that undertaking continues in operation in the year 2000. The relevant environmental standards that will be applicable will be those of the year 2000.[142]

Conclusions

The judgment in the *Case Concerning the Gabcikovo-Nagymaros Project* indicates the extent to which the concept of environmental assessment has developed and become established since the first edition of this book.[143] A broad range of international instruments now establishes general obligations requiring prior environmental assessment of projects which may cause environmental harm; a smaller number set forth more detailed criteria for the conduct of such assessments, whether in particular geographic areas, to protect particular resources, or in respect of particular categories of activities. The EC's experience under the 1985 Directive identifies some of the difficulties associated with environmental impact assessments, and as other regions and organisations formalise similar arrangements they could usefully draw upon the lessons learned in the EC. As noted in the introduction to this chapter, there is considerable support for the view that environmental impact assessments are required as a matter of customary law, particularly in respect of activities which may cause transboundary effects. Most multilateral development banks now require some form of environmental impact assessment, and they are now required by international law also to assess the environmental consequences of potentially damaging projects into which they consider putting financial resources.

   In the past decade, the limitations of the first generation of project-related environmental impact assessments has become apparent, and this has translated into a second generation of instruments revising earlier approaches and establishing strategic environmental assessments of programmes and plans. In respect of projects, the critical issues remain: the scope of the impacts to be assessed; the type of projects to be covered; the availability of information to the public and their participation in the process; and the requirement that the statement be taken into account *before* authorisation is granted. The unwillingness of states to subject themselves to what they consider to be unnecessary

---

[142] *Ibid.*, 114.
[143] See e.g. *Maffezini* v. *Spain*, ICSID Award of 9 November 2000, para. 67, 16 *ICSID Rev-FILJ*, 248 (2001).

and intrusive environmental assessments remains a problem, as illustrated by the differences between the United Kingdom and Ireland over the need to carry out an assessment on a nuclear reprocessing plant which led to the adoption of a Recommendation on the matter by PARCOM in June 1993,[144] and a similar dispute in 2001 concerning the quality of the assessment of the MOX plant. The decision of the UNEP Legal Experts Group, in 1993, to add to the Montevideo Programme a new programme area to promote the widespread use of environmental impact assessment procedures by governments and international organisations reflected the need to elaborate international criteria establishing generally agreed minimum standards.[145]

---

[144] See chapter 9, pp. 430–4 above.

[145] Programme for the Development and Periodic Review of Environmental Law, Programme 4, UNEP/GC 17/5, 2 February 1993, 14. The mandate includes the development of existing national and international methods and procedures; the preparation of regional agreements and guidelines; and the use of environmental impact assessment as a tool of international co-operation in case of activities and projects likely to have transboundary effects.

Environmental information

Introduction

Improving the availability of information on the state of the environment and on activities which have adverse or damaging effects are well-established objectives of international environmental law.[1] Information is widely recognised as a prerequisite to effective national and international environmental management, protection and co-operation. The availability of, and access to, information allows preventative and mitigation measures to be taken, ensures the participation of citizens in national decision-making processes, and can influence individual, consumer and corporate behaviour. Information also allows the international community to determine whether states are complying with their legal obligations.

Environmental impact assessment, addressed in chapter 16, is one important technique for acquiring environmental information. International agreements and practice have developed other techniques for ensuring that states and other members of the international community are provided with information on the environmental consequences of certain activities. Legal obligations developed with early treaty obligations requiring parties to provide information to the depository, or to other parties, on measures to implement commitments. Since then, environmental information has gradually emerged as a central issue of international environmental law. Principle 2 of the 1972 Stockholm Declaration called for the 'free flow of up-to-date scientific information and transfer

[1] On early practice, including at the national level, see OECD (Environment Committee), 'Application of Information and Consultation Practices for Preventing Transfrontier Pollution', in OECD, *Transfrontier Pollution and the Role of States* (1981); M. Baram, 'Risk Communication Law and Implementation Issues in the US and EC', 6 *Boston University International Law Journal* 21 (1988); R. Abrams and D. Ward, 'Prospects for Safer Communities: Emergency Response, Community Right-to-Know, and Prevention of Chemical Accidents', 14 *Harvard Environmental Law Review* 135 (1990); B. Nordenstam and J. F. DiMento, 'Right-to-Know: Implications of Risk Communication Research for Regulating Policy', 23 *University of California (Davis) Law Review* 333 (1990); M. Padgett, 'Environmental Health and Safety – International Standardisation of Right-to-Know Legislation in Response to Refusal of United States Multinationals to Publish Toxic Emissions Data for Their United Kingdom Facilities', 22 *Georgia Journal of International and Comparative Law* 701 (1992).

of experience'. The 1982 World Charter for Nature broadened the scope and extent of obligations relating to information, calling for the dissemination of knowledge of research, the monitoring of natural processes and ecosystems, and the participation of all persons in the formulation of decisions of direct concern to the environment.[2]

By the mid-1980s, numerous treaties addressed public education, information exchange and consultation. The Seveso accident in 1982 and the Chernobyl accident in 1986 focused attention on the need to improve the provision of information in emergency situations and, towards the end of the 1980s, eco-labelling and corporate environmental auditing and accounting had become issues addressed by law at the international level. By the time of UNCED in 1992, numerous treaties and other international instruments included substantive obligations relating to information: particularly noteworthy are the 1986 IAEA Notification Convention, the 1989 Basel Convention, the 1991 EC Directive on Environmental Information and the 1992 Industrial Accidents Convention. Notably, no fewer than four of the Rio Declaration's twenty-seven Principles are concerned with improving the provision of, and access to, environmental information. The Rio Declaration calls for: exchanges of knowledge (information); individual access to environmental information; public awareness; notification of emergencies; and prior and timely notification of certain potentially hazardous activities. Chapter 40 of Agenda 21, entitled 'Information for Decision-Making', recognises that the need for information arises at all levels, from senior decision-makers at international levels to the grass roots and individual level, and to that end calls for the development of two programme areas: to bridge the 'data gap' and to improve information availability.[3] The UNEP Legal Experts Group has also agreed a new programme area to promote public awareness, education, information and public participation, including the development of national rules, laws and standards.[4]

The period since the first edition of this book has seen numerous significant developments which consolidate and, in some respects, develop existing techniques. The 1998 Aarhus Convention establishes a Europe-wide regime, clarifying and, in certain respects, developing the EC rules. The 1998 Chemicals Convention is largely concerned with issues related to the access to, and exchange of, information; and other agreements, such as the 1997 Kyoto Protocol, the 2000 Biosafety Protocol and the 2001 POPs Convention, include prominent commitments to ensuring appropriate flows of information. The commitment to ensuring the adequacy of information is affirmed by the WSSD Plan of Implementation, and were reflected also in a trend to allow arbitration

---

[2] Paras. 15, 18, 19 and 23.   [3] Agenda 21, para. 40.1.

[4] Programme for the Development and Periodic Review of Environmental Law, Programme G; UNEP/GC 17/5, 2 February 1993, 14; also Programme for the Development and Periodic Review of Environmental Law for the First Decade of the Twenty-First Century (2001), section 7 (public participation and access to information), GC Res. 21/23 (2001).

proceedings concerning international environmental matters to be open to the public.[5]

A detailed consideration of relevant international instruments identifies at least nine separate but related techniques concerning the provision and dissemination of information. These provide for or require:

1. information exchange;
2. reporting and the provision of information;
3. consultation;
4. monitoring and surveillance;
5. notification of emergency situations;
6. public right of access to environmental information;
7. public education and awareness;
8. eco-labelling; and
9. co-auditing and accounting.

The examples cited in the following sections are intended to be illustrative rather than exhaustive, given the large number of instruments and examples of state practice relating to informational matters. The overlap between the obligations relating to information exchange, consultation, reporting and notification is often evident, and it is important to bear in mind that these different areas are interrelated, as reflected in many recent international environmental agreements. In addition to the multilateral instruments which are cited, there are many others which are not mentioned as well as literally hundreds, if not thousands, of bilateral instruments which also contribute significantly to the law in this area.

In this regard, the recently adopted ILC draft Articles on the Prevention of Transboundary Harm adopt, as a central element, requirements relating to information, and may be seen as 'codifying' general practice, in particular as reflected in treaty requirements. They provide that, where an assessment of risk has taken place and indicates a risk of causing significant transboundary harm, the state of origin

> shall provide the state likely to be affected with timely notification of the risk and the assessment and shall transmit to it the available technical and all other relevant information on which the assessment is based.[6]

The draft Articles then propose that the states concerned

> shall enter into consultations, at the request of any of them, with a view to achieving acceptable solutions regarding measures to be adopted in order to prevent significant transboundary harm or at any event to minimize the risk thereof.[7]

---

[5] As occurred in the UNCLOS Annex VII arbitral tribunal proceedings in the *Southern Bluefin Tuna* cases (1999) (see chapter 11, p. 580 above) and the OSPAR *MOX* case (2003) (see p. 857 below).
[6] Art. 8(1).   [7] Art. 9(1).

The states concerned are to seek solutions based on an equitable balance of interests, in the light of the factors set out in draft Article 10.[8] The state of origin should not take any decision on authorisation pending the receipt, within six months, of the response of the state likely to be affected, and if the consultations fail to produce an agreed solution the state of origin must take into account the interests of the state likely to be affected.[9] The draft Articles also provide for procedures in the event that there is no notification, require the exchange of timely information while the activity is being carried out, and call for information to be provided to the public likely to be affected by that activity, and to ascertain their views.[10]

Information exchange

The general obligation to exchange information is found, in one form or another, in virtually every international environmental agreement. 'Information exchange' can be characterised as a general obligation of one state to provide general information on one or more matters on an *ad hoc* basis to another state, especially in relation to scientific and technical information. 'Information exchange' may be distinguished from specific obligations to provide regular or periodic information on specified matters to a specified body (reporting) or to provide detailed information on the occurrence of a particular event or set of events, such as an accident or emergency or proposed activity (notification). 'Information exchange' of a general nature is endorsed by Principle 20 of the Stockholm Declaration and by Principle 9 of the Rio Declaration, which supports exchanges of scientific and technical knowledge as a means of strengthening 'endogenous capacity-building for sustainable development by improving scientific understanding'. Other relevant texts include: Principle 7 of the 1978 UNEP draft Principles of Conduct, which calls for the exchange of information based upon the principle of co-operation and the spirit of good-neighbourliness; Article 5 of the 1986 Legal Principles of the WCED Legal Experts Group, which supports the exchange of information between states upon request, and in a timely manner, concerning transboundary natural resources; Article 12 of the ILC's draft Articles on Prevention of Transboundary Harm; and the WSSD Plan of Implementation.[11]

---

[8] Art. 9(2). The factors listed in Art. 10 relate to the degree of risk and the availability of means to prevent or minimise risk; the importance of the activity; the risk of significant harm to the environment; the allocation of the costs of prevention; the economic viability of the activity and possible alternatives; and the standards of prevention applied by the state likely to be affected to equivalent activities.

[9] Arts. 8(2) and 9(3).

[10] Arts. 11–13.

[11] Supporting information exchange or scientific co-operation on, *inter alia*, clean technologies (para. 15(c)), fresh water and marine resource management (paras. 27, 32 (a) and 34(a)), climate change (para. 36(d)) and biotechnology and biosafety (para. 42(q)).

Under environmental treaties, the obligation to exchange information can be a requirement between states, between states and international organisations, and between international organisations and non-state actors. By way of an early example, the 1949 Inter-American Tropical Tuna Commission was granted the power to request information from 'official agencies of the contracting parties, and any international, public, or private institution or organisation, or any private individual'.[12] Many other international organisations are required to facilitate and encourage the exchange of information, which dates back to some of the earliest international environmental agreements. The 1933 London Convention requires information exchange on the adoption of certain implementation measures, including import and export.[13] The 1940 Western Hemisphere Convention requires parties to 'make available to all the American Republics equally through publication or otherwise the scientific knowledge resulting from . . . co-operative effort'.[14]

Information exchange can be required in respect of general and undefined matters or in relation to specific matters. Examples of the former include the obligation to exchange information on: general scientific, research and technical matters; helping 'align or co-ordinate' national policies;[15] research results and plans for science programmes;[16] appropriate technologies;[17] relevant national records;[18] national legislation; implementation;[19] relevant national authorities and bodies; and even the availability of professors and teachers.[20] Examples of more specific requirements include information exchange on: aspects of pest and plant diseases;[21] catches and migratory movements of fish;[22] tuna fisheries;[23] pollution from land-based sources;[24] the conservation of species of wild flora and fauna;[25] archaeological excavations and discoveries;[26] environmental modification techniques for peaceful purposes;[27] the protection of nuclear material;[28] certain environmentally harmful activities;[29] forest

---

[12] 1949 Inter-American Tropical Tuna Convention, Art. I(16).

[13] Arts. 8(6), 9 and 12(1).   [14] Art. VI.

[15] 1982 Benelux Conservation Convention, Art. 2(2).

[16] 1959 Antarctic Treaty, Art. III(1)(a) and (c); 1973 Polar Bears Agreement, Art. VII.

[17] 1988 NO$_x$ Protocol, Art. 3(1); under Agenda 21, UNEP is to facilitate 'information exchange on environmentally sound technologies, including legal aspects': para. 38.22(j).

[18] 1952 North Pacific Fisheries Convention, Art. VIII.

[19] 1958 Danube Convention, Art. 12(3); 1983 Cartagena Oil Spills Protocol, Art. 4.

[20] 1959 Plant Protection Agreement, Art. IV(3).

[21] 1951 European Plant Protection Convention, Art. V(a)(5).

[22] 1958 Danube Convention, Art. 8.   [23] 1966 Atlantic Tuna Convention, Art. IV(2)(d).

[24] 1983 Quito LBS Protocol, Art. IX(d).   [25] 1979 Berne Convention, Art. 3(3).

[26] 1969 European Archaeological Heritage Convention, Art. 4(1).

[27] 1977 ENMOD Convention, Art. III(2).

[28] 1980 Convention on the Physical Protection of Nuclear Material, Art. 5; Art. 6 provides for the protection of confidentiality of material so exchanged.

[29] 1974 Nordic Environmental Protection Convention, Art. 5.

management, research and development;[30] and the conservation and sustainable use of biological diversity.[31]

Several later conventions established more detailed rules on the type of information to be exchanged. The 1982 UNCLOS requires the exchange of scientific information and other data relevant to the conservation of fish stocks, on marine scientific research, and on marine pollution.[32] Article 8 of the 1979 LRTAP Convention requires the exchange of 'available information', through an executive body and bilaterally on emissions data at periods of time to be agreed upon of: certain air pollutants; major changes in national policies and general industrial development; control technologies for reducing air pollution; the projected cost of the emissions control; meteorological, and physico-chemical data relating to processes and effects; and national, sub-regional and regional policies. Article 4 of the 1985 Vienna Convention requires the exchange of 'scientific, technical, socio-economic, commercial and legal information', as further elaborated in Annex II to that Convention, as well as information on alternative technologies. The 1987 Montreal Protocol calls for information exchange on best technologies, possible alternatives to controlled substances and products, and costs and benefits of relevant control strategies.[33]

A widespread concern about the limited effectiveness of the traditional language on information exchange has resulted in the adoption, in some conventions of more focused language. The 1992 Climate Change Convention, for example, calls on parties to promote and co-operate in 'the full, open and prompt exchange of relevant scientific, technological, technical, socio-economic and legal information related to the climate system and climate change, and to the economic and social consequences of various response strategies'.[34] A number of conventions have established more formal institutional arrangements and procedures for information exchange. Examples include the establishment of a documentation service,[35] an information service,[36] and even a permanent committee of information.[37] International organisations may also play a role in ensuring information exchange. They may be required to prepare an annual report,[38] or to keep parties 'abreast of . . . theoretical and practical work',[39] or to convene international information exchange conferences.[40] Notwithstanding a greater willingness of states and the private sector

---

[30] 1992 Statement of Forest Principles, Principle 13(c).
[31] 1992 Biodiversity Convention, Art. 17(1). Art. 17(2) provides that information exchange shall include 'specialised knowledge [and] indigenous and traditional knowledge' and 'shall also, where feasible, include repatriation of information'.
[32] Arts. 61, 143, 200 and 244.   [33] Art. 9(1).   [34] Art. 4(1)(h).
[35] 1951 European Plant Protection Convention, Art. V(9).
[36] 1963 South-West Asia Locust Agreement, Art. II(1).
[37] 1954 African Phyto-Sanitary Convention, Art. 9.
[38] 1954 African Phyto-Sanitary Convention, Art. 3(b); 1990 EBRD Agreement, Art. 35.
[39] 1959 Latin American Forest Research Agreement, Art. II(1)(c) and (d).
[40] 1959 Plant Protection Agreement, Art. VIII.

to seek to improve flows of information, it is unclear how effective these general obligations to exchange information have been.

The apparently limited effectiveness of many of these earlier obligations was often due to the reluctance of states to share information which might have commercial value, and the obligation, usually raised by developed countries, to ensure respect for intellectual property rights. Under the Biodiversity Convention, this issue was addressed explicitly for the first time, although the language finally agreed may have raised more questions and uncertainties than it resolved.[41] Increasingly, agreements have therefore included express provisions on confidential information. The 2000 Biosafety Protocol, for example, requires information to be submitted to the clearing-house mechanism established under the Convention '[w]ithout prejudice to the protection of confidential information'.[42] Similarly, under the 1998 Chemicals Convention, the exchange of information is on condition that parties 'shall protect any confidential information as mutually agreed'.[43]

Reporting and provision of information[44]

The obligation to report or to notify certain information on a regular or periodic basis, outside the context of an emergency situation or the occurrence of a particular event or activity, is a regular feature of international environmental agreements. At least four types of reporting or information provision requirements are used in international environmental agreements. First, the provision of a periodic report provided by an international organisation to the parties to a treaty; secondly, a requirement that parties provide a periodic report to the institutional organs or to other parties to that treaty; thirdly, a party (or state) may be required to provide information to another party (or state) on the occurrence of a certain event or activity; and, fourthly, a treaty may allow for a report to be presented by a non-governmental actor to a party to a treaty, which may be subject to onward transmission by the latter.

Reports by organisations

Some environmental treaties require one or more of the institutional organs to provide regular reports to its parties. This technique is used to inform all the parties of relevant measures being taken under the Convention, or

---

[41] Chapter 11, pp. 519–23 above.

[42] Art. 20(3). The Cartagena Protocol also establishes modalities for dealing with confidential information under the notification provisions of the protocol: Art. 21.

[43] Art. 14(1) and (2). The category of confidential information is limited, however, to further the purposes of the Convention: Art. 14(3) and (4). See also 2001 POPs Convention, Art. 9(5).

[44] On the relationship between reporting and compliance see chapter 5, pp. 180–2 above.

to provide information on the activities of the organisation itself to ensure accountability. An early example is the 1949 Inter-American Tropical Tuna Convention, which requires the Inter-American Tropical Tuna Commission to 'submit annually to the government of each high contracting party a report on its investigations and findings, with appropriate recommendations'.[45] Other conventions provide that reports should be submitted every two years,[46] or for the transmission of 'periodic reports' or publications,[47] or at such time as the institutional organ 'may consider necessary'.[48] The 1990 Articles of Agreement establishing the European Bank for Reconstruction and Development requires the Bank to provide an annual report on the environmental import of its activities.[49] Occasionally, the institutional organ might be required to report to another international organisation;[50] this approach is reflected in the work of the UN Commission on Sustainable Development, which receives reports from relevant organs, organisations, programmes and institutions of the UN system dealing with various issues of environment and development to enable it to monitor the progress of the implementation of Agenda 21 by analysing and evaluating reports submitted by other international organisations.[51]

Reports under treaties or other agreements

The second type of reporting obligation arises where a party to a treaty is required to provide a periodic report to the institutions established under the treaty or to other parties to that agreement. These reporting requirements, which increasingly require detailed and regular information, are used to provide information on the implementation of treaty commitments. The 1933 London Convention was among the first, requiring parties to 'notify the Government of the United Kingdom . . . of the establishment of any national parks or strict natural reserves, . . . and of the legislation, including the methods of administration and control, adopted in connexion therewith', as well as measures adopted in regard to the grant of certain licences.[52] Similar reporting requirements exist for authorisations of licences for the killing and taking of living

---

[45] Art. I(2). See also the 1954 African Phyto-Sanitary Convention, Art. 3(b); 1983 ITTA, Art. 28 (ITTC).

[46] 1966 Atlantic Tunas Convention, Art. III(9).

[47] 1962 African Migratory Locust Convention, Art. 7(2)(a); 1973 CITES, Art. XII(2)(f) and (g).

[48] 1971 ILO Benzene Convention, Art. 20.   [49] Art. 35.

[50] 1979 Berne Convention, Art. 15 (from the Convention's Standing Committee to the Committee of Ministers of the Council of Europe).

[51] UNGA Res. 47/191 (1992).

[52] Arts. 5(1) and 8(6). The Government of the United Kingdom was required to communicate information so received to other governments: Arts. 5(3) and 8(6).

resources;[53] on the construction of certain installations or projects and works[54] or proposed expeditions;[55] statistical information concerning catches;[56] or the establishment of quotas.[57]

Often, parties must provide progress reports on implementation measures and their effectiveness, and other relevant national legislation,[58] including the adoption of import restrictions.[59] Parties may also be required to report infractions of conventions by persons within their jurisdiction[60] and the penalties they impose,[61] as well as information on persons liable to contribute to a pollution fund established in accordance with the terms of a convention.[62] Increasingly, parties are being called upon to provide inventories or statistics of their natural and cultural resources[63] or of the production of certain chemicals or products,[64] and to report on their emissions and discharges and the consequences thereof.[65]

In fulfilment of the functions of the UN Commission on Sustainable Development, governments are required to provide information on activities they undertake to implement Agenda 21, the problems they face, and other environment and development issues they find relevant.[66] Parties to a treaty can

---

[53] 1946 International Whaling Convention, Art. VIII(1); 1972 Antarctic Seals Convention, Art. 4.

[54] 1958 Convention on the Continental Shelf, Art. 5(5); 1980 Convention creating the Niger Basin Authority, Art. 4(4).

[55] 1972 Antarctic Seals Convention, Annex, para. 6(d).

[56] 1946 International Whaling Convention, Art. VII.

[57] 1969 Southeast Atlantic Convention, Art. VIII(3)(a) and (b).

[58] 1956 Plant Protection Agreement, Art. II(1)(b); 1989 Basel Convention, Art. 3(1); 1992 Biodiversity Convention, Art. 26; 1992 Climate Change Convention, Art. 12; 1992 OSPAR Convention, Art. 22.

[59] 1951 International Plant Protection Convention, Art. VI(2)(b) and (c); 1989 Basel Convention, Arts. 4 and 13.

[60] 1946 International Whaling Convention, Art. IX(4); 1973 MARPOL, Art. 4(3).

[61] 1954 Oil Pollution Convention, Art. VI(3).   [62] 1971 Oil Fund Convention, Art. 15(2).

[63] 1972 World Heritage Convention, Art. 11(1) (property forming part of the cultural and natural heritage); 1979 Bonn Convention, Art. VI(2) (migratory species of wild animals); 1983 ITTA, Art. 27(1) and (2) (tropical timber); 1992 Biodiversity Convention, Art. 7(a) and (b); 1992 Climate Change Convention, Art. 4(1)(a).

[64] 2001 POPs Convention, Art. 15.

[65] 1976 Rhine Chemical Pollution Convention, Art. 2(1) and (2) and Annex III (of certain substances into the Rhine); 1976 Rhine Chloride Pollution Convention, Art 3(5) (increase in chloride-ion concentrations); 1985 SO_2 Protocol, Art. 4 (sulphur dioxide emissions); 1988 NO_x Protocol, Art. 8(1)(a) (emissions of nitrogen oxides); 1987 Montreal Protocol, as amended in 1990, Art. 7 (production, imports and exports of certain ozone-depleting substances); 1992 Climate Change Convention, Art. 12(1); 1996 EC Directive 96/61/EC, Art. 16(1) and (2) (emissions limit values and the best available techniques for integrated pollution prevention and control); 1998 POP Protocol to the 1979 LRTAP Convention, Art. 9(b) (emissions of persistent organic pollutants); 1998 Heavy Metals Protocol, Art. 7(b) (emissions of heavy metals); 1999 Acidification, Eutrophication, Ground Ozone Protocol, Art. 7(b).

[66] UNGA Res. 47/191 (1992), para. 3(b).

also be required to report on particular situations or events, including the existence of certain hazardous facilities;[67] the transit of hazardous substances;[68] the actions they take in relation to certain pollution incidents;[69] substances dumped into the marine environment;[70] the existence of evidence suggesting that unlawful dumping may be taking place;[71] incidents or accidents involving oil or other harmful substances;[72] the discharge of land-based pollutants;[73] and accidents involving hazardous waste.[74] Other examples of specific reporting requirements arise upon the occurrence, outbreak and spread of pests and diseases,[75] on inadequate oil disposal facilities at ports,[76] and on conservation measures concerning fish stocks.[77]

The 1992 Climate Change Convention and its 1997 Kyoto Protocol illustrate the extent to which reporting requirements have become increasingly detailed and onerous. Reporting, which is described as 'the communication of information related to implementation', is a central technique for ensuring implementation of the 1992 Climate Change Convention. All parties must publish and make available to the conference of the parties 'national inventories of anthropogenic emissions by sources and removals by sinks of all greenhouse gases not controlled by the Montreal Protocol', and communicate to the conference of the parties 'information related to implementation'.[78] These reports must include a general description of steps taken or envisaged to implement the Convention and 'any other information the party considers relevant to the achievement of the objective of the Convention and suitable for inclusion in its communication including, if feasible, material relevant for calculations of global emission trends'.[79] The EC and parties which are members of the OECD are additionally required to include in their communications a detailed description of the policies and measures that they have adopted to implement their specific commitments under the Convention and a specific estimate of the effects that the policies and measures they have taken will have on anthropogenic emissions by its sources and removals by its sinks of greenhouses gases.[80] All developed country parties must provide information on the provision by them of 'new and additional financial resources', other assistance, and the transfer of and access to environmentally sound technologies and know-how.[81] The

---

[67] 1963 Brussels Supplementary Convention, Art. 13(a) to (e) (nuclear power plants).
[68] 1980 Convention on the Physical Protection of Nuclear Material, Art. 4(5).
[69] 1969 Bonn Agreement, Art. 8.
[70] 1972 Oslo Convention, Art. 11; 1972 London Convention, Art. VI(4).
[71] 1972 Oslo Convention, Art. 15(2); 1972 London Convention, Art. VII(3).
[72] 1973 MARPOL, Art. 8 and Protocol I; 1981 Abidjan Emergency Protocol, Art. 7 and Annex.
[73] 1974 Baltic Convention, Art. 6(4).   [74] 1989 Basel Convention, Art. 13(1).
[75] 1951 International Plant Protection Convention, Art. VII(a) (also calling for the establishment of a 'world reporting service on plant diseases and pests').
[76] 1954 Oil Pollution Convention, Art. VIII(3).
[77] 1952 North Pacific Fisheries Convention, Art. III(1)(c)(iii).
[78] Arts. 4(1)(a) and (j).   [79] Art. 12(1)(b) and (c).   [80] Art. 12(1) and (2).
[81] Arts. 12(3) and 4(3), (4) and (5).

Kyoto Protocol adds the additional burden on Annex I countries of reporting the progress made towards reaching greenhouse gas reduction commitments.[82] Differentiated timeframes are adopted for providing the communication. Developed country parties were required to provide their initial communication within six months of the Convention's entry into force; all other parties were required to provide their initial communication within three years of entry into force, except for least-developed countries which may make their initial communication available at their discretion.[83] Developed country parties are currently in the process of submitting their third communications. Other innovations of the 1992 Climate Change Convention include the possibility for two or more parties to make a 'joint communication' provided that such a communication includes information on: each individual party's fulfilment of its obligations;[84] rules on confidentiality;[85] the provision to developing countries of financial resources 'to meet the agreed full costs incurred . . . in complying with' their reporting requirements;[86] and the establishment of a subsidiary body for implementation to consider information provided by parties in accordance with Article 12.[87] The Convention and its Protocol thus reflect a more comprehensive effort to address reporting.

Reports of events other than emergencies

The third situation requiring the provision of information or a report (closely connected to the obligation to consult) arises on the occurrence of an event other than an emergency situation. Examples include the construction of an installation or advance notice of activities which may entail significant environmental risk. In such circumstances, the state in which the activity is taking place may be required to provide information either directly to states which may be affected or to an appropriate intergovernmental organisation. The need for the provision of such information has been widely recognised by the international community since the mid-1970s. In 1972, UN General Assembly Resolution 2995 recognised that co-operation towards implementation of the 1972 Stockholm Declaration

> will be effectively achieved if official and public knowledge is provided of the technical data relating to the work to be carried out by states within their national jurisdiction, with a view to avoiding significant harm that may occur in the environment of the adjacent area.

The 1974 OECD Recommendation on Principles Concerning Transfrontier Pollution similarly provides that:

---

[82] Arts. 3 and 7(1) and (4).   [83] Art. 12(5).   [84] Art. 12(8).
[85] Art. 12(9).   [86] Art. 4(3).   [87] Art. 10(2).

[p]rior to the initiation in a country of works or undertakings which might create a significant risk of pollution, this country should provide early information to other countries which are or may be affected.[88]

Similar provisions exist in the 1978 UNEP draft Principles of Conduct,[89] the 1986 WCED Legal Experts Group Report,[90] and Principle 19 of the Rio Declaration.[91] Several treaties require the provision of information on the construction of certain installations, including the siting of hazardous installations or the conduct of hazardous activities near border areas.[92] The 1980 Agreement Between Spain and Portugal on Co-operation in Matters Affecting the Safety of Nuclear Installations in the Vicinity of the Frontier provides in Article 2 that:

[t]he competent authorities of the constructor country shall notify the neighbouring country of applications for licences for the siting, construction or operation of nuclear installations in the vicinity of the frontier which are submitted to them . . .[93]

Article 3 requires comments by the neighbouring country to be taken into account before the licence is issued.

Is the provision of prior information regarding certain hazardous activities now required by customary international law? The 1982 ILA Montreal Rules[94] and the 1987 IDI Resolution on Transboundary Air Pollution[95] suggest that customary law does and should require states planning activities which might entail a significant risk of transfrontier pollution to give early notice to a state likely to be affected and to enter into good faith consultations at the request of such a state. Principle 19 of the Rio Declaration appears to restate that obligation in unequivocal terms, and this is also now confirmed by the 2001 ILC draft Articles on Prevention of Transboundary Harm.[96]

---

[88] OECD C(74)224, 21 November 1974, Annex, para. 6. See also OECD Council Recommendation, Implementation of a Regime of Equal Right of Access and Non-Discrimination in Relation to Transfrontier Pollution, OECD C(77)28, 23 May 1977, Annex, para. 9(a).

[89] Principle 6.   [90] Art. 16(1).   [91] See p. 839 below.

[92] 1958 Convention on the Continental Shelf, Art. 5(5) (installations for the exploration and exploitation of the natural resources of the continental shelf); 1991 Espoo Convention, Art. 3; 1992 Industrial Accidents Convention, Art. 4; 1992 Watercourses Convention, Art. 14; 1997 Watercourse Convention, Art. 12.

[93] 31 March 1980, in force 13 July 1981, UN registration No. 20356. See also Belgium–France, Convention on Radiological Protection Relating to the Installations at the Ardennes Nuclear Power Station, 23 September 1966, 988 UNTS 288; Austria–Czechoslovakia, Agreement on Questions of Common Interest in Relation to Nuclear Facilities, 18 November 1982, in force 1 June 1984, reprinted in *Bundesgesetzblatt* No. 208/1984.

[94] Arts. 6 and 7. The Rapporteur, Professor Dietrich Rauschning, observed that 'recent state practice shows that information is not usually withheld': ILA, *Report of the 59th Conference* (1982, London), 545.

[95] Art. 8(1).   [96] See p. 838 above.

Information to and from non-state organisations

A fourth type of reporting requirement, which may be considered to be in an emerging stage of development, relates to obligations allowing, or requiring, non-governmental actors to report certain information to states, possibly for onward transmission to other parties or to the agreement's institutional organ, or to provide informational reports to organisations. The UN Commission on Sustainable Development is mandated to 'receive and analyse relevant input from competent non-governmental organisations, including the scientific and private sector, in the context of the overall implementation of Agenda 21'.[97] Although this falls short of actually entitling non-governmental actors to provide reports, it clearly envisages a role for them in providing inputs which will, in all likelihood, resemble reports.[98]

Consultation

The international community has recognised the importance of information on activities and other circumstances which could affect the interests of states in relation to shared natural resources. Typically, this is provided for in international agreements by two related commitments: a requirement to provide information to potentially affected states on particular activities, and a requirement to engage in consultation. The latter presupposes the provision of certain information. The obligation of states to consult with each other in the context of the conduct of certain activities has been recognised by international courts and tribunals,[99] and is reflected in many international environmental instruments,[100] as well as in Article 9 of the ILC's draft Articles on Prevention of Transboundary Harm. In 2001, the ITLOS prescribed provisional measures ordering Ireland and the United Kingdom to co-operate and, for that purpose, to 'enter into consultations forthwith' to exchange further information on the possible consequences for the Irish Sea arising out of the commissioning of the MOX plant, to monitor the risks or the effects of the operation of the MOX plant for the Irish Sea, and to devise measures to prevent pollution of the marine environment which might result from the operation of the MOX

---

[97] UNGA Res. 47/191 (1992), para. 3(h).

[98] On the informal provision of information by NGOs, see chapter 3, pp. 112–13 above. Note also the 1998 Aarhus Convention, providing for the submission of reports from the public to decision-making bodies (at the national/EC level) when considering decisions on specific activities, or when considering executive regulations or other 'generally applicable legally binding normative instruments': Arts. 6(7) and 8(c) (cf. Art. 7, information on plans, programmes or policies related to the environment).

[99] *Lac Lanoux Arbitration*, chapter 10, pp. 463–4 above; *Fisheries Jurisdiction* cases, chapter 11, pp. 567–8 above.

[100] See also 1978 UNEP draft Principles, Principle 7; 1986 WCED Legal Principles, Art. 17.

plant.[101] The order was premised on 'prudence and caution' and the duty to co-operate under Part XII of UNCLOS.[102]

Principle 19 of the Rio Declaration reflects what many states have recognised as required practice in terms which reflect an obligation of customary international law:

> states shall provide prior and timely notification and relevant information to potentially affected states on activities that may have a significant adverse transboundary environmental effect and shall consult with those states at an early stage and in good faith.

Environmental treaties have required consultation to take place between a number of different actors, including between two or more states; between a state and an international organisation; between a state and a non-governmental actor; between two or more international organisations,[103] and between an international organisation and a non-governmental actor.[104] Many institutional arrangements established by environmental treaties, such as conferences or meetings of parties, serve as fora for consultations between parties.[105] Specialised institutional arrangements for environmental treaties have included a special Consultative Committee[106] and a Consultative Committee of Experts.[107]

The obligation to consult arises in many circumstances. As a general matter, consultation has been required on the implementation of an agreement,[108] or on 'all problems of common interest' raised by the application of a particular convention.[109] Consultation can also be required as part of the process for the peaceful settlement of disputes,[110] including by removing doubts concerning the fulfilment by a party of its treaty obligations.[111]

A second type of situation calling for consultation arises when the activities of one state are likely to affect the environment or the rights and interests of another state. Thus, a state may be obliged to enter into consultations when, for example, pollution caused by the activities of one party to an agreement is likely to affect adversely the interests of another party to that agreement;[112] or when there is a question of the 'permissibility of environmentally harmful activities

---

[101] Order of 3 December 2001, para. 89(1); chapter 9, p. 436 above.
[102] Paras. 82 and 84.   [103] 1983 ITTA, Art. 14(1).
[104] 1982 UNCLOS, Arts. 165(2)(c) and 169(1); 1983 ITTA, Art. 14(1).
[105] 1978 Northwest Atlantic Fisheries Convention, Art. VI(1)(a).
[106] 1985 South Pacific Nuclear Free Zone Treaty, Art. 10 and Annex 3.
[107] 1977 ENMOD Convention, Art. V(2).   [108] 1985 ASEAN Agreement, Art. 18(2)(e).
[109] 1963 Brussels Supplementary Convention, Art. 16(a); 1977 ENMOD Convention, Art. V(1) and (2).
[110] 1959 Antarctic Treaty, Art. VIII(2); 1988 CRAMRA, Art. 57(1); 1997 Watercourses Convention, Art. 17.
[111] 1971 Nuclear Weapons Treaty, Art. III(2).
[112] 1983 Quito LBS Protocol, Art. XII; 1980 Athens LBS Protocol, Art. 12(1).

which entail or may entail considerable nuisance' in another party;[113] or where a party is 'actually affected by or exposed to' a significant risk of pollution.[114]

A third category of situations requiring consultation arises over the use of shared natural resources. Thus, consultation can be required generally in respect of shared resource issues,[115] as well as in the following specific situations: to avoid infringement of the rights and interests of states where natural resource deposits (such as wetlands) lie across two or more jurisdictions;[116] where there are plans 'to initiate, or make a change in, activities which can reasonably be expected to have significant effects beyond the limits of national jurisdiction';[117] where a party 'intends to establish a protected area contiguous to the frontier or to the limits of the zone of national jurisdiction of another party';[118] where certain commercial activities may harm wildlife;[119] and for the dissemination of information on environmental impact assessments.[120]

A fourth category of situations requiring consultation arises in times of emergency. Consultations may be required: to ensure that appropriate action is taken in emergency situations;[121] prior to the issue of a special permit to permit the marine dumping of hazardous wastes and other matters in emergencies;[122] and to minimise the radiological consequences of a nuclear accident.[123] Consultations are also required between a party and the most representative organisations of employers and workers to implement national policies on protection of the working environment and in applying the provisions of relevant conventions.[124]

The obligation to consult in such situations is now widely recognised by customary international law, and the failure to engage in consultation may violate the principles of good faith and international co-operation under international law. This view is supported by the *Lac Lanoux Arbitration*, was further elaborated upon by the ICJ in the *Fisheries Jurisdiction* cases,[125] and was reflected in the order of ITLOS in the *MOX* case.

---

[113] 1974 Nordic Environmental Protection Convention, Art. 11; see also 1991 Espoo Convention, Art. 5, and 1992 Industrial Accidents Convention, Art. 4.

[114] 1979 LRTAP Convention, Art. 5.

[115] 1968 African Nature Convention, Art. V(2) (concerning 'underground water resources').

[116] 1971 Ramsar Convention, Art. 5; 1982 UNCLOS, Art. 142(2) (where consultation includes 'a system of prior informed consent').

[117] 1985 ASEAN Agreement, Arts. 19(2)(d) and (e) and 20(3)(b) and (c).

[118] 1982 Geneva SPA Protocol, Art. 6(1).   [119] 1972 Antarctic Seals Convention, Art. 6.

[120] 1985 Nairobi Convention, Art. 13(3).

[121] 1981 Abidjan Emergency Protocol, Art. 10(1)(b).

[122] 1972 London Convention, Art. V(2); 1986 Noumea Dumping Protocol, Art. 10(1).

[123] 1986 IAEA Notification Convention, Art. 6; 1986 IAEA Assistance Convention, Arts. 2 and 11.

[124] 1960 ILO Radiation Convention, Art. 1; 1981 ILO Occupational Safety Convention, Art. 4(1).

[125] Chapter 5, pp. 201–2 above.

Prior informed consent

The obligation to consult is closely linked to the principle of 'prior informed consent' (PIC).[126] This principle has achieved widespread support in relation to transboundary movements of hazardous wastes and, more recently, hazardous substances, and has been adopted in a range of instruments, including, *inter alia*, the 1985 FAO Pesticides Guidelines, the 1989 UNEP London Guidelines, the 1989 Basel Convention, the 1989 Lomé Convention, the 1991 Bamako Convention and the 1996 Mediterranean Hazardous Wastes Protocol.[127] It is also to be found in the EC Regulation on the Transfrontier Movement of Hazardous Substances[128] and non-binding instruments adopted by the OECD and the IAEA, as well as in Agenda 21.[129]

A second-generation formulation of the PIC procedures, developing the voluntary schemes of the FAO Pesticides Guidelines and the UNEP London Guidelines, is reflected in the 1998 Chemicals Convention. The 1998 Convention establishes a bifurcated PIC procedure. For chemicals listed under Annex III to the Convention, import countries must submit their approval, approval subject to limitations, or rejection of future imports to the Secretariat.[130] For banned or severely restricted chemicals not listed under the Convention, export countries are required to ensure that proper notification is given to the import country before export of the chemicals.[131] The 2000 Biosafety Protocol does not refer to a PIC procedure, as such, but rather an advance informed agreement (AIA) procedure prior to the 'first intentional transboundary movement of living modified organisms for intentional introduction into the environment of the Party of import'.[132] The party of export is required to notify or ensure notification of an intent to export certain living modified organisms, which the party of import must acknowledge.[133] The import may only proceed if the party of import has given written consent or, after not less than ninety days, where no such written consent is given.[134] The Protocol also provides for a 'simplified procedure' specifying in advance cases in which intentional movements may take place simultaneously with notification and imports which are to be exempted from the advance informed agreement procedure.[135]

Notification of emergency situations

The early availability of information on the escape of hazardous substances following an accident or event likely to have a significant effect on the environment

---

[126] For the definition, see chapter 12, p. 630 above.

[127] See chapter 11 and chapter 1, p. 12 above.　　[128] Chapter 13, pp. 630–7 above.

[129] Chapter 13, pp. 699–703 above.　　[130] Art. 10 (providing for final or interim responses).

[131] Art. 12.　　[132] Art. 7; chapter 12, pp. 705–8 above.　　[133] Arts. 8 and 9, and Annex I.

[134] Art. 11(2). The party of import must communicate its written consent to the Biosafety Clearing-House: Art. 10(3).

[135] Art. 13.

of another state or in areas beyond national jurisdiction is necessary to allow other states and members of the international community to take the necessary actions to minimise damage. Principle 18 of the Rio Declaration recognised this need, and declared that:

> states shall immediately notify other states of any natural disasters or other emergencies that are likely to produce sudden harmful effects on the environment of those states. Every effort shall be made by the international community to help states so afflicted.[136]

As a result of developments following the Chernobyl accident (see below) and other emergency incidents, Principle 18 reflects broadly held views and crystallises developments in treaties, non-binding instruments and the practice of states. The 1982 Montreal ILA Rules[137] and the 1987 Institut de Droit International Resolution[138] refer to the existence of such a rule although evidence of state practice is hardly overwhelming; in the *Nicaragua* case, the ICJ affirmed that a substantive legal rule can be derived from principles of humanitarian law:[139]

> if a state lays mines in any waters whatever in which the vessels of another state have rights of access or passage, and fails to give any warning or notification whatsoever, in disregard of the security of peaceful shipping, it commits a breach of the principles of humanitarian law.[140]

Although the facts leading up to this *dictum* differ from those relating to industrial or other accidents affecting the environment, particularly on the question of the intent of the acting state, underlying considerations of humanity could apply also to the danger to the security of citizens in foreign countries arising from a transboundary release of hazardous substances.

Numerous early treaties have required the provision of information, following the outbreak of 'especially dangerous' pests and diseases,[141] or where there is 'evidence of serious danger to the environment and particularly to the water table',[142] or in respect of oil pollution emergencies.[143] More general requirements are set out in the 1982 UNCLOS, which requires a state to immediately

---

[136] See also Art. 17 of the ILC draft Articles on Prevention of Transboundary Harm (2001).

[137] Art. 7.   [138] Art. 9(1)(a).

[139] *Case Concerning Military and Paramilitary Activities In and Against Nicaragua* (*Nicaragua v. United States*) (Merits), (1986) ICJ Reports 1.

[140] *Ibid.*, 112. The principles of humanity were expressed by the ICJ in the earlier *Corfu Channel* case, chapter 2, n. 62, p. 34 above.

[141] 1959 Plant Protection Agreement, Art. II.

[142] 1976 Rhine Chemical Pollution Convention, Art. 4(1).

[143] See 1969 Bonn Agreement, Art. 5(1); see also the UNEP Regional Seas Conventions, chapter 9, pp. 452–4 above.

notify other states it deems likely to be affected, and the competent international organisations, where the 'marine environment is in imminent danger of being damaged or has been damaged by pollution'.[144] Specific obligations have been adopted for accidents occurring during the transboundary movement of hazardous or other wastes;[145] under the 1992 Industrial Accidents Convention on transboundary accidents;[146] and in treaties governing general environmental matters.[147]

The 1992 Biodiversity Convention provides that each party shall, as far as possible and as appropriate,

> in the case of imminent or grave danger or damage, originating under its jurisdiction or control, to biological diversity within the area under jurisdiction of other states or areas beyond the limits of national jurisdiction, notify immediately the potentially affected states of such danger or damage, as well as initiate action to prevent or minimise such danger or damage;[148]

Similarly, the 2000 Biosafety Protocol requires that parties shall

> take appropriate measures to notify affected or potentially affected States, the Biosafety Clearing-House and, where appropriate, relevant international organizations, when it knows of an occurrence under its jurisdiction resulting in a release that leads, or may lead, to an unintentional transboundary movement of a living modified organism that is likely to have significant adverse effects on the conservation and sustainable use of biological diversity, taking also into account risks to human health in such States.[149]

Non-binding guidelines and recommendations also require the provision of such information. In 1974, the OECD recommended that '[c]ountries should promptly warn other potentially affected countries of any situation which may cause any sudden increase in the level of pollution in areas outside the country of origin of pollution'.[150] In 1988, the OECD Council adopted a Decision on the exchange of information in relation to accidents capable of causing transfrontier damage.[151] Principle 9 of the 1978 UNEP draft Principles of Conduct makes similar provision.[152]

---

[144] Art. 198.   [145] 1989 Basel Convention, Art. 13(1).
[146] See chapter 12, pp. 623–5 above.   [147] 1985 ASEAN Agreement, Art. 20(3)(d).
[148] Art. 14(1)(d).   [149] Art. 17(1).
[150] OECD Recommendation C(74)224, 21 November 1974, para. 9.
[151] See OECD Council Decision, Exchange of Information Concerning Accidents Capable of Causing Transfrontier Damage (Preamble and Appendices I–III), 8 July 1988, 28 ILM 247 (1989).
[152] See also 1986 WCED Legal Principles, Art. 19.

Nuclear accidents

Other treaties establish the duty to warn potentially affected states in case of nuclear and other emergencies,[153] and several states have bilateral agreements requiring emergency information to be provided in the event of a nuclear accident. Thus, the 1983 Exchange of Notes Between the United Kingdom and France Concerning Exchanges of Information in the Event of Emergencies Occurring in One of the Two States Which Could Have Radiological Consequences for the Other State provides that 'Each state-party shall inform the other without delay of any emergency which occurs in its state as a result of civil activities which may have radiological consequences liable to affect the other state.[154] The information is to be communicated through reciprocal warning centres capable of receiving and transmitting information twenty-four hours a day.

The question of whether a state must warn all other states which are or might be affected by a nuclear accident causing transboundary radioactive harm has been described as 'the main legal issue involved in the Chernobyl nuclear disaster'.[155] In 1985, the IAEA drew up Guidelines on Reportable Events, Integrated Planning and Information Exchange in a Transboundary Release of Radioactive Materials (IAEA Information Guidelines).[156] These recommend that in the event of a potential or actual release of radioactive material, which might cross or has crossed an international boundary and which could be of radiological safety significance, there should be a timely exchange of adequate information between the competent national authorities of the state in which the plant is situated and the authorities in neighbouring states.[157] The information should relate to the site, the facility, the emergency response plan, and in the event of an off-site emergency should include the nature and time of the accident, the characteristics of the release and meteorological and hydrological conditions.[158]

Following the Chernobyl accident, many states maintained that the obligation to provide emergency information was a rule of international law. Much of the criticism of the USSR's failure to provide information immediately after the accident was couched in legal terms.[159] The IAEA Director General noted

---

[153] 1972 Agreement Between the United States and Canada Concerning the Great Lakes' Water Quality, 508 UNTS 26; 1983 Agreement Between the Federal Republic of Germany and the German Democratic Republic on Principles Covering Damage at the Border, Bulletin Presse und Informationsamt der Bundesregierung, No. 115 (September 1983).

[154] For other such agreements, see P. Sands, *Chernobyl: Law and Communication* (1988), 199.

[155] Provisional Report of the Rapporteur, Twentieth Commission of the IDI, 'Air Pollution Across National Frontiers', 62 AIDI 178 (1987-I).

[156] IAEA Doc. INFCIRC/321.   [157] Paras. 3.1 and 4.1.1.   [158] Paras. 4.1.2 and 4.3.2.

[159] See e.g. the US Secretary of State: 'When an incident has cross border implications, there is an obligation under international law to inform others and do it promptly', in Final Report of the Rapporteur (do Nascimento e Silva), Twentieth Commission of the IDI, 'Air Pollution Across National Frontiers', 62 AIDI 259 (1987-I). See also the Statement

the failure of the Soviet system to inform its own citizens and neighbouring countries of a release which would affect them, the late implementation of the emergency measures and the apparent failure to warn immediately.[160] During the negotiation of the 1986 Notification Convention, support for the view that there was a legal obligation to provide information under customary law was expressed on several occasions,[161] and many writers have reached the same conclusion.[162] Humanitarian principles also justify the provision of information to people who might be affected by a nuclear or other accident.

1986 Notification Convention

The failure of the USSR to provide immediate information led to the 1986 Notification Convention, which was opened for signature within six months of the Chernobyl accident. It incorporates many of the recommendations set out in the IAEA Information Guidelines, and applies in the event of any 'accident involving facilities or activities of a state party or of persons or legal entities under its jurisdiction or control'.[163] In the event of such an accident, state parties must notify, directly or through the IAEA, those states which are or may be physically affected with details of the accident, its nature, the time of its occurrence and its exact location.[164] They must also promptly provide the states and the IAEA with relevant available information so as to minimise the radiological

of the Group of Seven: 'Each country . . . is responsible for prompt provision of detailed and complete information on nuclear emergencies and accidents, in particular those with potential transboundary consequences. Each of our countries accepts that responsibility.' Group of Seven, Statement on the Implications of the Chernobyl Nuclear Accident, 5 May 1986, 25 ILM 1005 (1986).

[160] Speech by the Director General of the IAEA to the International Press Institute, Vienna, 13 May 1986. Transcript provided by the IAEA.

[161] See Statement of the US representative at the Final Plenary Meeting of Governmental Experts on 15 August 1986, IAEA Doc. GC (SPL.I) 2, Annex V, 4; the Chinese representative, *ibid.*, 5; and the Japanese representative, *ibid.*, 21. The Chairman of the Meeting of Governmental Experts at the Final Plenary Session on 15 August 1986 stated, in his summing up, that 'the [Notification and Assistance] conventions are not intended to derogate from any international obligations on early notification and assistance that may already exist under international law': IAEA Doc. GC (SPL.1), 2, Annex VI, 2.

[162] Professor Dietrich Rauschning, as quoted in Final Report, Twentieth Commission of the IDI, n. 159 above, 259; see also W. Rudolf, *ibid.*, 280.

[163] Vienna, 26 September 1986, in force 27 October 1986, 25 ILM 1370 (1986), Art. 1(i). The Convention only applies to certain 'facilities and activities': Art. 1(2). In October 1987, an accident occurred in Brazil when abandoned radiotherapy equipment was broken open by a scrap metal dealer. This led to widespread radioactive contamination and the death of a number of people: see *Financial Times*, 8 October 1987. It is unclear whether the Convention applies to such 'activities': Art. 1(2)(e) (the loss of the Russian submarine, the *Kursk*, in August 2000, would appear to be covered by the Convention, which applies to 'any nuclear reactor wherever located').

[164] Art. 2.

consequences in those states. This includes the cause and foreseeable development of the accident, the general characteristics of the radioactive release (including its nature, form, quantity, composition and effective weight), current and future meteorological and hydrological conditions, planned or taken protective measures, and the predicted behaviour over time of the release.[165] Such information is to be supplemented at 'appropriate intervals' by the provision of relevant information including the foreseeable or actual termination of the emergency situation.[166] States should also respond 'promptly' to a request for further information or consultations sought by an affected state.[167] The Convention is the first multilateral agreement to provide detailed rules on the provision of information in emergency situations, involving a role for the national authorities of state parties[168] and the IAEA, as well as a binding dispute settlement mechanism.

The Convention is not, however, exhaustive or immune from criticism. First, the Convention does not appear to apply to accidents caused by nuclear weapons and their testing.[169] Secondly, certain of the recommendations contained in the IAEA Information Guidelines were not included. In particular, the recommendation in Chapter III that 'intervention levels for the introduction of protective measures such as sheltering and evacuation be set in advance by competent national authorities'[170] was not included in the Convention. In addition, the whole of Chapter V, on 'Integrated Planning', was excluded. Thirdly, the reference in Article 1(1) to an accident that 'could be of radiological safety significance for another state' leaves it to the discretion of the state in whose territory or under whose jurisdiction or control the accident has occurred to determine what is or is not of radiological safety significance and what are the chances that another state will be affected. Given the dangers of radioactivity, it would have been preferable that all radioactive releases be notified to the IAEA. Failing that, there should be an agreed level which would trigger the obligation to provide information. Fourthly, several states entered reservations restricting the application of the Convention. Most relate to the non-applicability of the dispute settlement provision, but some relate to the substantive provisions: the Government of the People's Republic of China stated that the Convention did not apply to cases caused by 'gross negligence'.[171] Finally, the Convention does not

---

[165] Art. 5(1).   [166] Art. 5(2).   [167] Art. 6.   [168] Art. 7.

[169] The five nuclear weapons states have declared that they will voluntarily apply the Convention to all nuclear accidents, irrespective of origin: see Statements of Voluntary Application, reprinted in P. Sands (ed.), *Chernobyl: Law and Communication* (1988), 244–5. On 6 October 1986, shortly after the Notification Convention was opened for signature, the USSR provided information about an accident on board one of its nuclear-powered submarines which might have radiological consequences: see *Independent*, 7 October 1987, 1.

[170] IAEA Doc. INFCIRC/321, para. 3.5.

[171] Declaration of 26 September 1986 of the Government of the People's Republic of China to the 1986 IAEA Notification Convention.

require states giving or receiving information to make it available to members of the public. The IAEA Information Guidelines noted that:

> Dissemination of information to the public is an important responsibility of the appropriate authorities in each state. Particular arrangements ensuring the necessary co-ordination across international borders should be established.[172]

The importance of public access to information is recognised in other treaties, including at least one adopted prior to the 1986 Notification Convention, namely, the 1974 Nordic Convention.[173] A final point concerning the provision of information in emergency situations relates to the responsibility of the mass media in the reporting of matters such as the Chernobyl accident. The reporting in the Western press was criticised by the USSR as being untruthful and creating mistrust, and the USSR subsequently proposed that the spreading of untrue information could entail liability for states.[174] The IAEA Secretariat has noted the possibility of including in a new instrument 'an obligation to refrain from actions which might exacerbate the consequences of a nuclear accident'.[175]

Monitoring and other information gathering

Recent international environmental agreements have often required information relevant to specific or general environmental obligations to be collected. The term most frequently used to describe that requirement is 'monitoring', although other terms which have been used include 'systematic observation', 'surveillance', 'inspection', and 'verification',[176] depending upon the precise activity which is envisaged. Monitoring can be carried out for a variety of purposes, of which the most usual include conducting research or identifying patterns and trends which reflect the state of the environment. Monitoring to ensure compliance with the objectives of an international treaty remains

---

[172] IAEA Doc. INFCIRC/321, para. 4.5.1.   [173] Art. 7.

[174] USSR, Proposed Programme for Establishing an International Regime for the Safe Development of Nuclear Power, 25 September 1986, IAEA Doc. GC (SPL.1)/8.

[175] IAEA Doc. GOV/INF/509, paras. 18–19. See the 1953 Convention on the International Right of Correction, 435 UNTS 191; this Convention provides states directly affected by a report which they consider false or distorted, and which is disseminated by an information agency, with the possibility of securing commensurate publicity for its correction.

[176] Verification procedures, including inspection, relate more to the issue of compliance than general information gathering. They are specifically permitted for the purposes of compliance in relation to nuclear weapons treaties: 1971 Nuclear Weapons Treaty. 'Verification' must not interfere with activities of other parties and must be conducted 'with due regard for rights recognised under international law, including the freedoms of the high seas and the rights of coastal States': Art. III(6).

somewhat controversial because of the suggestion that a third party may be-come involved in the compliance process, and it is principally for that reason that, with only limited exceptions, inspection or verification by foreign states or international organisations remains relatively undeveloped in international environmental agreements. Monitoring has been defined as the 'repeated mea-surement' of three separate, but related, factors:

(a) the quality of the . . . environment and each of its compartments . . . ;
(b) activities or natural and anthropogenic inputs which may affect the quality of the . . . environment; [and]
(c) the effects of such activities.[177]

Under international arrangements, monitoring and other forms of informa-tion gathering are carried out by states individually or jointly or by international organisations. Monitoring by international organisations for the purposes of research and the identification of trends and patterns is now a reasonably well-developed practice, with several international arrangements currently in op-eration. UNEP runs Earthwatch, a programme developed by the Stockholm Conference to provide a continuous assessment of the global environment. It comprises four parts: (1) review and evaluation of environmental conditions to identify gaps in knowledge and the need for action; (2) research on envi-ronmental problems; (3) monitoring of certain environmental variables; and (4) exchange of information among scientists and governments.[178] The princi-pal component of Earthwatch is the Global Environmental Monitoring System (GEMS), which is responsible for monitoring. UNEP also runs the Interna-tional Environmental Information System (INFOTERRA), a global network of national information centres for the exchange of environmental information. The World Weather Watch system of the WMO, which compiles global data on basic meteorological parameters related to weather, has three main compo-nents: the Global Observing System; the Global Telecommunications System; and the Global Data Processing System.[179] For the EU, the European Environ-ment Agency is charged with monitoring the overall state of the environment and gathering information.[180]

Treaty arrangements

Treaty arrangements require parties to carry out a range of monitoring and re-lated activities. Treaty obligations are particularly developed for the Antarctic region, the marine environment, and freshwater resources. The 1959 Antarctic

---

[177] 1992 OSPAR Convention, Annex IV, Art. 1.
[178] http://earthwatch.unep.net/; see L. K. Caldwell, *International Environmental Policy* (1990, 2nd edn), 75–6.
[179] WMO, *World Weather Watch: Fourteenth Status Report on Implementation* (1989).
[180] Chapter 15, pp. 739–40 above.

Treaty allows inspections by consultative parties of all areas of Antarctica, and rights of aerial observation.[181] The 1972 London Convention requires each party to designate an appropriate authority to monitor the condition of the seas for the purposes of the Convention.[182] Other treaties require the monitoring of concentrations of controlled substances[183] and levels of marine pollution,[184] and similar provision exists under UNEP Regional Seas Conventions.[185] Under the 1982 UNCLOS, states should 'observe, measure, evaluate and analyse' the risks or effects of pollution of the marine environment, and 'keep under surveillance the effects of any activities which they permit or in which they engage in order to determine whether these activities are likely to pollute the marine environment'.[186] The 1992 OSPAR Convention requires the parties to undertake and publish joint assessments of the quality status of the marine environment, including an evaluation of the effectiveness of the measures taken and planned and an identification of priorities for action.[187] Under the 1992 Watercourses Convention, riparian parties must implement joint programmes for monitoring the conditions of transboundary waters, as well as the assessment of the conditions and the effectiveness of implementing measures.[188]

In relation to air quality, the 1979 LRTAP Convention established a 'co-operative programme for the monitoring and evaluation of the long-range transmission of air pollutants in Europe' (known as EMEP);[189] the 1985 Vienna Convention requires parties to undertake 'systematic observation' of the state of the ozone layer and other relevant parameters;[190] and the 1992 Climate Change Convention commits all parties to develop and periodically update national inventories of anthropogenic emissions by sources and removals by sinks of all greenhouse gases not controlled by the Montreal Protocol and promote and co-operate in systematic observation.[191] Participants in the 1997 Kyoto Protocol's Clean Development Mechanism are required to monitor levels of greenhouse gas emissions related to clean development projects in order to calculate the proper emissions reductions credits to be issued to the party.[192]

Monitoring or its equivalent is also required for biological diversity. Examples include the 1946 International Whaling Convention, which provides for inspection of whaling ships and the measuring of whales,[193] and the 1992 Biodiversity Convention, which requires all parties to identify and monitor the components of biological diversity and the processes and categories of activities

---

[181] Art. VII. See also the provisions on observation and inspection established by the 1980 CCAMLR, Art. XXIV; 1988 CRAMRA, Arts. 11 and 12; and 1991 Antarctic Environment Protocol, Art. 14.

[182] Art. VI(1)(d).   [183] 1976 Rhine Chemical Pollution Convention, Art. 10(1).

[184] 1974 Paris LBS Convention, Art. 11.

[185] 1976 Barcelona Convention, Art. 10; 1978 Kuwait Convention, Art. X.

[186] Art. 204(1) and (2).   [187] Art. 6 and Annex IV.   [188] Art. 11.

[189] Art. 9 and 1984 EMEP Protocol.   [190] Arts. 2(2)(a) and 3(2) and Annex I.

[191] Arts. 4(1)(a) and (g) and 5.   [192] Conference of the Parties, Annex Decision 17/CP 7.

[193] Schedule, Section V.

which are likely to have significant adverse impacts on the conservation and sustainable use of biodiversity.[194] Other environmental treaties provide for monitoring or inspection of record books in relation to the carriage of oil;[195] certification for the carriage by sea of hazardous substances,[196] imported species and goods;[197] the health of workers;[198] the air quality of the working environment;[199] the composition of waste to be dumped;[200] the possible discharge by a ship of any harmful substances;[201] and fisheries conservation levels.[202] In certain circumstances, UNCLOS allows the physical inspection of foreign vessels,[203] and the 1974 Nordic Environment Convention is probably unique in allowing for the supervisory authorities of one state to carry out on-site inspections to determine damage caused by their environmentally harmful activities in another state.[204] Under the 1995 Straddling Stocks Agreement, states must ensure that fishing vessels flying their flag provide the information necessary to fulfil their obligations under the Agreement, and shall 'collect and exchange scientific, technical and statistical data with respect to fisheries for straddling fish stocks and highly migratory fish stocks', as well as ensuring that data are collected in sufficient detail to facilitate effective stock assessment and are provided in a timely manner to fulfil the requirements of subregional or regional fisheries management organisations or arrangements.[205]

Few international organisations are granted independent monitoring or other information gathering powers by treaty. The European Environment Agency provides the EC and the member states with 'objective, reliable and comparable information at European level enabling them to take the requisite measures to protect the environment, to assess the results of such measures and to ensure that the public is properly informed about the state of the environment'.[206] To that end, it is required to 'record, collate and assess data on the state of the environment', although it has no powers of on-site inspection of industrial sites or facilities.[207]

The Marrakech Accords to the 1997 Kyoto Protocol establish two separate independent monitoring bodies each with powers of oversight of the parties to

---

[194] Art. 7(b) and (c).   [195] 1954 Oil Pollution Convention, Art. IX(5).

[196] MARPOL 73/78, Art. 5(2).

[197] 1956 Plant Protection Agreement for the South East Asia and Pacific Region, Arts. III and V; 1970 Benelux Birds Convention, Art. 10.

[198] 1960 ILO Ionising Radiations Convention, Art. 11; 1981 ILO Occupational Safety Convention, Art. 9.

[199] 1986 ILO Asbestos Convention, Art. 20.   [200] 1972 Oslo Convention, Art. 10.

[201] MARPOL 73/78, Art. 6(2).

[202] 1978 Northwest Atlantic Fisheries Convention, Art. XI(4).

[203] Art. 226(1). On inspection, see also the 1994 Straddling Stocks Agreement, Arts. 21 and 22.

[204] Art. 10.

[205] Art. 14 and Annex 1 (standard requirements for collection and sharing of data).

[206] See chapter 15, pp. 739–40 above; Art. 1(2).   [207] Art. 2(iii).

the Protocol. The first body is an expert review team which will conduct reviews of each party's calculations of its assigned amount of greenhouse gas emissions and the party's various emissions credits, and also conduct in-country reviews and desk reviews of each party's national registry.[208] The second body, the Enforcement Branch of the Compliance Committee, is responsible for determining whether each Annex I country is in compliance with its quantified emissions limitation or reduction commitment, as well as with certain methodological and eligibility requirements set up under the Protocol.[209]

Some organisations may conduct factual investigations,[210] while other treaties merely permit the relevant international organisation to be entrusted with surveillance functions[211] or to prepare a document summarising the result of national monitoring efforts.[212] Regulatory Committees established under the 1988 CRAMRA would be required to monitor the compliance of operators with Management Schemes.[213]

UNCED

Despite the development and operation of these and other international arrangements, there is a widespread consensus on the need to improve data collection and use. Chapter 40 of Agenda 21, entitled 'Information for Decision-Making', establishes two programme areas. The first, called 'Bridging the Data Gap', aims: to promote more cost-effective and relevant data collection and assessment; to strengthen national and international capacity to use and collect data in decision-making; to ensure that planning for sustainable development is based on timely, reliable and usable information; and to make information accessible in form and time.[214] The statistical office of the UN Secretariat and other UN organs and organisations are called upon to develop and use indicators of sustainable development and indicators related to areas outside of national jurisdiction, such as the high seas, the upper atmosphere and outer space, and to recommend the harmonised development of indicators at the national, regional and global levels for use at the international level 'subject to national sovereignty considerations'.[215] Agenda 21 calls in particular for the development of inventories of environmental, resource and development data for the management of sustainable development and the strengthening of data collection activities, including Earthwatch and World Weather Watch, particularly for urban air, freshwater, land resources (including forests and rangelands),

---

[208] Decision 23/CP.7 Annex 1, Parts III and V.   [209] Decision 24/CP.7 Annex, Part V.4.

[210] See e.g. the International Tropical Tuna Commission, which is required to investigate the abundance, biology, biometry and ecology of certain tunas: 1949 Inter-American Tropical Tuna Convention, Art. II(1).

[211] See e.g. 1962 African Migratory Locust Convention, Art. 4(4).

[212] 1976 Rhine Chemical Pollution Convention, Art. 10(3).

[213] Art. 52.   [214] Agenda 21, para. 40.5.   [215] *Ibid.*, paras. 40.6 and 40.7.

desertification, other habitats, soil degradation, biodiversity, the high seas and the upper atmosphere.[216]

The second programme area ('Improving Availability of Information') calls for the strengthening of existing national and international mechanisms of information processing and exchange to ensure 'effective and equitable availability of information . . . subject to national sovereignty and relevant intellectual property rights'.[217] It also supports the strengthening of electronic networking capabilities to facilitate implementation of Agenda 21 and intergovernmental negotiations, to monitor conventions, and to transmit environmental alerts.[218]

In 2002, the WSSD reaffirmed the commitments of Agenda 21, but set up no new substantial commitments or programmes. Instead, the WSSD Plan of Implementation calls for increased access to information or the gathering and dissemination of information on a wide variety of subject areas.[219]

Access to environmental information

D. Partan, 'The "Duty to Inform" in International Environmental Law', 6 *Boston University International Law Journal* 43 (1988); M. Pallemaerts (ed.), *The Right to Environmental Information* (1991); H. Smets, 'The Right of Information on the Risks Created by Hazardous Installations at the National and International Levels', in F. Francioni and T. Scovazzi (eds.), *International Responsibility for Environmental Harm* (1991); W. Birtles, 'Environmental Issues: The Right to Know', 137 *Solicitors Journal* 408 (1993); R. Hallo, *Access to Environmental Information in Europe, The Implementation and Implications of Directive 90/313/EEC* (1996).

The duty to provide – and the right to obtain – access to information on the environment, whether to the public at large or to specific categories of persons (such as workers), is a recent but now firmly entrenched development in international law. The right is closely connected to participation rights in environmental impact assessment procedures, and goes further than obligations to ensure public awareness, education or publicity (discussed in the following

---

[216] *Ibid.*, para. 40.8.
[217] *Ibid.*, para. 40.19. The Chapter calls for a review and strengthening of existing programmes such as the Advisory Committee for the Co-ordination of Information Systems (ACCIS) and INFOTERRA: para. 40.24.
[218] *Ibid.*, para. 40.25.
[219] E.g. improving the scientific understanding and assessment of marine and coastal ecosystems (para. 34); exchange of scientific data and information related to climate change (para. 36(d)); and desertification and drought (para. 39). The Plan of Implementation also calls for bridging the 'digital divide' by providing access to infrastructure and technology transfer to developing countries and for implementing Agenda 21 by making full use of developments in the field of information and communication technologies (paras. 63 and 138).

section).[220] The 1990 EC Directive on Access to Environmental Information, the 1992 OSPAR Convention, and the Council of Europe's 1993 Civil Liability Convention were the first group of instruments to elaborate in detail the modalities for giving effect to the right of persons to access to information on the environment. More recently, the right has been extended – geographically and substantively – by the 1998 Aarhus Convention, which is also leading to revision of the EC Directive. It has also been recognised, in relation to activities which may affect the public, in Article 12 of the ILC's draft Articles on Prevention of Transboundary Harm.

In each instrument, the existence and exercise of such a right is subject to certain limitations, reflecting a reluctance on the part of states to allow an unlimited right of access to information, as previously illustrated by the two treaties adopted shortly after the Chernobyl accident: the 1986 IAEA Notification Convention, which failed to provide citizens with any right of access to environmental information, and the 1986 IAEA Assistance Convention, which provided that an assisting party must make every effort to co-ordinate with the requesting state before releasing information to the public on the assistance provided in connection with a nuclear accident.[221] Other treaties, such as the 1992 Industrial Accidents Convention, create a positive obligation on parties to provide information to the public rather than creating a citizen's right of access to information.[222] The 1992 Climate Change Convention does not create a public right of access to information, although it requires information communicated by the parties to be made 'publicly available' at the time it is submitted to the conference of the parties once it has been made available to bodies involved in communication and review of information.[223] The dissemination of this information will be subject to limitations on grounds of confidentiality in accordance with criteria to be established by the conference of the parties.[224]

The Rio Declaration recognises the important role of public participation in environmental decision-making and provides in Principle 10 that:

> Environmental issues are best handled with the participation of all concerned citizens, at the relevant level. At the national level, each individual shall have appropriate access to information concerning the environment that is held by public authorities, including information on hazardous materials and activities in their communities, and the opportunity to participate in decision-making processes.[225]

---

[220] On access to information in human rights law, see *Guerra v. Italy* (1998 26 EHRR 357), chapter 7, pp. 301–2 above; see also S. Weber, 'Environmental Information and the European Convention on Human Rights', 12 *Human Rights Law Journal* 177 (1991).

[221] Art. 6(2).   [222] Art. 9 and Annex VIII; see also 1991 Espoo Convention, Art. 3(8).

[223] Art. 12(9) and (10).   [224] Art. 12(9).

[225] See also WSSD, Plan of Implementation, para. 24(b); and OECD Council Decision/Recommendation, Provision of Information to Public and Public Participation in Decision-Making Processes Related to Prevention of, and Response to, Accidents Involving

The Rio Declaration is silent as to what information will be considered 'appropriate', although some guidance may be found in Agenda 21, which provides that 'individuals, groups and organisations should have access to information relevant to environment and development held by national authorities, including information on products and activities that have or are likely to have a significant impact on the environment, and information on environmental protection measures.[226]

Some early treaties sought to ensure that information on hazardous substances was made available to workers. The 1985 Occupational Health Services Convention does not create a right of access in so many words, but does provide that 'all workers shall be informed of health hazards involved in their work'.[227] The 1986 Asbestos Convention goes further by providing, without apparent qualification, that workers, their representatives and inspection services 'shall have access' to records of the monitoring of the working environment and of the exposure of workers to asbestos.[228]

EC Directive on Access to Environmental Information

The EC Directive on Access to Environmental Information as the first international instrument to create a right of access to environmental information.[229] It is intended to ensure free access to, and dissemination of, environmental information held by public authorities throughout the EC by setting out basic terms and conditions on which the information should be made available.[230] The Directive is also intended to ensure greater environmental protection and remove disparities in member states' laws which create unequal conditions of competition. In 2000, the EC Commission proposed amendments to the 1990 Directive, to give effect to the requirements which would arise from Community ratification of the 1998 Aarhus Convention.[231]

Under the 1990 Directive, any natural or legal person, anywhere in the EC, is entitled to access to information relating to the environment without having

---

Hazardous Substances, 8 July 1988, OECD C(88)85, 28 ILM 277 (1989); and 1998 Recommendation on Environmental Information, C(98)67.

[226] Agenda 21, para. 23.3.   [227] Art. 13.   [228] Art. 20.

[229] Council Directive 90/313/EEC, OJ L158, 23 June 1990, 56; J. Rowan-Robinson, 'Public Access to Environmental Information: A Means to What Ends?', 8 JEL 19 (1996); C. Kimber, 'Understanding Access to Environmental Information: The European Experience', in T. Jewell and J. Steele, *Law in Environmental Policy Making* (1998). See also Regulation (EC) No. 1049/2001 regarding public access to European Parliament, Council and Commission documents, OJ L145 , 31 May 2001, 43.

[230] Art. 1.

[231] See new Directive 2003/4/EC of 28 January 2003 on public access to environmental information and repealing Council Directive 90/313/EEC, OJ L 41, 14 February 2003, 26.

to show an interest,[232] at a charge not exceeding a reasonable cost, upon request.[233] Under the Directive, a public authority must 'respond' to a request within two months.[234] The right of access to environmental information is subject to certain limitations, including where a request affects: the confidentiality of proceedings of public authorities, international relations and national defence; public security; matters which are or have been *sub judice* or under enquiry or are the subject of preliminary investigation; commercial and industrial confidentiality, including intellectual property; confidentiality of personal files and data; material supplied by a third party without that party being under a legal obligation to do so; and requests which are 'manifestly unreasonable' or 'formulated in too general a manner'.[235] Moreover, requests for information may be refused where they would involve the supply of 'unfinished documents or internal communications'.[236]

The Directive provides that a person who considers that his request has been unreasonably refused or ignored or inadequately answered may 'seek a judicial or administrative review of the decision in accordance with the relevant national legal system'.[237] Member states were required to implement the Directive by 31 December 1992, and it has given rise to a discrete but significant case law in member states[238] and in the ECJ.[239] The leading ECJ case is *Wilhelm Mecklenburg* v. *Kreis Pinneberg*, which raised the question of whether a statement of views given to a countryside protection authority participating in development consent proceedings was environmental information within the meaning of Article 2(a) of the Directive. In answering that question in the affirmative, the ECJ ruled that the Community legislature intended the concept to be a broad

---

[232] Art. 3. 'Information relating to the environment' is defined as 'any available information in written, visual, aural, or data-base form on the state of water, air, soil, fauna, flora, land and natural sites, and on activities (including those which give rise to nuisances such as noise) or measures designed to protect these, including administrative measures and environmental management programmes': Art. 2(a).

[233] Art. 3(1) and (5).   [234] Art. 3(4).   [235] Art. 3(2) and (3).

[236] Art. 3(3).   [237] Art. 4.

[238] See e.g. (in the UK) *R.* v. *Secretary of State for the Environment, Transport and Regions and Another, ex parte Alliance Against the Birmingham Northern Relief Road and Others* [1999] JPL 231; [1999] Env LR 447 (holding, *inter alia*, that: whether a document contains information which relates to the environment, and whether it may or must be treated as confidential are matters to be determined on an objective basis by the court; the definition of information relating to the environment in Art. 2 of the Directive is 'very broad', and the fact that the document can be described as a commercial document does not mean that it does not contain information which relates to the environment; and any derogation contained in the Directive must be construed strictly and proportionately, in a manner which is consistent with achieving the underlying objective of the Directive).

[239] Case C-217/97, *Commission* v. *Germany* [1999] ECR I-5087 (failure to transpose Arts. 3(2) and 5).

one, embracing information and activities relating to the state of those aspects, and including all forms of administrative activity.[240] The Court ruled:

> In order to constitute information relating to the environment for the purposes of the directive, it is sufficient for the statement of views put forward by an authority, such as the statement concerned in the main proceedings, to be an act capable of adversely affecting or protecting the state of one of the sectors of the environment covered by the directive. That is the case, as the referring court mentioned, where the statement of views is capable of influencing the outcome of the development consent proceedings as regards interests pertaining to the protection of the environment.[241]

The ECJ also ruled that the exceptions set forth in Article 3 of the Directive should be interpreted restrictively, and should not be interpreted in such a way as to extend their effects 'beyond what is necessary to safeguard the interests which it seeks to secure', having regard to the aims pursued by the Directive.[242]

1992 OSPAR Convention

The 1992 OSPAR Convention, which was the first international treaty to provide specific rules on the right of access to environmental information, draws significantly from the provisions of the 1990 EC Directive. Article 9 of the 1992 Convention requires the competent authorities of the parties to make available to any legal or natural person

> any available information in written, visual, aural or data-base form on the state of the maritime area, on activities or measures adversely affecting or likely to affect it and on activities or measures introduced in accordance with the Convention.[243]

The information must be provided in response to any reasonable request, without the person seeking the information having to prove an interest, without unreasonable charges, and as soon as possible and at the latest within two months.[244] As with the 1990 EC Directive, certain limitations apply: requests for information may be refused 'in accordance with their national legal systems and applicable international regulations' where the information affects, *inter alia*, the confidentiality of proceedings of public authorities, international relations and national defence, public security, matters which are *sub judice* or under enquiry, commercial and industrial confidentiality (including intellectual property), and the confidentiality of personal data or files.[245]

---

[240] Case C-321/96, [1998] ECR I-3809, paras. 19 and 20; see also the Opinion of Advocate General La Pergola, *ibid.*, paras. 15–25.

[241] Para. 21.

[242] Para. 25, citing Case C-335/94, *Mrozek and Jager* [1996] ECR I-1573, para. 9.

[243] Art. 9(2).   [244] Art. 9(1).

[245] Art. 9(3). The reasons for a refusal must be given: Art. 9(4).

In June 2001, Ireland instituted arbitration proceedings (under Article 32 of the OSPAR Convention) against the United Kingdom seeking access to information which had been redacted from two independent reports related to the authorisation of the MOX nuclear plant at Sellafield. The two reports had been commissioned by the UK Government to assess the 'economic justification' of the plant, as required by EURATOM law, but the government only put into the public domain versions which omitted large amounts of information relating to the operation and costs of the plant. Ireland requested access to the information under Article 9 of the OSPAR Convention. The United Kingdom refused to provide the information, on the grounds that it did not constitute information within the meaning of Article 9(1), or, alternatively, that if it was such information the United Kingdom was entitled to rely on the 'commercial confidentiality' exception to refuse disclosure. Further, in the course of its pleadings, the United Kingdom argued that Ireland was not entitled to rely on Article 9 of the Convention, which only required parties to put in place domestic arrangements to ensure access to information but did not entitle another party to bring an international claim premised on a right of access to information.

The arbitral tribunal gave its award in July 2002.[246] The tribunal unanimously rejected the UK's arguments that the tribunal lacked jurisdiction and that Ireland's claims were inadmissible, and by a 2-1 majority (Mustill and Griffiths) rejected the UK's submission that the implementation of Article 9(1) was assigned exclusively to the competent authorities in the UK and not to a tribunal established under UNCLOS. But by a 2-1 majority (Reisman and Mustill) the tribunal found that Ireland's claim did not fall within Article 9(2), on the ground that Ireland had not demonstrated that the categories of redacted information 'insofar as they may be taken to be activities or measures with respect to the commissioning and operation of a MOX Plant at Sellafield, are "information . . . on the state of the maritime area" or, even if they were, are likely adversely to affect the maritime area' (Award, para. 179). The dissenting opinion of Griffiths objected to the majority's approach on the grounds that: it failed to address 'the admitted environmental harm to the marine environment of the Irish Sea, as well as the fact that Article 9(2) only speaks of the likelihood of adverse effects'; the burden of proof lay with the UK, in accordance with the precautionary principle; the majority conclusion appeared to be unfounded since no evidence was presented in support of its finding; and the available material militated in favour of the conclusion that the probability of adverse effect might be demonstrated (Dissenting Opinion, para. 92). The majority's textual and 'acontextual' approach suggests that environmental considerations – including international legal developments which have occurred since the

---

[246] Dispute Concerning Access to Information under Article 9 of the OSPAR Convention, Permanent Court of Arbitration, 2 July 2003 (Michael Reisman, Gavan Griffith QC and Lord Mustill).

1980s – have perhaps not yet fully permeated the reasoning processes of some classical international lawyers.

1993 Civil Liability Convention

Chapter III of the 1993 Civil Liability Convention, entitled 'Access to Information', includes provisions entitling persons to have access to environmental information held by public authorities on terms which are virtually identical to the 1990 EC Directive.[247] However, the Convention additionally entitles persons to have access to environmental information held by 'bodies with public responsibilities for the environment and under the control of a public authority' on the same terms and conditions as information held by public authorities, and access to specific information held by operators.[248] This latter entitlement introduces a novel approach which goes beyond the 1990 EC Directive and the 1992 OSPAR Convention. It would entitle a person who has suffered damage to request a court to order an operator to provide her with specific information necessary to establish the existence of a claim for compensation under the Convention, including the elements of information available to her and relating to the equipment and machinery used, the kind and concentration of the dangerous substances or waste, and the nature of genetically modified organisms.[249] Operators may request a court to order another operator to provide specific information which may be necessary to establish the extent of her obligation or of her own right to compensation from the other operator, and may also rely on defences including the restrictions set out in Article 14(2), or where such information would incriminate her, or place a disproportionate burden on her, taking into account all the interests involved.[250]

1998 Aarhus Convention

The 1998 Aarhus Convention is built on three pillars: access to information; public participation in environmental decision-making; and access to justice in environmental matters. On environmental information, the Convention introduces several innovations which clarify – or develop, depending upon one's perspective – the approaches reflected in the 1990 EC Directive and Article 9 of the 1992 OSPAR Convention, which it generally follows. The 1998 Aarhus Convention obliges parties to ensure that public authorities make available to the public 'environmental information' without any interest having to be stated, generally in the form requested, and without an unreasonable charge being made.[251] The definition of environmental information is broader than earlier instruments, making express reference, for example, to factors of biodiversity such as genetically modified organisms, and a broad range of measures

---

[247] Arts. 13 and 14.   [248] Arts. 15 and 16.   [249] Art. 16(1) and (3).
[250] Art. 16(2), (5) and (6).   [251] Art. 4(1) and (9).

(such as environmental agreements, policies, plans and programmes and cost–benefit and other economic analyses and assumptions used in environmental decision-making).[252] The time available for responding to requests is reduced to one month, and the exceptions are to be interpreted in a restrictive way and tightened (e.g. the commercial confidentiality exception may only be applied where 'legitimate economic interests' need to be protected, and a presumption is established in favour of disclosing information on emissions which is relevant for the protection of the environment).[253] A refusal to disclose information is to be subject to the Convention provisions on access to review.[254] The Convention also imposes a positive obligation on a public authority which does not hold the information to inform the applicant where it might be applied for, and makes provision for the separation of information which would be exempted from disclosure so that the remainder may be disclosed.[255]

Article 5 of the Convention imposes a range of positive (and innovative) obligations on parties, beginning with the requirement that public authorities 'possess and update' environmental information relevant to their functions, and to establish mandatory systems to ensure an adequate flow of information to public authorities about activities which may significantly affect the environment.[256] In the event of any imminent threat to human health or the environment (from any source), public authorities are also required to immediately disseminate all information which could enable the public to take measures to prevent or mitigate the harm arising from the threat.[257] Parties are also required to ensure that public authorities make environmental information available to the public in transparent and accessible ways, to ensure that such information progressively becomes available in electronic databases, to publish (at least every four years) a national report on the state of the environment, and to take measures to disseminate national and international legislation and measures, including treaties.[258] The private sector is also targeted, although via the state: parties

> shall encourage operators whose activities have a significant impact on the environment to inform the public regularly of the environmental impact of their activities and products, where appropriate within the framework of voluntary eco-labelling or eco-auditing schemes or by other means.[259]

Finally, each party must take steps to establish progressively a 'coherent, nation-wide system of pollution inventories or registers on a structured, computerized and publicly accessible database'.[260]

---

[252] Art. 2(3). [253] Art. 4(2), (3)(d) and (4).
[254] Arts. 4(7) and 9; see chapter 5, p. 177 above.
[255] Art. 4(5) and (6). [256] Art. 5(1)(a) and (b).
[257] Art. 5(1)(c). [258] Art. 5(2)–(4). [259] Art. 5(6); see also Art. 5(7), below.
[260] Art. 5(9). The systems should include inputs, releases and transfers of specified susbtances and products, including water, energy and resource use, from a specified range of activities to environmental media and to on-site and off-site treatment and disposal sites: *ibid.*

Public education and awareness

A number of international environmental agreements include positive obligations requiring states to improve public education and awareness on environmental matters and give due publicity to matters of environmental importance. Principle 10 of the Rio Declaration synthesises commitments adopted in a number of international treaties. It recognises the importance of public education and provides that 'states shall facilitate and encourage public awareness and participation by making information widely available'. Chapter 36 of Agenda 21 (Promoting Education, Public Awareness and Training) elaborates upon Principle 10, and establishes three programme areas: reorienting education towards sustainable development; increasing public awareness; and promoting training.[261] Article 5 of the 1998 Aarhus Convention – described above – goes far in this regard.

Several treaties include provisions on public awareness, education and publicity. One of the earliest was the 1987 Montreal Protocol, which calls on parties to co-operate in 'promoting public awareness of the environmental effects of the emissions of controlled substances and other substances that deplete the ozone layer'.[262] Similar provisions are repeated in subsequent global instruments.[263] Education and training are also addressed with increasing frequency,[264] particularly in relation to instruments addressing the protection of workers.[265] The 1989 Convention on the Rights of the Child specifies that education should include 'development of respect for the natural environment'.[266] The 2000 Biosafety Protocol requires parties to promote public awareness, education and participation 'concerning the safe transfer, handling and use of living modified organisms in relation to the conservation and sustainable use of biological diversity'.[267] Finally, certain treaties specifically require that publicity should be given to specially protected areas,[268] or to maritime navigation

---

[261] See also the WSSD Plan of Implementation, including para. 19(m) (energy sources and technologies for sustainable development) and para. 41(b) (eco-tourism).

[262] Art. 9(2).

[263] 1989 Basel Convention, Art. 10(4); 1992 Climate Change Convention, Art. 4(1)(i); 1992 Biodiversity Convention, Art. 13; 1998 POP Protocol to the 1979 LRTAP Convention, Art. 6; 1999 Protocol on Water and Health to the 1992 Watercourses Convention, Art. 9(1); 1999 Acidification, Eutrophication and Ground-Level Ozone (Gothenburg) Protocol, Art. 5(1) and (2); 2000 Cartagena Protocol, Art. 23; 2001 POPs Convention, Art. 10(1)(c) and (f).

[264] 1985 ASEAN Agreement, Art. 16(1) and (3); 1992 Biodiversity Convention, Arts. 12 and 13; 1992 Climate Change Convention, Art. 4(1)(i); Ramsar Convention Res. VII.9 (1999); and 2001 POPs Convention, Art 10(1)(e) and (g).

[265] 1986 ILO Asbestos Convention, Art. 22; 1988 Construction Convention, Art. 33.

[266] Art. 29(1)(e).   [267] Art. 23(1)(a).

[268] 1982 Geneva SPA Protocol, Art. 8(1) (applies also to buffer areas).

dangers,[269] or to particular requirements for the prevention, reduction and control of pollution of the marine environment.[270]

Eco-labelling

P. Menell, 'The Uneasy Case for Ecolabelling', 4 RECIEL 304 (1995); E. Staffin, 'Trade Barrier or Trade Boon? A Critical Evaluation of Environmental Labelling and Its Role in "Greening" of World Trade', 21 *Columbia Journal of Environmental Law* 205 (1996); A. Appleton, *Environmental Labelling Programmes: International Trade Law Implications* (1997); E. Bartenhagen, 'The Intersection of Trade and the Environment: An Examination of the Impact of the TBT Agreement on Ecolabelling Programs', 17 *Virginia Environmental Law Journal* 1 (1997); S. Subedi, 'Balancing International Trade with Environmental Protection: International Legal Aspects of Eco-labels', 2 *Brooklyn Journal of International Law* 373 (1999).

The labelling of environmental aspects of goods and services (eco-labelling) emerged as an international issue in the trade context, following Mexico's complaint that the US 1990 Dolphin Protection Consumer Information Act (allowing 'Dolphin Safe' labels to be placed on tuna products provided that dolphins had not been killed) was incompatible with the GATT. Although the GATT Panel upheld the legislation, it did so in terms which suggested that other eco-labelling rules might be incompatible with the GATT.[271] Although there have been no subsequent GATT or WTO rulings regarding eco-labelling, debate continues in the WTO Committee on Trade and the Environment on the propriety of eco-labelling schemes under GATT/WTO rules, with particular focus on the compatibility with the WTO rules of mandatory labelling requirements for genetically modified organisms.[272] For its parties, the matter will now be governed, in respect of living modified organisms, by the 2000 Biosafety Protocol, which requires living modified organisms intended for direct use as food, feed or for processing to be identified to show that they 'may contain' living modified organisms and are not intended for intentional introduction into the environment.[273] More generally, the 1998 Aarhus Convention requires parties

---

[269] 1982 UNCLOS, Art. 24(2).   [270] 1982 UNCLOS, Art. 211(3).

[271] Chapter 19, pp. 953–61 below.

[272] See S. Subedi, 'Balancing International Trade with Environmental Protection: International Legal Aspects of Eco-labels', 25 *Brooklyn Journal of International Law* 373 (1999); A. Appleton, 'GMOs: The Labelling of GMO Products Pursuant to International Trade Rules', 8 *New York University Environmental Law Journal* 566 (2000). On the WTO rules, see chapter 19, p. 949 below.

[273] Art. 18(2)(a) (the conference of the parties will decide on the detailed requirements no later than two years after the date of entry into force of the Protocol); see also Art. 18(2)(b) and (c) on identification of LMOs contained and intended for intentional introduction into the environment.

to develop mechanisms to ensure that product information is available to allow consumers to make informed environmental choices.[274]

The European Community's 1992 Regulation on a Community eco-labelling scheme was the first international instrument to establish an eco-labelling scheme, functioning for several years until it was revised in 2000.[275] The 2000 Regulation revises the Community eco-labelling scheme, the objective of which is to establish a voluntary scheme for the award of an EC eco-label for products and services that reduce negative environmental impacts and contribute to the efficient use of resources and a high level of environmental protection.[276] The eco-label may be awarded to any product or service that possesses 'characteristics that enable it to contribute significantly to improvements in relation to key environmental aspects', on the basis that no substances or preparations which are classified as very toxic, toxic, dangerous to the environment, carcinogenic, toxic for reproduction, or mutagenic may be awarded the eco-label, and excluding certain products – food, drink and pharmaceuticals – from the scheme.[277] The Regulation establishes a European Union Eco-labelling Board (EUEB), composed of the competent bodies of the member states and a Consultation Forum, which, in association with the EC Commission and the Regulatory Committee, is responsible for establishing the product groupings and detailed criteria for awarding the eco-label in each grouping.[278] The criteria for each product group are to be established according to specific environmental requirements set forth in an 'Indicative Environmental Matrix' in Annex I, and specific procedural requirements set out in Annex II. The Annex I Matrix requires account to be taken of pollution and contamination in eleven environmental fields, in five phases of the product's life cycle or three phases of the service's life cycle.[279] The Regulation establishes a four-part procedure for establishing the detailed criteria.[280] Applications for the eco-label are to be made to the competent body of the member states by manufacturers, importers,

---

[274] Art. 5(7).

[275] Council Regulation (EC) No. 92/880, OJ L99, 11 April 1992, 1; Art. 1.

[276] Regulation (EC) No. 1980/2000, OJ L237, 21 September 2000, 1, Art. 1(1). See also Commission Decisions 2002/18/EC (eco-label working plan); 2000/730/EC (establishing EU Eco-labelling Board); 2000/731/EC (rules of procedure of the Consultation Forum); 2000/729/EC (standard contract covering the use of the Community Eco-label); and 2000/728/EC (application and annual fees of the Community Eco-label).

[277] Arts. 2(4) and (5) and 3.

[278] Arts. 6 and 13.

[279] The environmental fields are: air, water, soil, waste, energy savings, natural resources consumption, global warming prevention, ozone layer protection, environmental safety, noise, and biodiversity. The product life cycle phases are: pre-production/raw materials, production, distribution and packaging, use, and reuse/recycling/disposal. The service life cycle phases are: acquisition of goods for service performance, service performance, and waste management.

[280] A study to assess product types; study of product life cycle (taking into consideration the principles in EN ISO 14040 and ISO 14024); improvement analysis; and proposal for the criteria. Detailed criteria have been established under the Regulation (or its

service providers, traders and retailers where the product originates or, where the product originates outside the EC, in any member state where the product is to be placed on the market in accordance with the established criteria for each product group. The label is to be awarded by contract limited to the remaining period of validity for the ecological criteria and covering the terms of the label's use, including withdrawal of authorisation, and will be subject to the payment of the costs of processing the application and the payment of an annual fee.[281]

Eco-auditing and accounting

H. Gleckman, 'Proposed Requirements for Transnational Corporations to Disclose Information on Product and Process Hazards', 6 *Boston University International Law Journal* 89 (1988); L. Spedding, 'Environmental Auditing and International Standards', 3 RECIEL 14 (1994).

Environmental considerations are addressed in regulatory and voluntary schemes designed to identify the environmental effects of the activities of companies or industrial sites. These measures suggest that current accounting practices and statements need to be transformed to take into account the environmental costs of production and other activities, which are currently treated for the most part as 'zero-priced' resources. The primary purpose of environmental accounting is to ensure that environmental costs are accurately reflected in the individual accounts and balance sheets of companies, or the national accounts of states. An important secondary purpose is to ensure that information on the use of environmental resources is disclosed; information provided in accounts may relate to environmental policies and programmes, environmental improvements, or the financial impacts of environmental measures, as well as responsibilities for environmental clean-up or related measures. Environmental auditing, or 'eco-auditing', describes a technique for allowing a company or a state to assess the impact of its activities on the environment which includes procedures beyond the scope of a traditional financial audit which can be performed by an internal consultant or by an independent third person. The most important developments relating to environmental accounting and auditing have been taken at the national level.[282] At the international level the most significant work on environmental accounting has been carried

---

predecessor) for, *inter alia*, light bulbs, copying and graphic paper, indoor paints and varnishes, textile products, hardfloor coverings, television, footwear, dishwashers, soil improvers, portable computers, dishwashing detergents, all-purpose cleaners, tissue paper products, and washing machines.

[281] Arts. 9 and 12.

[282] For a short survey of national practices, see Report of the Secretary General: Information Disclosure Relating to Environmental Measures, UN Doc. E/C.10/AC.3/1990/5, 16 January 1990, especially 7–14; see also Report of the Secretary General: International Survey of Corporate Reporting Practices, UN Doc. E/C.10/AC.3/1992/3, 13 January 1992.

out under the auspices of the former UN Centre on Transnational Corporations (UNCTC) and, subsequently, UNCTAD, while that relating to eco-auditing is reflected in the Regulation establishing a voluntary scheme, first adopted by the EC in April 1993 and revised in 2001. Additionally, the International Standards Organization (ISO) has developed its ISO 14000 series of standards for environmental management.

Environmental accounting

Although discussions regarding environmental accounting have taken place in the international community for over a decade, no international legal obligations, or soft law commitments, have been adopted by states or international organisations in relation to environmental accounting, and none appears imminent. The best guide to possible future developments at the international level is reflected in the work of the Intergovernmental Working Group of Experts on International Standards of Accounting and Reporting (ISAR), established under the auspices of the former UNCTC, and now functioning under UNCTAD. The work of the former UNCTC in this area was submitted as a report to the UNCED Preparatory Committee,[283] and was partly reflected in Principle 16 of the Rio Declaration, which calls on national authorities to 'endeavour to promote the internalisation of environmental costs', and in Agenda 21. The 1991 UNCTC Report recognised that the main challenge for environmental accounting was to develop an acceptable valuation method for quantifying the costs of non-sustainable economic activity, and identifies some of the flaws in traditional accounting rules and practices in relation to environmental resources:

> It does not account for the full costs of production, including the costs of consuming essential natural resources such as air, water and fertile land . . . In addition, accounting rules penalise, rather than encourage, the environmentally responsible corporation. The more a corporation spends on prevention and clean-up, the less per share it earns in the short run. Accounting lacks a vehicle for recording 'green assets' and monitoring their use, for distinguishing between the costs of renewable versus non-renewable resources and for providing accounting incentives to improve environmental protection.[284]

The UNCTC recognised the need to ensure that accounts reflect environmental costs so that stakeholders have information to enable them to make the best uses of resources, taking account of 'the rights and obligations of shareholders,

---

[283] UN Doc. A/CONF.15 1/PC/89, 22 August 1991; also Report of the Secretary General: Accounting for Environmental Protection Measures, UN Doc. E/C.10/AC.3/1991/5, 11 February 1991.
[284] *Ibid.*, 4.

customers, and local communities affected by environmental degradation, as well as the implicit rights of other species and other habitats'.[285] It also identified the need to improve traditional financial statements, principally to address the concerns of securities' regulators, insurance companies, banks and shareholders about unreported contingent liabilities which might have an adverse effect on the net worth of a corporation. This raises a major problem of access to, and dissemination of, information, described by the UNCTC report as 'unprecedented disclosure problems in how, and when, to account for the potential contingent liabilities'.[286] The report identified three obstacles to the taking or reporting of environmental protection measures by companies. First, the lack of incentive to record liabilities which results from the rule in many countries that expenses are only deductible for tax purposes when paid; secondly, the impact of environmental costs on short-term earnings; and, thirdly, the difficulty of separating environmental costs from other costs.[287] The report noted that accounting for environmental expenses is feasible, and raises reporting issues which are 'tractable and essentially of a definitional and classificatory nature'.[288] Environmental liabilities raised more problems, in large part because of the difficulty in determining a 'reasonable estimate' of future obligations in the face of environmental liabilities which are dependent upon 'inherent uncertainties in future legislation, technological change and extent or nature of environmental clean-up required'.[289]

Since 1990, ISAR has sought to address these and other accounting issues by proposing methods for integrating environmental costs and liabilities into traditional accounting methods, including incorporating environmental information into financial disclosures and annual reports. In 1998, it published a guidance document to provide assistance to enterprises, regulators and standard-setting bodies regarding best practice in accounting for environmental transactions and events in the financial statements and associated notes.[290] The guidance document urges financial statements to recognise environmental costs,[291] and to measure environmental liabilities,[292] and recommends methods

---

[285] *Ibid.*, 5.*Ibid.*, 5.   [286] *Ibid.*, 6.   [287] *Ibid.*, 6–7.   [288] *Ibid.*

[289] *Ibid.*; on potential future developments in the law of liability for environmental damage, see chapter 18, pp. 938–9 below.

[290] ISAR, *Accounting and Financial Reporting for Environmental Costs and Liabilities* (1998), para. 2.

[291] Defined as 'the costs of steps taken, or required to be taken, to manage the environmental impacts of an enterprise's activity in an environmentally responsible manner, as well as other costs driven by the environmental objectives and requirements of the enterprise': para. 9.

[292] Defined as 'obligations relating to environmental costs that are incurred by an enterprise and that meet the criteria for recognition as a liability. When the amount or timing of the expenditure that will be incurred to settle the liability is uncertain, "environmental liabilities" are referred to as "provisions for environmental liabilities"': *ibid.*

for recognising, measuring and disclosing environmental costs.[293] In association with UNCTAD, ISAR is expected next to develop guidance on integrating 'environmental performance indicators' into traditional financial reports.[294]

Environmental auditing

International legal developments on environmental auditing, which is a necessary component of environmental accounting, began with the adoption in April 1993 of the EC Regulation, revised in 2001. Multilateral development banks, led by the EBRD, have conducted environmental audits on certain projects as part of a screening process to determine their potential liability, as well as that of project sponsors, for environmental damage related to loans, and to enhance environmental management of the facility.[295]

The EC's eco-management and audit scheme (EMAS) is intended to improve the environmental performance of companies' industrial activities. The scheme encourages companies to: implement environmental policies, programmes and management systems in relation to their sites; evaluate their environmental performance; provide information on environmental performance to the public; and encourage employee participation within the management system.[296] The scheme, which is without prejudice to EC or national environmental laws or standards, allows organisations to participate voluntarily by registering with the scheme.[297] For an organisation to be registered, it must first conduct an environmental review of its activities, products and services, and, in light of that review, implement an environmental management system.[298] The organisation must also: carry out an environmental audit in accordance with Annex II; prepare an environmental statement in accordance with Annex III; have the environmental review, management system, audit procedure, and environmental statement reviewed and validated by an environmental verifier to meet the requirements of Annex III; and submit the validated environmental statement

---

[293] *Ibid.*, Part V, paras. 11–20; Part VI, paras. 21–9; Part VIII, paras. 34–42; Part IX, paras. 43–61.

[294] Additionally, UN foundation partnership organisations, such as the Global Reporting Initiative and the Global Compact, have also called for revisions to financial disclosure to take into account all aspects of sustainable development. These 'triple bottom line' reports would take into account the economic, environmental and social costs of an enterprise's activities.

[295] 3 *Yearbook of International Environmental Law* 545 (1992).

[296] Council Regulation (EC) No. 761/2001, OJ L114, 19 March 2001, 1, Art. 1(a)–(d).

[297] Art. 3(1) and (2). Art 2(s) defines an organisation as any company, corporation, firm, enterprise, authority or institution, or part or combination thereof, whether incorporated or not, public or private, that has its own functions and administrations. Organisations cannot exceed the boundary of a member state or be smaller than a site.

[298] Art. 2(2)(a), Annex I, Annex VI and Annex VII. Organisations that have an approved, certified environmental management system do not have to repeat the process when applying for EMAS certification: Arts. 2(2)(a) and 9.

to the competent body of a member state and, after registration, make the environmental statement publicly available.[299]

An organisation will be registered by a national body after a validated environmental statement and a completed form including the minimum information required by Annex VIII have been received, a registration fee paid, and the competent body is satisfied that the organisation is in compliance with all environmental legislation and requirements of the Regulation.[300] Under certain conditions, registration may be refused or suspended or deleted from the register. The environmental management system requirements chosen by the Regulation are those set forth in ISO 14001.[301]

Conclusions

There now exists an extensive body of international rules aiming to improve the availability of environmental information, broadly recognised as a central technique for the implementation of environmental standards and procedures set by treaties and other international agreements. The original reporting, consultation and notification obligations which are well established in international law have been supplemented by a second generation of rules. These aim to increase the public availability of information by enhancing access, encouraging greater dissemination to consumers at various levels and, in a more limited fashion, imposing a positive obligation on certain states (in the ECE region) to collect, report on and publish environmental information. Existing arrangements remain incomplete, however, and there are significant gaps within and across regions. The overall objective remains an increase in the quantity and quality of information available, greater dissemination among all relevant members of the international community, and ensuring that it is used to inform decision-making at all national and international levels. To that end, a number of tasks appear particularly important.

First, international co-operation on the gathering of information on the state of the environment needs to be further enhanced. New arrangements such as those reflected in the clearing-house and information exchange mechanisms

---

[299] Art. 2(2)(b)–(e). Under Annex III (Point 3.2), the environmental statement must: describe the organisation, its activities, products and services and relationship to any parent organisations; describe its environmental policy and environmental management system; describe and explain all significant environmental impacts of the organisation; describe the environmental objectives and targets in relation to the significant environmental impacts; and provide data on the performance of the organisation against its environmental objectives and targets.

[300] Art. 6(1).

[301] ISO standards represent a consensus agreement of manufacturers, vendors and users, consumer groups, testing laboratories, governments, engineering professions and research organisations. By the end of 2001, nearly 37,000 ISO 14001 certificates had been issued in 112 countries.

set up under the 2000 Biosafety Protocol and the 1997 Kyoto Protocol could be developed in other subject matter areas.

Secondly, compliance with basic reporting requirements under environmental treaties remains inadequate and should be improved, including by establishing arrangements for composite reports fulfilling obligations under two or more conventions: if states are unable or unwilling to fulfil these primary obligations then it is unlikely that they will comply with the more onerous and important substantive standards established by the same treaties. Clearly, the collection of national information necessary to fulfil international reporting obligations can place heavy burdens on limited and already over-stretched human, institutional and financial resources. The availability of financial resources for reporting under agreements such as the Climate Change and Biodiversity Conventions have gone some way towards improving compliance with reporting requirements, but these need to be coupled with education and training, and an enhanced role for international organisations in assisting with reporting.

Thirdly, the general obligation in international law to consult and notify certain potentially harmful activities – now reflected in the ILC's 2001 draft Articles on Prevention of Transboundary Harm – has broad support, but is not always complied with. Incidents such as the Chernobyl accident and the cyanide spillage (Baia Mare) in the Tisa River basin involving Hungary and Romania reflect the need for constant vigilance where emergency situations occur.

Fourthly, the duty of states to provide – and the right of legal and natural persons to receive – environmental information is more broadly recognised but requires further development in practice, not least by making citizens aware of their rights. The 1998 Aarhus Convention is an important development beyond the EC, and could provide a model for other regions. EC experience suggests that the demand for environmental information increases as citizens become aware of their rights, and that the processing of requests places significant demands on public authorities which encourages them to find ways to avoid providing information. Accordingly, it will be necessary to ensure that the access to justice provisions of the Aarhus Convention are properly implemented and that other effective means of administrative or judicial redress are available at the national or international level to ensure that states fulfil their obligations.

18

Liability for environmental damage

Introduction

General principles of international law imposing liability on actors for their illegal acts, or for the adverse consequences of their lawful activities, are relatively well developed at a general level, and are now reflected in the Articles on State Responsibility adopted by the ILC in 2001.[1] In relation to environmental damage, however, the liability rules are still evolving and in need of further development. Environmental damage refers here to damage to the environment, which has been defined in treaties and other international acts to include four possible elements: (1) fauna, flora, soil, water and climatic factors; (2) material assets (including archaeological and cultural heritage); (3) the landscape and environmental amenity; and (4) the interrelationship between the above factors.[2] Most legal definitions of environment do not, therefore, include people and their property.

Liability rules at the domestic or international level serve a variety of purposes. They may be a form of economic instrument which provides an incentive to encourage compliance with environmental obligations.[3] They may also be used to impose sanctions for wrongful conduct, or to require corrective measures to restore a given environmental asset to its pre-damage condition. Finally, they may provide a technique for internalising environmental and other social costs into production processes and other activities in implementation of the polluter-pays principle.[4]

This chapter follows the distinction which has been drawn in practice between the liability of states and other international persons under public international law, and the liability of actors (which could include states) under rules of national law adopted pursuant to treaties which aim to harmonise national civil liability rules, or set minimum standards. State liability refers here to the liability of international persons under the operation of rules of international

---

[1] Report of the ILC, UN Doc. A/56/10 (2001).
[2] Chapter 1, pp. 15–18 above.
[3] See in this regard C. Murgatroyd, 'The World Bank: A Case for Lender Liability', 1 RECIEL 436 (1992).
[4] Chapter 6, pp. 279–85 above.

law of state responsibility. Civil liability refers to the liability of any legal or natural person under the rules of national law adopted pursuant to international treaty obligations establishing harmonised minimum standards. However, the distinction between state and civil liability is becoming increasingly difficult to draw, as treaties and other international acts have established an obligation for the state to provide public funds where an operator cannot meet certain costs of environmental damage.[5]

States have long recognised the role of liability for environmental damage, as well as the gaps and inadequacies which exist. Principle 22 of the Stockholm Declaration recognised gaps and called on states to 'co-operate to develop further the international law regarding liability and compensation for victims of pollution and other environmental damage caused by activities within the jurisdiction or control of such states to areas beyond their jurisdiction'. The 1982 World Charter for Nature did not directly address liability, although it called for degraded areas to be rehabilitated and for individuals to have access to means of redress when 'their environment has suffered damage or degradation'.[6] The Rio Declaration reflects the limited progress which has been made since 1972. It emphasises the development of national rules in addition to the further development of international rules for all adverse effects of environmental damage including, implicitly, liability for damage to the environment itself. Principle 13 of the Rio Declaration provides that:

> states shall develop national law regarding liability and compensation for the victims of pollution and other environmental damage. States shall also co-operate in an expeditious and more determined manner to develop further international law regarding liability and compensation for adverse effects of environmental damage caused by activities within their jurisdiction or control to areas beyond their jurisdiction.

The shift in emphasis in the Rio Declaration reflects an unwillingness to establish rules of international law which might impose excessive costs. This was also evident following the Chernobyl accident in 1986, following which no claims were made although it provided a relatively clear-cut case on which an international liability claim could be made. That episode illustrated the inertia which has limited developments since 1972 in the development of state liability rules for environmental damage, although a significant number of treaties have been, or are being, developed which establish international civil liability rules, as considered below. Other treaties commit their parties to develop rules

---

[5] See 1960 Paris Convention and 1963 Brussels Supplementary Convention, pp. 906–8 below; 1988 CRAMRA, pp. 900 and 931 below; and the 2001 ILC Articles on State Responsibility, pp. 901–4 below. See also the 2002 proposed EC Directive, p. 926 below.

[6] Paras. 11(c) and 23.

on liability or responsibility,[7] or support international efforts.[8] For state and civil liability, international rules address certain substantive and procedural elements which determine the nature and extent of the liability. The common issues which emerge are:

- whether to designate environmental damage as a distinct head of damage (separate from personal injury and property damage);
- defining environmental damage;
- establishing the standard of care (absolute, strict or fault);
- establishing the measure of damages;
- identifying the person or persons against whom the claim should be brought;
- determining who may bring a claim;
- designating the forum or fora before which claims may be brought;
- determining the remedies which are available; and
- providing for the availability of certain defences.

Many similarities exist among the various instruments, although each of the civil liability regimes sets its own rules in relation to each of these and other issues. The same is true of state liability rules adopted by treaty. In respect of such rules as exist under customary or general international law it will be seen that, in the context of very limited state practice, defining the parameters of each aspect of state liability is not an easy task.

State liability

L. F. E. Goldie, 'Liability for Damage and the Progressive Development of International Law', 14 ICLQ 1189 (1965); W. Jenks, 'Liability for Ultra-Hazardous Activities in International Law', 117 RdC 99 (1966-I); L. F. E. Goldie, 'International Principles of Responsibility for Pollution', 9 *Columbia Journal of Transnational Law* 283 (1970); J. M. Kelson, 'State Responsibility and the Abnormally Dangerous Activity', 13 *Harvard International Law Journal* 197 (1972); K. R. Hoffman, 'State Responsibility in International Law and Transboundary Pollution Injuries', 25 ICLQ 509 (1976); P.-M. Dupuy, 'International Liability of States for Damage Caused by Transfrontier Pollution', in OECD, *Legal Aspects of Transfrontier Pollution* (1977), 345; UNEP, 'Report of the Group of Experts on Liability for Pollution and Other Environmental Damage and Compensation for Such Damage', Doc. UNEP/WG.8/3 (1977); OECD, *Responsibilities and Liability of States in Re-*

---

[7] 1972 London Convention, Art. X; 1978 Kuwait Convention, Art. XIII (civil); 1982 UNCLOS, Art. 235(3); 1982 Jeddah Convention, Art. XIII (civil liability); 1983 Cartagena de Indias Convention, Art. 14; 1986 Noumea Convention, Art. 20; 1992 Baltic Convention, Art. 25; 1996 Protocol to the London Convention, Art. 15; 2000 Biosafety Protocol, Art. 27; 2001 POPs Convention, Art. 17.

[8] 1992 Watercourses Convention, Art. 7; 1992 Industrial Accidents Convention, Art. 13.

lation to Transfrontier Pollution (1979); R. C. d'Arge and A. V. Kneese, 'State Liability for International Environmental Degradation: An Economic Perspective', 20 *Natural Resources Journal* 427 (1980); G. Handl, 'State Liability for Accidental Transnational Environmental Damage by Private Persons', 74 AJIL 525 (1980); P. Ballantyne, 'International Liability for Acid Rain', 41 *University of Toronto Faculty Law Review* 63 (1983); I. Brownlie, *System of the Law of Nations: State Responsibility* (1983); OECD, Report by the Environment Committee on 'Responsibility and Liability of States in Relation to Transfrontier Pollution' (1984); P. Allott, 'State Responsibility and the Unmaking of International Law', 29 *Harvard International Law Journal* 1 (1988); G. Doeker and T. Gehring, 'Private or International Liability for Transnational Environmental Damage – The Precedent of Conventional Liability Regimes', 2 JEL 1 (1990); F. Francioni and T. Scovazzi (eds.), *International Responsibility for Environmental Harm* (1991); A. Rosas, 'Issues of State Liability for Transboundary Environmental Damage', 60 *Nordic Journal of International Law* 5 (1991); K. Zemanek, 'State Responsibility and Liability', in K. Neuhold, W. Lang and K. Zemanek (eds.), *Environmental Protection and International Law* (1991), 187; A. Rest, 'Ecological Damage in Public International Law, 22 *Environmental Policy and Law* 31 (1992); R. Lefeber, *Transboundary Environmental Interference and the Origin of State Liability* (1996); 'Environmental Damage' 5 RECIEL (issue 4) (1996); P. Wetterstein (ed.), *Harm to the Environment* (1997); T. Vaissiere, 'L'Ethique de résponsabilité chez Hans Jonas a l'épreuve du droit international de l'environnement', *Revue Interdisciplinaire d'Etudes Juridiques* 135 (1999); E. Brans, *Liability for Damage to Public Natural Resources* (2001); M. Bowman and A. Boyle (eds.), *Environmental Damage in International and Comparative Law* (2002); J. Crawford, *The ILC's Articles on State Responsibility* (2002).

Introduction

It is a well established principle of international law, recognised in Article 1 of the ILC Articles on the Responsibility of States for Internationally Wrongful Acts (2001), that every internationally wrongful act of a state entails the international responsibility of that state.[9] The same principle applies to other international persons, including international organisations. A state responsible for an internationally wrongful act is under an obligation to cease that act, if it is continuing, and to offer appropriate assurances and guarantees of non-repetition if the circumstances so require, and to make full reparation for

---

[9] See n. 1 above; for background, see J. Crawford, First Report on State Responsibility, UN Doc. A/CN.4/490 and Add.1–7 (1998); Second Report, UN Doc. A/CN.4/498 and Add.1–4 (1999); Third Report, UN Doc. A/CN.4/507 and Add.1–4 (2000); and Fourth Report, UN Doc. A/CN.4/517 (2001). See generally J. Crawford, *The ILC's Articles on State Responsibility: Introduction, Text and Commentaries* (2002).

the injury caused by the internationally wrongful act.[10] The obligation to make reparation – sometimes referred to as a liability[11] – is well established. As the PCIJ stated as early as 1928 in the *Chorzow Factory* case,

> it is a principle of international law, and even a general conception of law, that any breach of an engagement involves an obligation to make reparation. In Judgment No. 8 (1927) (PCIJ, Ser. A, No. 9, 21) . . . the Court had already said that reparation was the indispensable complement of a failure to apply a convention, and there is no necessity for this to be stated in the convention itself.[12]

The approach has been affirmed – in the environmental context – by the ICJ in the *Case Concerning the Gabcikovo-Nagymaros Project*.[13] The operation of these principles refers to rules of state responsibility and liability, although the term 'state responsibility' is perhaps misleading as it emerged at a time when states alone were considered as subjects of international law. To the extent that international organisations and other legal and natural persons may also be subjects of international law, the concept of 'state responsibility' may also inform the principle of the liability of other international persons under the rules of public international law.[14]

In the environmental field, no single instrument sets forth the generally applicable international rules governing responsibility and liability. The ILC's Articles on State Responsibility bring together the rules of general international law, and they are applicable (to the extent they reflect customary law) with environmental rules established by treaties and other internationally applicable rules.

A number of non-binding instruments adopted in the environmental field have sought also to restate general principles. Principle 12 of the 1978 UNEP draft Principles affirms that states are responsible for the fulfilment of their international environmental obligations relating to the utilisation of shared natural resources, and that they 'are subject to liability in accordance with

---

[10] *Ibid.*, Arts. 30 and 31.

[11] The term 'liability' in international law has been described in a number of ways. For Dupuy and Smets, it means the 'international obligation to compensate': P. M. Dupuy and H. Smets 'Compensation for Damage Due to Transfrontier Pollution', in OECD, *Compensation for Pollution Damage* (1981), 182. For Goldie, the meaning is wider in that it designates more generally 'the consequences of a failure to perform [a] duty, or to fulfil the standards of performance required. That is, liability connotes exposure to legal redress once responsibility and injury arising from a failure to fulfil that legal responsibility have been established': L. F. E. Goldie 'Concepts of Strict and Absolute Liability and the Ranking of Liability in Terms of Relative Exposure to Risk', 16 *Netherlands Yearbook of International Law* 175 at 180 (1985).

[12] (1928) PCIJ, Ser. A, No. 17, at 47.   [13] (1997) ICJ Reports 226, paras. 149 *et seq.*

[14] The ILC is separately considering the responsibility of international organisations.

applicable international law for environmental damage resulting from violations of these obligations caused to areas beyond their jurisdiction'.[15] The WCED Legal Principles Group states that:

> [i]f one or more activities create a significant risk of substantial harm as a result of a transboundary environmental interference, and if the overall technical and socio-economic cost or loss of benefits involved in preventing or reducing such risks far exceeds in the long run the advantage which such prevention or reduction would entail . . . the state which carried out or permitted the activities shall ensure that compensation is provided should substantial harm occur in an area under national jurisdiction of another state or in an area beyond the limits of national jurisdiction.[16]

The Institut de Droit International (IDI) has made a singular contribution to this subject. Its 1987 resolution on transboundary air pollution recognised that 'states incur responsibility under international law for any breach of their international obligations with respect to transboundary air pollution', and calls on states to conclude international treaties and enact laws and regulations to ensure an effective system of prevention and compensation for victims of transboundary air pollution.[17] In 1997, the IDI unanimously adopted a resolution on responsibility and liability under international law for environmental damage, which seeks to 'identify, harmonize and to the necessary extent develop the principles of international law applicable to responsibility and liability in the context of environmental damage'.[18] The resolution affirms that 'the breach of an obligation of environmental protection established under international law engages responsibility of the State . . . entailing as a consequence the obligation to reestablish the original position or to pay compensation', the latter obligation also being capable of arising from a rule of international law providing for strict liability on the basis of harm or injury alone.[19]

General international law

State liability for environmental damage is premised upon a breach of an international legal obligation established by treaty, or by a rule of customary international law, or possibly under general principles of international law. Article 2 of the ILC Articles on State Responsibility states:

---

[15] Principle 12 calls on states to 'co-operate to develop further international law regarding liability and compensation for the victims of environmental damage arising out of utilisation of a shared natural resource and caused to areas beyond their jurisdiction'.

[16] Art. 11; Art. 11(2) provides that states 'shall ensure that compensation is provided for substantial harm caused by transboundary environmental interferences resulting from activities carried out or permitted by that state notwithstanding that the activities were not initially known to cause such interferences'.

[17] Arts. 6 and 7.   [18] 4 September 1997, 37 ILM 1473 (1998).   [19] Art. 1.

> There is an internationally wrongful act of a State when conduct consisting
> of an act or omission:
> (a) is attributable to the State under international law; and
> (b) constitutes a breach of an international obligation of the State.

The ILC Articles on State Responsibility elaborate on the circumstances in which an act or omission will be attributable to a state,[20] and indicate the circumstances in which a breach of an obligation will have occurred and that the state must be bound by the obligation in question 'at the time that act occurs'.[21] They elaborate on the conditions which must be satisfied for one state to incur responsibility in connection with the acts of another state, for example where one state aids or assists another in the commission of an internationally wrongful act.[22] And they indicate the circumstances in which wrongfulness may be precluded, including where a state invokes necessity to justify an action to safeguard an essential interest against a grave and imminent peril.[23]

For present purposes, the most pertinent international obligation is that requiring a state to prevent particular environmental harm, or to refrain from carrying out or permitting activities which could lead to environmental damage. As discussed in chapter 6 above, the ICJ has affirmed that customary international law establishes an obligation to respect the environment of other states or of areas beyond national jurisdiction.[24] To a large extent discussions of state liability are likely to be concerned with the consequences of a breach of this obligation, which encompasses the obligation not to cause significant harm. But responsibility and liability also arise in relation to other substantive obligations, as well as procedural requirements pertaining, for example, to access to information and the duty to carry out an environmental impact assessment. Additionally, some regimes (for example, the WTO system) establish their own

---

[20] Chapter II of the ILC's Articles (Arts. 4–11).

[21] Chapter III, Arts. 12 and 13. See also Arts. 14 (on breaches of a continuing character) and 15 (composite acts).

[22] Chapter IV, in particular Art. 16 (providing *inter alia* for the international responsibility where aid or assistance is provided with knowledge of the circumstances of an internationally wrongful act). This confirms that a state (or international organisation) may be internationally responsible if it provides financial support – for example in the form of an export credit guarantee or insurance – in relation to the construction of a project the operation of which might, for example, contribute to a breach of an obligation relating to the equitable use of an international watercourse.

[23] Chapter V, in particular Art. 25 (in the *Gabcikovo-Nagymaros* case, the ICJ confirmed that a state of ecological necessity may be invoked to preclude wrongfulness; see chapter 10, pp. 469–77 above). The other circumstances in which wrongfulness may be precluded are consent (Art. 20), self-defence (Art. 21), countermeasures (Art. 22), *force majeure* (Art. 23), distress (Art. 24) and compliance with a peremptory norm (Art. 26).

[24] Chapter 6, pp. 237–41 above.

rules and remedies governing the consequences of a failure to comply with the obligations there established.[25]

With regard to the obligation to prevent environmental damage, general international law requires at least four related issues to be addressed: is the obligation aiming to prevent any transboundary environmental damage, or only transboundary environmental damage which has serious, or significant, or appreciable consequences? Is the obligation based upon the need to prove fault or is it imposed by operation of absolute or strict liability? What reparation should be made for environmental damage? And what is the extent of liability and the measure of damages? Other legal requirements would need to be satisfied to bring an international claim, including (as appropriate) the exhaustion of local remedies rule, the nationality of claims rule, any rules governing limitation on the time within which a claim can be brought, and the rules governing attribution of state responsibility for the acts of public bodies and private persons.[26] In respect of these and other questions, state practice, case law, treaties and the writings of jurists do not provide conclusive answers. Each case must be judged on its own merits.

Defining environmental damage

Defining environmental damage remains a complex issue. Two related issues need to be distinguished: what constitutes environmental damage? And what level of environmental damage might give rise to liability?

In defining environmental damage, treaties and state practice reflect various approaches. A narrow definition of environmental damage is limited to damage to natural resources alone (air, water, soil, fauna and flora, and their interaction); a more extensive approach includes damage to natural resources *and* property which forms part of the cultural heritage; the most extensive definition includes landscape and environmental amenity. On each approach, environmental damage does not include damage to persons or damage to property, although such damage can be consequential to environmental damage. Loss of environmental amenity, which may be included under the provisions of the 1993 Council of Europe Convention on Liability for Environmental Damage (1993 Lugano Convention) referring to the 'characteristic aspects of the landscape', could be treated as environmental damage or damage to property, depending on the definition of the latter. Environmental damage has been defined in instruments establishing civil liability, particularly in relation to oil pollution.[27] In respect of state liability the only treaty definition is provided by the 1988 CRAMRA, which defines damage to the Antarctic environment or ecosystem very broadly, to include:

---

[25] Chapter 19, p. 947 below. See P. Mavroides, 'Remedies in the WTO Legal System: Between a Rock and a Hard Place', 11 *European Journal of International Law* 763 (2000).

[26] See generally *Oppenheim*, vol. I, Pt I, 511–27 and 540–54.

[27] See pp. 912–23 below; and the 2002 EC draft Directive, at p. 926 below.

any impact on the living or non-living components of that environment or those ecosystems, including harm to atmospheric, marine or terrestrial life, beyond that which is negligible or which has been assessed and judged to be acceptable pursuant to [the] Convention.[28]

The concept of 'pollution', which is defined in the 1979 LRTAP Convention, the 1982 UNCLOS and elsewhere, provides some assistance but cannot be used interchangeably with 'environmental damage'. 'Air pollution' in the 1979 LRTAP Convention is defined by reference to deleterious effects (which are themselves undefined) on living resources and ecosystems, human health and material property, as well as interference with amenities and other legitimate uses of the environment.[29] The distinction between environmental damage (and compensable environmental damage) and pollution is illustrated by the 1993 Lugano Convention which provides that an operator of a dangerous activity will not be liable for damage (impairment of the environment) caused by pollution at 'tolerable' levels under local relevant circumstances.[30] Other treaties require 'adverse effects', rather than pollution, to define the consequences of activities which are to be avoided. Like pollution, the term 'adverse effects' provides some assistance in establishing a basis for, but cannot be used interchangeably with, a general definition of environmental damage. The 1985 Vienna Convention defines 'adverse effects' in relation to ozone depletion as, *inter alia*, 'changes in the physical environment or biota, including changes in climate, which have significant deleterious effects on human health or on the composition, resilience and productivity of natural and managed ecosystems, or on materials useful to mankind'.[31] The 1992 Climate Change Convention introduces a similar definition, although it reverses the order by placing deleterious effects on the environment before effects on human health, and extends the definition to include effects on socio-economic systems and human welfare.[32] Thus, 'pollution' and 'adverse effects' help in determining the threshold beyond which environmental damage might trigger liability, but they do not actually define it.

Other state practice is limited. Environmental damage in the pure sense was not considered by the arbitral tribunal in the *Trail Smelter* case, although the *Lac Lanoux Arbitration* implicitly recognised the possibility of pure environmental damage when it referred to changes in the composition, temperature or other characteristics of the waters of the River Carol which injured Spanish interests.[33] Treating environmental damage as a separate head was recognised in the claims by Australia and New Zealand in the *Nuclear Tests* cases, and by Nauru in the *Case Concerning Certain Phosphate Lands in Nauru*. It has been recognised – implicitly – by the ICJ in the *Case Concerning the Gabcikovo-Nagymaros*

---

[28] Art. 1(15).   [29] Art. 1(a); see also 1982 UNCLOS, Art. 1(4).
[30] See pp. 933–7 below.   [31] Art. 1(2).   [32] Art. 1(1).
[33] See chapter 10, pp. 463–4 above.

Project.[34] Clear support for the provision of compensation for environmental damage under rules of state liability was provided by the UN Security Council in 1991 when it reaffirmed that Iraq was 'liable under international law for any direct loss, damage, including environmental damage and the depletion of natural resources, or injury to foreign Governments, nationals and corporations' occurring as a result of its unlawful invasion and occupation of Kuwait.[35] UN Security Council Resolution 687, which is binding on the world, unequivocally determines that a state can be liable for the environmental damage and depletion of natural resources which result from unlawful use of force. Resolution 687 does not, however, define environmental damage or depletion of natural resources, or provide guidance to the Compensation Commission on their assessment, or the measure, of reparation or compensation.[36] The practice of the Claims Commission in defining environmental damage could provide assistance to other international bodies, including courts and tribunals, which may be required to deal with this issue in the future.

Threshold at which environmental damage entails liability

Whilst all pollution or human activity having adverse effects might give rise to environmental damage, it is unlikely that all environmental damage results in state liability. There are no agreed international standards which establish a threshold for environmental damage which triggers liability and allows claims to be brought. State practice, decisions of international tribunals and the writings of jurists suggest that environmental damage must be 'significant' or 'substantial' (or possibly 'appreciable', which suggests a marginally less onerous threshold) for liability to be triggered.

A 1993 EC Commission Green Paper on Environmental Liability identified several possibilities for determining the level of environmental damage triggering liability. These include defining environmental damage by reference to 'critical loads', which describe the point at which a pollutant becomes concentrated in the environment at a level which cannot be diluted or broken down by natural processes;[37] or by reference to environmental indicators and environmental accounting to measure environmental performance, pressures and

---

[34] (1997) ICJ Reports 226, at para 152 ('Hungary is entitled to compensation for the damage sustained as a result of the diversion of the Danube, since Czechoslovakia, by putting into operation Variant C, and Slovakia, in maintaining it in service, deprived Hungary of its rightful part in the shared water resources, and exploited those resources essentially for their own benefit').

[35] Security Council Res. 687 (1991); see pp. 890–4 below.

[36] See p. 893 below; and UNEP, *Report of the Working Group of Experts on Liability and Compensation for Environmental Damage Arising from Military Activities* (1996). See also chapter 7, p. 315 above.

[37] COM (93) 47, 17 March 1993, at e.g. chapter 8; see also 1992 Climate Change Convention, Art. 2 (stabilisation of greenhouse gas concentrations); 1985 SO_2 Protocol, Art. 2; and 1991 VOC Protocol, Art. 2 (critical levels).

conditions;[38] or by reference to existing international legislation which establishes quality standards for flora and fauna, water and air quality and which might be considered to establish a threshold for environmental damage above which a person responsible for the increase would be considered liable for the consequences. International instruments which set environmental quality standards, or product, emissions or process standards, may also provide some guidance as to the level of environmental damage considered to be tolerable or acceptable by the international community.

Some guidance may also be found in the exchange between the then President of the ICJ, Sir Humphrey Waldock, and the Government of Australia in the *Nuclear Tests* case, reflecting a view that not every transmission of chemical or other matter into another state's territory, or into the global commons, will create a legal cause of action in international law.[39] The tribunal in the *Trail Smelter* case held that the injury must have a 'serious consequence' to justify a claim.[40] In its claim against Australia, Nauru argued for general principle based upon an obligation not to bring about changes in the condition of territory which will cause 'irreparable damage to, or substantially prejudice' the legal interest of another state.[41] A similar approach underlies Hungary's Original Application in the *Case Concerning the Gabcikovo-Nagymaros Project*.[42] The Canadian claim following the crash of Cosmos 954 was brought in the context of damage to land which made it 'unfit for use', a level of damage which supports the view that the impact on the environment must be more than nominal to establish a claim.[43] A number of the civil liability instruments discussed below establish thresholds for environmental damage or adverse effects which are 'significant',[44] or 'serious',[45] or above 'tolerable levels',[46] and the ILA Montreal Rules call on states to prevent 'substantial injury'.[47]

Establishing the appropriate threshold turns on the facts of each case, and may vary according to local or regional circumstances. The limited state practice supports the view that the threshold to be crossed may still be established at a relatively high level of environmental damage. The difficulty of agreeing a threshold is illustrated by the Chernobyl accident, which raised numerous issues over what constituted harmful levels of radioactivity in the absence of legally binding international standards. Several international guidelines establish radiation dose limits for the whole human body or for specific organs or tissues. The EC Commission had published recommendations on dose levels as guidelines for national authorities in setting specific levels at which products might be

---

[38] OECD Council Recommendation, Environmental Indicators and Information, C(90)165/final (1991).

[39] Chapter 8, pp. 319–21 above. [40] Chapter 8, pp. 318–19 above.

[41] Chapter 12, pp. 666–9 above. [42] Chapter 10, pp. 469–77 above.

[43] See pp. 897–8 below. [44] 1992 Watercourses Convention, Art. 1(2).

[45] 1992 Industrial Accidents Convention, Art. 1(d).

[46] 1993 Lugano Convention, Art. 8(d). [47] Art. 3(1).

deemed unsafe (intervention levels),[48] and similar guidelines had also been prepared by the International Commission on Radiological Protection (ICRP),[49]
the WHO,[50] the IAEA,[51] and UNSCEAR. At the time of the Chernobyl accident,
little consideration had been given to the control of foodstuffs contaminated
by an accidental release of radioactivity, and national authorities set their own
intervention levels according to a range of different standards,[52] which led to
disputes on the permissibility of intervention measures which affected international trade. The EC Commission initially suspended the import of certain
agricultural products from central and eastern Europe, and then laid down the
maximum permitted level of radioactivity for products originating from these
countries.[53] Individual EC member states adopted their own intervention levels
which were used as the basis for undertaking national compensation to affected
farmers and other businesses.[54]

The absence of generally accepted standards on safe levels of radioactivity
made it difficult to assess whether these measures were justified, and resulted
in confusion, concern and public suspicion, as well as constraints on international food trade.[55] The FAO subsequently proposed 'Interim International
Radionuclide Action Levels for Food' (IRALFs) to cover food being traded
internationally, which, while non-binding and *ex post facto*, provided a useful standard for assessing whether the increases in radioactivity caused by the
Chernobyl accident were harmful to foodstuffs and whether intervention levels
were justified under international law.[56]

Liability can be closely related to the adoption of regulatory standards. As
the international community adopts such standards, the task of identifying the
level of compensable environmental damage will become easier. In the absence

---

[48] Radiological Protection Criteria for Controlling Doses to the Public in the Event of Accidental Releases of Radioactive Material, A Guide on Emergency Reference Levels of Dose
from the Group of Experts Convened under Article 41 of the EURATOM Treaty (1982).

[49] 'Protection of the Public in the Event of Major Radiation Accidents: Principles for Planning',
40 *Annals of the ICRP*, No. 2, 5–7 and 12–14 (1984).

[50] Nuclear Power: Principles of Public Health Actions for Accidental Releases (1984).

[51] Principles for Establishing Intervention Levels for the Protection of the Public in the Event
of a Nuclear Accident or Radiological Emergency (IAEA Safety Series No. 72, 1985).

[52] See FAO, 'Report of the Expert Consultation on Recommended Limits for Radionuclide
Contamination of Foods' (1987), Table II, for examples of varying post-Chernobyl 'action
levels' applied by some countries for certain radionuclides (in terms of becquerels per
kilogram or litre (bq/kg or bq/l) in imported foods, as at December 1986.

[53] Council Regulation (EEC) No. 86/1707, OJ L146, 31 May 1986, 88; the Regulation was
extended.

[54] West Germany, Equity Guideline, *Bundesanzeiger* of 27 May 1986, No. 95, p. 6417; United
Kingdom, Food Protection (Emergency Prohibitions) (England) Order 1986 (SI 1986
No. 1411).

[55] FAO Report, n. 52 above, 3.

[56] The IRALF for Iodine-131 was set at 400 bq/kg; the EC imposed import restrictions on
milk of 500 bq/kg and on vegetables of 350 bq/kg.

of international standards concerning the quality of the environment, including conservation of flora and fauna, states will set their own standards, resulting in divergences with resulting economic and environmental consequences.

Standard of care

If there is an obligation to prevent significant, substantial or serious environmental damage, what is the standard of care applicable to that obligation? Options include fault (based upon intention or negligence), strict liability ('essentially a *prima facie* responsibility, and various qualifications or defences may be available')[57] and absolute liability ('for which there can be no mode of exculpation').[58] Although this question has received considerable attention from writers,[59] it is reasonable to conclude that there 'is probably no single basis of international responsibility, applicable in all circumstances, but rather several, the nature of which depends on the particular obligation in question'.[60] The obligation in question may distinguish between ultra-hazardous activities and other activities.[61] This approach can be justified on policy grounds: dangerous activities are more likely to cause serious environmental damage, and a strict or absolute obligation is more likely to provide an incentive to states to adopt special precautions when engaging in or permitting such activities.

International law remains inconclusive on general rules governing the standard of care to be shown in fulfilling international environmental obligations. Principle 21 of the Stockholm Declaration and Principles 2 and 13 of the Rio Declaration do not provide guidance either way, and the decisions of international tribunals in the *Trail Smelter* case, the *Corfu Channel* case, the *Lac Lanoux* case and the *Nuclear Tests* cases can be interpreted to support conclusions of absolute/strict liability or fault-based liability. In respect of ultra-hazardous activities, certain treaties do support a standard of absolute or strict, liability. The 1972 Space Liability Convention supports absolute liability,[62] and, in reliance on this provision and general principles of international law, following the Cosmos 954 accident Canada claimed that 'the principle of absolute liability applies to fields of activity having in common a high degree of risk . . . [and] has been accepted as a general principle of international law'.[63] The 1988 CRAMRA also supports liability without the need to prove fault.[64]

Strict liability for ultra-hazardous activities might also be considered a general principle of law as it is to be found in the national law of many states in

---

[57] I. Brownlie, *System of the Law of Nations*, Part 1, *State Responsibility*, 44 (1983).

[58] *Ibid.*; see L. F. E. Goldie, 'Concepts of Strict and Absolute Liability and the Ranking of Liability in Terms of Relative Exposure to Risk', 16 *Netherlands Yearbook of International Law* 175 (1985).

[59] See the discussion by Brownlie, n. 57 above, 40–6 and the literature there cited.

[60] Oppenheim, vol. I, 509.

[61] On 'ultra-hazardous' and 'dangerous' activities see chapter 12 generally.

[62] Art. II.   [63] 18 ILM 907 (1992).   [64] Art. 8.

relation to ultra-hazardous activities.[65] Under English law, 'a person who for his own purposes brings on his land and collects and keeps there anything likely to do mischief if it escapes, must keep it in at his peril, and, if he does not do so, is *prima facie* answerable for all the damage which is the natural consequence of its escape'.[66] Many civil liability treaties also adopt the principle of strict liability for hazardous activities, including nuclear activities and the carriage of oil by sea, as well as dangerous activities generally.[67] Strict liability is also supported by Jenks, who considered that in relation to nuclear damage the principle of absolute liability 'is generally accepted, but the expression is somewhat misleading in that it does not exclude the possibility of exceptions'.[68] The ILC draft Articles on International Liability for Injurious Consequences Arising Out of Acts Not Prohibited by International Law proposed that a state of origin would be strictly liable for harm to the environment and the resulting harm to property and persons.[69]

For general industrial and other activities which are not ultra-hazardous or dangerous, it is less easy to argue for a standard of care based upon strict or absolute liability. In considering this matter the OECD's Environment Committee has observed that there is a 'custom based rule of *due diligence* imposed on all states in order that activities carried out within their jurisdiction do not cause damage to the environment of other states', which includes establishing and applying an effective system of environmental law and regulations, and principles of consultation and notification.[70]

Reparation

The principle is well established that the perpetrator of an internationally wrongful act is under an obligation to make reparation for the consequences of the violation. As expressed in the judgment of the *Chorzow Factory* case, the PCIJ stated that:

> The essential principle contained in the actual notion of an illegal act – a principle which seems to be established by international practice and in particular by the decisions of arbitral tribunals – is that reparation must, as far as possible, wipe out all the consequences of the illegal act and re-establish the situation which would, in all probability, have existed if that act had not been committed. Restitution in kind, or, if this is not possible, payment of a sum corresponding to the value which a restitution in kind would bear; the award, if need be, of damages for loss sustained which

[65] A. Tunc (ed.), *International Encyclopedia of Comparative Law*, vol. XI, Chapter V.
[66] *Rylands* v. *Fletcher* (1868) LR 3 HL 330.   [67] See below.
[68] W. Jenks, 'The Scope and Nature of Ultra-Hazardous Liability in International Law', 117 RdC 99 at 144 (1966).
[69] See pp. 901–4 below; Arts. 24, 26 and 28.
[70] OECD, Report by the Environment Committee, 'Responsibility and Liability of States in Relation to Transfrontier Pollution' (1984), 4.

would not be covered by restitution in kind or payment in place of it – such are the principles which should serve to determine the amount of compensation due for an act contrary to international law.[71]

The approach is now reflected in the ILC Articles on State Responsibility (2001), which envisage that the reparation for the injury caused by an internationally wrongful act shall take the form of restitution, compensation and satisfaction, either singly or in combination.[72] Restitution is aimed at re-establishing the situation which existed before the wrongful act was committed, provided and to the extent that it is not materially impossible and does 'not involve a burden out of all proportion to the benefit deriving from restitution instead of compensation'.[73] Compensation is to be provided for damage which is not made good by restitution, and should cover 'any financially assessable damage including loss of profits insofar as it is established'.[74] Satisfaction is to be provided if the injury cannot be made good by restitution or compensation, for example by an acknowledgment of the breach, an expression of regret or a formal apology.[75]

In most environmental cases, the victim will be seeking an end to the harmful act, or restitution, or financial compensation to cover the costs associated with material damage to environmental resources (pure environmental damage) and consequential damage to people and property (consequential environmental damage), including restoration or reinstatement.[76] In relation to restitution, it will be necessary to identify the baseline conditions prior to which the damage occurred, which may be difficult. Compensation raises the problem of assessing the measure of environmental damage:[77] should it be by reference to the costs of measures of reinstatement, or on the basis of an abstract quantification calculated in accordance with a theoretical model, or on some other basis? The problem arises because environmental damage does not fit easily with the traditional approaches of civil and state liability which

---

[71] (1927) PCIJ Ser. A, No. 17, at 47.   [72] Part I, Chapter II, Art. 34.

[73] *Ibid.*, Art. 35.   [74] *Ibid.*, Art. 36.

[75] *Ibid.*, Art. 37. In the *Rainbow Warrior* (*New Zealand* v. *France*) case, France was required to give a 'formal and unqualified apology' to New Zealand for the sinking of Greenpeace's vessel in Auckland Harbour, and ordered to pay US$7million in compensation: 82 ILR 500 at 575–7 (1990); 33 AFDI 922–3 (1987) and 34 AFDI 896–8 (1988).

[76] For example, in its Original Application in the *Gabcikovo-Nagymaros Project* case Hungary claimed that Czechoslovakia was under an obligation to 'cease the internationally wrongful act, re-establish the situation which would have existed if the act had not taken place and provide compensation for the harm which resulted from the wrongful act': Hungary, Original Application, 22 October 1992, para. 32. The 1997 IDI Resolution states that '[t]he fact that environmental damage is irreparable or unquantifiable shall not result in exemption from compensation': Art. 29.

[77] See R. Stewart (ed.), *Natural Resource Damages: A Legal, Economic and Policy Analysis* (1995); P. Sands and R. Stewart, 'Valuation of Environmental Damage – US and International Law Approaches', 5 RECIEL 290 (1996).

are designed to compensate an injured person by requiring the responsible person to pay the economic costs of resulting damage, which is frequently calculated by reference to a depreciation of the economic value of the damaged item, or the cost of repairing the damage. Pure damage to the environment may be incapable of calculation in economic terms, although it may have a non-economic value requiring restoration to the state prior to the damage occurring.[78] Even here difficulties of law and policy will continue to exist, as the EC Commission's 1993 Green Paper on Environmental Liability recognised:

> An identical reconstruction may not be possible, of course. An extinct species cannot be replaced. Pollutants emitted into the air or water are difficult to retrieve. From an environmental point of view, however, there should be a goal to clean-up and restore the environment to the state which, if not identical to that which existed before the damage occurred, at least maintains its necessary permanent functions . . . Even if restoration or clean-up is physically possible, it may not be economically feasible. It is unreasonable to expect the restoration to a virgin state if humans have interacted with that environment for generations. Moreover, restoring an environment to the state it was in before the damage occurred could involve expenditure disproportionate to the desired results. In such a case it might be argued that restoration should only be carried out to the point where it is still 'cost-effective'. Such determinations involve difficult balancing of economic and environmental values.[79]

The rules of international law relating to reparation for environmental damage remain undeveloped, as evidenced by the lack of legal precedents. Similar limitations exist at the national level. In the United States, restoration of damaged environments has been described as a 'fledgling activity shot through with uncertainty and controversy'.[80] Alternatives to valuing the environment for the purpose of assessing claims include the price that the environmental resource commands in the market, the economic value attached to the use of environmental resources (such as methods of costing travel relying on expenditures made by an individual to visit and enjoy a resource, or a hedonic pricing method which takes the extra market value enjoyed by private property with certain environmental amenities and assumes that public resources with comparable amenities have similar economic values), or contingent valuation methods to measure the willingness of individuals to pay for environmental goods such

---

[78] M. Bowman, 'Biodiversity, Intrinsic Value, and the Definition and Valuation of Environmental Harm', in M. Bowman and A. Boyle (eds.), *Environmental Damage in International and Comparative Law* (2002), 42.

[79] Communication from the EC Commission to the EC Council and European Parliament on Environmental Liability, 32, para. 5.2 (1993).

[80] R. Stewart, 'Tort Liability for Injury to Publicly Owned Natural Resources: A Category Mistake' (manuscript on file with author), 21.

as clean air or water or the preservation of endangered species (usually taken from public opinion surveys).[81]

The efforts of the UN Compensation Commission in applying Security Council Resolution 687 (see below) are likely to go some way in developing this aspect of international law, building on the precedents established by the *Trail Smelter* case and limited state practice, including the submission of claims. The approach taken by some of the civil liability precedents may also provide useful analogies in relation to state liability.

Trail Smelter Case (1941)   The tribunal in the *Trail Smelter* case found that the smelter at Trail in Canada had caused damage in the United States. The tribunal was called upon to decide what indemnity should be paid for the damage.[82] In applying the 'law and practice followed in dealing with cognate questions in the United States of America as well as international law and practice',[83] the tribunal considered the indemnity claimed by the United States for damage occurring after January 1932 in respect of: (a) cleared land and improvements thereon; (b) uncleared land and improvements thereon; (c) livestock; (d) property; (e) the wrong done to the United States in violation of sovereignty; (f) interest on the US$350,000 awarded by the ICJ on 1 January 1932 but not paid until 2 November 1935; and (g) business enterprises. The United States did not put forward a pure environmental damage claim, although this could be read into the claim in respect of 'uncleared land'. In its 1938 award, the tribunal found that damage to cleared land used for crops had occurred in varying degrees from 1932 to 1936 but not in 1937, and adopted the measure of damages applied by the US courts for nuisance or trespass, namely, 'the amount of reduction in the value of use or rental value of the land caused by fumigations'.[84] The tribunal also recognised some evidence of 'special damage' (rust and destruction of metalwork) which entitled owners to a nominal amount.

As to damage for cleared land not used for crops and to all uncleared land other than that used for timber, the tribunal adopted the same measure of damages, and rejected the US claim to the value of uncleared land at a ratio of loss measured by the reduced crop yield on cleared land. No damages were awarded for pasture lands, and as to cleared land used for merchantable timber the measure of damages was also that applied by US courts, namely, 'the reduction in the value of the land due to such destruction of timber'. For growing timber, the measure of damages was 'the reduction in the value of the land itself due

[81]   See generally *ibid.*, 21–32. See also D. Pearce *et al.*, *Blueprint for a Green Economy* (1989), 51–81.

[82]   Chapter 8, pp. 318–19 above.

[83]   See 1935 Convention, Art. IV, chapter 8, pp. 318–19 above.

[84]   *Trail Smelter* award, 199; see chapter 8, pp. 318–19 above.

to such destruction and impairment',[85] but the tribunal rejected the claim for damages due to lack of reproduction. On the basis of these considerations, the tribunal awarded US$62,000 for damage to cleared and uncleared land (other than land used for timber), and US$16,000 for damage to uncleared land used for timber.

The tribunal rejected the claim for damage to livestock (due to the failure to prove injury from fumes from the smelter), damage to property in the town of Northport (lack of proof) and damage to business enterprises ('too indirect, remote and uncertain to be appraised and not such for which an indemnity can be awarded').[86] The tribunal also rejected the US claim for damages from the 'injurious effects' to the Columbia River caused by the disposal of waste slag. The tribunal held that it was 'unnecessary to decide whether the facts proven did or did not constitute an infringement or violation of the sovereignty of the United States under international law independent of the Convention establishing the tribunal, since the Convention only submitted to the tribunal the question of damages caused by the Trail Smelter in the state of Washington, and it interpreted the intention of the parties as evidenced in the Convention not to include moneys spent by the US in investigating the problems, since the Convention used the words 'damages caused by the Trail Smelter'.[87] For the same reason, the tribunal rejected the claim for interest on the earlier payment of US$350,000.

In its 1941 award, the tribunal held that the United States had failed to prove that any fumigation between 1 October 1937 and 1 October 1940 had caused injury to crops, trees or otherwise and that no indemnity was due.[88] As to any damage occurring after 1 October 1940, irrespective of compliance with the regime it had established, the tribunal held that an indemnity should be paid for such damage when and if the two governments arranged for the settlement of claims under Article XI of the Convention, as well as up to US$7,500 per year to be paid to the United States as compensation in order to ascertain whether damage had occurred, provided that the two governments had determined under Article XI of the Convention that damage had occurred in the year in question.

The two awards of the tribunal did not deal with pure environmental damage *per se*, and rejected the opportunity to assess damages in respect of injurious consequences to the Columbia River. The tribunal basically took a market value approach which did not take account of loss of environmental amenity. In so doing, the tribunal took the measure of damage used by US courts, an approach which would most likely produce a different result today because of changes in US law which reflect loss of environmental amenity or resources as a separate measure of damage.

---

[85] *Ibid.*, 204.   [86] *Ibid.*, 206.   [87] *Ibid.*, 207.   [88] *Ibid.*, 709 and 712.

Other developments   In January 1955, the US Government paid US$2 million to Japan for the 'purposes of compensation for the injuries or damage sustained' by Japanese nationals as a result of thermonuclear tests carried out by the US near the Marshall Islands in March 1954.[89] The payments were made *ex gratia* and 'without reference to legal liability', and it is unclear whether the compensation included an amount for damage to the marine environment or loss of environmental amenity.[90] In its argument in the *Nuclear Tests* case, Australia argued that, if the existence of harm or damage was essential to liability, it could point to, *inter alia*, the 'harm, all the more real for being incapable of precise evaluation, to which its population, both present and future, and environment have been subjected for no benefit to them'.[91] In April 1981, the USSR agreed to pay, and Canada agreed to accept, C$3 million in final settlement of the Canadian claim, under the 1972 Space Liability Convention and general principles of international law, for damage incurred by way of expense in locating, recovering, removing and testing radioactive debris and for cleaning up affected areas following the crash of Cosmos 954 in January 1978.[92] And Nauru claimed 'appropriate reparation' in respect of the losses it had suffered as a result of Australia's alleged breaches of legal obligations relating to, *inter alia*, changes in the condition of Nauru's territory causing irreparable damage.[93]

Following the Chernobyl accident, no state made a formal claim against the USSR for damage resulting from radioactive fallout, although several reserved their right to do so, including the Federal Republic of Germany,[94] as they subsequently paid large sums of compensation to persons within their jurisdictions affected by the fallout.[95] Their reasons for not bringing claims reflect political and legal uncertainties. According to the Swedish Government:

> In terms of treaties there is no international agreement existing, whether bilateral or multilateral, on the basis of which a Swedish claim for damages against the USSR could be conceived. Insofar as customary international law is concerned, principles exist which might be invoked to support a claim

---

[89] See E. Margolis, 'The Hydrogen Bomb Experiments and International Law', 64 *Yale Law Journal* 629 at 638–9 (1955).

[90] *Ibid.*, 639.

[91] Oral Arguments of Australia, *Australia* v. *France* ICJ Pleadings (Nuclear Tests) 481 (1973).

[92] See below.

[93] *Certain Phosphate Lands in Nauru* (*Nauru* v. *Australia*), Preliminary Objections, Judgment (1992) ICJ Reports 240 at 244.

[94] Communication between the Embassy of the Federal Republic of Germany in London and the author, 8 December 1987.

[95] By 1 December 1987, the United Kingdom had paid £4,950,199 compensation (figures supplied by Ministry of Agriculture, Fisheries and Food); the Federal Republic of Germany had paid DM390 million compensation (figures supplied by London Embassy of the Federal Republic of Germany); and Sweden had paid SK204 million compensation to farmers, up to 30 June 1987, and SK117 million to the reindeer industry during the budget year 1986/7 (figures supplied by Swedish Embassy in London).

against the USSR. The issues involved, however, are complex from the legal
as well as the technical point of view and warrant careful consideration.
In present circumstances, the Government has felt that priority should be
given, in the wake of the Chernobyl accident, to endeavours of another
nature.[96]

The position of the United Kingdom Government was complicated by outstanding disputes relating to the problem of acid rain in Scandinavia, contamination of the Irish Sea by nuclear waste from the Windscale/Sellafield nuclear
plant, and alleged damage to Australian territory, from the nuclear tests carried
out by the United Kingdom in the 1950s. On 21 July 1986, the Secretary of State
for Foreign and Commonwealth Affairs in a written answer in the House of
Commons said:

> On 10 July we formally reserved our right with the Soviet government
> to claim compensation on our own behalf on behalf of our citizens for
> any losses suffered as a consequence of the accident at Chernobyl. The
> presentation of a formal claim, should we decide to make one, would not
> take place until the nature and full extent of any damage suffered had been
> assessed.[97]

Three months later, the Minister of State for Agriculture, Fisheries and Food
stated that:

> We have reserved our position on whether the USSR will be required – as
> it should be if the case is proved – to pay compensation.[98]

More recently, the position has been put thus by the Parliamentary Under-
Secretary of State for Scotland:

> The USSR is not a party to any of the international conventions relating
> to third party liability in nuclear energy, and is therefore not subject to
> any specific treaty obligation to compensate for damage caused outside its
> national boundaries.[99]

Following the accident, the IAEA convened various meetings on liability for
nuclear damage, which ultimately led to the establishment of the Standing
Committee on Nuclear Liability.[100] The IAEA Board of Governors requested
the Director General to invite comments from member states on the question
of international liability, which elicited responses from thirty-two states representing a broad range of views on the current rules of international law.[101]

---

[96] Correspondence with the Swedish Embassy in London, 10 December 1987.
[97] *Hansard*, House of Commons, 21 July 1986, vol. 102, col. 5(W).
[98] *Hansard*, House of Commons, 24 October 1986, vol. 102, col. 1455.
[99] *Hansard*, House of Commons, 16 November 1987, vol. 122, col. 894.
[100] See pp. 909–12 below.
[101] IAEA Docs. GOV/INF/550 (1988); Add.1 (1988); and Add.2 (1989).

Responses of states can be categorised into four types: five states considered that principles or rules of international law existed upon which state liability for nuclear damage could be established;[102] one state saw lacunae;[103] twenty-four states expressed no view either way;[104] and two states considered or suggested that norms of liability could only be based upon treaty.[105] It is therefore difficult to discern firm principles arising from the Chernobyl experience.

In the *Case Concerning the Gabcikovo-Nagymaros Project*, the ICJ confirmed that Hungary was entitled to 'compensation for the damage sustained as a result of the diversion of the Danube', but did not specifically indicate that Hungary was entitled to reparation for purely environmental damages.[106] As regards the measure of compensation, the Court merely observed that 'the issue of compensation could satisfactorily be resolved in the framework of an overall settlement if each of the Parties were to renounce or cancel all financial claims and counter-claims'.[107] The judgment therefore provides no practical guidance on how to calculate the measure of such environmental damage as the Court appeared willing to take into account in proposing the settlement. The reluctance is consistent with the limited international practice concerning reparation for environmental damage at the inter-state level. The work of the UN Compensation Commission may, however, provide some guidance on the future development of this area.

In April 2002, the Marshall Islands Nuclear Claims Tribunal made an award of US$324,949,311 to the People of Enewatak, as 'just and adequate' settlement for claims of Marshall Islanders in respect of damages to land arising out of the nuclear testing programme carried out by the United States between 1946 and

---

[102] Canada ('the existence of such general principles has been recognised in diplomatic practice, by scholars, in judicial and arbitral decisions, in resolutions and declarations of international conferences, and in many bilateral and multilateral treaties': GOV/INF/550, 6); Chile; Federal Republic of Germany ('[i]t is undisputed that states are liable for nuclear damage caused by conduct that is contrary to international law': GOV/INF/550, 23); Thailand ('there exist principles of customary international law that can be applicable to an incident which results in radiological releases beyond the limits of national jurisdiction': GOV/INF/550, 35); and Guatemala (recognising the possibility: GOV/INF/550/ Add.2, 2).

[103] Austria.

[104] Algeria, Bulgaria, Cameroon, China, Colombia, Czechoslovakia, Egypt (supporting 'a widening of the scope of liability in time and place', GOV/INF/550, 21), Finland, German Democratic Republic, Hungary, Ireland, Italy (but noting 'the absence of a well-established set of customary rules accepted by the state community as such', GOV/INF/550, 25), Luxembourg, Mexico, Netherlands, Norway, Pakistan, Poland, Sweden, Switzerland, Turkey, USSR, United Kingdom and United States.

[105] Belgium ('the situation in international law is more or less comparable to what we find in ancient Roman law, which did not know any general principle of liability and which only penalised the acts contained in a legal list of illicit acts', citing J. A. Salmon, *International Liability* (1979–80, 3rd edn), vol. 1, 6, in GOV/INF/550, 5) and Spain.

[106] Para. 151.   [107] Para. 152.

1958.[108] The award included payments in respect of past and future loss of use (US$199,154,811), restoration to a 'safe and productive state' (US$91,710,000), and hardship as a result of relocation (US$34,084,500). The Tribunal applied standards agreed by the parties, in particular standards applicable under US law. In relation to restoration, the Tribunal accepted the position adopted by the IAEA to the effect that 'policies and criteria for radiation protection of populations outside national borders from releases of radioactive substances should be at least as stringent as those for the population within the country of release', and accordingly applied the current standards applied by the US Environmental Protection Agency.[109]

UN Compensation Commission[110]

The UN Compensation Commission was established in 1991 to provide reparation for the consequences of Iraq's unlawful invasion of Kuwait. The Commission has established criteria for claims in respect of environmental damage and the depletion of natural resources. The language was drawn from a Working Paper submitted by the United States, which drew upon its domestic legislation, including provisions of the Oil Pollution Act of 1990 adopted following the *Exxon Valdez* oil spill in 1989.[111] In paragraph 35 of Decision 7, the Commission's Governing Council decided that payments would be available for direct environmental damage and the depletion of natural resources, including losses or expenses resulting from:

    (a) abatement and prevention of environmental damage, including expenses directly relating to fighting oil fires and stemming the flow of oil in coastal and international waters;

    (b) reasonable measures already taken to clean and restore the environment or future measures which can be documented as reasonably necessary to clean and restore the environment;

    (c) reasonable monitoring and assessment of the environmental damage for the purposes of evaluating and abating the harm and restoring the environment;

---

[108] Award of 13 April 2000, 39 ILM (2000) 1214.

[109] *Ibid.*, 1220. The EPA standard was described in 'Establishment of Cleanup Levels for CERCLA Sites with Radioactive Contamination', providing that 'Cleanup should generally achieve a level of risk with the 10-4 to 10-6 carcinogenic range based on the reasonable maximum exposure for an individual . . . If a dose assessment is conducted at the site . . . then 15 millrem per year (mrem/yr) effective dose equivalent (EDE) should generally be the maximum dose limit for humans': *ibid.*, 1220–1.

[110] M. Kazazi, 'Environmental Damage in the Practice of the UN Compensation Commission', in M. Bowman and A. Boyle (eds.), *Environmental Damage in International and Comparative Law* (2002), 111.

[111] UN Security Council Doc. S/AC.26/1991/WP.20, 20 November 1991.

(d) reasonable monitoring of public health and performing medical screenings for the purposes of investigation and combating increased health risks as a result of the environmental damage; and

(e) depletion of or damage to natural resources.[112]

In addressing these claims, the Commission is directed to apply Security Council Resolution 687 (1991) and the above criteria and, where necessary, 'other relevant rules of international law'.[113] Claims relating to the environment are referred to as category 'F4' claims, and may only be made by states and international organisations. A first group comprises claims for environmental damage and the depletion of natural resources in the Persian Gulf region, including those resulting from oil-well fires and the discharge of oil into the sea. The Commission has received about thirty such claims, requesting some US$40 billion in compensation. A second group comprises claims for costs incurred by states outside the region in providing assistance to states that were directly affected by the environmental damage, including the alleviation of damage caused by oil-well fires and the prevention and clean-up of pollution. The Commission has received seventeen such claims seeking some US$23 million in compensation. To date, the Panel of Commissioners charged with processing F4 claims has addressed two instalments of claims relating to preliminary matters, namely, compensation of assessment and monitoring activities undertaken or to be undertaken to identify and evaluate damage, relating to air pollution, depletion of water resources, groundwater, cultural heritage, oil pollution, fisheries, wetlands and rangelands and public health. In relation to the first instalment, the claims related to investigations of whether environmental damage or depletion of natural resources had occurred, studies to quantify the loss, and assessment of methodologies to abate or mitigate the damage. All the remaining claims are, in principle, to be addressed by the end of 2003, although this may be an ambitious timetable. The Panel's initial work indicates the basis upon which they may proceed on the outstanding larger claims. It has indicated that conclusive proof of environmental damage was not a prerequisite for monitoring and assessment claims, but has excluded claims which were 'theoretical or speculative' or which had only a tenuous link with damage resulting from Iraq's invasion.[114] In assessing the link, the Panel has had regard to the particular circumstances of each case and four considerations:

1. whether there was a possibility that damage or depletion could have been caused as a result of the invasion;

---

[112] Governing Council, UN Compensation Commission, Decision 7, para. 35, UN Doc. S/23765, Annex (1992), 31 ILM 1051 (1992).

[113] UN Compensation Commission Provisional Rules for Claims Procedures, Art. 31, S/AC.26/1992/10, 26 June 1992.

[114] Report on First Instalment, S/AC.26/2001/16, 22 June 2001, paras. 30–1.

2. whether the areas or resources in respect of the activity claimed for could have been affected by pollutant released as a result of the invasion;

3. whether there was evidence of environmental damage or risk of such damage as a result of the invasion; and

4. whether there was a reasonable prospect that the activity could produce results that would assist the panel in reviewing claims.[115]

The Panel has identified the difficulty of ascertaining whether and to what extent damage which was identified was attributable to Iraq's invasion, and the inadequacy of documented baseline information on the state of the environment or of conditions and trends regarding natural resources prior to the invasion.[116] It has also confirmed that loss or damage occurring outside Kuwait and Iraq was compensable.[117] In respect of the first instalment, the Panel recommended compensation payments of US$243 million (out of US$1,007 million claimed) to Iran, Jordan, Kuwait, Saudi Arabia, Syria and Turkey.[118]

The second 'F4' instalment related to claims incurred for measures to abate and prevent environmental damage, to clean and restore the environment, to monitor and assess environmental damage, and to monitor public health risks alleged to have resulted from the invasion. Iran, Kuwait and Saudi Arabia claimed US$829 million compensation for measures to respond to environmental damage and health risks from mines and other remnants of war, oil lakes, oil spills and pollutants released from oil-well fires. From outside the region, Australia, Canada, Germany, the Netherlands, the UK and the US claimed compensation of US$43 million for expenses incurred in providing assistance to states in the Persian Gulf region to respond to environmental damage or the threat of damage to the environment or health. The Panel has determined that 'environmental damage' is not limited to losses or expenses resulting from the activities and events which are identified in paragraph 35 of Decision 7 (above), but could also cover other direct losses or expenses, such as measures undertaken to prevent or abate harmful impacts of airborne contaminants, provided that they were a direct result of the invasion.[119] The Panel has also decided that Iraq cannot be exonerated from liability because other factors may have contributed to the loss or damage,[120] and that expenses resulting from activities undertaken by military personnel will be compensable if there is evidence to show that the predominant purpose of the activity engaged in was to respond to

---

[115] Paras. 31–2.

[116] Paras. 33–4. The Panel applied 'generally accepted scientific criteria and methodologies' (para. 35).

[117] Paras. 53–4.

[118] *Ibid.* Iran (US$17 million recommended out of US$42.9 million claimed); Jordan (US$7 million/US$12.5 million; Kuwait (US$108.9 million/US$460.4 million; Saudi Arabia (US$109.5 million/US$482 million); Syria (US$0.67 million/US$5.6 million); Turkey (US$0/US$3.7 million).

[119] Report on First Instalment, S/AC.26/2002/26, 3 October 2002, para. 23.

[120] Para. 25.

environmental damage or threats of damage to the environment or health.[121] The Panel has further recommended that compensation should be payable to cover expenses resulting from assistance rendered to countries in the region to respond to damage or threats, provided it does not duplicate compensation paid to any country in the region.[122] In reviewing the second instalment of claims, the Panel was assisted by a multidisciplinary team of independent experts retained by the Commission, having regard to the complexity of the issues and the need to consider scientific, legal, social, commercial and accounting issues.[123] The Panel recommended compensation payments of US$711 million, out of US$872 million claimed.[124]

The claims yet to be processed – relating to paragraphs 35(b) and (e) of Decision 7 – are complex, requiring consideration, among other issues, of the 'reasonableness' of the claim, causality, and the methodology for assessing and valuing environmental damage. To the extent that the Panel applies 'other relevant rules of international law', as directed, the Panel may contribute to the elucidation of the international rules in this emergent – but important – area. Paragraph 35(b) recognises a liability in respect of 'reasonable measures . . . to clean and restore the environment', whereas paragraph 35(e) recognises what appears to be an additional liability in respect of loss relating to 'depletion of or damage to natural resources'. No guidance is provided as to the meaning of the distinction which is drawn between claims in respect of 'environmental damage' and those in respect of 'depletion of natural resources'. In 1995, a UNEP Working Group suggested that the distinction may relate to the idea that a 'natural resource' has, primarily, a commercial value, whereas 'environmental damage' relates to injury caused to components of the environment to which typically no commercial value attaches.[125] The UNEP Working Group suggested that environmental damage could relate to 'impairment of the environment', which may be defined as:

> A change which has a measurable adverse impact on the quality of a particular environment of any of its components including its use and non-use values and its ability to support and sustain an acceptable quality of life and a viable ecological balance.[126]

---

[121] Para. 29.   [122] Paras. 34–5.

[123] Paras. 42–3. Experts were retained in the fields of oil spill response, ordnance removal and disposal, accounting, civil engineering, electric power systems operations, fisheries, marine biology and oceanography.

[124] Para. 347. Iran (US$67,000 recommended out of US$64.3 million claimed); Kuwait (US$694 million/US$715 million); Saudi Arabia (US$8.2 million/US$49.7 million); Australia (US$7,000/US$20,000); Canada (US$529,000/US$1.25 million); Germany (US$2 million/US$28.7 million); Netherlands (zero/US$1.9 million); UK (US$1.8 million/US$2.2 million); US (US$3.8 million/US$9.1 million).

[125] See R. Mackenzie and R. Khalastchi, 'Liability and Compensation for Environmental Damage in the Context of the Work of the UNCC', 5 RECIEL 281 (1996).

[126] Note 36 above, para. 45.

On the definition of 'depletion of natural resources, the UNEP Working Group suggested that it could be desirable

> to treat depletion of natural resources as referring to the destruction of natural resource assets which occur in their natural state . . . and which have a primarily commercial use or commercial value rather than a non-commercial use or value.[127]

As regards methodology, the Commission will have to decide whether it will allow claims in accordance with methods of assessment which rely upon the abstract quantification of damage, or whether it will only allow claims in respect of clean-up costs of environmental damage which have been *actually* incurred, or are reasonably likely to be incurred. This was the issue faced by the International Oil Pollution Convention Fund, which decided in 1980 that the assessment of compensation would not be made on the basis of 'an abstract quantification of damage calculated in accordance with theoretical models', an approach which does not allow claims for loss of environmental amenity.[128] The approach of the International Oil Pollution Convention Fund has been reflected in certain other civil liability treaties: the 1993 Lugano Convention allows compensation for impairment of the environment damage, other than loss of profit from such impairment, limited to 'the costs of measures of reinstatement actually undertaken or to be undertaken'.[129]

International crimes

G. Gilbert, 'The Criminal Responsibility of States', 39 ICLQ 345 (1990); A. Vercher, 'The Use of Criminal Law for the Protection of the Environment in Europe: Council of Europe Resolution 77(28)', 10 *Northwestern Journal of International Law and Business* 442 (1990); R. Prévost, 'International Criminal Environmental Law', in G. Goodwin-Gill and S. Talmon (eds.), *The Reality of International Law: Essays in Honour of Ian Brownlie* (1999).

International responsibility may also trigger liability of a criminal nature. The ILC has proposed that certain environmental damage may be so serious in the eyes of the international community that it should be categorised as criminal, or delictual. In Article 19 of its 1980 draft Articles on State Responsibility, the ILC had proposed classifying as an international crime or delict 'a serious breach of an international obligation of essential importance for the safeguarding and preservation of the human environment, such as those prohibiting massive pollution of the atmosphere or of the seas'.[130] However, the Articles on State Responsibility adopted in 2001 eliminated Article 19, having regard to the fact

---

[127] *Ibid.*, para. 50.   [128] See pp. 915–22 below.
[129] Art. 2(8)(c), pp. 933–7 below; see also 1989 CRTD Convention, pp. 930–1 below.
[130] Part I, *Yearbook of the International Law Commission* (1980–II), part 2, 30, Art. 19.

that the responsibility with which it was concerned was that of a state, and not of individuals.[131] The provisions which were adopted – Articles 40 and 41 on serious breaches – identify the legal consequences for violations of peremptory norms of general international law, but do not state exhaustively what those norms are.[132] Massive pollution and other environmental catastrophes are not referred to as examples of serious breaches in the Articles or in the commentary on the Articles, although the commentary does not purport to be exhaustive.[133] It is plain also that Articles 40 and 41 were intended to be open-ended, so as not to preclude the development of rules detailing the consequences of serious breaches.[134]

Other ILC work has maintained a reference to environmental crimes, although in the context of individual (as opposed to statal) criminality. The ILC's Draft Code of Crimes Against the Peace and Security of Mankind, adopted on second reading in 1996, identifies widespread environmental damage as a crime against the peace and security of mankind.[135] By draft Article 20(g) (formerly Article 22), an individual who employs methods or means of warfare 'which are intended or may be expected to cause widespread, long-term and severe damage to the natural environment' would be liable to be guilty of an exceptionally serious war crime. The standard applicable to the level of environmental damage is taken from the 1977 ENMOD Convention and Protocol I Additional to the 1949 Geneva Conventions.[136] The draft Articles as adopted exclude draft Article 26 (from the first draft), which was stated to apply in times of peace as well as during armed conflict, and which provided that an individual who 'wilfully causes or orders the causing of widespread, long-term and severe damage to the natural environment' would also be guilty of a crime.

The ILC's work informed the drafting of the Statute of the International Criminal Court (ICC Statute), which defines as a war crime an intentional attack with the knowledge that it will cause 'widespread, long-term and severe damage to the natural environment which would be clearly excessive in relation to the concrete and direct overall military advantage anticipated'.[137] It remains to be seen whether the ICC Statute will be interpreted to include environmental crimes in relation to acts of genocide or crimes against humanity, as has been suggested.[138]

---

[131] See p. 874 above.

[132] *Yearbook of the International Law Commission* (2001), 292.

[133] See *ibid.*, 277–92.   [134] *Ibid.*, 292.

[135] Report of the ILC, 48th Session, UN Doc. A/51/10 (1996), Art. 20; the first draft (1991) is available at 30 ILM 1584 (1991).

[136] Chapter 7, pp. 313–16 above.

[137] Rome, 17 July 1998, in force 2 July 2002, 37 ILM 999 (1998), Art. 8(2)(b)(iv).

[138] See generally P. Sharp, 'Prospects for Environmental Liability in the International Criminal Court', 18 *Virginia Environmental Law Journal* 217 (1999).

It should also be noted that in 1998 the Council of Europe adopted a Convention on the Protection of the Environment Through Criminal Law, requiring parties to criminalise under their domestic law intentional (Article 2) or grossly negligent (Article 3) acts falling within certain categories which cause substantial environmental damage.[139] The Convention identifies certain categories of environmentally damaging acts as being especially serious,[140] and other acts in respect of which sanctions or other measures may be appropriate.[141] The Convention identifies as sanctions imprisonment, fines and reinstatement of the environment, and allows parties to establish criminal liability for corporations.[142]

Treaties

The liability of states for environmental damage in relation to particular activities or regions is addressed by a small number of treaties. These establish rules of state liability, or provide a basis for the development of such rules on state liability,[143] or deny that the treaty contains any such rule on liability.

Space Liability Convention[144]

R. E. Alexander, 'Measuring Damages under the Convention on International Liability for Damage Caused by Space Objects', 6 *Journal of Space Law* 151 (1978); C. Q.

---

[139] Strasbourg, 4 November 1998, not yet in force, ETS No. 172. Under Art. 6, on jurisdiction, states are to criminalise activities committed on their territory, on ships or aircrafts registered in their territory or flying their flags, or by their nationals if the offence is criminal where it is committed.

[140] Art. 2(1)(a)–(e). The intentional unlawful acts include: the discharge, emission or introduction of a quantity of substances or ionising radiation into air, soil or water which causes death or serious injury to any person, or creates a significant risk of causing death or serious injury to any person (Art. 2(1)(a)); unlawful discharge, emission or introduction of a quantity of substances or ionising radiation into air, soil or water which causes or is likely to cause their lasting deterioration or death or serious injury to any person or substantial damage to protected monuments, other protected objects, property, animals or plants (Art. 2(1)(b)); unlawful disposal, treatment, storage, transport, export or import of hazardous waste (Art. 2(1)(c)); unlawful operation of a plant in which a dangerous activity is carried out (Art. 2(1)(d)); and manufacture, treatment, storage, use, transport, export or import of nuclear materials or other hazardous radioactive substances (Art. 2(1)(e)). Art. 1(a) defines 'unlawful' as 'infringing a law, an administrative regulation or a decision taken by a competent authority, aiming at the protection of the environment'.

[141] Art. 4 (the acts include: unlawful introduction of substances or ionising radiation; causing of noise; disposal, treatment, storage, transport, export or import of waste; operation of a plant; manufacture, treatment, use, transport, export or import of nuclear materials, other radioactive substances or hazardous chemicals; causing of changes detrimental to natural components of a national park, nature reserve, water conservation area or other protected areas; and possession, taking, damaging, killing or trading of or in protected wild flora and fauna species).

[142] Arts. 6 and 9.   [143] See nn. 15 and 22 above.

[144] See also 1967 Outer Space Treaty, Art. VII; 1979 Moon Treaty, Art. XIV.

Christol, 'International Liability for Damage Caused by Space Objects', 74 AJIL 346 (1980); B. Schwartz and N. L. Berlin, 'After the Fall: An Analysis of Canadian Legal Claims for Damage Caused by Cosmos 954', 27 *McGill Law Journal* 676 (1982).

The Convention on International Liability for Damage Caused by Space Objects (1972 Space Liability Convention) is one of the few treaties to establish a clear rule of state liability.[145] Subject to the exceptions set out in Articles VI and VII, a state which launches a space object is 'absolutely liable to pay compensation for damage caused by its space object on the surface of the earth or to aircraft in flight'.[146] 'Damage' is defined as 'loss of life, personal injury or other impairment of health; or loss of or damage to property of states or of persons, natural or judicial, or property of international intergovernmental organisations'.[147] Although the definition does not refer to 'environmental' harm, it can be interpreted to allow compensation claims for the 'property of states' which are environmental assets or other natural resources:

> Compensation is to be determined in accordance with international law and the principles of justice and equity, in order to provide such reparation in respect of the damage as will restore the person, natural or judicial, state or international organisation on whose behalf the claim is presented to the condition which would have existed if the damage had not occurred.[148]

A party will be liable for damage other than on the surface of the earth to another space object or persons or property on board only if the damage is due to fault.[149] In some situations, states may be jointly and severally liable, notably where damage is caused on the surface of a third state as a result of damage by one space object to another.[150]

The only claim under the 1972 Convention was presented by Canada in 1979 to the former USSR for damage caused by the crash of Cosmos 954, a nuclear-powered satellite which disintegrated over Canada.[151] Canadian authorities took steps to locate, recover, remove and test the radioactive debris and to clean up the affected areas of the Northwest Territories and the Provinces of Alberta and Saskatchewan, claiming some C$6 million from the USSR. The Canadian claim was based on relevant international agreements (the 1972 Convention and Article VII of the 1967 Outer Space Treaty) and general principles of international law. Canada claimed that the deposit and presence of hazardous radioactive debris over large areas of Canadian territory rendering part of it unfit for use constituted damage to property within the meaning of the

---

[145] 29 March 1972, in force 1 September 1972, 961 UNTS 187. The Convention establishes procedures and timetables for the presentation of compensation claims.
[146] Art. II.   [147] Art. I(a).   [148] Art. XII.   [149] Art. III.   [150] Arts. IV and V.
[151] Canada, Claim Against the USSR for Damage Caused by Soviet Cosmos 954, 23 January 1979, 18 ILM 899–908 (1979).

1972 Convention.[152] Canada also claimed the USSR had failed to minimise the effects by providing timely and complete answers to its questions, and under general principles of international law the USSR was bound to prevent and reduce harmful consequences and mitigate damage.[153] The claim covered the costs of restoring Canadian territory, to the extent possible, to the condition which would have existed if the intrusion had not occurred. In calculating the costs, Canada applied 'the relevant criteria established by general principles of international law and has limited the costs included in the claim to those costs that are reasonable, proximately caused by the intrusion of the satellite and deposit of debris and capable of being calculated with a reasonable degree of certainty'.[154]

Canada also claimed under Article VII of the 1967 Outer Space Treaty that the USSR must compensate in accordance with international law for the consequences of the intrusion of the satellite into Canadian air space and the deposit on Canadian territory of hazardous radioactive debris.[155] Finally, Canada claimed under general principles of international law that the violation of its sovereignty was established by 'the mere fact of the trespass of the satellite, the harmful consequences of this intrusion, being the damage caused by the presence of hazardous radioactive debris and the interference with the sovereign right of Canada to determine the acts that will be performed on its territory'.[156] This violation gave rise to an obligation to pay compensation and was based on a standard of absolute liability for space activities, which applied to activities in common having a high degree of risk and had been accepted as a general principle of international law.[157] The measure of compensation under this head was the same as that applied under the 1972 Convention. Canada additionally reserved its rights to present additional claims for compensation for damage not yet identified, for the costs incurred in establishing a Compensation Commission under the 1972 Convention, and for interest.[158]

The matter was settled in 1981 when the USSR agreed to pay C$3 million in full and final compensation, and Canada agreed to accept such payment in full and final settlement of its claim.[159] Although the settlement agreement was silent as to the basis of the settlement, the reference in Article II of the agreement to Canada's claim allows a conclusion that the settlement was agreed on the basis of all the legal arguments proposed by Canada.[160]

---

[152] *Ibid.*, 905.   [153] *Ibid.*, 805–6.   [154] *Ibid.*, 906.

[155] *Ibid.*, 907.   [156] *Ibid.*, 908.   [157] *Ibid.*   [158] *Ibid.*, 909.

[159] Protocol Between Canada and the USSR, Arts. I and II, 2 April 1981, 20 ILM 689 (1981).

[160] Although in an earlier communication, pre-dating the Canadian claim, the USSR 'reaffirmed' that it was guided by 'the international agreements regulating the activities of states in the outer space', and that any compensation claim presented by Canada would be considered by the USSR in strict accordance with the provisions of the 1972 Convention: USSR Note of 21 March 1978, 18 ILM 902 at 923 (1979).

LRTAP Convention

The 1979 LRTAP Convention is of interest mainly because of a footnote entered in relation to Article 8, which commits parties to exchange available information on, *inter alia*, the extent of the damage which physico-chemical and biological data indicate can be attributed to long-range transboundary air pollution. The footnote provides that the Convention 'does not contain a rule on state liability as to damage', and reflects concern over inadvertently entering into an international agreement which may subsequently be used to establish their liability for damage. The footnote is neutral in its effect and does not prevent the application of general rules of international law concerning state liability for damage resulting from the breach of the terms of the 1979 LRTAP Convention itself.

UNCLOS

B. Kwiatkowska-Czechowksa, 'States' Responsibility for Pollution Damage Resulting from the Exploration for and Exploitation of Sea-Bed Mineral Resources', 10 *Polish Yearbook of International Law* 157 (1980); B. D. Smith, *State Responsibility and the Marine Environment* (1988); G. Kasoulides, 'State Responsibility and Assessment of Liability for Damage Resulting from Dumping Operations', 26 *San Diego Law Review* 497 (1989).

UNCLOS contains two rules on state liability for damage. Under Article 139, which applies to the 'Area' (i.e. the seabed and ocean floor and subsoil beyond the limits of national jurisdiction), states parties and international organisations have the responsibility to ensure that activities in the Area carried out by them, or by their nationals or by those effectively controlled by them or their nationals, comply with the UNCLOS rules on the Area.[161] Moreover:

> Without prejudice to the rules of international law and Annex III, Article 22, damage caused by the failure of a State Party or international organization to carry out its responsibilities under this Part shall entail liability; State Parties or international organizations acting together shall bear joint and several liability.[162]

A state party may argue, as a defence, that it has taken all necessary and appropriate measures to secure effective compliance under the relevant provisions of UNCLOS. State parties are also required to take appropriate measures to

[161] Art. 139(1).

[162] Art. 139(2). Art. 22 of Annex III provides, *inter alia*, that contractors shall have responsibility or liability for any damage arising out of wrongful acts in the conduct of operations in the 'Area', and that the authority shall have responsibility or liability for damage arising out of wrongful acts in the exercise of its powers and functions; in every case liability shall be 'for the actual amount of damage': Annex III, Art. 22.

ensure that international organisations of which they are members implement their responsibilities under Article 139.[163]

The second provision is Article 235, according to which states are themselves

> responsible for the fulfilment of their international obligations concerning the protection and preservation of the marine environment. They shall be liable in accordance with international law.[164]

Article 235 incorporates existing rules of state liability into the Convention and does not create a new rule of liability for damage to the marine environment. UNCLOS does not define 'damage' to the marine environment and, with the exception of the provision for the measure of damage in relation to the liability of contractors or the enterprise, does not establish a measure of compensation. The definition of marine 'pollution' in Article 1(4) provides some guidance as to the standard of damage which might be applied: 'deleterious effects' envisaged include harm to living resources and marine life, hazards to human health, hindrance to marine activities, impairment of water quality, and reduction of amenities.

CRAMRA

H. C. Burmester, 'Liability for Damage from Antarctic Mineral Resource Activities', 29 *Virginia Journal of International Law* 621 (1989); M. Poole, 'Liability for Environmental Damage in Antarctica', 10 *Journal of Environmental and Natural Resources Law* 246 (1992).

Under the 1988 CRAMRA, a sponsoring state will be liable, in accordance with international law, if damage under Article 8(2) of the Convention would not have occurred or continued if it had 'carried out its obligations under [the] Convention' with respect to the operator.[165] Although liability will be limited to that not satisfied by the operator or otherwise, this provision establishes potentially unlimited state liability for environmental damage.

Climate Change Convention

The 1992 Climate Change Convention does not contain a rule on the consequences of activities by states which harm the environment, although during the negotiations some states wanted to include a provision that the Convention did not prejudice the rules of international law concerning state responsibility and liability.[166] The Climate Change Convention defines 'adverse effects of

---

[163] Art. 139(2) and (3).   [164] Art. 235(1).

[165] Art. 8(3)(a); see chapter 14, pp. 716–21 above. Damage not covered under Art. 8(2) is subject to the applicable rules of international law: Art. 8(3)(b).

[166] See also the declarations adopted at the time of signature by Kiribati, Tuvalu and Nauru: chapter 4, pp. 135–6 above; and A. Jaitly and N. Khanna, 'Liability for Climate Change: Who Pays, How Much and Why?', 1 RECIEL 453 (1992).

climate change',[167] and under Article 4(4) requires developed country parties listed in Annex II and the EC to 'assist the developing countries parties that are particularly vulnerable to the adverse effects of climate change in meeting costs of adaptation to those adverse effects'.[168] While this novel provision is not a formal expression of liability under the principles of state responsibility, it reflects an admission of responsibility with financial consequences.

The work of the ILC

R. Quentin Baxter, ' "Schematic Outline" on International Liability for Injurious Consequences Arising out of Acts Not Prohibited by International Law, *Yearbook of the International Law Commission* (1982), II/1, 51–64; J. Barboza, 'Preliminary Report on International Liability for Injurious Consequences Arising out of Acts Not Prohibited by International Law', UN Doc. A/CN.4/394 (1985); D. B. Magraw, 'Transboundary Harm: The International Law Commission's Study of International Liability', 80 AJIL 305 (1986); S. C. McCaffrey, 'The Work of the International Law Commission Relating to Transfrontier Environmental Harm', 20 NYUJILP 608 (1988); A.Boyle, 'State Responsibility and International Liability for Injurious Consequences of Acts Not Prohibited by International Law: A Necessary Distinction?', 39 ICLQ 1 (1990); C. Tomuschat, 'International Liability for Injurious Consequences Arising Out of Acts Not Prohibited by International Law: The Work of the ILC', in F. Francioni and T. Scovazzi (eds.), *International Responsibility for Environmental Harm* (1991); J. Barboza, 'International Liability for the Injurious Consequences of Acts Not Prohibited by International Law and Protection of the Environment', 247 RdC 295 (1994-III).

Apart from its now completed work on state responsibility, the ILC began working in the late 1970s on the issue of the liability of states for acts not prohibited by international law, and in 1990 prepared a first set of draft Articles.[169] The draft Articles remain incomplete, and somewhat controversial. They were intended to supplement the rules on state responsibility and to establish principles governing state and civil liability in respect of transboundary harm which arises from activities which are not unlawful *per se*. In 1992, the ILC divided the topic of international liability into prevention and remedial measures and decided to focus initially on developing draft Articles on prevention.[170] In 2001, the Drafting Committee of the ILC adopted, upon second reading, final draft Articles on the Prevention of Transboundary Harm from Hazardous Activities,

---

[167] Note 32 above.   [168] See also 1997 Kyoto Protocol, Art. 2(3).

[169] J. Barboza, Sixth Report, UN Doc. A/CN.4/428, 39 (1990).

[170] P. Rao, First Report on Prevention of Transboundary Damage from Hazardous Activity, UN Doc. A/CN.4/487, 3–4 (1998).

completing its work on that part of the topic.[171] This part does not address liability and reparation, as earlier drafts had done, although some states expressed the view that liability and reparation were closely related to prevention and should be considered jointly.[172] The ILC has decided, nevertheless, to develop the topics separately. In 2002, the ILC returned to its work on the related topic of liability.[173] Initial consideration of the topic addressed its scope and the roles of the operator and the state in the allocation of loss. Other topics identified for future consideration include: inter-state or intra-state mechanisms for the consolidation of claims; issues arising out of the international representation of the operator; the processes for assessment, quantification and settlement of claims; access to the relevant forums; and the nature of available remedies.

The direction to be taken by the ILC remains unclear, so its earlier 1990 draft Articles may well turn out to be of historic interest only. Nevertheless, they repay consideration since they indicate an authoritative basis upon which to reflect upon some of the issues addressed in this chapter. The draft Articles were intended to establish basic principles applicable to the activities carried out in the territory of a state, or in other places under its jurisdiction, or under its control, the physical consequences of which cause, or create a risk of causing, transboundary harm throughout the process.[174] They envisaged five principles to govern such activities.[175] The first principle, reflecting elements of Principle 21 of the Stockholm Declaration, proposed that the sovereign freedom of states to carry out or permit human activities 'must be compatible with the protection of the rights emanating from the sovereignty of other states'. The second principle required states to co-operate in good faith and to 'take appropriate measures to prevent or minimise the risk of transboundary harm or, where necessary, to contain or minimise the harmful transboundary effects of such activities' by the 'best practicable, available means'. The third principle related to reparation, requiring a state of origin to make reparation

---

[171] Chapter 6, pp. 249–51 above. Prevention of Transboundary Harm from Hazardous Activities: Draft Preamble and Draft Articles Adopted by the Drafting Committee on second reading, 3 May 2001, UN Doc. 1/CN/4/L.601.

[172] P. Rao, Third Report on International Liability for Injurious Consequences Arising Out of Acts Not Prohibited by International Law (Prevention of Transboundary Damage from Hazardous Activities), UN Doc. A/CN.4/510 (2000).

[173] ILC, Report of its Fifty-Fourth Session, UN Doc. A/57/10, paras. 442 et seq. (2002).

[174] ILC draft Articles, Art. 1. The activities envisaged include those which involve 'the handling, storage, production, carriage, unloading or other similar operation of one or more dangerous substances; or [which] use technologies that produce hazardous radiation; or [which] introduce into the environment genetically altered organisms and dangerous micro-organisms': ibid., Art. 2(a); see also Art. 2(b), (c) and (d) for definitions of 'dangerous substances', 'genetically altered organisms' and 'dangerous micro-organisms'.

[175] Arts. 6–10.

for appreciable harm caused by activities following negotiation between states and guided by the criteria set out in the draft Articles. Such reparation should restore the balance of interests affected by the harm. Finally, a principle of non-discrimination would require state parties to 'treat the effects of an activity that arise in the territory or under the jurisdiction or control of another state in the same way as effects arising in their own territory'.

Chapter III of the ILC's 1990 draft Articles proposes procedural rules for the prevention of transboundary harm, including provisions on assessment, notification and information (including provision for industrial and other confidentiality) and consultations.[176] To assist in achieving an equitable balance of interests, draft Article 17 identified factors to be taken into account in negotiations or consultations. Although not binding, they reflect one considered approach to the identification and application of principles of equity in environmental matters, and provide a point of reference for courts or tribunals faced with a balancing exercise.[177] That said, they remained in draft form only.

Chapter IV of the ILC's 1990 draft Articles addresses the issue of liability if transboundary harm arises. Bearing in mind that the harm must, in principle, be fully compensated, concerned states would be required to negotiate to determine the legal consequences of the harm.[178] The draft Articles proposed that an affected state may agree a reduction in payments for which the state of origin is liable if it appears equitable for certain costs to be shared.[179] Under draft Article 24, a distinction was to be drawn between different harms. With regard to environmental harm, the state of origin would be required to 'bear the costs of any reasonable operation to restore, as far as possible, the conditions that existed prior to the occurrence of the harm' or, if that proved impossible, to reach agreement on monetary or other compensation for the deterioration suffered.[180] Harm to persons or property as a consequence of environmental harm would also be compensated.[181] The draft Articles do not settle on the consequences if there was more than one state of origin: two options considered were joint and several liability, or liability in proportion to the harm caused by each state.[182] The draft Articles also envisage certain exceptions to

---

[176] Arts. 11, 14 and 15; see chapter 16, pp. 801–3 above and chapter 17, pp. 838–41 and 852–4 above.

[177] On equity, see chapter 4, p. 152 above and chapter 6, pp. 261–3 above; the factors include: the degree of probability of transboundary harm and its possible gravity; the existence of means to prevent harm; alternative activities or locations; the importance and economic viability of the activity; the capacity of the state of origin to prevent harm, restore environmental conditions, compensate for harm, or undertake alternatives; national, regional and international protection standards; benefits related to the activity; the effect of harm on natural resources; the willingness of the affected state to contribute to costs; the interests of the community as a whole; the availability of assistance from international organisations; and the applicability of relevant principles of international law.

[178] Art. 21.   [179] Art. 23.   [180] Art. 24(a).   [181] Art. 24(b).   [182] Art. 25.

liability,[183] a limitation period for the bringing of claims,[184] and the exclusion of the exhaustion of local remedies rule.[185]

Chapter V of the ILC's 1990 draft Articles envisages civil claims being brought in the national courts of the state of origin as an alternative to inter-state claims for the same harm, and to provide access to affected states, individuals or legal entities.[186] Individuals or states would be able to institute proceedings in the courts of the affected state or the state of origin.[187] The draft Articles propose the non-discriminatory application of national law,[188] the recognition of judgments,[189] and a limitation on state immunity, except in respect of enforcement measures.[190] It remains to be seen whether, and if so to what extent, the ILC will return to these approaches as it reconsiders the subject in 2003 and beyond.

Civil liability for environmental damage under international law

S. C. McCaffrey, 'Private Remedies for Transfrontier Pollution Damage in Canada and the United States: A Comparative Survey', 15 *University of Western Ontario Law Review* 35 (1981); S. E. Gaines, 'International Principles for Transnational Environmental Liability: Can Developments in Municipal Law Help Break the Impasse?', 30 *Harvard International Law Journal* 311 (1989); Hague Conference on Private International Law, *Note on the Law Applicable to Civil Liability for Environmental Damage* (1992); G. Betlem, *Civil Liability for Transfrontier Pollution* (1993); C. Von Bar, 'Environmental Damage in Private International Law', 268 RdC 291 (1997); E. Reid, 'Liability for Dangerous Activities: A Comparative Analysis', 48 ICLQ 731 (1999).

A growing number of treaties establish rules on civil liability for environmental or related damage, although several are not yet in force, and some will probably never enter into force. This suggests that the willingness of states to establish and apply principles of civil liability turns on the nature of the activity to be regulated, and the content of the rules agreed upon. In broad terms, there appears to be an inverse relationship between the scope of application of the rules – in terms of the activity targeted and the potential financial consequences proposed – and the prospects that they will enter into force. Generally, the civil liability regimes have been developed in relation to specific activities which are

---

[183] Art. 26; they include war, hostilities, civil war, certain natural phenomena, acts or omissions of third parties, or contributory negligence.

[184] Art. 27; the proposal was for a limitation of three or five years from the date when the harm was known or could reasonably have been known, with an absolute limit of thirty years from the date of the accident or the last occurrence if the accident consists of a series of occurrences.

[185] Art. 28(a). [186] Arts. 28(b) and 29(a). [187] Art. 29(c).

[188] Arts. 29(b) and 30. [189] Art. 32. [190] Art. 31.

considered to be ultra-hazardous, and rules have been in force for some time for damage caused by nuclear activities and as a result of oil spills. International rules have also been adopted for damage caused by waste (including its international trade)[191] and for environmental damage resulting from certain dangerous activities. The current trend – not altogether successful – has been towards general rules of civil liability for damage arising from unspecified activities: the Council of Europe has recently adopted a convention which takes this approach, and rules which would be of relatively generalised application to hazardous activities are being considered by the EC and the ECE.

Typically, the civil liability regimes follow a similar approach, establishing rules which:

1. define the activities or substances covered;
2. define the damage (to persons, property and the environment);
3. channel liability;
4. establish a standard of care (usually strict liability);
5. provide for liability amounts;
6. allow exonerations;
7. require the maintenance of adequate insurance or other financial security;[192]
8. identify a court or tribunal to receive the claims; and
9. provide for the recognition and enforcement of judgments.

Nuclear installations

M. J. L. Hardy, 'Nuclear Liability: The General Principles of Law and Further Proposals', 36 BYIL 223 (1960); W. Berman and L. M. Hyderman, 'A Convention on Third Party Liability for Damage from Nuclear Incidents', 55 AJIL 966 (1969); OECD, *Nuclear Third Party Liability: Nuclear Legislation* (1976); L. A. Malone, 'The Chernobyl Accident: A Case Study in International Law Regulating State Responsibility for Transboundary Nuclear Pollution', 12 *Columbia Journal of Environmental Law* 203 (1987); P. Sands, *International Law of Liability for Nuclear Damage* (1990); O. Von Busekist, 'A Bridge Between Two Conventions on Civil Liability for Nuclear Damage: The Joint Protocol Relating to the Application of the Vienna Convention and the Paris Convention', 43 *Nuclear Law Bulletin* 10 (1990); L. de La Fayette, 'Nuclear Liability Revisited', 1 RECIEL 443 (1992).

Two conventions specifically regulate civil liability for risks from the peaceful use of nuclear energy: the 1960 Paris OECD Convention on Third Party Liability in the Field of Nuclear Energy (1960 Paris Convention);[193] and the 1963 IAEA Vienna Convention on Civil Liability for Nuclear Damage (1963 Vienna

---

[191] See the 1989 Basel Convention, Art. 12.
[192] See OECD, Pollution Insurance and Compensation Funds for Accidental Pollution (1991).
[193] 29 July 1960, in force 1 April 1968; 956 UNTS 251; fifteen states are party.

Convention).[194] Other agreements have been concluded in respect of damage caused by nuclear ships.[195] The Paris and Vienna Conventions generally follow the same approach, although the latter is potentially of global application. Both agreements are now obsolete, and in 1997 a Protocol amending the 1963 Vienna Convention was adopted,[196] together with a new Convention on Supplementary Compensation (1997 Supplementary Compensation Convention).[197] Compared to oil spill regimes, the recent 'improvements' are somewhat marginal, and it is likely that these instruments would be overwhelmed and inadequate in the event of a major nuclear accident.

1960 Paris Convention

The purpose of the Paris Convention is to harmonise national legislation with regard to third party liability and insurance against nuclear risks and establish a regime of minimum standards for liability and compensation in the event of a nuclear incident, as defined in Article 1(a)(i). The Paris Convention generally applies only to nuclear incidents occurring, and damage suffered, in the territory of contracting parties.[198] A party in whose territory the nuclear installation of the operator liable is situated is free to provide otherwise in its national legislation,[199] but the Convention is silent as to damage in areas beyond national jurisdiction.

The operator of the nuclear installation,[200] whether a private entity or the state, is strictly liable for injury to or loss of life of any person and damage to or loss of property; no provision is made for liability in respect of environmental damage.[201] Liability generally extends to damage caused by incidents outside

---

[194] Vienna, 21 May 1963, in force 12 November 1977, 1063 UNTS 265; thirty-two states are party.

[195] Brussels Convention on the Liability of Operators of Nuclear Ships, 25 May 1962, not in force, 57 AJIL 268 (1963); M. J. L. Hardy, 'The Liability of Operators of Nuclear Ships', 12 ICLQ 778 (1963); P. Szasz, 'The Convention on the Liability of Operators of Nuclear Ships', 2 *Journal of Maritime Law and Commerce* 541 (1970–1). See also 1963 Netherlands and United States Agreement on Public Liability for Damage Caused by the NS Savannah, The Hague, 6 February 1963, 487 UNTS 113.

[196] Protocol to Amend the Vienna Convention on Civil Liability for Nuclear Damage, Vienna, 12 September 1997, not yet in force, 36 ILM 1454 (1997).

[197] Convention on Supplementary Compensation for Nuclear Damage, Vienna, 12 September 1997, not yet in force, 36 ILM 1473 (1997).

[198] Art. 2.   [199] *Ibid.*

[200] 'Nuclear installation' includes reactors other than those used in a means of transport, factories for manufacturing or processing nuclear substances or separating isotopes of or reprocessing nuclear fuels, and storage facilities for nuclear substances: Art. 1(a)(ii); 'nuclear substances' means nuclear fuel and radioactive products or waste: Art. 1(a)(iv).

[201] Art. 3(a). Even this restrictive provision has been interpreted by the English High Court to exclude 'pure economic loss': see *Merlins* v. *British Nuclear Fuels plc* [1990] 3 All ER 711. Other countries, such as the Netherlands and Germany, have extended their domestic legislation to include 'environmental' damage.

the installation during carriage to another installation or to other persons.[202] This applies also to incidents involving nuclear substances in the course of carriage to or from that installation.[203] The operator's liability may be established by proving a causal connection between the damage and the nuclear incident; proof of fault on the part of the operator is not required, although the rule does not establish 'absolute' liability since exceptions to the operator's liability are provided by Articles 4 and 9. Unless a longer period is provided by national legislation, claims must be brought within ten years from the date of the nuclear incident.[204] Jurisdiction over actions will generally lie with the courts of the party in whose territory the nuclear incident occurred,[205] and a state may not, except in respect of measures of execution, invoke any jurisdictional immunities.[206] Judgments are enforceable in the territory of any party, and the Convention is to be applied without discrimination as to nationality, domicile or residence.[207]

The operator's maximum liability for damage caused by a nuclear incident is fifteen million European Monetary Agreement units of account (approximately US$15 million), although any party may establish a greater or lesser amount, but not less than five million units of account.[208] Operators are required to maintain insurance or other financial security.[209]

Recognising that in many cases the damage suffered might exceed the operator's liability, most parties have ratified the Brussels Supplementary Convention of 1963, which increases the total amount of compensation available to 120 million units of account per incident.[210] Under the 1963 Supplementary Convention, the operator's liability is unchanged, but the party in whose territory the installation is situated is required to provide additional compensation of up to seventy million units of account.[211] Should the damage exceed this amount, further compensation up to 120 million units of account is to be paid jointly by the parties to the 1963 Supplementary Convention according to a formula reflecting each party's gross national product and the thermal power

---

[202] Art. 4(b). See also the Convention Relating to Civil Liability in the Field of Maritime Carriage of Nuclear Material, 17 December 1971, in force 15 July 1975, Misc. 39 (1972), Cmnd 5094. The 1971 Convention is intended to ensure that the operator of a nuclear installation will be exclusively liable for damage caused by a nuclear incident occurring in the course of maritime carriage of nuclear material by exonerating any person apart from the operator of a nuclear installation from liability for such damage: Arts. 1 and 2.

[203] Art. 4.   [204] Art. 8.

[205] Art. 13(a). See also the 1962 Brussels Nuclear Ships Convention, which allows the claimant to bring a claim either to the courts of the licensing state or to the courts of the party in whose territory nuclear damage has been sustained: Art. X(1).

[206] Art. 13(e).   [207] Arts. 13(d) and 14.   [208] Art. 7(b).   [209] Art. 10.

[210] OECD Agreement Supplementary to the Paris Convention of 1960 on Third Party Liability in the Field of Nuclear Energy, 31 January 1963, in force 4 December 1974, 1041 UNTS 358 (as amended by 1964 Protocol), Art. 3(a).

[211] Supplementary Agreement, Art. 3(b)(ii); eleven states are party.

of reactors situated in its territory.[212] In 1982, further Protocols to the Paris Convention and the Brussels Supplementary Convention were adopted, which changed the unit of compensation to the 'special drawing rights' (SDR) of the IMF and increased the compensation payable by a party and by parties jointly to 175 million SDR and 300 million SDR respectively.[213]

1963 Vienna Convention[214]

The provisions of the 1963 Vienna Convention, which are not to be construed as 'affecting the rights, if any, of a contracting party under the general rules of public international law in respect of nuclear damage',[215] are generally to the same effect as those of the Paris Convention. The operator is liable for 'nuclear damage', which is defined as loss of life, personal injury or damage to property, upon proof that such damage was caused by a nuclear incident in the installation or, with certain limitations, in the course of carriage to or from the installation.[216] The Vienna Convention does not specifically provide for liability for environmental damage, although it allows the law of the competent court to provide for other damage.[217] Liability is stated to be absolute, although provision is made for certain defences and exceptions.[218] Generally, actions must be brought within ten years from the date of the nuclear incident, and jurisdiction over actions lies only with the courts of the party within whose territory the nuclear incident occurred.[219] If an action is brought against a state it may not, except in respect of measures of execution, invoke any jurisdictional immunities.[220] Final judgments which are recognised are enforceable in the territory of any party.[221] The Vienna Convention allows the installation state to limit the operator's liability, but in no event may it be limited to less than US$5 million for any nuclear incident.[222] Operators must maintain insurance or other financial security; however, if the security is inadequate to satisfy claims, Article VII provides that the installation state is required to meet any deficiencies up to the limit, if any, of the operator's liability as established under Article V. In contrast to the position under the 1963 Supplementary Convention, no provision is made for further compensation beyond this limit by either the installation state or the parties jointly.

The Chernobyl accident highlighted the inadequacies of the liability regime established by the Paris and Vienna Conventions. The accident on 26 April 1986 released large amounts of radioactivity and led to increased levels of

---

[212] Arts. 3(b)(iii) and 12.   [213] Paris, 16 November 1982, IELMT 963:101B.

[214] Note 194 above. See IAEA, 'Civil Liability for Nuclear Damage', Official Records, Legal Services No. 2, 149 *et seq.* (1964) (*travaux préparatoires*).

[215] Art. XVIII.

[216] Arts. I(1)(k) and II(1). See also the Convention Relating to Civil Liability in the Field of Maritime Carriage of Nuclear Material, p. 907 above.

[217] Art. I(1)(k)(ii).   [218] Art. IV.   [219] Arts. VI and XI.

[220] Art. XIV.   [221] Art. XII(1) and (2).   [222] Art. V.

radiation over an extensive area.[223] In the former USSR, more than 100,000 people were evacuated from a radius of twenty miles around the plant within thirty-six hours, and thirty-one people died as a direct result within a few weeks. Within six months of the accident, the IAEA had sponsored two new international conventions on emergency notification and assistance,[224] and the issue of nuclear liability returned to the international agenda. The Board of Governors of the IAEA, having considered a background paper by the IAEA secretariat on the question of international liability for nuclear damage,[225] asked the secretariat to 'consider whether it was necessary to devise a new instrument on state liability for nuclear damage . . . full account being taken of the work of the [ILC]'.[226] The secretariat concluded that 'there seems to be no doctrinal obstacle to the elaboration of special rules intended to regulate international liability for nuclear damage', the rules of which might result from the work of the ILC,[227] and suggested that a new instrument

> could complement the existing civil law conventions on nuclear liability . . .
> in those areas where their regimes are incomplete because of legal lacunae
> (claims between states, damage to the environment) and it could provide the
> necessary framework for possibly combining international liability aspects
> and the issues already covered by the Vienna and Paris Conventions into
> a comprehensive nuclear liability regime, giving the parties to either of
> these instruments the option of providing remedies in accordance with
> appropriate procedures to be embodied within the framework.[228]

In 1989, the IAEA established a Standing Committee on Nuclear Liability to revise the 1963 Vienna Convention, which resulted in the adoption of the 1997 Protocol to the 1963 Vienna Convention, and the 1997 Convention on Supplementary Compensation. The slow progress of the Standing Committee's work reflected political and economic sensitivities, and illustrated the difficulties in developing liability rules in other areas. A number of important nuclear power

---

[223] Increased radiation levels were subsequently observed, *inter alia*, in Sweden, Denmark, Finland and Poland (27 April); Austria, German Democratic Republic, Hungary, Italy, Norway and Yugoslavia (29 April); Federal Republic of Germany, Switzerland and Turkey (30 April); France (1 May); Belgium, Greece, the Netherlands and the United Kingdom (2 May); and Iceland (7 May). Low-level increases were also detected in Japan and the United States. Significant increases of particular danger to human health and the environment were observed in levels of iodine-131, caesium-134 and caesium-137 immediately after the accident; see Summary Report of 22 July 1986 of the Working Group on Assessment of Radiation Dose Contamination in Europe due to the Chernobyl Accident, noted in 28 IAEA *Bulletin*, No. 3 (1986) 27.

[224] See chapter 12, pp. 647–8 above.

[225] IAEA, Note by Director General, 'The Question of International Liability for Damage Arising from a Nuclear Accident', IAEA Doc. GOV/INF/509, Annex (1987).

[226] IAEA, Note by Director General, 'The Question of Liability for Damage Arising from a Nuclear Accident', IAEA Doc. GOV/2306, para. 1 (1987).

[227] *Ibid.*, Annex 2, paras. 2 and 3.   [228] *Ibid.*, Annex 2, para. 4.

states, including France, the United Kingdom and the United States, strongly opposed rules of state liability in the amendments.

Controversial issues in the negotiations included the extension of the 1963 Vienna Convention to military installations, its application to damage in areas outside the territory of parties (including areas beyond national jurisdiction), and liability for environmental damage. Two other difficult issues concerned the extent to which the limits on the operator's liability should be increased, and the differences between states supporting full compensation for the victim and restoration of the environment, and states wishing to limit liability to protect nuclear industries from insurance and other costs. Underlying the debate was concern that increases in the operator's maximum liability to adequately cover a Chernobyl-type accident would make the insurance of nuclear plants difficult (if not impossible) in many countries and could limit the further development of nuclear power. On the other hand, it was clear that any limitation on liability amounted to an interference with the application of the polluter-pays principle and a *de facto* subsidy to the nuclear industry.[229]

Another issue which caused difficulty at the IAEA Standing Committee was the question of whether to establish an international claims tribunal to handle claims which might follow a major nuclear incident.[230] Supporters of the original 1963 system, which requires all claims to be channelled to the courts (or a court) of the state in which the accident occurred, argued that this was the only way to achieve a uniform interpretation of the rules and an equitable disbursement of the funds in the context of the limited sums available. Opponents pointed out that it was unrealistic to expect individuals to file claims in a court located several thousand miles away and that no national court could cope with the deluge of claims which would follow a major accident. They also pointed out that the original system provided no incentive for countries such as Ireland and Luxembourg to join the conventions when their citizens could benefit from rights provided under the conventional rules of private international law, allowing them to choose their jurisdiction.[231] In the end, the proponents of the original arrangements prevailed.

When it enters into force, the 1997 Protocol will introduce several amendments for its parties.[232] As to the definition of 'nuclear damage', the Protocol specifies with greater particularity the types of damage which the laws of the competent court may treat as giving rise to liability, including economic loss, the costs of measures of reinstatement of impaired environment (unless

---

[229] See chapter 6, pp. 279–85 above; and chapter 19, pp. 1010–15 below.

[230] See in this regard the Marshall Islands Nuclear Claims Tribunal, and its decision in respect of US nuclear testing around the Marshall Islands (1946–58), p. 889 above.

[231] See 1968 Brussels Convention and 1988 Lugano Convention; chapter 5 above.

[232] A state which is a party to the Protocol but not to the 1963 Convention will be bound by the provisons of the Convention as amended, unless it expresses a different intent at the time of becoming a party, in which case it will not be bound by the 1963 Convention in relation to states which are parties only to the Convention: 1997 Protocol, Art. 19(1).

insignificant), the costs of preventive measures, and loss of income deriving from an economic interest in any use or enjoyment of the environment (as a result of a significant impairment of that environment).[233] It is important to note, however, that the amended Convention will not require environmental damage to be compensated: only loss of life or personal injury or damage to property must be compensated. Among the other clarifications is provision to the effect that nuclear installations used for 'non-peaceful purposes' are excluded from the Convention,[234] and that the Convention applies 'to nuclear damage suffered anywhere', subject to the right of a party to exclude damage suffered in the territory of a non-party or in any maritime zones established by a non-party in accordance with international law (provided these non-parties also possess nuclear installations within their territory and maritime zones but do not provide reciprocal benefits).[235] The ability of a party to limit the liability of an operator is amended to establish a floor of not less than 300 million SDRs,[236] with consequential changes to the provisions on financial security.[237] Prescription periods are amended to a minor extent.[238] The exclusive jurisdiction of the courts of the party in whose territory the nuclear incident occurred remains, but is extended to encompass damage occurring in the exclusive economic zone.[239] States will be able to bring an action (in the party's courts having jurisdiction) on behalf of persons who have suffered damage,[240] and the Protocol introduces a dispute settlement clause into the Convention.[241] These are modest amendments which do not modify the basic approach of the 1963 Convention or address the fundamental criticisms which have been levelled towards it.

Together with the 1997 Protocol there has also been adopted the new 1997 Convention on Supplementary Compensation. This is intended to supplement the system of compensation which is provided under national law pursuant to the 1960 and 1963 Conventions (and any amendments to them) or which complies with the standards established in the Annex to the 1997 Convention.[242]

---

[233] 1997 Protocol, Art. 2, amending Art. I(k) of the 1963 Convention. Art. 2(4) of the 1997 Protocol provides new definitions.

[234] 1997 Protocol, Art. 3, establishing a new Art. IB to the 1963 Convention.

[235] 1997 Protocol, Art 3, establishing a new Art. IA to the 1963 Convention.

[236] 1997 Protocol, Art. 7(1), replacing Art. V of the 1963 Convention. The Protocol provides for 'transitional arrangements' for up to fifteen years, during which limits may be 100 million SDRs (Art. 7(2)). See also new Arts. VA to VD, providing *inter alia* for: payment of interest and costs; enforcement; and amendments to limits of liability by decision of the parties.

[237] 1997 Protocol, Art. 9, amending Art. VI of the 1963 Convention.

[238] 1997 Protocol, Art. 8, amending Art. VI of the 1963 Convention.

[239] 1997 Protocol, Art. 12, establishing a new Art. XI(1*bis*) to the 1963 Convention.

[240] 1997 Protocol, Art. 13, establishing a new Art. XIA to the 1963 Convention.

[241] 1997 Protocol, Art. 17, establishing a new Art. XXA to the 1963 Convention.

[242] Art. II(1). The Convention is thereby potentially open to states such as the United States which are not party to the 1960 or 1963 Conventions.

Parties are to ensure the availability of 300 million SDRs or other amount as permitted and notified and, beyond that amount, additional public funds as required pursuant to a formula established under Article IV of the Convention.[243] The Convention provides detailed rules on the organisation of supplementary funding once it appears that damage caused by an incident exceeds the amount available under Article III(1)(a), as well as rules on jurisdiction and applicable law, generally following the approach in the 1960 and 1963 Conventions.[244]

1988 Joint Protocol

In 1988, a Joint Protocol Relating to the Application of the Vienna Convention and the Paris Convention[245] linked the operative parts of the Paris and Vienna Conventions by providing that the operator of a nuclear installation in the territory of a party to either the Paris or Vienna Convention will be liable under that Convention for nuclear damage suffered in the territory of a state which is a party to the other Convention and the Protocol.[246] The Joint Protocol provides for the exclusive application of each Convention and sets forth choice-of-law rules.[247]

Oil pollution

P. N. Swan, 'International and National Approaches to Oil Pollution Responsibility: An Emerging Regime for a Global Problem', 50 *Oregon Law Review* 504 (1971); S. Bergman, 'No Fault Liability for Oil Pollution Damage', 5 *Journal of Maritime Law and Commerce* 1 (1973); T. Treves, 'Les Tendences récentes du droit conventionnel de la responsabilité et le nouveau droit de la mer', 21 AFDI 767 (1975); R. E. Stein, 'Responsibility and Liability for Harm to the Marine Environment', 6 *Georgia Journal of International and Comparative Law* 41 (1976); G. Handl, 'International Liability of States for Marine Pollution', 21 *Canadian Yearbook of International Law* 85 (1983); M. Jacobsson and N. Trotz, 'The Definition of Pollution Damage in the 1984 Protocols to the 1969 Civil Liability Convention and the 1971 Fund Convention', 17 *Journal of Maritime Law and Commerce* 467 (1986); B. Maffei, 'The Compensation for Ecological Damage in the "Patmos" Case', in F. Francioni and T. Scovazzi (eds.), *International Responsibility for Environmental Harm* (1991); S. T. Smith, 'An Analy-

---

[243] Art. III(1). The formula is (i) the amount which is the product of the party's installed nuclear capacity multiplied by 300 SDRs per unit of installed capacity, plus (ii) the amount determined by applying the ratio between the party's UN rate of assessment as assessed for the year preceding that in which the nuclear incident occurs, and the total of such rates for all parties to 10 per cent of the sum of the amounts calculated for all parties under (i) above, subject to a maximum contribution and the principle that states on the minimum UN rate of assessment with no nuclear reactors will not be required to make a contribution: Art. IV(1).

[244] Arts. VI–XII and XIII–XIV.

[245] Vienna, 21 September 1988, in force 27 April 1992, 42 *Nuclear Law Bulletin* 56 1998.

[246] Arts. II and IV.   [247] Art. III.

sis of the Oil Pollution Act of 1990 and the 1984 Protocols on Civil Liability for Oil Pollution Damage', 14 *Houston Journal of International Law* 115 (1991); A. D. Cummings, 'The Exxon Valdez Oil Spill and the Confidentiality of Natural Resource Damage Assessment Data', 19 *Ecology Law Quarterly* 363 (1992); A. H. E. Popp, 'Legal Aspects of International Oil Spills in the Canada/US Context', 18 *Canada–US Law Journal* 309 (1992); P. Birnie, 'Liability for Damage Resulting from the Transport of Hazardous Cargoes by Sea', 25 *Law of the Sea Institute Proceedings* 377 (1993); C. B. Kende, 'Liability for Pollution Damage and Legal Assessment of Damage to the Marine Environment', 11 *Journal of Energy and Natural Resources Law* 105 (1993); D. J. Wilkinson, 'Moving the Boundaries of Compensable Damage Caused by Marine Oil Spills: The Effect of Two New International Protocols', 5 JEL 71 (1993); C. de la Rue, *Liability for Damage to the Marine Environment* (1993); P. Wetterstein, 'Trends in Maritime Environmental Impairment Liability', LMCLQ 230 (1994); G. Gauci, *Oil Pollution at Sea: Civil Liability and Compensation for Damage* (1997); M. Goransson, 'Liability for Damage to the Marine Environment', in A. Boyle and D. Freestone (eds.), *International Law and Sustainable Development* (1999), 345.

Civil liability for damage caused by oil pollution is principally governed by two well-developed and well-applied international instruments adopted under the auspices of the IMO: the Brussels International Convention on Civil Liability for Oil Pollution Damage (1992 CLC) and the Brussels International Convention on the Establishment of an International Fund for Compensation of Oil Pollution Damage (1992 Oil Fund Convention), together with a Convention on Civil Liability for Bunker Oil Pollution Damage, adopted in 2001. In the 1970s, three private arrangements were set up to increase the amounts of funding available, but two – TOVALOP and CRISTAL – were wound up in 1997, after the entry into force of the 1992 IMO Protocols.

1992 Civil Liability Convention[248]

The original 1969 CLC was adopted following the accident involving the Liberian-registered *Torrey Canyon*, which ran aground in the Atlantic off the south-west coast of Britain on 18 March 1967 while carrying nearly 120,000 tons of crude oil. The escape of oil caused widespread damage to the British coastline and to marine life, and eventually polluted the coast of France.[249]

[248] 29 November 1969, in force 19 June 1975, 973 UNTS 3; amended by the 1976 Protocol, 19 November 1976, in force 8 April 1981, 16 ILM 617 (1977); 1984 Protocol, 25 May 1984, not in force, 23 ILM 177 (1984); and 1992 Protocol, 27 November 1992, in force 30 May 1996, IMO LEG/CONF.9/15. The 1992 Liability Protocol replaced the 1984 Protocol and entered into force after it had been ratified by at least four states each with not less than one million units of gross tanker tonnage: Art. 13 (the 1984 Protocol required ratification by six such states). The consolidated text is available at www.iopcfund.org/engtextoc.pdf; ninety-one states are party.

[249] See the report prepared by the UK Home Office, *The Torrey Canyon*, Cmnd 3246 (1967); Gill, *The Wreck of the Torrey Canyon* (1967); Brown, 21 *Current Legal Practice* 216 (1968); *British Practice in International Law* 90–2 (1967).

The accident led to the Brussels Conference of 1969 and the adoption of two new conventions: the 1969 Intervention Convention[250] and the 1969 CLC. The latter has been the subject of three amending Protocols, most recently by the 1992 Liability Protocol. With the entry into force of the 1992 Protocol, the 1969 CLC is now known as the International Convention on Civil Liability for Oil Pollution Damage 1992 (1992 CLC).

The 1992 CLC establishes the liability of the owner of a ship for pollution damage caused by oil escaping from the ship as a result of an incident on the territory of a party (including its territorial sea), and covers preventive measures to minimise such damage.[251] Under the 1969 CLC, 'pollution damage' was defined as:

> loss or damage caused outside the ship carrying oil by contamination resulting from the escape or discharge of oil from the ship, wherever such escape or discharge may occur, and includes the cost of preventive measures and further loss or damage caused by preventive measures.[252]

The view that this includes environmental damage is supported by the amended text of the 1992 CLC, which defines pollution damage as:

(a) loss or damage caused outside the ship by contamination, resulting from the escape or discharge of oil from the ship, wherever such escape or discharge may occur, provided that compensation for impairment of the environment other than loss of profit from such impairment shall be limited to costs of reasonable measures of reinstatement actually undertaken or to be undertaken;

(b) the costs of preventative measures and further loss or damage caused by preventative measures.[253]

This current definition, which develops the 1969 definition, implies that the latter is intended to include compensation for impairment of the environment. However, in order for a claim for environmental damage to be brought, the 1992 definition requires measures taken to be 'reasonable' and to have actually been undertaken or to be undertaken. The 1992 CLC establishes joint and several liability for damage which is not 'reasonably separable', and allows a limited number of exceptions, including war and hostilities, intentional acts,

---

[250] Chapter 9, p. 449 above.

[251] Arts. II and III(1). The Convention does not apply to warships or other ships owned or operated by a state and being used at the time of the incident for non-commercial purposes: Art. XI(1). Art. 3 of the 1992 Protocol would extend the application of the Convention to pollution damage caused in the EEZ of a party or, if the party has not declared an EEZ, to the area extending to no more than 200 nautical miles from the baseline from which its territorial sea is measured.

[252] Art. I(6). 'Preventive measures' are limited to 'reasonable measures' to prevent or minimise pollution damage: Art. I(7).

[253] 1992 Protocol, Art. 2(3). The 1992 Protocol amended the definitions of other terms, including 'ship', 'oil' and 'incident': Art. 2.

governmental negligence and contributory negligence, and it extinguishes all other claims for compensation.[254] Under the original 1969 CLC, the owner could limit liability to 2,000 francs for each ton of the ship's net tonnage with an overall limit on liability of 210 million francs, but may not avail itself of the limit if the incident is the result of the owner's 'actual fault or privity'.[255] The permitted limits were increased by the 1992 Protocol to 3 million SDRs for ships not exceeding 5,000 units of tonnage, and 420 SDRs for each additional unit of tonnage to a maximum of 59.7 million SDRs.[256] The owner must maintain insurance or other financial security to cover its liability and, to limit its liability, establish a fund for the total sum of liability with the court in which action is brought.[257] Under the 1992 CLC, claims may be brought before the courts of any party or parties in which the pollution damage has occurred or the preventive measures have been taken, and judgments are generally recognisable and enforceable in the courts of all parties.[258] The court in which a fund is established is exclusively competent to apportion and distribute the fund.[259]

The 1992 Protocol makes a number of consequential changes to the 1992 CLC, and establishes a hierarchical relationship between the 1992 Liability Convention and the 1992 Fund Convention by providing for the prior application of the latter.[260]

The 1992 Fund Convention[261]

The 1992 (originally 1971) Fund Convention was adopted under the auspices of an International Legal Conference on Marine Pollution Damage to provide

---

[254] Arts. III(2) and (3) and IV.

[255] Art. V. The 1992 Protocol amended Art. V(2) by removing the owner's entitlement to limit liability if it is proved that the pollution damage resulted from the owner's 'personal act or omission, committed with the intent to cause such damage or recklessly and with knowledge that such damage would probably result': Art. 4(2). The 1992 Protocol established procedures for amending the limitation amounts: Art. 15.

[256] Art. 6(1). The IMO's Legal Committee increased the compensation limits by 'tacitly amending' Art. 6(1) to 4.51 million SDRs for ships not exceeding 5,000 units of gross tonnage and 631 SDRs for each additional unit of tonnage to a maximum, at 140,000 units of tonnage, of 89.77 million SDRs. The amendment will enter force on 1 November 2003: IOPC Funds, *Annual Report 2000*, 16, available at www.iopcfund.org/eng2000ar.pdf.

[257] Arts. V(3), VI and VII.   [258] Arts. IX(1) and X.   [259] Art. IX(3).

[260] 1992 Protocol, Art. 9, establishing a new Art. XII*bis* to the 1992 Convention.

[261] Brussels, 18 December 1971, in force 16 October 1978; 1110 UNTS 57; amended by Protocol, London, 19 November 1976, not yet in force; 16 ILM 621 (1977); 1984 Protocol, 25 May 1984, not yet in force; 1992 Fund Protocol, 27 September 1992, in force 30 May 1996, IMO LEG/CONF.9/16. The 1992 Protocol entered into force after ratification by eight states in which contributing importers had received a total of 450 million tons of oil in the preceding calendar year (the 1984 Protocol required eight states and 600 million tons). The text of the 1992 Fund Convention is available at www.iopcfund.org/engtextoc.pdf; eighty-five states are party. In May 2003 a diplomatic conference adopted a Protocol on the Establishment of a Supplementary Fund for Oil Pollution Damage, creating an additional, third tier of compensation.

additional compensation for victims of oil pollution and to transfer some of the economic consequences to the owners of the oil cargo, as well as the shipowner subject to the original 1969 CLC. The original 1971 Convention was amended by three Protocols, most recently by the 1992 Fund Protocol. With the entry into force of the 1992 Protocol, the 1971 Fund Convention is known as the International Convention on the Establishment of an International Fund for Oil Pollution Damage, 1992 (1992 Fund Convention). By May 2002, the 1971 Fund had been involved in the settlement of claims arising out of 107 incidents, and the total compensation paid amounted to £283 million, and the 1992 Fund had been involved in fifteen incidents and made compensation payments of £61 million.

In general, the 1992 Fund Convention adopts the same definitions as the 1992 CLC.[262] The 1992 Fund Convention, which establishes an International Oil Pollution Compensation Fund (IOPC Fund), has as its objective to provide compensation for pollution damage which is inadequately compensated by the 1992 CLC.[263] The 1971 Convention represented the first time that linkage in an international legal instrument was explicitly made between the extent of a person's liability and compliance with obligations found in other treaties.

To fulfil its objective, the Fund pays compensation to any person suffering pollution damage if that person has been unable to obtain 'full and adequate' compensation under the 1992 CLC because no liability arises under that Convention, or the owner cannot meet obligations under that Convention, or the liability exceeds the limit established by that Convention.[264] The 1992 Fund Convention limits the obligation of the Fund in certain situations, including war, lack of evidence that the damage resulted from an incident involving one or more ships, damage by warships or state operated non-commercial ships, and contributory negligence.[265] Originally, compensation payable under the Fund was limited to 450 million francs per incident, and an aggregate of 450 million francs for pollution damage 'resulting from a natural phenomenon of an exceptional, inevitable and irresistible character'.[266] At its ninth session, the Fund Assembly increased the aggregate amount of compensation payable by the Fund for any one incident to 900 million francs (60 million SDRs) for incidents occurring after 30 November 1987.[267] The 1976 Protocol amended the ceilings

---

[262] Art. 1. See also 1992 Protocol, Art. 2(3) to (6).

[263] Art. 2(1). The 1992 Protocol amended Art. 2(1) of the 1971 Fund Convention by removing a second objective (to relieve shipowners from additional financial burdens provided they have complied with safety at sea and other conventions) and extending the application of the Convention to include the EEZ or equivalent area: Arts. 3 and 4. The 1992 Protocol deleted Art. V of the 1971 Convention, whereby the Fund indemnified the owner and guarantor for that portion of the liability under the 1969 CLC which exceeded certain amounts: Art. 7.

[264] Art. 4(1).   [265] Art. 4(2) and (3); see also the 1992 Protocol, Art. 6(2).

[266] Art. 4(4).

[267] This is the maximum permitted under Art. 4(6) of the Fund Convention, and follows earlier increases to 675 million francs and 787.5 million francs.

to 30 million SDRs or 450 million monetary units and 60 million SDRs or 900 million monetary units respectively.[268] The 1992 Protocol replaced the entire text of Art. 4(4) of the 1971 Fund Convention with a new provision increasing the maximum liability to 135 million SDRs per incident or for certain natural damage, and to 200 million SDRs for any period when there are three parties to the Convention where the combined relevant quantities of contributing oil received by persons in the territories of those parties equalled or exceeded 600 million tons in the preceding year.[269]

The 1992 Fund Convention limits periods for the bringing of claims, and requires any action against the Fund for compensation to be brought only before a court competent under Article IX of the 1992 CLC.[270] Where an action has been brought before a court against an owner under the 1992 CLC, that court has exclusive competence over any action against the Fund under Article 4 of the 1992 Fund Convention in respect of the same damage.[271] Where that court is in a state which is not a party to the 1992 Fund Convention, the claimant may bring the case before the court where the Fund is headquartered (London) or any court of a party to the 1992 Fund Convention competent under Article IX of the 1992 CLC.[272] The 1992 Fund Convention also sets forth rules concerning the effect of judgments on the Fund, the recognition and enforcement of judgments, and rights of recourse and subrogation.[273]

Annual contributions to the Fund are made, in respect of each party, by any person (including associated persons) who has received a total of more than 150,000 tons of contributing oil in the ports or terminals in the territory of that party contributing oil carried by sea, and contributing oil first received in any installations situated in the territory of that party which has first been carried by sea and discharged in a port or terminal of a non-party.[274] The assessment of each person's annual contribution which may be needed to balance the budget comprises a proportion of the total amount of contributions required by the Fund to fulfil its estimated annual expenditure.[275] The 1992 Protocol's transitional provisions govern contributions and place a limit, for up to five years, on the contribution of any one party to a maximum of 27.5 per cent of the total contributions to the Fund.[276]

---

[268] Art. III(a). The 1984 Protocol would have amended Art. 4(6) by removing the right of the Assembly to increase the amounts of compensation, and provides for a new procedure for the amendment of compensation limits: Arts. 6(5) and 33.

[269] Art. 6(3).   [270] Arts. 6 and 7(1).   [271] Art. 7(3).   [272] *Ibid.*

[273] Arts. 7(6), 8 and 9.

[274] Arts. 10(1) and (2) and 12; 'contributing oil' means crude oil and fuel oil as defined in Art. 1(3)(a).

[275] Art. 12(2) and (3).

[276] 1992 Protocol, Art. 26, creating new Arts. 36(*bis*) and 36(*ter*) of the 1992 Fund Convention. This provision was included to encourage ratification by Japan, which in 1991 contributed 28.92 per cent of the Fund.

The IOPC Fund, which has legal personality under the laws of each party,[277] comprises an Assembly, a Secretariat and an Executive Committee.[278] The Assembly, in which all parties to the Convention are members, has overall responsibility for the administration of the Fund and for the proper execution of the Convention, and its functions include approving the settlement of claims, taking decisions in respect of distributions under Article 4(5) and provisional payments, and electing the Executive Committee.[279] There are fifteen members of the Executive Committee, elected on the basis of equitable geographic distribution, including parties particularly exposed to the risks of oil pollution and having large tanker fleets, and approximately one-half from those parties in whose territory the largest quantities of oil were received.[280] The functions of the Executive Committee include approving the settlement of claims and giving instructions to the Director.[281]

IOPC Fund Resolution No. 3   The IOPC Fund has received numerous claims for environmental damage, and its practice may prove instructive to the international community as it seeks to define environmental damage in other contexts. It will be recalled that the Fund pays compensation for pollution damage, which means 'loss or damage outside the ship carrying oil by contamination'. The first claim to the Fund, arising out of the grounding of the USSR-registered *Antonio Gramsci* off Ventspils, in the former USSR, on 27 February 1979, raised the question of whether this definition included environmental damage or damage to natural resources, as claimed by the USSR and others. The response of the Fund Assembly is to be found in Resolution No. 3, adopted in 1980, which determined that 'the assessment of compensation to be paid by the IOPC Fund is not to be made on the basis of an abstract quantification of damage calculated in accordance with theoretical models'.[282]

The Patmos claim   In 1985, on the basis of Resolution No. 3, the IOPC Fund addressed a £9.2 million claim (later reduced to £2.3 million) by the Italian Government for damage to the marine environment arising out of a spillage from the *Patmos*, a Greek-registered tanker, off the coast of Calabria on 21 March 1985. In the absence of any documentation from the Italian Government indicating the nature of the damage which had been caused or the basis

---

[277] Art. 2(2).
[278] Arts. 16 to 30. The 1992 Protocol discontinued the Executive Committee: Arts. 17 to 24.
[279] Arts. 17 and 18. Decisions of the Assembly and the Executive Conunittee are generally taken on the basis of a simple majority of those present and voting, with special provision for certain decisions to be taken on the basis of a three-fourths or two-thirds majority of those present: Arts. 32 and 33.
[280] Art. 22.   [281] Art. 26.
[282] 10 October 1980, FUND/A/ES 1/13, para. 11(a) and Annex (1980). An Intersessional Working Group used similar language in finding that compensation could only be granted if a claimant had suffered economic loss.

on which the amount claimed had been calculated, the IOPC Fund rejected the claim.[283] The Italian Government took the case to the Italian courts, and in 1986 the Court of First Instance rejected the government's claim for compensation for ecological damage to marine flora and fauna on the grounds that the territorial sea was not crown or patrimonial property of the state but a *res communis omnium* which could not be violated by private parties, and that even if it was the state had not incurred any direct or indirect loss as a result of the oil spill since no disbursements for the cleaning of the coastline had been incurred nor had any loss of profit occurred.[284] In 1989, the Court of Appeal overruled the decision, interpreting the Convention to include as environmental damage 'everything which alters, causes deterioration in or destroys the environment in whole or in part'.[285] The Court of Appeal interpreted the terms of the 1969 CLC by reference to the 1969 Intervention Convention, which defines the threat to 'related interests' justifying intervention as including 'the conservation of living marine resources and of wildlife'.[286] The Court of Appeal went on to hold that:

> the environment must be considered as a unitary asset, separate from those of which the environment is composed (territory, territorial waters, beaches, fish etc.) and it includes natural resources, health and landscape. The right to the environment belongs to the state, in its capacity as representative of the collectivities. The damage to the environment prejudices immaterial values, which cannot be assessed in monetary terms according to market prices, and consists of the reduced possibility of using the environment. The damage can be compensated on an equitable basis, which may be established by the Court on the grounds of an opinion of experts . . . The definition of 'pollution damage' as laid down in Article 1(6) is wide enough to include damage to the environment of the kind described above.[287]

The Court of Appeal held that the traditional view of property damage was no longer valid, and that the owner of the *Patmos*, the UK Club (an insurers' group) and the IOPC Fund were liable for the environmental damage claimed by the Italian Government.[288] It appointed three experts to ascertain the existence, if any, of damage to the marine resources resulting from the oil spillage.[289] In their March 1990 report, the experts found that, with the exception of damage to fishing activities which they valued at approximately £465,000, there was a lack

---

[283] FUND/EXC.16/8, 22 October 1986, para. 3.3.

[284] Joined Cases No. 676/86 and No. 337 and others, *General Nation Maritime Transport Company and Others* v. *Patmos Shipping Company and Others*, Court of Messina, 1st Civil Section, 30 July 1986, unofficial translation (on file with the author), 27, 28.

[285] Cases 391, 392, 393, 398, 426, 459, 460 and 570/1986, Court of Appeal of Messina, Civil Section, Judgment of 30 March 1989, unofficial translation (on file with the author), 57.

[286] *Ibid.*, 58; 1969 Intervention Convention, Art. II(4)(c); see chapter 9, p. 449 above.

[287] Summary of Judgment of the Court of Appeal, Doc. FUND/EXC.30/2, 29 November 1991, para. 4.15.

[288] *Ibid.*, 59–60.   [289] See *Annual Report 1991*, 30.

of data to evaluate the economic impact on other activities and that a precise assessment of damage to such activities was impossible. The experts also determined that the court was the appropriate body to carry out the evaluation.[290] In December 1993, the Court of Appeal awarded a final judgment of £827,000 for environmental damage.[291] The court decided that the lack of data and inability of the experts to determine a precise damage award for environmental harms were not reasons to refuse compensation. It found that the experts were wrong to calculate damages based only on market prices for fish. Because the environment and its natural resources were worth more to the community, the Court of Appeal determined damages according to principles of equity. The decision itself does not make clear exactly how the judge assessed and calculated the environmental damages beyond the £465,000 previously indicated by the panel of experts.[292]

The Haven case   Another case before the Fund indicated the differences of interpretation which may be applied to the concept of 'environmental damage'. On 11 April 1991, the *Haven*, a Cypriot-registered tanker, caught fire and broke apart seven miles from Genoa in Italy and released over 10,000 tonnes of oil, causing damage to the Italian and French coasts and necessitating extensive clean-up operations.[293] The Italian Government submitted a claim for damage to the marine environment, this time in the provisional amount of 100,000 million Italian lire (£47 million), a figure which the Region of Liguria requested should be doubled.[294] One thousand two hundred Italian claimants, the French Government, twenty-two French municipalities and two other public bodies also submitted claims. In the subsequent court proceedings at the Court of First Instance in Genoa, the question arose as to whether claims for damage to the marine environment could be pursued against the shipowners outside the Conventions under the relevant Italian law if such damage was not admissible under the 1969 CLC and the 1971 Fund Convention.[295] In his report on this matter, the Director of the Fund concluded that the 1969 and 1971 Conventions were designed to provide compensation to victims of pollution damage, that claims which did not relate to such compensation fell outside the scope of the Conventions, and that claims relating to non-quantifiable elements

---

[290] *Ibid.*

[291] E. Brans, *Liability for Damage to Public Natural Resources: Standing, Damage and Damage Assessment* (2001), 329–31.

[292] *Ibid.*, 330.   [293] See *Annual Report 1991*, 59–62.   [294] *Ibid.*, 63.

[295] *Ibid.*, 68. The relevant Italian legislation relating to the protection of the marine environment is the Act of 31 December 1982 (No. 979), containing provisions for the protection of the sea and the Act of 8 July 1986 (No. 349) establishing the Ministry of Environment. The issue also raised the question of the relationship under Italian law between the legislation implementing the 1969 and 1971 Conventions (Act No. 506 of 27 May 1978) and this later legislation.

of damage to the environment were of a punitive nature and beyond the scope of the Convention.[296] The Director took the view that the drafters of the 1971 Fund Convention could not have intended that the Fund should pay damages of a punitive character calculated on the basis of the seriousness of the fault of the wrongdoer or the profit earned by the wrongdoer, and that the result of including such damage would be unacceptable.[297] On this basis, the Director concluded that such claims could be pursued outside the Conventions on the basis of national law.[298] In rejecting the Director's analysis during a session of the Executive Committee, the Italian delegation maintained its view that the 1969 and 1971 Conventions did not exclude compensation for environmental damage which was non-quantifiable, that the state had a legal right to compensation for damage to the environment which had irreversible consequences or where the environment could not be reinstated, and that Italian law envisaged the possibility of compensation for damage to the marine environment for quantifiable and non-quantifiable elements.[299] The Director's point of view was supported by France, the United Kingdom, Japan and the observer delegation of the International Group of P&I Clubs (shipping, insurance and freight companies).[300]

On 5 April 1996, the Court of First Instance in Genoa ruled that 'pollution damage' in the 1969 CLC and 1971 Fund Convention had a wide enough meaning to include natural resource and environmental damage.[301] Because these could not be calculated according to commercial or economic valuations, the court awarded £13 million (40,000 million lire), about one-third of the clean-up cost, on the basis that the clean-up did not repair all the damage caused; the award essentially compensated the unremedied residual damage.[302] The IOPC Fund appealed, and in response Italy requested that the environmental damages be increased to £284 million (883,435 million lire). On 4 March 1999, the parties (Italy, the shipowner, the UK Mutual Steam Ship Assurance Association and the IOPC Fund) withdrew all legal action from Italian courts and signed

---

[296] The study is set out in Doc. FUND/EXC.30/2 and summarised in the *Annual Report 1991*, 68–9.

[297] *Ibid.*   [298] *Ibid.*

[299] See FUND/EXC.30/5, paras. 3.1.5 to 3.1.7. Art. 1226 of the Italian Civil Code allows for the possibility that the amount of damage could be determined in an equitable manner if it was not possible to achieve a precise quantification; see also the text of the Italian statement in Doc. FUND/EXC.30/WP.1, 16 December 1991.

[300] *Ibid.*, paras. 31.1.13–31.1.18.

[301] E. Brans, *Liability for Damage to Public Natural Resources: Standing, Damage and Damage Assessment*, 334. The court dismissed claims by provinces and municipalities because no economic loss was suffered: *ibid.* The IOPC Funds suggest that the judge meant that only Italy had standing to bring environmental claims. See IOPC Funds, *Annual Report 1999*, Section 10.2, Incidents Dealt with by the 1971 Fund During 1999, at www.iopcfund.org/99AR_English.htm.

[302] *Ibid.*

an agreement.[303] The shipowner and the UK club made an *ex gratia* payment of £9.1 million (25,000 million lire), in addition paying the amount indicated by the Court of First Instance to Italy, without admitting liability beyond the shipowner's limits under the 1969 CLC.[304]

2001 Bunker Oil Convention

In 2001, the IMO adopted the International Convention on Civil Liability for Bunker Oil Pollution Damage, filling a lacuna left by previous oil pollution conventions, which did not cover liability for fuel spills from ships' bunkers, except for tankers.[305] The 2001 Convention is largely based on the 1992 CLC, which makes shipowners strictly liable for fuel spills,[306] but also allows states to limit liability in accord with national or international regimes, such as the amended 1976 Convention on Limitation of Liability for Maritime Claims.[307] Article 7 of the 2001 Convention requires owners of ships registered in state parties to maintain insurance or other financial security equal to the limitation provided in Article 6. The 2001 Convention relies on the same approach to environmental damage as the 1992 CLC, limiting compensation for environmental damage to 'reasonable measures of reinstatement'.[308]

TOVALOP, CRISTAL and OPOL

In addition to these international treaty arrangements, shipowners and oil companies have entered into private agreements establishing compensation schemes. These are the 1969 Tanker Owners Voluntary Agreement Concerning Liability for Oil Pollution (TOVALOP),[309] the 1971 Contract Regarding a Supplement to Tanker Liability for Oil Pollution (CRISTAL)[310] and the 1974 Oil Companies Offshore Pollution Liability Agreement (OPOL).[311] TOVALOP and CRISTAL were wound up in 1997, as a result of greater acceptance by states of the IMO civil liability regimes.[312] OPOL is a voluntary agreement that came

---

[303] *Annual Report 1999*, n. 301 above.

[304] In June 1999, the 1971 Fund paid £26.4 million to Italy, £1.3 million to France and £28,000 to Morocco, as well as indemnifying the UK club for £2.5 million. However, none of the 1971 Fund payments related to environmental damage: *ibid*.

[305] London, 23 March 2001, not yet in force.   [306] 2001 Bunker Oil Convention, Art. 3.

[307] Art. 6.   [308] Art. 1(9)(a).

[309] 7 January 1969, in force 6 October 1969, 8 ILM 497 (1969); amended most recently on 20 February 1987. In October 1991, the duration of TOVALOP was extended to 20 February 1994. By 1990, 97 per cent of the world's tanker tonnage was covered by TOVALOP: see *TOVALOP (The International Tanker Owners Pollution Federation Ltd and CRISTAL Ltd)* (1990 2nd edn), 1.

[310] 14 January 1971 (most recently amended on 23 October 1989), 10 ILM 137 (1971). In October 1991, the duration of CRISTAL had been extended to 20 February 1994.

[311] 4 September 1974, 13 ILM 1409 (1974); see also Rules of OPOL, 2 October 1974, 14 ILM 147 (1975).

[312] See www.itopf.com/history.html; and the first edition of this book, at 665–6.

into effect on 1 May 1975, and originally applied only to offshore oil pollution incidents within the jurisdiction of the UK. All offshore oil operators working on the UK continental shelf are a party to OPOL.[313] However, OPOL has been extended to European Community states, Norway and the Isle of Man. The Agreement provides for a voluntary regime of strict liability, with limitations to liability, for pollution caused by offshore facilities engaging in oil exploration or production from the seabed and its subsoil. In 1996, OPOL was amended to require its operators to accept strict liability for up to US$120 million per pollution incident and US$240 million in aggregate.

Marine environment

Apart from the various marine environment conventions which encourage the development of liability and compensation rules,[314] two civil liability conventions have been adopted. The 1977 Convention on Civil Liability for Oil Pollution Damage Resulting from Exploration for and Exploitation of Seabed Mineral Resources,[315] which has not entered into force, provides for the liability of the operator of an installation under the jurisdiction of a party for pollution damage resulting from an incident occurring beyond the coastal low-water line.[316] Only states with coastlines on the North Sea, the Baltic Sea or northern parts of the Atlantic may become parties.[317] The pollution damage must be suffered in the territory of a party, including the internal waters and territorial sea, or in areas in which the party has sovereign rights over natural resources under international law, as well as in respect of preventive measures wherever taken.[318] The definition of 'pollution damage' as 'loss or damage outside the installation caused by contamination resulting from the escape or discharge of oil from the installation' is sufficiently broad to include environmental damage.[319] The Convention provides for strict liability, joint and several liability, the extinction of other claims against the operator for pollution damage, an entitlement to limit liability, an insurance requirement, and recognition and enforcement of judgments.[320] Liability may not be limited if it is proved that the damage occurred 'as a result of an act or omission by the operator himself, done deliberately with actual knowledge that pollution damage would result',[321] and there will be no liability in respect of abandoned wells where the damage occurred more than five years after abandonment 'under the authority and in accordance

---

[313] Offshore Pollution Liability Association Ltd, Summary of the OPOL Agreement, www.opol.org.uk/opolagreement.html.

[314] Note 7 above.

[315] London, 1 May 1977, not yet in force, 16 ILM 1450 (1977); W. N. Hancock and R. M. Stone, 'Liability for Transnational Pollution Caused by Offshore Oil Rig Blowouts', 5 *Hastings International and Comparative Law Review* 377 (1982).

[316] Arts. 2(a) and 3(a). Art. 1(2) defines 'installation'.   [317] Art. 18.

[318] Art. 2(b).   [319] Art. 1(6).   [320] Arts. 3–8 and 12.   [321] Art. 6(4).

with the requirements' of the controlling party.[322] Actions under the Convention are subject to an overall limitation period of four years.[323] By limiting actions to the courts of any party where the damage was suffered or in respect of an area in which 'in accordance with international law, a state has sovereign rights over natural resources', or the courts of the controlling party, the Convention appears to exclude the possibility of environmental claims concerning damage in areas beyond national jurisdiction.[324]

The 1992 Black Sea Convention requires each party to adopt rules and regulations on liability for damage caused by natural or juridical persons to the marine environment of the Black Sea, and to ensure that recourse is available for 'prompt and adequate' compensation or other relief for damage caused by pollution of the marine environment.[325] The object of the rules is to ensure the 'highest degree of deterrence and protection for the Black Sea as a whole', and to that end the parties are committed to co-operating on the development and harmonisation of their laws and procedures relating to liability, assessment and compensation for damage.[326]

Waste

General

Liability for damage caused by waste has been an international legal issue since Article X of the 1972 London Convention committed parties to 'develop procedures for the assessment of liability' regarding dumping, in accordance with the principles of international law regarding state responsibility for environmental damage.[327] The 1991 Bamako Convention requires each party to impose strict and unlimited liability, as well as joint and several liability, on hazardous waste generators, as well as committing the parties to develop a Protocol on liability and compensation.[328]

In 1999, pursuant to Article 12 of the 1989 Basel Convention, parties adopted the Protocol on Liability and Compensation for Damage Resulting from Transboundary Movements of Hazardous Wastes and Their Disposal.[329] The Protocol includes numerous innovative provisions, and compares favourably with other recently adopted instruments. It is intended to provide a comprehensive regime for liability and for adequate and prompt compensation for damage, defined to include damage to persons and property and loss of income deriving from an economic interest in the environment, costs of measures reinstating

---

[322] Art. 3(4).   [323] Art. 10.   [324] Art. 11(1).

[325] Art. XVI(2) and (3), chapter 9, pp. 454–5 above.   [326] Art. XVI(4).

[327] See now Art. 15 of its 1996 Protocol, committing parties to 'undertake to develop procedures regarding liability'.

[328] Art. 4(3)(b), see chapter 13, pp. 695–6 above.

[329] Basel, 10 December 1999, not yet in force; S. Choksi, 'The Basel Convention on the Control of Transboundary Movements of Hazardous Wastes and Their Disposal: 1999 Protocol on Liability and Compensation', 28 *Ecology Law Quarterly* 509 (2001).

the impaired environment, and preventive measures.[330] The Protocol expressly requires any person who is in operational control of the waste to take all reasonable measures to mitigate damage arising from an incident.[331]

The Protocol applies to damage due to an incident occurring during a transboundary movement, including illegal traffic and in respect of re-import, 'from the point where the wastes are loaded on the means of transport in an area under the national jurisdiction of the state of export'.[332] Its application is subject to certain other exclusions.[333] It covers all damage suffered in an area under the national jurisdiction of a party, but only damage to persons and property and preventive measures in areas beyond national jurisdiction, and provides particular rules where the state of import, but not the state of export, is a party to the Protocol.[334]

The Protocol provides generally for strict liability, with fault liability where there is a failure to comply with the Convention or damage occurs because of intentional, reckless or negligent acts or omissions.[335] The Protocol does not affect the rights and obligations of parties under general international law.[336] Under a regime of strict liability, the notifying entity is generally liable for damage until the disposer takes possession of the waste, at which point liability shifts to the disposer,[337] with a special rule governing hazardous waste within the meaning of Article 1(1)(b) of the Convention (wastes determined to be hazardous by a party but not included in Annex I to the Convention).[338] Liability is excluded upon proof of damage arising as a result of certain acts, including armed conflict and insurrection, certain natural phenomena, and the wrongful conduct of a third party.[339]

Liability is limited for non-fault-based incidents to amounts determined by domestic law,[340] but there are no liability limits for damage from fault-based incidents.[341] The Protocol sets minimum liability for damage,[342] and liable persons must also have insurance or financial guarantees covering these

---

[330] Arts. 1 and 2(2)(c). 'Measures of reinstatment' and 'preventive measures' are defined at Art. 2(2)(d) and (e).

[331] Art. 6.

[332] Art. 3(1) and (4). A party may notify the exclusion of the application of the Protocol, where it is the state of export, for incidents occurring within an area under its national jurisdiction, as regards damage in such area: *ibid.* The Protocol further defines its scope of application in relation to particular activities: Art. 3(2).

[333] Art. 3(6)(a) and (b), (7) and (8).

[334] Art. 3(3)(a), (b) and (c). Special provision is made for damage to states of transit: Art. 3(3)(d) and Annex A.

[335] Art. 5.   [336] Art. 16.   [337] Art. 4(1).   [338] Art. 4(2).   [339] Art. 4(5).

[340] Art. 12(1) and Annex B(1). Annex B(2)(b) does not allow the maximum liability for disposers to be less than 2 million units of account for any incident.

[341] Art. 12(2).

[342] Annex B(2)(a) (1 million SDRs for shipments of less than 5 tonnes; 2 million SDRs for shipments of 5–25 tonnes; 4 million SDRs for shipments of 25–50 tonnes; 6 million SDRs for shipments of 50–1,000 tonnes; 10 million SDRs for 1,000–10,000 tonnes; and 1,000 SDRs for each additional tonne beyond 10,000 up to a maximum of 30 million SDRs).

amounts.[343] Claims may be brought in the courts of the party where the damage was suffered, or where the incident occurred, or where the defendant has his habitual residence or principal place of business, and provision is made for the mutual recognition and enforcement of judgments.[344] Matters not regulated by Protocol are governed by the law of the competent court.[345] Claims under the Protocol are inadmissible unless brought within ten years of the incident and within five years from the date when the claimant knew or ought reasonably to have known of the damage.[346]

European Community

The EC has been deliberating the adoption of rules on civil liability for damage caused by waste since 1984.[347] In 1989, the EC Commission first proposed a Directive on civil liability for damage caused by waste, which was amended in 1991,[348] and in 1993 published a first Green Paper on liability for environmental damage.[349] The EC's Fifth Environmental Action Programme committed the EC 'as soon as practicable' to establish a mechanism whereby damage to the environment is restored by the person or body responsible for the damage incurred.[350] On 23 January 2002, the European Commission published a new proposed Directive on environmental liability with the objective of preventing and remedying environmental damage.[351] The proposal was based on principles set out in the Commission's White Paper on environmental liability, published in February 2000, taking into account comments received from member states,[352] and aims to apply an approach of strict liability without financial limits.

The draft Directive is notable, however, for its focused approach, and is distinguishable from existing arrangements in a number of significant respects. First, it is only intended to cover 'environmental damage', meaning damage to biodiversity, water and land, and does not extend to damage to persons and

---

[343] Art. 14.   [344] Arts. 17 and 21.   [345] Art. 19.   [346] Art. 13.

[347] Directive 84/631/EEC, OJ L326, 13 December 1984, 31, Art. 11(3), chapter 15, pp. 786–94 above. See also Fourth Environmental Action Plan, chapter 15, pp. 749–54 above, providing that work on civil liability and insurance is to be completed and proposals made: point 5.3.6.

[348] OJ C251, 4 October 1989, 3; amended proposal COM (91) 219 final, SYN 217, OJ C192, 23 July 1991, 6.

[349] EC Commission Communication, *Green Paper on Remedying Environmental Damage*, COM (93) 47, 17 March 1993.

[350] Chapter 15, p. 751 above.

[351] European Commission, Proposal for a Directive of the European Parliament and of the Council on Environmental Liability with Regard to the Prevention and Remedying of Environmental Damage, COM (2002) 17 final, adopted 23 January 2002, OJ C151E, 25 June 2002, 132, Art. 1.

[352] COM (2000) 66 final, adopted 9 February 2000.

property (which would continue to be governed by national law).[353] Secondly, the Directive would apply only to environmental damage caused by the operation of any of the activities expressly identified in an Annex to the Directive (and to imminent threats of such damage), although biodiversity damage would be covered irrespective of whether the activity causing it was listed in the Annex.[354] Thirdly, the scheme it proposes to establish is centred on the requirement that the member state must, in respect of prevention and remediation, either require the operator to take the necessary measures or itself take such measures.[355]

The proposed Directive includes other distinguishing features. For example, it includes detailed rules on the extent of remediation, with the objective of restoring 'the environment as a whole to its baseline condition';[356] it encourages – but does not require – operators to have insurance or other forms of financial security to pay for environmental damage;[357] and it provides that persons adversely affected or likely to be adversely affected by environmental damage will be entitled to request the member state to take action under the Directive, with a right of access to a court (or other independent and impartial public body) to review the procedural and substantive legality of the decisions, acts or failures to act of the member state.[358] The draft Directive also contains rules on the allocation of certain costs and limitation periods,[359] and permits member states to maintain or adopt more stringent provisions.[360] It is also notable for the broad range of exceptions proposed: it would not apply to damage regulated by various international agreements,[361] or to damage caused by certain nuclear activity regulated by certain agreements,[362] and would exclude the personal liability of an operator acting in his capacity as an insolvency

---

[353] Draft Arts. 3(1) and 2(18), and Annex I. Damage is broadly defined to include 'a measurable adverse change in a natural resource and/or measurable impairment of a natural resource service which may occur directly or indirectly and which is caused by any of the activities covered by this Directive': draft Art. 2(5).

[354] Draft Art. 3(1) and (2), and Annex 1.

[355] Draft Arts. 4 and 5. The member state is also required to ensure that necessary preventive and remedial measures are taken if the operator cannot be identified, cannot pay for some or all of the cost of prevention or restoration, or is not liable under the Directive (Art. 6(1)(a)–(d)). Draft Art. 7(1) requires the competent authority to recover from the operator who has caused the damage or the imminent threat of damage the costs it has incurred in relation to the taking of preventive or restorative measures.

[356] Draft Art. 5(3) and Annex II (at para. 2.1). Restoration is to be achieved on the basis of an identification of reasonable restorative options (para. 3.1) and the choice of the restorative options (para. 3.2).

[357] Draft Art. 16.   [358] Draft Arts. 14(1) and 15(1).

[359] Draft Arts. 8 and 10–12.   [360] Draft Art. 18(1).

[361] Draft Art. 3(3) (the 1992 CLC, the 1992 Oil Pollution Fund Convention, 2001 Bunker Oil Convention, 1996 HNS Convention, and 1989 Convention on Civil Liability for Damage Caused During Carriage of Dangerous Goods).

[362] Draft Art. 3(4) (1960 Paris Convention, 1963 Vienna Convention, 1988 Joint Protocol to the Paris and Vienna Conventions, and 1971 Brussels Convention on Civil Liability for Maritime Carriage of Nuclear Material).

practitioner.[363] And it would not apply to damage caused by pollution of a widespread, diffuse character, where it is impossible to establish a causal link between the damage and the activities of certain individual operators,[364] or to activities the sole purpose of which is to serve national defence,[365] or to damage caused by:

1. an act of armed conflict, hostilities, civil war or insurrection;
2. a natural phenomenon of exceptional, inevitable and irresistible character;
3. an emission or event allowed in applicable laws and regulations, or in the permit or authorisation issued to the operator;
4. emissions or activities which were not considered harmful according to the state of scientific and technical knowledge at the time when the emission was released or the activity took place.[366]

It remains to be seen whether the approach set forth in this new draft of the Directive will find favour with the member states. In the meantime, in 1991, the European Court of Justice adopted a ruling which may have blurred the distinction between civil and state liability and may have informed the potential development of the EC rules of environmental liability. In *Francovich v. Italian Republic*, the ECJ had to decide whether the failure by a member state to implement a Directive which protected the rights of employees in the case of insolvency of their employer gave rise to the liability of the state. Although the case did not relate to the environment, it established principles pertinent to violations of environmental obligations. The Court held that 'it is a principle of Community law that the member states are obliged to pay compensation for harm caused to individuals by breaches of Community law for which they can be held responsible'.[367] The Court considered that the full effectiveness of Community law, and the protection of rights thereunder, would be affected if individuals could not recover compensation when their rights were infringed, and that compensation by a member state was 'particularly indispensable' where 'the full effectiveness of Community rules is subject to prior action on the part of the state and consequently individuals cannot, in the absence of such action, enforce the rights granted to them by Community law before the national courts'.[368] The Court set forth three conditions which had to

---

[363] Draft Art. 9(4) (provided the person acts in accordance with the relevant national provisions governing insolvency, liquidation, winding-up or analogous proceedings, and is not otherwise at fault or negligent).

[364] Draft Art. 3(6).   [365] Draft Art. 3(7).

[366] Draft Art. 9(1). The proposed exception draft Art. 9(1)(c) and (d) would not apply if the operator had been negligent.

[367] Cases C-6/90 and C-9/90, Judgment of 19 November 1991 [1993] 2 CMLR 66 at 78, para. 37.

[368] Paras. 33–4; the Court also relied on Art. 5 of the 1957 EEC Treaty, which it interpreted as including 'the obligation to make good the unlawful consequences of a breach of Community law': para. 36.

be satisfied before a violation of EC law by a member state gave rise to liability: first, the result prescribed by the Directive in question should entail the grant of rights to individuals; secondly, it should be possible to identify the content of those rights on the basis of the provisions of the Directive; and, thirdly, there should be a causal link between the breach of the obligation by the state and the damage suffered by the persons affected.[369] These conditions could clearly be fulfilled in the case of a violation of an EC environmental obligation.

The Court went on to hold that in the absence of EC rules it was for the internal legal order of each member state to determine the competent courts and to lay down the procedural rules for legal proceedings intended to safeguard rights which individuals derive from law.[370] However, the Court did rule that national substantive and procedural conditions on compensation could not be 'less favourable than those relating to similar internal claims and may not be so framed as to make it virtually impossible or excessively difficult to obtain compensation'.[371]

The judgment establishes a basis for member states to be liable for damages resulting from their failure to implement environmental Directives which create individual rights, including obligations setting water or air quality standards, or creating participatory rights in environmental impact assessments, or granting rights of access to environmental information. Provided that environmental Directives confer rights for the benefit of individuals, the conditions established by the Court seem capable of opening up a new type of 'state liability' being applied in the civil or administrative courts of the EC or EFTA states.[372] Finally, it should be noted that, since the amendments introduced by the Amsterdam Treaty came into force, in 1999, the ECJ has been empowered to levy fines on member states which do not comply with earlier judgments of the Court.[373] In July 2000, the ECJ applied this provision, Article 228(2), for the first time, ordering Greece to pay a penalty of 20,000 euros for each day of delay in implementing the measures necessary to comply with a 1992 judgment concerning violations of Directive 75/442/EEC (on waste) and 78/319/EEC (on toxic and dangerous waste) which endangered human health and harmed the environment.[374] In setting the amount of the penalty, the Court noted that the failure to comply with 'the obligation resulting from Article 4 of Directive 75/442 could, by the very nature of that obligation, endanger human health

---

[369] Para. 40.   [370] Para. 42.   [371] Para. 43.

[372] On EC environmental law, see generally chapter 15 above.

[373] Art. 228(2) provides that 'If the Court of Justice finds that the Member State concerned has not complied with its judgment it may impose a lump sum or penalty payment on it'.

[374] Case C-387/97, *Commission* v. *Greece* [2000] ECR 1-5047; see L. Borzsak, 'Punishing Member States or Influencing Their Behaviour or Index (Non) Calculate', 13 JEL 244 (2001); and C. Hilson, 'Article 228 and the Enforcement of EC Environmental Law' 3 *Environmental Law Review* 131 (2001).

directly and harm the environment and must, in the sight of the other obligations, be regarded as particularly serious'.[375]

Transport

Transport issues are addressed by two instruments: the Geneva Convention on Civil Liability for Damage Caused during Carriage of Dangerous Goods by Road, Rail and Inland Navigation Vessels (1989 CRTD);[376] and the 1996 International Convention on Liability and Compensation for Damage in Connection with the Carriage of Hazardous and Noxious Substances by Sea (1996 HNS Convention).[377] Neither instrument is in force.

The 1989 CRTD was adopted under the auspices of the ECE, and provides for the liability of the carrier (the registered owner or person controlling the road vehicle or inland navigation vessel or operator of a railway line) for damage caused during the transport of dangerous goods.[378] Compensable damage includes loss of life or personal injury, loss of or damage to property, and:

> loss or damage by contamination to the environment caused by dangerous goods, provided that compensation for impairment of the environment other than for loss of profit caused from such impairment shall be limited to costs of reasonable measures of reinstatement actually undertaken or to be undertaken.[379]

The carrier may limit its liability in case of rail or road transport to 18 million SDRs for claims covering loss of life or personal injury and to 12 million SDRs for other claims, and in the case of inland navigation vessels to 8 million SDRs and 7 million SDRs respectively.[380] Under the CRTD, a victim has a choice of courts in which to bring actions: the courts of the party in which the accident occurred, or the damage or loss occurred, or where preventive measures were taken, or where the carrier has its habitual residence.[381]

The 1996 HNS Convention, adopted under the auspices of the IMO, provides a two-tiered system of liability and compensation similar to the 1992 CLC and 1992 Fund Convention, and uses the same definitions as the 1989 CRTD to determine compensable damage, including environmental damage.[382] The approach of the HNS Convention follows the 1992 CLC. Chapter II establishes a regime of strict liability for shipowners and a list of defences to liability, rules

---

[375] Case C-387/97, *Commission* v. *Greece* [2000] ECR 1-5047, para. 95.
[376] 10 October 1989, not yet in force; ECE/TRANS/79.
[377] London, 3 May 1996, 35 ILM 1404 (1996); not yet in force.   [378] Art. 5.
[379] Art. 1(10)(c). 'Damage' also includes the cost of preventive measures, defined as 'any reasonable measures taken by any person after an incident has occurred to prevent or minimise damage': Art. 1(10)(d) and (11).
[380] Art. 9.   [381] Art. 19.
[382] 1996 HNS Convention, Art. 1(6)(a)–(d); 1989 CRTD, Art. 1(10)(a)–(d).

for joint and several liability for damage that is not reasonably separable by shipowner, and compulsory shipowner's insurance.[383] Article 9(1) limits the shipowner's liability to specified amounts;[384] Article 9(2), however, imposes no limit to liability if the shipowner intended to cause damage or acted recklessly with knowledge that damage would result. Chapter III establishes the HNS Fund which, like the 1992 Fund Convention for oil pollution, will compensate any person who suffers damage under Chapter II but is unable to obtain compensation because the shipowner is not liable, the shipowner is incapable of meeting all its financial obligations, or the damages exceed the shipowner's liability under Chapter II.[385]

Antarctic

CRAMRA

The 1988 CRAMRA was the first Antarctic treaty to address liability, although it is now unlikely to enter into force.[386] Of particular note are the provisions concerning liability for environmental damage, and the relationship between the liability of the operator and the operator's sponsoring state. Under Article 8, the operator is under an obligation to take necessary and timely response action if its activities result in, or threaten, damage to the Antarctic environment or its dependent or associated ecosystems. Such action includes prevention, containment, clean-up and removal measures.[387] The operator will be strictly liable for damage to the Antarctic environment or dependent or associated ecosystems (including: payment in the event that there has been no restoration to the *status quo ante*); loss of or impairment to established use; loss of or damage to people and property; and reimbursement of reasonable costs relating to necessary response action to restore the *status quo ante* (including prevention, containment, clean-up and removal).[388] Environmental liability is widely defined.[389]

Where the damage would not have occurred if the sponsoring state had carried out its obligation under the Convention, that state will be liable for the part which remains unsatisfied by the operator.[390] This innovative approach links civil and state liability in a unique way. CRAMRA would allow limited

---

[383] Arts. 7, 8 and 12.

[384] The limitations for any one incident are: 10 million SDRs for ships under 2,000 units of tonnage; an additional 1,500 SDRs for each unit of tonnage between 2,001 and 50,000; and an additional 360 SDRs for every unit of tonnage over 50,000, provided that the total limit on liability does not exceed 100 million SDRs.

[385] Art. 14(1).   [386] Chapter 14 above.   [387] Art. 8(1).   [388] Art. 8(2).

[389] Art. 1(15). This definition appears to be the first in an international treaty which does not set the threshold for damage to be compensable at a level which is 'significant' or 'substantial'.

[390] Art. 8(3).

defences to liability,[391] and provides for the elaboration of further rules and procedures on liability in a supplementary Protocol.[392] Guidance is provided on the content of those rules and procedures, which are to be designed to enhance the protection of the Antarctic and discourage commercial activity. The rules and procedures could include provisions for appropriate limits on liability where they can be justified, means and mechanisms to assess and adjudicate claims, and means to provide immediate assistance for response action including where the operator is financially incapable of meeting its obligation in full or there is a defence to liability.[393]

Antarctic Environment Protocol

The 1991 Antarctic Environment Protocol dispensed with CRAMRA's substantive liability rules, and commits the parties to elaborate rules and procedures relating to liability for damage arising from activities taking place in the Antarctic and covered by the Protocol.[394] The rules will have to be consistent with the objectives of the Protocol for the comprehensive protection of the Antarctic environment and dependent and associated ecosystems. In 1998, the group of legal experts, convened under Article 16 of the 1991 Protocol, presented their Final Report to the twenty-second Antarctic Treaty Consultative Meeting (ATCM). Members of the ATCM were unable to reach a consensus on the key issues contained in the group's report, including whether to adopt a comprehensive liability annex or a set of specific liability annexes, whether to compensate irreparable environmental damage, whether to establish an environmental protection fund, and whether to exclude environmental damages resulting from activities found to be acceptable by national authorities after environmental impact assessments.[395] The ATCM member states decided to dissolve the group of legal experts and shift the responsibility for developing an Antarctic liability regime to its Working Group I.[396] By the twenty-fourth ATCM in 2001, the group seemed to be no closer to forming a consensus on the key issues of liability.[397]

---

[391] Art. 8(4) and (6) (including unforeseeable natural disaster; armed conflict or act of terrorism against which precautionary measures would not have been effective; and contributory negligence).

[392] Art. 8(7).   [393] Art. 8(7)(c).

[394] Art. 16, see chapter 14, pp. 721–6 above. The Final Act of the Eleventh Antarctic Treaty Special Consultative Meeting, which adopted the Protocol, underlined the commitment of the parties to develop at an early stage rules on liability, and their understanding that liability for damage to the Antarctic environment should be included in the rules: chapter 14, pp. 721–6 above.

[395] R. Lefeber, 'General 'Developments: International/Civil Liability and Compensation', 9 *Yearbook of International Environmental Law* 158 at 164 (1998).

[396] *Ibid.*

[397] Item 10, The Question of Liability as Referred to in Article 16 of the Protocol, Report of the XXIV Antarctic Treaty Consultative Meeting, 9–20 July 2001, www.24atcm.mid.ru/24atcm/official.html.

General instruments relating to dangerous goods or activities

Council of Europe

The 1993 Council of Europe Convention on Civil Liability for Damage Resulting from Activities Dangerous to the Environment (1993 Lugano Convention)[398] aims to provide adequate compensation for damage resulting from activities dangerous to the environment, and to provide for prevention and restitution.[399] Its far-reaching provisions have not commended themselves to many states, and it is unlikely to enter into force. Nevertheless, it is of interest in suggesting a different approach. In establishing rules of application beyond a particular industrial sector or activity or source of harm, the 1993 Lugano Convention moves beyond the earlier efforts described above, and is noteworthy as the first civil liability instrument to include provisions on access to information.[400] The Convention will not be construed as limiting or derogating from rights of persons who suffer damage, or as limiting provisions concerning environmental protection or reinstatement provided under the laws of any party or under any other treaty to which it is a party, and expressly provides that in their relations parties which are members of the EC are to apply EC rules and not the rules of the Convention except where there is no EC rule governing the subject concerned.[401]

The Convention is a regional instrument, which is open to signature by the members of the Council of Europe, non-member states which have participated in its elaboration, and the EC, although it is possible for any other state to become a party after its entry into force, and is potentially applicable regardless of where the damage is suffered when the incident occurs in the territory of a party.[402] Article 4 sets out exceptions to which the Convention will not apply, including damage arising from carriage or to the extent that it is incompatible with the rules of applicable law relating to workmen's compensation or social security schemes.[403] The Convention will not apply to damage caused by a nuclear substance which arises from a nuclear incident 'the liability of which is regulated either by' the 1960 Paris Convention (and its 1963 Additional Protocol) or by the 1963 Vienna Convention, or if liability for such damage is regulated by a specific internal law which is as favourable as these instruments.[404] The drafting of the nuclear exception leaves a certain ambiguity which arises through the use of the word 'regulated'. Article 4(2)(a) would appear to permit an interpretation allowing for the application of the 1993 Lugano Convention to the consequences of a nuclear incident in France which had effects in Luxembourg, or in the United Kingdom which had effects in Ireland (assuming all were parties to the 1993 Convention), since Luxembourg and Ireland are not parties to the 1960 Paris Convention or the 1963 Vienna

---

[398] Lugano, 21 June 1993, not in force, 32 ILM 480 (1993). C. de Sola, 'The Council of Europe Convention on Environmental Damage', 1 RECIEL 411 (1992).

[399] Art. 1.   [400] Arts. 13 to 16; see chapter 17, pp. 852–4 above.   [401] Art. 25.

[402] Arts. 32, 33(1) and 3(a).   [403] Art. 4(1) and (3).   [404] Art. 4(2).

Convention, and the liability in respect of damage in or to their territory would not appear to be 'regulated' by those treaties. Similarly, to the extent that a state is a party to the 1993 Lugano Convention and the 1960 Paris Convention or the 1963 Vienna Convention, the 1993 Convention may apply to damage caused by the disposal or permanent deposit (as opposed to storage) of nuclear waste, or in respect of environmental damage, not regulated by the 1960 or 1963 Conventions. However, Article 4(2)(b) creates further difficulty by excluding the application of the 1993 Convention if liability for damage caused by a nuclear substance 'is regulated by a specific internal law, provided that such law is as favourable' as the 1960 or 1963 Conventions: the issue is whether that specific internal law is that of the state in which the accident occurred, or that of the state in which the damage was suffered, or both. The text does not provide clear guidance.

The 1993 Convention channels liability to the operator in respect of incidents causing damage from a dangerous activity, and departs from earlier instruments by not including a provision allowing parties to limit liability.[405] The Convention does not require operators to be covered by mandatory insurance or other financial security, only requiring each party to ensure that operators are covered by a financial security scheme up to a certain limit where appropriate and taking due account of the risks of the activity.[406] An incident includes any 'sudden occurrence or continuous occurrence or any series of occurrences having the same origin, which causes damage or creates a grave and imminent threat of causing damage', leaving open the possibility that preventive measures taken by a potential victim, such as evacuation or prohibitive measures taken to prevent an activity from being carried out, could give rise to the liability of the operator.[407] The operator is the 'person who exercises control of a dangerous activity';[408] no guidance is provided by the Convention on what constitutes control. The Convention applies only to incidents occurring after its entry into force, and transitional provisions apply in respect of damage occurring before and after entry into force.[409] The Convention distinguishes between two sources of harm, and for both sources of harm the operator's right of recourse against third persons is not prejudiced.[410] For dangerous substances, genetically modified organisms and micro-organisms, and for certain waste installations or sites, the operator will be liable for damage caused by the activity as a result of any incident when he was exercising control of the activity.[411] Rules of joint and several liability apply for damage caused

---

[405] An earlier draft allowed internal law to limit the liability of the operator, taking account of the risks of the activity, the possible extent of damage and the aim of ensuring adequate compensation, and providing that the operator would not be entitled to limit his liability in certain circumstances: Council of Europe draft, 31 July 1992, DIR/JUR (92) 3, Art. 12.
[406] Art. 12.   [407] Art. 2(11).   [408] Art. 2(5).   [409] Art. 5.   [410] Arts. 6(5) and 7(4).
[411] Arts. 2(1)(a) to (c) and 6(1). 'Dangerous substance', 'genetically modified organism' and 'micro-organism' are defined at Art. 2(2) to (4) and Annex I; 'dangerous substance' is

by continuous occurrences, or a series of occurrences having the same origin, although if the operator can prove that the occurrence during the period when he was exercising control of the dangerous activity caused only a part of the damage he will be liable only for that part of the damage.[412] Where the damage becomes known after dangerous activity has ceased, the last operator of the activity will be liable, unless he or the person who suffered damage can prove that all or part of the damage occurred before he became the operator, in which case the provisions of Article 6(1) to (3) apply.[413]

The operator of a site for the permanent deposit of waste will be liable for damage caused by waste deposited at the site, and the last operator will be liable for damage caused by waste deposited before the closure of a site, which damage only becomes known after the site has closed.[414] Liability under this provision will generally preclude liability under Article 6.[415]

Damage   Damage includes loss of life or personal injury, loss of or damage to property, and the costs of preventive measures and any loss or damage caused by preventive measures.[416] The Convention also applies to environmental damage, which is:

> loss or damage by impairment of the environment in so far as this is not considered to be damage within the meaning of [Article 2(7)(a) or (b)] . . . provided that compensation for impairment of the environment, other than for loss of profit from such impairment, shall be limited to the costs of reasonable measures of reinstatement actually undertaken or to be undertaken . . .[417]

The environment includes natural resources, property forming part of the cultural heritage, and the characteristic aspects of the landscape. Measures of reinstatement means:

> any reasonable measures aiming to reinstate or restore damaged or destroyed components of the environment, or to introduce, where reasonable, the equivalent of these components into the environment. Internal law may indicate who will be entitled to take such measures.[418]

This definition must be read in the context of the Article 8 exceptions, which provides, *inter alia*, that the operator will not be liable for damage which he proves 'was caused by pollution at tolerable levels under local relevant circumstances'.[419] This approach calls for comment. It indicates clearly the distinction to be drawn between pollution and liability for environmental damage;

defined by reference to, *inter alia*, EEC Council Directives 67/548/EEC and 88/379/EEC, providing evidence of the growing international reach of EC environmental law. Annex II lists different types of waste installation or site.

[412] Art. 6(2) and (3).   [413] Art. 6(4).   [414] Arts. 2(1)(d) and 7(1).
[415] Art. 7(2) and (3).   [416] Art. 2(7)(a), (b) and (d).   [417] Art. 2(7)(c).
[418] Art. 2(8) and (10).   [419] Art. 8(d).

while all environmental damage is likely to be included in the definition of pollution, not all pollution will give rise to liability. Moreover, it does not define a 'tolerable level' of pollution, which is problematic in the absence of agreed international standards. Finally, it recognises that tolerable levels are not absolute and may vary between localities or regions, and implements a shift in the burden of proof requiring the operator to prove that the pollution is at a tolerable level, and not for the victim to prove that the level of pollution is intolerable.

Exemptions and other rules   The operator may benefit from exemptions if it is able to prove that damage was caused by, *inter alia*, war or a natural phenomenon of an 'exceptional, inevitable and irresistible character', or by the intent of a third party, or as a result of compliance with an order or compulsory measure of a public authority, or by a dangerous activity lawfully undertaken in the interests of the person who suffered the damage.[420] Contributory fault of the person suffering damage can result in a reduction or disallowance of compensation.[421] The Convention also includes a basic rule on proving causality, requiring the court to take due account of the increased danger of causing damage which is inherent in the dangerous activity.[422]

Actions for compensation and other claims   Under the Convention, claims may be brought to the court of the place where the damage was suffered, or where the dangerous activity was conducted, or where the defendant has his habitual residence.[423] The Convention envisages claims by environmental organisations. Under Article 18, any association or foundation whose statute aims at the protection of the environment and which complies with the requirements of the internal law of the party where the request is submitted may request the prohibition of a dangerous activity which is unlawful and poses a grave threat of damage to the environment, or that the operator be ordered to take measures to prevent an incident or damage (including after an incident), or that the operator be ordered to take measures of reinstatement.[424] Internal law may determine the admissibility of such requests, and the administrative or judicial body before which such a request should be made, and the Convention sets out rules governing requests by environmental organisations registered under the law of another party.[425] Requests by organisations for the prohibition of a dangerous activity may only be brought within a court or administrative authority of the place where the dangerous activity is or will be conducted, and

---

[420] Art. 8(a), (b), (c) and (e).   [421] Art. 9.   [422] Art. 10.
[423] Art. 19(1). The provisions on jurisdiction will not apply to parties bound by a treaty establishing rules for recognition and enforcement, such as the 1968 Brussels Convention and the 1989 Lugano Convention: Art. 24.
[424] Art. 18(1).   [425] Art. 18(2), (3) and (5).

other requests may be taken to such a court or to the court of the place where the measures are to be taken.[426] Provision is made for limitation periods, notification of proceedings, *lis pendens*, related actions, and the recognition and enforcement of judgments.[427]

The Convention establishes a Standing Committee to review problems related to the Convention and provides for amendment.[428] Of note is the procedure envisaged for amendment of the definition of dangerous substances set out in Annex I which is necessitated because of the definition by reference to EC Directives which are frequently amended by the EC member states.[429]

Reservations   The sensitive and legally complex nature of the 1993 Lugano Convention required the permissibility of reservations in relation to three matters. Reservations are permitted to allow a party: to apply the Convention to damage suffered in the territory of non-parties only on the basis of reciprocity; to provide in internal law that the operator will not be liable for damage caused by substances or genetically modified organisms or micro-organisms if he proves that the state of scientific and technical knowledge at the time of the incident was not such as to enable the existence of the dangerous properties of the substance or the significant risk involved in the operation dealing with the organism to be determined; and to refrain from applying Article 18 (requests by organisations).

UNECE

In 2001, the governing bodies of and parties to the UNECE's 1992 Watercourses Convention and 1991 Industrial Accidents Convention established a working group to develop a Draft Legally Binding Instrument on Civil Liability for Transboundary Damage Caused by Hazardous Activities, Within the Scope of Both Conventions. The working group's mandate is to develop draft Articles to be adopted by a joint special session of the parties to both the Watercourses and Industrial Accidents Conventions in 2003.[430] The proposal follows the work of an earlier UNECE Task Force, which considered rules on responsibility and liability for transboundary water resources.[431]

---

[426] Art. 19(3) and (4).

[427] Arts. 17 and 20 to 23. The provisions on recognition and enforcement will not apply to parties bound by a treaty establishing rules for recognition and enforcement, such as the 1968 Brussels Convention and the 1989 Lugano Convention.

[428] Arts. 26 to 31.   [429] Art. 31.

[430] ECE, Report of the Joint Special Session, UN Doc. ECE/MP.WAT/7 or ECE/CP.TEIA/5 (2001), 6.

[431] 'Report and Guidelines on Responsibility and Liability Concerning Transboundary Water Pollution', ENVWA/R.45 (1990), as described in A. Rest, 'Ecological Damage in Public International Law', 22 *Environmental Policy and Law* 31 (1992); see also G. Handl, 'Balancing of Interests and International Liability for the Pollution of International Watercourses:

Conclusions

With the exception of the oil pollution regime, the rules of international law governing liability for environmental damage remain in their early phases of development, particularly in relation to rules of state liability. States remain reluctant to put in place rules which have the potential to impose significant constraints on the conduct of potentially hazardous activities, as well as being aware of significant costs to the public sector. This is particularly reflected in the amendments to the 1963 Vienna Convention on civil liability for nuclear damage, and in the remote prospects for the entry into force of the 1993 Lugano Convention. States also appear unwilling to bring claims against other states for environmental and other damage even where there might be good legal grounds for doing so, as the practice following the Chernobyl accident indicated.

In relation to civil liability, Principle 13 of the Rio Declaration recognised the importance of national laws on liability and compensation. The failure of states to put such laws in place, or to enforce them, will increasingly be a matter of legitimate international concern for environmental and economic reasons. This applies equally at the regional level, as reflected in the continuing (and long-standing) efforts by the EC Commission to adopt minimum standards for all EC member states. The body of international civil liability instruments in force is now impressive, and the case law under some, such as the oil pollution rules, has established useful precedents on the basis of which further developments and innovations can be based. Significant developments in the past five years include the adoption of liability protocols to the 1989 Basel Convention and regimes on hazardous and noxious substances, as well as the entry into force of the IMO's two 1992 Protocols. Efforts are underway to establish new regimes, in particular in relation to the 1991 Antarctic Environment Protocol and the 2000 Biosafety Protocol, which poses particular challenges in respect of defining what constitutes damage. Gaps still need to be filled for activities which are not covered by liability rules, and the geographical coverage of existing instruments needs to be enhanced by bringing on board the large number of states who remain outside the liability regimes. A 'second generation' of civil liability rules will face new issues, including: the possibility of conflicting approaches to the definition of environmental damage; ensuring that such limitations on liability as are permitted do not serve to subsidise potentially harmful activities; establishing effective procedures before courts and tribunals for dealing with mass claims in the event of catastrophic accidents or events; and developing

Customary Principles of Law Revisited', 13 *Canadian Yearbook of International Law* 156 (1975); J. G. Polakiewicz, 'La Responsabilité de l'état en matière de pollution des eaux fluviales ou souterraines internationales', *Journal de Droit International* 283 (1991); A. Rest, 'New Tendencies in Environmental Responsibility/Liability Law: The Work of the UNECE Task Force on Responsibility and Liability Regarding Transboundary Water Pollution', 21 *Environmental Policy and Law* 135 (1991).

schemes to provide for supplementary funding in the event that a liable person runs out of funds, or cannot be located, or the damage exceeds a permitted financial limit of liability.

It is in regard to state liability that the 'expeditious and more determined' co-operation called for by Principle 13 of the Rio Declaration remains to be addressed. Since the 1972 Stockholm Conference, developments have been limited. Although the ILC's 2001 draft Articles on State Responsibility introduce a codified framework, the Commission's progress in its efforts to develop principles of state liability for environmental damage which are of general application remains limited. In view of the unwillingness of any state to bring a claim against the USSR following the Chernobyl accident in 1986 for environmental or other damage, the principal developments have been: the adoption and recent entry into force of Article 235 of the 1982 UNCLOS; the innovative approach of the 1988 CRAMRA towards the linkage of civil and state liability; and the affirmation in 1991 by Security Council Resolution 687 that Iraq was liable for the environmental damage caused by its unlawful invasion of Kuwait. Indeed, the UN Compensation Commission may well have the responsibility of defining an approach which may be applied more broadly. Few state claims have been made since 1972, notable exceptions being the successful Canadian claim against the USSR following the crash of Cosmos 954 in 1978 and the Hungarian claim against Slovakia in relation to the consequences of the operation of the Gabcikovo barrage (although the ICJ did not take up the opportunity to address the particularities of that claim). The legal issues which will need to be addressed in relation to state liability are broadly similar to those concerning civil liability, although the range of activities for which a state might be liable is extensive. Specific issues of particular concern include liability for damage to the environment in areas beyond national jurisdiction, the question of financial limits (if any) of a state's liability, and the distinction between liability for damage to the environment of a state and liability for damage to its property interests. In coming years, the fora for addressing these and other issues will include the ILC and those bodies dealing with civil liability which are coming under increasing pressure to further define the relationship between civil and state liability. Other bodies, such as the conference of the parties of the 1992 Climate Change Convention and – increasingly – international courts and tribunals, are likely to emerge as fora for addressing the responsibilities of states for new environmental challenges.

International trade and competition

S. J. Rubin and T. Graham, *Environment and Trade: The Relation of International Trade and Environmental Policy* (1982); E. Brown Weiss, 'Environment and Trade as Partners in Sustainable Development: A Commentary', 86 AJIL 700 (1992); J. Jackson, 'World Trade Rules and Environmental Policies: Congruence or Conflict?', 49 *Washington and Lee Law Review* 1219 (1992); R. B. Stewart, 'International Trade and Environment: Lessons from the Federal Experience', 49 *Washington and Lee Law Review* 1219 (1992); P. Callas, D. Esty and D. Van Hoogstraten, 'Environmental Protection and International Trade: Toward Mutually Supportive Rules and Policies', 16 *Harvard Environmental Law Review* 271 (1992); S. Charnovitz, 'The Environment vs. Trade Rules: Defogging the Debate', 23 *Environmental Law* 475 (1993); D. Esty, 'Beyond Rio: Trade and the Environment', 23 *Environmental Law* 387 (1993); OECD, *Trade and Environment: Processes and Production Methods* (1994); J. Cameron, P. Demaret and D. Geradin (eds.), *Trade and Environment: The Search for Balance* (1994); E.-U. Petersmann, *International and European Trade and Environmental Law after the Uruguay Round* (1995); D. Geradin, *Trade and the Environment: A Comparative Study of EC and US Law* (1997); M. J. Trebilcock and R. Howse, *The Regulation of International Trade* (1999, 2nd edn); WTO Secretariat, *Trade and Environment* (1999); J. Weiler (ed.), *The EU, the WTO, and the NAFTA: Towards a Common Law of International Trade* (2000); A. Batabyal and H. Beladi (eds.), *The Economics of International Trade and the Environment* (2001); C. Robb (ed.), *International Environmental Law Reports*, vol. 2, *Trade and Environment* (2001); G. P. Sampson and W. B. Chambers (eds.), *Trade, Environment, and the Millennium* (2002); 'International Trade and the Environment' 11 RECIEL (2002).

Introduction

UNCED marked a further stage towards the integration of economic and environmental aspects of international law, prompted in part by considerations of the relationship between differing environmental standards and economic competitiveness.[1] Principle 4 of the Rio Declaration reflects this

[1] R. Stewart, 'Environmental Regulation and International Competitiveness', 102 *Yale Law Journal* 2039 (1993); R. Hudec, 'Differences in International Environmental Standards: The

interdependence, providing that 'in order to achieve sustainable development environmental protection shall constitute an integral part of the development process and cannot be considered in isolation from it'. The theme of integration was central to the preparations for UNCED. Agenda 21 recognised that the international economy should provide a 'supportive international climate for achieving environment and development goals',[2] and identified the following as objectives for the international community:

- making trade and the environment mutually supportive;
- encouraging macroeconomic policies conducive to environment and development; and
- providing adequate financial resources to developing countries and dealing with international debt.[3]

This chapter considers the international legal aspects of the first two of these issues: the relationship between international trade and environmental protection, and the application of international rules of competition law to environmental issues. In chapter 20, other aspects of the relationship between international economic law and environmental protection are addressed, including financial resources, transfer of technology, and intellectual property rights. Chapter 21 addresses the relationship between rules of international law for the promotion of foreign investments and the protection of the environment.

One of the consequences of an emphasis on greater integration of economics and the environment has been to bring together two very different groups of international legal practitioners who have traditionally had very little to do with one another. International trade law in the past had been seen as a separate, self-contained field, dominated by the principles and ideology of free trade. More recently, environmentalists and others have challenged the dominance of free trade ideals and particularly their utility to achieve other international goals such as environmental protection.[4]

Greater integration between economics and the environment has manifested itself in many other ways than simply as a clash of intellectual cultures. A number of international legal issues relating to trade, competition and the environment have been controversial in recent years. Three principal issues concern the use in environmental treaties of international trade measures, the circumstances in which one or more states may lawfully adopt 'unilateral'

Level Playing-Field Dimension', 5 *Minnesota Journal of Global Trade* 1 (1995); R. Hudec and J. Bhagwhati (eds.), *Fair Trade and Harmonization* (1996); D. Esty and D. Garadin, 'Environmental Competitiveness and International Trade: A Conceptual Framework', 32 *Journal of World Trade* 5 (1998); O. Fauchald, *Environmental Taxes and Trade Discrimination* (1998).

[2] Agenda 21, para. 2.3.   [3] *Ibid.*   [4] See generally D. Esty, *Greening the GATT* (1994).

environmental protection measures (measures taken outside the context of an international agreement) which limit international trade and may conflict with obligations under global and regional free trade agreements, such as the GATT, the EC Treaty, the United States–Canada Free Trade Agreement, the NAFTA and the African Economic Community Treaty, and the requirements for states to adopt trade measures in furtherance of national goals of human, animal or plant health and safety protection. The chapter also addresses the emerging relationship between competition law and environmental protection.

Trade measures in international environmental agreements

J. Cameron and J. Robinson, 'The Use of Trade Provisions in International Environmental Agreements and Their Compatibility with GATT', 2 *Yearbook of International Environmental Law* 3 (1991); J. Cameron and J. Robinson, *The Use of Trade Provisions in International Environmental Agreements: A Report for the OECD* (1991); I. Cheyne, 'Environmental Treaties and the GATT', 1 RECIEL 14 (1992); T. Swanson, 'The Evolving Trade Mechanism in CITES', 1 RECIEL 52 (1992); J. Werksman, 'Trade Sanctions under the Montreal Protocol', 1 RECIEL 69 (1992); J. Dunoff, 'Reconciling International Trade with Preservation of the Global Commons: Can We Prosper and Protect?', 49 *Washington and Lee Law Review* 1407 (1992); R. Tarasofsky, 'Ensuring Compatibility Between Multilateral Environmental Agreements and GATT/WTO', 7 *Yearbook of International Environmental Law* 52 (1996); A. Qureshi, 'The Cartagena Protocol on Biosafety and the WTO – Coexistence or Incoherence?', 49 ICLQ 835 (2000); A. Bianchi, 'The Impact of International Trade Law on Environmental Law and Process', in F. Francioni (ed.), *Environment, Human Rights and International Trade* 105 (2001).

The use of trade measures in international environmental agreements has a long history. The 1933 London Convention controlled and regulated the import, export and traffic in certain trophies.[5] Other agreements establish quantitative restrictions on international trade to achieve environmental protection objectives.[6] Three types of environmental objectives have been addressed by trade regulations: agreements to protect wildlife, agreements to protect the

---

[5] Art. 9; chapter 11, p. 524 above.

[6] 1940 Western Hemisphere Convention, Art. IX; 1950 Birds Convention, Arts. 3, 4 and 9; 1968 African Nature Convention, Art. IX; 1973 CITES, Arts. III to V and VII; 1987 Montreal Protocol, Art. 4 (as amended); 2000 Biosafety Protocol, Arts. 10 and 11; 2001 POPs Convention (not yet in force) Art. 3. The 1997 Kyoto Protocol (not yet in force) to the 1992 Climate Change Convention also contemplates the use of trade measures to achieve the environmental objective of stabilising levels of greenhouse gases in the atmosphere. However, in the case of the Kyoto Protocol, trade is not restricted but instead facilitated, with Art. 17 permitting Annex B parties to participate in emissions trading for the purpose of fulfilling their emissions reduction commitments under the Protocol.

environment of the importing state from harmful organisms and products, and agreements to protect the global commons.

Agreements for the protection of wildlife usually make use of restrictions on export or import between parties,[7] often based on a permit system, as well as on transit through the territory of parties,[8] and restrictions on trade with non-parties.[9] Agreements to protect the environment of the importing state from harmful organisms or products, which have generally been concerned with plant pests, hazardous waste and pesticides, but which have more recently been extended to include genetically modified organisms, rely primarily on import restrictions,[10] although restrictions on transit through the territory of parties and on trade with non-parties are also used. Agreements to restrict exports and imports either establish a complete ban,[11] or make imports conditional upon the grant of a permit[12] or the prior informed consent of the relevant authorities of the importing state,[13] or a combination of techniques.[14] The 2000 Biosafety Protocol combines a prior informed consent procedure and risk assessment, while also allowing importing parties to restrict imports where there is a '[l]ack of scientific certainty due to insufficient relevant scientific information and knowledge regarding the extent of the potential adverse effects of a living modified organism on the conservation and sustainable use of biological diversity in the Party of import, taking also into account risks to human health'.[15] For hazardous waste, export restrictions supplement the import restrictions.[16]

To date, the only international agreement which has used trade measures to protect the global commons is the 1987 Montreal Protocol. Article 4 controls the import and export of certain ozone-depleting substances from and to non-parties, whereas Article 4B requires parties which are unable to phase out

---

[7] 1973 CITES, Arts. III, IV and V.

[8] 1940 Western Hemisphere Convention, Art. IX.   [9] 1973 CITES, Art. X.

[10] 1951 International Plant Protection Convention, Art. 1; 1954 African Phyto-Sanitary Convention, Preamble; 1956 Plant Protection Agreement for the South East Asia and Pacific Region, Preamble; 1976 North American Plant Protection Agreement; 2000 Biosafety Protocol, Arts. 10 and 11; 2001 POPs Convention, Art. 3.

[11] 1989 Lomé Convention, Art. 39; 1991 Bamako Convention, Art. 4; 1956 Plant Protection Agreement for the South East Asia and Pacific Region, Art. IV and Appendix B; 2001 POPs Convention, Art. 3.

[12] 1989 Basel Convention, Art. 4(1); 1951 International Plant Protection Convention, Art. VI(I).

[13] 1989 UNEP London Guidelines and 1985 FAO Pesticides Guidelines; 2000 Biosafety Protocol, Arts. 8–12 ('Advance Informed Agreement Procedure'). See also the 1998 Chemicals Convention, establishing a prior informed consent procedure for imports of pesticides and industrial chemicals that have been banned or severely restricted for health or environmental reasons by participating parties.

[14] Council Regulation (EC) No. 259/93 OJ L30, 6 February 1993, 1.

[15] 2000 Biosafety Protocol, Arts. 10(6) and 11(8).

[16] 1989 Basel Convention, Art. 4; 1991 Bamako Convention, Art. 4; 1989 Lomé Convention, Art. 39; 2001 POPs Convention, Art. 3.

production of controlled substances by the required phase-out dates to ban the export of used, recycled and reclaimed quantities of the substances, other than for the purpose of destruction. The 1992 Climate Change Convention and the 1992 Biodiversity Convention do not use trade provisions as an international enforcement measure, although, when it comes into force, the 1997 Kyoto Protocol will make use of such measures under its compliance mechanism.[17] As discussed below, both the climate change and biodiversity regimes address the permissibility of unilateral measures adopted by parties.

The use of trade sanctions to implement international environmental obligations raises possible conflicts between obligations under environmental agreements and those under free trade agreements. Such conflicts would be subject to the general rules of international law, as reflected in the 1969 Vienna Convention on the Law of Treaties.[18] Applying these rules, it follows that the trade restrictions established under post-1994 agreements, such as the 2000 Biosafety Protocol and the 2001 POPs Convention, will prevail over inconsistent obligations established under the 1994 GATT (to the extent that they are inconsistent) as between parties to both, but that the free trade obligations of the GATT might prevail where a state was not a party to the relevant multilateral agreement (to the extent that GATT obligations were inconsistent). The situation is slightly more complex in the case of pre-1994 multilateral environmental agreements, such as the 1987 Montreal Protocol and the 1989 Basel Convention. With GATT 1947 being re-adopted as GATT 1994 at the Uruguay Round of trade negotiations, the trade agreement is (at least technically) the *lex posterior*.[19] However, the ruling of the WTO Appellate Body in the *Shrimp/Turtle* dispute (discussed below) suggests that trade restrictions in multilateral environmental agreements like the 1987 Montreal Protocol and the 1989 Basel Convention are unlikely to fall foul of GATT 1994 requirements.[20]

Even for international environmental agreements concluded after 1994, the relationship between the trade measures used in environmental agreements and the requirements of trade treaties is sometimes unclear.[21] Despite the prominence of the issue of the relationship between trade and environmental

---

[17] Under the compliance regime for the Kyoto Protocol, elaborated by the Marrakesh Accords, the Enforcement Branch of the Compliance Committee will have the authority to impose trade restrictions on parties as a sanction for non-compliance. In the case of non-compliance with emissions targets, Annex I parties may be subject to a penalty of 30 per cent in the second commitment period and a bar on selling emissions reductions.

[18] Chapter 4, pp. 136–8 above.

[19] See C. Wold, 'Multilateral Environmental Agreements and the GATT: Conflict and Resolution?', 26 *Environmental Law* 841 (1996).

[20] See also J. Crawford and P. Sands, *The Availability of Article 11 Agreements in the Context of the Basel Convention's Export Ban on Recyclables* (International Council on Metals and the Environment, 1997).

[21] See A. H. Qureshi, 'The Cartagena Protocol on Biosafety and the WTO: Coexistence or Incoherence?', 49 ICLQ 835 (2000).

commitments during the negotiations for the 2000 Biosafety Protocol, the only clue as to the appropriate relationship is given by opaque language in the Protocol's Preamble.[22] Further clarification may be forthcoming if new negotiations on the relationship between trade rules and environmental agreements, being conducted under the auspices of the WTO's Committee on Trade and Environment, are successful (see below).

The GATT envisages certain exceptions to the prohibition on import restrictions, and support has been expressed for the view that import restrictions could be justified under the Article XX exceptions when they are based on measures adopted pursuant to a multilateral environmental agreement, such as the 1987 Montreal Protocol. In 1992, the EC suggested that, for an exception to be so justified, the multilateral environmental agreement should fulfil certain conditions, including:

1. the agreement should have been negotiated under the aegis of the UN and the procedures for negotiation should have been open to the participation of all GATT members; and
2. the agreement should be open for accession by any GATT members on terms which are equitable in relation to those which apply to original members.[23]

The EC also recognised that the same criteria should apply to regional agreements, but that in no circumstances could such agreements provide justification for applying extra-jurisdictional trade measures *vis-à-vis* countries outside the region.[24] The requirement for multilaterality in order to justify trade action for environmental purposes was stressed by the WTO Appellate Body in the *Shrimp/Turtle* dispute.[25]

The 1987 Montreal Protocol raises further legal issues by requiring parties to ban the import and export of controlled substances from non-parties and, following amendments adopted in 1991, 1992 and 1995, to ban the import from non-parties of certain products which contain controlled substances.[26] Here the question arises as to whether these bans can be enforced, under international law, against states which are not parties to the Montreal Protocol but which are parties to the GATT. The dispute settlement bodies of the WTO have not yet been called upon to consider the question; at first sight such a restriction might appear to be incompatible with Article XI of the GATT (elimination of quantitative restrictions) but might be brought within the exceptions established under Article XX.[27] A WTO Panel or the Appellate Body might find

---

[22] Chapter 11, p. 522 above.   [23] GATT Doc. TRE/W/5, 17 November 1992, 9.

[24] *Ibid.* The 1991 Bamako Convention, negotiated under the auspices of the OAU, might have difficulty in meeting this test.

[25] *United States – Import Prohibition of Certain Shrimp and Shrimp Products*, Report of the Appellate Body, WT/DS58/AB/R, 38 ILM 118 (1999), para. 168.

[26] 1987 Montreal Protocol, Art. 4(1) to (4); see further chapter 8, pp. 345–57 above.

[27] See below.

it difficult to hold that an import ban imposed pursuant to an international treaty (to which more than 180 states are party) was not 'necessary to protect human, animal or plant life or health' although the result would not be certain. Under the NAFTA, Mexico, Canada and the United States have adopted a different approach, expressly providing that trade sanctions in the 1973 CITES, the 1987 Montreal Protocol (and the 1990 amendments thereto) and the 1989 Basel Convention will prevail over the NAFTA.[28]

Unilateral environmental measures and international trade

Unilateral environmental measures are national environmental protection measures adopted by states which include an international trade limitation or prohibition and which are adopted in the absence of agreed international standards or rules, or go beyond agreed international standards. Examples of such measures include national laws establishing product-labelling requirements, import bans or quotas, and other environmentally related measures which can have the effect, directly or indirectly, of limiting international trade. The main international trade agreements of relevance to the adoption of environmental measures of this type are the 1994 GATT, the 1957 EC Treaty (as amended), the 1988 Free Trade Agreement between Canada and the United States and the 1992 North American Free Trade Agreement (NAFTA) between Mexico, Canada and the United States. The 1991 Treaty establishing the African Economic Community is also likely to be important.

The rapid development of national environmental legislation limiting imports and trade in the past few years, usually adopted outside the context of agreed international standards, has led to more trade-related disputes between states. This trend is likely to continue in the face of increased disparities between countries' environmental protection standards and the failure to adopt binding international standards. As a result, international courts, tribunals and other bodies find themselves increasingly called upon to determine the compatibility of national environmental protection measures with international legal obligations which prohibit restrictions or barriers to international trade.

WTO/GATT

K. W. Dam, *The GATT Law and International Economic Organisations* (1970); F. Kirgis, 'Effective Pollution Control in Industrialised Countries: International Economic Disincentives, Policy Responses and the GATT', 70 *Michigan Law Review* 860 (1972); O. Long, *Law and its Limitations in the GATT Multilateral Trade System* (1985); E.-U. Petersmann, 'Trade Policy, Environmental Policy and the GATT: Why

---

[28] See p. 999 below.

Trade Rules and Environmental Rules Should be Mutually Consistent', 46 *Aussenwirtschaft* 197 (1991); S. Charnovitz, 'Exploring the Environmental Exceptions in GATT Article XX', 25 *Journal of World Trade* 37 (1991); P. Sorsa, 'Environment – A New Challenge to GATT?' (World Bank, 1991); E.-U. Petersmann, 'International Trade Law and International Environmental Law – Prevention and Settlement of International Disputes in GATT', 27 *Journal of World Trade* 43 (1993); J. Cameron, 'The GATT and the Environment', in P. Sands (ed.), *Greening International Law* (1993), 100; D. Esty, *Greening the GATT: Trade, Environment, and the Future* (1994); S. Charnovitz, 'The World Trade Organization and the Environment', 8 *Yearbook of International Environmental Law* 98 (1997); D. McRae, 'Trade and Environment: The Development of WTO Law', 9 *Otago Law Review* 221 (1998); WTO Secretariat, *Guide to the Uruguay Round Agreements* (1999); M. Blakeney and F. MacMillan, *The WTO and the Environment* (2001).

The GATT was originally adopted in 1947 as the main international arrangement to encourage trade between states.[29] In December 1993, after seven years of negotiation, the Trade Negotiations Committee of the Uruguay Round adopted by consensus the Final Act. The Final Act includes the Agreement Establishing the World Trade Organization (WTO)[30] and annexed agreements on, *inter alia*: the General Agreement on Tariffs and Trade 1994 (GATT 1994),[31] the General Agreement on Trade in Services (GATS),[32] the Agreement on Trade-Related Aspects of Intellectual Property Rights (TRIPs)[33] and the Understanding on Rules and Procedures Governing the Settlement of Disputes (DSU).[34] These and related agreements were opened for signature at Marrakesh on 15 April 1994 and entered into force on 1 January 1995.

The entire package established a permanent organisation, the WTO, which, with a current membership of 144 states and the EC, has become an important forum for the development of international law on matters relating to trade and the environment. The WTO replaces the former GATT Council as 'the common institutional framework for the conduct of trade relations among its

[29] 30 October 1947, not yet in force, 55 UNTS 194; the GATT 1947 was brought into force on a provisional basis by the Protocol of Provisional Application, 30 October 1947, in force 1 January 1948, 55 UNTS 308. Eight multilateral trading rounds took place under the auspices of the GATT: 1947 (Geneva); 1949 (Annecy); 1951 (Torquay); 1956 (Geneva); 1960–1 (Geneva); 1964–7 ('Kennedy'); 1973–7 (Tokyo); and 1986–93 (Uruguay).

[30] 33 ILM 13 (1994).

[31] Annex 1A, 33 ILM 28 (1994). This Annex also includes Agreements on, *inter alia*, Agriculture, Sanitary and Phytosanitary Measures, Technical Barriers to Trade, Trade-Related Aspects of Investment Measures, and Subsidies and Countervailing Measures.

[32] Annex 1B, 33 ILM 44 (1994). The text makes no reference to sustainable development or environmental protection requirements, although a Decision on Trade in Services and the Environment was adopted.

[33] Annex 1C, 33 ILM 81 (1994). The text makes no reference to sustainable development or environmental protection requirements.

[34] Annex 2, 33 ILM 136 (1994).

Members in matters related to the agreements and associated legal instruments included in the Annexes [to the WTO Agreement].'[35] As a permanent multi-lateral institution, the WTO takes its place alongside the World Bank and the IMF. Although it does not have express environmental objectives, the Preamble recognises that the WTO must allow 'the optimal use of the world's resources in accordance with the objective of sustainable development' and seek 'both to protect and preserve the environment and enhance the means for doing so in a manner consistent with' the respective needs and concerns of the parties at different levels of economic development. The WTO's tasks are: to implement the WTO Agreement and the multilateral trade agreements; to provide the framework for the implementation of the plurilateral trade agreements; to ad-minister the DSU and the Trade Policy Review Mechanism; to provide a forum for the negotiations among members; and to co-operate with the World Bank and the IMF.[36] Despite the new institutional overlay, the GATT 1994 remains the central substantive agreement under the WTO umbrella, which is designed to encourage trade between WTO members by reducing tariffs and preventing trade barriers.

Article III(1) of the GATT 1994 prohibits the application to imported or do-mestic products of internal taxes and other internal charges, laws, regulations and requirements so as to afford protection to domestic products. Article III(2) prohibits the application, directly or indirectly, of internal taxes or other in-ternal charges of any kind in excess of those applied, directly or indirectly, to like domestic products or in a manner contrary to Article III(1). Under Article XI, prohibitions or restrictions, including quotas, import or export licences or other measures, on the import or export of any product from or to an-other contracting party are prohibited. Article XX permits exceptions to these limitations. It provides, *inter alia*:

> Subject to the requirement that such measures are not applied in a manner which would constitute a means of arbitrary or unjustifiable discrimina-tion between countries where the same conditions prevail, or a disguised restriction on international trade, nothing in this Agreement shall be con-strued to prevent the adoption or enforcement by any contracting party of measures:
>
> . . .
>
> (b) necessary to protect human, animal or plant life or health;
>
> . . .
>
> (g) relating to the conservation of exhaustible natural resources if such measures are made effective in conjunction with restrictions on do-mestic production or consumption.

---

[35] Note 30 above, Art. II(1).

[36] *Ibid.*, Art. III. The institutional arrangements comprise a ministerial conference, a general council (with authority to establish a Dispute Settlement Body), a secretariat and a number of specialist subsidiary councils and committees.

The GATT 1994 does not include a reference to environmental protection.[37] Efforts during the Uruguay Round to strengthen provisions on environmental protection, in particular by amending Articles XX(b) and (g), failed, although pursuant to Article 2.2 of the Agreement on Technical Barriers to Trade (discussed below) the contracting parties did identify 'environmental protection' as a 'legitimate objective' to be considered in evaluating the GATT compatibility of environmental regulations.

Technical barriers to trade

During the 1973–9 Tokyo Round, an Agreement on Technical Barriers to Trade (1979 TBT Agreement) was negotiated and adopted to deal with the growing problem of trade barriers resulting from disparate national regulations.[38] It established basic guidelines which governed, among other matters, the acceptability of national environmental regulations. The 1979 TBT Agreement did not attract widespread ratification by GATT contracting parties and during the Uruguay Round it was renegotiated. The result of the Uruguay Round negotiations was two new agreements dealing with national regulatory standards: the Agreement on the Application of Sanitary and Phytosanitary Measures (SPS Agreement),[39] which deals with measures designed to protect human, animal and plant life or health, and the Agreement on Technical Barriers to Trade (TBT Agreement),[40] which covers other technical standards not regulated by the SPS Agreement.[41] The main objective of the new TBT Agreement is to ensure that technical regulations and standards, including packaging, labelling and marking requirements and methods of certifying conformity with technical regulations and standards, are not adopted or applied so as to create unnecessary obstacles to trade. Environmental regulations may be technical barriers to trade. The TBT Agreement adopts the principles of national treatment and non-discrimination by stating that, in relation to such technical regulations or standards, imported products are not to receive less favourable treatment 'than that accorded to like products of national origin and to like products originating in any other country'.[42] WTO members must also ensure that technical regulations 'are not prepared, adopted or applied with a view to or with the effect of creating unnecessary obstacles to international trade'. Accordingly, technical regulations must not be 'more trade-restrictive than necessary to fulfil a legitimate objective, taking account of the risks non-fulfilment would create'.[43] The list of 'legitimate objectives' in Article 2.2 includes 'the protection of human health or safety, animal or plant life or health, or the environment'. In assessing

---

[37] But cf. the understanding of an 'environmental' interpretation of GATT Art. XX(b) and (g) of Canada, Mexico and the United States in the context of the NAFTA, pp. 999–1007 below.

[38] In force 1 January 1980, Misc. 20 (1979), Cmnd 7657; 31 UST 405, TIAS 9616.

[39] GATT Doc. MTN/FA II-A1A-4 (15 December 1993).

[40] GATT Doc. MTN/FA II-AIA-6 (15 December 1993).

[41] TBT Agreement, Art. 1.   [42] Art. 2.1.   [43] Art. 2.2.

the risks to health or the environment, the relevant factors for consideration include 'available scientific and technical information, related processing technology or intended end-uses of products'.[44] This formulation suggests that both characteristics of the product itself, and the process by which it is produced, are relevant in assessing the health or environmental risks posed by a product.

The main distinction between technical regulations and standards, which lay down technical specifications relating to the characteristics of a product, is that in the case of the former compliance is mandatory while in the case of the latter it is not. All products are subject to the provisions of the TBT Agreement, which recognises that technical regulations and standards would not pose problems to international trade if the parties used international standards as the basis for their adoption. The TBT Agreement obliges parties, where 'relevant international standards exist or their completion is imminent', to use them as a basis for their technical regulations, except when they are an inappropriate means for the fulfilment of the legitimate objective pursued, for example 'because of fundamental climatic or geographical factors or fundamental technological problems'.[45] The TBT Agreement thus explicitly recognises that environmental protection could allow deviation from international standards. Such a deviation would, however, be subject to the basic obligation of the TBT Agreement to ensure that technical regulations should not create unnecessary obstacles to international trade. The TBT Agreement also imposes certain procedural requirements. The members must publish technical regulations in draft form where they are not based on international standards, or where such standards do not exist, and where the technical regulation or standard that is being adopted is likely to have a significant effect on trade.[46] To ensure that exporting countries, particularly developing countries, have time to adapt their products or methods of production to the requirements of the importing country, the Agreement requires that there should be a reasonable interval between the publication of technical regulations and their entry into force.[47] However, where 'urgent problems of safety, health, environmental protection or national security arise or threaten to arise for a Member', the member may fast-track the introduction of a technical regulation, provided that other members are notified immediately through the WTO Secretariat and given an opportunity to present their comments in writing, discuss these comments upon request, and have their written comments and the results of discussions taken into account.[48] The TBT Agreement requires each party to set up enquiry points from which relevant information about technical regulations, standards and conformity assessment procedures can be obtained.[49]

The TBT Agreement also recognises that developing countries are entitled to special treatment and that technical assistance should be made available to them.[50] Such special treatment could include, *inter alia*, taking into account

---

[44] *Ibid.*   [45] Art. 2.4.   [46] Art. 2.9.   [47] Art. 2.12.   [48] Art. 2.10.   [49] Art. 10.
[50] Art. 12.

their trade and financial needs in the preparation of technical regulations, standards, test methods and certification systems, and ensuring that the adoption of technical regulations does not create unnecessary obstacles to exports from developing countries.[51] Additionally, the technical regulations and standards adopted should be based on scientific considerations and, to that end, in the event of a dispute arising, a WTO panel may establish a technical expert group to assist it with questions of a technical nature.[52] This assists the panel by advising whether the measure is necessary for the protection of human, animal or plant life or health and whether it was based on a legitimate scientific judgment.

Committee on Trade and the Environment

At Marrakesh, in April 1994, ministers adopted a Decision on Trade and the Environment to co-ordinate policies in the fields of trade and the environment within the competence of the multilateral trading system.[53] The Decision called for the establishment of a Committee on Trade and the Environment (CTE) to take over the role of the previous GATT Group on Environmental Measures and International Trade,[54] which, despite being established in 1971, was not activated until October 1991, in preparation for UNCED. The terms of reference of the CTE are to identify the relationship between trade and environmental measures to promote sustainable development, and to recommend whether there is a need for modifications to the multilateral trading system to (a) enhance positive interaction between trade and environment, (b) avoid protectionist trade measures while ensuring responsiveness to the environmental objectives of Agenda 21 and the Rio Declaration, and (c) provide for surveillance of trade measures for environmental purposes, of trade-related aspects of environmental measures, and of effective implementation of 'multilateral disciplines' governing such measures. The Decision identified seven matters to be initially addressed by the CTE.[55] To date, intergovernmental deliberations

---

[51] Art. 12.3.   [52] Art. 14.2 and Annex II.

[53] Communication from the Chairman of the GATT Trade Negotiations Committee, 'Decision on Trade and Environment', GATT Doc. MTN.TNC/W/141, 29 March 1994.

[54] GATT Doc. L/3622/Rev.1 and C/M/74.

[55] These issues were:

- the relationship between the provisions of the multilateral trading system and trade measures for environmental purposes, including those in environmental agreements;
- the relationship between certain environmental policies and measures and the multilateral trading system;
- the relationship between the multilateral trading system and environmental charges and taxes and requirements for environmental purposes relating to products (including standards and technical regulations, packaging, labelling and recycling);
- the transparency of trade measures for environmental purposes and environmental measures and requirements with significant trade effects;

have produced little progress on substantive issues.[56] However, the role of the CTE may potentially be revitalised by new negotiations taking place under its auspices dealing with the relationship between existing WTO rules and trade obligations in multilateral environmental agreements, as agreed in the Doha Ministerial Declaration in November 2001.[57] Following Doha, the first meeting of the CTE's Trade Negotiations Committee was held in February 2002.

WTO/GATT Dispute Settlement

R. E. Hudec, 'The New WTO Dispute Settlement Procedure: An Overview of the First Three Years', 9 *Minnesota Journal of Global Trade* 1 (1999); J. Jackson, *The Jurisprudence of GATT and the WTO* (2000); P. K. Rao, *World Trade Organization and the Environment* (2000).

In the event of a dispute between WTO members concerning environmental measures and agreements and trade obligations, the matter may be referred to dispute settlement in accordance with the procedures of the DSU.[58] The DSU introduced significant changes to the dispute settlement procedures formerly employed under the GATT. The Dispute Settlement Body (DSB) established under the WTO is responsible for administering the rules and procedures governing dispute settlement. The traditional approaches used under GATT 1947 (consultation, good offices, conciliation and mediation) remain in place,[59] with amended rules for the Dispute Settlement Panels and new provisions on appellate review and arbitration. Panels assist the DSB in making recommendations or in giving the rulings provided for in the relevant agreements.[60] Third parties

– the relationship between dispute settlement mechanisms in the multilateral trading system and those in environmental agreements;
– the effect of environmental measures on market access; and
– the issue of exports of domestically prohibited goods.

[56] See S. Charnovitz, 'A Critical Guide to the WTO's Report on Trade and Environment', 14 *Arizona Journal of International and Comparative Law* 341 (1997).

[57] Declaration of the Fourth Ministerial Conference, Doha, Qatar, WT/MIN(01)/DEC/1, 20 November 2001, paras. 31–3. By the Declaration, Ministers of WTO members agreed to negotiations, without prejudging their outcome, on:

(i) the relationship between existing WTO rules and specific trade obligations set out in multilateral environmental agreements (MEAs). The negotiations shall be limited in scope to the applicability of such existing WTO rules as among parties to the MEA in question. The negotiations shall not prejudice the WTO rights of any Member that is not a party to the MEA in question;

(ii) procedures for regular information exchange between MEA Secretariats and the relevant WTO committees, and the criteria for the granting of observer status;

(iii) the reduction or, as appropriate, elimination of tariff and non-tariff barriers to environmental goods and services (*ibid.*, para. 31).

[58] Chapter 5, pp. 220–2 above.   [59] DSU, paras. 4 and 5.   [60] *Ibid.*, para. 11.

having a substantial interest in a matter before a Panel are entitled to partici-pate in Panel proceedings.[61] Most significantly, Panel reports become binding unless one of the parties to the dispute decides to appeal or the DSB decides by consensus not to adopt the report.[62] Appeal is permitted only on points of law related to a panel ruling. The appeal is made to a standing Appellate Body, which is composed of seven independent persons, three of whom serve on any one case.[63] Appellate Body reports must be adopted by the DSB and unconditionally accepted by the parties to the dispute unless the DSB decides by consensus not to adopt the report within thirty days of its issuance.[64] The DSU also provides for rules on surveillance of implementation of recommen-dations and rulings of the DSB, compensation and suspension of concessions, and binding arbitration by mutual agreement of the parties as an alternative means of dispute settlement.[65]

Prior to the entry into force of the DSU in January 1995, six GATT panels had been established for disputes relating – directly or indirectly – to international environmental issues,[66] and many other panel decisions provided guidance on interpretation of relevant provisions of the GATT.[67] The most important of these decisions were two panel reports issued in 1991 and 1994[68] concerning the dispute between Mexico and the United States over the latter's ban of imports of yellow-fin tuna from Mexico and 'intermediary nations' which had been caught in a manner which harmed dolphins. The dispute was controversial and, unlike previous GATT panel decisions, subject to intense public scrutiny.

Tuna/Dolphin Cases (1991 and 1994)

M. Hurlock, 'The GATT, US Law and the Environment: A Proposal to Amend the GATT in Light of the Tuna/Dolphin Decision', 92 *Columbia Law Review* 2098 (1992); B. Kingsbury, 'The Tuna-Dolphin Controversy, the World Trade Organization and the Liberal Project to Reconceptualize International Law', 5 *Yearbook of International Environmental Law* 1 (1994); A. Ferrante, 'The Dolphin-Tuna Controversy and Environmental Issues', 5 *Journal of Transnational Law and Policy* 279 (1996).

---

[61] *Ibid.*, para. 10.   [62] *Ibid.*, para. 16.3.   [63] *Ibid.*, para. 17.

[64] *Ibid.*, para. 17.14.   [65] *Ibid.*, paras. 21, 22 and 25.

[66] See *Canadian Tuna Case* (Report of the Panel adopted on 22 February 1982, BISD/29S/91); *US Chemicals Tax Case* (Report of the Panel adopted on 17 June 1987, BSD/34S/160); *US Processed Herring Case* (Canada – Measures Affecting Exports of Unprocessed Herring and Salmon, Report of the Panel adopted on 22 March 1988, BISD/35S/98); *Thai Cigarette Case* (Thailand – Restriction on Importation of and Internal Taxes on Cigarettes, Report of the Panel adopted on 7 November 1990, BISD/37S/200); *Tuna/Dolphin I* (30 ILM 1594 (1991)); *Tuna/Dolphin II* (33 ILM, 839 (1994)).

[67] *US – Section 337 of the Tariff Act of 1930* (Panel Report, 7 November 1989, BISD/36S/345); *EEC – Regulation on Imports of Parts and Components* (Panel Report, 16 May 1990, BISD/37S/132).

[68] *Tuna/Dolphin I* (30 ILM 1594 (1991)); *Tuna/Dolphin II* (33 ILM 839 (1994)).

The *Tuna/Dolphin* dispute arose over regulations adopted under the US 1972 Marine Mammal Protection Act (MMPA), as amended. The MMPA regulates, *inter alia*, the harvesting of tuna by US fishermen and others who are subject to the jurisdiction of the US. Under the MMPA, US authorities granted licences for the fishing of yellow-fin tuna by United States vessels in the Eastern Tropical Pacific Ocean (ETPO), on condition that the domestic fleet did not exceed an incidental taking of a total of 20,500 dolphins per year in the ETPO. The MMPA also required the US Secretary of State

> to ban the importation of commercial fish or products from fish which have been caught with commercial fishing technology which results in the incidental kill or incidental serious injury of ocean mammals in excess of United States standards.[69]

The MMPA amounted to a requirement that US environmental standards should be applied to all countries in respect of their fishing activities. Under US law, fish caught by a vessel registered in a country is deemed to originate in that country. As a condition of access to the US market for the yellow-fin tuna or yellow-fin tuna products caught by its fleet, each country of registry of vessels fishing yellow-fin tuna in the ETPO was required to prove to the satisfaction of the US authorities that its overall regulatory regime regarding the taking of marine mammals was comparable to that of the US. To meet this requirement, the country in question needed to prove that the average rate of incidental taking of marine mammals by its tuna fleet operating in the ETPO was not in excess of 1.25 times the average incidental taking rate of US vessels operating in the ETPO during the same period.

The MMPA additionally provided that ninety days after imports of yellow-fin tuna and yellow-fin tuna products from a country had been prohibited in accordance with the rules set out above, the import of such tuna and tuna products from any 'intermediary nation' would also be prohibited, unless the intermediary nation could prove that it too had acted to ban imports of such tuna and tuna products from the country of origin subject to the direct import embargo. Finally, certification by the US Secretary of State to the President, which took place six months after the effective date of an embargo, triggered the operation of section 8(a) of the 1967 Fishermen's Protective Act (the 'Pelly Amendment'). This provides a discretionary authority for the US President to order a prohibition of imports of fish products 'for such duration as the President determines appropriate and to the extent that such prohibition is sanctioned by the [GATT]'.[70] Under the MMPA, the US prohibited the

---

[69] MMPA, section 101(a)(2), in Panel Report, para. 2.5.

[70] Panel Report, para. 2.9. The Panel held that the 'possible' extension of import prohibitions to all fish products of Mexico under the Pelly Amendment was not, in itself, inconsistent with Art. XI since it merely gave executive authorities the power to act inconsistently with the GATT, and did not require trade measures to be taken (para. 5.21).

import into its customs territory of yellow-fin tuna and yellow-fin tuna products from Mexico which were caught with purse-seine nets in the ETPO. An earlier embargo had been imposed on such tuna and tuna products in August 1990; a new embargo was put in place in March 1991, and from 24 May 1991 the US implemented an 'intermediary nations' embargo on products from several other countries, including those from the European Community.

The dispute also concerned labelling requirements. The 1990 Dolphin Protection Consumer Information Act (DPCIA) provided that, when a tuna product exported from or offered for sale in the US bears the optional label 'Dolphin Safe' or any similar label indicating it was fished in a manner not harmful to dolphins, this tuna product must not contain tuna harvested on the high seas by a vessel engaged in driftnet fishing, or harvested in the ETPO by a vessel using a purse-seine net, unless it is accompanied by documentary evidence showing that the purse-seine net was not intentionally deployed to encircle dolphins. The labelling provisions of the DPCIA took effect on 28 May 1991.

Tuna/Dolphin I (1991)

In January 1991, Mexico requested the GATT Council to establish a Panel to examine the compatibility of the MMPA and the DPCIA, and implementing regulations, with the GATT. The Panel examined the compatibility with GATT (under Articles III, IX, XI and XIII, and the exemptions under Article XX)[71] of:

1. the prohibition of imports of certain yellow-fin tuna and certain yellow-fin tuna products from Mexico imposed by the US and the provisions of the MMPA on which it was based;
2. the prohibition of imports of certain yellow-fin tuna and certain yellow-fin tuna products from 'intermediary nations' imposed by the US and the provisions of the MMPA on which it was based;
3. the possible extension of each of these import prohibitions to all fish products from Mexico and the 'intermediary nations', under the MMPA and the Pelly Amendment; and
4. the application to tuna and tuna products from Mexico of the labelling provisions of the DPCIA, as well as its provisions as such.

The Panel held that the US import restrictions were incompatible with the GATT and could not be justified under Article XX(b) or (g).[72] The measures prohibiting Mexican imports were classed as quantitative restrictions under Article XI. The Panel rejected the US argument that the prohibitions were

---

[71] Australia, the EC, Indonesia, Japan, Korea, the Philippines, Senegal, Thailand and Venezuela made oral presentations to the Panel; and Canada and Norway submitted their views in writing.

[72] GATT Doc. DS21/R, 3 September 1991 (30 ILM 1594 (1991)).

internal regulations under Article III, noting that, even if they were, the US import prohibitions were discriminatory and did not meet the requirements of Article III(4) which:

> calls for a comparison of the treatment of imported tuna as a product with that of domestic tuna *as a product*. Regulations governing the taking of dolphins incidental to the taking of tuna could not possibly affect tuna as a product. Article III.4 therefore obliges the [US] to accord treatment to Mexican tuna no less favourable than that accorded to [US] tuna, whether or not the incidental taking of dolphins by Mexican vessels corresponds to that of [US] vessels.[73]

Since the direct import prohibitions were inconsistent with Article XI(1) of GATT (the US had not presented a contrary argument), it was not necessary to make a finding on the consistency of the measures under Article XIII.[74]

At the heart of the case lay the question of whether these import prohibitions, which were contrary to Article XI, were permitted under Article XX(b) and (g). The Panel considered that the US was entitled to invoke Article XX, but noted that:

> the practice of panels has been to interpret Article XX narrowly, to place the burden on the party invoking Article XX to justify its invocation, and not to examine Article XX exceptions unless invoked.[75]

The principal issue relating to Article XX(b) was whether it covered measures necessary to protect human, animal or plant life *outside US jurisdiction*. Since the GATT text did not provide a clear answer, the provision had to be analysed 'in the light of its drafting history, its purpose, and the consequences that the interpretations proposed by the parties would have for the operation of the GATT as a whole'.[76] The Panel concluded that the concerns of the drafters focused on the use of measures 'within the jurisdiction of the importing country'.[77] The Panel further considered that measures taken under Article XX(b) must be 'necessary' and should not 'constitute a means of arbitrary or unjustifiable discrimination' and that Article XX(b) was intended to allow restrictions 'to pursue overriding public policy goals to the extent that such inconsistencies were unavoidable'.[78] The Panel held that to accept the US interpretation justifying measures under this provision would mean that:

> each contracting party could unilaterally determine the life or health protection policies from which other contracting parties could not deviate without jeopardising their rights under the General Agreement. The General Agreement would then no longer constitute a multilateral framework for trade among all contracting parties but would provide legal security only in respect of trade between a limited number of contracting parties with identical internal regulations.[79]

---

[73] Para. 5.15 (emphasis added).   [74] Para. 5.18.   [75] Para. 5.22.
[76] Para. 5.26.   [77] *Ibid.*   [78] *Ibid.*   [79] *Ibid.*

Even if Article XX(b) were interpreted to permit extra-jurisdictional protection of life and health, the Panel held that the US had not shown that its measures were necessary, or that it had exhausted all other options reasonably available to it to pursue its dolphin protection objectives in a manner which was compatible with the GATT, in particular through the negotiation of international co-operative arrangements. Moreover, even if an import prohibition was the only measure reasonably available, the conditions adopted were too unpredictable to be regarded as necessary to protect the health or life of dolphins.[80]

The Panel concluded that the direct import prohibitions were also unjustified under Article XX(g), which could not be interpreted to apply extra-jurisdictionally. It found that Article XX(g) required measures relating to the conservation of exhaustible natural resources to be taken 'in conjunction with restrictions on domestic production or consumption', which could only occur if the measure 'was primarily aimed at rendering effective these restrictions'.[81] The Panel considered that a

> country can effectively control the production or consumption of an exhaustible natural resource only to the extent that the production or consumption is under its jurisdiction[82]

and that to accept the extra-jurisdictional interpretation of the US would mean that

> each contracting party could unilaterally determine the conservation policies from which other contracting parties could not deviate without jeopardising their rights under the General Agreement.[83]

Finally, even if Article XX(g) could be applied extra-jurisdictionally, the US measures did not meet the conditions of the Article, since 'a limitation on trade based on such unpredictable conditions could not be regarded as being primarily aimed at the conservation of dolphins'.[84]

The Panel also rejected the 'intermediary nations' embargo. It held that the embargo was a quantitative restriction subject to, and in this case inconsistent with, Article XI. It fell outside Article III, as argued by the US, since the domestic regulations were not applied to tuna as a product. For the reasons set out above, Article XX(b) and (g) also were not applicable. The Panel found that, since the US restrictions were inconsistent with the GATT, Article XX(d) was also not applicable.

The Panel found that the labelling provisions of the DPCIA relating to tuna caught in the ETPO were compatible with GATT. The labelling provisions

---

[80] The Panel was referring to the linkage by the US of 'the maximum incidental dolphin taking rate which Mexico had to meet during a particular period in order to be able to export tuna to the United States to the taking rate actually recorded for the United States fishermen during the same period': para. 5.28.

[81] Para. 5.31.   [82] *Ibid.*   [83] Para. 5.32.   [84] Para. 5.33.

did not make the right to sell tuna or tuna products, or the access to a government-conferred advantage affecting the sale of tuna or tuna products, conditional upon the use of tuna harvesting methods. Moreover, the legislation was consistent with Article I(1) of the GATT, since it did not discriminate against countries fishing in the ETPO (which was the only geographic area in which the harvesting of tuna by intentionally encircling dolphins with purse-seine nets occurred, by reason of the particular nature of the association between dolphins and tuna observed only in that area) and did not distinguish between products originating in Mexico and products originating in other countries.

Tuna/Dolphin II (1994)

In the second *Tuna/Dolphin* dispute, the EC and the Netherlands challenged provisions of the MMPA which placed an embargo on tuna imports from 'intermediary nations'.[85] Although originally intended to prevent circumvention of the primary embargo by transhipment of dolphin-unsafe tuna through a third country, amendments made following a US court decision required each country which was identified as an 'intermediary nation' to prove that it had prohibited the import of any tuna that was barred from direct importation into the US, regardless of whether the tuna had in fact been caught in a dolphin-unsafe manner.[86] The EC and the Netherlands maintained that the intermediary nations embargo violated Article XI of the GATT and could not be excused under the Article XX exceptions. The Panel agreed that the measures were inconsistent with Article XI(1) and proceeded to analyse their compatibility with Article XX(b) and (g).[87]

In evaluating the compatibility of the US measures with Article XX(b) and (g), the Panel employed a three-step analysis. First, it had to be determined whether the policy underlying the measure fell within the range of policies mentioned in Article XX(b) or (g), i.e. policies to protect human, animal or plant life or health, or to conserve exhaustible natural resources. Secondly, it had to be determined whether the measure for which the exception was being invoked fulfilled the conditions of the relevant exception. Thirdly, it had to be determined whether the measure was applied in conformity with the requirement set out in the Preamble to Article XX, namely, that the measure not be applied in a manner which would constitute a means of arbitrary

---

[85] *Tuna/Dolphin II* (33 ILM 839 (1994)). Six other GATT parties made third party submissions to the panel: Australia, Canada, Japan, New Zealand, Thailand and Venezuela.

[86] *Ibid.*, para. 5.5.

[87] *Ibid.*, para. 5.10. The US also argued that the intermediary nations embargo was justified under Art. XX(d), on the basis that it was necessary to secure compliance with import prohibitions under the primary nation embargo provisions. However, this argument was rejected by the Panel (para. 5.41).

or unjustifiable discrimination between countries where the same conditions prevail or in a manner which would constitute a disguised restriction on international trade.[88]

Examining Article XX(g), the Panel accepted that a policy to conserve dolphins was a policy to conserve an exhaustible natural resource since dolphin stocks could potentially be exhausted, and the basis of a policy to conserve them did not depend on whether their stocks were presently depleted.[89] The EC and the Netherlands had argued (in line with the findings of the Panel in the first *Tuna/Dolphin* dispute) that the exhaustible natural resource to be conserved under Article XX(g) could not be located outside the territorial jurisdiction of the country taking the measure. However, this argument was firmly rejected by the Panel following an analysis of the text of the exception and the requirements of 'general international law'.[90]

The panel then turned to the requirements of the exception itself, namely, that the measure be 'related to' the conservation of an exhaustible natural resource and be made effective 'in conjunction' with restrictions on domestic production or consumption. In line with previous GATT Panel decisions on Article XX(g),[91] the Panel interpreted the phrases 'related to' and 'in conjunction with' to mean 'primarily aimed at'.[92] The Panel then proceeded to examine whether the embargoes imposed by the United States could be considered to be primarily aimed at the conservation of an exhaustible natural resource, and primarily aimed at rendering effective restrictions on domestic production or consumption.[93] The Panel noted that the intermediary nation embargo prohibited tuna imports from a country which imported tuna from countries maintaining harvesting practices and policies not comparable to those of the United States, whether or not the particular tuna was harvested in a dolphin-unsafe manner, and regardless of whether the country had tuna harvesting practices and policies that harmed or could harm dolphins.[94] These observations might have led the Panel to conclude that the US measure was arbitrary or unjustifiably discriminatory in violation of the Article XX *chapeau*. Instead, the Panel decided that the 'primary aim' of embargo was to force changes in policy and practice in other countries, an objective which could not be justified under Article XX(g).[95] The Panel held:

---

[88] *Ibid.*, paras. 5.12 and 5.29. [89] *Ibid.*, para. 5.13.

[90] *Ibid.*, paras. 5.15–5.17. However, the Panel rejected the argument that various bilateral and multilateral environment treaties cited by the parties were relevant as a primary or supplementary means of interpretation of the text of the GATT, under the principles of interpretation stipulated in Arts. 31 and 32 of the Vienna Convention on the Law of Treaties.

[91] Report of the Panel in *Canada – Measures Affecting the Exports of Unprocessed Herring and Salmon*, adopted 22 March 1988, BISD/35S/98, 114, para. 4.6.

[92] *Tuna/Dolphin II*, para. 5.22. [93] *Ibid.*, para. 5.23. [94] *Ibid.*

[95] *Ibid.*, para. 5.27.

If . . . Article XX were interpreted to permit Contracting Parties to take trade measures so as to force other Contracting Parties to change their policies within their jurisdiction, including their conservation policies, the balance of rights among Contracting Parties, in particular the right of access to markets, would be seriously impaired.[96]

The Panel suggested that not only the intermediary nations embargo, but also the primary embargo could not be justified under Article XX(g) on this basis.[97] The Panel applied similar reasoning in its analysis of the US measures under Article XX(b). Like Article XX(g), Article XX(b) was considered 'not [to] spell out any limitation on the location of the living things to be protected'.[98] However, the Panel concluded that 'measures taken so as to force other countries to change their policies, and that were effective only if such changes occurred, could not be considered 'necessary' for the protection of animal life or health in the sense of Article XX(b).[99]

Assessment

The GATT Panel decisions in the *Tuna/Dolphin* dispute placed significant limitations on the use of unilateral trade measures by states to achieve environmental goals. The *Tuna/Dolphin I* Panel rejected the use of trade restrictions seeking to give effect to national environmental protection measures relating to processes, operations or activities carried out beyond the jurisdiction of the contracting party adopting the measures. It also stipulated that national environmental provisions must be 'necessary', which was defined to mean 'predictable' and 'unavoidable', the latter in the sense that all reasonably available international co-operative arrangements must have been exhausted. The application of these principles required the contracting parties to focus on the limited issue of the environmental effects in its territory of the product itself, and not the process which constituted the finished product.

The *Tuna/Dolphin II* Panel rejected the extra-jurisdictional limitation on Article XX(b) and (g) formulated by the first Panel, but went on to devise a further restriction on the use of these exceptions. The Panel held that unilateral trade measures which aim to change the environmental policies or practices of other contracting parties undermined the multilateral trading system and could not be justified under Article XX. This interpretation, which has no apparent basis in the text of the GATT, created a test which could make it 'impossible for

---

[96] *Ibid.*, para. 5.26.   [97] *Ibid.*, para. 5.24.   [98] *Ibid.*, para. 5.31.

[99] *Ibid.*, para. 5.39. The Panel agreed with the interpretation of a previous panel in the *Thai Cigarettes Case* (Report of the Panel on *Thailand – Restrictions on Importation of and Internal Taxes on Cigarettes*, DS10/R, adopted 7 November 1990, 37S/200, 223 (30 ILM 1122 (1991))) that the term 'necessary' in Art. XX(b) means that there must be no other reasonably available, GATT-consistent alternative measure.

any nation to meet in the international trade arena'.[100] The Panel's approach seemed to deny the availability of trade measures for environmental purposes, regardless of the geographic scope of the adverse environmental effects, and irrespective of a shared interest in the resource which is the subject of protective measures. Where the adverse environmental effects complained of by the importing country are the consequence of lax environmental process standards in the exporting country, the effectiveness of the measure to achieve its environmental goal could be dependent upon creating incentives for the exporting country to change its environmental policies in order to maintain access to the importing country's market.

The decisions of the GATT Panels in the *Tuna/Dolphin* dispute were apparently motivated by policy considerations, including concern at the prospect of the adoption of unilateral measures and growing disparities in national environmental standards, and a desire to encourage an international regulatory response to the trade problems posed by national environmental disparities. The concluding remarks of the first Panel included a call for the contracting parties, in the event that they decided to permit trade measures such as those adopted by the US, to do so by amending or supplementing the GATT, or waiving obligations thereunder, rather than by interpreting Article XX. The Panel suggested this would enable the contracting parties to impose limits on the range of environmental policy differences justifying trade responses and to develop criteria to prevent abuse. In the end, neither of the *Tuna/Dolphin* Panel decisions was adopted by the GATT Council. The findings of the Panels in the *Tuna/Dolphin* dispute must now be read in the context of the subsequent jurisprudence of the WTO Appellate Body, described below, which render both decisions of historical – rather than practical – interest.

Reformulated Gasoline Case (1996)

The *Reformulated Gasoline* case[101] provided the new WTO Appellate Body with its first case, and its first opportunity to consider trade measures purporting to pursue environmental goals. The dispute arose out of a complaint brought by Brazil and Venezuela against regulations promulgated under the US Clean Air Act (CAA) dealing with the standards for reformulated and conventional gasoline. The function of the regulations, known as the 'Gasoline Rule', was to establish 'cleanliness' standards for gasoline sold throughout the US, based

---

[100] C. Wofford, 'A Greener Future at the WTO: The Refinement of WTO Jurisprudence on Environmental Exceptions to GATT', 24 *Harvard Environmental Law Review* 563 at 579 (2000).

[101] *United States – Standards for Reformulated and Conventional Gasoline*, Report of the Panel, 29 January 1996, WT/DS2/R (*Reformulated Gasoline*, Panel Report); *United States – Standards for Reformulated and Conventional Gasoline*, Report of the Appellate Body, 29 April 1996, WT/DS2/AB/R (*Reformulated Gasoline*, Appellate Body Report), 35 ILM 603 (1996).

on 1990 pollution levels. The Gasoline Rule made provision for the establishment of 1990 baselines for refiners, blenders and importers as an integral part of the process of compliance assessment for the programme. Domestic entities were permitted to establish individual baselines; no provision was made, however, to allow foreign refiners to establish individual baselines. Instead, all foreign refiners were required to use statutorily determined baselines as a basis for determining whether their gasoline met the requirements of the Gasoline Rule. The US argued that statutory baselines for foreign refiners were necessary because of the overwhelming administrative difficulties its Environmental Protection Agency (EPA) would face if required to verify compliance of foreign refiners with individual baselines.[102] The US also claimed that the measures were justified under the 'environmental exceptions' of Article XX as measures necessary for the protection of human health and relating to the conservation of an exhaustible natural resource (clean air).[103]

The WTO Panel, at first instance, concluded that the Gasoline Rule was inconsistent with the national treatment obligation of Article III(4) and was not justified under Article XX(b) or (g).[104] In reaching its conclusion in respect of Article XX(b), the Panel ruled that statutory baselines for foreign refiners were not 'necessary' because other GATT-consistent or less inconsistent measures, such as applying statutory baselines to domestic as well as foreign refiners or permitting foreign refiners to use individual baselines, were reasonably available to the US to achieve its policy goal.[105] The Panel considered that the US had not discharged its burden of proving that reasons of administrative complexity precluded the effective use of individual baselines for foreign refiners, noting particularly that the US had not shown that a determination of origin of the gasoline could not be achieved by standard means of documentary evidence and third party verification.[106] In respect of Article XX(g), the Panel concluded that clear air was a 'natural resource' that could be 'depleted', and hence a policy to reduce the depletion of clean air was a policy to conserve an exhaustible natural resource within the meaning of Article XX(g).[107] However, the Panel held that, as there was no direct connection between the less favourable treatment of imported gasoline and the US objective of improving air quality, the baseline establishment rules could not be 'primarily aimed at' the conservation of a natural resource.[108] In reaching this conclusion, the Panel appeared to rely

---

[102] *Reformulated Gasoline*, Panel Report, paras. 3.19 and 6.23.

[103] *Ibid.*, para. 3.37. The US also sought to justify its measures under Art. XX(d) but this argument was rejected by the Panel and its finding was not appealed by the US.

[104] The complainants also argued that the US measure amounted to a 'technical regulation' under the TBT Agreement but the Panel concluded that, in view of its findings under the GATT, it was not necessary to decide on the issues raised under the TBT Agreement: *ibid.*, para. 6.43.

[105] *Ibid.*, para. 6.25.   [106] *Ibid.*, para. 6.26.

[107] *Ibid.*, para. 6.37.   [108] *Ibid.*, para. 6.40.

on its earlier conclusion in respect of Article XX(b), namely, that the baseline establishment rules were not necessary for the protection of human, animal or plant life or health. The Panel read into Article XX(g) a 'least restrictive means' test.

The appeal to the Appellate Body was limited to the Panel's rulings in respect of the application of Article XX(g). The Appellate Body found a number of legal errors in the Panel's approach to Article XX(g). First, the Appellate Body noted that the Panel should have examined whether it was the *measure*, rather than the *less favourable treatment*, which aimed at the conservation of resources.[109] Secondly, the Panel had erred in applying a least restrictive means test (i.e. effectively whether the measure was 'necessary') rather than interpreting the actual words of the exception which simply required that the measure 'relate to' conservation. While the Appellate Body did not expressly overrule the interpretation of 'relating to' as equivalent to 'primarily aimed at' advanced in previous GATT Panel decisions, it noted that the phrase 'primarily aimed at' was not itself treaty language and 'was not designed as a simple litmus test for inclusion or exclusion from Article XX(g)'.[110] In this regard, the Appellate Body had concluded that 'the General Agreement is not to be read in clinical isolation from public international law', opening up the possibility of its reaching out to other rules of international law arising outside the WTO, including those in the environmental field.[111]

Overturning the Panel, the Appellate Body ruled that the Gasoline Rule was 'primarily aimed at' conservation as the baseline rules were necessary to allow scrutiny and monitoring of the level of compliance by refiners and others with the non-degradation requirements, which in turn were necessary to reach the objective of stabilising and preventing further deterioration of air quality.[112] The Appellate Body noted that the requirement in Article XX(g) for the measures to be made effective in conjunction with restrictions on domestic production and consumption amounted to a requirement of even-handedness that was satisfied in respect of the US measure.[113]

The Appellate Body then went on to analyse the US measure under the *chapeau* to Article XX. In doing so, it made the following general observations about the interpretation of the *chapeau*:

- It addresses not so much the questioned measure or its content but the manner in which the measure is applied.
- Its purpose and object are the prevention of abuse of the Article XX exceptions.

---

[109] *Reformulated Gasoline*, Appellate Body Report, 617–18.   [110] *Ibid.*, 623.

[111] *Ibid.*, 621; J. Cameron and K. R. Gray, 'Principles of International Law in the WTO Dispute Settlement Body', 50 ICLQ 248 (2001).

[112] *Reformulated Gasoline*, Appellate Body Report, 621.   [113] *Ibid.*, 625–6.

- It is animated by the principle that, while the exceptions of Article XX may be invoked as a matter of legal right, they should not be so applied as to frustrate or defeat the legal obligations of the holder of rights under the substantive rules of the GATT.
- Measures falling within the particular exceptions must be applied with due regard to the legal duties of the party claiming the exception and the legal rights of the other parties concerned.
- The burden of proof to justify the measure under the *chapeau* rests with the party advancing the measure.[114]

The Appellate Body noted that the US had alternative courses open to it to achieve its policy goal, namely:

1. setting statutory baselines for domestic refiners; or
2. allowing foreign refiners to use individual baselines.[115]

The Appellate Body did not accept that the use of individual baselines for foreign refiners was precluded by the administrative difficulties that would face the EPA. The Appellate Body noted that there are 'established techniques for checking, verification, assessment and enforcement of data relating to imported goods, techniques which in many contexts are accepted as adequate to permit international trade', and concluded that the US must have been aware that for these established techniques to work 'co-operative arrangements with both foreign refiners and the foreign governments concerned would have been necessary and appropriate'.[116] It appeared to the Appellate Body that the US had not pursued the possibility of entering into co-operative arrangements with foreign governments, or, if it had, then it had not reached 'the point where it encountered governments that were unwilling to co-operate'.[117]

In respect of the application of statutory baselines to domestic refiners, the US had argued that this would have been physically and financially impossible because of the magnitude of the changes required in almost all US refineries, causing substantial delay in implementing the programme. The Appellate Body noted, however, that similar considerations did not appear to have been taken into account *vis-à-vis* foreign refiners.[118]

There had been two omissions on the part of the US, namely:

1. the failure to explore adequately the means (including, in particular, co-operation with the governments of Venezuela and Brazil) of mitigating the administrative problems relied on as justification by the US for rejecting individual baselines for foreign refiners; and
2. the failure to count the costs for foreign refiners that would result from the imposition of statutory baselines.

---

[114] *Ibid.*, 626–9.   [115] *Ibid.*, 629.   [116] *Ibid.*, 631.   [117] *Ibid.*   [118] *Ibid.*, 632.

According to the Appellate Body, these resulted in the US measure giving rise to unjustifiable discrimination and amounting to a disguised restriction on international trade. The US measure thus could not be validated under Article XX(g).[119] The Appellate Body went out of its way, however, to note that:

> It is of some importance that the Appellate Body point out what this does not mean. It does not mean, or imply, that the ability of any WTO Member to take measures to control air pollution or, more generally, to protect the environment, is at issue. That would be to ignore the fact that Article XX of the General Agreement contains provisions designed to permit important state interests – including the protection of human health, as well as the conservation of exhaustible natural resources – to find expression. The provisions of Article XX were not changed as a result of the Uruguay Round of Multilateral Trade Negotiations. Indeed, in the preamble to the WTO Agreement and in the Decision on Trade and Environment, there is specific acknowledgment to be found about the importance of co-ordinating policies on trade and the environment. WTO Members have a large measure of autonomy to determine their own policies on the environment (including its relationship with trade), their environmental objectives and the environmental legislation they enact and implement. So far as concerns the WTO, that autonomy is circumscribed only by the need to respect the requirements of the General Agreement and the other covered agreements.[120]

Shrimp/Turtle Cases (1998 and 2001)

D. Brack, 'The Shrimp-Turtle Case: Implications for the Multilateral Environmental Agreement–World Trade Organization Debate', 9 *Yearbook of International Environmental Law* 13 (1998); H. Mann, 'Of Revolution and Results: Trade and Environmental Law in the Afterglow of the Shrimp Turtle Case', 9 *Yearbook of International Environmental Law* 28 (1998); D. Wirth, 'Some Reflections on Turtles, Tuna, Dolphin and Shrimp', 9 *Yearbook of International Environmental Law* 40 (1998); R. Howse, 'The Appellate Body Rulings in the Shrimp/Turtle Case: A New Legal Baseline for the Trade and Environmental Debate', 27 *Columbia Journal of Environmental Law* 491 (2002).

The second 'environmental' case to come before the dispute resolution bodies of the WTO raised similar legal issues to those considered by GATT Panels in the *Tuna/Dolphin* dispute. The case concerned an import prohibition imposed by the US on certain shrimp and shrimp products from India, Malaysia, Pakistan and Thailand, on the ground that they were harvested in a manner which adversely affected endangered sea turtles.[121] In 1987, the US had issued regulations (pursuant to its 1973 Endangered Species Act) requiring all US-registered shrimp trawl vessels to use approved turtle excluder devices (TEDs) in specified areas where there was a significant mortality of sea turtles in shrimp

---

[119] *Ibid.*, 633.   [120] *Ibid.*, 634.   [121] AB-1998-4, 12 October 1998, 33 ILM 118 (1999).

harvesting. TEDs allowed for shrimp to be harvested without harming other species, including sea turtles. The US regulations became fully effective in 1990, and were subsequently modified to require the general use of approved TEDs at all times and in all areas where there was a likelihood that shrimp trawling would interact with sea turtles. In 1989, the US enacted section 609 of Public Law 101-162, which addressed the importation of certain shrimp and shrimp products. Section 609 required the US Secretary of State to negotiate bilateral or multilateral agreements with other nations for the protection and conservation of sea turtles. Section 609(b)(1) imposed (not later than 1 May 1991) an import ban on shrimp harvested with commercial fishing technology which might adversely affect sea turtles. Further regulatory guidelines were adopted in 1991, 1992 and 1996, governing *inter alia* annual certifications to be provided by harvesting nations. In broad terms, certification was to be granted only to those harvesting nations which provided documentary evidence of the adoption of a regulatory programme to protect sea turtles in the course of shrimp trawling. Such a regulatory programme had to be comparable to the programme of the US, with an average rate of incidental taking of sea turtles by their vessels which should be comparable to that of US vessels. The 1996 guidelines further required that all shrimp imported into the US had to be accompanied by a shrimp exporter's declaration attesting that the shrimp was harvested either in the waters of the nation certified under section 609, or under conditions that did not adversely affect sea turtles, including through the use of TEDs. Section 609 also included a provision calling upon the US Secretary of State, in consultation with the Secretary of Commerce, 'to initiate negotiations as soon as possible for the development of bilateral or multilateral agreements with other nations for the protection and conservation of . . . sea turtles'. Acting under this provision, the US negotiated and concluded an Inter-American Convention for the Protection and Conservation of Sea Turtles with nations fishing for shrimp in the Western Atlantic. However, the US made no attempt to negotiate a similar agreement with the complainants prior to the imposition of the import ban.

From a WTO perspective, the difficulty with the approach taken by the US was that it was, in effect, applying its conservation laws extra-territorially to activities carried out within – or subject to the jurisdiction of – third states. This raises an issue of broader international legal interest, namely, the circumstances (if any) in which a state may apply its conservation measures to activities taking place outside its territory or jurisdiction, including by non-nationals. The US sought to justify its actions on the ground that the sea turtles it was seeking to protect were recognised in international law as being endangered.

The US legislation was challenged by India, Malaysia, Pakistan and Thailand. At first instance, a WTO Panel concluded that the import ban applied on the basis of section 609 was not consistent with Article XI(1) of GATT 1994 and could not be justified under any of the exceptions in Article XX of GATT 1994.[122]

---

[122] WT/DS58/R, 15 May 1998.

The US appealed to the WTO Appellate Body, invoking in particular Article XX(g) to justify the legality of its measures. In appraising section 609 under Article XX of GATT 1994, the Appellate Body followed a three-step analysis. First, the Appellate Body asked whether the Panel's approach to the interpretation of Article XX was appropriate; it concluded that the Panel's reasoning was flawed and 'abhorrent to the principles of interpretation we are bound to apply' (paras. 112–24). Secondly, the Appellate Body asked whether section 609 was 'provisionally justified' under Article XX(g). Invoking the concept of 'sustainable development', it found that it was so justified (paras. 125–45). Thirdly, it asked whether section 609 met the requirements of the *chapeau* of Article XX, and concluded that it did not because the US actions imposed an 'unjustifiable discrimination' and an 'arbitrary discrimination' against shrimp to be imported from India, Malaysia, Pakistan and Thailand. In relation to the second and third steps, the Appellate Body invoked the principle of 'sustainable development', as an aid to interpretation.

The Appellate Body's approach is premised upon an application of the 'customary rules of interpretation of public international law', as required by Article 3(2) of the DSU, which rules 'call for an examination of the ordinary meaning of the words of a treaty, read in their context, and in the light of the object and purpose of the treaty involved'.[123] It is these customary rules which the Panel had failed to apply, leading to the conclusion at step one that the Panel's approach was flawed.

In relation to step two, the Appellate Body invoked the principle of sustainable development in determining whether the measures taken by the US were 'provisionally justified'. As a threshold question, the Appellate Body had to decide whether section 609 was a measure *concerned with* the conservation of 'exhaustible natural resources', in the face of the argument that the term refers only to finite resource such as minerals, and not biological or renewable resources such as sea turtles (which, it was argued, fall to be covered by Article XX(b)). The Appellate Body rejected the argument, ruling that Article XX(g) extended to measures taken to conserve exhaustible natural resources, whether living or non-living, and that the sea turtles involved here 'constituted "exhaustible natural resources" for the purpose of Article XX(g)'.[124] In reaching that conclusion, the Appellate Body stated that Article XX(g) had to be read by a treaty interpreter 'in the light of contemporary concerns over the community of nations about the protection and conservation of the environment'.[125]

Referring to the Preamble to the 1994 WTO Agreement, the Appellate Body noted that its signatories were 'fully aware of the importance and legitimacy of environmental protection as a goal of national and international policy' and that the Preamble 'explicitly acknowledges "the objective of *sustainable*

---

[123] Para. 114.   [124] *Ibid.*, paras. 131 and 134.   [125] *Ibid.*, para. 129.

development.[126] This, said the Appellate Body, was a concept which 'has been generally accepted as integrating economic and social development and environmental protection'.[127] According to the Appellate Body, this conclusion was supported by modern international conventions and declarations, including the UN Convention on the Law of the Sea.[128] It followed that the sea turtles at issue were an 'exhaustible natural resource' and highly migratory animals, passing in and out of the waters subject to the rights of jurisdiction of various coastal states on the high seas.[129] The Appellate Body observed:

> Of course, it is not claimed that all populations of these species migrate to, or traverse, at one time or another, waters subject to United States jurisdiction. Neither the appellant nor any of the appellees claims any rights of exclusive ownership over the sea turtles, at least not while they are swimming freely in their natural habitat – the oceans. We do not pass upon the question of whether there is an implied jurisdictional limitation in Article XX(g), and if so, the nature or extent of that limitation. We note only that in the specific circumstances of the case before us, there is a sufficient nexus between the migratory and endangered marine populations involved and the United States for the purpose of Article XX(g).[130]

The concept of 'sustainable development' was not expressly invoked to justify this potentially far-reaching conclusion as to the nexus between the sea turtles and the United States. Nevertheless, the concept appeared to inform that conclusion, apparently establishing the necessary link between the interest of the United States in the proper conservation of a distant natural resource located from time to time outside its jurisdiction, and the finding that section 609 is 'provisionally justified' under Article XX(g). Although the Appellate Body claimed that it did 'not pass upon the question of whether there is an implied jurisdictional limitation in Article XX(g)', its conclusion appears hardly consistent with such a limitation. The concept of 'sustainable development' (and the need to integrate economic and social development and environmental protection) appears to have been implicitly invoked to extend (by interpretation) the jurisdictional scope of Article XX(g). This marks a significant move away from the approach of the earlier *Tuna/Dolphin* panels.

---

[126] *Ibid.*

[127] *Ibid.*, para. 129, at note 107 and the accompanying text. The Preamble to the WTO Agreements provides *inter alia* that 'the Parties to this Agreement, recognising that their relations in the field of trade and economic endeavour should be conducted with a view to raising standards of living, ensuring full employment and a large and steadily growing volume of real income and effective demand, and expanding the production of and trade in goods and services, while allowing for the optimal use of the world's resources in accordance with the objective of sustainable development, seeking both to protect and preserve the environment and to enhance the means of doing so in a manner consistent with their respective needs and concerns at different levels of economic development . . .'.

[128] *Ibid.*, para. 130, citing Art. 56(1)(a) of the 1982 UNCLOS.

[129] *Ibid.*, paras. 132 and 133.   [130] *Ibid.*, para. 133.

The third step of the Appellate Body's analysis addressed the issue of whether section 609 was consistent with the requirements of the *chapeau* to Article XX. Again, the Appellate Body invoked 'sustainable development', this time in the context of its conclusion that section 609 was an 'unjustifiable' discrimination.[131] The Appellate Body revisited the Preamble to the WTO Agreement, noting that it demonstrated that WTO negotiators recognised 'that optimal use of the world's resources should be made in accordance with the objective of sustainable development', and that the preambular language, including the reference to sustainable development

> must add colour, texture and shading to our interpretation of the agreements annexed to the WTO Agreement, in this case the GATT 1994. We have already observed that Article XX(g) of the GATT 1994 is appropriately read with the perspective embodied in the above preamble.[132]

In support of the relevance of 'sustainable development' to the process of interpretation of the WTO Agreements, the Appellate Body invoked the Decision of Ministers at Marrakesh to establish a permanent Committee on Trade and the Environment. That Decision refers, in part, to the consideration that 'there should not be . . . any policy contradiction between . . . an open, non-discriminatory and equitable multilateral trading system on the one hand, and acting for the protection of the environment, and the promotion of sustainable development on the other'.[133] The Appellate Body noted that the terms of reference for the establishment by this Decision of the Committee on Trade and the Environment (which made further reference to the concept of sustainable development) specifically referred to Principles 3 and 4 of the Rio Declaration on Environment and Development.[134]

It appears that 'sustainable development' informed the conclusion that the US measures constituted an unjustifiable discrimination: according to the Appellate Body, section 609 established a rigid standard by which US officials determined whether or not countries would be certified, and it was not acceptable 'for one WTO Member to use an economic embargo to require other Members to adopt essentially the same comprehensive regulatory programme, to achieve a certain policy goal, as that in force within that Member's territory, without taking into consideration different conditions which may occur in the territories of those other Members'.[135] Shrimp caught using identical

---

[131] Sustainable development is not invoked or referred to to justify the conclusion that section 609 constitutes an 'arbitrary discrimination'.

[132] *Ibid.*, para. 153.   [133] *Ibid.*, para. 154.

[134] Principle 3 of the Rio Declaration provides that 'the right to development must be fulfilled so as to equitably meet developmental and environmental needs of present and future generations'. Principle 4 states: 'In order to achieve sustainable development, environmental protection shall constitute an integral part of the development process, and cannot be considered in isolation from it.'

[135] *Ibid.*, para. 164.

methods to those employed in the US had been excluded from the US market solely because they had been caught in waters of countries that had not been certified by the US, and the resulting situation was 'difficult to reconcile with the declared [and provisionally justified] policy objective of protecting and conserving sea turtles'.[136] This suggested that the US was more concerned with effectively influencing WTO members to adopt essentially the same comprehensive regulatory regime as that applied by the US to its domestic shrimp trawlers. Moreover, the US had not engaged the appellees 'in serious, across-the-board negotiations with the objective of concluding bilateral or multilateral agreements for the protection and conservation of sea turtles, before enforcing the import prohibition'.[137] The failure to have *a priori* consistent recourse to diplomacy as an instrument of environmental protection policy produced 'discriminatory impacts on countries exporting shrimp to the US with which no international agreements [were] reached or even seriously attempted'.[138] The fact that the United States negotiated seriously with some but not other members that exported shrimp to the United States had an effect which was 'plainly discriminatory and unjustifiable'. Further, different treatment of different countries' certification was observable in the differences in the levels of efforts made by the US in transferring the required TED technology to specific countries.[139] Moreover, the protection and conservation of highly migratory species of sea turtles demanded 'concerted and co-operative efforts on the part of the many countries whose waters [were] traversed in the course of recurrent turtle migrations'.[140] Such 'concerted and co-operative efforts' were required by *inter alia* the Rio Declaration (Principle 12), Agenda 21 (para. 2.22 (i)), the 1992 Biodiversity Convention (Article 5) and the 1979 Berne Convention. Further, the 1996 Inter-American Convention for the Protection and Conservation of Sea Turtles provided a 'convincing demonstration' that alternative action was reasonably open to the US other than the unilateral and non-consensual procedures established by section 609.[141] And finally, while the US was a party to the 1973 CITES, it had not attempted to raise the issue of sea turtle mortality in relevant CITES committees, and had not signed the 1979 Berne Convention or the 1982 UNCLOS, or ratified the 1992 Biodiversity Convention.[142]

Shrimp/Turtle Case Phase II (2001)

The Appellate Body report in the *Shrimp/Turtle* dispute was adopted by the WTO's DSB on 6 November 1998, together with a recommendation that the

---

[136] *Ibid.*, para. 165.   [137] *Ibid.*, para. 166.   [138] *Ibid.*, para. 167.
[139] *Ibid.*   [140] *Ibid.*, para. 168.
[141] Ibid., para. 170. The 1996 Convention establishes obligations to reduce harm to sea turtles and encourages the appropriate use of TEDs (Art. IV(2)(h)). It also provides expressly that in implementing the Convention the parties shall act in accordance with the WTO Agreement, including in particular the Agreement on Technical Barriers to Trade and Art. XI of GATT 1994 (Art. XV).
[142] *Ibid.*, para. 171 and note 174 (and accompanying text).

US bring the import prohibition into conformity with its obligations under the WTO Agreement. In implementing the recommendations and rulings of the DSB, the US did not amend section 609, leaving its import prohibition on shrimp from uncertified states in effect. However, the US Department of State issued 'Revised Guidelines for the Implementation of Section 609 of Public Law 101-162 Relating to the Protection of Sea Turtles in Shrimp Trawl Fishing Operation'. Under the Revised Guidelines, a country could apply for certification even if it did not require the use of TEDs, provided it demonstrates that it had implemented and was enforcing, a 'comparably effective' regulatory programme to protect sea turtles without the use of TEDs.[143] Malaysia challenged the Revised Guidelines before another WTO panel, which found them to be in violation of Article XI but justified under Article XX as long as the conditions stated in the findings of the Panel's report, and in particular 'the ongoing serious good faith efforts to reach a multilateral agreement' remained satisfied.[144]

Malaysia subsequently appealed the Panel's ruling to the Appellate Body, on two principal grounds: first, the duty of the US to pursue international co-operation in protecting and conserving endangered sea turtles prior to implementing unilateral trade measures, and, secondly, whether the Revised Guidelines were sufficiently 'flexible' to meet the requirements of the Article XX *chapeau*. In its rulings on these issues, the Appellate Body clarified its approach to unilateral trade measures taken to achieve environmental goals. In relation to the duty to pursue international co-operation, Malaysia asserted that the US should have negotiated *and concluded* an international agreement on the protection and conservation of sea turtles before imposing a unilateral import prohibition.[145] In response, the US countered that it had made serious, good faith efforts to secure a multilateral sea turtle conservation agreement among Indian Ocean and South-East Asian states.[146] The Appellate Body confirmed

---

[143] *United States – Import Prohibition on Certain Shrimp and Shrimp Products*, Recourse to Article 21.5 of the DSU by Malaysia, Report of the Appellate Body, 22 October 2001, WT/DS58/AB/RW, para. 6 (requiring the US Department of State 'to take fully into account any demonstrated differences between the shrimp fishing conditions in the United States and those in other nations, as well as information available from other sources'). Under the Revised Guidelines, an exporting country may also be certified if its shrimp fishing environment does not pose a threat of incidental capture of sea turtles.

[144] *United States – Import Prohibition on Certain Shrimp and Shrimp Products*, Recourse to Article 21.5 of the DSU by Malaysia, Report of the Panel, 15 June 2001, WT/DS58/RW, para. 6.1 (*Shrimp/Turtle*, Panel Recourse report).

[145] *Shrimp/Turtle*, Appellate Body Recourse report, n. 143 above, para. 115.

[146] *Ibid*. These efforts included the following activities:

(a) A document communicated on 14 October 1998 by the United States Department of State to a number of countries of the Indian Ocean and the South-East Asia region containing possible elements of a regional convention on sea turtles in the region;

that the requirement for 'serious across-the-board negotiations' did not imply that agreements on environmental resources had to be actually concluded,
since that would, in effect, grant a veto to individual states.[147] The Appellate
Body considered that such a requirement would not be reasonable:

> For a variety of reasons, it may be possible to conclude an agreement with
> one group of countries but not another. The conclusion of a multilat-
> eral agreement requires the co-operation and commitment of many coun-
> tries. In our view, the United States cannot be held to have engaged in
> 'arbitrary or unjustifiable discrimination' under Article XX solely because
> one international negotiation resulted in an agreement while another did
> not.[148]

Although the *conclusion* of an agreement with all affected countries was preferable, it was not required: what was necessary was that negotiations in different
fora should be *comparable*.[149] The Appellate Body ruled that the Panel had
correctly concluded that the efforts made by the US in the Indian Ocean and
South-East Asia region constituted serious, good faith efforts to secure multilateral agreement on sea turtle conservation in that region, and the US measure
was not being applied in a manner constituting unjustifiable or arbitrary discrimination.[150]

On the issue of the 'flexibility' of the Revised Guidelines to take account of the
differing conditions prevailing in other members' territories, Malaysia argued
that the Revised Guidelines breached the Article XX *chapeau* by 'unilaterally'
imposing US domestic standards on exporters.[151] The Appellate Body rejected
this argument, noting that the Revised Guidelines contained provisions permitting the US authorities to take into account the specific conditions of Malaysian
shrimp production, and of the Malaysian sea turtle conservation programme,

(b) The contribution of the United States to a symposium held in Sabah on 15–17
July 1999. The Sabah Symposium led to the adoption of a Declaration calling
for the negotiation and implementation of a regional agreement throughout the
Indian Ocean and South-East Asia region;

(c) The Perth Conference in October 1999, where participating governments, including the United States, committed themselves to developing an international
agreement on sea turtles for the Indian Ocean and South-East Asia region;

(d) The contribution of the United States to the Kuantan round of negotiations, 11–
14 July 2000. This first round of negotiations towards the conclusion of a regional
agreement resulted in the adoption of the Memorandum of Understanding on
the Conservation and Management of Marine Turtles and their Habitats of the
Indian Ocean and South-East Asia (the 'South-East Asian MOU'). The Final Act
of the Kuantan meeting provided that before the South-East Asian MOU could
be finalised, a Conservation and Management Plan had to be negotiated and
annexed to the South-East Asian MOU.

---

[147] *Ibid.*, para. 123.   [148] *Ibid.*   [149] *Ibid.*, paras. 122 and 124.
[150] *Ibid.*, para. 134.   [151] *Ibid.*, para. 135.

should Malaysia decide to apply for certification.[152] The Appellate Body found that the Revised Guidelines, on their face, permitted a degree of flexibility which would enable the US to consider the particular conditions prevailing in Malaysia if and when Malaysia applied for certification.[153] The Appellate Body's approach appears to be intended to address concerns raised in the wake of its decisions in *Reformulated Gasoline* and the first phase of the *Shrimp/Turtle* dispute, to the effect that countries wishing to adopt unilateral trade measures for environmental purposes would face an extremely onerous task if required to consider the particular conditions prevailing in every potentially affected member before acting. It remains to be seen whether the changes to the US measure in issue will result in adequate consideration by US authorities of other countries' alternative approaches to achieving environmental goals, and the limitations those countries may face in addressing environmental concerns.

Asbestos Case (2000)

D. A. Wirth, 'GATT – Technical Barriers to Trade Agreement – Asbestos Import Ban', 96 AJIL 435 (2002); S. Charnovitz, 'The Law of Environmental "PPMs" in the WTO: Debunking the Myth of Illegality', 27 *Yale Journal of International Law* 59 (2002).

The most recent trade/environment case to come before a WTO panel and the Appellate Body involved a challenge by Canada to a French decree concerning asbestos and products containing asbestos. In the *Measures Affecting Asbestos and Asbestos-Containing Products* case, Canada requested a WTO panel to consider the consistency of a French decree with the TBT Agreement, and Articles III and XI of the GATT.[154] It also alleged, under Article XXIII(1)(b) of the GATT, that the French decree nullified or impaired advantages accruing to Canada directly or indirectly under the WTO Agreement, or impeded the attainment of an objective of that Agreement. The French decree law generally banned the use of asbestos and asbestos-containing products, subject to time-limited exceptions for certain existing materials, products or devices containing chrysotile fibres. In particular, chrysotile fibres and products containing them

---

[152] *Ibid.*, paras. 146–7. In addition, the provisions of the Revised Guidelines state that the import prohibitions imposed under section 609 do not apply to shrimp or products of shrimp 'harvested in any other manner or under any other circumstances that the Department of State may determine, following consultations with the [United States National Marine Fisheries Services], does not pose a threat of the incidental taking of sea turtles'.

[153] *Ibid.*, para. 148.

[154] *European Communities – Measures Affecting Asbestos and Asbestos-Containing Products*, Report of the Panel, WT/DS135/R, 18 September 2000 (*Asbestos*, Panel Report); *European Communities – Measures Affecting Asbestos and Asbestos-Containing Products*, Report of the Appellate Body, WT/DS135/AB/R, 12 March 2001 (*Asbestos*, Appellate Body Report).

could continue to be used but only where no substitute was available which 'in the present state of scientific knowledge, poses a lesser occupational health risk than chrysotile fibre to workers handling those materials, products or devices' and 'provides all technical guarantees of safety corresponding to the ultimate purpose of the use thereof'.[155]

In examining the French decree under the TBT Agreement, the Panel distinguished between its general prohibition in Article 1 of the decree and the exceptions established by Article 2, holding that the former did not fall within the scope of the TBT Agreement as the asbestos ban did not amount to a 'technical regulation'.[156] The Panel did not consider whether the exceptions amounted to a technical regulation under the TBT Agreement, on the basis that no claim had been made by Canada in relation to Article 2 of the decree.[157] The Panel found that the law violated Article III(4), but held that the French measures could be justified under Article XX(b).[158] Canada appealed the Panel's decision to the Appellate Body, challenging the Panel's interpretations of the TBT Agreement, and Articles III, XX(b) and XXIII(1)(b) of the GATT.

In reviewing the Panel's interpretation of the term 'technical regulation' in the TBT Agreement, the Appellate Body stated that the proper legal character of the measure at issue could not be determined unless the measure were examined as a whole, including both the ban and its exceptions.[159] The Appellate Body ruled that the French decree was a 'technical regulation' under the TBT Agreement,[160] but did not go on to complete the analysis under the TBT Agreement as it concluded that it did not have an adequate factual basis in the findings of the Panel to enable it to do so.[161]

For present purposes, the most important aspect of the Appellate Body's ruling relates to its interpretation of the 'like products' requirement in Article III(4). The question raised was whether chrysotile asbestos fibres were 'like' certain other fibres, namely, PVA fibres, or cellulose and glass fibres (collectively referred to as PCG fibres), and whether cement-based products containing asbestos fibres were 'like' those containing one of the PCG fibres. The Panel had concluded that the two categories of products – one containing asbestos and the other containing PCG alternatives – were 'like' within the meaning of Article III(4). The EC appealed, arguing that the 'likeness' test in Article III(4) called for an analysis of the health objective of the regulatory distinction made

---

[155] Décret no. 96-1133 relatif à l'interdiction de l'amiante, pris en application du code de travail et du code de la consommation, *Journal officiel*, 26 December 1996.

[156] *Asbestos*, Panel Report, n. 154 above, para. 8.63.

[157] *Ibid.*, paras. 8.70 and 8.72.   [158] *Ibid.*, paras. 8.158 and 8.241.

[159] *Asbestos*, Appellate Body Report, n. 154 above, para. 64.

[160] *Ibid.*, para. 77 (stressing that its finding should not be taken to mean that all internal measures covered by Art. III(4) of the GATT affecting sale, offering for sale, purchase, transportation, distribution or use of a product were necessarily technical regulations).

[161] *Ibid.*, paras. 82 and 83.

in the measure between asbestos fibres and other fibres. The Appellate Body accepted the EC's arguments and reversed the Panel's finding.

The Appellate Body considered the term 'like products' in Article III(4) by reference to dictionary definitions, the surrounding GATT provisions, and the general principle articulated in Article III(1) that members should ensure equality of competitive conditions for imported products in relation to domestic products. It concluded that 'likeness' was 'a determination about the nature and extent of a competitive relationship between and among products', and had to be made on a case-by-case basis.[162] The Appellate Body adopted the criteria taken by previous GATT panels, and the WTO Panel in the *Asbestos* case, to assess the question of likeness, namely: (1) the properties, nature and quality of the products; (2) the end-uses of the products; (3) consumers' tastes and habits in respect of the products; and (4) the tariff classification of the products.[163] In this case, for asbestos fibres 'evidence relating to the health risks associated with a product' could be pertinent in an examination of 'likeness' and needed to be evaluated under the criteria of physical properties, and of consumers' tastes and habits, having regard to their carcinogenicity.[164] The evidence had established that the products in issue were physically different, and, to overcome an indication that products were *not* 'like', 'a higher burden is placed on complaining members to establish that, despite the pronounced physical differences, there is a competitive relationship between the products such that *all* of the evidence, taken together, demonstrates that the products are 'like' under Article III: (4) of the GATT 1994'.[165] Considering the health risks posed by asbestos products, and the implications of such for the physical properties of the products and consumers' preferences in respect of them, the Appellate Body found that the evidence relied on by the Panel in finding 'likeness' was insufficient, and reversed the Panel's finding on this point.[166]

---

[162] *Ibid.*, paras. 99 and 101. The Appellate Body noted, however, that even if two products were 'like' it did not always follow that the measure at issue was inconsistent with Article III(4): the complaining member must still establish that the measure accorded to the group of 'like' imported products 'less favourable treatment' than it accorded to the group of 'like' domestic products: paras. 100 and 103.

[163] *Ibid.*, para. 102 (but noting that they were simply tools which were not treaty-mandated and did not form a closed list of criteria that would determine the legal characterisation of products). The criteria are derived from the Report of the Working Party on Border Tax Adjustments, adopted on 2 December 1970, BISD/18S/97, para. 18.

[164] *Asbestos*, Appellate Body Report, n. 154 above, paras. 113 and 114.

[165] *Ibid.*, para. 118. The Appellate Body criticised the Panel for failing to consider relevant consumer preferences, noting that 'consumers' tastes and habits regarding *fibres*, even in the case of commercial parties, such as manufacturers, are very likely to be shaped by the health risks associated with a product which is known to be highly carcinogenic': *ibid.*, para. 122.

[166] *Ibid.*, paras. 126 and 128. See also the separate concurring statement (at paras. 152–4), indicating the willingness of one member of the Appellate Body to attribute even greater significance to the health risks of asbestos-containing products, not requiring evidence

As to the meaning of 'necessity' under Article XX(b), the Appellate Body rejected Canada's three grounds of challenge. It ruled that Article XX(b) did not require the Panel to 'quantify' the risk associated with asbestos fibres: it was sufficient for the risk to be evaluated either in quantitative or qualitative terms.[167] On the question of the level of health protection selected by France in its law, the Appellate Body reiterated that WTO members have an undisputed right to determine their own level of health protection, and that the 'controlled use' of asbestos fibres and asbestos-containing products (as proposed by Canada) was not an alternative measure that would achieve the end sought by France. In determining whether any alternative measure was 'reasonably available', several factors had to be taken into account, besides the difficulty of implementation, including the interests or values pursued by the measure. The health protection objective pursued by the measure was a value 'both vital and important in the highest degree', and France could not reasonably be expected to employ any alternative measure if the measure would involve a continuation of the very risk that the law sought to halt because the alternative measure would effectively prevent France from achieving its chosen level of health protection.[168]

Finally, the Appellate Body made important observations about the standard of proof to be applied by Panels when evaluating scientific evidence advanced in justification of a measure taken under Article XX(b). It rejected Canada's argument that any such claim had to be made on the basis of the 'preponderant' weight of the evidence, ruling that it was sufficient for a member to rely, in good faith, on scientific sources which, at the time, may represent a divergent, but qualified and respected, opinion. Thus, a member was not obliged automatically to follow what, at any given time, constituted majority scientific opinion.[169]

Assessment

Overall, the 'trade and environment' disputes decided under the new WTO dispute resolution system have tended to give greater weight to the environmental and health concerns reflected in the Article XX(b) and (g) exceptions. In interpreting the provisions of the GATT 1994 and other WTO Agreements, the Appellate Body has demonstrated a commitment to refer to general international law arising outside the WTO system, including multilateral environmental treaties. It has also proposed a clearer legal framework for analysis of measures under Article XX and has clarified that the purpose of the *chapeau* is to prevent protectionist abuse of the Article's exceptions, not to limit the use of measures which are genuinely intended to achieve environmental objectives.

concerning end-uses and consumer preferences, and questioning the necessity or appropriateness of the majority's adoption of a 'fundamentally' economic interpretation of the 'likeness' criterion.

[167] *Ibid.*, para. 167.   [168] *Ibid.*, paras. 172 and 174.   [169] *Ibid.*, para. 178.

In the *Reformulated Gasoline* and *Shrimp/Turtle* cases, the Appellate Body has identified two preconditions necessary to ensure that a member's environmental measures do not fall foul of the requirements of the Article XX *chapeau*: first, the need to make serious efforts to secure a co-operative solution to the problem, prior to resorting to unilateral action; and, secondly, the need to consider the conditions prevailing in other members' territories in designing any trade-restricting measure. The *Asbestos* case provides important guidance on the meaning of 'likeness', indicating a willingness to permit greater consideration of potential health and environmental risks associated with a product in determining 'likeness' for the purpose of Article III(4).

Measures for health and safety protection

An increasingly important aspect of the relationship between trade and the environment in international law is that relating to the requirements for states to adopt trade measures in furtherance of national goals of human, animal or plant health and safety protection. Health and safety measures with the potential to impact trade are dealt with by the WTO's Agreement on Sanitary and Phytosanitary Measures (SPS Agreement).[170] The SPS Agreement lays down the conditions governing sanitary and phytosanitary (SPS) measures enacted by members, amplifying Article XX(b) and confirming that measures consistent with the SPS Agreement are deemed to meet the requirements of that Article.[171]

---

[170] Agreement on Sanitary and Phytosanitary Measures, Annex 1A, 33 ILM 28 (1994).

[171] Art. 2.4. SPS measures are defined in Annex A to the SPS Agreement as:

Any measure applied:

(a) to protect animal or plant life or health within the territory of the Member from risks arising from the entry, establishment or spread of pests, diseases, disease-carrying organisms or disease-causing organisms;

(b) to protect human or animal life or health within the territory of the Member from risks arising from additives, contaminants, toxins or disease-causing organisms in foods, beverages or feedstuffs;

(c) to protect human life or health within the territory of the Member from risks arising from diseases carried by animals, plants or products thereof, or from the entry, establishment or spread of pests; or

(d) to prevent or limit other damage within the territory of the Member from the entry, establishment or spread of pests.

Sanitary or phytosanitary measures include all relevant laws, decrees, regulations, requirements and procedures including, *inter alia*, end product criteria; processes and production methods; testing, inspection, certification and approval procedures; quarantine treatments including relevant requirements associated with the transport of animals or plants, or with the materials necessary for their survival during transport; provisions on relevant statistical methods, sampling procedures and methods of risk assessment; and packaging and labelling requirements directly related to food safety.

The SPS Agreement affirms the right of each WTO member to take SPS measures necessary for the protection of human, animal and plant life or health, subject to the provisions of the Agreement, in particular their trade restrictiveness and the need for scientific justification.[172] Members must observe national treatment and non-discrimination principles in the design of their measures, must accept the SPS measures of other members as equivalent if the exporting member objectively demonstrates equivalency, and must not apply SPS measures in a manner that would constitute a disguised restriction on international trade.[173] Members must also ensure that their SPS measures are applied only to the extent necessary, are based on scientific principles and are not maintained without sufficient scientific evidence.[174] To promote the harmonisation of SPS measures, members are encouraged to base their SPS measures on international standards where they exist.[175] SPS measures that 'conform to' international standards are deemed necessary to protect human, animal and plant life or health and are presumed to be consistent with the SPS Agreement.[176] Members are not prevented from introducing or maintaining SPS measures which are stricter than those reflected in international standards 'if there is a scientific justification, or as a consequence of the level of sanitary or phytosanitary protection a Member determines to be appropriate in accordance with the relevant provisions of paragraphs 1 through 8 of Article 5'.[177]

Article 5 provides that members are to ensure their SPS measures are based on a risk assessment which takes into account *inter alia* available scientific evidence and relevant processes and production methods, and relevant ecological and environmental conditions.[178] In assessing risk and determining the measure to achieve its appropriate level of SPS protection, a member must take into account as relevant economic factors the potential damage in terms of loss of production or sales in the event of entry, the establishment or spread of the pest or disease, the costs of control or eradication and the relative cost-effectiveness of alternatives to limiting risks.[179] Members must avoid arbitrary or unjustifiable distinctions in the levels of protection considered appropriate in different situations if the distinctions result in discrimination or a disguised restriction on international trade.[180] They must also ensure that measures are not more

---

[172] Art. 2.1.   [173] Arts. 2.3 and 2.4.   [174] Art. 2.2.   [175] Art. 3.1.   [176] Art. 3.2.

[177] Art. 3.3. A footnote to the Article explains that '[f]or the purposes of paragraph 3 of Article 3, there is a scientific justification if, on the basis of an examination and evaluation of available scientific information in conformity with the relevant provisions of this Agreement, a Member determines that the relevant international standards, guidelines or recommendations are not sufficient to achieve its appropriate level of sanitary or phytosanitary protection'.

[178] Arts. 5.1 and 5.2.   [179] Art. 5.3.

[180] Art. 5.5. To assist in determining the consistency of SPS measures to address different risks, the Committee on Sanitary and Phytosanitary Measures established by the SPS Agreement is to develop guidelines for the practical implementation of Art. 5.5, bearing

trade-restrictive than is required to achieve the appropriate level of SPS protection, taking into account technical and economic feasibility.[181] Where relevant scientific evidence is insufficient to allow a full risk assessment, Article 5.7 allows the adoption of provisional SPS measures by a member 'on the basis of available pertinent information' and subject to undertaking a subsequent risk assessment within a 'reasonable' period of time.[182]

Disputes between members over SPS measures are dealt with under the dispute settlement procedures of the WTO. To date, there have been three disputes before WTO Panels and the Appellate Body which raised issues under the SPS Agreement: the *Australian Salmon*, *Japanese Varietals* and *Beef Hormones* cases. One dispute which has not yet been taken to WTO dispute settlement is that between the United States and the European Union, concerning the latter's *de facto* moratorium on the approval of new genetically modified crops, which has been in place since mid-1998, as well as various EU and other schemes designed to require the labelling of products which contain, or may contain, GMOs.

Beef Hormones

J. McDonald, 'Big Beef Up or Consumer Health Threat?: The WTO Food Safety Agreement, Bovine Growth Hormone and the Precautionary Principle', 15 *Environmental and Planning Law Journal* 115 (1998); D. A. Wirth, 'European Communities Restrictions on Imports of Beef Treated with Hormones', 92 AJIL 755 (1998); J. Pauwelyn, 'The WTO Agreement on Sanitary and Phytosanitary Measures as Applied in the First Three SPS Disputes', 2 *Journal of International Economic Law* 641 (1999); T. Christoforou, 'Settlement of Science-Based Trade Disputes in the WTO: A Critical Review of the Developing Case Law in the Face of Scientific Uncertainty', 8 *New York University Environmental Law Journal* 622 (2000).

The *Beef Hormones* case presented the WTO Appellate Body with a first opportunity to consider the application of the provisions of the SPS Agreement. The dispute concerned an EC prohibition on imports of meat or meat products derived from cattle to which either natural hormones (oestradiol-17β, progesterone, testosterone) or certain synthetic hormones (trenbolone acetate, zeranol or melengestrol acetate (MGA)) had been administered for growth-promotion purposes.[183] The prohibition was set forth in a series of EC Directives[184] which covered both the placing on the EC market, and the import, of

---

in mind 'the exceptional character of human health risks to which people voluntarily expose themselves'.

[181] Art. 5.6.

[182] See J. Bohanes, 'Risk Regulation in WTO Law: A Procedure-Based Approach to the Precautionary Principle', 40 *Columbia Journal of Transnational Law* 323 (2002).

[183] *EC – Measures Concerning Meat and Meat Products (Hormones)*, Report of the Appellate Body, WT/DS26/AB/R and WT/DS48/AB/R, 16 January 1998.

[184] Culminating in Council Directive 96/22/EC of 29 April 1996, OJ L125, 23 May 1996, 3.

meat from animals to which such hormones had been administered. Exceptions were allowed in certain circumstances for meat of animals which had been administered substances having hormonal or thyrostatic action for therapeutic or zootechnical purposes.

Canada and the US challenged the EC measures primarily on the ground of the alleged failure of the EC to undertake a risk assessment, prior to adoption of the measures, as required by the SPS Agreement. The Panel upheld the challenges, holding that the EC measure was inconsistent with Article 5.1, and that the import prohibition was inconsistent with Articles 3.3 and 5.5 of the SPS Agreement.[185] Beyond its conclusion on the relevance of the precautionary principle,[186] the Appellate Body overturned the Panel's ruling that the SPS Agreement allocated the 'evidentiary burden' to the member imposing an SPS measure.[187] It found that the complaining parties bore the initial burden of showing *prima facie* inconsistency of the challenged measures with the SPS Agreement; only after such a *prima facie* case was made did the burden shift to the other party to provide evidence and arguments to disprove the complaining party's claim.[188] The standard of review was neither *de novo* review nor 'total deference' to national authorities, but rather the 'objective assessment of the matter' required by Article 11 of the DSU.[189]

As to Article 3.1 and 3.3 of the SPS Agreement, the Appellate Body overturned the Panel, ruling that Article 3.1 did not require members to harmonise their SPS measures, by conforming those measures to international standards. Instead, a measure which was 'based on' international standards (such as *Codex Alimentarius* standards) may adopt some but not necessarily all of the elements of the international standard.[190] Measures based on (rather than conforming to) international standards enjoyed no presumption of GATT consistency, but the burden was on the complainant to demonstrate *prima facie* inconsistency with the SPS Agreement.[191] The Appellate Body noted that Article 3.3 gave members an 'autonomous right' (which was neither unqualified nor absolute) to establish their own levels of SPS protection, which may be stricter than international standards.[192] In this regard it agreed with the Panel that a higher standard pursuant to Article 3.3 required a risk assessment (pursuant to Article 5.1).[193]

As to Article 5.1, the Appellate Body considered that the function of the Panel was simply to determine whether the measures were sufficiently supported or reasonably warranted by the risk assessment.[194] It was not necessary that the risk assessment come to a monolithic conclusion that coincided with the scientific

---

[185] *EC – Measures Concerning Meat and Meat Products (Hormones)*, Reports of the US and Canadian Panels, WT/DS26/R/USA and WT/DS48/R/CAN, 18 August 1997.
[186] Chapter 6, p. 277 above.   [187] *Ibid.*, para. 102.   [188] *Ibid.*, para. 109.
[189] *Ibid.*, para. 116.   [190] *Ibid.*, para. 163.   [191] *Ibid.*, paras. 170 and 171.
[192] *Ibid.*, paras. 172 and 173.   [193] *Ibid.*, paras. 175 *et seq.*   [194] *Ibid.*, para. 186.

conclusion or view implicit in the SPS measure.[195] The SPS measure might be based on a qualified but divergent minority scientific view:

> The risk assessment could set out both the prevailing view representing the 'mainstream' of scientific opinion, as well as the opinions of scientists taking a divergent view. Article 5.1 does not require that the risk assessment must necessarily embody only the view of a majority of the relevant scientific community. In some cases, the very existence of divergent views presented by qualified scientists who have investigated the particular issue at hand may indicate a state of scientific uncertainty. Sometimes the divergence may indicate a roughly equal balance of scientific opinion, which may itself be a form of scientific uncertainty. In most cases, responsible and representative governments tend to base their legislative and administrative measures on 'mainstream' scientific opinion. In other cases, equally responsible and representative governments may act in good faith on the basis of what, at a given time, may be a divergent opinion coming from qualified and respected sources. By itself, this does not necessarily signal the absence of a reasonable relationship between the SPS measure and the risk assessment, especially where the risk involved is life-threatening in character and is perceived to constitute a clear and imminent threat to public health and safety.[196]

The Appellate Body also addressed the preparation and content of the risk assessment.[197] It concluded that the EC's measures were not based on a risk assessment that reasonably supported or warranted the import prohibition. The various scientific studies the EC had adduced (produced by European committees, international organisations and individual scientists which it sought to rely upon as the basis for its measures) were too general in nature.[198] Accordingly, the measures were inconsistent with Article 5.1 and consequently also with Article 3.3.[199]

Australian Salmon

The *Salmon* dispute arose out of a Canadian complaint regarding Australia's prohibition on the importation of fresh, chilled or frozen salmon from

---

[195] *Ibid.*, para. 194.   [196] *Ibid.*   [197] *Ibid.*, paras. 187–90.
[198] *Ibid.*, paras. 195–200. For example, with regard to the synthetic hormone, MGA, the EC produced studies which dealt with the category of progestins (of which the hormone progesterone is a member) arguing that as MGA is an anabolic agent which mimics the action of progesterone, the studies were highly relevant. However, the Appellate Body considered that the studies were too general as they did not assess how closely related MGA is chemically and pharmacologically to other progestins or the effects of MGA when administered for growth promotion purposes. The Appellate Body did not insist on the production of studies on MGA by the complainants as this material 'was proprietary and confidential in nature'. Consequently, the Appellate Body upheld the Panel's finding that the EC had not based its measure with respect to MGA on a risk assessment (para. 201).
[199] *Ibid.*, paras. 208–9.

Canada.[200] The Australian restrictions, which had been in place since 1975, were maintained on the basis that importation of Canadian salmon could result in the introduction of exotic disease agents into Australia, with negative consequences for the health of fish in the country's waters. They prohibited the import of dead salmon into Australia unless, prior to importation, the fish had been 'subject to such treatment as in the opinion of the Director of Quarantine is likely to prevent the introduction of any infectious or contagious disease, or disease or pest affecting persons, animals or plants'.[201] The Director of Quarantine had permitted the entry of commercial imports of heat-treated salmon products for human consumption as well as non-commercial quantities of other salmon (primarily for scientific purposes) subject to prescribed conditions.[202] Australian authorities had conducted an import risk analysis for uncooked, wild, adult ocean-caught Pacific salmon which was initially set forth in a 1995 Draft Report, finalised in December 1996 (Final Report). The 1995 Draft Report had recommended allowing the importation of ocean-caught Pacific salmon under certain conditions but this was revised in the Final Report which recommended continuing the import prohibition for uncooked salmon products.[203] Acting on the basis of the Final Report, the Director of Quarantine decided to prohibit the importation of uncooked ocean-caught Pacific salmon.[204]

The WTO Panel found that the Australian prohibition was in breach of the SPS Agreement on the grounds that it was not based on a risk assessment and that the prohibition was more trade-restrictive than required to achieve Australia's chosen level of SPS protection. The Panel also held that Australia had adopted arbitrary or unjustifiable distinctions in the levels of SPS protection designated for salmon *vis-à-vis* non-salmonids in breach of Article 5.5.[205] Australia appealed the Panel's decision to the WTO Appellate Body, challenging the Panel's interpretation of Articles 5.1, 5.5 and 5.6 of the SPS Agreement.

As to Article 5.1, the Appellate Body conducted its own assessment of the consistency of the Australian measure with Article 5.1. It first examined whether the risk analysis conducted by Australian authorities amounted to a risk assessment for the purpose of Article 5.1, holding that a risk assessment on which quarantine restrictions are based must satisfy three conditions, namely, it must:

1. *identify* the diseases whose entry, establishment or spread a member wants to prevent within its territory, as well as the potential biological and economic consequences associated with the entry, establishment or spread of these diseases;

---

[200] *Australia – Measures Affecting Importation of Salmon*, Report of the Appellate Body, WT/DS18/AB/R, 20 October 1998.
[201] *Ibid.*, para. 2.   [202] *Ibid.*   [203] *Ibid.*   [204] *Ibid.*
[205] *Australia – Measures Affecting Importation of Salmon*, Report of the Panel, WT/DS18/R, 12 June 1998.

2. *evaluate* the likelihood of entry, establishment or spread of these diseases, as well as the associated potential biological and economic consequences; and

3. *evaluate* the likelihood of entry, establishment or spread of these diseases according to the SPS measures which might be applied.[206]

The Appellate Body stressed that it was not sufficient for a risk assessment to conclude that there was a possibility of entry, establishment or spread of diseases. Rather, a proper risk assessment had to evaluate the likelihood (i.e. the 'probability'), of entry, establishment or spread of diseases and associated biological and economic consequences, including by reference to the SPS measures which might be applied.[207] The likelihood or probability of an event could be expressed quantitatively or qualitatively and there was no requirement for a risk assessment to establish a certain magnitude or threshold level of degree of risk.[208] On this basis, the Appellate Body concluded that the 1996 Final Report was not a proper risk assessment within the meaning of Article 5.1.[209] With regard to Article 5.5, the Appellate Body found that the different levels of SPS protection adopted by Australia for imports of different fish and fish products were arbitrary,[210] and that the distinctions in the levels of protection imposed by Australia resulted in a disguised restriction on international trade.[211] As to Article 5.6, the Appellate Body reversed the Panel's finding but made no final determination as to the consistency of the import prohibition with Article 5.6.[212]

Japanese Varietals

The *Japanese Varietals* dispute concerned a challenge by the United States to a requirement imposed by Japan to test and confirm the efficacy of quarantine treatment for each variety of certain agricultural products prior to import.[213] Under its Plant Protection Law and Regulation, Japan prohibited the importation of eight agricultural products (apples, cherries, peaches, walnuts, apricots, pears, plums and quince) from, *inter alia*, the United States on the ground that these fruits were potential hosts of the codling moth, a pest of quarantine significance to Japan. Pursuant to the Japanese regulations, the import prohibition could be lifted if an exporting country proposed an alternative quarantine treatment which would achieve a level of protection equivalent to the import prohibition. Japan issued administrative guidelines concerning the

---

[206] *Ibid.*, para. 121.   [207] *Ibid.*, para. 123.   [208] *Ibid.*, para. 124.

[209] *Ibid.*, paras. 135 and 136.   [210] *Ibid.*

[211] *Ibid.*, para. 177. The Appellate Body made the same finding in relation to imports of other types of Canadian salmon: see para. 240.

[212] *Ibid.*, para. 213. The Appellate Body made the same finding in relation to imports of other types of Canadian salmon: see para. 242.

[213] *Japan – Measures Affecting Agricultural Products*, Report of the Appellate Body, WT/DS76/AB/R, 22 February 1999.

testing requirements which applied to initial lifting of the import prohibition
on a product and also to import approval for additional varieties of the product.
The testing requirement for additional varieties was the measure challenged by
the United States in the dispute. A WTO Panel found that Japan's measure
violated several provisions of the SPS Agreement, including Articles 2.2, 5.6
and 5.7.[214]

The Panel found that Japan's varietal testing requirement (as applied to
apples, cherries, nectarines and walnuts) was maintained without sufficient
scientific evidence and therefore inconsistent with Article 2.2.[215] Japan appealed
the Panel's findings, arguing that the requirement in Article 2.2 for a member
not to maintain an SPS measure 'without sufficient scientific evidence' should
be interpreted in light of the precautionary principle.[216] The Appellate Body
upheld the Panel's ruling, and reiterated its finding in *Beef Hormones* that the
precautionary principle, while finding reflection in the Preamble, Article 3.3
and Article 5.7, 'has not been written into the SPS Agreement as a ground for
justifying SPS measures that are otherwise inconsistent with the obligations of
Members set out in particular provisions of the Agreement'.[217]

The Panel had also rejected Japan's reliance on Article 5.7. Reviewing that
provision, the Appellate Body found that it establishes four requirements for
provisional SPS measures, all of which must be satisfied, namely, that the measure is:

1. imposed where 'relevant scientific information is insufficient';
2. adopted 'on the basis of available pertinent information';
3. not maintained unless the member 'seek[s] to obtain the additional information necessary for a more objective assessment of risk'; and
4. 'review[s] the . . . measure accordingly within a reasonable period of time'.[218]

The Appellate Body upheld the Panel's finding that additional information collected by Japan had failed to 'examine the appropriateness' of the SPS measure
at issue and had not addressed the core issue of whether 'varietal characteristics
cause a divergency in quarantine efficacy'.[219] It also confirmed that Japan had
not conducted the necessary review within a 'reasonable period of time'.[220]

Assessment

The decisions under the SPS Agreement indicate the extent of the limitations on
the ability of WTO members to adopt SPS measures with potential trade effects.
They emphasise the need for measures to be based on a scientific assessment of

---

[214] *Japan – Measures Affecting Agricultural Products*, Report of the Panel, WT/DS76/R, 27
     October 1998. The Panel also ruled that Japan had acted inconsistently with Art. 7 of the
     SPS Agreement by not publishing the varietal testing requirement.
[215] *Japanese Varietals*, Appellate Body Report, n. 213 above, para. 72.
[216] *Ibid.*, para. 81.   [217] *Ibid.*, paras. 81–4 and 113–14.
[218] *Ibid.*, paras. 89–90.   [219] *Ibid.*, para. 92.   [220] *Ibid.*, paras. 93 and 94.

potential risks, which comprehensively evaluates the probability (not the mere possibility) of adverse effects, on a case-by-case basis. 'Real world' risks can be taken into account as part of the assessment but there must be a rational relationship between any SPS measure and the scientific evidence. As to Article 5.5, the Appellate Body has affirmed that members have an autonomous right to determine their appropriate level of SPS protection for different risks.[221] The decisions in *Beef Hormones* and *Australian Salmon* emphasise the need for WTO members to pay greater attention to the issue of consistency between the SPS measures which they maintain for similar risks. In *Beef Hormones*, the Appellate Body appeared willing to accept differences in levels of SPS protection reflecting the socio-cultural environment of the adopting member state; the *Australian Salmon* case suggests that substantial differences between SPS measures for similar risks may be taken as an indication of a discriminatory or protectionist intent, especially in the absence of a scientific risk assessment justifying the measures adopted. With regard to Article 5.7, members must seek additional information germane to the conduct of a proper risk assessment and review any provisional measures within a reasonable period of time. The precautionary principle does not provide a separate basis for the adoption of SPS measures where the underlying science is uncertain, though a precautionary approach to risk assessment may be warranted in such circumstances. In particular, a member may be justified in basing its measures on qualified divergent scientific opinion 'where the risk involved is life-threatening in character and is perceived to constitute a clear and imminent threat to public health and safety'.[222]

European Community[223]

EC Commission, *1992: The Environmental Dimension – Task Force Report on the Environment and the Internal Market* (1990); P. Demaret, 'Trade-Related Environmental Measures (TREMs) in the External Relations of the European Community', in M. Maresceau (ed.), *The European Community's Commercial Policy After 1992: The Legal Dimension* (1993); A. Ziegler, *Trade and Environmental Law in the European Community* (1996); L. Gormley, 'Free Movement of Goods and the Environment', in J. Holder (ed.), *The Impact of EC Environmental Law in the United Kingdom* (1997); H. Temminck, 'From Danish Bottles to Danish Bees', 1 *Yearbook of European Law* 61 (2000); J. Scott, *EC Environmental Law* (2000), Chapter 4; J. Jans, *European Environmental Law* (2000), 121–34 and Chapter VI; L. Krämer, *EC Environmental Law* (2000, 4th edn), 74–89; V. Heyvaert, 'Balancing Trade and Environment in the European Union: Proportionality Substituted?', 13 *Journal of Environmental Law* 392 (2001).

---

[221] *Ibid.*, para. 194.   [222] *Beef Hormones*, Appellate Body Report, n. 183 above, para. 172.
[223] On EC environmental law generally, see chapter 15 above.

Similar provisions to those found in the GATT also exist in the EC Treaty, which was adopted in 1957 to create a 'common market' between the six original member states. Article 28 (formerly Article 30) of the EC Treaty prohibits quantitative restrictions on imports and all measures having equivalent effects (non-tariff barriers to trade). The express exceptions to Article 28, set out in Article 30 (formerly Article 36), include the protection of health and life of humans, animals or plants, provided that such prohibitions or restrictions do not constitute a means of arbitrary discrimination or a disguised restriction on trade between member states. Environmental protection is not expressly included as an exception. As set out in further detail in chapter 15 above, the EC began to legislate actively on environmental matters shortly after the 1972 Stockholm Conference, and in 1980 the ECJ endorsed the use of the EC Treaty to legislate on environmental matters.[224] In 1986, the EC Treaty was amended by the addition of a new Article 100a (now Article 95) and the specific provisions on environmental protection in Articles 130r to 130t (now Articles 174–176), but Article 30 was not amended to include environmental measures as a justifiable limitation on trade.[225] Following the conclusion of the Treaty of Amsterdam in 1997, the EC Treaty was again amended to include a further provision relating to environmental protection. Article 6 (formerly Article 3c) of the Treaty now provides that:

> Environmental protection requirements must be integrated into the definition and implementation of the Community policies and activities . . . in particular with a view to promoting sustainable development.

In relation to the trade and environment issue, the EC Treaty was amended to provide that where harmonisation measures are adopted by the EC under Article 95 (including environmental measures) to achieve the progressive establishment of the internal market then if

> a Member State deems it necessary to maintain national provisions on grounds of major needs referred to in Article 30, or relating to the protection of the environment or the working environment, it shall notify the Commission of these provisions as well as the grounds for maintaining them. Moreover, . . . if, after the adoption by the Council or by the Commission of a harmonisation measure, a Member State deems it necessary to introduce national provisions based on new scientific evidence relating to the protection of the environment or the working environment on grounds of a problem specific to that Member State arising after the adoption of the harmonisation measure, it shall notify the Commission of the envisaged provisions as well as the grounds for introducing them.[226]

---

[224] Joined Cases 91 and 92/79, *EC Commission* v. *Italy* [1980] ECR 1099 and 1115.
[225] See chapter 15, pp. 742–5 above.   [226] Art. 95(4) and (5) (formerly Art. 100a).

Where environmental protection measures are adopted under Article 175 of the EC Treaty, member states are not prevented from 'maintaining or introducing more stringent protective measures' which are compatible with the EC Treaty.[227] Even after the amendments introduced in 1986, 1992, 1997 and 2001, the EC Treaty is silent as to the permissibility of national environmental measures which restrict or limit trade where no EC measures have been adopted on a particular environmental matter under Articles 95 or 175.

Trade restrictions on environmental grounds: the role of the ECJ

The ECJ has played an important role in delimiting the conditions under which environmental protection measures adopted by EC member states will be permitted. In 1983, the ECJ upheld French legislation which restricted the export of waste oils from France to other EC member states.[228] Two years later, the ECJ held that the protection of the environment was one of the Community's 'essential objectives' which could, as such, justify certain limitations on the free movement of goods provided that they did not 'go beyond the inevitable restrictions which are justified by the pursuit of the objective of environmental protection'.[229] This was followed by two landmark cases which provided significant guidance on the position of the ECJ: the 1989 judgment in the *Danish Bottles* case[230] and the 1992 judgment in the *Belgian Waste Disposal* case.[231] Since then, the ECJ has decided a number of cases dealing with both environmental protection measures and measures concerned with the related goal of ensuring public health and safety.

Danish Bottles Case

P. Kromarek, 'Environmental Protection and Free Movement of Goods: The Danish Bottles Case', 2 JEL 89 (1990); P. Sands, 'Danish Bottles and Mexican Tuna', 1 RECIEL 28 (1992).

The *Danish Bottles* case was the result of an action commenced by the EC Commission under Article 226 (formerly Article 169) against Denmark, for a declaration that a Danish beer and soft drinks container law breached Article 28 (formerly Article 30) of the EC Treaty. In 1978, Danish legislation had been introduced to allow the relevant minister to adopt rules limiting, prohibiting or requiring the use of certain materials and types of container for drinks. The

---

[227] Art. 176 (formerly Art. 130t); under the 1992 Maastricht Treaty amendments, such measures must be notified to the Commission.

[228] Case 172/82, *Syndicat National des Fabricants d'Huile de Graissage* v. *Groupement d'Intérêt Économique 'Inter-Huiles'* [1983] ECR 555.

[229] Case 240/83, *Procureur de la République* v. *Association de Défenses des Brûleurs d'Huiles Usagées* [1985] ECR 531.

[230] Case 302/86, *EC Commission* v. *Denmark* [1989] 1 CMLR 619.

[231] Case C-2/90, *EC Commission* v. *Belgium* [1993] 1 CMLR 365.

legislation was presented as an anti-pollution measure, and empowered the National Agency for the Protection of the Environment (NAPE) to administer the law. In 1981, further legislation was adopted pursuant to the 1978 legislation requiring, first, that containers for gaseous mineral waters, lemonade, soft drinks and beer be subject to a compulsory deposit-and-return system, and, secondly, that such containers be approved by NAPE.

Producers of beverages and containers in other member states, and their trade associations, considered the Danish legislation to establish a non-tariff barrier to trade which restricted the import into Denmark of their products. Insofar as the Danish legislation affected production (bottling) techniques outside Danish jurisdiction, the legislation might be considered to have certain extra-territorial effects. The producers were supported in their view by the EC Commission, which called on the Danish Government to change its 1981 law. This led to a 1984 amendment to the 1981 legislation, which allowed beverages covered by the 1981 legislation to be sold in non-approved containers, provided that the quantity sold did not exceed 3,000 hectolitres per annum per producer, or that the beverage was being sold in the container normally used for that product in the country of production in order to 'test-market' it in Denmark. Additionally, the 1984 amendment required that no metal containers be used, that a return/recycling system for non-approved containers be set up, that the deposit for the container be equal to that normally charged on a similar approved container, and that the person marketing the product keep the NAPE fully informed to show compliance.

The EC Commission was not satisfied with the 1984 amendments and in 1986 brought Article 226 proceedings to have the compulsory deposit-and-return system and the NAPE bottle approval system declared incompatible with Article 28 of the EC Treaty. The United Kingdom intervened in support of the Commission. In his opinion, Advocate General Slynn supported the Commission's argument and found both the compulsory deposit-and-return system and the compulsory NAPE approval system to be in breach of Article 28. The ECJ did not follow the Advocate General's Opinion, holding that the deposit-and-return system was compatible with Article 28 but that the NAPE approval system was not compatible. In its first judgment after the 1986 Single European Act to address environmental limitations on free trade in the single market, but applying the pre-1986 rules, the ECJ stated that:

> in the absence of common rules relating to the marketing of the products concerned, obstacles to movement within the Community resulting from disparities between national laws must be accepted, in so far as such rules, applicable to domestic and imported products without distinction, may be recognised as being necessary in order to satisfy mandatory requirements of Community law. It is also necessary for such rules to be proportionate to the aim in view. If a member state has a choice between various measures to achieve the same objective, it should choose the means which least restrict

the free movement of goods . . . The protection of the environment is a
mandatory requirement which may limit the application of Article 30 of
the Treaty.[232]

The ECJ found that the deposit-and-return system established an obligation
which was:

> an essential element of a system aiming to secure the re-use of containers
> and therefore appears to be necessary to attain the objectives of the disputed
> regulations. In view of this finding, the restrictions which they impose on
> the free movement of goods should not be considered as disproportionate.

However, as regards the NAPE approval system, the ECJ found that by restricting the quantity of beer and soft drinks which could be marketed by a single
producer in non-approved containers to 3,000 hectolitres per year Denmark
had adopted measures with disproportionate consequences:

> the existing system of return for approved containers guarantees a maxi-
> mum percentage of re-use and therefore gives considerable protection to
> the environment because the empty containers can be returned to any re-
> tailer of beverages, whereas non-approved containers can only be returned
> to the retailer who sold the beverage because of the impossibility of setting
> up such a complete organisation for such containers also. However, the
> system for returning non-approved containers is capable of protecting
> the environment and, so far as imports are concerned, covers only lim-
> ited quantities of beverages by comparison with the quantity consumed
> in the country because of the restrictive effect of the compulsory return
> of containers on imports. Under these conditions, limiting the quantity of
> products which can be marketed by importers is disproportionate to the
> objective.[233]

In the absence of specific EC legislation establishing a rule of environmental
protection, national environmental rules to restrict trade between member
states will be permitted provided that

1. the rules are necessary to protect the environment;
2. the effect on trade is not disproportionate to the objective pursued; and
3. the rules are not discriminatory against producers in third countries.

The ECJ's approach is not dissimilar to the analysis applied to the Article XX
chapeau by the Appellate Body in the *Shrimp/Turtle* dispute, although the Appellate Body speaks in terms of the need to maintain a balance between the
right of a member to invoke an exception under Article XX and the rights of
the other members under GATT's substantive provisions, rather than in terms
of proportionality. The ECJ's approach recognises the widespread support for
weight to be given to legal aspects of environmental protection, even if this

---

[232] Note 230 above, 631.   [233] *Ibid.*, 632.

results in disparities in environmental standards and justifiable interference with the sanctity of free trade ideals. It focuses primarily on the nature of the legislation at issue, rather than the consequences for the 'single market'. As required by EC law, there is no consideration of the intentions of the drafters (who are unlikely to have imagined these types of disputes back in the mid-1950s), and the 'extra-jurisdictional' consequences of the Danish legislation were ignored.

Dead Red Grouse Case

The following year, the ECJ was called upon to consider the legality of a Dutch prohibition on the importation of red grouse lawfully killed in the United Kingdom. On an Article 234 (formerly Article 177) reference from the Netherlands, the Court held that the prohibition was incompatible with Article 30 (formerly Article 36) of the EC Treaty, read in conjunction with the 1979 EC Wild Birds Directive.[234] Although Article 14 of the Directive permitted member states to introduce stricter protective measures than those provided under the Directive, the import prohibitions could not be justified for a species of bird which did not inhabit the territory of the legislating member state but could be found in another member state where it could be lawfully hunted under the Directive. Since the red grouse was neither a migratory species nor a seriously endangered species listed in Annex I to the Directive, and was not an endangered species under EC legislation implementing CITES, the Dutch prohibition was held to be unlawful under EC law.

Belgian Waste Disposal Case

In July 1992, the ECJ ruled that Belgian legislation limiting the free movement of waste had been adopted in breach of an EC Directive but did not violate the provision on the free movement of goods. The judgment is an important one which established further principles to justify restrictions on free trade which are adopted for environmental protection purposes. The case was brought by the EC Commission against Belgium under Article 226 of the EC Treaty. The Commission took the view that legislation of the Wallonia region of Belgium which prohibited the disposal in Wallonia of waste originating from another state was incompatible with Directive 75/442/EEC (waste) and Directive 84/631/EEC (transboundary movement of waste), as well as Article 28 (formerly Article 30) and Article 30 (formerly Article 36) of the EC Treaty. The Court found that there had been no breach of Directive 75/442, since it did not include any provisions on trade in waste between member states or any express prohibition on adopting measures such as those taken by Belgium.[235]

---

[234] Case C-169/89, *Criminal Proceedings Against Gourmetterie Van den Burg* [1990] ECR 2143 at 2165; on the 1979 Directive, see chapter 11, pp. 602–5 above.

[235] Note 231 above, 394; on Directive 75/442/EEC, see chapter 15, pp. 787–9 above.

The Court did hold, however, that the Belgian legislation breached Directive 84/631, as amended. By introducing an absolute ban, the legislation went beyond the measures permitted by the Directive, which had established a 'complete system relating to transfrontier shipments of hazardous wastes for disposal in specified establishments' including a system of notification and the possibility of banning certain shipments of hazardous wastes which posed a threat to the environment and health, or to public security; the Directive did not permit a blanket prohibition.[236]

The question concerning the violation of Articles 28 and 30 raised interesting points which are analogous to issues raised in GATT/WTO disputes. It turned on whether the EC Treaty provisions governing the free movement of goods applied to wastes which could not be recycled or re-used. Belgium argued that such wastes were not goods within the meaning of Article 28, since they had no intrinsic commercial value and could not be the subject of a sale. The Court rejected this approach. It held that any objects which were transported across a boundary to give effect to a commercial transaction were subject to Article 28, whatever the nature of the transaction, and that recyclable or non-recyclable wastes were products subject to Article 28 whose free movement under that Article should not, as a matter of principle, be limited.[237] The Court held that the distinction between recyclable and non-recyclable wastes created serious practical difficulties of application, particularly in the context of constantly evolving technical progress; whether waste was recyclable or not depended also on the cost of recycling and the usefulness of the re-use envisaged.

Having decided that wastes were covered by Article 28, the Court considered whether the prohibition imposed by the limitation could nevertheless be justified. It accepted that the protection of the environment could justify the Belgian legislation, and rejected the Commission's argument that the legislation should be declared unlawful on the grounds that it was discriminatory because it treated wastes from other member states more restrictively than the same wastes which might have been produced in Wallonia having regard 'to the differences between waste produced in one place and that in another and its connection with the place where it is produced'.[238] The Court considered that waste had a special character and that the application of Article 174(2) (formerly Article 130r(2)) of the EC Treaty, which established the principle that environmental damage should as a priority be rectified at source, implied that it was a matter for each region, commune or other local authority to take appropriate measures to ensure the receipt, treatment and disposal of its own wastes: waste should be disposed of as close as possible to the place where it is produced in order to keep the transport of waste to the minimum practicable.[239] The Court thus endorsed an environmentally-based limitation on the free movement of

---

[236] *Ibid.*, 395.   [237] *Ibid.*, 396.   [238] *Ibid.*, 397.   [239] *Ibid.*

goods under EC law, justifying this on the grounds that it accorded with the principles of 'self-sufficiency' and 'proximity' as provided in the 1989 Basel Convention.[240]

Belgian Pesticides Case

The *Belgian Pesticides* case was brought before the ECJ on an Article 234 preliminary ruling reference from Belgium.[241] A Belgian law prohibited the sale of pesticides for non-agricultural use, where they had not been previously authorised by the Belgian authorities. A prosecution was brought under the Belgian law in respect of the sale of a prohibited pesticide which had nevertheless been approved in the Netherlands and satisfied all the requirements of existing EC Directives. The parties agreed that the Belgian law was incompatible with Article 28 (formerly Article 30) of the EC Treaty but sought guidance from the Court as to whether Belgium could rely on the public health exemption under Article 30 (formerly Article 36).

The ECJ found that Community legislation, as it stood, did not make any provision relating to the marketing of biocidal products.[242] The Court noted that, since biocidal products are used to combat organisms harmful to human or animal health and organisms liable to damage natural or manufactured products, they inevitably contain dangerous substances and that in the absence of harmonising rules, the member states are free to decide on their intended level of protection of human health and life and on whether to require prior authorisation for the marketing of such products.[243] The Court held that while a member state is free to require a product of the type in issue in the case, which had already received approval in another member state, to undergo a fresh procedure of examination and approval, the authorities of the member states are nevertheless required to assist in relaxing the controls existing in intra-Community trade and to take account of technical or chemical analyses or laboratory tests which have already been carried out in another member state.[244]

Aher-Waggon Case

In the *Aher-Waggon* case, a German court made an Article 234 preliminary reference to the ECJ seeking a ruling as to whether certain German legislation was incompatible with Article 28 (formerly Article 30) of the EC Treaty.[245] The German legislation, implementing Council Directive 80/51/EEC on the limitation of noise emissions from subsonic aircraft, made the first registration in

---

[240] *Ibid.* On the 1989 Basel Convention, see chapter 13, pp. 691–5 above.
[241] Case C-293/94, *Rechtbank van eerste aanleg Turnhout – Belgium* [1996] ECR I-3159.
[242] Para. 10.   [243] Para. 11.   [244] Para. 12.
[245] Case C-389/96, *Aher-Waggon GmbH* v. *Germany* [1998] ECR I-4473.

Germany of aircraft previously registered in another member state conditional upon compliance with stricter noise standards than those laid down by the Directive, while exempting from those standards aircraft which obtained registration in Germany before the Directive was implemented. The ECJ noted that the EC Directive merely laid down minimum requirements for noise emissions from aircraft and did not prevent member states from imposing stricter noise limits. Moreover, the Court found that, while the measure restricted intra-Community trade, it could be justified by considerations of public health and environmental protection such as those put forward by the German Government, namely, that Germany, which is a very densely populated state, attaches special importance to ensuring that its population is protected from excessive noise emissions.[246] The Court was satisfied that the measure was proportionate, accepting the explanation by the German Government that limiting noise emissions from aircraft was the most effective and convenient means of combating the noise pollution which they generate. The German Government argued that, without extremely costly investment, it was generally difficult to reduce noise emissions appreciably by carrying out works in the vicinity of airports.[247]

As for the exemption from stricter noise emissions standards for aircraft registered in Germany before the Directive was implemented, this did not violate Article 28 since those aircraft were also required to comply with the stricter noise standards when they underwent technical modification, even if such modifications had no bearing on noise emissions, or when they were temporarily withdrawn from service. Furthermore, the Court noted, the number of such aircraft could readily be determined by the German authorities.[248] The national authorities were thus entitled to consider that the number of aircraft not meeting the stricter noise standards was necessarily going to fall and that the overall level of noise pollution would diminish. Moreover, the ECJ held, the effectiveness of the German policy of progressively eliminating from the national fleet aircraft not meeting the stricter noise standards would be undermined if their number could be increased, to an extent not foreseeable by the national authorities, by aircraft from other member states.[249]

Danish Bees Case

The *Danish Bees* case arose out of criminal proceedings brought against Ditlev Bluhme for the infringement of Danish legislation prohibiting the keeping on the Danish island of Laeso of bees other than those of the subspecies *Apis mellifera mellifera* (Laeso brown bees).[250] The defendant argued that the legislation was a prohibition on importation, and constituted a measure having equivalent effect contrary to Article 28. A preliminary ruling on the question was sought from the ECJ under Article 234 of the EC Treaty. The Danish Government

---

[246] Paras. 18 and 19.   [247] Para. 21.   [248] Para. 23.   [249] Para. 24.
[250] Case C-67/97, *Criminal Proceedings Against Bluhme* [1998] ECR I-8033.

argued that its measure applied to bees indiscriminately, whatever their state of origin, and was justified by the aim of protecting biological diversity, such an aim being recognised, *inter alia*, by the 1992 Habitats Directive. The Danish Government argued that the measure was both necessary and proportionate as the Laeso brown bee sub-species was disappearing and could be preserved only on the island of Laeso. Moreover, the measure did not affect the possibility of carrying on bee-keeping on the island but merely regulated the species of bee which could be used for this purpose.[251] These contentions were disputed by the defendant and the Commission on the basis of a lack of scientific consensus as to whether Laeso brown bees were a distinct sub-species or in fact in danger of extinction. Notwithstanding the lack of conclusive scientific evidence establishing the nature of the sub-species and the risk of extinction, the Court considered that the threat of disappearance of the Laeso brown bee was 'undoubtedly genuine' if mating with golden bees occurred, given the recessive nature of the genes of the brown bee.[252] The measure was justified on environmental protection grounds since:

> measures to preserve an indigenous animal population with distinct characteristics contribute to the maintenance of biodiversity by ensuring the survival of the population concerned. By so doing, they are aimed at protecting the life of those animals and are capable of being justified under Article 36 [now Article 30] of the Treaty. From the point of view of such conservation of biodiversity, it is immaterial whether the object of protection is a separate subspecies, a distinct strain within any given species or merely a local colony, so long as the populations in question have characteristics distinguishing them from others and are therefore judged worthy of protection either to shelter them from a risk of extinction that is more or less imminent, or, even in the absence of such risk, on account of a scientific or other interest in preserving the pure population at the location concerned.[253]

The Court noted that the conservation of biodiversity through the establishment of areas in which a population enjoys special protection was a method recognised by Article 8(a) of the 1992 Biodiversity Convention, and was already put into practice in Community law by the Directives on wild birds and habitat protection.[254] Thus the establishment by Danish legislation of a protection area was a necessary and proportionate measure in relation to the aim pursued.[255]

Belgian Foodstuffs Labelling Case

The *Belgian Foodstuffs Labelling* case was the result of an action commenced by the EC Commission under Article 226 (formerly Article 169) against Belgium

---

[251] Para. 25.   [252] Para. 37.   [253] Paras. 33 and 34.
[254] Para. 36. On the 1992 Convention and the 1992 Directive, see chapter 11, pp. 515–23 and 536–40 above.
[255] Para. 37.

for a declaration that a Belgian Royal Decree concerning the placing on the market of nutrients and foodstuffs to which nutrients had been added was contrary to Article 28.[256] The Decree required the labelling of foodstuffs containing nutrients to include details of the notification number given to the product by the Inspection Service for Foodstuffs of the Ministry of Public Health and the Environment. Belgium sought to justify its labelling requirement on the ground of public health protection under Article 30 of the EC Treaty.

In its judgment, the ECJ reiterated that it had made clear in its case law that:

> in the absence of harmonisation of laws, Article 30 [now Article 28] of the Treaty prohibits, in principle, obstacles to intra-Community trade which are the consequence of applying, to goods coming from other Member States where they are lawfully manufactured and marketed, rules that lay down requirements to be met by such goods, such as those relating to presentation, labelling and packaging, even if those rules apply without distinction to domestic products and imported products.[257]

The Court found that the Belgian labelling obligation was 'of a nature such as to hinder intra-Community trade' as it had the potential to 'force the importer to alter the packaging of his products on the basis of the place where they are marketed and therefore to incur additional packaging and labelling costs'.[258] Notwithstanding the Belgian Government's contention that the extra costs associated with the packaging and labelling requirements would ultimately be borne by Belgian consumers, the Court found that 'the mere prospect of having to lay out those costs constitutes a barrier for traders since it is capable of acting as a disincentive to those of them who are contemplating marketing the products concerned in Belgium'.[259] The Court concluded that the measure was not justified on the grounds of public health protection, nor was it proportionate.[260]

Swedish Chemical Products Ban Case

In *Kemikalieinspektionen* v. *Toolex Alpha AB*, a Swedish court sought a preliminary ruling from the ECJ concerning whether a prohibition on the industrial use of the chemical trichloroethylene was consistent with Article 30 of the EC Treaty, even if it contravened Article 28.[261] The Swedish measure in issue banned the industrial use of trichloroethylene chemical products subject to certain exemptions which applied to allow the continued use of the chemical where no feasible substitutes were available. Sweden argued that the measure was justified under Article 30 as being necessary for the protection of human health and/or the environment. While the chemical was not a known carcinogen,

---

[256] Case C-217/99, *Commission of the European Communities* v. *Kingdom of Belgium* [2000] ECR I-10251.

[257] Para. 16.   [258] Para. 17.   [259] Para. 18.   [260] Para. 26.

[261] Case C-473/98, *Kemikalieinspektionen* v. *Toolex Alpha AB* [2000] ECR I-5681.

experimental and epidemiological studies had suggested a link between the chemical and cancer in humans.

The ECJ upheld the legislation as justified:

> [T]aking account of the latest medical research on the subject, and also the difficulty of establishing the threshold above which exposure to trichloroethylene poses a serious health risk to humans, given the present state of the research, there is no evidence in this case to justify a conclusion by the Court that national legislation such as that at issue in the case in the main proceedings goes beyond what is necessary to achieve the objective in view.[262]

Moreover, the exemptions established by the measure were appropriate and proportionate offering increased protection for workers while at the same time taking account of the difficulties faced by companies for which no feasible alternative for the chemical was available. This was ensured by strict conditions on the granting of exemptions which permitted use of the chemical only where no safer replacement product was available, and provided that the applicant continued to seek alternative solutions which were less harmful to public health and the environment.[263] Furthermore, in no case could the concern to avoid causing disruption to an undertaking where there was no alternative solution justify the grant of an exemption unless workers' exposure to trichloroethylene was maintained at acceptable levels.[264]

German Renewable Energy Case[265]

The *German Renewable Energy* case arose out of an Article 234 reference to the ECJ concerning, *inter alia*, the compatibility with Article 28 of a German law obliging electricity supply undertakings, which operated a general supply network, to purchase the electricity produced in their area of supply from renewable sources of energy. The ECJ noted that, according to the well-known *Dassonville* formula, 'any national measure which is capable of hindering, directly or indirectly, actually or potentially, intra-Community trade' is inconsistent with Article 28.[266] It recalled that its case law established that an obligation to obtain a certain percentage of supplies from a national supplier limited the possibility of importing the same product because purchasers are precluded from obtaining supplies, in respect of part of their needs, from suppliers situated in other member states.[267] Consequently, the German law was 'capable, at least potentially, of hindering intra-Community trade', since it expressly stated that the purchase obligation imposed on electricity suppliers applied only to electricity produced from renewable energy sources within the respective supply area.[268]

---

[262] Para. 45.   [263] Para. 47.   [264] Para. 48.
[265] Case C-379/98, *PreussenElektra AG v. Schleswag AG* [2001] ECR I-2099.
[266] Case 8/74, *Dassonville* [1974] ECR 837, para. 5.
[267] Note 265 above, para. 70.   [268] Para. 71.

Notwithstanding this finding, the Court ruled that the German measure was not incompatible with Article 28 given its aim and the features of the electricity market.[269] In particular, the Court noted that the:

> use of renewable energy sources for producing electricity, which a statute such as the amended *Stromeinspeisungsgesetz* is intended to promote, is useful for protecting the environment in so far as it contributes to the reduction in emissions of greenhouse gases which are among the main causes of climate change which the European Community and its Member States have pledged to combat.[270]

In contrast to the *Danish Bottles* case, the Court did not rely on environmental protection as a 'mandatory requirement' justifying a departure from Article 28. Rather, it pointed to a number of considerations supporting its conclusion that, 'in the current state of Community law concerning the electricity market', legislation such as the German law was not incompatible with Article 28 of the Treaty. These included the obligations assumed by the Community and individual member states under the 1992 Climate Change Convention and the 1997 Kyoto Protocol to promote growth in the use of renewable energy; the requirements of Article 6 of the EC Treaty (environmental protection requirements must be integrated into the definition and implementation of EC policies); various recitals of Council Directive 96/92/EC concerning common rules for the internal market in electricity, which expressly state that it is 'for reasons of environmental protection' that the Directive authorises member states to give priority to the production of electricity from renewable sources; and the fact that once electricity has been allowed into the transmission or distribution system, it is difficult to determine its origin and, in particular, the source of energy from which it was produced necessitating a system of certificates of origin for electricity produced from renewable sources, capable of being the subject of mutual recognition, in order to make intra-Community trade in that type of electricity both reliable and possible in practice.[271]

Canada–United States Free Trade Agreement

The Canada–United States Free Trade Agreement (FTA) aims to eliminate a large number of barriers to trade between the two countries.[272] Although it has been superseded by the NAFTA (see below), the FTA merits consideration because of the case law it has generated. Under the FTA, the parties affirm the 1979 GATT Agreement on Technical Barriers to Trade and agree not to

---

[269] Para. 72.   [270] Para. 73.   [271] Paras. 76–80.

[272] Ottawa, 22 December 1987 and 2 January 1988, and at Washington, DC and Palm Springs, 23 December 1987 and 2 January 1988, in force 2 January 1988, 27 ILM 281 (1988); M. Swenarchuk, *Environmental Impacts of the Canada–US Free Trade Deal* (Canadian Environmental Law Association, 1988).

'maintain or introduce standards-related measures or procedures for product approval that would create unnecessary obstacles to trade between the
territories of the parties'.[273] 'Unnecessary obstacles' are not deemed to be created if 'the demonstrable purpose of the measure or procedure is to achieve a
'legitimate domestic objective' and the measure or procedure does not exclude
goods of the other party that meet such an objective.[274] An objective whose
purpose is to protect the environment is a legitimate objective.[275] Exceptions
are also made for trade in goods by Article 1201 of the FTA, which incorporates
Article XX of the GATT. The FTA requires the parties to exchange full texts of
proposed federal standards-related measures and product approval procedures
prior to their adoption, except in urgent cases where delay would frustrate the
achievement of a legitimate domestic objective.[276]

The FTA has its own dispute settlement provisions, including the establishment of FTA Panels. In 1989, an FTA Panel interpreted Article XX(g) of the
GATT in the *Salmon and Herring* case, and in 1990 an FTA Panel considered
environmental issues the *Lobsters from Canada* case.[277] The latter dispute concerned the enactment by the US of an amendment to the Magnuson Fishery
Conservation and Management Act to prohibit, *inter alia*, the sale or transport
in or from the US of whole live lobsters smaller than the minimum possession
size in effect under US federal law. Canada considered that the application of
this law to Canadian lobster exports to the US was contrary to Article 407
of the FTA, which incorporates Article XI of the GATT. The US agreed that
even if the measures were contrary to Article XI, they fell within the exception
under Article XX(g) of the GATT, which was incorporated by Article 1201 of
the FTA. The Panel held, by a majority of three to two, that the US measures
imposed on live US and Canadian lobsters were not covered by Article XI but
by Article III of GATT, and that they came within the 'scope of laws, regulations and requirements affecting the internal sale, offering for sale, purchase,
transportation, distribution or use of products'. The Panel did not determine
whether these Article III measures were consistent with the national treatment requirements, since such determination lay outside its terms of reference.
Accordingly, the majority did not consider the applicability of Article XX of
the GATT.

The minority, however, found that Article XI was applicable and that the
US measures conflicted with that provision, since they had the effect of totally
denying access to the US market of Canadian live small lobsters. Accordingly,
they considered whether the US measures were permitted by the conservation
exception in Article XX(g). The minority relied on the interpretation of Article

---

[273] Arts. 602 and 603. The provisions apply to technical standards related to goods other than
agricultural, food, beverage and certain related goods as defined in Chapter Seven of the
FTA (Agriculture): Art. 601.

[274] Art. 603.   [275] Art. 609.   [276] Art. 607.

[277] *Lobsters from Canada*, Final Report of the Panel, 25 May 1990, USA 89–1807–01.

XX(g) adopted by the FTA Panel in the *Salmon and Herring* case,[278] which had held that Article XX(g) must be narrowly construed and that to qualify for an exemption:

- the measure must relate to an exhaustible natural resource;
- domestic production of the resource must be likewise restricted;
- the measure must not involve arbitrary or unjustifiable discrimination between foreign countries; and
- the measure must be primarily aimed at conservation.[279]

On this basis, the minority in the FTA *Lobsters from Canada* case concluded that the US measures were in the nature both of a conservation measure and of a trade restriction, and that therefore the 1989 Magnuson amendment was not 'primarily aimed at' conservation, since the US had not addressed the reasons why its conservation objections could not be met by alternative measures, such as the special marking of small Canadian lobsters, or the requirement that lobsters be sorted by size prior to importation into the US, or particular documentary requirements as to small lobsters of Canadian origin, or increased penalties for the possession of sub-sized lobsters, more vigilant enforcement efforts, or other requirements.[280]

North America Free Trade Agreement

G. C. Hufbauer *et al.*, *NAFTA and the Environment: Seven Years Later* (2000).

The North America Free Trade Agreement (NAFTA) between Canada, Mexico and the US entered into force in January 1994.[281] The NAFTA establishes a free trade area between the parties in accordance with Article XXIV of the GATT, and is intended to establish principles and rules (including national treatment and most-favoured nation treatment, which will, *inter alia*, eliminate barriers to trade in goods and services and promote competition between the parties) in a manner which is consistent with environmental protection and conservation and which will promote sustainable development.[282] In the event of inconsistencies between the NAFTA and the GATT, and except as otherwise provided in the NAFTA, the provisions of the NAFTA will prevail.[283] The NAFTA's provisions on foreign investment protection are addressed in chapter 20 below.

---

[278] *In the Matter of Canada's Landing Requirements for Pacific Coast Salmon and Herring*, Final Report of the FTA Panel, 16 October 1989, 30 ILM 181 (1991).

[279] *Ibid.*, paras. 7.02 and 7.04.   [280] *Lobsters from Canada*, n. 277 above, para. 1.9.1.

[281] Washington, 8 and 17 December 1992; Ottawa, 11 and 17 December 1992; Mexico City, 14 and 17 December 1992, in force 1 January 1994, 32 ILM 289 (1993) and 32 ILM 605 (1993).

[282] Preamble and Arts. 101 and 102(1)(a) and (b).   [283] Art. 103(2).

Environmental considerations were and remain a controversial aspect of the NAFTA, due to strong lobbying by environmental groups and labour unions in the US who were concerned by the potential effect of weaker Mexican environmental standards on the more stringent US environmental standards, and on the implications for labour. The NAFTA addresses environmental issues, and further measures to strengthen its commitment to environmental protection were set forth in the 1993 Agreement on Environmental Co-operation (see below). It expressly provides that trade obligations under the 1973 CITES, the 1987 Montreal Protocol (and its 1990 amendments), the 1989 Basel Convention (upon its entry into force for the parties), and the agreements set out in Annex 104.1 to the NAFTA, are to prevail to the extent of inconsistency 'provided that where a party has a choice among equally effective and reasonably available means of complying with such obligations, the party chooses the alternative that is least inconsistent with the other provisions of [NAFTA]'.[284] Moreover, for the purposes of Part Two (Trade in Goods) and Part Three (Technical Barriers to Trade) of the NAFTA, Article XX of the GATT is incorporated on the understanding that 'the measures referred to in GATT Article XX(b) include environmental measures necessary to protect human, animal or plant life or health, *and* that GATT Article XX(g) applies to measures relating to the conservation of living and non-living exhaustible natural resources'.[285]

The NAFTA requires each party to accord national treatment to the goods of the other parties in accordance with Article III of the GATT,[286] and provides for the elimination of tariffs.[287] Except as provided in the NAFTA, non-tariff measures such as prohibitions on imports or exports, which could include national environmental protection measures, are prohibited except in accordance with Article XI of the GATT.[288] Prohibited non-tariff measures include customs user fees, country of origin marking, standards and labelling of distinctive products, and export taxes and other export measures.[289] The NAFTA contains detailed provisions on sanitary and phytosanitary measures, and other non-technical barriers to trade, drawing a distinction between the rules applicable to each type of measure.

---

[284] Art. 104(1). The agreements identified in Annex 104.1 are the 1983 Agreement Between the United States of America and the United Mexican States on Co-operation for the Protection and Improvement of the Environment in the Border Areas, La Paz, Baja California Sur, 14 August 1983, and the 1986 Agreement Between Canada and the United States of America Concerning the Transboundary Movement of Hazardous Waste, Ottawa, 28 October 1986.

[285] Art. 2101.   [286] Art. 301; but on sanitary and phytosanitary measures, see below.

[287] Arts. 302 to 308.

[288] Art. 309; on sanitary and phytosanitary measures, see below: 'Measures' includes 'any law, regulation, procedure, requirement or practice': Art. 201(1). Annex 301.3 sets out measures to which this prohibition and that under Art. 301 do not apply, including controls by each of the parties on the export of logs of all species.

[289] Arts. 310 to 315 and Annexes.

Agricultural, sanitary and phytosanitary measures

The NAFTA establishes a framework of rules and disciplines to guide the development, adoption and enforcement of sanitary and phytosanitary measures that may directly or indirectly affect trade between the parties which is virtually identical to that of the WTO SPS Agreement.[290] The NAFTA SPS rules allow each party to adopt, maintain or apply any sanitary or phytosanitary measure which is 'necessary for the protection of human, animal or plant life or health in its territory, including a measure more stringent than an international standard, guideline or recommendation'.[291] Under Article 712(2), each party may establish appropriate levels of protection in accordance with protecting human, animal or plant life or health, but must ensure that any sanitary or phytosanitary measure that it adopts, maintains or applies:

1. is based on scientific principles (including a risk assessment) (Article 712(3));
2. does not arbitrarily or unjustifiably discriminate between its goods and like goods of another party or between goods of another party and like goods of any other country where identical or similar conditions prevail (Article 712(4));
3. is applied only to the extent necessary to achieve its appropriate level of protection (Article 712(5)); and
4. does not create a disguised restriction on trade (Article 712(6)).

Under NAFTA, international standards, guidelines or recommendations are to be used as the basis for sanitary and phytosanitary conditions.[292] The general objective of this section is to create equivalence in standards:

> Without reducing the level of protection of human, animal or plant life or health, the parties shall, to the greatest extent practicable and in accordance with this Section, pursue equivalence of their respective sanitary and phytosanitary measures.[293]

Article 715 sets out the factors which are to be taken into account in conducting risk assessments. These include: relevant techniques and methodologies of international standardising organisations; relevant scientific evidence; relevant

---

[290] Art. 709; Arts. 301 and 309 and Art. XX(b) of the GATT, as incorporated into Art. 2101, do not apply to any sanitary or phytosanitary measures.

[291] Art. 712(1).

[292] Art. 713(1). Article 713 also establishes a presumption that measures conforming to international standards are presumed to be consistent with Art. 712, but that measures which differ from such international standards shall not for that reason alone be presumed to be inconsistent with Chapter 7, subparagraph B: Art. 713(2). The parties are encouraged to participate in relevant international standardising organisations, including the *Codex Alimentarius* Commission, the International Office of Epizootics, the International Plant Protection Convention, and the North American Plant Protection Convention.

[293] Art. 714(1).

processes and production methods and inspection and testing methods; the prevalence of relevant diseases or pests; relevant ecological or other environmental conditions; relevant treatments such as quarantine; certain specified economic factors; and the objective of minimising negative trade effects and arbitrary or unjustifiable restrictions on trade which discriminate or constitute a disguised restriction on trade.[294] NAFTA provides for adaptation to regional conditions and the procedures for dealing with control, inspection and approval, and for the notification and publication of information on federal measures, and establishes an advisory Committee on Sanitary and Phytosanitary Measures to facilitate the enhancement of food safety and the improvement of sanitary and phytosanitary conditions, activities under Articles 713 and 714, technical co-operation and consultation.[295]

Non-technical barriers to trade

Chapter 9 of the NAFTA (Articles 901 to 915) establishes rules for any standards-related measure of a party other than sanitary and phytosanitary measures, that may directly or indirectly affect trade in goods or services between the parties, and to measures of the parties relating to such standards. This includes environmental measures other than those related to agriculture. Further to Article 103, the parties affirm their existing rights and obligations relating to standards-related measures under the 1979 GATT Agreement on Technical Barriers to Trade and all other international agreements, including environmental and conservation agreements, to which they are party.[296]

Under Article 904(1), the parties are allowed to adopt, maintain or apply any standards-related measure, which is defined as a standard, technical regulation, or conformity assessment procedure, including those 'relating to safety, the protection of human, animal and plant life or health, the environment or consumers, and any measure to ensure its enforcement or implementation'. Article 904(1) provides that such measures include those to prohibit the importation of a good of another party that fails to comply with the applicable requirements of those measures. Since the definition of standard and technical regulation includes 'processes and production methods' related to goods,[297] Article 904 would appear to permit US legislation prohibiting the import of yellow-fin tuna from Mexico on the ground that it was caught in a way which violated US environmental and fisheries standards, in effect superseding the ruling of the GATT Panel in the *Yellow-Fin Tuna* case. This would appear to be the correct interpretation, since in pursuing its legitimate environmental objectives each party may establish the level of protection that it considers appropriate, provided that those measures:

[294] Art. 715(1) and (2).   [295] Arts. 716 to 724.   [296] Art. 903.   [297] Art. 915(1).

avoid arbitrary or unjustifiable distinctions between similar goods or services in the level of protection it considers appropriate, where the distinctions:

(a) result in arbitrary or unjustifiable discrimination against goods or service providers of another party;
(b) constitute a disguised restriction on trade between the parties; or
(c) discriminate between similar goods or services for the same use under the same conditions that pose the same level of risk and provide similar benefits.[298]

Goods and service providers are entitled to national treatment and treatment no less favourable than that accorded to goods or service providers of any other country.[299] Standards-related measures are prohibited if they create an unnecessary obstacle to trade, but no such unnecessary obstacle will be deemed to be created if the demonstrable purpose of such measures is to achieve a legitimate objective and they do not exclude goods of another party that meet that legitimate objective.[300] However, the parties must use established international standards (or international standards whose completion is imminent) as a basis for their standards-related measures, except where such standards would be ineffective or inappropriate to fulfil legitimate objectives, including their failure to achieve a 'level of protection that the party considers appropriate'.[301] Measures based on international standards will be presumed to be consistent with Article 904(3) and (4).[302] Moreover, and crucially, Article 905(1) is not to be construed

> to prevent a party, in pursuing its legitimate objectives, from adopting, maintaining or applying any standards-related measure that results in a higher level of protection than would be achieved if the measures were based on the relevant international standard.[303]

In this context (and recognising the 'crucial role of standards-related measures in promoting and protecting legitimate objectives'), the parties agree to work jointly to enhance the level of the protection of the environment; without reducing such protection, and taking into account international standardisation activities, NAFTA commits the parties 'to the greatest extent practicable, [to] make compatible their respective standards-related measures'.[304] To that end, the parties undertake to seek to promote the compatibility of specific standard or conformity assessment procedures.[305] Each importing party agrees to treat

---

[298] Arts. 904(2) and 907(2).   [299] Art. 904(3).   [300] Art. 904(4).
[301] Art. 905(1).   [302] Art. 905(2).   [303] Art. 905(3).
[304] Art. 906(1) and (2). 'Make compatible' is defined as bringing 'different standards-related measures of the same scope approved by different standardising bodies to a level such that they are either identical, equivalent, or have the effect of permitting goods or services to be used in place of one another or fulfil the same purpose': Art. 915(1).
[305] Art. 906(3).

technical regulations adopted or maintained by an exporting party as equivalent to its own where the exporting party demonstrates to the satisfaction of the importing party that its technical regulation adequately fulfils the importing party's legitimate objectives.[306] In pursuing their legitimate objectives, a party may conduct a risk assessment on a good or service, which is to include: consideration of available scientific evidence; intended end uses; processes or production and other methods; and environmental conditions.[307]

Chapter 9 of NAFTA also provides for rules establishing the compatibility of conformity assessment, the notification and publication of proposals adopting or modifying technical regulations, inquiry points and technical co-operation.[308] A Committee on Standards-Related Measures is established to, *inter alia*: monitor implementation; facilitate the compatibility of measures and enhance the development, application and enforcement of measures; and consider non-governmental regional and multilateral developments regarding standards-related measures, including those under the WTO/GATT.[309]

Competition

The rules on competition are far less detailed than their equivalent in the EC and are unlikely, in the short or medium term, to provide a basis for the further development of international law rules on competition and the environment. The NAFTA requires each party to adopt or maintain measures to proscribe anti-competitive business conduct.[310] A monopoly must not act in a manner which is inconsistent with a party's obligations under the NAFTA, must act solely in accordance with commercial considerations, and must not use its monopoly position to engage in anti-competitive practices in a non-monopolised market in its territory.[311] The NAFTA establishes a Working Group on Trade and Competition, but has no rules on subsidies.[312] National laws on anti-dumping and countervailing duties are retained.[313]

Institutions and dispute settlement

NAFTA's principal organ is the Free Trade Commission, which is responsible for supervising implementation, overseeing its further elaboration, resolving disputes concerning interpretation and application, supervising the work of committees established under the Agreement and considering any other matters which arise.[314] The Commission, which comprises cabinet-level representatives or their designees, is assisted by a secretariat.[315] The system for the settlement of disputes under the NAFTA provides for a number of options. First, disputes arising under both the NAFTA and the GATT may be settled in

[306] Art. 906(4).   [307] Art. 907(1).   [308] Arts. 908 to 912.   [309] Art. 913.
[310] Art. 1501.   [311] Art. 1502(3).   [312] Art. 1504.
[313] NAFTA, Chapter 19 and Art. 1902.   [314] Art. 2001(1) and (2).   [315] Art. 2002.

either forum at the discretion of the complaining party.[316] However, where the responding party claims that its action is subject to Article 104 (Relation to Environmental and Conservation Agreements) and requests that the matter be dealt with under the NAFTA, only the procedures available under the NAFTA will be available.[317] Similar provisions apply in respect of disputes arising under the provisions on sanitary and phytosanitary measures and standards-related measures concerning, *inter alia*, measures to protect the environment or factual issues concerning the environment and directly related scientific matters.[318] If consultations between the parties and the good offices of the Free Trade Commission fail to resolve the matter, an arbitral panel of five members will be established by the Commission at the request of any consulting party.[319] The Panel's initial report will be based on the parties' submissions and arguments, and on information from experts and Scientific Review Boards, and may contain findings of fact, determinations, and recommendations for the resolution of the dispute.[320] Unless the parties agree otherwise, the Panel will present a final report within thirty days of the initial report, which will be published fifteen days after its transmission to the Commission.[321] The parties will then agree on the resolution of the dispute, which 'normally shall conform with the determinations and recommendations of the panel', and either not implement a measure or remove a measure which does not conform with the NAFTA, or provide compensation.[322] If no agreement is reached within thirty days, the complaining party may suspend the application to the party in breach of benefits of equivalent effect until agreement is reached.[323] Agreed interpretations of the NAFTA by the Commission may be submitted to national courts or bodies, but the NAFTA excludes rights of action before domestic courts on the ground that a measure by another party is inconsistent with the NAFTA.[324]

North American Agreement on Environmental Co-operation

To counter criticisms of the inadequate provisions of the NAFTA on environmental matters, in September 1993 the three NAFTA parties adopted a supplementary North American Agreement on Environmental Co-operation to support the environmental goals and objectives of NAFTA.[325] The Agreement's general objectives include protecting and improving the environment, promoting sustainable development, enhancing compliance with environmental laws and regulations, and promoting pollution prevention.[326] The Agreement's general commitments address information, education, environmental assessment

---

[316] Art. 2005(1).   [317] Art. 2005(3).   [318] Art. 2005(4).   [319] Art. 2008(1) and (2).
[320] Art. 2016.   [321] Art. 2017.   [322] Art. 2018.   [323] Art. 2019(1).
[324] Arts. 2020 and 2021.
[325] Washington, Ottawa and Mexico City, 8, 9, 12 and 14 September 1993, in force 1 January 1994, 32 ILM 1480 (1993). See also the North American Agreement on Labor Co-operation, 32 ILM 1499 (1993).
[326] Art. 1.

and promoting the use of economic instruments; it does not affect rights and obligations under other applicable international environmental agreements.[327] Marginally more substantive are the obligations which require each party to 'ensure that its laws and regulations provide for high levels of environmental protection' and to effectively enforce these laws and regulations through governmental action and the availability of judicial and administrative enforcement proceedings to sanction or remedy violations.[328] Each party is also required to ensure that 'persons with a legally recognised right under its law in a particular matter' have appropriate access to enforcement proceedings, and to ensure that such proceedings are fair, open and equitable and subject to procedural guarantees.[329]

The Agreement creates a Commission for Environmental Co-operation to oversee implementation of the Agreement and further development, comprising a Council, secretariat and Joint Public Advisory Committee.[330] The Council has limited powers to adopt non-binding recommendations on a wide range of matters, although it has a more substantive role in the enforcement process. The secretariat may consider submissions from any non-governmental organisation or person asserting that a party is 'failing to effectively enforce its environmental law' and can request a response from the party concerned if it determines that the submission so merits.[331] The secretariat may be instructed by the Council, by a two-thirds vote, to prepare a 'factual record' which may be made public by the Council.[332] The Council may also, upon request of any party and by a two-thirds vote, establish an Arbitral Panel to address an 'alleged persistent pattern of failure by the party complained against to effectively enforce its environmental law' involving companies or sectors which produce goods or provide services which are traded between the parties or which compete with the goods or services of another party.[333] Panel reports should lead to an agreement between the disputing parties on a mutually satisfactory action plan which will normally conform with the Panel's recommendations.[334] Non-implementation of the action plan may lead to the Panel being reconvened and a monetary enforcement assessment being imposed, the non-payment of which may lead to the suspension of benefits.[335]

---

[327] Arts. 2 and 40.   [328] Arts. 3 and 5(1) and (2).

[329] Arts. 6(2) and 7.   [330] Arts. 8 to 19. See www.cec.org.

[331] Art. 14. On CEC enforcement, see chapter 5, pp. 211–12 above.

[332] Art. 15. The procedure has been used by NGOs in all three of the NAFTA state parties to raise issues of non-compliance with environmental laws. Factual records have been produced in several cases but as yet no Arbitral Panel has been established to hear a complaint. Records of the submissions made and the factual reports and responses of NAFTA parties are made available by the Commission for Environmental Co-operation on its website, www.cec.org/citizen/index.cfm:?varlan=english.

[333] Arts. 22 to 37. 'Environmental law' is defined at Art. 45(2).   [334] Art. 34.

[335] Arts. 34 to 36 and Annexes 34 (Monetary Enforcement Assessments), 36A (Canadian Domestic Enforcement and Collection) and 36B (Suspension of Benefits).

Border Environment Co-operation Commission, and North American Development Bank

The United States and Mexico also adopted an Agreement Concerning the Establishment of a Border Environment Co-operation Commission and a North American Development Bank.[336] The Commission's purpose is to preserve, protect and enhance the environment of the border region by developing environmental infrastructure projects and arranging public and private financing for such projects.[337] The Bank will provide financing for projects certified by the Commission or for community adjustments and investments supporting the purposes of NAFTA which have been endorsed by the United States or Mexico.[338] The Bank is capitalised at US$3 billion, which is divided in equal shares between Mexico and the United States.

African Economic Community

The Treaty Establishing the African Economic Community was adopted in 1991 to promote interrelated objectives, including: economic, social and cultural development and the integration of African economies; co-operation in all fields of human endeavour to raise the standards of living of African peoples; and to 'co-ordinate and harmonise policies among existing and future economic communities in order to foster the gradual establishment of the [African Economic] Community'.[339] The Treaty sets forth a range of measures which are to be taken towards the achievement of those objectives. At their heart is the commitment to abolish customs duties and non-tariff barriers among member states, together with a commitment to the 'harmonisation and co-ordination of environmental protection policies'.[340] The Treaty is silent as to how it will address those environmental laws of its member states which are also non-tariff barriers, and it does not propose a basis upon which the balance between environmental objectives and free trade objectives is to be struck. It does, however, include several provisions which suggest that the environment will not necessarily be accorded a significantly lower status. By Article 58, the member states undertake to 'promote a healthy environment' and, to that end, agree to adopt national, regional and continental policies, strategies and programmes, and to establish institutions for the protection and enhancement of the environment. Moreover, member states commit themselves to accelerating the process leading to 'ecologically rational, economically sound and socially acceptable development

---

[336] Washington and Mexico City, 16 and 18 November 1993, in force 1 January 1994, 32 ILM 1545 (1993).

[337] Chapter I, Art. 1.   [338] Chapter II, Art. I.

[339] Abuja, 3 June 1991, in force May 1994, 30 ILM 1241 (1991).

[340] Art. 4(2)(d) and (o); see also Arts. 29 to 31 on the elimination of customs duties and non-tariff barriers.

policies', to take every appropriate step to ban the importation and dumping of hazardous wastes in their territories, and to co-operate in accordance with the yet-to-be-negotiated Protocol on the Environment.[341]

The Treaty therefore provides a basis for the development of regional and continental environmental policies, much in the same way that the original EC Treaty served, in the name of economic integration, as the basis for the development of an extensive body of environmental laws aimed both at establishing basic standards and at removing barriers to trade.

UNCED

Trade and the environment was one of the most controversial legal issues at UNCED. Four of the five instruments there adopted contain provisions on the permissibility of unilateral environmental measures. The most detailed is the consensus language adopted by 176 states in Agenda 21, which has served as an important point of reference in 'trade and environment' disputes. It commits states:

> To promote, through the gradual development of universally and multi-laterally negotiated agreements or instruments, international standards for the protection of the environment that take into account the different situations and capabilities of countries. States recognise that environmental policies should deal with the root causes of environmental degradation, thus preventing environmental measures from resulting in unnecessary restrictions to trade. Trade policy measures for environmental purposes should not constitute a means of arbitrary or unjustifiable discrimination or a disguised restriction on international trade. Unilateral actions to deal with environmental challenges outside the jurisdiction of the importing country should be avoided. Environmental measures addressing international environment problems should, as far as possible, be based on an international consensus. Domestic measures targeted to achieve certain environmental objectives may need trade measures to render them effective. Should trade policy measures be found necessary for the enforcement of environmental policies, certain principles and rules should apply. These could include, *inter alia*, the principle of non-discrimination; the principle that the trade measure chosen should be the least trade-restrictive necessary to achieve the objectives; an obligation to ensure transparency in the use of trade measures related to the environment and to provide adequate notification of national regulations, and the need to give consideration to the special conditions and development requirements of developing countries as they move towards internationally agreed environmental objectives.[342]

---

[341] Arts. 58(2), 59 and 60.

[342] Agenda 21, para. 39.3(d). The WSSD Plan of Implementation calls for continued efforts to 'enhance the mutual supportiveness of trade, environment and development with a view

Principle 12 of the Rio Declaration is compatible with the text of Agenda 21, but shorter, incorporating the central elements, but excluding reference to the principles. The text is drawn from Agenda 21, with one exception: 'international environmental problems' in the Agenda 21 text is replaced by 'transboundary or global environmental problems' in the Rio Declaration. Principle 12 and the Agenda 21 language were adopted by consensus, subject to the written statement of the US that trade measures may provide an effective and appropriate means of addressing environmental concerns, including those 'outside national jurisdiction, subject to certain disciplines'.[343] While establishing a presumption in favour of free trade obligations and against national environmental measures, these formulations nevertheless leave open the possibility that unilateral measures may be adopted, even where they may have 'extra-jurisdictional effect'.

The other instruments adopted at UNCED are less specific. The 1992 Climate Change Convention provides that measures to combat climate change 'should not constitute a means of arbitrary or unjustifiable discrimination or a disguised restriction on international trade', which also suggests that trade measures are permissible in certain circumstances.[344] The Forest Principles also address trade issues, calling for international trade in forest products to be facilitated on the basis of non-discriminatory and multilaterally agreed rules and procedures consistent with international trade law and practices.[345] The Forest Principles also provide that '[u]nilateral measures, incompatible with international obligations or agreements, to restrict and/or ban the international trade in timber or other forest products, should be removed or avoided'.[346]

Taken together, the UNCED instruments suggest the emergence of a consensus, reinforced in the subsequent WTO/GATT jurisprudence, that unilateral measures should be avoided but that they are not, *per se*, prohibited. The *Shrimp/Turtle (Phase II)* decision of the WTO Appellate Body provides particular guidance in this regard, suggesting that unilateral measures will be permissible where preceded by serious, though not necessarily successful, attempts to secure international agreement on an environmental issue, and provided that the measures are designed in such a manner that there is sufficient flexibility to take into account the specific conditions prevailing in any exporting WTO member. The WSSD Plan of Implementation restates the language of Agenda 21 and the Rio Declaration,[347] suggesting that states did not feel the need to revisit their approach in the light of WTO case law since 1992.

---

to achieving sustainable development' (para. 91), and to promote 'mutual supportiveness between the multilateral trading system and the multilateral environmental agreements, consistent with sustainable development goals . . . while recognizing the importance of maintaining the integrity of both sets of systems' (para. 92).

[343] UNCED Report, A/CONF.151/26/Rev.1/Vol. II (June 1993), 18.   [344] Art. 3(5).
[345] Principle 13(a) and (d); see also Principle 13(b).   [346] Principle 14.   [347] Para. 95.

Competition and subsidies

S. Budlong, 'Article 130r(2) and the Permissibility of State Aids for Environmental Compliance in the EC', 30 *Columbia Journal of Transnational Law* 431 (1992); OECD, *Subsidies and Environment: Exploring the Linkages* (1996); D. Geradin, 'EC Competition Law and Environmental Protection', 2 *Yearbook of European Environmental Law* 117 (2002).

Closely related to international trade obligations are the emerging rules which prohibit anti-competitive behaviour which distorts trade. These rules, established by the WTO/GATT and the EC, are potentially significant for environmental issues. They are intended, in large part, to supplement free trade obligations by limiting anti-competitive practices which might distort competition and consequently affect trade between states. As was seen in chapter 15 above, the development of environmental law in the EC was in large part justified by the desire to remove environmentally related distortions to competition and barriers to trade.[348]

Competition law has intersected with the environment in at least three ways. First, environmental considerations influence the application of rules prohibiting or limiting the grant by governments and other public authorities of subsidies (state aids). Secondly, environmental considerations are beginning to be taken into account in applying competition rules to agreements between companies, including 'environmental agreements'.[349] Thirdly, the failure to integrate environmental costs into production costs has led to charges of 'environmental dumping' in international trade. A fourth aspect of the relationship concerns the international instruments addressing the economic aspects of environmental policies, which have long recognised the relationship between environmental protection and competition. The development and application of the polluter-pays principle, described in chapter 6 above, is closely related to competition rules, since it is intended in part to ensure that the costs of the environmental measures necessary to protect the environment should be reflected in the costs of goods and services which cause pollution in production or consumption; as early as 1972, the OECD Council recommended that environmental protection measures should not be accompanied by subsidies that would create significant distortions in international trade and investment, although exceptions or special arrangements may occur.[350]

---

[348] Chapter 15, pp. 740–2 above.

[349] On environmental agreements, see chapter 4, p. 166 above; see generally R. Khalastchi and H. Ward, 'New Instruments for Sustainability: An Assessment of Environmental Agreements under Community Law', 10 JEL 257 (1998).

[350] OECD Council Recommendation on Guiding Principles Concerning International Economic Aspects of Environmental Policies, C(72)128 (1972), Annex, paras. 4 and 5.

Subsidies

The introduction of environmental considerations into the law of subsidies has at least two consequences. It may allow the grant of subsidies which would otherwise be prohibited for activities which are environmentally beneficial. And it may allow enforcement bodies to prevent subsidies from being granted to activities which are particularly harmful to the environment. Although Agenda 21 called for the removal or reduction of subsidies that do not conform with sustainable development objectives,[351] international legal developments have so far focused on the first of these two aspects. In 1974, the OECD Council recommended that in application of the polluter-pays principle the state should not, as a general rule, assist polluters in bearing the costs of pollution control whether by means of subsidies, tax advantages or other measures.[352] The OECD Council further recommended that the grant of such assistance for pollution control should be strictly limited and be notified to OECD member countries, and must comply with three conditions:

1. it should be selective and restricted to those parts of the economy, such as industries, areas or plants, where severe difficulties would otherwise occur;
2. it should be limited to well-defined transitional periods, laid down in advance and adapted to the specific socio-economic problems associated with the implementation of a country's environmental programme; and
3. it should not create significant distortions in international trade and investment.[353]

The OECD rules have influenced the EC. Article 87 (formerly Article 92) of the EC Treaty prohibits state aids (subsidies) which distort competition and affect trade between member states unless it has a social character, makes good damage caused by natural disasters or other exceptional occurrences, or is 'aid granted to the economy of certain areas of the Federal Republic of Germany affected by the division of Germany, insofar as such aid is required in order to compensate for the economic disadvantages caused by that division'.[354] However, state aid

---

[351] Agenda 21, para. 8.32(b). See also the WSSD Plan of Implementation, calling for completion of the work programme of the Doha Ministerial Declaration on subsidies so as to 'encourage reform of subsidies that have considerable negative effects on the environment and are incompatible with sustainable development': para. 91(b).

[352] OECD Council Recommendation C(74)223, Chapter 6, Part III, para. 1.

[353] Paras. 2 and 4.

[354] The ECJ has held that aid must involve a direct or indirect transfer of state resources to undertakings: see Case C-379/98, *PreussenElektra AG* v. *Schleswag AG* [2001] ECR I-2099 (provision requiring that private electricity supply undertakings must purchase electricity produced in their area of supply from renewable energy sources at minimum prices higher than the real economic value of that type of electricity, and that distributing the financial burden resulting from that obligation between those electricity supply undertakings and upstream private electricity network operators does not constitute state aid within the meaning of Art. 92(1) of the EC Treaty).

may be held compatible with the common market by the EC Commission if it:

1. promotes economic development in certain areas where the standard of living is abnormally low or where there is serious underemployment;
2. promotes the execution of an important project of common European interest;
3. remedies a serious disturbance in the economy of a member state;
4. facilitates the development of certain economic activities and does not adversely affect trading conditions to an extent contrary to the common interest;
5. promotes culture and heritage conservation where such aid does not affect trading conditions and competition in the Community to an extent that is contrary to the common interest; or
6. is otherwise decided by the EC Council.[355]

The EC Council Recommendation on cost allocation and action by public authorities on environmental matters allows exceptions to the polluter-pays principle, including: financial contributions for the construction of public installations for the protection of the environment which could not be wholly covered in the short term from charges paid by polluters using them; financing to meet particularly heavy costs to achieve 'an exceptional degree of environmental cleanliness'; and contributions towards research and development on processes and products causing less pollution.[356]

The EC approach is now governed by its 2001 Guidelines, although since 1975 the grant of environmental aid in the EC has been the subject of special rules and practice.[357] The original principles provided that aid had to specify the industry and geographical areas for which it was to be granted and should facilitate the adaptation of firms to new obligations for the elimination of pollution imposed by public authorities, with the aim of carrying out research and development or new investments. Moreover, aid could be granted only where a 'sudden major change' in pollution-related obligations and constraints had occurred and only to plant in service at the time of the change, unless international competition is such that their activities would be 'seriously handicapped by being subjected to differing obligations from those imposed in given non-member countries or where non-member countries are themselves granting environmental protection aid'.[358] This approach was justified as a compromise to reconcile the need to accelerate urgent pollution control investment

---

[355] Art. 87(3).   [356] Chapter 6, p. 283, n. 287 above, Annex, para. 7.

[357] EC Commission, 'Community Approach to State Aids in Environmental Matters', 7 November 1974, Fourth Report on Competition Policy, points 180–2.

[358] *Ibid.*, point 182. The approach was extended after 1980, subject to modifications: EC Commission Letter of 7 July 1980 to Member States, Tenth Report on Competition, points 225–6 (1980).

with the requirement of undistorted competition, and applied until the mid-1990s.[359]

Practice under the earlier rules was extensive. Examples of projects in which state aid had been granted for which the Commission did not raise objections included a Danish law on aid for environmental investments;[360] aid by the state of Baden-Württemberg in Germany to encourage air pollution control measures going beyond statutory requirements;[361] reductions in a Dutch special consumer tax for less-polluting cars;[362] a Spanish draft government programme to create an industrial, energy and environmental technology base; a Catalonian regional aid scheme to reduce atmospheric pollution;[363] and Dutch tax incentives for the purchase of buses and lorries that comply with stricter noise and exhaust emissions standards.[364] In 1992, the Commission approved, subject to the fulfilment of certain conditions, an aid scheme financed by a levy to stimulate the environmentally acceptable disposal of surplus manure, to prevent the contamination of surface and subterranean water supplies, gaseous emissions, and residual heavy metals.[365] Although the aid did not fall within the Commission's 1974 and 1980 guidelines, since it was not designed to finance investments, it was exempted under Article 87(3)(c) as it facilitated the economic development of Dutch animal husbandry

> by creating a system for an environmentally-sound disposal of its surplus manure. Having due regard to Article 130r of the Treaty the Commission notes that the environmental policy pursued by the Netherlands Government, in so far as it reduces manure pollution, is in the interest of the Community as a whole.[366]

However, the Commission did not always accept arguments by governments to approve the grant of aid on environmental grounds. For example, in 1989, the Commission objected to a French aid scheme providing grants of up to 50 per cent of investment costs with a total budget of FFr90 million, on the ground that the 'intensity of the aid and the size of the budget were liable to distort competition and affect intra Community trade'.[367]

---

[359] Sixteenth Competition Report, point 259 (1986).
[360] Tenth Competition Report point 227 (1980).
[361] Sixteenth Competition Report, point 260 (1986).
[362] Nineteenth Competition Report, point 199 (1989).
[363] Twentieth Competition Report, points 285–6 (1982).
[364] Twentieth Competition Report, point 288 (1990).
[365] Commission Decision 92/316/EEC, OJ L170, 25 June 1992, 34.
[366] *Ibid.*, 38. The aid was approved until 31 December 1994 in so far as it did not exceed the fixed cost of the administrative apparatus and the creation and maintenance of storage facilities.
[367] Nineteenth Competition Report, point 198 (1989). Proceedings were subsequently closed when France announced that it was discontinuing the scheme and introducing a new scheme for innovative investment in a non-productive plant that involved the first

In 1994, the Commission adopted new guidelines on state aid for environmental protection,[368] which remained in force until new guidelines were adopted at the start of 2001, having regard to (1) developments in the field of the environment; (2) state aid being granted more frequently in the energy sector; and (3) new forms of operating aid.[369] The 2001 Guidelines apply to aid to protect the environment in all sectors governed by the EC Treaty, including those subject to specific Community rules on state aid (e.g. steel processing, transport and fisheries) with the exception of agriculture. The Guidelines seek to encourage energy efficiency and the use of renewable energies. They identify the Commission's policy on the control of state aid for environmental purposes as having a double imperative, namely:

1. to ensure the competitive functioning of markets; and
2. to ensure that the requirements of environmental protection are integrated into the definition and implementation of competition policy, to promote sustainable development, recognising that the internalisation of costs is a priority objective.

The 2001 Guidelines mark a significant shift in approach. The 1994 Guidelines had permitted aid either to encourage firms to adapt to new environmental standards, or to act as an incentive to improve on standards or undertake further investment to reduce pollution. The 2001 Guidelines reflect the Commission's position that aid will only now be justified on the second ground and will no longer be used to make up for the absence of cost internalisation, so that aid will no longer be justified for investments to bring companies into line with new or existing standards.[370] The 2002 Guidelines set out the general and detailed conditions for authorising aid (pursuant to Article 87(3)(c) of the EC Treaty) of three kinds:

1. investment aid;
2. aid to small and medium-sized enterprises for advisory and consultancy services in the environmental field; and
3. operating aid.

The Commission maintains a register of state aid decisions on environmental aid.[371]

industrial application of a new technology, which the Commission approved on the grounds that the measures proposed encouraged industry to go further than EC environmental standards required: Twentieth Competition Report, point 287 (1990).

[368] OJ C72, 10 March 1994, 3. These expired on 31 December 1999 and were extended to 31 December 2000: OJ C184, 1 July 2000, 25.

[369] OJ C37, 3 February 2001, 3.

[370] Para. 20. Aid may be granted to small and medium-sized enterprises for a period of up to three years to enable them to adapt to new standards.

[371] http://europa.eu.int/comm/competition/state_aid/register/ii/by_primary_obj_environmental_aid.html.

Article XVI(1) of the GATT has a similar objective to Article 87 of the EC Treaty, although the former does not prohibit subsidies or declare them void *per se*. Rather, Article XVI(1) requires any contracting party to notify the other contracting parties on the nature and extent of any subsidisation and its estimated effect on imports or exports, and requires discussions between the parties concerned, or with the contracting parties, about the possibility of limiting subsidies which are determined to cause or threaten serious prejudice to the interests of any other contracting party. To date, the provision has not apparently led to any disputes between contracting parties over environment-related subsidies. The increased attention being given by states to their international competitiveness in the face of increased national and international environmental regulation makes it likely, however, that Article XVI(1) could become a contentious issue.

Under the auspices of the GATT Uruguay Round, a Subsidies Agreement was negotiated which is binding on all WTO members. The Agreement defines certain 'non-actionable' subsidies, including those related to environmental protection. It states, quite specifically, that non-actionable environmental subsidies cover:

> assistance to promote adaptation of existing facilities to new environmental requirements imposed by law and/or regulations which result in greater constraints and financial burden on firms, provided that the assistance:
>
> (i) is a one-time non-recurring measure; and
> (ii) is limited to 20 per cent of the cost of adaptation; and
> (iii) does not cover the cost of replacing and operating the assisted investment, which must be fully borne by firms; and
> (iv) is directly linked to and proportionate to a firm's planned reduction of nuisances and pollution, and does not cover any manufacturing cost savings which may be achieved; and
> (v) is available to all firms which can adopt the new equipment and/or production processes.[372]

Anti-competitive agreements

The second area of competition law with environmental implications relates to rules which prohibit anti-competitive agreements and practices by companies and other persons. The WTO does not yet have rules on this subject, but Article 81 (formerly Article 85) of the EC Treaty prohibits agreements, decisions and concerted practices which affect trade between member states

---

[372] Art. 8.2(c) of the Agreement on Subsidies and Countervailing Measures. The provision does not appear to have been the subject of any action by the WTO or attention by its DSB. In November 2001, the WTO Doha Ministerial Declaration agreed to negotiations (to be completed by 1 January 2005) aimed at clarifying and improving disciplines under the Subsidies Agreement, in particular fisheries subsidies.

and prevent, restrict or distort competition. Under Article 82 (formerly Article 86), similar prohibitions apply to abuses by companies of dominant positions, such as price-fixing and limiting markets and technical developments. Under Article 81(3), the EC Commission may find that the Article 81 prohibition is not applicable to agreements, decisions or practices, or categories thereof, which are considered to bring public benefits; these public benefits include improving the production or distribution of goods or promoting technical or economic progress, while allowing consumers a fair share of the resulting benefit, provided that the agreement does not impose restrictions which are not indispensable to the attainment of these objectives or eliminate competition in respect of a substantial part of the products in question. This is broad enough language to justify exemptions for technical or economic progress which contributes to environmental protection, thereby benefiting consumers.[373] In *Cali v. Servizi ecologici porto di Genova SpA*, the ECJ ruled that Article 82 (formerly Article 86) of the EC Treaty is not applicable to anti-pollution surveillance with which a body governed by private law has been entrusted by the public authorities in an oil port of a member state, even where port users must pay dues to finance that activity.[374] The EC Commission has been willing to take into account environmental considerations in applying Articles 81 and 82, and has also applied Article 81 to 'environmental agreements' between companies.[375] By way of example, in *Re Independent Power Generators*, which concerned a joint venture agreement in the energy sector which included certain restrictive practices (agreement not to compete), one of the factors the Commission took into account in deciding not to object to a long-term exclusive purchase agreement, which might otherwise have been caught, was the intended use by the joint venture of combined cycle gas turbine generators or clean coal-fired systems, which was considered to be efficient generating technology offering environmental advantages.[376]

Anti-dumping

The third area of competition law which is likely to become relevant in relation to environmental protection is that on dumping. Under Article VI(1) of the GATT, as elaborated by the Uruguay Round Anti-Dumping Agreement,[377]

---

[373] EC Commission, Guidelines on the Applicability of Article 81 of the EC Treaty to Horizontal Co-operation Agreements, OJ C3, 6 January 2001, 2, paras. 179 *et seq.*; also Decision 94/322, Exxon/Shell, OJ L144, 9 June 1994, 20, and other examples cited in D. Geradin, 'EC Competition Law and Environmental Protection: Conflict or Compatibility', 2 *Yearbook of European Environmental Law* 117 (2002).

[374] Case C-343/95, *Diego Cali and figli Srl* v. *Servizi Ecologici Porto di Genova SpA* [1997] ECR I-1547.

[375] See the examples cited in Geradin, n. 373 above.

[376] EC Commission Notice (Case IV/34.078) [1992] 5 CMLR 88 at 89.

[377] Agreement on the Implementation of Article VI of the General Agreement on Tariffs and Trade 1994.

dumping (which is defined as the introduction of products into the market of another country at 'less than normal value of the products') will be condemned if it causes or threatens material injury to an established industry in the territory of a contracting party or materially retards the establishment of a domestic industry. The product is introduced at less than normal value if the price of the product exported from one country to another:

1. is less than the comparable price, in the ordinary course of trade, for the like product when destined for consumption in the exporting country; or
2. in the absence of such domestic price, is less than either:
   (i) the highest comparable price for the like product for export to any third country in the ordinary course of trade; or
   (ii) the cost of production of the product in the country of origin plus a reasonable addition for selling cost and profit.

These provisions, which are applied also in the EC,[378] allow for 'environmental dumping' arguments to be raised in respect of price differentials resulting from the failure to integrate environmental costs into production costs. Article VI does require due allowance to be made for, *inter alia*, 'other differences affecting price comparability', and this raises the question of whether, and if so to what extent, environmental costs must be reflected in production costs.[379] It will be recalled that the Rio Declaration sends out conflicting messages which call for a balancing of interests: Principle 11 states that environmental standards should reflect the environmental and developmental context to which they apply and that standards applied by some countries may be inappropriate and of unwarranted social cost to other countries, particularly developing countries. Principle 16, on the other hand, calls on states to promote the internalisation of environmental costs.

Conclusions

As this chapter shows, a large body of international legislation and case law has developed over the past ten years as the international community seeks, at the regional and global level, to find an acceptable balance between trade liberalisation objectives and environmental objectives. If anything, the legal situation has become increasingly complex. On the one hand, the international community has furthered its efforts to liberalise and deregulate international trade; on the other hand, it has redoubled efforts to develop international environmental agreements, many of which rely upon trade sanctions to achieve their

---

[378] Council Regulation (EC) No. 384/96 of 22 December 1995 on protection against dumped imports from countries not members of the European Community, OJ L56, 6 March 1996, 1.
[379] See the Agreement on Subsidies and Countervailing Measures above.

objectives. These international initiatives have been accompanied by domestic legislation, mostly in industrialised countries, which tightens up national environmental regulations, including restrictions on imports. In the midst of these political and legal controversies, international courts and other bodies find themselves increasingly being called upon to adjudicate on the basis of bilateral, regional and global legal arrangements, and it is hardly surprising that they will apply different tests and reach different conclusions on the appropriate balance between environmental objectives and trade objectives. It is one of the ironies of the trade/environment tension that the free trade ideal based upon deregulation has required a new layer of international regulation to set minimum standards; the experience in each region and globally has been that free trade inevitably points to a degree of harmonisation of environmental standards, at least in the sense that minimum standards are to be met. The challenge for the international community is to ensure that those harmonised standards do not lead to a general weakening of environmental protection. In this regard, it is notable that many international environmental agreements explicitly recognise the right of a party to maintain more stringent standards, subject to certain requirements.[380]

While it can be argued that the GATT/WTO rules do not give adequate weight to the environment, the jurisprudence of, in particular, the new WTO Appellate Body has significantly expanded the potential for the 'environmental exceptions' available under Article XX of the GATT. This development reflects a recognition that legitimate environmental measures can, in certain circumstances, lawfully restrict international trade, provided that certain conditions are met. The international community faces two challenges here. One relates to standards, the other to institutions. With regard to standards, further efforts will be needed to refine and clarify (through practice, presumably) the emerging rules to assist governments, international organisations and adjudicative bodies to determine when environmental considerations can be allowed. In view of the approach taken by the Appellate Body, it may no longer be necessary to reconsider and modernise Article XX of the GATT, as the previous edition of this book suggested. It is apparent that the WTO Appellate Body has been inspired by rules of international law arising outside the WTO, including the approach taken by the ECJ in the *Danish Bottles* and *Belgian Waste Disposal* cases, and reflected in Principle 12 of the Rio Declaration. With regard to institutions, significant advances have been made with the establishment of the WTO and the conclusion of new agreements relating to SPS measures and technical barriers to trade. However, the concept of sustainable development (and its practical consequences) remains to be defined, and the relationship between international trade law and multilateral environmental agreements remains less certain than it should be. The level of controversy and debate stimulated by the

---

[380] 1998 Chemicals Convention, Art. 15(4); 2000 Biosafety Protocol, Art. 2(4).

Appellate Body's decision in *Beef Hormones* suggested that the interaction of international trade obligations with domestic health and environmental standards may be a new frontier on which the 'trade and environment' battle is fought out in the twenty-first century.

In many ways, the trade/environment debate reflects a broader issue as to how far environmental considerations can go in bringing about a restructuring of established international economic organisations, how far environment and development can (as a matter of law) be integrated, and whether it is the environment which will ultimately be subsumed into economic approaches, or whether it will be the other way round.

In the meantime, if the late 1980s to the early years of the new millennium were about trade and environment, the next related international legal issue looming on the horizon is the relationship between competition law and the environment. It is likely that environmental arguments will increasingly be raised to justify commercial agreements which might otherwise be caught by anti-trust laws. It is equally foreseeable that the law on subsidies and the environment will expand, and that environmental dumping (selling goods whose prices do not fully reflect their environmental costs and impacts) will be subject to international legal scrutiny. It is at this interface between international environmental law and international economic law that the effectiveness of the standards which have been meticulously developed to protect flora, fauna and other environmental resources will be judged.

Financial resources, technology and intellectual property

Introduction

The establishment by the 1990 amendments to the 1987 Montreal Protocol of a financial mechanism to address ozone depletion marked an important turning point in international environmental law. In the subsequent decade the rules on finance and technology transfer have developed significantly and substantively, together with legislative and judicial consideration of the relationship between intellectual property rights and environmental protection. This has occurred notwithstanding the early concerns of some industrialised countries that the establishment of the Montreal Fund would adversely prejudice future developments. Financial resources, technology transfer and intellectual property were central issues at UNCED and of the two treaties signed at UNCED. As described in this chapter, the 1992 Climate Change and Biodiversity Conventions – as well as subsequent instruments on drought and desertification (1994), climate change (1997), biosafety (2000) and persistent organic pollutants (2001) have further elaborated the principles established under the Montreal Protocol and its amendments. Related developments – particularly in the context of the activities of the multilateral development banks, the WTO Agreement on Trade Related Aspects of Intellectual Property Rights (TRIPs), the European Patent Convention, and the 2001 International Treaty on Plant Genetic Resources for Food and Agriculture – have added to the broadening range of legal issues which are touched by, and increasingly integrated with, international environmental concerns.

These three subjects – financial resources, technology and intellectual property – occupy a central place in the legal arrangements of international environmental law, at the regional and global levels, and will determine to a considerable extent whether the substantive protections put in place can be achieved (in that regard, the experience with the Montreal Protocol provides some grounds for optimism). The consequence is that international environmental lawyers will necessarily find themselves facing the complex (and often black letter) legal issues which emerge as a result of an increasingly integrated approach to environmental protection and economic development. It remains to be seen, in the process of cross-fertilisation, what the nature of the integrated relationship will be, and the manner in which balance will be achieved.

Financial resources and mechanisms

The provision of international financial resources related to the environment has two main aspects. The first concerns the extent to which overseas development assistance granted bilaterally by states (or collectively by a group of states) or by international organisations is subject to compliance with international environmental law. The second relates to the body of international institutional and substantive law which has arisen out of the establishment and development of international mechanisms to provide financial assistance for global environmental objectives. These include the Global Environment Facility (GEF) and the Montreal Protocol Multilateral Fund, as well as earlier mechanisms such as the Wetlands Fund, the World Heritage Fund, and the International Fund for Plant Genetic Resources. Complex legal issues have also arisen in the context of the relationship between the GEF and international conventions on biodiversity, climate change, desertification and POPs. Other efforts to support international conservation include 'debt-for-nature swaps', trust funds and endowments.[1]

Chapter 33 of Agenda 21, 'Financial Resources and Mechanisms', deals with the financing of Agenda 21 and the global consensus integrating environmental considerations into an accelerated development process. In the context of the estimated US$600 billion annual cost over the period 1993–2000 of implementing in developing countries the activities set out in Agenda 21, Chapter 33 identifies three objectives for the international community: adopting measures concerning financial resources and mechanisms for the implementation of Agenda 21; providing new and additional financial resources that are adequate and predictable; and seeking full use and improvement of the funding mechanisms to be utilised for the implementation of Agenda 21, including the provisions on environmental protection.[2] The main sources of financial resources will be bilateral overseas development aid and funds from the multilateral development banks and specialised environmental funds; other sources are likely to include private funding, debt relief, direct foreign investment and what Agenda 21 terms 'innovative financing', including debt swaps,[3] the use of

---

[1] See e.g. the Rainforest Trust Fund, below; see also Royal Government of Bhutan, UNDP and WWF, 'Prospectus Trust Fund for Environmental Conservation in Bhutan' (WWF, 1991).

[2] Agenda 21, paras. 33.11, 33.12 and 33.13; see also WSSD Plan of Implementation, para. 80.

[3] See generally T. J. Hrynik, 'Debt for Nature Swaps: Effective but Not Enforceable', 22 *Case Western Reserve Journal of International Law* 141 (1990); D. Barrans, 'Promoting International Environmental Protections through Foreign Debt Transactions', 24 *Cornell*

economic and fiscal incentives and tradeable permits.[4] Agenda 21 also supports
the reallocation of resources committed to military purposes.[5]

Overseas development assistance

J. Hornberry, 'The Accountability of Development Assistance Agencies: The Case
of Environmental Policy', 12 *Ecology Law Quarterly* 675 (1985); P. Muldoon, 'The
International Law of Eco-Development: Emerging Norms for Development Assistance Agencies', 22 *Texas International Law Journal* 1 (1987); P. Kohona, 'UNCED –
The Transfer of Financial Resources to Developing Countries', 1 RECIEL 307 (1992).

At UNCED – and again at the WSSD – the developed countries reaffirmed their
political commitment to reach the accepted UN target of 0.7 per cent of GNP
for overseas development assistance (ODA) and, to the extent that they had
not yet reached that target, agreed to augment their aid programme to reach
that target as soon as possible.[6] The developed countries have not, however,
accepted any international legal obligations or other international commitments to apportion ODA, or any part of it, to environmental programmes and
projects. As a matter of domestic policy, a number of developed countries have
committed themselves to the objective of allocating a proportion of ODA to
environmental activities. The grant of ODA is subject to any obligations which
the granting state may have under relevant international environmental law,
including treaty obligations. Such obligations might include compliance with
certain minimum standards, and the conduct of environmental assessments
in respect of projects likely to damage the environment. Several bilateral and
regional development assistance treaties include specific environmental obligations, which either require assistance to be directed towards environmental
protection programmes or projects, or that development assistance should be
subjected to some form of environmental assessment. Thus, environment and
development are closely interwoven throughout the 1989 Lomé Convention,
which provided that the support to be provided in the ACP–EC co-operation for
the ACP states' efforts to achieve comprehensive self-reliant and self-sustained
development must be based on development which achieves a 'sustainable
balance between its economic objectives, the rational management of the environment and the enhancement of natural and human resources'.[7] To the extent
that overseas development assistance is subject to compliance with the national

International Law Journal 65 (1991); F. G. Minujin, 'Debt-for-Nature Swaps: A Financial
Mechanism to Reduce Debt and Preserve the Environment', 21 *Environmental Policy and
Law* 146 (1991); K. Von Moltke, 'Debt-for-Nature: The Second Generation', 14 *Hastings
International and Comparative Law Review* 973 (1991).
[4] Chapter 4, pp. 158–67 above.
[5] Agenda 21, paras. 33.16, 33.17 and 33.18; WSSD Plan of Implementation, para. 79(a).
[6] Para. 33.15.   [7] Art. 4.

environmental laws of the assisting state, the possibility arises that such assistance could in effect apply national environmental laws extra-territorially.[8] In practice, the political and economic requirements of the assisted state have limited the scope of making such types of 'green conditionality' arguments, and Principle 4 of the Rio Declaration provides a powerful basis for arguing that environmental protection must be an integral part of all development assistance.

The OECD Council has recommended that development assistance projects and programmes which could significantly affect the environment should be subjected to an environmental assessment at an early stage.[9] The Recommendation identifies the issues which should be considered in an environmental assessment, and requires an in-depth environmental assessment for certain very fragile environments, such as wetlands, mangrove swamps, coral reefs, tropical forests and semi-arid areas.[10] Other projects or programmes in need of environmental assessment include substantial changes in renewable resource use or farming and fishing practices, exploitation of hydraulic resources, infrastructure, industrial activities, extractive industries and waste management and disposal.[11] Similar requirements have been applied in relation to public schemes aiming to insure or guarantee foreign investments from political and other risks, including regulatory change.[12]

Multilateral development banks

R. E. Stein and B. Johnson, *Banking on the Biosphere? Environmental Procedures and Practices of Nine Multilateral Development Agencies* (1979); B. Rich, 'The Multilateral Development Banks, Environmental Policy and the United States', 12 *Ecology Law Quarterly* 69 (1985); S. Schwartzmann, *Bankrolling Disasters: International Development Banks and the Global Environment* (Sierra Club, 1986); V. Nanda, 'Human Rights and Environmental Considerations in the Lending Policies of International Development Agencies: An Introduction', 17 DJILP 29 (1988); Z. Plater, 'Damming the Third World: Multilateral Banks, Environmental Diseconomies, and International Reform Pressures on the Lending Process', 17 DJILP

---

[8] On extra-territoriality, see chapter 6, pp. 237–41 above. See also *R. v. Secretary of State for Foreign Affairs, ex parte World Development Movement Ltd* [1995] 1 All ER 611 (judgment declaring unlawful a decision of UK Foreign Secretary to provide finance for the construction of the Pergau dam in Malaysia, on the ground that the grant of aid was so economically unsound that it violated section 1 of the Overseas Development Co-operation Act 1980). The Environmental Procedures of the United States Agency for International Development have generated controversy by tying the grant of development assistance by the United States to compliance with its national environmental laws, including in relation to assistance channelled through the multilateral development banks and other funds.

[9] Recommendation on Environmental Assessment of Development Assistance Projects and Programmes, C(85)104 (1985).

[10] Appendix. para. 2.   [11] Appendix, para. 3.   [12] Chapter 21, p. 1071 below.

121 (1988); B. Rich, 'The Emperor's New Clothes: The World Bank and Environmental Reform', 10 *World Policy Journal* 305 (1990); I. Shihata, *The World Bank in a Changing World: Selected Essays* (1991) (especially Chapter 4); I. Shihata, 'The World Bank and the Environment: A Legal Perspective', 16 *Maryland Journal of International Law and Trade* 1 (1992); K. Piddington, 'The Role of the World Bank', in A. Hurrell and B. Kingsbury (eds.), *The International Politics of the Environment* (1992), 212; 'Financial Mechanisms for the Protection of the Environment', 3 RECIEL 81 (1994); C. Redgwell, *Intergenerational Trusts and Environmental Protection* (1999); G. Handl, *Multilateral Development Banking: Environmental Principles and Concepts Reflecting General International Law and Public Policy* (2001).

The World Bank and the six regional development banks have played an important role in the elaboration of rules of international environmental law. In 1980, largely as a result of strong criticism targeted at their environmentally unsound lending activities, the World Bank, five of the regional development banks, the EC, the OAS, UNEP and UNDP adopted a Declaration of Environmental Policies and Procedures Relating to Economic Development.[13] The Declaration reaffirmed their support for the principles and recommendations of the Stockholm Conference and agreed to institute procedures for the 'systematic examination' of all development activities under consideration for financing to ensure that appropriate measures are proposed for compliance with the Stockholm instruments. They also undertook to provide technical assistance to developing countries on environmental matters, and, if appropriate, to support project proposals which protect, rehabilitate or otherwise enhance the human environment.[14] This early commitment to achieving environmental protection is now reflected in more detailed requirements forming part of the internal laws of multilateral development banks and other funding agencies.

The World Bank and the regional banks are established by international treaty. As such, and having been endowed by their constituent instruments with certain capacities and functions on the international plane, they have a degree of international personality from which certain consequences flow: the power to make treaties and, to undertake legal proceedings; and certain privileges and immunities under international law. As international legal persons, the multilateral development banks may also have rights and obligations under international law. In the *Reparations for Injuries* case, the ICJ ruled that the UN was 'a subject of international law and capable of possessing international rights and duties, and that it has the capacity to maintain its rights by bringing international claims'.[15] From the Advisory Opinion of the Court, it is clear

---

[13] 1 February 1980, 19 ILM 524 (1980).   [14] Paras. 3 and 4.

[15] *Reparation for Injuries Suffered in the Service of the United Nations*, Advisory Opinion (1949) ICJ Reports 174.

that the multilateral development banks will have a sufficient degree of inter-national personality to subject them to certain duties under international law, including duties which arise under the operation of general and specific rules of international environmental law. Multilateral development banks are under an obligation to comply with general principles of international law relating to the protection of the environment, and any failure to comply with such obli-gations might entail their international responsibility, as well as liability for damages.[16] This possibility is important in the context of the attention which has been given to the development lending activities of multilateral develop-ment banks which have contributed to environmental despoliation and which have led to the adoption of measures to limit and prevent the adverse effects of their activities, including requirements for environmental impact assess-ment and environmental audits. Other, emerging approaches to dealing with the potential liability of the multilateral lender for the adverse environmental consequences of its activities include the use of 'environmental covenants'[17] and agreements channelling liability to the recipient.

World Bank (www.worldbank.org)

The World Bank group comprises the International Bank for Reconstruction and Development (IBRD), the International Development Association (IDA) and the International Finance Corporation (IFC).[18] The IBRD was established in 1945 to promote the international flow of financial resources for productive purposes and to assist in the reconstruction of states after the Second World War. Its Articles of Agreement do not include any provisions specifically refer-ring to environmental protection objectives or to the sustainable or rational use of natural resources.[19] Its main objective today is to provide financial sup-port, usually in the form of loans, for productive projects or to finance reform programmes which will lead to economic growth in its less developed member countries. By the end of 2002, its outstanding disbursed loans totalled US$371 billion, with loans of US$11.5 billion in 2002.

---

[16] Chapter 18, pp. 869–904 above. This raises the possibility of multilateral development banks being subjected to the application of 'lender liability' rules for the adverse or illegal environmental consequences of their loans.

[17] 'Environmental covenants' have been used by the EBRD to obtain assurances that, for the duration of the period in which it is supervising implementation of a loan, the environ-mental measures specified in the loan agreement are being met; see G. Rose, 3 *Yearbook of International Environmental Law* 545 (1992).

[18] Three other associated organisations are based within the World Bank: the Consulta-tive Group on International Agricultural Research (CGIAR); the International Centre for the Settlement of Investment Disputes (ICSID) (see chapter 21, p. 1062 below); and the Multilateral Investment Guarantee Agency (MIGA): (see chapter 21, p. 1071 below). In 1990, the Global Environment Facility was established by the World Bank, UNEP and UNDP; see pp. 1032–6 below.

[19] Washington, 27 December 1945, in force 27 December 1945, 2 UNTS 143 (as amended).

The IDA was established in 1959 to promote economic development in the least-developed countries by providing concessionary finance on more concessionary terms than the conventional loans provided by the IBRD.[20] The IDA finances projects and reform programmes in countries which would otherwise not be able to service loans from the IBRD. The IDA's resources come from contributions from developed and developing countries, including original subscriptions and nine replenishments, amounting to total resources of US$135 billion by the end of 2002. The IDA is subject to the World Bank's Directive on Environmental Assessment, and, in 1989, the Ninth Replenishment called for all IDA recipients to complete Environmental Action Plans by June 1993. The IDA has just been subject to its thirteenth replenishment.

The IFC was established in 1956, and became a specialised agency of the UN in 1957. The IFC is affiliated to the IBRD but has separate legal personality and maintains its capital separately from the IBRD.[21] The IFC invests in private or partly governmental enterprises together with private investors, with a commitment to providing finance in the private sector; its Environment and Social Development Department ensures that IFC-financed projects meet the IFC's environmental policies and guidelines. Since its founding, the IFC has committed more than US$34 billion of its own funds and has arranged US$21 billion in syndications for 2,825 companies in 140 developing countries.

The World Bank group provides financial support for a wide range of projects, some of which have had notorious adverse environmental consequences. Large infrastructure projects, particularly relating to energy, transport and other infrastructure, such as the construction of the Polonoreste dam in Brazil, have often resulted in significant environmental damage at the national and regional levels.[22] Smaller-scale projects, including in particular those relating to agriculture, transportation and energy, have also been criticised for failing to take into account long-term environmental costs, and for contributing to environmental degradation and unsustainable development in developing countries. In the late 1980s, the Bank embarked on a programme of restructuring, which included the creation of an Environment Department and the adoption of a number of Operational Directives (now Operational Policies, accompanied by Bank Policies) related to the environment. These included Directives on involuntary resettlement,[23] indigenous people,[24] the involvement of non-governmental organisations in World Bank supported activities,[25] and

---

[20] Washington, 26 January 1960, in force 26 September 1960, 439 UNTS 249.

[21] Washington, 25 May 1955, in force 20 July 1956, 264 UNTS 117, www.ifc.org/enviro/.

[22] See B. Rich, 'The Multilateral Development Banks, Environmental Policy and the United States', 12 *Ecology Law Quarterly* 681 at 705 (1985); see generally P. Le Prestre, *The World Bank and the Environment Challenge* (1989).

[23] Operational Directive 4.30 (1989); now Operational Policy (OP) 4.12.

[24] Operational Directive 4.20 (1989); now OP 4.20.

[25] Operational Directive 14.70 (1990); now OP 14.70.

environmental assessment.[26] In 1992, new environmental Operational Directives were issued in relation to National Environmental Action Plans[27] and agricultural pest management,[28] and subsequently policies have been adopted on natural habitats,[29] forests,[30] the safety of dams,[31] and projects on international waterways.[32] Also in 1992, the Executive Directors of the World Bank established a Rainforest Trust Fund, for which the Bank will act as trustee, to support a Pilot Programme to Conserve the Brazilian Rainforest.[33] In 2001, the Bank's directors adopted a five-year Environment Strategy. One of the Bank's eleven thematic groups is 'Environment and Natural Resources Management'.[34]

Regional and sub-regional development banks

The regional development banks also provide large-scale financial support in the form of loans to developing countries, which are used on a range of projects. Agenda 21 limits itself to calling for these banks and funds to play 'an increased and more effective' role in providing resources on concessional or other favourable terms to implement the activities set out in Agenda 21.[35]

The African Development Bank was established in 1963 under the auspices of the UN Economic Commission for Africa to 'contribute to the economic development and social progress of its members – individually and jointly'.[36] In 1987, an Environment Unit was established, and in 1990 the Board of Directors approved the Bank's Environment Policy Paper, which established guidelines for the environmental impact assessment of project and non-project loans.

The Inter-American Development Bank was established under the auspices of the Economic Conference of the OAS in 1959 to 'contribute to the acceleration of the process of economic and social development of the regional developing member countries'.[37] The Bank has a Sustainable Development Department (formerly an Environment Committee and an Environmental Protection Division established in 1990) to ensure that the Bank's operations comply with the environmental legislation of recipient countries and its own environmental impact assessment and related requirements.

---

[26] Operational Directive 4.01 (1991); now OP 4.01. See chapter 16, pp. 807–13 above.

[27] Operational Directive 4.02 (1992); now OP 4.02.

[28] Operational Directive 4.03 (1992); now OP 4.09.   [29] OP 4.04; chapter 11, p. 537 above.

[30] OP 4.36.   [31] OP 4.37.   [32] OP 7.50; chapter 10, p. 477 above.

[33] World Bank, *World Development Report 1992* (1992), 170.

[34] The portfolio is valued at approximately US$5.2 billion and addresses the following themes: biodiversity; climate change; environmental policies and institutions; land management; pollution management and environmental health; water resources management; other environmental and natural resources management.

[35] Para. 33.16(a)(ii); see also WSSD Plan of Implementation, para. 80.

[36] Khartoum, 4 August 1963, in force 10 September 1964, 510 UNTS 3 (www.afdb.org).

[37] Washington DC, 8 April 1959, in force 30 December 1989, 389 UNTS 69 (www.iadb.org); see IDB, *IDB and the Environment* (1990–2002).

The Asian Development Bank was established in 1965 under the auspices of the predecessor organisation to ESCAP.[38] It has had an Office of the Environment for some time, and in November 2002 adopted a new Environmental Policy paper which recommends means to adopt the new environmental policy.[39] It has guidelines for incorporating environmental impact assessments into its project cycles.

The Caribbean Development Bank was established in 1970 under the auspices of UNDP 'to contribute to the harmonious economic growth and development of the member countries in the Caribbean and to promote economic co-operation and integration among them, having special attention and urgent regard to the needs of the less developed member countries of the region'.[40] The Bank requires its borrowers to undertake an impact assessment of project proposals to ensure that they are environmentally sound and sustainable, and that any environmental consequences are taken into account in the project design.

The Islamic Development Bank was established in 1973 to foster the economic development and social progress of member countries and Muslim communities in accordance with the principles of *Shari'ah* (Islamic law).[41] The Bank participates in equity capital and grants loans for projects and enterprises and provides financial assistance to members for economic and social development. It requires the prior environmental assessment of projects before funds will be disbursed.

The European Bank for Reconstruction and Development was established in 1990 to contribute to the economic progress and reconstruction of the countries of Central and Eastern Europe and to apply the principles of multi-party democracy, pluralism and market economics.[42] The EBRD is the first multilateral development bank to include in its constitution a specific commitment to environmental protection. The EBRD is required to 'promote in the full range of its activities environmentally sound and sustainable development'.[43] This language implies that all of its activities must comply with environmental standards, although the Articles of Agreement do not specify the source of

---

[38] Manila, 4 December 1965, in force 22 August 1966, 571 UNTS 123 (www.adb.org).

[39] The ADB's Environment Policy contains five main elements: (1) promoting environment and natural resource management interventions to reduce poverty directly; (2) assisting developing member countries to mainstream environmental considerations in economic growth; (3) helping maintain global and regional life-support systems that underpin future development prospects; (4) building partnerships to maximise the impact of ADB lending and non-lending activities; and (5) integrating environmental considerations across all ADB operations.

[40] Kingston, 18 October 1969, in force 26 January 1970, 712 UNTS 217 (www.caribank.org).

[41] www.isdb.org.

[42] 23 ILM 1083 (1990). Art. 1 (www.ebrd.org); P. Sands, 'Present at the Creation: A New Development Bank for Europe in the Age of Environment Awareness', 84 *Proceedings of the American Society of International Law* 77 at 88–91 (1990).

[43] Art. 2(1)(vii).

these standards. Possible sources of environmental standards include those established by general international law, those established by the national law of
donor and/or recipient countries, or any applicable regional rules such as those
of EC environmental law. In performing its functions, the Bank is expressly
mandated to make loans and to provide technical assistance for the reconstruction or development of infrastructure, including environmental programmes.[44]
The Bank is also required to report annually on the environmental impact of
its activities.[45] The Bank has an Environmental Department, and since January
1992 the Bank has adopted detailed environmental procedures, including the
use of environmental assessments, environmental audits and environmental
covenants. The Bank administers three funds for nuclear safety.[46]

In the context of the EC, financial support of a general nature is provided
to projects both inside and outside the member states by the European Investment Bank, and to projects in EC member states by the general programme on
structural funds. The European Investment Bank is established by the EC Treaty
and has as its task to contribute to the 'balanced and steady development of the
common market' in the interest of the EC.[47] It operates on a non-profit-making
basis and provides loans and guarantees to facilitate the financing of three categories of projects: for developing less developed regions; for modernising or
converting companies or developing fresh activities where these projects are
too large or complex to be financed by individual member states; and projects
of common interest to several member states which cannot be financed entirely
by those member states. The protection of the environment is stated to be one
of its five operational priorities, and it currently has an Environmental Assessment Group, an Environmental . . . Unit and . . . an Environmental Steering
Committee. As an institution of the EC, the Bank is subject to compliance with
the standards and procedures established under EC environmental law.[48]

Environment funds

The establishment of the Multilateral Fund (under the 1990 amendments to the
1987 Montreal Protocol) and the Global Environmental Facility highlights the
growing connection between the development and application of environmental rules and standards and the provision of financial resources to ensure their
implementation, particularly by developing countries. In fact, the provision of

[44] Art. 11(1)(v).   [45] Art. 35(2).

[46] A Nuclear Safety Account (to improve safety at nuclear plants); International Decommissioning Support Funds for Bulgaria, Lithuania and the Slovak Republic (to support the decommissioning of high-risk nuclear plants); and the Chernobyl Shelter Fund
(to contribute to the costs of a Chernobyl Shelter Implementation Plan, at a cost of
US$768 million).

[47] Arts. 266 and 267 (formerly Arts. 198d and 198e) of the EC Treaty (www.eib.org).

[48] On those standards, see generally chapter 15 above.

international financial resources dedicated to international environmental protection goals, and the establishment of the necessary mechanisms, dates back at least to 1972 when the World Heritage Convention established the World Heritage Fund. This was followed in 1972 by the creation of the voluntary UNEP Environment Fund, and subsequently by funds established under the UNEP Regional Seas Programme.[49] In 1990, a Wetlands Fund was established under the 1971 Ramsar Convention, and the 1989 Basel Convention allows the parties to decide on the establishment of 'appropriate funding mechanisms of a voluntary nature' and to consider the establishment of a revolving fund to assist on an interim basis in case of emergency situations to minimise damage from accidents.[50] The EC has a financial instrument (LIFE) and a cohesion financial instrument which is to provide financial assistance for environmental projects; both instruments supplement the activities of the EC Structural Funds, the European Investment Bank and funds dedicated to Central and Eastern Europe under the PHARE programme. Other funds which provide financial resources in the form of compensation for environmental damage include the Kuwait Compensation Fund,[51] and the International Oil Pollution Fund.[52]

UNEP Environment Fund

The voluntary Environment Fund established by General Assembly Resolution 2997 was established to enable the UNEP Governing Council to fulfil its policy guidance role for the direction and co-ordination of activities.[53] It finances the whole or partial costs of new environmental initiatives within the UN system, including monitoring and data-collection, environmental research, information exchange, research on appropriate technologies, and such other programmes as the Governing Council may decide upon.[54] In 2002, the Fund received contributions of about US$45 million.

World Heritage Fund

The Fund for the Protection of the World Cultural and Natural Heritage was established under Article 15 of the World Heritage Convention.[55] It is a trust fund which grants financial assistance to protect cultural and natural heritage of outstanding universal value, and is administered by the World Heritage Committee. In 2002, the Fund administered a budget of approximately US$3.5 million, raised by a combination of voluntary and compulsory contributions. The majority was spent on technical co-operation and training, with the remainder spent on preparatory assistance and regional studies, emergency assistance and advisory services.

---

[49] Chapter 9, pp. 426–7 above.   [50] Art. 14.
[51] Chapter 18, pp. 890–4 above.   [52] Chapter 18, p. 894 above.
[53] UNGA Res. 2997 (XXVII) (1972).   [54] Part III, paras. 2 and 3.
[55] Chapter 11, pp. 611–15 above (http://whc.unesco.org/ab_fund.htm).

Wetlands Fund

The Wetland Conservation Fund was established in 1990 by the conference of the parties to the 1971 Ramsar Convention to assist developing country parties to implement their obligations under the Convention.[56] The Fund is operated in a similar way to the World Heritage Fund, and provides assistance to developing countries, upon their request, to support wetland conservation in one of four fields: improving the management of sites on the Ramsar List; designating new sites; promoting 'wise use'; and supporting regional and promotional activities. Developing countries which are not parties may request support for the designation of a site for the List, which is a condition for becoming a party. The Fund is administered by the Standing Committee to the Convention and by the Bureau.

Montreal Protocol Multilateral Fund

R. Bowser, 'History of the Montreal Protocol's Ozone Fund', 14 *International Environmental Reporter* 6356 (1991); P. Lawrence, 'Technology Transfer Funds and the Law: Recent Amendments to the Montreal Protocol on Substances that Deplete the Ozone Layer', 4 JEL 15 (1992); J. Patlis, 'The Multilateral Fund of the Montreal Protocol: A Prototype for Financial Mechanism in Protecting the Global Environment', 25 *Cornell International Law Journal* 181 (1992); F. Biermann, 'Financing Environmental Policies in the South: Experiences from the Multilateral Ozone Fund', 9 *International Environmental Affairs* 179 (1997).

The 1990 amendments to the 1987 Montreal Protocol established a mechanism, including a Multilateral Fund, to provide financial and technical co-operation, including the transfer of technologies, to developing country parties to enable their compliance with the control measures established under the Protocol.[57] The Multilateral Fund operates under the authority of the parties who decide on its overall policies.[58] The Fund meets on a grant or concessional basis the 'agreed incremental costs' of developing country parties in order to enable their compliance with the control measures of the Montreal Protocol; finances

---

[56] Conf. Res. C.4.3; on the 1971 Ramsar Convention, see chapter 11, pp. 543–5 above. In 1997, the Ramsar secretariat and the United States established a separate 'Wetlands for the Future Fund'.

[57] 1987 Montreal Protocol, as amended in 1990, Art. 10(1)–(3) (www.unmfs.org). The parties have adopted an Indicative List of Categories of Incremental Costs: Appendix I to Decision II/8 ('Financial Mechanism') adopted by the Second Meeting of the Parties, UNEP/OzL.Pro.2/3, Annex IV, 29 June 1990.

[58] The amount was raised to US$240 million when India and China became parties (for 1991–3). It has subsequently been replenished in the amount of US$455 million (1994–6), US$466 million (1997–9) and US$440 million (2000–2). It has funded about 3,850 projects in 124 developing countries, and is estimated to have resulted in the phase-out of the consumption of some 150,000 tonnes of ozone-depleting products and the production of nearly 50,000 tonnes of ozone-depleting products.

clearing-house functions to assist in identifying co-operation needs, to facilitate technical co-operation, to distribute information and relevant materials, to hold workshops, and to facilitate and monitor other co-operation available; and finances the secretarial services of the Fund.[59] An Executive Committee, comprising seven developed and seven developing country parties, implements specific operational policies guidelines and administrative arrangements, including the disbursement of resources, with the co-operation and assistance of the World Bank, UNEP, UNDP and UNIDO.[60] The Fund is administered by the World Bank as the implementing agency under the agreement between the Fund's Executive Committee and the World Bank. The Fund is financed by countries not operating under Article 5(1) (i.e. by developed countries) in currency or in kind on the basis of the United Nations scale of assessments, and allows bilateral and agreed regional co-operation to be considered as a contribution to the Fund provided that such co-operation, as a minimum, relates to compliance with the Montreal Protocol, provides additional resources and meets incremental costs.[61] The concurrence of the beneficiary party is required, and decisions taken under the Fund are to be taken by consensus whenever possible, but otherwise by a two-thirds majority of the parties present and voting, including a 'double majority' of developed country parties and of developing country parties.[62]

Global Environment Facility

J. Helland-Hansen, 'The Global Environment Facility', 3 *International Environmental Affairs* 137 (1991); L. Boisson de Chazournes, 'Le Fonds pour l'environnement mondial: recherche et conquête de son identité', AFDI 612 (1995).

The Global Environment Facility (GEF) was established in 1990 as a three-year 'experiment' to provide grants for investment projects, technical assistance and research to developing countries to protect the global environment and to transfer environmentally benign technologies.[63] The establishment of the GEF followed a proposal by France in September 1989 and materials prepared in 1990 by the World Bank in consultation with UNEP and UNDP, on the understanding that no new institutional structures would be created and only

---

[59] Art. 10(1), (3) and (4); see Terms of Reference of the Multilateral Fund, Appendix IV to Decision IV/8 ('Financial Mechanism'), n. 57 above.

[60] Art. 10(5). See *Terms of Reference of the Executive Committee*, Appendix II to Decision II/8 ('Financial Mechanism'), n. 57 above.

[61] Art. 10(6).   [62] Art. 10(8) and (9).

[63] Res. No. 91-5 of the Executive Directors of the World Bank, November 1991. See also World Bank Operational Directive 9.01 on investment operations under the GEF. The GEF Secretariat has suggested that the restructured GEF should be established in the same legal manner as the GEF in its first phase: see GEF, 'Legal Framework', draft of 6 November 1992, para. 2. See 'Global Environment Facility: The Pilot Phase and Beyond', Working Paper Series No. I, May 1992 (World Bank, UNDP, UNEP).

minimal changes would be made to the three implementing agencies.[64] The first meeting of participating countries was held in May 1991. The resolution provided for the establishment of the GEF, comprising the Global Environment Trust Fund (GET), co-financing arrangements with the GET, the Ozone Projects Trust Fund and such other trust funds and agreements as the World Bank may from time to time establish or agree to administer under the GET.

In March 1994, representatives of the then seventy-three states participating in the GEF's pilot phase and of other states wanting to participate in the restructured GEF accepted an Instrument for the Establishment of the Restructured GEF.[65] The Instrument entered into force through subsequent adoption by the governing bodies of UNDP, UNEP and the World Bank. The World Bank serves as trustee of the GEF Trust Fund, which receives and administers contributions.[66] Any member of the UN or its specialised agencies may become a participant in the restructured GEF. The arrangements for the governance of the GEF reflect the complexities of dividing responsibilities between donor and recipient participant states: it comprises an Assembly, a Council and a secretariat, and a Scientific and Technical Advisory Panel (STAP) provides advice.[67] The Assembly consists of representatives of all of the participants, and has responsibility for reviewing the general policies of the GEF and its operation, and for adopting amendments to the Instrument.[68] The Council has responsibility for operational policies and programmes, and consists of thirty-two members (sixteen from developing countries, fourteen from developed countries, and two from countries from Central and Eastern Europe and the former USSR), some of which represent a constituency of states.[69] The Implementing Agencies are UNDP, UNEP and the World Bank (which collaborate in accordance with an inter-agency agreement),[70] and they are accountable to the Council for their GEF-financed activities, which is itself under an obligation to ensure that the GEF operate, *inter alia*, in conformity with the policies, programme priorities and eligibility criteria decided by the conferences of the parties of

---

[64] The establishment of the GEF was endorsed by Res. 16/47 of the UNEP Governing Council, 13 May 1991, and Decision 92/16 of the UNDP Governing Council, 26 May 1992. Procedural arrangements for operational co-operation under the GEF were signed by the Executive Heads of the World Bank, UNDP and UNEP: see Res. No. 91-5, Annex C.

[65] Instrument Establishing the GEF, Geneva, 16 March 1994, 33 ILM 1273 (1994).

[66] See Annex B (Role and Fiduciary Responsibility of the Trustee of the GEF Trust Fund), providing that the Trustee is accountable to the Council: para. 2.

[67] Paras. 7, 11 and 24. The Assembly comprises representatives of all Participants, whereas the Council consists of representatives of thirty-two members representing constituency groups (sixteen from developing countries, fourteen from developed countries and two from Central and Eastern Europe: paras. 13 and 16, and Annex E (Constituencies of the GEF Council).

[68] Paras. 13–14.   [69] Paras. 15–20.

[70] Annex D (Principles of Co-operation Among the Implementing Agencies).

the conventions which it supports.[71] To that end, the Council has approved co-operative arrangements or agreements with the conferences of the parties to the conventions.[72]

According to the Instrument, the GEF is to provide 'new and additional grant and concessional funding to meet the agreed incremental costs of measures to achieve agreed global environmental benefits' in the following areas: climate change; biodiversity; international waters; and ozone layer depletion. Also eligible for funding are the agreed incremental costs of activities concerning land degradation, primarily desertification and deforestation.[73] The GEF has been designated as the financial mechanism under three conventions (the 1992 Climate Change Convention, the 1992 Biodiversity Convention and the 2001 POPs Convention); it funds projects that combat desertification and protect international watercourses and the ozone layer; and it has been designated to manage other funds, such as the Adaptation Fund, the Least Developed Countries Fund and the Special Convention Fund (all under the 1992 Climate Change Convention).

The restructured GEF was originally capitalised at US$2 billion (over three years); in August 2002, thirty-two donor states pledged nearly US$3 billion to finance the GEF over the following four years. Allocation of the GEF's resources has been principally directed towards climate change and biodiversity.[74]

UNCED and the relationship with the Biodiversity and Climate Change Conventions

On an interim basis and subject to its restructuring, the GEF was confirmed as the financial mechanism for Agenda 21 and the Climate Change and Biodiversity Conventions. Agenda 21 identified the GEF as the financial mechanism to cover the 'agreed incremental costs of relevant activities under Agenda 21' subject to the fulfilment of six conditions. The GEF should: be restructured to encourage universal participation; have sufficient flexibility; ensure transparent and democratic governance; ensure new and additional financial resources on grant and concessional terms; ensure predictability in the flow of funds; and ensure access to and disbursement of funds under mutually agreed criteria without introducing new forms of conditionality.[75] The 1994 Instrument achieved that restructuring.

---

[71] Paras. 12, 22, 26 and 27, and Annex D.   [72] Para. 27.   [73] Paras. 2 and 3.

[74] Between 1991 and 1999, the GEF allocated US$991 million in grants, and mobilised an additional US$1.5 billion in co-financing for biological diversity projects (addressing US$884 million to 227 climate change projects and enabling activities, which was matched by more than US$4.7 billion in co-financing; US$360 million to international waters initiatives; US$155 million to projects to phase out ozone-depleting substances; US$350 million on projects relating to deforestation and desertification.

[75] Agenda 21, Chapter 33, para. 33.16(a)(iii).

The 1992 Biodiversity Convention requires developed country parties to provide 'new and additional' financial resources to enable developing country parties to meet the agreed full incremental cost of implementing their commitments under the Convention, and links such implementation with the effective implementation by developed country parties of their financial commitments under the Convention.[76] The Convention establishes a mechanism for the provision of financial resources to developing countries on a grant or concessional basis which 'shall function under the authority and guidance of, and be accountable to, the conference of the parties for the purpose of this Convention'.[77] The conference of the parties designated the GEF as the institutional structure to carry out the operations of the mechanisms and will determine the 'policy, strategy, programme priorities and eligibility criteria' relating to access to and use of the resources.[78]

The 1992 Climate Change Convention also requires the developed country parties to provide new and additional financial resources to developing country parties, and links the implementation by developing country parties of their commitments to the fulfilment by developed country parties of their financial commitments.[79] It establishes a mechanism for the provision of financial resources on a grant or concessional basis which shall function 'under the guidance of and be accountable to' the conference of the parties, which will decide on its policies, programme priorities and eligibility criteria related to the Convention.[80] The financial mechanism under the Climate Change Convention is not defined as being under the 'authority' of the conference of the parties, unlike the financial mechanism to be established by the Biodiversity Convention. The financial mechanism of the Climate Change Convention is to have an 'equitable and balanced representation of all parties within a transparent system of governance', and the conference of the parties and the entity entrusted with the operation of the mechanism will agree upon the working arrangements, including: the modalities to ensure that funded projects conform with the policies, programme priorities and eligibility criteria established by the conference of the parties and that particular funding decisions may be reconsidered; the provision of regular reports to the conference of the parties on funding operations; and the determination of the amounts of funding necessary

---

[76] 1992 Biodiversity Convention, Art. 20(2) and (4), and its 2000 Biosafety Protocol, Art. 28; see chapter 12, pp. 653–8 above. The 2001 Treaty on Plant Genetic Resources commits parties to 'implement a funding strategy' to ensure 'the effective allocation of predictable and agreed resources' for the implementation of the Treaty, but calls for the establishment of a 'Trust Account' rather than a financial mechanism, and no express reference is made in the Treaty to the GEF: Arts. 18(1) and (4) and 19(3)(f) (chapter 11, p. 553 above). The 1994 Desertification Convention calls for 'the availability of financial mechanisms' and establishes a Global Mechanism to 'promote actions leading to the mobilization and channelling of substantial financial resources': Art. 21(1) and (4).
[77] Art. 21(1).   [78] *Ibid.*   [79] Art. 4(3) and (7).   [80] Art. 11(1).

and available in a predictable and identifiable manner.[81] The conference of the parties has designated the GEF as the international entity entrusted with the operation of the financial mechanism.[82]

The 2001 POPs Convention similarly requires developed country parties to provide new and additional financial resources to enable developing country parties and economies in transition to 'meet the agreed full incremental costs of implementing' measures required by the Convention, as agreed between the recipient party and the financial mechanism.[83] The GEF is entrusted with the operations of the financial mechanisms (pending designation by the conference of the parties), which is to provide 'adequate and sustainable financial resources . . . on a grant or concessional basis'.[84]

An important issue which has emerged is the legal relationship between the conferences of the parties of the various Conventions and the GEF Participants' Assembly, and in particular whether the conferences of the parties will have the final say on individual funding decisions or more general decisions taken by the GEF. Under the Conventions, the ultimate decision-making power rests with the conferences of the parties, which are granted the right to decide on the 'policies, programme priorities and eligibility criteria' of the financial mechanism (the Biodiversity Convention also grants power over 'strategies'), and in the event that the financial mechanism is not being operated to the satisfaction of the conferences of the parties each will be free to take a decision redesignating the international institution operating the mechanism. In that sense, the GEF and its Participants' Assembly are, ultimately, accountable to the conferences of the parties and, in the case of the Biodiversity and POPs Conventions, under the 'authority' of the respective conferences of the parties. Whether the GEF and the Participants' Assembly are accountable to the conferences of the parties for each individual funding decision is less clear, but the ultimate sanction of 'redesignation' provides an incentive to the GEF to ensure that the wishes of the conferences of the parties are followed, or at least of those parties comprising the particular majority of parties which may be required to adopt a decision on the designation or redesignation of the financial mechanism.[85]

EC financial resources

Apart from the general programme on structural funds (which are not dedicated to environmental-protection-related issues),[86] the EC has created two specialised instruments to provide financial resources for environmental protection. The financial instrument for the environment (LIFE) was created in 1992

---

[81] Art. 11(2) and (3).   [82] Art. 21(3).   [83] Art. 13(2).   [84] Arts. 13(6) and 14.

[85] See 1992 Climate Change Convention, Art. 7(3); 1992 Biodiversity Convention, Art. 23(3); 2001 POPs Convention, Art. 13(8).

[86] See above; see also *Greenpeace* v. *EC Commission*, chapter 5, p. 177 above.

and, as revised in 2000, aims to contribute to 'the implementation, updating and development of Community environment policy and of environmental legislation, in particular as regards the integration of the environment into other policies, and to sustainable development in the Community'.[87] It is divided into three components – LIFE-Nature, LIFE-Environment and LIFE-Third Countries – and provides financial assistance in those three fields.[88] Assistance is provided in the form of co-financing of actions and interest rebates, with 640 million euros available for the period 2000–4 (LIFE III).[89]

The second instrument established by the EC is a cohesion financial instrument established in 1993 to provide financial contributions to projects in the field of the environment and trans-European transport infrastructures in low-income EC member states (Greece, Spain, Ireland and Portugal). The instrument was established on an interim basis pending the establishment of the Cohesion Fund envisaged in ex Article 104c of the Treaty on European Union.[90] The cohesion financial instrument now provides assistance of approximately 2.6 billion euros per annum, for the period 2000–6, *inter alia*, for environmental projects contributing to the achievement of the objective of Article 174 (formerly Article 130r) of the EC Treaty.[91] Assistance for projects will be provided at a rate of 80–85 per cent of public or similar expenditure, and financial projects must be in conformity with the provisions of the EC Treaty, including those concerning environmental protection.[92]

Technology transfer and technical assistance[93]

C. Okolie, *Legal Aspects of the International Transfer of Technology to Developing Countries* (1975); C. P. Jeffries, 'Regulation of the Transfer of Technology: An Evaluation of the UNCTAD Code of Conduct', 18 *Harvard International Law Journal* 309 (1977); S. K. Agrawala, 'Transfer of Technology to LDCs: Implications of the Proposed Code', 23 *Indian Journal of International Law* 246 (1983); M. A. Bent, 'Exporting Hazardous Industries: Should American Standards Apply?', 20 NYUJILP 777 (1988); R. E. Lutz, 'The Export of Danger: A View from the Developed World', 20 NYUJILP 629 (1988); M. Blakeney, *Legal Aspects of Technology Transfer to*

---

[87] Regulation (EC) No. 1655/2000 on the Financial Instrument for the Environment (LIFE), OJ L192, 28 July 2000, 1, Art. 1.

[88] Arts. 3–5. LIFE projects must meet the following general criteria: be of Community interest; be carried out by technically and financially sound participants; and be feasible in terms of technical proposals, timetable, budget and value for money.

[89] Art. 8.

[90] Council Regulation (EC) No. 93/792 OJ L79, 1 April 1993, 74, Art. 1; now Council Regulation (EC) No. 1164/94 establishing a Cohesion Fund, OJ L130, 25 May 1994, 1 (as amended by Council Regulation (EC) No. 1264/99, OJ L161, 26 June 1999, 57).

[91] Arts. 2(1) and 3.   [92] Arts. 7 and 8.

[93] See M. Blakeney, *Legal Aspects of the Transfer of Technology to Developing Countries* (1989).

Developing Countries (1989) (and bibliography cited at 190–202); T. A. Cinti 'The Regulator's Dilemma: Should Best Available Technology or Cost Benefit Analysis Be Used to Determine the Applicable Hazardous Waste Treatment, Storage, and Disposal Technology?', 16 *Rutgers Computer and Technology Law Journal* 145 (1990); M. Lachs, 'Thoughts on Science, Technology and World Law', 86 AJIL 673 (1992); G. MacDonald, 'Technology Transfer: The Climate Change Challenge', 1 *Journal of Environment and Development* 1 (1992); L. Gundling, 'Compliance Assistance in International Environmental Law: Capacity Building Through Financial and Technology Transfer', 56 ZaöRV 796 (1996).

One of the major problems facing the international community is the use of obsolete, environmentally damaging techniques by industry in many countries. The wider dissemination and use of state-of-the-art technologies, including 'clean technologies', would go a long way to reducing the damaging effects of certain activities, and international law is now grappling with the problem of how to encourage or require the transfer of environmentally-sound technologies, particularly to developing countries. Until recently, the provisions of international environmental treaties concerning the transfer of technology and know-how, as well as the provision of technical assistance, particularly from developed to developing countries, established only vague and general commitments of limited value and effect. The inadequacy of many treaty provisions on technology transfer has been widely recognised, and developments reflected in the provisions of recent treaties suggest that technology transfer provisions are acquiring an enhanced legal and practical significance, with renewed efforts to address the issues properly.

A first development is the broad recognition of the need to ensure that financial resources are available to meet the costs of transferring environmentally-sound technologies and know-how, which has contributed to the establishment of the international mechanisms to channel resources. A second development is the linkage which has been made between the implementation by developing country parties of their treaty commitments with the transfer of technology and know-how from developed country parties in fulfilment of their treaty obligations. A third development, which seeks to address the problem that the application of intellectual property rights might raise barriers to the transfer of environmentally sound technologies, is considered in a later section of this chapter.

As early as 1972, Principle 12 of the Stockholm Declaration recognised the need to make international technical assistance available to developing countries, and Principle 20 called for 'environmental technologies to be made available to developing countries on terms which would encourage their wide dissemination without constituting an economic burden'. Twenty years later, Agenda 21 devoted an entire chapter to the subject of technology transfer and related issues.

Technology transfer is a term which is frequently used, with little consideration given to what it actually means. In general terms, 'technology transfer' describes the specific communication of a body of knowledge which is enshrined in a particular transaction, comprising an integrated sequence of commercial or non-commercial transactions, which might include the following:

> the grant or assignment of industrial property rights; the communication of technical know-how in a documentary form; the communication of technical or other know-how in the supply of services; assistance in the commissioning of an industrial plant; the sale or lease of machinery or the provision of services in relation to the sale or lease of machinery; providing services to assist in the recruitment and training of staff and the institutions of managerial and accounting procedures; providing services in relation to the marketing and distribution of the product of the plant.[94]

In the context of international environmental agreements, technology transfer could include each one of these aspects, as well as larger infrastructure projects and technologies and services specifically related to environmental know-how.

Treaty provisions

The lack of real progress in establishing practical and effective means to ensure the transfer of environmentally-sound technology is evident from the unsuccessful efforts of the international community to elaborate an International Code of Conduct on the Transfer of Technology to establish basic rules of general application governing the transfer of technology, under the auspices of UNCTAD and the World Intellectual Property Organization (WIPO).[95] Progress on the subject was equally limited under early international environmental agreements. Early treaties included general language on the exchange of information on appropriate technologies.[96] UNCLOS included a more detailed commitment to technology transfer, in particular to developing countries. Part XIV contains thirteen Articles on the development and transfer of marine technology, and adopts language subsequently relied upon in the UNCED

[94] *Ibid.*, 3.

[95] The Code would establish rules on, *inter alia*: objectives and principles; national regulations; restrictive business practices; responsibilities and obligations of parties to technology transfer transactions; special treatment for developing countries; international collaboration; and institutional and dispute settlement mechanisms. For recent developments, see UNGA Res. 46/214 (1991); UNCTAD, 'A New Partnership for Development: The Cartagena Commitment', UN Doc. TD(VIII)/Misc. 4, 27 February 1992, paras. 173–4; Agenda 21, Chapter 34, para. 34.18(f). By 1993, it became clear that agreement on a Code would not be forthcoming: UNGA Res. 48/167 (1993). On the history of the Code, see M. Blakeney, *Legal Aspects of the Transfer of Technology to Developing Countries* (1989), 131–61.

[96] See 1979 LRTAP Convention, Art. 8(c); 1988 NO_x Protocol, Art. 3 (Exchange of Technology); 1991 VOC Protocol, Art. 4 (Exchange of Technology).

instruments. UNCLOS calls for the development and transfer of science and marine technology on 'fair and reasonable terms and conditions' as a principal objective, taking into account the capabilities of states with regard to, *inter alia*, the conservation and management of marine resources and the protection and preservation of the marine environment, and should seek to accelerate the social and economic development of the developing states.[97] Under UNCLOS, states commit themselves to: foster favourable economic and legal conditions for technology transfer for the benefit of all parties concerned on an equitable basis;[98] promote the acquisition, evaluation and dissemination of marine technological knowledge; facilitate access to information and data; develop appropriate marine technology; and develop the necessary infrastructure to facilitate the transfer of technology.[99] Under Article 269, states are required to endeavour to, *inter alia*:

> establish programmes of technical co-operation for the effective transfer of all kinds of marine technology to states which may need and request technical assistance in this field, particularly the developing land-locked and geographically disadvantaged states, as well as other developing states which have not been able either to establish or develop their own technological capacity in marine science and in the exploration and exploitation of marine resources or to develop the infrastructure of such technology

and to promote 'favourable conditions for the conclusion of agreements, contracts and other similar arrangements, under equitable and reasonable conditions'.[100] Further commitments are adopted to foster international co-operation and to establish national and regional marine scientific and technological centres whose function will include compiling information on the marketing of technology and on contracts and other arrangements concerning patents.[101] The UNEP Regional Seas Conventions include rather more general commitments on scientific and technical co-operation.[102] Other conventions providing for the promotion of clean technologies include the 1994 Desertification Convention[103] and, in relation to technical assistance, the 2001 POPs Convention.[104]

The ozone regime

More concrete legal developments in relation to the transfer of technology occurred under the regime established by the 1985 Vienna Convention and the

---

[97] Art. 266(1) and (2).   [98] Art. 266(3).   [99] Art. 268.   [100] Art. 269.

[101] Arts. 270 to 278, especially Art. 277(h). See also Art. 144 (technology transfer relating to activities in the Area) and Art. 202 (technical assistance to developing countries).

[102] 1980 Athens LBS Protocol, Arts. 9 and 10; 1983 Cartagena Convention, Art. 13; 1985 Nairobi Convention, Art. 14; 1986 Noumea Convention, Arts. 17 and 18; see chapter 9, p. 399 above.

[103] Art. 18.   [104] Art. 12.

1987 Montreal Protocol. The earlier treaty required parties to facilitate and en-courage the exchange of scientific, technical, socio-economic, commercial and legal information and to co-operate, in consistency with their national laws, in promoting the 'development and transfer of technology and knowledge'.[105] The original 1987 Montreal Protocol provided for co-operation in information exchange and in promoting technical assistance to developing countries to fa-cilitate participation in and implementation of the Protocol.[106] It was only with the 1990 amendments that the Montreal Protocol required each party to take steps to ensure that the 'best available, environmentally safe substitutes and re-lated technologies are expeditiously transferred to' developing country parties and that those transfers occur under 'fair and most favourable conditions'.[107] The establishment of the Multilateral Fund, providing financial resources to meet the incremental costs of enabling compliance by developing country par-ties with their obligations, has provided significant funds to meet the cost of supplying substitutes to controlled substances.[108] The Montreal Protocol may also be interpreted as prohibiting the transfer of technologies which do not satisfy the standards of being 'environmentally safe', without expressly stating that commitment.

Biodiversity Convention

The 1992 Biodiversity Convention establishes a range of provisions which will go some way to encouraging, but still not actually requiring, the transfer of technology. The Convention also addresses the relationship between technol-ogy transfer and intellectual property rights. The Convention links the effective implementation by developing countries of their commitments with the effec-tive implementation by developed country parties of their commitments related to, *inter alia*, transfer of technology.[109] The appropriate standard which tech-nologies should satisfy are also elaborated: parties must provide and/or facilitate access for and transfer to other parties of 'technologies that are relevant to the conservation and sustainable use of biological 'diversity or make use of genetic resources and do not cause significant damage to the environment'.[110] The ac-cess and transfer to developing country parties of those technologies should take place under 'fair and most favourable terms, including on concessional and preferential terms where mutually agreed' and on terms which recognise

---

[105] 1985 Vienna Convention, Art. 4 and Annex II.

[106] 1987 Montreal Protocol, Arts. 9 and 10.

[107] 1987 Montreal Protocol as amended in 1990, Art. 10A.

[108] Art. 10(1); see now Annex VIII, Indicative List of Categories of Incremental Costs, UNEP/OzL.Pro.4/15, 25 November 1992, 51; on the Fund see pp. 1031–2 above.

[109] Art. 20(4). The definition of 'technology' simply states that it includes 'biotechnology': Art. 2.

[110] Art. 16(1). See also conference of the parties Decisions II/5 and III/16.

and are consistent with the adequate and effective protection of intellectual property rights.[111] Technologies which make use of genetic resources provided by parties, in particular developing country parties, are to be accessed by and transferred to those parties on 'mutually agreed terms', including technology protected by patents and other intellectual property rights, where necessary, through the provision of the Convention relating to financial resources and the financial mechanism.[112] Moreover, each party must take appropriate measures with the aim that the private sector facilitates access to, joint development of and transfer of these technologies.[113] The Convention's financial mechanism should meet some of the costs of technology transfer as 'agreed full incremental costs'.[114]

Climate Change Convention

Similar provisions appear in the 1992 Climate Change Convention, which requires all parties to promote and co-operate in 'full, open and prompt' exchange of relevant scientific, technical, socio-economic and legal information related to the climate system and climate change.[115] The provision of financial resources by developed country parties includes resources for the transfer of technology, and those parties undertake to take 'all practicable steps to promote, facilitate, and finance, as appropriate, the transfer of, or access to, environmentally sound technologies and know-how to other parties, particularly developing country parties, to enable them to implement the provisions of the Convention'.[116] This process includes support for the enhancement of endogenous capacities and technologies of developing country parties. Developing country parties are also encouraged to voluntarily propose projects, including specific technologies needed to implement projects.[117] The Clean Development Mechanism established under Article 12 of the 1997 Kyoto Protocol will go a considerable way towards facilitating the transfer of environmental technologies, particularly in the energy sector.[118]

UNCED and WSSD

Chapter 34 of Agenda 21 ('Transfer of Environmentally Sound Technology, Co-operation and Capacity-Building') reflects the commitment, albeit a limited one, of the international community concerning technology transfer and technical assistance. The main objectives of Agenda 21 in this regard are to help ensure access to scientific and technological information, and to:

[111] Art. 16(2).   [112] Art. 16(3). See also Arts. 20 and 21.   [113] Art. 16(4).
[114] Art. 20(1) and (2).   [115] Art. 4(1)(h).   [116] Arts. 4(5) and 11(1).
[117] Art. 4(1).   [118] Chapter 8, p. 373 above.

> promote, facilitate and finance, as appropriate, the access to and the transfer of environmentally sound technologies and corresponding know-how, in particular to developing countries, on favourable terms, including on concessional and preferential terms, as mutually agreed, taking into account the need to protect intellectual property rights as well as the special needs of developing countries for the implementation of Agenda 21.[119]

Further objectives include: promoting environmentally sound indigenous technologies; supporting endogenous capacity-building; and promoting long-term partnerships between holders of technologies and potential users.[120] Similar provisions are reflected in Principle 9 of the Rio Declaration, which declares that:

> states should co-operate to strengthen endogenous capacity-building for sustainable development by improving scientific understanding through exchanges of scientific and technological knowledge, and by enhancing the development, adaptation, diffusion and transfer of technologies, including new and innovative technologies.

Both of these instruments set out 'safe' commitments, and it will be left for more formal treaty arrangements to translate the objectives into the actual transfer of technology. The WSSD Plan of Implementation does little more than restate the 1992 commitments.[121]

Intellectual property

S. Lall, 'The Patent System and the Transfer of Technologies to Less Developed Countries', 10 *Journal of World Trade Law* 1 (1976); W. R. Cornish, *Intellectual Property: Patents, Copyright, Trade Marks and Allied Rights* (1990); M. Gollin, 'Using Intellectual Property to Improve Environmental Protection', 4 *Harvard Journal of Law and Technology* 193 (1991); N. Atkinson and B. Sherman, 'Intellectual Property and Environmental Protection', 13 *European Intellectual Property Review* 165 (1991); G. Winter, 'Patent Law Policy in Biotechnology', 4 JEL 167 (1992); R. Margulies, 'Protecting Biodiversity: Recognizing International Intellectual Property Rights in Plant Genetic Resources', 14 *Michigan Journal of International Law* 322 (1993); D. Alexander, 'Some Themes in Intellectual Property and the Environment', 2 RECIEL 113 (1993); F. Yamin and D. Posey, 'Indigenous Peoples, Biotechnology and Intellectual Property Rights', 2 RECIEL 141 (1993); M. Footer, 'Intellectual Property and Agrobiodiversity: Towards Private Ownership of Genetic Commons', 10 *Yearbook of International Environment Law* 48 (1999); G. Dutfield, *Intellectual Property Rights, Trade and Biodiversity: Seeds and Plant Varieties* (2000); UK Department for International Development, *Integrating Intellectual Property*

---

[119] Agenda 21, Chapter 34, para. 34.14(a) and (b).
[120] Para. 34.14(c)–(e).   [121] Paras. 99–100.

Rights and Development Policy: Report of the Commission on Intellectual Property Rights (2002); P. Drahos and M. Blakeney, *Intellectual Property, in Biodiversity and Agriculture* (2001).

'Intellectual property' refers to property rights protected by laws which protect the application of thoughts, ideas and information which are of commercial value, including the law relating to patents, copyrights, trademarks, trade secrets and other similar rights.[122] Legal issues arising out of the application of patent and other intellectual property rights have been raised in the development of international environmental law and policy, in three broad areas: first, the extent to which intellectual property rights granted, for example, in accordance with the WTO Agreement on Trade-Related Aspects of Intellectual Property Rights (TRIPs), may limit the transfer of environmentally sound technology as required by international conventions; secondly, whether intellectual property rights should be granted to potentially environmentally damaging technologies, for example the grant of patents in respect of living organisms (biotechnology); and, thirdly, the extent to which intellectual property rights can or should protect indigenous environmental knowledge which has been in the public domain for decades or more.

Technology transfer

The first issue concerns the claim by developed states, in the negotiation of international environmental agreements, that they are precluded from imposing technology transfer requirements on persons within their jurisdiction or control because of their obligations under national and international laws for the protection of intellectual property,[123] patents[124] and biotechnology.[125]

---

[122] See W. R. Cornish, *Intellectual Property: Patents, Copyright, Trade Marks and Allied Rights* (1990). See also M. Blakeney, *Legal Aspects of Technology Transfer to Developing Countries* (1989).

[123] The principal international agreements include the Convention for the Protection of Industrial Property, Paris, 20 March 1883, in force 6 July 1884, 10 Martens (2d) 133 (as revised, see 828 UNTS 305).

[124] The relevant agreements include the Patent Co-operation Treaty, Washington DC, 19 June 1970, in force 24 January 1978, 9 ILM 978 (1970); Convention on the Grant of European Patents, Munich, 5 October 1973, in force 7 October 1977, 13 ILM 270 (1973), (1973 European Patent Convention); Convention for the European Patent for the Common Market, Luxembourg, 15 December 1975, not in force, 15 ILM 5 (1975); agreement Concerning International Patent Classification, Strasbourg, 24 March 1971, in force 7 October 1975, Cmnd 6238, UKTS 113 (1975).

[125] The relevant agreements include the International Convention for the Protection of New Varieties of Plants (UPOV Convention), Brussels, 2 December 1961, in force 10 August 1968, 815 UNTS 89; Treaty on the International Recognition of the Deposit of Micro-organisms for the Purposes of Patent Procedure, Budapest, 28 April 1977, in force 19 August 1980, 17 ILM 285 (1977).

This issue has been particularly acute in the context of the development of biotechnology and the conservation of biodiversity, and is also addressed by Agenda 21 in relation to technology transfer, where the international community declared the need to consider the role of patent protection and intellectual property rights and to examine their impact on the access to and transfer of environmentally sound technology, particularly to developing countries.[126] Significantly, Agenda 21 recognises the bar which intellectual property rights might place on the transfer of technologies: in a passage which balances competing interests, Agenda 21 calls for measures to be taken (including acquisition through compulsory licensing and the provision of 'equitable and adequate compensation') which are in 'compliance with and under the specific circumstances recognised by the relevant international conventions adhered to by states'.[127]

The 1992 Biodiversity Convention was the first international environmental treaty to tackle the issue of intellectual property, its provisions reflecting a concern about the possible threat to intellectual property rights posed by technology transfer obligations, as well as the need to ensure the equitable allocation of 'ownership' rights in biological materials. Taken together, the various provisions are inconclusive as to which rights will prevail in the event of a conflict. The Biodiversity Convention recognises the need to protect property rights, providing in Article 16(2) that the access to and transfer of technology which is subject to patents and other intellectual property rights is to be provided 'on terms which recognise and are consistent with the adequate and effective protection of intellectual property rights'.[128] However, in Article 16(5) the Convention also recognises that rights in intellectual property may have an influence on the implementation of the Convention, and calls on parties to co-operate on intellectual property rights 'subject to national legislation and international law in order to ensure that such rights are supportive and do not run counter to [the Convention's] objectives'. In this regard, the conference of the parties has recognised that intellectual property rights may have implications for the implementation of the Convention and the achievement of its objectives.[129] Finally, the language of Article 22 of the Convention suggests that intellectual property rights and obligations deriving from an existing international agreement might actually be overridden 'where the exercise of those rights and obligations would cause a serious damage or threat to biological diversity'. The language of this latter provision, if interpreted to provide for the supremacy of the Biodiversity Convention, raises the possibility that it might conflict with the international treaties protecting intellectual property rights, which conflict would fall to be resolved by recourse to the ordinary rules of

---

[126] Agenda 21, Chapter 34, paras. 34.10 and 34.18.   [127] Para. 34.18(e)(iv).
[128] See also Bonn Guidelines (2002), chapter 11, p. 520 above.   [129] Decision III/17 (1996).

public international law.[130] In the meantime, the Biodiversity Convention introduces a note of uncertainty into the debate about the primacy of intellectual property rights which caused sufficient concern to the United States to contribute to a delay in signing and an unwillingness to ratify. The United States may be reassured by the ECJ decision declining to recognise an inherently adverse link between the patentability of certain inventions and compliance with obligations to promote technology transfers, under the 1992 Biodiversity Convention.[131]

The 2001 Treaty on Plant Genetic Resources aims to ensure the conservation and sustainable use of plant genetic resources and the fair and equitable sharing of benefits.[132] It includes provisions designed to facilitate the transfer of technologies for the conservation of genetic resources. The heart of the Treaty is a 'Multilateral System' of access and benefit-sharing in respect of plant genetic resources for the food and agriculture listed in Annex I to the Convention and which are under the management and control of parties and in the public domain.[133] The parties agree to facilitate access to resources forming part of the Multilateral System, and to that end recipients agree not to claim any intellectual property or other rights that limit access to the resources or their genetic parts or components.[134] Access to resources protected by intellectual and other property rights are to be consistent with relevant international agreements and with relevant national laws.[135] The Treaty also provides that benefits accruing from the Multilateral System are to be shared fairly and equitably, including through the exchange of information and access to and transfer of technology.[136] Additionally, the parties undertake to provide and facilitate access to technologies for the conservation and use of resources under the Multilateral System and, recognising that some technologies can only be transferred through genetic material, to do so in conformity with the requirements of Article 12 'while respecting applicable property rights and access laws'.[137] Technology which is protected by intellectual property rights is to be transferred to developing countries and countries with economies in transition under

> fair and most favourable terms, in particular in the case of technologies for use in conservation as well as technologies for the benefit of farmers in developing countries . . . including on concessional and preferential terms where mutually agreed. Such access and transfer shall be provided on terms which recognise and are consistent with the adequate and effective protection of intellectual property rights.[138]

---

[130] See chapter 4, pp. 136–8 above.   [131] See n. 164 below and the accompanying text.
[132] Chapter 11, p. 553 above (not yet in force).
[133] Arts. 10 and 11(1)–(2). The Multilateral System will also include plant genetic resources held in specified *ex situ* collections: Art. 11(5).
[134] Art. 12(1) and (2) and (3)(d).   [135] Art. 12(3)(f).
[136] Art. 13(1) and (2).   [137] Art. 13(2)(b)(i).   [138] Art. 13(2)(b)(iii).

Patents and other rights[139]

A second – and related – issue raised by intellectual property rights in the context of international environmental law concerns the extent to which environmental considerations may limit or prevent the grant of patent (or other intellectual property rights) to products which may have adverse consequences for the environment. The 1973 European Patent Convention (establishing the European Patent Office (EPO)) provides that European patents will not be granted for inventions the publication or exploitation of which would be contrary to *ordre public* or morality, provided that the exploitation shall not be deemed to be so contrary merely because it is prohibited by law or regulation in some or all of the parties.[140] It also prohibits the grant of patents in respect of 'plant or animal varieties or essentially biological processes for the production of plants or animals'.[141]

The jurisdiction to refuse patent protection for environmentally damaging technologies as contrary to *ordre public* also receives indirect support from the Opinion of Advocate General Jacobs, in a case challenging the validity of the Biotechnology Directive (see below). He said:

> Preservation of the environment must be regarded in the present state of Community law as one of the fundamental interests of society. That was recognised by the Court as long ago as 1988 in *Commission* v. *Denmark* . . . and is now enshrined in Article 2 of the Treaty which includes the promotion of 'a high level of protection and improvement of the quality of the environment among the Community's tasks. The 'fundamental interests of society' referred to by the Court in *Bouchereau* . . . must to my mind now be understood as extending to the environment. A genuine and sufficiently serious threat to the environment would thus fall squarely within the concept of *ordre public*.[142]

The case law relating to Article 53 of the 1973 European Patent Convention illustrates the circumstances in which there may exist a certain tension between the grant of patents and the protection of the environment. In *Lubrizol Genetics Inc.*, objections were made to the grant of a patent on the grounds, among others, that such a grant would lead to a loss of biodiversity. The EPO stated that environmental arguments could be addressed within the *ordre public*/morality exception, and decided that a 'fair test to apply is to consider whether it is probable that the public in general would regard the invention as so abhorrent that the grant of a patent right would be inconceivable', noting that Article 53(a)

---

[139] For an excellent review of the issues, see UK Department for International Development, *Integrating Intellectual Property Rights and Development Policy: Report of the Commission on Intellectual Property Rights* (2002).

[140] See p. 1044 above; Art. 53(a).   [141] Art. 53(b).

[142] Case C-377/98, *Netherlands* v. *European Parliament and EU Council* [2001] ECR I-7079.

was 'likely to be invoked only in rare and extreme cases'.[143] On the facts, the EPO rejected the challenge, noting in respect to the loss of biodiversity argument that biotechnology increased genetic diversity by increasing new plant varieties, that traditional breeding techniques could also result in loss of biodiversity, and that biotechnology should not be singled out among various factors causing loss of biodiversity. The EPO also expressed the view that 'patent law is not an appropriate instrument for regulating the development of new technologies and that the legislature should determine whether a certain technology is so dangerous and unacceptable to the public that it should be suppressed'.[144]

In *Hormone Relaxin*, the test applied by the EPO in relation to the morality test was whether the grant of a patent for an invention 'would universally be regarded as outrageous', and noting that the existence of a draft EU Biotechnology Directive indicated that the patenting of human gene sequences was not universally considered to be outrageous.[145] That case was appealed to the EPO Technical Board of Appeal since the passing of the EU Biotechnology Directive 98/44/EC of 6 July 1998, and the earlier decision was upheld[146] in light of the interpretation provided by the Directive of the concept of *ordre public*.

In *Plant Genetic Systems*, Greenpeace challenged the grant of a patent in respect of an invention for developing plants and seeds resistant to certain types of herbicide, on the grounds that such plants and seeds would be environmentally harmful. The EPO's Technical Board of Appeal confirmed that *ordre public* encompasses environmental protection and that 'inventions, the exploitation of which is not in conformity with the conventionally accepted standards of conduct pertaining to [the culture inherent in European society and civilisation] are to be excluded from patentability as being contrary to morality'.[147] The Board of Appeal ruled that the revocation on environmental grounds of a patent under Article 53(a) of the 1973 Convention required the environmental hazards to be sufficiently substantiated, that the evidence submitted by Greenpeace demonstrated possible risk, but that it would not be possible to deny a patent 'on the basis of possible, yet not conclusively documented hazards'.[148] The Board of Appeal also confirmed earlier case law to the effect that seeds and plants shall not *per se* constitute an exception to patentability on the ground that plant genetic resources should remain the 'common heritage of mankind'.[149]

The *Oncomouse/Harvard* case has attracted particular attention. The applicants sought the grant of a European patent for the US-patented Harvard oncomouse, the genetic make-up of which had been manipulated by the introduction of a single specified oncogene making it abnormally sensitive to

---

[143] Case T320/87, [1990] OJEPO 71.   [144] Para. 000.   [145] [1995] 6 OJEPO 388.
[146] Case T272/95, 29 October 2002.   [147] Case T356/93, [1995] 8 OJEPO 545.
[148] Para. 18.7. The Board also noted that it was for regulatory bodies and not the EPO to evaluate whether risks should lead to a prohibition in the patenting of an invention.
[149] Para. 18; on 'common heritage' see chapter 11, p. 552 above.

carcinogenic substances and stimuli and, consequently, prone to develop tumours, which necessarily caused suffering. The patent was challenged on the grounds that it was incompatible with Article 53(a) of the 1973 Convention. On appeal, the Examining Division of the European Patent Office considered that the invention was not immoral or contrary to public order. The Examining Division held that each individual invention requires the question of morality to be examined, and that the possible detrimental effects and risks, including those of an environmental nature, had to be weighed and balanced against the merits and advantages.[150] Three different interests were involved and required balancing in deciding whether to grant a patent:

> there is a basic interest of mankind to remedy widespread and dangerous diseases, on the other hand the environment has to be protected against the uncontrolled dissemination of unwanted genes and, moreover, cruelty to animals has to be avoided. The latter two aspects may well justify regarding an invention as immoral and therefore unacceptable unless the advantages, i.e. the benefit to mankind, outweigh the negative aspects.[151]

The Examining Division decided that the invention was useful to mankind, that it contributed to the reduction of the overall extent of animal suffering, and that animal test models were at present indispensable. As to 'possible risks to the environment', the Examining Division found that:

> No release is intended into the general environment. Therefore the risk of an uncontrolled release is practically limited to intentional misuse or blatant ignorance on the part of the laboratory personnel carrying out the tests. The mere fact that such uncontrollable acts are conceivable cannot be a major determinant for deciding whether a patent should be granted or not. Exclusion of patentability cannot be justified merely because technology is dangerous.[152]

The grant was followed by renewed challenge, in proceedings that lasted several years and which were only concluded after the coming into force of the EU Biotechnology Directive. In November 2001, the EPO Examination Division decided to maintain the 'oncomouse' patent in amended form.[153]

---

[150] Decision of the Examining Division, 3 April 1992 (Onco-mouse/Harvard), Application No. 85 304 490.7, [1992] OJEPO 589 at 591. The Decision followed the ruling by the European Patent Convention Technical Board of Appeal in Decision T 19/90 (*Re Harvard College (President and Fellows)*) that the danger of unforeseeable and irreversible effects following the release of genetically-manipulated organisms into the environment was to be considered in applying Art. 53(a) (*European Patents Handbook* (1991), 103 (release 9): T 19/90–1); overruling the decision of first instance that patent law was not the right tool for regulating, *inter alia*, the problem of drastically disrupting evolution: Onco-mouse, Decision of 14 July 1989, [1989] OJEPO 451 at 458–9.

[151] *Ibid.*, 591–2.   [152] *Ibid.*, 592–3.

[153] EPO Press Release, 7 November 2001 (as at 16 December 2002, the reasons had not yet been published).

However, the cases indicate that, although it is possible to raise arguments against the grant of a patent based upon environmental grounds, the prospects of success are limited. The decisions indicate a tendency to focus on the environmental consequences flowing from the intended use, rather than the environmental consequences of misuse, whether accidental or otherwise. They also indicate a relatively high threshold of proof of environmental damage, in terms not dissimilar to the approach taken by the ICJ in the *Gabcikovo-Nagymaros* case. Further, no decision appears, thus far at least, to have invoked the precautionary principle (or approach), at least expressly.

The EPO adjudicatory bodies have been careful to avoid establishing general rules of wholesale application, thus requiring each case to be dealt with on its own merits. The 1973 Convention has been joined by a number of new international instruments since the first edition of this book appeared. It remains to be seen what their influence might be on the EPO's approach, although (as will be seen) their thrust is broadly neutral in seeking to achieve a balance between the protection of the environment, on the one hand, and of intellectual property rights, on the other.

At the global level, the 1994 WTO TRIPs Agreement establishes a regime requiring WTO members to make patents available for any inventions, whether products or processes, in all fields of technology without discrimination, subject to the normal tests of novelty, inventiveness and industrial applicability. It also requires that patents be available and patent rights be enjoyable without discrimination as to the place of invention and regardless of whether products are imported or locally produced.[154]

Like the 1973 European Convention, the TRIPs Agreement allows exceptions to the general rule on patentability, of which two are environmentally relevant. The first is that patents should not be granted to inventions which are contrary to *ordre public* or morality (including inventions dangerous to human, animal or plant life or health or seriously prejudicial to the environment).[155] The second exception is that members may exclude plants and animals other than micro-organisms and essentially biological processes for the production of plants or animals other than non-biological and microbiological processes.[156]

Neither of these exceptions have yet been the subject of proceedings in an environmental case, but it is likely that the term *ordre public* would be held to mean the same in the TRIPs Agreement as in the 1973 European Patent

---

[154] Art. 27(1).

[155] Art. 27(2). The exception is subject to the condition that the commercial exploitation of the invention must also be prevented, and this prevention must be necessary for the protection of *ordre public* or morality.

[156] Art. 27(3)(b). Any country excluding plant varieties from patent protection must, however, provide an effective *sui generis* system of protection.

Convention from which it derives.[157] If so, it will remain open to states bound by TRIPs to deny patent protection to environmentally damaging inventions.

A second new instrument is EC Directive 98/44/EC on the legal protection of biotechnological inventions, which commits member states to protecting biotechnological inventions under national patent law, without prejudice to their obligations under international agreements, in particular the TRIPs Agreement and the 1992 Biodiversity Convention.[158] The Directive, which took over a decade to legislate, and which seeks in part to clarify the application of the 'ordre public and morality' exception in the 1973 European Patent Convention, provides that new inventions which are susceptible of industrial application are patentable 'even if they concern a product consisting of or containing biological material or a process by means of which biological material is produced, processed or used'.[159] However, plant and animal varieties and 'essentially biological processes for the production of plants or animals' are not patentable unless, in respect of inventions which concern plants or animals, the technical feasibility of the invention is 'not confined to a particular plant or animal variety'.[160] And inventions the commercial exploitation of which would be contrary to ordre public or morality remain unpatentable.[161]

The Netherlands challenged the legality of the Directive on the basis, among other grounds, that its provisions violated the TRIPs Agreement and the 1992 Biodiversity Convention. The ECJ ruled that Article 4 of the Directive did not violate Article 27(3)(b) of the TRIPs Agreement, which allows (but does not require) member states not to grant a patent for plants and animals other than micro-organisms.[162] The Court also rejected the Dutch argument that the Directive's purpose – of making biotechnological inventions patentable in all the member states – was counter to the principle of equitable sharing of the benefits arising out of the utilisation of genetic resources, one of the objectives of the 1992 Biodiversity Convention. The Court ruled:

[157] As to the meaning of which, see the opinion of Advocate General Jacobs in Case C-377/98, *Netherlands* v. *European Parliament and EU Council* [2001] ECR I-7079.

[158] OJ L213, 30 July 1998, 13, Art. 1.

[159] Art. 3(1). Further, a 'biological material which is isolated from its natural environment or produced by means of a technical process may be the subject of an invention even if it previously occurred in nature': Art. 3(2).

[160] Art. 4(1)(a) and (b) and (2). Inventions which concern 'a microbiological or other technical process or a product obtained by means of such a process' are patentable: Art. 4(3).

[161] Art. 6; for the view that *ordre public* encompassed the protection of the environment, see the Opinion of Advocate General Jacobs in Case C-377/98, *Netherlands* v. *European Parliament and Council* [2001] ECR 1-7079 paras. 108–9 (a 'genuine and sufficiently serious threat to the environment would thus fall squarely within the concept of *ordre public*').

[162] Case C-377/98, *Netherlands* v. *European Parliament and EU Council*, [2001] ECR I-7079, paras. 57–8.

> It cannot be assumed, in the absence of evidence, which is lacking in this case, that the mere protection of biotechnological inventions by patent would result, as is argued, in depriving developing countries of the ability to monitor their biological resources and to make use of their traditional knowledge, any more than it would result in promoting single-crop farming or in discouraging national and international efforts to preserve biodiversity.[163]

The Court also found that, while the Article 1 objective of the 1992 Convention is the fair and equitable sharing of the benefits arising out of the utilisation of genetic resources, including by appropriate access to genetic resources and by appropriate transfer of relevant technologies, the provision specifies that this must be done taking into account all rights over those resources and technologies. The Court identified no provision of the Convention which requires that 'the conditions for the grant of a patent for biotechnological inventions should include the consideration of the interests of the country from which the genetic resource originates or the existence of measures for transferring technology'.[164]

Traditional knowledge[165]

It is broadly recognised that traditional knowledge may contribute to the conservation of the environment, biodiversity and sustainable agricultural practices.[166] However, the international community has only now begun to consider whether there is a need to take steps to protect such knowledge, and whether the existing system of intellectual property or new forms of protection will be required.

In 1996, the conference of the parties to the 1992 Biodiversity Convention called for case studies on the impact of intellectual property rights on the

---

[163] Para. 65.

[164] Para. 66 (see also the Opinion of Advocate General Jacobs, noting that the Convention is 'in the nature of a framework agreement', that its 'suggested measures are rather varied and in most cases couched in general terms' and that 'nowhere does the Convention prohibit or restrict the patentability of biotechnological materials, or even of genetic resources': Opinion, paras. 179 and 183). The ECJ also rejected the argument that the Directive was an obstacle to international co-operation: para. 67.

[165] UK Department for International Development, *Integrating Intellectual Property Rights and Development Policy: Report of the Commission on Intellectual Property Rights* (2002), Chapter 4.

[166] C. Correa, *Traditional Knowledge and Intellectual Property* (Quater United Nations Office, Geneva, 2001), cited in the report of the UK Department for International Development, n. 165 above. The author notes the other benefits which flow from such protection: the custodians of traditional knowledge could receive fair compensation if the traditional knowledge leads to commercial gain; the profile of the knowledge and the people entrusted with it may be raised, both within and outside communities; it may prevent appropriation by unauthorised parties and may avoid 'biopiracy'; and may promote development.

achievement of the Convention's objectives, including relationships between such rights and the knowledge, practices and innovations of indigenous and local communities embodying traditional lifestyles relevant for the conservation and sustainable use of biological diversity.[167] There has also been extensive work by WIPO in the field of traditional knowledge, but there has been no international harmonisation of standards of protection in this area and none is in sight. Practice differs among national jurisdictions: in some traditional knowledge may be protected by regular intellectual property rights, and in others *sui generis* regimes have been put in place.[168] Recent international developments include the introduction of farmers' rights into the FAO International Undertaking on Plant Genetic Resources and the 2001 Treaty,[169] and Article 8(j) of the 1992 Biodiversity Convention. These efforts provide a starting point for the development of international rules governing the protection of traditional knowledge, recognising the tension between the objective of facilitating access to environmental benefits, on the one hand, and providing appropriate financial and other benefits to the holders of the knowledge, including through sharing of the monetary and other benefits of commercialisation.

Conclusions

The legal relationship between environmental protection and financial resources, technology transfer, and intellectual property rights is well established and becoming increasingly complex. This results from the developments at the regional and global levels in the period shortly before UNCED, and is now reflected in the two conventions and other international acts adopted at UNCED, and subsequent legislative and judicial developments. The consequence is a two-way interchange, also reflected in recent developments relating to the interplay of trade and environment: on the one hand, international environmental law and lawyers must take account of, and apply, legal concepts and rules deriving from the rules relating to the international economic system, including the protection of intellectual property rights; on the other hand, international economic institutions and their legal systems must integrate environmental considerations across the range of their activities.

This is a logical step in the progressive development of international environmental law, and follows earlier phases in which standards were set, institutions created, and procedural requirements put in place. There are four fundamental challenges which will need to be properly addressed if environmental considerations are to be moved from the periphery of international

---

[167] Decision III/17 (1996), Preamble. See also Doha WTO Ministerial Declaration, para. 19 (2001); 1992 Biodiversity Convention Conference of the Parties Decision VI/10 (2002).

[168] UK Department for International Development reports, n. 165 above.

[169] Art. 9.

legal and institutional arrangements to their centre. First, international development assistance resources, and in particular those provided by the multilateral development banks, must be subjected to a regime which: (1) sets forth clear international legal obligations which ensure that adequate environmental standards are applied; (2) ensures that procedural obligations relating to environmental information and assessment are put in place and complied with; and (3) allows efficient and effective mechanisms to be put in place which will ensure that decisions which do not satisfy basic environmental requirements are reviewed and rejected if found wanting. With regard to review mechanisms, the system of international administrative tribunals provides an independent forum for reviewing employment decisions taken by international organisations and is a useful mechanism which has been tried and tested over time and found to be effective. To a significant extent these objectives have been met in the past decade. The second challenge for the law is posed by the creation of new mechanisms which have been established to provide financial resources dedicated to addressing regional or global environmental objectives, such as the GEF, the Ozone Fund and the EC Cohesion and LIFE Funds. Others may follow, under the NAFTA and possibly even under the WTO. The creation of these new arrangements raises complex constitutional issues, as the early wrangling over the establishment of the GEF illustrates. It will therefore be important to ensure that their creation takes a long-term view; that their activities reflect the needs of the communities which they are intended to serve; that their decision-making structures continue to be broadly acceptable to donors and recipients and allow the effective participation of interested and affected members of the international community; and that they target real environmental needs on the basis of internationally agreed environmental obligations. The considerations outlined above for bilateral and multilateral development assistance apply equally to the new, dedicated environmental funds, the successful operation of which will play a large part in determining whether new international environmental obligations are implemented.

The third challenge, which is closely linked to the need to provide international funds, will be the development of effective modalities to ensure the transfer of environmentally sound technologies which will allow developing countries to 'leapfrog' the dirty and obsolete technologies which have been used to underwrite mass industrialisation. Without international funding, it is unlikely that the technology transfer provisions set forth in recent environmental agreements can amount to very much. Additionally, however, international institutional questions will need to be addressed. One of the major institutional gaps, which UNCED did not fill, has been the absence of international institutional arrangements which can identify and assess appropriate technologies, provide information to buyers and sellers, and act as a conduit for independent advice on appropriate technologies. The idea of an international 'clearing house' is now reflected in the 1997 Kyoto Protocol, the 1998 Chemicals Convention and the 2000 Biosafety Protocol. These arrangements, and others such as the Kyoto Protocol's Clean Development Mechanism and the 2001 Plant Treaty's Multilateral System, should go some way towards achieving greater transfers of clean technologies.

Finally, the fourth challenge relates to intellectual property rights which raise a variety of international legal issues of relevance to the environmental agenda. The challenge here will be to construct a system which can fulfil at least three environmental functions: to ensure that technologies or practices which are likely to lead to significant damage to the environment will not be granted protected status; to contribute to the efficient transfer of environmentally sound technologies; and to allow the knowledge of indigenous peoples to be adequately protected.

Foreign investment

R. Buckley, 'International Trade, Investment and Environmental Regulation: An Environmental Management Perspective', 27 *Journal of World Trade Law* 101 (1993); H. Ward and D. Brack, *Trade, Investment and the Environment* (1999); Permanent Court of Arbitration/Peace Palace Papers, *International Investments and the Protection of the Environment* (2000); T. Waelde and A. Kobo, 'Environmental Regulation, Investment Protection and "Regulatory Taking" in International Law', 50 ICLQ 811 (2001); R. Barsh, 'Is the Expropriation of Indigenous Peoples' Land Gatt-able?', 10 RECIEL 13 (2001); E. Neumayer, *Greening Trade and Investment: Environmental Protection Without Protectionism* (2001); Symposium on Regulatory Takings in National and International Law, 11 *New York University Environment Law Journal* 1 (2003).

Introduction

Foreign direct investment is now the largest source of external finance for developing countries, having outstripped public sector overseas development assistance since the early 1990s. In 2002, the WSSD Plan of Implementation called on states to:

> [f]acilitate greater flows of foreign direct investment so as to support sustainable development activities, including the development of infrastructure, of developing countries, and enhance the benefits that developing countries can draw from foreign investment, with particular actions to:
>
> (a) Create the necessary domestic and international conditions to facilitate significant increases in flows of [foreign direct investment] to developing countries . . .
> (b) Encourage foreign direct investment in developing countries and countries with economies in transition through export credits that could be instrumental to sustainable development.[1]

---

[1] Para. 78.

The objective of increasing foreign investment in areas of environmental need is reflected in mechanisms established under various environmental agreements, such as the Clean Development Mechanism established by the 1997 Kyoto Protocol,[2] as well as in provisions of various environmental agreements promoting the transfer of technology.[3] Among the international mechanisms available to encourage foreign direct investment, two are especially important for present purposes: the first comprises investment treaties – bilateral and multilateral – which seek to protect foreign investments against certain governmental acts, in particular expropriation and unfair treatment; the second comprises arrangements – domestic and international – which seek to provide guarantees (insurance and other) against the acts prohibited by investment treaties. Both mechanisms are becoming increasingly connected to international environmental rules, in the sense that they may impact upon states' abilities to adopt certain environmental measures at the national level or through multilateral environmental agreements, or encourage states to reduce their environmental standards in order to attract foreign investment.[4] In recent international cases (discussed below) the principal issue has been the manner in which the protections that investment treaties are intended to afford against expropriation and other prohibited acts are applied when such acts are motivated by environmental (or other social) objectives, including those which are taken in accordance with international environmental obligations. In relation to export credit insurance, the principal issues concern the extent to which such arrangements should be available to projects which may be environmentally harmful, and what mechanisms are available to identify such projects at an early stage of their development.

Investment treaties

The rules of international law protecting the property rights of foreigners (traditionally referred to as 'aliens') are well established. Customary international law grants states a broad measure of discretion in relation to the treatment they accord to the property of aliens on their territory, including foreign investment. According to one leading commentator, 'far-reaching interference with private property, including that of aliens, is common in connection with such matters as taxation, measures of police, public health, the administration of public

---

[2] Chapter 8, p. 373 above.

[3] Chapter 20, p. 1037 above; see also H. French, 'Harnessing Private Capital Flows for Environmentally Sustainable Development' (Worldwatch Paper 139, 1998).

[4] For a review of literature on the environmental effects of foreign investment, see Note by the OECD Secretariat, DAFFE/MAI/RD(97)33/Rev1 (www1.oecd.org/daf/mai/pdf/ng/ng9733r1e.pdf).

utilities and the planning of urban and rural development'.[5] To the list may be added measures intended to protect the environment, which could have the effect of limiting the economic benefits of an investment, or of bringing such benefits to an end altogether. It is accepted, however, that the state's discretion is not unlimited, and customary law requires a state to observe certain minimum international standards in respect of alien property. These standards are relatively well developed in relation to acts of expropriation and due process rights (including a right of access to courts and the principle of equality before the law). In assessing the legality of such acts, it is apparent that a balance must be struck between the legitimate interests of the state hosting the investment and the need to protect such investments from excessive interference.[6]

The minimum standards set by customary international law are supplemented by more specific rules established by treaties. More than 2,000 bilateral investment treaties (BITs) have now been adopted,[7] and they have recently been joined by a growing number of multilateral agreements applicable within a region or to a particular economic activity, such as the 1994 North American Free Trade Agreement (NAFTA) and the 1994 Energy Charter Treaty. Efforts to establish a global regime – in the mid-1990s under the auspices of the OECD – failed, although these have recently been renewed under the auspices of the WTO. Bilateral and multilateral treaties establish specific rules providing substantive protections, together with procedures for resolving disputes between foreign investors and host states, usually in the form of international adjudicatory arrangements.

Substantive rules

Each BIT and multilateral agreement establishes its own substantive rules governing the extent of the protection to be granted to foreign investments. In general terms, however, the protection extends to two kinds of act: a prohibition on acts or measures which expropriate or relatedly interfere with the investment, and a prohibition on acts or measures which constitute 'unfair treatment'.

In relation to rules prohibiting expropriation, it is important to note that the obligations imposed on the host state will not be identical in each bilateral treaty, so that each one must be considered on its own merits and interpreted

[5] Oppenheim, 912; see generally M. Sornarajah, *The International Law on Foreign Investment* (1994).
[6] Oppenheim, 913–15.
[7] See generally R. Dolzer and M. Stevens, *Bilateral Investment Treaties* (1995). See also F. Mann, 'British Treaties for the Promotion and Protection of Investments', 52 BYIL 242 (1981); G. Sacerdoti, 'Recent Developments in Bilateral Treaties on Investment Protection', 269 RdC 251 (1997).

and applied in accordance with the normal rules of treaty interpretation.[8] As one leading commentary has put it:

> The most common terms . . . are expropriation and nationalization, but in addition some BITs refer to 'dispossession', 'taking', 'deprivation' or 'privation'. These latter terms are considered quite wide in scope and would include expropriation, nationalization and the transfer of property to nationals of the host state (i.e. indigenisation). BITs generally do not define the term expropriation or any of the other terms denoting similar measures of forced dispossession . . . Such apparent reluctance to attempt a definition of 'expropriation' in the BITs may be explained by the fact that a host state, as is well known, can take a number of measures which have a similar effect of expropriation or nationalization, although they do not *de jure* constitute an act of expropriation; such measures are generally termed 'indirect', 'creeping', or 'de facto' expropriation. The expropriation clause in most BITs therefore commonly includes expropriation and nationalization as well as a reference to indirect measures, and accords to them all the same legal treatment.[9]

In broad terms, the approach taken by bilateral treaties is followed by multilateral agreements seeking to promote and protect foreign investments. The approach taken by Chapter 11 of the NAFTA is not unusual in this regard, although its language has led to varied approaches from the growing number of arbitral tribunals charged with resolving disputes. Article 1102 imposes a 'national treatment' requirement,[10] and Article 1106 prohibits certain 'performance requirements'.[11] Additionally, Article 1105(1) provides:

> Each Party shall accord to investments of investors of another Party treatment in accordance with international law, including fair and equitable treatment and full protection and security.

---

[8] On the 1969 Vienna Convention on the Law of Treaties, see chapter 4, p. 130 above.

[9] On 'indirect takings', see R. Higgins, 'The Taking of Property by the State', 176 RdC 267 (1982-III).

[10] Art. 1102(1) provides: 'Each Party shall accord to investors of another Party treatment no less favourable than that it accords, in like circumstances, to its own investors with respect to the establishment, acquisition, expansion, management, conduct, operation, and sale or other disposition of investments.'

[11] Article 1106(1) provides that no party may impose or enforce certain performance requirements in relation to investments, including requirements to transfer technology, a production process or other proprietary knowledge to a person in its territory, except when the requirement is imposed or the commitment or undertaking is enforced by a court, administrative tribunal or competition authority to remedy an alleged violation of competition laws or to act in a manner not inconsistent with other provisions of NAFTA (Art. 1106(1)(f)). Art. 1106(2) provides: 'A measure that requires an investment to use a technology to meet generally applicable health, safety or environmental requirements shall not be construed to be inconsistent with paragraph 1(f).'

And Article 1110(1) provides:

> No Party may directly or indirectly nationalize or expropriate an investment of an investor of another Party in its territory or take a measure tantamount to nationalization or expropriation of such an investment ('expropriation'), except:
>
> (a) for a public purpose;
> (b) on a non-discriminatory basis;
> (c) in accordance with due process of law and Article 1105(1); and
> (d) on payment of compensation in accordance with paragraphs 2 through 6.[12]

Article 1114(1) of NAFTA (Environmental Measures) provides that nothing in Chapter 11

> shall be construed to prevent a Party from adopting, maintaining or enforcing any measure otherwise consistent with this Chapter that it considers appropriate to ensure that investment activity in its territory is undertaken in a manner sensitive to environmental concerns.

This language indicates a hierarchy between the Article 1105 and 1110 obligations of the NAFTA parties and their rights in relation to environmental protection measures, and does not suggest that environmental objectives can inform the interpretation or application of Article 1105 and 1110 obligations. However, Article 1114(2) directs parties not to relax their environmental rules to attract foreign investment, indicating the parties' recognition that:

> it is inappropriate to encourage investment by relaxing domestic health, safety or environmental measures. Accordingly, a Party should not waive or otherwise derogate from, or offer to waive or otherwise derogate from, such measures as an encouragement for the establishment, acquisition, expansion or retention in its territory of an investment of an investor. If a Party considers that another Party has offered such an encouragement, it may request consultations with the other Party and the two Parties shall consult with a view to avoiding any such encouragement.

The 1994 Energy Charter Treaty reflects a similar approach, although it is limited to investments relating to the energy sector. Part 3 addresses investment promotion and protection, and Article 10(1) provides:

---

[12] Art. 1110(2) provides: 'Compensation shall be equivalent to the fair market value of the expropriated investment immediately before the expropriation took place ("date of expropriation"), and shall not reflect any change in value occurring because the intended expropriation had become known earlier. Valuation criteria shall include going concern value, asset value including declared tax value of tangible property, and other criteria, as appropriate, to determine fair market value.'

Each Contracting Party shall, in accordance with the provisions of this Treaty, encourage and create stable, equitable, favourable and transparent conditions for Investors of other Contracting Parties to make Investments in its Area. Such conditions shall include a commitment to accord at all times to Investments of Investors of other Contracting Parties fair and equitable treatment. Such Investments shall also enjoy the most constant protection and security and no Contracting Party shall in any way impair by unreasonable or discriminatory measures their management, maintenance, use, enjoyment or disposal. In no case shall such Investments be accorded treatment less favourable than that required by international law, including treaty obligations. Each Contracting Party shall observe any obligations it has entered into with an Investor or an Investment of an Investor of any other Contracting Party.

Article 13(1) provides:

Investments of Investors of a Contracting Party in the Area of any other Contracting Party shall not be nationalized, expropriated or subjected to a measure or measures having effect equivalent to nationalization or ex-propriation (hereinafter referred to as 'Expropriation') except where such Expropriation is:

(a) for a purpose which is in the public interest;
(b) not discriminatory;
(c) carried out under due process of law; and
(d) accompanied by the payment of prompt, adequate and effective com-pensation.[13]

Dispute settlement

Beyond the substantive obligations imposed in the bilateral and multilateral agreements, the arrangements almost always provide a means for internation-alising the settlement of disputes.[14] The investor will usually wish to avoid the national courts of the host state, and the host state will wish to avoid the national courts of the investor, or of a third state. The preferred option is therefore to

---

[13] It goes on to provide: 'Such compensation shall amount to the fair market value of the Investment expropriated at the time immediately before the Expropriation or impending Expropriation became known in such a way as to affect the value of the Investment (here-inafter referred to as the "Valuation Date"). Such fair market value shall at the request of the Investor be expressed in a Freely Convertible Currency on the basis of the market rate of exchange existing for that currency on the Valuation Date. Compensation shall also include interest at a commercial rate established on a market basis from the date of Expropriation until the date of payment.'

[14] On settlement of disputes in BITs, see R. Dolzer and M. Stevens, *Bilateral Investment Treaties* (1995), Chapter 5.

provide for the settlement of disputes relating to claims of expropriation or un-fair treatment to be addressed by international arbitration. Numerous options are available, but the tendency is either resort to the World Bank's International Centre for Settlement of Investment Disputes (ICSID)[15] or recourse to arbitra-tion under the rules of the United Nations Commission on International Trade Law (UNCITRAL).[16] The attraction of ICSID is that it provides an established institutional structure, which the UNCITRAL rules do not. It is to be noted that initiation of the procedure is almost invariably at the instigation of the investor alone; since the host state generally has no express rights granted under the BIT or the multilateral treaty, *vis-à-vis* the investor, no right is generally granted to it to invoke proceedings.

The NAFTA and the Energy Charter Treaty illustrate the options. Under Article 1120(1) of the NAFTA, once six months have elapsed since the events giving rise to a claim

> a disputing investor may submit the claim to arbitration under:
>
> (a) the ICSID Convention, provided that both the disputing Party and the Party of the investor are parties to the Convention;
> (b) the Additional Facility Rules of ICSID, provided that either the disputing Party or the Party of the investor, but not both, is a party to the ICSID Convention; or
> (c) the UNCITRAL Arbitration Rules.

Article 26 of the 1994 Energy Charter Treaty allows the investor to choose to submit dispute to a marginally wider choice of procedures. Three months after the parties' failure to settle a dispute amicably, the investor may submit the dispute: to the courts or administrative tribunals of the state party to the dis-pute; to any applicable, previously agreed dispute settlement procedure; or to international arbitration or conciliation under the ICSID rules, or the ICSID Additional Facility rules (where the state is not a party to the ICSID Conven-tion), or UNCITRAL rules, or an arbitral proceeding under the Arbitration Institute of the Stockholm Chamber of Commerce.[17]

Global rules

In 1995, negotiations began under the auspices of the OECD towards agreeing a Multilateral Agreement on Investment (MAI), which would establish invest-ment rules of global application. The negotiations foundered in 1998, by which

---

[15] www.worldbank.org/icsid; see generally C. Schreuer, *The ICSID Convention: A Commen-tary* (2001).

[16] www.uncitral.org/english/texts/arbitration/adrindex.htm.

[17] Art. 26 provides certain limited exceptions in relation to states making declarations under the 1994 Treaty.

time considerable progress had been made towards agreement on the rules relating to investment protection and the procedures to govern the settlement of disputes between an investor and a contracting party. On both of these aspects, the draft text generally followed the approach taken in the NAFTA and the Energy Charter Treaty.[18] However, one of the central sticking points concerned the relationship between the obligation not to expropriate or otherwise interfere with an investment, on the one hand, and the maintenance, adoption or enforcement of domestic environmental standards, on the other. By the time the negotiations collapsed in 1998, four draft texts sought to address the general agreement that states should not lower environmental standards; other draft texts addressed related environmental matters.[19] One of the draft texts proposed a 'general exception Article' (reflecting Article XX(b) and (g) of the GATT 1994) stating:

> Subject to the requirement that such measures are not applied in a manner which would constitute a means of arbitrary or unjustifiable discrimination or a disguised restriction on investment, nothing in this agreement shall be construed to prevent the adoption, maintaining or enforcement by any Contracting party of measures:
>
> (a) necessary to protect human, animal or plant life or health;
> (b) relating to the conservation of living or non-living exhaustible natural resources.[20]

Another state (unnamed) proposed a full-scale 'environmental review' of the MAI, addressing *inter alia* the following questions:

1. Could MAI obligations affect parties' implementation and enforcement of their existing national and regional environmental laws?
2. Could the MAI affect a party's ability to address environmental problems in the future (i.e. the creation of new policy means to tackle new problems or the creation of new policies/regulations to deal with problems yet to be identified)?
3. Would MAI obligations conflict with any existing obligations under existing multilateral environmental agreements?[21]
4. Could MAI obligations constrain the future development of existing or new multilateral environmental agreements?
5. Could the MAI encourage either MAI parties or non-parties to slacken environmental regulation in order to attract investment?[22]

---

[18] OECD, 'The MAI Negotiating Text' (as of 24 April 1998), available at www.oecd.org/pdf/M00003000/M00003291.pdf.
[19] *Ibid.*, 54–5.   [20] *Ibid.*, 56.
[21] See Note by the OECD Secretariat, 'Relationships Between the MAI and Selected MEAs', DAFFE/MAI/(98)1 (www1.oecd.org/daf/ mai/pdf/ng/ng981e.pdf).
[22] DAFFE/MAI/RD(97)43/Final (www1.oecd.org/daf/mai/ pdf/ng/ngrd9743fe.pdf).

The MAI negotiations did not lead to agreement on these or other issues. In 2001, however, the Doha WTO Ministerial Declaration revived the idea of global rules, within the framework of the WTO. Ministers recognised 'the case for a multilateral framework to secure transparent, stable and predictable conditions for long-term cross-border investment, particularly foreign direct investment, that will contribute to the expansion of trade', and agreed that negotiations would commence in 2003 with a view to concluding the negotiations by 1 January 2005. It is unlikely that the environmental issues raised in the MAI negotiation will not re-emerge in future WTO negotiations.

Case law

Within the past five years a number of cases have been arbitrated internationally that address the relationship between domestic environmental protection measures and obligations to protect foreign investments from expropriatory and other practices. The cases have largely – but not exclusively – arisen in the NAFTA context, and in certain respects mirror the case law of the European Court of Human Rights in relation to the protection of property rights.[23] A number of NAFTA cases are of particular interest for their implications on national and international environmental rules.[24]

Ethyl Corporation v. *Canada* was the first arbitral decision under Chapter 11 of NAFTA, although it settled after the jurisdiction phase. The United States investor challenged Canada's ban on inter-provincial trade in and commercial imports of MMT, a manganese-based compound which enhances the octane value of unleaded gasoline. Ethyl Corporation claimed that the ban (which had been adopted on environmental grounds) violated *inter alia* national treatment requirements and represented an act 'tantamount to an expropriation' without compensation, as required by Article 1110 of NAFTA, and claimed damages of US$251 million. After the arbitrators found that the NAFTA/UNCITRAL tribunal had jurisdiction,[25] and after a Canadian procedure had found that the ban violated Canada's Agreement on Internal Trade, the parties settled the

---

[23] Chapter 6, p. 278 above. It will be apparent that the approach taken by the European Court of Human Rights is less protective of property rights than some of the arbitral tribunals that have addressed investment disputes: see H. Mountfield, 'Regulatory Expropriations in Europe: The Approach of the European Court of Human Rights', 11 NYUELJ 136 (2002).

[24] For information on all NAFTA cases, see www.naftalaw.org. Beyond the cases discussed here, a number of others cases also touch on environmental subjects: see *Azinian, Davitian and Baca* v. *Mexico*, Award of 1 November 1998, 5 ICSID Reps 269 (no violation of Arts. 1105 and 1110 in dispute relating to waste collection and disposal concession contract); *Waste Management Inc.* v. *Mexico*, Award of 2 June 2000, 5 ICSID Reps 443 (declining jurisdiction in a claim relating to Arts. 1105 and 1110 in a dispute relating to a waste collection and disposal concession contract; the case has subsequently been renewed and is pending on the merits following a decision of 26 June 2002 upholding jurisdiction).

[25] *Ethyl Corporation* v. *Canada*, Jurisdiction Phase, 38 ILM 708 (1999).

dispute, with Canada paying Ethyl US$13 million. It is not clear why Canada settled the case. The settlement indicated that the claim might have had some merit, and apparently encouraged other Article 1110 claims premised on the view that domestic environmental regulations could unlawfully interfere with investors' rights under NAFTA.

In *S. D. Myers, Inc.* v. *Canada,* the United States investor challenged a Canadian legislative order banning exports of PCBs and PCB wastes, on the ground *inter alia* of violations of Articles 1102, 1105, 1106 and 1110 of NAFTA. The Canadian ban had been adopted in November 1995 purportedly on the ground of 'a significant danger to the environment and to human life and health'; government views supporting the ban included a statement to the effect that Canada was obliged by the terms of the 1989 Basel Convention to dispose of its own PCBs.[26] The ban was lifted in 1997, while the proceedings were pending. The arbitral tribunal found that the ban was intended primarily to protect the Canadian PCB disposal industry from US competition and that 'there was no legitimate environmental reason for introducing the ban'.[27] In interpreting the NAFTA rules, the arbitral tribunal had regard to a range of environmental agreements, including the 1986 US–Canada Agreement Concerning the Transboundary Movement of Hazardous Waste, the 1989 Basel Convention and the 1994 North American Agreement on Environmental Co-operation, stating that:

> the NAFTA should be interpreted in the light of the following general principles:
>
> • Parties have the right to establish high levels of environmental protection. They are not obliged to compromise their standards merely to satisfy the political or economic interests of other states;
> • Parties should avoid creating distortions to trade;
> • Environmental protection can and should be mutually supportive.[28]

The tribunal considered that the logical corollary of these principles was that:

> Where a state can achieve its chosen level of environmental protection through a variety of equally effective and reasonable means, it is obliged to adopt the alternative that is most consistent with open trade. This corollary also is consistent with the language and the case law arising out of the WTO family of agreements.[29]

Taking into account these principles, the arbitral tribunal held that Canada had violated Article 1102 of NAFTA by not treating US and Canadian companies

---

[26] Partial Award, 11 November 2000, paras. 184–5; on the 1989 Basel Convention, see chapter 13 above.

[27] Paras. 194–5 (noting that 'there were other equally effective means of encouraging the development and maintenance of a Canadian-based PCBs remediation industry').

[28] Para. 220.   [29] Para. 221.

involved in the destruction of PCBs in 'like circumstances', an assessment of which should take into account circumstances that would justify governmental regulations that treat entities differently in order to protect the public interest (i.e. the environment).[30] A majority of the arbitral tribunal ruled that the breach of Article 1102 additionally gave rise to a breach of Article 1105, by failing to provide 'fair and equitable treatment'.[31] However, the arbitral tribunal found no breach of Articles 1106 and 1110.[32] The tribunal awarded the claimant US$6.05 million in damages, with interest.[33]

Metalclad Corporation v. *Mexico* is the most notorious of the NAFTA environmental cases.[34] The facts bear careful consideration, indicating the context of environmental and federalism issues against which the arbitral tribunal's approach is to be assessed. A Mexican company (COTERIN) owned a site in the valley of La Pedrera in the municipality of Guadalcazar, located in the Mexican state of San Luis Potosi. COTERIN began operating a hazardous waste transfer station at the site in 1990, pursuant to an authority granted by the federal government of Mexico. However, 20,000 tons of waste were unlawfully deposited on the site without treatment or separation, and in September 1991 the federal government ordered the closure of the transfer station, which remained in effect until February 1996. Also in 1991, COTERIN applied to the municipality for a permit to construct a hazardous waste landfill at the site, but the application was refused, and the municipality's opposition to any further use of the site for the storage of hazardous wastes was reaffirmed in 1992. In 1993, COTERIN received two federal permits in respect of a hazardous waste landfill at the site, two federal environmental impact authorisations in respect of the construction and operation of the landfill, and a land use permit issued by the state of San Luis Potosi. In 1993, Metalclad Corporation (a US investor) purchased COTERIN (and the site), without a municipal construction permit having been granted, or a decision having been given by the Mexican courts that no such permit was needed.[35] It was well aware of the municipal permit issue, having made three-quarters of the purchase price contingent upon its resolution. COTERIN commenced construction of the landfill at the site without a

---

[30] Paras. 249–57.

[31] Paras. 258–66 (Arbitrator Chiasson dissented, on the ground that a finding of a violation of Art. 1105 had to be based on a demonstrated failure to meet the fair and equitable requirements of international law).

[32] On Art. 1110 the tribunal concluded: 'Canada realised no benefit from the measure. The evidence does not support a transfer of property or benefit directly to others. An opportunity was delayed. This is not an expropriation case' (paras. 287–8).

[33] Second Partial Award (Damages), 21 October 2002.

[34] Award, 25 August 2000, 40 ILM 35 (2001).

[35] In the arbitration proceedings, Metalclad alleged, and the tribunal found, that Mexican federal officials had assured Metalclad that COTERIN had all the authorisations required to undertake the landfill project.

municipal construction permit (although a further federal construction permit was issued in January 1995). In October 1994, the municipality issued a 'stop work' order due to the lack of a municipal permit. COTERIN applied for a municipal construction permit in November 1994, but it was denied by the municipality in December 1995.[36] By March 1995, construction of the landfill facility at the site had been completed. In November 1995, Metalclad entered into an agreement (*convenio*) with two sub-agencies of the Secretariat of the Environment of the Mexican Government, permitting operation of the landfill for an initial period of five years.[37] In February 1996, the federal authorities issued a further permit to COTERIN increasing the annual permitted capacity of the facility from 36,000 tons to 360,000 tons. In April 1996, the municipality rejected a renewed application for a construction permit. The refusal was challenged in the Mexican federal court but dismissed on the ground that COTERIN had not exhausted its administrative remedies. An appeal to the Mexican Supreme Court was subsequently abandoned. In October 1996, Metalclad initiated NAFTA arbitration proceedings, alleging breaches of Articles 1105 and 1110 of NAFTA. On 20 September 1997, the governor of the state of San Luis Potosi issued an ecological decree declaring an area of 188,758 hectares within the municipality, including the site, to be an ecological preserve for the protection of cacti.

The arbitral tribunal found that Mexico could be internationally responsible for the acts of the municipality and the state of San Luis Potosi.[38] As to Article 1105, it found that Mexico had not treated Metalclad fairly and equitably, having regard to the requirements of transparency imposed by Articles 102 and 1802 of NAFTA. The tribunal ruled that the denial of the construction permit by the municipality – by reference to environmental impact and other considerations – was improper, since the federal authority's jurisdiction was controlling and the authority of the municipality extended only to 'appropriate construction considerations'.[39] It found that Mexico had failed to ensure the transparent and predictable framework for Metalclad's investment, and that the lack of orderly process and timely disposition was inconsistent with the investor's

---

[36] The municipality denied the application on the grounds, *inter alia*, that; (1) COTERIN had been denied a construction permit in 1991; (2) COTERIN had commenced construction before applying for the permit and finished the construction while the permit application was pending; (3) there were environmental concerns; and (4) a great number of the municipality's inhabitants were opposed to the granting of the permit.

[37] The municipality challenged the *convenio*, by means of administrative complaint to the federal Secretariat of the Environment and by filing a writ of *amparo* with the Federal Court in January 1996. In the *amparo* proceedings, the municipality obtained an injunction in respect of the *convenio* in February 1996, but the *amparo* proceedings were dismissed in May 1999.

[38] Award, 25 August 2000, 40 ILM 35 (2001), para. 73.

[39] Paras. 86–97; the conclusion was not affected by Art. 1114 of NAFTA: para. 98.

expectation that it would be treated fairly and justly.[40] With regard to Article 1110, the tribunal ruled that Mexico had indirectly expropriated Metalclad's investment:

> By permitting or tolerating the conduct of Guadalcazar in relation to Metalclad which the Tribunal has already held amounts to unfair and inequitable treatment breaching Article 1105 and by thus participating or acquiescing in the denial to Metalclad of the right to operate the landfill, notwithstanding the fact that the project was fully approved and endorsed by the federal government, Mexico must be held to have taken a measure tantamount to expropriation in violation of NAFTA Article 1110(1) . . . [The municipality's denial of a construction permit], taken together with the representations of the Mexican federal government, on which Metalclad relied, and the absence of a timely, orderly or substantive basis for the denial by the Municipality of the local construction permit, amount to an indirect expropriation.[41]

For good measure, the tribunal added:

> Although not strictly necessary for its conclusion, the Tribunal also identifies as a further ground for a finding of expropriation the Ecological Decree issued by the Governor of [San Luis Potosi] on September 20, 1997. The Decree covers an area of 188,758 hectares within the 'Real de Guadalcazar' that includes the landfill site, and created therein an ecological preserve. This Decree had the effect of barring forever the operation of the landfill . . . The Tribunal need not decide or consider the motivation or intent of the adoption of the Ecological Decree. Indeed, a finding of expropriation on the basis of the Ecological Decree is not essential to the Tribunal's finding of a violation of NAFTA Article 1110. However, the Tribunal considers that the implementation of the Ecological Decree would, in and of itself, constitute an act tantamount to expropriation.[42]

---

[40] Para. 99.

[41] Paras. 104 and 107. In reaching this conclusion, the tribunal relied on a generous, broad and unprecedented definition of expropriation: 'expropriation under NAFTA includes not only open, deliberate and acknowledged takings of property, such as outright seizure or formal or obligatory transfer of title in favour of the host state, but also covert or incidental interference with the use of property which has the effect of depriving the owner, in whole or in significant part, of the use or reasonably-to-be-expected economic benefit of property even if not necessarily to the obvious benefit of the host state': para. 103.

[42] Paras. 109 and 111. In reaching this conclusion, the tribunal appears to have relied on the Decree's ninth Article (forbidding 'any work inconsistent with the Ecological Decree's management programme'); the fourteenth Article (forbidding 'any conduct that might involve the discharge of polluting agents on the reserve soil, subsoil, running water or water deposits and prohibit[ing] the undertaking of any potentially polluting activities'); and the fifteenth Article (forbidding 'any activity requiring permits or licences unless such activity is related to the exploration, extraction or utilisation of natural resources'). It does not appear from the award that the tribunal had regard to any evidence as to whether the Ecological Decree did in fact 'bar forever' the operation of the landfill site.

The tribunal awarded Metalclad US$16.685 million in damages. Mexico challenged the award before the Supreme Court of British Columbia (which had jurisdiction on the basis that Vancouver, British Columbia, had been the place of arbitration and on British Columbia's International Arbitration Act 1996). The Supreme Court annulled that part of the award relating to Article 1105, on the ground that by incorporating principles and obligations concerning transparency under Chapter 18 into Article 1105 the Tribunal had made a decision which went beyond the scope of the submission to arbitration (limited to Chapter 11).[43] The Supreme Court found that the tribunal's analysis of Article 1105 infected its analysis of Article 1110, so that by relying on transparency to conclude that there had been an expropriation the tribunal had also gone beyond the scope of the submission to arbitration.[44] The Supreme Court did not, however, consider that the tribunal's decision on the effects of the 1997 Ecological Decree had been infected by its analysis of Article 1105. It noted that the tribunal had given 'an extremely broad definition of expropriation for the purposes of Article 1110', but that the definition of expropriation was a question of law which the Supreme Court was not entitled to interfere with under section 34 of the International Commercial Arbitration Act, from which it derived its jurisdiction, and concluded that any error by the tribunal in relation to its decision on the Ecological Decree was not 'patently unreasonable'.[45] Consequently that part of the arbitral award was upheld.

It should be noted, however, that the broad definition of expropriation applied by the *Metalclad* arbitral tribunal has not been utilised or adopted in other awards.[46]

In *Methanex* v. *United States* (which is pending on the merits), a Canadian investor brought proceedings challenging Californian legislation restricting the use of MTBE, a methanol-based source of octane and oxygenate for gasoline, on the grounds that it 'presents a significant risk to the environment', by the possibility of contaminating drinking water. Methanex's claim, as amended, is that the Californian legislation was arbitrary and went beyond what was necessary to protect a legitimate public interest, and violated Articles 1105 and 1110 of NAFTA, as well as Article 1102 (prohibiting discrimination). In relation to Article 1110, Methanex claims that the legislation would end sales of methanol

---

[43] 2 May 2001, [2001] *British Columbia Trail Cases* 664; 5 ICSID Reps 236, paras. 68–76.

[44] Paras. 77–80.   [45] Paras. 99–103.

[46] Awards finding no violation of Art. 1110 include: *S. D. Myers* v. *Canada*, n. 26 above; *Pope and Talbot* v. *Canada*, Interim Merits Award, 26 June 2000, paras. 96–105 (the test is whether the interference is sufficiently restrictive to support a conclusion that the property has been 'taken' from the owner' (para. 102)); *Marvin Feldman* v. *Mexico*, Award, 9 December 2002, paras. 96 *et seq.* (noting that 'the ways in which governmental authorities may force a company out of business, or significantly reduce the economic benefits of its business are many . . . At the same time, governments must be free to act in the broader public interest through protection of the environment, . . . imposition of zoning restrictions and the like': para. 103).

for use in MTBE in California and contribute to the extended closure of a plant, amounting to a substantial taking of Methanex's investment in two companies. Methanex claims that MTBE is safe and has not been prohibited in the European Union. The tribunal has ruled that it cannot make a final determination of whether it has jurisdiction until a fresh pleading is filed; it held that as the pleadings stood it would be likely to find that it did *not* have jurisdiction on the ground that the measures at issue did not 'relate to' Methanex in the sense of Article 1101 (Scope and Coverage) of NAFTA. It therefore gave Methanex another opportunity to file a pleading, together with all supporting evidence showing how the measures relate to Methanex such as to confer standing to commence the claim.[47] It remains to be seen whether the tribunal will adopt a broad definition of expropriation, or follow other decisions which have taken a more traditional approach. The tribunal has already made a significant contribution to the participation rights of non-state actors: in January 2001, it ruled that it had the power pursuant to Article 15(1) of the UNCITRAL rules (governing the proceedings) to accept *amicus* written submissions from the International Institute of Sustainable Development.[48] This appears to be the first time that the possibility of an *amicus* submission has been recognised in international arbitral proceedings.

Beyond the NAFTA system, in *Compania del Desarrollo de Santa Elena SA* v. *Costa Rica*, an ICSID tribunal applying a Costa Rica/US bilateral investment treaty had to determine the amount of compensation to be paid to the investor for the expropriation of its property in Costa Rica. The property in question had been acquired in 1973 for the purpose of building a tourist resort, and comprised tropical dry forest which was 'home to a dazzling variety of flora and fauna' and located next to the Santa Rosa National Park.[49] The property was expropriated in 1978 for the purpose of adding to the area of the Santa Rosa National Park and to conserve flora and fauna, including the protection of jaguars, pumas and sea turtles.

The parties were not in dispute that the object of the expropriation was lawful and for a public purpose, namely, to protect biodiversity; they disagreed as to the amount of compensation to be paid. In presenting its claim, Costa Rica invited the tribunal to have regard to the environmental objectives of the expropriation, and the concern that setting too high an amount would provide a disincentive for states, in particular developing states, to adopt legitimate environmental objectives such as the establishment and extension of national parks. Costa Rica also claimed that its expropriation was taken pursuant to and

---

[47] First Partial Award (Jurisdiction and Admissibility), 7 August 2002 (www.state.gov/s/l/c5818.htm).
[48] Order, 15 January 2001 (www.state.gov/documents/organization/ 6039.pdf).
[49] Award of 17 February 2000, 39 ILM 1317 (2000), paras. 15–18.

in accordance with its obligations under various international environmental agreements, including the 1940 Western Hemisphere Convention.[50] The tribunal did not accept that the standard of compensation (applying the principle of full compensation for fair market value) could be affected by environmental considerations. It ruled:

> While an expropriation or taking for environmental reasons may be classified as a taking for a public purpose, and thus may be legitimate, the fact that the Property was taken for this reason does not affect either the nature or the measure of the compensation to be paid for the taking. That is, the purpose of protecting the environment for which the Property was taken does not alter the legal character of the taking for which adequate compensation must be paid. The international source of the obligation to protect the environment makes no difference. Expropriatory environmental measures – no matter how laudable and beneficial to society as a whole – are, in this respect, similar to any other expropriatory measures that a state may take in order to implement its policies: where property is expropriated, even for environmental purposes, whether domestic or international, the state's obligation to pay compensation remains.[51]

The tribunal accordingly declined to analyse the detailed evidence regarding what Costa Rica referred to as 'its international legal obligation to preserve the unique ecological site that is the Santa Elena property'.[52]

Insurance

With a view to encouraging direct foreign investment, various national and international governmental arrangements have been established to insure foreign investors (and provide other guarantees) against certain risks which may befall their investments. The approach of the Multilateral Investment Guarantee Agency (MIGA) draws upon that applied at the national level, including in particular the approach of the United States' Overseas Private Investment Corporation.[53]

Increasingly, such arrangements require prior environmental assessment of the project in order to ensure that financial support is not provided to projects which are harmful to the environment.

The leading international scheme is that provided by MIGA, which is part of the World Bank family.[54] MIGA provides investment guarantees against certain

---

[50] On the 1940 Convention, see chapter 11, p. 527 above.
[51] Award of 17 February 2000, 39 ILM 1317 (2000), paras. 71–2.   [52] *Ibid.*
[53] For national arrangements, see e.g. the United States' Overseas Private Investment Corporation (OPIC) (www.opic.gov).
[54] www.miga.org.

non-commercial risks (i.e. political risk insurance) to eligible foreign investors for qualified investments in developing member countries. MIGA's coverage is against the following risks: transfer restrictions, expropriation, breach of contract, and war and civil disturbance. MIGA has an environmental assessment policy (Annex B to its Operational Regulations), which requires environmental assessment of proposed projects to help ensure that it provides guarantees only to projects that are environmentally sound and sustainable. It also applies various other environmental and social policies – drawn from the World Bank's Operational Policies – to determine a project's contribution to the development of the host country.[55]

Conclusions

This aspect of international environmental law has emerged since the publication of the first edition of this book, and it is clear from the not altogether consistent jurisprudence that it is yet to find its centre of gravity. A number of broad conclusions may be drawn. First, it has been confirmed that national environmental regulations (and their application) are susceptible to challenge on the grounds that they might interfere inappropriately with the property rights of foreign investors, either because they are expropriatory in character, or they fail to treat the foreign investor fairly, or they discriminate as between a domestic entity and a foreign investor. Secondly, it appears from the case law thus far that foreign investors may have a greater degree of protection than nationals, whose property is protected by human rights conventions.[56] Too great a gulf between the two systems should be avoided. Thirdly, in the one decided case on point there has been a reluctance to have regard to international environmental obligations in determining the level of compensation to be paid for a lawful expropriation: the *Santa Elena* v. *Costa Rica* decision does not indicate a willingness to address environment and development in an integrated manner, as the requirements of sustainable development require[57] and the jurisprudence of the WTO Appellate Body has done.[58] Fourthly, the cases indicate that the relationship between the protection of investments and the protection of the environment touches upon the delicate issue of subsidiarity or federalism, namely, the level of government and decision-making at which environmental decisions (for example, on the siting of hazardous facilities) are to be taken.[59] International adjudicators will need to be alert to the possibility of undermining support for foreign investment by inadvertently upsetting the

---

[55] Chapter 20, p. 1025 above; MIGA applies policies in relation to: natural habitats; forestry; pest management; safety of dams; involuntary resettlement; indigenous peoples; safeguarding cultural property; and projects on international waterways.

[56] See Chapter 7 above.   [57] Chapter 6, p. 252 above.   [58] Chapter 19, p. 946 above.

[59] See in this regard the approach taken by the 1998 Aarhus Convention to rights of public participation in decision-making; chapter 3, p. 118 above.

delicate balance which many states have achieved, or are struggling with, in relation to this aspect.

These conclusions coalesce around a broad theme, which suggests the broad challenge for the next phase of this lively area of the law. There is a need for balance: between the domestic, the regional and the global; between the legitimate interests of investors and legitimate environmental and other social interests; and between the state and its constituent parts.[60]

---

[60] P. Sands, 'Searching for Balance', 11 NYUELJ 198 (2002).

INDEX

Aarhus Convention 1998
  Compliance Committee, 209–10
  eco-labelling, 861
  information rights, 292, 297, 827,
    858–9
  and NGOs, 113
  non-compliance mechanism, 118,
    177–8
Aarhus Protocol on Heavy metals,
  334–5
Aarhus Protocol on POPs, 334–5, 628
Abidjan Convention 1981, 403
abuse of rights doctrine, 138–51
access to justice
  Aarhus Convention, 297
  OECD recommendations, 196
  Rio Declaration, 119–20
accidents
  Amoco Cadiz, 394, 450
  Bahia Paraiso, 711
  Chernobyl. *See* Chernobyl accident
  consultation, 840
  Cosmos 954, 202, 887, 897–8
  Exxon Valdez, 394, 442, 890
  Haven, 920–2
  industrial. *See* industrial accidents
  and information, 827
  nuclear emergencies, 647–8, 794
    notification, 844–5
  Patmos, 918–20
  Prestige, 438
  prevention
    agreements, 620–1
    generally, 620–5
    industrial. *See* industrial accidents
    Seveso Directives, 622–3, 785
  reporting requirements, 835, 841–3

Sandoz, 479–80, 481
Seveso, 827
Torrey Canyon, 394, 448, 913–15
UN Centre for Urgent
    Environmental Assistance, 84
ACCOBAMS, 596
accounting, environmental accounting,
    864–6
acid rain, 324, 327, 335–6, 478, 729, 757
acquiescence, 149
actio popularis, 187–90
Action Aid, 115
Action Plans, 143
actors, 15, 70. *See also* international
    organisations; NGOs, non-state
    actors; states
adjudication, international
    adjudication, 26
Afghanistan, 308
Africa
  African Nature Convention 1968, 34,
    243, 258, 524–6
  Bamako Convention. *See* Bamako
    Convention
  biodiversity agreements, 524–7
  East Africa, regional seas, 404–5
  hazardous waste, 150, 156
  international organisations, 106–7
  Lomé Convention, 254, 259, 295,
    680, 695, 753, 1022
  Lusaka Agreement, 525–6
  Nairobi SPA Protocol, 404, 526–7
  nuclear weapons, 651
  Pelindaba Treaty, 651
  rivers, 489–91
  sea dumping, 685
  wildlife, 28

African Charter of Human and
   Peoples' Rights, 106, 294, 298
African Development Bank, 107, 1027
African Economic Community, 107,
   1007–8
African Nature Convention 1968, 34,
   243, 258, 524–6
African Union, 106
Agenda 21
   agriculture, 58
   atmosphere, 58
   biodiversity, 58
   biotechnology, 58, 652, 672
   development banks, 1027
   economics and environmental law,
      941, 942–6
   education, 860
   environmental impact assessments,
      802–3
   financial mechanisms, 1021–2
   fisheries, 573
   forests, 58, 547
   free trade and environment, 1008
   freshwater resources, 58, 494–6
   generally, 57–9
   hazardous products, 670–2
   implementation, 59, 87–9, 226
   information rights, 827, 851–2, 854
   institutions, 59–60, 75
   intellectual property, 1045
   international law objectives, 62
   marine pollution, 428, 455–7
   national law objectives, 60–1
   non-binding instrument, 53
   and non-state actors, 71, 112–13
   public education, 860
   straddling stocks, 58
   sustainable development, 57–9
   technology transfer, 1042–3,
      1045
   toxic chemicals, 58, 619
   waste, 59, 676, 705–8
agriculture
   Agenda 21, 58
   ammonia emissions, 336, 757
   generally, 5, 669–70
   hazardous waste, 679–81
   sustainable agriculture, 96
   tractor engines, 759

air pollution
   aircraft emissions, 157, 341
   Canada–US Air Quality Agreement,
      339–41
   Combustion Directive, 336–9
   conventions, 41
   customary law, 321–2
   definition, 240, 325, 877
   early agreements, 34
   and environmental rights, 301–2
   EU law, 755–68
   gases, 323
      ECE Regulations, 324
   generally, 322–42
   international organisations, 109
   long-range transboundary pollution,
      324–36
      definition, 325
   LRTAP Convention, 324–36
   Thirty Per Cent Club, 327
   Trail Smelter case, 241–2, 318–19,
      885–6
   transboundary pollution, 388
      state liability, 874
   working environment, 638–9
aircraft
   emission standards, 157, 341–2
   emissions, ICAO Convention, 341
   EU environmental law, 759
   noise, 300–1, 302–3, 341, 992–3
   sovereign immunity, 417
airports, 300–1, 302–3
airspace, sovereignty over, 13
albatrosses, 610
Aleutians, 727
Alliance of Small Island States (AOSIS),
   361
Alps, 27
Alps Convention 1991, 535–6
Amazonian Treaty 1978, 265, 529–30
American Convention on Human
   Rights (ACHR), 107, 294,
   298
Americas
   Amazonian Treaty 1978, 265,
      529–30
   biodiversity agreements, 527–31
   international organisations, 107
   Kingston SPS Protocol 1990, 530–1

Americas (*cont.*)
  watercourses, 484–9
  Western Hemisphere Convention
    1940, 527–9
amicus curiae, 115, 1070
ammonia emissions, 336, 757
Amoco Cadiz, 394, 450
Amsterdam Treaty
  environmental law, 748–9
  generally, 739
  precautionary principle, 271
animal diseases, 29
animal experimentation, 779
Antarctic, 14, 17
  Antarctic Environment Protocol
    1991
    civil liability, 932
    environmental impact
      assessments, 818–19
    generally, 721–6
    institutions, 725
  Antarctic Mineral Resources
    Commission, 192–3
  Antarctic Seals Convention 1972,
    713–14
  Antarctic Treaty 1959, 712–13
  CCAMLR 1980, 714–15
  civil liability, 931–2
  compliance, 726
  CRAMRA 1988
    civil liability, 721, 931–2
    compliance, 721
    definition of damage, 876–7
    dispute settlement, 721
    generally, 716–21
    institutions, 718
    state liability, 900
  description, 711
  environmental impact assessments,
    723, 804, 818–19
  exploration, 719–20
  fish conservation, 586
  global commons, 710
  mineral resources, 155, 665, 716–21,
    722
  natural reserve, 712, 723
  ozone layer, 343
  Scientific Committee for Antarctic
    Research (SCAR), 114, 714–20

  seals, 713–14
  ship pollution, 442, 724
  sites of special scientific interest, 717
  special protection areas, 713
  specially managed areas, 724–5
  specially protected areas, 713, 717,
    724–5
  tourism, 725
  treaties, 33, 41, 711–12, 726
  waste, 723–4
    incineration, 687
    landfill, 688
    radioactive waste, 34
  whales, 595
anti-dumping, 1016
Apia Convention 1976, 531–2, 685
arbitration
  early international cases, 29–30
  generally, 212–14
archaeological excavations, 830
archipelagic states, 569–70
Arctic
  Action Plan, 730
  Arctic Council, 711, 727
  Arctic Environmental Protection
    Strategy, 727, 728–30
  generally, 727–30
  indigenous peoples, 727
  jurisdiction, 711, 727
  polar bears, 605–6
asbestos
  Convention, 639
  EU law, 766, 785
  information rights, 854
  WTO dispute, 7, 973–7
ASCOBANS, 595–6
ASEAN Convention
  biodiversity, 540–2
  development and environment, 265
  environmental impact assessments,
    804
  generally, 108
  sustainable use of resources, 46,
    258
  transboundary damage, 199
Asia
  ASEAN. *See* ASEAN Convention
  Asia-Pacific Fisheries Commission,
    585

biodiversity agreements, 540–2
international organisations, 108
sea turtles, 610
South Asia, nuclear weapons, 651
watercourses, 491–4
Asian Development Bank, 108, 210,
    1028
Athabaskans, 728
Atlantic
    cetaceans, 609
    fisheries
        research, 584
        tuna, 598–9
    North Atlantic
        marine mammals, 596
        salmon, 586
    North-East Atlantic
        fisheries, 586
        NEAFC, 586
        Oslo Convention, 423–5
        OSPAR. See OSPAR Convention
        seabed activities, 445
        treaties, 409
    North-West Atlantic
        fisheries, 585
        NAFO, 585
    sea turtles, 609
    South-East Atlantic
        fisheries, 585
        SEAFO, 585
atmosphere. See also air pollution;
        climate change; outer space;
        ozone depletion
    Agenda 21, 58
    global commons, 14
    international organisations,
        109
    landmarks, 317
    pollution, oceans and seas, 437–8
    protection, 4
    and sustainable development, 386–8
    UNCED, 385–9
Atmospheric Research and
        Environment Programme, 98
auditing, eco-auditing, 167, 863–7
    development banks, 1025
Australia
    and Antarctic, 716, 722
    British nuclear tests, 888

compensation from Iraq, 892
    French nuclear tests. See nuclear tests
    Great Barrier Reef Marine Park,
        505
    and Kyoto Protocol, 372, 374
    Nauru phosphates, 94, 666–9, 879,
        887
    ozone layer, 343
    Salmon case, 981–3
    Southern Bluefin Tuna cases, 137–8,
        213, 220, 275–6, 580–1
    territorial waters, 569
    tuna regulation, 600
    Volga case, 220
    world heritage areas, 612–14
Austria, 337, 659

Bahia Paraiso, 711
Baia Mare, 868
Bali Partnership Fund, 548
Balkans, 308
Baltic Sea
    cetaceans, 609
    fisheries, 585
    HELCOM, 413
    seabed activities, 448
    ship pollution, 442
    treaties, 412–15
    whaling, 595–6
Baltic Sea Convention 1974,
        413–14
Baltic Sea Convention 1992
    adoption, 395
    atmospheric pollution, 437
    generally, 413–15
    non-state actors, 271
Bamako Convention 1991
    chemicals, 637
    civil liability, 924
    generally, 695
    hazardous waste, 680
    incineration, 686
    precautionary principle, 270
    radioactive waste, 651
    scope, 619
    waste prevention, 683
Bangkok Declaration, 90
Bangladesh, Ganges River, 492–3
banks. See development banks

Basel Convention 1989
  Antarctic, 726
  'Basel Ban', 694–5
  enforcement, 187
  generally, 679–80, 691–5
  Liability Protocol 1999, 924–6
  recycling, 689
  waste prevention, 682, 692
bathing water, 772–3
bats, 609
batteries, 785, 792
bears, 605–6, 729
Beef Hormones case, 7, 277–8, 979–81
bees, 993–4
Belgium, 337, 433
  Foodstuffs Labelling case, 994–5
  Pesticides case, 992
  Waste Disposal case, 990–2
  wild birds, 604
Belize, 203
Benelux Convention 1970, 602
Benelux Convention 1982, 535
benzene, 638, 760
Bergen Declaration, 160, 269, 272
Bering Sea, 561–6
Berlin Mandate, 369
Berne Convention, 532, 686–7
biocides, 786
biodiversity
  1992 Convention. See Biodiversity
    Convention 1992
  Agenda 21, 58
  categories, 499
  CITES. See CITES
  common concern of humankind,
    516
  conservation, 5, 517–19
  EU law, 779–83
  global treaties, 505–23
  information exchange, 831
  international organisations, 110–11
  and land use. See land use
  loss of habitats and species, 499–501
  regional treaties, 523
    Africa, 524–7
    Americas, 527–31
    Asia, 540–2
    Europe, 532–40
    South Pacific, 531–2

  regulatory techniques
    bioregional management, 505
    generally, 503–5
    identification of ecosystems, 517
    identification of species, 518
    inventories, 503
    protected areas, 503
  specific habitats and species,
    543–615
    birds. See birds
    forests. See forests
    marine living resources, 558–600
    migratory species, 606–11
    plants, 551–4
    polar bears, 605–6
    vicunas, 606
    wetlands. See wetlands
  sustainable use, 517–19
  threats, 499–501
  treaties, 501–3
  UN priority, 51
Biodiversity Convention 1992
  access to genetic resources, 519–21
    Bonn guidelines, 520
  Annex I, 517–18
  biotechnology, 516, 520–3, 652
  and Biotechnology Directive, 1051–2
  commitments, 517–19
  environmental impact assessments,
    819–20
  equity, 263
  financial mechanisms, 523, 1034,
    1035
  generally, 515
  identification of ecosystems, 517
  institutions, 523
  intellectual property, 521, 1045–6
  jurisdiction, 516–17
  monitoring, 849
  notification of emergencies, 519, 843
  objectives, 516
  precautionary principle, 270
  principles, 234
  protected areas, 518
  reservations, 516
  scope, 516–17
  sovereignty rights, 237
  technology transfer, 520–1, 1041–2
biological resources, meaning, 18

biological weapons, 312
bioregional management, 505
Biosafety Protocol
  environmental impact assessments,
    820–1
  and GATT, 945
  generally, 653–8
  ICCP, 523
  import restrictions, 943
  information rights, 841
  living modified organisms (LMOs),
    861
  notification of emergencies, 843
  precautionary principle,
    270–1, 653
  public education, 860
Biosphere Conference, 35
biosphere reserves, 505
biotechnology, 5
  Agenda 21, 58, 652, 672
  Biodiversity Convention, 516,
    520–3, 652
  Biosafety Protocol 2000, 653–8
  EU law, 658–62, 1051
  generally, 651–62
  GMOs. *See* genetically modified
    organisms
  living modified organisms (LMOs),
    653–8, 861
  standards, 157
birds
  Benelux Convention 1970, 602
  Birds Convention 1950, 601–2
  conventions, 601
  generally, 601–5
  migratory birds, early conventions,
    27–8
  sea birds, 96, 588
  waterbirds, 609, 610
  Wild Birds Directive, 537
    case law, 604–5
    derogations, 604
    generally, 602–5, 779
Black Sea
  cetaceans, 609
  civil liability, 924
  ship pollution, 442
  UNEP Regional Seas Programme,
    405

bogs, 537
Bonn Agreements, 370, 377, 452–3
Botswana, 500
Brazil, 323, 361, 595, 961–73, 1027
Brundtland Report
  generally, 48–50
  Hague Declaration, 74
  Legal Experts Group, 260
  objectives, 11, 48
  organisational gaps, 74
  priority areas, 49–50
  regional organisations, 102
  state liability, 874
  sustainable development, 10–11, 46,
    252–3
  and UNCED, 48, 52, 53
Brunei, 541
buffer zones, 505
Buffon, Count, 26
Bulgaria, 735
Bunker Oil Convention 2001, 454, 922
Bush, George W., 370
business community, 70, 115–17
bustards, 610

cadmium, 333, 773
Cambodia, 491, 541
Canada
  Arctic jurisdiction, 727
  Asbestos case, 973–6
  Australian Salmon case, 981–3
  Beef Hormones case, 277–8, 979–81
  Boundary Waters Treaty, 203
  Canada–US Air Quality Agreement,
    339–41
  Canada–US Free Trade Agreement
    1991, 107
  Canada–US free trade agreements,
    997–9
  compensation from Iraq, 892
  Cosmos 954, 202, 879, 881, 887,
    897–8
  emission targets, 371
  Estai case, 578–80
  fisheries conservation, 217
  Great Lakes Water Quality
    Agreement 1978, 487–9, 685–6
  Gut Dam arbitration, 486–7
  and Kyoto Protocol, 372, 376

Canada (*cont.*)
  MMT ban, 1064–5
  NAFTA. *See* NAFTA
  PCBs, 1065–6
  territorial waters, 569
  Trail Smelter case, 241–2, 318–19,
    885–6
  US–Canada Boundary Waters Treaty
    1909, 485–6
  whaling, 595
carbon dioxide emissions
  agreements, 166
  climate change, 357–8, 372
  EU law, 758, 767, 768
carbon monoxide, 328–9, 759
carbon tax, 756
carbon tetrachloride, 350
carcinogens, 638, 784, 995–6
Caribbean
  biodiversity agreements, 527–31
  Caribbean Development Bank, 107,
    1028
  international organisations, 107
  monk seals, 591
  UNEP Regional Seas Programme,
    404
Caring for the Earth, 47–8, 62
Cartagena Commitment, 89
Cartagena Convention 1983, 404
Cartagena Protocol, 7, 404
case law, 153
caves, 537
cedar groves, 546
cetaceans 609, 779. *See also* dolphins;
  whaling
CFCs, 137, 343, 349, 357–8, 388–9
charges, as economic instruments,
  161
chemical installations, 808
chemical weapons, 295, 628
chemicals
  Agenda 21, 58, 619
  Chemicals Convention 1998
    generally, 635–6
    information rights, 827, 841
  classification, 626–7
  EU law, 784–6
  generally, 625–37
  health and safety at work, 640–1

  installations, 808
  international organisations, 111
  international trade, 630–5
    UNEP London Guidelines, 633–5
  labelling, 626–7
  packaging, 626–7
  prior informed consent, 630–1,
    634–5, 841
  production and use, 628
  regional agreements, 637
  registration, 626–7
  regulation, 155
  toxic chemicals, 5
  transport, 637
  UNCED, 670–2
  weapons, 295, 628
  WSSD, 672
Chernobyl accident, 191, 242, 292, 318,
    322, 647, 729, 794
  contaminated food, 880
  inadequacy of conventions, 908–9
  information failure, 844–5, 847
  lack of compensation, 870
  reparation, 879, 887–9
Chile, 582–3
China, 108
  air pollution, 323
  and climate change, 361
  and Kyoto Protocol, 373, 376
  and Notification Convention,
    846
  Trusteeship Council, 94
chlordane, 728
CIEL, 115
circuses, 509–11
CITES
  amendments, 141
  definitions, 507
  enforcement, 514–15
  generally, 505–15
  institutions, 506–7
  listed species, 508–9
    amendments, 509–10
    bluefin tuna, 599
  quotas, 513–14
  reservations, 510–11, 513
  trade in listed species, 508–9
    exemptions, 509–11, 513
citizen suits, 177

civil liability for environmental damage
  Antarctic, 931–2
  Caring for the Earth, 48
  Council of Europe, 64, 905
  generally, 904–37
  issues, 871
  Lugano Convention, 933–7
  marine pollution, 454–5, 923–4
  meaning, 870
  nuclear installations
    1988 Joint Protocol, 912
    1997 Protocol, 910–11
    generally, 905–12
    Paris Convention 1960, 906–8
    Vienna Convention 1963, 908–12
  oil pollution. See oil pollution
  rules, 165, 905
  Stockholm Conference, 38
  transport, 930–1
  waste. See waste
civil rights, 305–7
Clean Air Strategy, 756
Clean Development Mechanism,
    373–4, 379–80, 1042,
    1057
clean technology, 411, 787
climate change
  adverse effects, 877, 901
  and aircraft, 342
  Berlin Mandate, 369
  Bonn Agreements, 370, 377
  EU law, 767–8
  generally, 357–81
  Geneva Declaration, 369–70
  greenhouse gases, 357
  international organisations, 109
  IPCC, 101, 358
  Kyoto Protocol, 368–81
  Marrakesh Accords, 370, 377–81
  priority, 4
  scientific reports, 358
Climate Change Convention 1992
  amendment, 368
  Berlin Mandate, 369
  commitments, 362–3
  common but differentiated
    responsibility, 286, 362
  developed/developing countries,
    360–1

dispute settlement, 368
economic interests, 360–1
environmental impact assessments,
    805
equity, 263
financial assistance, 180, 366–8,
    1034, 1035–6
and free trade, 1009
generally, 359–68
Geneva Declaration, 369–70
implementation, 368
information rights, 853
institutions, 367–8
joint implementation, 365
monitoring requirements, 849
objectives, 361–2
Preamble, 361
precautionary principle, 271
principles, 233–4, 362
Protocol. See Kyoto Protocol
reporting requirements, 363–4,
    835–6
reservations, 368
sinks, 346–60, 361, 362, 364–6
sources, 360, 364–6
state liability, 900–1
technology transfer, 366–8,
    1042
climate system, meaning, 18
coastal states
  exclusive economic zones, 570–2
  general rights, 569–70
  Iceland, 567
  rights over continental shelf, 566,
    570
  rights over high sea fishing, 567
  straddling stocks, 576
  UNCLOS, 572
  UNCLOS I, 566
Coastal Zone Management, 781
Codex Alimentarius, 95, 99–100, 627,
    671
Colombia, 149
Columbia River, 886
Combustion Directive
  existing plants, 337
  generally, 336–9
  new plants, 338–9
command and control, 155, 170

common but differentiated
    responsibility
    Climate Change Convention 1992,
        362
    Combustion Directive, 337
    principle, 55–6, 231, 285–9
    UNCLOS, 397
common concern, 287, 547
common heritage of humankind, 547,
        552
common law, 142
Commonwealth Secretariat, 102
compensation
    case law, 887–90
    environmental damage, 883–4
    liability. See civil liability for
        environmental damage; state
        liability for environmental
        damage
    Trail Smelter case, 885–6
    UN Compensation Commission,
        885, 890–4
competition
    anti-competitive agreements,
        1015–16
    anti-dumping, 1016
    environmental dumping, 1010
    EU law, 1011–14
    generally, 1010–17
    NAFTA, 1004
    and subsidies, 1011–15
compliance
    generally, 171
    role of international organisations,
        78
conciliation, 203–5
conflict resolution. See dispute
        resolution
construction, health and safety, 639–40
consultation
    customary law, 840
    generally, 838–40
consumer information, 167
contemporaneity principle, 824
continental shelf
    1958 Convention, 566
    exploitation, 448
    rights of coastal states, 566, 570
    sovereignty over, 14

contributory negligence, 916, 936
Convention on Rights of the Child
        1989, 299, 860
co-operation
    Montreal Protocol 1987, 355–6
    principle, 231, 249–51
    Stockholm Conference, 38
    Vienna Convention 1985, 345
COPUOS, 90
coral bleaching, 393
coral reefs, 499, 500, 1023
Cosmos 954, 202, 879, 881, 887, 897–8
COSPAR, 114
Costa Rica, 1070–1
cost-effectiveness, 8
Cotonou Agreement, 695–6, 753
Council of Europe
    air pollution, 34
    civil liability for environmental
        damage, 64, 905
    environmental crimes, 896
    generally, 105–6
    Lugano Convention, 177, 933–7
covenants, environmental covenants,
        1025
cradle-to-grave concept, 168
CRAMRA 1988, 716–21, 876–7, 900,
        931–2
cranes, 609
criminal liability, states, 894–6
CRISTAL, 922–3
crocidolite, 639
CRTD 1989, 930
curlews, 609
customary law
    acquiescence, 149
    air pollution, 321–2
    consultation rights, 840
    generally, 143–50
    instant customary law, 58
    opinio juris, 146, 147
    persistent objectors, 149
    regional custom, 149–50
    reporting requirements, 837, 845
    state practice, 144–6
    and treaties, 145–6, 147–8
    treatment of aliens, 1057–8
cyanide, 868
cyprinids, 775

Cyprus, 733, 735
Czech Republic, 412, 735

dams, 312, 463–4, 469–77, 486–7,
    612–14, 1023, 1027
dangerous substances. *See* hazardous
    substances
Danube, 65, 191, 217, 462, 469–77,
    478, 822–4, 889
Dassonville Formula, 996
DDT, 728
demography
    Rio Declaration, 56
    Stockholm Conference, 39
    UN Commission on Population and
        Development, 93
Denmark
    air pollution, 304
    Arctic jurisdiction, 727
    Danish Bees case, 993–4
    Danish Bottles case, 987
    environmental standards, 412, 795
    and Sellafield, 433
    state aids, 1013
deposit-refund systems, 164
desertification. *See* drought and
    desertification
detergents, 768
developed countries
    Climate Change Convention 1992,
        360–1
    common but differentiated
        responsibility, 287–9
    generally, 71
    overseas development assistance,
        1022–3
    verification mechanisms, 9
developing countries
    air pollution, 323
    Beijing Symposium, 62
    Climate Change Convention 1992,
        360–1, 366–7, 688
    common but differentiated
        responsibility, 287–9
    compliance with conventions, 180
    financial assistance, 9
    generally, 71–2
    integration of environment and
        development, 266

Kyoto Protocol, 375
living modified organisms (LMOs),
    657–8
Lomé Convention, 41
Montreal Protocol 1987, 354–5
POPs Convention 2001, 629
right to development, 55
technology. *See* technology transfer
development and environment
    looming issue, 34
    overseas development assistance,
        1022–3
    planning, 49
    Rio Declaration, 54–5
    Stockholm Conference, 39
    World Conservation Strategy, 47
development banks
    African Development Bank, 107,
        1027
    Asian Development Bank, 108, 210,
        1028
    Caribbean Development Bank, 107,
        1028
    dispute procedures, 210–11
    environmental audits, 866–7, 1025
    environmental impact assessments,
        821–2
    environmental policy, 41–2
    European Bank for Reconstruction
        and Development (EBRD), 42,
        102, 1028–9
    European Investment Bank, 1029
    generally, 1023–9
    Inter-American Development Bank,
        107, 210, 1027
    Islamic Development Bank, 1028
    regional banks, 1027–9
    World Bank. *See* World Bank
diesel engines, 759
direct effect doctrine, 734
discrimination, environmental
    discrimination, 298
dispute resolution
    arbitration, 212–14
    Climate Change Convention 1992,
        368
    conciliation, 203–5
    CRAMRA 1988, 721
    development banks, 210–11

dispute resolution (*cont.*)
  diplomatic means, 201–12
  foreign direct investment, 1061–2
    Energy Charter Treaty, 1062
    NAFTA, 1062
  generally, 200–26
  ICSID, 1037, 1062
  international courts, 214. *See also*
    specific courts
  ITLOS. *See* ITLOS
  legal means, 212–26
  mechanisms, 200–1
  mediation, 203–5
  NAFTA, 211–12, 1004–5
  negotiation, 201–2
  non-compliance procedures,
    205–10
  role of international organisations,
    78
  treaty provisions, 137–8
  UNCLOS. *See* UNCLOS
  WTO, 220–2
dolphins, 16, 190, 588, 590–2
  EU law, 779
  Mediterranean sanctuary, 597
  Tuna/Dolphin cases, 185, 190, 238,
    861, 953–61
driftnet fishing, 42, 151, 157
  1989 Convention, 588–9
  generally, 588
  UN Resolution, 589
drinking water, 771–2
drought and desertification
  Action Plan, 556
  generally, 58, 64
  UNCCD, 557–8
  UNCED, 556–7
Dubrovnik, 312
ducks, 607
dugongs, 591
dumping
  anti-dumping, 1016
  environmental dumping, 1010,
    1017
Dumpwatch, 696
dunes, 537
dust, 765
Dworkin, R., 234
dykes, 312

Earth Charter, 54
Earthwatch, 37, 848
East Africa, regional Seas, 404–5
eco-auditing, 167, 863–7, 1025
eco-labelling, 17, 167, 861–3
ecological necessity, 472–4, 477
ecology, meaning, 15
economic instruments
  charges and taxes, 161
  civil liability, 165
  consumer information incentives,
    167
  deposit-refund systems, 164
  enforcement incentives, 165
  environmental agreements, 166
  form of regulation, 154
  generally, 158–67
  investment incentives, 166
  joint implementation, 161–4, 170
  subsidies, 164–5
  trade measures, 165–6
  tradeable permits, 161–4, 312, 378
economic rights, 297–305
economics
  Climate Change Convention 1992,
    360–1
  cost-effectiveness, 8
  and environmental law, 940–2
  and international law, 8–9
  and sustainable development, 259,
    941
  trade measures. *See* trade restrictions
    on environmental grounds
economies in transition, 71, 366
ECOSOC, 79, 91
ecosystems
  early conventions, 33
  identification and monitoring, 517
  meaning, 15
Ecuador, 598
education
  Agenda 21, 860
  public education and awareness,
    860–3
  Rio Declaration, 860
  World Charter for Nature, 46
eels, 571, 775
effects doctrine, 240
El Salvador, 598

Elbe, 478
electricity, 996–7
elephants, 135, 140, 509–11, 513, 514, 607
EMAS, 866–7
EMEP, 849
emergencies. *See* accidents
emission standards, 157, 341–2
endangered species
  African Nature Convention, 525
  Berne criteria, 509–10
  CITES. *See* CITES
  EU law, 780
  international organisations, 110
  international trade, 41, 508–9
    exemptions, 509–11, 513
  lists, 507, 508–9
    amendments, 509–10
    bluefin tuna, 599
  marking of specimens, 513
  meaning of species, 507
  quotas, 513–14
  ranching, 513
  sea turtles, 588, 607, 609, 961–73
energy
  efficiency, EU law, 767–8, 1014
  Energy Charter Treaty 1994, 664–5
  generally, 663–5
  International Atomic Energy
    Authority (IAEA), 100
  international organisations, 74
  renewable energy, 996–7
  UN Committee on Energy and
    Natural Resources for
    Development, 93
  UNCED, 663
  WSSD, 663
Energy Charter Treaty 1994, 1060–1, 1062
enforcement
  by international organisations, 191–5
  by non-state actors, 195–200
    in internal courts, 198–200
    in national courts, 195–8
  international enforcement, 182
  state enforcement, 182–91
    areas beyond national
      jurisdictions, 184–91

  damage to other states, 184
    within state territories, 184
ENMOD Convention, 111, 313–14
environment
  and development, looming issue, 34
  and human rights, 38, 117, 294–7
  meaning, 15
environment funds
  European Union, 1030, 1036–7
  GEF. *See* Global Environmental
    Facility
  generally, 1029–37
  Kuwait Compensation Fund, 1030
  LIFE, 1030, 1036–7
  Montreal Protocol Multilateral
    Fund, 355–6, 1021, 1029,
    1031–2, 1041
  oil pollution. *See* oil pollution
  UNEP Environment Fund, 1030
  Wetlands Fund, 545, 1021, 1030,
    1031
  World Heritage Fund, 614, 1021,
    1030
environmental agreements, 166
environmental audits, 167, 863–7, 1025
environmental covenants, 1025
environmental damage, definition,
    869, 876–8, 897, 935–6
environmental discrimination, 298
environmental dumping, 1010, 1017
environmental impact assessments
  Agenda 21, 802–3
  Antarctic, 723, 804, 818–19
  Caring for the Earth, 48
  and development banks, 821–2, 1025
  emergence, 799–802
  EU law, 803, 807–13
    contents, 809–10
    disputes, 810–11
    mandatory assessments, 808–9
    non-mandatory assessments, 809
    strategic environmental
      assessments, 812–13
  Gabcikovo-Nagymaros case, 822–4
  ILC, 803
  international organisations, 111
  landfill, 687
  marine pollution, 433–4
  nuclear tests, 187

environmental impact assessments
(*cont.*)
  Rio Declaration, 795, 800
  scope, 17
  Stockholm Declaration, 801
  treaties
    Antarctic Environment Protocol,
      818–19
    ASEAN Agreement, 804
    Biodiversity Convention, 819–20
    Biosafety Protocol, 820–1
    Climate Change Convention, 805
    Espoo Convention, 42, 803,
      814–17
    generally, 803–21
    Noumea Convention 1986,
      813–14
    UNCLOS, 805–7
  UNEP principle, 44, 801
  World Charter for Nature, 46, 802
  WSSD, 803
environmental law. *See* international
    environmental law
environmental modifications, 17,
    314
equity, 152, 262
erga omnes obligations, 185, 188–9
Espoo Convention, 687
  dispute resolution, 205
  generally, 814–17
  global commons, 187
  landfill, 687
Estai case, 578–80
Estonia, 412, 735
EU
  Commission, 193–5, 736–8
  Council of Ministers, 736–7, 738
  disputes with US, 7
  environmental law. *See* EU
    environmental law
  institutions, 736–7
  and Kyoto Protocol, 372, 374, 376
  law. *See* EU law
  Parliament, 737, 738
EU environmental law
  Action Programmes on
    Environment, 750–3
  air quality
    aircraft and ships, 759

assessment and management,
    756–8
  CAFE Programme, 756
  Clean Air Strategy, 756
  CO_2 emissions, 767, 768
  diesel engines, 759
  generally, 755–68
  industrial plants, 763–4
  lead in fuels, 760
  mobile equipment, 759
  monitoring, 767
  motor cars, 758–9, 766
  ozone, 766–7
  ozone layer, 761–2
  sulphur and nitrogen dioxides,
    478, 762–3
  waste incineration, 764–6
asbestos, 766
biodiversity, 779–83
biotechnology, 658–62, 1051
carbon dioxide emissions, 151, 156,
    166
carbon tax, 756
chemicals, 637, 784–6
coastal zones, 781
Cohesion Fund, 746
consistency with international law,
    762
eco-labelling, 167, 862–3
EMAS, 866–7
emission targets, 371
energy efficiency, 767
Environmental Action Programmes,
    65, 787, 926
environmental auditing, 866–7
environmental impact assessments,
    803, 807–13
financial resources, 1030, 1036–7
fisheries, 781–3
forests, 766
greenhouse gas emissions, 164
Habitats Directive, 536–40
hazardous substances, 784–6
history, 740–2
  Amsterdam Treaty, 748–9
  EEA Agreement, 747
  Maastricht Treaty, 745–6
  Single European Act, 742–5
implementation, 175

information rights, 17, 854–6
integrated pollution prevention and
  control (IPPC), 168, 754–5, 764
meaning of environment, 17–18
noise, 783–4
non-economic factors, 8, 746,
  748–9
packaging of dangerous goods, 34
polluter-pays principle, 283–5, 742
precautionary principle, 232, 271,
  279, 746
  Beef Hormones case, 277–8,
    979–81
principles, 749–54
radioactive substances, 793–4
Seveso Directives, 622–3, 785
soil issues, 556
standards, 795
subsidiarity, 751
sustainable development, 748
Swordfish case, 582–3
tax incentives, 759
tax on fossil fuel products, 161
waste
  civil liability, 926–30
  electric and electronic equipment,
    792
  Framework Directive, 787–9
  generally, 786–92
  hazardous waste, 680–1, 699–703,
    764–5, 789–91
  incineration, 686, 687, 764–6, 792
  landfill, 687, 792
  packaging waste, 792
  particular wastes, 791–2
  prevention, 681–2
  radioactive waste, 441, 703–5, 711
  recycling, 689
  treaties, 792
water quality, 477
  bathing water, 772–3
  dangerous substances, 773–4
  drinking water, 771–2
  generally, 768–79
  groundwater, 774–5
  marine pollution, 778–9
  protection of fish, 775–6
  river basin management, 769–71
  urban waste water, 776–8

Water Framework Directive,
  769–71
Wild Birds Directive, 537, 602–5, 779
EU law
  Amsterdam Treaty, 271, 739, 748–9
  competition
    anti-competitive agreements,
      1015–16
    anti-dumping, 1017
    subsidies, 1011–14
  Court of First Instance, 224
  ECJ. *See* European Court of Justice
  enforcement of state obligations by
    other states, 185–6
  environmental law. *See* EU
    environmental law
  European Patent Convention,
    1047–50
  founding treaties, 734, 736
  implementation, 737, 738
  jurisdiction, 732–3
  legal order, 734
  Maastricht Treaty, 259, 271, 739,
    745–6
  Nice Treaty, 735, 739
  non-economic factors, 10–11
  non-tariff barriers, 986–7
  principles, 735
  Single European Act, 739, 742–5
  sources of law, 736–8
  state aids, 1011–14
  state liability, failure to implement
    EU law, 928–9
  supremacy over national law, 734,
    736–7, 738
  taxation, 735
  Tuna/Dolphin case, 958–60
  unilateral trade restrictions on
    environmental grounds
    Aher-Waggon case, 992–3
    Belgian Foodstuffs Labelling case,
      994–5
    Belgian Pesticides case, 992
    Belgian Waste Disposal case, 990–2
    Danish Bees case, 993–4
    Danish Bottles case, 987
    Dassonville formula, 996
    Dead Red Grouse case, 990
    ECJ jurisprudence, 987

EU law (*cont.*)
    generally, 985–97
    German renewable energy, 996–7
    Swedish ban on chemical
        products, 995–6
EURATOM, 641, 642, 734
EURATOM Treaty, 793
Europe
    bats, 609
    biodiversity agreements, 532–40
        Alps Convention 1991, 535–6
        Benelux Convention 1982, 535
        Berne Convention 1979, 532
        Habitats Directive, 536–40
    international organisations, 102–6
    watercourses agreements, 477–85
European Bank for Reconstruction and
        Development (EBRD), 42, 102,
        1028–9
European Commission on Human
        Rights, 203
European Convention on Human
        Rights, 106, 198, 245, 294,
        299–304
European Court of Human Rights, 65,
        225
European Court of Justice
    fines on member states, 929–30
    generally, 222–4, 737–9
    jurisdiction, 737–9
    jurisprudence, 153
    preliminary references, 224
European Environment Agency,
        739–40, 843–8, 850
European Investment Bank, 1029
European Patent Convention, 1047–50
European Social Charter, 106, 294
eutrophication, 335–6, 392, 757
exclusive economic zones, 14, 569,
        570–2
explosives, 784
export restrictions, 943, 948, 1065–6
expropriation, 1058, 1068–9, 1070–1
Exxon Valdez, 394, 442, 890

Fabre, Jean Henri, 26
Faroe Islands, 596
fens, 537
FIELD, 115

Fiji, 135
financial assistance
    Brundtland Report, 50
    Climate Change Convention 1992,
        366–8
    development banks, 1023–9
    funds. *See* environment funds
    generally, 1021
    Montreal Protocol 1987, 355–6, 1020
    overseas development assistance,
        1022–3
Finland, 337, 412, 727
fires, 505
fish
    common responsibility, 286
    protection, water quality, 775–6
fisheries
    anadromous species, 571, 572, 585,
        607
    archipelagic states, 569–70
    catadromous stocks, 571, 572
    catches, information exchange, 830
    coastal states, 569–70
    conservation, generally, 560–1
    driftnets. *See* driftnet fishing
    early conventions, 27
    EU law, 781–3
    exclusive economic zones, 569,
        570–2
    FAO Code of Conduct, 577–8
    high seas, 572–8
    international cases, 578–83
    international organisations, 111
    legal history, 560–1, 568
        Fisheries Jurisdiction case, 567–8
        Pacific Fur Seal arbitration, 253,
            561–6
        UNCLOS I, 566–7
    marine mammals, 571, 572, 573,
        590–2
    migratory species, 569, 571–2
    overfishing, 559–60
    regional agreements, 584–7
        ineffectiveness, 586–7
    straddling stocks. *See* straddling
        stocks
    UNCED, 573
    UNCLOS, 568–73
    WSSD Plan of Implementation, 600

fishing zones, sovereignty over, 14
flag states, and straddling stocks, 577
flora and fauna
    1958 Geneva Conventions, 32
    Arctic, 729–30
    endangered species. See CITES
    export restrictions, 943
    information exchange, 830
    Stockholm Declaration, 501–2
    terminology, 16
Food and Agriculture Organization
        (FAO)
    environmental role, 31
    fisheries, 565–6, 577–8
    food contaminated by radiation, 880
    generally, 95–6
    genetic resources, 552–4
    pesticides, 631–3
    Tropical Forestry Action Plan, 85,
        96, 548
    World Soil Charter, 555
Food Standard Programme, 99
foreign direct investment
    case law, 1064–71
    dispute settlement, 1061–2
    Energy Charter Treaty, 1060–1, 1062
    expropriation, 1058, 1068–9, 1070–1
    insurance, 1071–2
    MIGA, 1071–2
    Multilateral Agreement on
        Investment (MAI), 1062–4
    NAFTA, 1059–60, 1062
    treaties, 1057–64
    WSSD, 1056
forestry equipment, 760
forests
    Agenda 21, 58, 547
    ASEAN Agreement, 541
    carbon sinks, 374, 381
    and climate change, 361
    deforestation, 4, 27, 499, 546
    EU law, 766, 781
    fires, 318
    forestry equipment, 759
    generally, 545–51
    International Tropical Timber
        Agreement 1994, 547–8
    land-use change and forestry
        (LUCUF) activities, 377, 380

management, information exchange,
    830
Marrakesh Accords, 379
Rain Forest Trust Fund, 1027
research, 96
Tropical Forestry Action Plan, 85,
    96, 548
tropical forests, 500, 1023, 1070–1
UN Forum on Forests, 92
UNCED Forest Principles, 52, 54,
    546, 548–51, 1009
and World Bank, 1027
fossil fuel products, 161
France
    Amoco Cadiz, 450
    and Antarctic, 716, 722
    Asbestos case, 973–6
    dumping of radioactive waste, 426
    and GEF, 1032
    GMOs, 659
    Haven claim, 920–2
    Lac Lanoux arbitration, 184, 202,
        463–4
    marine pollution, 433
    Mediterranean marine mammals,
        596–7
    nuclear emergencies, notification,
        844
    and nuclear liability, 910
    nuclear tests. See nuclear tests
    pollution of Rhine, 198, 213
    prawn fisheries, 185
    Rhine pollution, 479–80
    South Pacific nuclear activities, 650
    state aids, 1013
    sulphur and nitrogen dioxides, 337
    sulphur dioxide emissions, 304
    Torrey Canyon, 448, 913–15
    trade restrictions, waste oils, 987–90
    Trusteeship Council, 94
    wild birds, 604
free trade. See trade restrictions on
        environmental grounds
freedom of expression, 292
freshwater resources
    Agenda 21, 58, 494–6
    case law. See Gabcikovo-Nagymaros
        case
    community of interests, 461, 463

freshwater resources (*cont.*)
  customary law, 461–77
  Helsinki Rules, 464–5
  human rights issue, 497
  international organisations, 110
  issues, 460–1
  Lac Lanoux arbitration, 184, 202,
      463–4
  protection, 5, 51
  regional agreements, 477–94
    Africa, 489–91
    Americas, 484–9
    Asia, 491–4
    Europe, 477–85
  treaties, 459–60
  US–Canada Boundary Waters Treaty
      1909, 485–6
  Watercourses Convention 1992,
      482–5
  Watercourses Convention 1997,
      466–8
  WSSD, 496
Friends of the Earth, 114
fuels, lead in, 760
Fund Convention 1992, 688, 915–22
furs, 28

G-77, 55, 72, 360, 373
Gabcikovo-Nagymaros case, 65, 174,
      184, 217
  co-operation principle, 250–1
  environmental impact assessments,
      822–4
  generally, 469–77
  precautionary principle, 274–5
  prevention principle, 248
  reparation, 889
  threshold of damage, 879
  use of shared natural resources, 263,
      462
Galapagos Agreement, 583
Galapagos fur seals, 591
Ganges River, 492–3
garbage, ship pollution, 443–4
gas emissions, 148
GATS, 947
GATT. *See* WTO/GATT
geese, 607
genetic resources

  access to, 519–21
  Bonn guidelines, 520
  genetic diversity, 47
  Global System on Plant Genetic
      Resources, 95
  intellectual property, 1046
  International Fund for Plant Genetic
      resources, 1021
  meaning, 18
  protection, 552–4
  Treaty on Plant Genetic Resources,
      1046
genetically modified organisms
      (GMOs)
  civil liability, 937
  EU law, 10–11, 659–62
  issue, 652
  release, 14
  scientific opinion, 7
  trade restrictions, 943
Geneva Conventions, 314–15
Geneva Declaration, 369–70
Germany
  Aher-Waggon case, 992–3
  and Basel Convention, 135
  Chernobyl reparations, 887
  and Climate Change Convention
      1992, 360
  compensation from Iraq, 892
  environmental rights, 299
  environmental standards, 412, 795
  Fisheries Jurisdiction case, 567–8
  GMOs, 659
  nuclear plants, 306
  precautionary principle, 267
  renewable energy, 996–7
  state aids, 1011, 1013
  sulphur and nitrogen dioxides, 337
  and Wild Birds Directive, 194, 604
GESAMP, 101, 392, 393
Global Atmosphere Watch (GAW), 99,
      386
global commons
  Antarctic, 710
  enforcement of treaty obligations in,
      187–9
  and extra-territoriality, 240
  meaning, 14
  trusteeship, 94

Global Compact, 116
Global Environment Facility (GEF)
  assistance to developing countries, 9,
    1021
  Biodiversity Convention, 1035
  Climate Change Convention 1992,
    368, 1034, 1035–6
  creation, 42, 1029
  generally, 1032–4
  POPs Convention, 1034, 1036
  UNCED, 1034–6
  and UNDP, 85
Global Environmental Monitoring
    System (GEMS), 37, 84, 848
Global Ozone Observing System
    (GOOS), 98–9, 344, 386, 388
globalisation, 4
good faith, 150–1, 902
good-neighbourliness, 242–3, 249
Gorbachev, Mikhail, 94
gorillas, 607
Gothenburg Protocol 1999, 335–6
grasslands, 500, 537
grayling, 775
Great Lakes
  1909 Treaty, 485–6
  1978 Great Lakes Water Quality
    Agreement, 487–9
  Gut Dam arbitration, 486–7
Greece, 337, 659, 795, 929, 1037
greenhouse gases
  EU law, 756, 767
  generally, 357
  inventories, 101
  ozone molecules, 343
  sources and sinks, 364–6, 374–5
  stabilisation objective, 156
  tradeable permits, 164, 767, 768
Greenland, 596
Greenland halibut, 578
Greenpeace, 114, 1048
ground-level ozone, 335–6
groundwaters, 465, 774–5
Guadeloupe fur seals, 591
Guatemala, 203
Gulf of Aden, 403–4, 442
Gulf of Guinea, 402–3
Gut Dam arbitration, 486–7
Gwich'in, 728

habitats
  conventions, 41
  and World Bank, 1027
Habitats Directive
  criteria, 537
  derogations, 540
  financing, 539
  generally, 536–40, 779
  habitat types, 537
  Natura 2000, 537, 539
  protection of species, 539–40
  special areas of conservation, 537
  special conservation measures,
    538–9
  species list, 537
Hague Declaration 1989, 74, 295
halibut, 578, 585
halons, 343, 349
Hawaii, monk seals, 591
hazardous activities
  agriculture, 669–70
  civil liability, 937
    Europe, 933–7
  energy, 663–5
  generally, 662–70
  ILC draft articles, 234
  mining, 665–9
  tourism, 670
hazardous substances
  2000 HNS Protocol, 452
  Agenda 21, 670–2
  Chemicals Convention 1998, 635–6
  civil liability, 65
    carriage by sea, 454
    Europe, 933–7
    strict liability, 48
  classification, 626–7
  EU law, 784–6
    water quality, 773–4
  generally, 625–37
  health and safety at work, 640–1
  international trade, 630–5
    UNEP London Guidelines, 633–5
  labelling, 626–7
  packaging, 626–7
  prior informed consent, 630–1,
    634–5
  production and use, 628
  regional agreements, 637

hazardous substances (*cont.*)
  registration, 626–7
  reporting requirements, 835
  sea dumping, 34, 155
  transport, 637, 930–1
  US–Mexico agreement, 621
hazardous waste. *See* waste
HCFCs, 350–1, 761
health and safety at work, 638–41, 646
health and safety measures, and free
      trade, 977–85
heavy metals
  Aarhus Protocol 1998, 333–4
  Arctic, 729, 730
  at sea, 430
  EU law, 765
HELCOM, 413
Helsinki Rules, 464–5
heritage. *See* world heritage
hexachlorocyclohexane, 773
high seas
  1958 Convention, 566
  diminishing area, 560
  fishing rights, 1958 Convention,
      566–7
  UNCLOS, 572–8
history
  after UNCED, 63–9
  from Stockholm to Rio, 40–52
  international organisations, 73–4
  pre-UN conventions, 26–30
  stages, 25–6
  Stockholm Conference, 35–9
  UN period, 30–1
  UNCCUR period, 31–5
  UNCED, 52–63
HNS Convention 1996, 930–1
Honduras, 203
human rights
  African Charter on Human and
      Peoples' Rights, 106, 294, 298
  American Convention on Human
      Rights, 107, 294, 298
  civil rights, 305–7
  development of international
      human rights law, 293–4
  economic and social rights, 297–305
  and environmental protection, 38,
      117, 294–7

European Convention on Human
      Rights, 106, 198, 245, 294,
      299–304
  freshwater resources, 497
  ICCPR, 293
  ICESCR, 293
  indigenous peoples, 299
  international courts, 225
  political rights, 305–7
  property rights, 303–4
  UN Commission on Human Rights,
      93
  Universal Declaration of Human
      Rights, 293
  and waste, 295, 675, 691
  water, 497
humanitarian law, 152
Humboldt, Alexander von, 27
Hungary, 735, 868
      See also Gabcikovo-Nagymaros
      case
hydrobromofluorocarbons, 350–1
hydrocarbons, 430, 759
hydrofluorocarbons, 372

ICAO Convention, 341
Iceland
  Arctic jurisdiction, 727
  Fisheries Jurisdiction case, 567–8
  whaling, 135, 593, 594, 595,
      596
ICSID, 1037, 1062
ICSU, 114
IMF, 101
implementation
  conflict. *See* dispute resolution
  developing countries, 180
  enforcement by non-state actors,
      195–200
  generally, 174
  international enforcement, 182
  national compliance, 176–80
  national law, 175
  private enforcement, 177
  reporting, 180–2, 834
  role of international organisations,
      77–8
  state enforcement, 182–91
  techniques, 69

import restrictions
  asbestos, 973–6
  beef hormones, 979–81
  bees, 993–4
  Canadian lobsters, 998–9
  chemical products, 995–6
  Danish bottles, 987
  EU states, 986–7
  food labelling, 994–5
  generally, 943
  grouse, 990
  Japanese varietals, 983–4
  MMT, 1064–5
  pesticides, 992
  reformulated gasoline, 961–5
  salmon, 981–3
  Shrimp/Turtle cases, 961–73
  Tuna/Dolphin cases, 953–61
  and WTO, 948
incendiary weapons, 312
incineration
  at sea, 156, 419, 422, 424,
      426
  Baltic Sea, 414
  generally, 686–7
  hazardous waste, 157, 792
  municipal waste, 679
  on board ships, 444
India
  air pollution, 323
  and climate change, 361
  precautionary principle,
      279
  river treaties, 492–3
  shrimps, 965–6
Indian Ocean
  Indian Ocean Tuna Commission
      Agreement 1993, 599–600
  sea turtles, 610
  UNEP Regional Seas Programme,
      404–5
  whales, 595
indigenous peoples
  Arctic, 727
  civil and political rights, 306
  environmental and human rights,
      299
Indonesia, 541
industrial accidents

1992 Convention, 42, 64, 111, 621,
    623–5
civil liability, 937
co-operation, 249
ILO code of conduct, 621
UN priority, 51
industrial plants, 763–4
information
  access to, 826
  consultation, 838–40
  customary law, 845
  eco-auditing, 863–7
  eco-labelling, 17, 167, 861–3
  exchange
    air pollution protocols, 336
    Canada–US Air Quality
        Agreement, 341
    chemicals, 633–5
    generally, 829–32
    pesticides, 632–3
    role of international
        organisations, 77
  gathering, 847–51
  monitoring
    international organisations,
        847–51
    treaty obligations, 851
  Notification Convention 1986, 687,
      845–7
    limitations, 846–7
    reservations, 801, 846
  notification of emergencies
    generally, 841–3
    nuclear accidents, 844–5
  prior informed consent
    generally, 841
    hazardous substances, 630–1,
        634–5, 841
  public education, 860–3
  reporting, 832–8
  rights
    Aarhus Convention, 292, 297,
        827, 858–9
    Agenda 21, 7, 827, 851–2, 854
    Caring for the Earth, 48
    EU law, 17, 854–6
    generally, 852–9
    Lugano Convention, 858
    OSPAR Convention, 411, 856

information (*cont.*)
  restrictions, 292
  Rio Declaration, 118, 853–4
  Stockholm Declaration, 39, 40,
    826
  UNEP principle, 44
  World Charter for Nature, 46, 827
  UNCED, 851–2
INFOTERRA, 37, 84, 848
Institut de Droit International, 29, 115,
    154, 321–2, 874
insurance
  EU waste operators, 927
  foreign direct investments, 1071–2
  Lugano Convention, 934
  nuclear installations, 907, 908, 910
  oil pollution, 915
integrated pollution control, 154,
    167–9
  IPPC Directive, 754–5, 764
intellectual property
  Agenda 21, 7, 1045
  Biodiversity Convention 1992, 521,
    688, 1045–6
  generally, 1043–53
  patents, 1047
  technology transfer, 1044–6
  and traditional knowledge, 1052–3
  Treaty on Plant Genetic Resources,
    1046
  TRIPs, 947, 1020, 1044, 1050–2
Inter-American Development Bank,
    107, 210, 1027
international arbitral tribunals, 65, 153
International Atomic Energy Authority
    (IAEA), 100, 880, 888, 909–10
International Chamber of Commerce
    (ICC), 115
International Civil Aviation
    Organization (ICAO), 99
International Commission on
    Radiological Protection
    (ICRP), 880
International Congress for the
    Protection of Nature, 29
International Council for Bird
    Protection, 28
International Council for the
    Exploration of the Sea, 584

International Court of Justice
  advisory opinions, 217–18
  Chamber for Environmental
    Matters, 172
  contentious cases, 215–17
  generally, 215–18
  interim measures of protection,
    218
  jurisdiction, 579
  jurisprudence, 94–5, 153
  role, 51
International Covenant on Civil and
    Political Rights (ICCPR), 91
international crimes, 894–6
International Criminal Court, 313,
    315, 895
International Development
    Association (IDA), 1026
International Energy Agency, 102
international environmental law
  actors, 26, 70
  conflicts. *See* dispute resolution
  contemporaneity principle, 824
  during war, 308–11
  and economics, 8–9, 940–2
  emergence, 3–4
  general principles, 231
  history. *See* history
  issues, 3–5
  non-legal factors, 5–11
  participants, 15, 70
  scientific factors, 6–8
  Sienna Forum 1990, 62
  social objectives, 9–10
  terminology, 15–18
International Finance Corporation
    (IFC), 1026
international human rights. *See* human
    rights
International Labor Organization
    (ILO)
  conventions, 638–41
  generally, 98
  nuclear safety, 638, 646
  working environment, 34, 638–41
international law
  adjudicative function, 13
  administrative function, 12
  and Agenda 21, 7, 62

functions, 12–13
general principles, 150–2
generally, 11–18
legislative function, 12
parties, 15
regulatory approaches, 154–5
sources. *See* sources of international
law
sustainable development, 53,
56
International Law Association, 115,
154, 234, 236, 313, 321
International Law Commission
creation, 82
environmental impact assessments,
803
generally, 86
information rights, 39
prevention of transboundary
damage, 234, 322, 828–9
state liability. *See* state liability for
environmental damage
warfare, 313
International Maritime Organization
(IMO), 33, 97–8
international organisations
African organisations, 106–7
Agenda 21 implementation, 59–60
American organisations, 107
arising from Stockholm Conference,
37, 74
Asian organisations, 108
common law, 142
dispute resolution role, 204
early institutions, 29
enforcement of treaties, 191–5
established by environmental
treaties, 108–11
European organisations, 102–6
gaps, 74
generally, 72–8
global institutions, 78–101
history, 73–4
post-Stockholm impact, 42–3
regional organisations, 102–8
reporting requirements, 832–3
role, 76–8
source of law, 140–2
International Seabed Authority, 101

International Tropical Timber
Agreement (ITTA) 1994, 547–8
International Union for the Protection
of Nature (IUPN), 31
interpretation of treaties, 130–3
Inuits, 727
investment. *See* foreign direct
investment
investment incentives, 166
IPCC, 101, 358
Iran, 892
Iraq, Kuwait damages, 93, 140, 315,
402, 878, 890–4
Ireland
environmental resources, 1037
MOX case. *See MOX* case
property rights, 303–4
and Sellafield, 433
sulphur and nitrogen dioxides,
337
wild birds, 604
iron works, 808
ISAR, 864–6
Islamic Development Bank, 1028
islands, 500
Isle of Man, 923
Israel–Jordan Peace Treaty, 494
Italy
environmental rights, 301–2
environmental standards, 795
Haven claim, 920–2
Mediterranean marine mammals,
596–7
oil pollution, 204
Patmos claim, 918
wetlands, 392
wild birds, 604
ITLOS
Estai case, 578–80
generally, 65, 218–20
MOX case. *See MOX* case
prompt release cases, 578
role, 101
Seabed Disputes Chamber, 219
Southern Bluefin Tuna cases, 137–8,
213, 220, 275–6, 580–1
Swordfish case, 582–3
IUCN, 114, 115, 296, 503, 516
ivory, 8, 42, 140, 509–11, 514, 779

Japan
  carbon dioxide emissions, 166
  and Climate Change Convention
      1992, 360
  driftnet fishing, 151
  emission targets, 371
  and Kyoto Protocol, 376
  Marshall Islands tests, 887
  ratification of Kyoto Protocol, 370
  sea lions, 591
  Southern Bluefin Tuna cases, 137–8,
      213, 220, 275–6, 580–1
  tuna regulation, 600
  Varietals case, 983–4
  whaling, 37, 135, 593, 594, 595
Jeddah Convention 1982, 403, 408,
      686
Jenks, W., 882
joint implementation
  Climate Change Convention 1992,
      365
  generally, 161–4, 170
  Kyoto Protocol, 372–3
Jordan, 494, 892
Jordan River, 494
Juan Fernandez fur seals, 591
jurisdiction
  Biodiversity Convention 1992,
      516–17
  Brussels Convention 1968, 197
  European Convention on Human
      Rights, 198
  fishing rights, 567–8
  Lugano Convention, 198
  territorial jurisdiction, 13–16
  transboundary natural resources,
      29–30
  victims, 197
jurisprudence, 153
jurists' writings, 154
jus cogens, 320

Kingston SPA Protocol 1990, 530–1
Kiribati, 135, 420
Korea, 166, 600
Kosovo, 308
krill, 711
Kuwait
  Compensation Fund, 1030

  damages from Iraq, 93, 140, 315,
      385, 402, 878, 890–4
Kuwait Convention 1978, 402, 407
Kyoto Protocol
  adoption, 64
  amendments, 376
  Clean Development Mechanism,
      166, 373–4, 849, 1042
  common but differentiated
      responsibility, 289
  compliance procedures, 199–200,
      376
  developing countries, 375
  emission trading, 372–3
  entry into force, 376
  generally, 368–81
  joint implementation, 161–2, 372–3
  Marrakesh Accords, 370, 377–81
  monitoring requirements, 849
  policies and measures, 372
  reporting requirements, 375–6, 836
  sinks, 374–5
  targeted gases, 371
  targets and timetables, 365, 371–2
  trade measures, 944
  tradeable permits, 161–2, 378

labelling
  eco-labelling, 17, 167, 861–3
  LMOs, 861
  trade barriers, 946, 949, 957–8,
      994–5
Lake Constance, 478
Lake Geneva, 478
Lake Ontario, 486–7
land resources
  Agenda, 7, 58
  protection, 4
land use
  African Nature Convention, 525
  ASEAN Agreement, 542
  and climate change, 377
  generally, 555–8
  land-use change and forestry
      (LUCUF) activities, 377, 380
landfill, 678–9, 687–8, 792, 1066–9
Laos, 491, 541
Latin America, nuclear weapons, 650
Latvia, 412, 735

Lauterpacht, Sir Hersch, 146
lead, 333, 760
League of Arab States, 102
Lebanon, 546
legal definitions, and international law, 15–18
legal groups, 115
leopard skins, 513–14
liability. *See* civil liability for environmental damage, state liability for environmental damage
Liberia, flags, 448
Libya, 385
LIFE, 1030, 1036–7
Lima Convention 1981, 244, 403
liquefied gases, 452
Lithuania, 412, 735
litigation, growth of international litigation, 65
litter, 430
living modified organisms (LMOs), 653–8, 861
lobsters, 998–9
locus standi, 306
locusts, 29, 96
Lomé Convention
  and EU, 753
  hazardous waste, 680, 695
  sustainable development, 254, 259, 265, 1022
London Convention 1972, 685
  1996 Protocol, 420–3
  amendments, 141
  civil liability, 454, 924
  generally, 416–22, 685
  incineration, 686
  monitoring requirements, 849
  resolutions, 141
Lowe, A. V.
LRTAP Convention
  Aarhus Protocol on Heavy Metals 1998, 333–4
  Aarhus Protocol on Persistent Organic Pollutants 1998, 334–5, 628
  generally, 324–36
  Gothenburg Protocol 1999, 335–6

Monitoring and Evaluation Protocol, 326–7
monitoring requirements, 849
NO_x Protocol, 328–9
protocols, 240, 325
state liability, 899
Sulphur Protocol 1985, 327
Sulphur Protocol 1994, 332–3
Volatile Organic Compounds Protocol 1991, 329–32
Lugano Convention 1993
  claims, 936–7
  enforcement, 177
  exemptions, 936
  generally, 933–7
  information rights, 858
  reservations, 937
Lusaka Agreement, 525–6
Luso-Spanish river basins, 478
Luxembourg, 648, 659
Lyster, Simon, 607, 616

Maastricht Treaty
  common but differentiated responsibility, 288
  generally, 739, 745–6
  precautionary principle, 271
  sustainable development, 259
Madagascar, 500
Mahakali River, 492, 493–4
Malaysia, 361, 541, 712, 965–6, 971–3
Malta, 733, 735
manatees, 591
mangroves, 1023
manure pollution, 1013
margins of appreciation, 7, 302
marine environment. *See* seas and oceans
marine mammals, 571, 572, 573
  generally, 590–2
  Mediterranean sanctuary, 596–7
  treaties, 591
  whales. *See* whaling
markhors, 513–14
MARPOL 73/78
  Annex I, 441–2
  Annex II, 442–3
  Annex III, 443
  Annex IV, 443

MARPOL 73/78 (*cont.*)
  Annex V, 443–4
  Annex VI, 444, 448
  definitions, 440–1
  generally, 440–5
Marrakesh Accords, 370, 377–81, 850–1
Marshall Islands, 274, 887, 889–90
Martens Clause, 311
media, 120
mediation, 203–5
Mediterranean
  cetaceans, 609
  marine mammal sanctuary, 596–7
  Mediterranean Action Plan,
    400
  monk seals, 591
  scientific exploration, 584
  seabed activities, 445, 448
  ship pollution, 442
  tuna, 598–9
  UNEP Regional Sea Programme,
    400–2
Mekong River, 491
Mendes, Chico, 292
mercury, 333, 773
methane, 372
methylbromide, 350–1, 761
methylchloroform, 350
Meuse, 478
Mexico
  hazardous substances, US border,
    621
  hazardous waste, 1066–9
  Mexico–US Hazardous Waste
    Agreement, 680, 697
  NAFTA. *See* NAFTA
  tuna regulation, 598
  Tuna/Dolphin cases, 185, 238, 861,
    953–61
  whaling, 595
Micronesia, 274
MIGA, 1071–2
migratory species
  Bonn Convention 1979, 607–11
  categories, 607
  generally, 41, 606–11
  international convention, 110
military activities, 299, 310. *See also*
    war and environment

mining
  Antarctic, 155, 665, 716–21, 722
  and development assistance, 1023
  generally, 665–9
  hazardous waste, 679–81
  Nauru phosphates case, 94, 217,
    666–9, 879, 887
  and UN, 74
mires, 537
Monaco, 596–7
monk seals, 591
Montevideo Programme, 44–5, 62,
    67–9, 84, 556
Montreal Protocol 1987
  adjustments and amendments,
    346–7
  amendment procedure, 139–40, 141
  Beijing Adjustments, 349
  compliance procedures, 165, 180,
    206–7
  conflict with WTO, 136, 945–6
  control of production and
    consumption, 348–52
    carbon tetrachloride, 350
    CFCs, 349–50
    halons, 349
    HCFCs, 350–1
    hydrobromofluorocarbons, 350–1
    methylbromide, 350–1
    methylchloroform, 350
    transfer of production, 351–2
  control of trade, 352–3
  controlled substances, 348
  developing countries, 354–5
  enforcement, 187
  equity, 263
  generally, 345–7
  institutions, 356–7
  landmark, 345
  Multilateral Fund, 355–6, 1021,
    1029, 1031–2, 1041
  precautionary approach, 268, 346
  public awareness, 860
  recycling, 689
  reporting requirements, 181, 356
  technical and financial assistance,
    355–6, 1020
  technology transfer, 1041
  trade restrictions, 943

moon, 286
Moon Treaty 1979, 178, 384, 686–7
Mosel, 478
motor vehicles
    carbon dioxide emissions,
        166
    diesel engines, 759
    emission standards, 157
    end of life, 792
    environmentally friendly vehicles
        (EEV), 759
    EU environmental law, 758–9, 766
    gaseous pollutant emissions, 324
motorways, 808
mountains, Agenda 21, 58
MOX case, 213, 251, 428, 436
    environment statement, 806–7
    information rights, 857–8
    ITLOS arbitration, 138
    precautionary principle, 276
MTBE, 1069–70
Mururoa, 319
Myanmar, 541

NAFTA, 107, 115
    Agreement on Environmental
        Co-operation, 1005–6
    Border Environment Co-operation
        Commission, 1007
    case law, 1064–70
    Commission on Environmental
        Co-operation, 211–12, 1006
    competition rules, 1004
    conflicts with environmental
        treaties, 1000
    dispute settlement, 211–12, 1004–5
    environmental considerations, 946,
        999–1000
    foreign direct investment, 1059–60,
        1062
    Free Trade Commission, 1004–5
    and GATT, 999, 1000, 1004
    generally, 999–1007
    health and safety measures, 1001–2
    institutions, 1004–5, 1006
    non-technical trade barriers, 1002–4
    North American Development Bank,
        1007
Nairobi SPA Protocol 1985, 404, 526–7

NAMMCO, 596
national courts, jurisprudence, 153
national law
    and Agenda, 7, 60–1
    implementation of international
        obligations, 175
national parks, 155, 499, 528, 833,
    1070–1
Natura 2000, 537, 539
natural reserves, 833
natural resources
    equitable use, 261–3
    jurisdiction over, 29–30
    shared. *See* shared natural resources
    state sovereignty over, 54
    Stockholm Conference, 39
    sustainable use, 257–61
Nauru, 135
    phosphate mining case, 94, 217,
        666–9, 879, 887
    preventive action, 248
    radioactive waste dumping at sea,
        420
necessity, 472–4, 475, 477
negotiation, dispute resolution, 201–2
Nepal, Mahakali River, 492, 493–4
Netherlands
    car pollution, 1013
    compensation from Iraq, 892
    Dead Red Grouse case, 990
    environmental standards, 795
    legality of Biotechnology Directive,
        1051–2
    manure pollution, 1013
    pollution of Rhine, 198, 213, 480
    sulphur and nitrogen dioxides, 337
    Tuna/Dolphin case, 958–60
    wild birds, 604
New Delhi Declaration, 234
New Zealand
    biodiversity, 500
    Nauru phosphates, 94, 667–8
    nuclear tests cases. *See* nuclear tests
    Southern Bluefin Tuna cases, 213,
        220, 275–6, 580–1
    tuna regulation, 600
NGOs
    generally, 114–15
    participation, 70

NGOs (*cont.*)
  role, 87–8
  watchdog role, 199–200
Nicaragua, 598, 842
Nice Treaty, 735, 739
Niger, 489–90
nitrogen oxides
  Canada–US Air Quality Agreement,
    340
  Combustion Directive, 337
  EU law, 478, 757, 759, 762–3
  ship emissions, 444
noise
  airports and aircraft, 300–1, 302–3,
    341, 992–3
  Arctic, 729
  EU law, 783–4
  working environment, 638–9
non-discrimination
  ILC principle, 903
  UNEP principle, 44
  WTO principle, 965, 970
non-state actors
  business community, 115–17
  enforcement of treaties, 195–200
  generally, 112–13
  individuals, 117–20
  information to and from, 838
  legal groups, 115
  media, 120
  NGOs. *See* NGOs
  participation, 70
  role, 87–8
  scientific community, 113–14
non-tariff barriers. *See* import
  restrictions
Nordic Environment Convention,
  850
North American Development Bank,
  1007
North Sea
  cetaceans, 609
  incineration, 686
  oil pollution, Bonn Agreements,
    452–3
  Oslo Convention, 423–5
  OSPAR. *See* OSPAR Convention
  sea dumping, 685
  seabed activities, 445

sewage sludge, 685
  treaties, 409
  whaling, 595–6
Norway
  Arctic jurisdiction, 727
  oil pollution, 923
  territorial waters, 569
  whaling, 135, 593, 595
Notification Convention 1986,
  845–7
Noumea Convention 1986, 405, 407,
  531, 688, 813–14
NO_x, EU law, 765
NO_x Protocol 1988, 328–9
nuclear accidents, 647–8, 794
  Chernobyl. *See* Chernobyl accident
  civil liability, 905–12
  definition of nuclear damage, 908,
    910
nuclear installations
  civil liability, 905–12
    1988 Joint Protocol, 912
    1997 Protocol, 910–11
    Paris Convention 1960, 906–8
    Vienna Convention 1963, 908–12
  environmental impact assessments,
    808
  reporting requirements, 837
  and war, 312–13
nuclear safety
  border co-operation, 646–7
  conventions, 63, 64, 644–5
  emergencies, 647–8
  EU law, 793–4
  generally, 642–51
  IAEA, 100
  ILO Convention, 638, 646
  information exchange, 830
  reporting requirements, 837, 846
  spent fuel, 644–5, 697–9
  transport, 645–6
  UNSCEAR, 90, 641
nuclear tests
  actio popularis, 188
  British nuclear tests, 888
  CTBT 1996, 649
  generally, 318–19
  information requirements, 846
  Marshall Islands, 889–90

Nuclear Tests cases, 120, 184–5, 188, 242, 245–6, 310
  damage threshold, 879
  environmental impact assessments, 813–14
  facts, 319–21
  ICJ interim measures, 218
  precautionary principle, 273–4
  reparation, 887
  Test Ban Treaty 1963, 243, 319–21, 438, 649
  United Nations, 33
nuclear weapons
  Africa, 651
  enforcement mechanisms, 193
  and environmental obligations, 311
  generally, 649–51
  information requirements, 846
  Latin America, 650
  legality, 218, 310, 312, 315
  ocean floor, 649
  outer space, 383
  South Asia, 651
  South Pacific, 650–1
  Stockholm Declaration, 309
nutrients, at sea, 430

occupational health, 639
oceans. *See* seas and oceans
OECD
  and Climate Change Convention 1992, 360
  energy, 664
  Environment Committee, 41, 103
  environmental agreements, 166
  generally, 102–4
  integrated pollution control, 168–9
  member states, 72
  Multilateral Agreement on Investment (MAI), 1062–4
  Nuclear Energy Agency, 641, 642
  overseas development assistance, 1023
  polluter-pays principle, 281–3
  reporting recommendations, 836
  and subsidies, 1011
  use of economic instruments, 160
  waste management, 676, 688
offshore drilling, 447

offshore mining, 447
Oil Fund Convention 1992, 192, 915–22, 1030
oil pollution
  1969 Intervention Convention, 449
  Bonn Agreements, 452–3
  civil liability
    Bunker Oil Convention 2001, 454, 922
    Civil Liability Convention 1992, 299, 454, 913
    Fund Convention 1992, 915–22
    generally, 912–23
    private agreements, 922–3
  early convention, 28
  EU law, 779
  North Sea, 452–3
  Oil Pollution Compensation Fund, 915–22, 1030
    Antonio Gramsci claim, 918
    Haven claim, 920–2
    Patmos claim, 918–20
  post-war conventions, 33
  preparedness, 451–2
  United Nations, 33
oncomouse, 1048–9
OPEC, 102
opinio juris, 146, 147
OPOL, 922–3
Organization for Security and Co-operation in Europe (OSCE), 106
Organization of African Unity (OAU), 106
Organization of American States (OAS), 107
Organization of the Islamic Conference, 102
OSCOM, 424–5
Oslo Convention 1972
  generally, 423–5, 685
  incineration, 686
  OSCOM, 424–5
OSPAR Convention
  adoption, 395
  atmospheric pollution, 437
  compliance, 193
  ecosystem approach, 410–11
  generally, 409–12

OSPAR Convention (*cont.*)
 incineration, 686
 information rights, 411, 856
 monitoring requirements, 849
 non-state actors, 113
 OSPAR Commission, 411, 412
 pollution from land-based sources,
  300, 434–6
 precautionary principle, 271,
  273
 sea dumping, 425–6
 seabed activities, 447
outer space
 common responsibility, 286
 COPUOS, 90
 exploration, 383
 generally, 382–5
 global commons, 14
 Moon Treaty, 384
 Outer Space Principles 1992, 382,
  384–5
 Outer Space Treaty 1967, 383
 province of all mankind, 383
 space debris, 383
 Space Liability Convention 1972,
  896–8
 treaties, 382
Outer Space Treaty 1967, 383
Oxfam, 115
oysters, 27
ozone depletion, 4
 adverse effects, 877
 Arctic, 730
 cause, 343
 conventions, 343–4
 evidence, 318
 generally, 342–57
 Global Ozone Observing System
  (GOOS), 98–9, 344, 386, 388
 ground-level ozone, 335–6
 Montreal Protocol 1987, 345–57
 technology transfer, 1040–1
 UNCED, 388
 Vienna Convention 1985, 344–5
  technology transfer, 1040–1
ozone layer
 EU environmental law, 761–2
 international organisations,
  109

 meaning, 18, 343
 UN priority, 51
ozone pollution, 766–7

Pacific Fur Seals arbitration, 253, 561–6
Pacific Region
 Asia-Pacific Fisheries Commission,
  585
 Eastern Pacific Convention 1989, 598
 halibut, 585
 North Pacific Anadromous Fish
  Commission, 585
 North-East Pacific, UNEP Regional
  Seas Programme, 405
 radioactive materials, 150
 South Pacific, 531–2
  Apia Convention 1976, 531–2
  biodiversity agreements, 531–2
  fisheries, 585
  Noumea Convention 1986, 531
  nuclear free zone, 650–1
  sea dumping, 427, 685
  SPFFA, 585
  UNEP Regional Seas Programme,
   405
 South Pacific Commission, 108
 South Pacific Regional Environment
  Programme (SPREP), 108
 South-East Pacific, UNEP Regional
  Seas Programme, 403
packaging
 trade barriers, 949
 waste, 792
pacta sunt servanda, 151
Pakistan, 965–6
PARCOM, 432–4, 825
Paris Convention 1960, 906–8
Paris Convention 1974, 430–4
participation. *See* public participation
patents
 and Biodiversity Convention, 521
 European Patent Convention,
  1047–50
 generally, 1047
 TRIPs, 1050–2
Patmos incident, 918–20
PCBs, 432, 444, 728, 1065–6
Pelindaba Treaty, 651
perches, 775

perfluorocarbons, 372
Pergau dam, 1023
Permanent Court of Arbitration, role,
    51
Permanent Court of International
    Justice, 216–17
permanent sovereignty over natural
    resources, 81
Persian Gulf, 308, 402, 442, 445
persistent objectors, 149
persistent organic pollutants (POPs)
    Aarhus Protocol 1998, 334–5, 628
    Arctic, 730
    at sea, 430
    disposal, 688
    POPs Convention 2001, 628–30, 683
        financial assistance, 1034, 1036
Perspective 2000, 50–1, 690–705
Peru, 598
pesticides
    Belgian Pesticides case, 992
    Chemicals Convention 1998, 635–6
    classification, 626–7
    code, 95
    EU law, 786
    FAO Code of Conduct, 631–3
    generally, 625–37
    health and safety at work, 640–1
    international trade, 630–5
    issues, 625–6
    labelling, 626–7
    packaging, 626–7
    prior informed consent, 630–1,
        632–3, 634–5
    production and use, 627, 628
    regional agreements, 637
    registration, 626–7
    transport, 637
    UNEP London Guidelines, 633–5
pests, 842, 983
petrels, 610
petrol, 331, 760
PHARE, 1030
Philippines, 541
phosphate mining. See Nauru
phylloxera, 28
pikes, 775
plants
    breeders' rights, 552–3

diseases, 243
    information exchange, 830
    reporting requirements, 835, 842
    generally, 551–4
    International Fund for Plant Genetic
        resources, 1021
    patents, 1048
    protection of genetic resources,
        552–4
    Treaty on Plant Genetic Resources,
        1046
plastics, 443, 787
poaching, 505
poisonous substances, 29
Poland, 412, 735
polar bears, 605–6, 729
political rights, 305–7
polluter-pays principle
    ASEAN Agreement, 542
    and competition, 1010
    and conservation, 537
    emergence, 51, 103, 159
    EU, 742
    EU waste, 789, 790
    generally, 231, 279–85
    and subsidies to polluters, 1011
porpoises, 592
ports, 808, 835
Portugal, 337, 795, 837, 1037
precautionary principle
    Biodiversity Convention, 270
    Biosafety Protocol 2000, 270–1, 653
    burden of proof, 273
    definition, 142
    driftnet fishing, 589
    emergence of concept, 48, 51
    endangered species, 510–11, 513
    EU law, 232, 746
    Gabcikovo-Nagymaros case, 477
    generally, 231, 266–79
    London Convention 1972, 419
    Paris Convention 1974, 432
    Rio Declaration, 56
    sea dumping, 423
    state of science, 6
    straddling stocks, 575, 576, 581
    WTO/GATT, 7–8, 277–8, 984, 985
press censorship, 292
Prestige, 438

preventive action principle, 231, 246–9
Pribilov Islands, 563
principles
    international environmental law, 231
    status, 232–4
prior informed consent (PIC), 630–1,
        632–3, 634–5, 841
process standards, 157–8
product standards, 156–7
property rights, 303–4
proportionality, 462, 475, 988–9, 993
protected areas
    Antarctic, 713, 717, 724–5
    Biodiversity Convention, 518
    generally, 503
    special areas of conservation, 537
    specially protected areas, 713, 717,
        724–5
public participation
    Aarhus Convention, 111
    generally, 117–20
    Rio Declaration, 64, 306–7
public procurement, 104

quotas
    endangered species, 513–14
    and free trade, 946, 948

radioactive substances
    Arctic, 729, 730
    at sea, 430
    EU law, 793–4
    generally, 641–51
    moon, 384
radioactive waste. *See* waste
railway lines, 808
Rain Forest Trust Fund, 1027
Ramsar Convention, 97, 543–5
ranching, 513
recycling, 688–9
Red Sea, 403–4, 442
refugees, environmental refugees, 292
regulation
    approaches, 154–5
    direct regulation, 155–8
    economic instruments, 154, 158–67
    emission standards, 157
    environmental quality standards,
        155–6

integrated pollution control, 154,
        167–9
process standards, 157–8
product standards, 156–7
remedies
    Caring for the Earth, 48
    remediation, EU waste liability, 927
    UNEP principle, 44
reparation
    Gabcikovo-Nagymaros case, 476–7
    international law, 872–96
    liability. *See* civil liability for
        environmental damage; state
        liability for environmental
        damage
    state reparations
        civil claims, 904
        generally, 882–90
        ILC principle, 902–3
reporting
    by international organisations,
        832–3
    customary international law, 837
    emergencies, 841–3
    general requirements, 832–8
    non-emergency events, 836–7
    non-state organisations, 838
    treaty requirements, 833–6
research
    NO_x Protocol, 329
    UNEP principle, 44
    Vienna Convention 1985, 345
restitution, 883–4
restoration of sites, 48
Rhine
    1999 Convention, 481
    2001 Programme on Sustainable
        Development, 481–2
    Berne Agreement, 479–80
    generally, 191, 198, 478–82
    Rhine Action Programme, 481
    Rhine Chlorides Convention, 480
    Sandoz accident, 479–80, 481
Rio Declaration
    anthropocentric approach, 293
    common but differentiated
        responsibility, 55–6, 285–6, 288
    consultation, 839
    demography, 56

development and environment, 54–5
education, 860
environmental impact assessment,
    795, 800
free trade and environment, 1009
generally, 54–7
information rights, 827, 853–4
liabilities, 870
non-binding instrument, 52
and non-state actors, 71, 112–13
notification of emergencies, 842
polluter-pays principle, 280–1
precautionary principle, 272
Principle 2, 231, 232, 241, 246, 310
public education, 860
public participation, 118–20
regulatory approaches, 154–5
sustainable development, 55, 259–60
technology transfer, 1043
warfare, 309
risk assessments, 8
river basin management, 769–71
rivers. See watercourses
roads, 808
Romania, 735, 868
Roosevelt, F. D., 32
Russia
    Arctic jurisdiction, 727
    Bering Sea fishing rights, 562–3
    emission targets, 371
    environmental standards, 412
    and Kyoto Protocol, 370, 376
    Trusteeship Council, 94
    Volga, 220

Saamis, 727
SAARC, 108
SADC Protocol 1999, 527
Sahel, 610
salmon, 571, 586, 775, 981–3
Salvage Convention 1989, 450–1
Samoa, 274
Sandoz accident, 479–80, 481
Saudi Arabia, 360, 361, 385, 451, 892
Saussure, Horace de, 27
savannahs, 500
SAVE, 767
SCAR, 114, 714–20
Scheldt, 478

science
    definitions, 16
    and international law, 6–8
    pre-20C scientists, 26
scientific community, 70, 113–14
SCOPE, 114
scrub, 537
sea birds, 96, 588
sea dumping
    conventions, 41, 415
    definition, 416–17, 423, 425
    generally, 415–27, 684–5
    hazardous substances, 34, 155
    incineration, 156, 419
    London Convention 1972, 416–22
        1996 Protocol, 422–3
    Oslo Convention, 423–5
    OSPAR Convention, 425–6
    permits, 418
    radioactive waste, 420–1, 426
        customary law, 148
        moratorium, 140, 419
        sub-seabed disposal, 421–2
    regional agreements, 426–7
    UNCLOS, 416
    waste, 417
sea lions, 591
sea turtles, 588, 607, 609
seabed
    activities
        causes of pollution, 445
        generally, 445–8
        mining, 665–9
        OSPAR Convention, 447
        other treaty obligations, 447–8
        UNCLOS, 445
    Baltic Sea, 414
    civil liability, 923–4
    common responsibility, 287
    disputes, 192
    nuclear weapons, 649
    sovereignty over, 14
    sub-seabed disposal of radioactive
        wastes, 421–2, 433
seals, 29–30, 607
    Antarctic Seals Convention 1972,
        713–14
    EU law, 779
    exclusive economic zones, 571

seals (*cont.*)
   fur seals, 591
   generally, 590–2
   monk seals, 591
   Pacific Fur Seals arbitration, 253,
      561–6
   Wadden Sea, 609
seas and oceans
   Agenda 21, 58, 1017
   atmospheric pollution, 437–8
   coastal states. *See* coastal states
   development of international law,
      33, 393–5
   dumping. *See* sea dumping
   emergencies, 448–54
      1969 Intervention Convention,
         449
      1973 Intervention Protocol,
         449–50
      Bonn Agreements, 452–3
      hazardous and noxious
         substances, 452
      non-oil substances, 449
      oil pollution, 449
      oil pollution preparedness, 451–2
      regional agreements, 453–4
      salvage, 450–1
   exclusive economic zones, 14, 569,
      570–2
   general issues, 391–3
   global and regional treaties, 395
   incineration, 156
   international organisations,
      109–10
   living resources
      Antarctic, 714–15
      fisheries. *See* fisheries
      generally, 558–600
      history of legal developments,
         560–1, 568
      UNCLOS, 568–73
   marine environment
      meaning, 17
      UN priority, 51
   marine pollution
      civil liability, 454–5, 923–4
      definition, 398, 406, 900
      EU law, 778–9
   marine resources, protection, 5

pollution from land-based sources,
      427–38
   1995 Global Programme of
      Action, 429–30
   Agenda 21, 428
   definitions, 431, 434
   information exchange, 830
   OSPAR Convention, 300, 434–6
   Paris Convention 1974, 430–4
   treaties, 428–9
   UNCLOS, 429
   UNEP Regional Seas Protocols,
      436–7
pollution from vessels. *See* ship
      pollution
protection, 5
regional agreements, 399–415
   Antarctic. *See* Antarctic
   Baltic Sea, 412–15
   North-East Atlantic and North
      Sea, 409
   UNEP. *See* UNEP Regional Seas
      Programme
   waste dumping, 426–7
seabed. *See* seabed
territorial waters, 569–70
UNCED, 455–7
UNCLOS. *See* UNCLOS
sediment, 430
Sellafield, 433–4, 857–8
Seveso accident, 827
Seveso Directives, 622–3, 785
sewage, 5, 430, 443, 456, 679–81, 685,
      792
Sharda River, 493–4
shared natural resources
   consultation, 840
   and extra-territoriality, 238–9
   fish, 560
   legal limitations, 464
   meaning, 14, 43
   UNEP draft principles, 43–4, 560
sharks, 96
shellfish, 776
ship pollution
   Antarctic, 442, 724
   EU environmental law, 759
   generally, 438–45
   MARPOL 73/78, 440–5

nitrogen oxides, 444
noxious liquid substances in bulk, 442
oil. *See* oil pollution
packaged harmful substances, 443
sewage, 443
ship waste, 443–4, 685
sulphur oxide, 444
UNCLOS, 439
ships
    carriage of nuclear materials, 646
    pollution from. *See* ship pollution
    safety, 444–5
    sovereign immunity, 417
Shrimp/Turtle cases, 190, 255, 965–73
Sienna Forum 1990, 62
Singapore, 541
Single European Act, 739, 742–5
sinks
    Climate Change Convention, 346–60, 361, 362, 364–6
    Kyoto Protocol, 374–5
    Marrakesh Accords, 381
sites of special scientific interest, Antarctic, 717
skins, 28
Slovakia, 412, 735. *See also* *Gabcikovo-Nagymaros* case
Slovenia, 735
social objectives, 9–10
social rights, 297–305
soft law
    development, 77
    meaning, 124, 140
    UNEP activities, 44
soil erosion, 525, 555–8
Solomon Islands, 274
sources of international law
    Action Plans, 143
    acts of international organisations, 140–2
    conference declarations, 142–3
    customary international law. *See* customary law
    general principles, 150–2
    generally, 123
    international acts, 140–3

jurisprudence, 153
    secondary legislation, 140–2
    subsidiary sources, 153–4
    treaties. *See* treaties
    writings of jurists, 153
South Korea, 600
Southern Africa Development Community (SADC), 490–1, 527
Southern Bluefin Tuna cases, 137–8, 213, 220, 275–6, 580–1
sovereign immunity, ships, 417
sovereignty. *See* state sovereignty
Soviet Union
    Chernobyl. *See* Chernobyl accident
    Cosmos 954, 202, 287–9, 887, 897–8
    whaling, 135, 593
space debris, 383
Space Liability Convention, 896–8
Spain
    air pollution, 1013
    environmental resources, 1037
    environmental rights, 301
    environmental standards, 795
    environmental technology, 1013
    Estai case, 578–80
    Fisheries Jurisdiction case, 217, 239
    Lac Lanoux arbitration, 184, 202, 463–4
    nuclear installations, 837
    radioactive waste dumping at sea, 420
    Santona Marshes case, 602–3
special areas of conservation, 537
specially protected areas, Antarctic, 713, 717, 724–5
species, meaning, 507
St Lawrence River, 486–7
standards
    best available scientific knowledge, 366
    best available techniques, 158, 410, 412, 434, 755
    best available technology, 142, 158, 432, 448
    best available technology economically feasible (BATEF), 158, 330

standards (*cont.*)
    best available technology not
        entailing excessive costs
        (BATNEEC), 158, 763, 764, 789
    best environmental practice, 158,
        410, 412, 434, 448, 483
    best scientific evidence available, 575
    best technical facilities available, 479
    clean production methods, 158
    emission standards, 157
    environmental management, 864
    environmental quality standards,
        155–6
    environmentally sound
        management, 158
    ISO 14000, 864
    ISO 14001, 867
    minimum environmental standards,
        299
    nuclear safety, 642
    process standards, 157–8
    product standards, 156–7
state aids, 164–5, 1011–15
state liability for environmental
        damage
    criminal liability, 894–6
    definition of environmental damage,
        869, 876–8
    generally, 871–904
    ILC articles, 65, 86, 182–3, 873,
        874–5
        civil claims, 904
        criminal liability, 894–5
        forms of reparation, 883
        generally, 901–4
        strict liability, 882
    international law, 872–96
    Iraq–Kuwait, 890–4
    issues, 871
    jurisprudence, 887–90
    meaning, 869
    reparation, 882–90
    standard of care, 881–2
    strict liability, 881–2
    threshold of damage, 878–81
    Trail Smelter case, 885–6
    treaties
        Climate Change Convention,
            900–1

CRAMRA, 900
        generally, 896–901
        LRTAP Convention, 899
        Space Liability Convention, 896–8
        UNCLOS, 899–900
    UN Compensation Commission,
        885, 890–4
state of necessity, 472–4, 477
state sovereignty
    and enforcement of international
        treaties, 191
    meaning of territory, 13–14
    over natural resources
        and extra-territoriality, 237–41,
            1023
        principle, 231, 232, 235–41
        UNCLOS, 397
    principle, 13–14
states
    categories, 71–2
    coastal. *See* coastal states
    enforcement of international
        obligations, 182–3
        extra-territorial damage, 184
        within own territories, 184
    regional groupings, 72
    role, 71–2
steel works, 808
Stockholm Conference
    Action Plan, 37
    civil liability, 38
    context, 35
    demography, 39
    development and environment, 39
    environmental impact assessment,
        801
    follow-up, 40
    generally, 35–9
    influence on EU, 741
    institutions arising from, 37, 40
    landmark, 25
    origins, 32
Stockholm Declaration
    environmental impact assessments,
        801
    environmental protection as human
        right, 294
    generally, 38–9
    institutions arising from, 74

liability for environmental damage,
    870
nuclear weapons, 309
Principle 21, 51, 54, 145, 148, 151,
    189, 231, 232, 235–6, 241,
    246
    and armed conflict, 310
technical assistance, 1038
wildlife, 501–2
straddling stocks
    Agenda 21, 58
    conference, 64, 574
    conservation measures, 575–6
    Estai case, 578–80
    exclusive economic zones, 571
    flag states, 577
    Greenland halibut, 578–80
    international cases, 578–83
    international co-operation, 576–7
    monitoring, 850
    precautionary approach, 575, 576,
        581
    Southern Bluefin Tuna cases,
        580–1
Straddling Stocks Agreement 1995
    compliance and enforcement, 186
    generally, 64, 574–8
    non-state actors, 271
Strategy for Sustainable Living, 47–8,
    53
strict liability
    Basel Protocol, 925
    hazardous substances, 48
    Lugano Convention, 146–56
    state liability, 881–2
strict wilderness reserves, 155
Strong, Maurice, 36
Suarez, J. L., 584
subsidiarity, 751, 1072
subsidies, 164–5, 1011–15
subsistence fishermen, 576
subsoil, 14, 287
sulphur
    Canada–US Air Quality Agreement,
        340
    Combustion Directive, 337
    EU law, 478, 757, 760, 762–3
    OECD, 664
    ships, 444

sulphur hexafluoride, 372
Sulphur Protocol 1985, 327
Sulphur Protocol 1994, 332–3
Surrell, 26
sustainable development
    Agenda 21, 57–9
    and atmospheric protection,
        386–8
    Brundtland Report, 49, 252–3
    Business Charter on Sustainable
        Development, 116
    Climate Change Convention 1992,
        362
    Commission for Sustainable
        Development, 53
    concept, 10–11
    emergence of concept, 9, 46, 47
    equitable use of natural resources,
        261–3
    EU law, 748
    future generations, 256–7
    Gabcikovo-Nagymaros case, 476
    integration of environment and
        development, 263–6
    international law, 53, 56
    New Delhi Declaration, 234
    objectives, 11
    principle, 231, 252–66
    Rio Declaration, 55, 259–60
    Strategy for Sustainable Living,
        47–8, 53
    sustainable use of resources,
        257–61
        Biodiversity Convention 1992,
            517–19
    UNCED, 386–8
    World Summit on Sustainable
        Development (WSSD), 66–7
    and WTO, 259, 967, 968–9
Sweden
    Arctic jurisdiction, 727
    chemical products ban, 995–6
    Chernobyl reparations, 887–8
    environmental rights, 303
    environmental standards, 412
    sulphur dioxides, 337
Switzerland, 277–8, 479
Swordfish case, 582–3
Syria, 892

taxes
    as economic instruments, 161
    as trade barriers, 948
    EU law, 735, 759
technical assistance. *See* technology
    transfer
technology exchange, 329, 336
technology transfer
    Agenda 21, 1042–3, 1045
    Biodiversity Convention 1992,
        520–1, 1041–2
    Climate Change Convention 1992,
        366–8, 1042
    code of conduct, 1039
    generally, 1037–43
    and intellectual property, 1044–6
    Montreal Protocol 1987, 354, 355–6,
        1041
    ozone regime, 1040–1
    Rio Declaration, 1043
    UNCLOS, 1039–40
    UNEP Regional Seas Conventions,
        1040
    Vienna Convention 1985, 1041
    WSSD, 1043
terminology, 15–18
territorial waters, 13, 567, 569–70
Thailand, 491, 541, 965–6
Thirty Per Cent Club, 327
THORP, 433–4
timber, 547–8
Tisa River, 868
Torrey Canyon, 394, 448, 913–15
tortoises, 514
tourism, 670, 725
TOVALOP, 922–3
toxaphene, 728
toxic chemicals. *See* chemicals
toxic waste, dumping, and human
    rights, 295
trade associations, 116
trade restrictions on environmental
    grounds
    African Economic Community,
        1007–8
    environmental treaties, 941, 942–6
        export restrictions, 943
        import restrictions, 943
        v. free trade treaties, 944

free trade agreements, 946
    unilateral measures
        and Canada–US Free Trade
            Agreement, 997–9
        EU law. *See* EU law
        generally, 946–1009
        and NAFTA. *See* NAFTA
        UNCED, 1008–9
        and WTO. *See* WTO/GATT
tradeable permits
    EU law, 767, 768
    generally, 161–4
    Kyoto Protocol, 372–3
    Marrakesh Accords, 378
traditional knowledge, 1052–3
Trail Smelter case, 241–2, 318–19,
    885–6
transboundary damage
    enforcement by states, 184
    ILC principles, 322, 902–3
    state responsibility not to cause, 34,
        38, 231, 232, 235–6, 241–6, 902
transfer of technology. *See* technology
    transfer
transport
    chemicals, 637
    civil liability, 930–1
        CRTD 1989, 930
        HNS Convention 1996, 930–1
    generally, 670
    nuclear materials, 645–6
    and UN, 74
    waste, 690–705
travaux préparatoires, 132, 138, 144
treaties
    amendment, 138–40
    classification, 126–7
    and customary law, 145–6, 147–8
    dispute settlement provisions, 137–8
    entry into force, 133–4
    environmental treaties, 127–8
    implementation. *See*
        implementation
    interpretation, 130–3
    interpretative declarations, 135
    inter-treaty conflicts, 136–8
    pacta sunt servanda, 151
    ratification, 133–4
    reservations, 134–6

source of international law, 125–40
trade measures in environmental
    treaties, 941, 942–6
travaux préparatoires, 132, 138
treaty-making process, 128–30
Vienna Convention 1969, 130,
    131–2, 137
TRIPs, 947, 1020, 1044, 1050–2
Tropical Forestry Action Plan, 85, 96,
    548
tropical forests, 500, 1023, 1070–1
tropical timber, 547–8
Truman, Harry, 32
trusteeship, 564
Trusteeship Council, 94
tuna
    1949 Tropical Tuna Convention, 598
    1966 Tuna Convention, 598–9
    1989 Eastern Pacific Convention, 598
    1993 CCSBT, 600
    1993 Indian Ocean Tuna
        Commission Agreement,
        599–600
    conservation organisations, 586
    information exchange, 830
    international regulation, 597–600
    overfishing, 572
    Southern Bluefin Tuna cases, 137–8,
        213, 220, 275–6, 580–1, 600
    Tuna/Dolphin cases, 185, 190, 238,
        861, 953–61
Turkey, 735, 892
turtles, 588, 606–11
    Shrimp/Turtle cases, 190, 255,
        961–73
Tuvalu, 135

UN. *See also* specific agencies
    Centre for Urgent Environmental
        Assistance, 84
    Charter, 31, 293
    Commission on Human Rights, 295
    Commission on Social
        Development, 93
    Commission on Sustainable
        Development (CSD), 53, 64, 82,
        86–9
    Committee on Economic, Social and
        Cultural Rights, 298

    Compensation Commission, 885,
        890–4
    co-operative arrangements, 101
    co-ordination, 79–80
    creation, 30–1
    ECOSOC, 79, 91
    General Assembly, 79, 80–3
    generally, 78–80
    organs, 79
    Perspective 2000, 50–1
    Population Fund, 90
    Regional Economic Commissions,
        91–2
    Security Council, 93–4, 193
    specialised agencies, 95
    subsidiary bodies, 89–91
    System Wide Medium-Term
        Environment Programmes,
        44
    Trusteeship Council, 94
UNCCUR, 31–5, 91
UNCED. *See also* Agenda 21; Rio
        Declaration
    anthropocentric approach, 293
    atmospheric protection, 385–9
    chemicals, 670–2
    energy, 663
    equity, 262
    fisheries, 573
    Forest Principles, 52, 54, 546,
        548–51, 1009
    freshwater resources, 494–6
    generally, 52–63
    implementation, 225–6
    landmark, 26
    marine protection, 455–7
    negotiating processes, 53
    non-binding instruments, 52
    organisational framework, 74–6
    origins, 32
    ozone depletion, 388
    participation rights, 306–7
    priorities, 4, 169
    rationalisation of law-making,
        124–5
    sustainable development, 386–8
    treaties, 53
    waste, 705–8
UNCITRAL, 1062, 1070

UNCLOS
  adoption, 395
  Antarctic, 726
  civil liability, 454
  dispute settlement, 218–20
  enforcement rules, 178–80, 192
  environmental impact assessments,
      805–7
  fishing rights, 568–73
    exclusive economic zones, 570–2
    high seas, 572–8
    maritime zones, 561
    territorial waters, 569–70
  generally, 41, 395–9
  implementation rules, 175
  institutions, 101
  monitoring requirements, 849
  pollution
    atmospheric pollution, 437
    objectives, 396–7
    obligations, 396–9
    pollution from land-based
        sources, 429
    sea dumping, 416
    seabed activities, 445
    ship pollution, 439
    transboundary damage, 244–5
  technology transfer, 1039–40
UNCLOS I, 566–7
UNCTAD, 89–90, 864
UNDP, 82, 85
UNECE, 34, 42
UNEP
  chemicals, London Guidelines 1987,
      633–5, 687
  creation, 40, 74, 82
  Draft Principles, 43–4, 234, 568
    environmental impact
        assessments, 801
    state liability, 873
  emergencies, 621
  Environment Fund, 1030
  generally, 83–5
  information rights, 827
  Montevideo Programme, 44–5, 62,
      67–9, 84, 556
  recommendations, 141
  seas programme. See UNEP
      Regional Seas Programme
  World Soils Policy, 555

UNEP Regional Seas Programme
  Arabian Gulf, 402
  areas, 400
  Black Sea and North-East Pacific,
      405
  Caribbean, 404
  emergencies, 453–4
  framework conventions, 406
  generally, 83, 395, 399–408
  Gulf of Guinea, 402–3
  Indian Ocean and East Africa,
      404–5
  institutions, 407–8
  Mediterranean, 400–2
  obligations, 406–7
  pollution from land-based sources,
      436–7
  procedures, 407
  Red Sea and Gulf of Aden,
      403–4
  South Pacific, 405
  South-East Pacific, 403
  technology transfer, 1040
  waste dumping, 426–7
UNESCO, 31, 35, 96, 505, 611–15
UN-Habitat, 90
UNITAR, 90
United Kingdom
  and Biodiversity Convention, 135,
      234
  Chernobyl reparations, 888
  and Combustion Directive, 339
  compensation from Iraq, 892
  dumping of radioactive waste,
      426
  environmental rights, 300–1, 302–3
  Fisheries Jurisdiction case, 567–8
  MOX case. See MOX case
  and Nauru phosphates, 94, 667–8
  nuclear emergencies, notification,
      844
  and nuclear liability, 910
  offshore oil operators, 923
  Pacific Fur Seals arbitration, 561–6
  Sellafield, 433–4
  sewage sludge, 151
  South Pacific nuclear activities,
      650
  Torrey Canyon, 448, 913–15
  Trusteeship Council, 94

United States
  access to genetic resources, 520
  Adiron regional park, 505
  Arctic jurisdiction, 727
  Beef Hormones case, 7, 277–8, 979–1
  biodiversity, 500
  and Biodiversity Convention 1992,
    516, 688, 1046
  Boundary Waters Treaty, 203
  Canada–US Air Quality Agreement
    1991, 339–41, 687
  Canada–US Free Trade Agreement,
    997–9
  and Climate Change Convention
    1992, 233–4, 360, 688
  compensation from Iraq, 892
  disputes with EU, 7
  emission targets, 371
  environmental discrimination, 298
  environmental impact assessments,
    806
  and extra-territoriality, 238
  foreign aid, 37
  Great Lakes Water Quality
    Agreement, 487–9, 685–6
  Gut Dam arbitration, 486–7
  hazardous substances, Mexican
    border, 621
  Japanese Varietals case, 983–4
  and Kyoto Protocol, 370, 372, 374,
    376
  marine pollution, 394
  Marshall Islands reparation, 887,
    889–90
  Mexico–US Hazardous Waste
    Agreement, 680, 697
  MTBE, 1069–70
  NAFTA. *See* NAFTA
  and nuclear liability, 910
  Pacific Fur Seals arbitration, 253,
    561–6
  precautionary principle, 279
  Reformulated Gasoline case, 961–5
  restoration of damaged
    environment, 884
  right to development, 149
  Shrimp/Turtle cases, 190, 255,
    961–73
  South Pacific nuclear activities, 650
  territorial waters, 569
  tradeable permits, 161–2, 373
  Trail Smelter case, 184, 318–19,
    885–6
  Trusteeship Council, 94
  Tuna/Dolphin cases, 185, 190, 861,
    953–61
  and UN Compensation
    Commission, 890
  US–Canada Boundary Waters Treaty
    1909, 485–6, 649
  wetlands, 392, 544
Universal Declaration of Human
  Rights, 293
UNSCEAR, 90, 641, 880

Valdez principles, 116
Venezuela, 27, 323, 961–73
vibration, working environment, 638–9
victims
  enforcement in national courts, 197
  European Convention on Human
    Rights, 198
vicunas, 606
Vienna Convention, 681, 908–12
  1988 Joint Protocol, 912
  1997 Protocol, 910–11
Vienna Convention, 130, 131–2, 137,
  684–8
Vienna Convention, 686
  amendment procedure, 139–40
  generally, 344–5
  implementation, 345
  monitoring requirements, 849
  Protocol. *See* Montreal Protocol
  technology transfer, 1040–1
Vietnam, 308, 491, 541
volatile organic compounds (VOCs),
  329–32, 757, 766
Volga, 220

Wadden Sea, 481, 609
war and environment. *See also* weapons
  ENMOD Convention, 111, 313–14
  generally, 307–16
  international environmental law
    during war, 308–11
  rules of environmental protection,
    311–13
  special rules of environmental
    protection, 313–16

war crimes, 313, 895
waste
  Agenda 21, 7, 59, 676, 706–7
  Antarctic, 723–4
    incineration, 687
    landfill, 688
    radioactive waste, 34
  civil liability
    Bamako Convention, 924
    Basel Protocol, 689, 924–6
    EU law, 926–30
    generally, 924–30
    London Convention, 924
  definition, 425, 677–8
  and development assistance, 1023
  disposal, 684–8
    at sea. See sea dumping
    Belgian Waste Disposal case, 990–2
    incineration, 679, 686–7, 764–6
    installations, 808
    lakes and rivers, 685–6
    landfill, 678–9, 687–8, 792
  EU law, 786–92
  hazardous waste, 5
    Agenda 21, 7, 59, 705–6
    Bamako Convention, 695
    Basel Convention, 687, 691–5
    Cairo Guidelines, 676–7
    EU law, 699–703, 764–5, 789–91
    generally, 679–81
    import into Africa, 156
    incineration, 157, 792
    Mexico, 1066–9
    UN priority, 51, 72
  and human rights, 295, 675, 691
  international organisations, 111
  municipal waste, 678–9
  prevention, 681–4, 787
  radioactive waste, 5
    Agenda 21, 7, 59, 707–8
    Bamako Convention, 651, 687
    ban on sea dumping, 140, 148
    early convention, 33
    EIAs, 808
    EU law, 441, 703–5, 711, 794
    generally, 681
    IAEA Code of Conduct, 697–9
    legal regime, 679–80
    management, 644–5

    sea dumping, 419, 420–1, 426,
      685
    spent fuel, 644–5, 697–9
    sub-seabed disposal, 421–2, 433
  recycling, 688–9
  solid waste, 5
  transport and trade, 690–705
    Bamako Convention, 695
    Basel Convention, 687, 691–5
    EU law, 699–703
    IAEA Code of Conduct, 697–9
    Lomé Convention, 695
    Mexico–US Agreement, 697
  waste water, 776–8
Water Framework Directive, 769–71
water quality
  EU law, 768–79
  European rivers, 484–9
  Great Lakes, 488
  waste water, 776–8
water, right to water, 298
watercourses. See also specific rivers
  1992 Convention, 42, 270
  Africa, 489–91
  Americas, 484–9
  Asia, 491–4
  case law, 34
  early conventions, 28–9
  Europe, 477–85
  Helsinki Rules, 464–5
  reasonable use, 148
  regional agreements, 34, 477–94
  river basin management, 769–71
  US–Canada Boundary Waters
    Treaty, 485–6, 649
  and World Bank, 463, 1027
Watercourses Convention 1992
  1999 Protocol, 484–5
  civil liability, 937
  generally, 482–5
  monitoring requirements,
    849
Watercourses Convention 1997, 689
  armed conflicts, 310
  dispute resolution, 204
  generally, 466–8
waterfowl, 286
WCED. See Brundtland Report
WCED Legal Principles, 50, 62

weapons
    biological weapons, 312
    chemical weapons, 295, 628
    enforcement of agreements, 193
    incendiary weapons, 312
    nuclear. *See* nuclear tests, nuclear
        weapons
Western Hemisphere Convention 1940,
        527–9, 670
wetlands
    assessment, 1023
    definition, 543
    designation, 544
    destruction, 499, 544
    generally, 543–5
    Italy, 392
    Ramsar Convention, 33, 110,
        543–5
    United States, 392, 544
    Wetlands Fund, 545, 1021, 1030,
        1031
whaling
    ACCOBAMS, 596
    ASCOBANS, 595–6
    conservation, 590–2
    conventions, 27, 110, 592,
        595–7
    definition of whale, 16, 592
    EU law, 779
    exclusive economic zones, 571
    International Whaling Commission,
        141, 592–5
        competence, 597
    Japan, 37
    Mediterranean sanctuary, 597
    monitoring, 849
    moratorium, 42, 65, 135, 140, 155,
        594–5
    NAMMCO, 596
    reporting requirements, 181
    scientific exception, 593
    sustainable use, 258
whistleblowers, 292
whitefish, 775
Wild Birds Directive, 537, 602–5,
        779
wilderness reserves, 528
wildlife. *See* flora and fauna
working environment, 638–41, 646

World Bank
    assistance to developing countries, 9
    and environmental impact
        assessments, 821–2
    environmental policy, 41–2, 1026–7
    environmentally damaging projects,
        1026
    generally, 1025–7
    ICSID, 1037, 1062
    Inspection Panel, 118, 210–11
    and international waterways, 463,
        1027
    MIGA, 1071–2
    role, 101
World Charter for Nature
    biodiversity, 502
    education, 46
    environment and development,
        265
    environment and human rights, 294
    environmental impact assessments,
        46, 802
    generally, 45–7
    information rights, 46, 827
    liabilities, 870
    principles, 16
    warfare, 309
    waste, 675
World Climate Programme, 98
World Commission on Environment
        and Development (WCED). *See*
        Brundtland Report
World Conservation Strategy 1980, 47,
        686
World Food Summit, 96
World Health Organization (WHO),
        99–100, 880
world heritage
    common responsibility, 286
    conventions, 611
    extra-territorial damage, 243
    generally, 611–15
    underwater heritage, 97
    and war
    World Heritage Convention 1972,
        41, 97, 111, 611–15
    World Heritage Fund, 614, 1021,
        1030
World Heritage Sites, 504

World Meteorological Organization
(WMO)
  generally, 98–9
  Global Ozone Observing System
    (GOOS), 98–9, 344, 386,
    388
  IPCC, 101, 358
World Soil Charter, 96, 555
World Soil Policy and Plan of Action,
  96
World Summit on Sustainable
    Development (WSSD)
  chemicals, 672
  energy, 663
  environmental impact assessments,
    803
  fisheries, 600
  foreign direct investment, 1056
  free trade, 1009
  freshwater resources, 496
  generally, 66–7
  information rights, 852
  ocean issues, 80
  Programme of Implementation, 81,
    116, 388–9, 600
  technology transfer, 1043
World Weather Watch, 98, 848
Worldwide Fund for Nature (WWF),
  114
WTO/GATT
  annexed agreements, 947
  and Biodiversity Convention,
    522–5
  Committee on Trade and
    Environment, 951–2, 969
  competition
    anti-dumping, 1016–17
    subsidies, 1015
  dispute settlement, 204, 220–2,
    952–3
  disputes, 7, 946–85
  environmental definitions, 16
  Environmental Group, 41, 42
  environmental protection, 949

extra-territorial measures, 238,
    965–6
  functions, 947–8
  health and safety restrictions, 977–85
    Australian Salmon case, 981–3
    Beef Hormones case, 7, 277–8,
      979–81
    Japanese Varietals case, 983–4
    precautionary principle, 7–8,
      277–8, 984, 985
  history, 947
  importance, 101
  and NAFTA, 999, 1000, 1004
  non-discrimination principle, 970
  SPS Agreement, 977–9
  sustainable development, 259, 967,
    968–9
  trade restrictions
    eco-labelling, 167, 861
    in environmental treaties, 136–8,
      944–6
    prohibition, 948–9
    technical barriers, 949–51
  unilateral environmental
      restrictions, 31, 166, 238, 241
    Asbestos case, 973–6
    generally, 946–85
    jurisprudence, 1018–19
    Reformulated Gasoline case, 961–5
    Shrimp/Turtle cases, 190, 255,
      961–73
    Shrimp/Turtle II case, 970–3
    Tuna/Dolphin cases, 953–61
    Tuna/Dolphin I, 955
    Tuna/Dolphin II, 958–60
  Uruguay Round, 115
WTO Appellate Body, 65

Yarmouk River, 494
Yosemite National Park, 499
Yugoslavia, 218, 312

Zambezi, 83, 258, 490–1
zoos, 509–11, 780